| | |
|---|---|
| **15. Introduction to Macroeconomics** | Macroeconomic coverage begins with Chapter 15, which introduces macroeconomic issues and GDP accounting. |
| **16. Measuring Inflation and Unemployment** | Chapter 16 follows with its attention on measuring inflation and unemployment. |
| **17. Economic Growth**<br>**18. Keynesian Macroeconomics**<br>**19. Aggregate Demand and Supply** | Chapters 17, 18, and 19 contain the core of macroeconomic theory. Chapter 17 includes a brief overview of classical theory before the 1930s and an expanded discussion of the importance and sources of economic growth. Keynesian macroeconomics, with its focus on aggregate expenditures, is covered in Chapter 18. And Chapter 19 introduces students to the modern macroeconomics of aggregate supply and demand. *One important note:* These three chapters can be [illegible] or studied in any sequence, adding flexibility for instructors [illegible]efer to include or exclude one chapter or another. |
| **20. Fiscal Policy**<br>**21. Federal Deficits and Public Debt**<br>**22. Money and the Financial System**<br>**23. Monetary** | Fiscal and monetary policy is the focus of Chapters 20 to 23. Discretionary fiscal policy, automatic stabilizers, and how fiscal policy affects aggregate supply constitute most of Chapter 20. Chapter 21 discusses deficits and the public debt, how they are financed, their burden on future generations, and their implications for macroeconomic policy in an open economy. Money—its nature, measurement, and creation by banks—and the institutional aspects of the Federal Reserve are the focus of Chapter 22. Monetary theory and policy are covered in Chapter 23, with an emphasis on how money and monetary policy affect interest rates, investment, and the economy. This chapter includes a detailed concluding section on the causes of the recent recession. |
| **24. Macroeconomic Policy Challenges** | Chapter 24 covers macroeconomic challenges facing policymakers. Phillips curves, inflationary expectations, and the implications of rational expectations on macroeconomic policy are the main issues presented in Chapter 24. In addition, theory is applied to the last three recessions and their "jobless recovery" aspects. |
| **25. International Trade**<br>**26. Open Economy Macroeconomics** | The final two chapters of the book are devoted to the international economy. Chapter 25 covers the classic issues of international trade, including the gains from trade (the Ricardian perspective), the terms of trade, a discussion of the impacts of tariffs and quotas, and an expanded discussion and evaluation of the arguments against trade. Chapter 26 examines the traditional topics of international finance (the balance of payments and exchange rates), along with an examination of fixed and flexible exchange rate systems. The final section of this chapter looks at the effect of these exchange rate systems on monetary and fiscal policy in an open economy. |

second edition

# CoreEconomics

second edition

# CoreEconomics

Gerald W. Stone
Metropolitan State College, Denver

Worth Publishers

*To Josephine and Sheila*

Senior Publisher: Catherine Woods
Executive Editor: Charles Linsmeier
Development Editor: Bruce Kaplan
Media and Supplements Editor: Tom Acox
Executive Marketing Manager: Scott Guile
Associate Managing Editor: Tracey Kuehn
Project Editors: Vivien Weiss and TSI Graphics
Art Director: Babs Reingold
Senior Designer: Kevin Kall
Interior Designer: Lissi Sigillo
Photo Editor: Christine Buese
Photo Researcher: Deborah Anderson
Production Manager: Barbara Anne Seixas
Composition: TSI Graphics
Printing and Binding: RR Donnelley
Cover Photo Credits: Mike Kemp/Rubberball/Corbis

Library of Congress Cataloging in Publication Data: 2010940229

ISBN-13: 978-1-4292-3711-6
ISBN-10: 1-4292-3711-2



Printed in the United States of America

First printing 2011

Worth Publishers
41 Madison Avenue
New York, NY 10010
www.worthpublishers.com
www.wortheconomics.com

# About the Author

**Gerald W. Stone** was Emeritus Professor of Economics at Metropolitan State College of Denver. He taught principles of economics to over 10,0000 students throughout his career, and he also taught courses in labor economics and law and economics. He authored or coauthored over a half dozen books and numerous articles that have been published in economic journals, such as the *Southern Economic Journal* and the *Journal of Economics and Sociology.* He earned his Bachelor's and Master's degrees in economics at Arizona State University, his Ph.D. in economics at Rice University, and a J.D. in law at the University of Denver.

# Preface

For many years I taught two classes that met only on Saturday for three hours each. Two problems arose. First, many of my students were business people who were more vocal than other students and were not afraid to voice any concerns they might have. Because I could effectively cover only maybe two-thirds of the standard principles of macroeconomics or microeconomics text, these students conti[illegible]omplained that they were not getting full value with their textbooks. They thoug[illegible]xts too expensive, too long, too encyclopedic, and they often resented paying for [illegible] unused extra material. The *CoreEconomics* text grew out of this experience.

Second, it soon became clear that students needed more feedback than what a once-a-week meeting could provide. I gave short quizzes on Saturday, analyzed each student's responses on Sunday, and sent each student a personalized set of study suggestions and additional exercises on Monday. The *CourseTutor* supplement evolved from this approach and is intended to help students who need something more than just a traditional study guide.

One thing more. My experience with my students at Metropolitan State College of Denver, who come from varied backgrounds in an urban setting, led me to produce a text that is interesting and usable for a broad group of instructors and students alike. My concern to give a broad range of students more help led me to produce a unique student supplement (*CourseTutor*) that is integrated with this text and that contains a wide variety of material, from tutorials and hints to practice problems and essay questions as well as standard assessment questions. Together, the *CoreEconomics* textbook and *CourseTutor* supplement provide instructors and students with something that no one else provides.

## What Does *Core* Mean?

*CoreEconomics* is not an encyclopedic offering. It does not cover every topic, but is partly based on a survey of economics professors to determine what they actually covered in their courses. Two important points emerged from this survey:

- **One chapter per week.** Instructors typically cover one chapter per week, or 15 chapters in a 15-week semester.
- **The majority of instructors teach roughly the same two-thirds of a standard economics textbook.** The overwhelming majority of instructors covers the same chapters in their course and then spends minimal time covering additional chapters. Over 90% of professors cover roughly 15 chapters in their microeconomics or macroeconomics text, which typically includes 19–22 chapters.

In this sense, "core" does not mean brief or abridged. Rather, it means that the textbook contains the chapters that most instructors need with only a few additional chapters on special-interest topics.

## The Core Text

Having a class meet only on Saturdays left my students more reliant on a text than usual. This text is written with these students in mind. I set out to provide a text that reduced student anxiety and made the material more accessible and interesting.

*CoreEconomics* follows a traditional organization. Coverage is concise. Concepts are thoroughly explained and illustrated with contemporary examples and issues integrated into the text with the aim of enhancing the reading–learning experience. A conscious effort has been made to resist putting too much information—more than students need and unnecessarily detailed—to keep students honed in on the most important concepts. The goal has been to give students what is needed and no more.

A number of elements have been included to pique and sustain the interest of a broad range of students. Several of these are unique to this book.

### By the Numbers

"By the Numbers" is a new feature of the second edition. It grew out of the fact that my students were bombarded with data and data graphs in the popular press and online, and they wanted some help dealing with them. The "By the Numbers" feature appears on the third page of select chapters and presents data, data graphs, and pictures focused around a theme, such as the possibility of creating a sustainable environment or how to compare the recent recession with previous downturns. The goal is to help students feel comfortable with data. The "By the Numbers" feature can be found in:



### Issues

The second edition contains a set of varied applications throughout, called Issues. Some are obviously related to economic theory, such as the latest empirical work on the strength of various multipliers or the value of brands. Other issues take the student further from normal pursuits, showing how economic theory can be applied in surprising ways. Here is a small sample of the issues that can be found in every chapter:

- In chapter 1 (page 8), the behavior of hummingbirds is looked at from the perspective of economic theory. Hummingbirds make good economists.
- In chapter 3 (page 49), census data from 1910 is used to show that supply and demand did matter in the marriage market in the old West.
- In chapter 5 (page 126), we look at Hubbert's Peak, the 1950s prediction by Marion King Hubbert that *U.S.* oil production would peak in the 1970s. This in fact happened. Hubbert's model predicts that *world* oil production will peak within the next decade. If true, what will happen? How will markets adjust?
- In chapter 11 (page 266), we examine the effects of cell phones, WiFi, and smart phones on the way we work and where we work.
- In chapter 16 (page 395), we consider whether it matters if the Consumer Price Index overstates inflation.
- In chapter 20 (page 482), empirical work on spending and tax multipliers is analyzed in the context of the effectiveness of fiscal policy.

- In chapter 21 (page 508), the federal deficit is approached by asking whether the United States is heading into a debt trap.
- In chapter 23 (page 554), we tackle the standard economic but important issue of assessing the Fed's performance.

### End-of-Chapter Questions and Problems

The second edition has grouped the end-of-chapter questions and problems into four categories to help in student assessment of concept mastery. Check Your Understanding questions test understanding of basic concepts and definitions. Apply the Concepts check if students can apply chapter concepts. In the News questions take quotes on recent issues found in the popular press and ask students to analyze them, extending chapter concepts in unique ways. Finally, Solving Problems test analytical skills and often stretch student understanding.

### History of Economics as a Discipline

The text incorporates the historical development of economics so students see how ideas and theories evolve with the times. Eleven historical figures are highlighted in biographies and, in addition, the biographies of Nobel Prize winners are included when their contributions are of particular importance to the chapter.

### Descriptive Art

Time series graphs can be visually boring so I have tried to make this book more visually appealing by including a photo or drawing with many of these graphs. Some of these can be whimsical. See, for example, the figures on poverty rates (page 352), inflation (page 392), and the interest on the public debt (page 500). The photos and drawings help students see what is sitting behind the data.

## What Is the *CourseTutor?*

As mentioned above, the *CourseTutor* evolved from the need to give my Saturday students more help than can be found in a traditional study guide.

Each chapter of the *CourseTutor* is divided into two basic sections: a six-step detailed walk through the material to help each student check his or her individual progress, followed by a section with standard study material such as fill-in, true/false, multiple-choice, and short essay questions. Both sections are designed for interactivity.

The first part of the *CourseTutor* is divided into six self-paced steps:

- **STEP ONE:** What You Need to Know
  - Lists the chapter objectives as they appear in the text.
- **STEP TWO:** Review the Key Terms
  - Outlines vocabulary words and definitions.
- **STEP THREE:** Work Through the Chapter Tutorials
  - This step includes solved problems, self quizzing, and a student-directed worked example that asks the student to draw graphs.
- **STEP FOUR:** Consider These Hints, Tips, and Reminders
  - Studying tips
- **STEP FIVE:** Do the Homework
  - Additional practice questions—the only section of the *CourseTutor* where students are not provided with the answers. Ideal for homework assignments.
- **STEP SIX:** Use the ExamPrep to Get Ready for Exams
  - Boils down key concepts of the chapter to help students prepare for exams—a favorite for students.

The second part of the *CourseTutor* provides extensive questions and problems—standard study guide material—that students can use to test their mastery of concepts. Answers are provided for all questions and problems.

Students learn by many different methods. *CourseTutor* addresses this by providing a **buffet of learning choices.** Students select those methods that best help them learn. Students having problems with specific material can turn to that particular section in the *CourseTutor* for help. It is important to note that students are not expected to work through all of the material unless they absolutely need this level of additional help.

*CourseTutor* should save you time if students work through the tutorial before they come to see you; they should have fewer unfocused questions when they show up at your office for help. I believe you will find the *CourseTutor* a very worthwhile addition for your students.

Together, I think *CoreEconomics* and *CourseTutor* provide something to you and your students that no one else in the market provides.

## Outline of the Book

*CoreEconomics* follows a traditional organizational sequence with microeconomics covered before macroeconomics. This serves students better because they are used to dealing in markets with firms, and microeconomic issues are part of their everyday lives. Macroeconomics, while fascinating, deals in billions and trillions of dollars and is more abstract than microeconomics. Within these two divisions, *CoreEconomics* follows, as you will see, a very traditional outline for chapters.

### Microeconomics

Students are introduced to economics in the first five chapters that focus on the nature of economics, trade, markets, supply, demand, and elasticity. Chapters 1 and 2 provide a foundation for the study of economics along with a brief look at production and trade. Chapter 3 lays out supply, demand, and market equilibrium and details the efficiency of markets. Chapter 4 provides a balance to chapter 3 by introducing the requirements for efficient markets, what happens when markets fail and how they tend to fail, and what government can do, along with a brief economic history of the United States over the past 150 years. These two chapters give students a good grounding in the benefits of markets along with some of the caveats. Chapter 5 introduces elasticity with its ramifications for total revenue and tax policy.

Chapters 6 and 7 provide students with an understanding of what's behind supply and demand curves. Chapter 6 on consumer decision-making covers marginal utility analysis with an indifference curve appendix. Chapter 7 lays out production and cost analysis for both the short run and long run.

The next three chapters (8–10) take students through market structure analysis plus a discussion of antitrust issues and an expanded coverage of game theory. The ability to discern behavior from market structure data is a fundamental aspect of microeconomics and these three chapters cover that material in detail.

Chapters 11 and 12 discuss the theory and issues surrounding input markets, especially labor markets. Chapter 11 uses market structure analysis to examine input markets and chapter 12 goes into more detail on issues of human capital, economic discrimination, labor unions, and collective bargaining.

Market failures, public goods, and environmental economics are the issues in chapter 13, while poverty and income distribution are covered in Chapter 14. These two chapters provide the economic background to several of the most widely discussed issues in microeconomics today including poverty, growing income inequality, and global climate change.

## Macroeconomics

Macroeconomic coverage begins with chapter 15 that introduces students to macroeconomic issues and GDP accounting. Chapter 16 follows with its attention on measuring inflation and unemployment. These two chapters give students the background needed for our discussion of macroeconomic theory in the next three chapters.

Chapter 17, 18, and 19 contain the core of macroeconomic theory. Chapter 17 introduces students to a brief overview of classical theory before the 1930s and an expanded discussion of the importance and sources of economic growth. Keynesian macroeconomics with its focus on aggregate expenditures is covered in Chapter 18. The last chapter in this sequence, Chapter 19, introduces students to the modern macroeconomics of aggregate supply and demand. One important note: These three chapters can be read or studied in any sequence, adding flexibility for instructors who prefer to include or exclude one chapter or another.

Fiscal and monetary policy is the focus of chapters 20 to 23. Discretionary fiscal policy, automatic stabilizers, and how fiscal policy affects aggregate supply constitute most of Chapter 20. Chapter 21 discusses deficits and the public debt, how they are financed, and their burden on future generations. Money, its nature, measurement, and creation by banks, and the institutional aspects of the Federal Reserve are the focus of chapter 22. Monetary theory and policy are covered in Chapter 23, with an emphasis on how money and monetary policy affect interest rates, investment, and the economy. This chapter includes a detailed concluding section on the causes of the recent recession.

Chapter 24 covers macroeconomic challenges facing policymakers. Phillips curves, inflationary expectations, and the implications of rational expectations on macroeconomic policy are the main issues presented in Chapter 24. In addition, theory is applied to the last three recessions and their "jobless recovery" aspects.

The final two chapters of the book are devoted to the international economy. Chapter 25 covers the classical issues of international trade including the gains from trade (the Ricardian perspective), the terms of trade, along with a discussion of the impacts of tariffs and quotas, and an expanded discussion and evaluation of the arguments against trade. The last chapter (Chapter 26) examines the traditional topics of international finance (the balance of payments and exchange rates) along with an examination of fixed and flexible exchange rate systems. The final section of this chapter looks at the effect of these exchange rate systems on monetary and fiscal policy in an open economy.

# Supplements: *By* Educators, *For* Students

A useful and seamless supplements package has been developed by instructors who actively teach the principles of economics course. Most of the supplements authors have taught for many years. The result: a supplements package crafted with instructors and students in mind.

## For Instructors

### Teaching Manual with Suggested Answers to Problems

The Teaching Manual prepared by Dr. Mary H. Lesser (Iona College) is an ideal resource for instructors trying to enliven their classroom lectures while teaching the CORE concepts. The Teaching Manual focuses on highlighting varied ways to bring real-world examples into the classroom by expanding on examples and real-world problem material within the text. Portions of the Teaching Manual have been designed for use as student handouts.

Every chapter of the Teaching Manual includes:

- ***Chapter Overview:*** A brief summary of the main topics covered in each chapter is provided.

- ***Ideas for Capturing Your Classroom Audience:*** Written with both the experienced and novice instructor in mind, this section provides ideas for introducing the chapter material. The suggestions provided can be used in a number of ways—they can be in-class demonstrations or enrichment assignments, and can be used in on-site, distance-learning, or hybrid course formats.
- ***Chapter Check Points:*** Each chapter of the text has Chapter Check Point sections that provide both bulleted review points and a question designed to assess whether students have mastered the main points of the section material. The TM provides the instructor with suggested answers to those questions, notations about points to emphasize, and suggestions about reinforcing the assessment of student learning.
- ***Debate the Issues in the Chapter:*** The TM reproduces the issues used in each chapter and provides a discussion of these examples. As with the Chapter Check Point material, teachers will find that these sections delineate points to emphasize and provide additional resources for spurring student debate.
- ***Examples Used in the End-of-Chapter Questions:*** A number of the end-of-chapter questions refer to specific articles in major newspapers or particular real-world examples. The TM provides the instructor with a succinct overview of those questions and cites additional resources that can be used to develop more in-depth analysis of the topics involved. Note that this is in addition to the sample answers that are also provided.
- ***For Further Analysis:*** Each TM chapter contains an additional extended example that can be used in a variety of ways. *Formatted as a one-page handout,* it can be duplicated and distributed in-class (or posted online), and is designed for use either as an in-class group exercise or as an individual assignment in both the on-site and on-line class format. Asking students to document research allows the instructor to use the example as a case study or group project as well. Learning objectives are specified and a one-page answer key is also available for reference or distribution.
- ***Web-based Exercise:*** Each TM chapter includes a Web-based example that requires students to obtain information from a web site and use it to answer a set of questions. This Web-based Exercise can be used in a variety of ways, as in-class group exercises or as individual assignments. Learning objectives are specified and suggested answers to questions are provided that can be used for reference or distribution.
- ***Tips from a Colleague:*** Each chapter of the TM concludes with a "tips" section which shares ideas about classroom presentation, use of other resources, and insights about topics that students typically find difficult to master.
- ***New to this edition*** are "Economics Is Everywhere" sections for the common and microeconomics chapters. These contain short synopses selected from the many vignettes in *Economics is Everywhere* by Daniel S. Hamermesh that correspond to the material covered in the chapter. The question that accompanies each vignette appears as an essay-type question in the Hamermesh book; for use with the Stone text those questions are adapted to a multiple-choice format and are assignable in EconPortal (see below for an explanation of Portal). The correct answers are indicated and feedback is provided. For the macroeconomics chapters, "Under the Macroscope" sections relate content to everyday experiences or situations that will be familiar to students. Each Section is accompanied by a multiple choice question to help the instructor assess student understanding of the key concept addressed in the section. Both features are also available and assignable in the EconPortal for *CoreEconomics.*

## Test Bank

***Coordinator and Contributor:*** Richard Croxdale (Austin Community College). ***Test bank contributors:*** Emil Berendt (Siena Heights University), Dennis Debrecht (Carroll College), Fred W. May (Trident Technical College), Tina A. Carter (Flagler College and University of Phoenix), Thomas Rhoads (Towson University), TaMika Steward (Tarrant County College), and Michael Fenick (Broward College).

This Test Bank contains nearly 9,000 carefully constructed questions to help you assess your students' comprehension, interpretation, analysis, and synthesis skills. Questions have been checked for this continuity with the text content and reviewed extensively for accuracy.

The Test Bank features include the following:

- ***New to this edition*** are skill descriptors. To aid instructors in building tests, each question has been categorized according to their skill descriptor geared for economics and based upon Bloom's Taxonomy. The skill descriptor was designed in order to aid in the evaluation both of students' abilities to "think like an economist" and to apply knowledge to the real world desirable for accredited business programs.
- Each question has also been categorized according to their general *degree of difficulty.* The three levels are: easy, moderate, or difficult. *Easy* questions require students to recognize concepts and definitions. These are questions that can be answered by direct reference to the textbook. *Moderate* questions require some analysis on the student's part. These questions may require a student to distinguish between two or more related concepts, to apply a concept to a particular situation, or to use an economic model to determine an answer. *Difficult* questions will usually require more detailed analysis by the students.
- To further aid instructors in building tests, each question is referenced by the specific topic heading in the textbook. Questions are presented in the order in which concepts are presented in the text.
- Questions have been designed to correlate with the questions and problems within the text and *CourseTutor.* A beginning set of *Objectives Questions* are available within each chapter. These questions focus directly on the key concepts from the text that students should grasp after reading the chapter. These questions can easily be used for brief in-class quizzes.
- The test bank includes questions with tables that students must analyze to solve for numerical answers. It contains questions based on the graphs that appear in the book. These questions ask students to use the graphical models developed in the textbook and to interpret the information presented in the graph. Selected questions are paired with scenarios to reinforce comprehension.

## Computerized Test Bank

Diploma was the first software for PCs that integrated a test-generation program with grade-book software and an on-line testing system. Diploma is now in its fifth generation. The printed Test Banks for *CoreEconomics* are available in CD-ROM format for both Windows and Macintosh users.

With Diploma, you can easily create and print tests and write and edit questions. You can add an unlimited number of questions, scramble questions, and include figures. Tests can be printed in a wide range of formats. The software's unique synthesis of flexible word-processing and database features creates a program that is extremely intuitive and capable.

## Instructor's Resource CD-ROM

Using the Instructor's Resource CD-ROM, instructors can easily build classroom presentations or enhance online courses. This CD-ROM contains two alternate sets of classroom presentation PowerPoints, all text figures (in JPEG and GIF formats), the Teaching Manual and detailed solutions to all End-of-the-Chapter Questions. You can choose from the various resources, edit, and save for use in your classroom.

## Two Sets of PowerPoints

***New to this edition*** is the **Dynamic PowerPoint Presention:** PowerPoint slides designed by Solina Lindahl (California Polytechnic State University) with front of the classroom presentation and visual learning experience in mind. This set of PowerPoints contains fully animated graphs, visual learning images, additional examples, links, and embedded questions suitable both for classroom discussion and assessment. These slides may be customized by instructors to suit individual needs. These files may be accessed on the instructor's side of the Web site or on the Instructor's Resource CD-ROM.

**Lecture PowerPoint Presentation** consist of PowerPoint slides designed by Debbie Evercloud (University of Colorado, Denver) that provide graphs from the textbook, data tables, and bulleted lists of key concepts suitable for lecture presentation. Key figures from the text are replicated and animated to demonstrate how they build. The *CheckPoints* from the text have been included to facilitate a quick review of key concepts. These slides may also be customized by instructors to suit individual needs. These files may be accessed on the instructor's side of the Web site or on the Instructor's Resource CD-ROM.

## For Instructors and Students

### Companion Web Site: bcs.worthpublishers.com/stoneecon2

The Companion site is a virtual study guide for students and an excellent resource for instructors. The tools on the site include:

**Student Resources**

- ***Self-test Quizzes:*** this quizzing engine provides a set of quiz questions per chapter with appropriate feedback and page references to the textbook. All student answers are saved in an online database that can be accessed by instructors.
- ***Key Term Flashcards:*** Students can test themselves on the key terms with these pop-up electronic flashcards.
- ***Web Links:*** Key Web sites, online data bases and online news articles selected and categorized by chapter to help students further access key concepts and principles.
- ***Learning Objectives:*** The Key concepts from each chapter listed out for easy access to students to evaluate whether they have grasped each objective after completing each chapter.

**Instructor Resources**

- ***Quiz Gradebook:*** The site gives you the ability to track students' work by accessing an online gradebook. Instructors have the option to have student results emailed directly to them.
- ***Both Dynamic PowerPoint and Lecture Outline PowerPoint Presentations:*** These two sets of PowerPoint slides are designed to assist instructors with lecture preparation and presentation by providing bulleted lecture outlines suitable for large lecture presentation. Instructors can customize these slides to suit their individual needs.
- ***Textbook Illustrations:*** A complete set of figures and tables from the textbook in JPEG and PowerPoint format.
- ***Teaching Manual and Suggested Solutions to End-of-Chapter Questions:*** The teaching manual and solutions are posted electronically for easy access.

### EconPortal—*AVAILABLE FOR FALL 2011*

**EconPortal** is the digital gateway to *CoreEconomics*, designed to enrich your course and improve your students' understanding of economics. EconPortal provides a powerful, easy-to-use, completely customizable teaching and learning management system complete with the following:

- ***An Interactive eBook with Embedded Learning Resources:*** The eBook's functionality will provide for highlighting, note-taking, graph and example enlargements, and a full text and glossary search. Embedded icons will link students directly to resources available to enhance their understanding of the key concepts.
- ***A Personalized Study Plan for Students, Featuring Diagnostic Quizzing:*** Students will be asked to take the PSP: Self-Assessment Quiz after they have read the chapter

and before they come to the lecture that discusses that chapter. Once they've taken the quiz, a personalized study plan (PSP) based on the quiz results is created for them. This PSP will provide a path to the appropriate eBook materials and resources for further study and exploration, helping students learn and retain the course material.

- ***A Fully Integrated Learning Management System:*** EconPortal is meant to be a fully customizable and highly interactive one-stop shop for all the resources tied to the book. The system will carefully integrate the teaching and learning resources for the book into an easy-to-use system. EconPortal will enable you to create assignments from a variety of question types to prepare self-graded homework, quizzes, or tests, saving many hours of preparation time.
- Instructors can assign and track any aspect of their students' EconPortal activities. The Gradebook will capture students' results and allow for easily exporting reports as well as importing grades from offline assignments.

This dynamic virtual homework and course management system enables students to gauge their comprehension of concepts and provides a variety of resources to help boost their performance within the course. This is an alternative to the pen and paper version of the *CourseTutor*. Instead, students can work through the *CourseTutor* content and additional resources online. In this online format, students can follow their own pace and complete any or all steps of the *CourseTutor*. All of this is possible with or without instructor involvement.

EconPortal includes the following *CourseTutor* **Interactive Resources:**

- ***Solved Problems:*** problems designed for this online environment using a graphing and assessment engine. Students may be asked to draw, interpret, or interact with a graph to provide an answer. Students will receive detailed feedback and guidance on where to go for further review.
- ***Core Graphs:*** animated versions of these key graphs *with assignable questions.*
- ***Core Equations:*** animated versions of the key equations *with assignable questions.*

**STUDENTS: What can they do with the EconPortal?**

- Test mastery of important concepts from the text.
- Access *The Economist* news feed within EconPortal.
- Improve understanding of difficult topics by working with interactive tutorials, graphing questions, flashcards, as well as the assets that make up the printed *CourseTutor.*
- Take notes on any of the resources.
- Browse by chapter or search by topic if they need quick information about a specific concept.

**INSTRUCTORS: What can you do with the EconPortal?**

- Interact with your students as little or as much as you like! You can assign the exercises as out-of-class activities, or allow your students to work independently.
- If you so desire, monitor your students' progress within the EconPortal using a sophisticated online gradebook.
- Export grades to your current Course Management System.

## Additional Online Offerings

### Aplia—Integrated Textbook Solution

**aplia.com/worth**

Aplia is the leading homework management solution in principles of economics. Worth was the first publisher to partner with Aplia in 2004 and continues to offer full Aplia integration for all of our principles of economics texts.

Our premium Aplia solution includes:

- ***Full eBook integration.*** The Stone Aplia course includes a full eBook.

- ***Homework sets correlated to the text.*** Online homework is easy to assign, and it grades automatically. The course gradebook quickly puts results at your fingertips.
- ***Algorithmic problem sets.*** All homework problem sets offer Grade It Now. Students can attempt any problem set up to three times with variables that randomize on each attempt.
- ***Multiple purchase options.*** Aplia access can be packaged with any version of the text, or purchased separately online as a less expensive alternative to the book because it includes an eBook. Students who purchase on-line access can also buy a physical textbook directly from Aplia at a significant discount.

Visit www.aplia.com/worth for demos and information on Worth Aplia. Contact your campus rep or support@aplia.com for access to a course for your class.

### Blackboard and WebCT

The Stone WebCT & Blackboard e-Packs enable you to create a thorough, interactive, and pedagogically sound online course or course Web site. The e-Packs, provided free, give you cutting-edge online materials that facilitate critical thinking and learning, including Test Bank content, preprogrammed quizzes, links, activities, animated graphs, and a whole array of other materials. Best of all, this material is pre-programmed and fully functional in the WebCT or Blackboard environment. Pre-built materials eliminate hours of course-preparation work and offer significant support as you develop your online course. The result: an interactive, comprehensive online course that allow for effortless implementation, management, and use. The files can be easily downloaded from our Course Management System site directly onto your department server.

## Further Resources Offered

### i>clicker

Developed by a team of University of Illinois physicists, i>clicker is the most flexible and reliable classroom response system available. It is the only solution created *for* educators, *by* educators—with continuous product improvements made through direct classroom testing and faculty feedback. You'll love i>clicker no matter your level of technical expertise, because the focus is on *your* teaching, *not the technology.* To learn more about packaging i>clicker with this textbook, please contact your local sales rep or visit www.iclicker.com.

### *Financial Times* Edition

For adopters of the Stone textbook, Worth Publishers and the *Financial Times* are offering a 15-week subscription to students at a tremendous savings. Instructors also receive their own free *Financial Times* subscription for one year. Students and instructors may access research and archived information at www.ft.com.

### Dismal Scientist

A high-powered business database and analysis service comes to the classroom! Dismal Scientist offers real-time monitoring of the global economy, produced locally by economists and professionals at Economy.com's London, Sydney, and West Chester offices. Dismal Scientist is *free* when packaged with the Stone textbook. Please contact your local sales rep for more information or go to www.economy.com.

### *The Economist*

*The Economist* has partnered with Worth Publishers to create an exclusive offer that will enhance the classroom experience. Faculty receive a complimentary 15-week subscription when 10 or more students purchase a subscription. Students get 15 issues of *The Economist* at a huge savings. Inside and outside the classroom, *The Economist* provides a global perspective that helps students keep abreast of what's going on in the world, and gives insight into how the world views the United States. *The Economist* ignites dialogue, encourages debate, and enables readers to form well-reasoned opinions—while providing a deeper understanding of key political, social, and business issues. Supplement your textbook with the knowledge and insight that only *The Economist* can provide. To get 15 issues of *The Economist,* go to www.economistacademic.com/worth.

## Acknowledgements

No project of this scope is accomplished alone. Many people have helped make this package a better resource for students, and I sincerely appreciate their efforts. These include reviewers of blocks of manuscript chapters, focus group participants, reviewers of the *CourseTutor* chapters, accuracy reviewers, and the production and editorial staff of Worth Publishing.

First, I want to thank those reviewers of the second edition who read through chapters in manuscript and offered many important suggestions that have been incorporated into this project. They include:

Innocentus Alhamis, Southern New Hampshire University
Scott Beaulier, Mercer University
Margot Biery, Tarrant County College, South Campus
Andrea Borchard, Hillsborough Community College
Stacey Brook, University of Iowa
Gary Campbell, Michigan Technological University
Kevin Coyne, Southern New Hampshire University
Michael Fenick, Broward College
Aaron Finkle, California State University, San Marcos
Michael Forney, Austin Community College
Adam Gifford, Lake-Sumter Community College
Jane Himarios, University of Texas at Arlington
Janis Y. F. Kea, West Valley College
Delores Linton, Tarrant County College
Fred May, Trident Technical College
Jaishankar Raman, Valparaiso University
Tom Rhoads, Towson University
Richard Rouch, Volunteer State Community College
Peter Schwarz, University of North Carolina, Charlotte
Lea Templer, College of the Canyons
Wesseh Wollo, Lincoln University

Reviewers of the first edition manuscript gave many useful suggestions. They include:

Dwight Adamson, South Dakota State University
Norman Aitken, University of Massachusetts, Amherst
Fatma Wahdan Antar, Manchester Community College
Anoop Bhargava, Finger Lakes Community College
Craig Blek, Imperial Valley College
Mike W. Cohick, Collin County Community College
Kathleen Davis, College of Lake County
Dennis Debrecht, Carroll College
Christopher Erickson, New Mexico State University
Shaikh M.Ghanzanfar, University of Idaho
Lowell Glenn, Utah Valley State College
Jack Hou, California State University, Long Beach
Charles Kroncke, College of Mt. St. Joseph
Laura Maghoney, Solano Community College
Pete Mavrokordatos, Tarrant County College
Philip Mayer, Three Rivers Community College
John McCollough, Penn State University, Lehigh
Pat Mizak, Canisius College
Jay Morris, Champlain College
Jennifer Offenberg, Loyola Marymount University
Joan Osborne, Palo Alto College
Diana Petersdorf, University of Wisconsin, Stout
Oscar Plaza, South Texas Community College
Mary Pranzo, California State University, Fresno
Mike Ryan, Gainesville State College
Supriya Sarnikar, Westfield State College
Lee Van Scyoc, University of Wisconsin, Oshkosh
Paul Seidenstat, Temple University
Ismail Shariff, University of Wisconsin, Green Bay
Garvin Smith, Daytona Beach Community College
Gokce Soydemir, University of Texas, Pan America
Martha Stuffler, Irvine Valley College
Ngoc-Bich Tran, San Jacinto College
Alan Trethewey, Cuyahoga Community College

Chad Turner, Nicholls College
Va Nee L. Van Vleck, California State University, Fresno
Dale Warnke, College of Lake County

Second, I would like to take this opportunity to thank those focus group participants who devoted a lot of time and effort to discussing the elements of this project before it was published in its first edition. Their thoughts and suggestions (and criticisms) contributed immensely to the development of this project. They include:

Emil Berendt, Friends University
Harmanna Bloemen, Houston Community College, Northeast
Mike Cohick, Collin County Community College
Rohini Divecha, San Jacinto College, South
Bob Francis, Shoreline Community College
John Kane, State University of New York, Oswego
Sukanya Kemp, University of Akron
Charlene Kinsey, Houston Community College, Northwest
Delores Linton, Tarrant Community College, Northwest
Fred May, Trident Tech
Saul Mekies, Kirkwood Community College
Diego Mendez-Carbajo, Illinois Wesleyan
Cyril Morong, San Antonio College
Oscar Plaza, South Texas Community College
Michael Polcen, Northern Virginia Community College
Jaishankar Raman, Valparaiso University
Belinda Roman, Palo Alto College
Greg Rose, Sacramento City College
Ted Scheinman, Mt. Hood Community College
Marianna Sidoryanskaya, Austin Community College, Cypress
Lea Templer, College of the Canyons
Bich Tran, San Jacinto College, South
Don Weimer, Milwaukee Area Technical College, Downtown

Third, my thanks go out to those who took the time to review single chapters of the first edition text and the *CourseTutor* together, and to those who class-tested single chapters. Thanks for the reviews and the suggestions. These reviewers included:

Shawn Abbott, College of the Siskiyous
Roger Adkins, Marshall University
Richard Agesa, Marshall University
Ali Akarca, University of Illinois—Chicago
Frank Albritton, Seminole Community College
Anca Alecsandru, Louisiana State University
Innocentus Alhamis, Southern New Hampshire University
Basil Al-Hashimi, Mesa Community College
Samuel Andoh, Southern Connecticut State University
William Ashley, Florida Community College at Jacksonville
Rose-Marie Avin, University of Wisconsin—Eau Claire
Sukhwinder Bagi, Bloomsburg University
Dean Baim, Pepperdine University
Joanne Bangs, College of St. Catherine
Abby Barker, University of Missouri—St. Louis
Perry Barrett, Chattahoochee Technical College
David Bartram, East Georgia College
Robert Beekman, University of Tampa
Emil Berendt, Siena Heights University
Gerald Bialka, University of North Florida
Paul Biederman, New York University
Richard Bieker, Delaware State University
Tom Birch, University of New Hampshire—Manchester
John Bockino, Suffolk Community College
Orn Bodvarsson, St. Cloud State University
Antonio Bos, Tusculum College
Laurette Brady, Norwich University
Bill Burrows, Lane Community College
Rob Burrus, University of North Carolina—Wilmington
Tim Burson, Queens University of Charlotte
Dean Calamaras, Hudson Valley Community College
Charles Callahan, State University of New York—Brockport
Colleen Callahan, American University
Dave Cauble, Western Nebraska Community College
Henrique Cezar, Johnson State College
Matthew Chambers, Towson University
Lisa Citron, Cascadia Community College
Ray Cohn, Illinois State University
Kevin Coyne, Southern New Hampshire University
Tom Creahan, Morehead State University
Richard Croxdale, Austin Community College
Rosa Lea Danielson, College of DuPage

Amlan Datta, Cisco Junior College
Helen Davis, Jefferson Community & Technical College
Susan Davis, Buffalo State College
Dennis Debrecht, Carroll College
Robert Derrell, Manhattanville College
Julia Derrick, Brevard Community College
Jeffrey Dorfman, University of Georgia
Justin Dubas, St. Norbert College
Harold Elder, University of Alabama
G. Rod Erfani, Transylvania University
William Feipel, Illinois Central College
Rick Fenner, Utica College
James Ford, San Joaquin Delta College
Marc Fox, Brooklyn College
Lawrence Fu, Illinois College
Mark Funk, University of Arkansas, Little Rock
Mary Gade, Oklahoma State University
Khusrav Gaibulloev, University of Texas—Dallas
Gary Galles, Pepperdine University
Lara Gardner, Florida Atlantic University
Kelly George, Florida Community College at Jacksonville
Lisa George, Hunter College
J. P. Gilbert, Mira Costa College
Chris Gingrich, Eastern Mennonite University
James Giordano, Villanova University
Susan Glanz, St. John's University
Devra Golbe, Hunter College
Michael Goode, Central Piedmont Community College
Gene Gotwalt, Sweet Briar College
Glenn Graham, State University of New York—Oswego
David Gribbin, East Georgia College
Phil Grossman, St. Cloud State University
Marie Guest, North Florida Community College
J. Guo, Pace University
N. E. Hampton, St. Cloud State University
Deborah Hanson, University of Great Falls
Virden Harrison, Modesto Junior College
Fuad Hasanov, Oakland University
Scott Hegerty, University of Wisconsin—Milwaukee
Debra Hepler, Seton Hill College
Jim Henderson, Baylor University
Jeffrey Higgins, Sierra College
Jannett Highfill, Bradley University
Harold Hotelling, Lawrence Technological University
Wanda Hudson, Alabama Southern Community College
Terence Hunady, Bowling Green University
Mitchell Inman II, Savannah Technical College
Anisul Islam, University of Houston—Downtown
Eric Jamelske, University of Wisconsin—Eau Claire
Russell Janis, University of Massachusetts, Amherst
Andres Jauregui, Columbus State University
Jonathan Jelen, The City College of New York
George Jouganatos, California State University—Sacramento
David Kalist, Shippensburg University
Jonathan Kaplan, California State University—Sacramento
Nicholas Karatjas, Indiana University of Pennsylvania
Janis Kea, West Valley College
Deborah Kelly, Palomar College
Kathy Kemper, University of Texas—Arlington
Brian Kench, University of Tampa
Mariam Khawar, Elmira College
Young Jun Kim, Henderson State University
T. C. Kinnaman, Bucknell University
Paul Koch, Olivet Nazarene College
Andy Kohen, James Madison University
Lea Kosnik, University of Missouri—St. Louis
Charles Kroncke, College of Mount Saint Joseph
Craig Laker, Tri-State University
Carsten Lange, California Polytechnic State University—Pomona
Gary Langer, Roosevelt University
Leonard Lardaro, University of Rhode Island
Daniel Lawson, Drew University
Bill Lee, St. Mary's College
Mary Jane Lenon, Providence College
Mary Lesser, Iona College
Bozena Leven, The College of New Jersey
Ralph Lim, Sacred Heart University
Anthony Liuzzo, Wilkes University
Jennifer Logan, Southern Arkansas University
Dening Lohez, Pace University
Ellen Magenheim, Swarthmore College
Y. Lal Mahajan, Monmouth University
Mary Ellen Mallia, Siena College
Don Mathews, Coastal Georgia Community College
Phil Mayer, Three Rivers Community College
Norman Maynard, University of Oklahoma
Kimberly Mencken, Baylor University

John Messier, University of Maine, Farmington
Randy Methenitis, Richland College
Charles Meyer, Cerritos College
David Mitchell, Missouri State University
Ilir Miteza, University of Michigan—Dearborn
Jay Morris, Champlain College
Charles Myrick, Dyersburg State Community College
Natalie Nazarenko, State University of New York—Fredonia
Tim Nischan, Kentucky Christian University
Tom Odegaard, Baylor University
Jennifer Offenberg, Loyola Marymount University
Jack Peeples, Washtenaw Community College
Don Peppard, Connecticut College
Elizabeth Perry, Randolph-Macon Women's College
Dean Peterson, Seattle University
John Pharr, Cedar Valley College
Chris Phillips, Somerset Community College
Mary Pranzo, California State University—Fresno
Joseph Radding, Folsom Lake College
Jaishankar Raman, Valparaiso University
Donald Richards, Indiana State University
Bill Ridley, University of Oklahoma
William Rieber, Butler University
Dave Ring, State University of New York—Oneonta
Paul Robillard, Bristol Community College
Denise Robson, University of Wisconsin—Oshkosh
Rose Rubin, University of Memphis
Chris Ruebeck, Lafayette University
Randy Russell, Yavapai College
Marty Sabo, Community College of Denver
Hedayeh Samavati, Indiana University-Purdue University—Fort Wayne
Julia Sampson, Malone College
Paul Schoofs, Ripon College
Peter Schwarz, University of North Carolina—Charlotte
Paul Seidenstat, Temple University
T. M. Sell, Highline Community College
Chad Settle, University of Tulsa
Bill Seyfried, Rollins College
Maurice Shalishali, Columbus State
R. Calvin Shipley, Henderson State University
William Simeone, Providence College
Geok Simpson, University of Texas—Pan American
Noel Smith, Palm Beach Community College
Phil Smith, Georgia Perimeter College, Lawrenceville
Dennis Spector, Naugatuck Valley Community College
Todd Steen, Hope College
Richard Stratton, University of Akron
Stuart Strother, Azusa Pacific University
Martha Stuffler, Irvine Valley College
Boo Chun Su, Santa Monica Community College
Della Lee Sue, Marist College
Abdulhamid Sukar, Cameron University
Thomas Swanke, Chadron State College
Thomas Sweeney, Des Moines Area Community College
Michael Tansey, Rockhurst University
Henry Terrell, University of Maryland
Thomas Tiemann, Elon College
Dosse Toulaboe, Fort Hays State University
Christine Trees, State University of New York—Cobbleskill
Andrew Tucker, Tallahassee Community College
David Tufte, Southern Utah University
Jennifer VanGilder, Ursinus College
Yoav Wachsman, Coastal Carolina University
Craig Walker, Oklahoma Baptist University
Elizabeth Wark, Springfield College
Jonathan Warner, Dordt College
Roger White, Franklin & Marshall College
Jim Wollscheid, Texas A&M University—Kingsville
John Yarber, NE Mississippi Community College
Haichun Ye, University of Oklahoma
Anne York, Meredith College
Nazma Zaman, Providence College
Madeline Zavodny, Agnes Scott College

Fourth, I owe a special debt and want to give a special thanks to Eric Chiang of Florida Atlantic University and Greg Rose of Sacramento City College for their tireless examination of the page proofs to ensure accuracy. Together, they caught errors that none of us want to see. Thanks again!

Fifth, a huge debt of gratitude is owed to Tom Acox and the supplements authors. Tom coordinated the development of the supplements and our online presence. He did a remarkable job and was able to get some great people to author the supplements. They include Mary H. Lesser from Iona College who authored the Teaching Manual. Among other things, she did a wonderful job of adding real-world examples designed for use as student handouts. My thanks to Richard Croxdale from Austin Community College who coordinated the development of the Test Bank along with creating questions. Emil Berendt (Siena Heights University), Dennis Debrecht (Carroll College), Fred W. May (Trident Technical College), Tina A. Carter (Flagler College and University of Phoenix), Thomas Rhoads (Towson University), TaMika Steward (Tarrant County College), and Michael Fenick (Broward College) all contributed questions. Thanks to all of you for creating a Test Bank with nearly 9,000 questions.

Sixth, the production team at Worth is outstanding. My thanks to the entire team including Kevin Kall, Senior Designer, for a great set of interior and cover designs; Babs Reingold, the Art Director; Tracey Kuehn, Associate Managing Editor, Vivien Weiss, Project Editor, Susie Bothwell, Project Supervisor, and Barbara Anne Seixas, the Project Manager—all who made sure each part of the production process went smoothly. Thanks for a job well done.

I want to thank Charles Linsmeier, executive editor of economics, for his help and guidance. Thanks to Paul Shensa for his support and ideas on editorial changes and marketing; he is a valuable resource for any author. There is no way that I can thank Bruce Kaplan enough for what he has meant to this project and me. He has kept me focused and has suggested so many good ideas that I could fill several pages with his contributions. Thanks Bruce, you are the best!

You couldn't ask for a better marketing manager than Scott Guile. His enthusiasm is infectious and I appreciate the huge effort he has put into this project. Steven Rigolosi created an extensive pre-launch marketing review program that was very helpful at an important juncture of the text's development. Also I want to thank Tom Kling for helping sales reps see many of the benefits of this project. He is an incredible personality and I appreciate his efforts.

Finally, I am grateful to my wife, Sheila, for putting up with the forgone vacations given the demands a project like this requires. I hope it lives up to her expectations.

Gerald W. Stone

# Memorial

Worth Publishers regrets to inform you that Jerry Stone passed away after a difficult battle with cancer at the end of August 2010, as *CoreEconomics* and its accompanying *CourseTutor* were finishing up in the production process. Jerry Stone had a remarkable career as a longtime teacher at Metropolitan State College of Denver and as an author of two successful principles of economics textbooks. Those who knew Jerry will miss his steadfast commitment to the teaching of economics, a legacy that lives on in each new edition of *CoreEconomics*.

Jerry Stone long-believed that the best principles of economics textbooks are authored by people invested in their students' classroom experience. The decisions made in the shaping of the second edition were educated by Jerry's thirty-plus years in the classroom and by the team of instructors that contributed to every aspect of the media and supplements package. The second edition is Jerry's accomplishment: a book envisioned, designed, and executed to be the principles of economics book that teaches better than any other textbook on the market.

## A Look Ahead

In the months preceding his passing, Jerry was very conscious of ensuring a successful future for *CoreEconomics* at Worth. Earlier this year, Jerry and the economics team at Worth worked to find the perfect candidate to lead *CoreEconomics* in its subsequent editions. We found that person in Eric Chiang, associate professor of economics at Florida Atlantic University. Eric is a young, dynamic teacher, and a 2009 recipient of FAU's highest teaching honor, the Distinguished Teacher of the Year. He also received the Stewart Distinguished Professorship awarded by the College of Business, and has been a recipient of numerous other teaching awards. Eric embodies Jerry's belief that *CoreEconomics* should be a book written "by educators, for students." Eric is currently contributing two online chapters to the second edition—one on health care economics and another on the economics of network goods and services. He is also the lead academic on EconPortal, available with *CoreEconomics*, 2e, and he will assume all authorial responsibilities on the third edition of the textbook.

# Brief Contents

# Contents

# Production, Economic Growth, and Trade 2

# Supply and Demand 3

# 5 Elasticity

# Consumer Choice and Demand

# 7 Production and Cost

## 8 Competition



## 9 Monopoly

## 13 Public Goods, Externalities, and Environmental Economics

# 14 Poverty and Income Distribution

# Introduction to Macroeconomics 15

# Measuring Inflation and Unemployment 16

# Economic Growth 17



# Keynesian Macroeconomics 18

# Federal Deficits and Public Debt 21



# Money and the Financial System 22

# 25 International Trade

# Open Economy Macroeconomics 26

# Exploring Economics

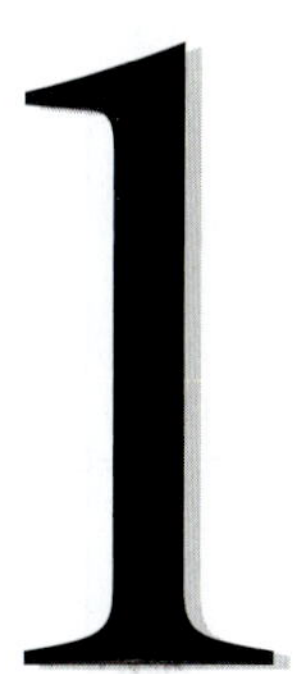

Jack Hollingsworth/Getty Images

**Ideas are important.** They change civilizations. Most of the world in the last half-century has renewed its interest in economic ideas. The two most recent U.S. presidential administrations (Bush and Obama) and the Federal Reserve have turned to ideas from the 1930s to provide policy guidance for the 2008–2009 financial crisis and subsequent recession. In 1936, British economist John Maynard Keynes created the field of macroeconomic analysis—analysis of the broad economy—and suggested the solution to the Great Depression. He argued that increased government spending and lower taxes were needed to replace falling consumer spending and declining business investment. Additional government spending was necessary to return the economy to its long-run trend of economic growth.

Why are governments so preoccupied with economic growth? Our level of economic growth today largely determines the standards of living for our children, and their children, and then their children.

How important is economic growth, really? To put this in perspective, let's conduct the following experiment. Today, our real gross domestic product (GDP; it represents all the goods and services produced annually) is roughly $15 trillion (that's a 15 with 12 zeros—a very big number). The United States has the largest economy in the world, with the European Union a close second. To see the importance of economic growth rates on our standard of living, let's assume that from 1930 to today our growth rate was just *1 percentage point less* every year. So, for example, if our economy grew at a 7% rate between 1953 and 1954, we will assume that it really only grew at a 6% rate.

Simply subtracting 1 percentage point from our growth rate every year over the last 80 years *would cut in half the size of our economy today.* Since we have removed the effects of

**After studying this chapter you should be able to:**

- ☐ Explain the scope of economics and economic analysis.
- ☐ Differentiate between microeconomics and macroeconomics.
- ☐ Describe how economists use models.
- ☐ Describe the *ceteris paribus* assumption.
- ☐ Discuss the difference between efficiency and equity.
- ☐ Describe the key ideas in economics.

inflation from our estimates, this small adjustment in economic growth rates each year would give us real (adjusted for inflation) aggregate income of roughly $7 trillion today—not the $15 trillion we actually have.

While real GDP for the total economy is not a perfect measure of our standard of living, real GDP per capita, a better measure, would also roughly be cut in half. So, toss out half your stuff and move to an apartment half the size you are in today. Note that we have *ignored* a bunch of complementary impacts like reduced education, as well as reduced research and development, that are closely associated with lower incomes. These impacts probably would have reduced these numbers and our standard of living even further. If we were to conduct this little experiment going back to the beginning of the century rather than from 1930, we would likely have the standard of living of Mexico today.

This calculation shows that economic growth makes the world a better place to live. This example leads to an obvious question: What causes economic growth? Why have some countries leaped ahead, while others have made little progress at all?

Economist John Kay[1] examined 19 highly productive countries with the highest living standards in the world. He found that they were distinguished from the other countries in the world by numerous complex relationships. Highly productive countries have the following characteristics:

- Most are democracies.
- Most have high environmental standards.
- Most have cool climates.
- Most enjoy freedom of expression.
- Women's rights and freedoms are better protected.
- Most enjoy better health.
- Population is taller.
- Government is less corrupt.
- Income inequality is lower.
- Inflation is lower.
- Population is more literate.
- Most have fewer restrictions on trade (more open).
- Population growth is lower.
- Property rights are more secure.

John Kay noted that "correlation does not imply causation." Some of these characteristics follow from a nation being more productive and rich; some, like literacy and health, help promote productivity. These are clearly complex relationships. As Jared Diamond[2] has argued, development in Europe and the United States benefited from immense luck with the weather and the types of flora and fauna native to those regions. Without all three, he argued, we would probably not have seen the high level of economic growth that has transpired.

This is why the structure of the society and the economy are so important, and why politicians and governments focus so much of their attention on economic issues. Economies do not develop overnight; it can take 50 years or more to produce modern living standards. For many countries of the world, even beginning today with the right economic programs and policies might mean it would not be until the end of this century before their living standards reach our standards of today. And by that time, much of the world will have moved on.

[1] John Kay, *The Truth About Markets: Their Genius, Their Limits, Their Follies* (London: Allen Lane), 2003, pp. 27–31. The highly productive countries are United States, Singapore, Switzerland, Norway, Canada, Denmark, Belgium, Japan, Austria, France, Hong Kong, Netherlands, Germany, United Kingdom, Finland, Italy, Australia, Sweden, and Ireland.

[2] Jared Diamond, *Guns, Germs, and Steel: The Fates of Human Societies* (New York: Norton), 1999.

## By the Numbers

# Economic Issues Are All Around Us

So much of what we do and the issues we face ultimately involve economics.

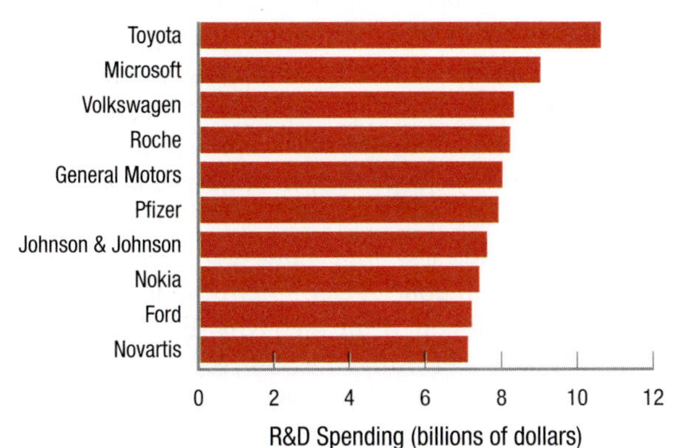


**New products come from research and development (R&D)** and carmakers and drug and technology firms spend the most on R&D. Half of the top 310 companies based on R&D spending are in the United States.

**25%**
Percent of all U.S. companies in the last decade founded by immigrants.

**403,000**
Estimate of the number of ATM machines in the United States

**Market Shares (%)**

| | 1960 | 2008 |
|---|---|---|
| Big Three | 85 | 45 |
| Others | 15 | 55 |

Ean Taylor/Illustration Works/Corbis

**The market share of America's Big Three automakers**—General Motors, Ford, and Chrysler—have fallen consistently and dramatically since 1960. Asian automakers have gained substantial ground, and Toyota now is the leading seller in America.

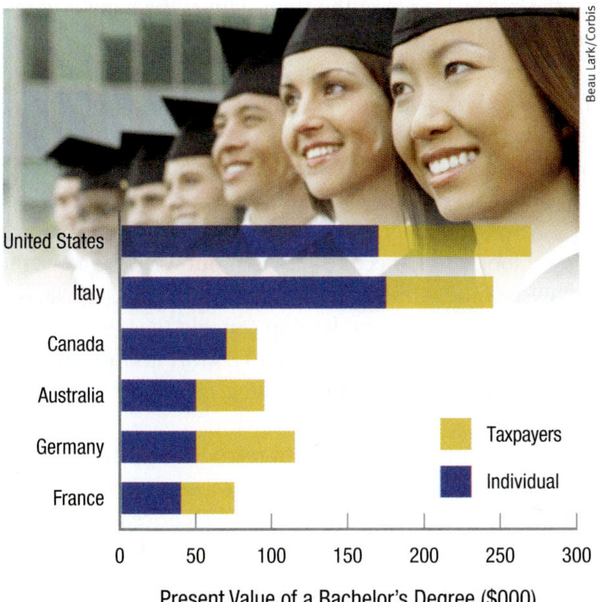


**A college degree** in the United States is worth over $250,000 on the day you graduate. This takes into account the added funds you get and what taxpayers receive in the form of higher tax payments over your working life. Graduates in other countries do not fare as well.

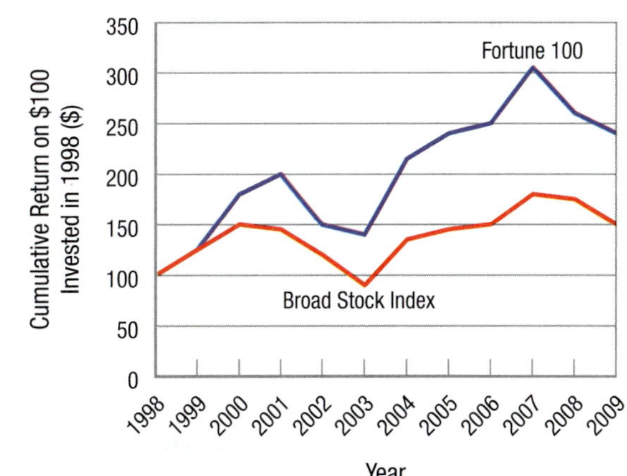


**Companies that are good to work for** are also good investments. Fortune magazine's top 100 firms to work for saw higher returns than a broad stock market index of all firms on the Nasdaq, New York Stock Exchange, and the American Stock Exchange.

**Sources:** Research and development spending: *The Economist*, 11-20-2009. Automobile market shares: *The Economist*, 4-30-2009. Companies founded by immigrants: *The Economist*, 3-13-2009. ATM machines: Business Week, 9-2009. Value of a college degree: *The Economist*, 9-8-2009. Companies that are good to work for: *The Economist*, 2-17-2009.

Today, many are concerned about outsourcing, globalization, and international trade. Look at this from an undeveloped country's point of view. These things can help them rise from abject poverty to attain modern living standards. After all, the United States was once underdeveloped, and trade with richer nations like France and Britain helped us develop.

Modern technologies and improvements in computing, transportation, and communications all are accelerating the development process. For example, cellular phone infrastructure is so much cheaper to install than the landline technology of the past. This has meant that developing nations can now get a state-of-the-art communications network at a fraction of the price that the United States paid to string telephone wires and lay cables over the last century. Future communications will undoubtedly be wireless, so many developing nations will be up to speed in a decade. We will see early in this book what countries can do to accelerate their economic growth.

This is the broad picture. Living standards are important, and economic growth improves living standards. Certain programs and policies can foster economic growth. So far, so good. But you are probably asking: What is in it for me? Why should I study economics if I am never going to be an economist? Probably the best reason is that you will spend roughly the next 40 years working in an economic environment. You will have a job; you will pay taxes; you will see the overall economy go from recession to a growth spurt and then maybe stagnate; you will have money to invest; and you will have to vote on economic issues affecting your locality, your region, and your country. It will benefit you to know how the economy works, what to expect in the future, and how to correct the economy's flaws.

But more than that—much more, in fact—economic analysis gives you a structure from which you can make decisions in a more rational manner. This course may well change the way you look at the world. It can open your eyes to how you make everyday decisions from what to buy to whom to marry. It may even make you reconsider your major.

Notice that we have just talked about economic analysis as a way of analyzing decisions that are not "economic" in the general sense of the term. This is the benefit of learning economic analysis. It can be applied all over the map. Sure, learning economic thinking may change your views on spending and saving, on how you feel about government deficits and public debt, and on your opinion of globalization and international trade. You may also reflect differently on environmental policies and what unions do. But you also may develop a different perspective on how much time to study each of your courses this term, or how much to eat at an all-you-can-eat buffet. Such is the broad scope of economic analysis.

In this introductory chapter, we look at what economics is about. We take a brief look at a key method of economic analysis: model building. Economists use stylized facts and the technique of holding some variables constant to develop testable theories about how consumers, businesses, and governments act. Second, we turn to a short discussion of some key principles of economics to give you a sense of the guiding concepts you will meet throughout this book.

The purpose of this introductory chapter is just that: an introduction. It seeks to give you a sense of what economics is, what concepts it uses, and what it finds to be important. Do not go into this chapter thinking you have to memorize these concepts. You will be given many opportunities to understand and use these concepts throughout this course. Rather, use this chapter to get a sense of the broad scope of economics. Then return to this chapter at the end of the course and see if everything has now become crystal clear.

## What Is Economics About?

Economics is a very broad subject, and often it seems that economics has something important to say about almost everything.

For example, economics has some important things to say about crime and punishment. On first glance, you might think we are talking about the cost of a prison system when we apply economic analysis here. But if we categorize economics as a way of thinking about how people make rational decisions, we can broaden the discussion. Economics considers criminals and potential criminals as rational people who follow their incentives. Criminals are concerned with getting caught and being punished: That is their cost. Longer prison sentences potentially raise the cost of committing a crime. Possibly more important than longer prison sentences is the probability of being convicted for an offense: A long sentence is not an effective deterrent if it is rarely used. This is why wounding or killing police officers is prosecuted aggressively and publicized: Potential criminals know they will pay a high cost if a police officer is harmed. Thus, economics looks at all of those factors that raise the cost of crime to criminals. Economics is a way of thinking about an issue, not just a discipline that has money as its chief focus.

Economists tend to have a rational take on nearly everything. Now all of this "analysis/speculation" may bring only limited insight in some cases, but it gives you some idea of how economists think. We look for rational responses to incentives. We begin most questions by considering how rational people would respond to the incentives that specific situations provide. Sometimes (maybe even often) this analysis leads us down an unexpected path.

## Microeconomics Versus Macroeconomics

Economics is split into two broad categories: microeconomics and macroeconomics. **Microeconomics** deals with decision making by individuals, business firms, industries, and governments. It is concerned with issues such as which orange juice you should buy, which job to take, and where to go on vacation; which products a business should produce and what price it should charge; and whether a market should be left on its own or be regulated.

Microeconomics: The decision making by individuals, businesses, industries, and governments.

We will see that markets—from flea markets to real estate markets to international currency markets—are usually efficient and promote competition. This is good for society. The opposite of competitive markets—monopoly, where one firm controls the market—leads to high prices, and it is bad for society. There is also a vast middle area between the extremes of competition and monopoly, and we will spend some time on those.

Microeconomics extends to such things as labor markets and environmental policy. Labor market analysis looks at both the supply (how much we as individuals are willing to work and at what wage) and demand (how much business is willing to hire and at what wage) of labor to determine market salaries. Designing policies to mitigate environmental damage uses the tools of microeconomics.

**Macroeconomics,** on the other hand, focuses on the broader issues we face as a nation. Most of us don't care whether an individual buys Nike or Merrell shoes. We *do* care whether prices of *all* goods and services rise. Inflation—a general increase in prices economy-wide—affects all of us. And as we have already seen, economic growth is a macroeconomic issue that affects everyone.

Macroeconomics: The broader issues in the economy such as inflation, unemployment, and national output of goods and services.

Macroeconomics uses microeconomic tools to answer some questions, but its main focus is on the broad aggregate variables of the economy. Macroeconomics has its own terms and topics: business cycles, recession, depression, unemployment, and job creation rates. Macroeconomics looks at policies that increase economic growth, the impact of government spending and taxation, the effect of monetary policy on the economy, and inflation. It also looks closely at theories of international trade and international finance. All of these topics have broad impacts on our economy and our standard of living.

Economics is a social science that uses many facts and figures to develop and express ideas. After all, economists try to explain the behavior of the economy and its participants. This inevitably involves facts and numbers. For macroeconomics, this means getting used to talking and thinking in huge numbers: billions (9 zeros) and trillions (12 zeros). Today we are talking about a federal government budget approaching $4 trillion. To wrap your mind around such a huge number, consider how long it would take to spend a trillion dollars if you spent a dollar every second, or $86,400 per day. To spend $1 trillion would require over 31,000 years. And the federal government now spends nearly 4 times that much in one year.

Although we break economics into microeconomics and macroeconomics, there is considerable overlap in the analysis. We use simple supply and demand analysis to understand both individual markets and the general economy as a whole. You will find yourself using concepts from microeconomics to understand fluctuations in the macroeconomy.

## Economic Theories and Reality

If you are like me, the first thing you do when you buy a book is flip through the pages to see what's inside. If the number of charts and graphs in this book, along with the limited number of equations, started to freak you out, relax. All of the charts and graphs become relatively easy to understand since they all basically read the same way. The few equations in this book stem from elementary algebra. Once you get through one equation, the rest are similar.

Graphs, charts, and equations are often the simplest and most efficient ways to express data and ideas. Simple equations are used to express relationships between two variables. Complex and wordy discussions can often be reduced to a simple graph or figure. These are efficient techniques for expressing economic ideas.

### Model Building

As you study economics this semester or quarter, you will encounter stylized approaches to a number of issues. By *stylized,* we mean that economists boil down facts to their basic relevant elements and use assumptions to develop a stylized (simple) model to analyze the issue. While there are always situations that lie outside these models, they are the exception. Economists generalize about economic behavior and reach generally applicable results.

We begin with relatively simple models, then gradually build in more difficult issues. For example, in the next chapter we introduce one of the simplest models in economics, the production possibilities frontier that illustrates the limits of economic activity. This simple model has profound implications for the issue of economic growth. We can add in more dimensions and make the model more complex, but often this complexity does not provide any greater insight than the simple model.

### *Ceteris Paribus:* All Else Held Constant

*Ceteris paribus:* Assumption used in economics (and other disciplines as well), where other relevant factors or variables are held constant.

To aid in our model building, economists use the ***ceteris paribus*** assumption: "Holding all other things equal" means we will hold some important variables constant. For example, to determine how many songs you might be willing to download from iTunes in any given month, we would hold your monthly income constant. We then would change song prices to see the impact on the number purchased (again holding your monthly income constant).

Though model building can lead to surprising insights into how economic actors and economies behave, it is not the end of the story. Economic insights lead to economic theories, but these theories must then be tested. We will see many instances where economic predictions turned out to be false. One of the major errors was the classical notion that economy-wide contractions would be of short duration. The Great Depression that lasted a decade turned this notion on its head. New models were then developed to explain what had happened. So it may be best to think of model building as a *process* of understanding economic actors and the general economy: Models are created and then tested; if they fail to explain reality, new models are constructed. Some models have met the test of time. Others have had to be corrected or discarded. Progress, however, has been made.

## Efficiency Versus Equity

Efficiency: How well resources are used and allocated. Do people get the goods and services they want at the lowest possible resource cost? This is the chief focus of efficiency.

**Efficiency** deals with how well resources are used and allocated. No one likes waste. Much of economic analysis is directed toward ensuring that the most efficient outcomes result from public policy. *Production efficiency* occurs when goods are produced at the lowest possible cost, and *allocative efficiency* occurs when individuals who desire a product the most (as measured by their willingness to pay) get those goods and services. It would not make sense for society to allocate to me a large amount of cranberry sauce—I would not eat the stuff. Efficient policies are generally good policies.

The other side of the coin is **equity,** or fairness. Is it fair that the CEOs of large companies make hundreds of times more money than rank-and-file workers? Many think not. Is it fair that some have so much and others have so little? Again, many think not. There are many divergent views about fairness until we get to extreme cases. When just a few people earn nearly all of the income and control nearly all of a society's wealth, most people agree that this is unfair.

**Equity:** The fairness of various issues and policies.

Throughout this course you will see instances where efficiency and equity collide. You may agree that a specific policy is efficient, but think it is unfair to some group of people. This will be especially evident when you consider tax policy and its impact on income distribution. Fairness or equity is a subjective concept, and each of us has different ideas about what is just and fair. Economists generally stay out of discussions about fairness, leaving that issue to philosophers and politicians. When it comes to public policy issues, economics will help you see the tradeoffs between equity and efficiency, but you will ultimately have to make up your own mind about the wisdom of the policy given these tradeoffs.

**CHECKPOINT**

### WHAT IS ECONOMICS ABOUT?

- Economics is separated into two broad categories: microeconomics and macroeconomics.
- *Microeconomics* deals with individuals, firms, and industries and how they make decisions.
- *Macroeconomics* focuses on broader economic issues such as inflation, employment and unemployment, and economic growth.
- Economics uses a stylized approach, creating simple models that hold all other relevant factors constant (*ceteris paribus*).
- Economists and policymakers often face a tradeoff between efficiency and equity. Economists have much to say about efficiency.

**QUESTION:** In each of the following situations, determine whether it is a microeconomic or macroeconomic issue.

1. Hewlett-Packard announces that it is lowering the price of printers by 15%.
2. The president proposes a tax cut.
3. You decide to look for a new job.
4. The economy is in a recession, and the job market is bad.
5. The Federal Reserve announces that it is raising interest rates because it fears inflation.
6. You get a nice raise.
7. Average wages grew by 2% last year.

Answers to the Checkpoint questions can be found at the end of this chapter.

## Key Ideas of Economics

Economics has a set of key principles that show up continually in economic analysis. Some are more restricted to specific issues, but most apply universally. As mentioned earlier, these principles should give you a sense of what you will learn in this course. Do not try to memorize these principles at this juncture. Rather, read through them now, and return to them later in the course to assess your progress. By the end of this course, these key principles should be crystal clear.

## Choice and Scarcity Force Tradeoffs

Wouldn't it be grand if we all had the resources of Bill Gates or if nanotechnology developed to the point where any product could be made with sand and thus was virtually costless? But we don't, and it hasn't, so back to reality.

We all have limited resources. Some of us are more limited than others, but each of us has time limitations: There are only 24 hours in a day, and some of that must be spent in sleep. Our wants are always greater than our resources. Therefore, we face **scarcity.**

**Scarcity:** Our unlimited wants clash with limited resources, leading to scarcity. Everyone faces scarcity (rich and poor) because, at a minimum, our time is limited on earth. Economics focuses on the allocation of scarce resources to satisfy unlimited wants.

The fact that we have limited resources (scarcity) means that we must make tradeoffs in nearly everything we do. In fact, *economics is often defined as the study of the allocation of scarce resources to competing wants.* We have to decide between alternatives.

Such decisions as which car to buy, which school to attend (this may be constrained by factors other than money), and whether to study or party all involve tradeoffs. We cannot do everything we would like if for no other reason than our time on earth is limited.

## Opportunity Costs Dominate Our Lives

Economics is often categorized as the discipline that always weighs benefits against costs. This is straightforward enough. What makes this task harder is that if we undertake to do one activity, some other highly valued activity must be given up, a special concept economists use called **opportunity costs.** For example, when you wait hours in line to buy a concert ticket and then attend the concert, your total costs are your time in line *plus* the price of the ticket *plus* your time at the concert. That time and money could have been spent on another highly valued activity. Economists refer to these total costs (hours in line plus ticket price plus time at concert) as opportunity costs.

**Opportunity costs:** The next best alternative; what you give up to do something or purchase something. For example, to watch a movie at a theater, there is not just the monetary cost of the tickets and refreshments, but the time involved in watching the movie. You could have been doing something else (knitting, golfing, hiking, or studying economics).

We have limited resources. College students have limited budgets. Say we can purchase that new music CD we want or have ice cream for a week, but not both. Ice cream for a week is the opportunity cost of purchasing that music CD.

Every activity we do involves opportunity costs. Sleeping, eating, studying, partying, running, hiking, and so on, all require that we spend resources that could be used in another activity. This other activity represents the opportunity costs of the current activity chosen. Opportunity costs apply to us as individuals and to societies as a whole. The next chapter focuses on this issue in detail.

## *Issue:* Do Hummingbirds Make Good Economists?

**Black-chinned** hummingbirds found in the Sonoran desert of Arizona are models of economy when it comes to battling for territory and resources. Nectar feeders on flowers of the saguaro cactus, they defend a feeding territory against other hummingbirds by vocalizations and aerial combat against intruders. But as John Alcock has noted, "No knee-jerk aggressiveness for them; they want a payoff, and they somehow know when fighting is counterproductive."

Studies by researchers have shown that these hummingbirds are extremely sensitive to the cost and benefits of defending a nectar territory. They will fiercely defend a rich source and significantly reduce their efforts for a less ideal territory. Even juveniles who would normally be at a disadvantage against adults will be sufficiently aggressive to successfully defend a nectar-rich territory.

The birds use vocalization (chatter) to both defend and signal to others their willingness to defend their territories, and they conduct aerial duels with their dagger-like bills. Defending nectar-rich territories involves noisier and longer aerial combat than in less favorable territory. According to Alcock, "hummingbirds chatter and squeak in their hot-blooded struggle, fashioning an aerial ballet based on cold-blooded economics."

Arthur Morris/Corbis

Source: John Alcock, *Sonoran Desert Summer* (Tucson: The University of Arizona Press), 1990.

## Rational Behavior Requires Thinking at the Margin

Have you ever noticed that when you eat at an all-you-can-eat buffet, you always go away fuller than when you order and eat at a normal restaurant? Is this phenomenon unique to you, or is there something more fundamental? Remember, economists look at facts to find incentives to economic behavior.

In this case, people are just rationally responding to the price of *additional* food. They are thinking at the margin. In a restaurant, dessert costs extra, and you make a decision as to whether the dessert is worth the extra cost. At the buffet, dessert is free. So now you don't have to ask yourself if dessert is worth the extra money since it costs nothing. Where you might be nearly full and decline dessert in a restaurant, you will often have dessert in the buffet even if you are stuffed afterwards.

Throughout this book, we will see examples of thinking at the margin. Businesses use marginal analysis to determine how much of their products they are willing to supply to the market. People use marginal analysis to determine how many hours to work. And governments use marginal analysis to determine how much pollution should be permitted.

## People Follow Incentives

Tax policy rests on the idea that people follow their incentives. Do we want to encourage people to save for their retirement? Then let them deduct a certain amount that they can put in an individual retirement account (IRA), and let this money compound tax free. Do we want businesses to spend more to stimulate the economy? Then give them tax credits for new investment. Do we want people to go to college? Then give them tax advantages for setting up education savings accounts when their children are young, and provide tuition tax credits.

Tax policy is an obvious example in which people follow incentives. But this principle can be seen in action wherever you look. Want to encourage people to use commuter trains during non-rush-hour times? Provide an off-peak discount. Want to spread out the dining time at restaurants? Give Early-Bird Special discounts for those willing to consider a 5:00 P.M. dinner time slot rather than the more popular 8:00 P.M. slot. Want to fill up airplanes during the slow travel days of Tuesday and Wednesday? Offer price discounts or additional frequent flyer miles for flying on those days.

Note that in saying that people follow incentives, economists do not claim that everyone follows each incentive at every time. You may not want to eat dinner at 4:30 P.M. But there might be a sufficient number of people who are willing to accept an earlier time slot in return for a cheaper meal.

If not properly constructed, incentives may not work to our economy's advantage. In the recent financial crisis, it became clear that the incentives for executives and traders set by Wall Street investment banks were perverse. Traders and executives were paid bonuses based on short-term (annual) profits. This encouraged them to take extreme risks to generate quick profits and high bonuses with little regard for the long-term viability of the bank. The bank may be gone tomorrow, but these people still have those huge (often seven-figure) bonuses.

## Markets Are Efficient

Private markets and the incentives they provide are the best mechanisms known today for providing products and services. There is no government food board that makes sure that bread, cereal, coffee, and all the other food products you demand are on your plate during the day. The vast majority of products we consume are privately provided, assuming, of course, that we have the money to pay for them.

Markets bring buyers and sellers together. Competition for the consumer dollar forces firms to provide products at the lowest possible price, or some other firm will undercut their high price. New products enter the market and old products die out. Such is the dynamic characteristic of markets. Starbucks has made latte drinkers of us all, whereas just a short time ago, few of us could even spell the word.

What drives and disciplines markets? Prices and profits are the keys. Profits drive entrepreneurs to provide new products (think of pharmaceutical firms or Apple) or existing products at lower prices (think of Wal-Mart). When prices and profits get too high in any market, new firms jump in with lower prices to grab away customers. This competition, or sometimes even the threat of competition, keeps markets from exploiting consumers.

## Government Must Deal With Market Failure

As efficient as markets usually are, there are some classes of products and services that markets fail to provide efficiently. Where consumers have no choice but to buy from one firm (local utility, telephone, or cable companies), the market will fail to provide the best solution, and government regulation is often used to protect consumers. Another example is pollution: Left on their own, companies will pollute the air and water—we will see why later in this book. Governments then intervene to deal with this market failure.

## Information Is Important

Markets are efficient because people tend to make rational choices. To help make these choices, people rely on information. Each of us has to decide when we have enough information: Complete information may not be possible to obtain, and too much information can be debilitating. Some decisions require little information: What brand of table salt should you buy? Other decisions require more information: What type of automobile should you buy? Information is valuable.

Strange things happen to markets when one side of a transaction has a consistently superior information advantage. Martha Stewart was convicted of lying about selling stock based on inside information. The top officials of a business know much more quickly than anyone else if their company is developing business problems. These problems might lead to a fall in the price of the company's stock. If the officials act on this inside information while it is still secret, they can sell their stock before the price dips. This information gives them an unfair advantage over the other stockholders or people who may want to own the stock. This is why there are laws preventing insiders from taking undue advantage of their privileged position.

Markets work best when both sides of a transaction can weigh carefully the costs and benefits of goods and services. Superior information can provide significant advantages. We will see what markets can do to correct for information problems, and what government can do when the market cannot provide an acceptable solution.

## Specialization and Trade Improve Our Lives

Trading with other countries leads to better products for consumers at lower prices. David Ricardo laid out the rationale for international trade almost two centuries ago, and it still holds true today. We will expand on this in the next chapter.

As you will learn, economies grow by producing those products where they have an advantage over other countries. This is why few of us grow our own food, sew our own clothes, make our own furniture, or write the books we read. We do those things we do best and let others do the same. In nearly all instances, they are able to do it cheaper than we can. The next time you come back from a shopping trip, look closely to discover where every product was made. More than likely, over half will have come from another country.

## Productivity Determines Our Standard of Living

*You can see the computer age everywhere but in the productivity statistics.*

ROBERT SOLOW

*If you want jobs for jobs' sake, trade in bulldozers for shovels. If that doesn't create enough jobs, replace shovels with spoons. Heresy! But there will always be more work to do than people to work. So instead of counting jobs, we should make every job count.*

ROBERT MCTEER, JR.[3]

[3] Past president of the Federal Reserve Bank of Dallas.

## Adam Smith (1723–1790)

When Adam Smith was a four year-old boy, he was kidnapped by gypsies and held for ransom. Had the gypsies not taken fright and returned the boy unharmed, the history of economics might well have turned out differently.

Born in Kirkaldy, Scotland in 1723, Smith graduated from the University of Glasgow at age 17 and was awarded a scholarship to Oxford—time he considered to be largely wasted. As he so succinctly put it, "professors have, for these many years, given up altogether even the pretense of teaching". Returning to Scotland in 1751, Smith was named Professor of Moral Philosophy at the University of Glasgow. His health from an early age was never good. He suffered from a "shaking in the head", was notoriously absent-minded, had an unusual walk (wavy, worm-like). Rising early, he began his daily lectures at 7:30am and these lectures were well liked and well attended.

After twelve years at Glasgow, Smith, who never married, began tutoring the son of a wealthy Scottish nobleman. This job provided him with a life-long income, as well as the opportunity to spend several years touring the European continent with his young charge. In Paris, Smith met some of the leading French economists of the day, which helped stoke his own interest in political economy. While there, he wrote a friend, "I have begun to write a book in order to pass the time."

Returning to Kirkaldy in 1766, Smith spent the next decade finishing *An Inquiry Into the Nature and Causes of the Wealth of Nations.* Before publication in 1776, he read sections of the text to Benjamin Franklin. Smith's genius was in taking the disparate forms of economic analysis his contemporaries were then developing and putting them together in systematic and comprehensive fashion, thereby making sense of the national economy as a whole. Smith further demonstrated numerous ways in which individuals left free to pursue their own economic interests end up acting in ways that enhance the welfare of all. This is Smith's famous "invisible hand." In Smith's words: "By directing that industry in such a manner as its produce may be of the greatest value, he intends only his own gain, and he is in this, as in many other cases, led by an invisible hand to promote an end which was no part of his intention."

How important was Adam Smith? He has been called the "father of political economy", but that is inadequate. As Wilhelm Roscher has argued, ". . . the whole of political economy might be divided into two parts—before and since Adam Smith; the first part being a prelude and the second a sequel (in the way either of continuation or opposition to him)."

Sources: Howard Marshall, *The Great Economists: A History of Economic Thought,* (New York: Pitman Publishing Corporation), 1967; Paul Strathern, *A brief History of Economic Genius,* (New York: Texere), 2002; Ian Ross, *The Life of Adam Smith,* (Oxford: Clarendon Press), 1995.

Imagine you need to hire someone in your own business (you've finished college and you are now an entrepreneur). You have narrowed the field down to two candidates who are equal in all respects except two. One person can do twice as much as the other (assume you can accurately measure these things), and this same person wants a salary that is 50% higher. Other than that they are equal. Whom should you hire?

The answer is obvious in this situation, because the more productive person is actually the best buy since she produces twice as much as the other candidate, but only wants half again as much pay. In this case, you would be willing to pay even more to get this person. Productivity and pay go together. Highly paid movie stars get high pay because they are worth it to the movie producer. The same is true of professional athletes, corporate executives, rocket scientists, and heart surgeons.

The same is true for nations. Those countries with the highest average per capita income are also the most productive. Their labor forces are highly skilled, and firms are willing to place huge amounts of capital with these workforces because this results in immense productivity. In turn, these workers earn high wages. So, high productivity growth results in solid economic growth, high wages and income, and large investments in education and research. All of this leads to higher standards of living.

### Government Can Smooth the Fluctuations in the Overall Economy

All of us have heard of recessions and depressions. These terms refer to downturns in the general economy. The general movement of the economy from good times to bad and back again is called the business cycle.

Early economists viewed the overall economy as a self-correcting mechanism that would quickly adjust to disturbances in the business cycle if only it was left to itself. Along came the Great Depression of the 1930s, which showed that the overall economy could get stuck in a downturn. The solution was government intervention. Just as government can intervene successfully in individual markets when market failure occurs, so too can government intervene successfully when the overall economy gets stuck in a downturn. You can observe this principle at work when you hear discussions of using increased government spending or a tax cut to pull an economy out of a recession.

The intricacies of what government can do to smooth out the business cycle are a major part of your study of macroeconomics. Remember, saying the government *can* successfully intervene does not mean it *always* successfully intervenes. The macroeconomy is not a simple machine. Successful policymaking is a tough task.

You will learn more about these important ideas as the semester progresses. For now, realize that economics rests on the foundation of a limited number of important concepts.

**CHECKPOINT**

KEY IDEAS OF ECONOMICS

- Choice and scarcity force tradeoffs.
- Opportunity costs dominate our lives.
- Rational behavior requires thinking at the margin.
- People follow incentives.
- Markets are efficient.
- Government must deal with market failure.
- Information is important.
- Specialization and trade improve our lives.
- Productivity determines our standard of living.
- Government can smooth the fluctuations in the overall economy.

**QUESTION:** McDonald's introduced a premium blend of coffee that sells for more than its standard coffee. How does this represent thinking at the margin?

Answers to the Checkpoint question can be found at the end of this chapter.

## Key Concepts

Microeconomics, p. 5
Macroeconomics, p. 5
*Ceteris paribus*, p. 6
Efficiency, p. 6
Equity, p. 7
Scarcity, p. 8
Opportunity costs, p. 8

## Chapter Summary

### What Is Economics About?

Economic analysis can be usefully applied to topics as diverse as how businesses make decisions, how college students allocate their time between studying and relaxing, and how government deals with electric utilities that pollute nearby rivers.

Economics is separated into two broad categories: microeconomics and macroeconomics. *Microeconomics* deals with individual, firm, industry, and public decision making.

*Macroeconomics,* on the other hand, focuses on the broader economic issues confronting the nation. Issues such as inflation (a general increase in prices economy-wide), employment and unemployment, and economic growth affect all of us.

Economics uses a *stylized* approach to a number of issues. Stylized models boil issues and facts down to their basic relevant elements. To build models means that we make use of the *ceteris paribus* assumption and hold some important variables constant. This useful device often provides surprising insights about economic behavior.

Economists and policymakers often confront the tradeoff between efficiency and equity. Efficiency reflects how well resources are used and allocated. Equity (or fairness) of an outcome is a subjective matter; there are differences of opinion about fairness except in extreme cases where people tend to come to a general agreement. Economics illuminates the tradeoffs between equity and efficiency.

## Key Ideas of Economics

1. Choice and scarcity force tradeoffs because we face limited resources and limitless wants. We must make tradeoffs in nearly everything we do. Economics is often defined as the study of the allocation of scarce resources to competing wants.
2. Opportunity costs—resources (e.g., time and money) that could be used in another activity—dominate our lives. Everything we do involves opportunity costs.
3. Rational behavior requires thinking at the margin.
4. People follow incentives.
5. Markets are efficient. Markets bring buyers and sellers together. Competition forces firms to provide products at the lowest possible price, or some other firm will undercut the price. New products are introduced to the market and old products disappear. This dynamism makes markets efficient.
6. Government must deal with market failure. Though markets are usually efficient, there are recognized times when they are not. Pollution is an example.
7. Information is important. Superior information gives economic actors a decided advantage. Sometimes information advantages can result in dysfunctional markets.
8. Specialization and trade improve our lives. Trading leads to better products at lower prices. Economies grow by producing those products where they have an advantage over other countries.
9. Productivity determines our standard of living. Countries with the highest average per capita income are also the most productive.
10. Government can smooth the fluctuations in the overall economy.

# Questions and Problems

## Check Your Understanding

1. Does your going to college have anything to do with expanding choices or reducing scarcity? Explain.
2. You normally stay at home on Wednesday nights and study. Next Wednesday night, the college is having a free concert on the main campus. What is the opportunity cost of going to the free concert?

## Apply the Concepts

3. Gregg Easterbrook, in his book *The Progress Paradox* (New York: Random House, 2003), noted that life in the United States is significantly better today than in the past and provided many statistical facts, including:
   a. Nearly a quarter of households (or 60+ million people) have incomes of at least $75,000 a year.
   b. Real (inflation adjusted) per capita income has more than doubled since 1960—people on average have twice the real purchasing power now as in 1960.
   c. In 1956, the typical American had to work 16 weeks for each 100 square feet of new housing. Today that number is 14 weeks, and new houses are considerably more luxurious.
   d. The United States accepts more legal immigrants than all other nations of the world combined.

e. The quality of health care improved substantially over the last half-century, and life spans have grown dramatically.

This is just a sampling of the improvements in living standards Easterbrook catalogued. However, his book is subtitled *How Life Gets Better While People Feel Worse*, and this is a paradox he set out to explain. What reasons might explain why even though our lives have improved, people feel that life was better in an earlier time?

4. In 2001 Nobel Prize winner Robert Solow noted that "the computer age is seen everywhere except in productivity data." More recent studies suggest that it takes roughly seven years for investment in computers to have an impact on productivity. Why do you think this is the case?
5. In contrasting equity and efficiency, why do high-tech firms seem to treat their employees better (better wages, benefits, working environments, vacations, etc.) compared to how landscaping or fast-food franchises treat their employees? Is this fair? Is it efficient?
6. People talk about a big fall in the housing market. Who specifically is hurt by this fall? Consider real-estate agents, current homeowners, home builders, banks or financing institutions, and newly married couples who want to buy a home. Now consider what happens if the economy is booming. What happens to these groups?
7. In 2006 the Nobel Peace Prize went to economist Muhammad Yunus and the Grameen Bank "for their efforts to create economic and social development from below." Yunus led the development of micro loans to poor people without financial security: loans of under $200 to people so poor they could not provide collateral, to use for purchasing basic tools or other basic implements of work. This helped to pull millions of people out of poverty. Discuss how economic prosperity and security for everyone can result in a more peaceful planet.

### In the News

8. *The Wall Street Journal* recently noted that bachelor's degrees in economics were up 40% between 1999 and 2004: "There is a clear explosion in economics as a major," and "the number of students majoring in economics has been rising even faster at top colleges." What might be some reasons for this now? (Jessica E. Vascellaro, "The Hot Major for Undergrads Is Economics," *Wall Street Journal*, July 5, 2005, p. A11.)

### Solving Problems

9. The black rhinoceros is extremely endangered. Its horn is considered a powerful aphrodisiac in many Asian countries, and a single horn fetches many thousands of dollars on the black market, creating a great incentive for poachers. Unlike other stories of endangered species, this one might have a simple solution. Conservationists could simply capture as many rhinos as possible and remove their horns, reducing the incentive to poach. Do you think this will help reduce poaching? Why or why not?
10. With higher gasoline prices, the U.S. government wants people to buy more hybrid cars that use much less gasoline. Unfortunately, hybrids are approximately $4,000 to $5,000 more expensive to purchase than comparable cars. If people follow incentives, what can the government do to encourage the purchase of hybrids?
11. The By the Numbers box suggests that the stocks of companies that are good to work for (such as Google, Cisco, Genentech, Goldman Sachs, and Adobe) also tend to outperform general stock market averages. What factors or characteristics of these companies might account for their stellar stock market performance?

## Answers to Questions in CheckPoints

### Check Point: What Is Economics About?

(1) microeconomics, (2) macroeconomics, (3) microeconomics, (4) macroeconomics, (5) macroeconomics, (6) microeconomics, (7) macroeconomics.

### Check Point: Key Ideas of Economics

McDonald's is adding one more product (premium coffee) to its line. Thinking at the margin entails thinking about how you can improve an operation (or increase profits) by adding to your existing product line or reducing costs.

# Appendix: Working With Graphs and Formulas

**You can't watch the news on** television or read the newspaper without looking at a graph of some sort. If you have flipped through this book, you have seen a large number of graphs, charts, and tables, and a few simple equations. This is the language of economics. Economists deal with data for all types of issues. Just looking at data in tables often doesn't help you discern the trends or relationships in the data.

Economists develop theories and models to explain economic behavior and levels of economic activity. These theories or models are simplified representations of real-world activity. Models are designed to distill the most important relationships between variables, and then these relationships are used to predict future behavior of individuals, firms, and industries, or to predict the future course of the overall economy.

In this short section, we will explore the different types of graphs you are likely to see in this course (and in the media) and then turn to an examination of how graphs are used to develop and illustrate models. This second topic leads us into a discussion of modeling relationships between data and how to represent these relationships with simple graphs and equations.

## Graphs and Data

The main forms of graphs of data are time series, scatter plots, pie charts, and bar charts. Time series, as the name suggests, plots data over time. Most of the figures you will encounter in publications are time series graphs.

### Time Series

Time series graphs involve plotting time (minutes, hours, days, months, quarters, or years) on the horizontal axis and the value of some variable on the vertical axis. Figure APX-1 on the next page illustrates a time series plot for civilian employment of those 16 years and older. Notice that since the early 1990s, employment has grown by almost 20 million for this group. The vertical strips in the figure designate the last two recessions. Notice that in both cases when the recession hit, employment fell, then rebounded after the recession ended.

### Scatter Plots

Scatter plots are graphs where two variables (neither variable is time) are plotted against each other. Scatter plots often give us a hint if the two variables are related to each other in some consistent way. Figure APX-2 on the next page plots one variable, the number of strikes, against another variable, union membership as a percent of total employment.

Two things can be seen in this figure. First, these two variables appear to be related to each other in a positive way. A rising union membership as a percent of employment leads

**After studying this appendix you should be able to:**

- ☐ Describe the four simple forms of data graphs.
- ☐ Make use of a straightforward approach to reading graphs.
- ☐ Read linear and nonlinear graphs and know how to compute their slopes.
- ☐ Use simple linear equations to describe a line and a shift in the line.
- ☐ Explain why correlation is not the same as causation.

**FIGURE APX-1—Civilian Employment, 16 Years and Older**

This time series graph shows the number of civilians 16 years and older employed in the United States since 1990. Employment has grown steadily over this period, except in times of recession, indicated by the vertical strips. Note that employment fell during the recession, and then bounced back after each recession ended.

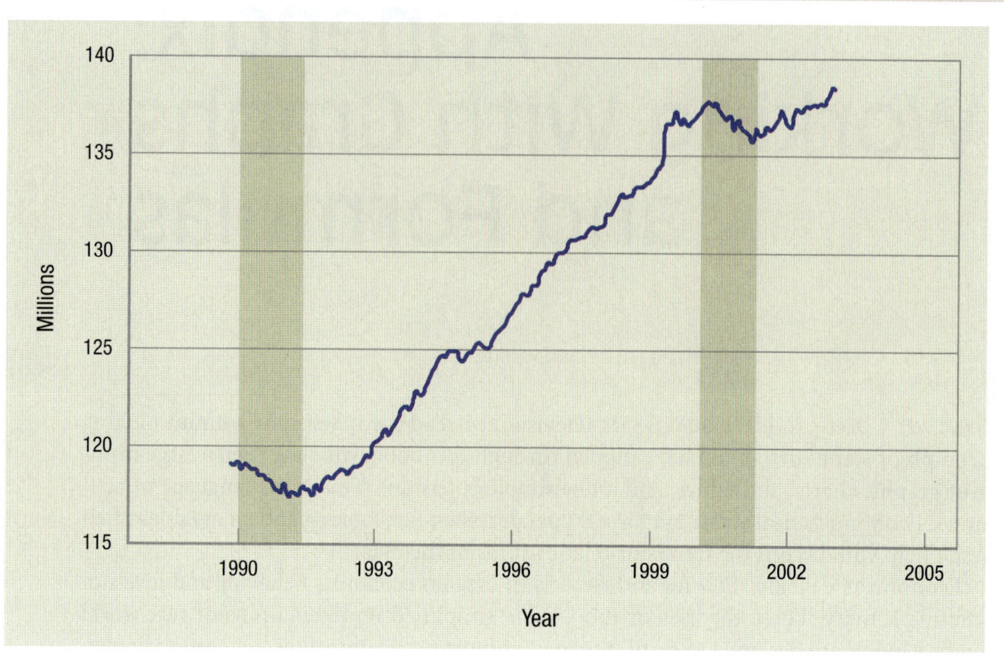


to a greater number of strikes. It is not surprising that greater union membership and more strikes are related, because greater union membership means more employees are covered by collective bargaining agreements, and thus we would expect more strikes. Also, greater union membership means that unions would be more powerful, and strikes represent a use of this power. Second, given that the years for the data are listed next to the dots, we can see that union representation as a percent of total employment has fallen significantly over the last half century. From this simple scatter plot, we get a lot of information and ideas about how the two variables are related.

**FIGURE APX-2—The Relationship Between the Number of Strikes and Union Membership as a Percent of Total Employment**

This scatter diagram plots the relationship between the number of strikes and union membership as a percent of total employment. The number of strikes increased as union membership became a larger percentage of those employed. Note that union membership as a percentage of those employed has fallen in the last half century.

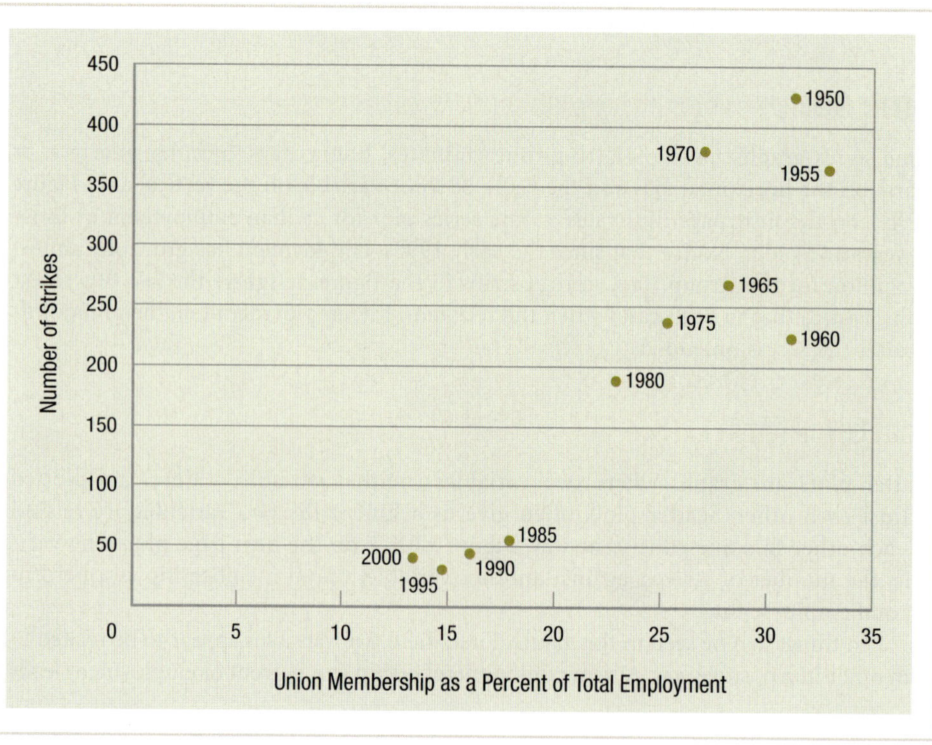

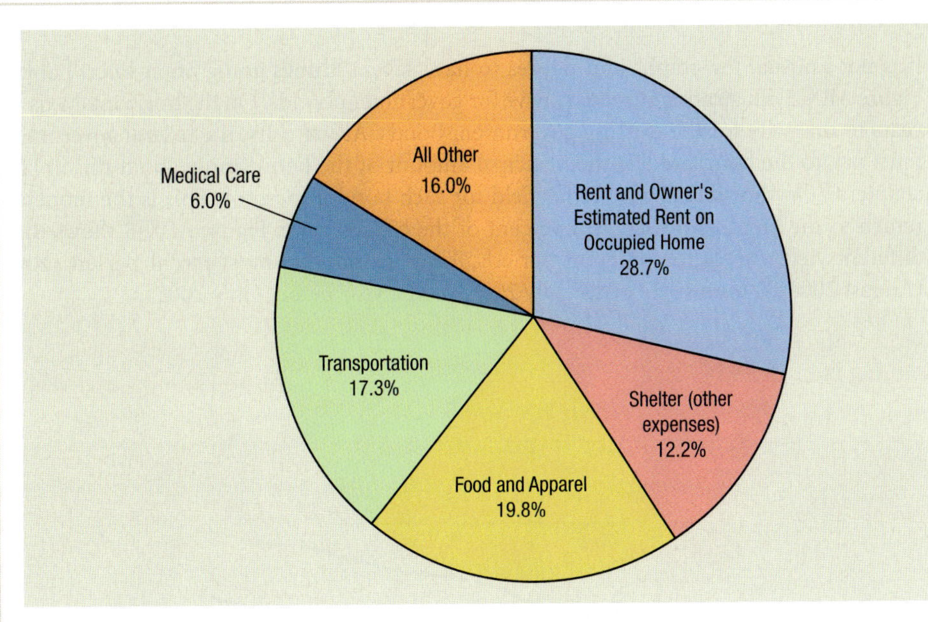


**FIGURE APX-3—Relative Importance of Consumer Price Index (CPI) Components (2003)**

This pie chart shows the relative importance of the components of the consumer price index, showing how typical urban households spend their income.

## Pie Charts

Pie charts are simple graphs that show data that can be split into percentage parts that combined make up the whole. A simple pie chart for the relative importance of components in the consumer price index (CPI) is shown in Figure APX-3. It reveals how the typical urban household budget is allocated. By looking at each slice of the pie, we get a picture of how typical families spend their income.

## Bar Charts

Bar charts use bars to show the value of specific data points. Figure APX-4 is a simple bar chart showing the annual changes in real (adjusted for inflation) gross domestic product (GDP). Notice that over the last 40+ years the United States has had only 5 years when GDP declined.

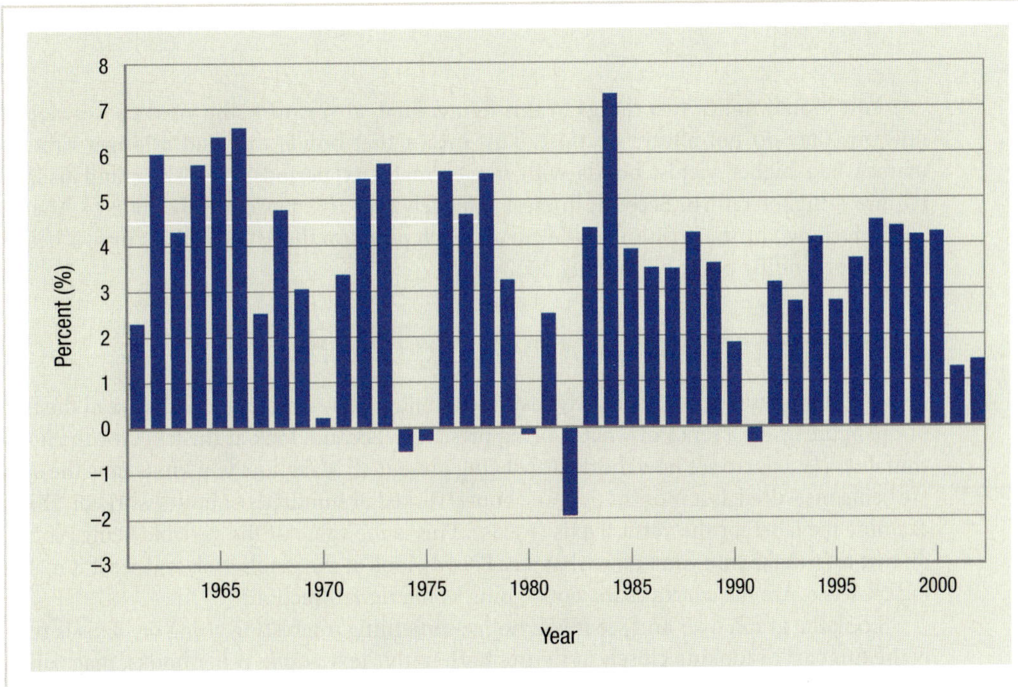


**FIGURE APX-4—Percent Change in Real (Inflation Adjusted) GDP**

This bar chart shows the annual percent change in real (adjusted for inflation) gross domestic product (GDP) over the last 40 years. Over this period, GDP has declined only five times.

## Simple Graphs Can Pack In a Lot of Information

It is not unusual for graphs and figures to have several things going on at once. Look at Figure APX-5, illustrating the yield curve for government bonds. On the horizontal axis are years to maturity for the existing government bonds. At maturity, the federal government must pay to the bond holders the principal amount of the bond (more about this in later chapters). On the vertical axis is the yield for each bond in percent. This is the monetary return to the bond expressed as a percent of the bond's price. Figure APX-5 shows three different yield curves for different periods. They include the most recent period shown (August 2003), a month previous (July 2003), and a year before (July 2002).

**FIGURE APX-5—Yield Curve**

This yield curve for government bonds shows that interest rates fell between the middle of 2002 and the middle of 2003, shown by each point on the August 2003 curve being below the corresponding point on the July 2002 curve. Also, this figure shows that the yield (rate of return) for each bond grew as the time to maturity grew. This is due to higher risk associated with longer term bonds.

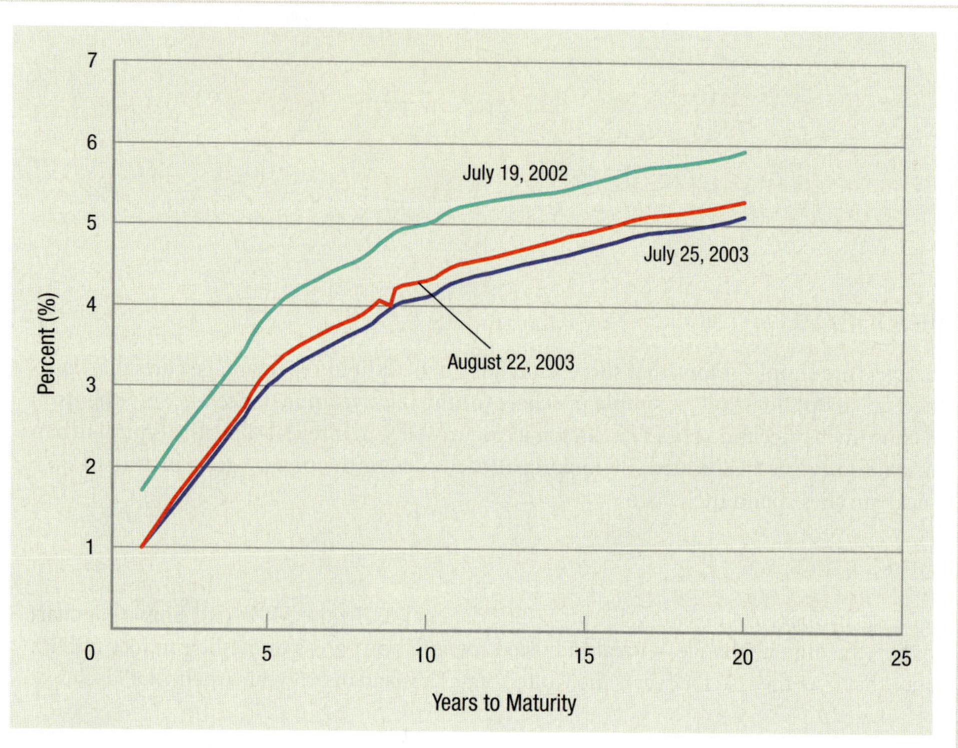


You should notice two things in this figure. First, at this time the yield curves sloped upward (they do not always do this). This meant that bonds that had a longer time to mature had higher yields; bonds with longer maturity periods are riskier and usually require a higher return. Second, interest rates fell over this period (July 2002 to August 2003) as shown by the position of the curves. Each point on the August 2003 curve is below the corresponding point on the July 2002 curve.

## A Few Simple Rules for Reading Graphs

Looking at graphs of data is relatively easy if you follow a few simple rules. First, read the title of the figure to get a sense of what is being presented. Second, look at the label for the horizontal axis (*x* axis) to see how the data are being presented. Make sure you know how the data are being measured. Is it months or years, hours worked or hundreds of hours worked? Third, examine the label for the vertical axis (*y* axis). This is the value of the variable being plotted on that axis; make sure you know what it is. Fourth, look at the graph itself and see if it makes logical sense. Are the curves (bars, dots) going in the right direction?

Look the graph over and see if you notice something interesting going on. This is really the fun part of looking closely at figures both in this text and in other books, magazines, and newspapers. Often simple data graphs can reveal surprising relationships between variables. Keep this in mind as you examine graphs throughout this course.

One more thing. Graphs in this book are always accompanied by explanatory captions. Examine the graph first, making your preliminary assessment of what is going on. Then carefully read the caption, making sure it accurately reflects what is shown in the graph. If the caption refers to movement between points, follow this movement in the graph. If you think there is a discrepancy between the caption and the graph, reexamine the graph to make sure you have not missed something.

## Graphs and Models

Let's now take a brief look at how economists use graphs and models, also looking at how they are constructed. Economists use what are called *stylized graphs* to represent relationships between variables. These graphs are a form of modeling to help us simplify our analysis and focus on those relationships that matter. Figure APX-6 is one such model.

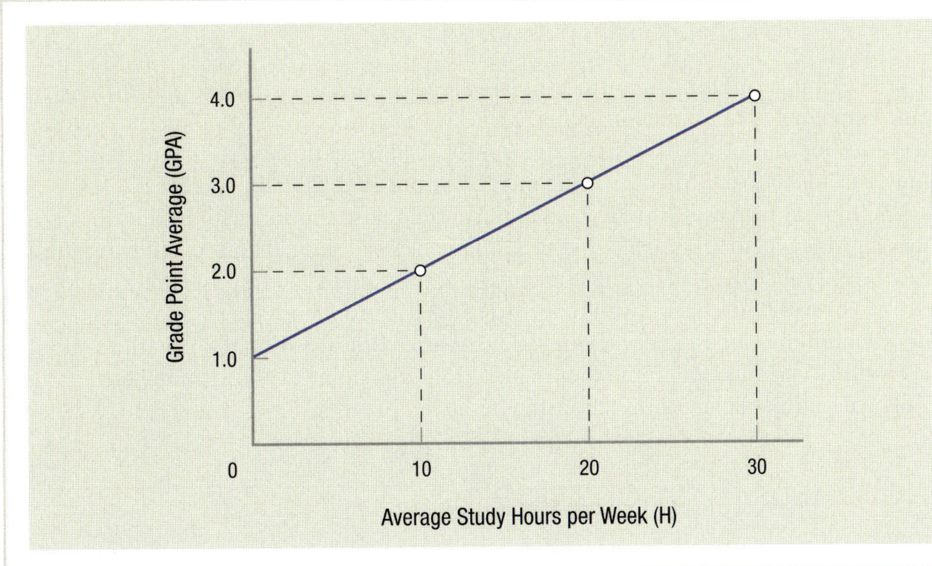


**FIGURE APX-6—Studying and Your GPA**

This figure shows a hypothetical linear relationship between average study hours and GPA. Without studying, a D average results, and with 10 hours of studying, a C average is obtained, and so on.

## Linear Relationships

Figure APX-6 shows a linear relationship between average study hours and grade point average (GPA). The more you study, the higher your GPA (duh!). By a linear relationship, we mean that the "curve" is a straight line. In this case, if you don't study at all, we assume you are capable of making Ds and your GPA will equal 1.0, not enough to keep you in school for long. If you hit the books for an average of 10 hours a week, your GPA rises to 2.0, a C average. Studying for additional hours raises your GPA up to its maximum of 4.0.

The important point here is that the curve is linear; any hour of studying yields the same increase in your GPA. All hours of studying provide equal yields from beginning to end. This is what makes linear relationships unique.

### Computing the Slope of a Linear Line

Looking at the line in Figure APX-6, we can see two things: The line is straight, so the slope is constant, and the slope is positive. As average hours of studying increase, GPA increases. Computing the slope of the line tells us how much GPA increases for every hour that studying is increased. Computing the slope of a linear line is relatively easy and is shown in Figure APX-7 on the next page.

**FIGURE APX-7—Computing Slope for a Linear Line**

Computing the slope is based on a simple rule: rise over run (rise divided by run). In the case of this straight line, the slope is equal to 0.1 because every 10 additional hours of studying yields a 1.0 increase in GPA.

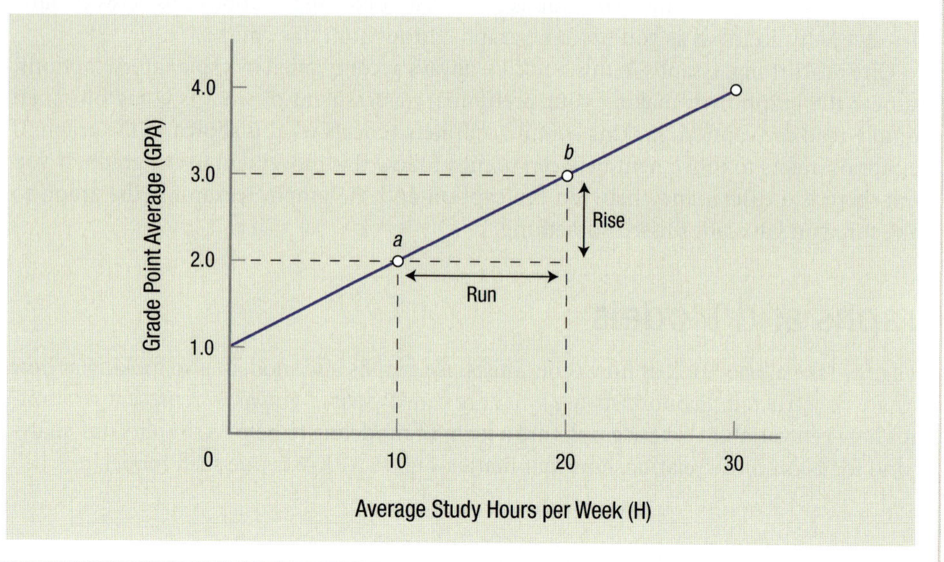


The simple rule for computing slope is: Slope is equal to rise over run (or rise ÷ run). Since the slope is constant along a linear line, we can select any two points and determine the slope for the entire curve. In Figure APX-7 we have selected points *a* and *b* where GPA moves from 2.0 to 3.0 when studying increases from 10 to 20 hours per week.

Your GPA increases (rises) by 1.0 for an additional 10 hours of study. This means that the slope is equal to 0.1 (1.0 ÷ 10 = 0.1). So for every additional hour of studying you add each week, your GPA will rise by 0.1. Thus, if you would like to improve your grade point average from 3.0 to 3.5, you would have to study five more hours per week.

Computing slope for negative relations that are linear is done exactly the same way, except that when you compute the changes from one point to another, one of the values will be negative, making the relationship negative.

## Nonlinear Relationships

It would be nice for model builders if all relationships were linear, but that is not the case. It is probably not really the case with the amount of studying and your GPA either. Figure APX-8 depicts a more realistic nonlinear and positive relationship between studying and

**FIGURE APX-8—Studying and Your GPA (nonlinear)**

This nonlinear graph of study hours and GPA is probably more typical than the one shown in Figures APX-6 and APX-7. Like many other things, studying exhibits diminishing returns. The first hours of studying result in greater improvements to GPAs than further hours of studying.

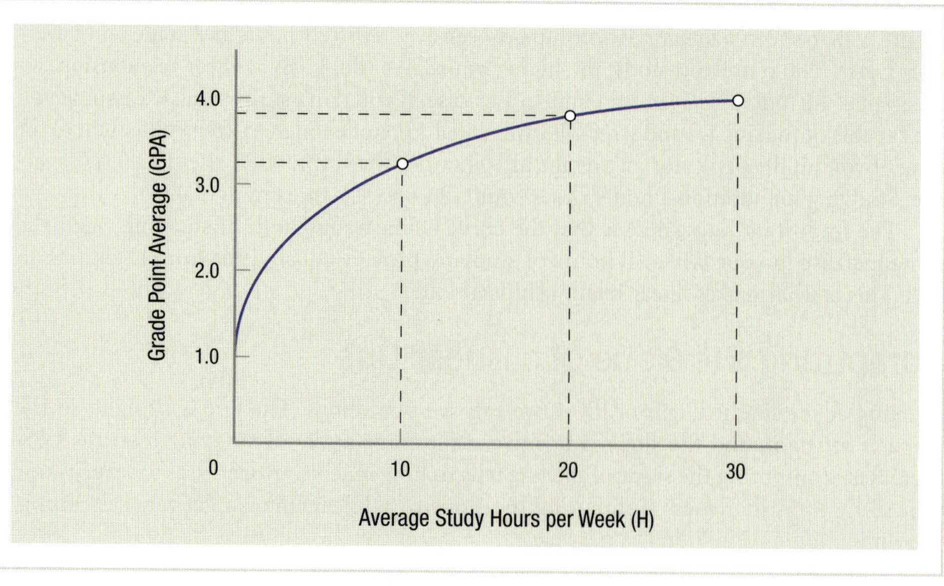

GPA. Again, we assume that you can get a D average (1.0) without studying and reach a maximum of straight As (4.0) with 30 hours per week.

Figure APX-8 suggests that your first few hours of study per week are more important to raising your GPA than are the others. Your first 10 hours of studying yields more than the last 10 hours: You go from 1.0 to 3.3 (a gain of 2.3), as opposed to going only from 3.8 to 4.0 (a gain of only 0.2). This curve exhibits what economists call diminishing returns. Just as the first bite of pizza tastes better than the one-hundredth, so the first 5 hours of studying brings a bigger jump in GPA than the 25th to 30th hours.

## Computing the Slope of a Nonlinear Curve

As you might suspect, computing the slope of a nonlinear curve is a little more complex than for a linear line. But it is not that much more difficult. In fact, we use essentially the same rise over run approach that is used for lines.

Looking at the curve in Figure APX-8, it should be clear that the slope varies for each point on the curve. It starts out very steep, then begins to level out above 20 hours of studying. Figure APX-9 shows how to compute the slope at any point on the curve.

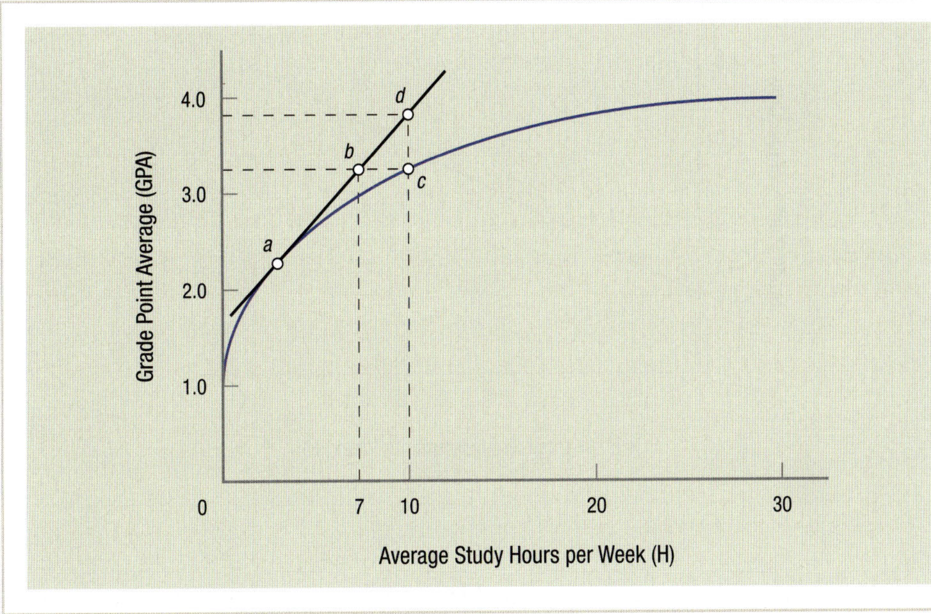


**FIGURE APX-9—Computing Slope for a Nonlinear Curve**

Computing the slope of a nonlinear curve requires that you compute the slope of each point on the curve. This is done by computing the slope of a tangent to each point.

Computing the slope at point *a* requires drawing a line tangent to that point, then computing the slope of that line. For point *a*, the slope of the line tangent to it is found by computing rise over run again. In this case, it is length $dc \div bc$ or $[(3.8 - 3.3) \div (10 - 7)] = 0.5 \div 3 = 0.167$. Notice that this slope is significantly larger than the original linear relationship of 0.1. If we were to compute the slope near 30 hours of studying, it would approach zero (the slope of a horizontal line is zero).

## *Ceteris Paribus*, Simple Equations, and Shifting Curves

Hold on while we beat this GPA and studying example into the ground. Inevitably, when we simplify analysis to develop a graph or model, important factors or influences must be controlled. We do not ignore them, we hold them constant. These are known as *ceteris paribus* assumptions.

## *Ceteris Paribus:* All Else Equal

By *ceteris paribus* we mean other things being equal or all other relevant factors, elements, or influences are held constant. When economists define your demand for a product, they want to know how much or how many units you will buy at different prices. For example, to determine how many DVDs you will buy at various prices (your demand for DVDs), we hold your income and the price of movie tickets constant. If your income suddenly jumped, you would be willing to buy more DVDs at all prices, but this is a whole new demand curve. *Ceteris paribus* assumptions are a way to simplify analysis; then the analysis can be extended to include those factors held constant, as we will see next.

## Simple Linear Equations

Simple linear equations can be expressed as: $Y = a + bX$. This is read as, $Y$ equals $a$ plus $b$ times $X$, where $Y$ is the variable plotted on the $y$ axis and $a$ is a constant (unchanging), and $b$ is a different constant that is multiplied by $X$, the value on the $x$ axis. The formula for our studying and GPA example introduced in Figure APX-6 is shown in Figure APX-10.

**FIGURE APX-10—Studying and Your GPA: A Simple Equation**

The formula for a linear relationship is $Y = a + bX$, where $Y$ is the $y$ axis variable, $X$ is the $x$ axis variable, and $a$ and $b$ are constants. For the original relationship between study hours and GPA, this equation is $Y = 1.0 + 0.1X$.

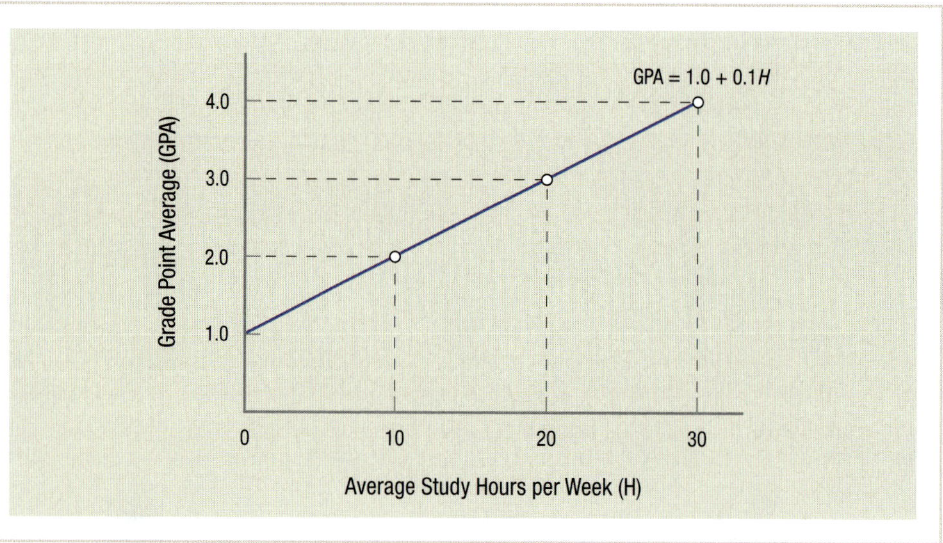


The constant $a$ is known as the vertical intercept because it is the value of your GPA when study hours ($X$) is zero, and therefore when it cuts (intercepts) the vertical axis and is equal to 1.0 (D average). Now each time you study another hour on average, your GPA rises by 0.1, so the constant $b$ (the slope of the line) is equal to 0.1. Letting $H$ represent hours of studying, the final equation is: GPA $= 1.0 + 0.1H$. You start with a D average without studying and as your hours of studying increase, your GPA goes up by 0.1 times the hours of studying. If we plug in 20 hours of studying into the equation, the answer is a GPA of 3.0 ($1.0 + (0.1 \times 20) = 1.0 + 2.0 = 3.0$).

## Shifting Curves

Now let's introduce a couple of factors we have been holding constant (the *ceteris paribus* assumption). These two elements are tutoring and partying. So, our new equation now becomes GPA $= 1.0 + 0.1H + Z$, where $Z$ is our variable indicating whether you have a tutor or whether you are excessively partying. When you have a tutor, $Z = 1$, and when you party too much, $Z = -1$. Tutoring adds to the productivity of your studying (hence $Z = 1$), while excessive late-night partying reduces the effectiveness of studying because

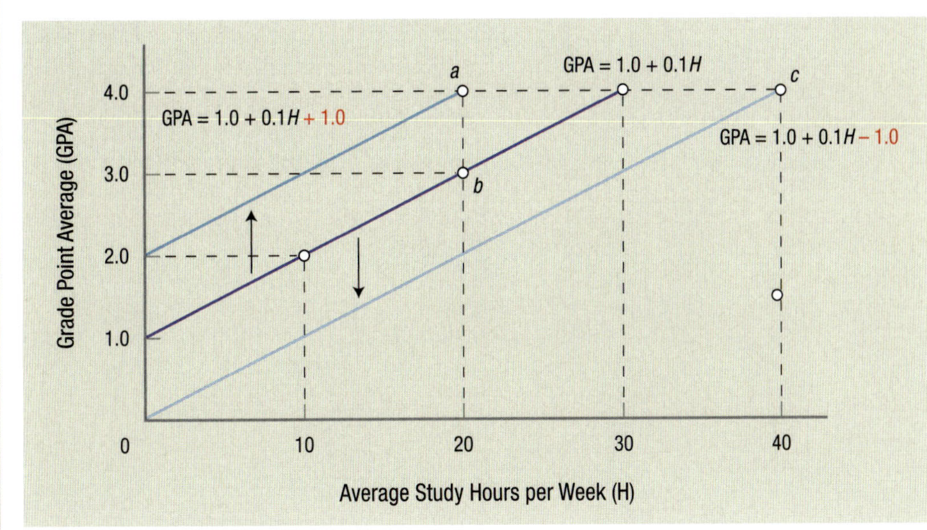


**FIGURE APX-11—The Impact of Tutoring and Partying on Your GPA**

The effect of tutoring and partying on our simple model of studying and GPA is shown. Partying harms your academic efforts and shifts the relationship to the right, making it harder to maintain your previous average (you now have to study more hours). Tutoring, on the other hand, improves the relationship (shifts the curve to the left).

you are always tired (hence $Z = -1$). Figure APX-11 shows the impact of adding these factors to the original relationship.

With tutoring, your GPA-studying curve has moved upward and to the left. Now, because $Z = 1$, you begin with a C average (2.0), and with just 20 hours of studying (because of tutoring) you can reach a 4.0 GPA (point *a*). Alternatively, when you don't have tutoring and you party every night, your GPA-studying relationship has worsened (shifted downward and to the right). Now you must study 40 hours (point *c*) to accomplish a 4.0 GPA. Note that you begin with failing grades.

The important point here is that we can simplify relationships between different variables and use a simple graph or equation to represent a model of behavior. In doing so, we often have to hold some things constant. When we allow those factors to change, the original relationship is now changed and often results in a shift in the curves. You will see this technique applied over and over as you study economics this semester.

## Correlation Is Not Causation

Just because two variables seem related or appear related on a scatter plot does not mean that one causes another. Economists a hundred years ago correlated business cycles (the ups and downs of the entire economy) with sunspots. Because they appeared related, some suggested that sunspots caused business cycles. The only rational argument was that agriculture was the dominant industry and sunspots affected the weather; therefore, sunspots caused the economy to fluctuate.

Another example of erroneously assuming that correlation implies causality is the old Wall Street saw that related changes in the Dow Jones average to women's hem lines. Because two variables appear to be related does not mean that one causes the other to change.

Understanding graphs and using simple equations is a key part of learning economics. Practice helps.

## Correlation Is Not Causation

# Production, Economic Growth, and Trade

Boris Lyubner/Getty Images

**We live in a consumer world.** Everywhere you look, people are purchasing and consuming things. Everything from plastic wrap to baseballs, from artichokes to cellular phones, gets produced, traded, and consumed. Whether an economy is a capitalist market economy as in the United States, a capitalist marketplace with a strong touch of socialism as in many European countries, or a predominately communist economy as is true of many of China's markets, goods and services must change hands. Several centuries ago, individuals produced most of what they consumed. Today, most of us produce little of what we consume. Instead, we work at specialized jobs, then use our wages to purchase the goods we need. And purchase we do.

Though newspapers frequently report consumption excesses—and these excesses occur in rich *and* poor countries around the globe—we should not let these excesses obscure the fact that consumption is a great driver of economic growth. In many respects, consumption is simply a way for people to better themselves, to make their lives less of a drudgery, or to enrich their lives. Farmers in poor countries move from a precarious existence as subsistence farmers to producers of cash crops—keeping enough to live on but generating a surplus to sell—to obtain those consumption goods that better their lives.

Another great driver of economic growth is technological change. Technological advances have led to a telecommunications industry that simply was not dreamed of 50 years ago. In 1950, long distance phone calls were placed with the assistance of live operators, every minute costing the average consumer several hours' worth of pay. Today, fiber-optic cables allow thousands of calls to be made on one cable, thus drastically reducing the cost of telephone service. Cell phones, meanwhile, have become necessities because they are convenient and raise productivity. The globe is shrinking as communications bring us closer together.

**After studying this chapter you should be able to:**

- ☐ Describe the three basic questions that must be answered for any economy.
- ☐ Describe production and the factors that go into producing various goods and services.
- ☐ Describe the opportunity cost an economy incurs to increase the production of one product.
- ☐ Use a production possibilities frontier (PPF) or curve to analyze the limits of production.
- ☐ Describe economic growth and the impacts of expanding resources through increasing human resources, capital accumulation, and technological improvements.
- ☐ Describe the concepts of absolute and comparative advantage and explain what they tell us about the gains from trade when countries specialize in certain products.
- ☐ Describe the practical constraints on free trade and how some industries might be affected.

Another driver of economic growth—trade—is less obvious. Yet its effect is clear. Nearly every country engages in commercial trade with other countries to expand the opportunities for consumption and production by its people. As products are consumed, new products must be produced, so increased consumption in one country can spur economic growth in another. Given the ability of global trade to open economic doors and raise incomes, it is vital for growth in developing nations. China's per person income has jumped dramatically in the decades since it opened its doors to trade.

This chapter gives you a framework for understanding economic growth. It provides a simple model for thinking about production, then applies this model to economies at large so you will know how to think about economic growth and its determinants. It then goes on to analyze international trade as a special case of economic growth. By the time you finish this chapter, you should understand the importance of economic growth and what drives it. To start, we turn to an examination of the three basic questions that every economy, no matter how it is organized, must solve.

## Basic Economic Questions and Production

Regardless of the country, its circumstances, or its precise economic structure, every economy must answer three basic questions.

### Basic Economic Questions

The three basic economic questions that each society must answer are:

- What goods and services are to be produced?
- How are these goods and services to be produced?
- Who will receive these goods and services?

The response an economy makes to the first question—What to produce?—depends on the goods and services a society wants. In a communist state, the government decides what a society wants, but in a capitalist economy, consumers signal what products they want by way of their demands for specific commodities. In the next chapter, we investigate how consumer demand for individual products is determined and how markets meet these demands. For now, we assume that consumers, individually and as a society, are able to decide on the mix of goods and services they most want, and that producers supply these items at acceptable prices.

Once we know what goods a society wants, the next question its economic system must answer is how these goods and services are to be produced. In the end, this problem comes down to the simple question of how labor, capital, and land should be combined to produce the desired products. If a society demands a huge amount of corn, say, we can expect its utilization of land, labor, and capital will be different from a society that demands digital equipment. But even an economy devoted to corn production could be organized in different ways, perhaps relying on extensive use of human labor, or perhaps relying on automated capital equipment.

Once an economy has determined what goods and services to produce and how to produce them, it is faced with the distribution question: Who will get the resulting products? *Distribution* refers to the way an economy allocates to consumers the goods and services it produces. How this is done depends on how the economy is organized.

### Economic Systems

All economies have to answer the three basic economic questions. How that is done depends on who owns the factors of production (land, labor, capital, and entrepreneurship) and how decisions are made to coordinate production and distribution.

In *capitalist* or *market* economies, private individuals and firms own most of the resources. The what, how, and who decisions are determined by individual desires

## By the *Numbers*

### Growth, Productivity, and Trade Are Key to Our Prosperity

In the last half-century, average annual working hours fell by 13% but productivity has risen 200%, so real (adjusted for inflation) GDP per person and our standard of living have risen dramatically.

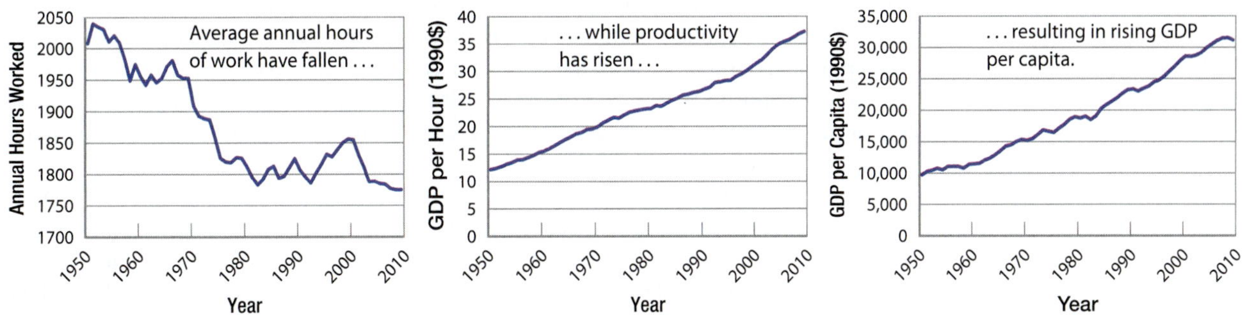


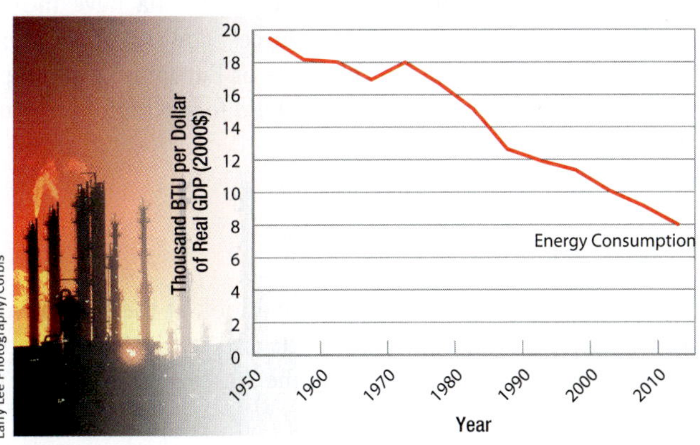


**Energy in BTU per dollar** of real (inflation adjusted) GDP has been steadily declining over the last 60 years. Today it is less than half of what it was in 1950.

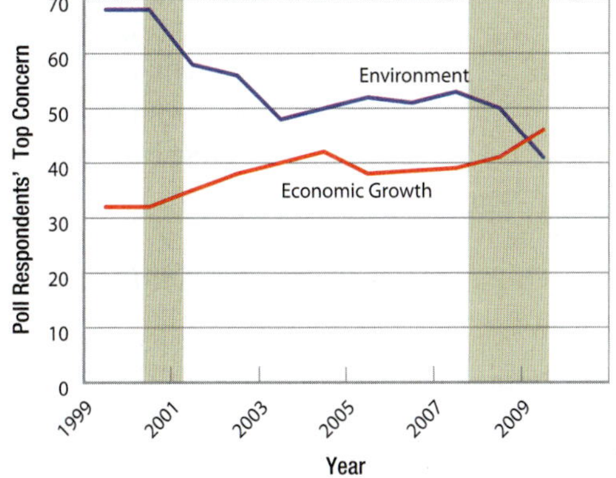


**American attitudes** about concerns for the environment or a preference for economic growth vary based on the state of the economy. As the economy enters a recession (shaded areas), the desire for economic growth grows while concern for the environment ebbs.

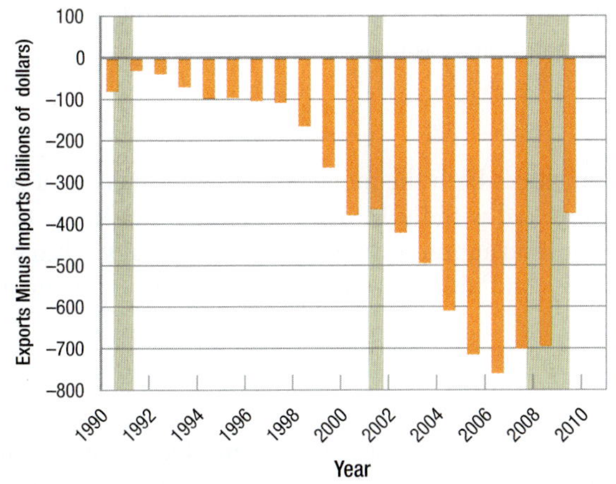


**Our trade balance (exports minus imports)** has grown steadily negative over the last 20 years. During the current recession, however, we cut our purchases of imported goods by 25% while exports held steady, balancing exports and imports.

**Firing workers can be costly** in some countries. Firing a full-time worker with 20 years at the company costs roughly 70 weeks pay in Germany, but it is even more costly in China.

**Chapter 2** Hours worked, Productivity and GDP: The Conference Board, Total Economy Database, 1-2009. Energy use per dollar of GDP, *The Economist*, 5-8-2008. Exports and imports: U.S Department of Commerce. American attitudes on environment and economic growth, *The Economist*, 12-5-2009. Cost of firing workers, *The Economist*, 9-16-2008.

for products and profit-making decisions by firms. Product prices are the principal mechanism for communicating information in the system. Based on prices, consumers decide whether to buy or not, and firms decide how to employ their resources and what production technology to use. This competition between many buyers and sellers leads to highly efficient production of goods and services. Producers are free to survive or perish based on their efficiency and the quality of their products. The government's primary roles are protecting property rights, enforcing contracts between private parties, providing public goods such as national defense, and establishing and ensuring the appropriate operating environment for competitive markets. Today the U.S. economy is not a pure *laissez-faire* ("leave it alone," or minimal government role) market economy but more of a mixed economy with many regulations and an extended role for government.

In contrast, *planned* economies (socialist and communist) are systems where most of the productive resources are owned by the state and most economic decisions are made by central governments. Big sweeping decisions for the economy, often called "five-year plans," are centrally made and focus productive resources on these priorities. Both the former Soviet Union and China (until quite recently) were highly centrally planned, and virtually all resources were government owned. Although Russia and China have moved toward market economies, a large portion of each country's resources is owned by the communist state. Socialist countries (e.g., the Scandinavian countries of Europe) enjoy a high degree of freedom with a big role both for government services paid for by high taxes, and for highly regulated private businesses.

## Resources, Production, and Efficiency

Having examined the three basic economic questions, let's take a look at the production process. **Production** involves turning **resources** into products and services that people want. Let's begin our discussion of this process by examining the scarce resources used to produce goods and services.

**Production:** The process of converting resources (factors of production)—land, labor, capital, and entrepreneurial ability—into goods and services.

**Resources:** Productive resources include land (land and natural resources), labor (mental and physical talents of people), capital (manufactured products used to produce other products), and entrepreneurial ability (the combining of the other factors to produce products and assume the risk of the business).

### Land

For economists, the term **land** includes both land in the usual sense, but it also includes all other natural resources that are used in production. Natural resources like mineral deposits, oil and natural gas, and water are all included by economists in the definition of land. Economists refer to the payment to land as *rent.*

**Land:** Includes natural resources such as mineral deposits, oil, natural gas, water, and land in the usual sense of the word. The payment to land as a resource is called rent.

### Labor

**Labor** as a factor of production includes both the mental and physical talents of people. Few goods and services can be produced without labor resources. Improvement to labor capabilities from training, education, and apprenticeship programs, typically called human capital, all add to labor's productivity and ultimately to a higher standard of living. Labor is paid *wages.*

**Labor:** Includes the mental and physical talents of individuals who produce products and services. The payment to labor is called wages.

### Capital

**Capital** includes all manufactured products that are used to produce other goods and services. This includes equipment such as drill presses, blast furnaces for making steel, and other tools used in the production process. It also includes trucks and automobiles used by businesses, as well as office equipment such as copiers, computers, and telephones. Any manufactured product that is used to produce other products is included in the category of capital. Capital earns *interest.*

Note that the term *capital* as used by economists refers to real capital—actual manufactured products used in the production process—not money or financial capital. Money and financial capital are important in that they are used to purchase the real capital that is used to produce products.

**Capital:** Includes manufactured products such as welding machines, computers, and cellular phones that are used to produce other goods and services. The payment to capital is referred to as interest.

## Entrepreneurial Ability

**Entrepreneurs** *combine* land, labor, and capital to produce goods and services, and they assume the *risks* associated with running a business. Entrepreneurs combine and manage the inputs of production, and manage the day-to-day marketing, finance, and production decisions. Today, the risks of running a business are huge, as the many bankruptcies and failures testify; and globalization has opened many opportunities as well as risks. For undertaking these activities and assuming the risks associated with business, entrepreneurs earn *profits*.

**Entrepreneurs:** Entrepreneurs combine land, labor, and capital to produce goods and services. They absorb the risk of being in business, including the risk of bankruptcy and other liabilities associated with doing business. Entrepreneurs receive profits for this effort.

## Production and Efficiency

*Production* turns *resources*—land, labor, capital, and entrepreneurial ability—into products and services. The necessary production factors vary for different products. To produce corn, for instance, one needs arable land, seed, fertilizer, water, farm equipment, and the workers to operate that equipment. Farmers looking to produce corn would need to devote hundreds of acres of open land to this crop, plow the land, plant and nurture the corn, and finally harvest the crop. Producing digital equipment, in contrast, requires less land but more capital and highly skilled labor.

As we have seen, every country has to decide what to produce, how to produce it, and decide who receives the output. Countries desire to do the first two as efficiently as possible, but this leads to two different aspects of efficiency.

**Production efficiency** occurs when the mix of goods society decides to produce is produced at the lowest possible resource or opportunity cost. Alternatively, production efficiency occurs when as much output as possible is produced with a given amount of resources. Firms use the best technology available and combine the other resources to produce products at the lowest cost to society.

**Production efficiency:** Goods and services are produced at their lowest resource (opportunity) cost.

**Allocative efficiency** occurs when the mix of goods and services produced is the most desired by society. In capitalist countries this is determined by consumers and businesses and their interaction through markets. The next chapter explores this interaction in some detail. Needless to say, it would be inefficient (a waste of resources) to be producing vinyl records in the age of digital music players. Allocative efficiency requires that the right mix of goods be produced at the lowest cost.

**Allocative efficiency:** The mix of goods and services produced is just what the society desires.

Every economy faces constraints or limitations. Land, labor, capital, and entrepreneurship are all limited. No country has an infinite supply of available workers or the space and machinery that would be needed to put them all to work efficiently; no country can break free of these natural restraints. Such limits are known as production possibilities frontiers, and they are the focus of the next section.

### CHECKPOINT

### BASIC ECONOMIC QUESTIONS AND PRODUCTION

- Every economy must decide what to produce, how to produce it, and who will get what is produced.
- Production is the process of converting factors of production (resources)—land, labor, capital, and entrepreneurial ability—into goods and services.
- Land includes land and natural resources. Labor includes the mental and physical resources of humans. Capital includes all manufactured products used to produce other goods and services. Entrepreneurs combine resources to produce products, and they assume the risk of doing business.
- Production efficiency requires that products be produced at the lowest cost. Allocative efficiency occurs when the mix of goods and services produced is just what society wants.

**QUESTION:** The one element that really seems to differentiate entrepreneurship from the other resources is the fact that entrepreneurs shoulder the *risk* of failure of the enterprise. Is this important? Explain.

Answers to the Checkpoint question can be found at the end of this chapter.

# Production Possibilities and Economic Growth

As we discovered in the previous section, all countries, and all economies, face constraints on their production capabilities. Production can be limited by the quantity of the various factors of production in the country and its current technology. Technology includes such considerations as the country's infrastructure, its transportation and education systems, and the economic freedom it allows. Though perhaps going beyond the everyday meaning of the word *technology,* for simplicity, we will assume all of these factors help determine the state of a country's technology.

To further simplify matters, production possibilities analysis assumes that the quantity of resources available and the technology of the economy remain constant. Moreover, all economic agents—workers and managers—are assumed to be technically efficient, meaning that no waste will occur in production. Finally, we will examine an economy that produces only two products. While keeping our analysis simple, altering these assumptions will not fundamentally change our general conclusions.

## Production Possibilities

Assume our sample economy produces leather jackets and microcomputers. Figure 1 with its accompanying table shows the production possibilities frontier for this economy. The table shows seven possible production levels (*a–g*). These seven possibilities, which range from 12,000 leather jackets and zero microcomputers to zero jackets and 6,000 microcomputers, are graphed in Figure 1.

**Production possibilities frontier (PPF):** Shows the combinations of two goods that are possible for a society to produce at full employment. Points on or inside the PPF are feasible, and those outside of the frontier are unattainable.

When we connect the seven production possibilities, we delineate the **production possibilities frontier (PPF)** for this economy (some economists refer to this curve as the production possibilities curve). All points on the PPF curve are considered *attainable* by our economy. Everything to the left of the PPF curve is also attainable, but is an inefficient use of resources—the economy can always do better. Everything to the right of the

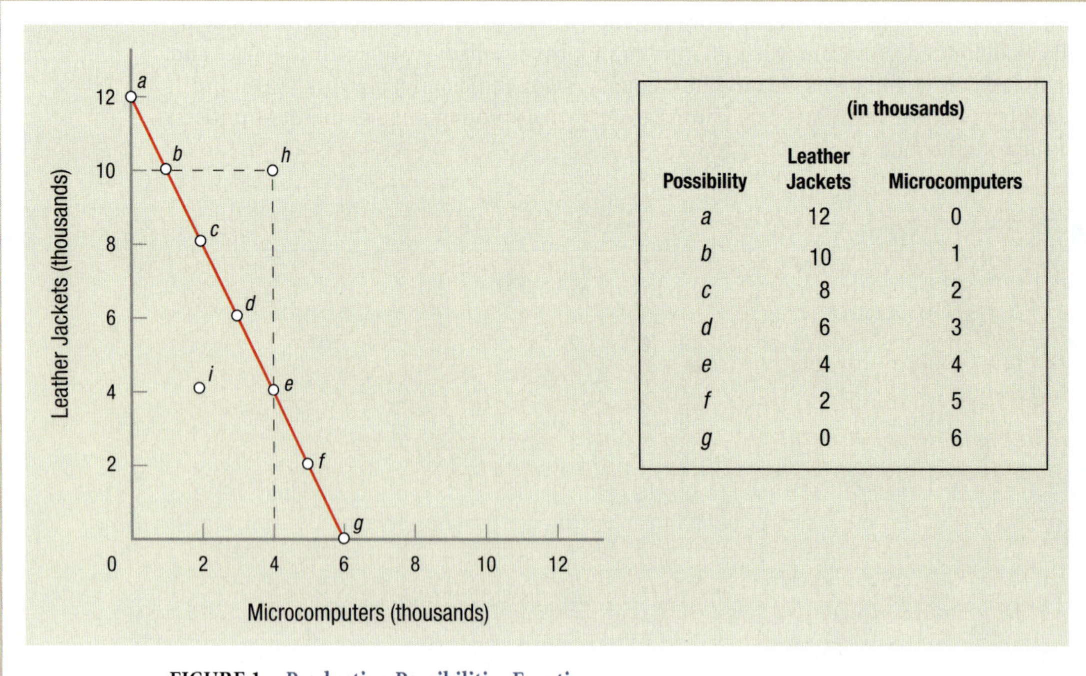


| | (in thousands) | |
|---|---|---|
| Possibility | Leather Jackets | Microcomputers |
| *a* | 12 | 0 |
| *b* | 10 | 1 |
| *c* | 8 | 2 |
| *d* | 6 | 3 |
| *e* | 4 | 4 |
| *f* | 2 | 5 |
| *g* | 0 | 6 |

**FIGURE 1—Production Possibilities Frontier**

Using all of its resources, this stylized economy can produce many different mixes of leather jackets and microcomputers. Production levels on, or to the left of, the resulting PPF are attainable for this economy. Production levels to the right of the PPF curve are unattainable.

curve is considered *unattainable.* Therefore, the PPF maps out the economy's limits; it is impossible for the economy to produce at levels beyond the PPF. What the PPF in Figure 1 shows is that, given an efficient use of limited resources and taking technology into account, this economy can produce any of the seven combinations of microcomputers and leather jackets listed. Also, the economy can produce any combination of the two products on or within the PPF, but not any combinations beyond it.

## Full Employment

As Figure 1 further suggests, all of the points along the PPF represent points of maximum output for our economy, that is, points at which all resources are being fully used. Therefore, if the society wants to produce 1,000 microcomputers, it will only be able to produce 10,000 leather jackets, as shown by point *b* on the PPF curve. Should the society decide Internet access is important, it might decide to produce 4,000 microcomputers, which would force it to cut leather jacket production down to 4,000, shown by point *e.*

Contrast points *c* and *e* with production at point *i.* At point *i* the economy is only producing 2,000 microcomputers and 4,000 jackets. Clearly, some resources are not being used and unemployment exists. When fully employed, the economy's resources could produce more of both goods (point *d*).

Because the PPF represents a maximum output, the economy could not produce 4,000 microcomputers and still produce 10,000 leather jackets. This situation, shown by point *h,* lies to the right of the PPF and hence outside the realm of possibility. Anything to the right of the PPF is impossible for our economy to attain; all points along the curve represent full employment.

## Opportunity Cost

Whenever a country reallocates resources to change production patterns, it does so at a price. This price is called **opportunity cost.** Opportunity cost is the price an economy or an individual must pay, measured in units of one product, to increase its production (or consumption) of another product. In moving from point *b* to point *e* in Figure 1, microcomputer production increases by 3,000 units, from 1,000 units to 4,000 units. In contrast, our country must forgo producing 6,000 leather jackets because production falls from 10,000 jackets to 4,000 jackets. Giving up 6,000 jackets for 3,000 more computers represents an opportunity cost of 6,000 jackets, or two jackets for each microcomputer.

**Opportunity cost:** The cost paid for one product in terms of the output (or consumption) of another product that must be forgone.

Opportunity cost thus represents the tradeoff required when an economy wants to increase its production of any single product. Governments must choose between guns and butter, or between military spending and social spending. Since there are limits to what taxpayers are willing to pay, spending choices are necessary. Think of opportunity costs as what you or the economy must give up to have more of a product or service.

Every day, everyone faces tradeoffs based on opportunity cost. A day has only 24 hours: You must decide how much time to spend eating, watching movies, going to class, sleeping, playing golf, partying, or studying—more time partying means less time for study. If you set aside a certain amount of time for studying, more time studying biology means less time studying history. But time is not the only constraint we face. Money restricts our choices as well. Should you buy a new computer, move to a nicer apartment, or save up for next semester's tuition? Indeed, virtually every choice in life involves tradeoffs or opportunity costs.

## Increasing Opportunity Costs

In most cases, land, labor, and capital cannot easily be shifted from producing one good or service to another. You cannot take a semi truck and use it to plow a farm field, even though the semi and a top-notch tractor cost about the same. The fact is that some resources are suited to specific sorts of production, just as some people seem to be better suited to performing one activity over another. Some people have a talent for music or art, and they would be miserable—and inefficient—working as accountants or computer programmers. Some people find they are more comfortable working outside, while others require the amenities of an environmentally controlled, ergonomically designed office.

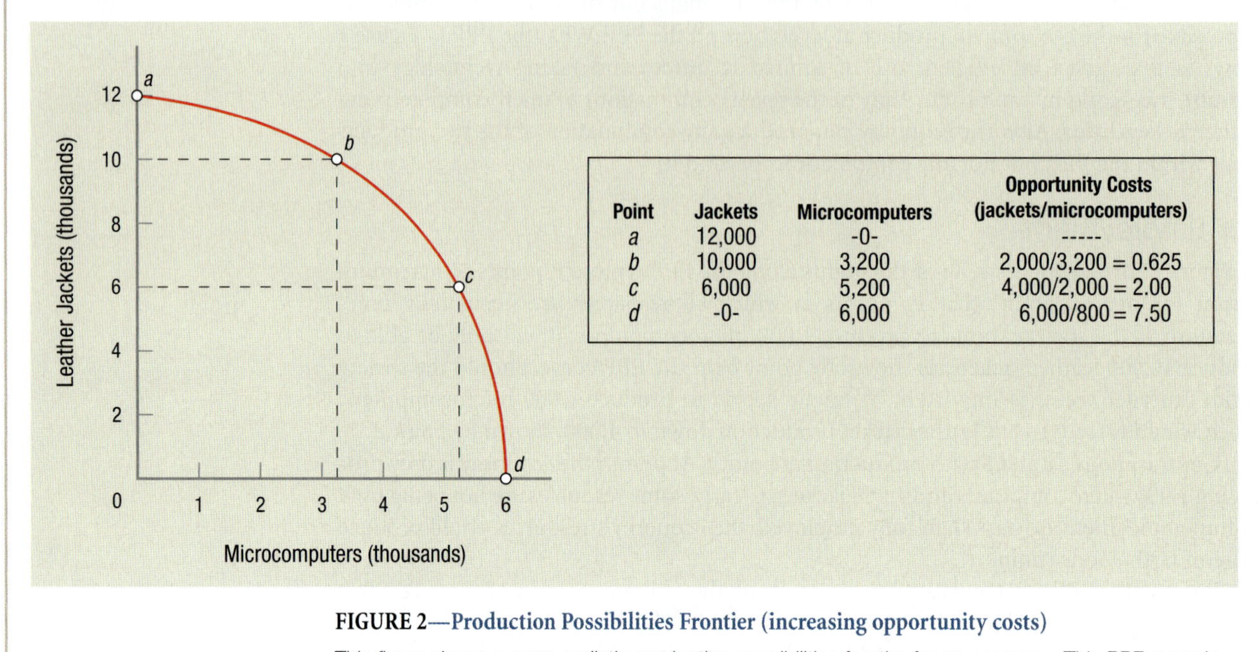


| Point | Jackets | Microcomputers | Opportunity Costs (jackets/microcomputers) |
|---|---|---|---|
| *a* | 12,000 | -0- | ----- |
| *b* | 10,000 | 3,200 | 2,000/3,200 = 0.625 |
| *c* | 6,000 | 5,200 | 4,000/2,000 = 2.00 |
| *d* | -0- | 6,000 | 6,000/800 = 7.50 |

**FIGURE 2—Production Possibilities Frontier (increasing opportunity costs)**

This figure shows a more realistic production possibilities frontier for an economy. This PPF curve is bowed out from the origin since opportunity costs rise as more factors are used to produce increasing quantities of one product or the other.

Thus, a more realistic production possibilities frontier is shown in Figure 2. This PPF curve is bowed out from the origin, since opportunity costs rise as more factors are used to produce increasing quantities of one product. Let's consider why this is so.

Let's begin at a point where the economy's resources are strictly devoted to leather jacket production (point *a*). Now assume that society decides to produce 3,200 microcomputers. This will require a move from point *a* to point *b*. As we can see, 2,000 leather jackets must be given up to get the added 3,200 microcomputers. This means the opportunity cost of 1 microcomputer is 0.625 leather jackets (2,000 ÷ 3,200 = 0.625). This is a low opportunity cost, because those resources that are better suited to producing microcomputers will be the first ones shifted into this industry, resulting in rapidly increasing returns from specialization.

But what happens when this society decides to produce an additional 2,000 computers, or moves from point *b* to point *c* on the graph? As Figure 2 illustrates, each additional computer costs 2 leather jackets since producing 2,000 more computers requires the society to sacrifice 4,000 leather jackets. Thus, the opportunity cost of computers has more than tripled due to diminishing returns on the computer side, which arise from the unsuitability of these new resources as more resources are shifted to microcomputers.

To describe what has happened in plain terms, when the economy was producing 12,000 leather jackets, all its resources went into jacket production. Those members of the labor force who are engineers and electronic assemblers were probably not well suited to producing jackets. As the economy backed off jackets to start producing microcomputers, the opportunity cost of computers was low, since the resources first shifted, including workers, were likely to be the ones most suited to computer production and least suited to jacket manufacture. Eventually, however, as computers became the dominant product, manufacturing more computers required shifting leather workers to the computer industry. Employing these less suitable resources drives up the opportunity costs of computers.

You may be wondering which point along the PPF is the best for society. Economists have no grounds for stating unequivocally which mixture of goods and services would be ideal. The perfect mixture of goods depends on the tastes and preferences of the members of society. In a capitalist economy, resource allocation is determined largely by individual choices and the workings of private markets. We consider these markets and their operations in the next chapter.

## Economic Growth

We have seen that PPFs map out the maximum that an economy can produce: Points to the right of the PPF curve are unattainable. But what if that PPF curve can be shifted to the right? This shift would give economies new maximum frontiers. In fact, we will see that economic growth can be viewed as a shift in the PPF curve outward. In this section, we use the production possibilities model to determine some of the major reasons for economic growth. Understanding these reasons for growth will enable us to suggest some broad economic policies that could lead to expanded growth.

The production possibilities model holds resources and technology constant to derive the PPF. These assumptions suggest that economic growth has two basic determinants: expanding resources and improving technologies. The expansion of resources allows producers to increase their production of all goods and services in an economy. Specific technological improvements, however, often affect only one industry directly. The development of a new color printing process, for instance, will directly affect only the printing industry.

Nevertheless, the ripples from technological improvements can spread out through an entire economy, just like ripples in a pond. Specifically, improvements in technology can lead to new products, improved goods and services, and increased productivity.

Sometimes, technological improvements in one industry allow other industries to increase their production with existing resources. This means producers can produce more output without using added labor or other resources. Alternately, they can get the same production levels as before while using fewer resources than before. This frees up resources in the economy for use in other industries.

When the electric lightbulb was invented, it not only created a new industry (someone had to produce lightbulbs), but it also revolutionized other industries. Factories could stay open longer since they no longer had to rely on the sun for light. Workers could see better, thus improving the quality of their work. The result was that resources operated more efficiently throughout the entire economy.

The modern-day equivalent to the lightbulb might be the cellular phone. Widespread use of these mobile devices enables people all across the world to produce goods and services more efficiently. Insurance agents can file claims instantly from disaster sites, deals can be closed while one is stuck in traffic, and communications have been revolutionized. Thus, this new technology has ultimately expanded time, the most finite of our resources. A similar argument could be made for the Internet. It has profoundly changed how many products are bought, sold, and delivered, and has expanded communications and the flow of information.

### Expanding Resources

The PPF represents the constraints on an economy at a specific time. But economies are constantly changing, and so are PPFs. Capital and labor are the principal resources that can be changed through government action. Land and entrepreneurial talent are important factors of production, but neither is easy to change by government policies. The government can make owning a business easier or more profitable by reducing regulations, or by offering low-interest loans or favorable tax treatment to small businesses. However, it is difficult to turn people into risk takers through government policy.

***Increasing Labor and Human Capital*** A clear increase in population, the number of households, or the size of the labor force shifts the PPF outward, as shown in Figure 3 on the next page. With added labor, the production possibilities available to the economy expand from $PPF_0$ to $PPF_1$. Such a labor increase can be caused by higher birthrates, increased immigration, or an increased willingness of people to enter the labor force. This last type of increase has occurred over the past several decades as more women have entered the labor force on a permanent basis. America's high level of immigration (legal and illegal) fuels a strong rate of economic growth.

Rather than simply increasing the number of people working, however, the labor factor can also be increased by improving workers' skills. Economists refer to this as *investment in human capital.* Activities such as education, on-the-job training, and other

**FIGURE 3—Economic Growth by Expanding Resources**

A clear increase in population, the number of households, or the size of the labor force shifts the PPF outward. In this figure, a rising supply of labor expands the economy's production possibilities from $PPF_0$ to $PPF_1$.

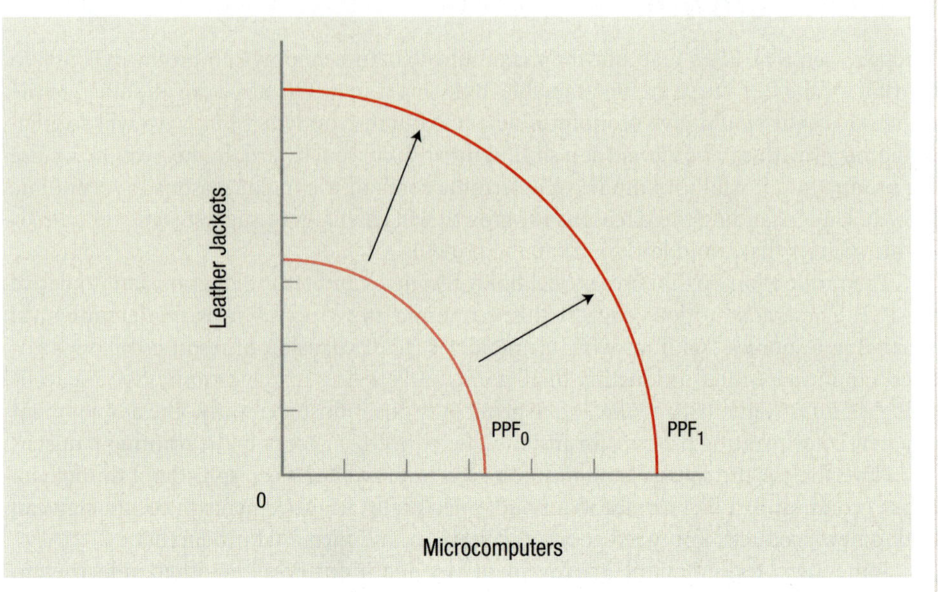


professional training fit into this category. Improving human capital means people are more productive, resulting in higher wages, a higher standard of living, and an expanded PPF for society.

***Capital Accumulation*** Increasing the capital used throughout the economy, usually brought about by investment, similarly shifts the PPF outward, as shown in Figure 3. Additional capital makes each unit of labor more productive and thus results in higher possible production throughout the economy. Adding robotics and computer-controlled machines to production lines, for instance, means each unit of labor produces many more units of output.

The production possibilities model and the economic growth associated with capital accumulation suggest a tradeoff. Figure 4 illustrates the tradeoff all nations face between current consumption and capital accumulation.

**FIGURE 4—Consumption Goods and Capital Goods and the Expansion of the Production Possibilities Frontier**

If a nation selects a product mix where the bulk of goods produced are consumption goods, it will initially produce at point *b*. The small investment made in capital goods has the effect of expanding the nation's productive capacity only to $PPF_b$ over the following decade. If the country decides to produce at point *a*, however, devoting more resources to producing capital goods, its productive capacity will expand much more rapidly, pushing the PPF curve out to $PPF_a$ over the following decade.

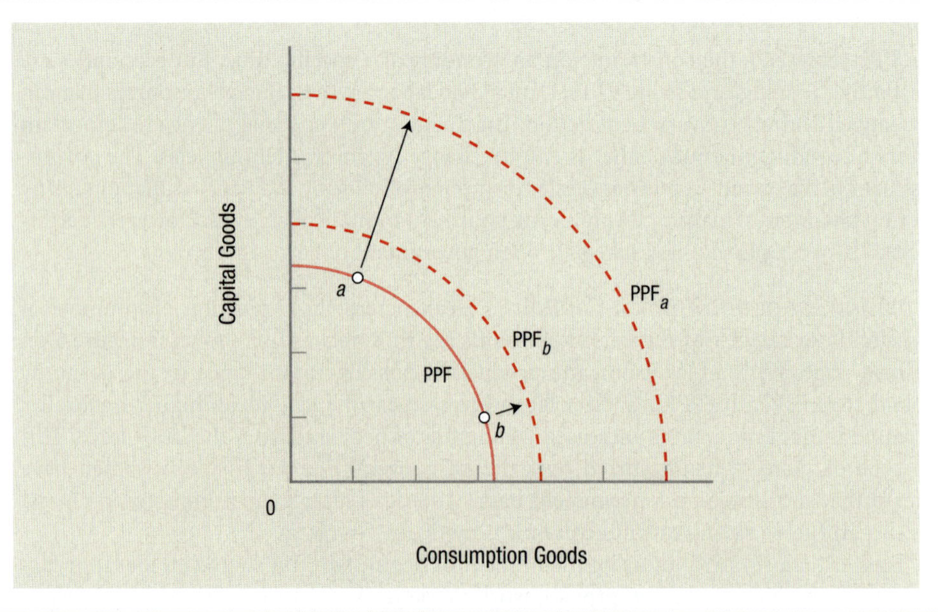

Let's first assume a nation selects a product mix where the bulk of goods produced are consumption goods—that is, goods that are immediately consumable and have short life spans, such as food and entertainment. This product mix is represented by point *b* in Figure 4. Consuming most of what it produces, a decade later the economy is at $PPF_b$. Little growth has occurred, since the economy has done little to improve its productive capacity—the present generation has essentially decided to consume rather than to invest in the economy's future.

Contrast this decision to one where the country at first decides to produce at point *a*. In this case, more capital goods such as machinery and tools are produced, while fewer consumption goods are used to satisfy current needs. Selecting this product mix results in the much larger PPF curve a decade later ($PPF_a$), since the economy steadily built up its productive capacity during those 10 years.

## Technological Change

Figure 5 illustrates what happens when an economy experiences a technological change in one of its industries, in this case the microchip industry. As the diagram shows, the economy's potential output of microcomputers expands greatly, though its maximum production of leather jackets remains unchanged. The area between the two curves represents an improvement in the society's standard of living. People can produce and consume more of both goods than before: more microcomputers because of the technological advance, and more jackets because some of the resources once devoted to microcomputer production can be shifted to leather jacket production, even as the economy is turning out more computers than before.

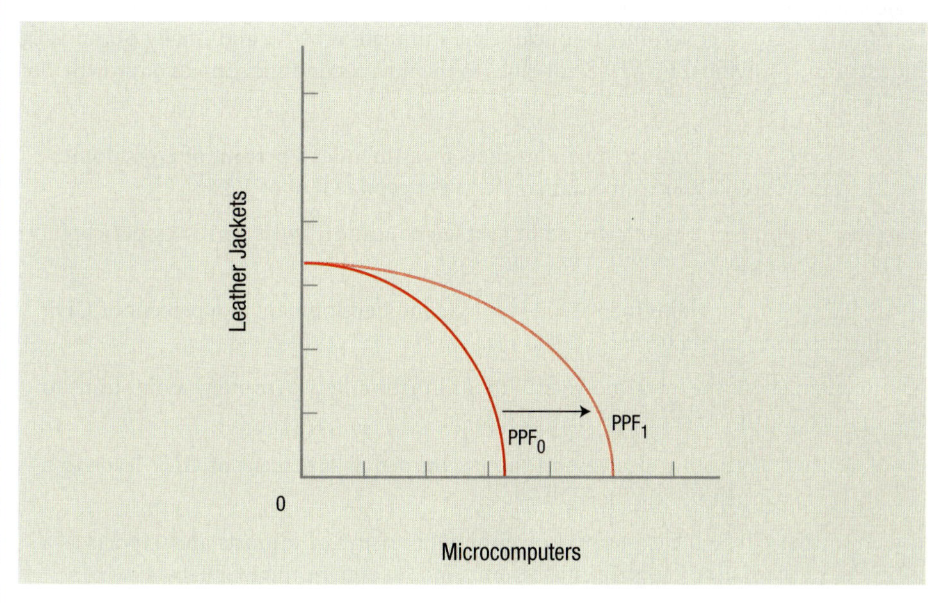


**FIGURE 5—Technological Change and Expansion of the Production Possibilities Frontier**

In this figure, an economy's potential output of microcomputers has expanded greatly, while its maximum production of leather jackets has remained unchanged. The area between the two curves represents an improvement in the society's standard of living, since more of both goods can be produced and consumed than before. Some of the resources once used for microcomputer production are diverted to leather jackets, even as the number of microcomputers increases.

This example reflects the United States today, where the computer industry is exploding with new technologies. Intel Corporation, the largest microprocessor manufacturer in the world, leads the way. Intel relentlessly develops newer, faster, and more powerful chips, setting a target time of 18 months for the development, testing, and release of each new generation of microprocessors. Consequently, consumers have seen home computers go from clunky conversation pieces to powerful, fast, indispensable machines. Today's microcomputers are more powerful than the mainframe supercomputers of just a few decades ago! And the latest developments in smart phones that allow users to surf the Web and play music, videos, and games do what powerful microcomputers did a decade ago.

Besides new products, technology has dramatically reduced the cost of microprocessor production. These cost reductions have permitted the United States to produce and consume more of other products as our consumption of high-tech items has soared. Our whole PPF has expanded outward.

But technological improvements result not only in smaller and cheaper microchips. An economy's technology also depends on how well its important trade centers are linked together. If a country has mostly dirt paths rather than paved highways, you can imagine how this deficiency would affect its economy: Distribution will be slow, and industries will be slow to react to changes in demand. In such a case, improving the roads might be the best way to stimulate economic growth.

As you can see, there are many ways to stimulate economic growth. A society can expand its output by using more resources, perhaps encouraging more people to enter the workforce or raising educational levels of workers. The government can encourage people to invest more, as opposed to devoting their earnings to immediate consumption. The public sector can spur technological advances by providing incentives to private firms to do research and development or underwrite research investments of its own.

## Estimating the Sources of Economic Growth

Adrian Hillman

How important are each of these factors? A recent study by the Organisation for Economic Co-operation and Development (OECD)[1] focused on what has been driving economic growth in 21 nations over the last several decades. The study first looked at contributions to economic growth from the macroeconomic perspective of added resources and technological improvements as we have been discussing in this chapter. It then looked at some benefits from good government policies that stimulate growth, and finally examined the industry and individual firm level for clues to the microeconomic sources of growth. Some of the findings include:

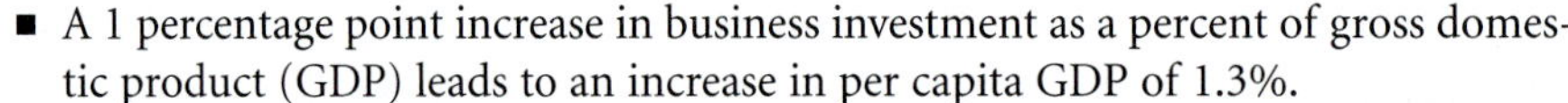

- A 1 percentage point increase in business investment as a percent of gross domestic product (GDP) leads to an increase in per capita GDP of 1.3%.
- An additional one-year increase in average education levels increases per capita GDP by 4 to 7%.
- A 0.1 percentage point increase in research and development as a percent of GDP increases per capita GDP by 1.2%.
- Reducing both the level and variability of inflation by 1 percentage point leads to an increase in per capita GDP of 2.3%.
- A 1 percentage point decrease in the tax burden as a percent of GDP leads to a 0.3% increase in per capita GDP.
- An increase in trade exposure (a combined measure of imports and exports as a percent of GDP) of 10 percentage points increases per capita GDP by 4%.

In less numerical terms, greater investment by business (physical capital), higher levels of education (human capital), high levels of research and development, lower inflation rates, reduced tax burdens, and greater levels of international trade all result in higher standards of living (per capita GDP).

One important point to take away from this discussion is that our simple stylized model of the economy using only two goods gives you a good first framework upon which to judge proposed policies for the economy. While not overly complex, this simple analysis is still quite powerful.

[1] *The Sources of Economic Growth in the OECD Countries* (Paris: Organisation for Economic Co-operation and Development), 2003.

## *Issue:* Is There a Moral Dimension to Economic Growth?

**As Benjamin M. Friedman** has stated, "Why do we care so much about economic growth? When we talk about microeconomic issues in economics, the conversation boils down to efficiency: How can we best organize economic activity—production, buying, selling, consuming—in order to keep the economy as close as possible to the frontier that represents the maximum possible production and satisfaction of the desires of all."

Clearly, economic growth expands the economy's production possibilities frontier and improves our standard of living, but does it improve the quality of life? Benjamin Friedman[2] made a compelling argument that we also care so much about growth because there are moral consequences to growth. This is the other side of the coin that is rarely discussed.

Looking back at two centuries of historical evidence pertaining to our country and others, Friedman found that when the economy is growing and the general population feels they are getting ahead, they are more likely to protect and enhance their basic moral values. These, he argued, include providing greater opportunity for all; expanding tolerance for people of other races, ethnic groups, and religions; and improving a sense of fairness to those in need. As a result, Americans become more committed to their democratic institutions.

Robin Jareaux/Getty Images

His analysis also brings a warning: When economic growth stagnates for an extended period, the evidence suggests that "predictable pathologies have flourished in American society in ways that we all regret." Friedman's analysis of the moral implications provides another dimension of economic growth to add to our toolbox.

### CHECKPOINT

### PRODUCTION POSSIBILITIES AND ECONOMIC GROWTH

- A production possibilities frontier (PPF) depicts the different combinations of goods that a fully employed economy can produce, given its available resources and current technology (both assumed fixed in the short run).
- Production levels inside and on the frontier are possible, but production mixes outside the curve are unattainable.
- Because production on the frontier represents the maximum output attainable when all resources are fully employed, reallocating production from one product to another involves *opportunity costs*: The output of one product must be reduced to get the added output of the other. The more of one product that is desired, the higher its opportunity costs because of diminishing returns and the unsuitability of some resources for producing some products.
- The PPF model suggests that economic growth can arise from an expansion in resources or improvements in technology. Economic growth is an outward shift of the PPF curve.

**QUESTION:** Having abundant resources such as oil or diamonds would seem to be a benefit to an economy, yet some people have considered it a curse. Why would plentiful resources like these be a curse?

Answers to the Checkpoint question can be found at the end of this chapter.

## Specialization, Comparative Advantage, and Trade

As we have seen, economics is all about voluntary production and exchange. People and nations do business with one another because all expect to gain from the transactions. Centuries ago, European merchants ventured to the Far East to ply the lucrative spice trades. These days, American consumers buy wines from Italy, cars from Japan, electronics from Korea, and millions of other products from countries around the world.

[2] Benjamin M. Friedman, *The Moral Consequences of Economic Growth* (New York: Knopf), 2005.

Many people assume that trade between nations is a zero-sum game—a game in which, for one party to gain, another party must lose. This is how poker games work. If one player walks away from the table a winner, someone else must have lost money. But this is not how voluntary trade works. Voluntary trade is a positive-sum game: Both parties to a transaction score positive gains. After all, who would voluntarily enter into an exchange if he or she did not believe there was some gain from it? To understand how all parties to an exchange (whether individuals or nations) can gain from it, we need to consider the concepts of absolute and comparative advantage developed by David Ricardo roughly 200 years ago.

## Absolute and Comparative Advantage

**Absolute advantage:** One country can produce more of a good than another country.

Figure 6 shows hypothetical production possibilities curves for the United States and Mexico. Both countries are assumed to produce only crude oil and microcomputer chips. Given the PPFs in Figure 6, the United States has an **absolute advantage** over Mexico in

### David Ricardo (1772–1823)

David Ricardo's rigorous, dispassionate evaluation of economic principles influenced generations of theorists, including such vastly different thinkers as John Stuart Mill and Karl Marx. The son of Dutch-Jewish immigrants, Ricardo was born in London as the third of 17 children. At age 14 he joined his father's trading business on the London Stock Exchange, but after he married a Quaker and converted to Christianity, his father disowned him. At 21 he borrowed money from friends, started his own brokerage, and within five years had amassed a small fortune.

While vacationing in Bath, England, he chanced on a copy of Adam Smith's *The Wealth of Nations,* and decided to devote his energies to studying economics and writing. He once wrote to his lifelong friend Thomas Malthus (of *Essay on Population* fame) that he was "thankful for the miserable English climate because it kept him at his desk writing." Ricardo and Malthus corresponded on a regular basis, and their exchanges were so important that John Maynard Keynes considered them " . . . the most important literary correspondence in the whole development of political economy."

Later, as a member of the British Parliament, Ricardo was an advocate of sound monetary policies and an outspoken critic of the 1815 Corn Laws, which placed high tariffs on imported grain to protect British landowners. His arguments were sound, but his oration was awful because he had a high-pitched squeal of a voice. His political views would also figure prominently in his economic writings.

Despite a pessimistic streak, Ricardo was an optimist when it came to free trade. His theory of "comparative advantage" suggested that countries would mutually benefit from trade by specializing in export goods they could produce at a lower opportunity cost than another country. His classic example was trade between Britain and Portugal. If Britain specialized in producing cloth and Portugal in exporting wine, each country would gain from a free exchange of goods. Ricardo died in 1823 of an ear infection, leaving an enduring legacy of classical (pre-1930s) economic analysis and his huge estate to his friend Thomas Malthus.

Arco Images Gmbh/Alamy

Sources: E. Ray Canterbery, *A Brief History of Economics* (New Jersey: World Scientific), 2001; Howard Marshall, *The Great Economists: A History of Economic Thought* (New York: Pitman Publishing Corporation), 1967; Steven Pressman, *Fifty Major Economists, 2d ed.,* (New York: Routledge), 2006; John Maynard Keynes, *Essays in Biography* (New York: Norton), 1951.

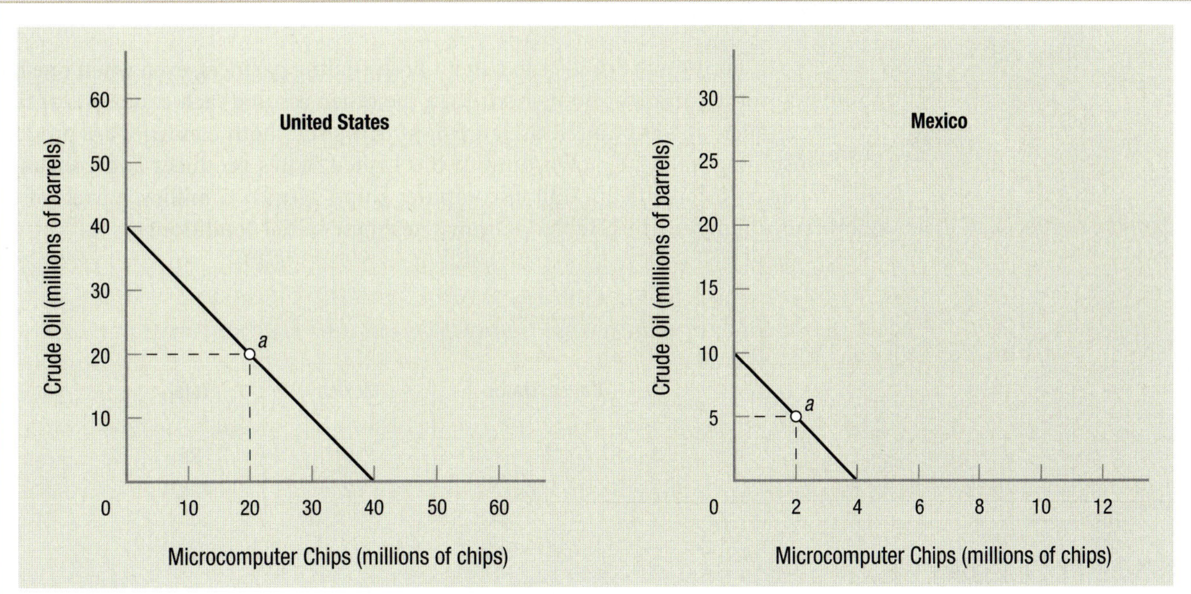


**FIGURE 6—Production Possibilities for the United States and Mexico**

One country has an absolute advantage if it can produce more of a good than another country. In this case, the United States has an absolute advantage over Mexico in producing both microchips and crude oil—it can produce more of both goods than Mexico can. Even so, Mexico has a comparative advantage over the United States in producing oil, since it can increase its output of oil at a lower opportunity cost than can the United States. This comparative advantage leads to gains for both countries from specialization and trade.

producing both products. An absolute advantage exists when one country can produce more of a good than another country. In this instance, the United States can produce 4 times more oil (40 million vs. 10 million barrels) and 10 times as many microcomputer chips (40 million vs. 4 million microchips) as Mexico. Note that the scales on the axes of the two panels in Figure 6 are different to make them easier to read.

At first glance you might wonder why the United States would even consider trading with Mexico. The United States has so much more productive capacity than Mexico, so why wouldn't it just produce all of its own crude oil and microcomputer chips? The answer lies in comparative advantage.

One country has a **comparative advantage** in producing a good if its opportunity cost to produce that good is lower than the other country's. In Figure 6, Mexico has a comparative advantage over the United States in producing oil. For the United States to produce an additional million barrels of crude oil, the *opportunity cost* is a million microcomputer chips. Each barrel of oil therefore costs the American economy one computer chip.

**Comparative advantage:** One country has a lower opportunity cost of producing a good than another country.

Contrast this with the situation in Mexico. For every microchip Mexican producers forgo, they are able to produce an additional 2.5 barrels of oil. This means one barrel of oil costs the Mexican economy only 0.4 computer chip. Therefore, Mexico has a comparative advantage in the production of crude oil, since a barrel of oil costs Mexico only 0.4 microchip, but to produce the same barrel of oil costs one microchip in the United States.

Conversely, the United States has a comparative advantage over Mexico in producing computer chips: Producing a microchip in the United States costs one barrel of oil, whereas the same chip in Mexico costs 2.5 barrels of oil. These relative costs suggest that the United States should pour its resources into producing computer chips, while Mexico specializes in crude oil. The two countries can then engage in trade to their mutual benefit.

## The Gains from Trade

To see how specialization and trade can benefit both trading partners, even when one has the ability to produce more of both goods than the other, assume each country is at first (before trade) operating at point *a* in Figure 6. At this point, both countries are producing and consuming only their own output; the United States produces and consumes 20 million barrels of oil and 20 million computer chips; Mexico, 5 million barrels of oil and 2 million computer chips. Table 1 summarizes these initial conditions.

**TABLE 1** Initial Consumption-Production Pattern

| | United States | Mexico | Total |
|---|---|---|---|
| Oil | 20 | 5 | 25 |
| Chips | 20 | 2 | 22 |

Now assume Mexico focuses on oil, producing the maximum it can: 10 million barrels. We also assume both countries want to continue consuming 25 million barrels of oil between them. So the United States only needs to produce 15 million barrels of oil since Mexico is now producing 10 million barrels. For the United States, this frees up some resources that can be diverted to producing computer chips. Since each barrel of oil in the United States costs one microchip, reducing oil output by 5 million barrels means that 5 million more microcomputer chips can be produced.

Table 2 shows each country's production after Mexico has begun specializing in oil production.

**TABLE 2** Production after Mexico Specializes in Producing Crude Oil

| | United States | Mexico | Total |
|---|---|---|---|
| Oil | 15 | 10 | 25 |
| Chips | 25 | 0 | 25 |

Notice that the combined production of crude oil has remained constant, but the total output of computer chips has risen by 3 million chips. Assuming the two countries agree to share the added 3 million computer chips between them equally, Mexico will now ship 5 million barrels of oil to the United States in exchange for 3.5 million computer chips. From the 5 million additional computer chips the United States produces, Mexico will receive 2 million (its original production) plus 1.5 million for a total of 3.5 million, leaving 1.5 million additional chips for U.S. consumption. The resulting mix of products consumed in each country is shown in Table 3. Clearly, both countries are better off, having engaged in specialized production and trade.

**TABLE 3** Final Consumption Patterns after Trade

| | United States | Mexico | Total |
|---|---|---|---|
| Oil | 20 | 5 | 25 |
| Chips | 21.5 | 3.5 | 25 |

## *Issue:* Is Trade Really So Important? Neanderthals vs. Homo Sapiens

**Neanderthals** *(Homo neanderthalensis)* lived 200,000 years before Homo sapiens arrived on the scene. Both species then lived together in roughly the same ranges for another 10,000 years, at which time the Neanderthals died out. Modern evidence suggests that Neanderthals were roughly as intelligent as *Homo sapiens,* stronger, and also capable of speech. Until recently, the generally accepted reason for the Neanderthals' extinction was that *Homo sapiens* had more sophisticated tools, developed modern symbolic thinking, and created a more sophisticated language.

Digging in prehistoric *Homo sapiens'* caves has uncovered such items as paintings, spear points, stone tools made from materials not found in the same location, and seashell jewelry found in inland locations far from the ocean. These discoveries have produced a new theory of why *Homo sapiens* came to dominate the land: They were trading with other colonies of humans. The theory is that trade led to specialization, whereby the best hunters hunted, and the others made weapons, clothes, and other necessities.

To test this theory, several anthropologists created a computer population simulation model that included such variables as rates of fertility and mortality, specialization and trade, hunting ability, and the same number of skilled hunters and craftsmen in each population. They gave *Homo sapiens* an edge in the ability to specialize and trade. As the model ran, *Homo sapiens* had superior hunting success, giving them more meat and driving up fertility and population. The model assumed the number of animals was fixed, so the available meat for the Neanderthals declined, and so did their population. Depending on the model's parameters, the time it took for Neanderthals to die out roughly coincided with that estimated by other anthropologists. Ancient humans may have known the benefits of trade long before David Ricardo developed his theory of absolute and comparative advantage.

Source: "Human Evolution: Homo Economicus?" *The Economist,* April 9, 2005, pp. 67–68; and "Mrs. Adam Smith," *The Economist,* December 9, 2006, p. 85, and Matt Ridley, *The Rational Optimist: How Prosperity Evolves* (New York: HarperCollins) 2010.

The important point to remember here is that even when one country has an absolute advantage over another country, both countries still benefit from trading with one another. In our example, the gains were small, but such gains can grow; as two economies become more equal in size, the benefits of their comparative advantages grow.

## Limits on Trade and Globalization

Before leaving the subject of international trade, we should take a moment to note some practical constraints on trade. First, every transaction involves costs, including transportation, communications, and the general costs of doing business. Even so, over the last several decades, transportation and communication costs have been declining all over the world, resulting in growing global trade.

Second, the production possibilities curves for nations are not linear, but rather governed by increasing costs and diminishing returns. Therefore, it is difficult for countries to specialize in producing one product. Complete specialization would be risky, moreover, since the market for a product can always decline, perhaps because the product becomes technologically obsolete. Alternatively, changing weather patterns can wreak havoc on specialized agriculture products, adding further instability to incomes and exports in developing countries.

Finally, though two countries may benefit from trading with one another, expanding this trade may well hurt some industries and individuals within each country. Notably, industries finding themselves at a comparative disadvantage may be forced to scale back production and lay off workers. In such instances, government may need to provide workers with retraining, relocation, and other help to ensure a smooth transition to the new production mix.

When the United States signed the North American Free Trade Agreement (NAFTA) with Canada and Mexico, many people experienced what we have just been discussing. Some American jobs went south to Mexico because of low production costs. By opening up more markets for American products, however, NAFTA did stimulate economic growth, such that retrained workers may end up with new and better jobs.

**CHECKPOINT**

**SPECIALIZATION, COMPARATIVE ADVANTAGE, AND TRADE**

- An absolute advantage exists when one country can produce more of some good than another.
- A comparative advantage exists if one country has lower opportunity costs of producing a good than another country. Both countries gain from trade if each focuses on producing those goods at which it has a comparative advantage.
- Thus, voluntary trade is a positive-sum game, because both countries benefit from it.

**QUESTION:** Unlike most people, why do Hollywood stars (and many other rich people) have full-time personal assistants who manage their personal affairs?

Answers to the Checkpoint question can be found at the end of this chapter.

## Key Concepts



## Chapter Summary

### Basic Economic Questions and Production

Every economy must decide what to produce, how to produce it, and who will get the goods produced. How these questions are answered depends on how an economy is organized (capitalist, socialist, or communist).

Production is the process of converting factors of production—land, labor, capital, and entrepreneurial ability—into goods and services. Production efficiency occurs when goods and services are produced at the lowest possible resource cost. Allocative efficiency occurs when the mix of goods and services produced is that desired by society.

### Production Possibilities and Economic Growth

The PPF curve shows the different combinations of goods that a fully employed economy can produce, given its available resources and current technology (both assumed to be fixed in the short run). Production levels inside and on the frontier are possible, but production mixes lying outside the curve are unattainable.

Production on the frontier represents the maximum output attainable by the economy when all resources are fully employed. At full employment, reallocating production from one product to another involves opportunity costs: the output of one product that must be reduced to get the added output of the other. As an economy desires more of one product, the opportunity costs for this product rises because of diminishing returns and the unsuitability of some specialized resources to be devoted to producing some products.

The production possibilities model suggests that economic growth can arise from an expansion in resources or from improvements in technology. Expansions in resources expand the production possibilities frontier for all commodities. New technology allows previous output to be produced using fewer resources, thus leaving some resources available for use in other industries.

Economic growth can be enhanced by increasing the quantity or quality of labor available for production. Population growth, caused by higher birthrates or immigration, increases the quantity of labor available. Investments in human capital improve labor's quality. Greater capital accumulation further improves labor's productivity and thus increases growth rates.

### Specialization, Comparative Advantage, and Trade

An absolute advantage exists when one country can produce more of some good than another. A country has a comparative advantage if its opportunity costs to produce this good are lower than in the other country. Countries gain from voluntary trade if each focuses on producing those goods at which it enjoys a comparative advantage. Voluntary trade is thus a positive-sum game: Both countries stand to benefit from it.

## Questions and Problems

### Check Your Understanding

1. When can an economy increase the production of one good without reducing the output of another?
2. Explain the important difference between a straight line PPF and the PPF that is concave (bowed out) to the origin.
3. List the ways an economy can grow, given the discussion in this chapter.
4. Describe how opportunity cost is shown on a PPF.
5. In which of the three basic questions does technology play the greatest role?
6. How would unemployment be shown on the PPF?

### Apply the Concepts

7. Describe how a country producing more capital goods rather than consumer goods ends up in the future with a PPF that is larger than a country that produces more consumer goods and fewer capital goods.
8. The United States has an absolute advantage in making many goods, such as short-sleeve cotton golf shirts. Why do Costa Rica and Bangladesh make these shirts and export them to the United States?
9. As individuals, we all know what scarcity means: not enough time (even the rich face a scarcity of time), or insufficient income so we are unable to buy that new car, vacation home, or water-ski boat we want. But for nations as a whole, what does it mean to face scarcity?
10. Why is it that America uses heavy street cleaning machines driven by one person to clean the streets, while China and India use many people with brooms to do the same job?
11. China has experienced levels of economic growth in the last decade that have been 2 to 3 times that of the United States (10% vs. 3 to 4% per year in the United States). Has China's high growth rate eliminated scarcity in China?
12. If specialization and trade as discussed in this chapter lead to a win-win situation where both countries gain, why is there often opposition to trade agreements and globalization?
13. The By the Numbers box at the beginning of this chapter detailed the costs of firing workers in various countries. If the costs of *firing* workers are high, how does this affect the *hiring* of workers?
14. American attitudes about the tradeoff between the environment and economic growth shown in the By the Numbers box at the beginning of the chapter changed

significantly when the economy entered a recession. However, during the recession in 2009, Americans were roughly equally split between their concerns for the environment and economic growth. What would you expect to find in a similar survey in a relatively poor developing nation?

## Solving Problems

15. Political commentators often make the argument that growth in another country (most notably China) is detrimental to the economic interests of the United States. Look back at Tables 1 to 3 in the Gains from Trade section of the chapter. Then, assume that Mexico doubles in size, and make those changes to Table 1. Reconstruct Tables 2 and 3 given Mexico's greater capacity. Has the United States benefited by Mexico being able to produce more?

16. The table shows the potential output combinations of oranges and jars of prickly pear jelly (from the flower of the prickly pear cactus) for Florida and Arizona.
    a. Compute the opportunity cost for Florida of oranges in terms of jars of prickly pear jelly. Do the same for prickly pear jelly in terms of oranges.
    b. Compute the opportunity cost for Arizona of oranges in terms of jars of prickly pear jelly. Do the same for prickly pear jelly in terms of oranges.
    c. Would it make sense for Florida to specialize in producing oranges and for Arizona to specialize in producing prickly pear jelly and then trade? Why or why not?

| Florida | | Arizona | |
|---|---|---|---|
| Oranges | Prickly Pear Jelly | Oranges | Prickly Pear Jelly |
| 0 | 10 | 0 | 500 |
| 50 | 8 | 20 | 400 |
| 100 | 6 | 40 | 300 |
| 150 | 4 | 60 | 200 |
| 200 | 2 | 80 | 100 |
| 250 | 0 | 100 | 0 |

17. Complete the following sentences based on the figure below where three different production possibilities frontiers are shown.

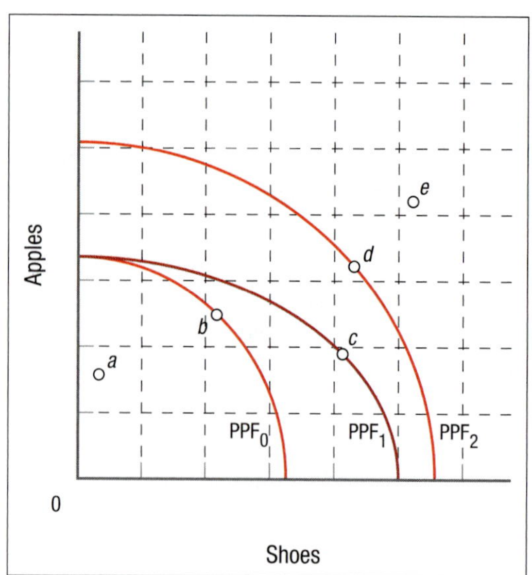

a. If the production possibilities frontier for this nation is $PPF_0$, then point *a* represents ________________________________.

b. If the production possibilities frontier for this nation is $PPF_0$, then point *e* represents ________________________________.

c. $PPF_1$ represents ________________________________.

d. If the initial production possibilities frontier is $PPF_0$, then $PPF_2$ represents ____________________________________________ and is caused by ____________________________________________.

# Answers to Questions in CheckPoints

## Check Point: Basic Economic Questions and Production

Typically, entrepreneurs put not only their time and effort into a business but also their money, often pledging private assets as collateral for loans. Should the business fail, they stand to lose more than their jobs, rent from the land, or interest on capital loaned to the firm. Workers can get other jobs, land owners can rent to others, and capital can be used in other enterprises. But the entrepreneur must suffer the loss of personal assets and move on.

## Check Point: Production Possibilities and Economic Growth

Abundant resources like oil or diamonds can be a curse because the economy often depends only on these resources for income and develops little else in terms of commerce. Many of the countries in the Middle East and Africa face this situation. Because their major source of income is concentrated in one resource, corruption often results, harming development in other sectors of the economy.

## Check Point: Specialization, Comparative Advantage, and Trade

For Hollywood stars and other rich people, the opportunity cost of their time is high. As a result, they hire people at lower cost to do the mundane chores that each of us is accustomed to doing because our time is not as valuable.

# Supply and Demand 

Illustration Works/Alamy

**Imagine you are going to build a house.** Your plans are drawn up, the land is purchased, and you are all set to begin construction. What is the first thing you do? Do you immediately start putting up walls or set the painters to work? Of course not! Before you can build any walls, much less start painting, you must lay a foundation. The same is true in economics: Before you can understand more complex economic concepts, you need a foundation. This chapter provides the basic foundation on which all other economic theory rests. This foundation—supply and demand analysis—explains how market economies operate. In the previous chapter on economic growth, we took markets for granted. Here we start examining markets in detail.

In our economy, most goods and services (including labor) are bought and sold through private markets. These products include everything from iPods to airline flights, from haircuts to new homes. Most markets offer consumers a wide variety of choices. The typical Walmart, for instance, features over 500,000 different items, while even a small town has numerous competing choices of hair salons, movie theaters, and shoe stores.

In any given market, prices are determined by "what the market will bear." Which factors determine what the market will bear, and what happens when events that occur in the marketplace cause prices to change? For answers to these questions, economists turn to supply and demand analysis. The basic model of supply and demand presented in this chapter will allow you to determine why product sales rise and fall, what direction prices move in, and how many goods will be offered for sale when certain events happen in the marketplace. Later chapters use this same model to explain complex phenomena such as how personal income is distributed.

**After studying this chapter you should be able to:**

- ☐ Describe the nature and purposes of markets.
- ☐ Describe the nature of demand, demand curves, and the law of demand.
- ☐ Describe the determinants of demand and be able to forecast how a change in one or more of these determinants will change demand.
- ☐ Describe the difference between a change in demand and a change in quantity demanded.
- ☐ Describe the nature of supply, supply curves, and the law of supply.
- ☐ Describe the determinants of supply and be able to forecast how a change in one or more of these determinants will change supply.
- ☐ Describe the difference between a change in supply and a change in quantity supplied.
- ☐ Determine market equilibrium price and output.
- ☐ Determine and predict how price and output will change given changes to supply and demand in the market.
- ☐ Understand the impacts of government intervention in markets.

This chapter introduces some of the basic economic concepts you need to know to understand how the forces of supply and demand work. These concepts include markets, the law of demand, demand curves, the determinants of demand, the law of supply, supply curves, the determinants of supply, equilibrium, surpluses, and shortages. Lastly, we look at what happens when governments attempt to alter market outcomes by setting limits on prices.

## Markets

A **market** is an institution that enables buyers and sellers to interact and transact with one another. A lemonade stand is a market because it allows people to exchange money for a product, in this case lemonade. Ticket scalping, though illegal in many states, similarly represents market activity since it leads to the exchange of money for tickets. The Internet, without a physical location, permits firms and individuals to sell a large number of low-volume niche products and still make money.[1] This includes students who resell their textbooks on Amazon.com and Half.com.

Even though all markets have the same basic component—the transaction—they can differ in a number of ways. Some markets are quite limited because of their geographical location, or because they offer only a few different products for sale. The New York Stock Exchange serves as a market for just a single type of financial instrument, stocks, but it facilitates exchanges worth billions of dollars daily. Compare this to the neighborhood flea market, which is much smaller and may operate only on weekends, but offers everything from food and crafts to T-shirts and electronics. Cement manufacturers are typically restricted to local markets due to high transportation costs, whereas Internet firms can easily do business with customers around the world.

### The Price System

When buyers and sellers exchange money for goods and services, accepting some offers and rejecting others, they are also doing something else: They are communicating their individual desires. Much of this communication is accomplished through the prices of items. If buyers sufficiently value a particular item, they will quickly pay its asking price. If they do not buy it, they are indicating they do not believe the item to be worth its asking price.

Prices also give buyers an easy means of comparing goods that can substitute for each other. If margarine falls to half the price of butter, this will suggest to many consumers that margarine is a better deal. Similarly, sellers can determine what goods to sell by comparing their prices. When prices rise for tennis rackets, this tells sporting goods stores that the public wants more tennis rackets, leading these stores to order more. Prices, therefore, contain a huge amount of useful information for both consumers and sellers. For this reason, economists often call our market economy the **price system.**

**Markets:** Institutions that bring buyers and sellers together so they can interact and transact with each other.

**Price system:** A name given to the market economy because prices provide considerable information to both buyers and sellers.

**CHECKPOINT**

**MARKETS**

- Markets are institutions that enable buyers and sellers to interact and transact business.
- Markets differ in geographical location, products offered, and size.
- Prices contain a wealth of information for both buyers and sellers.
- Through their purchases, consumers signal their willingness to exchange money for particular products at particular prices. These signals help businesses decide what to produce, and how much of it to produce.

[1] Chris Anderson, *The Long Tail: Why the Future of Business Is Selling Less of More* (New York: Hyperion), 2006.

- The market economy is also called the price system.

**QUESTION:** What are the important differences between the markets for financial securities such as the New York Stock Exchange and your local farmer's market?

Answers to the Checkpoint question can be found at the end of this chapter.

## *Issue:* Are There Markets in Everything, Even Marriage?

***All else equal,*** would a woman want to marry a man with greater social status and more resources (wealth)? Of course.

Economic theory suggests the answer is obvious, but proof is difficult to tease from marriage data, and many social scientists scoff at the idea. Two evolutionary psychologists, Thomas Pollet and Daniel Nettle, examined data from the 1910 census and discovered that supply and demand do matter in the marriage market.

In the early part of the last century, the West was relatively unsettled. Because many men moved west, communities often had a scarcity of women. Most of the eastern states had a male/female ratio of one, while in much of the West it was greater than one.

Pollet and Nettle set out to test the proposition that "when men are locally abundant, women will be able to demand a higher 'price' in terms of SES [socio-economic status] for entering a marriage than they can when men are locally scarce."

They found that in states where the ratio of men to women was equal, the marriage rate of high SES and low SES men were roughly the same. In states where men outnumbered the women, nearly twice the percentage of high SES men were married compared to low SES men. Women had the edge and they were pickier.

Pollet and Nettle concluded, "Marriage can be seen as partly involving a trade of female fertility and nurturance for male genes, resources and paternal investment, and, as in any trade, prices are affected by supply and demand." As most economists would expect, there are markets in everything, even marriage.

Sources: Thomas V. Pollet and Daniel Nettle, "Driving a hard bargain: sex ratio and male marriage success in a historical US population," *Biology Letters*, published online, 2007, and "A Buyers' Market," *The Economist*, December 15, 2007, p. 88.

Jupiterimages/Getty Images

# Demand

Whenever you purchase a product, you are voting with your money. You are selecting one product out of many and supporting one firm out of many, both of which signal to the business community what sorts of products satisfy your wants as a consumer.

Economists typically focus on wants rather than needs because it is so difficult to determine what we truly need. Theoretically, you could survive on tofu and vitamin pills, living in a lean-to made of cardboard and buying all your clothes from thrift stores. Most people in our society, however, choose not to live in such austere fashion. Rather, they want something more, and in most cases they are willing and able to pay for more. These wants—the desires consumers have for particular goods and services, which they express through their purchases—are known as demands.

## The Relationship between Quantity Demanded and Price

**Demand** refers to the goods and services people are willing and able to buy during a certain period of time at various prices, holding all other relevant factors constant (the *ceteris paribus* condition). Given the current popularity of television, most people would probably love to own a flat-panel HDTV with surround sound and hook it to a digital satellite or cable system that features hundreds of channels. And, indeed, if the products needed for such a setup were priced low enough, virtually everyone owning a television would opt for this system.

**Demand:** The maximum amount of a product that buyers are willing and able to purchase over some time period at various prices, holding all other relevant factors constant (the *ceteris paribus* condition).

As your television gets bigger and as you upgrade from basic television to cable or digital satellite, the cost of your home entertainment system increases. Yet, as the price of these services increases, the quantity demanded will decrease, since fewer and fewer people will be willing to spend their money on such things.

Thus, in a survey of households with television sets, we would expect to find a few people with virtually no service. A few people would have digital satellite hookups giving them access to sports channels, movie channels, and every other channel imaginable. The vast majority of consumers, however, would fall between these two categories, receiving some, but not all, of the services and channels available, in accord with their tastes and means.

In a market economy, there is a negative relationship between price and quantity demanded. This relationship, in its most basic form, states that as price increases, the quantity demanded falls, and conversely, as prices fall, the quantity demanded increases.

## The Law of Demand

**Law of demand:** Holding all other relevant factors constant, as price increases, quantity demanded falls, and as price decreases, quantity demanded rises.

This principle, that as price increases, quantity demanded falls, and as price decreases, quantity demanded rises—all other factors held constant—is known as the **law of demand.** The law of demand states that the lower a product's price, the more of that product consumers will purchase during a given time period. This straightforward, commonsense notion happens because, as a product's price drops, consumers will substitute the now-cheaper product for other, more expensive products. Conversely, if the product's price rises, consumers will find other, cheaper products to substitute for it.

To illustrate, when videocassette recorders first came on the market 30 years ago, they cost $3,000, and few homes had one. As VCRs became less and less expensive, however, more people bought them, and others found more uses for them. Today, DVD players and digital video recorders (DVRs) are everywhere, and VCRs are essentially consigned to museums. Digital music players have altered the structure of the music business, and digital cameras have essentially replaced film cameras.

Time is an important component in the demand for many products. Consuming many products—watching a movie, eating a pizza, playing tennis—takes some time. Thus, the price of these goods includes not only their money cost, but also the opportunity cost of the time needed to consume them. It follows that, all other things being equal, including the cost of a ticket, we would expect more consumers to attend a two-hour movie than a four-hour movie. The shorter movie simply requires less of a time investment.

## The Demand Curve

Several decades ago, computers filling entire air-conditioned rooms laboriously churned out data. Now, inexpensive laptop computers and smart phones can perform even more complex operations in a fraction of the time. This advance in computer technology has led to the widespread use of computers for both business and pleasure. Once offering only Pong, game companies now take millions of players a year into mythical adventures, space battles, military campaigns, and rounds of championship golf. Indeed, games on the three main platforms—Sony's Playstation 3, Microsoft's XBox 360, and Nintendo's Wii—are a driving force behind the development of faster microprocessor technology, because games are voracious users of speed.

**Demand curve:** Demand schedule information translated to a graph.

The law of demand states that as price decreases, quantity demanded increases. When we translate demand information into a graph, we create a **demand curve.** This demand curve, which slopes down and to the right, graphically illustrates the law of demand.

For example, consider Betty and her demand for computer games. Figure 1 depicts her annual demand in both table (the demand schedule) and graphical (the demand curve) form. Looking at the table and reading down Betty's demand schedule, we can see that Betty is willing to buy more computer games as the price decreases, from zero games at a price of $100 to 20 games at a price of $20. It makes sense that Betty will buy more computer games as the price decreases.

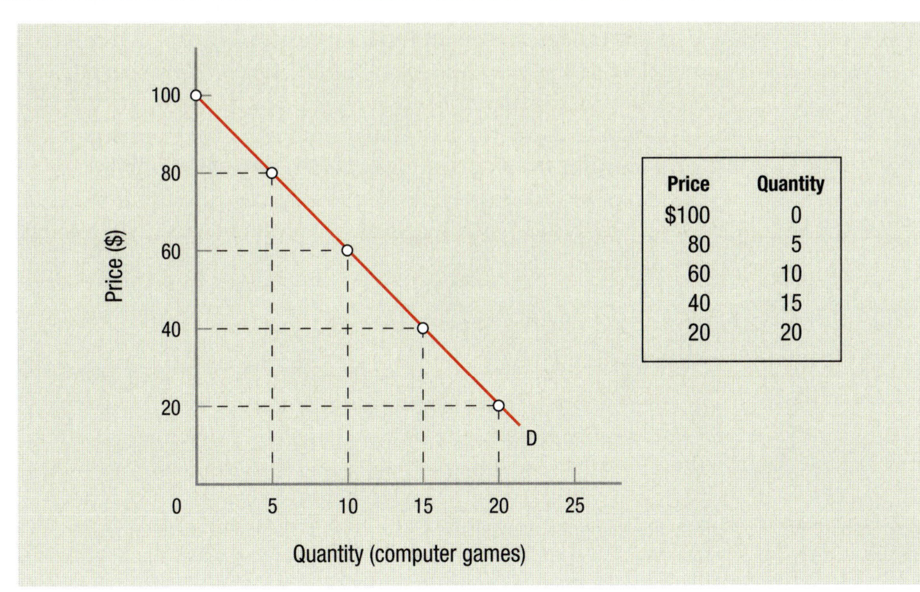


| Price | Quantity |
|---|---|
| $100 | 0 |
| 80 | 5 |
| 60 | 10 |
| 40 | 15 |
| 20 | 20 |

**FIGURE 1—Betty's Demand for Computer Games**

This figure shows Betty's demand schedule (the table) and her demand curve (the graph) for computer games over a year. Betty will purchase 5 computer games when the price is $80, buy 10 when the price falls to $60, and buy more as prices continue to fall. The demand curve D is Betty's demand curve for computer games.

We can take the values from the demand schedule in the table and graph them in a figure, with price as the vertical axis and computer games as the horizontal axis, following the convention in economics of always placing price on the vertical axis and quantity demanded on the horizontal axis. This line is the demand curve. Comparing the table with the graph, we can see that they convey the same information. For instance, find the price of $60 on the vertical axis in the graph and look to the right to the point on the curve; then look down to locate the quantity of 10 computer games. This is the same information conveyed in the table: locating a price of $60 and looking to the right gives you the quantity of 10 computer games demanded.

Both the table and the graph portray the law of demand. As the price decreases, Betty demands more computer games. If the price of each game is $100, Betty will not purchase any games; they are just too expensive. Let the price drop to $40, however, and she will buy 15 games during the year.

## Market Demand Curves

Though individual demand curves, like the one showing Betty's demand for computer games, are interesting, market demand curves are far more important to economists, as they can be used to predict changes in product price and quantity. Market demand is the sum of individual demands. To calculate market demand, economists simply add together how many units of a product all consumers will purchase at each price. This process is known as **horizontal summation.**

**Horizontal summation:** Market demand and supply curves are found by adding together how many units of the product will be purchased or supplied at each price.

Figure 2 on the next page shows an example of horizontal summation of individual demand curves to obtain a market demand curve. Two individual demand curves for Abe and Betty, $D_a$ and $D_b$, are shown. For simplicity, let's assume they represent the entire market, but recognize this process would work for a larger number of people. Note that at a price of $100 a game, Betty will not buy any, though Abe is willing to buy 10 games at $100. Above $100, therefore, the market demand is equal to Abe's demand. At $100 and below, however, we add both Abe's and Betty's demands at each price to obtain market demand. Thus, at $80, individual demand is 15 for Abe and 5 for Betty, so the market demand is equal to 20 (point *c*). When the price is $40 a game, Abe buys 25 and Betty buys 15, for a total of 40 games (point *e*). The heavier curve, labeled $D_{Mkt}$, represents this market demand; it is a horizontal summation of the two individual demand curves.

**FIGURE 2—Market Demand: Horizontal Summation of Individual Demand Curves**

Individual demand curves $D_a$ and $D_b$ are horizontally summed to get market demand, $D_{Mkt}$. Horizontal summation involves adding together the quantities demanded by each individual at each possible price.

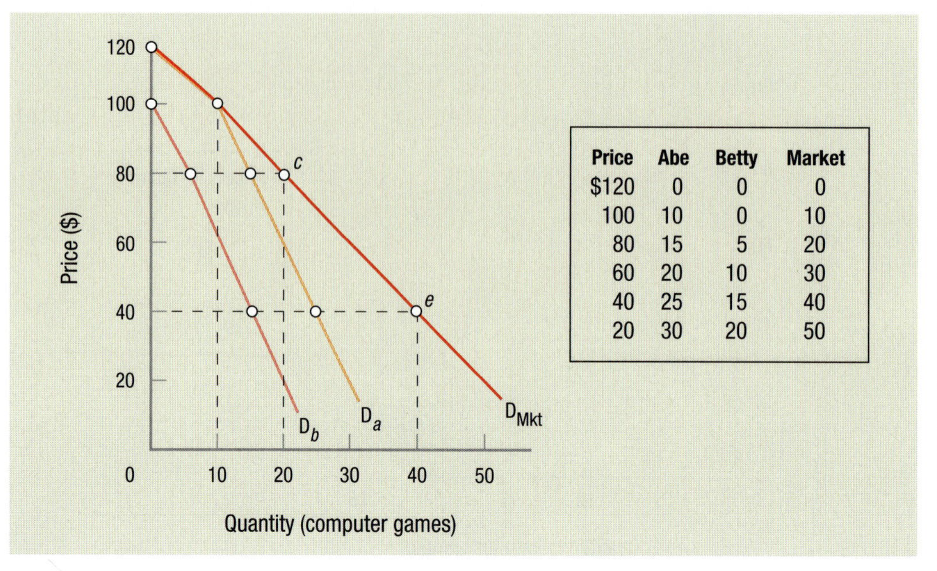


| Price | Abe | Betty | Market |
|---|---|---|---|
| $120 | 0 | 0 | 0 |
| 100 | 10 | 0 | 10 |
| 80 | 15 | 5 | 20 |
| 60 | 20 | 10 | 30 |
| 40 | 25 | 15 | 40 |
| 20 | 30 | 20 | 50 |

This all sounds simple in theory, but in the real world estimating market demand curves is a tricky business, given that many markets contain millions of consumers. Marketing professionals use sophisticated statistical techniques to estimate the market demand for particular goods and services.

The market demand curve shows the maximum amount of a product consumers are willing and able to purchase during a given time period at various prices, all other relevant factors being held constant. Economists use the term determinants of demand to refer to these other, nonprice factors that get held constant. This is another example of the use of *ceteris paribus:* holding all other relevant factors constant.

## Determinants of Demand

**Determinants of demand:** Nonprice factors that affect demand, including tastes and preferences, income, prices of related goods, number of buyers, and expectations.

Up to this point, we have discussed only how price affects the quantity demanded. When prices fall, consumers purchase more of a product, so quantity demanded rises. When prices rise, consumers purchase less of a product, so quantity demanded falls. But several other factors besides price also affect demand, including what people like, what their income is, and how much related products cost. More specifically, there are five key **determinants of demand:** (1) tastes and preferences, (2) income, (3) prices of related goods, (4) the number of buyers, and (5) expectations regarding future prices, income, and product availability. When one of these determinants change, the *entire* demand curve changes. Let's see why.

### Tastes and Preferences

We all have preferences for certain products instead of others, easily perceiving subtle differences in styling and quality. Automobiles, fashions, phones, and music are just a few of the products that are subject to the whims of the consumer.

Remember Crocs, those brightly colored rubber sandals with the little air holes that moms, kids, waitresses, and many others have been favoring for the past several years? They were an instant hit. Initially, demand was $D_0$ in Figure 3. They then became such a fad that demand jumped to $D_1$ and for a short while Crocs were hard to find. Eventually Crocs were everywhere. Fads come and go, and now the demand for them has settled back to something like $D_2$, less than the original level. Notice an important distinction here: More Crocs weren't sold because the *price* was lowered; the entire demand curve shifted rightward when they were hot and more Crocs could be sold at *all* prices. Now that the fad has subsided, fewer can be sold at all prices. It is important to keep in mind that when one of the determinants change, such as tastes and preferences in this case, the *entire* demand curve shifts.

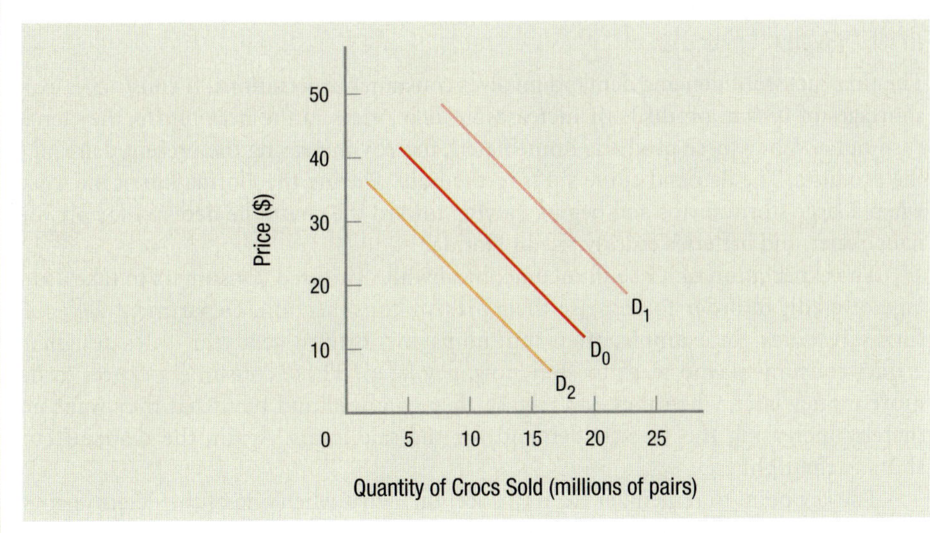


**FIGURE 3—Shifts in the Demand Curve**

The demand for Crocs originally was $D_0$. When they became a fad, demand shifted to $D_1$ as consumers were willing to purchase more at *all* prices. Once the fad cooled off, demand fell (shifted leftward) to $D_2$ as consumers wanted less at each price. When a determinant such as tastes and preferences changes, the *entire* demand curve shifts.

## Income

Income is another important factor influencing consumer demand. Generally speaking, as income rises, demand for most goods will likewise increase. Get a raise, and you are more likely to buy a nice car. Your demand curve will shift to the right (such as from $D_0$ to $D_1$ in Figure 3). Products for which demand is positively linked to income—when income rises, demand for the product also rises—are called **normal goods.**

There are also some products for which demand declines as income rises, and the demand curve shifts to the left. Economists call these products **inferior goods.** As your income grows, for instance, your consumption of public transportation will likely fall since you will probably own a car. Similarly, when you graduate from college and your income rises, your consumption of ramen noodles will fall as you begin dining in restaurants.

**Normal good:** A good for which an increase in income results in rising demand.

**Inferior good:** A good for which an increase in income results in declining demand.

## Prices of Related Goods

The prices of related commodities also affect consumer decisions. You may be an avid concert-goer, but with concert ticket prices often topping $100, if your local movie theater drops its ticket price to $8, you will probably end up seeing more movies than concerts. Movies, concerts, plays, and sporting events are good examples of **substitute goods,** since consumers can substitute one for another depending on their respective prices. When the *price* of concerts rises, your *demand* for movies increases, and vice versa. These are substitute goods.

Movies and popcorn, on the other hand, are examples of **complementary goods.** These are goods that are generally consumed together, such that an increase or decrease in the consumption of one will similarly result in an increase or decrease in the consumption of the other—see fewer movies, and your consumption of popcorn will decline. Other complementary goods include cars and gasoline, hot dogs and hot dog buns, and Windows System 7 and DRAM (dynamic random access memory) chips. Thus, when the *price* of movies increases, your *demand* for popcorn declines (shifts to the left), and vice versa.

**Substitute goods:** Goods consumers will substitute for one another depending on their relative prices. When the *price* of one good rises and the *demand* for another good increases, they are substitute goods, and vice versa.

**Complementary goods:** Goods that are typically consumed together. When the *price* of a complementary good rises, the *demand* for the other good declines, and vice versa.

## The Number of Buyers

Another factor influencing market demand for a product is the number of potential buyers in the market. Clearly, the more consumers there are who would be likely to buy a particular product, the higher its market demand will be (the demand curve will shift rightward). As our average life span steadily rises, the demands for medical services, rest homes, and retirement communities likewise increase. As more people want smart phones, fewer people want plain-vanilla cell phones, and their demand declines.

### Expectations about Future Prices, Incomes, and Product Availability

The final factor influencing demand involves consumer expectations. If consumers expect shortages of certain products or increases in their prices in the near future, they tend to rush out and buy these products immediately, thereby increasing the present demand for the products. The demand curve shifts to the right. During the Florida hurricane season, when a large storm forms and begins moving toward the coast, the demand for plywood, nails, water, and batteries quickly rise in Florida.

The expectation of a rise in income, meanwhile, can lead consumers to take advantage of credit in order to increase their present consumption. Department stores and furniture stores, for example, often run "no payments until next year" sales designed to attract consumers who want to "buy now, pay later." These consumers expect to have more money later, when they can pay, so they go ahead and buy what they want now, thereby increasing the present demand for the sale items. Again, the demand curve shifts to the right.

The key point to remember from this section is that when one of the determinants of demand changes, the *entire* demand curve shifts rightward (an increase in demand) or leftward (a decline in demand). A quick look back at Figure 3 shows that when demand increases, consumers are willing to buy more at all prices, and when demand declines, they will buy less at all prices.

## Changes in Demand Versus Changes in Quantity Demanded

When the price of a product rises, consumers simply buy fewer units of that product. This is a movement along an existing demand curve. However, when one or more of the determinants change, the entire demand curve is altered. Now at any given price consumers are willing to purchase more or less depending on the nature of the change. This section focuses on this important distinction between *changes in demand* versus *changes in quantity demanded.*

**Change in demand:** Occurs when one or more of the determinants of demand changes, shown as a shift in the entire demand curve.

**Changes in demand** occur whenever one or more of the determinants of demand change and demand curves shift. When demand changes, the demand curve shifts either to the right or to the left. Let's look at each shift in turn.

Demand increases when the entire demand curve shifts to the right. At all prices, consumers are willing to purchase more of the product in question. Figure 4 shows an increase

**FIGURE 4—Changes in Demand Versus Changes in Quantity Demanded**

A shift in the demand curve from $D_0$ to $D_1$ represents an *increase in demand,* and consumers will buy more of the product at each price. A shift from $D_0$ to $D_2$ reflects a *decrease in demand.* Movement along $D_0$ from point *a* to point *c* indicates an *increase in quantity demanded;* this type of movement can only be caused by a change in the price of the product.

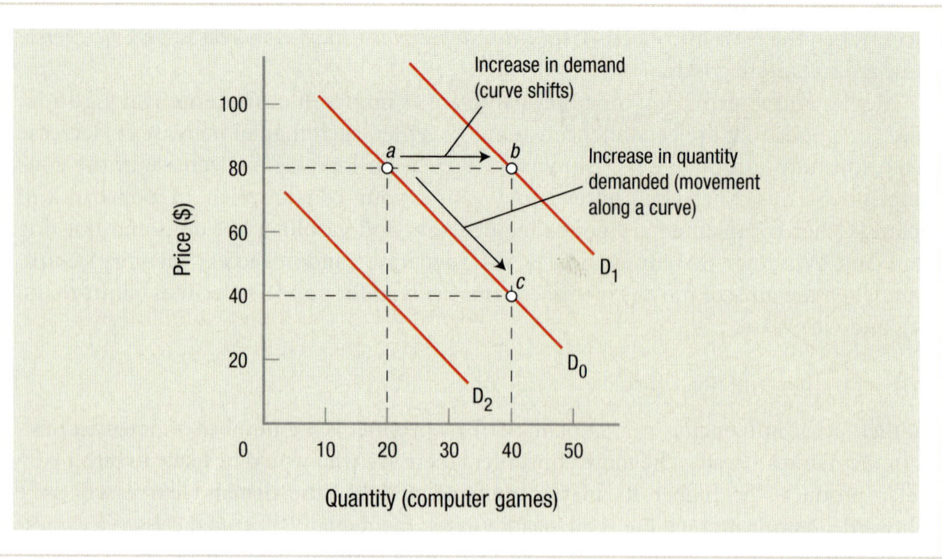

in demand for computer games; the demand curve shifts from $D_0$ to $D_1$. Notice that more computer games are purchased at all prices along $D_1$ as compared to $D_0$.

Now look at a decrease in demand, when the entire demand curve shifts to the left. At all prices, consumers are willing to purchase less of the product in question. A drop in consumer income is normally associated with a decline in demand (the demand curve shifts to the left). This decrease in demand is shown in Figure 4 as the demand curve shifting from $D_0$ to $D_2$.

Whereas a change in demand can be brought about by many different factors, a **change in quantity demanded** can be caused by only one thing: *a change in product price.* This is shown in Figure 4 as a reduction in price from \$80 to \$40, resulting in sales (quantity demanded) increasing from 20 (point *a*) to 40 (point *c*) games annually. This distinction between a change in demand and a change in quantity demanded is important. Reducing price to increase sales is different from spending a few million dollars on Super Bowl advertising to increase sales at all prices!

**Change in quantity demanded:** Occurs when the price of the product changes, shown as a movement along an existing demand curve.

These concepts are so important that a quick summary is in order. As Figure 4 illustrates, given the initial demand $D_0$, increasing sales from 20 to 40 games can occur in either of two ways. First, changing a determinant (say, increasing advertising) could shift the demand curve to $D_1$ so that 40 games would be sold at \$80 (point *b*). Alternatively, 40 games could be sold by reducing the price to \$40 (point *c*). Selling more by increasing advertising causes an increase in demand, or a shift in the whole demand curve that brings about a movement from point *a* to point *b*. Simply reducing the price, on the other hand, causes an increase in quantity demanded, or a movement along the existing demand curve, $D_0$, from point *a* to point *c*.

## CHECKPOINT

### DEMAND

- Demand refers to the quantity of products people are willing and able to purchase at various prices during some specific time period, all other relevant factors being held constant.
- Price and quantity demanded have an inverse (negative) relation: As price rises, consumers buy fewer units; as price falls, consumers buy more units. This inverse relation is known as the law of demand. It is depicted as a downward-sloping (from left to right) demand curve.
- To find market demand curves, simply horizontally sum all of the individual demand curves.
- Demand curves shift when one or more of the determinants of demand change.
- The determinants of demand are consumer tastes and preferences, income, prices of substitutes and complements, the number of buyers in a market, and expectations about future prices, incomes, and product availability.
- A shift of a demand curve is a *change in demand*. An increase in demand is a shift to the right. A decrease in demand is a shift to the left.
- A *change in quantity demanded* occurs only when the price of a product changes, leading consumers to adjust their purchases along the existing demand curve.

**QUESTION:** Sales of hybrid cars are on the rise. The Toyota Prius, while priced above comparable gasoline-only cars, is selling well. Other manufacturers are adding hybrids to their lines. What has been the cause of the rising sales of hybrids? Is this an increase in demand or an increase in quantity demanded?

Answers to the Checkpoint questions can be found at the end of this chapter.

# Supply

As mentioned earlier, the analysis of a market economy rests on two foundations: supply and demand. So far, we've covered the demand side of the market. Let's focus now on the decisions businesses make regarding production numbers and sales. These decisions cause variations in product supply.

## The Relationship between Quantity Supplied and Price

**Supply:** The maximum amount of a product that sellers are willing and able to provide for sale over some time period at various prices, holding all other relevant factors constant (the *ceteris paribus* condition).

**Supply** is the maximum amount of a product that producers are willing and able to offer for sale at various prices, all other relevant factors being held constant. The quantity supplied will vary according to the price of the product.

What explains this relationship? As we saw in the previous chapter, businesses inevitably encounter rising opportunity costs as they attempt to produce more and more of a product. This is due in part to diminishing returns from available resources, and in part to the fact that when producers increase production, they must either have existing workers put in overtime hours (at a higher hourly pay rate) or hire additional workers away from other industries (again at premium pay).

Producing more units, therefore, makes it more expensive for producers to produce each individual unit. These increasing costs give rise to the positive relationship between product price and quantity supplied to the market.

## The Law of Supply

**Law of supply:** Holding all other relevant factors constant, as price increases, quantity supplied will rise, and as price declines, quantity supplied will fall.

Unfortunately for producers, they can rarely charge whatever they would like for their products; they must charge whatever the market will permit. But producers can decide how much of their product to produce and offer for sale. The **law of supply** states that higher prices will lead producers to offer more of their products for sale during a given period. Conversely, if prices fall, producers will offer fewer products to the market. The explanation is simple: The higher the price, the greater the potential for higher profits and thus the greater the incentive for businesses to produce and sell more products. Also, given the rising opportunity costs associated with increasing production, producers need to charge these higher prices to profitably increase the quantity supplied.

## The Supply Curve

**Supply curve:** Supply schedule information translated to a graph.

Just as demand curves graphically display the law of demand, **supply curves** provide a graphical representation of the law of supply. The supply curve shows the maximum amounts of a product a producer will furnish at various prices during a given period of time. While the demand curve slopes down and to the right, the supply curve slopes up and to the right.[2] This illustrates the positive relationship between price and quantity supplied: the higher the price, the greater the quantity supplied.

## Market Supply Curves

As with demand, economists are more interested in market supply than in the supplies offered by individual firms. To compute market supply, use the same method used to calculate market demand, horizontally summing the supplies of individual producers. A hypothetical market supply curve for computer games is depicted in Figure 5.

[2] There are some exceptions to positively sloping supply curves. But for our purposes, we will ignore them for now.

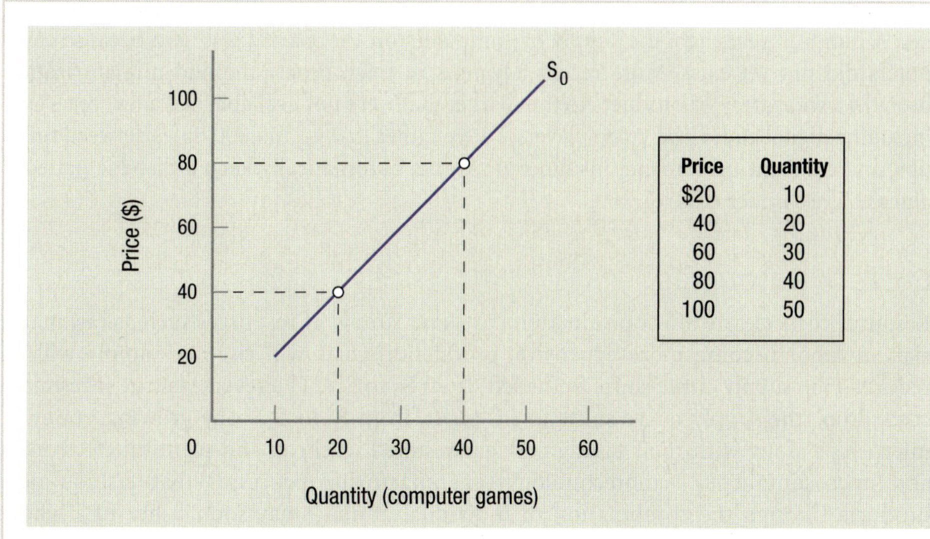


**FIGURE 5—Supply of Computer Games**

This supply curve graphs the supply schedule and shows the maximum quantity of computer games that producers will offer for sale over some defined period of time. The supply curve is positively sloped, reflecting the law of supply. In other words, as prices rise, quantity supplied increases; as prices fall, quantity supplied falls.

## Determinants of Supply

Like demand, several nonprice factors help to determine the supply of a product. Specifically, there are six **determinants of supply:** (1) production technology, (2) costs of resources, (3) prices of other commodities, (4) expectations, (5) the number of sellers (producers) in the market, and (6) taxes and subsidies.

**Determinants of supply:** Nonprice factors that affect supply, including production technology, costs of resources, prices of other commodities, expectations, number of sellers, and taxes and subsidies.

### Production Technology

Technology determines how much output can be produced from given quantities of resources. If a factory's equipment is old and can turn out only 50 units of output per hour, then no matter how many other resources are employed, those 50 units are the most the factory can produce in an hour. If the factory is outfitted with newer, more advanced equipment capable of turning out 100 units per hour, the firm can supply more of its product at the same price as before, or even at a lower price. In Figure 6, this would be represented by a shift in the supply curve from $S_0$ to $S_1$. At every single price, more would be supplied.

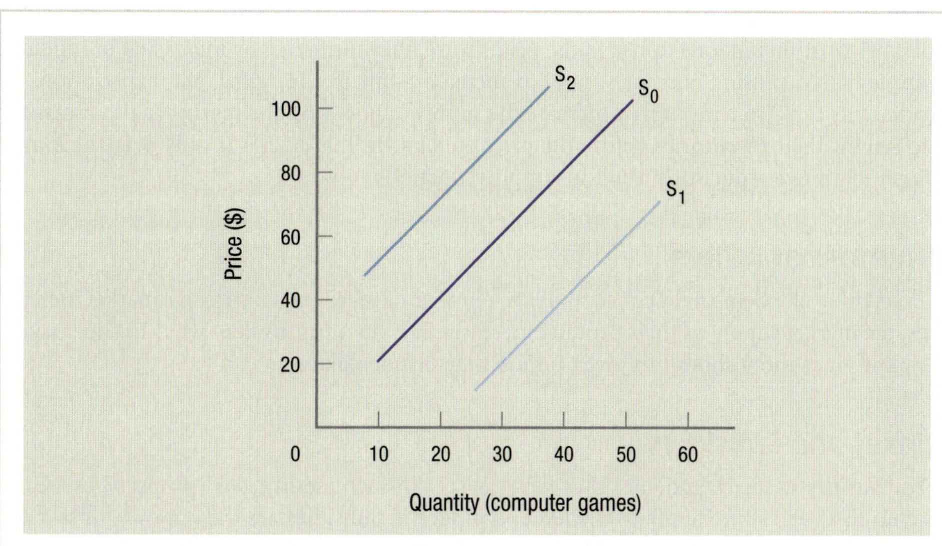


**FIGURE 6—Shifts in the Supply Curve**

The supply of computer games originally is $S_0$. If supply shifts to $S_1$, producers are willing to sell more at *all* prices. If supply falls, supply shifts leftward to $S_2$. Now firms are only willing to sell less at each price. When a determinant of supply changes, the *entire* supply curve shifts.

Technology further determines the nature of products that can be supplied to the market. A hundred years ago, the supply of computers on the market was zero because computers did not yet exist. More recent advances in microprocessing and miniaturization brought a wide array of products to the market that were not available just a few years ago, including digital audio and video players, auto engines that go 100,000 miles between tune-ups, and constant-monitoring insulin pumps that automatically keep a diabetic patient's glucose levels under control.

## Costs of Resources

Resource costs clearly affect production costs and supply. If resources such as raw materials or labor become more expensive, production costs will rise and supply will be reduced (the supply curve shifts to the left, from $S_0$ to $S_2$). The reverse is true if resource costs drop (the supply curve shifts to the right, from $S_0$ to $S_1$). The growing power of microchips along with their falling cost has resulted in cheap and plentiful electronics and microcomputers. Nanotechnology—manufacturing processes that fashion new products through the combination of individual atoms—may soon usher in a whole new generation of inexpensive products.

On the other hand, if the cost of petroleum goes up, the cost of products using petroleum in their manufacture will go up, leading to the supply being reduced (the supply curve shifts leftward). If labor costs rise because immigration is restricted, this drives up production costs of California vegetables (fewer farm workers) and software in Silicon Valley (fewer software engineers from abroad) and leads to a shift in the supply curve to the left in Figure 6.

## Prices of Other Commodities

Most firms have some flexibility in the portfolio of goods they produce. A vegetable farmer, for example, might be able to grow celery, radishes, or some combination of the two. Given this flexibility, a change in the price of one item may influence the quantity of other items brought to market. If the price of celery should rise, for instance, most farmers will start growing more celery. And since they all have a limited amount of land on which to grow vegetables, this reduces the quantity of radishes they can produce. Hence, in this case, the rise in the price of celery may well cause a reduction in the supply of radishes (the supply curve for radishes shifts leftward).

## Expectations

The effects of future expectations on market supplies can be complicated, and it often is difficult to generalize about how future supplies will be affected. When producers expect the prices of their goods to rise in the near future, they may react by increasing production immediately, causing current supply to increase (shift to the right). Yet, expectations of price cuts can also temporarily increase the supply of goods on the market as producers try to sell off their inventories before the price cuts hit. In this case, it is only over the longer term that price reductions result in supply reductions.

## Number of Sellers

Everything else being held constant, if the number of sellers in a particular market increases, the market supply of their product increases. It is no great mystery why: 10 shoemakers can produce more shoes in a given period than 5 shoemakers.

## Taxes and Subsidies

For businesses, taxes and subsidies affect costs. An increase in taxes (property, excise, or other fees) will shift supply to the left and reduce it. Subsidies are the opposite of taxes. If the government subsidizes the production of a product, supply will shift to the right and rise. A luxury tax on powerboats in the 1990s reduced supply (the tax was the equivalent of an increase in production costs), while today's subsidies to ethanol producers are expanding ethanol production.

## Changes in Supply Versus Changes in Quantity Supplied

A **change in supply** results from a change in one or more of the determinants of supply; it causes the entire supply curve to shift. An increase in supply of a product, perhaps because advancing technology has made it cheaper to produce, means that more of the commodity will be offered for sale at every price. This causes the supply curve to shift to the right, as illustrated in Figure 7 by the shift from $S_0$ to $S_1$. A decrease in supply, conversely, shifts the supply curve to the left, since fewer units of the product are offered at every price. Such a decrease in supply is here represented by the shift from $S_0$ to $S_2$.

**Change in supply:** Occurs when one or more of the determinants of supply change, shown as a shift in the entire supply curve.

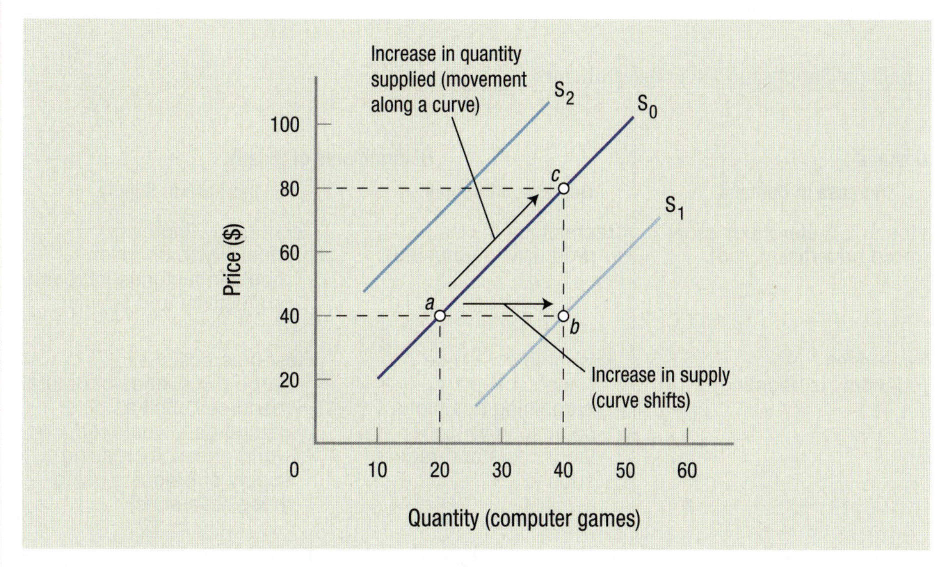


**FIGURE 7—Changes in Supply Versus Changes in Quantity Supplied**

A shift in the supply curve from $S_0$ to $S_1$ represents an *increase in supply,* since businesses are willing to offer more of the product to consumers at *all* prices. A shift from $S_0$ to $S_2$ reflects a decrease in supply. A movement along $S_0$ from point *a* to point *c* represents an *increase in quantity supplied;* it results from an increase in the product's market price from $40 to $80.

A change in supply involves a shift of the entire supply curve. In contrast, the supply curve does not move when there is a **change in quantity supplied.** Only a change in the price of a product can cause a change in the quantity supplied; hence, it involves a movement along an existing supply curve rather than a shifting to an entirely different curve. In Figure 7, for instance, an increase in price from $40 to $80 results in an increase in quantity supplied from 20 to 40 games, represented by the movement from point *a* to point *c* along $S_0$.

**Change in quantity supplied:** Occurs when the price of the product changes, shown as a movement along an existing supply curve.

In summary, a change in supply is represented in Figure 7 by the shift from $S_0$ to $S_1$ or $S_2$, which involves a shift in the entire supply curve. For example, an increase in supply from $S_0$ to $S_1$ results in an increase in supply from 20 computer games (point *a*) to 40 (point *b*) provided at a price of $40. More games are provided at the same price. In contrast, a change in quantity supplied is shown in Figure 7 as a movement along an existing supply curve, $S_0$, from point *a* to point *c* caused by an increase in the price of the product from $40 to $80.

As on the demand side, this distinction between changes in supply and changes in quantity supplied is crucial. It means that when a product's price changes, only quantity supplied changes—the supply curve does not move. A summary of how the determinants affect both supply and demand is shown in Figure 8 on the next page.

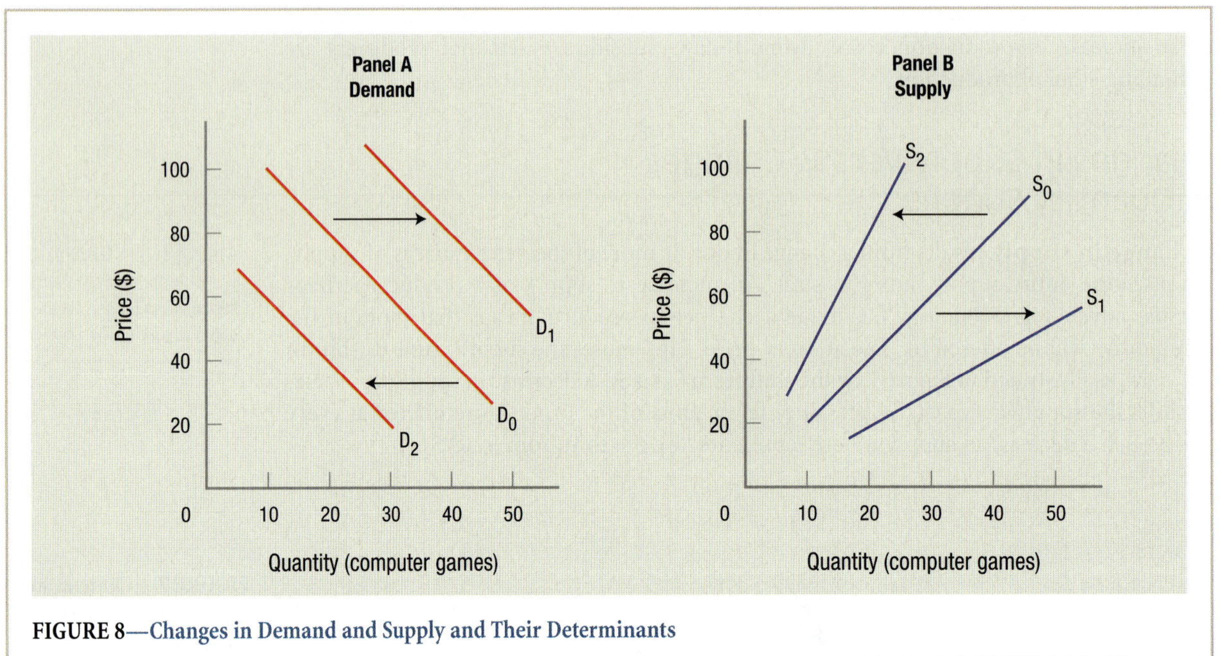


FIGURE 8—Changes in Demand and Supply and Their Determinants

| Determinants of Demand | | Determinants of Supply | |
|---|---|---|---|
| **Decrease in Demand** | **Increase in Demand** | **Decrease in Supply** | **Increase in Supply** |
| Tastes and preferences decline (less advertising, out of fashion). | Tastes and preferences grow (more advertising, fad). | Technology harms productivity (unusual). | Technology improves productivity (production robots in factories increase productivity and supply). |
| Income falls (economy is in a recession). | Income rises (economy is booming). | Resource costs rise (tough collective bargaining by unions could lead to higher labor costs and reduce supply). | Resource costs fall (large discoveries of natural resources such as oil or natural gas, would reduce world prices, increasing supply of products using these resources). |
| Price of substitute falls (price of tea falls, coffee demand declines). Price of complement rises (price of gasoline rises, demand for big SUVs drops). | Price of substitute rises (chicken prices rise, demand for beef increases). Price of complement falls (price of DVD players falls, demand for DVD movies increases). | Price of a production substitute rises (cucumber prices rise, reducing the supply of radishes as more cucumbers are planted). | Price of a production substitute falls (price of apples falls, landowners plant grapes instead and eventually the supply of wine rises). |
| Number of buyers falls. | Number of buyers grows. | Decreasing number of sellers | Rising number of sellers |
| Expecting future glut; expected surplus in future leads to lower prices so consumers hold off buying now (some consumers wait for after-Christmas sales of unsold—surplus—merchandise). | Expecting future shortages; leads to stocking up now to avoid higher prices in future (predicted gasoline shortages lead to filling of tanks now—an increase in current demand). | Expectation of a rise in future price of product (unsettled world conditions lead to expectations that gold will jump in price, which may lead to a withholding of gold from the market, reducing current supply). | Falling future price expectations for product (if beef prices are expected to fall, producers may sell more cattle now). |
| | | Increase in taxes or reduction in subsidies (increasing taxes on cigarettes or reducing subsidies for ethanol will reduce supplies of both products). | Decrease in taxes or an increase in subsidies (reductions in excise taxes on luxury vehicles and increases in subsidies for education will increase the supply of both). |

**CHECKPOINT**

## SUPPLY

- Supply is the quantity of a product producers are willing and able to put on the market at various prices, all other relevant factors being held constant.
- The law of supply reflects the positive relationship between price and quantity supplied: the higher the market price, the more goods supplied, and the lower the market price, the fewer goods supplied.
- As with demand, market supply is arrived at by horizontally summing the individual supplies of all of the firms in the market.
- A change in supply occurs when one or more of the determinants of supply change.
- The determinants of supply are production technology, the cost of resources, prices of other commodities, expectations, the numbers of sellers or producers in the market, and taxes and subsidies.
- A *change in supply* is a shift in the supply curve. A shift to the right reflects an increase in supply, while a shift to the left represents a decrease in supply.
- A *change in quantity supplied* is only caused by a change in the price of the product; it results in a movement along the existing supply curve.

**QUESTION:** What has been the impact of the iPod, iTunes, and MP3 players in general on high-end stereo equipment production?

Answers to the Checkpoint question can be found at the end of this chapter.

# Market Equilibrium

Supply and demand together determine the prices and quantities of goods bought and sold. Neither factor alone is sufficient to determine price and quantity. It is through their interaction that supply and demand do their work, just as two blades of a scissors are required to cut paper.

A market will determine the price at which the quantity of a product demanded is equal to the quantity supplied. At this price, the market is said to be cleared or to be in **equilibrium,** meaning the amount of the product that consumers are willing and able to purchase is matched exactly by the amount that producers are willing and able to sell. This is the **equilibrium price** and the **equilibrium quantity.** The equilibrium price is also called the market-clearing price.

**Equilibrium:** Market forces are in balance when the quantities demanded by consumers just equal the quantities supplied by producers.

**Equilibrium price:** Market equilibrium price is the price that results when quantity demanded is just equal to quantity supplied.

**Equilibrium quantity:** Market equilibrium quantity is the output that results when quantity demanded is just equal to quantity supplied.

Figure 9 on the next page puts together Figures 2 and 5, showing the market supply and demand for computer games. It illustrates how supply and demand interact to determine equilibrium price and quantity. Clearly, the quantities demanded and supplied equal one another only where the supply and demand curves cross, at point *e.* Alternatively, you can see this in the table that is part of the figure: Quantity demanded and quantity supplied are the same at only one particular point. At $60 a game, sellers are willing to provide exactly the same quantity as consumers would like to purchase. Hence, at this price, the market clears, since buyers and sellers both want to transact the same number of units.

The beauty of a market is that it automatically works to establish the equilibrium price and quantity, without any guidance from anyone. To see how this happens, let us assume that computer games are initially priced at $80, a price above their equilibrium price. As we can see by comparing points *a* and *b,* sellers are willing to supply more games at this price than consumers are willing to buy. Economists characterize such a situation as one of excess supply, or **surplus.** In this case, at $80, sellers supply 40 games to the market (point *b*), yet buyers want to purchase only 20 (point *a*). This leaves an excess of 20 games overhanging the market; these unsold games ultimately become surplus inventories.

**Surplus:** Occurs when the price is above market equilibrium, and quantity supplied exceeds quantity demanded.

Here is where the market kicks in to restore equilibrium. As inventories rise, most firms cut production. Some firms, moreover, start reducing their prices to increase sales.

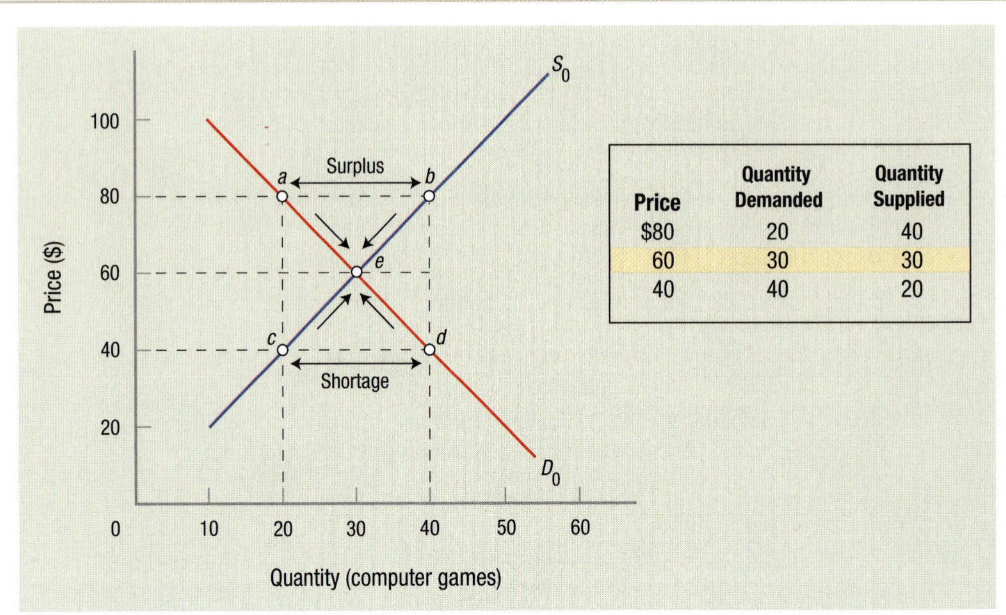


| Price | Quantity Demanded | Quantity Supplied |
|---|---|---|
| $80 | 20 | 40 |
| 60 | 30 | 30 |
| 40 | 40 | 20 |

**FIGURE 9—Equilibrium Price and Quantity of Computer Games**

Market equilibrium is achieved when quantity demanded and quantity supplied are equal. In this graph, that equilibrium occurs at point *e*, at an equilibrium price of $60 and an equilibrium output of 30. If the market price is above equilibrium ($80), a surplus of 20 computer games will result (*b* − *a*), automatically driving the price back down to $60. When the market price is too low ($40), a shortage of 20 computer games will result (*d* − *c*), and businesses will raise their offering prices until equilibrium is again restored.

Other firms must then cut their own prices to remain competitive. This process continues, with firms cutting their prices and production, until most firms have managed to exhaust their surplus inventories. This happens when prices reach $60 and quantity supplied equals 30, since consumers are once again willing to buy up the entire quantity supplied at this price, and the market is restored to equilibrium.

**Shortage:** Occurs when the price is below market equilibrium, and quantity demanded exceeds quantity supplied.

In general, therefore, when prices are set too high, surpluses result, which drive prices back down to their equilibrium levels. If, conversely, a price is initially set too low, say at $40, a **shortage** results. In this case, buyers want to purchase 40 games (point *d*), but sellers are only providing 20 (point *c*), creating a shortage of 20 games. Because consumers are willing to pay more than $40 to get hold of the few games available on the market, they will start bidding up the price of computer games. Sensing an opportunity to make some money, firms will start raising their prices and increasing production, once again until equilibrium is restored. Hence, in general, excess demand causes firms to raise prices and increase production.

When there is a shortage in a market, economists speak of a tight market or a seller's market. Under these conditions, producers have no difficulty selling off all their output. When a surplus of goods floods the market, this gives rise to a buyer's market, since buyers can buy all the goods they want at attractive prices.

We have now seen how changing prices naturally work to clear up shortages and surpluses, thereby returning markets to equilibrium. Some markets, once disturbed, will return to equilibrium quickly. Examples include the stock, bond, and money markets, where trading is nearly instantaneous and extensive information abounds. Other markets react very slowly. Consider the labor market, for instance. For various psychological reasons, most people have an inflated idea of their worth to both current and future employers. It is only after an extended bout of unemployment, therefore, that many people will face reality and accept a position at a salary lower than their previous job. Similarly, real estate markets can be slow

## Alfred Marshall (1842–1924)

British economist Alfred Marshall is considered the father of the modern theory of supply and demand—that price and output are determined by both supply *and* demand. He noted that the two go together like the blades of a scissors that cross at equilibrium.

He assumed that changes in quantity demanded were only affected by changes in price, and that all other factors remained constant. Marshall also is credited with developing the ideas of the laws of demand and supply, and the concepts of consumer surplus and producer surplus—concepts we will study in the next chapter.

As a boy, he suffered from severe headaches, which could only be cured by playing chess. He later swore off chess because "otherwise I would have been tempted to spend all my time on it." When his uncle went to Australia and made a fortune as a farmer, he was able to give Alfred financial support.

With financial help from this uncle, Marshall attended St. John's College, Cambridge, to study mathematics and physics. But after long walks through the poorest sections of several European cities and seeing their horrible conditions, he decided to focus his attention on political economy.

PRINCIPLES
OF
ECONOMICS
BY
ALFRED MARSHALL,
PROFESSOR OF POLITICAL ECONOMY IN THE UNIVERSITY OF CAMBRIDGE;
HONORARY FELLOW OF BALLIOL COLLEGE, OXFORD.
VOL. I.
*Natura non facit saltum.*
London:
MACMILLAN AND CO., LIMITED.
NEW YORK: THE MACMILLAN COMPANY.
1898

In 1890, he published *Principles of Economics* at the age of 48. In it he introduced many new ideas for the first time, though as Ray Canterbery noted, ". . . without any suggestion that they are novel or remarkable." During his lifetime, the book went through eight editions. In hopes of appealing to the general public, Marshall buried his diagrams in footnotes. And, although he is credited with many economic theories, he would always clarify them with various exceptions and qualifications. He expected future economists to flesh out his ideas.

Above all, Marshall loved teaching and his students. According to John Maynard Keynes, it was impossible to take coherent notes from Marshall's lectures. They were never orderly or systematic since he tried to get students to think *with* him and ultimately think for themselves. At one point near the turn of the twentieth century, essentially all of the leading economists in England had been his students.

More than anyone else, Marshall is given credit for establishing economics as a discipline of study. Keynes, the most influential economist of the last century and Marshall's student, wrote a 70-page, 20,000-word memorial to Marshall, published in the *Economic Journal* 3 months after his death in 1924.

Sources: E. Ray Canterbery, *A Brief History of Economics: Artful Approaches to the Dismal Science* (New Jersey: World Scientific), 2001; Robert Skidelsky, *John Maynard Keynes: Volume Two The Economist as Saviour 1920–1937* (New York: The Penguin Press), 1992; and John Maynard Keynes, *Essays in Biography* (New York: Norton), 1951.

to adjust since sellers will often refuse to accept a price below what they are asking for, until the lack of sales over time convinces sellers to adjust the price downward.

These automatic market adjustments can make some buyers and sellers feel uncomfortable: It seems as if prices and quantities are being set by forces beyond anyone's control. In fact, this phenomenon is precisely what makes market economies function so efficiently. Without anyone needing to be in control, prices and quantities naturally gravitate toward equilibrium levels. Adam Smith was so impressed by the workings of the market that he suggested it is almost as if an "invisible hand" guides the market to equilibrium.

Given the self-correcting nature of the market, long-term shortages or surpluses are almost always the result of government intervention, as we will see later in this chapter. First, however, we turn to a discussion of how the market responds to changes in supply and demand, or to shifts of the supply and demand curves.

## Moving to a New Equilibrium: Changes in Supply and Demand

Once a market is in equilibrium and the forces of supply and demand balance one another out, the market will remain there unless an external factor changes. But when the supply curve or demand curve shifts (some determinant changes), equilibrium also shifts, resulting in a new equilibrium price and/or output. The ability to predict new equilibrium points is one of the most useful aspects of supply and demand analysis.

### Predicting the New Equilibrium When One Curve Shifts

When only supply or only demand changes, the change in equilibrium price and equilibrium output can be predicted. We begin with changes in supply.

***Changes in Supply*** Figure 10 shows what happens when supply changes. Equilibrium initially is at point *e*, with equilibrium price and quantity at $P_0$ and $Q_0$, respectively. But let us assume a rise in wages or the bankruptcy of a key business in the market (the number of sellers declines) causes a decrease in supply. When supply declines (the supply curve shifts from $S_0$ to $S_2$), equilibrium price rises to $P_2$, while equilibrium output falls to $Q_2$ (point *a*).

**FIGURE 10—Equilibrium Price, Output, and Shifts in Supply**

When supply alone shifts, the effects on both equilibrium price and output can be predicted. When supply grows ($S_0$ to $S_1$), equilibrium price will fall and output will rise. When supply declines ($S_0$ to $S_2$), the opposite happens: Equilibrium price will rise and output will fall.

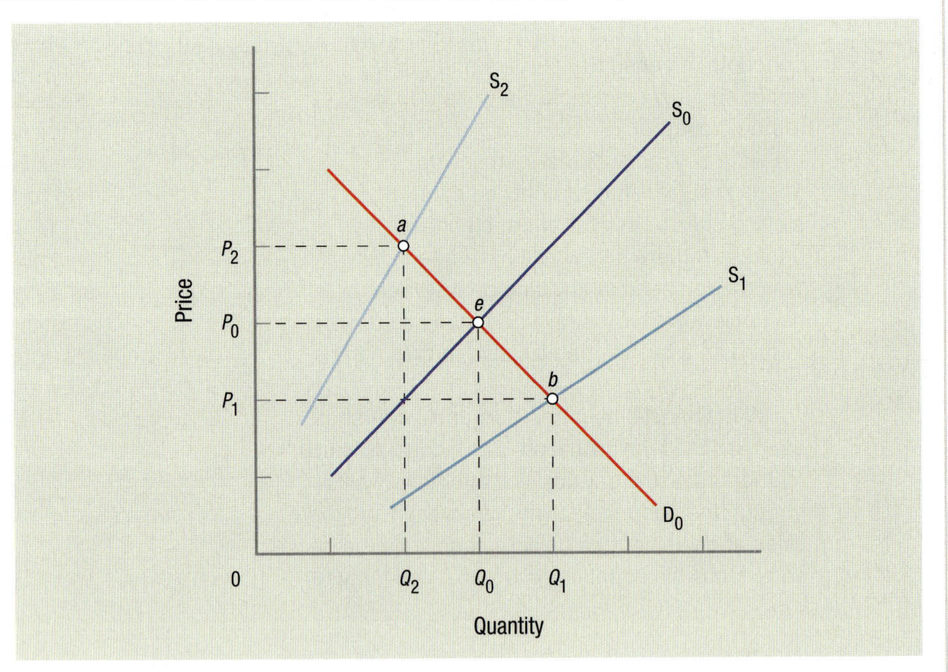


If, on the other hand, supply increases (the supply curve shifts from $S_0$ to $S_1$), equilibrium price falls to $P_1$, while equilibrium output rises to $Q_1$ (point *b*). This is what has happened in the electronics industry: Declining production costs have resulted in more electronic products being sold at lower prices.

***Changes in Demand*** The effects of demand changes are shown in Figure 11. Again, equilibrium is initially at point *e*, with equilibrium price and quantity at $P_0$ and $Q_0$, respectively. But let us assume the economy then enters a recession and incomes sink, or perhaps the price of some complementary good soars; in either case, demand falls. As demand declines (the demand curve shifts from $D_0$ to $D_2$), equilibrium price falls to $P_2$, while equilibrium output falls to $Q_2$ (point *a*).

## *Issue:* Two-Buck Chuck: Will People Drink $2 a Bottle Wine?

**The great California** wines of the 1990s put California vineyards on the map. Demand, prices, and exports grew rapidly. Overplanting of new grape vines was a result. Driving along Interstate 5 or Highway 101 north of Los Angeles, grape vineyards extend as far as the eye can see, and most were planted in the mid- to late 1990s. The 2001 recession reduced the demand for California wine, and a rising dollar made imported wine relatively cheaper. The result was a sharp drop in demand for California wine and a huge surplus of grapes.

Bronco Wine Company President Fred Franzia made an exclusive deal with Trader Joe's (an unusual supermarket that features exotic food and wine products), bought the excess grapes at distressed prices, and with his modern plant produced inexpensive wine under the Charles Shaw label. Selling for $1.99 a bottle, Two-Buck Chuck, as it is known, is available in chardonnay, merlot, cabernet sauvignon, shiraz, and sauvignon blanc. Consumers have flocked to Trader Joe's and literally haul cases of wine out by the carload. In less than a decade, 400 million bottles have been sold. This is not rotgut: the 2002 shiraz beat out 2,300 other wines to win a double gold medal at the 28th Annual International Eastern Wine Competition in 2004. Still, to many Napa Valley vintners it is known as Two-Buck Upchuck.

Donald Gruener

Two-Buck Chuck was such a hit that other supermarkets were forced to offer their own discount wines. This good, low-priced wine has had the effect of opening up markets. People who previously avoided wine because of the cost have begun drinking more. As *The Economist* has noted, the entire industry may benefit because "wine drinkers who start off drinking plonk often graduate to upmarket varieties."[3]

During the same recession just described, the demand for inferior goods (beans and baloney) will rise, as declining incomes force people to switch to cheaper substitutes. For these products, as demand increases (shifting the demand curve from $D_0$ to $D_1$), equilibrium price rises to $P_1$, and equilibrium output grows to $Q_1$ (point *b*).

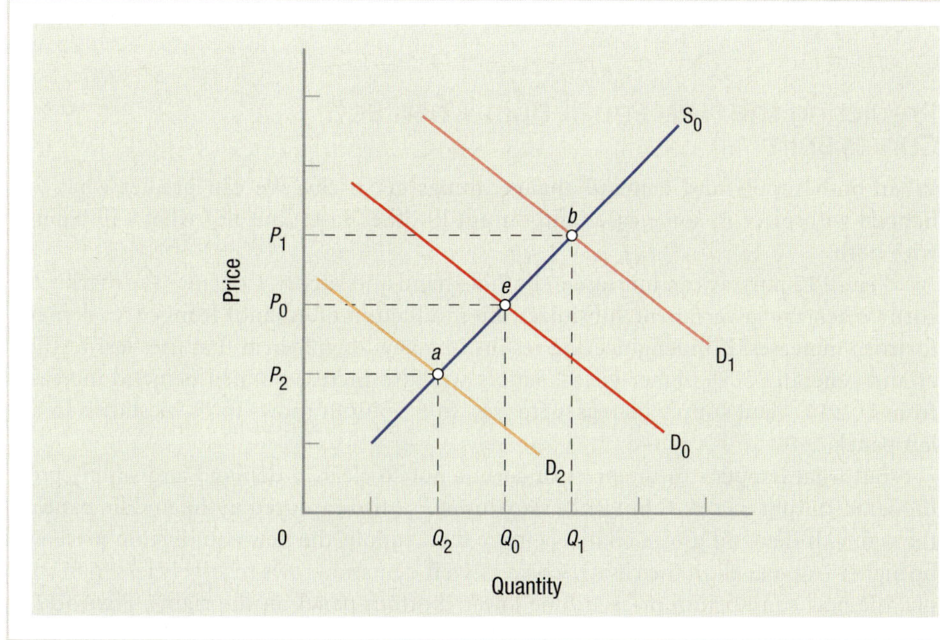


**FIGURE 11—Equilibrium Price, Output, and Shifts in Demand**

When demand alone changes, the effects on both equilibrium price and output can again be determined. When demand grows ($D_0$ to $D_1$), both price and output rise. Conversely, when demand falls ($D_0$ to $D_2$), both price and output fall.

[3] "California Drinking," *The Economist*, June 7, 2003, p. 56, and Dana Goodyear, "Drink Up: The Rise of Really Cheap Wine", *The New Yorker*, May 18, 2009, pp. 59–65.

## *Issue:* What Happened When the Price of Jumbo Tires Quadrupled?

**In mid-2006,** as prices for commodities such as copper, coal, oil, zinc, and silver doubled and tripled, the price of one input needed to mine these commodities *quadrupled.* That resource? Supersized tires used on dump trucks and other heavy equipment.

Lester Lefkowitz/CORBIS

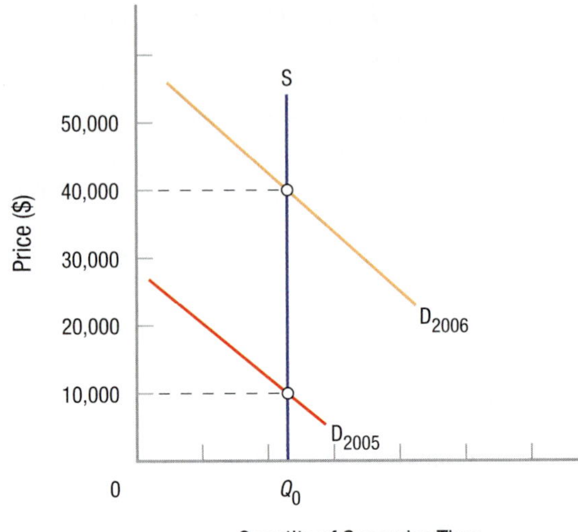


Producing these 4-foot-wide, 12-foot-diameter jumbo tires has always been considered a specialized business, and there have been relatively few manufacturers with limited capacity. Further, these tires require a 24-hour cooling period in the mold, limiting the number that can be produced in a day to two or three.

This leaves the market looking like the accompanying figure. In 2005 jumbo tires were selling for one-fourth their $40,000 cost in 2006. Because the production process is time consuming and the cooling process requires the use of the mold for a day, the quantity of tires available for sale is essentially fixed in the short run. Existing firms tried to expand capacity as well as build new factories, but estimates are that this capacity will not come on line for several years.

Because of the shortage of production capacity, mining firms are trying to extend the useful life (roughly 6,000 hours) of these expensive tires by training drivers to avoid rocks and smoothing the surface of mine roads. Retread companies are also finding they can't meet the demand for these jumbo tires. Commodity prices stayed high until late 2008, when tire prices fell back to normal levels.

Source: Simon Romero, "Big Tires in Short Supply," *The New York Times,* April 20, 2006.

## Predicting the New Equilibrium When Both Curves Shift

When both supply and demand change, things get tricky. We can predict what will happen with price in some cases and output in other cases, but not what will happen with both.

Figure 12 portrays an increase in both demand and supply. Consider the market for corn. When the government subsidizes the production of ethanol from corn, demand for corn increases. If bioengineering results in a new corn hybrid that uses less fertilizer and generates 50% higher yields, supply will also increase. When demand increases from $D_0$ to $D_1$ and supply increases from $S_0$ to $S_1$, output grows to $Q_1$ as shown in the left panel.

But what happens to the price of corn is not so clear. If demand and supply grow the same, output increases but price remains at $P_0$ (also captured in the middle panel to the right). If demand grows relatively more than supply, the new equilibrium price will be higher (top panel on the right). Conversely, if demand grows relatively less than supply, the new equilibrium price will be lower (bottom panel on the right). Figure 12 is just one of the four possibilities when both supply and demand change. The other three possibilities are shown in Table 1, and all four possibilities are discussed in detail in the *CourseTutor.*

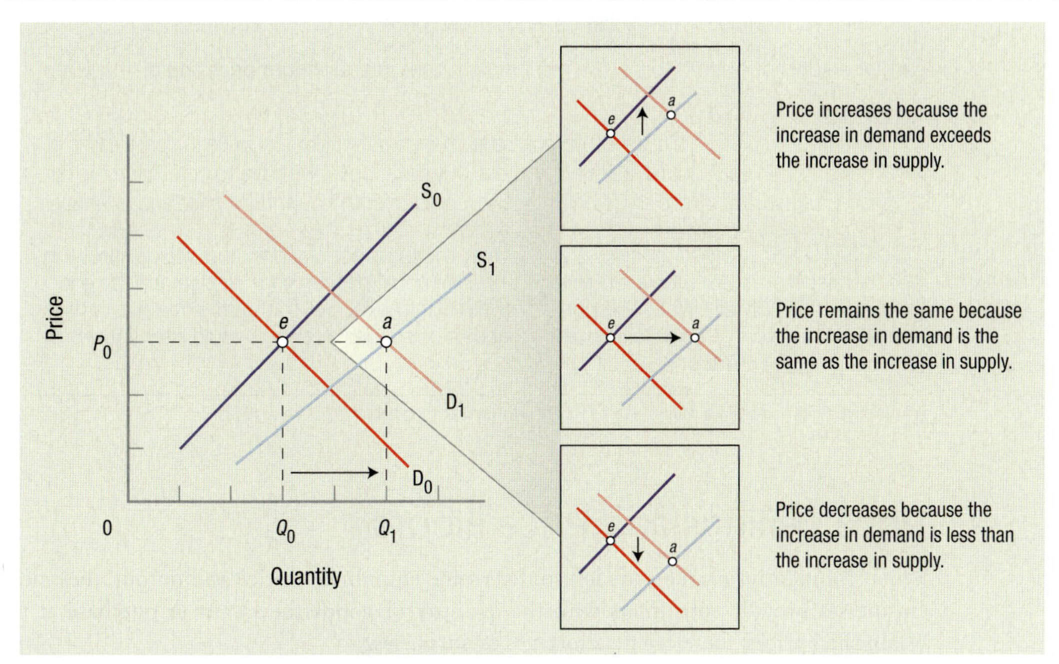


**FIGURE 12—Increase in Supply, Increase in Demand, and Equilibrium**

When both demand and supply increase, output will clearly rise, but what happens to the new equilibrium price is uncertain. If demand grows relatively more than supply, price will rise, but if supply grows relatively more than demand, price will fall.

**TABLE 1** The Effect of Changes in Demand or Supply on Equilibrium Prices and Quantities

| Change in Demand | Change in Supply | Change in Equilibrium Price | Change in Equilibrium Quantity |
|---|---|---|---|
| No change | Increase | Decrease | Increase |
| No change | Decrease | Increase | Decrease |
| Increase | No change | Increase | Increase |
| Decrease | No change | Decrease | Decrease |
| Increase | Increase | Indeterminate | Increase |
| Decrease | Decrease | Indeterminate | Decrease |
| Increase | Decrease | Increase | Indeterminate |
| Decrease | Increase | Decrease | Indeterminate |

## CHECKPOINT

### MARKET EQUILIBRIUM

- Together, supply and demand determine market equilibrium.
- Equilibrium occurs when quantity supplied exactly equals quantity demanded.
- The equilibrium price is also called the market-clearing price.

- When supply and demand change, equilibrium price and output change.
- When only one curve shifts, the resulting changes in equilibrium price and quantity can be predicted.
- When both curves shift, we can predict the change in equilibrium price in some cases or the change in equilibrium quantity in others, but never both. We have to determine the relative magnitudes of the shifts before we can predict both equilibrium price and quantity.

**QUESTIONS:** As China and India (both with huge populations and rapidly growing economies) continue to develop, what do you think will happen to their demand for energy and specifically oil? What will suppliers of oil do in the face of this demand? Will this have an impact on world energy (oil) prices? What sort of policies or events could alter your forecast about the future price of oil?

Answers to the Checkpoint questions can be found at the end of this chapter.

# Price Ceilings and Price Floors

When competitive markets are left to determine equilibrium price and output, they clear. Businesses provide consumers with the quantity of goods they want to purchase at the established prices; there are no shortages or surpluses.

But, there are times when the equilibrium price may not be what many people consider to be a desired or fair price. For political or social reasons—not economic ones—governments will intervene in the market by setting limits on such things as wages, apartment rents, electricity, or agricultural commodities. Government uses price ceilings and price floors to keep prices below or above market equilibrium. But, what happens when government sets prices below or above market equilibrium?

## Price Ceilings

Price ceiling: A government-set maximum price that can be charged for a product or service. When the price ceiling is set below equilibrium, it leads to shortages.

When the government sets a **price ceiling,** it is legally mandating the maximum price that can be charged for a product or service. This is a legal maximum; regardless of market forces, price cannot exceed this level.

Figure 13 shows an *effective* price ceiling, or one in which the ceiling price is set below the equilibrium price. In this case, equilibrium price is at $P_e$, but the government

**FIGURE 13—Price Ceiling Below Equilibrium Price Creates Shortages**

A price ceiling is a maximum sales price for a product. When the government enacts a price ceiling below equilibrium, it creates shortages. Consumers will demand $Q_1$ output at a price of $P_c$, but businesses will supply only $Q_2$, creating a shortage equal to $Q_1 - Q_2$. The product's price cannot rise to restore equilibrium because of the legal price ceiling.

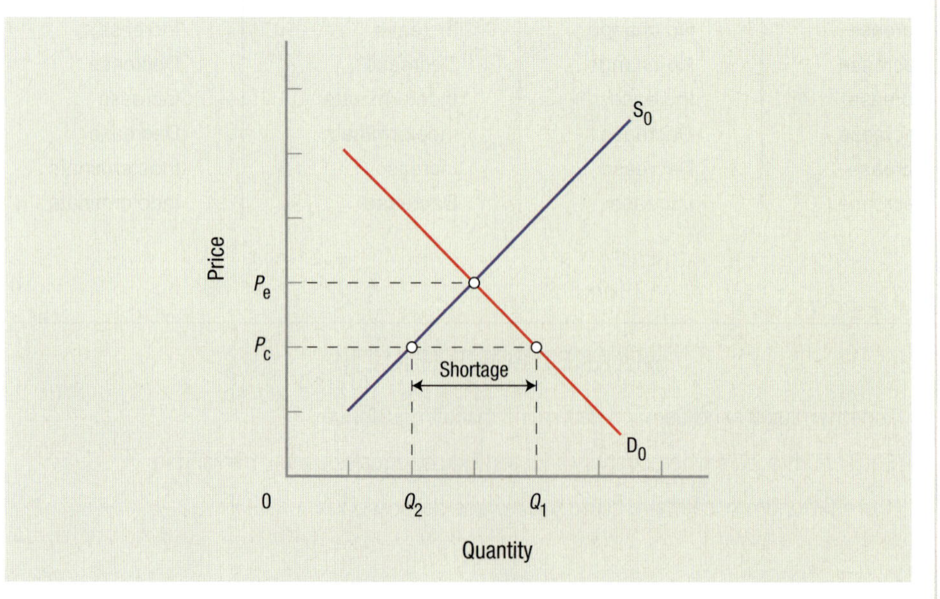

has set a price ceiling at $P_c$. Quantity supplied at the ceiling price is $Q_2$, whereas consumers want $Q_1$, so the result is a shortage of $Q_1 - Q_2$ units of the product. Note that if the price ceiling is set above $P_e$, the market simply settles at $P_e$, and the price ceiling has no impact.

Rent controls are a classic example of price ceilings. Many local governments have decided affordable housing is a priority and that tenants need protection from high rental rates (presumably protection from greedy landlords). And in the short run, rent controls work. Landlords cannot easily convert apartment units to alternative uses, so they have little choice but to rent out these units at the lower rates. But as soon as they can, landlords will convert their real estate holdings to condominiums or offices. Other landlords, facing a ceiling on the rents they can charge, will not incur additional upkeep charges and so will let their properties deteriorate. Few landlords, meanwhile, will invest in more rental units. So the shortage we see in Figure 13 will come from a reduced number of rental units due to condo conversion and no new units, while current units are allowed to deteriorate.

Okay, you might say, there will be a shortage of rental units over time, but at least the rents charged will be "fairer." The question is, fairer to whom? The chief beneficiaries are the people already renting. Over time, their rents will be much lower than the equilibrium price. Sufferers include people moving to the area who cannot find a place to rent, or growing families that are trapped in small apartments. When these people do find a potential place, there is a huge incentive for landlords to ask for under-the-table payments, such as a $5,000 payment for keys to the apartment. In New York City, rent control instituted during World War II is still in place: The beneficiary class is not the poor, but people lucky enough to be renters during the early phases of the rent control and who have passed on their apartments to their family. This has led to the gruesome habit of would-be renters reading obituaries to discover renters who died with no obvious heirs. This behavior is a far cry from the normal act of looking for an apartment when markets work freely.

More recently, the federal government has begun placing a form of price ceiling on the Medicare payments to doctors and hospitals. Doctors who accept Medicare patients are not allowed to charge patients more than what is allowed by Medicare for specific procedures. These maximum prices have been getting lower as the Medicare budget has been squeezed. As a result, some doctors no longer accept new Medicare patients, since the fees they can charge will no longer cover their costs. For some patients who are just retiring and joining Medicare, finding a doctor can be difficult. The price ceilings have created a shortage of doctors willing to treat Medicare patients.

The key point to remember here is that price ceilings are intended to keep the price of a product below its market or equilibrium level. The ultimate effect of a price ceiling, however, is that the quantity of the product demanded exceeds the quantity supplied, thereby producing a shortage of the product in the market.

## Price Floors

A **price floor** is a government-mandated minimum price that can be charged for a product or service. Regardless of market forces, product price cannot legally fall below this level.

**Price floor:** A government-set minimum price that can be charged for a product or service. When the price floor is set above equilibrium, it leads to surpluses.

Figure 14 on the next page shows the economic impact of price floors. In this case, the price floor, $P_f$, is set above equilibrium, $P_e$, resulting in a surplus of $Q_2 - Q_1$ units. At price $P_f$, businesses want to supply more of the product ($Q_2$) than consumers are willing to buy ($Q_1$), thus generating a surplus. Again, note that if the price floor is set below equilibrium, it has no impact on the market.

For over a half-century, agricultural price supports or price floors have been used to try to smooth out the income of farmers, which often fluctuates wildly due to wide annual variations in crop prices. Government acts as a buyer of last resort, and if surpluses result, the government purchases these commodities. Since these price supports

**FIGURE 14—Price Floor Above Equilibrium Price Creates Surpluses**

A price floor is the lowest price at which a product can be sold. When the government sets a price floor above equilibrium, it creates surpluses. Businesses try to sell $Q_2$ at a price of $P_f$, but consumers are willing to purchase only $Q_1$ at that price. The result is a market surplus equal to $Q_2 - Q_1$. The price floor prevents the product's price from falling to equilibrium.

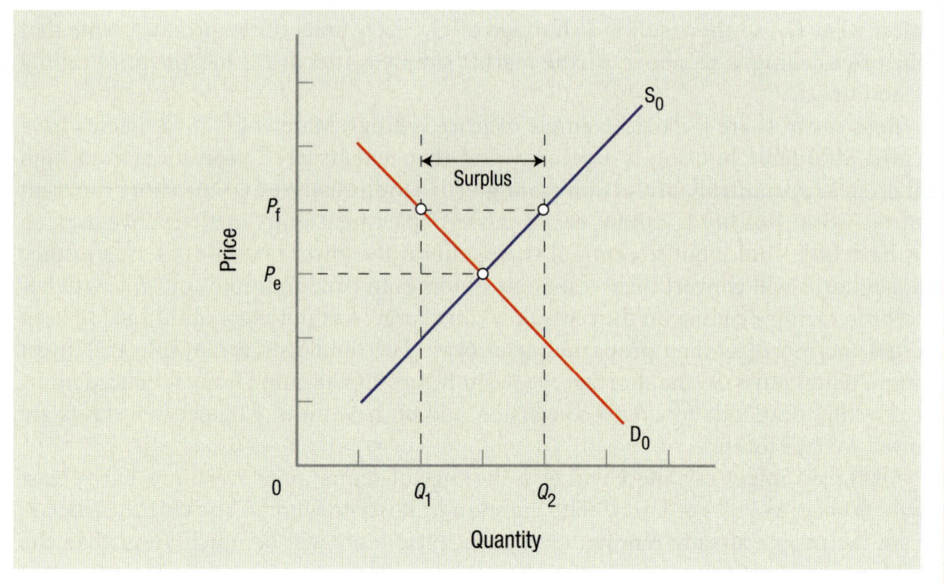


typically are above market equilibrium prices, frequent surpluses have resulted. These surpluses have been stored and earmarked for use in the event of future shortages, but few such shortages have arisen due to improvements in farm technology and rising crop yields. Consumers pay more for agricultural commodities, and surpluses arise and often rot, all in the expectation that the income of farmers will be steady. Despite their questionable economic justification, political pressures have ensured that agricultural price supports and related programs still command a sizable share of the discretionary domestic federal budget.

Another area in which price floors are used is the minimum wage. To the extent that the minimum wage is set above the equilibrium wage, unemployment—a surplus of labor—will result. The groups most affected by this unemployment tend to be low-skilled workers and teenagers, groups that already suffer high unemployment rates. Such people might have been able to find jobs had employers been allowed to pay them the equilibrium wage rate, but these jobs go uncreated when employers are forced to pay the higher minimum wage.

Governments must be careful when setting price ceilings and price floors to avoid creating shortages or surpluses.

## CHECKPOINT

### PRICE CEILINGS AND PRICE FLOORS

- Governments use price floors and price ceilings to intervene in markets.
- A price ceiling is a maximum legal price that can be charged for a product. Price ceilings set below equilibrium result in shortages.
- A price floor is the minimum legal price that can be charged for a product. Price floors set above market equilibrium result in surpluses.

**QUESTION:** Rent controls are found in cities such as New York and Santa Monica, California, where land prices are at a premium and the city is relatively builtout (very little vacant land remains). Why is rent control not found in cities such as Phoenix, Arizona, or Denver, Colorado?

Answers to the Checkpoint question can be found at the end of the chapter.

## Key Concepts



## Chapter Summary

### Markets

Markets are institutions that enable buyers and sellers to interact and transact business with one another. Markets differ in geographical location, products offered, and size. Prices contain an incredible amount of information for both buyers and sellers. Through their purchases, consumers signal their willingness to exchange money or other valuables for particular products at particular prices. These signals help businesses to decide what to produce and how much of it to produce. Consequently, the market economy is often called the price system.

### Demand

Demand refers to the quantity of products people are willing and able to purchase during some specific time period, all other relevant factors being held constant. Price and quantity demanded stand in a negative (inverse) relationship: as price rises, consumers buy fewer units; and as price falls, consumers buy more units. This is known as the law of demand and is depicted in a downward-sloping demand curve.

Market demand curves are found by horizontally summing individual demand curves.

The determinants of demand include (1) consumer tastes and preferences, (2) income, (3) prices of substitutes and complements, (4) the number of buyers in the market, and (5) expectations regarding future prices, incomes, and product availability. Demand changes (the demand curve shifts) when one or more of these determinants change. A shift to the right reflects an increase in demand, whereas a shift to the left represents a decline in demand.

A change in quantity demanded occurs only when the price of a product changes, leading consumers to adjust their purchases by moving along the existing demand curve.

### Supply

Supply is the quantity of a product producers are willing and able to put on the market at various prices, all other relevant factors being held constant. The law of supply reflects the positive relationship between price and quantity supplied: The higher the market price, the more goods supplied; and the lower the market price, the fewer goods supplied. It is depicted in an upward-sloping supply curve. Market supply, as with market demand, is arrived at by horizontally summing the individual supplies of all of the firms in the market.

The six determinants of supply are (1) production technology, (2) the costs of resources, (3) prices of other commodities, (4) expectations, (5) the number of sellers or producers in the market, and (6) taxes and subsidies. When one or more of the determinants of supply change, a change in supply results, causing a shift in the supply curve. A shift to the right reflects an increase in supply, whereas a shift to the left represents a decline in supply. A change in quantity supplied is only caused by a change in the price of the product; it results in a movement along the existing supply curve.

### Market Equilibrium

Supply and demand together determine market equilibrium. Equilibrium occurs when quantity demanded and quantity supplied are precisely equal: producers are bringing precisely the quantity of some good to market that consumers wish to purchase. The price at which equilibrium is reached is called the equilibrium price, or the market-clearing price.

If prices are set too high, surpluses result, which drive prices back down to equilibrium levels. If prices are set too low, a shortage results, which drives prices up until equilibrium is reached.

When supply and demand change (a shift in the curves), equilibrium price and output change. When only one curve shifts, then both resulting changes in equilibrium price and quantity can be predicted.

When the two curves both shift, the change in equilibrium price can be forecasted in some instances, and the change in equilibrium output in others, but never both.

### Price Ceilings and Price Floors

Governments sometimes use price ceilings or price floors to keep prices below or above the market equilibrium.

A price ceiling is the maximum legal price that can be charged for a product. Price ceilings set below equilibrium result in shortages.

A price floor is the minimum legal price that can be charged for a product. Price floors set above market equilibrium result in surpluses.

## Questions and Problems

### Check Your Understanding

1. Product prices give consumers and businesses a lot of information besides just the price. What are they?
2. As the world population ages, will the demand for cholesterol drugs [increase/decrease/remain the same]? Assume there is a positive relationship between aging and cholesterol levels. Is this change a change in demand or a change in quantity demanded?
3. Describe some of the reasons why supply changes. Improved technology typically results in lower prices for most products. Why do you think this is true? Describe the difference between a change in supply and a change in quantity supplied.
4. Both individual and market demand curves have negative slopes and reflect the law of demand. What is the difference between the two curves?
5. Describe the determinants of demand. Why are they important?
6. Describe a price ceiling. What is the impact of an effective price ceiling? Show this on the figure on the next page. Give an example. Describe a price floor. What

is the impact of an effective price floor? Show this on the figure below. Give an example.

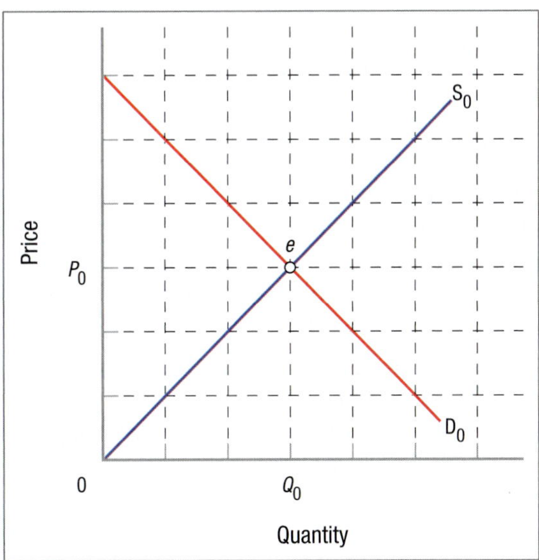


## Apply the Concepts

7. Demand for tickets to sports events such as the Super Bowl has increased. Has supply increased? What does the answer to this tell you about the price of these tickets compared to a few years ago?
8. In 2006 rental car companies often charged more to rent a compact car than an SUV or a luxury vehicle. Why do you think rental companies turned their normal pricing structure on its head?
9.

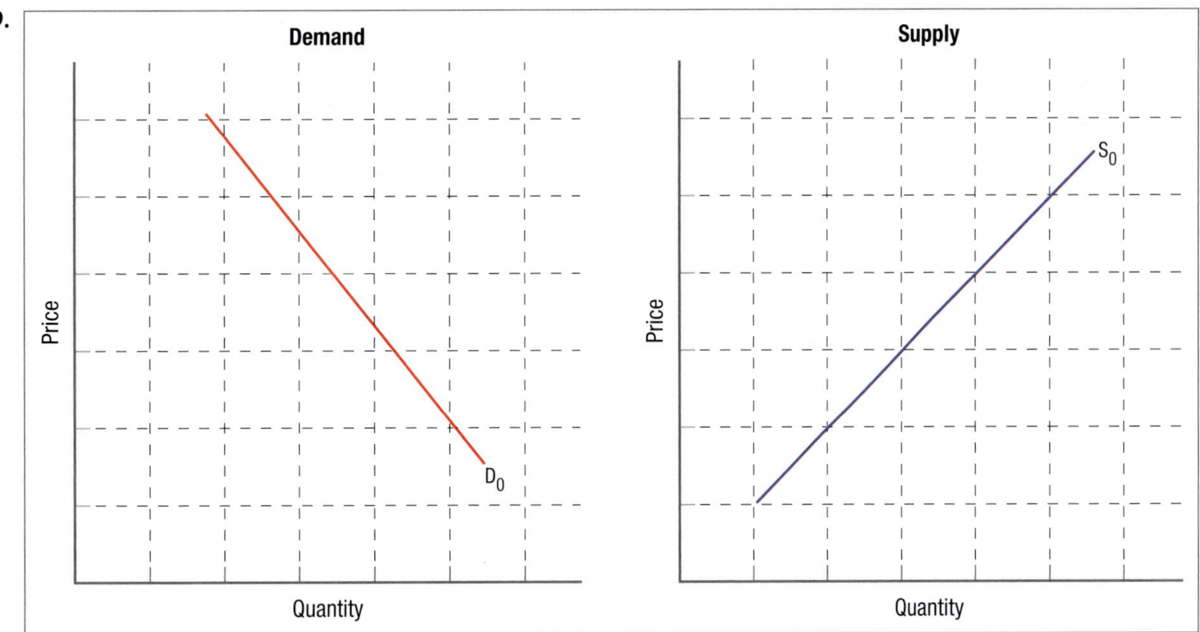


Using the figures above, answer the following questions:

a. On the Demand panel:

- Show an increase in demand and label it $D_1$.
- Show a decrease in demand and label it $D_2$.
- Show an increase in quantity demanded.

- Show a decrease in quantity demanded.
- What causes demand to change?
- What causes quantity demanded to change?

b. On the Supply panel:
- Show an increase in supply and label it $S_1$.
- Show a decrease in supply and label it $S_2$.
- Show an increase in quantity supplied.
- Show a decrease in quantity supplied.
- What causes supply to change?
- What causes quantity supplied to change?

**10.** Several medical studies have shown that red wine in moderation is good for the heart. How would such a study affect the public's demand for wine? Would it have an impact on the type of grapes planted in new vineyards?

**11.** Assume initially that the demand and supply for premium coffees (one-pound bags) are in equilibrium. Now assume Starbucks introduces the world to premium blends, and so demand rises substantially. Describe what will happen in this market as it moves to a new equilibrium. If a hard freeze eliminates Brazil's premium coffee crop, what will happen to the price of premium coffee?

## In the News

**12.** Norrath is a place in the online game EverQuest II. It is a virtual world with roughly 350,000 players "arrayed over worlds that are tethered to dozens of servers." As Rob Walker noted, "EverQuest is filled with half-elves, castles, sword fights and such, and involves a fairly complex internal economy, whose currency is platinum pieces used to buy weapons, food and other goods." This virtual market, however, has led to a real-world market, with real dollars for virtual goods. Players sell weapons, complete characters, and other virtual items on EverQuest's internal market called Station Exchange and on eBay. Common items sell for $10 to $25, while extensive characters or weapons can fetch a thousand dollars or more. (Based on Rob Walker, "The Buying Game: A real market, overseen by a real corporation, selling things that don't really exist," *New York Times Magazine,* October 16, 2005, p. 28.)

Why would someone buy virtual goods? Does supply and demand play any role in this real market for virtual goods? If there were virtual games similar to EverQuest II where everything is free, would any real markets exist for their virtual goods? How does paying for a virtual product differ from the situation where a buyer could purchase a nice watch for a reasonable price, but decides to buy a luxury brand for 10 to 20 times as much?

**13.** In December 2005, the *Wall Street Journal* reported that Clark Foam, a major supplier of polyurethane cores (blanks) for hand-shaped surfboards, closed its plant and went out of business (Peter Sanders and Stephanie Kang, "Wipeout for Key Player in Surfboard Industry," *The Wall Street Journal,* December 8, 2005, p. B1). Clark Foam was the Microsoft of surfboard blank makers, and had been supplying foam blanks to surf shops for over 50 years. Polyurethane blanks, while light and sturdy, contain a toxic chemical, toluene diisocyanate (TDI). Over the last two decades the Environmental Protection Agency has increasingly been restricting the use of TDI. Clark Foam's owner Gordon "Grubby" Clark indicated in a letter to customers that he was tired of fighting environmental regulators, lawsuits over injury to employees, and fire regulations. Surf historian and author of *The Encyclopedia of Surfing,* Matt Warshaw said, "It's the equivalent of removing lumber for the housing industry."

a. If you owned a retail surfboard shop and read this article in the *Wall Street Journal,* would you change the prices on the existing surfboards you have in the shop? Why or why not?

b. If the demand for surfboards remains constant over the next few years, what would you expect to see happen on the supply side in this industry?

14. Polysilicon is used to produce computer chips and solar photovoltaics. Currently, more polysilicon is used to produce computer chips, but the demand for ultrapure polysilicon for solar panels is rising. According to a 2006 *Business Week* article (John Carey, "What's Raining on Solar's Parade," *Business Week,* February 6, 2006, p. 78), this has created a shortage, and prices have more than doubled between 2004 and 2006.

    a. High oil and energy prices, along with subsidies from U.S. and European governments for solar power, have increased demand, but suppliers are reluctant to build new factories or expand existing facilities, because they fear governments can easily eliminate incentives and at this point they do not know if solar energy is just a fad. Are these legitimate concerns for business?

    b. Given the uncertainty associated with building additional production capacity in the polysilicon industry, what might these manufacturers do to reduce the risk?

15. Nobel Prize winner Gary Becker and Judge Richard Posner ("How to Make the Poor Poorer," *The Wall Street Journal,* January 26, 2007, p. A11) suggested that "unions strongly favor the minimum wage because it reduces competition from low-wage workers (who, partly because most of them work part time, tend not to be unionized) and thus enhances unions' bargaining power." They further argued that "although some workers benefit—those who were paid the old minimum wage but are worth the new higher one to the employers—others are pushed into unemployment, the underground economy or crime. The losers are therefore likely to lose more than the gainers gain; they are also likely to be poorer people." Are both of these statements consistent with the model of price floors discussed in this chapter? Why or why not?

16. Professor Donald Boudreaux wrote (*Wall Street Journal,* August 23, 2006, p. A11) that "there are heaps of bad arguments for raising the minimum wage. Perhaps the worst . . . is that a minimum wage increase is justified if a full-time worker earning the current minimum wage cannot afford to live in a city such as Chicago." He then asked "why settle for enabling workers to live only in the likes of Chicago? Why not raise the minimum wage so that everyone can afford to live in, say, Nantucket, Hyannis Port or Beverly Hills, within walking distance of Rodeo Drive?" Should the minimum wage be a "living wage," so a full-time worker can live comfortably in a given locale? What would be the impact if minimum wages were structured this way?

## Solving Problems

17. The table below represents the world supply and demand for natural vanilla in thousands of pounds. A large portion of natural vanilla is grown in Madagascar and comes from orchids that require a lot of time to cultivate. The sequence of events described below actually happened, but the numbers have been altered to make the calculations easier (See James Altucher, "Supply, Demand, and Edible Orchids," *Financial Times,* September 20, 2005, p.12). Assume the original supply and demand curves are represented in the table below.

| Price ($/pound) | Quantity Demanded (thousands) | Quantity Supplied (thousands) |
|---|---|---|
| 0 | 20 | 0 |
| 10 | 16 | 6 |
| 20 | 12 | 12 |
| 30 | 8 | 18 |
| 40 | 4 | 24 |
| 50 | 0 | 30 |

a. Graph both the supply ($S_0$) and demand ($D_0$) curves. What is the current equilibrium price? Label that point *a*.

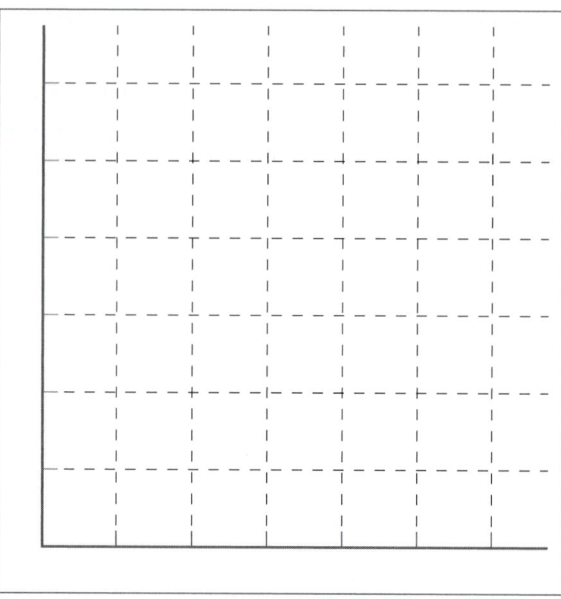

b. Assume that Madagascar is hit by a hurricane (which actually occurred in 2000), and the world's supply of vanilla is reduced by 5/6, or 83%. Label the new supply curve ($S_1$). What will be the new equilibrium price in the market? Label that point *b*.

c. Now assume that Coca-Cola announces plans to introduce a new "Vanilla Coke," and this increases the demand for natural vanilla by 25%. Label the new demand curve ($D_1$). What will be the new equilibrium price? Label this new equilibrium point *c*. Remember that the supply of natural vanilla was reduced by the hurricane earlier.

d. Growing the orchids that produce natural vanilla requires a climate with roughly 80% humidity, and the possible grower countries generally fall within 20° north or south of the equator. A doubling of prices encouraged several other countries (e.g., Uganda and Indonesia) to begin growing orchids or up their current production. Within several years, supply was back to normal ($S_0$), but by then, synthetic vanilla had replaced 80% of the original demand ($D_0$). Label this new demand curve ($D_2$). What is the new equilibrium price and output?

**18.** In late 2006 and early 2007, orange crops in Florida were smaller than expected, and the crop in California was put in a deep freeze by an Arctic cold front. As a result, the production of oranges was severely reduced. In addition, in early 2007, President Bush called for the United States to reduce its gasoline consumption by 20% in the next decade. He proposed an increase in ethanol produced from corn and the stalks and leaves from corn and other grasses. What was the likely impact of these two events on food prices in the United States?

## Answers to Questions in CheckPoints

### Check Point: Markets

The market for financial securities is a huge, well-organized, and regulated market compared to local farmer's markets. Trillions of dollars change hands each week in the financial markets, and products are standardized.

## Check Point: Demand

Rising gasoline prices have caused the demand for hybrids to swell. This is a change in demand.

## Check Point: Supply

Since iPods and other MP3 players are substitutes for high-end stereo equipment, production and sales of high-end stereo equipment have declined.

## Check Point: Market Equilibrium

Demand for both energy and oil will increase. Suppliers of oil will attempt to move up their supply curve and provide more to the market. Since all of the easy (cheap) oil has been found, costs to add to supplies will rise, and oil prices will gradually rise; in the longer term, alternatives will become more attractive, keeping oil prices from rising too rapidly.

## Check Point: Price Ceilings and Price Floors

Cities with a lot of vacant land do not have rents high enough to support activists who try to get people to control rents. Only in cities with little vacant land and high population densities are rents high enough that enough people think it "unfair," resulting in rent controls. If rent controls are introduced where a lot of vacant land exists, the land simply remains vacant because development is stymied.

# Market Efficiency, Market Failure, and Government

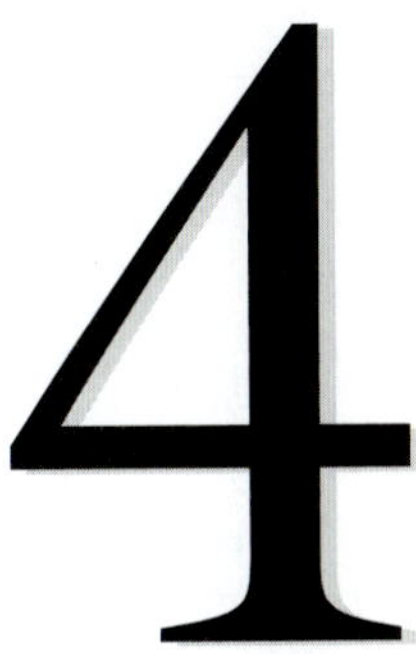

Panoramic Images/Getty Images

**Everywhere we look in the world** there are markets, from the Tokyo fish markets, where every morning 20,000 flash-frozen tuna weighing 400 to 500 pounds each are auctioned off in a few hours; to Aalsmeer, Holland, where millions of fresh flowers are flown in from all over the world every day, auctioned off, and then shipped to firms in other parts of the world; to Chicago, where billions of dollars of derivative securities and commodities are bought and sold on the futures market daily. Beyond these big markets, moreover, countless smaller markets dot our local landscapes, and many new virtual markets are springing up on the Internet.

In earlier chapters, we saw that every economy faces tradeoffs in the use of its resources to produce various goods and services, as represented graphically by the production possibilities frontier. The last chapter considered how supply and demand work together to determine the quantities of various products sold and the equilibrium prices consumers must pay for them in a market economy. As we saw, Adam Smith's invisible hand works to ensure that, in a market society, consumers get what they want.

Thus far, the markets we have studied have been stylized versions of competitive markets: they have featured many buyers and sellers, a uniform product, consumers and sellers who have complete information about the market, and few barriers to market entry or exit.

In this chapter, we consider some of the complexities inherent to most markets. The typical market does not meet all the criteria of a truly competitive market. That does not mean the supply and demand analysis you just absorbed will not be useful in analyzing economic events. Often, however, you will need to temper your analysis to fit the specific conditions of the markets you study. As we will find, some markets need constraints or rules to ensure that society gets the best results.

**After studying this chapter you should be able to:**

- ☐ Understand how markets allocate resources.
- ☐ Define the conditions needed for markets to be efficient.
- ☐ Understand how markets impose discipline on producers and consumers.
- ☐ Understand and be able to use the concepts of consumer and producer surplus.
- ☐ Understand what market failure is, and when it occurs.
- ☐ Describe the different types of market failure.
- ☐ Understand the history of the changing landscape between free markets and government intervention.

This chapter begins by considering the efficiency of the market system. We look at the conditions needed for a market to exist and be efficient. We also present a tool for determining economic efficiency. Efficient markets are rationing devices, ensuring that those who value a product the most are the ones who get it. Prices and profits help to carry out this rationing by serving as important market signals.

Markets rarely live up to our definition of the competitive market ideal. The second section of this chapter discusses markets in light of real-world experience, specifically focusing on market failures, or deviations from conditions of perfect competition. If a market is not competitive, this does not mean it collapses or is no longer a market. It just means that the market fails to contain the mechanisms for allocating resources in the best possible way, from the perspective of the larger society. In this section, we also consider several common solutions to market failures. Some failures require just a minor fix, such as a new regulation or law, but others may require that the government take over and provide products.

In the final section of this chapter, we consider this interplay between markets, market failure, and government intervention during the last century and a half. You will see that the borders between the two have changed over time. Issues like regulating commercial and investment banks, mitigating the impact of climate change, taming globalization, and providing health care all bring markets and government into conflict. The history of the American economy has been one of periodic market failures followed by the growth of government and regulation.

## Markets and Efficiency

Markets are efficient mechanisms for allocating resources. Just think how much information a government bureaucrat would need to decide how many plasma HDTVs should be produced, what companies should produce them, and who should get them. When you consider that our country has many millions of people who might want such televisions and several thousand possible suppliers, it becomes clear the likelihood of a lone bureaucrat or agency developing an efficient plan for HDTV production and distribution is extremely small. This was the problem the Soviet Union faced with virtually every good it produced, and it goes a long way toward explaining that nation's economic and political collapse.

The prices and profits characteristic of the market system provide incentives and signals that are nonexistent or seriously flawed in other systems of resource allocation. The old Soviet joke that "They pretend to pay us and we pretend to work" illustrates this problem. But efficient markets do not just spontaneously develop. They need reasonable laws and institutions to ensure their proper functioning.

### Efficient Market Requirements

For markets to be efficient, they must have well-structured institutions. John McMillan[1] suggests five institutional requirements for workable markets: (1) information is widely available, or in McMillan's words, "information flows smoothly"; (2) property rights are protected; (3) private contracts are enforced such that "people can be trusted to live up to their promises"; (4) spillovers from other actors are limited, or "side effects of third parties are curtailed"; and (5) competition prevails. Let's briefly discuss each of these requirements.

#### Accurate Information Is Widely Available

For markets to work efficiently, transactions costs must be kept low. One factor that reduces transactions costs is accurate and readily available information. Negotiations between the parties will be smoother if each party has adequate information about the product.

[1] John McMillan, *Reinventing the Bazaar: A Natural History of Markets* (New York: Norton), 2002.

Without good information, one party will not have the confidence needed to value the product, so that party will be reluctant to enter into a transaction. Many products today are highly sophisticated, and consumers need high-quality information in order to make good choices. This is important for buyers and sellers.

## Property Rights Are Protected

"Imagine a country where nobody can identify who owns what, addresses cannot be easily verified, people cannot be made to pay their debts, resources cannot be conveniently turned into money, ownership cannot be divided into shares, descriptions of assets are not standardized and cannot be easily compared, and the rules that govern property vary from neighborhood to neighborhood or even from street to street."[2] These are the conditions Hernando de Soto found throughout most of the developing world.

Most of us are accustomed to elaborate title and insurance provisions that govern the transfer of automobiles, real estate, and corporate shares in this country. In many developing nations, however, no such provisions exist. When a government fails to establish and protect **property rights,** more informal economic mechanisms will evolve. Even so, the absence of clear title prevents assets from being used as capital. You cannot borrow against your home, for instance, to purchase the sewing machine needed to start a small tailoring business if your family's long-standing ownership of this home has never been legally documented.

Property rights: The clear delineation of ownership of property backed by government enforcement.

Property rights provide a powerful incentive for the optimal use of resources. With ownership comes the incentive to use resources efficiently, not to waste.

## Contract Obligations Are Enforced

A well-functioning legal system makes doing business easier, and it is absolutely essential for large-scale business activity. Without the safeguards of a legal system, firms must rely on discussions with one another to determine whether customers are credit-worthy, or whether a customer's production order is trustworthy.

Still, even when a legal system is operating well, markets require some informal rules to create the general presumption that bargains will be kept. Most civil court systems in developed nations take several years to hear and decide disputes. Lawsuits, moreover, are never cheap.

The more valuable the contract, the more a legal instrument is needed to ensure that it is honored. Business relationships involving small amounts can usually rely on simple honesty. But cheating on a large loan, contract, or shipment might be worth the sacrifice of one's reputation, so something more than a handshake is needed to ensure compliance. Large and complex markets need a well running legal system that enforces contracts and agreements.

## There Are No External Costs or Benefits

When you drive your car on a crowded highway, you are inflicting *external costs* on other drivers and the larger society by adding to congestion and pollution. By attending a private college, conversely, you are conferring *external benefits* on the rest of us. You are more likely to become a better citizen, be less likely to commit a crime, and pay a greater share of the tax bill. Thus, we all benefit from your education, even though we do not have to bear the cost of it. These external costs and benefits are called *externalities,* as we will see later in this chapter. Markets operate most efficiently when externalities are minimized.

## Competitive Markets Prevail

When a market has many buyers and sellers, no one seller has the ability to raise its price above that of its competitors. To do so would be to lose most of its business. In competitive markets, products are close substitutes, so an increase in price by one firm would simply lead consumers to shift their purchases to other firms.

---

[2] Hernando de Soto, *The Mystery of Capital: Why Capitalism Triumphs in the West and Fails Everywhere Else* (New York: Basic Books), 2000, p. 15.

Competitive markets, moreover, tend to aggregate individual appraisals of value into market information. Without a market, values are determined in one-on-one encounters between buyer and seller. Competitive bargaining between many buyers and sellers gives rise to aggregate market prices and values much like prices are set in an auction. Therefore, competitive markets must be open to entry and exit.

Good information, protection of property, an efficient and fair legal system, the absence of externalities, and competition are all required if society is to get the best from its markets. These elements all work together to make markets efficient, as we will now see.

## The Discipline of Markets

Markets impose discipline on consumers and producers. Sellers would like to get away with charging higher prices while producing shoddier goods, thereby earning greater profits. Few manufacturers or service providers turn out terrific goods and services simply to feel good. Rather, their economic survival depends on it.

As for us consumers, we all would like to drive better cars, wear nothing but designer clothes, drink the finest wines, and smoke Cuban cigars. (Well, some of us would like the cigars.) For the superrich, such consumption is not only possible, but commonplace. For the rest of us, the market rations us out of such goods, except on very special occasions.

This is another function of the market: rationing. Given our limited resources, each of us must decide which products are most important to us, since we cannot have unlimited quantities. Everyone chooses based on their tastes, preferences, and limited incomes.

High prices in a market indicate that consumers value a product highly. Higher prices are usually accompanied by higher profits, and these higher profits attract new firms into the market. These new firms increase supply, and this reduces prices. The solution for high prices is high prices. As we saw in the last chapter, however, if something keeps above-market prices from falling, surpluses will accrue. Conversely, if something keeps low prices from rising to their equilibrium level, shortages will result.

Markets can also be useful tools for the government, since markets allocate resources to those individuals or firms that are most efficient. For example, the government uses markets to allocate the radio and cellular spectrum, to supply the nation's electricity, and to reduce pollution. Central planning is difficult for governments, but private firms can use planning effectively, since a firm's management and stockholders have a vested interest in the firm's success. Product and financial markets, moreover, force a discipline on private firms that is absent when governments centrally plan. If a firm fails to innovate, consumers will quit buying its products, financial markets will reduce or call in its loans, and stock markets will decimate its shares.

## Consumer and Producer Surplus: A Tool for Measuring Economic Efficiency

Markets determine equilibrium prices and outputs. Both consumers and businesses get extra benefits economists call consumer and producer surplus.

Figure 1 illustrates both in a simple diagram. In both panels, the market determines equilibrium price to be $6 (point *e*), at which 6 units of output are sold when $S_0$ and $D_0$ are the original curves. Assume that each point on the demand curve represents an individual consumer. Some people value the product highly. For instance, the consumer at point *a* in panel A thinks the product is worth $11. This consumer clearly gets a bargain, for although she would be willing to pay $11 for the product, the market determines that $6 is the price everyone pays. Economists refer to this excess benefit that these consumers get ($11 – $6) as **consumer surplus.** So for the consumer who purchases the first unit of output, consumer surplus is equal to $5 ($11 – $6). For the consumer

**Consumer surplus:** The difference between market price and what consumers (as individuals or the market) would be willing to pay. It is equal to the area above market price and below the demand curve.

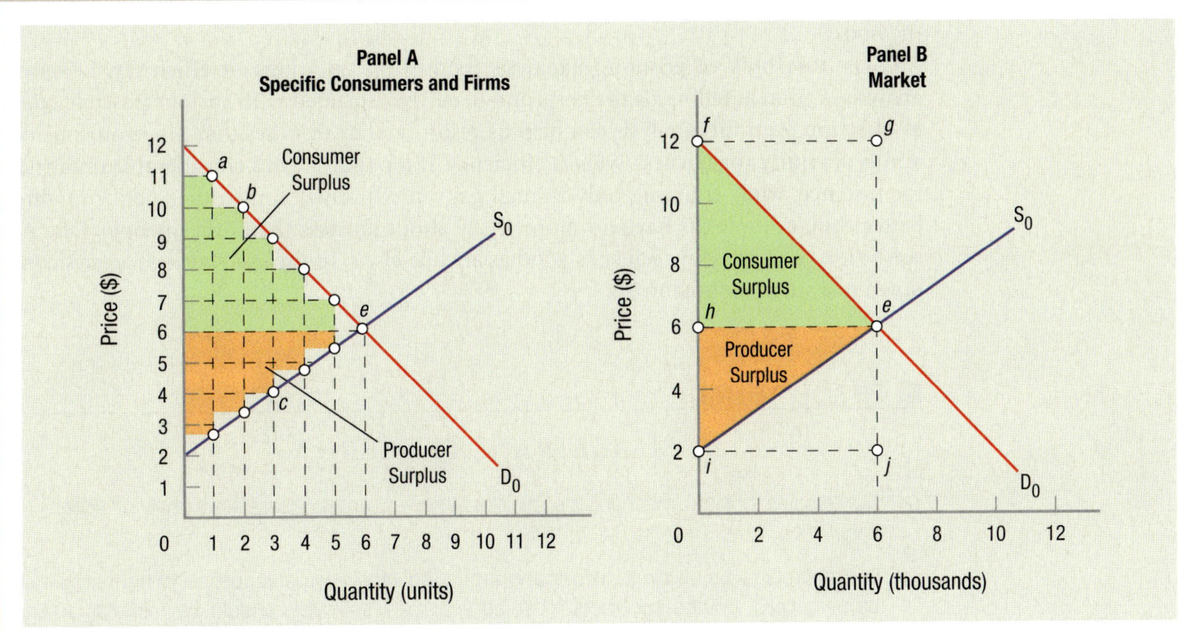


**FIGURE 1—Consumer and Producer Surplus**

Panel B shows a market consisting of the specific consumers and firms shown in panel A. This market determines equilibrium price to be $6 (point e), and total sales for each firm is 6 units. Consumer surplus is equal to the area under the demand curve but above the equilibrium price of $6. Producer surplus is the area under the equilibrium price but above the supply curve.

purchasing the second unit (point *b*), consumer surplus is a little less, $4 ($10 – $6). And so on for buyers of the third through fifth units of output. Total consumer surplus for the consumers in panel A is found by adding all of the individual consumer surpluses for each unit purchased. Thus, total consumer surplus in panel A is equal to $5 + $4 + $3 + $2 + $1 = $15.

In a similar way, assume that each point on the supply curve represents a specific firm. Notice at point *c* that this supplier is willing to provide the third unit to the market at a price of $4. Equilibrium price is $6, so this producer receives a **producer surplus** equal to $2 ($6 – $4). Total producer surplus in panel A is equal to the sum of each firm's producer surplus.

**Producer surplus:** The difference between market price and the price at which firms are willing to supply the product. It is equal to the area below market price and above the supply curve.

Panel B illustrates consumer and producer surplus for an entire market. For convenience we have simply assumed that the market is 1,000 times larger than that shown in panel A, so the *x* axis is output in thousands. Whereas in panel A we had discrete individuals and firms, we now have one big market, so consumer surplus is equal to the area under the demand curve above equilibrium price, or the area of the shaded triangle labeled "consumer surplus."

To put a number to the consumer surplus triangle (*feh*) in panel B, we can compute the value of the rectangle *fgeh* and divide it in half. Thus, total market consumer surplus in panel B is [($12 – $6) × 6,000] ÷ 2 = ($6 × 6,000) ÷ 2 = $18,000. The shaded triangle labeled "producer surplus" (area *hei*) is found in the same way by computing the value of the rectangle *heji* and dividing it in half. Producer surplus is equal to [($6 – $2) × 6,000] ÷ 2 = ($4 × 6,000) ÷ 2 = $12,000.

Markets are efficient from the standpoint that all consumers willing to pay $6 or more got the product from those firms willing to supply it for $6 or less. For demand and supply curves $D_0$ and $S_0$, total consumer and producer surplus is maximized. To see why, pick any price other than $6 and *total* consumer and producer surplus is less.

These two concepts are important in helping us to understand the impacts of market shocks and policy changes on consumer and producer well-being. We will use consumer and producer surplus as a way to evaluate the efficiency of policies throughout the rest of the book.

The vast bulk of economic analysis focuses on questions of efficiency. Economic analysis is good at telling us the costs and benefits associated with various possible courses of action. And this analysis can help us resolve policy disputes that hinge on considerations of equity (or fairness) versus efficiency. If a policy creates considerable unfairness, for instance, while spurring only a small gain in efficiency, some other policy might be better. Still, economists have no more to say about fairness than other people. One person's view of what is fair is just as good as anyone else's. In the end, fairness always comes down to a value judgment.

CHECKPOINT

### MARKETS AND EFFICIENCY

- Markets are efficient mechanisms for allocating resources. Prices are signals of potential profit.
- For markets to be efficient, information must be widely available, property rights must be protected, private contracts must be enforced, spillovers should be minimal, and competition should prevail.
- Markets impose discipline on producers and consumers.
- Consumer surplus occurs when consumers would have been willing to pay more for a good or service than the going price. Producer surplus occurs when businesses would have been willing to provide products at prices lower than the going price. Together, consumer and producer surplus can be used to understand the effects of public policies.

**QUESTION:** A *Current Affairs* broadcast by BBC Radio 4 in December 2007 focused on "repugnant markets." The program discussed markets for kidneys, prostitutes, and human cannonballs. For example, many people donate a kidney to a friend or relative, or earmark their kidneys for donation upon death, actions which are considered noble. But a market for kidneys—where people sell one of their kidneys for money—seems to disgust and outrage many of us. Because it is universally illegal to buy or sell kidneys, shortages result, and many people die each year for lack of a donation.

The program also provided the less dramatic example of Manuel Wackenheim, a "professional human missile." He is a dwarf who made his living being "hurled around for public entertainment." When a French government entity banned his performances, he pursued the case in court, eventually to the UN Commission on Human Rights. He argued that the essence of human dignity is "having a job and this is my job." The human cannonball lost. It was just too repugnant an occupation for the Commission.

Assuming that no one is forced to participate in any of these markets, what arguments can you make for and against these repugnant markets?

Answers to the Checkpoint question can be found at the end of this chapter.

## Market Failures

For markets to be efficient, they must operate within solid institutional structures. As we saw, these institutional requirements include: accurate information for buyers and sellers, protection of property rights, a legal system that enforces private contracts, an absence of externalities or spillovers, and a fostering of competition. This is a tall order, and many markets do not meet these requirements. When one or more of these conditions are not met, the market is said to fail. Market failure does not mean a market totally collapses or stops existing as a market, but that it fails to provide the socially optimal amount of goods and services. As we will see later, there is one exception: in one particular category of cases, private markets provide no goods whatsoever. In this section, we examine market failures.

## Accurate Information Is Not Widely Available: Asymmetric Information

For markets to operate efficiently, accurate information must be widely available. In many markets, one party to a transaction almost always has better information than the other, which is referred to as **asymmetric information.** Many buyers at garage sales have more information about the value of the antiques being sold than their sellers.

**Asymmetric information:** Occurs when one party to a transaction has significantly better information than another party.

More often, however, it is sellers who have the superior knowledge. Let us consider the used car market, which Nobel Prize winner George Akerlof studied many years ago.[3] Would you buy a used car from someone you do not know? If you hesitate, it is because of asymmetric information problems: the seller knows much more about the car than you do. Does the car burn oil? Was it in an accident? Fear of undisclosed information makes you hesitant or may keep you from buying at all.

What happens when sellers have better information than buyers? Buyers cannot differentiate good cars from lemons. Since buyers cannot tell lemons from good cars, they must assume that each car is a lemon.

In this case, the market does not collapse. Instead, dealers will start offering warranties in an attempt to get higher prices for their used cars and to assure buyers that their cars are not lemons. Consumers can then be more confident of getting higher quality used cars from a dealer, since offering a warranty on lemons would be a losing proposition for dealers.

Additionally, car owners can keep scrupulous records of oil changes and repairs, or buyers, trying to reduce their risk, may take used cars to mechanics for inspection before agreeing to purchase them. The lemons problem explains why many high-quality used cars are bought by the friends of the people who sell them: Sometimes only personal trust can overcome asymmetric information.

### Adverse Selection

**Adverse selection** is a type of asymmetric information that occurs when products of different qualities are sold at the same price. Adverse selection is most apparent in insurance markets. People who purchase health insurance or life insurance know far more about their lifestyles and general states of their health than can an insurance company, even if the insurance company requires a physical.

**Adverse selection:** Occurs when products of different qualities are sold at the same price because of asymmetric information.

Insurance rates are determined using averages, but the market includes some people who are higher than average risks and some people who are below average. Who do you think is more likely to purchase insurance? Overwhelmingly, it is those people above the average risk level who buy insurance, while those below the average risk level are more likely to "self-insure." The insurance pool therefore tends to be filled with higher risk individuals, which can lead to payouts exceeding projections and insurance companies losing money. In this case, then, adverse selection skews the insurance pool, giving it a risk level higher than the social average.

How can insurance underwriters deal with this problem? The answer is that they offer policies at different prices to different groups. Health insurance companies, for instance, use deductibles and co-payments to attract low-risk individuals. A deductible means that you must pay the first, say, $1,000 in medical expenses, then the insurance company begins covering a part, or even all, of the remaining costs. Co-payments are small cash payments paid for each visit to the doctor. These policies are attractive to low-risk clients since they have lower monthly premiums. For low-risk people, the likelihood of their needing to cover co-payments or pay their full deductible is low.

Conversely, a policy with a high deductible is not attractive to high-risk individuals, since they can project that the cost of the policy will be too high. They know they will probably have to pay all their monthly premiums, many co-payments, and their full deductible. These people tend to opt for policies with higher premiums but lower deductibles. This ensures that people who are high risk will select policies that accurately reflect their true state of health and lifestyle.

[3] George Akerlof, "The Market for Lemons: Quality, Uncertainty and the Market Mechanism," *Quarterly Journal of Economics,* 1970, pp. 488–500.

## Moral Hazard

**Moral hazard:** Asymmetric information problem that occurs when an insurance policy or some other arrangement changes the economic incentives and leads to a change in behavior.

**Moral hazard** occurs when an insurance policy or some other arrangement changes the economic incentives we face, thus leading us to change our behavior, usually in a way that is detrimental to the market. Think about what happens when you get comprehensive coverage, which includes theft insurance, on your car. Does this affect how scrupulously you lock your car doors? Of course it does. The moral hazard occurs because the insurance policy, which compensates you in case of loss, changes your behavior to make loss *more* (not *less*) likely.

Insurance companies place restrictions on individual behavior in some contracts. For example, insurance designed to protect the ability of professional athletes to honor multiyear contracts often prohibits dangerous activities such as skiing, rollerblading, hang gliding, and mountain climbing. In this way they reduce the moral hazard aspects of the policy. Some rental car companies, knowing that you won't check the oil in a rental car, rarely rent cars for more than a month at a time. They want to get their cars back into the shop to ensure all is well.

When high-quality information is not equally available to buyers and sellers, markets must adapt. The less complex the product and the better the information, the more efficient the market will be.

# Problems with Property Rights

Property rights provide a powerful incentive to use resources wisely. Incentives to waste are much stronger when property ownership is fuzzy or resources are owned in common. There are two general instances of market failure caused by property right issues: public goods and common property resources.

## Public Goods

Most of the goods we deal in are private goods: airline seats, meals at restaurants, songs on iTunes, and bicycles. When we purchase such goods, we consume them, and no one else can benefit from them. To be sure, when you buy an airline ticket, other passengers will be on the same flight, but no one else can sit in your seat for that flight—only you can enjoy its benefits. Thus, private goods are those the buyer consumes, and this precludes anyone else from similarly enjoying them.

**Public goods:** Goods that, once provided, no one person can be excluded from consuming (nonexclusion), and one person's consumption does not diminish the benefit to others from consuming the good (nonrivalry).

**Free rider:** When a public good is provided, consumers cannot be excluded from enjoying the product, so some consume the product without paying.

Contrast private goods with **public goods,** which are goods that one person can consume without diminishing what is left for others. My watching PBS does not mean that there is less PBS for you to watch. Economists refer to such a situation as one of *nonrivalry*. Public goods are also *nonexclusive,* meaning that once such a good has been provided for one person, others cannot be excluded from enjoying it. Normally, public goods are both nonrival and nonexclusive, whereas private goods are rival and exclusive.

Public goods give rise to the **free rider** problem. Once a public good has been provided, other consumers cannot be excluded from it, so many people will choose to enjoy the benefit without paying; they will free ride. National Public Radio and PBS are public goods. They exist because they receive donations from individuals, foundations, and governments, but their week-long begging and guilt transference sessions notwithstanding, most listeners and viewers (maybe as high as 90%) still choose to enjoy their services without pledging support.

Other public goods include weather forecasts, national defense, lighthouses, flood control projects, GPS satellites, World Court rulings, mosquito eradication, and immunization. Because these goods are nonrival and nonexclusive, they invariably end up being provided by governments.

This is the one case mentioned above where market failure can lead to no goods at all being provided by private markets. Government must step in. Who would contribute—or contribute adequately—to the costs of providing accurate weather forecasts if your neighbors were free riders? Contributions would soon dry up, and the public good in question would not be provided at all.

## Common Property Resources

Another market failure caused by problems with property rights occurs when a good is a **common property resource** or open-access resource. The market failure associated with commonly owned properties is often referred to as "the tragedy of the commons,"[4] where the tendency is for commonly held resources to be overused and overexploited. Because these resources are held in common, individuals have little incentive to use them in a sustainable fashion, so each person races to "get theirs" before others can do the same.

**Common property resources:** Resources that are owned by the community at large (parks, ocean fish, and the atmosphere) and therefore tend to be overexploited because individuals have little incentive to use them in a sustainable fashion.

Ocean fisheries are a good example. Fish in the ocean were once in excess supply; there was no need for use of this resource to be restricted. Very often people fished one species until it was exhausted and then moved on to fish another. Since the ocean was so big and fish species so plentiful, no one noticed. As the global demand for fish has risen, improved fishing technologies and boats have allowed fishing boats to increase their hauls and to range around the world. Because many of the world's fisheries are still unregulated, one population after another has been fished out, so much so that it has been estimated that nearly 90% of the ocean's predators are gone. The situation is clearly unsustainable, and indeed, as fish populations have shrunk, so have fishing fleets.

The solution to the problem of common property resources and overexploitation has typically focused on assigning property rights or using government regulation to protect these assets. Nobel Prize winner Elinor Ostrom studied small communities in the developing world and reported that these societies and groups regularly develop and enforce their own rules to prevent overusing their resources. Without formal government in place, the requirements for self-policing were: rules that defined what each party received (implicit property rights), good conflict resolution rules, the acknowledged duty of users to maintain

### *Issue:* Tragedy of the "Anticommons"

**When the community** holds property in common, overuse is often the result. Examples include overfishing, congestion, and the unnecessary use of antibiotics that results in drug-resistant infections. This is the tragedy of the commons.

The opposite is gridlock that occurs when too many people own a given property, often stifling innovation and leading to *underuse*. Spotting overuse is easy, but spotting underuse is more difficult. As Michael Heller[5] tells it, "A few years ago, a drug company executive presented me with an unsettling puzzle. His scientists had found a treatment for Alzheimer's disease, but they couldn't bring it to market unless the company bought access to dozens of patents. Any single patent owner could demand a huge payoff; some blocked the whole deal. This story does not have a happy ending. The drug sits on the shelf though it might have saved millions of lives and earned billions of dollars."

It is difficult to know when we have missed some technological advance because patent rights were held by so many. Heller notes that since airlines were deregulated in 1975, airport congestion has grown because the number of flyers has tripled, but only one new airport (Denver) has been built. In addition, numerous communities and landowners have been able to prevent most runway expansion projects at other congested airports.

Google has faced similar issues in its attempt to develop a database of out-of-print books that would represent a huge online library. Sued by the Author's Guild, Google reached a tentative multimillion-dollar agreement, permitting any author or publisher to "opt-out" of the system. Locating and getting agreement with all copyright holders is complicated by the fact that a copyright lasts for 75 years beyond the death of the author. Locating each heir would have been cost prohibitive and doomed the project from the start. This project will likely be in the courts for years. A smaller firm with fewer resources would have dropped it long ago.

Solutions to gridlock will likely involve legislation that makes it easier to assemble groups of property owners. This may involve forcing patent and copyright holders into pools, in much the same way ASCAP and BMI represent property holders in the music industry. For a fee, radio stations and businesses are permitted to play music, and ASCAP and BMI distribute these revenues to songwriters, musicians, and record labels based on the amount of play. Such a solution may require redefining these property rights.

[4] Garrett Hardin, "The Tragedy of the Commons," *Science* 162, 1968, pp. 1243–48.

[5] Michael Heller, *The Gridlock Economy: How Too Much Ownership Wrecks Markets, Stops Innovation, and Costs Lives* (New York: Basic Books), 2008.

the common resource in proportion to their benefits, monitoring and enforcement of the rules by the participants, and users taking part in the rule-making process.

In summary, when property rights are clearly defined, people have an incentive to use resources efficiently. But property rights are not always clearly defined, and this leads to market failure and waste. In the case of public goods, the free rider problem means that these goods may not be provided at all if left to private devices—government needs to step in. With common property resources, there is an incentive for individuals to grab as much as they can. Government must protect these resources.

## Contract Enforcement Is Problematical

When an efficient legal system for the enforcement of contracts is lacking, contracts will inherently be small, given that large contracts with complex financial provisions are difficult to enforce informally. Only if the parties to a contract have long histories together and want to continue doing business will an informal system work. Enforcement mechanisms for contracts are essential for widespread business and commercial expansion.

## There Are Significant External Costs or Benefits: Externalities

Markets rarely produce the socially optimal output when external costs or benefits are present. The market tends to overproduce goods with external costs, providing them at too low a price. To see why, consider Figure 2, keeping in mind that an **external cost** (or **negative externality**) is some socially undesirable effect of economic activity, such as pollution, overfishing, or traffic congestion.

**External cost** (or **negative externality**): Occurs when a transaction between two parties has an impact on a third party not involved with the transaction. External costs are negative, such as pollution or congestion. The market provides too much of a product with negative externalities at too low a cost.

Demand curve $D_P$ and supply curve $S_P$ represent the private demand and supply for some product. Market equilibrium is at point *a*. Assume this good's production creates pollution—an external cost. If its producer were forced to clean up its production process, the firm's costs would rise and the supply curve would decrease to $S_{P\,+\,\text{Cleanup Costs}}$. The result is a new equilibrium at point *b* with a higher price and lower output.

Output $Q_1$ is the socially desirable output for this product. But left on its own, this market will produce at $Q_0$ because consumers and producers of this product will not take

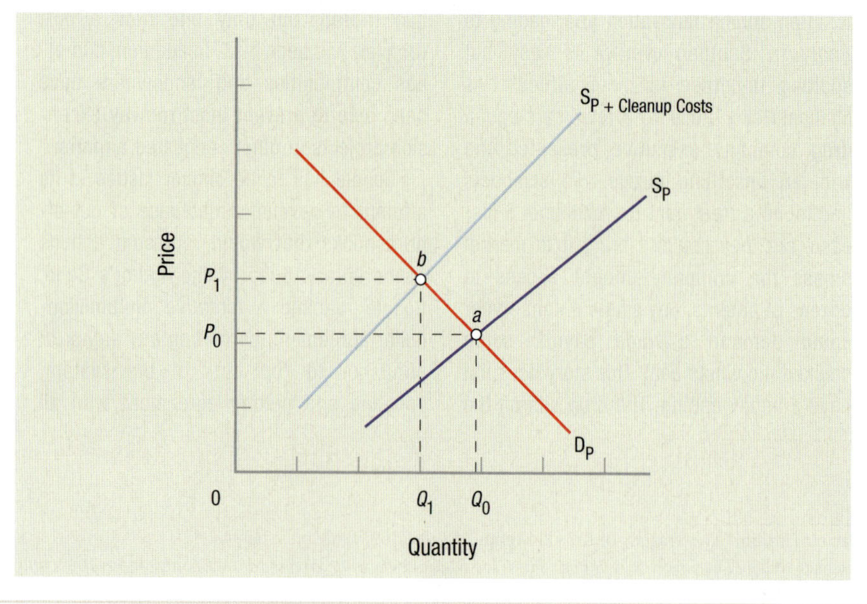


**FIGURE 2—Markets with External Costs**

Markets tend to overproduce goods with external costs. Demand curve $D_P$ and supply curve $S_P$ represent private demand and supply. Market equilibrium is at point *a*. If a good's production creates pollution (an external cost) and the producer was forced to clean up the production process, the firm's costs would rise, and the supply curve would decrease to $S_{P\,+\,\text{Cleanup Costs}}$. The result is the socially optimal equilibrium at point *b* with a higher price and lower output. Producers and consumers are now paying the full costs associated with the good's production. Markets do not inherently contain mechanisms that force firms or consumers to pay for external costs.

the pollution (and cleanup costs) into consideration. The society as a whole bears the brunt of the pollution. Markets fail because they do not contain mechanisms forcing firms to eliminate external costs. Left unregulated, the firm in this example will produce more of its product than the society wants, pushing the increased costs of this production off onto the larger society as an undesirable externality.

In a similar way, markets tend to provide too little of products that have **external benefits.** College education provides benefits not only to students but to the society as a

**External benefits:** Positive externalities, such as education and vaccinations. Private markets provide too little at too high a price of goods with external benefits.

## *Nobel Prize*

### Paul A. Samuelson

In 1970, Paul Samuelson became the first American to win the Nobel Prize in Economics. One could say that Paul Samuelson literally wrote the book on economics. In 1948, when he was a young professor at the Massachusetts Institute of Technology, the university asked him to write a text for the junior year course in economics. Sixty years later more than 4 million copies of his textbook, *Economics,* have been sold.

Samuelson once described himself as one of the last "generalists" in economics. His interests are wide ranging, and his contributions include everything from the highly technical and mathematical to a popular column for *Newsweek* magazine. He made breakthrough contributions to virtually all areas of economics. Steven Pressman sums up Samuelson's main contributions in macroeconomics and international trade this way: "They have involved explaining how domestic economies work, how they are impacted by engaging in trade with other nations, and how economic policies could be used to improve economic performance."

Courtesy The Samuelson Family

Born in Gary, Indiana, in 1915, Samuelson attended the University of Chicago as an undergraduate. He received the university's Social Science Medal and was awarded an innovative graduate fellowship that required that he study at another school. He chose Harvard, and while in the graduate program published 11 papers. Over the next several decades he earned every major award open to an economist.

He wanted to remain at Harvard, but was only offered an instructor's position. However, MIT soon made a better offer and, as he describes it, "On a fine October day in 1940 an *enfant terrible emeritus* packed up his pencil and moved three miles down the Charles River, where he lived happily ever after." He often remarked that a pencil was all he needed to theorize. Seven years later, he published his Ph.D. dissertation, the *Foundations of Economic Analysis,* a major contribution to the area of mathematical economics. Robert Lucas, another Nobel winner, declared, "Here was a graduate student in his twenties reorganizing all of economics in four or five chapters right before your eyes . . ."

Harvard made several attempts to lure him back, but he spent his entire career at MIT and is often credited with developing a department as good as or better than Harvard's. Samuelson was an informal advisor to President John F. Kennedy (he turned down an offer to head Kennedy's Council of Economic Advisers). A prolific writer, he averaged one technical paper each month during his active career, and often said "a day spent in committee meetings are for me a day lost." He has written that he "has always been incredibly lucky, throughout his lifetime overpaid and underworked." Quite a modest statement for a man whose *Collected Works* takes up five volumes and includes more than 350 articles. He was an active economist until his death in 2009 at the age of 93. As you read through this book, keep in mind that in virtually every chapter, Paul Samuelson has created or added to the analysis in substantial ways.

Sources: Steven Pressman, *Fifty Major Economists,* 2d ed. (New York: Routledge), 2006; David Warsh, *Knowledge and the Wealth of Nations: A Story of Economic Discovery* (New York: Norton), 2006; Paul Samuelson, "Economics in My Time," in William Breit and Roger Spencer, *Lives of the Laureates: Seven Nobel Economists* (Cambridge, MA: The MIT Press), 1986.

whole. But there is no incentive for an individual to take into consideration this external benefit when deciding to go to college. Government subsidies for higher education address the positive externalities aspect of education.

Externalities lead to market failure. To ensure that products are available at the socially desirable price and output, some government intervention may be required. Regulation or taxation can be used, for instance, to give markets the incentives they need to produce what society wants.

## Competitive Markets Do *Not Always* Prevail

In theory, a market left to itself should be competitive. In practice, however, the government often must promote competition in the marketplace if it wants to see the most efficient outcomes. One problem is that one or two firms can dominate some markets, and when this happens, prices rise above what would be the competitive price. We will learn more about this when we examine industrial structure in microeconomics.

In all of these cases of market failure (except in the case of pure public goods), markets do not collapse. Rather, markets do not provide the most efficient distribution of goods and services. They need some ameliorative device, often something provided by government such as laws or incentives, but often provided by private firms and individuals acting on their own behalf (remember used car warranties). The important point to keep in mind is the need for correctives when market failure is present. We will have a lot more to say about these issues in a later chapter.

In this section we have considered market failures and the need for government action. The next section looks at the tension between free markets and government intervention in the United States throughout the last century and a half.

### CHECKPOINT

#### MARKET FAILURES

- When markets fail, they usually do not totally collapse—they simply fail to provide the socially optimal amount of goods and services.
- Asymmetric information—when one party to a transaction has better information than another—can lead to market failure. Adverse selection occurs when products of different qualities are sold at one price. Moral hazard occurs when an insurance policy or other arrangement changes the economic incentives people face and so leads them to change their behaviors.
- Private goods can be consumed only by the person who purchases them: they are rival and exclusive. Public goods are nonrival and nonexclusive: my consumption does not diminish your consumption, and others cannot be excluded from enjoying it. Public goods give rise to the free rider problem. Public goods may not be provided at all by markets.
- Common property resources are typically subject to overexploitation.
- Markets rarely produce the socially optimal output when externalities (external benefits or costs) are present.
- Noncompetitive markets result in prices higher than what is socially optimal.

**QUESTION:** Tony Jackson (*Financial Times,* June 29, 2009) offers the following example about markets and market prices: "Suppose I offer to buy a picture from you, knowing (as you do not) that I have a buyer who will pay twice as much. You accept, knowing (as I do not) that the picture is a fake." Will these two parties reach an agreement despite the fact that neither has complete information? Does this simple scenario reflect our day-to-day transactions?

Answers to the Checkpoint questions can be found at the end of this chapter.

## Market Failure, Government Intervention, and U.S. Economic History

So far in this chapter and the last one we have seen how markets work and why they are generally efficient, and we have introduced the concepts of producer and consumer surplus. We also looked at the situations in which markets can fail to provide the optimal levels of goods and services to society. But studying economics is not just about acquiring a bunch of terms or theories, it is also about having a sense of how we got here and why the institutions that govern our economy exist. The kind of economy we have today did not happen instantaneously; it has evolved over the last several hundred years in response to specific events. This section briefly highlights the history of our economy and the events that have shaped it.

Throughout the past century and a half, tension has existed between free markets, market failure, and government intervention. Sometimes the market can be creative in solving problems and generating growth, but sometimes markets lead to unbridled excess and cause trouble. In contrast, sometimes government intervention has helped set down the rules of the game and made the economy work more efficiently, and sometimes government intervention has stifled the market and growth. American economic history has witnessed a changing interplay between free markets and government, with the pendulum swinging first one way, then the other.

### Industrialization

The era of industrialization was characterized by tremendous growth, with a small role for government. After the Civil War, the U.S. economy went from being a 97-pound weakling to a 250-pound industrial superstar in just a little over three decades. In less than five years (1861–1865), the number of manufacturers in the United States doubled to a quarter of a million and its output tripled. By 1869, the transcontinental railway was complete, giving the West access to eastern markets. In the three decades after the Civil War, railroad track gauge (width) was standardized, bringing the entire country into the system. Rail mileage increased by 6 times and freight tonnage increased by 30 times.

This tremendous growth brought with it some problems. Because rail companies had no local competition, they charged high prices. These high prices gave momentum to the Granger movement, which lobbied for laws favorable to farmers on freight and warehousing charges. Congress agreed, and in 1887 established the Interstate Commerce Commission (ICC) to regulate the railroads.

Other industries, including oil, steel, mining, and agriculture, grew just as rapidly. But as industry developed virtually unchecked and as firms combined into massive industrial giants, Americans became concerned with the "robber barons" who ran these companies. John D. Rockefeller absorbed many firms to create Standard Oil, which by 1890 was just about the only firm refining and distributing kerosene (more important than gasoline at the time). Others, such as Andrew Carnegie and J. P. Morgan, became wealthy by building colossal firms in steel and banking. The benefits of competition were lost as these large firms exploited their market power through high prices to generate huge profits. Ultimately, Congress passed the Sherman Antitrust Act in 1890 to break up these huge firms.

Labor unions were beginning to develop during this period, but the legal system was not supportive of their efforts. Union were mostly guilds of craftsmen until 1870 when the Knights of Labor was formed for all who worked for wages (excluding lawyers and those who sold liquor).[6] By the end of the nineteenth century, Samuel Gompers and the American Federation of Labor had only 500,000 members, but the union would grow dramatically in the first half of the twentieth century. Unions gradually won the right to bargain, and favorable legislation during the Great Depression led to unions representing a third of all workers by 1950.

[6] George Tindall and David Shi, *America: A Narrative History* (New York: Norton), 1993, p. 519.

## Rise of Consumerism and World War I

The tremendous growth fostered by industrialization raised living standards, which in turn made the consumer more powerful. Henry Ford's Model T made automobiles affordable for a growing number of Americans. In 1908, Ford sold 10,000 cars for a price of $850; ten years later he was selling 1 million at $350 each. Electric appliances were introduced, piggybacking on the electrification of urban areas. By 1920 the automobile industry was the largest industry in America, and ten years later more than 600,000 miles of road had been paved.

The National Bank Act (passed during the Civil War) guided banks for nearly six decades, but financial crises were common and banks went in and out of business much like restaurants today. An attempt by some financiers to corner the copper market caused a deep financial crisis in 1907. It would have been far deeper except J. P. Morgan stepped in, acted like a central banker, and convinced other New York banks to loan cash to the Knickerbocker Trust to stem a bank run. That experience led to the Federal Reserve Act in 1913, which created a central bank to regulate banks and manage the money supply.

In late summer 1914, the assassination of Archduke Franz Ferdinand, heir to the throne of Austria-Hungary, seemed inconsequential, but just over a month later all of Europe was at war. This "War to End All Wars" resulted in more than 10 million casualties. Europe had been the center of Western culture for many centuries, but when the war was over, it was America that became an economic and financial powerhouse and the leader of the free world. The 1919 Treaty of Versailles ended the war by assessing huge reparations on Germany that ultimately led to hyperinflation in the early 1920s and the rise of Hitler during the 1930s.

During the 1920s, Wall Street grew 5 times faster than the economy. The stock market was growing so fast that a poem[7] printed in the *Saturday Evening Post* in the summer of 1929 expressed the speculative fever of the time:

*Oh, hush thee, my baby, granny's bought some more shares,*
*Daddy's gone out to play with bulls and the bears,*
*Mother's buying on tips, and she simply can't lose,*
*And Baby shall have some expensive new shoes!*

Black Tuesday—the stock market crash—came on October 29, 1929, and within a year nearly 90% of the wealth created by the soaring stock market would be history. America plunged into the Great Depression, forever changing the American economy.

## The Great Depression: 1930–1941

We have seen that in the 1920s, the economy boomed as auto sales took off, consumerism began to blossom, and electricity became part of urban life, spurring on the creation of modern appliances. All of this growth encouraged the stock market, which exploded by more than 600%. What happened next had major implications not only for the United States but also the world.

The stock market collapse in late October 1929 created a financial crisis as margin calls went out to investors who had only put 10% down to buy stock and borrowed (margined) the remaining 90%. When stock prices fell, investors had to come up with additional cash to cover their losses or their accounts would be liquidated. Most investors were wiped out. The prevailing view was that the declines in 1929 would be temporary, after which the market would resume its upward trend. For a while, the irrational exuberance continued and investors kept pouring money into their accounts. When the market did not turn around, but instead got worse, investors ran out of money and their accounts (and wealth) evaporated. By the time the stock market bottomed out, losses equaled 87%.

SZ Photo/Scherl/The Image Works

Bankrupt investor Walter Thornton tries to sell his luxury roadster ($1,500 new) for $100 cash on the streets of New York City following the 1929 stock market crash.

[7] John Steel Gordon, *An Empire of Wealth: The Epic History of American Economic Power* (New York: HarperCollins Publishers), 2004, p. 314.

Over the next three years, income and output would be cut in half, 25% of workers would become unemployed, and more than 10,000 banks would fail. The nation's economy was in freefall. Was government the cure? Early on, the government exacerbated the problem by enacting policies that many argue turned a difficult recession into a depression.

In 1930, Congress passed the Smoot-Hawley Tariff Act, putting tariffs (charges) on imported goods, which raised their prices by an average of 60%. Despite a letter signed by 1,000 economists asking President Hoover to veto the act, he signed it. In retaliation, other countries raised tariffs on their imported goods (U.S. exports) and world trade collapsed. The Federal Reserve took several actions that led to a decline in prices and tightened credit. As a result of these actions, banks called in loans to maintain their solvency, increasing farm and home foreclosures.

Finally, President Hoover asked Congress to increase taxes to balance the budget. While unemployment took money out of people's hands, the tax increases took money out of the hands of people who still had jobs. This compounded the problems the country faced.

All three of these government actions made a bad situation much worse. Could government action make things better?

Running for president in 1932, candidate Franklin D. Roosevelt promised a "New Deal" for Americans. By March 1933, when Roosevelt was inaugurated, the country was at the bottom of the Depression and bank failures were so catastrophic that the president, in his genius, euphemistically called for a "bank holiday." He closed all banks for four days while he and his staff drafted emergency legislation. The legislation and assistance he proposed permitted most banks to reopen safely. Later that summer, passage of the Glass-Steagall Act created the Federal Deposit Insurance Corporation (FDIC) that protected depositor's funds and separated commercial banking from the more speculative investment banking. Since its passage, bank runs have been rare.

Library of Congress

Frances Perkins was secretary of labor from 1933 to 1945. As a member of Roosevelt's cabinet, she helped create much of the New Deal labor legislation.

A little known economist and sociologist, Frances Perkins, Roosevelt's secretary of labor and the first female cabinet member in U.S. history, played a crucial role in writing New Deal legislation. She helped develop federal relief programs such as the Civilian Conservation Corps, which provided federal aid to states for unemployment relief that eventually became the system of unemployment compensation we know today. She also helped create the federal minimum wage law; the Fair Labor Standards Act; the National Labor Relations Act, which made it easier to organize a union; and the Social Security Act. As labor secretary for 12 years, she pushed for many of the rights workers take for granted today.

During his first 100 days in office, Roosevelt signed more than a dozen Acts that brought new or additional federal government regulation of such industries as agriculture, banking, electric power, securities trading, home mortgages, and railroads. He also spent billions through the National Recovery Administration (NRA), which ultimately created the Works Progress Administration (WPA) that built more than 100,000 schools, post offices, and other public buildings, a half million miles of roads, 600 airports, and more than 10,000 bridges. The WPA also funded other projects for writers, artists, photographers, actors, and musicians. Many murals you see in post offices today were sponsored by WPA projects during the Depression. Other than the banking Acts that finally stabilized the banking system, the most lasting legacy of the Depression is the Social Security Act of 1935.

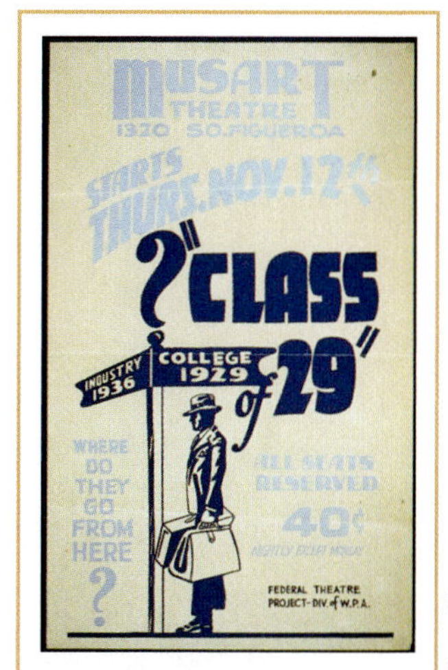


Library of Congress

A 1936 WPA poster for the Federal Theatre Project play "Class of 29."

## World War II 1942–1945

The U.S. buildup of armaments for World War II began right after the Germans invaded France in the summer of 1940. Unemployment was still high at 15% and this slack made the buildup easier. Within a few years, unemployment dropped to just over 1% as *real* (adjusted for inflation) GDP almost doubled in just five years. Virtually all of this additional output was military armaments, but by early 1942, America had left the Great Depression behind. The general consensus is that even though the economy was slowly climbing out of the Depression, war spending greatly accelerated the process. Much of the infrastructure used to build war materiel was quickly turned into civilian production after the war.

## The Postwar Economy: 1946–1960

World War II resulted in tremendous devastation for much of Europe. Ultimately, the U.S. economy was strengthened. However, most goods and services were in short supply as manufacturing capacity fed the war effort. Labor shortages dramatically changed the working status of both women and African Americans. During the war, taxes were raised to pay some of the war expenses, but selling war bonds raised more money. To keep inflation in check, government controls over wages and prices were implemented, along with rationing. Coupons were issued to limit the amount of sugar, shoes, and gasoline that people could legally buy.

In 1944, delegates from 44 countries met in Bretton Woods, New Hampshire, to create a "new world order" for the postwar economies. Out of this meeting came the International Monetary Fund (IMF) to help promote and finance world trade. Because the American economy was the strongest coming out of the war, American funds provided through the Marshall Plan helped to rebuild postwar Europe.

When the war ended, most people, including many economists, expected the economy to drop back into a depression. They were surprised by the ensuing growth. Pent-up demand from consumers for appliances, new homes, and cars spurred the market. Business investment skyrocketed, and wartime manufacturing capacity was rapidly converted to civilian use.

This economic growth did not go unchecked. The Great Depression and World War II had fundamentally changed our view of economic policy. Congress passed the Employment Act of 1946 that made it the *responsibility of government* to "promote maximum employment, production and purchasing power." The Act established the Council of Economic Advisers (CEA) and the Joint Economic Committee of Congress and required an annual Economic Report of the President. All three exist today.

Before the war, labor unions had grown under the Depression-era Wagner Act, but their bargaining power and wages were heavily limited during the war by the War Labor Board. Union strife came to a head in 1946 with 5,000 strikes involving 5 million workers. The result was the passage of the Taft-Hartley Act in 1947 that made it more difficult for unions to organize workers, outlawed closed shops where union membership was a requirement for work, and permitted employers to actively campaign against an organizing attempt. Taft-Hartley put unions on the defensive and is partly responsible for their decline over the last half century.

In the early 1950s, the United States fought the Korean War to a stalemate. The economy suffered a few recessions, but "creeping inflation" was beginning to be viewed as a long-term problem that might stifle future economic growth. Budget surpluses were seen as the solution, and federal taxes and expenditures were brought into line.

American consumerism and suburbanization expanded after World War II, setting off rapid economic growth and the rise of the middle class. Despite the good times, there was a growing awareness that a large part of America was not sharing in the benefits. The Supreme Court in 1954 concluded that segregation of public schools on the basis of race was unconstitutional, setting in motion the civil rights movement.

## Growing Government and Stagflation: 1960–1980

Economists emerged from the Great Depression with a new macroeconomic theory from John Maynard Keynes that justified a crucial role for government in managing the economy. This is called fiscal policy, or using taxing and spending to affect the economy. Using these Keynesian ideas, economists in the early 1960s declared an end to business cycles. If the economy headed into a recession, government could step in and spend more or reduce taxes, thereby stimulating the economy and short-circuiting the recession. Thus, business could always depend on a growing demand for their products and would therefore continue to invest in new factories, creating economic growth. Government would run deficits during an economic downturn and then surpluses when the economy was booming.

President John F. Kennedy adopted the Keynesian approach to economic policy. He cut taxes and expanded government programs designed to grow the economy. Before the Kennedy administration, the emphasis was on balancing the federal budget, which restricted fiscal policy's role. With the new administration (and this carried over to the Johnson years), deficits were less of a concern. Two tax-reduction packages were passed (in 1962 and 1964) even though the budget was in deficit (spending exceeded tax revenues). The focus of the "new economics" was on economic growth through tax rate cuts for individuals and reductions for business using investment tax credits to stimulate new investments in plant and equipment. In the early 1960s, the economy responded to these policies as incomes, investment, and economic growth all rose. As Figure 3 shows, the downside was a "creeping up" of the rate of inflation that was to become a serious problem in the next decade.

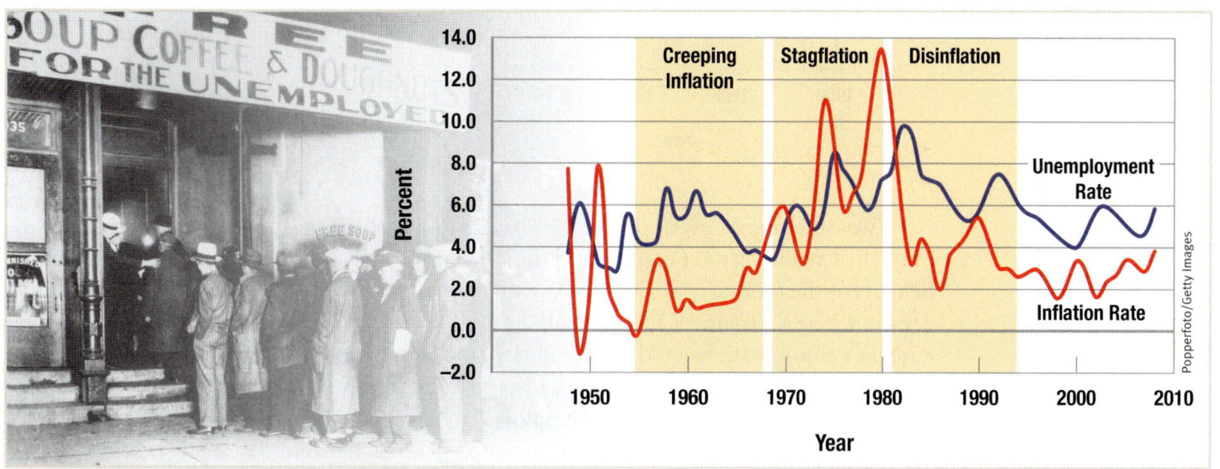


**FIGURE 3—Unemployment and Inflation, 1947–2009**

The economic policies of the 1960's resulted in creeping inflation, while in the 1970s many new government programs, new and costly business regulations along with Vietnam war spending brought on stagflation. Disinflation in the 1980s resulted from tight monetary policy that brought down inflation rates. Stable and low inflation along with lower tax rates and reduced regulation resulted in solid economic growth throughout the period.

President Kennedy's assassination brought Lyndon Johnson to the presidency, who established a host of new "Great Society" and "War on Poverty" government programs and departments, including the following:

- Medicare was created to provide medical care to the elderly, because illness is a principal cause of poverty in older populations. Medicare shifted the cost of their care to the government.
- Medicaid (in cooperation with the states) was created to provide health care to the indigent.
- The Office of Economic Opportunity created new bureaucracies to deal with education, housing, and employment issues.
- The Department of Housing and Urban Development (HUD), a cabinet-level department, was added to promote urban redevelopment.
- The Department of Transportation was established.
- The Open Housing Act prohibited discrimination in the sale or rental of housing.
- The Truth-in-Lending Act added transparency to borrowing.
- The Clear Water Restoration Act dealt with the nation's rivers.
- The Air Quality Act was passed to reduce pollution.

Although many of these "Great Society" government programs were controversial, Figure 4 on the next page shows that the poverty rate was cut in half in less than a decade and has stayed roughly constant over the last 40 years.

FIGURE 4—The Poverty Rate, 1960–1975

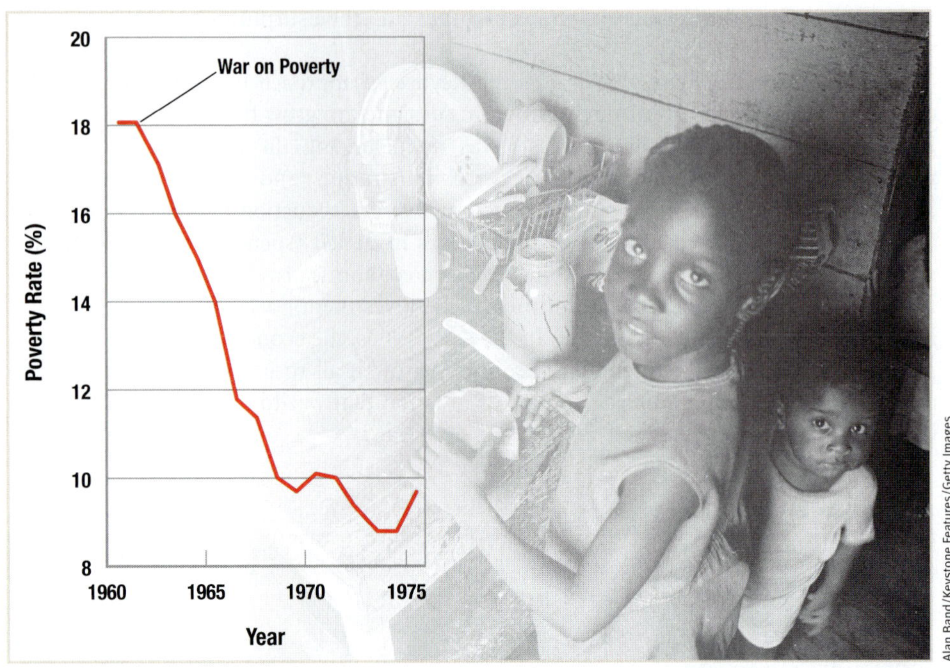


Two other major events in the 1960s were to have big long-term impacts on our economy: the Civil Rights Act of 1964 and the Vietnam War. The Civil Rights Act opened up the benefits of the economy to all and was a major achievement of President Johnson's administration. The Vietnam War, on the other hand, was controversial, was met with continual antiwar demonstrations, and eventually lost the support of the American people.

But the 1970s would go down in history as a period of *stagflation*: high rates of inflation coupled with high rates of unemployment along with slowing economic growth (see Figure 3). Confidence in the economy declined to such an extent that many economists, for the first time, predicted a lower standard of living for the next generation.

Globalization pressures were advancing as Japan and Western Europe became tough competitors to American business. The Organization of Petroleum Exporting Countries (OPEC) colluded to increase crude oil prices 500% in 1973 and increased them again in the latter part of the decade. Given America's dependence on oil, these price increases resulted in two deep recessions with continued inflation.

In the summer of 1971, President Nixon, in an attempt to deal with a growing problem of rising unemployment and inflation, instituted a 90-day *freeze* on wages, prices, and rents. He followed with wage and price controls later in the year. A regulatory body, the Pay Board, set limits on pay, while a Price Commission set limits on prices and profit increases. Generally viewed as a failure, controls were removed in early 1974. This ended our nation's first and last experiment with peacetime wage and price controls since World War II. Government intervention had gone too far.

The 1970s were also a period of increased government regulation, when the following legislation was passed:

- National Environmental Policy Act (1970)
- Water Quality Improvement Act (1970)
- Occupational Safety and Health Act (1970)
- Supplemental Security Income (added to Social Security in 1972)
- Federal Water Pollution Act (1972)
- Employee Retirement Income Security Act (1974)

Despite all of this new federal governance—or maybe because of it—public opinion was turning. In 1978, the Carter administration substantially deregulated the airline, trucking, and railroad industries. The 1970s ended with the first, and what was considered at the time a successful government bailout of the Chrysler Corporation, but almost 30 years later both Chrysler and General Motors would need federal help to remain in business.

Overall, the 1960s and 1970s were a period of rising government intervention in the economy, both through regulation and higher levels of government spending and taxation. It was also a period of rising inflation accompanied by rising unemployment and slow growth. Not a pretty picture.

To many observers, these events were connected, and economists would spend the next decade untangling the reasons for the stagflation that developed over these two decades. Was government the problem rather than the solution?

## Disinflation and Bubbles: 1980 to the Present

When Ronald Reagan took office in 1981, the economy was a mess. Inflation was 14% and rising, unemployment was over 7% and rising, 30-year home mortgage rates were 15%, and real economic growth (adjusted for inflation) was negative, so the economy was declining. Reagan believed intrusive government was the problem. He set out to halt the growth of federal spending, reduce personal and business tax rates, and to repeal burdensome regulations. He saw all of these goals as ways to release the power of markets and get the economy back on track. With the help of the Federal Reserve and especially its chairman, Paul Volcker, inflation began to ease and interest rates began to drop.

We now know that when people and business expect inflation, this can set off an inflationary cycle and these *inflationary expectations* were driving the economy in the early 1980s. To wring these expectations out of the system may require a severe recession, and the recession in the early 1980s was the deepest since the Depression as unemployment reached nearly 11%.

To get economic growth going again, taxes were cut and the deregulation push started by the Carter administration was expanded. This "supply-side" approach, Reagan argued, was needed to provide incentives for business to produce and hire more. Further, reducing personal income tax rates would increase work effort, since families could keep more of what they earned and would be willing to save more. As they saved, interest rates would fall, encouraging business investment in new plant and equipment. This supply-side approach was the opposite of the Keynesian demand-management approach of using government spending to drive (or try to drive) economic growth.

Although President Johnson's War on Poverty cut the poverty rate in half, by 1981 it had produced a political backlash against what many viewed as a welfare state that encouraged dependency rather than encouraging people to escape the cycle of poverty through decent-paying jobs. Social welfare eligibility criteria were tightened, the length of time people could draw benefits shortened, and benefits were reduced. The focus of aid programs shifted to putting people back to work. By the end of the 1980s, "workfare" programs were required of all state welfare systems.

When the air traffic controllers illegally went on strike early in Reagan's presidency, they were fired and the union decertified. Reagan could do this because federal law forbids federal workers from striking. But the unprecedented firing set the tone for labor relations across the country, and unions have not fared well since.

Although Reagan was successful at getting tax rate cuts, he was unable (or unwilling) to persuade Congress to hold down domestic spending in the face of increased military expenditures. As a result, annual federal deficits began an uphill march, roughly doubling to $153 billion during his two terms.

Federal deficits shrank during the 1990s as a technology-fueled boom swelled federal coffers and then turned to surpluses in President Clinton's second term. Clinton continued the restructuring of welfare programs, increased income tax rates on upper-income taxpayers, and pressed for trade legislation, implementing the North American Free Trade Agreement (NAFTA).

In 1999, Congress passed and President Clinton signed the landmark Financial Services Modernization Act that repealed the portion of the 1933 Glass-Steagall Act separating commercial and investment banking. The not-unexpected result was a rapid consolidation of banks, insurance companies, and investment underwriting services into giant conglomerates.

What *was* unexpected was how fast financial firms grew and the level of risk undertaken by commercial banks because of their new investment arms. Many observers attribute part of the severity of the 2008–2009 financial crisis to this Act.

What is most notable about the last quarter-century is the steady reduction in inflation from nearly 14% to about 2% (look back at Figure 3). This feat had as its foundation a policy of purposely putting the economy into a deep recession in the early 1980s to wring out inflation and inflationary expectations. Until just recently, the economy enjoyed steady growth, low inflation, amazingly low unemployment, and just two minor recessions. Much of the credit for this performance is due to a steady hand at the Federal Reserve and a better understanding by economists about inflation dynamics.

How quickly things change! As President Obama took office in January 2009, the economy was in a real mess. Stocks markets plunged, credit markets were frozen, and the nation's biggest banks were on the verge of collapse. General Motors and Chrysler were shells of their former selves, and home mortgage defaults, at unheard of levels, sent home prices falling. Consumer spending dropped, resulting in huge layoffs that pushed unemployment to the highest levels in more than two decades. Many were calling it the "worst recession since the Great Depression."

The reasons for this downturn are complex and are detailed later in this book. But mitigating the impact called for extraordinary measures by both the Federal Reserve and the federal government. The Federal Reserve used every tool available (and then some) to restore credit markets, lowering interest rates to historic levels and injecting massive amounts of liquidity into financial markets. The Obama administration passed a massive stimulus package, running the deficit for fiscal 2009 to nearly $2 trillion, with projections of substantial deficits over the next several years. As Figure 5 illustrates, based on these projections by the Congressional Budget Office, the national debt will nearly double over the near future to

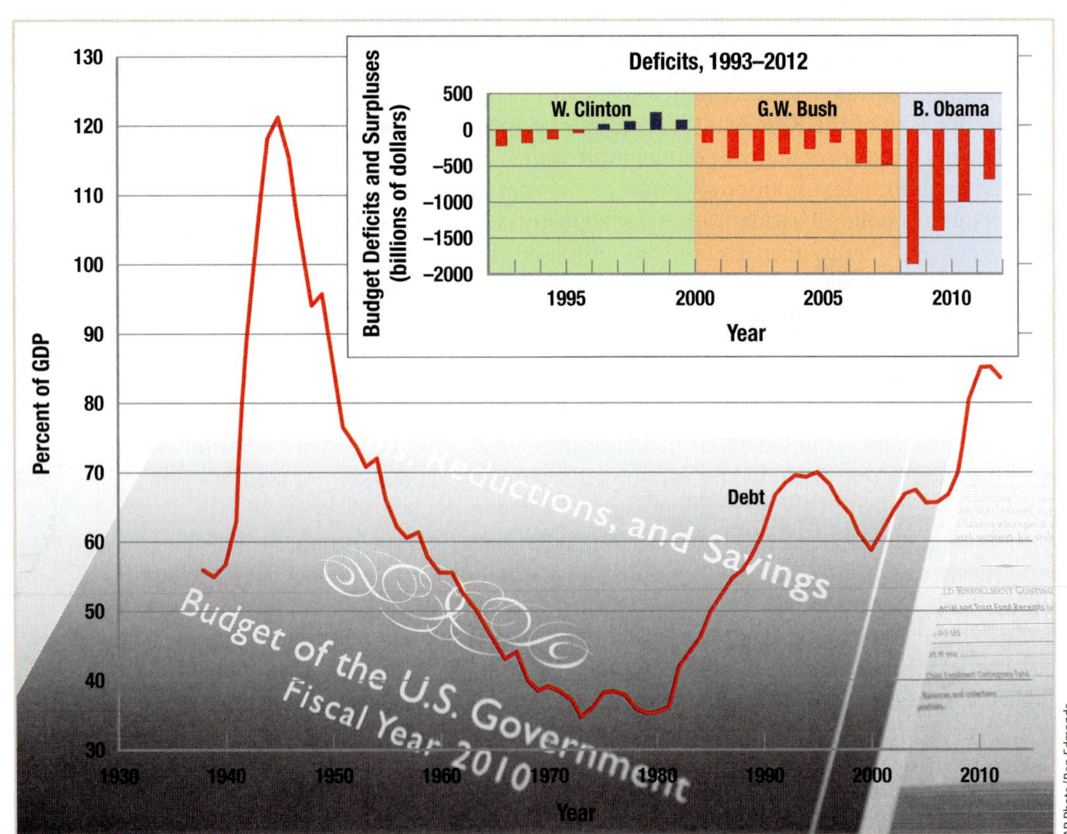


**FIGURE 5—Gross Public Debt as a Percent of GDP, and Deficits, 1993–2012**

Recent high deficits are pushing the gross public debt to levels not seen since World War II. Note that the 2010–2012 deficits are those projected by the Obama administration.

more than 80% of GDP. Undoubtedly, dealing with these huge deficits and their potential for raising inflation levels will quickly draw the focus of the Obama administration.

The history of our economy has been one of relying mostly on markets to provide and distribute goods and services. But, as we have seen, markets can fail. These failures bring forth a call for another round of government intervention, typically in the form of regulations or new government financing or provision of services. This process has resulted in government (federal, state, and local) growing from a single-digit percentage of GDP in the early 1900s to more than 40% today. We are a capitalist economy with a heavy dose of government.

Since World War II, our economy has endured a long cycle involving rising government intervention and regulation of the economy, accommodative (and sometimes erratic) monetary policy, and rising inflation (1960s and 1970s). This was followed by reductions in government involvement through deregulation, reduced taxes, and steady monetary policy that reduced inflation and kept it down (1980s to 2007). We are now in another period of increased government spending, re-regulation, and greater government involvement in the economy. Whether we will suffer another round of crippling inflation depends on how well we have learned the lessons of the past.

## CHECKPOINT

### MARKET FAILURE, GOVERNMENT INTERVENTION, AND U.S. ECONOMIC HISTORY

- After the Civil War, the economy grew dramatically. Railroads stretched from coast to coast, and the oil, steel, mining, and agriculture industries flourished.
- The early 1900s saw the rise of consumerism as automobiles, appliances, and electricity became common in households.
- The Great Depression brought misery to the country as stock prices fell 90%, unemployment reached 25%, and many thousands of banks failed, wiping out the savings of many families.
- President Roosevelt's New Deal, including the National Recovery Administration, the Works Progress Administration, and many other additions to the federal government, helped employ people and reduce the impact of the Depression.
- The buildup for World War II is generally credited with helping the economy pull out of the Depression.
- The Great Depression changed America's view of the role of government in economic affairs as Congress passed the Employment Act of 1946, making maximum employment, production, and purchasing power the responsibility of the government.
- The stagflation of the 1970s turned Americans away from government intervention in the economy and back toward markets.
- The reduction in government regulation seemed to work well because from the early 1980s until just recently, the economy enjoyed relative price stability, low unemployment, and steady growth.
- The recession of 2008–2009 has Americans debating a bigger role for government in regulating business and stimulating the economy.

**QUESTION:** Today, many of us pay our bills electronically, use our debit cards, and pay tolls on toll roads with E-ZPass (a little box attached to the windshield). All of these systems clearly make life less hectic and complicated. Economist Amy Finkelstein (*The New York Times*, July 4, 2007, p. B1) examined years of toll records from around the country. What she found was a clear pattern: "After an electronic system is put in place, tolls start rising sharply." Within 10 years, electronic tolls were roughly 30% higher than comparable tollbooth fees. The implication, of course, is that when bills are paid automatically and we don't pay cash or write a check, markets may not work effectively to control prices. What implications does this have for taxes and the possible tradeoff between growth of government versus private activity in our economy?

Answers to the Checkpoint question can be found at the end of this chapter.

## Key Concepts

Property rights, p. 81
Consumer surplus, p. 82
Producer surplus, p. 83
Asymmetric information, p. 85
Adverse selection, p. 85
Moral hazard, p. 86
Public goods, p. 86
Free rider, p. 86
Common property resources, p. 87
External cost (or negative externality), p. 88
External benefits, p. 89

## Chapter Summary

### Markets and Efficiency

Markets are efficient mechanisms for allocating resources. The prices and profits characteristic of market systems provide incentives and signals that are nonexistent or seriously flawed in other systems of resource allocation.

For markets to be efficient, they must have well-structured institutions. These include the following requirements: (1) Information is widely available; (2) property rights are protected; (3) private contracts are enforced; (4) spillovers are minimal; and (5) competition prevails.

Markets impose discipline on producers and consumers. Producers would like to charge higher prices and earn greater profits, but their economic survival depends on turning out quality goods at reasonable prices. As consumers, we would all like to engage in frequent extravagant purchases, but given our limited resources, each of us must decide which products are most important to us. As a result, markets are also rationing devices.

Because many consumers are willing to pay more than market equilibrium prices for many goods and services, they receive a consumer surplus. In a similar way, since many businesses would be willing to provide products at prices below equilibrium prices, they receive a producer surplus. The concepts of consumer and producer surplus are helpful when we wish to examine the impacts of public policy.

### Market Failures

If markets do not meet the five institutional requirements they will not be efficient. When one or more of these conditions is not met, the market is said to fail. Market failure does not mean that a market totally collapses or fails to exist, but that it fails to provide the socially optimal amount of goods and services.

In some markets, one party to a transaction almost always has better information than the other. In this case, the market is said to fail because of asymmetric information. Asymmetric information can result in the inability of sellers to find buyers for their products, but it usually just involves adjustments in contracting methods. Adverse selection occurs when products of different qualities are sold at one price and involve asymmetric information. Moral hazard occurs when an insurance policy or some other arrangement changes the economic incentives people face, leading people to change their behavior, usually in a way detrimental to the market.

Private goods are those goods that can be consumed only by the individuals who purchase them. Private goods are rival and exclusive. Public goods, in contrast, are nonrival and nonexclusive, meaning my consumption does not diminish your consumption and that once such a good has been provided for one person, others cannot be excluded from enjoying it.

Public goods give rise to the free rider problem. Once a public good has been provided, other consumers cannot be excluded from it, so many people will choose to enjoy the benefit without paying for it: they will free ride. And because of the possibility of free riding, the danger is that no one will pay for the public good, so it will no longer be provided by private markets, even though it is publicly desired. Pure public goods usually require public provision.

Common property resources are owned in common by the community and are subject to the "tragedy of the commons" and overexploitation.

When an efficient legal system for the enforcement of contracts is lacking, contracts will be small because large contracts with complex financial provisions are difficult to enforce informally.

Markets rarely produce the socially optimal output when external costs or benefits are present. The market overproduces goods with external costs, selling them at too low a price. Conversely, markets tend to provide too little of products that have external benefits.

Some markets tend toward noncompetition, so prices go up.

### Market Failure, Government Intervention, and U.S. Economic History

After the Civil War, the economy grew dramatically. Railroads stretched from coast to coast, and the oil, steel, mining, and agriculture industries flourished.

The early 1900s saw the rise of consumerism as automobiles, appliances, and electricity became common in households.

The Great Depression brought misery to the country as stock prices fell 90%, unemployment reached 25%, and many thousands of banks failed, wiping out the savings of many families.

President Roosevelt's New Deal, including the National Recovery Administration, the Works Progress Administration, and many other additions to the federal government, helped employ people and reduce the impact of the depression. The buildup for World War II is generally credited with helping the economy pull out of the Depression.

The Great Depression changed America's view of the role of government in economic affairs as Congress passed the Employment Act of 1946, making maximum employment, production, and purchasing power the responsibility of the government.

The stagflation of the 1970s turned Americans away from government intervention in the economy and back toward markets. The reduction in government regulation seemed to work well because from the early 1980s until just recently, the economy enjoyed relative price stability, low unemployment, and steady growth.

The recession of 2008–2009 has Americans debating a bigger role for government in regulating business and stimulating the economy.

## Questions and Problems

### Check Your Understanding

1. When professors get tenure, essentially guaranteeing them lifetime jobs, does this affect the effort they expend on teaching and research? What concept might be used to explain your answer?
2. Are buying brands (e.g., Coke, Sony, and Dell) a way consumers compensate for asymmetric information? Explain.
3. Describe consumer surplus. Describe producer surplus. Using the graph on the next page show both. Now assume that a new technology reduces the cost of

production. What happens to consumer surplus? Show the impact of the change in the graph.

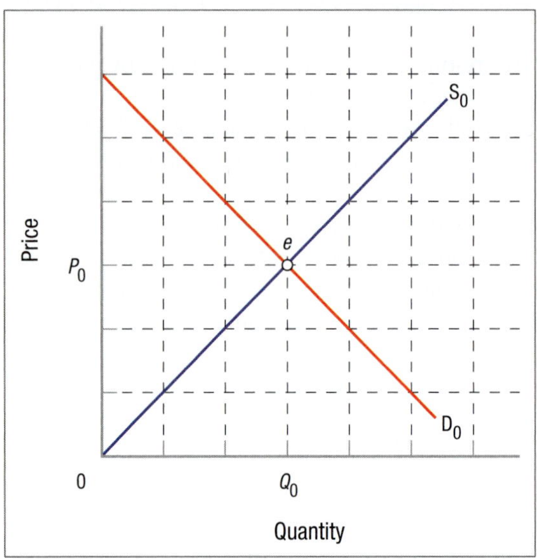


4. Define public goods. What is the free rider problem? Give several examples of public goods.

## Apply the Concepts

5. Many observers consider it a market failure when the pharmaceutical industry refuses to do research and development on what are known as neglected diseases: cures for malaria and tuberculosis and vaccines for other diseases in developing countries where the profit potential is small. Further, many drug firms are unwilling to make vaccines for illnesses such as influenza and other biohazards such as anthrax and smallpox. Vaccines are especially prone to large lawsuits because when they are administered, they are administered to millions of people in an emergency, and if there are serious unanticipated side effects, settlement costs can be huge. With anthrax vaccine, ethical considerations prevent exposing someone to anthrax and then injecting the medicine, so these types of vaccines often are used in emergencies without sufficient testing.

   a. One of the solutions currently used for neglected diseases is the public–private partnership (PPP). Grants by the Bill & Melinda Gates Foundation currently fund most of the PPPs that are conducted on a "no profit, no loss" basis. The firm's research and development costs are covered, but firms must sell the drugs at cost to developing countries. Why would pharmaceutical firms be willing to spend time on these types of projects?

   b. Since lawsuits are an important impediment to research and development of vaccines, what policies could the government institute to solve this problem?

   c. Besides the use of the PPP, what other policies might the government introduce to encourage drug firms to do research and development on neglected diseases and orphan diseases (diseases that affect only a few people and thus have extremely limited markets)?

6. "If millions of people are desperate to buy and millions more desperate to sell, the trades will happen, whether we like it or not." This quote by Martin Wolf[8] refers to trades in illicit goods like narcotics, knockoffs (counterfeit goods), slaves, organs, and other goods we generally refer to as "bads." He suggests that the only way to eliminate traffic in these illicit goods is to eliminate their profitability. Do you agree? Why or why not?

7. Academic studies suggest that the amount people tip at restaurants is only slightly related to the quality of service, and that tips are poor measures of how happy people are with the service. Is this another example of market failure? What might account for this situation?

8. The U.S. Department of Labor reports that of the roughly 145 million people employed, just over half (73.9 million) are paid hourly, but less than 3% earn the minimum wage or less; 97% of wage earners earn more. And of those earning the minimum wage or less, 25% are teenagers living at home. If so few people are affected by the minimum wage, why does it often seem to be such a contentious political issue?

9. Adam Smith, in his famous book *The Wealth of Nations,* noted, "Every individual . . . neither intends to promote the public interest, nor knows how much he is promoting it. By preferring the support of domestic to that of foreign industry he intends only his own security; and by directing that industry in such a manner as its produce may be of the greatest value, he intends only his own gain, and he is in this, as in many other cases, led by an invisible hand to promote an end which was no part of his intention." What was he describing and what did it do?

10. What is the purpose of a warranty given by a used-car dealer? Evaluate one used-car warranty that gives your money back if not satisfied in a certain time period, and one that does not give you back your money but lets you put this money toward the purchase of another used car. Which warranty would you prefer?

11. In 2006 Medicare recipients were permitted to sign up for a federally subsidized drug benefit plan. The sign-up phase had a May 15 deadline, and those signing up after that date faced a premium penalty. Does this deadline have anything to do with adverse selection? Explain.

## In the News

12. Economist N. Gregory Mankiw is quoted (*The New York Times,* March 18, 2008, p. C9) as suggesting, "If you have flood insurance, you are more likely to build your house on a flood plain, and: if you have fire insurance, you'll be less careful about smoking on the couch." What concept is Professor Mankiw describing?

13. Information would seem to be the ultimate public good. As *The Economist* (February 5, 2005, p. 72) noted, "It is a 'non-rival' good: i.e., your use of it does not interfere with my use. Better still, there are network effects: i.e., the more people who use it, the more useful it is to any individual user. Best of all, the existence of the Internet means that the costs of sharing are remarkably low." Is information a public good? Why then do we have copyright and patent laws to restrict the dissemination of some information?

[8] Martin Wolf, "The Profit Motive May Be Universal but Virtue Is Not," *Financial Times,* November 16, 2005, p. 13.

## Solving Problems

**14.** Consider the market shown in the figure below.

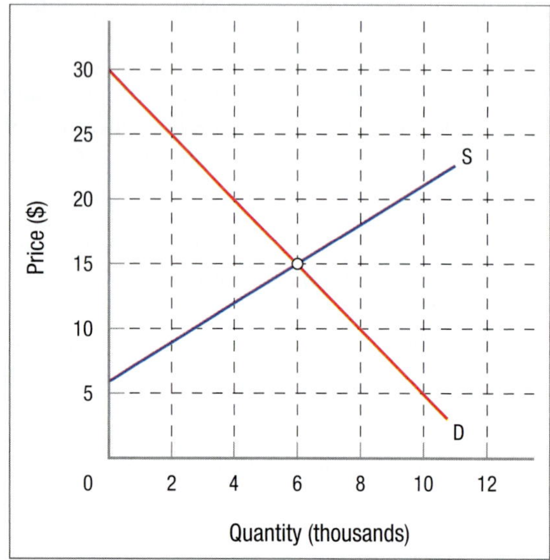


a. Compute the consumer surplus. ________________

b. Compute the producer surplus. ________________

Now assume that government puts a price floor on this product at $20 a unit.

c. Compute the new consumer surplus. ________________

d. Compute the new producer surplus. ________________

e. What group would tend to have their advocates or lobbyists support price floors?

# Answers to Questions in CheckPoints

## Check Point: Markets and Efficiency

Economists generally believe in the benefits of free trade between consenting adults. If trade did not benefit each party, they would not trade. Even in these markets, there is a demand for goods and services. As long as no one is forced to participate and everyone is fully informed, markets will be more efficient (e.g., more kidneys will be available than when relying on donations alone).

These markets are mainly repugnant on moral grounds. Markets for kidneys may result in the poor being targeted, since their opportunities in life are limited, and the equilibrium price for a kidney would be so low as to suggest they might have been exploited. Although illegal, this trade goes on today. The argument against the human cannonball is that his performance was considered demeaning and could bring disrespect and humiliation to other people of restricted growth. Besides the moral argument, prostitution faces health issues and is considered a demeaning occupation by many.

## Check Point: Market Failures

Yes, they will probably reach an agreement. Both will go forward on the basis of the information they have at hand. A price will likely be agreed upon, but that price will reflect some uncertainty on the buyer's part. There is always an element of asymmetric information in our transactions, especially those between two individuals who do not know each other and will not likely see each other again. One way most retailers have eliminated this uncertainty for buyers is through warranties and money-back guarantees. The 60-day money-back offer from General Motors was designed to remove the fear of purchasing a car from a company emerging from bankruptcy.

## Check Point: Market Failure, Government Intervention, and U.S. Economic History

Only a minority of Americans writes checks to the IRS or state governments on a regular basis. Most have income taxes automatically withdrawn from their paycheck (electronically transferred to the bank) and property taxes are automatically paid as part of their mortgage payments. So most people do not directly feel the pain of writing a large check to pay their bill for government services. Milton Friedman wrote that he came to regret his role in designing the income tax withholding scheme during World War II. "It never occurred to me at the time that I was helping to develop machinery that would make possible a government that I would come to criticize severely as too large, too intrusive, too destructive of freedom" (*The New York Times,* July 4, 2007, p. B1). It seems likely that when consumers (or taxpayers) do not see (or feel) the cost of what they purchase or pay for government services, they may demand more than if they had to directly confront the cost.

# Elasticity 5

Russ Schelpman/Corbis

**In 2008, gasoline prices started to climb.** Driven by problems in the Middle East and increased demand from China and India, gasoline prices kept climbing. By the summer, gasoline had reached a price of over $4.00 per gallon, almost three times as high as two years previously.

If you drove a car during this period, what did you do? At first, you probably did nothing but bear with it and pay the higher price. What *could* you do? It is not as if gasoline is the same as chewing gum: A large rise in the price of chewing gum might cause you to give it up. Things are not so easy with gasoline. Maybe you drove a little less. Over time, however, you may have considered alternatives such as buying a smaller car or a hybrid that gets much better gas mileage. Or you may have considered car pooling or public transportation. The drop in sales of large gas-guzzling sport utility vehicles (SUVs) tells us that over time, people responded to the steady rise in gasoline prices by cutting their quantity of gasoline purchased.

*Elasticity*—the responsiveness of one variable to changes in another—is the term economists use to measure this change. In this gasoline example, we know that the price of gasoline is one variable and the quantity of gasoline demanded is the other variable. The amount of gasoline we buy does not change very much in the short run even though the price might rise. Over the long run, the rise in the price of gasoline has led to some attempts to cut back usage. We can speculate that there will be greater attempts to use less gasoline as prices rise. But how much does the price have to rise before quantity demanded falls significantly? The concept of elasticity lets us measure the relative change in quantity demanded for various changes in the price of gasoline.

Elasticity can be measured for many different items. If the price of cancer-preventing drugs rises, how much will their sales fall? As well as price elasticity, we can look at another

**After studying this chapter you should be able to:**

- ☐ Understand the concept of elasticity and why percentages are used to measure it.
- ☐ Describe the difference between elastic and inelastic demand.
- ☐ Compute price elasticities of supply and demand.
- ☐ Use income elasticity of demand to define normal, inferior, and luxury goods.
- ☐ Describe cross elasticity of demand and use this concept to define substitutes and complements.
- ☐ Describe the relationship between total revenue and price elasticity of demand.
- ☐ Describe the determinants of elasticity of demand and supply.
- ☐ Use the concept of price elasticity of supply to measure the relationship between quantity supplied and changes in product price.
- ☐ Describe the time periods economists use to study elasticity, and describe the variables that companies can change during these periods.
- ☐ Describe the relationship between elasticity and the burden and incidence of taxes.

elasticity measure, income elasticity, which measures changes in consumer demand in response to changes in consumer income. In a slowing economy, with consumer incomes falling, will the public's purchases of cars and trucks fall off? By how much? When an economy enters a recession, automobile makers want to know how much sales of trucks and cars will decline in response to a fall in consumer income.

Elasticity is a simple economic concept that nonetheless contains a tremendous amount of information about demand for specific products. In the last two chapters, we saw that when prices rise, quantity demanded falls. But how much will quantity demanded fall? If a firm raises its price by 50 cents, will it end up with more in revenue, or will the increase in price lead to a drop in quantity demanded that more than offsets the price increase? If gasoline goes up by 50 cents per gallon, will you still vacation by car? What if the price increase is $2 per gallon?

Knowing a product's price elasticity allows economists to predict the amount by which quantity demanded will drop in response to a price increase, or grow in response to a price decline. Measures of elasticity have a further benefit: By putting changes in a relative (percentage) context, economists can compare the supply and demand curves for different products without worrying about their absolute magnitudes. In essence, the concept of elasticity helps you to put supply and demand concepts to work.

## Elasticity of Demand

We know by the law of demand that as prices rise, quantity sold falls. More importantly, *how much* will sales decline? If a small price increase results in *all* of your customers switching to your competitors, it is clearly not a good idea; you are out of business. And if a small price increase still results in a large reduction in quantity sold, then raising prices probably is not a good idea. However, if a large price increase elicits only a small loss in sales, then raising prices may make sense. As we will see, the concept of elasticity and the impact of changing price on a firm's sales revenue help to determine the answer.

**Price elasticity of demand** ($E_d$) is a measure of how responsive quantity demanded is to a change in price and is defined as

$$E_d = \frac{\text{Percentage Change in Quantity Demanded}}{\text{Percentage Change in Price}}$$

For example, if prices of strawberries rise by 5% and sales fall by 10%, then the price elasticity of demand for strawberries is

$$E_d = -10 \div 5 = -2$$

Alternately, if a 5% reduction in strawberry prices results in a 10% gain in sales, the price elasticity of demand also is $-2$ ($E_d = 10 \div -5 = -2$).

Often we are not given percentage changes. Rather, we are given numerical values and have to convert them into percentage changes. For example, to compute a change in price, take the new price ($P_{new}$) and subtract the old price ($P_{old}$), then divide this result by the old price ($P_{old}$). Finally, to put this ratio in percentage terms, multiply by 100. In equation form:

$$\text{Percentage Change} = \frac{(P_{new} - P_{old})}{P_{old}}$$

For example, if the old price of gasoline ($P_{old}$) was $2.00 a gallon and the new price goes up by $1.00 to $3.00, then the percentage change is

$$\text{Percentage Change} = \frac{\$3.00 - \$2.00}{\$2.00} = \frac{\$1.00}{\$2.00} = 0.50, \text{ or } 50\%$$

Just a reminder: 0.50 times 100 is 50%.

**Price elasticity of demand:** A measure of the responsiveness of quantity demanded to a change in price, equal to the percentage change in quantity demanded divided by the percentage change in price.

## Price Elasticity of Demand as an Absolute Value

The price elasticity of demand is always a negative number. This reflects the fact that the demand curve's slope is negative: As prices increase, quantity demanded falls. Price and quantity demanded stand in an inverse relationship to one another, resulting in a negative value for price elasticity. Economists nevertheless frequently refer to price elasticity of demand in positive terms. They simply use the *absolute value* of the computed price elasticity of demand. Recalling our examples, where $E_d = -2$, we can take the absolute value of $-2$, written as $|-2|$, and simply refer to $E_d$ as 2. For most comparisons, we can use the absolute value of elasticity and ignore the minus sign.

What does this elasticity value of 2 tell us? Quite simply, that for every 1% increase in price, quantity demanded will decline by 2%. Conversely, for every 1% decline in price, quantity demanded will increase by 2%.

## Measuring Elasticity with Percentages

Measuring elasticity in percentage terms rather than specific units enables economists to compare the characteristics of various unrelated products. Comparing price and sales changes for jet airplanes, cars, and hamburgers in dollar amounts would be so complex as to be meaningless. Because a dollar increase in the price for gasoline is different from a dollar increase in the price of a BMW, by using percentage change, we can compare the sensitivity of demand curves of different products. Percentages allow us to compare changes in prices and sales for any two products, no matter how dissimilar they are; a 100% increase is the same percentage change for any product.

We have seen how to compute the elasticity of demand, and we have seen why working with percentage changes is so important. Elasticity is a relative measure giving us a way to compare products with widely different prices and output measures.

## Elastic and Inelastic Demand

All products have some price elasticity of demand. When prices go up, quantity demanded will fall. That is the basis of the negative slope of the demand curve. But people are more responsive to changes in the prices of some products than in others. Economists label goods as being *elastic, inelastic,* or *unitary elastic.*

### Elastic

When the absolute value of the computed price elasticity of demand is greater than 1, economists refer to this as **elastic demand.** An elastic demand curve is one that is responsive to price changes. At the extreme is the *perfectly elastic* demand curve shown in panel A of Figure 1 on the next page. Notice that it is horizontal, showing that the slightest increase in price will result in zero output being sold.

**Elastic demand:** The absolute value of the price elasticity of demand is greater than 1. Elastic demands are very responsive to changes in price. The percentage change in quantity demanded is greater than the percentage change in price.

In reality, no branded product—Coca-Cola, Apple iPod, or Toyota Prius—ever has a perfectly elastic demand curve, but for many of us, no other products can perfectly substitute for these products. Still, products with many close substitutes face highly elastic demand curves. One recent study of several brands of bath tissue found the price elasticities of demand for Scott, Kleenex, Charmin, Northern, and other brands ranged from 2.0 to 4.5—highly elastic.[1] Raise the price of Charmin, and watch how quickly sales fall as people switch to Northern or Scott. Canned peaches, nuts and bolts, cereal, and bottled water are all examples of products facing highly elastic demands. If one bottled water company were to raise its price by much, many consumers would simply switch to other brands, since bottled water is nearly identical.

[1] Lawrence Wu, "Two Methods of Determining Elasticities of Demand and Their Use in Merger Simulation," in Lawrence Wu, *Economics of Antitrust: New Issues, Questions, and Insights* (New York: National Economic Research Associates), 2004, pp. 21–33.

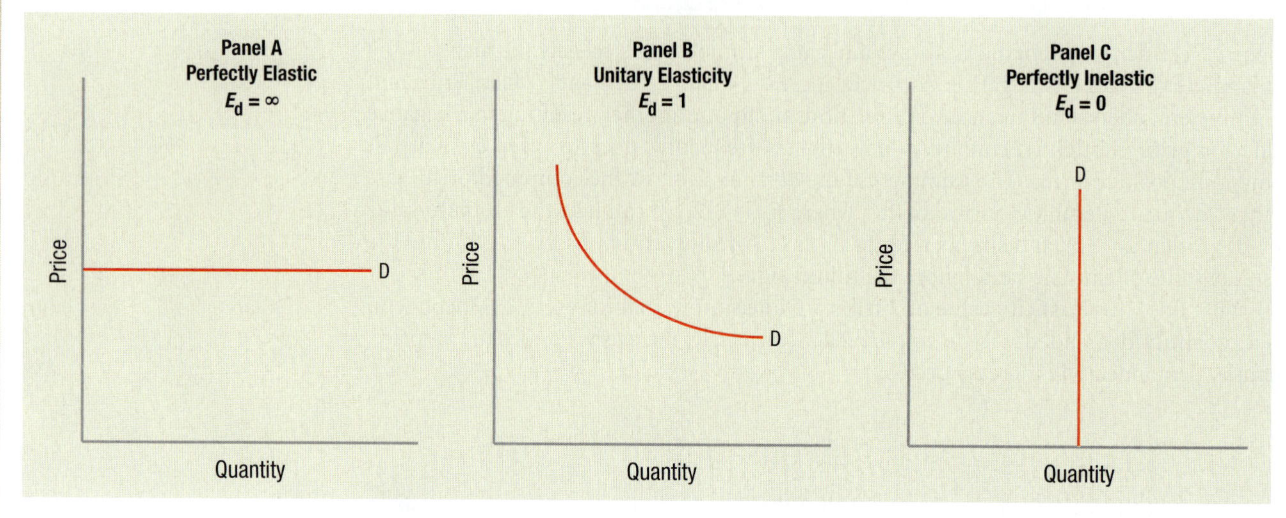


**FIGURE 1—Perfectly Elastic, Unitary Elastic, and Perfectly Inelastic Demand Curves**

The horizontal demand curve in panel A represents perfectly elastic demand because when price increases, quantity demanded drops to zero. Panel C, on the other hand, illustrates a perfectly inelastic demand curve where quantity demanded is insensitive to changes in price. Panel B shows that if elasticity of demand is unitary, then a 1% increase in price will result in a 1% decrease in quantity demanded. Note that the unitary elastic demand curve is not a straight line.

## Inelastic

At the other extreme, what about products that see little change in sales even when prices change dramatically? The opposite of the perfectly elastic demand curve is the curve showing no response to changes in price. Economists call this a *perfectly inelastic* demand curve. An example appears in panel C of Figure 1. This curve is vertical, not horizontal as in panel A. For products with perfectly inelastic demands, quantity demanded does not change when price changes.

What products might be inelastically demanded? Consider products that are immensely important to our lives but have few substitutes—for example, drugs that ameliorate life-threatening illnesses such as heart disease or stroke, and insulin for diabetics. If people who need these products have the money, they will buy them, no matter how high their price. Some products that are relatively, though not perfectly, inelastic include gasoline, tobacco, and most spices. If gasoline prices rise too sharply, some consumers will curtail their driving. Still, it takes a fairly drastic rise in gasoline prices before most people curtail their driving significantly. A doubling of the price of cinnamon will probably not reduce our demand since it is such a small fraction of our overall food budget. Economists define **inelastic demand** as demand curves with elasticity coefficients that are less than 1.

Inelastic demand: The absolute value of the price elasticity of demand is less than 1. Inelastic demands are not very responsive to changes in price. The percentage change in quantity demanded is less than the percentage change in price.

Note that the demand for gasoline is inelastic, but the elasticity for specific brands of gasoline is elastic. Brand preferences for homogeneous commodities such as gasoline are weak, and many different outlets exist for buying gas. If your Shell dealer raises gasoline prices by a significant amount, you probably will go to the Texaco dealer down the street. Giving up using gasoline altogether, on the other hand, is much harder. Over time, public transportation or electric (or hybrid) cars may be possible substitutes for gas-powered cars, but few people will be able to adopt these substitutes in the short run. On the contrary, many people are highly dependent on their gas-powered cars, so gas purchases do not drop substantially when prices rise. Thus, demand for a particular brand of gas (Exxon, Shell) is elastic, while the demand for gasoline as a commodity is inelastic.

### Unitary Elasticity

Elastic demand curves have an elasticity coefficient that is greater than 1, while inelastic demand curves have a coefficient of less than 1. That leaves those products with an elasticity coefficient just equal to 1. This condition is called *unit* or **unitary elasticity of demand.** It means the percentage change in quantity demanded is precisely equal to the percentage change in price. Panel B of Figure 1 shows a demand curve where price elasticity equals 1. Note that this demand curve is not a straight line. The reasons for this will become clear in our discussion later on in the chapter.

**Unitary elasticity of demand:** The absolute value of the price elasticity of demand is equal to 1. The percentage change in quantity demanded is just equal to the percentage change in price.

## Determinants of Elasticity

Price elasticity of demand measures how sensitive sales are to price changes. But what determines elasticity itself? The four basic determinants of a product's elasticity of demand are (1) the availability of substitute products, (2) the percentage of income or household budget spent on the product, (3) the time period being examined, and (4) the difference between luxuries and necessities.

### Substitutability

The more close substitutes, or possible alternatives, a product has, the easier it is for consumers to switch to a competing product and the more elastic the demand. Beef and chicken are substitutes for many people, as are competing brands of cola such as Coke, Pepsi, and RC Cola. All have relatively elastic demands. Conversely, if a product has few close substitutes, such as insulin for diabetics or tobacco for heavy smokers, its elasticity of demand tends to be lower.

### Proportion of Income Spent on a Product

A second determinant of elasticity is the proportion (percentage) of household income spent on a product. In general, the smaller the percent of household income spent on a product, the lower the elasticity of demand. For example, you probably spend little of your income on salt, cinnamon, or other spices. As a result, a hefty increase in the price of salt, say, 25%, would not affect your salt consumption because the impact on your budget would be tiny. But if a product represents a significant part of household spending, elasticity of demand tends to be greater, or more elastic. A 10% increase in your rent, for example, would put a large dent in your budget, significantly reducing your purchasing power for many other products. Such a rent increase would likely lead you to look around earnestly for a cheaper apartment.

### Time Period

The third determinant of elasticity is the time period under consideration. When consumers have some time to adjust their consumption patterns, the elasticity of demand becomes more elastic. When they have little time to adjust, the elasticity of demand tends to be more inelastic. Thus, as we saw earlier, when gasoline prices rise suddenly, most consumers cannot immediately change their transportation patterns, so gasoline sales do not drop significantly. However, as gas prices continue to remain high, we see shifts in consumer behavior, to which automakers respond by producing smaller, more fuel-efficient cars.

### Luxuries Versus Necessities

Luxuries tend to have demands that are more elastic than do necessities. Necessities like food, electricity, health care, and tobacco for smokers are more important to everyday living, and quantity demanded does not change significantly when prices rise. Luxuries like trips to Hawaii, yachts, and Johnny Walker Blue label scotch, on the other hand, can be

**TABLE 1** Selected Estimates of Price Elasticities of Demand

| Inelastic | | Roughly Unitary Elastic | | Elastic | |
|---|---|---|---|---|---|
| Salt | 0.1 | Movies | 0.9 | Restaurant meals | 2.3 |
| Cigarettes | 0.24 | Private education | 1.1 | Air travel | 2.4 |
| Medical care | 0.3 | Shoes | 0.9 | Foreign travel | 4.0 |
| Taxi service | 0.6 | Automobiles | 1.2 | Furniture | 1.5 |
| Gasoline (short run) | 0.2 | Tires | 1.0 | Fresh vegetables | 2.5 |
| Medical prescriptions | 0.3 | | | Commuter rail service (long run) | 1.6 |
| Pesticides | 0.2–0.5 | | | Shrimp | 1.25 |

**Source:** Compiled from numerous studies reporting estimates for price elasticity of demand.

postponed or forgotten when prices rise. Table 1 provides a sampling of estimates of elasticities for specific products. Note that as we might expect, medical care and taxi service have relatively inelastic price elasticities of demand, while foreign travel and restaurant meals have relatively elastic demands.

## Computing Price Elasticities

When elasticity is computed between two points, the calculated value will differ depending on whether price is increasing or decreasing. For example, in Figure 2, if the price *increases* from $1.00 to $2.00, elasticity is equal to

$$
\begin{aligned}
E_d &= \frac{300 - 500}{500} \div \frac{2.00 - 1.00}{1.00} \\
&= \frac{-200}{500} \div \frac{1.00}{1.00} \\
&= -0.4 \div 1.00 \\
&= |-0.4| \\
&= 0.4
\end{aligned}
$$

**FIGURE 2—Computing Elasticity of Demand Using Midpoints**

A problem can occur when calculating elasticity over a range of prices. The calculated value can vary depending on whether price is increasing or decreasing. To avoid getting different results when approaching the same analysis from different directions, economists use midpoint price and midpoint quantity.

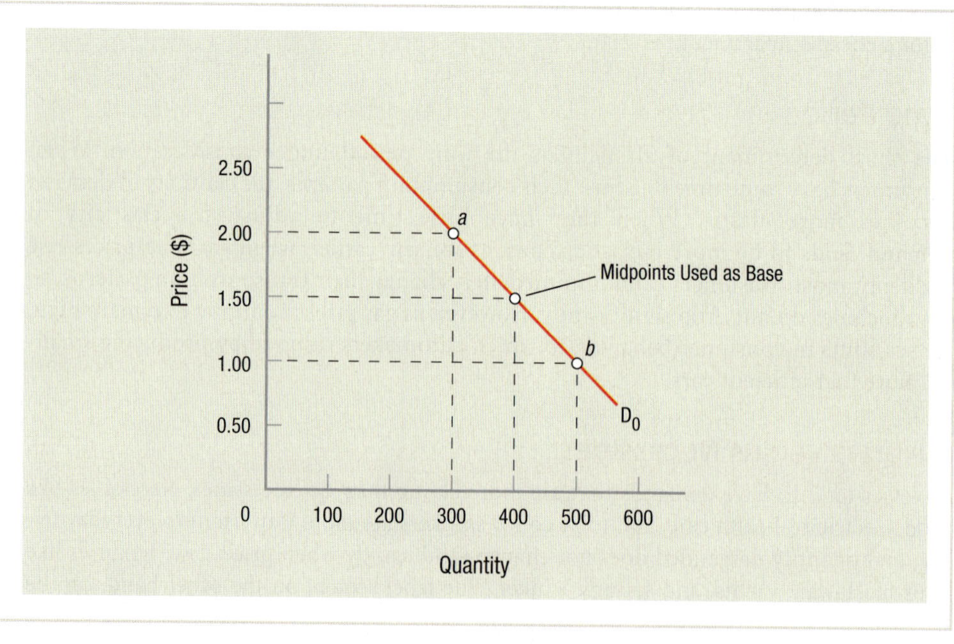

But when price *decreases* from \$2.00 to \$1.00, elasticity is equal to

$$\begin{aligned} E_d &= \frac{500 - 300}{300} \div \frac{1.00 - 2.00}{2.00} \\ &= \frac{200}{300} \div \frac{-1.00}{2.00} \\ &= 0.67 \div -0.5 \\ &= |-1.34| \\ &= 1.34 \end{aligned}$$

## Using Midpoints to Compute Elasticity

To avoid getting different results computing elasticity from different directions, economists compute price elasticity using the midpoints of price $[(P_1 + P_0)/2]$ and the midpoints of quantity demanded $[(Q_1 + Q_0)/2]$ as the base.

Therefore, the *price elasticity of demand* formula (assuming price falls from $P_0$ to $P_1$ and quantity demanded rises from $Q_0$ to $Q_1$) is

$$E_d = \frac{Q_1 - Q_0}{(Q_1 + Q_0)/2} \div \frac{P_1 - P_0}{(P_1 + P_0)/2}.$$

Using the midpoints of price and quantity to compute the relevant percentage changes essentially gives us the average elasticity between point *a* and point *b*. Price elasticity of demand is the difference in quantity over the sum of the two quantities divided by 2, divided by the difference in price over the sum of the two prices divided by 2. In Figure 2, the price elasticity of demand between points *a* and *b* would equal

$$\begin{aligned} E_d &= \frac{500 - 300}{(500 + 300)/2} \div \frac{1.00 - 2.00}{(1.00 + 2.00)/2} \\ &= \frac{200}{400} \div \frac{-1.00}{1.50} \\ &= 0.50 \div -0.67 \\ &= |-0.75| \\ &= 0.75 \end{aligned}$$

Check for yourself to see that this elasticity formula yields the same results whether you compute elasticity for a price increase from \$1.00 to \$2.00 or for a price decrease from \$2.00 to \$1.00.

Now that we have seen what price elasticity of demand is and how to calculate it, let's put this knowledge to work by looking at how elasticity affects total revenue.

**CHECKPOINT**

### ELASTICITY OF DEMAND

- Elasticity summarizes how responsive one variable is to a change in another variable.
- Price elasticity of demand summarizes how responsive quantity demanded is to changes in price.
- Price elasticity of demand is defined as the percentage change in quantity demanded divided by the percentage change in price.
- Inelastic demands are relatively unresponsive to changes in price, while quantity demanded is more responsive with elastic demands.
- Elasticity is determined by a product's substitutability, its proportion of the budget, whether it is a luxury or a necessity, and the time period considered.
- Economists use midpoints to derive consistent estimates whether price rises or falls.

**QUESTION:** According to a report from the Federal Trade Commission (FTC), in the first three weeks of August 2003, gas prices in Phoenix, Arizona, jumped from $1.52 to $2.11 a gallon, roughly a 40% increase, due to a ruptured pipeline between Tucson and Phoenix. The pipeline normally brought 30% of Phoenix's fuel from a Texas refinery. During this period, Phoenix gas stations were able to buy gas from West Coast refineries at higher prices. By the end of the month, the rupture was repaired and prices returned to normal. During this three-week period of supply disruption, gasoline sales fell by 8%. What was the approximate price elasticity of demand for gasoline during this period? If the gas stations were unable to get additional gas from the West Coast and supplies fell by the full 30%, how high might have prices risen during that three-week period?

Answers to the Checkpoint questions can be found at the end of this chapter.

## Elasticity and Total Revenue

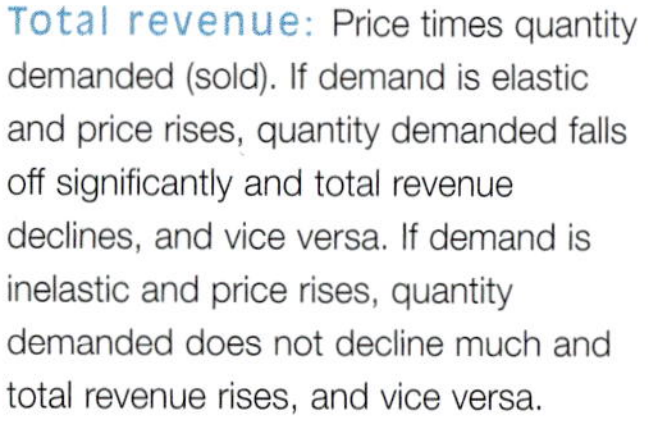

**Total revenue:** Price times quantity demanded (sold). If demand is elastic and price rises, quantity demanded falls off significantly and total revenue declines, and vice versa. If demand is inelastic and price rises, quantity demanded does not decline much and total revenue rises, and vice versa.

Elasticity is important to firms because elasticity measures the responsiveness of quantity sold to changes in price, which has an impact on the total revenues of the firm. **Total revenue** *TR* is equal to the number of units sold *Q* times the price of each unit *P*, or

$$TR = P \times Q$$

The sensitivity of output sold to price changes greatly influences how much total revenue changes when price changes.

### Inelastic Demand

When consumers are so loyal to a product or so few substitutes exist that consumers continue to buy the product even when its price goes up, the product is inelastically demanded. Panel A of Figure 3 shows the impact such a price increase has on total revenue when the demand for a product is inelastic. Price rises from $2.00 to $4.00, and sales decline from

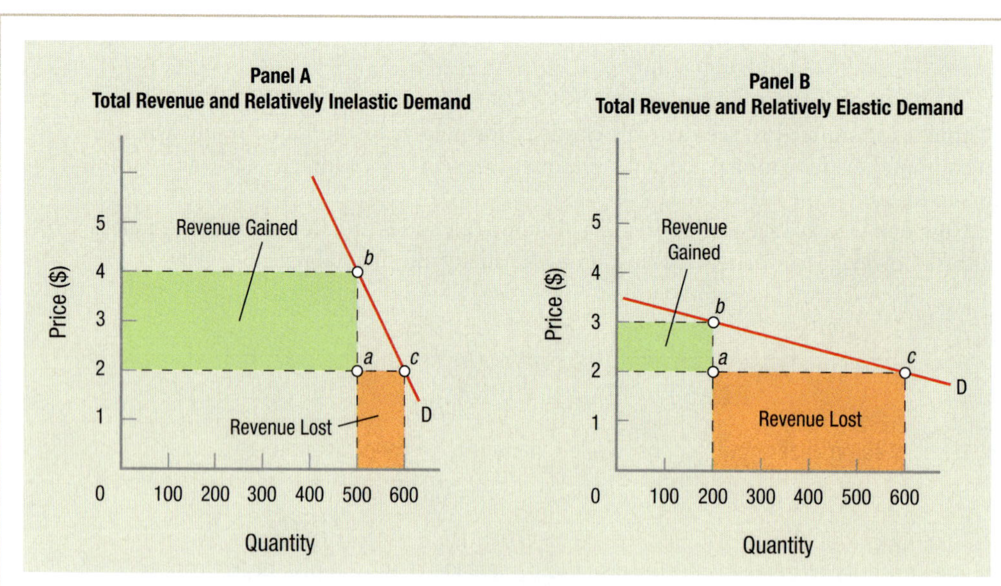


**FIGURE 3—Total Revenue and Elasticity of Demand**

Given inelastic demand in panel A, when price rises from $2 to $4, revenue rises because the revenue gained from the price hike ($1,000) is greater than the revenue lost from fewer sales ($200). The price hike may have driven off a few customers, but the firm's many remaining customers are paying a much higher price, thus increasing the firm's revenue. When products have elastic demands as shown in panel B, usually because many substitutes are available, firms feel a greater impact from changes in price. A small rise in price causes sales to fall off dramatically.

600 to 500 units. In this case, total revenue *rises.* We know this because the revenue gained from the price hike [(4.00 − 2.00) × 500 = $1,000] is greater than the revenue lost [(2.00 × (600 − 500) = $200]. We can see this by comparing the size of the Revenue Lost area with the Revenue Gained area in the figure. What has happened here? The price hike has driven off only a few customers (a small percent), but the firm's many remaining customers are paying a much higher price (a larger percent), thus driving up the firm's total revenue. This is to be expected: Demand for the firm's product is inelastic, so price increases will be accompanied by smaller declines in sales. The percentage change in quantity (16.7%) is smaller than the percentage change in price (100%).

This may suggest firms would always want the demand for their products to be inelastic. Unfortunately for them, inelastic demand has a flip side. Specifically, if supply increases (due to a technical advance, say), sales will rise only moderately, even as prices fall dramatically. This leads to a drop in total revenue: Consumers indeed buy more of the product at its new lower price, but not enough more to pay the firm for the decline in price.

## Elastic Demand

Elastic demand is the opposite of inelastic demand. Firms with elastically demanded products will see their sales change dramatically in response to small price changes. Panel B of Figure 3 shows what happens to total revenue when a firm increases the price of a product with elastic demand. Although price does not increase much, sales fall significantly. Revenue lost greatly exceeds the revenue gained from the price increase, so total revenue falls.

The opposite occurs when prices fall and demand is elastic. The high elasticity of demand faced by restaurants helps explain why so many of them offer "buy one get one free" specials and other discounts. As prices fall to their discounted levels, sales have the potential to expand rapidly, thus increasing revenue.

## Unitary Elasticity

We have looked at the impact of changing prices on revenue when demand is elastic and inelastic. When the elasticity of demand is unitary ($E_d = 1$), a 10% increase in price results in a 10% reduction in quantity demanded. As a result, total revenue is unaffected.

Table 2 summarizes the effects price changes have on total revenue for different price elasticities of demand.

**TABLE 2** Total Revenue, Price Changes, and Price Elasticity of Demand

| | Elasticity | | |
|---|---|---|---|
| **Price Change** | **Inelastic** | **Elastic** | **Unitary** |
| Price increases | TR increases | TR decreases | No change in TR |
| Price decreases | TR decreases | TR increases | No change in TR |

## Elasticity and Total Revenue Along a Straight-Line Demand Curve

Elasticity varies along a straight-line demand curve. Figure 4 on the next page shows a linear demand curve in panel A and graphs the corresponding total revenue points in panel B. Table 3 on the next page shows the raw data for the figure. In panel A, the elastic part of the curve is that portion above point *e.* Notice that when price falls from $11 to $10, the revenue gained ($100) is much larger than the revenue lost ($10), and thus total revenue rises. This is shown in panel B, where total revenue rises when output grows from 10 to 20 units.

As we move down the demand curve, elasticity will eventually equal 1 (at point *e*) where elasticity is unitary. Price was falling up to this point, while total revenue kept rising

**FIGURE 4—Price Elasticity and Total Revenue Along a Straight Line (Linear) Demand Curve**

Price elasticity varies along a straight line demand curve. In panel A, the elastic part of the curve lies above point *e*. Thus, when price falls from $11 to $10, revenue rises, as shown in panel B. As we move down the demand curve, elasticity equals 1 (at point *e*) where elasticity is unitary. Revenue is maximized at this point. As price continues to fall below $6, demand moves into an inelastic range. When price falls from $3 to $2, revenue declines, as shown in panel B.

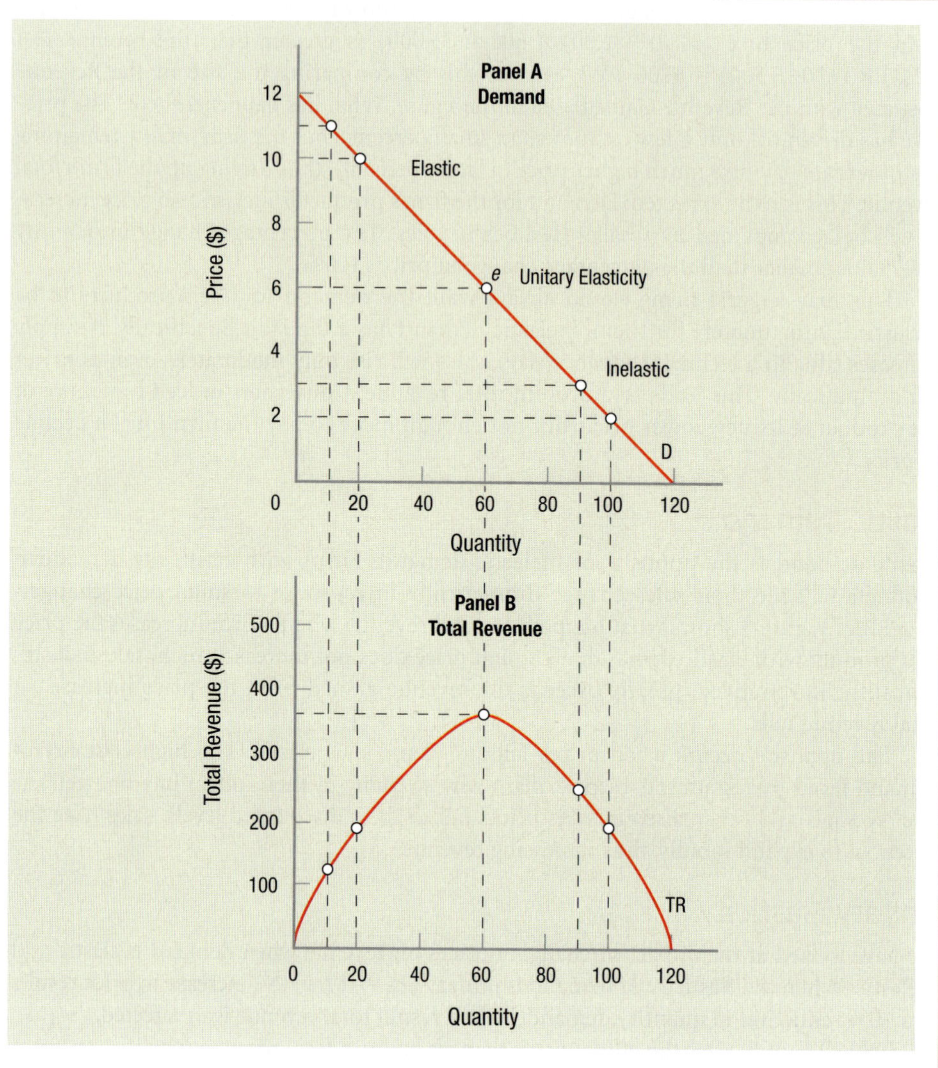


**TABLE 3** Data for Demand, Elasticity, and Total Revenue for Figure 4

| Price | Quantity | Elasticity | Description | Total Revenue |
|---|---|---|---|---|
| 12 | 0 | | | 0 |
| 11 | 10 | 23.00 | Elastic | 110 |
| 10 | 20 | 7.00 | Elastic | 200 |
| 9 | 30 | 3.80 | Elastic | 270 |
| 8 | 40 | 2.43 | Elastic | 320 |
| 7 | 50 | 1.67 | Elastic | 350 |
| 6 | 60 | 1.18 | Unitary elastic | 360 |
| 5 | 70 | 0.85 | Inelastic | 350 |
| 4 | 80 | 0.60 | Inelastic | 320 |
| 3 | 90 | 0.41 | Inelastic | 270 |
| 2 | 100 | 0.26 | Inelastic | 200 |
| 1 | 110 | 0.14 | Inelastic | 110 |
| 0 | 120 | 0.04 | Inelastic | 0 |

until the last price reduction just before \$6, where revenue did not change. Revenue is at its maximum at point *e* or a price of \$6 in both panels.

As price continues to fall below \$6, the demand curve moves into an inelastic range because the percentage change in quantity demanded is less than the percentage change in price. Therefore, when price falls from \$3 to \$2, revenue declines. The revenue gained (\$20) is less than the revenue lost (\$90). This decline in revenue is shown in panel B, as total revenue falls as output rises from 90 to 100 units sold.

To summarize, all negatively sloped linear demand curves have an upper portion that is elastic, a midpoint where elasticity is unitary, and a lower part that is inelastic. The logic underlying this fact is straightforward. The slope is constant along the demand curve, so each \$1 change in price leads to a 10-unit change in quantity demanded. Slope is the ratio of *change* in one variable to another. Elasticity is the ratio of the *percentage* change in one variable to another. Thus, when the price of a product is low, a 1-unit change in price is a large percentage change while the percentage change in quantity demanded is small. When the price is high, a 1-unit change in price is a small percentage change but the percentage change in quantity is large.

## Other Elasticities of Demand

Besides the price elasticity of demand, two other elasticities of demand are important. The first, *income elasticity of demand,* measures how responsive quantity demanded is to changes in income. Incomes vary as the economy expands and contracts. To plan their future employment and production, many industries want to know how the demand for their products will be affected when the economy changes. How much will airline travel be affected if the economy moves into a recession? What will happen to automobile sales? What will happen to sales of lattes at Starbucks? Each business faces a different situation.

Another type of demand elasticity registers changes that occur when competitors change the prices of their products. This is called *cross elasticity of demand.* If Toyota is planning a price reduction, what impact will this have on the sale of Fords? Ford will want to estimate this to decide whether to ignore Toyota or lower its own automobile prices.

Let's consider these two elasticities of demand more closely, beginning with income elasticity of demand.

### Income Elasticity of Demand

The **income elasticity of demand** ($E_Y$) measures how responsive quantity demanded is to changes in consumer income. We define the income elasticity of demand as

$$E_Y = \frac{\text{Percentage Change in Quantity Demanded}}{\text{Percentage Change in Income}}$$

Depending on the value of the income elasticity of demand, we can classify goods in three ways. First, a **normal good** is one where income elasticity is positive, but less than 1 ($0 < E_Y < 1$). As income rises, quantity demanded rises as well, but not as fast as the rise in income. Most products are normal goods. If your income doubles, you will probably buy more sporting equipment and restaurant meals, but not twice as many.

A second category, *income superior goods* or **luxury goods,** includes products with an income elasticity greater than 1 ($E_Y > 1$). As income rises, quantity demanded grows faster than income. Goods and services such as Mercedes automobiles, caviar, fine wine, and visits to European spas are luxury or income superior goods.

Finally, **inferior goods** are those goods for which income elasticity is negative ($E_Y < 0$). When income rises, the quantity demanded for these goods falls. Inferior goods include potatoes, beans, compact cars, and public transportation. Get yourself a nice raise, and you will probably be taking the bus a lot less. Note that this is an instance where a minus sign conveys important information.

**Income elasticity of demand:** Measures how responsive quantity demanded is to changes in consumer income.

**Normal goods:** Goods that have positive income elasticities of less than 1. When consumer income grows, quantity demanded rises for normal goods, but less than the rise in income.

**Luxury goods:** Goods that have income elasticities greater than 1. When consumer income grows, quantity demanded of luxury goods rises more than the rise in income.

**Inferior goods:** Goods that have income elasticities that are negative. When consumer income grows, quantity demanded falls for inferior goods.

Understanding how product sales are affected by changing incomes and economic conditions can help firms to diversify their product lines so sales and employment can be stabilized to some extent over the course of the business cycle. For example, firms that produce all three types of goods can try to switch production toward the good that current economic conditions favor: In boom times, production is shifted more toward the making of luxury goods. Ford will produce more Lincoln town cars in boom times, and more compact cars during economic slowdowns.

## Cross Elasticity of Demand

**Cross elasticity of demand:** Measures how responsive the quantity demanded of one good is to changes in the price of another good. Substitute goods have positive cross elasticities: An increase in the price of one good leads consumers to substitute (buy more) of the other good whose price has not changed. Complementary goods have negative cross elasticities: An increase in the price of a complement leads to a reduction in sales of the other good whose price has not changed.

**Substitutes:** Goods consumers substitute for one another depending on their relative prices, such as coffee and tea. Substitutes have a positive cross elasticity of demand.

**Complements:** Goods that are typically consumed together, such as coffee and sugar. Complements have a negative cross elasticity of demand.

**Cross elasticity of demand** ($E_{ab}$) measures how responsive the quantity demanded of one good (product a) is to changes in the price of another (product b):

$$E_{ab} = \frac{\text{Percentage Change in Quantity Demanded of Product a}}{\text{Percentage Change in Price of Product b}}$$

Using cross elasticity of demand, we can classify goods in two ways. Products a and b are **substitutes** if their cross elasticity of demand is positive ($E_{ab} > 0$). Common sense tells us that chicken and beef are substitutes. Therefore, if the price of beef rises, people will substitute away from beef and toward chicken, so the quantity demanded for chicken will grow. This illustrates a positive cross elasticity. Similar relationships exist between Toyota and Honda cars, cell phone services provided by AT&T and Sprint, the price of gas and public transportation, and film and digital cameras.

Second, products a and b are **complements** if their cross elasticity of demand is negative ($E_{ab} < 0$). Complementary products are those goods and services that are consumed together, such as gasoline and large SUVs. When the price of gasoline rises, the result is that the quantity demanded for SUVs declines. Other complementary goods include coffee and cream, hamburgers and french fries, and suntan lotion and flip-flops. Finally, two goods are *not related* if a cross elasticity of demand is zero, or near zero.

This is a good place to stop and reflect on what we have discovered so far. We have seen that elasticity measures the responsiveness of one variable to changes in another. Elasticity measures changes in percentage terms so that products of different magnitudes—a bottle of Coca-Cola and an airplane—can be compared. Products that have a price elasticity of demand greater than 1 have elastic demand; products with price elasticity of demand less than 1 have inelastic demand; and products with a price elasticity of demand equal to 1 have unitary elastic demand. We saw that a negatively sloped straight line demand curve has elastic and inelastic ranges, and we also saw that total revenue changes with elastic or inelastic demand. Finally, we saw that as well as price elasticity of demand, we can also look at income elasticity of demand and cross elasticity of demand.

### CHECKPOINT

#### ELASTICITY AND TOTAL REVENUE

- When demand is inelastic and prices rise, total revenue rises. When demand is inelastic and prices fall, total revenue falls.
- When demand is elastic and prices rise, total revenue falls. When demand is elastic and prices fall, total revenue rises.
- Straight line demand curves have elastic (at higher prices) and inelastic (at lower prices) ranges.
- Income elasticity of demand is a measure of how responsive quantity demanded is to changes in income. This determines whether a good is a luxury, normal, or inferior good.
- Cross elasticity of demand measures how responsive the quantity demanded of one product is to price changes of another. Substitutes have positive cross elasticities while complements have negative ones.

**QUESTION:** Two clothing stores are located in the same shopping center. Both stores have a big sale: 20% off on everything in the store. After the sale, store 1 finds that its total revenue has increased, while store 2 finds that total revenue has decreased. What does this tell you about the price elasticity of demand for the clothes in stores 1 and 2?

Answers to the Checkpoint question can be found at the end of this chapter.

# Elasticity of Supply

So far, we have looked at the consumer when we looked at the elasticity of demand. Now let us turn our attention to the producer, and look at elasticity of supply.

**Price elasticity of supply** ($E_s$) measures the responsiveness of quantity supplied to changes in the price of the product. Price elasticity of supply is defined as

$$E_s = \frac{\text{Percentage Change in Quantity Supplied}}{\text{Percentage Change in Price}}$$

**Price elasticity of supply:** A measure of the responsiveness of quantity supplied to changes in price. An elastic supply curve has elasticity greater than 1, whereas inelastic supplies have elasticities less than 1. Time is the most important determinant of the elasticity of supply.

Note that since the slope of the supply curve is positive, the price elasticity of supply will always be a positive number. Economists classify price elasticity of supply in the same way they classify price elasticity of demand. Classification is based on whether the percentage change in quantity supplied is greater than, less than, or equal to the percentage change in price. When price rises just a little and quantity increases by much more, supply is elastic, and vice versa. The output of many commodities such as gold and seasonal vegetables cannot be quickly increased if their price increases. In summary:

**Elastic supply:** $E_s > 1$
**Inelastic supply:** $E_s < 1$
**Unitary elastic supply:** $E_s = 1$

**Elastic supply:** Price elasticity of supply is greater than 1. The percentage change in quantity supplied is greater than the percentage change in price.

**Inelastic supply:** Price elasticity of supply is less than 1. The percentage change in quantity supplied is less than the percentage change in price.

**Unitary elastic supply:** Price elasticity of supply is equal to 1. The percentage change in quantity supplied is equal to the percentage change in price.

Looking at the three supply curves in Figure 5 on the next page, we can easily determine which curve is inelastic, which is elastic, and which is unitary elastic. First, note that all three curves go through point *a*. As we increase the price from $P_0$ to $P_1$, we see that the response in quantity supplied is different for all three curves. Consider supply curve $S_1$ first. When price changes to $P_1$ (point *b*), the change in output ($Q_0$ to $Q_1$) is the smallest for the three curves. Most important, the percentage change in quantity supplied is smaller than the percentage change in price, so $S_1$ is an inelastic supply curve.

Contrast this with $S_3$. In this case, when price rises to $P_1$ (point *d*), output climbs from $Q_0$ all the way to $Q_3$. Because the percentage change in output is larger than the percentage change in price, $S_3$ is elastic. And finally, curve $S_2$ is a unitary elastic curve because the percentage change in output is the same as the percentage change in price.

Here is a simple rule of thumb. When the supply curve is linear, like those shown in Figure 5, you can always determine if the supply curve is elastic, inelastic, or unitary elastic by extending the curve to the axis and applying the following rules:

- Elastic supply curves always cross the price axis, as does curve $S_3$.
- Inelastic supply curves always cross the quantity axis, as does curve $S_1$.
- Unitary elastic supply curves always cross through the origin, as does curve $S_2$.

## Time and Price Elasticity of Supply

The primary determinant of price elasticity of supply is time. To adjust output in response to changes in market prices, firms require time. Firms have both variable inputs, such as labor, and fixed inputs, such as plant capacity. To hire more labor, firms must recruit, interview, and hire more workers. This can take as little time as a few hours—a call to a

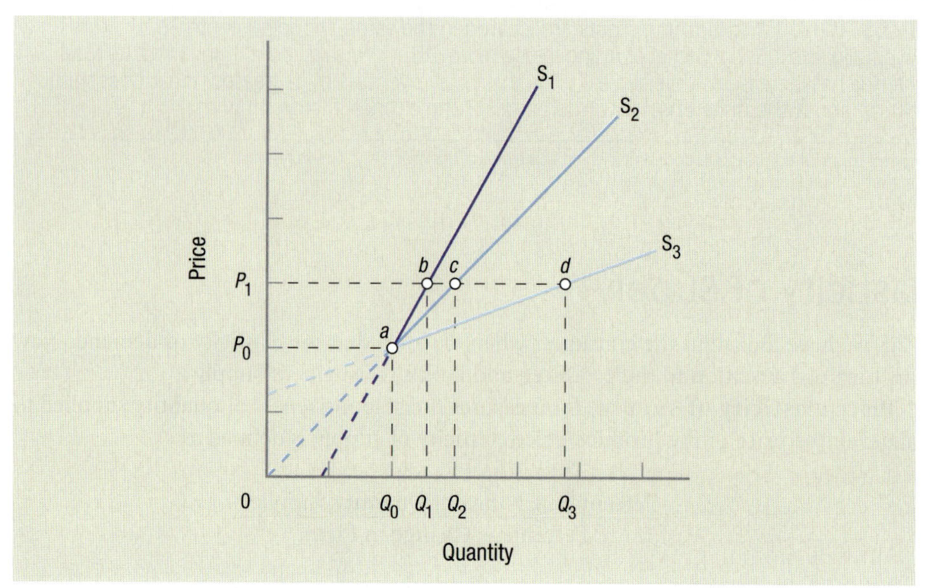


**FIGURE 5—Price Elasticity of Supply**

All three supply curves in this figure run through point *a,* but they respond differently when price changes from $P_0$ to $P_1$. Considering supply curve $S_1$ first, when price changes, the percentage change in quantity supplied is smaller than the percentage change in price, so $S_1$ is an inelastic supply curve. Curve $S_2$ is a unitary elastic supply curve, since the percentage change in output is the same as the percentage change in price. For supply curve $S_3$, the percentage change in output is greater than the percentage change in price, so $S_3$ is elastic. Elastic linear supply curves cross the price axis, inelastic linear curves cross the quantity axis, and unitary elastic linear curves go through the origin.

temporary agency—or as long as a few months. On the other hand, building another plant or expanding the existing plant to increase output involves considerably more time and resources. In some industries, such as building a new oil refinery or a computer chip plant, it can take as long as a decade, with environmental permits alone often requiring years of study and costing millions of dollars. Economists typically distinguish among three types of time periods: the market period, the short run, and the long run.

## The Market Period

**Market period:** Time period so short that the output and the number of firms are fixed. Agricultural products at harvest time face market periods. Products that unexpectedly become instant hits face market periods (there is a lag between when the firm realizes it has a hit on its hands and when inventory can be replaced).

The **market period** is so short that the output and the number of firms in an industry are fixed; firms simply have no time to change their production levels in response to changes in product price. Consider a raspberry market in the summer. Even if consumers flock to the market, their tastes having shifted in favor of fresh raspberries, farmers can do little to increase the supply of raspberries until the next year. Figure 6 on the next page shows a market period supply curve ($S_{MP}$) for agricultural products like raspberries. During the market period, the quantity of product available to the market is fixed at $Q_0$. If demand changes (shifting from $D_0$ to $D_1$), the only impact is on the price of the product. In Figure 6, price moves from $P_0$ (point *e*) to $P_1$ (point *a*). In summary, if demand grows over the market period, price will rise, and vice versa.

Changes in demand over the market period can be devastating for firms selling perishable goods. If demand falls, cantaloupes cannot be kept until demand grows; they must either be sold at a discount or trashed.

## The Short Run

**Short run:** Time period when plant capacity and the number of firms in the industry cannot change. Firms can employ more people, use overtime with existing employees, or hire part-time employees to produce more, but this is done in an existing plant.

The **short run** is defined as a period of time when plant capacity and the number of firms in the industry cannot change. Firms can, however, change the amount of labor, raw materials, and other variable inputs they employ in the short run to adjust their output to

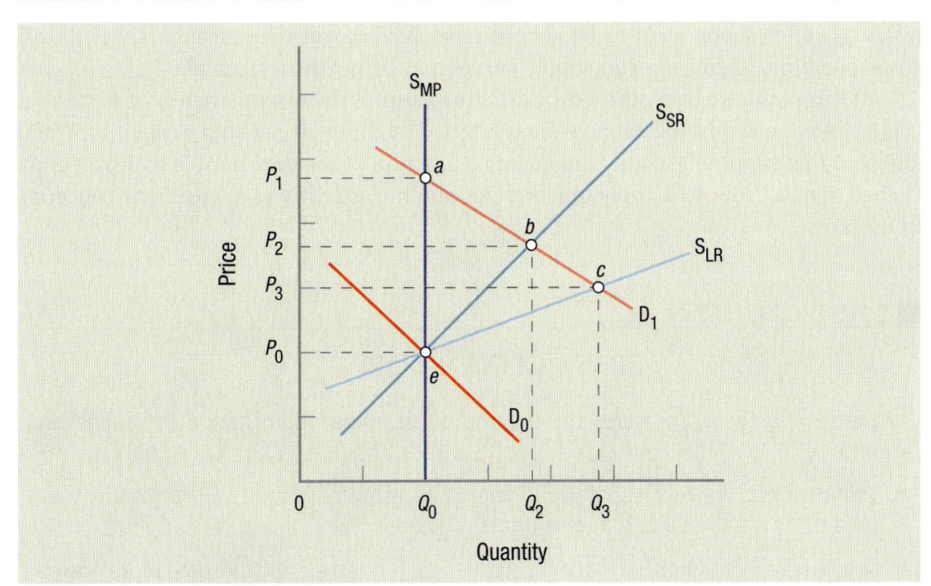


**FIGURE 6—Time and Price Elasticity of Supply**

During the market period, the quantity of output available to the market is fixed and the only impact will be on the price of the product, which will rise from $P_0$ to $P_1$. Over the short run, firms can change the amount of inputs they employ to adjust their output to market changes. Thus, the short-run supply curve ($S_{SR}$) is more elastic than the market period curve; and price increases are more moderate. In the long run, firms can change their plant capacity and enter or exit an industry. Long-run supply curve $S_{LR}$ is elastic and a rise in demand leads to only a small increase in price.

changes in the market. Note that the short run does not imply a specific number of weeks, months, or years. It simply means a period short enough that firms cannot adjust their plant capacity, but long enough for them to hire more labor to increase their production. A restaurant with an outdoor seating area can hire additional staff and open this area in a relatively short time frame when the weather gets warm, but manufacturing firms usually need more time to hire and train new people for their production lines. Clearly, the time associated with the short run differs depending on the industry.

This also is illustrated in Figure 6. The short-run supply curve, $S_{SR}$, is more elastic than the market period curve. If demand grows from $D_0$ to $D_1$, output expands from $Q_0$ to $Q_2$ and price increases to $P_2$ as equilibrium moves from point *e* to point *b*. Because output can expand in the short run in response to rising demand, the price increase is not as drastic as it was in the market period (from $P_0$ to $P_1$).

## The Long Run

Economists define the **long run** as a period of time long enough for firms to alter their plant capacity and for the number of firms in the industry to change. In the long run, some firms may decide to leave the industry if they think the market will be unfavorable. Alternatively, new firms may enter the market, or existing firms can alter their production capacity. Because all these conceivable changes are possible in the long run, the long-run supply curve is more elastic, as illustrated in Figure 6 by supply curve $S_{LR}$. In this case, a rise in demand from $D_0$ to $D_1$ gives rise to a small increase in the price of the product, while generating a major increase in output, from $Q_0$ to $Q_3$ (point *c*).

**Long run:** Time period long enough for firms to alter their plant capacities and for the number of firms in the industry to change. Existing firms can expand or build new plants, or firms can enter or exit the industry.

In giving long-run supply curve $S_{LR}$ a small but positive slope, we are assuming an industry's costs will increase slightly as it increases its output. Firms must compete with other industries to expand production. Wages and other input prices rise in the industry as firms attempt to draw resources away from their immediate competitors and other industries.

Some industries may not face added costs as they expand. Fast-food chains, copy centers, and coffee shops seem to be able to reproduce at will without incurring increasing costs. Therefore, their long-run supply curves may be nearly horizontal.

At this point, we have seen how elasticity measures the responsiveness of demand to a change in price and how total revenue is affected by different demand elasticities. We have also seen that supply elasticities are mainly a function of the time needed to adjust to price change signals. Now, let's apply our findings about elasticity to a subject that concerns all of us: taxes.

**CHECKPOINT**

**ELASTICITY OF SUPPLY**

- Elasticity of supply measures the responsiveness of quantity supplied to changes in price.
- Elastic supplies are very responsive to price changes. With inelastic supply, quantity supplied is not responsive to changing prices.
- Supplies are highly inelastic in the market period, but can expand (become more elastic) in the short run because firms can hire additional resources to raise output levels.
- In the long run, supplies are relatively elastic since firms can enter or exit the industry, and existing firms can expand their plant capacity.

**QUESTION:** Rank the following industries and businesses in how elastic you think supply is in the long run, from most elastic to least elastic: (a) fast food, (b) nuclear power, (c) crude oil production, (d) Hollywood (movies), (e) computer microchips, (f) grocery stores, (g) airlines, (h) Starbucks.

Answers to the Checkpoint question can be found at the end of this chapter.

## Taxes and Elasticity

On average, families pay more than 40% of their income in taxes. These taxes include income, property, estate, sales, and excise taxes. (An excise tax is a sales tax applied to a specific product, such as gasoline or tobacco.) It often seems the government taxes everything! We saw in the last chapter that supply and demand analysis is helpful in analyzing the impact of taxes on markets. In this section we use elasticity to help policymakers determine the impact of these various taxes on individuals, families, and businesses. Again, to simplify the analysis, we will continue to focus on excise taxes.

**Incidence of taxation:** Refers to who bears the economic burden of a tax. The economic entity bearing the burden of a particular tax will depend on the price elasticities of demand and supply.

Economists studying taxes are interested in the **incidence of taxation** and in *shifts* in the tax burden. The incidence of a tax simply refers to who bears its economic burden. Statutes determine what is taxed, who must pay various taxes, and what agencies are responsible for collecting taxes and remitting the revenue collected. Even so, the individuals, firms, or groups who pay a tax may not be the ones bearing its economic burden. As we will see, this burden, or the incidence of a tax, can be shifted onto others. Considering the elasticities of demand and supply will help us determine the incidence of various taxes—who really bears the tax burden—and thus the ultimate impact of various tax policies.

### Elasticity of Demand and Tax Burdens

Let us consider what happens when an excise tax is levied on a product with elastic demand such as strawberries. Panel A of Figure 7 shows the market before an excise tax is imposed. The initial supply curve ($S_0$) is supply before the tax and demand curve $D_0$ reflects demand. Originally, the market is in equilibrium at point *e*, where 5,000 baskets are sold for 65 cents each.

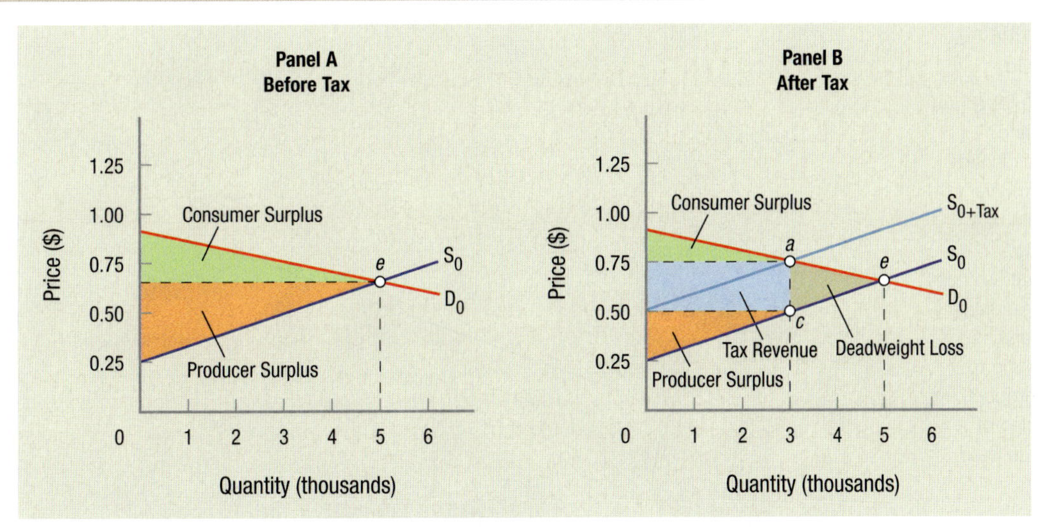


**FIGURE 7—Tax Burden with Relatively Elastic Demand**

$S_0$ is the initial supply curve for a product with elastic demand (panel A). When a 25 cent excise tax is placed on the product, the supply curve shifts upward by the amount of the tax, $S_{0+Tax}$ (panel B. With demand remaining constant at $D_0$, equilibrium moves to point *a* (3,000 units). In this case, output falls substantially when the tax is imposed because elastic demand means extreme price sensitivity. As a result, sellers end up bearing most of the burden of this tax, and the deadweight loss is relatively large (area *cae*).

In panel B, we now add a per unit tax—say, $0.25 a basket—paid by the grower. This, in effect, adds 25 cents to the cost for each basket and adds a wedge between what consumers pay and what growers receive. Supply curve $S_0$ therefore shifts upward by this amount, to $S_{0+Tax}$. The new supply curve runs parallel to $S_0$, with the distance the curve has shifted (*ac*) equaling the 25 cent tax per basket.

Assuming demand remains constant at $D_0$, the new equilibrium is at point *a*, with 3,000 baskets sold for a price of 75 cents each. The firm receives 75 cents per basket, of which it must send 25 cents to the government, keeping 50 cents for itself. Keep in mind that, because this demand is elastic, many consumers are not really willing to pay a higher price for the product; this is why output declines so much and why sellers bear most of the burden of this tax.

Before the tax, both consumer and producer surplus in panel A (discussed in Chapter 4) was substantial. After the tax, the government collects revenue equal to the tax (25 cents) times the number of baskets sold (3,000), or $750 (the blue area), consumer surplus now equals the area above the blue section, and producer surplus equals the area below it. Note that consumers and producers lose surplus equal not only to the revenue gained by the government but also to area *cae*. Economists refer to this area as a **deadweight loss** because this area is lost to society—the government, consumers, and business lose this—because of the tax.

**Deadweight loss:** The loss in consumer and producer surplus due to inefficiency because some transactions cannot be made and therefore their value to society is lost.

Contrast this situation with the impact of an excise tax when the demand is inelastic (e.g., cigarettes), as in Figure 8 on the next page. Initially, 23,000 packages are sold at $3.00 per package. With a $1.25 tax, supply shifts to $S_{0+Tax}$, market equilibrium moves to point *g*, price increases from $3.00 to $4.00 per pack, and output declines from 23,000 to 20,000. Inelastic demands are price insensitive, so output hardly declines when this tax is imposed. The $1.25 tax in this case is *gh*, with consumers paying *gi* (a dollar), sellers paying *ih* (25 cents), and a deadweight loss equal to area *hge*. In general, deadweight losses are small when demand is inelastic. A small quantity reduction given a higher price means that nearly all the excise tax is shifted forward to consumers. In this case, consumers pay an additional $1.00 for each unit, but firms end up bearing only a small burden (25 cents).

**FIGURE 8—Tax Burden with Relatively Inelastic Demand**

$S_0$ is the initial supply curve for a product with inelastic demand. When a $1.25 excise tax is placed on the product, the supply curve shifts upward by the amount of the tax, to $S_{0+Tax}$. Assuming demand remains constant at $D_0$, the new equilibrium will be at point *g*. Because this demand curve is inelastic, consumers are willing to pay a higher price for the product, and bear nearly all the burden of the tax. The deadweight loss (area *hge*) is relatively small when demand is inelastic.

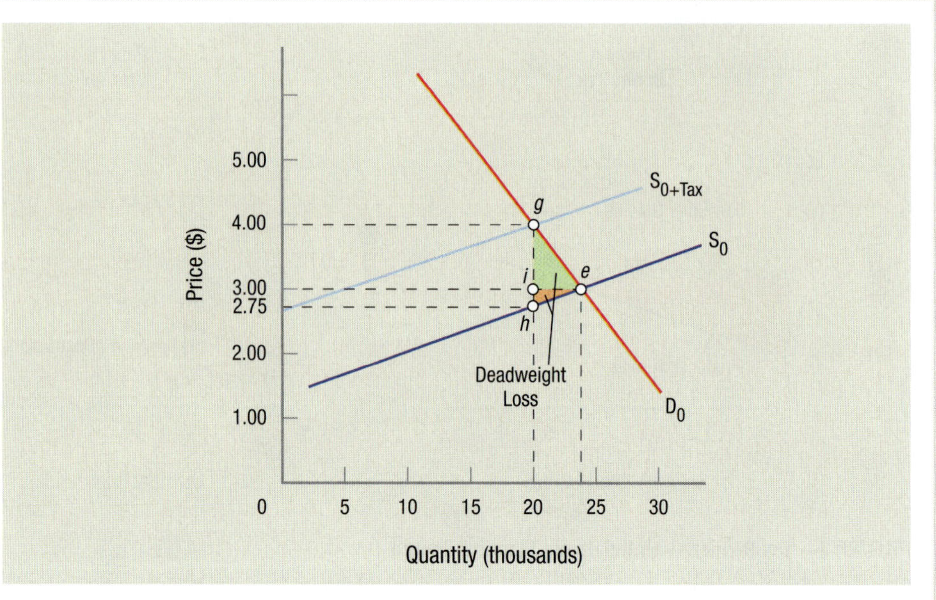


We can generalize about the effects of elasticity of demand on the tax burden. For a given supply of some product, the greater the price elasticity of demand, the lower the share of the total tax burden shifted to consumers and the greater the share borne by sellers, and vice versa.

This simple analysis shows why proposals to raise excise taxes usually focus on such inelastically demanded commodities such as luxury cars, jewelry, tobacco, gasoline, and alcohol. For products with inelastic demands, the reduction in output is lower when prices rise because of the tax—most smokers keep smoking even when the tobacco tax goes up, and the rich will still buy fancy cars even if they must pay a bit more for them. Therefore, these taxes generate more revenue than would excise taxes on elastically demanded products because the quantity demanded will drop considerably when prices rise on elastically demanded products. Proposals to raise excise taxes are often cloaked in public health and welfare rhetoric, politicians finding it easier to sell the idea of taxes that punish sins or soak the rich. But, if the products in question did not have inelastic demands, the tax revenues generated by such taxes would be small. Because consumers substantially reduce their purchases when demand is elastic, many workers in the industries with such elastically demanded products would become unemployed. As a result, such taxes are rarely ever enacted.

## Elasticity of Supply and Tax Burdens

In a similar way, the elasticity of supply is an important determinant of who bears the ultimate burden of taxation. In panel A of Figure 9, demand is held constant at $D_0$ and equilibrium is initially at point *e*. Supply curve $S_0$ is perfectly elastic, or horizontal. When a per unit tax is added to the product, supply shifts vertically to $S_{0+Tax}$ and the new market equilibrium moves to point *d*, with $Q_1$ units sold at price $P_1$. Notice that in this limiting situation of perfectly elastic supply, the full monetary burden of the tax ($P_1 - P_0$) is borne by consumers in the form of higher prices, though industry bears an indirect burden of reduced output and employment. The deadweight loss, area *cde*, is relatively large with elastically supplied products.

Now consider the case when the supply curve is inelastic, as with $S_0$ in panel B of Figure 9. When we add the same tax as before to this supply curve, market equilibrium moves to point *a*. Price increases less than before ($P_2$ in panel B is lower than $P_1$ in panel A) and the reduction in output is also less than before ($Q_0 - Q_2$ in panel B is less than $Q_0 - Q_1$ in panel A).

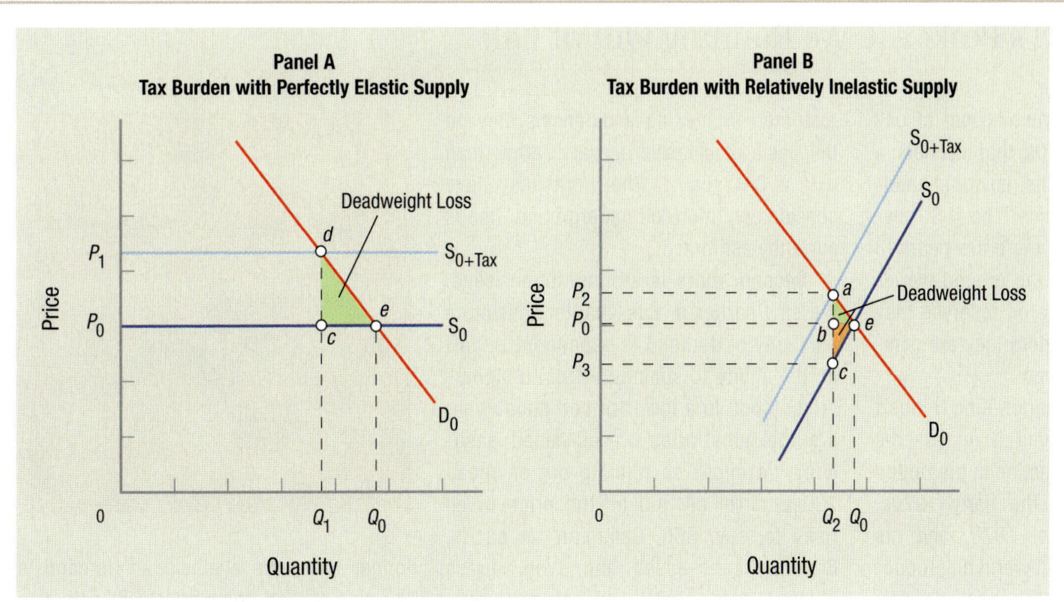


**FIGURE 9—Tax Burden and Supply Elasticities**

When supply curve $S_0$ is perfectly elastic as shown in panel A, a per unit excise tax added to the product shifts supply vertically to $S_{0+Tax}$. In this limiting case of perfectly elastic supply, the full burden of the tax ($P_1 - P_0$) is borne by consumers through higher prices. The deadweight loss is relatively large with elastic supply curves and equal to area *cde.* When supply is inelastic as in panel B, with the same excise tax (*ac* in panel B = *cd* in panel A), price increases are less, and the reduction in output is also less than before. Consumers pay only part of the tax, *ab,* and the deadweight loss to society is equal to area *cae,* less than with the elastic supply shown in panel A.

Consumers pay only part of the tax, *ab,* while sellers must absorb *bc,* and the deadweight loss *cae* is relatively small.

Note what happens in all of these tax cases. Figures 7 to 9 show that whenever a tax is added, the tax moves the market away from its equilibrium point, regardless of whether the tax is borne by consumers, producers, or both. All taxes generate a tax wedge, resulting in a deadweight loss to society. The more elastic the demand or supply, the greater is this deadweight loss. Table 4 summarizes these general results.

These last three chapters have given us the powerful tools of supply and demand analysis. Elasticity is important because it encapsulates the complex relationships among prices, quantity demanded, and total revenues in just two words: elastic and inelastic. When demands are inelastic and some incident marginally reduces supply, policymakers (and

**TABLE 4** Summary of Elasticity and Taxes

| Elasticity | | Tax Burdens | | | |
|---|---|---|---|---|---|
| Demand | Supply | On Consumers | On Business | Deadweight Loss | Figure Where Shown |
| Elastic | No change | Lower | Higher | Large | 7 |
| Inelastic | No change | Higher | Lower | Small | 8 |
| No change | Elastic | Higher | Lower | Large | 9A |
| No change | Inelastic | Lower | Higher | Small | 9B |

## *Issue:* Hubbert's Peak: Are We Running Out of Oil?

**Is the world** running out of oil? Ever since the early 1970s, that has been a popular refrain by pundits, environmentalists, and some academics. The U.S. government estimates that there are nearly 3 trillion barrels of oil in the ground worldwide, but some of these oil reserves may require higher prices before they are commercially feasible to pump.

In the mid-1950s, Marion King Hubbert created a model of known U.S. oil reserves and predicted that production in the United States would peak in the early 1970s. Production did peak in 1970, and his model now suggests that world oil production will peak within the next decade. Hubbert's model marks the point where half of the recoverable oil has been pumped out and half remains, so production has peaked. If world economic growth continues, world oil demand will continue to grow, oil production will slow, and the gap between supply and demand will grow, with oil prices correspondingly rising. Several authors suggest that production declines and rapid increases in oil prices will lead to a worldwide recession or even a depression.[2]

There are many reasons to believe that oil prices will continue to be high in the future, but our analysis of markets and elasticity suggests that we are unlikely to run out of oil for a long time, if ever.

First, there is a measurement issue. Controversy surrounds the accurate measurement of world oil reserves. Many experts argue that current estimates understate "proven reserves," and as Daniel Yergin has noted, the reporting system is based on 30-year-old technology and is "roughly analogous to a doctor restricted to making a diagnosis only on the basis of invasive surgery rather than with a CAT scan."[3] The world may have considerably more oil underground than is currently estimated.

Second, there is a substitution issue. We saw earlier in this chapter that price elasticity of demand is dependent in part on the ability to substitute from a higher-priced good to a lower-priced good. What are the substitutes for oil-based gasoline? We might be running out of cheap $30-a-barrel oil, but as the price of oil rises to, say, $60, Canadian tar sands, Brazilian cane-based and switch-grass ethanol, and natural gas and coal converted to liquid become economical. When oil prices reach $80 a barrel, shale and corn-based ethanol become competitive. If prices go higher, biodiesel and other forms of alternative energy become attractive. These are substitutes for oil-based gasoline.

Third, there is an adjustment issue based on time. Over time, the higher price of oil should lead to an increase in supply as newer, more costly technologies such as steam injection permit the recovery of oil still in the ground that earlier technologies couldn't recover.[4] Also over time, consumers will adjust their demands for oil. The short-term elasticity of gasoline is roughly 0.2, making short-term price changes quite responsive to small changes in supplies. The price of crude oil is particularly sensitive in the short run to the political stability of exporting nations (particularly in the Middle East and Africa), natural disasters (hurricanes along the Gulf Coast), and accidents (ruptures in pipelines). In the longer term, the elasticity of demand is 0.7 to 0.9, and consumers will adjust to rising prices through conservation in its various forms.

Elnur Amikishiyev

Thus, even if we reach Hubbert's peak in the next decade, it will not be like falling off a precipice where prices skyrocket. Prices will rise gradually, especially in the futures markets that reach out five to seven years. This will give us plenty of time to begin adjusting to higher prices and using the alternatives described earlier.

Long before we run out of oil, the world will begin substituting alternative energy sources, and petroleum will be used only for high-valued uses such as manufacturing. The problems of global warming may force this change sooner rather than later. Modern oil companies are becoming less exploration oriented and are focusing more on manufactured oil products. Pure fossil-based fuels will, in the future, need to be blended with other products to reduce their greenhouse emissions. Given all the substitutes for oil, we will never run out. Just what constitutes "oil" will change.

---

[2] See Kenneth S. Deffeyes, *Hubbert's Peak: The Impending World Oil Shortage* (Princeton: Princeton University Press), 2001. Two other books suggest that Saudi Arabia's major oil fields are hitting their peak; see Paul Roberts, *The End of Oil: On the Edge of a Perilous New World* (New York: Houghton Mifflin), 2004, and Matthew R. Simmons, *Twilight in the Desert: The Coming Saudi Oil Shock and the World Economy* (Hoboken, NJ: John Wiley & Sons), 2005.

[3] Daniel Yergin, "How Much Oil Is Really Down There?" *Wall Street Journal,* April 27, 2006, p. A18.

[4] See "Steady as She Goes: Why the World Is Not About to Run Out of Oil," *Economist,* April 22, 2006, pp. 65–67.

now you) know that price will go up substantially, though consumers will continue to purchase the product. Again, this is what happens when gasoline prices rise—consumers continue to purchase roughly the same amount as before, so oil industry revenue and profits rise substantially in the short run.

If, however, demand is elastic and the same incident reduces supply, prices will rise, but by a smaller amount, and output and employment will fall a lot more. If weather conditions in California and Florida ruin the orange crop, reducing the supply and increasing the price of orange juice, consumers will readily substitute other juices. As a result, output, employment, revenues, and profits will decline in the orange industry.

**CHECKPOINT**

### TAXES AND ELASTICITY

- When price elasticity of demand is elastic, consumers bear a smaller burden of taxes while more is borne by sellers. When demands are inelastic a higher share of the total tax burden is shifted to consumers.
- When the price elasticity of supply is elastic, buyers bear a larger burden of taxes. Elastic supplies also lead to a larger deadweight loss. When supply is inelastic, more of the tax burden is shifted to sellers, but the deadweight loss is less.

**QUESTION:** Excise taxes were the principal taxes levied for the first hundred years or so after the Revolutionary War. Today, excise taxes fall mainly on cigarettes, liquor, luxury cars and boats, telephones, gasoline, diesel fuel, aviation fuel, bows and arrows, gas-guzzling vehicles, and vaccines. What do all of these products seem to have in common?

Answers to the Checkpoint question can be found at the end of this chapter.

## Key Concepts

Price elasticity of demand, p. 108
Elastic demand, p. 109
Inelastic demand, p. 110
Unitary elasticity of demand, p. 111
Total revenue, p. 114
Income elasticity of demand, p. 117
Normal goods, p. 117
Luxury goods, p. 117
Inferior goods, p. 117
Cross elasticity of demand, p. 118
Substitutes, p. 118
Complements, p. 118
Price elasticity of supply, p. 119
Elastic supply, p. 119
Inelastic supply, p. 119
Unitary elastic supply, p. 119
Market period, p. 120
Short run, p. 120
Long run, p. 121
Incidence of taxation, p. 122
Deadweight loss, p. 123

## Chapter Summary

### Elasticity of Demand

Price elasticity of demand measures how sensitive the quantity demanded of a product is to price changes. Price elasticity of demand typically is expressed as an absolute value. It is determined by dividing the percentage change in quantity demanded by the percentage change in price. Elasticity measures permit comparisons among diverse products because they are based on percentages.

When the absolute value of the price elasticity of demand is greater than 1, that product has an *elastic* demand. Elastically demanded products have many substitutes and their demand is quite sensitive to price changes. When elasticity is less than 1, demand is *inelastic.* Quantity demanded is not very sensitive to price changes. Necessities such as gasoline, prescription drugs, and tobacco have relatively inelastic demands.

There are four major determinants of elasticity. Elasticity is influenced by the availability of substitute products, the percentage of income spent on the product, the length of time consumers have to adjust, and the difference between luxuries and necessities.

Total revenue is affected by price elasticity of demand. With an inelastically demanded product, quantity demanded is less sensitive to price changes. When prices rise, total revenue rises since quantity demanded falls off less than price increases. When price declines, total revenue falls since quantity sold increases less than price declines.

If a product is elastically demanded, a small price change can lead to large changes in quantity demanded. Thus, when prices fall for an elastically demanded good, sales surge and total revenue rises. However, when price rises, consumers quickly find substitutes and sales plunge, resulting in lower total revenues.

Income elasticity of demand measures how quantity demanded varies with consumer income. Normal goods have a positive income elasticity of demand, but less than 1. Luxury goods have income elasticities greater than 1. Inferior goods have negative income elasticities. As income rises, spending on luxury goods grows faster than income, while spending on inferior goods falls. When income rises, spending on normal goods rises, but at a pace that is less than the increase in income.

Cross elasticity of demand measures how responsive quantity demanded of one good is to changes in the price of another good. If cross elasticity of demand is positive, the two goods are substitutes. If negative, the two goods are complements.

## Elasticity of Supply

The price elasticity of supply measures how sensitive the quantity of a product supplied is to changes in price for that product. It is found by taking the percentage change in quantity supplied and dividing it by the percentage change in price (essentially the same formula as that for the price elasticity of demand). The slope of the supply curve is positive, so price elasticity of supply is always positive. An elastic supply curve has a price elasticity of supply greater than 1. Price elasticity is less than 1 for inelastic supply curves, and equal to 1 for unitary elastic supply curves.

The market period, short run, and long run are the three basic time periods economists use to study elasticity. The market period is so short that the output of firms is fixed, or perfectly inelastic. In the short run, companies can change the amount of labor and other variable factors to alter output, but the physical plant and the number of firms in the industry are assumed to be fixed. In the long run, companies have time to build new production facilities, and to enter or exit the industry.

## Taxes and Elasticity

Elasticity affects the burden and incidence of taxes. The more elastic the demand, the less a company can shift part of a sales or excise tax to consumers in the form of price increases. This is because consumers can readily substitute for elastically demanded products that rise in price. Elastic demand and supplies generate relatively large deadweight losses for society. An inelastically demanded product, however, can absorb the price increase due to a tax without much impact on quantity demanded. Producers can therefore pass most of the burden for such taxes on to consumers, and the deadweight loss is relatively small. When supply is elastic, the tax burden is higher on consumers, and the deadweight loss is larger. With inelastic supplies, the burden on consumers is less, and the deadweight loss is less.

# Questions and Problems

## Check Your Understanding

1. When the demand curve is relatively inelastic and the price falls, what happens to revenue? If the demand is relatively elastic and price rises, what happens to revenue?
2. Why is the demand for gasoline relatively inelastic, while the demand for Exxon's gasoline is relatively elastic?
3. Describe cross elasticity of demand. Why do substitutes have positive cross elasticities? Describe income elasticity of demand. What is the difference between normal and inferior goods?
4. Describe the impact of time on price elasticity of supply.
5. Why would the demand for business airline travel be less elastic than the demand for vacation airline travel by retirees?

## Apply the Concepts

6. One major rationale for farm price supports is that demand is inelastic and that rapidly improving technology, better crop strains, improved fertilizer, and better farming methods increased supply so significantly that farm incomes were severely depressed. Explain why this rationale would seem to be correct.
7. If the price of chicken rises by 15% and the sales of turkey breasts expand by 10%, what is the cross elasticity of demand for these two products? Are they complements or substitutes?
8. For which of the following pairs of goods and services would the cross elasticity of demand be negative: (a) iPods and songs downloaded from iTunes, (b) digital satellite service and digital video recorders, (c) recreational vehicles and camping tents, (d) bowling and co-ed softball, (e) textbooks and study guides.
9. Consider chip plants: potato and computer. Assume there is a large rise in the demand for computer chips and potato chips.
   a. How responsive to demand is each in the market period?
   b. Describe what a manufacturer of each product might do in the short run to increase production.
   c. How does the long run differ for these products?
10. If one automobile brand has an income elasticity of demand of 1.5 and another has an income elasticity equal to −0.3, what would account for the difference? Give an example of a specific brand for each type of car.
11. Suppose you estimated the cross elasticities of demand for three pairs of products and came up with the following three values: 2.3, 0.1, −1.7. What could you conclude about these three pairs of products? If you wanted to know if two products from two different firms competed with each other in the marketplace, what would you look for?
12. In the 1990s, the government charged Microsoft with being a monopolist (the only seller of operating systems for PCs) with its Windows operating system. Could estimates of cross elasticity of demand help Microsoft defend itself against the charges?

## In the News

13. In 2003, London instituted a £5 congestion charge for cars or trucks entering the central city. The levy is said to have reduced congestion by 30% and raised nearly £80 million its first year. London increased the levy to £8 a day, and London's

mayor had this to say: "Congestion charging has achieved its key objective of reducing congestion and has also provided an additional stream of revenue to help the funding of other transport measures within my transport strategy. The charge increase will maintain the benefits currently witnessed in the zone and build upon its success, cutting congestion even further and raising more revenue to be invested in London's transport system." Given what the mayor had to say about the increase in congestion charges and the change in revenue, what must he believe about the elasticity of demand for driving into central London?

14. Alan Greenspan, the former chairman of the Federal Reserve, speaking before the National Petrochemical and Refiners Association in April 2005, made reference to rising oil prices by noting that "higher prices have only brought a modest slowdown in demand for crude oil reflecting a low short-term elasticity of demand. However, the response on the demand side should be more pronounced in the longer term." Is Alan Greenspan correct? Why or why not?

15. Nobel Prize–winning economist, Gary Becker (*Economist,* May 31, 2008) estimated that in the past, "over periods of less than five years, oil *consumption* in the OECD [Organization for Economic Co-operation and Development] dropped by 2–9% when the price doubled. Likewise, oil *production* in countries outside OPEC [Organization of Petroleum Exporting Countries] grew by only 4% every time the price doubled. But over longer periods consumption dropped by 60% and supply rose by 35%." Assume the short-term drop in oil consumption in OECD countries was 5% (not a range of 2 to 9% as Becker estimates). Using these numbers, compute the short- and long-term elasticities of demand and supply of oil. Do your estimates seem roughly consistent with what we have recently seen as oil (and gasoline) prices rose?

## Solving Problems

16. Betty's Bakery estimates that they can sell 400 cookies at 60¢ a cookie and will be able to sell 500 if the price drops to 50¢. Using the midpoint formula, what is the elasticity of demand for Betty's cookies? Will total revenue rise or fall if the price of cookies is lowered?

17. Used music CDs rise in price from $7 to $8, and total revenue falls from $700 to $640.
    a. Is the demand curve over this range elastic or inelastic? Why?
    b. Using the midpoint formula, what is the value of the elasticity of demand over this range?

18. Rising world wholesale fair-trade coffee bean prices force the local Dunkin' Donuts franchise to raise its price of coffee from 89 cents to 99 cents a cup. As a result, management notices that donut sales fall from 950 to 850 a day. Shortly after the coffee price spike, the local Cinnabon franchise reduced its price on cinnamon rolls from $1.89 to $1.69. This resulted in a further decline in Dunkin' Donuts donut sales to 750 a day.
    a. What is the cross elasticity of demand for coffee and donuts? Are these two products complements or substitutes?
    b. What is the cross elasticity of demand for Dunkin' Donuts donuts and Cinnabon cinnamon rolls? Are these two products complements or substitutes?

19. Many health plans pay for dental care. If the elasticity of demand for dental care is 0.8, and the health plan increases the price for dental care by 10%, what will be the impact?

20. Your boss, who is the general manager of the Pontiac Rangers, an adequate AA baseball team, has heard that you are taking a principles of economics course

and has asked you to research the demand for summer night games. She has surveyed a sample of 10 people whom she feels accurately represent the potential market. We will assume that they do as well. The results of the survey are presented below:

**Number of Night Games Willing to Attend at Various Prices**

| Name | $5.00 | $4.50 | $4.00 | $3.50 | $3.00 | $2.50 | $2.00 |
|---|---|---|---|---|---|---|---|
| Arvilla | 1 | 2 | 2 | 3 | 3 | 4 | 5 |
| Quintha | 3 | 4 | 5 | 6 | 7 | 7 | 8 |
| Mary | 0 | 0 | 1 | 2 | 3 | 5 | 5 |
| Ray | 5 | 5 | 5 | 5 | 5 | 6 | 7 |
| Vern | 0 | 0 | 0 | 1 | 3 | 3 | 3 |
| Fran | 5 | 5 | 5 | 5 | 5 | 5 | 5 |
| Jerry | 2 | 2 | 2 | 2 | 3 | 3 | 3 |
| Richard | 5 | 5 | 6 | 6 | 6 | 7 | 8 |
| Whitey | 3 | 6 | 8 | 8 | 8 | 8 | 8 |
| Windy | 6 | 6 | 6 | 7 | 7 | 7 | 8 |

a. What ticket price will maximize total revenue for the team?

b. Using the midpoint formula, what is the price elasticity of demand between $2.50 and $2.00?

c. The local bowling alley has extended league play on Wednesday night. Is the cross elasticity of demand positive or negative between night baseball and bowling? If the manager schedules night games on Wednesday, will that affect attendance at the games?

**21.** J. Crew sells sweaters, pants, and other clothes to college students, among other groups. Many like its clothing, but the company had financial problems nearly a decade ago. In the belief that these problems stemmed from simple merchandising issues—styles, colors, price—J. Crew started to reposition itself in 2003. While some current and potential customers urged the company to lower prices and thereby expand its appeal, in fact prices were raised on many products. For example, a sweater selling for $48 in 2002 sold for $88 at the end of 2003.

a. By raising prices so much, what did J. Crew's management conclude about the price elasticity of demand of its customers?

b. Assume J. Crew sold 100,000 sweaters at the $48.00 price. How many sweaters would they have to sell at the new $88.00 price to have the same total revenue? Assume they sold 80,000 sweaters at the $88.00 price. Using the midpoint formula, what is the price elasticity of demand?

**22.** Coca-Cola in dispensers located on a golf course sells for $1.25 a can, and golfers buy 1,000 cans. Assume the course raises the price to $1.26 (assume a penny raise is possible) and sales fall to 992 cans.

a. Using the midpoint formula, what is the price elasticity of demand for Coke at these prices?

b. Assume the demand for Coke is a linear line. Would the elasticity of demand be elastic or inelastic at 75 cents a can?

c. At $2.00 a can?

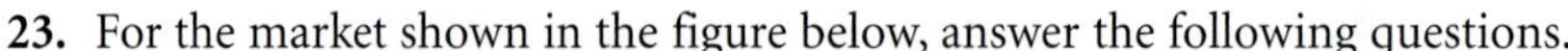

**23.** For the market shown in the figure below, answer the following questions.

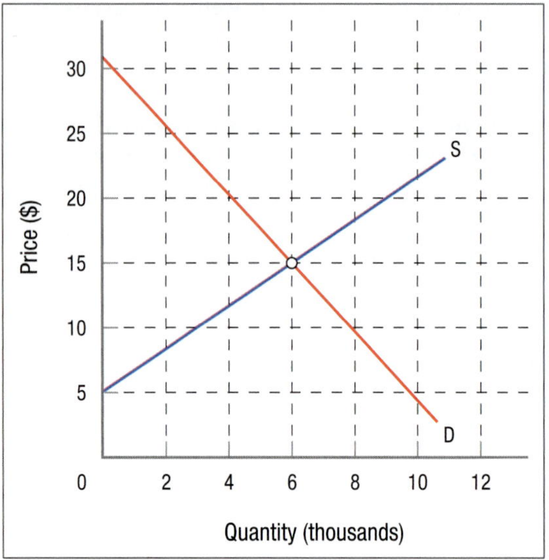


a. Compute the consumer surplus: ______________

b. Compute the producer surplus: ______________

Now assume that government puts a price ceiling on this product at $10 a unit.

c. Compute the new consumer surplus: ______________

d. Compute the new producer surplus: ______________

e. What group would tend to have their advocates or lobbyists support price ceilings?

f. How large is the deadweight loss associated with this price ceiling?

## Answers to Questions in CheckPoints

### Check Point: Elasticity of Demand

If prices in Phoenix rose by 40% and sales fell by 8%, then elasticity is $-0.2 = -0.08/0.40$. Now, if supplies fell by 30% and elasticity is 0.2, then prices could have risen by roughly 150% ($0.30/0.2 = 1.5$) to clear the market.

### Check Point: Elasticity and Total Revenue

Store 1 has an elastic demand for its clothes, while store 2 faces an inelastic demand. Look back at Table 2.

### Check Point: Elasticity of Supply

There are some close calls in this list, but here is our answer from most to least elastic: Starbucks, fast food, grocery, Hollywood, airlines, microchips, crude oil, nuclear power.

### Check Point: Taxes and Elasticity

They all appear to have relatively inelastic demands. This reduces the impact on the industries and leads to higher tax revenues.

# Consumer Choice and Demand

AP Photo/Middletown Journal, Pat Auckerman, file

**Demand analysis rests on an** important assumption: People are rational decision makers. Do people always act rationally? Of course not. A number of economists, called behavioralists, have been studying certain situations where people make irrational decisions. For example, what explains the fact that people often hold on to common stocks long after they rationally recognize that the stocks are dogs and they probably will never make back their losses? It seems that people just do not want to admit—to themselves and others—they have made a stock-picking mistake, and so hold on for years in the vain hope that prices will eventually right themselves.

Important though this work on the irrational is, it does not invalidate the assumption that people choose rationally. If there were a preponderance of irrationality, society would come to a halt because we could not predict anything. In a trivial example, what pedestrian would cross the street even if the light said "walk" if there was a modicum of fear that many drivers would act irrationally and ignore a red light? People *do* miss or ignore red lights, but not often.

So we are left with an underlying assumption of rational decision making that is not bedrock, but is reasonable and powerful nonetheless. We can use it to delve into demand analysis a little more. We know that people determine what price they will pay for various products. How do they make this determination?

We have to choose. We all have a finite quantity of resources at our command. The kinds of products we can purchase are determined, to an extent, by the resources we possess or our income level. For most of us, buying an exotic sports car, a luxury yacht, or a large mansion is simply out of the question—we lack the resources to make such purchases. Making consumer choices, therefore, comes down to buying and enjoying

**After studying this chapter you should be able to:**

- ☐ Use a budget line to determine the constraints on consumer choices.
- ☐ Describe the difference between total and marginal utility.
- ☐ Describe the law of diminishing marginal utility.
- ☐ Understand consumer surplus.
- ☐ Use marginal utility analysis to derive demand curves.

those products that we can, given the fact that we are not Bill Gates or part of his immediate family.

In this chapter, we are going to see what lies behind demand curves by looking at how consumers choose. In the next chapter, we will examine what lies behind supply curves by looking at how producers choose to produce what they do.

There are two major ways to approach consumer choice. We will cover both in this chapter.

The first theory explaining what people choose to buy, given their limited incomes, is known as *utility theory* or *utilitarianism.* This theory holds that rational consumers will allocate their limited incomes so as to maximize their happiness or satisfaction. The clear implication of this theory is that higher incomes should lead to more choices and greater happiness.

Consumer decision making has fascinated economists and philosophers for centuries. Jeremy Bentham (1748–1832), an extraordinary eccentric, argued that every human action is submitted to a "Felicific Calculus"—before acting, we ask ourselves which action would bring the most happiness. That calculus, wrote economic historian Robert Heilbroner,[1] treated "humanity as so many living profit-and-loss calculators, each busily arranging his life to maximize the pleasure of his psychic adding machine."

Bentham's writings were so voluminous that they fill 40 volumes. Still, though Bentham wrote massive draft manuscripts and carried out a correspondence with countless contemporaries, he published little. His influence depended not on publications, but on his personal contacts. Bentham's ideas were so far ahead of their time, moreover, that most of them were not fully developed until well after his death. Forty years after Bentham died, his ideas were rediscovered, refined, and published in *The Theory of Political Economy* by William Stanley Jevons (1835–1882). This work of 1871 marked the beginning of the "marginal revolution."

The second approach, *indifference curve analysis,* is covered in the Appendix to this chapter. Developed by Francis Ysidro Edgeworth, a mathematician who wrote for economists (1845–1926), it added analytical rigor to utility analysis by developing *indifference curves,* which portray combinations of two goods of equal total utility. Edgeworth was a shy man who studied in public libraries because he saw material possessions as a burden. Nevertheless, he brought the precision of mathematics to bear on utility theory and international trade and contributed to statistical analysis by developing the correlation coefficient, which numerically shows the relationship between two variables.

## Marginal Utility Analysis

The work of Bentham and Jevons solved the riddles of consumer behavior by developing **marginal utility analysis.** To begin, let's consider more carefully how a limited income puts constraints on our choices.

**Marginal utility analysis:** A theoretical framework underlying consumer decision making. This approach assumes that satisfaction can be measured and that consumers maximize satisfaction when the marginal utilities per dollar are equal for all products and services.

### The Budget Line

As a student, you came to college to improve your life not only intellectually but also financially. As a college graduate, you can expect your lifetime earnings to be triple those of someone with only a high school education. Even once you have achieved these higher earnings, there will be limits on what you can buy. But first, let us return to the present. Assume you have $50 a week to spend on pizza and wall climbing. This is a proxy for a more general choice between food and entertainment. We could use different goods or

[1] Robert Heilbroner, *The Worldly Philosophers: The Lives, Times, and Ideas of the Great Economic Thinkers,* 6th ed. (New York: Simon & Schuster), 1986, p. 174.

## Jeremy Bentham (1748–1832)

Jeremy Bentham was a social philosopher, legal reformer, and writer who founded the philosophy known as utilitarianism. As an economic theorist, his most valuable contribution was the idea of *utility,* which explained consumer choices in terms of maximizing pleasure and minimizing pain.

Born in 1748, Bentham was the son of a wealthy lawyer. At age 12 he entered Oxford University, then studied for the bar. After hearing Blackstone's famous lectures on English common law, however, Bentham decided not to practice. In 1792, his father died, leaving him a considerable fortune, which allowed him to spend his time writing and thinking. Derided by Karl Marx as the ultimate British eccentric, Bentham dreamed up reform proposals that were both imaginative and remarkably detailed. One of his best-known inventions was the design of a model prison, known as a "Panoptican," which he described as a "mill for grinding rogues honest."

But his primary contribution was analyzing the notion of utility as a driving force in social and economic behavior. Bentham disapproved of notions such as *natural law,* believing that the aim of society and government should be to maximize utility or to promote the "greatest happiness for the greatest number," a phrase Bentham borrowed from a book by Joseph Priestly. In 1789, he published his most famous work, *Introduction to the Principles of Morals,* which laid out his utilitarian philosophy. Bentham believed it was possible to derive a "Felicific Calculus" to compare the various pleasures or pains.

Although modern economists have cast doubt on the notion that utility could be measured or calculated, Bentham had many ideas that were ahead of his time, including the notion of cost-benefit analysis, which logically followed from his utilitarian views on government policies. Bentham also formulated the contemporary notion of marginal utility. After reading this chapter, it will be hard for you to avoid thinking in Bentham's terms about your own consumer choices, and you'll find yourself asking questions like "Do I really get $12 worth of satisfaction out of a Coke and popcorn at the movies, or do I have better alternatives for that money?"

Brand X/SuperStock

more goods, but the principle would still be the same. In our specific example, if pizzas cost $10 each and an hour of wall climbing costs $20, you can climb walls for 2.5 hours or consume 5 pizzas each week, or do some combination of these two. Your options are plotted in Figure 1 on the next page.

This **budget line** (constraint) is a lot like the production possibilities frontier (PPF) discussed in Chapter 2. Though you might prefer to have more of both goods, you are limited to consumption choices lying on the budget line, or inside the budget line if you want to save any part of your $50 weekly budget. As with the PPF curve, however, any points to the right of the line are unattainable for you—they exceed your available income.

**Budget line:** Graphically illustrates the possible combinations of two goods that can be purchased with a given income, given the prices of both products.

In this example, the budget line makes clear that many different combinations of wall climbing and pizzas will exhaust your $50 budget. But which of these possible combinations will you select? That depends on your personal preferences. If you love pizza, you will probably make different choices than if you are a fitness fanatic who rarely consumes fatty foods. Your own preferences determine how much pleasure you can expect to get from the various possible options. Economists call this pleasure the *utility* of an item.

**FIGURE 1—The Budget Constraint or Line**

When pizzas cost $10 each, wall climbing costs $20 per hour, and you have $50 a week to spend, you could buy 5 pizzas per week, 2.5 hours of wall climbing, or some combination of the two. The budget line makes clear all of the possible purchasing combinations of two products on a particular budget.

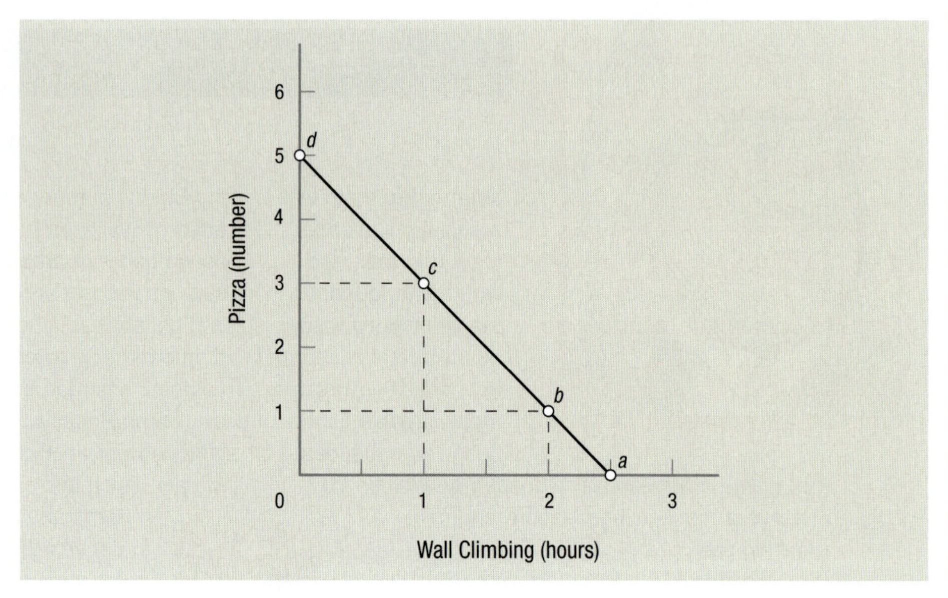


## Preferences and Utility

**Utility:** A hypothetical measure of consumer satisfaction.

**Utility** is a hypothetical measure of consumer satisfaction. It was introduced by early economists attempting to explain how consumers make decisions. The utilitarian theory of consumer behavior assumes, first of all, that utility is something that *can* be measured. It assumes, in other words, that we can quantifiably determine how much utility (satisfaction) you derive from consuming one or more pizzas, and how much utility you derive from spending one or more hours on the climbing wall. Table 1 provides estimates of the utility you derive from both pizzas and wall climbing, measured in *utils,* hypothetical units of satisfaction or utility. Compare columns 1 and 2 with columns 4 and 5.

At first glance, it might seem that if you wanted to maximize your utility, you would simply go wall climbing for 2.5 hours, thereby maximizing your total utility at 270 utils. If you spent a little time with the table, you would notice that combinations give you more total utility. If you went wall climbing for 2 hours and had 1 pizza, your total utility would be 330 utils (260 + 70 = 330), much more than concentrating on one item alone.

Other than trial and error, how do we determine the best combination? Before we can see just which combination of these two goods would actually bring you the most happiness, we need to distinguish between *total utility* and *marginal utility.*

**TABLE 1** Total and Marginal Utility from Pizzas and Wall Climbing

| Pizza | | | Wall Climbing | | |
|---|---|---|---|---|---|
| (1) Quantity | (2) Total Utility | (3) Marginal Utility | (4) Quantity | (5) Total Utility | (6) Marginal Utility |
| 0 | 0 | 0 | 0.0 | 0 | 0 |
| 1 | 70 | 70 | 0.5 | 90 | 90 |
| 2 | 130 | 60 | 1.0 | 170 | 80 |
| 3 | 180 | 50 | 1.5 | 230 | 60 |
| 4 | 220 | 40 | 2.0 | 260 | 30 |
| 5 | 250 | 30 | 2.5 | 270 | 10 |

## Total and Marginal Utility

**Total utility** is the total satisfaction that a person receives from consuming a given quantity of goods and services. In Table 1, for example, the total utility received from consuming 3 pizzas is 180 utils, whereas the total utility from 4 pizzas is 220 utils. Marginal utility is something different.

**Total utility:** The total satisfaction that a person receives from consuming a given amount of goods and services.

**Marginal utility:** The satisfaction received from consuming an additional unit of a given product or service.

**Marginal utility** is the satisfaction derived from consuming an *additional* unit of a given product or service. It is determined by taking the difference between the total utility derived from, say, consuming 4 pizzas and consuming 3 pizzas. The total utility derived from 4 pizzas is 220 utils, and that from 3 pizzas is 180 utils. Hence, consuming the fourth pizza yields only an additional 40 utils of satisfaction (220 − 180 = 40 utils).

The marginal utility for both pizza eating and wall climbing is listed in Table 1. Notice that as we move from one quantity of pizza to the next, total utility rises by an amount exactly equal to marginal utility. This is no coincidence. Marginal utility is nothing but the change in total utility obtained from consuming one more pizza (the marginal pizza), so as pizza eating increases by one pizza, total utility will rise by the amount of additional satisfaction derived from consuming that additional pizza. Also note that, for both pizzas and wall climbing, marginal utility declines the more a particular product or activity is consumed.

## The Law of Diminishing Marginal Utility

Why does marginal utility decline as the consumption of one product or activity increases? No matter our personal tastes and preferences, we eventually become sated once we have consumed a certain amount of any given commodity. Most of us love ice cream. As youngsters, some of us imagined a world in which meals consisted of nothing but ice cream—no casseroles, no vegetables, just ice cream. To children this might sound heavenly, but as adults, we recognize we would quickly grow sick of ice cream. Human beings simply crave diversity; we quickly tire of the same product or service if we consume it day after day.

This fact of human nature led early economists to formulate the **law of diminishing marginal utility.** This law states that as we consume more of a product, the rate at which our total satisfaction increases with the consumption of each additional unit will decline. And if we continue to consume still more of the product after that, our total satisfaction will eventually begin to decline.

**Law of diminishing marginal utility:** As we consume more of a given product, the added satisfaction we get from consuming an additional unit declines.

This principle is illustrated by Figure 2 on the next page, which graphs the total utility and marginal utility for pizza eating, as listed in Table 1. Notice that total utility, charted in panel A, rises continually as we move from 1 pizza per week to 5 pizzas. Nevertheless, the rate of this increase declines as more pizzas are consumed. Accordingly, panel B shows that marginal utility declines with more pizzas eaten. On your student budget, you could not afford any more than 5 pizzas a week, but we can imagine that if you were to keep eating pizzas—50 pizzas in a week—your total utility would actually start to drop with each additional pizza. At some point, it simply hurts to stuff any more pizzas down your throat.

It is one thing to grasp the obvious fact that consumers have limited budgets and that the products they can choose among provide them increasing satisfaction but are subject to diminishing marginal utility. It is another thing to figure out exactly how consumers allocate their limited funds so as to maximize their total level of satisfaction or utility. We now turn our attention to how early economists solved the problem of maximizing utility and the analytic methods that flowed out of their work.

## Maximizing Utility

Let's take a moment to review everything we need to know to plot the budget line in Figure 1: your total income and the prices of all the products you could purchase. In our example, the weekly budget is $50, pizzas cost $10 apiece, and wall climbing is $20 per hour or $10 per half hour. This is enough information to plot all of the options open to you.

**FIGURE 2—Total and Marginal Utility for Pizza**

Total utility, charted in panel A, rises continually as we move from 1 pizza per week to 5 pizzas. Nevertheless, the rate of this increase declines as more pizzas are consumed. Accordingly, panel B shows that marginal utility declines with more pizzas eaten.

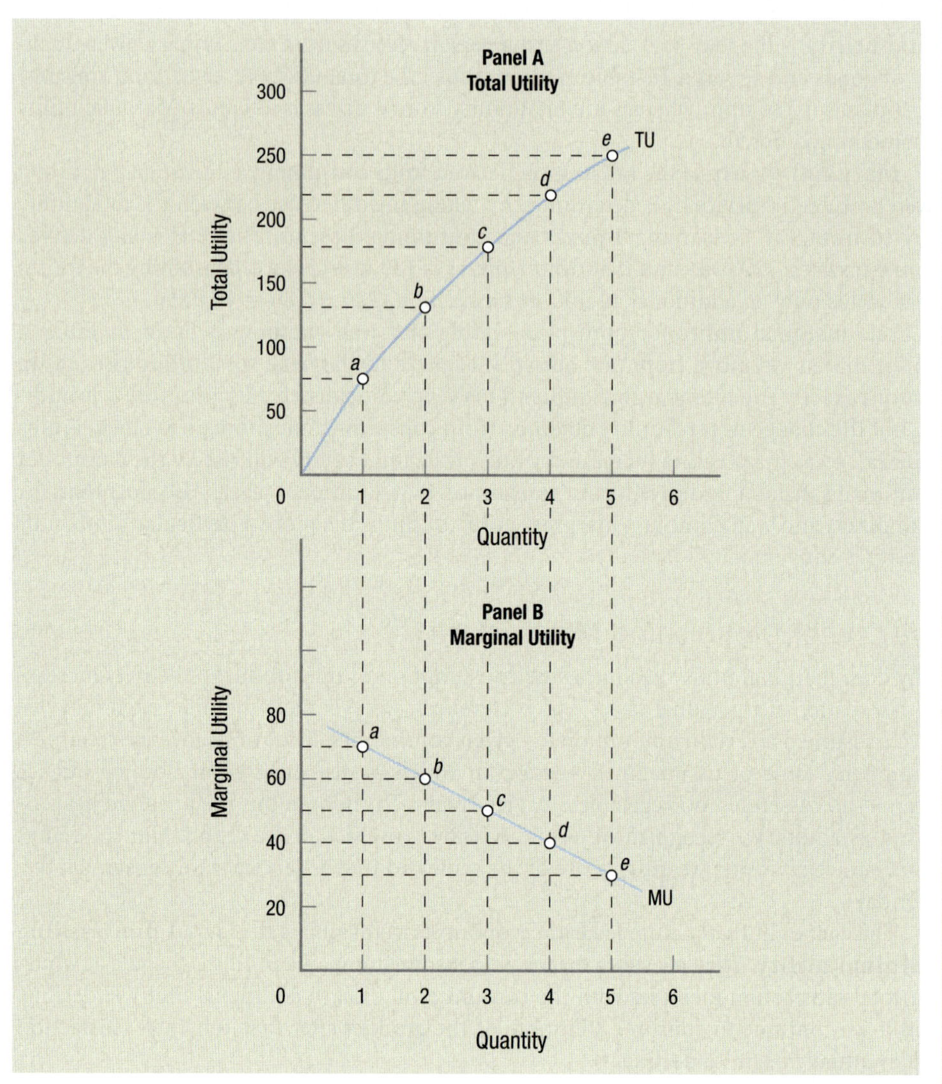


Now, we need to consider the utility we receive from our various levels of consumption of these two products. Take a look at columns (4) and (8) of Table 2. These two columns express the marginal utilities of pizzas and wall climbing, respectively, in terms of marginal utility per dollar; these amounts are computed by dividing the marginal utility of each product by the product's price.

To see the importance of computing marginal utility per dollar, consider the following. Given the figures in columns (4) and (8), and assuming you want to get the most for your money, on which activity would you spend the first $10 of your weekly budget? You can spend the first $10 on a pizza or a half-hour of wall climbing. A pizza returns 70 utils of satisfaction, whereas a half-hour of wall climbing yields 90 utils. Since 90 is greater than 70, clearly the first $10 would be better spent on wall climbing.

Now, for the sake of simplicity, let's keep your spending increments constant. On what will you spend your next $10—pizza or climbing? Look again at the table. Your first pizza still gives you 70 utils, while the second half-hour of wall climbing returns 80 utils. Wall climbing again is the obvious choice. If your total budget had only been $20 per week, you would have been inclined to give up pizzas completely.

TABLE 2 Total and Marginal Utility per Dollar from Pizzas and Wall Climbing

| Pizza | | | | Wall Climbing | | | |
|---|---|---|---|---|---|---|---|
| (1) Quantity (units of pizza) | (2) Total Utility | (3) Marginal Utility | (4) Marginal Utility per Dollar (price = $10) | (5) Quantity (units of wall climbing) | (6) Total Utility | (7) Marginal Utility | (8) Marginal Utility per Dollar (price = $10 per half hour) |
| 0 | 0 | 0 | 0 | 0.0 | 0 | 0 | 0 |
| 1 | 70 | 70 | 7 | 0.5 | 90 | 90 | 9 |
| 2 | 130 | 60 | 6 | 1.0 | 170 | 80 | 8 |
| 3 | 180 | 50 | 5 | 1.5 | 230 | 60 | 6 |
| 4 | 220 | 40 | 4 | 2.0 | 260 | 30 | 3 |
| 5 | 250 | 30 | 3 | 2.5 | 270 | 10 | 1 |

Proceeding in the same way, using your third $10 to buy your first pizza will yield an additional 70 utils of satisfaction, whereas using this money to purchase a third half-hour of wall climbing will bring only 60 utils. (Wall climbing is starting to get a bit boring.) Thus, because 70 is greater than 60, with your third $10 you buy your first pizza.

Finally, using the remaining $20 of your budget to buy either additional pizzas or additional half-hours of wall climbing would yield an additional 120 utils of satisfaction. Thus, you split the remaining $20 evenly between these two activities. When the consumption of additional units of two products provides equal satisfaction, economists say consumers are *indifferent* to which product they consume first.

By following this incremental process, therefore, we have determined that you will spend your $50 on 2 pizzas ($20) and 1.5 hours of wall climbing ($30). This results in a total utility of 360 utils (130 for pizza and 230 for wall climbing). *No other combination of pizzas and wall climbing will result in total satisfaction this high,* as you can prove to yourself by trying to spend the $50 differently.

Note also for the last two units of each product consumed, the marginal utilities per dollar were equal at 6. This result is to be expected. Simple logic tells us that if one activity yields more satisfaction per dollar than some other, you will continue to pursue the activity with the higher satisfaction per dollar until some other activity starts yielding more satisfaction. This observation leads to a simple rule for maximizing utility: You should allocate your budget so that the marginal utilities per dollar are equal for the last units of the products consumed. This **utility maximizing rule,** in turn, leads to the following equation, where $MU$ = marginal utility and $P$ = price.

**Utility maximizing rule:** Utility is maximized where the marginal utility per dollar is equal for all products, or $MU_a/P_a = MU_b/P_b = \ldots = MU_n/P_n$.

$$\frac{MU_{\text{Pizza}}}{P_{\text{Pizza}}} = \frac{MU_{\text{Wall Climbing}}}{P_{\text{Wall Climbing}}}$$

This equation and the analyses described earlier can be generalized to cover numerous goods and services. For all goods and services *a, b, . . . n:*

$$\frac{MU_a}{P_a} = \frac{MU_b}{P_b} = \cdots = \frac{MU_n}{P_n}$$

The important point to remember is that, according to this theory of consumer behavior, consumers approach every purchase by asking themselves which of all possible additional acts of consumption would bring them the most satisfaction per dollar.

## *Issue:* Tipping and Consumer Behavior

**If consumers maximize** their utility with a given (limited) budget, why would they ever tip? Consider that tips come at the end of a meal. How can tips affect the quality of service already given?

Many reasons might explain tipping. First, if it is a restaurant you frequent, tips might assure better service in the future. Second, you might consider tips to be rewards for higher-quality service. Third, tipping is a custom and is part of the wages for several dozen occupations.

What would happen if many people refused or neglected to tip? Would various occupations seek to make tipping legally binding? It is likely this would be the result, if a recent case in New York is any guide. If you have ever gone to a restaurant with a large party, you will notice that menus and bills often state that a set tip will be added for large parties. One large party gave a very small tip after what they considered to be inadequate service. The restaurant sued, claiming that the 18% tip was mandatory. The court's decision for the tipper turned on the phrasing in the menu. This could be viewed as a first shot: If too many people refuse to tip or tip poorly, we can expect legal redress.

We can establish, then, that tipping is a custom that leads to better service, and so is followed even though the tip comes after the service is performed. In this way, it seems to run counter to the idea of people tipping based on a calculation of marginal utility. And how much we tip raises questions about how we calculate marginal utility.

Economists have found only a weak statistical link between quality of service and size of the tip. Tipping also appears to be unrelated to the number of courses in the meal, and whether or not people intend to return to the restaurant. The table at left shows some of the things that do affect the size of the tip.

Obviously, a waiter or waitress cannot do all of these things and expect to see their tips increase by the sum of all the percentages, but we all have experienced many of these techniques in restaurants. Interestingly, if a waitress draws a smiley face on the bill, her tips go up, but if a waiter does the same, his tips go down. Suggestive selling raises the tip because people tend to tip based on the size of the bill. After having read about this study, you probably will find yourself being a little cynical when some of these techniques are used the next time you dine out.

Banana Stock/Jupiter Images

**Percentage Increase in Tips from Specific Behavior by Wait Staff**

| Tip Enhancing Action | Change in Tip |
|---|---|
| Wearing a flower in hair | 17% |
| Introducing yourself by name | 53% |
| Squatting down next to the table | 20–25% |
| Repeat order back to customers | 100% |
| Suggestive selling | 23% |
| Touching customer | 22–42% |
| Using tip trays with credit card insignia | 22–25% |
| Waitress drawing a smiley face on check | 18% |
| Writing "thank you" on the check | 13% |

See Michael Lynn, *Mega Tips: Scientifically Tested Techniques to Increase Your Tips,* 2004, p. 25. This publication is available free (in PDF format) on the Internet. The author suggests a tip if you find the study helpful.

Source: Based on Raj Persaud, "What's the tipping point?" *Financial Times,* April 9, 2005, p. w3.

**CHECKPOINT**

### MARGINAL UTILITY ANALYSIS

- The budget constraint graphically illustrates the limits on purchases for a given income (budget).
- Utility is a hypothetical measure of consumer satisfaction.
- Total utility is the total satisfaction a person gets from consuming a certain amount of goods.
- Marginal utility is the additional satisfaction a consumer gets from consuming one more unit of the good or service.
- The law of diminishing marginal utility states that as consumption of a specific good increases, the increase in total satisfaction will decline.

- Consumers maximize satisfaction by purchasing goods up to the point where the marginal utility per dollar is equal for all goods.

**QUESTIONS:** Let's apply the theory of diminishing marginal utility to an all-you-can-eat restaurant meal. First, do you think you will eat more than at a normal restaurant? Why? Second, consider the quality of the food offered at a buffet or an all-you-can-eat restaurant. Recalling what you answered to the first question, what can you predict about the quality of food offered?

Answers to the Checkpoint questions can be found at the end of this chapter.

## Using Marginal Utility Analysis

You have seen how the marginal utility analysis of consumer behavior works when we assume that satisfaction or well-being can be measured directly (in utils). We can now use this theory of consumer behavior to derive the demand curve for wall climbing and to examine consumer surplus in a little more depth than when we first introduced this concept in Chapter 4.

### Deriving Demand Curves

We know consumers will maximize their utility by spending each dollar of their limited budgets on the goods and services yielding the highest marginal utility per dollar. In our previous example, with pizzas costing $10 each and an hour of wall climbing costing $20, this meant you bought 2 pizzas and 1.5 hours of wall climbing. Would your consumption choices change if these prices changed? Let us consider what happens when the cost of wall climbing rises to $30 per hour.

Now that wall climbing costs $30 per hour or $15 per half hour, column (8) of Table 3 has been altered to reflect this new rate for wall climbing. The first half hour of climbing yields 90 utils and now costs $15, so each dollar yields 6 utils. Now your first $10 will be spent on a pizza ($MU/P = 7$ for pizza versus $MU/P = 6$ for wall climbing).

The next $25 is split between another pizza and a half-hour of wall climbing since $MU/P = 6$ for both. Your final $15 is spent on wall climbing since its marginal utility per dollar (5.33) is higher than for a third pizza (5).

Thus, your final allocation is 2 pizzas and 1 hour of wall climbing. Clearly, consumer choices respond to changes in product prices. With wall climbing at $20 per hour, you consumed 1.5 hours of climbing and 2 pizzas. When the price of wall climbing rose to $30 per

**TABLE 3** Total and Marginal Utility per Dollar from Pizzas and Wall Climbing (price of wall climbing increases to $30 per hour or $15 per half hour)

| Pizza | | | | Wall Climbing | | | |
|---|---|---|---|---|---|---|---|
| (1) Quantity (units of pizza) | (2) Total Utility | (3) Marginal Utility | (4) Marginal Utility per Dollar (price = $10) | (5) Quantity (units of wall climbing) | (6) Total Utility | (7) Marginal Utility | (8) Marginal Utility per Dollar (price = $15 per half hour) |
| 0 | 0 | 0 | 0 | 0.0 | 0 | 0 | 0.00 |
| 1 | 70 | 70 | 7 | 0.5 | 90 | 90 | 6.00 |
| 2 | 130 | 60 | 6 | 1.0 | 170 | 80 | 5.33 |
| 3 | 180 | 50 | 5 | 1.5 | 230 | 60 | 4.00 |
| 4 | 220 | 40 | 4 | 2.0 | 260 | 30 | 2.00 |
| 5 | 250 | 30 | 3 | 2.5 | 270 | 10 | 0.67 |

hour you altered your consumption. Now, instead of 1.5 hours and 2 pizzas, you consume 1 hour and 2 pizzas. This new level is shown in the shaded area of Table 3.

Figure 3 plots both your budget constraint and your demand for wall climbing based on the results of Tables 2 and 3. Panel A shows the effect of increasing the price of wall climbing from \$20 to \$30 per hour. At the increased price of wall climbing, if you were to spend your entire budget on this activity, you could only climb for 1.66 hours (\$50/\$30 = 1.66). This price increase rotates the budget line leftward, reducing your consumption opportunities, as the figure illustrates.

When the price of wall climbing was \$20 per hour, you climbed for 1.5 hours (points *b* in both panels of Figure 3). When the price was increased to \$30 per hour, marginal utility analysis led you to reduce your consumption of wall climbing to 1 hour (point *a* in both panels). Connecting these points in panel B of Figure 3 yields the demand curve for wall climbing.

Thus, the marginal utility theory of consumer behavior helps explain both how consumers allocate their income according to their personal preferences and the law of demand. Remember that the law of demand posited an inverse (negative) relationship between price and quantity demanded. This negative relationship is shown in panel B. In addition, this analysis shows why consumers almost always get more than they pay for in terms of the goods and services they buy. This surprising phenomenon that we have seen before is known as **consumer surplus.**

**Consumer surplus:** The difference between what consumers are willing to pay and what they actually pay for a product in the market.

**FIGURE 3—Deriving the Demand for Wall Climbing Using Marginal Utility Analysis**

With the price of wall climbing at \$20 per hour, you climb for 1.5 hours (point *b* in both panels). When the price increases to \$30 per hour, you reduce your consumption of wall climbing to 1 hour (point *a* in both panels). Connecting these points in panel B yields the demand curve for wall climbing.

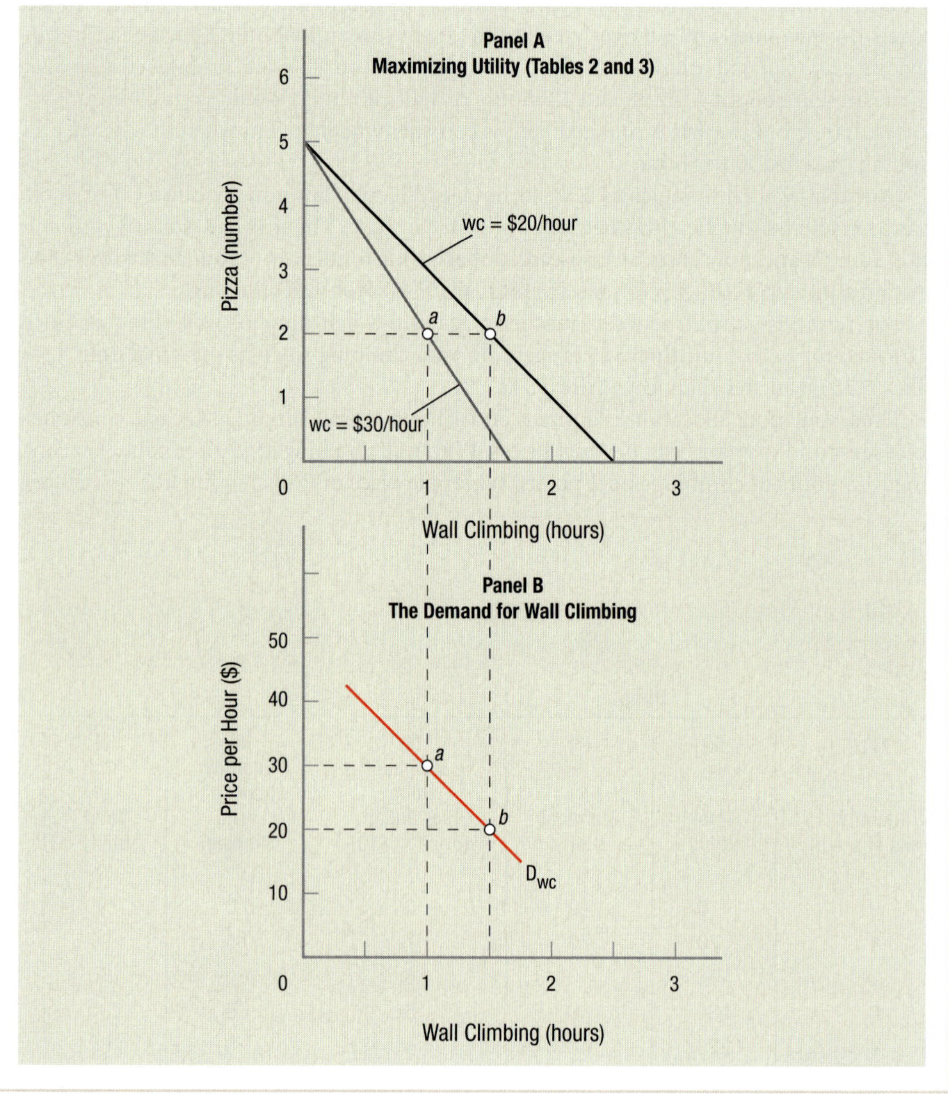

## Consumer Surplus

Consumer surplus is another example of the gains that accrue from markets, which we discussed in Chapter 4. Remember, it is the difference between what consumers would be willing to pay for a product and what they must actually pay for the product in the market. Typically, when you purchase something, you can buy all you want of it (within your budget) at the market price. In our initial example, we assumed that the market price of wall climbing was $20 per hour and concluded that you would climb for 1.5 hours per week. When the cost rose to $30 per hour, you reduced your climbing to 1 hour per week. Figure 4 reproduces panel B from Figure 3, highlighting your demand curve for wall climbing for all prices above $20 per hour. Additionally, a supply curve has been superimposed that provides a market equilibrium price of $20 per hour.

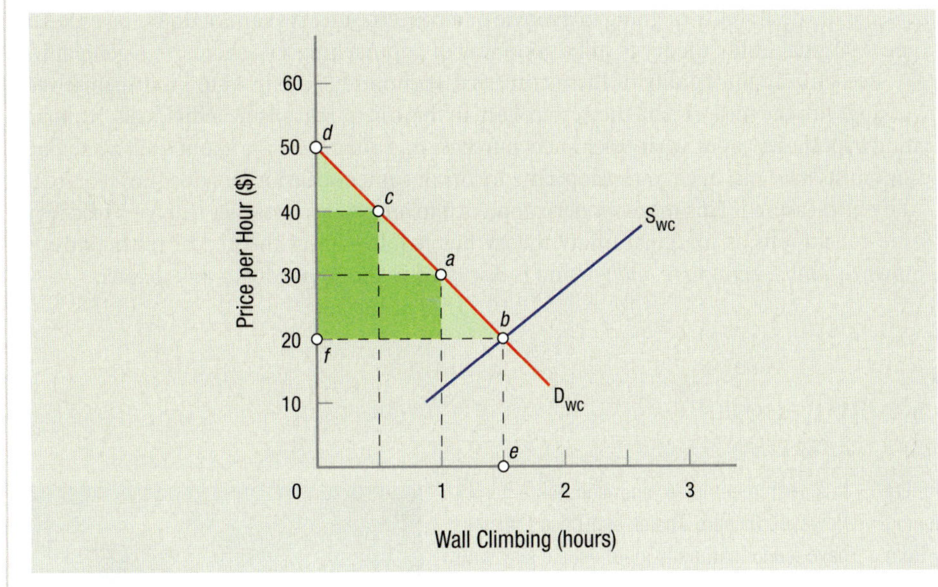


**FIGURE 4—Consumer Surplus**

Consumer surplus is the difference between what consumers are willing to pay and what they actually pay for a product in the market. When looking at a large market, it is represented by the shaded area *fdb,* the area under the demand curve and above the market price.

Notice that for the first half-hour of climbing, your demand curve shows that you would have been willing to pay $40 per hour (point *c*). Nevertheless, you received that first half-hour for the market price of $20 per hour. That represents a nice gain for you; it is your consumer surplus for the half-hour of climbing. For the next half-hour, you still would have been willing to pay $30 per hour (point *a*), but again you got it for the market price of $20 per hour—not quite as good a deal, but still a nice bargain. Only by the time you are purchasing your third half-hour of climbing must you pay exactly what you would have been willing to pay for this activity, $20 per hour, thus marking the end of your consumer surplus. For this specific instance, your consumer surplus is equal to $30 ($20 + $10 + $0) because we are dealing with a small number of discrete half-hour increments of wall climbing.

The shaded area marked out by triangle *fdb* in Figure 4 represents a more general measure of consumer surplus when we look at large markets.

The total amount spent on climbing in Figure 4 is equal to area 0*fbe.* Total satisfaction from climbing is area 0*dbe.* Consequently, consumer surplus is equal to shaded area *fdb*—that is, area 0*dbe* minus area 0*fbe.* Consumer surplus is a nice "bonus."

## Marginal Utility Analysis: A Critique

Marginal utility analysis explains not only how consumers purchase goods and services but also how all household choices are made. We can analyze the decision of whether or not to get a job, for example, by comparing the marginal utility of work versus the marginal utility of leisure. As a college student, you are familiar with having many demands made on your time.

More work means more money but less time for leisure, and vice versa. Marginal utility theory helps us to identify that point where work and leisure (and hopefully study) balance out.

Though marginal utility theory is an elegant and logically consistent theory that helps us understand how consumers behave, it has faced some important criticisms. First and foremost, it assumes that consumers are able to measure the utility they derive from various sorts of consumption. Yet, this is virtually impossible in everyday life—how many utils do you get out of eating a bowl of ice cream? This is not to suggest that marginal utility theory is invalid. It simply requires one very restrictive assumption, namely, that people are able to measure their satisfaction for every purchase. Clearly, this is an assumption that finds little empirical confirmation in everyday life.

Others have argued that it is absurd to think that we could carry out the mental calculus required to compare the ratios of marginal utility to price for all possible goods and services. This is no doubt true, but even if we do not compare all possible goods and services in this way, we do draw some comparisons. After all, we somehow need to be able to distinguish between the desirability of going to a movie or a concert, since we cannot do both at the same time. Marginal utility theory is still a good way of approaching this choice, in a general way.

Recognizing the validity of these criticisms, economists have tried to limit themselves to working with the sorts of data they can collect, in this case purchases by individuals. By formulating hypotheses about what consumers purchase and what this says about their preferences, economists have managed to develop a theory of consumer behavior that does not require that utility be measured. This more modern approach to analyzing consumer behavior reaches the same conclusions as marginal utility theory but requires fewer theoretical restrictions; it is known as *indifference curve analysis* and is discussed in the Appendix to this chapter.

## *Issue:* Are Consumers Really Rational?

**Are people really** rational utility maximizers? As mentioned at the beginning of this chapter, the challenge comes from behavioral economists. Chief among them are Daniel Kahneman and Richard Thaler.

Let's start with an example. Many companies have retirement plans in which an employee can deduct money tax-free from a paycheck and invest it in a company-sponsored plan where the returns also compound tax-free until retirement. Normally, the various plans are set up with an opt-in feature: When someone is hired, he or she decides whether to set aside any money for the retirement plan (whether to opt in) and how much to contribute. Some companies recently have changed the way employees become part of the retirement plan: Rather than opt in, the companies have automatically enrolled each new employee at a set percentage of pay deducted and employees specifically have to request not to be included (they opt out).

Here is the key: If people are rational utility maximizers, it should make no difference whether they opt in or opt out. The decision should be the same: Should I become part of this retirement plan and contribute to it? However, Richard Thaler and Cass Sunstein have found that many more people stay with the program if they have to opt out than sign up if they opt in. What accounts for this large difference in behavior for the same decision?

Two explanations have been given for this curious behavior. First, behavioral economists have discovered a "status quo bias," a tendency to go along with a default option. David Laibson claims that the vast majority of U.S. households would save more for retirement if they were rational utility maximizers, and they do not because people have limited rationality, limited self-control, but unbounded optimism.

Thaler and Sunstein suggest a policy prescription for this systematic failure of people to be rational utility maximizers. In a book entitled *Nudge,* they suggest using little nudges to push people in certain preferred directions.

Of course, as soon as companies see the power of the nudge, it is open to abuse. If the default option is set in the wrong way, people can be nudged to do things that might not be in their best interest. In

Ken Bohn/San Diego Zoo/HO/Reuters/Corbis

2008, Frontier Airlines began adding a $10.95 travel insurance charge to all tickets as the default option. Customers had to explicitly opt out of this charge before final purchase. At the same time, Frontier raised fees for changing flights after the time of sale. A Frontier spokesman said: "We believe it's a value to our customers . . . and we think it's in their best interests to buy it." Clearly, there are instances where consumers have biases and act in irrational ways, but it seems unlikely that the bulk of our behavior is irrational.

Sources: Richard Thaler and Cass Sunstein, *Nudge: Improving Decisions about Health, Wealth, and Happiness* (New Haven: Yale University Press), 2008; and Chris Walsh, "Frontier Flier Bolts over Travel Insurance," *Rocky Mountain News,* August 2, 2008, p. 2.

**CHECKPOINT**

### USING MARGINAL UTILITY ANALYSIS

- Demand curves for products can be derived from marginal utility analysis simply by changing the price of one good and plotting the resulting changes in consumption.
- Consumer surplus is the difference between what you would have been willing to pay for a good and what you actually have to pay.
- Even though marginal utility analysis requires us to measure utility explicitly, it still offers significant insight into how consumers make decisions between products, how consumers react when one product's price changes, and when income drops.

**QUESTIONS:** Even though convenience stores have significantly higher prices than normal grocery stores such as Safeway, they seem to do well, judging by their numbers. Why are people willing to pay these higher prices? If a Safeway began to operate 24/7, would this affect the sales of a nearby convenience store?

Answers to the Checkpoint questions can be found at the end of this chapter.

## Key Concepts



## Chapter Summary

### Marginal Utility Analysis

The budget line shows the different combinations of goods that can be purchased at a given level of income. Because consumer budgets are limited, consumption decisions often require making tradeoffs—more of one good can be purchased only if less of another is bought.

The utility of a product is a hypothetical measure of how much satisfaction a consumer derives from the product. Though not something that can be measured directly like weight or length, economists estimate the utility of various products at different levels of consumption to understand consumer preference and predict consumer behavior. The standard unit of utility is the *util.*

Total utility is the entire amount of satisfaction a consumer derives from consuming some product; it is equal to the sum of the utility derived from the consumption of each individual unit of this product.

Marginal utility is the amount of utility derived from consuming one more unit of a given product. Note that as a person consumes more units of a product, marginal utility changes—consuming the ninth unit of a product may lead to a different increase in total utility than did consuming the third unit.

The law of diminishing marginal utility states that as more units of any product are consumed, marginal utility declines.

Marginal utility analysis provides a theoretical framework that helps economists understand how consumers make their consumption decisions among different products at varying price levels. It assumes that consumers try to maximize the utility they receive on their limited budgets, by adjusting their spending to the point where the utility derived from the last dollar spent on any product is equal to the utility from the last dollar spent on other products.

### Using Marginal Utility Analysis

*Consumer surplus* is the difference between what consumers are willing to pay for a product and what they must actually pay for the product in the market.

The applicability of marginal utility analysis to the real world is restricted by the fact that it assumes consumers can measure utility accurately and perform complex calculations regarding utility in their heads—both of which are difficult to measure empirically.

## Questions and Problems

### Check Your Understanding

1. Describe the utility-maximizing condition in words. Explain why it makes sense.

### Apply the Concepts

2. Describe the conditions necessary for total utility to be positive but marginal utility is negative. Give an example of such a situation.
3. One luxury goods manufacturer noted that "Our customers do not want to pay less. If we halved the price of all our products, we would double our sales for six months, and then we would sell nothing." Is there something about luxury goods that suggests consumers are irrational? Do luxury goods not follow the law of demand?
4. Advertisements on television both inform consumers and persuade them to purchase products in differing proportion depending on the ad. But today, digital video recorders can be found in 50 to 60 million households, and much of what these households watch is recorded, and the vast bulk of the ads are skipped. If this trend continues, where will consumers find out about new products?
5. Critics of marginal utility analysis argue that it is unrealistic to assume that people make the mental calculus of marginal utility per dollar for large numbers of products. But when you are making a decision to either go to a first-run movie or buy a used DVD of last summer's blockbuster, does this analysis seem so complex? Is it a reasonable representation of your thought process?

### In the News

6. A new field called neuroeconomics studies brain activity as people make decisions while trading stocks, gambling, and playing games designed for experiments. The *Wall Street Journal* (April 20, 2006, p. C3) reports that researchers have found that people are particularly afraid of ambiguous risk with unknown odds. Could this simple insight go a long way toward showing why terrorism seems so effective?
7. Harvard economist David Laibson (*Economist,* January 15, 2005, p. 71) has found that "people tend much to prefer, say $100 now to $115 next week, but they are indifferent between $100 a year from now and $115 in a year and a week" Does this seem rational? Using brain scans, he and colleagues found that short-term decisions are governed by the emotional (limbic system) side of the brain, whereas longer-term decisions are governed by the prefrontal cortex, which is associated with reason and calculation. Why might longer-term decisions be more consistent with the consumer choice theories we discussed earlier in this chapter?
8. Richard Layard, in his book *Happiness: Lessons from a New Science,* found that once a country's annual income exceeds $20,000 per capita, there is little relationship between happiness and income. But if you are poor, more money does make you happy. Does this fact suggest that the marginal utility from more income above $20,000 per capita is small?
9. In the summer of 2009, Chrysler announced that beginning with its 2010 models it is dropping the current lifetime powertrain (engine and transmission parts)

warranty and replacing it with a 5-year, 100,000-mile guarantee. The *Wall Street Journal* (August 20, 2009) reported that "Chrysler spokesman Rick Deneau said that the decision was driven by market research that showed customers prefer warranties with a fixed time period." The new five-year warranty will be transferable if the vehicle is sold, while the prior lifetime warranty applied only to the original owner.

Given marginal utility analysis, does it seem reasonable that consumers really prefer a 5-year, 100,000-mile warranty to a lifetime warranty? What customers actually benefit from this new warranty?

## Solving Problems

**10.** Assume a consumer has $20 to spend and for both products the marginal utilities are shown in the table below:

| Quantity | $MU_A$ | $MU_B$ |
|---|---|---|
| 1 | 20 | 30 |
| 2 | 10 | 10 |
| 3 | 5 | 2 |

Assume that each product sells for $5 a unit.

a. How many units of each product will the consumer purchase?

b. Assume the price of product B rises to $10 a unit. How will this consumer allocate her budget now?

c. If the prices of both products rise to $10 a unit, what will be the budget allocation?

**11.** Answer the questions following the table below.

| First-Run Movies | | | Bottles of Wine | | |
|---|---|---|---|---|---|
| Quantity | Total Utility | Marginal Utility | Quantity | Total Utility | Marginal Utility |
| 0 | 0 | ______ | 0 | 0 | ______ |
| 1 | 140 | ______ | 1 | 180 | ______ |
| 2 | 260 | ______ | 2 | 340 | ______ |
| 3 | 360 | ______ | 3 | 460 | ______ |
| 4 | 440 | ______ | 4 | 510 | ______ |
| 5 | 500 | ______ | 5 | 540 | ______ |

a. Complete the table.

b. Assume that you have $50 a month to devote to entertainment (column labeled First-Run Movies) and wine with dinner (column labeled Bottles of Wine). What will be your equilibrium allocation if the price to see a movie is $10 and a bottle of wine cost $10 as well?

c. A grape glut in California results in Napa Valley wine dropping in price to $5 a bottle, and you view this wine as a perfect substitute for what you were drinking earlier. Now what will be your equilibrium allocation between movies and wine?

d. Given this data, calculate your elasticity of demand for wine over these two prices (see the midpoint equation in Chapter 5).

# Answers to Questions in CheckPoints

## Check Point: Marginal Utility Analysis

As a general rule, you will eat more because the price for any additional item is zero, so theoretically you eat until the marginal utility is zero. The quality of food, in general, will be lower.

## Check Point: Using Marginal Utility Analysis

Convenience stores offer a small set of products at high prices nearer to home and have extended hours of operation. They also provide quicker service in that customers are in and out of the store quickly with what they need. The marginal utility of convenience overcomes the higher prices, so people shop because time is money. A 24/7 Safeway would have an impact on convenience store sales. At off-hours, supermarkets might be as fast as convenience stores, but cheaper.

# Appendix: Indifference Curve Analysis

**Marginal utility analysis provides** a good theoretical glimpse into the consumer decision-making process, yet it requires that utility be measured and that marginal utility per dollar be computed for innumerable possible consumption choices. In reality, measuring utility is impossible, as is mentally computing the marginal utility of thousands of products. To get around these difficulties, economists have developed a modern explanation of consumer decisions that does not require measuring utility. The foundation of this analysis is the indifference curve.

## Indifference Curves and Consumer Preferences

If consumers cannot precisely measure the exact satisfaction they receive from specific products, economists reason that people can distinguish between different bundles of goods and decide whether they prefer one bundle to another. This analysis entirely eliminates the idea of consumer satisfaction. It instead assumes that consumers will either be able to choose between any two bundles, or else be *indifferent* to which bundle is chosen. An **indifference curve** shows all points at which consumers' choices are indifferent—points at which consumers express no preference between two products.

**Indifference curve:** Shows all the combinations of two goods where the consumer is indifferent (gets the same level of satisfaction).

To illustrate how an indifference curve works, let us return to our original example of pizzas and wall climbing, now graphed in Figure APX-1. Compare the combination represented by point *b* (2 pizzas and 1.5 hours of climbing) and the combination at point *e* (2 pizzas and 0.5 hour of wall climbing). Which would you prefer, assuming you enjoy both of

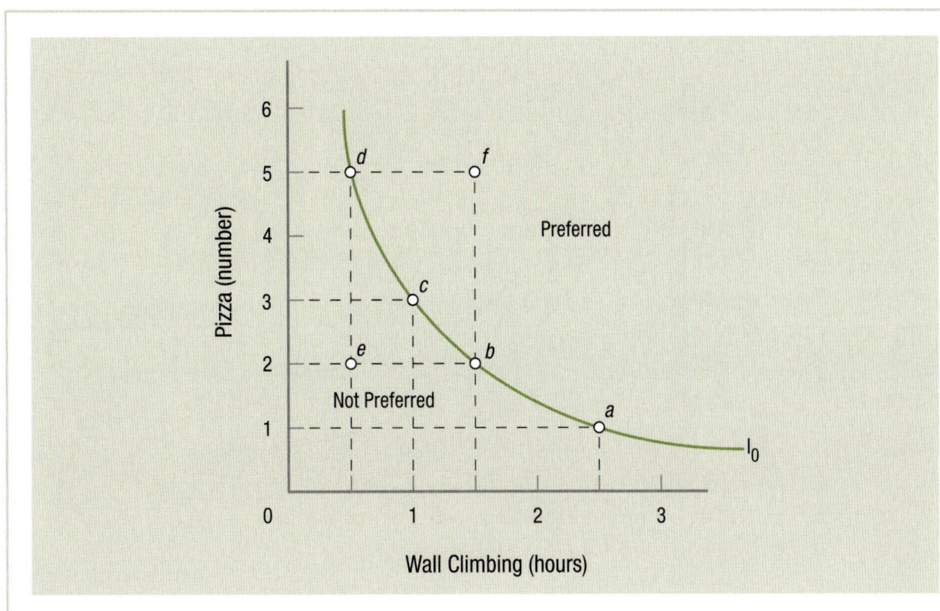


**FIGURE APX-1—An Indifference Curve**

All of the different possible combinations lying on the indifference curve $I_0$ represent bundles of goods for which you are indifferent—you would just as soon have any one of these combinations as any other. But compare the combination represented by point *b* and the combination at point *e*. Which would you prefer? Point *b*, of course, because you get more. All points upward and to the right are preferred to all points on indifference curve $I_0$.

these activities? Clearly, the combination at point *b* is preferable to the combination at point *e* since you get the same amount of pizza but more wall climbing. By the same logic, bundle *f* is preferable to bundle *b* because you get the same amount of climbing, but 3 more pizzas.

These choices have all been easy enough to make. But now assume you are offered bundles *d* and *b*. Bundle *d* contains more pizzas than bundle *b*, but bundle *b* has more climbing time. Given this choice, you may well conclude that you do not care which bundle you get—you are indifferent. In fact, all of the different possible combinations lying on the indifference curve $I_0$ represent bundles for which you are indifferent, such that you would just as soon have any one of these combinations as any other. And this tells us what an indifference curve is: It identifies all possible combinations of two products that offer consumers the same level of satisfaction or utility. Notice that this mode of analysis does not require us to consider the precise quantity of utility that various bundles yield, but only whether one bundle would be preferable to another.

## Properties of Indifference Curves

Indifference curves have negative slopes and are convex to the origin; they bow inward, that is. They have negative slopes because we assume consumers will generally prefer to have more, rather than less, of each product. Yet, to obtain more of one product and maintain the same level of satisfaction, consumers must give up some quantity of the other product. Hence, the negative slope.

Indifference curves are bowed inward toward the origin because of the law of diminishing marginal utility discussed earlier. When you have a lot of pizzas (point *d*), you are willing to give up 2 pizzas to obtain another half-hour of climbing (moving from point *d* to point *c*). But once you have plenty of wall time, yet few pizzas (point *b*), you are unwilling to give up as many pizzas to get more climbing time. This is the law of diminishing marginal utility at work: As we consume more of any particular product, the satisfaction we derive from consuming additional units of this product declines.

## Indifference (or Preference) Maps

**Indifference map:** An infinite set of indifference curves where each curve represents a different level of utility or satisfaction.

An indifference curve is a curve that represents a set of product bundles to which a consumer is indifferent. An **indifference map,** or *preference map,* is an infinite set of indifference curves, each representing a different level of satisfaction. Three possible indifference curves, forming part of a preference map, are shown in Figure APX-2.

**FIGURE APX-2—Three Indifference Curves for Pizza and Wall Climbing (An Indifference Map)**

An indifference map, or preference map, contains an infinite set of indifference curves, each representing a different level of satisfaction. Three possible indifference curves for pizzas and wall climbing, forming part of a preference map, are shown here.

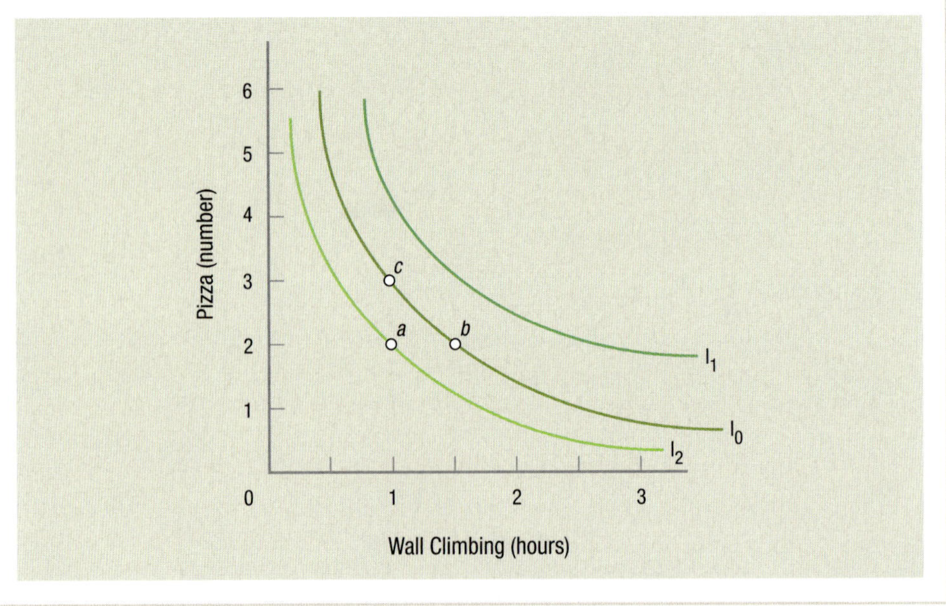

## *Issue:* Auto Advertisements: Utility Versus Indifference Curves

**Contrast ads for** luxury autos with ads for more prosaic autos such as minivans (denigrated by the trendsetters as the vehicle for "soccer moms"). Why do ads for luxury autos often have few words but instead have images of fancy houses and deserted beaches, while ads for minivans show a passenger door behind the driver's seat, or cup holders, or ways to fold up seats?

The luxury auto ads use an indifference curve approach. For this higher-priced item that often has a status component to it, the ads in effect ask consumers to compare in broad terms the luxury experience with the experience they have with their current auto. There is no intent to have consumers calculate utility for the various components of the luxury auto—consumers are not asked to calculate the utils received from their current auto's seat with the utils to be received from the high-priced leather seat of the luxury auto.

The less-expensive minivan's ads, in contrast, seem more in line with a marginal utility approach. Individual features are enumerated. Potential customers are pushed into doing at least some mental calculation for each feature. How many utils does one receive from an auto that has cup holders that handle juice boxes as well as cups, since juice boxes are part of a young child's normal equipment? So, for a less expensive product in the same product category, we see more of a marginal utility approach than an indifference curve approach.

We should be a little cautious in our hypothesis. Soft drinks are inexpensive, yet their ads use an indifference curve approach, probably because the differences between competitors are so small that a marginal utility approach does not make sense. Can you enumerate specific differences between Coca-Cola and Pepsi? Nevertheless, it is useful to look at advertisements for products and use the approaches discussed in this chapter to better understand what advertisers are trying to do.

Indifference curve $I_0$ is the same curve shown in Figure APX-1. Indifference curve $I_1$ provides consumers with greater satisfaction than $I_0$ since it is located farther from the origin. In general, utility rises as curves move outward from the origin, since these curves represent larger quantities of both goods. Conversely, indifference curve $I_2$ offers consumers less total satisfaction since it is located closer to the origin and represents smaller amounts of both products than $I_0$.

To confirm the observations just made, compare point *a* on indifference curve $I_2$ with point *b* on indifference curve $I_0$. Points *a* and *b* contain the same amount of pizza, but point *b* contains more climbing time. Hence, point *b* offers a higher level of satisfaction than point *a*. An analysis of points *a* and *c* yields a similar conclusion. Since both points *c* and *b* on indifference curve $I_0$ are preferred to point *a* on $I_2$, indifference curve $I_0$ must generally offer higher levels of satisfaction than the points on indifference curve $I_2$.

This result leads us to one final property of indifference curves: They do not intersect. Since all of the points on any indifference curve represent bundles of goods to which consumers are indifferent, if two indifference curves were to cross, this would mean some of the bundles they represent offered the same level of satisfaction (where the curves meet), but others did not (where the curves do not touch). Yet, this is a logical impossibility, since each indifference curve is defined as a set of bundles offering exactly the same level of satisfaction.

We now turn now to the question of how consumers use such preference maps to optimize their satisfaction within their budget constraints.

## Optimal Consumer Choice

Figure APX-3 on the next page superimposes a budget line of $50 per week onto a preference map that assumes pizzas cost $10 each and wall climbing costs $20 per hour. Maximizing your satisfaction on your limited income requires that you purchase some bundle of goods on the highest possible indifference curve. In this example, the best you can do is indicated by point *b:* 2 pizzas and 1.5 hours of wall climbing. Clearly, if you were to pick any other point on the budget line, your satisfaction would be diminished because you would end up on a lower indifference curve (points *a* or *c* in Figure APX-3). It follows that the indifference curve running tangent to the budget line identifies your best option, in this case the indifference curve that just touches the budget line at point *b*.

**FIGURE APX-3—Optimal Consumer Choice**

Maximizing your satisfaction on your limited income requires purchasing some bundle of goods on the highest possible indifference curve. The best you can do in this situation is indicated by point *b:* 2 pizzas and 1.5 hours of wall climbing. Indifference curve $I_0$ is the highest indifference curve that can be reached with the budget line shown.

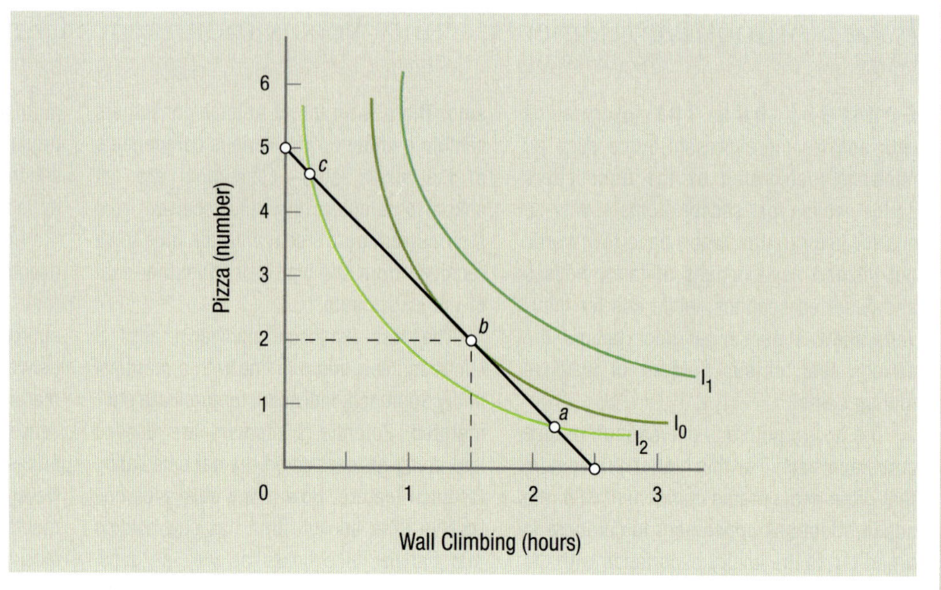


Of course, this is the same result we reached earlier using marginal utility analysis, specifically in Table 2. Notice, however, that using indifference curve analysis, we did not have to assume that utility can be measured. We were able to understand how you would allocate your budget between two goods so as to achieve the highest possible level of satisfaction, even without knowing exactly how high that level might be.

## Using Indifference Curves

Indifference curves are a useful device to help us understand consumer demand. Economists use indifference curves, for instance, to shed light on the impact of changes in consumer income and product substitution resulting from a change in product price. Indifference curve analysis, moreover, provides some insight into how households determine their supply of labor (this analysis, however, is left to a later chapter). Before we move on to applications of indifference curve analysis, however, we first need to derive a demand curve from an indifference map.

### Deriving Demand Curves

We derive the demand curve using indifference curve analysis in much the same way we did using marginal utility analysis. Panel A of Figure APX-4 restates the results of Figure APX-3: When you have a budget of $50 per week, the price of pizza is $10, and climbing is $20 per hour, your optimal choice is found at point *b*. In panel B, we want to plot the demand curve for wall climbing. We know that when wall climbing costs $20 per hour, you will climb for 1.5 hours, so let us indicate this on panel B by marking point *b*.

To fill out the demand curve, let us now increase the price of wall climbing to $30 per hour. This produces a new budget line, *cd.* (Point *d* is located at 1.66 hours because $50/$30 = 1.66 hours of possible wall climbing.) This shift in the budget line yields a new optimal choice at point *a* on indifference curve $I_2$, now indicating the highest level of satisfaction you can attain. As panel A shows, the ultimate result of this hike in the price of wall climbing to $30 an hour is a reduction in your climbing to 1 hour per week. Transferring this result to panel B, we mark point *a* where price = $30 and climbing hours = 1. Now connecting points *a* and *b* in panel B, we are left with the demand curve for wall climbing.

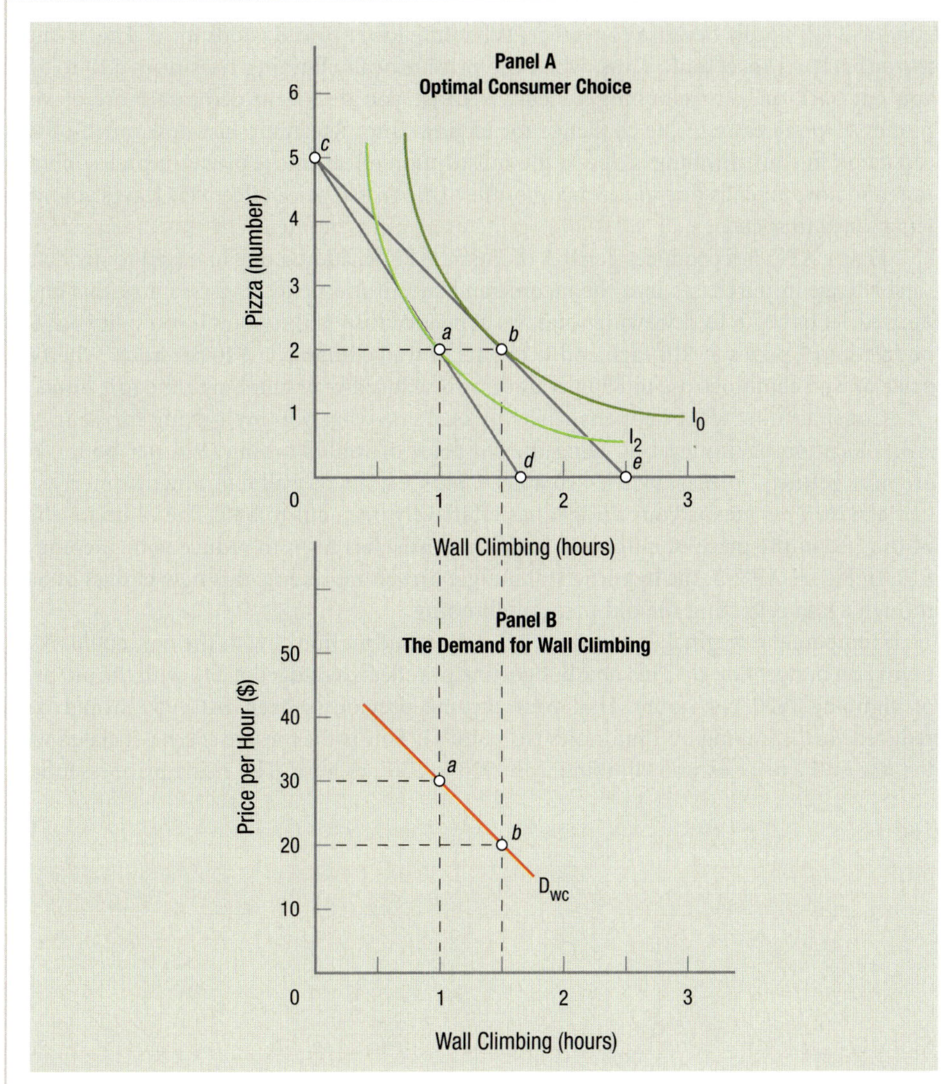


**FIGURE APX-4—Deriving the Demand for Wall Climbing Using Indifference Curve Analysis**

In panel A, when wall climbing costs \$20 per hour, your optimal choice is found at point *b*. When the price of wall climbing rises to \$30 per hour, this produces a new budget line, *cd*, shifting the optimal choice to point *a*. Transferring points *a* and *b* down to panel B and connecting the points generates the demand curve for wall climbing.

Once again, therefore, we arrive at the same conclusion using indifference curve analysis as we did earlier using marginal utility analysis. Both approaches are logical and elegant, and both approaches tell us something about the thought processes consumers must use as they make their spending decisions. Indifference curve analysis, however, arrives at its conclusion without requiring that utility be measurable or that consumers perform complex arithmetic computations.

## Income and Substitution Effects

Another way economists use indifference curves is to separate income and substitution effects when product prices change. First we need to distinguish between these two effects.

When the price of some product you regularly purchase goes up, your spendable income is thereby essentially reduced. If you always buy a latte a day, for instance, and you continue to do so even when the price of lattes goes up, you must then reduce your consumption of other goods. This essentially amounts to a reduction in your income. And we know that when income falls, the consumption of normal goods likewise declines. Hence, when higher prices essentially reduce consumer incomes, the quantity demanded for normal goods generally falls. Economists call this the **income effect.**

Income effect: When higher prices essentially reduce consumer income, the quantity demanded for normal goods falls.

**Substitution effect:** When the price of one good rises, consumers will substitute other goods for that good, so the quantity demanded for the higher priced good falls.

When the price of a particular good rises, meanwhile, the quantity demanded of that good will fall simply because consumers substitute lower priced goods for it. This is called the **substitution effect.** Thus, when the price of wall climbing rises from $20 to $30, you cut back on your climbing, in part, because you decide to dedicate more of your money to pizza eating. The challenge for us now is to determine just how much of this reduction in your climbing is due to the substitution effect (more pizzas mean less climbing) and how much is due to the income effect (the rise in price effectively leaves you with less money to spend).

Figure APX-5 reproduces panel A of Figure APX-4, adding one line (*gh*) to divide the total change in purchases into the income and substitution effects. To see how this line is derived, let us begin by reviewing what has happened thus far. At point *b* you split your $50 budget into 2 pizzas at $10 each and 1.5 hours of wall climbing at $20 per hour. When the price of wall climbing rose to $30 per hour, you reduced your climbing time to 1 hour.

Consider now what happens when we evaluate what you are getting for your *current* allocation of money, but using the *old* price of wall climbing ($20 per hour). You are now getting 2 pizzas, worth $10 apiece, plus 1 hour of wall climbing, formerly valued at $20. This means your budget has effectively been cut to $40. The ultimate effect of the rise in the price of climbing, in other words, has been to reduce your income by $10. In Figure APX-5, the hypothetical budget line *gh* represents this new budget of $40, though again reflecting the old price of climbing.

Compare the original equilibrium point *b* on budget line *ce* with the new equilibrium point *f* on budget line *gh*. This new budget line *gh* reflects a budget of $40 with the old price of climbing ($20 per hour). Had your income previously been $40, you would have reduced your climbing by 15 minutes (to point *f*). This is the *income effect* associated with the rise in the price of wall climbing from $20 to $30 per hour. The rising price essentially

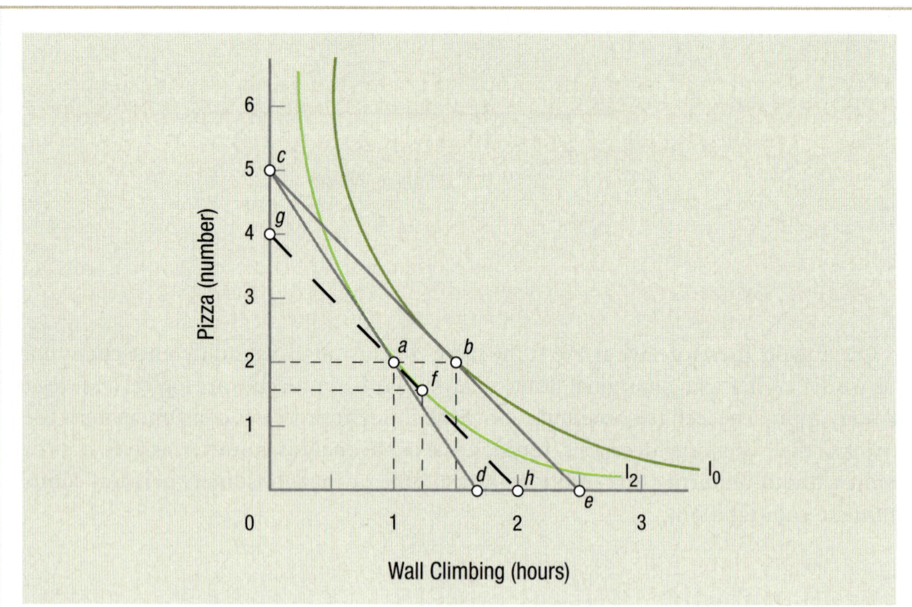


**FIGURE APX-5—Income and Substitution Effects**

Panel A of Figure APX-4 is reproduced in this figure. The price of climbing having risen to $30 per hour, this effectively reduces your budget to $40 per week, assuming you continue climbing as much as you did before. Line *gh* represents a new budget of $40, though reflecting the old price of climbing. This new budget line *gh* allows us to divide the total change in purchases into the income and substitution effects. Increasing the price of wall climbing from $20 to $30 an hour would mean a reduction in wall climbing (holding income constant at $40) from point *f* to point *a*. This is the substitution effect. The income effect is thus the reduction in consumption from point *b* to point *f*. Adding both effects together yields the total reduction.

reduced your income, and your reduction in wall climbing due to this income reduction alone is 15 minutes.

The change in price is the only thing that differentiates equilibrium point *a* from point *f*, income having been held constant. This difference of 15 minutes between point *f* and point *a* therefore represents a *substitution effect*. It is the effect that comes from changing the price of climbing, while holding income constant.

Combined, the substitution and income effects constitute the entire change in quantity demanded when the price of wall climbing rises by $10 per hour. The income effect (movement from point *b* to point *f*) is a movement from one budget line to another. The substitution effect (movement from point *f* to point *a*) is a movement along the new budget line. Together, they represent the total change in quantity demanded. In this case the income and substitution effects were the same, 15 minutes, but this will not always be the case.

This chapter examined how consumers and households make decisions. Households attempt to maximize their well-being or satisfaction within the constraints of limited incomes. We have seen that the analysis of consumer decisions can be approached in two different ways, using marginal utility analysis or indifference curve analysis.

Marginal utility analysis assumes that consumers can readily measure utility and make complex calculations regarding the utility of various possible consumption choices. Both of these assumptions are empirically rather dubious. This does not, however, invalidate marginal utility analysis; it just makes it difficult to use and test in an empirical context. Indifference curve analysis gives us a more powerful set of analytical tools without these restrictive assumptions.

## *Issue:* Economic Analysis of Terrorism

**Since the attack** on the World Trade Center on September 11, 2001, combating terrorism has taken center stage in national politics and was an important issue in the 2008 election. Combating terrorism is a complicated, difficult problem that will confront the country for several generations to come. In this brief section, the household indifference curve model outlined in this appendix is applied to this problem. This discussion is based on work by Professors Enders and Sandler. Using the household model, terrorists are treated as rational actors who maximize a set of goals subject to constrained resources.

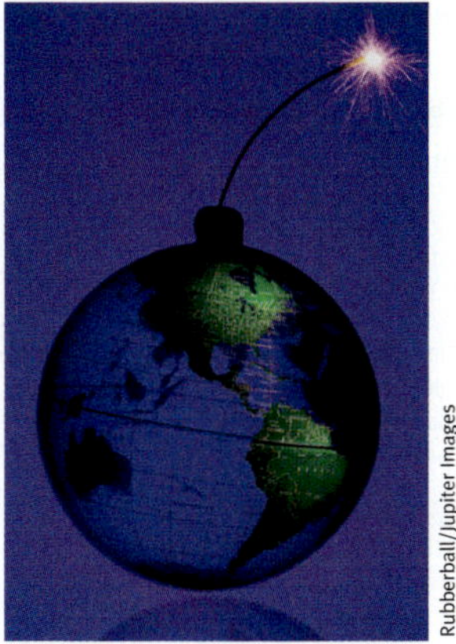


Terrorist campaigns are not new and extend back to the French Revolution, Russian Revolutions, the IRA campaign in Northern Ireland, and the Palestinian (PLO) struggle against Israel. In essence, as Enders and Sandler note, "Terrorists want to circumvent the normal political channels/procedures and create political change through threats and violence." Terrorism tactics include bombings, assassinations, threats, suicide attacks, and kidnappings all designed to garner support for their cause through extensive media coverage.

Let's apply our household indifference curve model to terrorist activities. Every terrorist organization can achieve its goals using violent terrorist activities *V* and nonviolent political means *N*. The violent means were just described; the nonviolent means include running candidates for political election and acts of civil disobedience. These activities can be modeled using the indifference curves shown in the figure below. Violent activities can be substituted for nonviolent activities along the indifference curves shown. As long as the goal of more support is reached, terrorists would be indifferent between violent terrorist

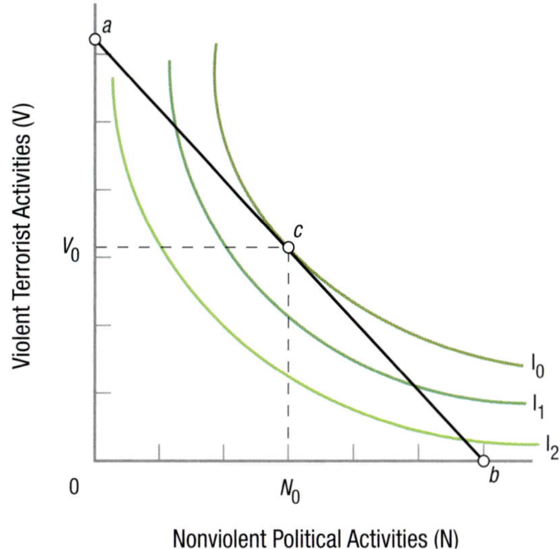


*continued*

activity and nonviolent political activity. The level of the group's utility (or support for their cause) increases for indifference curves moving away from the origin ($I_2 < I_1 < I_0$). From the perspective of terrorist groups, being able to engage in more of both activities is preferable.

Similar to the households we described earlier, terrorist groups do not have unlimited resources (terrorist activities require funding) and face a budget constraint similar to line *ab* shown in the figure. Given the groups' limited resources, if all of their activities are devoted to nonviolent activity, they can engage in 0*b* nonviolent acts, and if all their energies are devoted to terrorism, they can complete 0*a* levels of terrorism. Terrorists maximize their "utility" by engaging in $V_0$ violent terrorist acts and undertaking $N_0$ political activities (point *c*). This is the best they can do with their limited resources; any other combination will put them on a lower indifference curve. If terrorists can shift their budget constraint out, they will find themselves on a higher indifference curve, with greater opportunities for both violent and nonviolent activities.

## Policy Implications

What can this simple model tell policymakers about how to fight terrorism? Simply, just as terrorist groups want to shift their budget constraints out, governments want to shift the terrorists' budget (or resource) constraints in.

Governments have two general approaches to fighting terrorism, defensive and offensive (proactive). Defensive policies include elaborate airport screening procedures, inspection activities at ports for cargo, and sophisticated protections or barriers at likely targets. Proactive policies include military campaigns against terrorist strongholds, intelligence activities intended to infiltrate terrorist cells, and cooperation with other governments to freeze financial resources and block transfers of funds to potential terrorist cells.

First, let's look at defensive antiterrorist policies. For example, heightening security measures at airports raises the cost of using airplanes to perpetrate violent terrorist actions. Terrorists have to engage in more elaborate planning, or they might shift resources from targets harder to attack before but now easier because of the relative shift in what is now a hard target or a soft target. If defensive antiterror measures increase the cost (price) of violent acts, the resource constraint rotates from *ab* to *db* in the next figure. There is a rotation of the resource constraint because the cost of violent terrorist activities rises, but there is no change in the cost of nonviolent political activities. The increase in the price of violent activities establishes a new equilibrium at point *e* with a reduction in violence to $V_1$ and an increase of political activities to $N_1$.

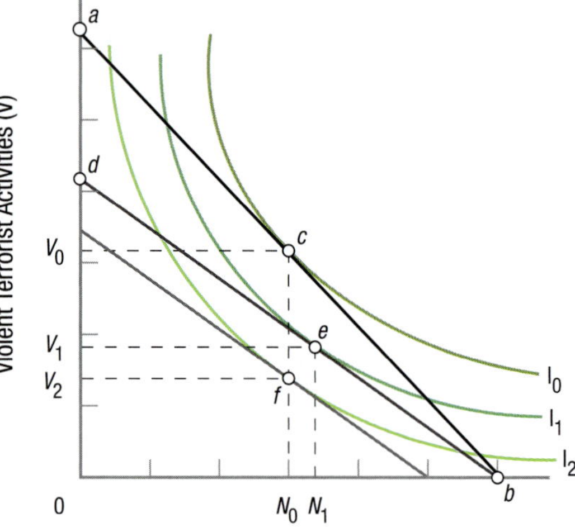


In a similar way, if government restricts nonviolent political activities, the result is fewer nonviolent activities, but an upsurge in violent terrorist activities. Try this yourself by tilting the original budget line *ab* inward at the bottom so that point *b* moves toward the origin. Then look at the new equilibrium point. This result is consistent with a study by Alan Krueger showing that terrorists tend to come from countries with low levels of civil liberties. He concludes, "When nonviolent means of protest are curtailed, malcontents appear to be more likely to turn to terrorist tactics." Professor Krueger's research also goes a long way to debunk the widely held, often-repeated belief that "instead of being drawn from the ranks of the poor . . . terrorists tend to be drawn from well educated, middle class or high income families."

Alternatively, proactive antiterror measures affect the terrorist resource (or budget) constraint, but in a different way. Proactive intelligence and infiltration of terrorist cells will increase the costs of maintaining a terrorist cell and so rotate the terrorist resource constraint as we saw with defensive antiterrorist measures, but other proactive measures have a different effect. Military campaigns, freezing of financial assets, and making transfers of purported terrorist funds more difficult reduce the resources available for terrorist activities and nonviolent political activities. This shifts the entire budget constraint in, and a new equilibrium is established at point *f*. Now, compared to the previous equilibrium at point *e*, terrorism declines to $V_2$ and in this case nonviolent political activities also decline to $N_0$.

What comes from this analysis is confirmation of the commonsense notion that both defensive and proactive antiterrorist measures reduce terrorism. What we see a little clearer is the different effects of each type of measure. Using the basic household model to describe terrorist activities, we can conclude that a successful antiterrorist campaign will most likely include both defensive and proactive elements that work in tandem to make terrorist activities more costly and reduce the resources available to terrorist groups.

Sources: Walter Enders and Todd Sandler, *The Political Economy of Terrorism* (New York: Cambridge University Press), 2006. Enders and Sandler, *The Political Economy of Terrorism*, p. 4. Alan Krueger, *What Makes a Terrorist: Economics and the Roots of Terrorism* (Princeton, NJ: Princeton University Press), 2007; and David Wessel, "Princeton Economist Says Lack of Civil Liberties, Not Poverty, Breeds Terrorism," *Wall Street Journal*, July 5, 2007, p. A2.

**CHECKPOINT**

### INDIFFERENCE CURVE ANALYSIS

- Indifference curve analysis does not require utility measurement. All it requires is that consumers can choose between different bundles of goods.
- An indifference curve shows all the combinations of two goods where the consumer has the same level of satisfaction.
- Indifference curves have negative slopes, are convex to the origin due to the law of diminishing marginal utility, and indifference curves do not intersect.
- An indifference map is an infinite set of indifference curves.
- Consumer equilibrium occurs where the budget line is tangent to the highest indifference curve.
- When the price of one product rises, not only will your consumption of that product fall (the substitution effect), but also your relative income will be reduced as well, and for normal goods you will consume less (the income effect). The opposite occurs when price falls.

**QUESTION:** Consumers face a set of goods called "credence goods." These are goods where customers must "take it on faith that the supplier has given them what they need and no more."[2] Examples include surgeons, auto mechanics, and taxis. These experts tell us what medical procedures, repairs, and routes we require to satisfy our needs, and very often we don't know the price until the work is done. If we do not know the price and cannot establish whether we actually need some of these goods, how does this square with our indifference curve analysis?

Answers to the Checkpoint question can be found at the end of this chapter.

## Appendix Key Concepts



## Appendix Summary

### Indifference Curve Analysis

An indifference curve graphically represents all of the combinations of two products that represent the same level of satisfaction to consumers. An indifference curve, in other words, identifies a set of possible consumption combinations that leaves the consumer indifferent.

Like marginal utility analysis, indifference curve analysis helps economists understand how consumers allocate their limited budgets among diverse goods. In fact, indifference curve analysis leads to the same theoretical conclusions as marginal utility analysis. It is subject to less restrictive assumptions, however, in that it does not require that consumers actually measure utility or calculate marginal utility per dollar; instead, consumers can decide which bundles of goods they would prefer to consume under varying circumstances.

The income effect is a change in quantity demanded that comes about as a result of a change in income due to a change in price. When the price of some regularly purchased

[2] "Economic Focus: Sawbones, Cowboys and Cheats," *Economist,* April 15, 2006.

good rises, this leaves consumers with less money to spend buying goods of all sorts. The rise in price, therefore, effectively reduces consumer income, resulting in a drop in demand for most normal goods, often including the good whose price has risen.

When the price of some good rises, quantity demanded for the good will typically fall as consumers begin purchasing cheaper substitute products; this is the substitution effect. Note that when the price of a product rises, quantity demanded for it will typically fall, partially due to the income effect, and partially due to the substitution effect; indifference curve analysis helps us determine how much of this drop in quantity demanded is due to each effect.

# Appendix Questions and Problems

## Check Your Understanding

1. Indifference curves cannot intersect. Why not?
2. Explain why the following bundles of apples (A) and bananas (B) cannot be on the same indifference curve: (4A, 2B); (1A, 5B); (4A, 3B).
3. Answer the following questions using the figure below:

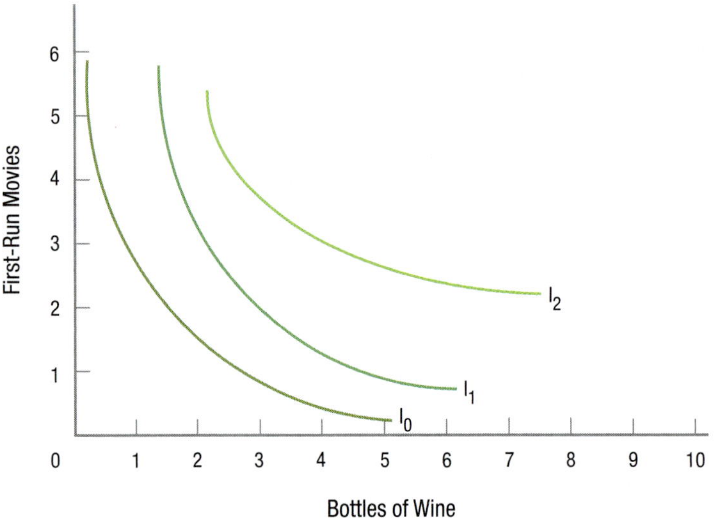


a. Assume that you have $50 a month to devote to entertainment (First-Run Movies) and wine with dinner (Bottles of Wine). What will be your equilibrium allocation if the price to see a movie or buy a bottle of wine is $10? Graph the equilibrium on the figure and label it point *a*.

b. A grape glut in California results in Napa Valley wine dropping in price to $5 a bottle, and you view this wine as a perfect substitute for what you were drinking earlier. Now what will be your equilibrium allocation between movies and wine? Graph that on the figure and label the new equilibrium as point *b*.

# Answers to Appendix Checkpoint Question

## CheckPoint: Indifference Curve Analysis

Not very well. They are largely a problem of incomplete information and a challenging problem for consumers. If doctors make more money on complex operations, they will be inclined to prescribe them more often. One study found that doctors elect surgery for themselves less often than nondoctors. As long as consumers are aware of the incentive structure of these transactions, they can build this into the decision calculus, but ultimately, information asymmetries are not adequately represented in this model.

# Production and Cost

Robert Gilhooly/Alamy

**Twenty five years ago,** coffee was a commodity product. In the United States, coffee obtained in corporate settings was often dispensed in horrid vending machines: You put your 50 cents in, pressed the button, hoped the paper cup that dropped on the grill would not tip too much the wrong way or even fall out, and waited for the usually tasteless liquid to pour into the paper cup. Coffee brands such as Maxwell House ("good to the last drop") and Folger's advertised on television, but the difference between each was minimal. Not very satisfying, but no great pressure for change, either: How could a new company make any money in such a commodity market?

As you sip your latte or Frappuccino now, it may be hard to imagine a world without Starbucks. Howard Schultz, the key person in the development and growth of Starbucks, was touring the coffee houses in Rome when he wondered why coffee in the United States did not come up to European standards. He thought people would appreciate a superior product that brought with it the coffee-house experience. The number of Starbucks establishments in major cities in the United States shows he was right. So does the almost inconceivable notion of a world without double-shot espressos and lattes.

With entrepreneurs such as Howard Schultz, the idea comes first. They perceive a market need. The next thing that probably goes through their minds is: Can I make a profit out of it? To gauge profits, entrepreneurs have to estimate revenues and costs.

In this chapter, we look at what motivates firms to do what they do—profits. We then look at the production and cost part of the profit equation. In further chapters, we add the revenue part to the production part. In this way, we begin to examine what lies behind supply curves.

**After studying this chapter you should be able to:**

- ☐ Describe the nature of firms and markets.
- ☐ Describe the nature of economic costs and profits.
- ☐ Differentiate between the short run and long run.
- ☐ Describe the nature of short-run production, total product, marginal product, and average product.
- ☐ Differentiate between increasing, constant, and decreasing returns.
- ☐ Describe the nature of short-run costs, fixed costs, variable costs, average costs, and marginal costs.
- ☐ Use graphs to show the relationship between short-run average fixed cost, average variable cost, average total cost, and marginal cost curves.
- ☐ Describe long-run costs.
- ☐ Describe the reasons for economies and diseconomies of scale.

# Firms, Profits, and Economic Costs

Firms produce the products and services that you purchase. Most of the business news you see or read concerns giant corporations, but consumers deal most often with small family-owned firms in their neighborhoods. These small firms run the gamut from pizza parlors and CD shops to barber and beauty shops, small garages, and locally owned McDonald's franchises.

As consumers, we take for granted many of the things producers *voluntarily* provide in the market. We all expect businesses to provide us with our morning lattes, fuel for our cars, and up-to-date books for us to read. In fact, it is entrepreneurs in the pursuit of profits who meet all of our needs as consumers.

## Firms

A **firm** is an economic institution that transforms inputs, or factors of production, into outputs, or products for consumers. Most firms begin as family enterprises or small partnerships. When successful, these firms can evolve into corporations of considerable size.

**Firm:** An economic institution that transforms resources (factors of production) into outputs for consumers.

In the process of producing goods for consumers, firms must make numerous decisions. First, they have to determine a market need. Then, most broadly, firms must decide what quantity of output to produce, how to produce it, and what inputs to employ. The latter two decisions depend on the production technology the firm selects.

Any given product can typically be produced in a wide variety of ways. Some businesses, like McDonald's franchises and Dunkin' Donuts shops, use considerable amounts of capital equipment, whereas others, such as T-shirt shops and wok eateries, require very little. Even among similar firms, the quality and quantity of resources available often determine what technologies are used. Firms located in areas with an abundance of low-cost labor tend to use low-technology, labor-intensive production methods. In areas where high-skill, high-wage labor is the norm, production is more often done by high-technology, capital-intensive processes.

## Entrepreneurs

If a product or service is to be provided to the market, someone must first assume the risk of raising the required capital, assembling workers and raw materials, producing the product, and, finally, offering it for sale. Markets provide incentives and signals, but it is entrepreneurs who provide products and services by taking risks in the hopes of earning profits.

Recent research in neuroscience has shown that "entrepreneurs' brains were more active in the region responsible for taking risky or 'hot' decisions.[1] The research compared entrepreneurs who had founded at least two high-tech firms with senior managers from the private and public sectors. When the decisions were "emotionally neutral," the groups performed the same, but when the decisions were "hot" or risky, the entrepreneurs were more impulsive and more mentally flexible. It is this willingness to take risk to earn profits that distinguishes entrepreneurs from the rest of us.

In the United States, 12% of people ages 18 to 64 classify themselves as entrepreneurs. This means they are running start-up businesses or businesses less than 42 months old. Entrepreneurial rates in Europe are only half the American rate, and Japanese entrepreneurship is less than 2%.[2]

Entrepreneurs can be divided into three basic business structures: sole proprietorships (one owner), partnerships (two or more owners), and corporations (many stockholders). The United States has more than 25 million businesses, over 70% of them sole

[1] Andrew Lawrence, et al., "The Innovative Brain," *Nature,* November 13, 2008, pp. 168–69.

[2] *The Economist,* "Enterprising Rising," January 8, 2004, p. 55.

## By the *Numbers*

### Innovation, Productivity, and Costs Rule Business

To remain in business, firms must innovate not only by improving the products they make but also by controlling their costs. Controlling costs is done by introducing new technologies in production and increasing their productivity. This holds for the service sector as well.

**The cost of industrial robots** has fallen over 70% since 1990.

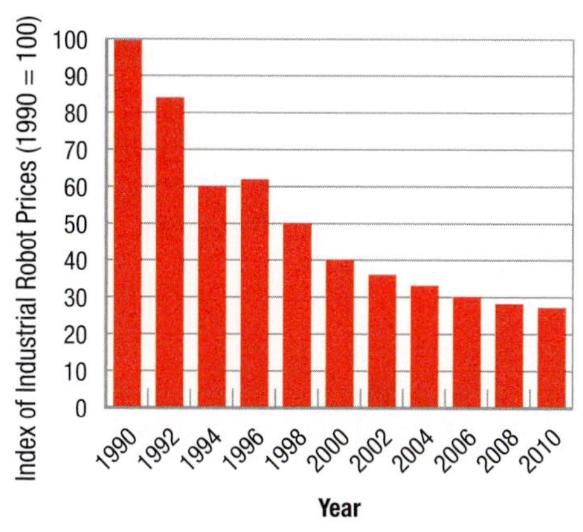

Christopher Honeywell/Alamy

**Productivity has risen** over 50% since 1990.

**$9 Billion**
Annual revenue needed to support a new semiconductor fabrication plant

**9.17 hours**
Time spent by the average American on government paperwork

**Domestic Content of Autos**

| | |
|---|---|
| Domestic manufacturers | 80% |
| Foreign owned | 65% |

We've found the key to productivity. It's Fred, down in the shop. He makes the stuff."

From the Wall Street Journal, Permission Cartoon Features Syndicate

**Cost Breakdown for an iPod**

| | |
|---|---|
| Retail Price | $299 |
| Costs: | |
| Hard drive | 73 |
| Display module | 20 |
| Video processor chip | 8 |
| Controller chip | 5 |
| Misc. components | 34 |
| Assembly | 4 |
| Distribution costs | 75 |
| Profit for Apple | 80 |

**Capacity utilization and employment cost growth** have both fallen in recent years. Notice how both fall during recessions (dark bands).

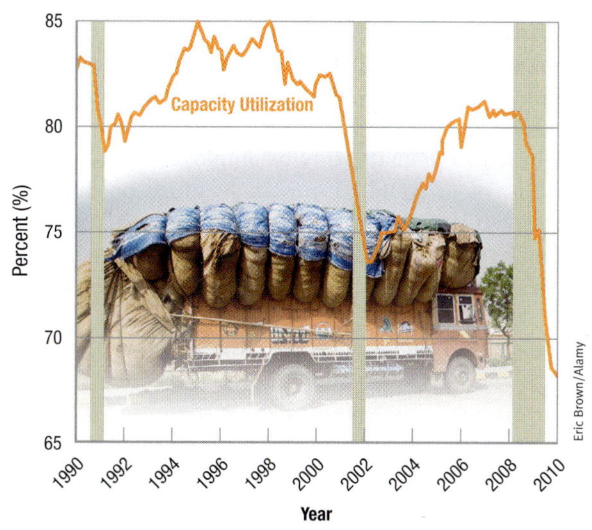


Eric Brown/Alamy

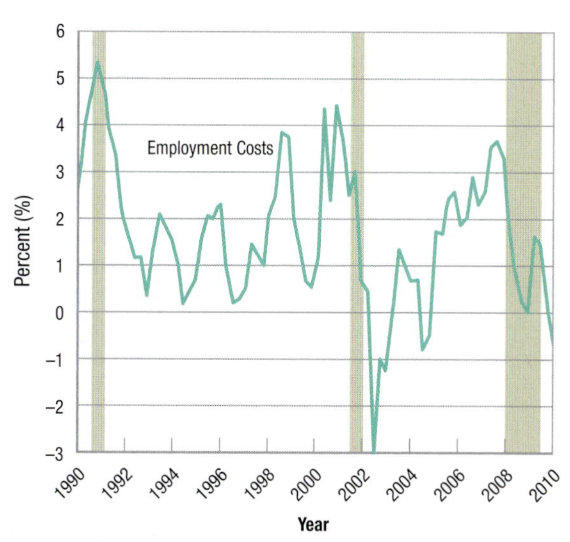

proprietorships or small businesses. Only 20% of American businesses are corporations. Nevertheless, corporations sell nearly 90% of all products and services in the United States. Likewise, around the world, the corporate form of business has become the dominant form. To see why, we must first take a brief look at the advantages and disadvantages of each business structure.

## Sole Proprietors

**Sole proprietor:** A type of business structure composed of a single owner who supervises and manages the business and is subject to unlimited liability.

The **sole proprietor** represents the most basic form of business organization. A proprietorship is composed of one owner, who usually supervises the business operation. Local restaurants, dry cleaning businesses, and auto repair shops are often sole proprietorships. A sole proprietorship is easy to establish and manage, having much less paperwork associated with it than other forms of business organization. But the proprietorship has disadvantages. Single owners are often limited in their ability to raise capital. In many instances, all management responsibilities fall on this single individual. And most important, the personal assets of the owner are subject to unlimited liability. If you as a sole proprietor own a pizza shop and someone slips on your floor, he or she can sue you and take away your house and your life savings if you do not have sufficient insurance.

## Partnerships

**Partnership:** Similar to a sole proprietorship, but involves more than one owner who shares the management of the business. Partnerships are also subject to unlimited liability.

**Partnerships** are similar to sole proprietorships except that they have more than one owner. Establishing a partnership usually requires signing a legal partnership document. Partnerships find it easier to raise capital and spread around the management responsibilities. Like sole proprietors, however, partners are subject to unlimited liability, not only for their share of the business, but for the entire business. If your partner takes off for Bermuda, you are left to pay all the bills, even those your partner incurred. The death of one partner dissolves a partnership, unless other arrangements have been concluded ahead of time. In any case, the death of a partner often creates problems for the continuity of the business.

## Corporations

**Corporation:** A business structure that has most of the legal rights of individuals, and in addition, the corporation can issue stock to raise capital. Stockholders' liability is limited to the value of their stock.

The **corporation** is today the premier form of business organization in most of the world. Roughly 5,000 American corporations sell nearly $20 trillion worth of goods and services every year. This is an amazing statistic when you consider that the country's nearly 20 million sole proprietorships have sales totaling just over $1 trillion. Clearly, corporations are structured in a way that enhances growth and efficiency.

Corporations possess most of the legal rights of individuals; in addition, they are able to issue stock to raise capital, and most significantly, the liability of individual owners (i.e., stockholders) is limited to the amount they have invested in (or paid for) the stock. This is what distinguishes corporations from the other forms of business organization: the ability to raise large amounts of capital because of limited liability.

Some scholars argue that corporations are the greatest engines of economic prosperity ever known.[3] Daniel Akst wrote, "When I worked for a big company, there was a miracle in the office every couple of weeks, just like clockwork. It happened every payday, when sizable checks were distributed to a small army of employees who also enjoyed health and retirement benefits. Few of us could have made as much on our own, and somehow there was always money left over for the shareholders as well."[4] Without the corporate umbrella, most of the jobs we hold would not exist; most of the products we use would not have been invented; and our standard of living would be a fraction of what it is today.

Business owners of all types are people who react to the profit incentives of the market.

[3] John Micklethwait and Adrian Wooldridge, *The Company: A Short History of a Revolutionary Idea* (New York: The Modern Library), 2003.

[4] Daniel Akst, "Where Those Paychecks Come From," *Wall Street Journal*, February 3, 2004.

## *Issue:* Innovation and the Development of the iPod

**Your grandmother** may have one of those big, heavy radios that were so popular in the 1950s. If you removed the back, you would see a bunch of vacuum tubes. Manufacturers sought to increase the power of each vacuum tube, or get more tubes into the back of each radio. In the early 1960s, Akio Morita of Sony developed the transistor radio, a flimsy-looking yet portable handheld radio that could be taken with you wherever you went. The old-style radio manufacturers pooh-poohed the Sony transistor radio, saying that it was cheap and looked cheap. Maybe more importantly, the manufacturers were bothered aesthetically by the transistor radio: It just was not as elegant as the radio box. Consumers thought otherwise, and the transistor radio was a big hit. And the transistor radio begat the Sony *Walkman.* And the *Walkman* probably had a role in inspiring the creation of the iPod.

The iPod moved consumers away from albums to individual songs. As the iPod, iPhone, and Microsoft's Zune develop, these devices' capabilities are being expanded to carry music, video, cell service, email, PDA functionality, and so on. So when you are walking along listening to your iPod or using your iPhone, consider for a moment how entrepreneurs searching for market needs in the hope of generating profits create these new products for you.

Radius/Jupiter Images

## Profits

Entrepreneurs and firms employ resources and turn out products with the goal of making profits. **Profit** is simply the difference between total revenue and total cost.

**Profit:** Equal to the difference between total revenue and total cost.

*Total* **revenue** is the amount of money a firm receives from the sales of its products. It is equal to the price per unit times the number of units sold (TR $= p \times q$). Note, we use lower case p and q when we are dealing with an individual firm and use upper case when describing a market. *Total cost* includes both out-of-pocket expenses and opportunity costs; we will discuss this concept shortly.

**Revenue:** Equal to price per unit times quantity sold.

Economists explicitly assume that firms proceed rationally and have the maximization of profits as their primary objective. Alternative behavioral assumptions for firms have been tested, including sales maximization, "satisfactory" profits, and various goals for market share. The biography of Nobel Prize winner Herbert Simon discusses these. Although these more complex assumptions for firm behavior often predict different outcomes, economists have not been persuaded that any of them yield results superior to those of the profit maximization approach. Profit maximization has stood the test of time, and thus we will assume it is the primary economic goal of firms.

## Economic Costs

Economists approach business costs and profits from the opportunity cost perspective discussed in Chapter 2. They separate costs into explicit costs, or out-of-pocket expenses, and implicit costs, or opportunity costs. **Economic costs** are the sum of explicit and implicit costs.

**Economic costs:** The sum of explicit (out-of-pocket) and implicit (opportunity) costs.

**Explicit costs** are those expenses paid directly to some other economic entity. These include wages, lease payments, expenditures for raw materials, taxes, utilities, and so on. A company can easily determine its explicit costs by summing all of the checks it has written during the normal course of doing business.

**Explicit costs:** Those expenses paid directly to another economic entity, including wages, lease payments, taxes, and utilities.

**Implicit costs** refer to all of the opportunity costs of using resources that belong to the firm. These include depreciation, the depletion of business assets, and the opportunity cost of a firm's capital. In any business, some assets are depleted over time. Machines, cars, and office equipment depreciate with use and time. Finite oil or mineral deposits are depleted as they are mined or pumped. Even though firms do not actually pay any cash as

**Implicit costs:** The opportunity costs of using resources that belong to the firm, including depreciation, depletion of business assets, and the opportunity cost of the firm's capital employed in the business.

these assets are worn down or used up, these costs nonetheless represent real expenses to the firm.

Another major component of implicit costs is the capital firms have invested. Even small firms incur large implicit costs from their capital investment. Small entrepreneurs, for example, must invest both their own capital and labor into their businesses. Such people could normally be working for someone else, so their "lost salary" must be treated as an implicit cost when determining the true profitability of their businesses. Similarly, any capital invested in a business enterprise could just as well be earning interest in a bank account or returning dividends and capital gains through the purchase of stock in other enterprises. Though not directly paid out as expenses, these forgone earnings nonetheless represent implicit costs for the firm.

## Sunk Costs

**Sunk costs:** Those costs that have been incurred and cannot be recovered, including, for example, funds spent on existing technology that have become obsolete and past advertising that has run in the media.

**Sunk costs** are costs that have already been incurred and *cannot* be recovered. Examples include previous bets in a poker hand, the tuition you paid this semester, and expenditures on advertising that have run in the media. For example, beyond some point in the term, tuition is a sunk cost. If you drop a course near the beginning of the term and pay by credit hour, you might get a refund for some of the cost of this course. After several weeks in the term, however, most colleges do not provide any refund for dropped courses. Should you *not* drop a course you are doing poorly in and likely will not get better in simply because you paid tuition you cannot get back? Of course not—the tuition is a sunk cost and should be irrelevant to your decision to drop the course or not.

Sunk costs are costs that have been incurred in the past, and you are unable to get them back. These expenses are gone, and future decisions should ignore them. The future benefits from the decision either exceed the future costs or the project is not undertaken, no matter how much has already been spent. The decision to advertise a product in a new magazine depends on the benefits and costs of that advertising, not how much has been spent on television ads in the past. You will hear the phrase that "sunk costs are sunk," meaning ignore them; they are gone.

## Economic and Normal Profits

Economists define a *normal rate of return* on the capital invested in a firm as the return just sufficient to keep investors satisfied, and thus just sufficient to keep capital in the business over the long run. The normal rate of return therefore represents the opportunity cost of capital. If a firm's rate of return on capital falls below this rate, investors will put their capital to use elsewhere, and the firm will likely perish; at a minimum, the firm will find it virtually impossible to raise any additional capital. For example, if you could obtain 5% interest in a bank's savings account, why would you invest in a firm that pays less than this rate of return?

**Economic profits:** Profits in excess of normal profits. These are profits in excess of both explicit and implicit costs.

**Normal profits:** The return on capital necessary to keep investors satisfied and keep capital in the business over the long run.

Economists include both explicit and implicit costs in their analysis of business profits. They say a firm is earning **economic profits** if it is generating profits in excess of zero once implicit costs are factored in. Economic profits of zero therefore mean a firm is earning just the normal rate of return on its capital, or just enough to cover the opportunity cost of this capital. *Zero economic profits* and **normal profits** thus being equated, anything above zero economic profits represents a true economic profit, and anything below an economic loss. Note that a firm may be earning *accounting profits* as defined by the Internal Revenue Service for tax purposes, yet still be suffering economic losses, since taxable income does not reflect all implicit costs. Table 1 lists some examples of both explicit and implicit costs.

For example, an entrepreneur who opens a small restaurant and earns a $30,000 accounting profit after deducting her out-of-pocket (explicit) costs may or may not have really earned an economic profit. If she could have earned $35,000 a year working

**TABLE 1** Examples of Explicit and Implicit Costs

| Explicit | Implicit |
|---|---|
| • Salaries | • Earnings that an owner could have made in an alternative job |
| • Lease payments | • Interest on capital invested in business that could have been made by putting the capital in a bank account |
| • Cost of goods sold | |
| • Utilities | |
| • Insurance | |
| • Office supplies | |

elsewhere, she has suffered a $5,000 economic loss, and we haven't even considered the implicit cost of her capital yet.

Hence, economists designate normal profits as economic profits equal to zero. Normal profits are the profits necessary to keep a firm in business over an extended period of time, or over the long run. This brings us to an important economic distinction, between the short run and the long run.

## Short Run Versus Long Run

Although the short and the long run generally differ in their temporal spans, they are *not* defined in terms of time. Rather, economists define these periods by the ability of firms to adjust the quantities of various resources they are employing.

The **short run** is a period of time over which at least one factor of production is fixed, or cannot be changed. For the sake of simplicity, economists typically assume that plant capacity is fixed in the short run. Output from a fixed plant can still vary depending on how much labor the firm employs. Firms can, for instance, hire more people, have existing employees work overtime, or run additional shifts. For discussion purposes, we focus here on labor as the variable factor, but changes in the raw materials used can also result in output changes.

Short run: A period of time over which at least one factor of production (resource) is fixed, or cannot be changed.

The **long run,** conversely, is a period of time sufficient for a firm to adjust all factors of production, including plant capacity. Since all factors can be altered in the long run, existing firms can even close and leave the industry, and new firms can build new plants and enter the market.

Long run: A period of time sufficient for firms to adjust all factors of production, including plant capacity.

In the short run, therefore, with plant capacity and the number of firms in an industry being fixed, output varies only as a result of changes in employment. In the long run, as plant capacity and other factors are made variable, the industry may grow or shrink as firms enter or leave the business, or some firms alter their plant capacity.

Because all industries are unique, the time required for long-run adjustment varies by industry. Family-owned restaurants, lawn-mowing services, and roofing firms can come and go fairly rapidly. High-capital industries on the other hand, such as the chemical, petroleum, and semiconductor industries, face obstacles to change that require a long time to overcome, whether these be strenuous environmental regulation, immense research and development requirements, or huge capital costs for plant construction. Adding plant capacity in one of these industries can take a decade or more and cost billions of dollars.

The important point to note is that firms seek economic profits and determine profits by first calculating their costs. These costs may differ over the short run versus the long run. Therefore, we look first at production and costs in the short run, then consider costs in the long run.

**CHECKPOINT**

## FIRMS, PROFITS, AND ECONOMIC COSTS

- Firms are economic institutions that convert inputs (factors of production) into products and services.
- Entrepreneurs provide goods and services to markets. Entrepreneurs can be organized into three basic business structures: sole proprietorships, partnerships, and corporations.
- Corporations are the premier form of business organization because they give owners (shareholders) limited liability, unlike sole proprietorships and partnerships.
- Profit is the difference between total revenues and costs.
- Total revenue is price per unit times the number of units sold ($TR = p \times q$).
- Total cost includes both out-of-pocket and opportunity costs.
- Explicit costs are those expenses paid directly to some other economic entity, such as taxes, utilities, and the cost of raw materials. Explicit costs can be determined by adding up the checks paid out by a firm.
- Implicit costs represent the opportunity costs of doing business, including depreciation, depletion, and the firm's capital costs.
- Economic profits are those in *excess* of a normal rate of return (that return required to keep capital in the firm over a long term).
- Normal profits are equal to zero economic profits. The firm is earning just enough to keep capital in the firm over the long run.
- The short run is a period of time where one factor of production (usually plant capacity) is fixed. In the long run all factors can vary and the firm can enter or exit the industry.

**QUESTION:** Assume for a moment you want to go into business for yourself and you have a good idea. What are the pros and cons of buying an existing business versus starting your own from scratch?

Answers to the Checkpoint question can be found at the end of this chapter.

# Production in the Short Run

**Production:** The process of turning inputs into outputs.

**Production** is the process of turning inputs into outputs. Most products can be produced using a variety of different technologies. As discussed earlier, these can be either capital-intensive or labor-intensive. Which technology a firm chooses will depend on many things, including ease of implementation and the relative cost of each input into the process.

Again, in the simplified model we are working with, firms can vary their output in the short run only by altering the amount of labor they employ, because plant capacity is fixed in the short run. An individual firm's production possibilities follow the same general pattern as the production function for the entire economy introduced in Chapter 2. Hence, in the short run, output for an existing plant will vary by the amount of labor employed. This output is referred to as *total product.*

## Total Product

Imagine you decide to begin manufacturing windsurfing rigs in the unused barn of the farmhouse you rent. (You do not farm the acreage, you just rent the buildings.) Your physical plant is constrained in the short run by the size of the barn. Table 2 lists your firm's total output as you hire more workers.

**TABLE 2** Production Data for Windsurfing Sail Firm

| (1) L labor | (2) Q (total product) | (3) MP (marginal product) | (4) AP (average product) |
|---|---|---|---|
| 0 | 0 | 0 | — |
| 1 | 7 | 7 | 7.00 |
| 2 | 15 | 8 | 7.50 |
| 3 | 25 | 10 | 8.33 |
| 4 | 40 | 15 | 10.00 |
| 5 | 54 | 14 | 10.80 |
| 6 | 65 | 11 | 10.83 |
| 7 | 75 | 10 | 10.71 |
| 8 | 84 | 9 | 10.50 |
| 9 | 90 | 6 | 10.00 |
| 10 | 95 | 5 | 9.50 |
| 11 | 98 | 3 | 8.91 |
| 12 | 100 | 2 | 8.33 |
| 13 | 98 | −2 | 7.54 |
| 14 | 95 | −3 | 6.79 |
| 15 | 85 | −10 | 5.67 |

Panel A of Figure 1 on the next page displays your total product curve for windsurfing equipment, based on the data in columns 1 and 2 of Table 2. Output of rigs varies with the number of people you employ. Output rises from 0 to 40 when four people are working (point *a* in panel A) to a maximum of 100 when 12 people are employed (point *c*). As you continue to hire employees beyond 12, you encounter *negative returns.* Total output actually begins to fall, possibly because your barn has become overly crowded, confusing, hazardous, or noisy. Clearly, hiring any more than 12 employees would be counterproductive, since output falls but costs rise.

## Marginal and Average Product

**Marginal product** (column 3 in Table 2) is the change in output that results from a change in labor input. Marginal product is computed by dividing the change in output (ΔQ) by the change in labor (ΔL). The delta (Δ) symbol is used to denote "change in." Thus, marginal product (MP) is equal to ΔQ/ΔL; it is the change in output that results from adding additional workers.

Marginal product: The change in output that results from a change in labor (ΔQ/ΔL).

Notice that when employment rises from three to four workers, output grows from 25 to 40 rigs. Marginal product is therefore 15 rigs at this point (point *a* in panel B of Figure 1). Contrast this with a change in employment when 12 people are already employed. Adding the 13th employee actually reduces the total output of windsurfing rigs from 100 to 98, so marginal product is −2.

**Average product** (AP) or output per worker is found by dividing total output by the number of workers employed to produce that output (Q/L). Average product is shown in panel B of Figure 1. When employment is four people and output is 40, for instance, average product is 10 (point *d*).

Average product: Output per worker, found by dividing total output by the number of workers employed to produce that output (Q/L).

## Increasing and Diminishing Returns

As panel B of Figure 1 shows, when four people are employed, marginal product is 15 (point *a*), exceeding the average product of 10 (point *d*). This portion of the total product curve, where average and marginal products are both rising, is called the **increasing marginal returns**

Increasing marginal returns: A new worker hired adds more to total output than the previous worker hired, so that both average and marginal products are rising.

**FIGURE 1—Total Product Curve, Marginal Product, and Average Product**

These two panels show the relationship between additional labor and productivity. The top panel shows how increasing labor increases productivity, up to a point. The bottom panel shows marginal and average product. Once you add more than four workers, marginal product starts decreasing. Total product keeps increasing, however, until you hit 12 employees. At that point, marginal product is negative, meaning that each additional employee actually reduces production.

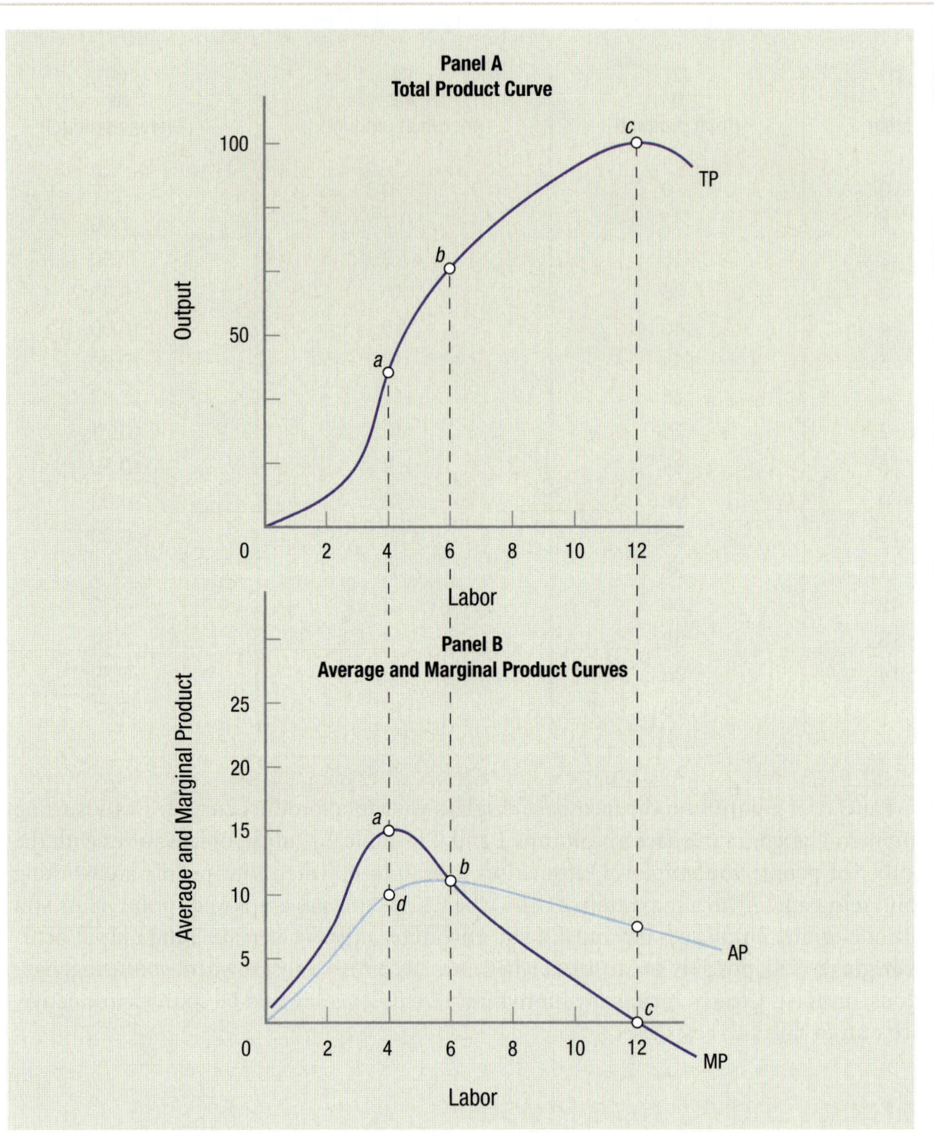


portion of the curve. Each of your first four employees adds more to output than the previous worker hired; thus, in this range, output grows faster as you employ additional labor.

Now note that as you hire your first six employees, average product continues to rise, and the marginal product remains higher than average product. When marginal product exceeds average product—when a new worker adds more to output than the average of the previous workers—hiring an additional worker increases average productivity. This might be because hiring more people allows you to establish more of a production line, say, thus heightening specialization and thereby raising productivity.

**Diminishing marginal returns:** An additional worker adds to total output, but at a diminishing rate.

Note, however, that after you have employed four people, *marginal productivity* begins to trail off. Between 4 and 12 workers (points *a* to *c*), you face **diminishing marginal returns** since each additional worker adds to total output, but at a diminishing rate. Note that at point *b* (six employees), both marginal and average product are roughly equal and average product is at its maximum (nearly 11 rigs).

Finally, note that once you have hired 12 employees, if you hire any more, this will result in negative marginal returns. Hiring additional people will actually reduce output, so rational firms never operate in this range.

The typical production curves shown in Figure 1 embody the *law of diminishing returns.* Given that your barn size is fixed in the short run, adding more labor will eventually—in this case, once four people have been hired—result in diminishing marginal returns, each additional worker adding to total production by a smaller and smaller amount.

**CHECKPOINT**

### PRODUCTION IN THE SHORT RUN

- Production is the process of turning inputs into outputs.
- Total product is the total output produced by the production process.
- Marginal product (MP) is the change in output that results from a change in labor input and is equal to $\Delta Q/\Delta L$.
- Average product (AP) is output per worker and is equal to Q/L.
- Increasing marginal returns occur when adding a worker adds *more* to output than the previous worker hired.
- Diminishing marginal returns occur when adding a worker adds less to output than the previous worker hired.
- Negative marginal returns occur when adding a worker actually leads to *less* total output than with the previous worker hired.

**QUESTIONS:** Microsoft has developed, updated, and sold Microsoft Office over the last 30 years, and it accounts for a significant portion of Microsoft revenues. Most users have barely scratched the surface on this product, probably using no more than 10% of the program's features. Has Microsoft reached diminishing returns with this product? Are the free Web-based word processors (e.g., Google Docs and Spreadsheets), which have most of the features people use, a threat to the Microsoft Office franchise?

Answers to the Checkpoint questions can be found at the end of this chapter.

# Costs of Production

Production tells only part of the story. We have to calculate how much it costs to produce this output. Let's now bring resource prices, including labor costs, into our analysis to develop the typical cost curves for the firm.

## Short-Run Costs

In a very straightforward way, production costs are determined by the productivity of workers. Ignoring all costs except wages, if you, by yourself, were to produce 10 pizzas an hour and you were paid $8 an hour, then each pizza would cost an average of 80 cents to produce—the cost of your labor. Yet, to ignore any other costs would be to neglect a significant portion of business expenses known as *overhead.*

To begin developing the concept of overhead specifically, and production costs more generally, remember that production periods are split into the short run and the long run. In the short run, at least one factor is fixed, whereas in the long run, all factors are variable. This has led economists to define costs as fixed and variable.

**Fixed costs:** Costs that do not change as a firm's output expands or contracts, often called overhead. These include items such as lease payments, administrative expenses, property taxes, and insurance.

**Variable costs:** Costs that vary with output fluctuations, including expenses such as labor and material costs.

### Fixed and Variable Costs

**Fixed costs,** or overhead, are those costs that do not change as a firm's output expands or contracts. Lease or rental payments, administrative overhead, and insurance are examples of fixed costs—they do not rise or fall as a firm alters production to meet market demands. **Variable costs,** on the other hand, do fluctuate as output changes. Labor and material costs are examples of variable costs, since making more products requires hiring more workers and purchasing more raw materials. To keep things simple, let us assume all costs fit into one of these two categories, such that total cost (TC) is equal to total fixed cost (TFC) plus total variable cost (TVC), or

$$TC = TFC + TVC$$

Note that, in the long run, all costs are variable (TFC = 0), since given enough time, a firm can expand or close its plant, and enter or leave an industry.

## Average Costs

When a firm produces a product or service, it typically wants a breakdown of how much labor, raw material, plant overhead, and sales costs are imbedded in each unit of the product. Modern accounting systems permit a detailed breakdown of costs for each unit of production. For our purposes, however, that level of detail is not necessary. For us, cost per unit of output (or *average cost*), average fixed cost, and average variable cost is sufficient.

If we divide the previous equation determining TC by total output Q, we get

$$TC/Q = TFC/Q + TVC/Q$$

**Average fixed cost:** Equal to total fixed cost divided by output (TFC/Q).

**Average variable cost:** Equal to total variable cost divided by output (TVC/Q).

**Average total cost:** Equal to total cost divided by output (TC/Q). Average total cost is also equal to AFC + AVC.

Economists refer to total fixed costs divided by output (TFC/Q)as **average fixed cost** (AFC). This represents the average amount of overhead for each unit of output. Total variable costs divided by output is known as **average variable cost** (AVC). It represents the labor and raw materials expenses that go into each unit of output. Adding AFC and AVC together results in **average total cost** (ATC), and thus the equation above can be rewritten as

$$ATC = AFC + AVC$$

Hence, average cost per unit (ATC) is the sum of average fixed cost (AFC) and average variable cost (AVC).

Table 3 provides us with more complete production and cost data for your windsurfing business. Note that we have assumed you pay $1,000 per month for rent of the barn, so total fixed costs equal $1,000 (column 5). Wages per worker are assumed to be $11 per hour, or $88 per day, for 20 days a month, and thus $1,760 per month per employee. Note also that, for the sake of simplicity, we have included all material and other variable costs under your labor costs.

Let's go through one row so you can be sure about how we arrived at the numbers in columns 3 to 11. Let's take the row where four workers are hired and therefore 40 windsurfing rigs are produced. Moving right through the table, we see the following. The marginal product of the additional worker as we move from three workers to four is 15 windsurfing rigs because the quantity produced has grown from 25 to 40. Note that this marginal product is more than the third worker produced, but also note that the marginal product peaks with this worker. Since average product is Q/L, average product for four workers is 10.

We now move to columns 5–7. As noted above, you pay $1,000 per month for the barn, and this is your total fixed cost—it does not change with the addition of more workers. Total variable cost does change, rising by $1,760 for each additional worker because this is the wage you need to pay for each worker. For four workers, you pay $1,760 × 4 = $7,040. Total cost is simply total fixed cost plus total variable cost, so when the fourth worker is added, total cost is $1,000 + $7,040 = $8,040.

Now let's move to columns 8–10. Average total cost is total cost divided by quantity produced, so when four workers are hired, $8,040 in total cost is divided by 40 windsurfing rigs produced to equal $201 in ATC. Average variable cost takes the total variable cost of $7,040 for four workers and divides it by 40 windsurfing rigs to equal $176 in AVC. We can calculate average fixed costs in two ways. First, we can take total fixed costs of $1,000 and divide it by 40 windsurfing rigs to equal $25 in AFC. Second, we know that

**TABLE 3** Production and Cost Data for Windsurfing Sail Firm

| (1) L | (2) Q | (3) MP | (4) AP | (5) TFC | (6) TVC | (7) TC | (8) ATC | (9) AVC | (10) AFC | (11) MC |
|---|---|---|---|---|---|---|---|---|---|---|
| 0 | 0 | — | — | 1000 | 0 | 1000 | — | — | — | — |
| 1 | 7 | 7 | 7 | 1000 | 1760 | 2760 | 394.29 | 251.43 | 142.86 | 251.43 |
| 2 | 15 | 8 | 7.50 | 1000 | 3520 | 4520 | 301.33 | 234.67 | 66.67 | 220.00 |
| 3 | 25 | 10 | 8.33 | 1000 | 5280 | 6280 | 251.20 | 211.20 | 40.00 | 176.00 |
| 4 | 40 | 15 | 10.00 | 1000 | 7040 | 8040 | 201.00 | 176.00 | 25.00 | 117.33 |
| 5 | 54 | 14 | 10.80 | 1000 | 8800 | 9800 | 181.48 | 162.96 | 18.52 | 125.71 |
| 6 | 65 | 11 | 10.83 | 1000 | 10560 | 11560 | 177.85 | 162.46 | 15.38 | 160.00 |
| 7 | 75 | 10 | 10.71 | 1000 | 12320 | 13320 | 177.60 | 164.27 | 13.33 | 176.00 |
| 8 | 84 | 9 | 10.50 | 1000 | 14080 | 15080 | 179.52 | 167.62 | 11.90 | 195.56 |
| 9 | 90 | 6 | 10.00 | 1000 | 15840 | 16840 | 187.11 | 176.00 | 11.11 | 293.33 |
| 10 | 95 | 5 | 9.50 | 1000 | 17600 | 18600 | 195.79 | 185.26 | 10.53 | 352.00 |
| 11 | 98 | 3 | 8.91 | 1000 | 19360 | 20360 | 207.76 | 197.55 | 10.20 | 586.67 |
| 12 | 100 | 2 | 8.33 | 1000 | 21120 | 22120 | 221.20 | 211.20 | 10.00 | 880.00 |
| 13 | 98 | −2 | 7.54 | 1000 | 22880 | 23880 | 243.67 | 233.47 | 10.20 | −880.00 |
| 14 | 95 | −3 | 6.79 | 1000 | 24640 | 25640 | 269.89 | 259.37 | 10.53 | −586.70 |

ATC = AVC + AFC, so if we know that \$201 = \$176 + AFC, we can solve for AFC and obtain \$25 in AFC. Thus, we see that we can calculate average total cost and its components.

Average total cost is an important piece of information for business firms. ATC does not, however, tell us how much costs will rise or fall if output changes. For this, we need to look at marginal cost.

## Marginal Cost

Because of increasing and decreasing returns associated with typical production processes, average costs vary with the level of output. Assume for a moment that your firm has orders for, and is producing, 98 windsurfing rigs per month. Now assume you get an order for one more rig. Just how much does this additional windsurfing rig cost to produce? Or, in the language of economics, what is the *marginal cost* of the next rig produced?

**Marginal cost** is the change in total cost arising from the production of additional units of output. Marginal cost (MC) is equal to the change in total cost (ΔTC) divided by the change in output (ΔQ), or

**Marginal cost:** The change in total costs arising from the production of additional units of output (ΔTC/ΔQ). Since fixed costs do not change with output, marginal costs are the change in variable costs associated with additional production (ΔTVC/ΔQ).

$$MC = \Delta TC/\Delta Q = \Delta TFC/\Delta Q + \Delta TVC/\Delta Q$$

Note that, for simplicity, we have been discussing changes of one unit of output, but we can calculate MC for a change in output of any amount by plugging in the appropriate value for ΔQ. Note that because fixed costs do not vary with changes in output, $\Delta TFC/\Delta Q = 0$, and thus the equation above can be rewritten as

$$MC = \Delta TVC/\Delta Q$$

Let us now examine Table 3 to determine approximately what the marginal cost would be for producing one more rig if you are currently producing 98 rigs.

As Table 3 suggests, at 98 rigs, you are employing 11 people, but producing an additional rig will require hiring a 12th worker. This will actually raise your output by two rigs, to 100—that is, one rig for the new customer and one additional rig for inventory. Paying this new employee's wages increases your costs by \$1,760 per month. And since you produce two additional windsurfing rigs, each rig effectively costs you \$880

(\$1,760 ÷ 2 = \$880). Consequently, the marginal cost to produce these additional rigs is \$880 per rig, as shown in column 11 in Table 3. Marginal cost again is the change in variable cost associated with producing one more unit of a product.

## Short-Run Cost Curves

Table 3 provides the numerical values for costs. Let us now translate these costs into figures to make their analysis simpler.

### Average Fixed Cost (AFC)

The average fixed cost (AFC) for your business is shown in Figure 2. Note that AFC falls continuously as more output is produced; this is because your overhead expenses are getting spread out over more and more units of output. At point *a,* for instance, when only 25 rigs are produced, AFC is \$40, and TFC is equal to area 0*fad* = \$1,000. When output grows to 100, however, TFC remains equal to area 0*ebc* = \$1,000, but AFC drops to \$10, since the TFC is being spread over 100 units. (Keep in mind that because AFC = TFC/Q, then TFC = AFC × Q. This will be helpful when we only have graphical analysis to work with.)

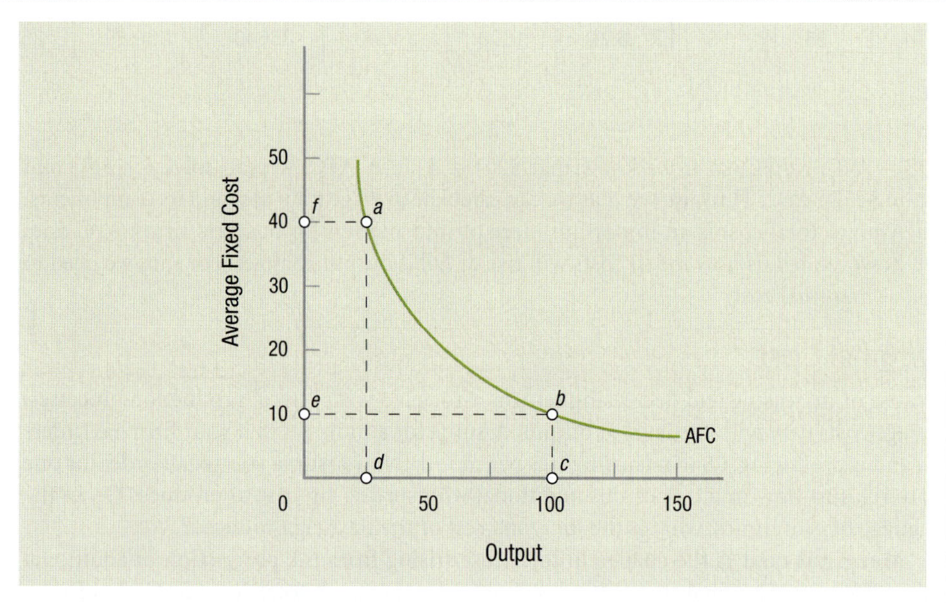


**FIGURE 2—The Average Fixed Cost Curve**

The average fixed cost (AFC) curve always decreases as production increases. This is because, in the short run, total fixed costs do not change, so that increasing production spreads the fixed costs over more units of output.

### Average Variable Cost (AVC)

Borrowing the data from Table 3, Figure 3 shows the AVC, ATC, and AFC for your hypothetical windsurfing firm. Notice that both the AVC and ATC curves are bowl-shaped. At relatively low levels of output, the curves slope downward, reflecting an increase in returns as average costs drop. As production levels rise, however, diminishing returns set in, and average costs start to climb back up. We get some sense of this by examining Table 3, but the figure makes it far easier to see.

In Figure 3, the average variable cost curve reaches its minimum where 65 rigs are produced (point *c*). Since AVC = TVC/Q, then TVC = AVC × Q. Thus, at point *c,* TVC is equal to the rectangular area 0*ace,* or \$10,560 (\$162.46 × 65).

### Average Total Cost (ATC)

Average total cost equals average fixed costs plus average variable cost (ATC = AFC + AVC). At an output of 65 rigs in Figure 3, ATC(*ed*) = AFC(*ef*) + AVC(*ec*). (Note that *cd* = *ef,* since we are adding AFC to AVC to yield ATC.) We know that ATC = TC/Q, so

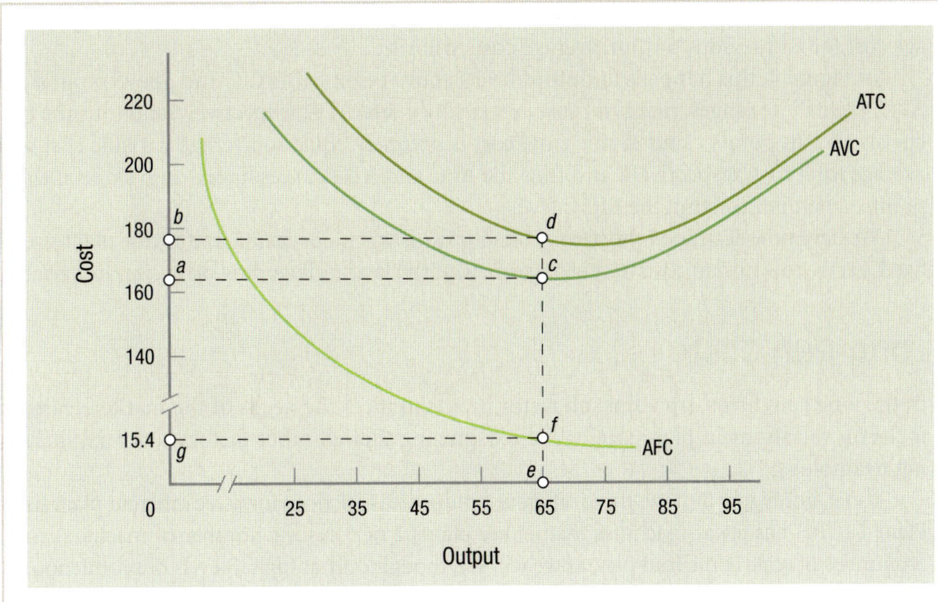


**FIGURE 3—Average Total Cost, Average Variable Cost, and Average Fixed Cost**

Curves for average total cost and average variable cost have been added to average fixed cost. The bowl shape of these curves demonstrates the law of diminishing returns: Beyond a certain level of output (65 units in this case), average variable costs increase. Total costs are equal to average total costs times output.

TC = ATC × Q. Hence, when output is 65, ATC = \$177.85 and TC = \$11,560 (\$177.85 × 65), or the rectangular area 0*bde* in Figure 3.

It is important to note that TC, TFC, and TVC can be found for *any point* on their respective curves by multiplying the average cost at that point by the output produced.

## Marginal Cost (MC)

Drawing our discussion of short-run costs to a close, Figure 4 plots the marginal cost curve, adding it to the AVC and ATC curves we have plotted already.

Notice that the marginal cost curve intersects the minimum points of both the AVC and ATC curves. This is not a coincidence. Marginal cost is the cost necessary to produce another unit of a given product. When the cost to produce another unit is *less* than the average of the previous units produced, average costs will *fall*. For the AVC curve in Figure 4, this happens at all output levels below point *c* (65 units); for the ATC curve, it happens at all output

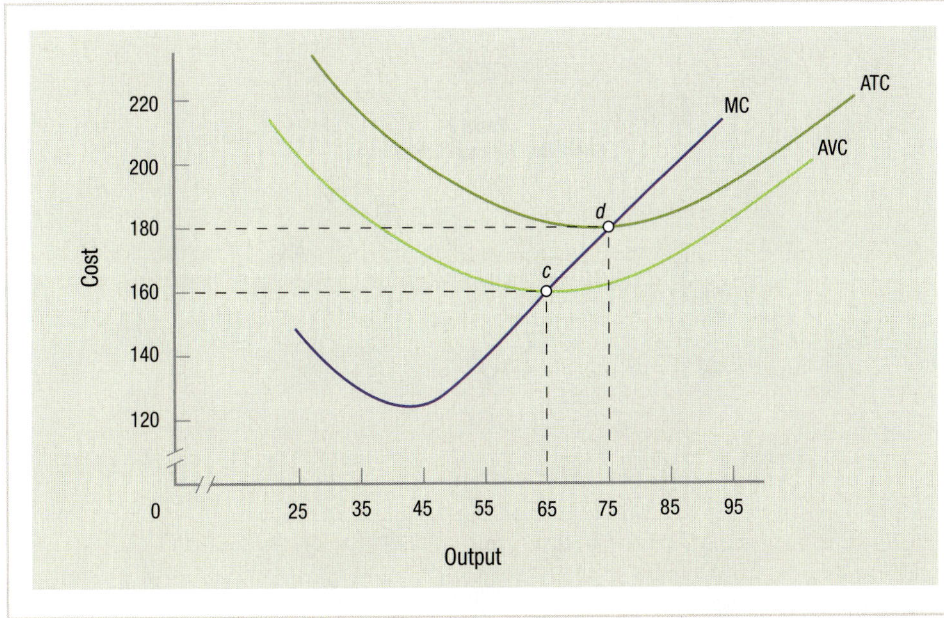


**FIGURE 4—Average Total Cost, Average Variable Cost, and Marginal Cost**

Marginal costs represent the added cost of producing one more unit of output. Note that the marginal cost curve passes through the minimum points on both the AVC and ATC curves.

levels below point *d* (75 units). But when the cost to produce another unit *exceeds* the average cost for all previous output, average costs will *rise*.

In Figure 4, this happens at output levels above point *c* for AVC and above point *d* for ATC. Over these ranges, marginal cost exceeds AVC and ATC, respectively, and thus the two curves rise. At points *c* and *d*, marginal cost is precisely equal to average variable cost and average total cost, respectively, and thus the AVC and ATC curves have a zero slope at these points, when intersecting the MC curve.

We have now examined short-run costs for firms when one factor, in this case plant size, is fixed. Let us now turn to costs in the long run, when all factors, including plant size, are variable.

## Long-Run Costs

In the long run, firms can adjust all factor inputs to meet the needs of the market. Here we focus on variations in plant size, while recognizing that all other factors can vary, including technology.

Panel A of Figure 5 shows three different production functions for three different plant sizes. Plant 1 ($TP_1$) has fewer machines than either plants 2 or 3. As the number of machines rises, economies of scale come into play, as we will see, though only at higher levels of production.

**FIGURE 5—Total Product Curves and Various Short-Run Average Cost Curves**

This figure shows the relationship between average total cost and plant size. In panel A, plant 1 ($TP_1$) has the fewest machines and the least output capacity; plant 3 ($TP_3$) has the most equipment, or capital, and hence the most capacity. Panel B shows the average total cost curve for each of the three plants. The larger plants have relatively high average total costs at lower levels of output, but much lower average total costs at higher output levels.

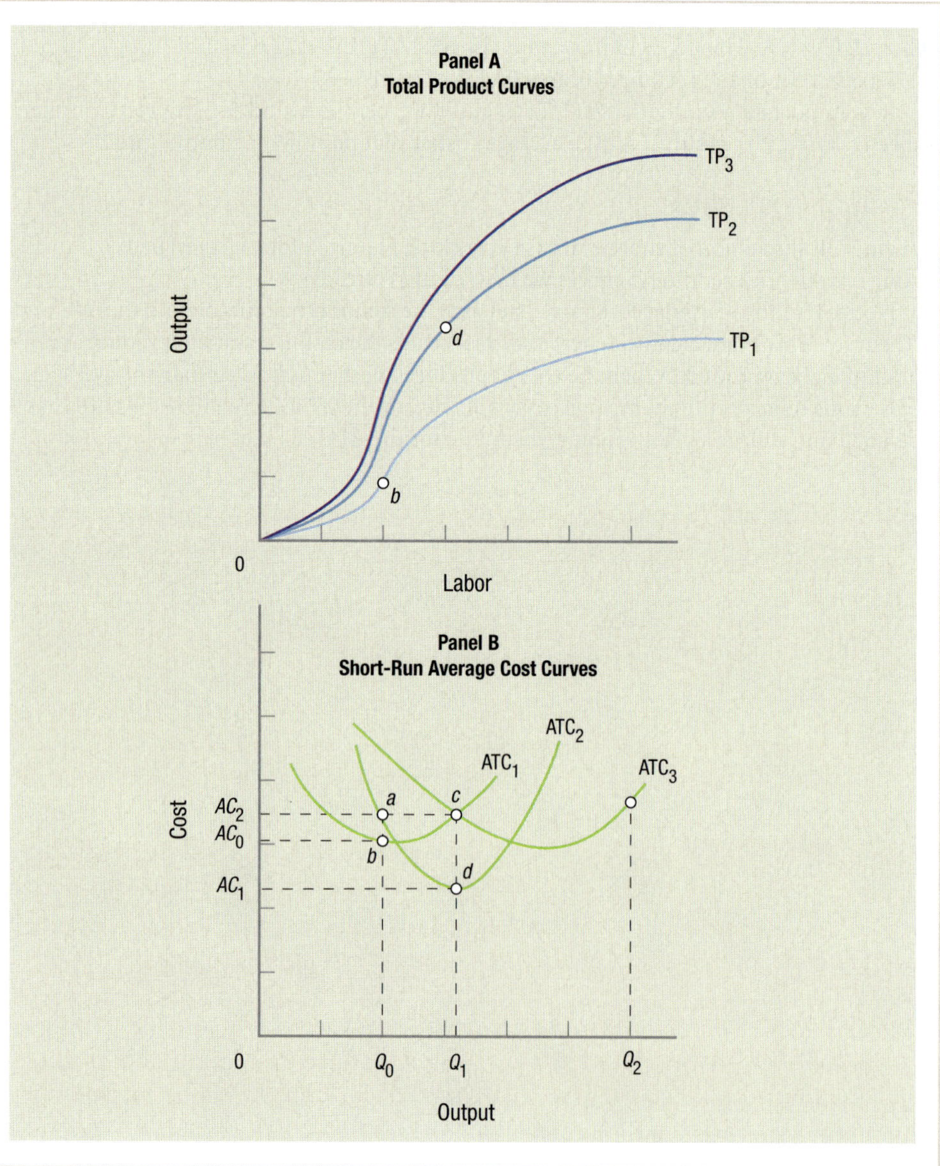

At lower levels of production, the average costs for plants 2 and 3 are quite high, since they have higher fixed costs than plant 1—more expensive machines and more square feet of space to house these machines. This is shown in panel B of Figure 5. For a small output, say $Q_0$, plant 1 produces for an average cost of $AC_0$ (point *b* in panel B). Plant 2, with its additional overhead, can produce $Q_0$ output, but only for an average cost of $AC_2$ (point *a* in panel B).

Once output rises to $Q_1$, however, plant 2 begins to enjoy the benefits of economies of scale. The additional machines mean that plant 2 can produce $Q_1$ for $AC_1$ (point *d*), whereas the machines in plant 1 get overwhelmed at this level of output, resulting in an average cost of $AC_2$ (point *c*). Similarly, if a firm expects market demand eventually to reach $Q_2$, it would want to build plant 3 because plants 1 and 2 are too small to efficiently accommodate that level of production.

## Long-Run Average Total Cost

The **long-run average total cost (LRATC)** curve represents the lowest unit cost at which any specific output can be produced in the long run, when a firm is able to adjust the size of its plant. Figure 6 is equivalent to panel B of Figure 5. In this figure, the LRATC curve is indicated by the green segments of the various short-run cost curves; these are the segments of each curve where output can be produced at the lowest per unit cost (the envelope curve). In short, the concept of LRATC assumes that, in the long run, firms will build plants of the size best fitting the levels of output they wish to produce.

**Long-run average total cost (LRATC):** In the long run, firms can adjust their plant sizes so LRATC is the lowest unit cost at which any particular output can be produced in the long run.

While the LRATC curve in Figure 6 is relatively bumpy, it will tend to smooth out as more plant size options are considered. In some industries, such as agriculture and food service, the options for plant size and production methods are virtually unlimited. In other industries, such as semiconductors, however, sophisticated plants may cost several billion dollars to build and require being run at near capacity to be cost effective.

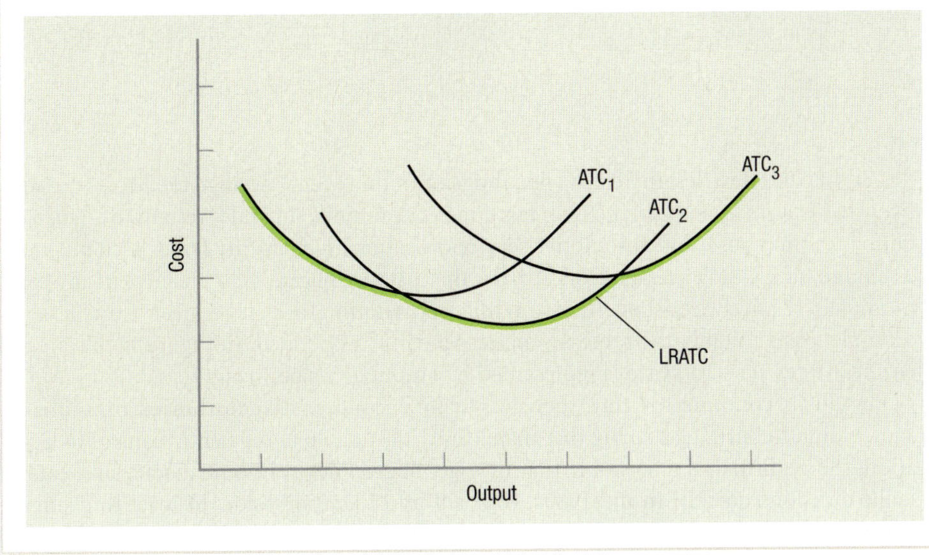


**FIGURE 6—The Long-Run Average Total Cost Curve**

This figure shows the long-run average total cost (LRATC) for three plants. Firms are free to adjust plant size in the long run, so they can switch from one plant type to the next to minimize their costs at each production level. The heavy envelope curve represents the firm's lowest cost to produce any given output in the long run and represents the LRATC curve.

These huge, sophisticated plants are so complex that Intel Corporation has dedicated teams of engineers that build new plants and operate them exactly as all others. These teams ensure that any new plant is a virtual clone of the firm's other operating facilities. Even small deviations from this standard have proven disastrous in the past.

## Economies and Diseconomies of Scale

As a firm's output increases, its LRATC tends to decrease. This is because, as the firm grows in size, **economies of scale** result from such items as specialization of labor and management, better use of capital, and increased possibilities for making several products that utilize complementary production techniques.

**Economies of scale:** As a firm's output increases, its LRATC tends to decline. This results from specialization of labor and management, and potentially a better use of capital and complementary production techniques.

A larger firm's ability to have workers specialize on particular tasks reduces the costs associated with shifting workers from one task to another. Similarly, management in larger operations can use technologies not available to smaller firms, for instance computers to remotely supervise workers. It is true that today's powerful personal computer networks have begun to narrow the gap in this arena. Larger firms, though, can still afford to purchase larger, more specialized capital equipment, whereas smaller firms must often rely on more labor-intensive methods. This equipment typically requires large production runs to be efficient, and only larger firms with correspondingly large marketing efforts can generate the sales necessary to satisfy these production volume requirements. Finally, larger firms are better able to engage in complementary production and use by-products more effectively.

The area for *economies of scale* is shown in Figure 7 as levels of output below $Q_0$ (average costs are falling).

**FIGURE 7—Economies, Diseconomies, and Constant Returns to Scale**

The curve in this figure shows how increasing production affects long-run average total cost (LRATC). Up to $Q_0$, economies of scale reduce LRATC as production increases. Over the range $Q_0$ to $Q_1$, the firm enjoys constant returns to scale, meaning that it can expand without affecting LRATC. Past $Q_1$, however, diseconomies of scale kick in, such that any further expansion causes an increase in LRATC.

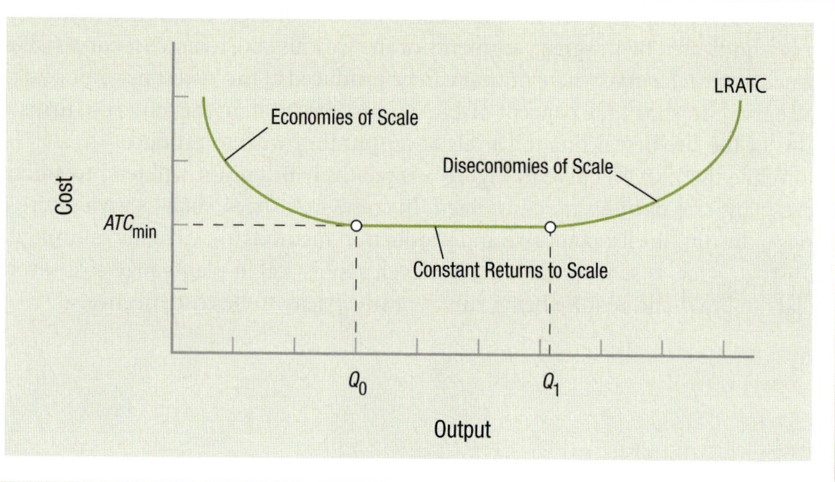


In many industries, there is a wide range of output where average total costs are relatively constant. Examples include fast-food restaurants, upscale restaurants such as Outback Steakhouse, and automotive service operations such as Jiffy Lube. Such businesses tend to have steady average costs because the cost to replicate their business in any community is relatively constant. Constructing and running a Dairy Queen franchise, for example, costs roughly the same no matter where it is operated. In Figure 7, this area of **constant returns to scale** is represented by output levels between $Q_0$ and $Q_1$.

As firms continue to grow, they eventually encounter **diseconomies of scale.** At some point, the firm gets so big that management is unable to efficiently control its operations. Some firms become so big that they get bogged down in bureaucracy and cannot make decisions quickly. In the 1980s, IBM fell into this trap—slow to react to changing market conditions for mainframe, mini, and microcomputers, the company was left behind by smaller, sleeker competition. Only through downsizing, reorganizing, refocusing, and a management change did IBM get back on track in the 1990s. Diseconomies of scale—the area where increased output increases costs disproportionately—are shown at outputs above $Q_1$ in Figure 7.

Constant returns to scale: A range of output where average total costs are relatively constant. Fast-food restaurants and movie theatres are examples.

Diseconomies of scale: A range of output where average total costs tend to increase. Firms often become so big that management becomes bureaucratic and unable to efficiently control its operations.

Economies of scope: By producing a number of products that are interdependent, firms are able to produce and market these goods at lower costs.

## Economies of Scope

When firms produce a number of products, it is often cheaper for them to produce another product when the production processes are interdependent. These economies are called **economies of scope.** For example, once a company has established a marketing department, it can take on the campaign of a new product at lower costs. It has developed the expertise and contacts necessary to sell the product. Book publishers can introduce a new book into the market more quickly and cheaply, and with more success than can a new firm starting in the business.

Some firms generate ideas for products, then send the production overseas. After they have been through this process, they become more efficient. Economists refer to this as *learning by doing.* Economies of scope often play a role in mergers as firms look for other firms with complementary products and skills.

## Role of Technology

We know that technology creates products that were the domain of science fiction writers of the past. Dick Tracy's wrist radio, first introduced in the comics of 1940s, has now morphed into the many wireless products we see today.

But we should mention in passing the role technology plays in altering the shape of the LRATC curve. The output level where diseconomies of scale are reached has significantly and continuously expanded since the beginning of the industrial revolution.

Enhanced production techniques, instantaneous global communication, and the use of computers in accounting and cost control are just a few recent examples of ways in which technology has permitted firms to increase their scale beyond what anyone had imagined possible 50 years earlier. Who would have imagined a century ago that one firm could have hundreds of thousands of employees and billions of dollars in annual sales? Today, IBM has more than 400,000 employees and sales of over $80 billion.

What spurs firms and entrepreneurs to develop new technologies and bring new products to market? Three words: profits, profits, and profits. In this chapter, we took a large step in analyzing where profits come from by looking at what firms do, how they measure profits, and how they determine the production and cost side of the profit equation. In the next chapter, we will look at revenues, as well as examine how firms can maximize their profits by adjusting output to market demand.

**CHECKPOINT**

### COSTS OF PRODUCTION

- Fixed costs (overhead) are those costs that do not vary with output, including lease payments and insurance. Fixed costs occur in the short run—in the long run, firms can change plant size and even exit an industry.
- Variable costs rise and fall as a firm produces more or less output. These include raw materials, labor, and utilities.
- Total cost equals total fixed cost plus total variable cost (TC = TFC + TVC).
- Average total cost equals total cost divided by output (ATC = TC/Q).
- Average fixed cost is total fixed cost divided by output (AFC = TFC/Q).
- Average variable cost is total variable cost divided by output (AVC = TVC/Q).
- Marginal cost is the change in total cost divided by the change in output (MC = $\Delta$TC/$\Delta$Q).
- Because total fixed cost does not change with output in the short run, then marginal cost is just the change in total variable cost divided by the change in output (MC = $\Delta$TVC/$\Delta$Q).
- The long-run average total cost curve (LRATC) represents the lowest unit cost at which specific output can be produced in the long run. Remember, firms can vary plant size in the long run, so this curve incorporates different plants to achieve the lowest average cost for a given level of output.
- As a firm grows in size, economies of scale result from specialization of labor, better use of capital, and the potential to produce many different products using complementary techniques.

- Diseconomies of scale occur because a firm gets so big that management loses control of its operations, and the firm becomes bogged down in bureaucracy.
- Economics of scope result when firms produce a number of interdependent products, so it is cheaper for them to add another product to the line.
- Modern communications and computers have permitted firms to become huge before diseconomies are reached.

**QUESTION:** In the late 1990s, Boeing reported that it takes roughly 12 years and $15 billion to bring a new aircraft from the design stage to a test flight. Boeing signed a 20-year exclusive agreement to supply aircraft to Delta, American, and Continental Airlines. The rationale for the agreement was that every time production of the plane doubled, a fifth was cut off the cost of the plane to the commercial airlines.[5] Why would doubling production cut costs per unit by 20%?

Answers to the Checkpoint question can be found at the end of this chapter.

# Key Concepts

Firm, p. 160
Sole proprietor, p. 162
Partnership, p. 162
Corporation, p. 162
Profit, p. 163
Revenue, p. 163
Economic costs, p. 163
Explicit costs, p. 163
Implicit costs, p. 163
Sunk costs, p. 164
Economic profits, p. 164
Normal profits, p. 164
Short run, p. 165
Long run, p. 165
Production, p. 166
Marginal product, p. 167
Average product, p. 167
Increasing marginal returns, p. 167
Diminishing marginal returns, p. 168
Fixed costs, p. 169
Variable costs, p. 169
Average fixed cost, p. 170
Average variable cost, p. 170
Average total cost, p. 170
Marginal cost, p. 171
Long-run average total cost (LRATC), p. 175
Economies of scale, p. 175
Constant returns to scale, p. 176
Diseconomies of scale, p. 176
Economies of scope, p. 176

# Chapter Summary

## Firms, Profits, and Economic Costs

*Firms* produce the products and services we consume. Firms are economic institutions that transform inputs (factors of production) into outputs (products and services).

Entrepreneurs provide goods and services to the market. Entrepreneurs are organized into three basic business structures: sole proprietorships, partnerships, and corporations.

*Corporations* are the premier form of business organization in most of the world. Corporations possess most of the legal rights of individuals, and in addition, they are able to issue stock to raise capital. Most significantly, the liability of individual owners (stockholders) is limited to the amount they have invested in the stock, unlike *sole proprietors* and *partnerships*.

[5] "Peace in our Time," *Economist*, July 26, 1997.

*Profits* comprise the difference between total revenue and total costs. Firms are assumed to seek to maximize their profits.

Economic costs are separated into *explicit* (out-of-pocket) and *implicit* (opportunity) costs. Explicit costs are those costs paid to some other entity, including wages, lease expenses, and taxes. Implicit costs include those items for which the firm does not directly pay others, but still incurs a cost, such as the depreciation and depletion of company assets, as well as the cost of the capital the firm employs. Sunk costs are expenses that have been incurred and are not recoverable.

Economists define a *normal return* as that return on capital that keeps investors willing to invest their capital in an industry over the long run. Firms earning just this level of profit are said to be earning normal profits. Firms earning more than this are earning *economic profits,* and firms earning less are taking *economic losses.*

The *short run* is a period of time during which at least one factor of production is fixed, usually plant capacity. Firms can vary output in the short run by hiring more labor or changing other variable factors. In the *long run,* firms are able to vary all factors, including plant size. Moreover, existing firms can leave the industry and new firms can enter.

## Production in the Short Run

In the short run, firms can vary the output they produce by varying their labor inputs. The *total product curve* relates labor inputs to outputs. *Marginal product* is the change in output resulting from a change in labor input ($\Delta Q/\Delta L$). Marginal product is thus the change in output associated with hiring one additional worker. *Average product* or output per worker is equal to total output divided by labor input ($Q/L$).

Typical production functions exhibit both increasing and decreasing returns. When *increasing returns* are present, each additional worker adds more to total output than previous workers. This can occur because of specialization, for instance. All production is eventually subject to the *law of diminishing returns,* whereby additional workers add less and less to total output.

## Costs of Production

In the short run, firms have fixed and variable costs. *Fixed costs,* or overhead, are those costs the firm incurs whether it produces anything or not. These costs include administrative overhead, lease payments, and insurance. *Variable costs* are those costs that vary with output, such as wages, utilities, and raw materials costs. Total cost is equal to total fixed cost plus total variable cost ($TC = TFC + TVC$).

*Average total cost* (ATC) represents cost per unit of total production, or $TC/Q$. *Average fixed cost* (AFC) is equal to $TFC/Q$, and *average variable cost* (AVC) is equal to $TVC/Q$. Consequently, $ATC = AFC + AVC$. *Marginal cost* (MC) is the change in total cost associated with producing one additional unit. Since fixed cost does not change in the short run ($\Delta TFC = 0$), marginal cost is equal to the change in variable costs when one additional unit is produced; hence, $MC = \Delta TVC/\Delta Q$.

In the long run, all factors of production are variable, and firms can enter or leave the industry. The *long-run average total cost* curve (LRATC) represents the lowest unit costs for any specific output level in the long run. *Economies of scale* associated with larger firm size result from such factors as specialization in labor and management. As a firm grows, the average cost of production falls. Eventually, however, a firm encounters *diseconomies of scale* when its size becomes so large that efficient management becomes impossible. At this point, average costs begin to rise. Today, advanced computer and communications technologies have radically increased the size of firms that can be efficiently managed. *Economies of scope* result from the ability of firms producing many interdependent products to add another at substantially lower costs.

## Questions and Problems

### Check Your Understanding

1. What is the difference between explicit and implicit costs? What is the difference between economic and accounting profits? Are these four concepts related? How?
2. How does the short run differ from the long run? Is the long run the same for all industries? Why or why not?
3. For business, are accounting profits or economic profits more important?
4. Why is the average fixed cost curve not bowl-shaped? Why does it not turn up like the average variable cost and average total cost curves?
5. What is the difference between average total cost and average variable cost?

### Apply the Concepts

6. Skype, the Internet phone company, uses peer-to-peer network principles to enable people to make free phone calls over the Internet anywhere in the world. Skype forwards calls through users' computers without having any central infrastructure. Users agree to let their computer's excess capacity be used as transfer nodes. In this way, Skype does not have to invest in more infrastructure as it adds users, and the system is highly robust and scalable. What is the marginal cost to Skype to add another user to its system?
7. List some of the reasons why the long-run average total cost curve has sort of a flat bowl shape. It declines early on, then is rather flat over a portion, and finally slopes upward.
8. The Finger Lakes region in New York State produces wine. The climate favors white wines, but reds have been produced successfully in the past 15 years. Categorize the following costs incurred by one winery as either fixed or variable:
   a. the capital used to buy 60 acres of land on Lake Seneca
   b. the machine used to pick some varieties of grapes at the end of August and the beginning of September
   c. the salary of the chief vintner, who is employed year-round
   d. the wages paid to workers who bind the grape plants, usually in April, and usually over a period of three to four days
   e. the wages paid to the same workers who pick the grapes at the end of August or early September
   f. the costs of the chemicals sprayed on the grapes in July
   g. the wages of the wine expert who blends the wine in August and September, after the grapes have been picked
   h. the cost of the building where wine tastings take place from April to October
   i. the cost of the wine used in the wine tasting
9. Why should sunk costs be ignored for decision making?
10. If marginal cost is less than average total cost, are average total costs rising or falling? Alternatively, if marginal cost is more than average total cost, are average total costs rising or falling? Give an example outside of economics to explain your answer.
11. Describe how marginal cost is related to marginal product.

### In the News

12. Economies of scope occur in big organizations with diversified product lines where innovation in one area feeds into others. In his book, *An Army of Davids,* Glenn Reynolds argued that "The balance of advantage—in nearly every aspect of society—

is shifting from big organizations to small ones. Economies of scale and scope matter much less in the information age than in the industrial one" (published by Nelson Current, 2006). Does this statement seem correct?

## Solving Problems

**13.** Using the table below, answer the following questions.

| Labor | Output | Marginal Product | Average Product |
|---|---|---|---|
| 0 | 0 | ______ | ______ |
| 1 | 7 | ______ | ______ |
| 2 | 15 | ______ | ______ |
| 3 | 25 | ______ | ______ |
| 4 | 33 | ______ | ______ |
| 5 | 40 | ______ | ______ |
| 6 | 45 | ______ | ______ |

a. Complete the table, filling in the answers for marginal and average products.

b. Over how many workers is the firm enjoying increasing returns?

c. At what number of workers do diminishing returns set in?

d. Are negative returns shown in the table?

**14.** Use the table below to answer the following questions. Assume that fixed costs are $100 and labor is paid $80 per unit (employee).

| L | Q | MP | AP | TFC | TVC | TC | ATC | AVC | AFC | MC |
|---|---|---|---|---|---|---|---|---|---|---|
| 0 | 0 | ___ | ___ | ___ | ___ | ___ | ___ | ___ | ___ | ___ |
| 1 | 7 | ___ | ___ | ___ | ___ | ___ | ___ | ___ | ___ | ___ |
| 2 | 15 | ___ | ___ | ___ | ___ | ___ | ___ | ___ | ___ | ___ |
| 3 | 25 | ___ | ___ | ___ | ___ | ___ | ___ | ___ | ___ | ___ |
| 4 | 40 | ___ | ___ | ___ | ___ | ___ | ___ | ___ | ___ | ___ |
| 5 | 45 | ___ | ___ | ___ | ___ | ___ | ___ | ___ | ___ | ___ |
| 6 | 48 | ___ | ___ | ___ | ___ | ___ | ___ | ___ | ___ | ___ |
| 7 | 50 | ___ | ___ | ___ | ___ | ___ | ___ | ___ | ___ | ___ |

a. Complete the table.

b. Graph ATC, AVC, AFC, and MC on a piece of paper.

**15.** After the Enron and other business scandals in the early 2000s, the United States passed the Sarbanes-Oxley Act, adding a number of rules and reporting requirements for U.S. corporations. The business community argues that these reporting requirements are extremely costly and cumbersome with only minimal benefit. Most companies, they argue, were not engaged in illegal or unethical behavior, and they are being punished because of a few. As Jane Sasseen and Joseph Weber (*Business Week,* March 26, 2006) note, one apparent impact of this law was that in 2005, "of the top 25 global initial public offerings (when companies first offer their stock to the general market for purchase), only one was in the United States." This was business lost to the New York Stock Exchange (NYSE) and NASDAQ. Are these kinds of compliance costs established by Sarbanes-Oxley fixed or variable costs? Why would firms care so much about these regulations? Can we expect to see the NYSE and NASDAQ try to buy or merge with other foreign stock exchanges in the near future?

## Answers to Questions in CheckPoints

### Check Point: Firms, Profits, and Economic Costs

Buying an existing business has several benefits, including that the business has existing customers and a location. In addition, it can generate cash and profits immediately. One downside is that determining a fair price may be difficult and potentially more than you can afford. Starting your own firm is cheaper in the beginning, but it involves doing everything from scratch. It typically takes three to four years for a firm to get a good foothold in the market.

### Check Point: Production in the Short Run

Microsoft may well have reached diminishing returns with its Office product. Many firms with a large number of users have been reluctant to upgrade, given the licensing costs and the added training required. The bigger and more complex Office becomes, the more it is best suited for specialized professional jobs, not for the majority of the market. Some have suggested that Microsoft's focus on future products may need to concentrate on ease of use, although its word processor is relatively easy to use even though it has a lot of power. Yes, the Web-based word processors and other open office programs are a threat to the domination of this market by Microsoft.

### Check Point: Costs of Production

This immense $15 billion development cost is spread over more planes, and rising volume creates economies. Producing commercial aircraft has huge economies of scale and scope.

# Competition

Panoramic Images/Getty Images

**In his classic economic treatise,** *The Wealth of Nations,* Adam Smith wrote of a "hidden hand" that guides businesses in their pursuit of self-interest, or profits, allowing only the efficient to survive. Some observers have noted similarities between Smith's work, written in 1776, and Charles Darwin's *Origin of Species,* published in 1872. The late biologist and zoologist Stephen Jay Gould wrote that "the theory of natural selection is, in essence, Adam Smith's economics transferred to nature," and that Darwin's account of the struggle for existence and reproductive success is the same "causal scheme applied to nature" as Smith's account of the competitive market.[1] Clearly, the notions of competition and the competitive market have played a prominent role in the history of ideas. In this chapter, we explore some of the implications competition has for markets and consider why the competitive market structure is so central to the thinking of economists. What you learn in this chapter will give you a benchmark to use when we consider other market structures in the following chapters.

Being engaged in stiff competition is the norm for lawn care companies, retail stores, Internet service providers, and restaurants. Large firms such as General Electric or Wal-Mart compete in many different markets, but some smaller firms—for example, the local newspaper or an oral surgeon—have only a few competitors. Firms specializing in standard products such as lumber, fertilizer, and cement tend to face stiff competition, while those focusing on unique services such as stained glass restoration, Web design, or organ transplants tend to have fewer competitors.

[1] Stephen Jay Gould, *The Structure of Evolutionary Theory* (Cambridge, MA: Belknap Press of Harvard University Press), 2002, pp. 121–25.

**After studying this chapter you should be able to:**

- ☐ Name the primary market structures and describe their characteristics.
- ☐ Define a competitive market and the assumptions that underlie it.
- ☐ Distinguish the differences between competitive markets in the short run and the long run.
- ☐ Analyze the conditions for profit maximization, loss minimization, and plant shutdown for a firm.
- ☐ Derive the firm's short-run supply curve.
- ☐ Use the short-run competitive model to determine long-run equilibrium.
- ☐ Describe why competition is in the public interest.

To economists, *competition* means more than just competing against one or two other firms. The model of competition in this chapter focuses on an idealized market structure containing so many small businesses that any one firm's behavior is irrelevant to its competitors. Firms in this competitive climate lack discretion over pricing and must perform efficiently merely to survive.

In this and the next two chapters, keep in mind the profitability equation developed in the previous chapter. Profits equal total revenues minus total costs. Total revenues equal price times quantity sold. So keep in mind the three items that determine profitability: price, quantity, and cost. In the next three chapters, we will see how firms try to control each one of these.

## Market Structure Analysis

To appreciate intensely competitive markets, we need to look at competition within the full range of possible market structures. Economists use **market structure analysis** to categorize industries based on a few key characteristics. By simply knowing simple industry facts, economists can predict the behavior of firms in that industry in such areas as pricing and sales.

Market structure analysis: By observing a few industry characteristics such as number of firms in the industry or the level of barriers to entry, economists can use this information to predict pricing and output behavior of the firm in the industry.

Below are the four factors defining the intensity of competition in an industry and a few questions to give you some sense of the issues behind each one of these factors.

- **Number of firms in the industry:** Is the industry composed of many firms, each with limited or no ability to set the market price, such as local pizza places, or is it dominated by a large firm such as Wal-Mart that can influence price regardless of the number of other firms?
- **Nature of the industry's product:** Are we talking about a homogeneous product such as salt for which no consumer will pay a premium, or are we considering leather handbags (Coach, Gucci) where consumers may think that some firms produce better goods than other firms?
- **Barriers to entry:** Does the industry require low start-up and maintenance costs such as found in a roadside fruit and vegetable stand, or is it a computer-chip business that may require a billion dollars to build a new chip plant?
- **Extent to which individual firms can control prices:** For example, pharmaceutical companies can set prices for new medicines, at least for a set period of time, because of patent protection. Farmers and copper producers have virtually no control and get their prices from world markets.

Possible market structures range from competition, characterized by many firms, to monopoly, where an industry contains only one firm. These market structures will make more sense to you as we consider each one in the chapters ahead. Right now, use this list and the descriptions below as reference points. You can always come back to this point and put the discussion in context.

### Primary Market Structures

The primary market structures economists have identified, along with their key characteristics, are as follows:

#### Competition

- Many buyers and sellers
- Homogeneous (standardized) products
- No barriers to market entry or exit
- No long-run economic profits
- No control over price

### Monopolistic Competition

- Many buyers and sellers
- Differentiated products
- No barriers to market entry or exit
- No long-run economic profits
- Some control over price

### Oligopoly

- Fewer firms (such as the auto industry)
- Mutually interdependent decisions
- Substantial barriers to market entry
- Potential for long-run economic profits
- Shared market power and considerable control over price

### Monopoly

- One firm
- No close substitutes for product
- Nearly insuperable barriers to entry
- Potential for long-run economic profit
- Substantial market power and control over price

Putting off discussion of the other market structures for later chapters, we turn to an extended examination of the requirements for a competitive market. In the remainder of this chapter, we explore short-run pricing and output decisions, and also the importance of entry and exit in the long run. Moreover, we use the conditions of competition to establish a benchmark for efficiency as we turn to evaluate other market structures in the following chapters.

## Defining Competitive Markets

The theory of **competition** rests on the following assumptions:

**Competition:** Exists when there are many relatively small buyers and sellers, a standardized product, with good information to both buyers and sellers, and no barriers to entry or exit.

1. Competitive markets have many buyers and sellers, each of them so small that none can individually influence product price.
2. Firms in the industry produce a homogeneous or standardized product.
3. Buyers and sellers have all the information about prices and product quality they need to make informed decisions.
4. Barriers to entry or exit are insignificant in the long run; new firms are free to enter the industry if so doing appears profitable, while firms are free to exit if they anticipate losses.

One implication of these assumptions is that competitive firms are **price takers.** Market prices are determined by market forces beyond the control of individual firms. That is, firms must simply take what they can get for their products. Paper for copy machines, most agricultural products, DRAMs (dynamic random access memory chips), and many other goods are produced in highly competitive markets. The buyers or sellers in these markets are so small that their ability to influence market price is nil. These firms must simply accept whatever price the market determines, leaving them to decide only how much of the product to produce or buy.

**Price taker:** Individual firms in competitive markets get their prices from the market since they are so small they cannot influence market price. For this reason, competitive firms are price takers and can produce and sell all the output they produce at market-determined prices.

Panel A of Figure 1 on the next page portrays the supply and demand for windsurfing sails in a competitive market; the market is in equilibrium at price $200 and industry

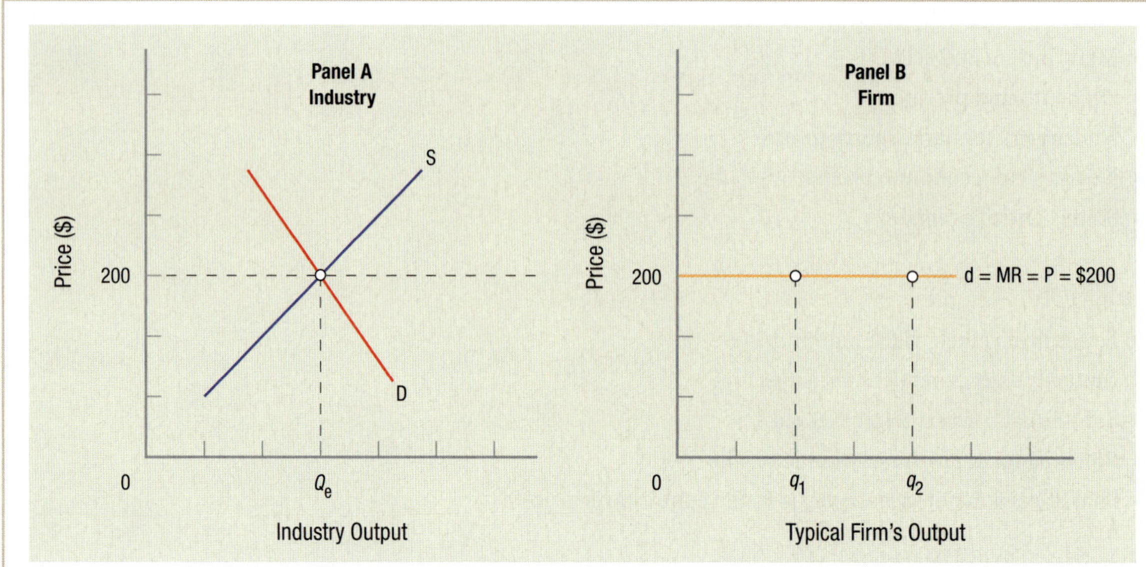


**FIGURE 1—The Market for Competitive Products with an Equilibrium Price of $200**

Panel A shows a market for standardized windsurfing sails in equilibrium at price $200 and industry output $Q_e$. This price is determined by the market's many buyers and sellers. Panel B illustrates product demand for an individual seller. The individual firm can sell all it wants to at $200 and has no reason to set its price below that. If it tries to sell at prices higher than $200, it sells nothing. The demand curve for the individual firm is horizontal at $200.

output $Q_e$. Remember that this product is a standardized sail (similar to two-by-four lumber, crude oil, and DRAMs) and that the market contains many buyers and sellers, who collectively set the product price at $200.

Panel B shows the demand for a seller's products in this market. The firm can sell all it wants at $200 or below. Yet, what firm would set its price below $200 when it can sell everything it produces at $200? Were the firm to set its price above $200, however, it would sell nothing. What consumer, after all, would purchase a standardized sail at a higher price when it can be obtained elsewhere for $200? The individual firm's demand curve is horizontal at $200. The firm can still determine how much of its product to produce and sell, but this is the only choice it has. The firm cannot set its own price, therefore it is a *price taker.*

Recall the profitability equation. Profits equal total revenues minus total costs. Total revenues equal price times quantity sold. In competitive markets, a firm's profitability is based on a given market price, quantity sold, and its costs. So how does it determine how much to sell?

## The Short Run and the Long Run (A Reminder)

Before turning to a more detailed examination of how firms decide how much output to produce in a competitive market, we need to recall a distinction introduced in the last chapter between the *short run* and the *long run.*

Again, in the *short run,* one factor of production is fixed, usually the firm's plant size, and firms cannot enter or leave an industry. Thus, in the short run, the number of firms in a market is fixed. Firms may earn economic profits, break even, or suffer losses, but still they cannot exit the industry, nor can new firms enter.

In the *long run,* all factors are variable, and thus the level of profits induce entry or exit. When losses prevail, some firms will leave the industry and invest their capital elsewhere. When economic profits are positive, new firms will enter the industry. The long run is far more dynamic than the short run.

**CHECKPOINT**

## MARKET STRUCTURE ANALYSIS

- Market structure analysis allows economists to categorize industries based on a few characteristics and use this analysis to predict pricing and output behavior.
- The intensity of competition is defined by the number of firms in the industry, the nature of the industry's product, the level of barriers to entry, and how much firms can control prices.
- Market structures range from competition (many buyers and sellers), to monopolistic competition (differentiated product), to oligopoly (only a few firms that are interdependent), to monopoly (a one-firm industry).
- Competition is defined by four attributes: Many buyers and sellers who are so small that none individually can influence price, firms that produce and sell a homogeneous (standardized) product, buyers and sellers who have all the information necessary to make informed decisions, and barriers to entry and exit that are insignificant.
- Firms in competitive markets get the product price from national or global markets. Therefore, competitive firms are price takers.
- In the short run, one factor (usually plant size) is fixed. In the long run, all factors are variable, and firms can enter or leave the industry.

**QUESTIONS:** Wal-Mart is a huge international firm with over 2,000,000 employees worldwide and sales of many billions of dollars. Where does Wal-Mart fit in our market structure approach? Microsoft? Starbucks? Toyota?

Answers to the Checkpoint questions can be found at the end of this chapter.

# Competition: Short-Run Decisions

Figure 1 represents a competitive market with an equilibrium price of $200. This translates into a demand curve for individual firms shown in panel B. Individual firms are price takers in this competitive situation: They can sell as many units of their product as they wish at $200 each.

## Marginal Revenue

Economists define **marginal revenue** as the change in total revenue that results from the sale of one added unit of a product. Marginal revenue (MR) is equal to the change in total revenue ($\Delta$TR) divided by the change in quantity sold ($\Delta q$); thus,

**Marginal revenue:** The change in total revenue from selling an additional unit of output. Since competitive firms are price takers, P = MR for competitive firms.

$$MR = \Delta TR/\Delta q$$

*Total revenue* (TR), meanwhile, is equal to price per unit ($p$) times quantity sold ($q$); thus:

$$TR = p \times q$$

In a competitive market, we know that price will not change. And since marginal revenue is defined as the change in revenue that comes from selling one more unit, in a competitive market, marginal revenue is simply equal to price. The added revenue a competitive firm receives from selling another unit is product price, or $200 in Figure 1. So determining marginal revenue in a competitive market is easy. As we will see in later chapters, this gets more complicated in market structures where firms have some control over price.

## Profit Maximizing Output

Figure 2 shows the price and marginal cost curve for a firm seeking to maximize its profits. As the price and cost curve show, the firm can sell all it wants at $200 a sail. Our first instinct might be to conclude that the firm will produce all it can, but this is not the case. Given the marginal cost curve shown in Figure 2, if the firm produces 85 units, profit will be less than the maximum possible. This is because revenue from the sale is $200, but the 85th sail costs $210 to produce (point *b*). This means producing this last sail reduces profits by $10.

**FIGURE 2—Profit Maximization in the Short Run in Competitive Markets**

If the firm produces 85 standardized windsurfing sails, the marginal cost to produce the last sail exceeds the revenue from its sale, thus reducing the firm's profits. For the 84th unit produced, marginal cost and price are both equal to $200, so the firm earns a normal return from producing this unit. Producing only 83 units means relinquishing the normal return that could have been earned from the 84th sail. Hence, the firm maximizes profits at an output of 84 (point e) where MC = MR = P = $200.

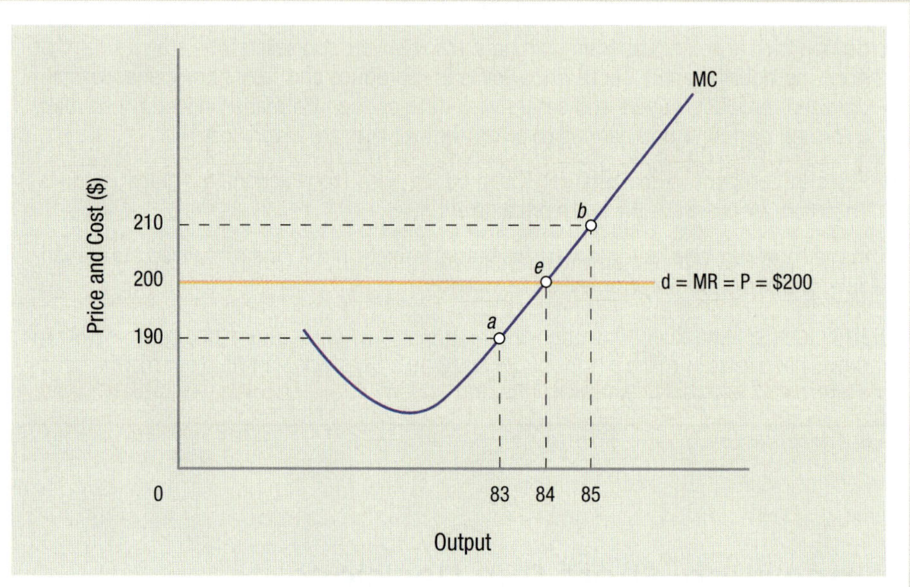


Assume the firm produces 84 sails. The revenue from selling the 84th unit (MR) is $200. This is precisely equal to the added cost (MC) of producing this unit, $200 (point *e*). Therefore, the firm earns zero economic profits by producing and selling the 84th sail. Zero economic profits, or normal profits, mean that the firm is earning a normal return on its capital by selling this 84th sail. If the firm starts producing only 83 sails, however, the additional cost (point a) will be less than the price, and the firm will have to relinquish the normal return associated with the 84th sail. Profits from selling 83 sails will therefore be lower than if 84 sails are sold because the normal return on the 84th sail is lost.

**Profit maximizing rule:** Firms maximize profit by producing output where MR = MC. No other level of output produces higher profits.

These observations lead us to a **profit maximizing rule:** *A firm maximizes profit by continuing to produce and sell output until marginal revenue equals marginal cost (MR = MC).* As we will see in subsequent chapters, this rule applies to all firms, regardless of market structure.

## Economic Profits

Let us return to our example from the previous chapter of your windsurfing sail manufacturing firm. We will assume the market has established a price of $200 for each sail. Your marginal revenue and cost curves are shown in Figure 3. (Incidentally, the MR and MC curves are the same as those shown in Figure 2.) Complete price, production, and cost data are shown in Table 1.

Earlier, we found that profits are maximized when the firm is producing output such that MR = MC, in this case, 84 sails. As Table 1 shows, profit is $1,720 when 84 windsurfing sails are produced and sold at $200 a sail.

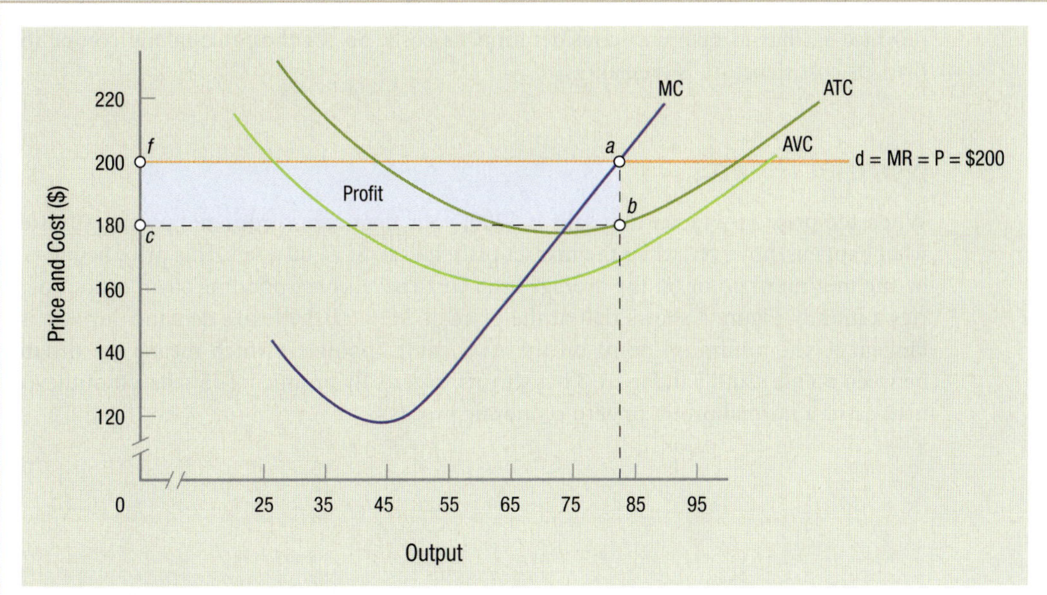


**FIGURE 3—Competitive Firm Earning Economic Profits**

The marginal revenue and cost curves derived from the data in Table 1 are shown here. As we can see, profits are maximized where MR = MC, or at an output of 84 and a price of $200. Price minus average total cost equals average profit per unit, represented by the distance *ab*. Average profit per unit times the number of units produced equals total profit; this is represented by area *cfab*.

Looking at Figure 3, we see that profits are maximized at point *a*, because this is where MR = MC. (This also can be seen in Table 1, where marginal costs of $195.56 closely approximates marginal revenue of $200.00.) We can also compute the profit in this scenario by multiplying average profit (profit per unit) by output. Average profit equals price minus average total costs (P − ATC). Thus, when 84 sails are produced, average profit is the distance *ab* in Figure 3, or $200 − $179.52 = $20.48. Total profit, or average profit times output, is $20.48 × 84 = $1,720; this is represented in Figure 3 by area *cfab*.

**TABLE 1 Production, Cost, and Price for Windsurfing Sail Firm**

| L | Q | MP | AP | TFC | TVC | TC | ATC | AVC | MC | AFC | P | TR | Profit |
|---|---|---|---|---|---|---|---|---|---|---|---|---|---|
| 0 | 0 | 0 | | 1000 | 0 | 1000 | | | | | 200.00 | 0 | −1000 |
| 1 | 7 | 7 | 7.00 | 1000 | 1760 | 2760 | 394.29 | 251.43 | 251.43 | 142.86 | 200.00 | 1400 | −1360 |
| 2 | 15 | 8 | 7.50 | 1000 | 3520 | 4520 | 301.33 | 234.67 | 220.00 | 66.67 | 200.00 | 3000 | −1520 |
| 3 | 25 | 10 | 8.33 | 1000 | 5280 | 6280 | 251.20 | 211.20 | 176.00 | 40.00 | 200.00 | 5000 | −1280 |
| 4 | 40 | 15 | 10.00 | 1000 | 7040 | 8040 | 201.00 | 176.00 | 117.33 | 25.00 | 200.00 | 8000 | −40 |
| 5 | 54 | 14 | 10.80 | 1000 | 8800 | 9800 | 181.48 | 162.96 | 125.71 | 18.52 | 200.00 | 10800 | 1000 |
| 6 | 65 | 11 | 10.83 | 1000 | 10560 | 11560 | 177.85 | 162.46 | 160.00 | 15.38 | 200.00 | 13000 | 1440 |
| 7 | 75 | 10 | 10.71 | 1000 | 12320 | 13320 | 177.60 | 164.27 | 176.00 | 13.33 | 200.00 | 15000 | 1680 |
| 8 | 84 | 9 | 10.50 | 1000 | 14080 | 15080 | 179.52 | 167.62 | 195.56 | 11.90 | 200.00 | 16800 | 1720 |
| 9 | 90 | 6 | 10.00 | 1000 | 15840 | 16840 | 187.11 | 176.00 | 293.33 | 11.11 | 200.00 | 18000 | 1160 |
| 10 | 95 | 5 | 9.50 | 1000 | 17600 | 18600 | 195.79 | 185.26 | 352.00 | 10.53 | 200.00 | 19000 | 400 |
| 11 | 98 | 3 | 8.91 | 1000 | 19360 | 20360 | 207.76 | 197.55 | 586.67 | 10.20 | 200.00 | 19600 | −760 |
| 12 | 100 | 2 | 8.33 | 1000 | 21120 | 22120 | 221.20 | 211.20 | 880.00 | 10.00 | 200.00 | 20000 | −2120 |
| 13 | 98 | −2 | 7.54 | 1000 | 22880 | 23880 | 243.67 | 233.47 | −880.00 | 10.20 | 200.00 | 19600 | −4280 |

Note that there *is* a profit maximizing point. The competitive firm cannot produce and produce—it has to take into consideration its costs. So for the price-taking competitive firm, its cost structure is crucial.

## Normal Profits

When the price of windsurfing sails is $200, your firm earns economic profits. Consider what happens, however, when the market price falls to $177.60 a sail. This price happens to be the minimum point on the average total cost curve, corresponding to an output of 75 rigs a month. Figure 4 shows that at the price of $177.60, the firm's demand curve is just tangent to the minimum point on the ATC curve (point *e*), which means the distance between points *a* and *b* in Figure 3 has shrunk to zero. By producing 75 sails a month, your firm earns a normal profit, or zero economic profits.

**FIGURE 4—Competitive Firm Earning Normal Profits (Zero Economic Profits)**

If the market sets a price of $177.60, the firm's demand curve is tangent to the minimum point on the ATC curve (point *e*). The best the firm can do under these circumstances is to earn normal profits on the sale of 75 windsurfing rigs.

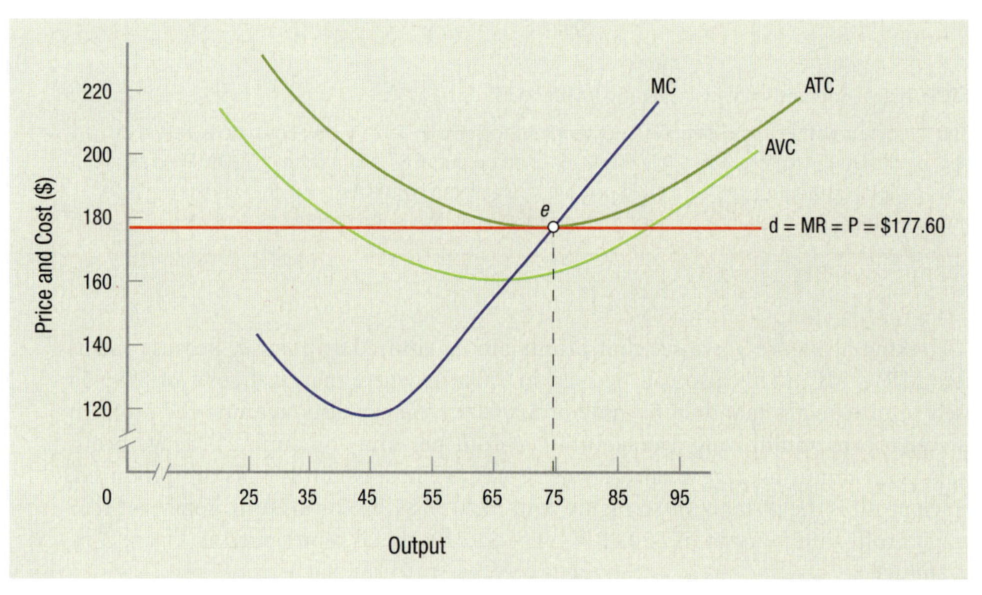


Remember that when a firm earns zero economic profits, it is generating just enough income to keep investor capital in the business. When the typical firm in an industry is earning **normal profits,** there are no pressures for firms to enter or leave the industry. As we will see in a later section, this is an important factor in the long run.

**Normal profits:** Equal to zero economic profits; where P = ATC.

## Loss Minimization and Plant Shutdown

Assume for a moment that an especially calm summer with few winds leads to a decline in the demand for windsurfing equipment. Assume also that, as a consequence, the price of windsurfing sails falls to $170. Figure 5 illustrates the impact on your firm. Market price has fallen below your average total costs of production, but remains above your average variable costs. Profit maximization—or, in this case, *loss minimization*—requires that you produce output at the level where MR = MC. That occurs at point *e*, where output falls somewhere between 65 and 75 units.

For the sake of simplicity, we will assume you cannot hire a partial employee (ignoring the possibility of part-time workers). From Table 1, we know that producing 65 rigs

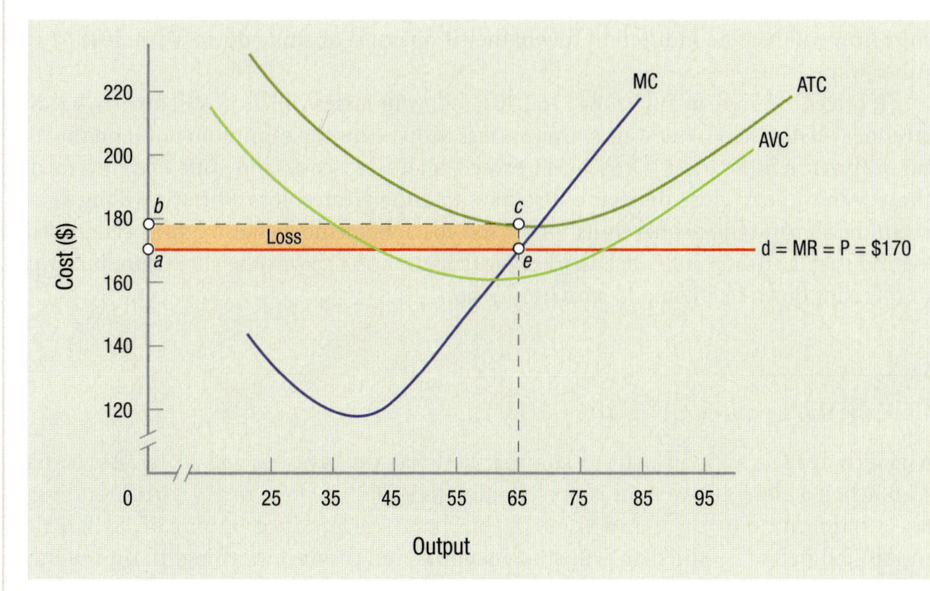


**FIGURE 5—Competitive Firm Minimizing Losses**

Assume that the price of windsurfing sails falls to $170 a sail. Loss minimization requires an output where MR = MC, in this case at 65 units (point e). Average total cost is $177.85 (point c) so loss per unit is equal to $7.85. Total loss is equal to $7.85 3 65 5 $510.25. Notice that this is less than the fixed costs ($1,000) that would have to be paid even if the plant was closed.

requires six employees. Again referring to Table 1, average total cost at this production level is $177.85, so with a market price of $170, loss per unit is $7.85. The total loss on 65 units is $7.85 × 65 = $510.25, corresponding to area *abce* in Figure 5.

These results may look grim, but consider your alternatives. If you were to produce more or fewer sails, your losses would just mount. You could, for instance, furlough your employees. But you will still have to pay your fixed costs of $1,000, and without revenue, your losses would be $1,000. Therefore, it is better to produce and sell 65 rigs, taking a loss of $510.25, thereby cutting your losses nearly in half.

But what happens if the price of windsurfing sails falls to $162.46? Such a scenario is shown in Figure 6. Your revenue from the sale of sails has fallen to a level just equal to variable costs. If you produce and sell 65 units of output (where MR = MC), you will be able to pay your employees their wages, but have nothing left over to pay your overhead;

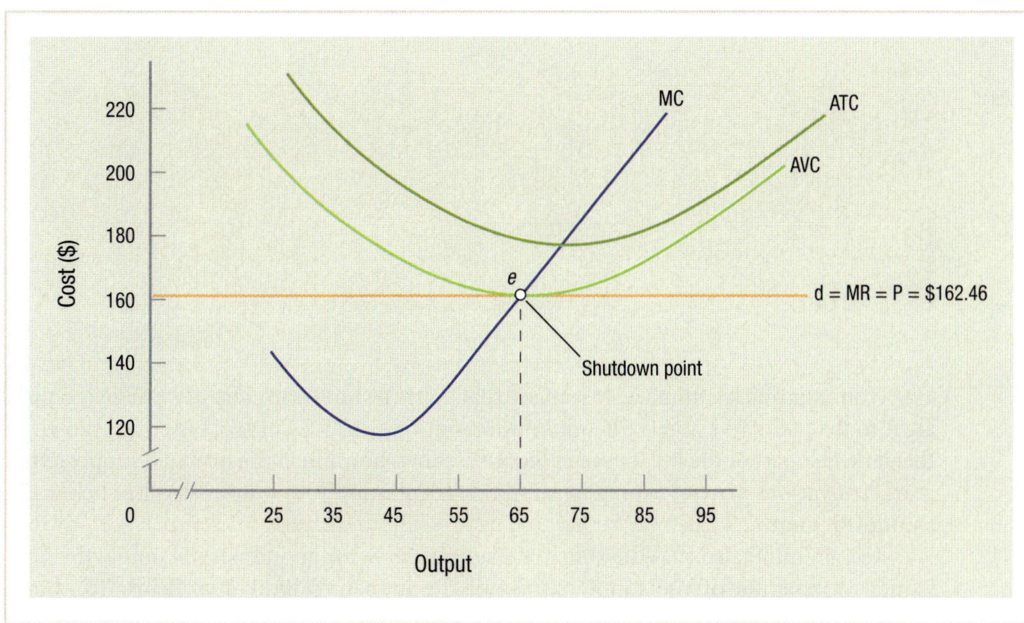


**FIGURE 6—Plant Shutdown in a Competitive Industry**

When prices fall below $162.46, or below the minimum point of the AVC curve, losses begin to exceed fixed costs. The firm will close if price falls below this minimum point (point *e*); this is the firm's shutdown point.

**Shutdown point:** When price in the short run falls below the minimum point on the AVC curve, the firm will minimize losses by closing its doors and stopping production. Since P < AVC, the firm's variable costs are not covered, so by shutting the plant, losses are reduced to fixed costs only.

thus your loss will be $1,000. Point *e* in Figure 6 represents a **shutdown point,** since your firm will here be indifferent to whether it operates or shuts down—you lose $1,000 either way.

If prices continue to fall below $162.46 a sail, your losses will grow still further, because revenue will not even cover wages. Once prices drop below the minimum point on the AVC curve (point *e* in Figure 6), losses will exceed total fixed costs and your loss minimizing strategy must be to close the plant. It follows that the greatest loss a firm is willing to suffer in the short term is equal to its total fixed costs. Remember that the firm cannot leave the industry at this point, since market participation is fixed in the short run, but it can simply shut down its plant and stop production.

## The Short-Run Supply Curve

A glance at Figure 7 will help to summarize what we have learned so far. As we have seen, when a competitive firm is presented with a market price of $P_0$, corresponding to the minimum point on the AVC curve, the firm will produce output of $q_0$. If prices should fall below $P_0$, the firm will shut its doors and produce nothing. If, on the other hand, prices should rise to $P_1$, the firm will sell $q_1$ and earn normal profits (zero economic profits). And if prices continue climbing above $P_1$, say, to $P_2$, the firm will earn economic profits by selling $q_2$. In each instance, the firm produces and sells output where MR = MC.

**FIGURE 7—The Short-Run Supply Curve for a Competitive Firm**

If prices fall below $P_0$, the firm will shut its doors and produce nothing. For prices between $P_0$ and $P_1$, the firm will incur losses, but these losses will be less than fixed costs, so the firm will remain in operation and produce where MR = MC. At a price of $P_1$, the firm earns a normal return. If price should rise above $P_1$ (e.g., to $P_2$), the firm will earn economic profits by selling an output of $q_2$. The portion of the MC curve above the minimum point on the AVC curve, here darkened, is the firm's short-run supply curve.

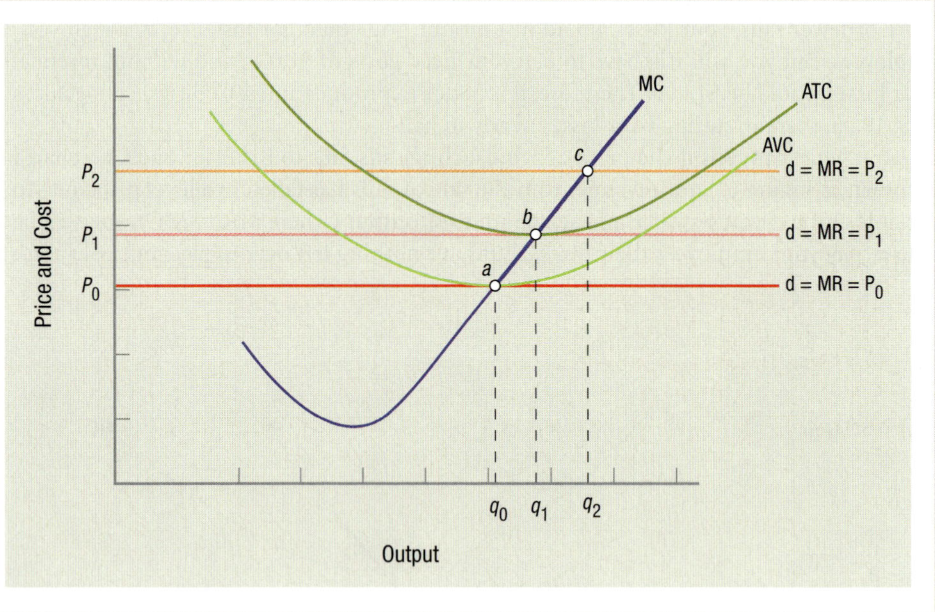


**Short-run supply curve:** The marginal cost curve above the minimum point on the average variable cost curve.

From this quick summary, we can see that a firm's **short-run supply curve** is equivalent to the MC curve above the minimum point on the AVC curve. This curve, shown as the darkened part of the MC curve in Figure 7, shows how much the firm will supply to the market at various prices, keeping in mind that it will supply no output at prices below the shutdown point.

Keep in mind also that the short-run supply curve for an industry is simply the horizontal summation of the supply curves of the industry's individual firms. To obtain industry supply, in other words, we simply add together the output of every firm at various price levels.

## Nobel Prize

### Herbert Simon

When he was awarded the Nobel Prize for Economics in 1978, Herbert Simon (1916–2001) was an unusual choice on two fronts. First, he wasn't an economist by trade; he was a professor of computer science and psychology at the time of his award. Second, Simon's major contribution to economics was a direct challenge to one of the basic tenets of economics: firms, in fact, do not always act to maximize profits.

In his book *Administrative Behavior,* Simon approached economics and the behavior of firms from his outsider's perspective. Simon thought real-world experience showed that firms are not always perfectly rational, in possession of perfect information, or striving to maximize profits.

AP Photo/Paul Sakuma

Rather, he proposed, as firms grow larger and larger, the access to perfect information becomes a fiction. As a rule, firms always have to make do with less than perfect information. Furthermore, since firms are run by individuals with both personal and social ties, these individuals' decisions are further altered by their inability to remain perfectly and completely rational in their decision making.

To Simon, the reality is not that firms tilt at the mythical windmill of maximizing profits, but that, as he said in his Nobel Prize acceptance speech, they recognize their limitations and instead try to come up with an "acceptable solution to acute problems." In short, each decision maker in each firm tries to come up with the best solution for his or her problems. By recognizing this approach to decision making, firms can then set realistic goals and make reasonable assessments of their successes or failures.

Simon's views attacked the basic presumption that drives our market structure models and theories. Simon brought data, theories, and knowledge from other disciplines into economics, broadening its scope and applying more realistic conditions actually found in the marketplace. Although the competitive model in this chapter is based on profit maximization (an admitted simplification), its conclusions steer you in the right direction, even though Simon's analysis must always be considered. Today's challenge to profit maximization and rational decisions are coming from behavioral economists.

## CHECKPOINT

### COMPETITION: SHORT-RUN DECISIONS

- Marginal revenue is the change in total revenue from selling an additional unit of a product.
- Competitive firms are price takers, getting their price from markets, so they can sell all they want at the going market price. As a result, their marginal revenue is equal to product price and the demand curve facing the competitive firm is a horizontal straight-line demand at market price.
- Competitive firms maximize profit by producing that output where marginal revenue equals marginal cost (MR = MC).
- When price is greater than the minimum point of the average total cost curve, firms earn economic profits.
- When price is just equal to the minimum point of the average total cost curve, firms earn normal profits.

- When price is below the minimum point of the average total cost curve, but above the minimum point of the average variable cost curve, the firm continues to operate, but earns an economic loss.
- When price falls below the minimum point on the average variable cost curve, the firm will shut down and incur a loss equal to total fixed costs.
- The short-run supply curve of the firm is the marginal cost curve above the minimum point on the average variable cost curve.

**QUESTION:** Describe why profit maximizing output occurs where MR = MC. Does this explain why competitive firms do not sell "all they can produce"?

Answers to the Checkpoint question can be found at the end of this chapter.

## Competition: Long-Run Adjustments

We have seen that competitive firms can earn economic profits, normal profits, or losses in the short run because their plant size is fixed, and they cannot exit the industry. We now turn our attention to the long run. In the long run, firms can adjust all factors, even to the point of leaving an industry. And if the industry looks attractive, other firms can enter it in the long run.

### Adjusting to Profits and Losses in the Short Run

If firms in the industry are earning short-run economic profits, new firms can be expected to enter the industry in the long run, or existing firms may increase the scale of their operations. Figure 8 illustrates one such possible adjustment path when the firms in an industry are earning short-run economic profits. To simplify the discussion, we will assume there are no economies of scale in the long run.

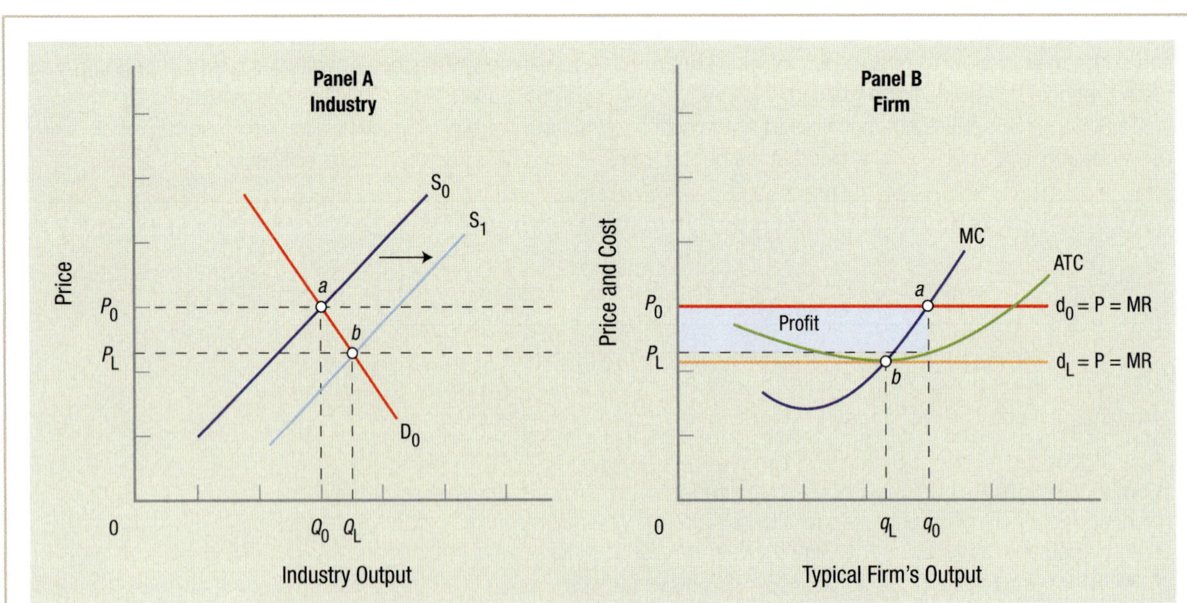


**FIGURE 8—Long-Run Adjustment With Short-Run Economic Profits**

Panel A shows a market initially in equilibrium at point *a*. Industry supply and demand equal $S_0$ and $D_0$, and equilibrium price is $P_0$. This equilibrium leads to the short-run economic profits shown in the shaded area in panel B. Short-run economic profits lead other firms to enter the industry, thus raising industry output to $Q_L$ in panel A, while forcing prices down to $P_L$. The output for individual firms declines as the industry moves to long-run equilibrium at point *b* in both panels. In the long run, firms in competitive markets can earn only normal profits, as shown by point *b* in panel B.

In panel A, the market is initially in equilibrium at point *a*, with industry supply and demand equal to $S_0$ and $D_0$, and equilibrium price equal to $P_0$. For the typical firm shown in panel B, this translates into a short-run equilibrium at point *a*. Notice that, at this price, the firm produces output exceeding the minimum point of the ATC curve. The shaded area represents economic profits.

These economic profits (sometimes called supernormal profits) will attract other firms into the industry. Remember that in a competitive market, entry and exit are easy in the long run; so, many firms decide to get in on the action when they see these profits. As a result, industry supply will shift to the right, to $S_1$, where equilibrium is at point *b*, resulting in a new long-run industry price of $P_L$. For each firm in the industry, output declines to $q_L$ and is just tangent to the minimum point on the ATC curve. Thus, all firms are now earning normal profits and keeping their investors satisfied. There are no pressures at this point for more firms to enter or exit the industry.

Consider the opposite situation—that is, firms in an industry that are incurring economic losses. Figure 9 depicts such a scenario. In panel A, market supply and demand are $S_0$ and $D_0$, with equilibrium price at $P_0$. In panel B, firms suffer economic losses equal to the shaded area. These losses cause some firms to reevaluate their situations and some decide to leave the industry, thus shifting the industry supply curve to $S_1$ in panel A, generating a new equilibrium price of $P_L$. This new price is just tangent to the minimum point of the ATC curve in panel B, expanding output for those individual firms remaining in the industry. Firms in the industry are now earning normal profits, so the pressures to leave the industry dissipate.

Notice that in Figures 8 and 9, the final equilibrium in the long run is the point at which industry price is just tangent to the minimum point on the ATC curve. At this point, there are no net incentives for firms to enter or leave the industry. If industry price rises above this point, the economic profits being earned will induce other firms to enter the industry; the opposite is true if price falls below this point. We will now evaluate this long-run equilibrium.

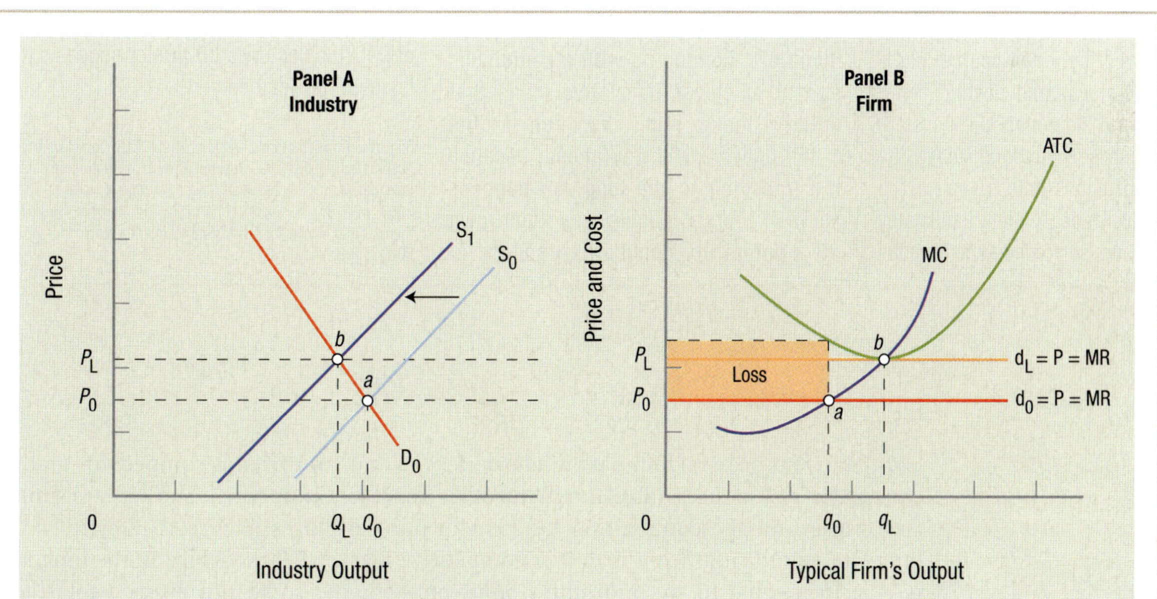


**FIGURE 9—Long-Run Adjustment With Short-Run Losses**

Panel A shows a market initially in equilibrium at point *a*. Industry supply and demand equal $S_0$ and $D_0$, and equilibrium price is $P_0$. This equilibrium leads to the short-run economic losses shown in the shaded area in panel B, thus inducing some firms to exit the industry. Industry output contracts to $Q_L$ in panel A, raising prices to $P_L$ and expanding output for the individual firms remaining in the industry, as the industry as a whole moves to long-run equilibrium at points *b* in both panels. Again, in the long run, firms in competitive markets will earn normal profits, as shown by point *b* in panel B.

## *Issue:* Can Businesses Survive in an Open-Source World?

**Open-source** software can be downloaded for free, used for free, and altered by anyone provided that any changes made can also be freely used and altered by anyone else. Open-source systems like Linux and Apache server software are used to run many of the Internet's biggest sites. Other software, including word-processing, spreadsheets, and photo manipulation, is now becoming open source. Because it is digital, the marginal cost of downloading, using, and duplicating this software approaches zero. Making a profit selling open-source software, even with enhanced features, is therefore a difficult process.

But now there is a movement to open-source *hardware.* Ardvino, a simple micro-controller board; Chumby, a device using software to display weather, play music, and so on; and Bug, a modular system that can be used to make many computing devices, are all open-source hardware products and plans that are available for free, which anyone can duplicate, alter if they wish, and sell.

What happens when open-source software is followed by open-source hardware? Cory Doctorow, in his novel *Makers,* imagines a world in which the "system makes it hard to sell anything above the marginal cost of goods unless you have a really innovative idea, which can't stay innovative for long, so you need continuous invention and reinvention, too." This sounds eerily similar to the battles going on today with smart phones, televisions, video games, ebooks, and other high-tech products. As soon as one company presents a game-changing product (think iPod, iPhone, and iPad), other firms work feverishly to clone it and competition pushes prices and margins down to lower levels. Imagine what would happen if these products were both hardware and software open source.

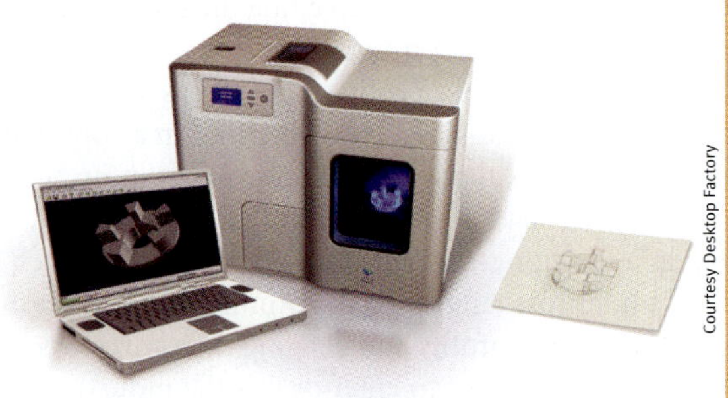

Courtesy Desktop Factory

*Makers* presents a world where two engineers make three-dimensional (3D) desktop printers that can produce any product consumers want from inexpensive "goop." This is essentially the same way that 3D printers today "print" small parts with overlapping layers of resins to serve as 3D versions of design drawings to check dimensions and fit. In *Makers,* the economy collapses, department stores vanish, and unemployment approaches depression levels of more than 20%. Coming up with a continuous stream of clever innovative ideas that initially make high short-run profits is the only way to stay ahead, because the transition to the long run happens so fast. Worse, people use their own 3D printers to duplicate products or designs for virtually nothing (the cost of the goop).

Technology of the kind we are seeing now has the possibility of driving markets to these kinds of levels where marginal cost and profit margins are low. Many companies have thousands of employees that make products from toothbrushes to plastic ware to nearly everything you see at dollar stores. If households had the capability to produce their own products from some cheap substance, many companies we know today would disappear. Cory Doctorow explores what happens when the printers can produce other printers and other open-source machines. Although *Makers* is science fiction, the photo above of Desktop Factory's 3D printer suggests it is not so far-fetched.

Sources: Cory Doctorow, *Makers* (New York: Tom Doherty Associates), 2009; L. Gordon Crovitz, "Technology Is Stranger Than Fiction," *Wall Street Journal,* November 23, 2009, p. A19; and Justin Lahart, "Taking an Open-Source Approach to Hardware," *Wall Street Journal,* November 27, 2009, p. B8.

## Competition and the Public Interest

Competitive processes dominate modern life. You and your friends compete for grades, concert tickets, spouses, jobs, and many other benefits. Competitive markets are simply an extension of the competition inherent in our daily lives. Figure 10 illustrates the long-run equilibrium for a firm in a competitive market. Market price in the long run is $P_{LR}$; it is equal to the minimum point on both the short-run average total cost (SRATC) curve and the long-run average total cost (LRATC) curve. At point *e,* the following is true:

$$P = MR = MC = SRATC_{min} = LRATC_{min}$$

This equation illustrates why competitive markets are the standard (benchmark) by which all other market structures are evaluated. First, competitive markets exhibit

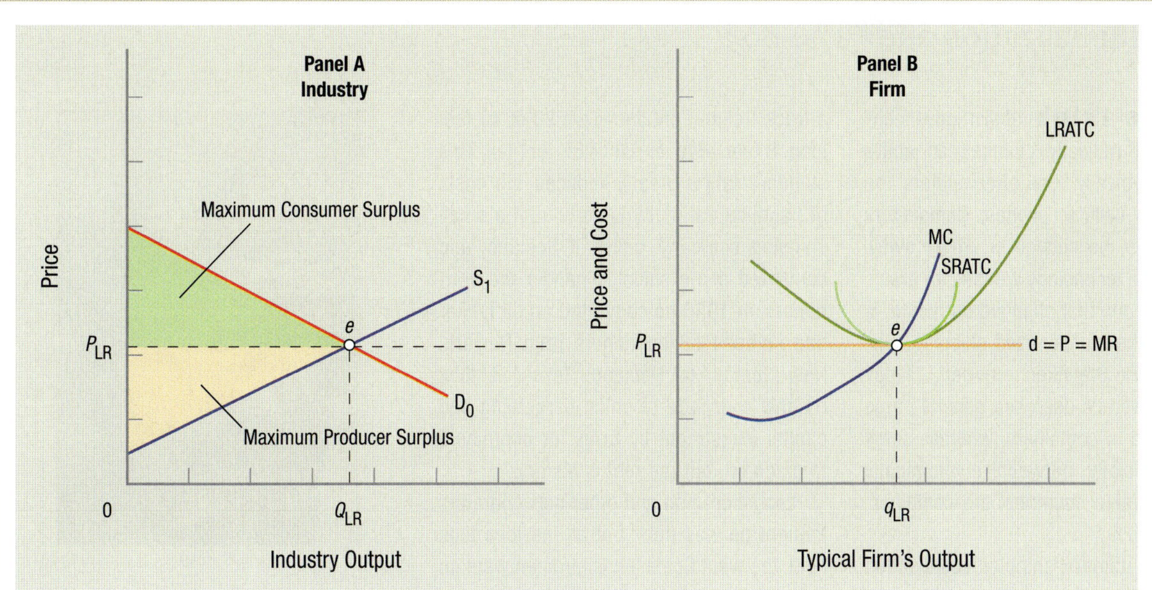


**FIGURE 10—Long-Run Equilibrium for the Competitive Firm**

Market price in the long run is $P_{LR}$, corresponding to the minimum point on the SRATC and LRATC curves. At point *e*, P = MR = MC = $SRATC_{min}$ = $LRATC_{min}$. This is why economists use competitive markets as the benchmark when comparing the performance of other market structures. With competition, consumers get just what they want since price reflects their desires, and they get these products at the lowest possible price ($LRATC_{min}$). Further, as panel A illustrates, consumer and producer surplus is maximized. Any reduction in output reduces the sum of consumer and producer surplus.

**productive efficiency.** Products are produced and sold to consumers at their lowest possible opportunity cost, the minimum SRATC and LRATC. Given the existing technology, firms cannot produce these products more cheaply. For consumers, this is an excellent situation: They pay no more than minimum production costs plus a profit sufficient to keep producers in business, and consumer surplus shown in panel A is maximized. When we look at monopoly firms in the next chapter, consumers will not get such a good deal.

**Productive efficiency:** Goods and services are produced and sold to consumers at their lowest resource (opportunity) cost.

Second, competitive markets demonstrate **allocative efficiency.** The price consumers pay for a given product is equal not only to the minimum average total cost but also to marginal cost. As panel A illustrates, consumer and producer surplus are maximized. Thus, the last unit purchased in the market is sold for a price equal to the opportunity costs required to produce that unit. Because price represents the value consumers place on a product, and marginal cost represents the opportunity cost to society to produce that product, when these two values are equal, the market is allocatively efficient. This means that the market is allocating the production of various goods according to consumer wants.

**Allocative efficiency:** The mix of goods and services produced are just what society desires. The price that consumers pay is equal to marginal cost and is also equal to the least average total cost.

The flip side of these observations is that if a market falls out of equilibrium, the public interest will suffer. If, for instance, output falls below equilibrium, marginal cost will be less than price. Therefore, consumers place a higher value on that product than it is costing firms to produce. Society would be better off if more of the product were put on the market. Conversely, if output rises above the equilibrium level, marginal cost will exceed price. This excess output costs firms more to produce than the value placed on it by consumers. We would be better off if those resources were used to produce another commodity more highly valued by society.

## *Issue:* Globalization and "The Box"

**When we think** of disruptive technologies that radically changed an entire market, we typically think of computers, the Internet, and cellular phones. Competitors must adapt to the change or wither away. One disruptive technology we take for granted today, but one that changed our world, is "the box"—the standardized shipping container. As Dirk Steenken reported, "Today 60% of the world's deep-sea general cargo is transported in containers, whereas some routes, especially between economically strong and stable countries, are containerized up to 100%."

Before containers, shipping costs added about 25% to the cost of some goods and represented over 10% of U.S. exports. The process was cumbersome; hundreds of longshoremen would remove boxes of all sizes, dimensions, and weight from a ship and load them individually onto trucks (or from trucks to a ship if they were going the other way). This process took a lot of time, was subject to damage and theft, and was costly and inconvenient for business.

In 1955 Malcom McLean, a North Carolina trucking entrepreneur, got the idea to standardize shipping containers. He originally thought he would drive a truck right onto a ship, drop a trailer, and drive off. Realizing that the wheels would consume a lot of space, he soon settled on a standard container that would stack together, but would also load directly onto a truck trailer. Containers are 20 or 40 feet long, 8 feet wide, and 8 or 8½ feet tall. This standardization greatly reduced the costs of handling cargo. McLean bought a small shipping company, called it Sealand, and converted some ships to handle the containers. In 1956 he converted an oil tanker and shipped 58 containers from Newark, New Jersey, to Houston, Texas. It took roughly a decade of union bargaining and capital investment by firms for containers to catch on, but the rest is history.

Longshoremen and other port operators thought he was nuts, but as the idea took hold, the West Coast longshoremen went on strike to prevent the introduction of containers. They received some concessions, but containerization was inevitable. Containerization was so cost effective that it could not be stopped. It set in motion the long-run adjustments we see in competitive markets. Ports that didn't adjust went out of business, and trucking firms that failed to add containers couldn't compete. The same was true for ocean shipping companies.

Much of what we call globalization today can be traced to "the box." Firms producing products in foreign countries can fill a container, deliver it to a port, and send it directly to the customer or wholesaler in the United States. The efficiency, originally seen by McLean, was that the manufacturer and the ultimate customer would be the only ones to load and unload the container, keeping the product safer, more secure, and cutting huge chunks off the cost of shipping. Before containers, freight often represented as much as 25% of a product's price. Today, a 40-foot container with 32 tons of cargo shipped from China to the United States costs roughly $5,000, or 7 cents a pound! This efficient, disruptive technology has facilitated the expansion of trade worldwide and increased the competitiveness of many industries.

Youssouf Cader

Sources: Based on Tim Ferguson, "The Real Shipping News," *Wall Street Journal,* April 12, 2006, p. D12; and on Mark Levinson, *The Box* (Princeton, NJ: Princeton University Press), 2006. Dirk Steenken, et al., "Container Terminal Operation and Operations Research," in Hans-Otto Gunther and Kap Hwan Kim, *Container Terminals and Automated Transport Systems* (New York: Springer), 2005. p. 4. Christian Caryl, "The Box Is King," *Newsweek International,* April 10–17, 2006; and Larry Rather, "Shipping Costs Start to Crimp Globalization," *New York Times,* August 3, 2008, p.10.

## Long-Run Industry Supply

Economies or diseconomies of scale determine the shape of the long-run average total cost (LRATC) curve for individual firms. A firm that enjoys significant economies of scale will see its LRATC curve slope down for a wide range of output. Firms facing diseconomies of scale will see their average costs rise as output rises. The nature of these economies and diseconomies of scale determines the size of the competitive firm.

Long-run industry supply is related to the degree to which increases and decreases in industry output influence the prices firms must pay for resources. For example, when all firms in an industry expand or new firms enter the market, this new demand for raw materials and labor may push up the price of some inputs. When this happens, it gives rise to an **increasing cost industry** in the long run.

**Increasing cost industry:** An industry that in the long run, faces higher prices and costs as industry output expands. Industry expansion puts upward pressure on resources (inputs), causing higher costs in the long run.

To illustrate, panel A of Figure 11 shows two sets of short-run supply and demand curves. Initially, demand and supply are $D_0$ and $S_0$, and equilibrium is at point *a*. Assume demand increases, shifting to $D_1$. In the short run, price and output will rise to point *b*. As we have seen earlier, economic profits will result and existing firms will

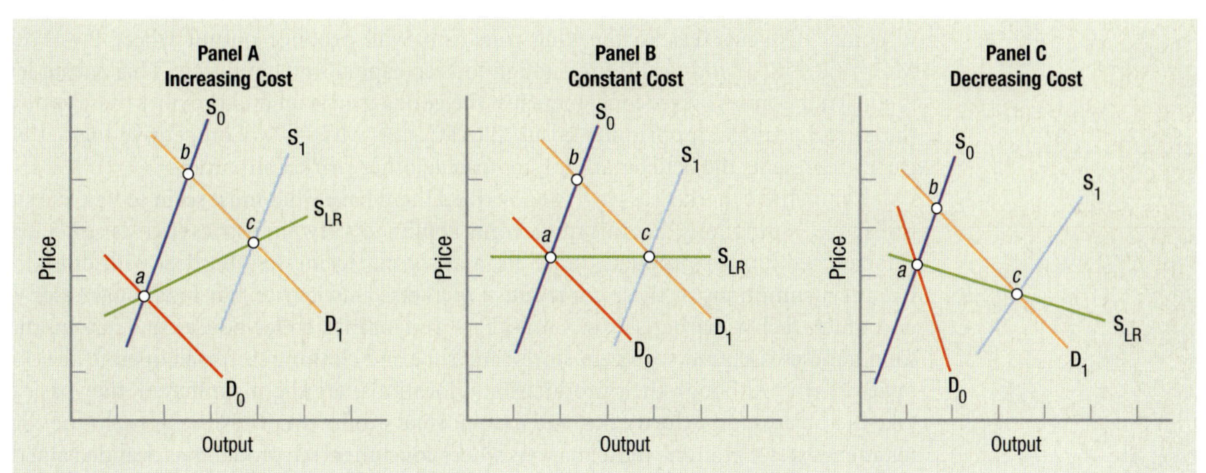


**FIGURE 11—Long-Run Industry Supply Curves**

Panel A shows an increasing cost industry. Demand and supply are initially $D_0$ and $S_0$, with equilibrium at point *a*. When demand increases, price and output rise in the short run to point *b*. As new firms enter the industry, they drive up the cost of resources. Supply increases in the long run to $S_1$ and the new equilibrium point *c* reflects these higher resource costs. In constant cost industries (panel B), firms can expand in the long run without economies or diseconomies, so costs remain constant in the long run. In decreasing cost industries (panel C), expansion leads to external economies and thus to a long-run equilibrium at point *c*, with lower prices and a higher output than before.

expand or new firms will enter the industry, causing product supply to shift to $S_1$ in the long run. Note that at the new equilibrium (point *c*), prices are higher than at the initial equilibrium (point *a*). This is caused by the upward pressure on the prices of industry inputs, notably raw materials and labor that resulted from industry expansion. Industry output has expanded, but prices and costs are higher. This is an *increasing cost industry.*

Alternatively, an industry might enjoy economies of scale as it expands, as suggested by panel C of Figure 11. In this case, price and output initially rise as the short-run equilibrium moves to point *b.* Eventually, however, this industry expansion leads to lower prices; perhaps raw materials suppliers enjoy economies of scale as this industry's demand for their product increases. The semiconductor industry seems to fit this profile: As the demand for semiconductors has risen over the past few decades, their price has fallen dramatically. In the long run, therefore, a new equilibrium is established at point *c,* where prices are lower and output is higher than was initially the case. This illustrates what happens in a **decreasing cost industry.**

Finally, some industries seem to expand in the long run without significant change in average cost. These are known as **constant cost industries** and are shown in panel B in Figure 11. Some fast-food restaurants and retail stores like Wal-Mart seem to be able to clone their operations from market to market without a noticeable rise in costs.

**Decreasing cost industry:** An industry that in the long run, faces lower prices and costs as industry output expands. Some industries enjoy economies of scale as they expand in the long run, typically the result of technological advances.

**Constant cost industry:** An industry that in the long run, faces roughly the same prices and costs as industry output expands. Some industries can virtually clone their operations in other areas without putting undue pressure on resource prices, resulting in constant operating costs as they expand in the long run.

## Summing Up

This chapter has focused on markets in which there is competition—that is, in which industries contain many sellers and buyers, each so small that they ignore the others' behavior and sell a homogeneous product. Sellers are assumed to maximize the profits they earn through sale of their products, and buyers are assumed to maximize the satisfaction they receive from the products they buy. Further, we assume that buyers and sellers have all the information necessary for informed transactions, and that sellers can sell as much of their products as they want at market equilibrium prices.

These assumptions allow us to reach some clear conclusions about how firms operate in competitive markets. In the long run, firms will produce output where P = MR = MC = $LRATC_{min}$ and profits are enough to keep capital in the industry. This output level is efficient because it gives consumers just the goods they want and provides these goods at the lowest possible opportunity costs ($LRATC_{min}$ = MC = P). Competitive market efficiency represents the benchmark for comparing other market structures.

Competitive markets as we have described them have what must seem to you like such restrictive assumptions that this model only applies to a few industries such as agriculture, standardized lumber products, minerals, and so on. Businesses you deal with don't look like the assumptions of these competitive markets. This is true, but most businesses you encounter, such as barber shops, salons, bars, restaurants, coffee houses, gas stations, fast-food franchises, cleaners, grocery stores, and shoe and clothing stores, all operate like competitive firms. Although their products (and locations) are slightly different, they basically take their prices from the market and earn normal profits over the long term. In the chapter after next, we examine those markets where consumers see products as branded and different and see how that industry's behavior is different from competitive markets.

Because the competitive market model is so clearly in the public interest and is the benchmark for comparing other market structures, we can ponder the answer to the following question: Do firms seek the competitive market structure? The answer is: Generally, no. Why? Recall the profit equation. In competitive markets, firms are price takers. They can achieve economic profits in the short run but find it almost impossible to have long-run economic profits. And crucially, the only way competitive firms can be profitable at all is to be efficient productively and continually so. There are some firms, such as Intel, that seem to thrive on competitive pressures. But most firms want long-run economic profits without facing such continual pressures to minimize costs. They want some ability to control price. In the next chapter, we will see what firms do to mitigate these competitive pressures.

## CHECKPOINT

### COMPETITION: LONG-RUN ADJUSTMENTS

- When competitive firms are earning short-run economic profits, these profits attract firms into the industry. Supply increases and market price falls until firms are just earning normal profits, and no firms are attracted into the industry.
- The opposite occurs when firms are making losses in the short run. Losses mean some firms will leave the industry. This reduces supply, thus increasing prices until profits return to normal.
- Competitive markets are efficient because P = MR = MC = $SRATC_{min}$ = $LRATC_{min}$.
- Competitive markets are productively efficient because products are produced at their lowest possible opportunity cost.
- Competitive markets are allocatively efficient because P = MC, and consumer and producer surplus are at a maximum.
- An industry where prices rise as the industry grows is an increasing cost industry, and increased costs may be caused by rising prices of raw materials or labor as the industry expands.
- Decreasing cost industries see their prices fall as the industry expands, possibly due to huge economies of scale or rapidly improving technology.
- Constant cost industries seem to be able to expand without facing higher or lower prices.

**QUESTION:** Most of the markets and industries in the world are highly competitive, and presumably most CEOs of businesses know that competition will mean they will only earn normal profits in the long run. Given this analysis, why do they bother to stay in business, since any economic profits will vanish in the long run?

Answers to the Checkpoint question can be found at the end of this chapter.

## Key Concepts

Market structure analysis, p. 184
Competition, p. 185
Price taker, p. 185
Marginal revenue, p. 187
Profit maximizing rule, p. 188
Normal profits, p. 190
Shutdown point, p. 192
Short-run supply curve, p. 192
Productive efficiency, p. 197
Allocative efficiency, p. 197
Increasing cost industry, p. 198
Decreasing cost industry, p. 199
Constant cost industry, p. 199

## Chapter Summary

### Market Structure Analysis

Market structure analysis enables economists to quickly categorize industries by looking at a few key characteristics. Once an industry has been properly categorized, its behavior in such areas as pricing and output can be predicted.

Economists have identified four basic market structures: competition, monopolistic competition, oligopoly, and monopoly. They are defined by the following factors: the number of firms in the industry, the nature of the product produced, the scope of barriers to entry and exit, and the extent to which individual firms can control prices.

The competitive market structure assumes, first, that the market has many buyers and sellers, each so small that they cannot influence product prices. Second, a competitive industry is assumed to produce a homogeneous or standardized product. Third, all buyers and sellers have all relevant information about prices and product quality. Fourth, barriers to entry and exit are assumed to be insignificant.

Competitive firms are price takers; they cannot significantly alter the sales price of their products. Product prices are determined in broad markets.

In the short run, at least one factor of production, usually plant capacity, is fixed. Also in the short run, firms cannot exit an industry, nor can new firms enter. In the long run, all factors of production are variable, with short-run profit levels inducing entry or exit.

### Competition: Short-Run Decisions

Total revenue equals price per unit times quantity sold (TR $= p \times q$). Marginal revenue is equal to the change in total revenue that comes from producing an added unit of the product (MR $= \Delta$TR/$\Delta q$). Since, in a competitive market, a firm can sell all it wants at the market price, marginal revenue is equal to market price for the competitive firm.

Firms maximize their profits by selling that level of output at which marginal revenue is just equal to marginal cost (MR = MC). For the competitive firm this translates into MC = MR = P. In the short run, a firm can earn economic profits, normal profits, or economic losses, depending on its product's market price.

If price is above the minimum point on the ATC curve, a firm will earn economic profits in the short run. If price is just equal to the minimum point on the ATC curve, the firm will earn normal profits. If price should fall below the minimum ATC, the firm will earn economic losses. Finally, if the price falls below the minimum point on the AVC curve, the firm will shut down and incur a loss equal to its fixed costs, since firms will not operate if they cannot cover their variable costs.

The short-run supply curve for the competitive firm is the marginal cost curve above the minimum point on the AVC curve.

## Competition: Long-Run Adjustments

In the long run, all factors of production are variable, including the ability to exit or enter an industry. When the firms in an industry earn economic profits in the short run, this attracts new firms to the industry, thus reducing product price until firms are earning just normal profits. A corresponding adjustment occurs when the firms in an industry suffer short-term economic losses: Some firms leave the industry, thus raising prices until the remaining firms are again earning normal returns.

Competitive markets serve the public interest by ensuring that firms price their products at their marginal cost, which also equals $LRATC_{min}$. Therefore, just the quantity of products that consumers want is provided at the lowest possible opportunity cost ($LRATC_{min}$). In addition, competitive market equilibrium maximizes consumer and producer surplus.

An industry may be an increasing cost industry, a decreasing cost industry, or a constant cost industry depending on the industry's precise structure, the current state of technology, and the degree of economies and diseconomies of scale.

# Questions and Problems

## Check Your Understanding

1. Why must price cover average variable costs if the firm is to continue operating?
2. Describe the role that easy entry and exit play in competitive markets over the long run.
3. Why are marginal revenue and price equal for the competitive firm?
4. Why, if competitive firms are earning economic profits in the short run, are they unable to earn them in the long run?
5. Describe the reasons why an industry's costs might increase in the long run. Why might they decrease over the long run?

## Apply the Concepts

6. The media reports each quarter on industry profits and losses. Some firms (most notably the airlines) seem to post losses quarter after quarter. Why do they keep operating?
7. Why do competitive firms sell their products only at the market price? Why not try to raise prices to make more profit or lower them to garner market share (more sales)?
8. How is the short-run supply curve for the competitive firm determined?
9. How has the development of the Internet affected small competitive businesses such as used bookstores and antique shops?
10. Of the characteristics that are used to define the four market structures discussed at the beginning of the chapter, which two characteristics intuitively seem to be the most important?
11. Assume a competitive industry is in long-run equilibrium and firms in the industry are earning normal profits. Now assume that production technology improves such that average total costs decline by $5 a unit. Describe the process this industry will go through as it moves to a new long-run equilibrium.
12. When a competitive firm is earning economic profits, is it also maximizing profit per unit? Why or why not?
13. In this chapter we suggested that whenever market price fell below average variable costs that the firm would shut down. At that point revenue is not covering its variable costs and the firm is losing more money than if it just shut down and lost fixed costs. Clearly, shutting the firm is more complicated than that. Under what circumstances might the firm continue to operate even though prices are below average variable costs?

## In the News

**14.** Michelle Slatalla (*New York Times,* February 3, 2005) stated, "The conventional wisdom a few years back was that the Internet would erase price differences among retailers by giving customers instant access to the best deals. Merchants who charged more would be driven out of business." She further quoted Professor Michael Baye, who noted, "The prediction was price-comparison sites would create perfectly competitive environments in which all firms would have to charge the same price." These forecasts for the Internet creating "perfectly competitive" markets were based on the competitive model we have presented in this chapter. Do you think the Internet has helped create more competitive markets or less? Why?

## Solving Problems

**15.** Use the table below to answer the following questions. Assume that fixed costs are $100, and labor is paid $80 per unit (per employee).

| L | Q | MP | AP | TFC | TVC | TC | ATC | AVC | AFC | MC |
|---|---|---|---|---|---|---|---|---|---|---|
| 0 | 0 | | | ___ | ___ | ___ | | | | |
| 1 | 7 | ___ | ___ | ___ | ___ | ___ | ___ | ___ | ___ | ___ |
| 2 | 15 | ___ | ___ | ___ | ___ | ___ | ___ | ___ | ___ | ___ |
| 3 | 25 | ___ | ___ | ___ | ___ | ___ | ___ | ___ | ___ | ___ |
| 4 | 40 | ___ | ___ | ___ | ___ | ___ | ___ | ___ | ___ | ___ |
| 5 | 45 | ___ | ___ | ___ | ___ | ___ | ___ | ___ | ___ | ___ |
| 6 | 48 | ___ | ___ | ___ | ___ | ___ | ___ | ___ | ___ | ___ |
| 7 | 50 | ___ | ___ | ___ | ___ | ___ | ___ | ___ | ___ | ___ |

a. Complete the table.

b. Graph ATC, AVC, AFC, and MC in the blank grid below.

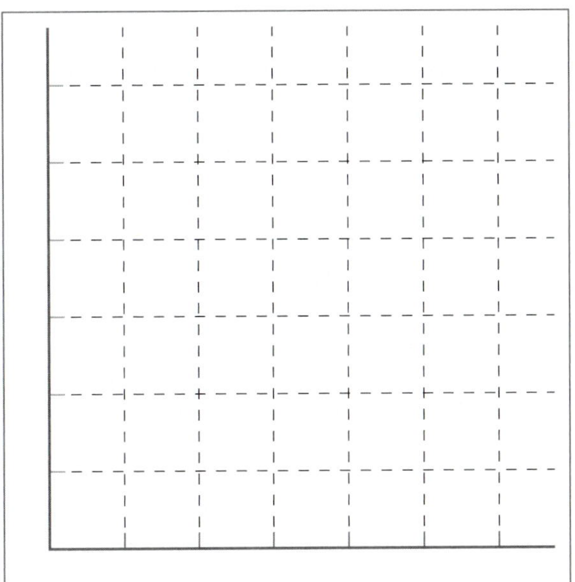

c. Assume the market sets the price at $16 a unit. How much will the firm produce, and what will its profit equal?

d. Assume now that price falls to $10.50. How much will the firm produce, and what will be its profits?

e. Now assume that the price falls to $7.50. Again, how much will the firm produce, and what will be its profits?

**16.** Use the figure below to answer the following true/false questions:

a. If market price is $25, the firm earns economic profits.

b. If market price is $20, the firm earns economic profit equal to roughly $100.

c. If market price is $9, the firm produces roughly 55 units.

d. If market price is $12.50, the firm produces roughly 70 units and makes an economic loss equal to roughly $175.

e. Total fixed costs for this firm are roughly $100.

f. If market price is $15, the firm sells 80 units and makes a normal profit.

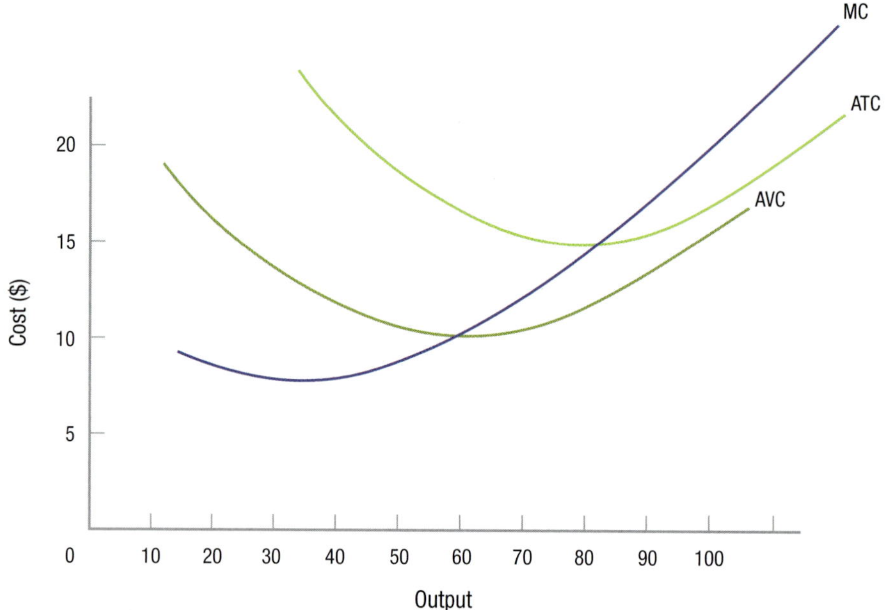


## Answers to Questions in CheckPoints

### Check Point: Market Structure Analysis

Wal-Mart is clearly a very competitive firm. But does this mean it is a competitor in the market structure sense: In some cases, yes, and probably in others, no. When Wal-Mart opens a store in a rural setting, it takes on a dominant retailing role in the local area and looks more like a monopolist with a large market share. When it opens stores in urban areas, it has a lot of competition, and its market share is small, so it looks more like just another retailer in a competitive environment. If we look at the market internationally, Wal-Mart is just one of many large retailers around the world, so it looks like it fits the competitive market structure in the international market. Microsoft is more toward the monopoly end of the spectrum. Who are its competitors? Starbucks has many competitors but its products are considered somewhat unique by consumers so it is a monopolistic competitor. Toyota and the automobile industry are more oligopolistic, with only a few auto manufacturers of importance in the market.

## Check Point: Competition: Short-Run Decisions

Keep in mind that marginal cost is the additional cost to produce another unit of output, and price equals marginal revenue and is the additional revenue from selling one more unit of the product. If MR is greater than MC, the firm earns more revenue than cost by selling that next unit, so the firm will sell up to where MR = MC. At that last unit where MR = MC, the firm is earning a normal profit on that unit (a positive accounting profit). When MC > MR, the firm is spending more to produce that unit than it receives in revenue and is losing money on that last unit, lowering overall profits. Thus, firms will not produce and sell all they can produce: They will produce and sell up to the point where MR = MC.

## Check Point: Competition: Long-Run Adjustments

All businesses are looking for the "next new thing" that will generate economic profits and propel them to monopoly status. Even normal profits are not trivial. Remember, normal profits are sufficient to keep investors happy in the long run. When firms do find the right innovation, such as the iPod, Windows operating system, or a blockbuster breakthrough drug, the short-run returns are huge.

# Monopoly 9

AP Photo/Jens Meyer, file

**In the previous chapter,** we constructed a model of competitive markets in which many sellers compete against one another for the business of many buyers. This model assumed that different firms sell almost identical products, produce where price equals marginal cost, and face no significant barriers to entry, entering or exiting industries easily.

In this chapter, we turn to the theory of monopoly. Unlike competitive firms, monopolies have pricing power. For example, consider Microsoft's Word program. The marginal cost of printing a CD-ROM with Word on it, putting it in a package, and earning a normal profit on its capital is maybe $15 per package. Yet Microsoft charges more than 10 times this amount. Why?

Monopoly is at the other extreme from the competitive model. Whereas the competitive model is in the public interest, we can guess at the outset that monopolies are not. We will see why monopolies exist and how they act. Then we will see what it means to have monopoly power. After that, we will see what can be done to mitigate the powers of monopolies that must exist, and how the United States tries to prevent monopolies from arising.

## Monopoly Markets

The very word *monopoly* almost defines the subject matter: a market in which there is only one seller. Here again, however, economists have attached a more extensive meaning to the word by specifying the types of products sold and the barriers to entry and exit. For economists, a **monopoly** is defined as follows:

Monopoly: A one-firm industry with no close product substitutes and with substantial barriers to entry.

- The market has just one seller—one firm *is* the industry. This contrasts sharply with the competitive market, where many sellers comprise the industry.

**After studying this chapter you should be able to:**

- ☐ Describe the characteristics of a monopoly and monopoly power.
- ☐ Describe the ways in which monopoly power is maintained.
- ☐ Use monopoly market analysis to determine the equilibrium level of output and price for a monopoly.
- ☐ Describe the differences between monopoly and competition.
- ☐ Describe the different forms of price discrimination.
- ☐ Describe the different approaches to regulating a natural monopoly.
- ☐ Relate the history and purpose of antitrust legislation to monopoly analysis.
- ☐ Apply concentration ratios and the Herfindahl-Hirshman index to analyze the likelihood of regulation in a given market.
- ☐ Describe the conditions of a contestable market and its significance.

- No close substitutes exist for the monopolist's product. Consequently, buyers cannot easily substitute other products for that sold by the monopolist. If you want anything like the product in question, you must purchase it from the monopolist.
- A monopolistic industry has significant barriers to entry. Though competitive firms can enter or leave industries in the long run, monopoly markets are considered nearly impossible to enter. So monopolists face no competition, even in the long run.

This gives pure monopolists what economists call monopoly power. Unlike competitive firms, which are price takers, monopolists are *price makers.* Their monopoly power, in other words, allows monopolists to adjust their output in ways that give them significant control over product price.

As we will see, nearly every firm has some monopoly power, or some control over price. Your neighborhood dry cleaner, for instance, has some control over price since it is found close to you, and you are probably not going to want to drive 5 miles just to save a few cents. This control over price becomes minor, however, as markets approach more competitive conditions.

## Sources of Monopoly Power

Monopoly and monopoly power do not mean the same thing. *Monopoly* is defined as one firm serving a market in which there are no close substitutes and entry is nearly impossible. **Monopoly power** (often referred to as market power) implies that a firm has some control over price. As a market structure approaches monopoly, one firm gains the maximum monopoly power possible for that industry. The key to monopoly power is significant barriers to entry. These barriers can be of several forms.

**Monopoly power:** A firm with monopoly power has some control over price.

**Economies of scale:** As the firm expands in size, average total costs decline.

### Economies of Scale

The **economies of scale** in an industry (when average total costs decline) can be so large that demand supports only one firm. Figure 1 illustrates this case. Here the long-run average total cost curve (LRATC) shows extremely large economies of scale. With industry demand at $D_0$, one firm can earn economic profits by producing between $Q_0$ and $Q_1$. If the industry were to contain two firms, however, demand for each would be $D_2$, and neither firm could remain in business without suffering losses. Economists refer to such cases as *natural monopolies.*

Some contemporary natural monopolies include microprocessors, electric utilities, and local newspapers. Though Intel is not a pure monopolist, it sells most of the world's microprocessors. Opening a production plant for its Core processors costs Intel more than a billion dollars, and it needs over $9 billion in annual sales just to support the plant. In addition, Intel spends billions of dollars each year on research, development, and marketing. The market for microprocessors is huge, but so are the development, production, and marketing scales a firm must attain to be successful. Still, the microprocessor market is so large that Intel does face some competition from another large firm (Advanced Micro Devices, AMD, with annual revenues about one-sixth of Intel's) and from smaller niche firms.

Utilities have traditionally been considered natural monopolists because of the high fixed costs associated with power plants and the inefficiency of several different electric companies stringing their wires throughout a city. Recent technology, however, is slowly changing the utilities industry, as smaller plants, solar units, and wind generators permit a smaller yet efficient scale of operations. Smaller plants can be quickly turned on and off, and the energy from the sun and wind is beginning to be stored and transported to where it is needed in the system.

### Control over a Significant Factor of Production

If a firm owns or has control over an important input into the production process, that firm can keep potential rivals out of the market. This was the case with Alcoa Aluminum 50 years ago. The company owned nearly all the world's bauxite ore, one of the key

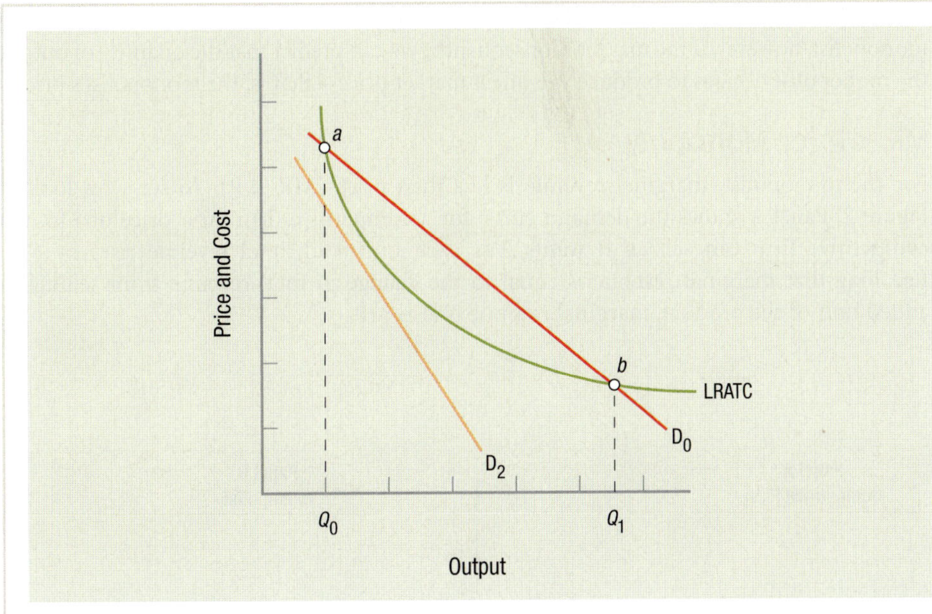


**FIGURE 1—Economies of Scale Leading to Monopoly**

The economies of scale in an industry can be so large that demand supports only one firm. In the industry portrayed here, one firm could earn economic profits (by producing output between $Q_0$ and $Q_1$ when faced with demand curve $D_0$). If the industry were to contain two firms, however, demand for each would be $D_2$, and neither firm could remain in business without suffering losses.

ingredients for aluminum production. In the end, the Justice Department moved against Alcoa to break up this monopoly. We discuss policies to combat monopolies later in this chapter.

### Government Franchises, Patents, and Copyrights

Some barriers to market entry extend from legal government mandates. A government franchise grants a firm permission to provide specific goods or services, while prohibiting others from doing so, thereby eliminating potential competition. The United States Postal Service, for instance, has an exclusive franchise in the delivery of first-class mail to your mailbox. Similarly, some public utilities and cable companies have been granted special franchises by state or local governments.

Patents are extended to firms and individuals who invent new products and processes. For a limited period, usually 20 years, the patent holder is legally protected from competition in production of the patented product. The basic reason behind the patent system is to give firms and individuals the incentive to invent and innovate. If entrepreneurs had to worry about their ideas being stolen by competitors as soon as they brought new products to the market, fewer new products would be developed. Patents are immensely important to many industries, including pharmaceuticals, computers, and chemicals. Many firms in these industries spend huge sums of money each year on research and development—money they might not spend if they could not protect their investments through patenting.

In a similar vein, copyrights give individuals or firms the exclusive right to produce or reproduce certain types of intellectual property for an extended period. A book, a piece of art, or a piece of software code can all be copyrighted. Copyright protection lay at the heart of the Microsoft legal case of the late 1990s. If Microsoft's Windows operating system had not been protected by copyright, Microsoft would not have enjoyed the monopoly power that sparked the government's lawsuit against it. Some firms guard trade secrets to protect their assets for even longer periods than the limited times provided by patents and copyrights. Only a handful of the top executives at Coca-Cola, for instance, know the secret to blending Coke.

## Monopoly Pricing and Output Decisions

We have seen how monopoly power is first attained: barriers to entry. Shortly we will discuss some ways it is maintained. First, however, let us consider monopoly pricing and output decisions. In the previous chapter, we saw that competitive firms maximize profits by producing at a level of output where MR = MC, selling this output at the established market price. The monopolist, however, *is* the market. Consequently, we can predict that the quantity of output the monopolist decides to produce will affect market price—that is, the monopolist's price.

## MR < P for Monopoly

For the monopolist, marginal revenue is less than price (MR < P). To see why, look at Figure 2. Panel A shows the demand curve for a competitive firm. At a price of $10, the competitive firm can sell all it wants. For each unit sold, total revenue rises by $10. Recalling that marginal revenue is equal to the change in total revenue from selling an added unit of the product, marginal revenue is also $10.

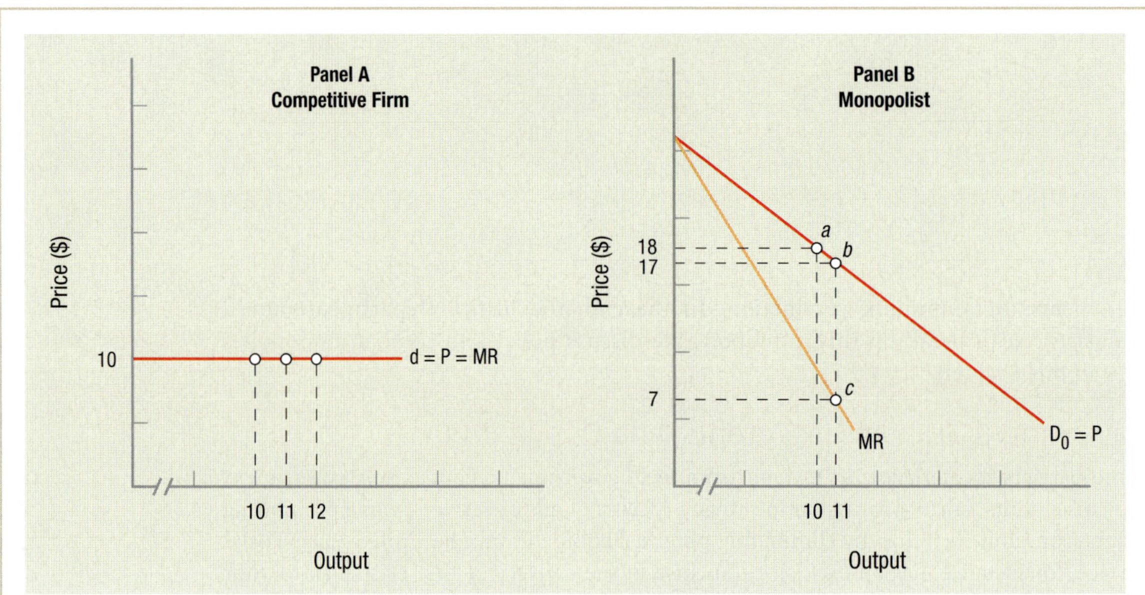


**FIGURE 2—Marginal Revenue for Monopolies and Competitive Firms**

Panel A shows the demand curve for a competitive firm. At a price of $10, the competitive firm can sell all it wants. For each unit sold, revenue rises by $10; hence, marginal revenue is $10. Panel B shows the demand curve for a monopolist. Because the monopolist constitutes the entire industry, it faces a downward sloping demand curve ($D_0$). If the monopolist decides to sell 10 units at $18 each (point *a*), total revenue is $180. Alternatively, if the monopolist wants to sell 11 units, price must be dropped to $17 (point *b*). This raises total revenue to $187 (11 × $17), but marginal revenue falls to $7 ($187–$180, point *c*). Gaining the added $17 in revenue from the sale of the 11th unit requires the monopolist to give up $10 in additional revenue that would have come from selling the previous 10 units for $18 each.

Contrast this with the situation of the monopolist in panel B. Because the monopolist constitutes the entire industry, it faces the downward sloping demand curve ($D_0$). If the monopolist decides to produce and sell 10 units, they can be sold in the market for $18 each (point *a*), generating total revenue of $180. Alternatively, if the monopolist wants to sell 11 units, their price must be dropped to $17 (point *b*). This raises total revenue to $187 (11 × $17). Notice, however, that marginal revenue, or the revenue gained from selling this added unit, falls to $7 ($187–$180). Gaining the additional $17 in revenue from the sale of the 11th unit requires that the monopolist give up $10 in revenue that would have come from selling the previous 10 units for $18 each. Marginal revenue for the 11th unit is shown as $7 (point *c*) in panel B.

Notice that we are assuming the monopolist cannot sell the 10th unit for $18 and then sell the 11th unit for $17; rather, the monopolist must offer to sell a given quantity to the market for a standard price. We are assuming, in other words, that there is no way for the monopolist to separate the market by specific individuals who are willing to pay different prices for the product. In the next section, we will relax this assumption and discuss *price discrimination.*

In summary, we can see from panel B of Figure 2 that MR < P, and the marginal revenue curve is always plotted below the demand curve for the monopolist. This contrasts with the situation of the competitive firm, for which price and marginal revenue are always the same. We should also note that marginal revenue can be negative. In such an instance, total revenue falls as the monopolist tries to sell more output. However, no profit maximizing monopolist would produce in this range because costs are rising even as total revenue is declining, thus reducing profits.

## Equilibrium Price and Output

As noted earlier, product price is determined in a monopoly by how much the monopolist wishes to produce. This contrasts with the competitive firm that can sell all it wishes, but only at the *market-determined price.* Both types of firms wish to make profits. Finding the monopolist's profit maximizing price and output is a little more complicated, however, since competitive firms have only output to consider.

Like competitive firms, the profit maximizing output for the monopolist is found where MR = MC. Turning to Figure 3, we find that marginal revenue equals marginal cost at point *e,* where output is 120 units. Now we must determine how much the monopolist will charge for this output. This is done by looking to the demand curve. An output of 120 units can be sold for a price of $30 (point *a*).

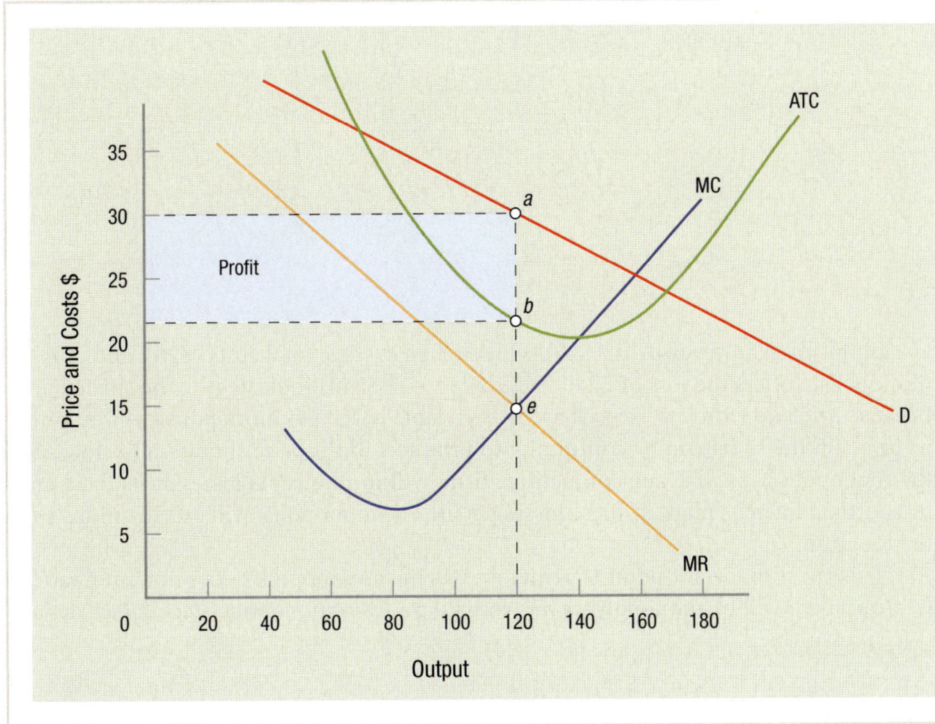


**FIGURE 3—Monopolist Earning Economic Profits**

Profit maximizing output is found for monopolists, as for competitive firms, at the point where MR = MC. In this figure, marginal revenue equals marginal cost at point *e,* where output is 120 units. These 120 units are sold for $30 each (point *a*). Profit is equal to average profit per unit times units sold: Profit = (P − ATC) × Q = ($30 − $22) × 120 = $8 × 120 = $960. The shaded area represents profit.

Profit for each unit is equal to $8, the difference between price ($30) and average total costs ($22). Profit per unit times output equals total profit ($8 × 120 = $960), as indicated by the shaded area in Figure 3. Following the MR = MC rule, profits are maximized by selling 120 units of the product at $30 each.

In summary, to find the equilibrium level of output and price, first find the point where MR = MC. This point determines the profit maximizing output on the horizontal axis, and by extending a vertical line through the point to the demand curve, it determines price on the vertical axis. The difference between this price and average total costs, multiplied by the number of units sold, equals total profit.

## Monopoly Does Not Guarantee Economic Profits

We have seen that competitive firms may or may not be profitable in the short run, but in the long run, they must earn at least normal profits to remain in business. Is the same true for monopolists? Yes. Consider the monopolist in Figure 4. This firm maximizes profits by producing where MR = MC (point *e*) and selling 80 units of output for price $25.

**FIGURE 4—Monopolist Firm Making Economic Losses**

Like competitive firms, monopolists may or may not be profitable in the short run, but in the long run, they must at least earn normal profits to remain in business. The monopolist shown here maximizes profits (minimizes losses) by producing at point *e*, selling 80 units of output at $25 each. Price is lower than average total costs, so the monopolist suffers the loss indicated by the shaded area. Because price still exceeds average variable cost (AVC), in the short run the monopolist will minimize its losses by continuing to produce.

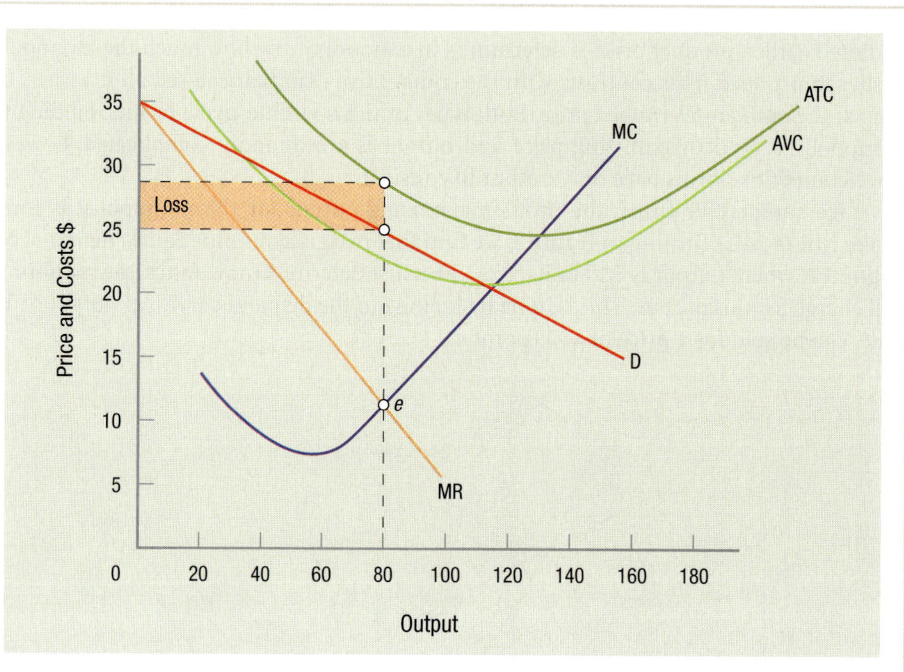


In this case, however, price ($25) is lower than average total costs ($28), and thus the monopolist suffers the loss of $240 ($-\$3 \times 80 = -\$240$) indicated by the shaded area. Because price nonetheless exceeds average variable costs, the monopolist will minimize its losses in the short run by continuing to produce. But if price should fall below AVC, the monopolist, just like any competitive firm, will minimize its losses at its fixed costs by shutting down its plant. If these losses persist, the monopolist will exit the industry in the long run.

This is an important point to remember. Being a monopolist does not automatically mean there will be monopoly profits to haul in. Even monopolies face *some* cost and price pressures.

## Comparing Monopoly and Competition

Would our economy be better off with more or fewer monopolies? This question almost answers itself. Who would want more monopolies—except the few lucky monopolists? The answer is, we want fewer monopolies and more competition. The reasons for this have to do with the losses associated with monopoly markets and monopoly power. As we will discuss in the next two sections, monopoly losses include reduced output at higher prices, deadweight losses, rent-seeking behavior of monopolists, and x-inefficiency losses.

## Higher Prices and Lower Output from Monopoly

Imagine for a moment that a competitive industry is monopolized, and the monopolist's marginal cost curve happens to be the same as the competitive industry's supply curve. Figure 5 illustrates such a scenario. The competitive industry produces where MC = P, and thus where price and output are $P_C$ and $Q_C$ (point *b*). Monopoly price and output, however, as determined as before, are $P_M$ and $Q_M$ (point *a*).

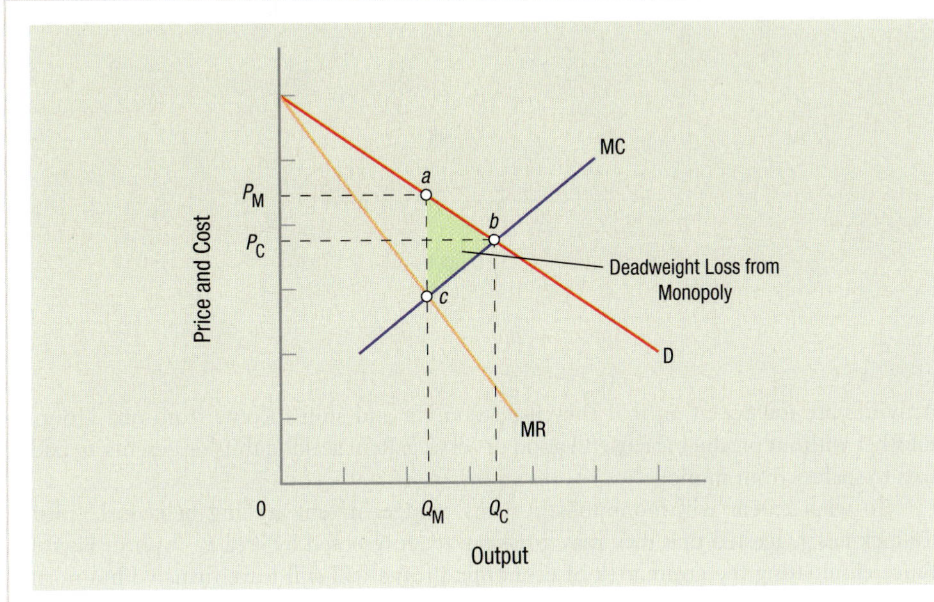


**FIGURE 5—Monopoly Inefficiency**

This figure shows what would happen if a competitive industry were monopolized and the new monopolist's marginal cost curve was the same as the competitive industry's supply curve. When the industry was competitive, it produced where MC = P, and thus where price and output are $P_C$ and $Q_C$ (point *b*). Monopoly price and output, however, are $P_M$ and $Q_M$ (point *a*); output is lower and price is higher than the corresponding values for competitive firms. Shaded area *cab* represents the deadweight loss suffered from monopoly.

Clearly, monopoly output is lower, and monopoly price is higher, than the corresponding values for competitive industries. Notice that at monopoly output $Q_M$, consumers value the $Q_M$th unit of the product at $P_M$ (point *a*), even though the cost to produce this last unit of output is considerably less (point *c*). The *deadweight loss,* otherwise known as the *welfare loss,* from monopoly is shown as the shaded area *cab.* This area represents the deadweight loss to society from a monopoly market.

## Rent Seeking and X-Inefficiency

Monopolies earn economic profits by charging more and producing less than competitive firms. This inefficiency results in a loss of consumer surplus. Figure 6 on the next page resembles Figure 5, except that we are assuming constant-cost conditions. As a result, MC is equal to ATC. Again, the monopolist produces $Q_M$ and sells this output for $P_M$, while the competitive firm sells $Q_C$ at price $P_C$. This results in a deadweight loss equal to area *cab.*

Economic profits in Figure 6 are equal to $P_C P_M ac$. Clearly, this is something monopolists will wish to protect. If entry to the market were eased, this economic profit would soon evaporate, just as it does in competitive markets. How, then, can a monopolist protect itself from potential competition? One way is to spend resources that could have been used to expand its production on efforts to protect its monopoly position.

Economists call this behavior **rent seeking**—behavior directed toward avoiding competition. Firms hire lawyers and other professionals to lobby governments, extend patents, and engage in a host of other activities intended solely to protect their monopoly position. Taxis in New York City, for instance, require licenses; restricting the number of licenses drives up their price and gives license holders a further incentive to restrict the number of new licenses, by lobbying and other means. Many industries spend significant resources lobbying Congress for tariff protection to reduce foreign competition. All these

**Rent seeking:** Resources expended to protect a monopoly position. These are used for such activities as lobbying, extending patents, and restricting the number of licenses permitted.

**FIGURE 6—Rent Seeking and Deadweight Loss in Monopoly**

Economic profits are equal to $P_C P_M ac$. To protect these lucrative profits, the typical monopolist will engage in a variety of rent-seeking behaviors—hiring lawyers and other professionals to lobby the government, for instance, or obtaining patents. Some economists argue that monopolistic firms may engage in so much rent-seeking behavior that all monopoly profits are eliminated.

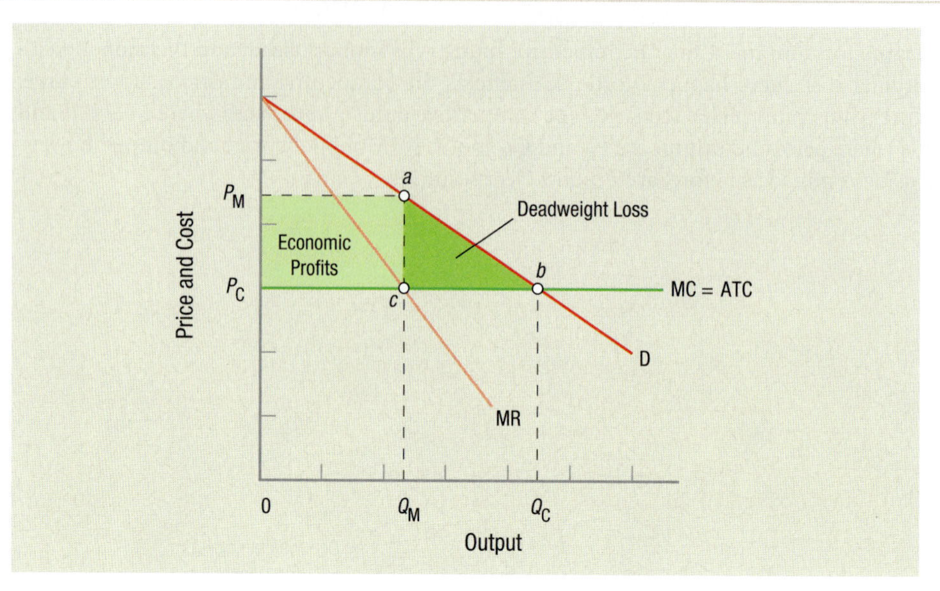


activities are inefficient, in that they use resources and shift income from one group to another without producing a useful good or service. Rent seeking thus represents an added loss to society from monopoly.

To what extent will monopolistic firms engage in rent seeking behavior? Gordon Tullock has suggested that they may go as far as represented by area $P_C P_M ac$ in Figure 6. Since eliminating the entire area of economic profits will still leave firms with a normal return, they may be willing to spend up to this total amount on rent seeking.

X-inefficiency: Protected from competitive pressures, monopolies do not have to act efficiently. Spending on corporate jets, travel, and other perks of business represent x-inefficiency.

Another area where society might lose from monopolies is called **x-inefficiency**. Some economists suggest that because monopolies are protected from competitive pressures, they do not have to operate efficiently. Management can offer itself perks, for instance, without worrying about whether costs are kept at efficient levels. Executive travel in corporate jets, even for private vacations, has been criticized "as a symbol of excess," even though the trip is treated as income for tax purposes (but some companies even pay the taxes for the executives).[1] Deregulation over the last several decades, particularly in the airline and trucking industries, has provided ample evidence of inefficiencies arising when firms are protected from competition by government regulations. Many firms in these industries found it tough sledding when competitive pressures were reintroduced into their industries.

Are there any benefits to monopolies? The answer to this question is, "Possibly yes, though generally no." If the economies associated with an industry are so large that many small competitors would face substantially higher marginal costs than a monopolist, a monopolist would produce and sell more output at a lower price than could competitive firms. Larger firms, moreover, can allocate more resources to research and development than smaller firms, and the possibility of economic profits may be the incentive monopolists require to invest.

Still, economists tend to doubt that monopolies are beneficial enough to outweigh their disadvantages.

In actuality, pure monopolies are rare, in part because of public policy and antitrust laws—more about this later in this chapter—and in part because rapidly changing technologies limit most monopolies to short-run economic profits—witness the battle among Google, Yahoo, and Microsoft for domination of search services, and Sony,

[1] See Geraldine Fabrikant, "Executives Take Company Planes as if Their Own," *New York Times*, May 10, 2006, p. C1.

Amazon, Apple, and several other firms to dominate the eBook market. Even so, all firms seek to increase their market or monopoly power and gain some ability to influence price.

We have seen what monopolies are and how they arise. We also saw why a monopolist produces less than the socially optimal quantity at a higher than socially necessary price, and witnessed how monopoly compares unfavorably to the competitive model. Furthermore, we looked at an expensive drawback of monopolies: the amount of resources wasted in maintaining a monopolist's position. In the next section, we look at what monopolists especially would like to do, and how a society might regulate a natural monopoly.

CHECKPOINT

### MONOPOLY MARKETS

- Monopoly is a market with no close substitutes, high barriers to entry, and one seller; the firm is the industry. Hence, monopolists are price makers.
- Monopoly power can result from economies of scale, control over an important input, or from government franchises, patents, and copyrights.
- For the monopolist, MR < P because the industry's demand is the monopolist's demand.
- Profit is maximized by producing that output where MR = MC and setting the price off the demand curve.
- Being a monopolist does not guarantee economic profits if demand is insufficient to cover costs.
- Monopoly output is lower and price is higher when compared to competition, resulting in a deadweight loss from monopoly.
- Monopolies are subject to rent-seeking behavior directed toward avoiding competition (lobbying and other activities to extend the monopoly).
- Because monopolies are protected from competitive pressures, they often engage in x-inefficiency behavior—extending perks to management and other inefficient activities.

**QUESTIONS:** Google has 85% of the search business on the Internet and generates a lot of advertising revenue. Microsoft has 90% of the operating system business and 80% or so of the Internet browsers in use. In early 2006, Google, the search monopolist, asked the government to rein in Microsoft's new browser, which has a search box in the upper right hand corner, similar to Firefox and Apple's Safari. The default, of course, is that when you type a search term, you go through Microsoft's search engine. Changing the default is, however, quite easy; Google has the instructions on its Web site. Does Google's effort feel a little like monopolistic rent seeking? Should the government step in, or is this just competition between giants?

Answers to the Checkpoint questions can be found at the end of this chapter.

# Monopoly Market Issues

When firms have some monopoly power, they will try to charge different customers different prices. This is called **price discrimination** and it is used to increase their profits. When monopolies must exist, there are policies that can be enacted to mitigate their power. We look at these issues in this section.

**Price discrimination:** Charging different consumer groups different prices for the same product.

## Price Discrimination

When firms with monopoly power price discriminate, they charge different consumers different prices for the same product. For example, senior citizens might pay less for a movie ticket than you do. Remember, unlike monopolies, competitive firms cannot price discriminate because they get their prices from the market (they are price takers). Several conditions are required for successful price discrimination.

- Sellers must have some monopoly (or market) power, or some control over price.
- Sellers must be able to separate the market into different consumer groups based on their elasticities of demand.
- Sellers must be able to prevent arbitrage; that is, it must be impossible or prohibitively expensive for low-price buyers to resell to higher-price buyers.

There are three major types of price discrimination. The first is known as perfect, or first-degree, price discrimination. It involves charging each customer the *maximum price* each is willing to pay. Second-degree price discrimination involves charging different customers different prices based on the *quantities* of the product they purchase. Firms may charge a high price for initial purchases, for instance, and then reduce the price after customers have bought a certain quantity.

The final and most common form of price discrimination is third-degree price discrimination. This occurs when firms *charge different groups of people different prices.* This is an everyday occurrence with airline, bus, and theater tickets.

## Perfect Price Discrimination

When perfect price discrimination can be employed, a firm will charge each customer the maximum price each is willing to pay. This type of price discrimination is perhaps best exemplified by the flea market, where sellers and buyers haggle over the price of each product. Figure 7 portrays such a scenario. Every point on the demand curve represents a price. The first few customers—those who value the product most—are charged a high price. The next customers are charged slightly lower prices, the $Q_M$th customer is charged $P_M$ (point *a*), and so on, until the last unit is sold to the $Q_C$th customer for $P_C$ (point *b*). As a result, a perfectly discriminating monopolist earns profits equal to the shaded area $P_C P_T b$.

Figure 7 shows why firms would want to price discriminate. Typical monopoly profits in this case, assuming the monopolist sells $Q_M$ units at price $P_M$, would be the rectangle area $P_C P_M ac$ (the lighter shaded area). This area is considerably smaller than profit triangle $P_C P_T b$, earned by the perfectly price discriminating monopolist. That is why price discrimination exists—it is profitable. Note also that the *last* unit of the product

**FIGURE 7—Perfect Price Discrimination**

With perfect price discrimination, firms charge each customer the maximum price each is willing to pay. Thus, every point on the demand curve in this figure represents a price. The first few customers—those who value the product most—are charged a high price. The next customers are charged a slightly lower price, and so on, until the last unit is sold for $P_C$ (point *b*). As a result, a perfectly discriminating monopolist earns profits represented by the shaded area $P_C P_T b$. This is considerably more profit than the monopolist would earn by selling $Q_M$ units at price $P_M$, represented by area $P_C P_M ac$.

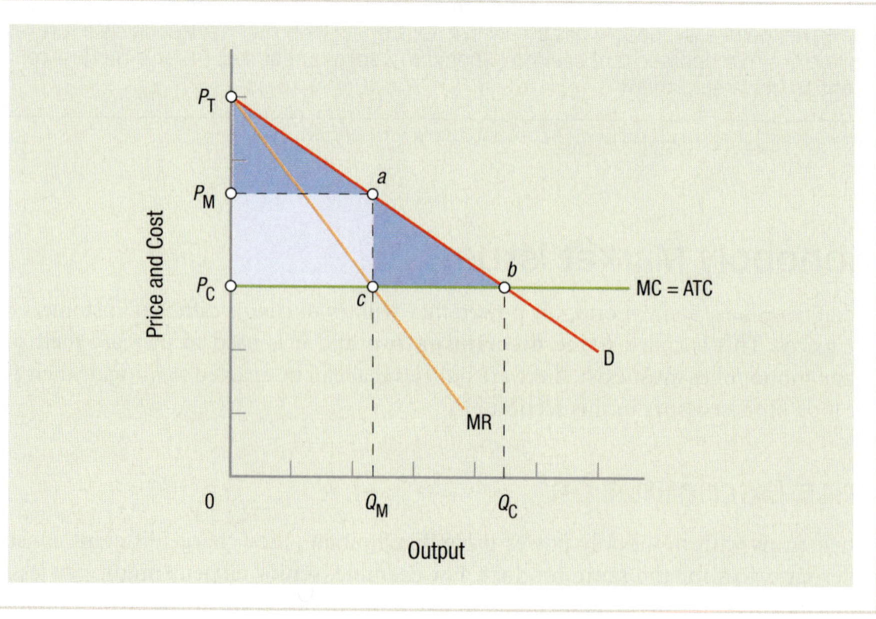

sold by this monopolist is priced at $P_C$, the competitive price. In this limited sense, then, the monopolist who can perfectly price discriminate is as efficient as a competitive firm. Notice that perfectly price discriminating monopolists manage to expropriate the entire consumer surplus.

## Second-Degree Price Discrimination

Second-degree price discrimination involves charging consumers for different blocks of consumption. Producers of electric, gas, and water utilities often incorporate block pricing. You pay one rate for the first so many kilowatt-hours of electricity and a lower rate for more, and so on. This block pricing scheme is shown in Figure 8.

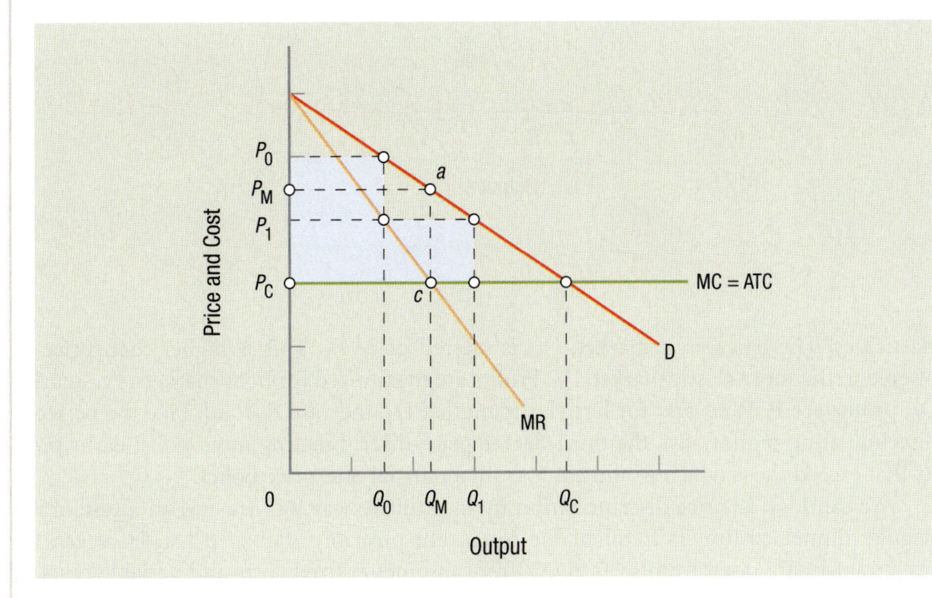


**FIGURE 8—Second-Degree Price Discrimination**

Second-degree price discrimination involves charging different customers different prices based on the quantities of the product they purchase. A nondiscriminating monopolist would earn economic profits equal to $P_C P_M ac$, but by charging three different prices—$P_0$, $P_1$, and $P_C$—profits increase, as shown by comparing the shaded area with area $P_C P_M ac$.

For the first $Q_0$ units of the product, consumers are charged $P_0$; between $Q_0$ and $Q_1$, the price falls to $P_1$; and after that, price is reduced to $P_C$. This results in profit to the firm equal to the shaded area. The shaded profit area for the discriminating monopolist is greater than that of the monopolist charging just one price $P_M$ (area $P_C P_M ac$): Compare the shaded profit area that does not overlap with this area. The most common price discrimination scheme, however, is third-degree, in which groups of consumers are charged different prices.

## Third-Degree Price Discrimination

Third-degree, or imperfect, price discrimination involves charging different groups of people different prices. An obvious example would be the various fares charged for airline flights. Business people have much lower elasticities of demand for flights than do vacationers, so airlines place all sorts of restrictions on their tickets to separate people into distinct categories. Purchasing a ticket several weeks in advance, for instance—which vacationers can usually do, but businesspeople may not be able to—often results in a significantly lower fare. Arbitrage (preventing low-cost buyers from selling to higher-price buyers) is prevented, meanwhile, by rules stipulating that passengers can only travel on tickets purchased in their name. Other examples of third-degree price discrimination include different ticket prices for children, adults, and seniors at movies; student discounts for many services; and even ladies night at clubs.

Third-degree price discrimination is illustrated in Figure 9 on the next page. The two demand curves, $D_0$ and $D_1$, represent two segments of a market with different demand

**FIGURE 9—Third-Degree Price Discrimination**

This figure illustrates third-degree price discrimination. The two demand curves, $D_0$ and $D_1$, represent two segments of a market with different demand elasticities. The less elastic market, $D_1$, is offered price $P_1$, which is higher than price $P_0$, offered to the more elastic market, $D_0$, thus maximizing the profits for both markets.

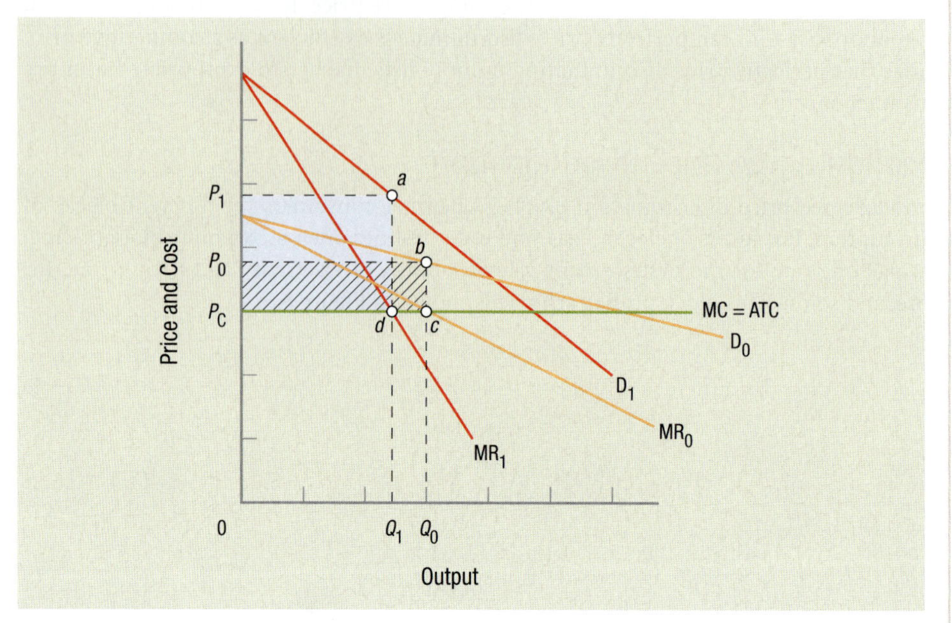


elasticities. The less elastic market, $D_1$, is offered price $P_1$. This is higher than price $P_0$ offered to the more elastic market, $D_0$. Profits are maximized for both markets. For market $D_0$, profits are $P_CP_0bc$, and for less elastic market $D_1$, they are $P_CP_1ad$. Like the perfectly discriminating monopolist, the third-degree price-discriminating monopolist earns profits that exceed those which would come from a normal one-price policy.

We can look at price discrimination in an intuitive way by focusing on a restaurant. Regular dinner customers frequent the restaurant probably after 6:30 P.M. However, the restaurant is still open from 4:30 to 6:30 P.M. and incurs fixed costs and variable costs (if workers start their shifts before the 6:30 rush). It is in the restaurant's interest to offer early bird specials, discounting dinners purchased before 6:30, as long as this policy attracts new customers and does not pull in too many of its later-appearing regular diners. In this way, the restaurant generates profits from two separate groups, while charging two separate prices. As long as the restaurant has some monopoly power—it can offer these two prices without driving its regular customers from higher-priced meals to lower-priced meals—it makes sense for it to act this way. Therefore, we can conclude that firms with some monopoly power will always try to price discriminate.

## Regulating the Natural Monopolist

Natural monopoly: Large economies of scale mean that the minimum efficient scale of operations is roughly equal to market demand.

A **natural monopoly** exists when economies of scale are so large that the minimum efficient scale of operation is roughly equal to market demand. In this case, efficient production can only be accomplished if the industry lies in the hands of one firm—a monopolist. Public utilities and water departments are examples. How can policymakers prevent natural monopolists from abusing their positions of market dominance? There are various approaches to dealing with natural monopolies:

> *First the firm can be publicly owned . . . , the expectation being that the mechanics of political direction and accountability will be sufficient to meet public interest goals. Secondly, the firm may remain in, or be transferred to, private ownership but be subjected to external constraints in the form of price and quantity regulation . . . thirdly, firms desiring to obtain a monopoly right may be forced to compete for it. . . . As part of their competitive bid, they are required to*

*stipulate proposed conditions of supply, relating especially to prices and quality; and those conditions then become terms of the license or franchise under which they exercise the monopoly right.*[2]

A market representing a natural monopoly is shown in Figure 10. Notice that the average cost and marginal cost curves decline continually because of large economies of scale.

If the monopolist were a purely private firm, it would produce only output $Q_M$ and sell this for price $P_M$ (point *a*). Accordingly, the monopolist would earn economic or monopoly profits, and consumers would be harmed, receiving a lower output at a higher price. This is the major argument for regulation.

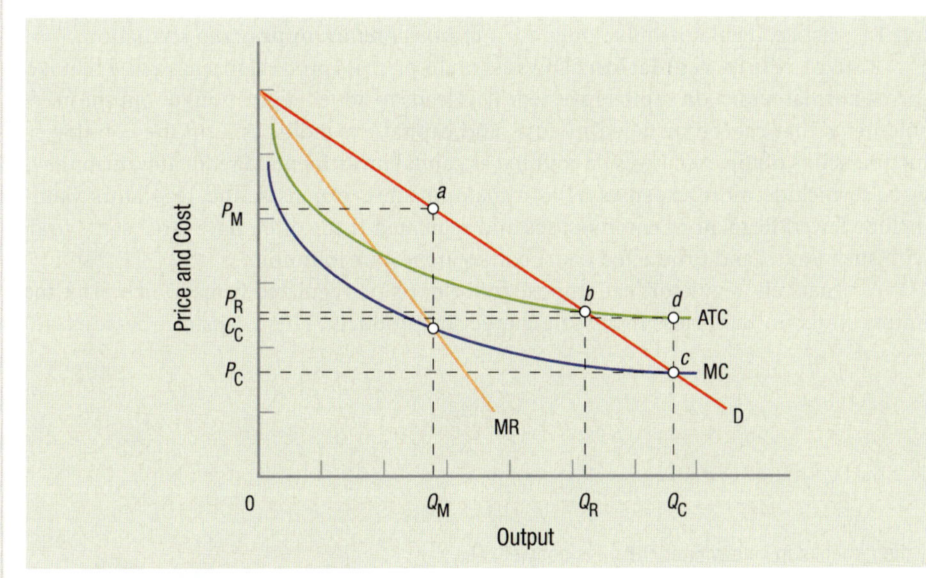


**FIGURE 10—Regulating a Natural Monopoly**

A natural monopoly exists when economies of scale are so large that the minimum efficient scale of operation is roughly equal to market demand. In this case, efficient production can only be accomplished if the industry lies in the hands of one firm—a monopolist. Yet, if the monopolist is a purely private firm, it will produce only output $Q_M$, selling it for price $P_M$ (point *a*). This is the principal rationale for regulating natural monopolies to produce output $Q_R$ for a price of $P_R$ (point *b*).

## Marginal Cost Pricing Rule

Ideally, regulators would like to invoke the P = MC rule of competitive markets and force the firm to sell $Q_C$ units for a price of $P_C$. This is the **marginal cost pricing rule** and would be the optimal resource allocation solution. Yet, because price $P_C$ is below the average cost of production for output $Q_C$, this would force the firm to sustain losses of *cd* per unit, ultimately driving it out of business. The public sector could subsidize the firm by an amount equal to area $P_C C_C dc$; this subsidy allows the firm to supply the socially optimal output at the socially optimal price, while earning a normal return. This approach has not been used often in the United States. However, Amtrak, with its history of heavy subsidies for maintaining rail service, may be the one major exception.

**Marginal cost pricing rule:** Regulators would prefer to have natural monopolists price where P = MC, but this would result in losses (long term) because ATC > MC. Thus, regulators often must use an average cost pricing rule.

## Average Cost Pricing Rule

The more common approach to regulation in the United States has been to insist on an **average cost pricing rule.** Such a rule requires that the monopolist produce and sell output where price equals average total costs. This is illustrated by point *b* in Figure 10, where the demand curve intersects the ATC curve and the firm produces output $Q_R$ and sells it for price $P_R$. The result is that the firm earns a normal return. Consumers do lose

**Average cost pricing rule:** Requires a regulated monopolist to produce and sell output where price equals average total costs. This permits the regulated monopolist to earn a normal return on investment over the long term and so remain in business.

[2] A. I. Ogus, *Regulation: Legal Form and Economic Theory* (Oxford: Oxford University Press), 1996, p. 5, cited in J. Lipczynski and J. Wilson, *Industrial Organization: An Analysis of Competitive Markets* (New York: Prentice Hall—Financial Times), 2001.

something, in that they must pay a higher price for less output than they would under idealized competitive conditions. Still, the normal profits keep the firm in business, and the losses to consumers are significantly less than if the firm were left unregulated.

## Regulation in Practice

America has a long history of public utility regulation. For most of this history, regulation has been accepted as a lesser of two evils. Monopolists have long been viewed with distrust, but regulators have just as often been portrayed as incompetent and ineffectual, if not lapdogs of the industries they regulate.[3] This is probably unfair: Regulating a large enterprise always presents immense difficulties and tradeoffs.

For one thing, finding a point like *b* in Figure 10 is difficult in practice, given that estimating demand and cost curves is an inexact science, at best, and markets are always changing. In practice, regulators must often turn to *rate of return* or *price cap* regulation.

**Rate of return regulation:** Permits product pricing that allows the firm to earn a normal return on capital invested in the firm.

**Price caps:** Maximum price at which a regulated firm can sell its product. They are often flexible enough to allow for changing cost conditions.

**Rate of return regulation** allows a firm to price its product in such a way that it can earn a normal return on capital invested. This leads to added regulations about the acceptable items that can be included in costs and capital expenditures. Can the country club memberships of top executives be counted as capital investments? Predictably, firms always want to include more expenses as legitimate business expenses, and regulators want to include fewer. Regulatory commissions and regulated firms often have large staffs to deal with such issues, and protracted court battles are not uncommon.

Alternatively, regulators can impose **price caps** on regulated firms, which place maximum limits on the prices firms can charge for products. These caps can be adjusted in

### *Issue:* Re-regulation Pressures

**Deregulation** began during the Carter administration in the 1980s and then in earnest with the election of Ronald Reagan. Over the years, trucking, airlines, telecommunications, and banking are among those industries that have seen regulations reduced. All of this was done with the aim of removing burdensome regulations from business, thereby stimulating economic activity and reducing prices to consumers.

Under airline regulation, 10 major air carriers controlled 90% of the market. The Civil Aeronautics Board regulated routes and set fares that guaranteed airlines a 12% return on flights that were on average 55% full. Deregulation intended to let new airlines enter and succeed (like Southwest) or fail (150 airlines have failed over the last 30 years). Advocates of deregulation saw success and failure as normal parts of competitive market dynamics.

When you look at freight rates, the price of airline tickets, and the cost of communications (both data and voice), deregulation looks to be a winner. But all is not well. The mortgage and financial crunch that came to a head in late 2008 capped off an already growing movement to re-regulate utilities, Internet services, student loans, and union organizing rules.

The recent bailout of the financial sector and the political success of Democrats sets the stage for a growing host of new regulations in finance, housing, energy, environmental affairs, and health care.

The re-regulate–deregulate–re-regulate pendulum seems to swing every several decades. The Great Depression ushered in a host of new agencies that covered almost all major industries. This was followed up in the 1960s and 1970s with new bureaucracies to regulate education, the environment, and many other industries. Ronald Reagan's election was partly based on "getting government off our backs," and over the last 30 years market discipline has substituted for government control. The recent financial and credit crunch has resulted in a growing chorus for re-regulation and we can expect to see just that. One ironic note, however, is the general consensus to use a market-based emissions trading system (markets) rather than regulation to cap our greenhouse gas emissions. The fight over markets versus government has been around since the country's inception and will continue.

Stockbyte/Getty Images

Source: Micheline Maynard, "Did Ending Regulation Help Flyers?," *New York Times*, April 17, 2008, p. C1.

[3] See George Stigler, "The Theory of Economic Regulation," *Bell Journal of Economics*, 1971, pp. 3–21.

response to changing cost conditions, including changes in labor costs, productivity, technology, and raw material prices. When a large part of a regulated firm's output is not self-produced but purchased on the open market, price caps can have disastrous results. This was seen in the California energy market, when wholesale prices for energy went through the roof, but price caps prevented private utilities from raising the retail price of electricity; several firms had to file for bankruptcy.

In sum, though regulation imposes costs on the market, these costs are less than the costs of private monopolies. Today, however, the pace of technological change is so rapid that regulation has lost some of its earlier luster and is not used as often. Rather than regulate the few natural monopolies that do arise, government has sought to prevent monopolies and monopolistic practices from arising at all—a topic we cover in the next section.

**CHECKPOINT**

### MONOPOLY MARKET ISSUES

- Firms with monopoly power price discriminate to increase profits.
- To price discriminate, firms must have some control over price and must be able to separate the market into different consumer groups based on their elasticity of demand, and sellers must be able to prevent arbitrage.
- With perfect price discrimination the firm can charge each customer a different price and expropriate the entire consumer surplus for itself.
- Second-degree price discrimination involves charging customers different prices for different quantities of the product.
- Third-degree price discrimination (the most common) involves charging different groups of people different prices.
- Regulating monopolies may involve a marginal cost pricing rule (have the monopolist set price equal to marginal cost) or an average cost rule (have the monopolist set price equal to average total cost).
- In practice, regulation often involves setting an acceptable rate of return on capital or setting price caps on charges.

**QUESTIONS:** Researchers at Yale University and the University of California, Berkeley found that minorities and women pay about $500 more on average for a car than white men when bargaining directly with car dealers. However, when minorities and women used Internet services such as Autobytel.com to purchase a car, the price discrimination disappeared. Is this price discrimination the same as that discussed in this section? Why or why not?

Answers to the Checkpoint questions can be found at the end of this chapter.

## Antitrust Policy

*Like all antitrust cases, this one must make economic sense.*

—United States v. Syufy Enterprises

Competition is the market structure that offers consumers the greatest product selection at the lowest prices. Monopolies and firms with substantial monopoly power have the potential to restrict output and increase prices, resulting in significant allocative inefficiencies. The economic model of monopoly forms the basis for the bulk of **antitrust law,** the goal of which is to preserve competition and prevent monopolies and monopoly power from arising.

**Antitrust law:** Laws designed to maintain competition and prevent monopolies from developing.

Antitrust cases can be filed by the Antitrust Division of the Department of Justice, the Federal Trade Commission (FTC), states' attorneys general, or lawyers for private plaintiffs. Currently, there is debate about the extent of efficiency losses that stem from monopoly power, and how often antitrust action is needed.[4] Even so, Americans have a visceral sense that monopolies are bad, and historically, antitrust policy has targeted monopolies as threats to economic efficiency.

## Brief History of Antitrust Policy

The American economy began to change dramatically after the Civil War. Many people left the farm to seek factory jobs in the cities, and the western territories were opened up as rail lines joined them to the rest of the country. Communications expanded along with transportation, the telephone replacing the telegraph. Markets grew from local to regional in size, and many firms dramatically expanded their size. Unfettered competition led many large firms to engage in brutal practices meant to drive competitors from the market. The largest firms established trusts, which brought many firms under one organizational structure that could set price and output levels, extract concessions from railroads, and act as we would expect monopolies to act. By the end of the century, trusts had become so powerful—and so hated—that Congress passed the first antitrust act, the Sherman Act, in 1890. Antitrust laws and policies, thus, had their origins in trust-busting activity.

Most of the legislators who voted for antitrust laws in the late 1800s and early 1900s were more concerned with equitably distributing income and wealth, and the health of small businesses, than with competition and allocative efficiency. The massive accumulations of wealth by such "robber barons" as John D. Rockefeller (Standard Oil) and Jay Gould (railroads and stock manipulation) sparked resentment and fear. Nobel Prize laureate George Stigler has argued, however, that the economists of the day had little enthusiasm for antitrust policy, viewing all limits placed on business as stifling free enterprise. Today, most economists agree that some antitrust legislation is needed, but that its primary role should be to prevent the allocative inefficiency associated with monopoly behavior.

## The Major Antitrust Laws

Several major statutes form the core of the country's antitrust laws. The most important provisions of these laws (as amended) are described in the following sections.

### The Sherman Act (1890)

> ***Section 1:*** *Every contract, combination in the form of trust or otherwise, or conspiracy, in restraint of trade or commerce among the several states, or with foreign nations, is hereby declared to be illegal.*
> ***Section 2:*** *Every person who shall monopolize, or attempt to monopolize, or combine or conspire with any other person or persons, to monopolize any part of the trade or commerce among the several states, or with foreign nations, shall be deemed guilty of a felony.*

Conviction in either section is a felony and carries a fine of up to $10,000,000 for corporations and $350,000 for individuals, and/or a prison sentence of up to 3 years. Section 1 focuses on the "restraint of trade," whereas Section 2 targets "monopolization" and the "attempt to monopolize." Congress purposefully left these terms undefined, thus requiring the courts to flesh them out.

### The Clayton Act (1914)

> ***Section 2:*** *It shall be unlawful for any person engaged in commerce . . . to discriminate in price between different purchasers of commodities of like grade and quality . . . where the effect of such discrimination may be substantially to lessen competition or tend to create a monopoly in any line of commerce, or to injure, destroy, or prevent competition.*

[4] See Richard A. Posner, *Antitrust Law*, 2d ed. (Chicago: University of Chicago Press), 2001.

## Nobel Prize

### George Stigler

Few modern economists have broken ground in so many different areas as George Stigler, described by some admirers as the "ultimate empirical economist." His 1982 Nobel Prize cited seminal work in industrial structure, the functioning of markets, and the causes and effects of public regulation.

Born in 1911 in the Seattle suburb of Renton, Washington, Stigler attended graduate school at the University of Chicago, a center of great intellectual ferment during the late 1930s, with fellow students and Nobel Prize winners Milton Friedman and Paul Samuelson. Professors like Frank Knight and Henry Simons encouraged what he would later describe as "an irreverence toward prevailing ideas bordering on congenital skepticism." Stigler was a professor at the University of Chicago from 1958 until his death in 1991.

AP Photo/George Ruhe

Exploring the relationship between size and efficiency led him to the "Darwinian" conclusion that by observing competition in an industry, he could determine the most efficient sizes for firms, a method he called "the survivor technique." In the 1960s, Stigler studied the impacts of government regulation on the economy, arriving at negative conclusions about its potential value to consumers. He later turned to the causes of regulation, observing that government interventions were often designed to optimize market conditions for producers instead of protecting the public interest. This work opened up a new field known as "regulation economics" and kindled greater interest in the relationship between law and economics.

Stigler considered his work on information theory his greatest contribution to economics. Conventional wisdom suggested that prices for homogeneous industries should be uniform, but in the real world, prices often varied. His research suggested that the variation could be explained by the costs of gathering and diffusing information about goods and prices. The Internet was supposed to bring a convergence of prices for nearly every product because the Internet's low information costs and competition would force firms to quickly meet the lowest seller's price. The fact that there are still widely varying prices for many products suggests that Stigler's insights are still important.

> ***Section 3:*** *It shall be unlawful for any person engaged in commerce [to] make a sale or contract for sale of goods . . . or other commodities . . . on the condition . . . that the lessee or purchaser thereof shall not use or deal in the goods . . . or other commodities of a competitor or competitors of the seller, where the effect of such lease, sale or contract . . . may be to substantially lessen competition or tend to create a monopoly in any line of commerce.*
>
> ***Section 7:*** *That no corporation engaged in commerce shall acquire, directly or indirectly, the whole or any part of the stock or other share capital and no corporation subject to the jurisdiction of the Federal Trade Commission shall acquire the whole or any part of the assets of another corporation engaged also in commerce, where in any line of commerce in any section of the country, the effect of such acquisition may be substantially to lessen competition, or tend to create a monopoly.*

The act goes on to forbid "tying contracts," agreements whereby the sale of one product is contingent upon the purchase of another product. The act further makes it illegal to acquire a competing company's stock and have interlocking directorates, the directors of one company sitting on the boards of competing companies. These practices are deemed illegal if they substantially lessen competition or tend to create a monopoly.

### The Federal Trade Commission Act (1914)

> ***Section 5.(a)(1)****: Unfair methods of competition in or affecting commerce, and unfair or deceptive acts or practices in or affecting commerce, are hereby declared unlawful.*

This act established an independent regulatory body, the Federal Trade Commission (FTC), and gave it the power to enforce the Clayton Act and the Robinson-Patman Act (discussed in the next section). Amended in 1938 by the Wheeler-Lea Amendments to add "unfair or deceptive acts or practices," this FTC Act is the centerpiece of federal consumer protection. The Supreme Court has given the FTC the power to enforce antitrust laws, except the Sherman Act.

### Other Antitrust Acts

The Robinson-Patman Act amended the Clayton Act in 1936 to prohibit price discrimination. Passed in the middle of the Depression, this Act was designed to protect mom and pop stores from the growing menace of chain stores and supermarkets. Chain stores have tremendous buying and bargaining power with manufacturers. This bargaining power translates into price discounts that chains can pass on to their customers, putting small businesses at a disadvantage. This same logic is often used today to prevent a Wal-Mart from opening stores in some towns. Today, the federal government rarely enforces these provisions, viewing them as outdated.

The 1950 Celler-Kefauver Antimerger Act closed a merger loophole in the Clayton Act. The original Clayton Act intended to forbid holding companies, and thus it outlawed one company from holding the stock of its competitors. But the Clayton Act did not prohibit anticompetitive mergers through asset acquisition. The Celler-Kefauver Act closed this loophole, and set up elaborate premerger notification requirements for mergers exceeding a certain size.

The intensity of antitrust enforcement has varied with presidential administrations and courts over the past century. Early on the focus was on monopolies and on attempts to monopolize, with actions brought against Standard Oil, American Tobacco, and Alcoa (Aluminum Company of America). Attention then turned to mergers and prenotification issues discussed earlier. More recently, antitrust enforcement has been concentrated on price fixing—conspiracies by firms to agree on industry prices to suppress or eliminate competition. In 2008 the U.S. Justice Department levied fines of $1.27 billion against a dozen airlines, including Air France-KLM, Cathay Pacific, SAS Scandinavian Airlines, British Airways, and Qantas, for fixing cargo rates for international air shipments to and from the United States. To date, this is the largest fine levied against an industry for price fixing.

Although price-fixing cases were of particular interest to the Bush administration, it is merger policy developed in the 1950s that has really stood the test of time. Economists and judges generally agree that the reason for antitrust enforcement is to prevent the inefficiencies associated with significant monopoly power. Premerger notification for approval or challenge by the Justice Department is designed to prevent mergers that have a reasonable likelihood of creating monopoly power. However, the first problem facing the enforcement community involves defining monopoly power. This entails defining the relevant product market and then agreeing on a proper measuring device of monopoly power.

## Defining the Relevant Market and Monopoly Power

We have seen that, as an industry moves from competition to monopoly, pricing power rises from zero to total. One of the challenges economists have faced is developing one measure that accurately reflects market power or concentration for all these market structures.

Industries that become more concentrated increase the losses to society. Therefore, any measure of concentration should accurately reflect the ability of firms to increase prices above that point which would prevail under competitive conditions. Such an index would help the Justice Department, for instance, determine when to bring a Sherman Act case against a firm for monopolizing or attempting to monopolize. It could further be used to determine whether two firms should be permitted to merge. Coming up with such a number requires, first, that we define the relevant market, and then that we compute an index number for this market.

## Defining the Market

To measure market power and the concentration of a market, we need to determine the limits of the market, geographically and as defined by the product itself.

Some markets can be severely limited geographically, such as concrete, with its extremely high transport costs, and dry cleaning, limited by the unwillingness of consumers to travel far for this service. Other markets are national in scope, like airlines, breakfast cereals, and electronics. Still others extend beyond the borders of a country, with the forces of global competition increasingly reducing domestic market power.

Economists have been unable to reduce the empirical definition of a relevant market to a simple rule. Nearly 50 years ago, George Stigler suggested that "all products or enterprises with large long-run cross-elasticities of supply or demand should be combined into a single industry."[5] This would mean that an industry or market should be regarded as containing those products that are ready substitutes for the main product in the long run. Stigler's suggestion by no means makes delineating a relevant market neat and easy, but at least it gives economists something to work with.

## Concentration Ratios

The most widely used measure of industry concentration is the **concentration ratio.** The $n$-firm concentration ratio is the share of industry sales accounted for by the industry's $n$ largest firms. Typically, four- and eight-firm concentration ratios (CR-4 and CR-8) are reported.

Concentration ratio: The share of industry shipments or sales accounted for by the top four or eight firms.

Though useful in giving a quick snapshot of an industry, concentration ratios express only one piece of the market power distribution picture: the market share enjoyed by the industry's four or eight largest firms. Yet, consider the following two 4-firm concentration ratios. In the first industry, the four largest firms have market shares equal to 65, 10, 5, and 5. This means the concentration ratio is 85; that is, the top four firms control 85% of industry sales. The second industry has market shares equal to 25, 20, 20, 20. This industry's concentration ratio also equals 85. But do the two industries exhibit the same level of monopoly power? Hardly! The second industry, whose top four firms are roughly equal in size, would be expected to be more competitive than the first, where 65% of the market is controlled by one firm.

Without more information about each industry, concentration ratios are not overly informative, except to point out extreme contrasts. If one industry's four-firm concentration ratio is 85, for instance, and another's is 15, the first industry has considerably more monopoly power than the second.

Economists and antitrust enforcers, however, need finer distinctions than concentration ratios permit. For this reason, the profession has developed the Herfindahl-Hirshman index.

## Herfindahl-Hirshman Index

The **Herfindahl-Hirshman index (HHI)** is the principal measure of concentration used by the Justice Department to evaluate mergers and judge monopoly power. The HHI is defined by the equation:

Herfindahl-Hirshman index (HHI): A way of measuring industry concentration, equal to the sum of the squares of market shares for all firms in the industry.

$$\text{HHI} = (S_1)^2 + (S_2)^2 + (S_3)^2 + \ldots + (S_n)^2,$$

[5] George J. Stigler, "Introduction," in National Bureau of Economic Research, *Business Concentration and Price Policy* (Princeton, NJ: Princeton University Press), 1955, p. 4.

where $S_1, S_2, \ldots Sn$ are the percentage market shares of each firm in the industry. Thus, the HHI is the sum of the squares of each market share. In a five-firm industry, for instance, in which each firm enjoys a 20% market share, the HHI is

$$\begin{aligned} HHI &= 20^2 + 20^2 + 20^2 + 20^2 + 20^2 \\ &= 400 + 400 + 400 + 400 + 400 \\ &= 2{,}000 \end{aligned}$$

The HHI ranges from roughly zero (a huge number of small firms) to 10,000 (a one-firm monopoly: $100^2 = 10{,}000$). By squaring market shares, the HHI gives greater weight to those firms with large market shares. Thus, a five-firm industry with market shares equal to 65, 15, 10, 5, 5 would have an HHI equal to

$$\begin{aligned} HHI &= 65^2 + 15^2 + 10^2 + 5^2 + 5^2 \\ &= 4{,}225 + 225 + 100 + 25 + 25 \\ &= 4{,}600 \end{aligned}$$

The HHI is consistent with our intuitive notion of market power. It seems clear that an industry with several competitors of roughly equal size will be more competitive than an industry in which one firm controls a substantial share of the market.

### Applying the HHI

In 1976, Congress passed the Hart-Scott-Rodino Act. This Act requires prenotification of large proposed mergers to the FTC and the antitrust division of the Justice Department. Prenotification gives federal agencies a chance to review proposed mergers for anticompetitive impacts. This approach prevents some mergers from taking place that would ultimately have to be challenged by Sherman Act litigation, a far more costly alternative for the government and for the firms involved.

During the prenotification review, the Justice Department or FTC can approve the proposed merger or else negotiate a settlement that introduces restrictions designed to reduce anticompetitive outcomes. Sometimes these agreements involve complex rules and reporting requirements that amount to government regulation. If no agreement is reached, the agencies can challenge the merger in court. When agreements cannot be reached, the merger is usually called off.

The Justice Department and FTC in 1992 issued merger guidelines based on the HHI. These guidelines classify industries as follows:

- HHI $<$ 1,000: Industry is unconcentrated.
- 1,000 $<$ HHI $<$ 1,800: Industry is moderately concentrated.
- HHI $>$ 1,800: Industry is highly concentrated.

Mergers where the resulting HHI is below 1,000 will often be approved. Mergers with postmerger HHIs between 1,000 and 1,800 will be closely evaluated; they are often challenged if the proposed merger raises the HHI by 100 points or more. When the HHI for the industry exceeds 1,800, a postmerger rise in the HHI of 50 points is enough to spark a challenge.

These guidelines have worked well, giving businesses a good idea of when the government will challenge mergers. Most mergers are rapidly approved; the remainder often require only minor adjustments or more information to satisfy government agencies. In the end, only a few proposed mergers are seriously challenged. Clearly, most firms that want to merge will ensure their companies and industries fit in the specified guidelines.

## Contestable Markets

**Contestable markets:** Markets that look monopolistic but where entry costs are so low that the sheer threat of entry keeps prices low.

Sometimes what looks like a monopolist does not act like a monopolist. Markets that are contestable fit this description. **Contestable markets** are those markets with entry costs so low that the sheer threat of entry keeps prices in contestable markets low. Potential competition constrains firm behavior. For example, Microsoft might charge more for its latest version of Windows if Linux was not nipping at its heels.

Many software firms argue, however, that new software innovations are stifled because once a new product has been released, Microsoft can simply clone the product and package it with Windows for free, thus rendering investment in new products unprofitable for smaller companies. It is far easier and cheaper to copy and enhance a software product than to conceive of the idea and bring it to market in the first place. A significant part of the arguments in the original Microsoft legal case revolved around just this issue. Still, the relative ease with which new operating systems can be developed to challenge Windows—witness Linux, Mac OS X, Unix—probably keeps Microsoft from significantly overcharging for Windows.

## The Future of Antitrust Policy

American antitrust legislation grew out of economic concentration and the resulting predatory behavior over a century ago. The laws passed to nullify these abuses have resulted in some fascinating legal cases, but in the end, antitrust legislation is rooted in the basic economics and market structure analysis discussed in the last two chapters.

As the United States transitioned from an agrarian to an industrial economy, public policy changed. As our economy today moves from its domestic manufacturing roots to more of a global information and service base, public policy again must adapt.

The Microsoft case was the first real attempt to apply the old antitrust rules to the newly emerging circumstances of the "new economy." The government met with some success in this case, but mostly failure.

The new economy differs from the old economy in many ways. The old economy was grounded in manufacturing and distributing physical goods such as steel, automobiles, appliances, and shoes. These old economy industries enjoyed economies of scale in production, often requiring huge capital requirements and modest rates of innovation.

New economy industries turn these requirements on their heads. Such industries as software, telecommunications infrastructure, and e-commerce operate with modest capital, extremely high rates of innovation, easy entry and exit, and economies of scale in consumption known as **network externalities.**

**Network externalities:** Markets in which the network becomes more valuable as more people are connected to the network.

One phone or Internet connection is worthless; it cannot be used to communicate with anyone. As more people become connected to the network, however, the network becomes more valuable—hence, the term "network externalities." Every firm therefore has a tremendous interest in seeing its innovation adopted as the industry standard, providing the firm with a monopoly in that technology. Witness the recent format war over high-definition optical disc standards eventually won by Blu-ray technology when Sony decided to include a Blu-ray player in its PlayStation video console.

Consumers and the society as a whole may benefit from monopoly standards—how could we exchange computer files if we all used different word-processing programs? But what, then, will keep temporary monopolists from charging excessive prices? To some degree, the answer lies in the contestability of the industry (low capital requirements, easy entry and exit, and rapid innovation). The Linux challenge to Microsoft Windows came from a university student who wrote this operating system as a school project. Often, it is low prices (free, in the case of Linux) that extend markets and create standards. Low prices mean more users, and more users lead to the creation of standards.

Now the Internet itself is presenting a challenge to the dominance of Microsoft Windows and Office. Google introduced its "Chrome" browser, which is designed to run Office-type programs over the Web without loading them physically on each computer. This "cloud" computing has led to inexpensive netbook computers intended to take advantage of Web computing without hard drives for storage. This approach is changing the way software is delivered and used.

Much of what new economy firms produce is intellectual property. In large measure, it is computer code of one form or another. Most of the costs to produce the programs are fixed, already sunk once the product is completed. To produce and distribute the product

## *Issue:* Oil and Gas—The Rise of Community Monopolies

**When we think** of monopoly power, we typically think of a large company selling an important product without reasonable substitutes. Rarely would we consider a community of homeowners as a single *seller* or a monopolist. However, rising commodity prices (especially oil and natural gas) in 2008 caused communities of homeowners to band together to bargain with natural gas companies for the drilling rights to their land.

By banding together and presenting a monopoly to the drilling companies, they were able to offer a larger tract of land as well as their use of social pressure to help the companies bring holdouts to the table. Higher gas prices and new drilling techniques allow companies to drill without disturbing the character of neighborhoods, making areas (suburbs) that were previously undrillable now quite profitable.

Getty Images

By forming these voluntary neighborhood bargaining groups (some as large as 7,000 homeowners), communities have been able to increase their offers from $1,000 to $3,000 an acre with a small (5%) royalty override to more than $20,000 an acre and 25% royalty rates. These neighborhood groups create a bargaining situation where the homeowners have monopoly power and the power of the oil companies is limited, resulting in a more favorable contract for homeowners.

Source: Ben Casselman, "Homeowners Unite, Get More for Drilling Rights," *Wall Street Journal,* June 6, 2008, p. A4.

costs only a fraction of the product's value; if the Internet is used, distribution costs can approach zero. This means markups and profits are high, which creates a strong incentive to clone successful products. Monopolies, therefore, tend to be transitory in the new economy. The travails of Lotus 123, WordPerfect, Borland, and Netscape all testify to the vulnerability of temporary monopolists in the software industry. All were industry leaders at one point, only to be displaced by some new kid on the block.

Antitrust laws and policy need to be adjusted to new market realities. In our global information and service economy, many of the old rules are irrelevant. One federal judge and economist, Richard Posner, argues that we should repeal all the old antitrust laws, chiefly because of the "gross redundancy of their manifold provisions." He suggests these laws be replaced with a simple statute that prohibits "unreasonably anti-competitive practices."[6]

When a firm's market share approaches monopoly levels, turning to antitrust laws is the obvious response. This and the last chapter looked at the polar opposites of market structures, competition and monopoly. The next chapter looks at the market structures in the middle and also looks at a more modern approach to analyzing firm behavior, game theory.

### CHECKPOINT

#### ANTITRUST POLICY

- The Sherman Act (1890) prohibited monopolization and attempts to monopolize.
- The Clayton Act (1914) prohibited price discrimination that lessened competition, prohibited tie-in sales, and prohibited corporate directors from serving on competing boards if this would lessen competition.
- The Federal Trade Commission Act (1914) prohibited unfair or deceptive business practices and established the Federal Trade Commission.
- Defining the relevant market is often difficult, but a focus on cross elasticity of demand is useful.

[6] Richard A. Posner, *Antitrust Law,* 2nd ed. (Chicago: University of Chicago Press), 2001, p. 260.

- Concentration ratios measure market concentration by looking at the share of industry sales accounted for by the top n firms.
- The Herfindahl-Hirshman index (HHI) measures concentration by computing the sum of the squares of market shares for all firms in the industry.
- The Justice Department uses the HHI to set premerger guidelines.
- Contestable markets are markets with low entry costs so that the potential threat of entry keeps prices low.

**QUESTION:** Assume the following table represents the sales figures for the eight largest firms in the auto industry in the United States:

| Company | Sales (billions of dollars) |
|---|---|
| General Motors | 2.063 |
| Toyota | 1.77 |
| Ford | 1.616 |
| Honda | 1.151 |
| Chrysler | 0.931 |
| Nissan | 0.77 |
| Hyundai | 0.435 |
| Mazda | 0.208 |
| **Total** | **8.944** |

a. Compute the four-firm concentration ratio for the industry.
b. Compute the HHI for the industry.
c. Assuming the industry is represented by these 8 firms, if Toyota and Ford wanted to merge, and you were the head of the Justice Department, would you permit the merger? Why or why not? How about if Hyundai and Mazda wanted to merge?

Answers to the Checkpoint questions can be found at the end of this chapter.

## Key Concepts



## Chapter Summary

### Monopoly Markets

A firm can *be* a monopoly; it can *have* monopoly power. For economists, a monopoly is defined by three key characteristics. First, the market has just one seller, thus the monopolistic firm *is* the industry. Second, no close substitutes exist for the monopolist's product, so consumers cannot easily substitute other products for the product sold by the monopolist. Third, significant barriers to entry keep other firms from entering the industry. This means the monopolist faces no competition, even in the long run.

Monopoly power is the degree to which a firm can control the price of its product by adjusting output. Competitive firms are price takers, meaning that they have no monopoly power; the prices for their products are determined by competitive markets. Monopolists, in contrast, are price makers. They enjoy considerable monopoly power and much freedom in deciding what to charge for their products.

The key to monopoly power is significant barriers to entry, which can take several forms. The economies of scale in an industry can be so large that demand will support only one firm. If a firm owns or has control over an important input into the production process, that firm can keep potential rivals out of the market.

Some barriers to market entry extend from the power of government. A government franchise grants a firm permission to provide specific goods or services while prohibiting others from doing so. Patents are extended to firms and individuals that invent new products and processes. For a limited period, the patent holder is legally protected from competition in the production of the patented product. Copyrights give firms or individuals the exclusive right to intellectual products for a long period.

Because the monopolist constitutes the entire industry, it faces a downward sloping demand curve. Product price is determined in a monopoly by how much the monopolist wishes to produce. This contrasts with the competitive firm, which can sell all it wishes, but only at the market determined price.

Like the competitive firm, the monopolist maximizes its profit at output where MR = MC. Because of the monopolist's downward sloping demand curve, however, marginal revenue does not equal price at this point; rather, MR < P. To determine the monopolist's profit maximizing price, extend a vertical line through the point where MR = MC to the demand curve; where this line intersects the demand curve determines the price to be found on the vertical axis. The monopolist's profit equals the difference between this price and average total costs, multiplied by the number of units sold.

Being a monopoly does not guarantee economic profits. If a monopolist's profit maximizing price is lower than average total costs, it will suffer a loss. As long as price exceeds average variable costs, the monopolist will minimize its losses in the short run by continuing to produce. But if price should fall below average variable costs, the monopolist will minimize its losses (equal to its fixed costs) by shutting down. If these losses persist, the monopolist will exit the industry in the long run.

Monopoly output is lower and monopoly price is higher, compared to competitive markets. As a result, monopolies earn economic profits at the expense of consumers: monopoly reduces consumer surplus. The loss to society from monopoly output and pricing is known as deadweight loss, or welfare loss.

To maintain their advantageous position, monopolists often engage in rent-seeking behavior. Rent seeking represents an added loss to society from monopoly because it shifts resources from one group to another without producing a useful good or service.

Some economists argue that monopolies do not have to operate efficiently because they are protected from competitive pressures. This is known as x-inefficiency.

## Monopoly Market Issues

When firms with monopoly power price discriminate, they charge different consumers different prices for the same product. The goal is to maximize profits by charging each customer as much as each is willing to pay. Several conditions are required for successful price discrimination: sellers must have some monopoly power, sellers must be able to separate the market into different consumer groups based on their elasticities of demand, and sellers must be able to prevent arbitrage—that is, it must be impossible or prohibitively expensive for low-price buyers to resell to higher-price buyers.

There are three major types of price discrimination. First-degree price discrimination involves charging each customer the maximum price each is willing to pay. Second-degree price discrimination involves charging different customers different prices based on the quantities of the product they purchase. The most common form of price discrimination is third-degree price discrimination: charging different groups of people different prices.

A natural monopoly exists when economies of scale are so large that the minimum efficient scale of operation is roughly equal to market demand. In such cases, policymakers employ a variety of measures to prevent natural monopolists from abusing their positions of market dominance.

## Antitrust Policy

Since 1890, the U.S. Congress has passed a series of major statutes that form the core of the country's antitrust laws. These include the Sherman Act (1890), the Clayton Act (1914), the Federal Trade Commission Act (1914), the Robinson-Patman Act (1936), and the Celler-Kefauver Antimerger Act (1950).

The early antitrust laws were passed with the intention of promoting an equitable distribution of wealth and protecting small businesses against predatory monopolies. The intensity of antitrust enforcement has varied with presidential administrations and courts over the past century. There is general agreement among economists and judges, however, that some antitrust regulation is needed, and that its basic purpose is to prevent the inefficiencies associated with significant monopoly power.

Economists have developed several means of measuring market concentration. The $n$-firm concentration ratio reports the share of industry sales accounted for by the $n$ largest firms. The Herfindahl-Hirshman index (HHI) is the principal measure of concentration used by the Justice Department to evaluate mergers and judge monopoly power.

Contestable markets are those with entry costs so low that firms can enter or leave the industry rapidly. If a firm is earning economic profits, new firms will enter the market until returns have been driven back down to normal levels. The sheer threat of entry, therefore, keeps prices in contestable markets low, even if the market is now a monopoly.

# Questions and Problems

## Check Your Understanding

1. Are McDonald's and Starbucks monopolies? Why or why not?
2. Explain why MR < P for the monopolist, but MR = P for competitive firms.
3. What do economists mean when they call monopolies inefficient? What is the deadweight loss of monopoly?

## Apply the Concepts

4. Synthetic diamonds are getting better, and starting to give De Beers a lot of competition in the diamond market. What will be De Beers' response?
5. How important is the existence of a significant barrier to entry to maintaining a monopoly? What would be the result if a monopoly market could easily be entered? Why might a monopoly in a high-tech field such as computers, the Internet, and consumer electronics be rather short-lived?
6. The monopoly model we discussed in this chapter suggests that monopolies have little incentive to innovate. In contrast, firms in competitive markets need to keep innovating to continue to exist. Some economists have suggested that if barriers to entry are not large, this is sufficient to keep a monopolist innovating to maintain its monopoly. Does the computer technology industry seem to fit this argument?
7. If cable television services were completely deregulated today, what would happen to the monthly charges?
8. My dentist recently recommended that I have a tooth replaced with a titanium pin inserted in my jaw and capped with a crown. I went to an oral surgeon to have the tooth removed and the pin inserted. The bill for the procedure was $300 to remove

the tooth and $1,500 to insert the titanium pin. Removing the tooth and inserting the pin each took roughly the same amount of time. Since the cost of the pin is negligible and both parts of the procedure took the same time why would the oral surgeon charge 5 times as much to set the pin as to pull the tooth? (Hint: Monopoly power and level of competition underlies the answer.)

## In the News

9. According to Peter Marsh (*Financial Times,* September 10, 2005) Swatch, the Swiss watchmaker famous for its inexpensive watches, announced in 2005 that it will no longer supply high-end mechanical movements (parts) to upscale manufacturers. Swatch manufactures and sells roughly 75% of the mechanical movements to such watchmakers as Lacroix, Nardin, and Breitling and has its own brands Omega, Longines, and Breguet. The change did not take place until 2010, but it sent many manufacturers scrambling to replace Swatch as a supplier. Swatch was only earning $3 million from the sale of movements to competitors, who turned them into watches worth several billions of dollars. One manufacturer suggested that "Swatch's decision was driven by its desire to reduce competition." Does this seem correct? Why or why not?
10. In 2006, Maryland passed a law requiring that any company with 10,000 or more employees must spend 8% of its payroll on health care, or must remit the difference to the state. Wal-Mart, the only employer approaching that employment level, was the target of the legislation. George Will's column (*Rocky Mountain News,* January 22, 2006) about this development said, "Maryland's grasping for Wal-Mart's revenues opens a new chapter in the degeneracy of state governments that are eager to spend more money than they have the nerve to collect straightforwardly in taxes. Fortunately, as labor unions and allied rent-seekers in 30 or so other states contemplate mimicking Maryland, Wal-Mart can contemplate an advantage of federalism." What does he mean by "labor unions and allied rent-seekers"? What do they have to gain?
11. Economists Robert Crandall and Clifford Winston (*Wall Street Journal,* March 9, 2006) asked, "Would consumer welfare seriously be threatened if Ford and General Motors merged?" In 1960, together they would have had almost 75% of the automobile and truck market, but today have only a third of the market. How would you answer their question if this was 1960? Today?
12. Being number one in any business attracts a lot of attention. As *The Economist* (December 17, 2005) has noted,

    *As soon as a firm climbs above the sharp elbows of its rivals, it starts getting pelted with the eggs of anti-business activities. People who hate big business aim high. So while big, bad Wal-Mart is pilloried, Target has in the past couple of years blithely cut the benefits of its non-union workers. And when was the last time you saw an anti-globalization mob destroy a Burger King outlet?*

    Describe some of the benefits of being number two in a large industry. In terms of total revenues (sales), name the number one and two firms in the following industries: major auto manufacturers, semiconductors, major drug manufacturers, banks, and major integrated oil and gas.
13. We often think that government-enforced patents and copyrights are the most frequently used public policies to create (or assist) monopolies. But economist Edward Glaeser (*New York Times,* March 5, 2006) argues that zoning laws and other regulatory hurdles have been a major force in escalating housing prices in many cities. He suggests that zoning and other restrictions on development have made "boutique" cities out of Manhattan, Boston, and San Francisco, where only the skilled and privileged can afford to live. As he notes, "Homeowners have a strong incentive to stop new development, both because it can be an inconvenience and also because, like any monopolist, stopping supply drives up the price of their own homes. Lack of affordable housing isn't a problem to homeowners; that's exactly what they want.

The thing you want most is to make sure that your home is not affordable if you own it." Is Professor Glaeser right in that homeowners are not monopolists, but often act like them to enhance the value of their houses? Would elimination of zoning laws and building codes result in a greater supply of affordable housing?

**14.** Professor Andrew Zimbalist is quoted (*Wall Street Journal,* November 24, 2007, p. B7) as wondering, "Imagine walking into a department store to buy a pair of slacks and being told by the salesman that in order to buy the pair you like, you would also have to buy a particular shirt, a particular tie and two pairs of socks. Department stores do not attempt such bundling, because the consumer would not stand for it." But this is exactly how the cable and satellite TV industry operates.

Cable networks are often monopolies in their local markets but typically face direct competition from the two satellite providers (DISH Network and DIRECTV). Does the cable provider's monopoly power explain the various bundling options that cable operators offer? Most networks charge the cable and dish providers a fee per subscriber to carry their programming. Might consumers be better off with an à la carte option where consumers select and pay for just the channels they want? If an à la carte option were offered, what would probably happen to the smaller, less popular channels?

## Solving Problems

**15.** Using the figure for a monopoly firm below, answer the following questions.

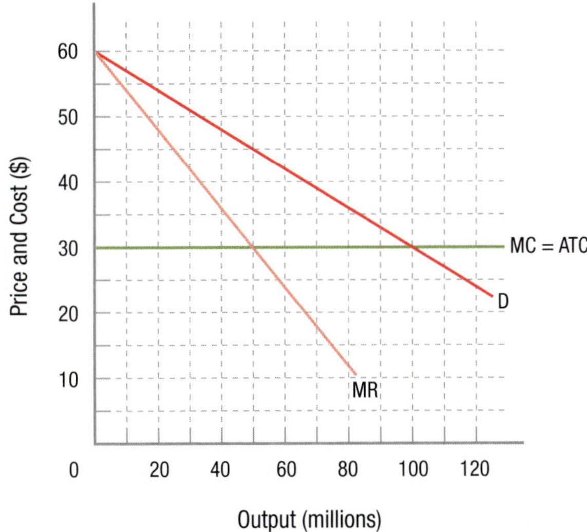


a. What will be the monopoly price, output, and profit for this firm?

b. If this monopolist could perfectly price discriminate, what would profit equal?

c. If this industry was competitive, what would be the price, output, and profit?

d. How large (in dollars) is the deadweight loss from this monopolist?

**16.** Using the figure for a natural monopoly firm below, answer the following questions.

a. Roughly what would be the monopoly price, output, and profit for this unregulated natural monopolist?

b. Assume that regulators use the competitive P = MC for regulation. Roughly how high would the total subsidy have to be to keep this firm in the industry over the long run?

c. Using P = ATC as the regulatory approach, approximately what would be the price, output, and profits for this monopolist?

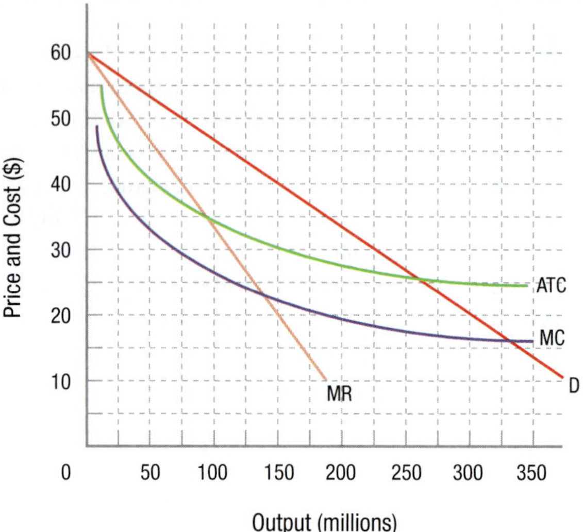


*The table below shows data for selected industries. Use this table to answer questions 17–19.*

| Industry | Number of Companies | CR-4 | CR-8 | HHI-50 Largest |
|---|---|---|---|---|
| Dental labs | 6,923 | 12.7 | 17.8 | 54.2 |
| Office furniture, mfg. | 4,129 | 24.2 | 32.4 | 178.7 |
| Lead pencil and art goods, mfg. | 138 | 58.3 | 73.1 | 1,276.1 |
| Aircraft engine and parts, mfg. | 296 | 76.9 | 82.4 | 2,527.7 |
| Electric lamp bulb and parts, mfg. | 57 | 88.5 | 94.1 | 2,757.6 |
| Household appliance, mfg. | 251 | 62.2 | 70.8 | 1,131.9 |
| Household vacuum cleaners, mfg. | 29 | 77.9 | 96.1 | 2,096.3 |
| Electronic computer, mfg. | 465 | 75.5 | 89.2 | 2,662.4 |
| Pharmaceutical and medicine, mfg. | 1,444 | 34.0 | 49.1 | 506.0 |
| Petroleum refineries | 88 | 41.2 | 63.5 | 639.7 |

**17.** If two firms, one in the CR-4 category and another in the CR-8 category, decided to merge, which of the industries in the table would the Justice Department almost automatically permit?

**18.** Why do you think that there are so many dental labs and that the concentration is so small?

**19.** What industries in the table would the Justice Department probably reject if any proposed mergers of two firms in the top eight? In these industries, would the Justice Department be likely to permit two small firms to merge?

# Answers to Questions in CheckPoints

## Check Point: Monopoly Markets

Yes, this is rent seeking. Google has a huge capital base and cash flow, and could compete with Microsoft in the browser market if it really saw the search box as a threat. The Justice Department announced in May 2006 that it did not feel the search box was a threat to competition.

## Check Point: Monopoly Market Issues

No, this is not the same type of price discrimination discussed in this section. This type of discrimination occurs because of information problems, racism, or other factors. The authors conclude that a large part of the price differences between Internet buying and bargaining in the showroom comes from the fact that Internet purchasers have better information. Price discrimination in this section of the chapter is based on consumers with different elasticities of demand, not information problems or racism. Examples include student, senior, and adult pricing in movie theaters.

## Check Point: Antitrust Policy

| Company | Sales (billions of dollars) | Share of Market | Share Squared |
|---|---|---|---|
| General Motors | 2.063 | 23.07 | 532.03 |
| Toyota | 1.77 | 19.79 | 391.64 |
| Ford | 1.616 | 18.07 | 326.45 |
| Honda | 1.151 | 12.87 | 165.61 |
| Chrysler | 0.931 | 10.41 | 108.35 |
| Nissan | 0.77 | 8.61 | 74.12 |
| Hyundai | 0.435 | 4.86 | 23.65 |
| Mazda | 0.208 | 2.33 | 5.41 |
| **Totals** | **8.944** | **100.00** | **1,627.26** |

a. The four-firm concentration ratio is 73.8.

b. The HHI for this industry is 1,627.26.

c. You probably would not permit Ford and Toyota to merge, since that would change the upper mix so significantly. Hyundai and Mazda would not be a problem since combined they would only be 7.19% of the market.

# Monopolistic Competition, Oligopoly, and Game Theory

# 10

Dirk Döring/agefotostock

**Pure competition and pure monopoly** rarely exist in actual practice. Both models provide the two extremes of market structure and provide direction for public policy when markets approach one or the other. However, the vast majority of markets are somewhere in between the extremes. In this chapter, we focus on the market structures between these polar opposites: monopolistic competition and oligopoly. We look at some of the classic models used to determine imperfectly competitive pricing and output decisions, then turn to the more modern analysis of game theory.

Competitive markets are defined by homogeneous products. This restricted our analysis to products that essentially are commodities: microchips and agricultural products such as wheat, for example. But most of the products we purchase are clearly not homogeneous. Hamburgers from Burger King, McDonald's, Wendy's, and Hardee's are similar, but for many consumers they are quite distinct. The same is true for computers, mobile phones, and cars.

Monopoly analysis required only one firm, and competition required a standardized product, but most of the markets that we encounter have only a few firms offering different products. We are now going to relax these monopoly and competition assumptions and look at markets where many firms offer products that are different (monopolistic competition) and at markets where only a few firms operate (oligopoly). Then we are going to look at game theory as an additional way to understand the behavior of oligopolists.

It is worth taking a moment to remember that most firms begin small in highly competitive environments. Some bring unique products to the market like Facebook, while others add something special to existing markets as is the norm in the restaurant business. Unique products are often exciting at their launch, but they eventually mature, and the firm grows by developing newer versions of older products or introducing new products to begin the cycle anew.

**After studying this chapter you should be able to:**

- ☐ Describe product differentiation and its impact on the firm's demand curve.
- ☐ Describe short-run pricing and output decisions for monopolistically competitive firms.
- ☐ Describe the reasons why, in the long run, monopolistically competitive firms only earn normal profits.
- ☐ Compare the efficiency of monopolistic competition to competition.
- ☐ Describe and recognize oligopolistic industries.
- ☐ Describe cartels and the reasons for their instability.
- ☐ Describe the kinked demand curve model and why some economists feel prices are relatively stable in oligopoly industries.
- ☐ Describe the Prisoner's Dilemma and determine the outcome of other games using the approach of minimizing your maximum loss.
- ☐ Understand the nature of Nash equilibria and their importance to economists.

Over time, some firms grow through further internal investment, franchising individual operations, or merger with other firms. Only the rare firm begins as a monopolist or even as an oligopolist (typically through a government franchise like local cable TV companies). They emerge as huge, dominant firms in many different ways.

## Monopolistic Competition

Until the 1920s, competition and monopoly were the only models of market structure that economists had in their toolbox. During the 1920s, economists began debating the effects of economies of scale on the competitive model. If economies were large relative to the market, one or a few firms would expand and eventually take over the market. Competition could not survive large economies of scale. Firms would then become large enough to affect prices in the market by their supply decisions.

Edward Chamberlin (1899–1967), as a graduate student at Harvard in 1922, decided to write a dissertation on the problems of the competitive model. Chamberlin was a tireless and tenacious person who wanted to alter the way economists thought about market structure. His 1933 book *The Theory of Monopolistic Competition* was not immediately warmly received, but all recognized the originality of his effort. Six months after the publication of Chamberlin's work, a British economist, Joan Robinson (1903–1983), published her *Economics of Imperfect Competition* and stole some of Chamberlin's thunder.

While Chamberlin was famous for this one contribution to economics, Joan Robinson is remembered for a huge variety of work and its radical nature. She was one of the economists who worked alongside John Maynard Keynes during the 1930s when he was developing *The General Theory.* She was responsible for the analysis of price discrimination discussed in the previous chapter, and she was the first woman to be a finalist for the Nobel Prize in Economics. Today, both Chamberlin and Robinson are generally given equal credit for discovering "imperfect" markets.

**Monopolistic competition** is nearer to the competitive end of the spectrum and is defined by the following:

- A large number of small firms. Like competition, these firms have an insignificantly small market share. They and their competitors cannot appreciably affect the market and, therefore, ignore the reactions of their rivals. They are thus independent of a competitor's reactions.
- Entry and exit is easy.
- Unlike competition, products are different. Each firm produces a product that is different from its competitors or is perceived to be different by consumers. What distinguishes monopolistic competition from competitive markets is product differentiation.

**Monopolistic competition:** Involves a large number of small firms and is similar to competition, with easy entry and exit, but unlike the competitive model, the firms have differentiated their products. This differentiation is either real or imagined by consumers and involves innovations, advertising, location, or other ways of making one firm's product different from that of its competitors.

## Product Differentiation and the Firm's Demand Curve

Most firms sell products that are differentiated from their competitors. This differentiation can simply take the form of a superior location. Your local dry cleaner, restaurant, grocery, and gas station can have slightly higher prices, and you will not abandon them altogether. Other companies have branded products that give them some ability to increase price without losing all of their customers, as would happen under competition.

Product differentiation gives the firm some (however modest) control over prices. This is illustrated in Figure 1. Demand curve $d_c$ is the competitive demand curve, and $d_{mc}$ is the demand faced by a monopolistic competitor. This is similar to the monopolist's demand, but the demand curve is considerably more elastic. Because a monopolistic competitor is small relative to the market, there are still a lot of substitutes. Thus, any increase in price is accompanied by a substantial decrease in output demanded.

Like a monopolist, the monopolistically competitive firm faces a downward sloping marginal revenue curve, shown in Figure 1 as $MR_{mc}$.

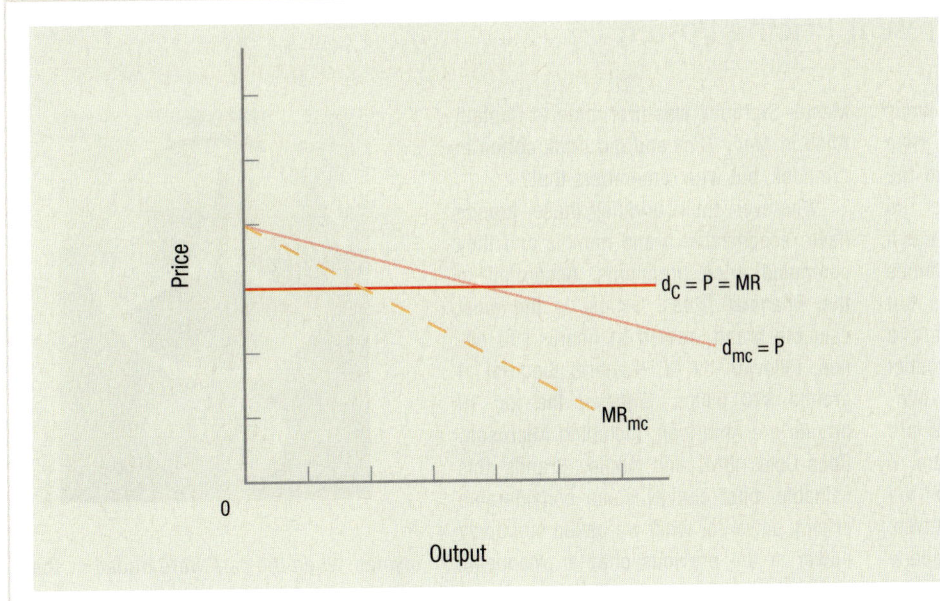


**FIGURE 1—Product Differentiation and Demand**

Product differentiation means that the firm has some leeway in its pricing policies. Demand curve $d_{mc}$ is the demand curve for a monopolistically competitive firm with modest price-making ability. Marginal revenue curve $MR_{mc}$ also slopes downward, reflecting the weak negative slope of the demand curve.

**Product differentiation** can be the result of a superior product, a better location, superior service, clever packaging, or advertising. All of these factors are intended to increase demand or reduce the elasticity of demand and generate loyalty to the product or service.

**Product differentiation:** One firm's product is distinguished from another's through advertising, innovation, location, and so on.

For some products, packaging is paramount; bulk, bagged, and bottled teas seem to fit this mold with their ornate packages and names to fit any mood or occasion. Olive oil—virgin and extra virgin—are sold in bottles and tins covered with pictorial farms, landscapes, animals, and other European scenes. Even wines have succumbed to pictorial animal packaging. Yellow Tail, a good inexpensive Australian wine, has a very attractive label featuring a yellow-tailed rock wallaby that looks like Australian aboriginal art. In five years, Yellow Tail sales in the United States have gone from nothing to over 100 million bottles annually. At least a large chunk of Yellow Tail's success has been due to the unique label, and other vintners have begun adding animals to their bottle labels.

Dan Galic/Alamy

## The Role of Advertising

Another important way to differentiate products is through advertising. Economists generally classify advertising in two ways: informational and persuasive. The informational aspects of advertising let consumers know about products and reduce search costs. Advertising is a relatively inexpensive way to let customers know about quality and price of a company's products. It can also enhance competition by making consumers aware of substitute or competitive products. Advertising also has the potential to reduce costs by increasing sales, bringing about economies of scale.

But advertising does have a negative side as well. Because so much of advertising is persuasive, designed to shift buyers among competitors of similar products, the result is that the cost of advertising simply drives up the price of many products. Persuasive ads often have little informational content and may result in consumers purchasing inferior products. With all the advertising we see, a significant portion probably cancels each other out.

Advertising is another area where technology has transformed the medium: Digital video recorders permit ad-skipping and have significantly reduced the impact of TV ads. A lot of advertising dollars are shifting away from conventional media (newspapers, magazines, and television) and moving to the Internet, where consumers can be targeted more inexpensively and efficiently.

All of these ways to differentiate their products gives monopolistically competitive firms some control over price. This means that their profit maximizing decisions will be a little different from competitive firms.

## *Issue:* Do Brands Represent Pricing Power?

**What is a brand?** All of us know brands through their names and logos. Nike has the swoosh, Intel has a logo and the four-note jingle you hear whenever its processors are advertised, Coca-Cola has a distinctive way of spelling its name. Names and logos are communication devices, but brands are more than this. They are a promise of performance. A branded product or service raises expectations in a consumer's mind. If these expectations are met, consumers pay a price premium. If expectations are not met, the value of the brand falls as consumers seek alternatives.

Brand names start with the company that makes the product or provides the service. In the past, this meant that brand names came from a limited number of sources. Some companies were named after their founders, such as Walt Disney; some companies were named after what they supplied, such as IBM (International Business Machines); and some have also been named by their main product, such as the Coca-Cola Company. Sometimes the company name has a tenuous link with the product but is strong nevertheless, such as the Starbucks name for coffee products: Master Starbuck was first mate to Captain Ahab in *Moby-Dick* and did drink coffee in the book, but who remembers that?

Whatever their origins, these brands have recognizable brand names, and they command price premiums. According to the *Financial Times,* Google is the most valuable brand, valued at nearly $90 billion, followed by GE (General Electric) at around $70 billion. Eight of the top 10 brands are American, including Microsoft, Coca-Cola, IBM, and Apple. Brands this valuable must convey some considerable pricing power, or what we called monopoly power in the previous chapter. Monopoly power is what companies want.

Toyota is now the highest valued brand in the auto industry at over $35 billion. Toyota has built its business and brand on the basis of an efficient production system, concentration on consistent high quality, a commitment to customer service, and continuous improvement of the product line. The Toyota brand has cachet: At the California plant that until 2009 Toyota shared with General Motors, *identical* cars came off the production line. Some were branded as GM cars, others Toyotas. When the cars were traded in, the Toyotas had a much higher trade-in value. The Toyota brand conveys quality, which gives Toyota its pricing power. How much will the Toyota brand be tarnished by the gas pedal problem that led to the worldwide recall of over 7 million cars in 2010?

Kaplonski/Alamy

Sources: F. O'Donnell, "Make It a Brand New Year," Life Insurance Marketing and Research Association *MarketFacts* 18:1, January/February, 1999, p. 18; Richard Tomkins, "Branding Consultants Get a Chance to Tell It Like It Is," *Financial Times,* January 30, 2004, p. 14; "The Car Company in Front," *Economist,* January 29, 2005; and John Gapper, "Holding Firm as Downturn Looms," *Financial Times,* April 21, 2008, Special Report, p. 1.

## Price and Output under Monopolistic Competition

Profit maximization in the short run for the monopolistically competitive firm is a lot like that for a monopolist, but given the firm's size, profit will tend to be less. Short-run profit maximizing behavior is shown in Figure 2. The firm maximizes profit where MR = MC (point *c*) by selling output $q_0$ for a price of $P_0$. Total profits are the shaded area $C_0P_0ab$. All of this should look very familiar from the last chapter. The difference is that the monopolistically competitive demand curve is quite elastic, and economic profits are diminished. The level of profits is dependent on the strength of demand, but in any event will be considerably lower than that of a monopolist.

This does not mean that profits are trivial. Many huge global firms sell their products in even larger global markets, and their profits are significant. They are large firms, but do not have significant monopoly power. Many companies such as Armani, Nike, and Sony are all quite large but relative to their markets face daunting competition.

If firms in the industry are earning economic profits like the firm shown in Figure 2, new firms will want to enter. Since there are no restrictions on entry or exit, new firms will enter, soaking up some industry demand and reducing the demand to each firm in the market. Demand will continue to decline as long as economic profits exist. At equilibrium in the long run, the typical firm in the industry will look like the one shown in Figure 3.

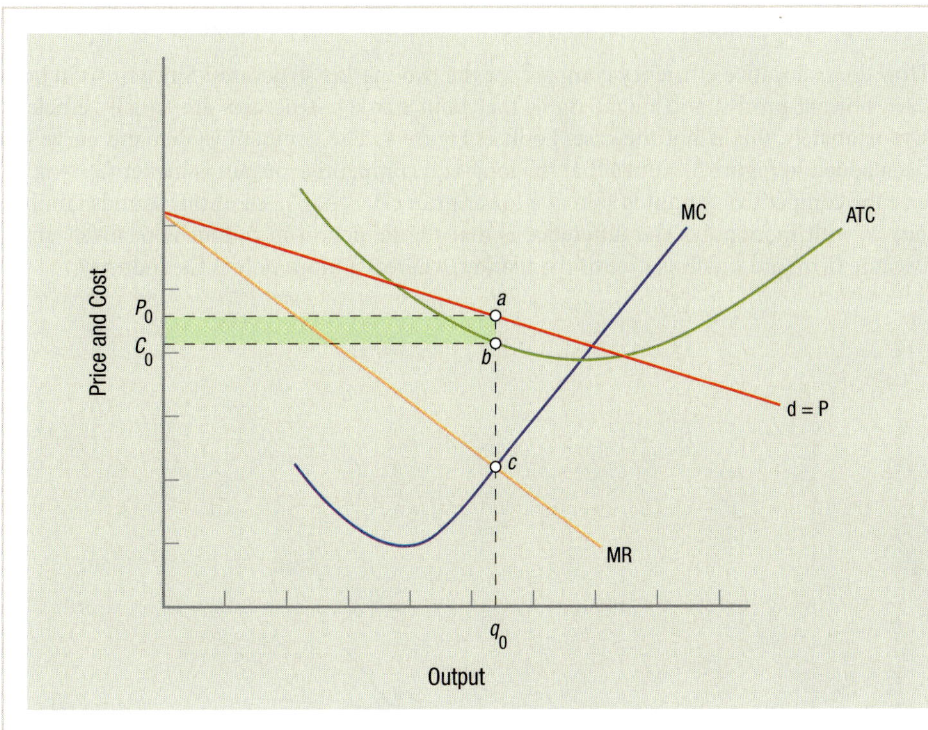


**FIGURE 2—Short-Run Equilibrium for Monopolistic Competition**

This monopolistically competitive firm will maximize profits in the short run by producing where MR = MC (point *c*). Profits are equal to the shaded area.

Notice that the demand curve is just tangent to the long-run average total cost (LRATC) curve, resulting in the firm earning normal profits in the long run. The firm produces and sells $q_L$ output at a price of $P_L$ (point *a*). Once the typical firm reaches this point, there is no longer any incentive for other firms to enter the industry. Just as the competitive firm does, monopolistically competitive firms earn normal profits in the long run.

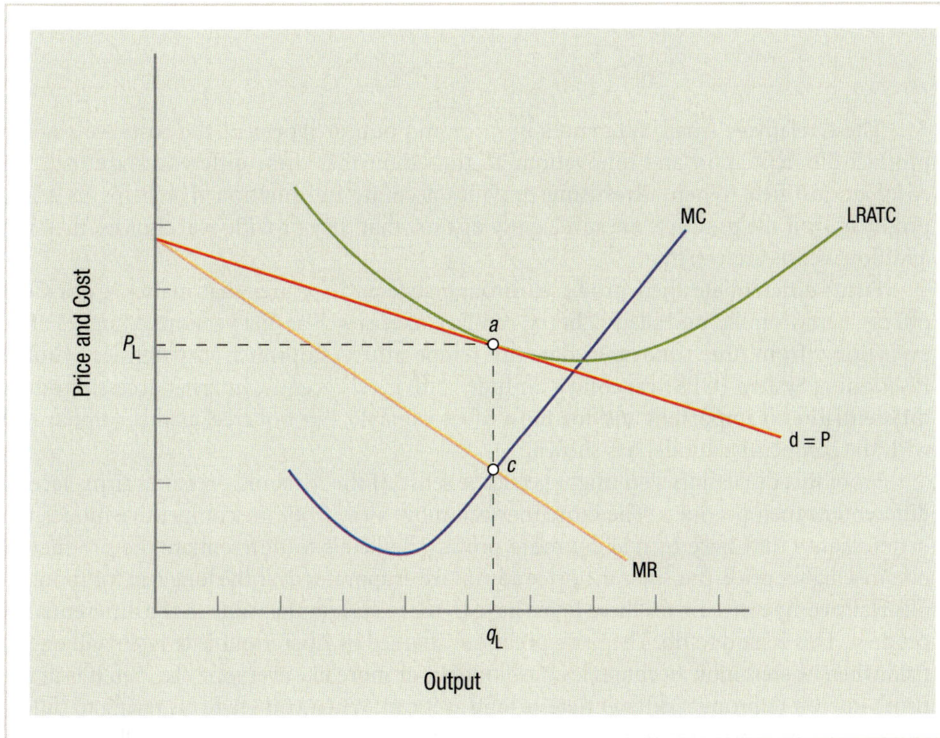


**FIGURE 3—Long-Run Equilibrium for Monopolistic Competition**

In the long run, easy entry and exit will adjust the demand for each firm so that the demand curve will be tangent (at point *a* in this case) to the long-run average total cost curve. This is long-run equilibrium because existing firms are earning normal profits and there is no incentive for further entry or exit.

## Comparing Monopolistic Competition to Competition

How does allocative efficiency compare for the two market structures? Since firms in both earn normal profits, you might think that both market structures are equally efficient. Unfortunately, this is not the case. Look at Figure 4. The competitive demand curve has been added to Figure 3. Notice that the long-run competitive output is higher ($q_c > q_{mc}$), and the competitive output is sold at a lower price ($P_c < P_{mc}$). All of this sounds familiar, just as with monopoly. The difference is that the reduction in output is relatively small because firms are small relative to the market, whereas a monopoly is the industry.

**FIGURE 4—Comparing the Long Run for Monopolistically Competitive and Competitive Firms**

Long-run equilibrium is at point *b* for competitive firms and at point *a* for monopolistically competitive firms. Equilibrium price is a little higher, and output is a little lower for the monopolistically competitive firm when compared to the competitive firm. These represent the real costs we, as consumers, pay for product differentiation.

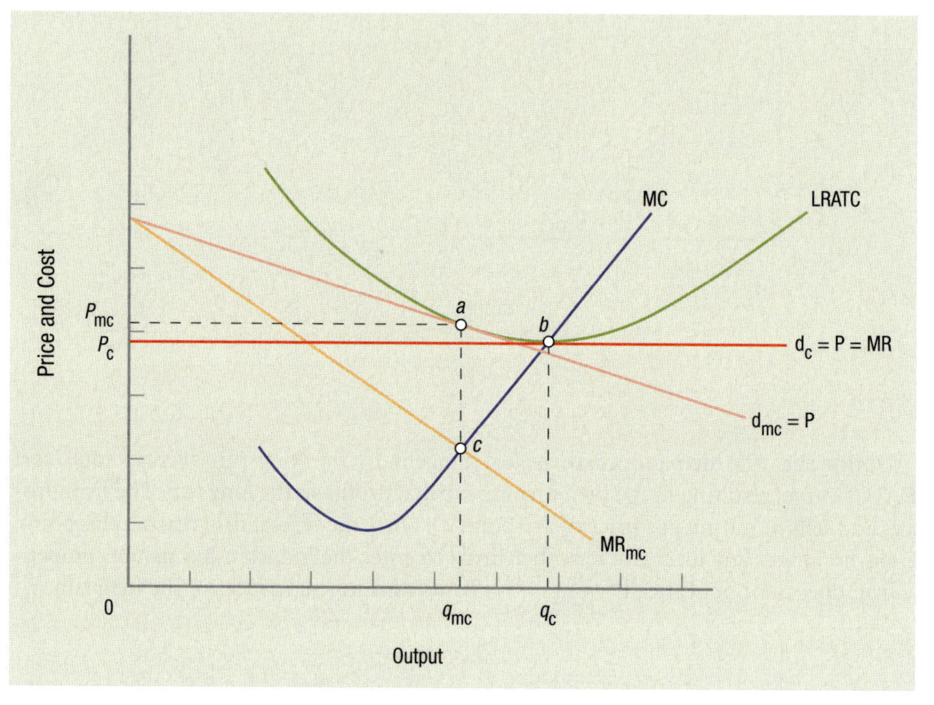


These relatively small differences in price and output represent the costs we pay for product differentiation and innovation. To the extent that these differences are real, the costs are justified. When advertising provides accurate information that helps us select products, or if the products are sufficiently distinct that they provide real choices, then the additional costs are worth it.

Firms differentiate their products through style and features that matter. Coca-Cola offers Cherry, Vanilla, and Black Cherry Vanilla Coke, as well as diet versions. Watches offer everything from the time and date to temperature, stopwatch capabilities, Global Positioning System (GPS) capability, altitude, and, most recently, Internet access. Product differentiation is important and for most of us valuable, but not free, as this comparison with the competitive model has shown.

From this discussion, you might get some sense of the dynamic pressures firms face to differentiate their products. The more they can move away from the competitive model, the better chance they have of making more profit. The key is to differentiate the product to obtain a higher price. But since the price advantage evaporates over the long run for monopolistically competitive firms, these firms have to try to sustain the value in the differentiated product. This is hard to do. The price premium charged by Abercrombie & Fitch will not be paid when Abercrombie becomes less fashionable, or more like everyone else. Yet, it is in the firm's interest to product differentiate as long as it can. When you see firms trying to differentiate their products, ask yourself if the products really are so different after all.

**CHECKPOINT**

## MONOPOLISTIC COMPETITION

- Monopolistically competitive firms look like competitive firms (large number of small firms in a market where entry and exit is unrestricted) but have differentiated products.
- Monopolistically competitive firms have very elastic demands.
- Short-run equilibrium output for the monopolistic competitor (like the monopolist) is at an output where MR = MC, but economic profits will be relatively small compared to an industry monopolist because demand is very elastic for the monopolistic competitor.
- In the long run, easy entry and exit result in monopolistically competitive firms earning only normal profits.
- Output is lower and price is higher for monopolistically competitive firms when compared to price and output for competitive firms.

**QUESTION:** Kelly Crow reports in the *Wall Street Journal* (August 12, 2005) that many of the 40 or so traveling circuses in America have celebrity clowns as their headline acts. These clowns earn high six-figure salaries plus royalties from souvenir sales. Why would circuses emphasize clowns over animal and trapeze acts?

Answers to the Checkpoint question can be found at the end of this chapter.

# Oligopoly

**Oligopoly** markets are those where a large market share is controlled by just a few firms. What constitutes a few firms controlling a large market share is not rigidly defined. Further, these firms can sell either a homogeneous product (e.g., gasoline, sugar) or a differentiated product (e.g., automobiles and pharmaceuticals).

**Oligopoly:** A market with just a few firms dominating the industry where (1) each firm recognizes that it must consider its competitors' reactions when making its own decisions (mutual interdependence), and (2) there are significant barriers to entry into the market.

Industries can be composed of a dominant firm with a few smaller firms making up the rest of the industry (e.g., microcomputer operating systems and cell phones), or the industry can be composed of a few similarly sized firms (e.g., automobiles and tobacco). The point of this discussion is that oligopoly models are numerous and varied, and we will explore only a few. Oligopoly models do, however, have several common characteristics.

## Defining Oligopoly

All oligopoly models share several common assumptions:

- There are only a few dominant firms in the industry.
- Each firm recognizes that it must take into account the behavior of its competitors when it makes decisions. Economists refer to this as **mutual interdependence.**
- There are significant barriers to entry into the market.

**Mutual interdependence:** When only a few firms constitute an industry, each firm must consider the reactions of its competitors to its decisions.

Since there are only a few firms, the actions of one will affect the ability of the others to successfully sell or price their output. If one firm changes the specifications of its product or increases its advertising budget, this will have an impact on its rivals, and they can be expected to respond in kind. Thus, one firm cannot forecast its change in sales for a new promotion without first making some assumption about the reaction of its rivals. For example, when after 10 years of development Mercedes adds a new driver attention assist system to detect fatigue and advertises this feature, it has to consider whether a competitor such as Lexus will immediately offer this feature as well.

In an industry composed of just a few firms, entry scale is often huge. Plus, with just a few firms, typically brand preferences are quite strong on the part of consumers, and a new firm may need a substantial marketing program just to get a foot in the door. For example, the investment in plant for a new automaker is huge, and the marketing effort also must be large to get people to even consider a new auto brand. Newer car manufacturers like Kia often must resort to long warranties (10 year, 100,000 miles) to entice customers to try its products.

## Cartels: Joint Profit Maximization

*Cartels are theft—usually by well-dressed thieves.*

GRAEME SAMUEL, HEAD OF AUSTRALIA'S ANTITRUST OFFICE

**Cartel:** An agreement between firms (or countries) in an industry to formally collude on price and output, then agree on the distribution of production.

The first oligopoly model we examine is *collusive* joint profit maximization, or a **cartel** model. Here we assume a few firms collude (combine secretly) to operate like a monopolistic industry, setting the monopoly price and output and sharing the monopoly profits. Cartels are illegal in the United States, though international laws do not ban them. However, this situation may change in the European Union.

As *The Economist* noted, "Just a few years ago, America seemed uniquely obsessed with price-fixing. Today, new measures against cartel behavior (which includes bid-rigging and deals to carve up market share, as well as price-fixing) are being taken from Sweden to South Korea, where the competition body levied its first fine against a foreign firm earlier this year [2002]."[1] Europe, in 2006, fined seven firms for running a cartel in bleaching chemicals.[2] Recently, Europe broke up and fined six firms nearly $500 million for a 20-year-old cartel in zippers.

The most famous cartel operating today is OPEC, the Organization of Petroleum Exporting Countries. OPEC countries meet to establish the price that members can charge and an output level that each individual member can produce, thus carving up shares of the profits. OPEC, formed principally of Middle Eastern countries in the early 1960s, really didn't become effective until 1973. Since then, it has had many successes and some failures.

## *Issue:* Why Did the Government Sponsor an Aluminum Cartel in the 1990s?

**What can a** CEO of a major American corporation do when foreign firms sell so much aluminum on the world market that the price decline threatens the corporation? Ask the government for help, of course. In the early 1990s, Russia sold more aluminum in world markets. This increase in supply was matched by a fall in demand brought about by slower worldwide economic growth and Russia's reduced production of aircraft. Prices fell by *half.*

Alcoa's CEO, Paul O'Neill, went to the Clinton administration for help. With its approval and the help of government antitrust lawyers, the Overseas Private Investment Corporation (OPIC), and the State Department, an agreement was made limiting aluminum production. In other words, a cartel was formed. With a $250 million equity investment from OPIC, Russian companies were persuaded to reduce their output. Prices rose from roughly 50 cents a pound to nearly 90 cents, and Alcoa's profits rose.

By 1995, worldwide demand for aluminum increased, and problems enforcing the agreement arose; shortly thereafter, the cartel fell apart. Because cartels are normally illegal in the United States, this "aluminum product–overseas investment agreement" was challenged, but dismissed by the courts. Export cartels are permitted in the United States as long as they do not adversely impact competition in domestic markets.

Robert Brook/Photo Researchers

Source: Based on Joseph E. Stiglitz, *Globalization and Its Discontents* (New York: Norton), 2003, pp. 173–176 and p. 268.

[1] See "Cartels: Fixing for a Fight," *Economist,* April 20, 2002, p. 63.

[2] William Echikson, "Europe Fines 7 Chemical Firms $489.8 Million for Bleach Cartel," *Wall Street Journal,* May 4, 2006, p. A2.

Cartels are inherently unstable because of the incentive to cheat by individual members. Even though each firm and the cartel jointly are earning economic profits, they are not being maximized. If all other members of the cartel continue to sell their authorized output, any one firm that can sell additional output for a price above marginal cost can earn additional profits. For oil producing countries, additional production is particularly profitable because a $100 barrel of oil may only cost $10 to $20 to produce. Each firm in the cartel faces these incentives, and if many attempt to sell additional output, the cartel agreement will break down. This analysis has led some economists to lose interest in cartels, since cartels are likely to fail in the long run.

Cartel stability is enhanced with fewer members with similar goals. Further, stability is improved if the cartel is maintained with legal provisions (government protection) and if nonprice competition is not possible. If the firm can give nonprice discounts (enhanced service or some other product as an inducement to purchase), the likelihood of stability is reduced. If their products and cost structures are similar and they are not secretive with each other, stability is enhanced. Finally, if there are significant barriers to entry, the cartel need not worry about new entrants, and the chances improve for the cartel to survive.

## The Kinked Demand Curve Model

One early oligopoly model that considered the reactions of other firms is the kinked demand curve model jointly developed by Sweezy, Hall, and Hitch in the late 1930s. These authors noticed that prices tended to be stable for extended periods in oligopolistic industries. It was in an effort to model this price stability that they settled on the idea of a kinked demand curve.

Demand curve d in Figure 5 represents the demand for one firm when all other firms in the industry *do not follow* its price changes. Demand curve D represents demand when all other firms raise or lower prices *in concert.* Demand curve d is relatively more elastic than demand curve D because when the firm raises prices and others do not follow, quantity demanded declines rapidly as customers substitute to the now lower-priced products from competitors. Similarly, when one firm's prices fall and the others ignore this change, demand for the lower-priced products grows rapidly. Hence, demand curve d is relatively elastic.

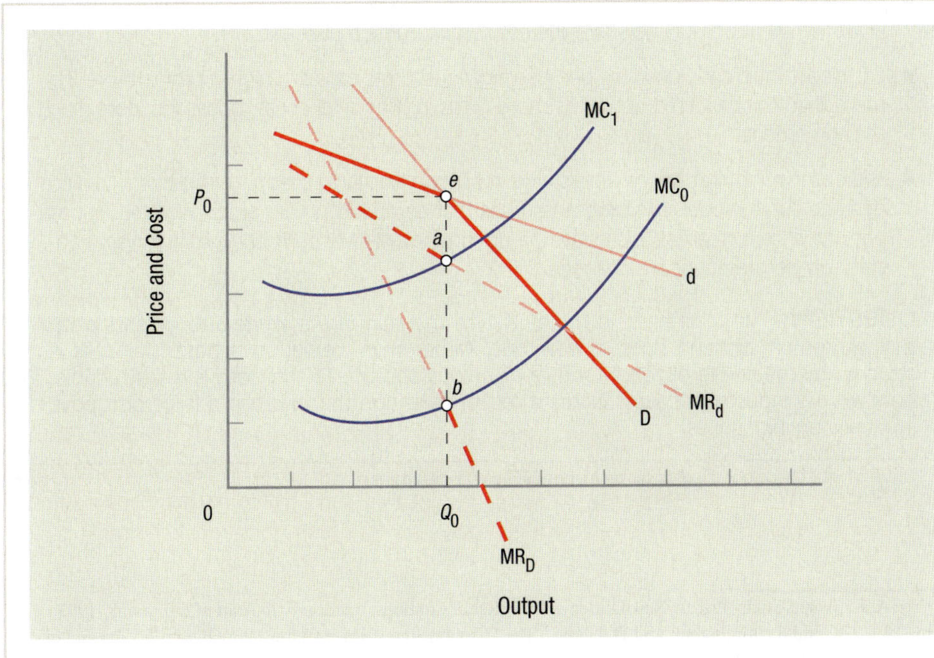


**FIGURE 5—The Kinked Demand Curve Model of Oligopoly**

The kinked demand curve model of oligopoly shows why oligopoly prices appear stable. The model assumes that if the firm raised its price, competitors will not react and raise their prices, but if the firm lowers prices, other firms will lower theirs in response. These reactions create a "kink" in the firm's demand curve at point *e*, and a discontinuity in the MR curve equal to the distance between points *a* and *b*. This discontinuity permits marginal costs to vary from $MC_0$ to $MC_1$ before the firm will change its price.

**Kinked demand curve:** An oligopoly model that assumes that if a firm raises its price, competitors will not raise theirs; but if the firm lowers its price, all of its competitors will lower their price to match the reduction. This leads to a kink in the demand curve and relatively stable market prices.

Demand curve D, on the other hand, is more like the industry demand. When all firms raise and lower their prices together, demand will be less elastic than demand curve *d*.

The **kinked demand curve** model assumes the following:

- If the firm raises prices for its products, its competitors will not react by raising prices, expecting to see their market share rise.
- If the firm lowers its prices, its competitors will meet the new prices with lower ones of their own to make sure that they do not lose market share.

As a result, the relevant demand curve facing the firm is the darkened portion of demand curves d and D that is kinked at point *e*. The relevant portion of the marginal revenue curve is the darkened dashed curve MR with the discontinuity between points *a* and *b*. Notice, we are just using the relevant portions of $MR_d$ and $MR_D$. As shown, marginal cost crosses through the discontinuity, resulting in an equilibrium price and output of $P_0$ and $Q_0$.

It is, of course, the discontinuity in the MR curve that gives this model its price stability. The marginal cost curve can vary anywhere between points *a* and *b* before the firm will have any incentive to change prices to maximize profits.

Critics of this model suggest that price stability can be explained by other factors, and that the model doesn't explain how prices were initially determined. It explains the existence of the kink but not how it was determined in an oligopoly context. George Stigler argued that the evidence of price stability was weak at best. However, more recent empirical investigations of retailing and others found price declines were more readily followed than price increases in oligopolistic industries.[3]

One clear result of the search for realistic oligopoly models was the realization by economists that the mutual interdependence of firms and their reactions to each other's policies were important. How one firm reacts to a competitor's market strategy determined the nature of competition in the industry. These ideas led to game theory.

## CHECKPOINT

### OLIGOPOLY

- Oligopolies are markets (a) with only a few firms, (b) where each firm takes into account the reaction of rivals to its policies or firms recognize their mutual interdependence, and (c) where there are significant barriers to entry.
- Cartels result when several firms collude to set market price and output. Cartels typically act like monopolists and share the economic profits that result.
- Cartels are inherently unstable because individual firms can earn higher profits by selling more than their allotted quota. As more firms in the cartel cheat, prices fall, defeating the agreement.
- The observation that prices were stable in oligopolistic industries gave rise to the kinked demand curve model. The model assumes that competitors will follow price reductions but not price increases. This leads to a discontinuity in MR permitting cost to vary substantially before prices are changed.

**QUESTION:** Alec Guinness, in the 1951 film *The Man in the White Suit*, invents cloth that shrugs off dirt and doesn't wear out. Rather than treated as a hero, Guinness is attacked by the textile oligopoly and labor unions because "if the cloth is indestructible, how will the industry survive?" Name a recent invention that has had a large disruptive influence on oligopolies.

Answers to the Checkpoint question can be found at the end of this chapter.

[3] See A. Kashyap, "Sticky Prices: New Evidence from Retail Catalogs," *Quarterly Journal of Economics*, 1995, pp. 245–274; and S. Domberger, and D. Fiebig, "The Distribution of Price Changes in Oligopoly," *Journal of Industrial Economics*, 1993, pp. 295–313.

## Game Theory

*If you say why not bomb them tomorrow, I say why not today? If you say today at 5 o'clock, I say why not one o'clock?*

—John von Neumann

**Game theory** developed from analysis of imperfect competition. The earliest analysis was done by French economist Antoine Cournot (pronounced core-no), in which he examined pricing principles for a duopolist (two firms). He analyzed how one firm would react to output changes from its rival. His analysis led to reaction curves (or functions) for each firm representing the best strategy that each firm could adopt given the behavior of the other firm. This model of mutual interdependence was the precursor to game theory.

Game theory: An approach to analyzing oligopoly behavior using mathematics and simulation by making different assumptions about the players, time involved, level of information, strategies, and other aspects of the game.

Modern game theory owes its origins to John von Neumann (1903–1957), who published a paper titled "Theory of Parlor Games" in 1928 and subsequently published (in 1944) the *Theory of Games and Economic Behavior* with Oskar Morganstern. Born in Hungary at the turn of the century, von Neumann was a brilliant mathematician who was able to divide two 8-digit numbers in his head and by his senior year in high school was

### Antoine Augustin Cournot (1801–1877)

Antoine Cournot is one of the great unsung heroes of microeconomics. He was the first economist to derive a demand curve. He pioneered the use of mathematics in analyzing market structures, prices, and equilibrium. Throughout his career, however, Cournot was bitterly disappointed by the lack of appreciation of his work. It was only near the end of his life that other economists began to notice the importance of what he had written.

Born in 1801 in Gray, a small town in central France, Cournot completed his math degree at the Sorbonne in 1823. Cournot spent the next 10 years assisting a French official prepare his memoirs. In his free time, he earned a doctorate in science and began publishing articles on mathematics. His work brought him to the attention of the mathematician Simeon-Denis Poisson. With the help of Poisson, he obtained an appointment as a professor at Lyon and later an administrative position at the Academy of Grenoble. In 1838, he was appointed Inspector General of Education in Paris.

That same year he published his most important work, *Researches into the Mathematical Principles of the Theory of Wealth,* which introduced differential calculus to economic analysis. He was the first to describe the downward slope of a demand curve, suggesting that the quantity demanded of a good such as wine depended on the price of that good. In other words, increasing the price of wine would reduce the quantity demanded. Cournot demonstrated that the equilibrium price was reached at the point where demand and supply were equal.

Corbis Premium RF/Alamy

Cournot made other surprising discoveries, which he described in his book. He explained how, under conditions of monopoly, sellers could maximize profits by producing output where marginal costs equaled marginal revenue. The economist Alfred Marshall later adapted this notion in his *Principles of Economics* in 1890. Cournot also explored the dynamics of duopolies, and his ideas were later used by John Nash in his Nobel Prize–winning work on game theory.

considered a professional mathematician.[4] Von Neumann worked on the Manhattan Project during the Second World War, and it has been suggested that he probably was the model for Dr. Strangelove in Stanley Kubrick's 1963 film *Dr. Strangelove, Or How I Learned to Stop Worrying and Love the Bomb.*[5]

Modern game theory has developed into a sophisticated mathematical and simulation science. Five people have been awarded the Nobel Prize in Economics for their work in game theory. To get a feel for the potential richness that game theory offers, let's look at some of the types of games economists use to model oligopolistic market behavior.

## Types of Games

Games can be simple or complicated depending on the various characteristics of the market they represent. As you will see by the following breakdown, we can have nearly as many games as we have different markets. Game theory characteristics include the following:

- **Cooperation:** *Cooperative* games permit players to collude on prices, output, or other variables, much as OPEC does in setting output quotas for each producer. *Noncooperative* games are the opposite in that they prevent player communication and collusion.
- **Players:** Simple games involve only two players, but many modern simulation games involve multiplayer environments.
- **Time:** In *static* games, all players choose their strategies at the same time. *Dynamic* games involve sequential decision making; for example, one firm sets a price, and the other responds to this price.
- **Information:** Players could have *complete (perfect)* information about the game or they could have *incomplete (imperfect)* information. Exact payoffs may be unknown or subject to uncertainty. Firms often have good information about their own costs but may not have equal information about their competitor's costs. *Asymmetric* information is also possible (in the case of used cars—sellers usually have better information than buyers).
- **Strategies:** Many games have *discrete* strategies where players choose from a few choices such as "advertise or do not advertise," "confess or do not confess," "enter the industry or not." *Continuous* strategies typify business-constant-pricing decisions where firms often have a large number of prices and products that are subjected to various (and sometimes random) events.
- **Repetition:** Whether the game is a *one-off* decision or will be *repeated* introduces another level of complexity. In a one-off game (as in the Prisoner's Dilemma, described later) players only have to consider the payoffs (impacts) on that one decision. In repeated games, players can react to the other player's past strategies. In one round where one player makes a choice that harms the other player, that harmed player can be expected to change strategies in the future.
- **Profit-Loss:** In a *zero-sum* game (poker, duels, and most sporting events), each winner is essentially paired with a loser. If the game is a *non-zero-sum* game, both players can stand to benefit.

These characteristics permit simple and complex games covering nearly all economic situations and reflect the importance of game theory's analytic method in modern economics. In the remainder of this chapter, we focus on several simple games and apply the general analysis to price discounting and advertising, then take a brief look at the strategies introduced with repeated games. The Prisoner's Dilemma is our first widely applicable game.

[4]Steven Pressman, *Fifty Major Economists* (New York: Routledge), 1999, pp. 124–128.

[5]See William Poundstone, *Prisoner's Dilemma* (New York: Doubleday), 1992, p. 5.

## The Prisoner's Dilemma

In *noncooperative* games, each player imagines how his opponent intends to play the game, then uses this information to help formulate his own strategy. However, it is impossible for players to communicate or collaborate in making their decisions or strategies. The classic static, noncooperative game is the **Prisoner's Dilemma.**

**Prisoner's Dilemma:** A noncooperative game where players cannot communicate or collaborate in making their decisions about whether to confess or not, which results in inferior outcomes for both players. Many oligopoly decisions can be framed as a Prisoner's Dilemma.

Two criminal suspects (Chris and Matthew) are apprehended for robbery. They are separated, put in solitary confinement, and are unable to speak to each other. Each prisoner is offered the same bargain: Testify against your partner and you will go free while your partner will go to prison for three years. If neither confesses, the state likely will convict them both on lesser charges resulting in a one-year sentence. Finally, if both confess, they each will go to prison for two years.

The dilemma facing each prisoner is shown in Table 1. The payoff table is arranged so that Matthew's payoff (time in prison) is the first number, and Chris's payoff is the second number. Thus, a payoff of 3,0 represents three years in prison for Matthew while Chris goes free.

**TABLE 1** The Prisoner's Dilemma

| | Chris | |
|---|---|---|
| **Matthew** | Do not confess | Confess |
| Do not confess | 1,1 | 3,0 |
| Confess | 0,3 | 2,2 |

The prisoners must make a decision, but each cannot find out what the other has done, and both decisions are irrevocable. Each prisoner is only concerned with his own welfare—minimizing his time in prison. Is there a unique solution?

Consider Matthew's situation, shown as the *first* payoff in each cell. Suppose Chris *confesses.* Matthew is better off confessing since two years in prison is better than three. This is read vertically in the "Confess" column of the payoff table. Now suppose that Chris *does not confess.* Matthew is still better off confessing since going free is preferred to one year in prison. Thus, from Matthew's perspective, no matter which strategy Chris selects, Matthew is better off confessing because his sentence is reduced by a year in both cases.

Similarly, no matter what Matthew does, Chris is better off confessing. The logical result is that both will confess despite the fact that both would be better off if neither did: 1 year served in prison versus two.

Von Neumann referred to this strategy and its outcome as a *minimax* solution; both prisoners are minimizing their maximum prison sentences. They are minimizing their worst outcome in this instance. Notice that this is not the best outcome for both prisoners. They would be better off not confessing, but neither could trust the other to not confess given the structure of the payoffs. It is important to note that this result (confess, confess) is due to the structure of the payoffs, not the absolute levels.

The Prisoner's Dilemma is not simply an idle game dreamed up by mathematicians and economists. Robert Harris[6] noted that

> *In robberies where murders occur, for example, there is often more than one criminal involved and thus more than one person who may be eligible for the death penalty. But for a prosecutor, "what's important is that you score one touchdown," in the form of a death sentence, said Franklin R. Zimring, University of California, Berkeley, law professor and a capital punishment expert.*
>
> *Frequently, a race ensues in which the robbers try to be the first to point the finger at an accomplice and make a deal with the prosecutor to testify in return for leniency.*
>
> *Sometimes, Zimring said, it never becomes clear whether the person who got leniency or the person on trial for his life actually pulled the trigger.*

[6] R. A. Harris, *Los Angeles Times,* January 29, 1990, cited in William Poundstone, *Prisoner's Dilemma* (New York: Doubleday), 1992, p. 119.

## John von Neumann (1903–1957)

The economist Nicholas Kaldor once described fellow Hungarian John von Neumann as "the nearest thing to a genius" he had ever encountered. In addition to being one of the leading mathematicians of his day, von Neumann made important contributions to quantum physics and helped develop the first computer. Von Neumann is best known, however, as the originator of game theory, which has many important uses in economics.

Born in Budapest in 1903, von Neumann was a math prodigy with a photographic memory. He entertained his parents' dinner guests by reciting pages from the phone book by memory. By the age of 8, he had learned calculus. During his final year in high school, he was publishing professional mathematical papers.

Photo courtesy of National Nuclear Security Administration/Nevada Site Office

According to Tim Harford, von Neumann was "asked to assist with the design of a new supercomputer required to solve a new and important mathematical problem, which was beyond the capabilities of existing supercomputers. He asked to have the problem explained to him, solved it in moments with pen and paper, and turned down the request."

In 1944, von Neumann and Oskar Morganstern published the *Theory of Games and Economic Behavior,* a seminal work that has inspired a generation of mathematicians and economists, including Kenneth Arrow, Gerard Debreu, and John Nash.

In game theory, individuals compete with one another without knowing what strategies the other will employ. Many economic interactions involve similar dynamics between groups and individuals. For example, von Neumann and Morganstern wrote about situations in which players would form coalitions to gain advantage over players, which is comparable to markets in which two firms in an oligopolistic industry combine to overcome other competitors. Other analogies might be the decision for individuals to form a union or for industry groups to form lobbying organizations to push for favorable legislation from government.

During World War II, von Neumann helped the U.S. military develop the first computer and later worked on the Manhattan Project with Robert Oppenheimer. A strong supporter of the nuclear weapons program, he served as an advisor to President Truman and was appointed to the Atomic Energy Commission by President Eisenhower. Von Neumann died in 1957.

Source: Tim Harford, *The Undercover Economist* (Oxford: Oxford University Press), 2006, p. 156.

## Nash Equilibrium

John von Neumann's focus was on two-person zero-sum games and was the initial building blocks for game theory. In a zero-sum game, the amount won equals the amount lost, as in a poker game where one person's winnings have to come at the expense of another person, or other people. While zero-sum games are realistic for poker, they are not as fruitful for strategic business interactions. It is not always the case that where one firm gains, another must lose. Other possibilities include mutually beneficial or mutually destructive strategies. Sometimes the most interesting economic games are complex multiperson, non-zero-sum games.

In 28 lines (a one-page paper), John Nash (of *A Beautiful Mind* fame) was able to prove that an *n*-person game where each player chooses his optimal strategy, given that all other players have done the same, has a solution. Nash assumed that each player would imagine what all other players would select as their best strategy. Then each player would select a strategy that represented his best strategy given the other players' intended strategies. Nash was able to show that given these conditions, equilibrium (a **Nash equilibrium**) would always exist for any *n*-person non-zero-sum game.

This is a very important result. Economists could now develop realistic (and often complex) games or models of market interactions and know that a solution for the game existed.

**Nash equilibrium:** An important proof that an *n*-person game where each player chooses his optimal strategy, given that all other players have done the same, has a solution. This was important because economists now knew that even complex models (or games) had an equilibrium, or solution.

## One-Off Games: Applying Game Theory

In this section, we examine some examples of how game theory can be used to model oligopoly decisions. First we look at static games where the decisions are made simultaneously, then we take a brief look at dynamic games where decisions are make sequentially.

### Static Games

**Static games** involve simultaneous decisions, and we will focus on those with perfect information and certain payoffs. In addition, these games are one-off and are not repeated.

**Static games:** One-off games (not repeated) where decisions by the players are made simultaneously and are irreversible.

***Price Discounting: Dairy Queen and Foster's Freeze*** The game shown in Table 2 is a straightforward extension of the Prisoner's Dilemma applied to business. This example could represent dueling advertising campaigns, decisions about research and development expenditures, or price changes. The game in Table 2 represents the decision to lower price facing two oligopolists.

**TABLE 2** Payoff Matrix for Price Change Game

| | Foster's Freeze's Price | |
|---|---|---|
| **Dairy Queen's Price** | $3 | $2 |
| $3 | $100,000,$100,000 | $60,000,$150,000 |
| $2 | $150,000,$60,000 | $75,000,$75,000 |

We assume that the two firms Dairy Queen and Foster's Freeze are currently charging $3 for banana splits and face roughly the same costs and demand curves. Now assume that both are thinking about reducing price to gain market share.

Notice that both are currently making $100,000 profit on this product. If only one firm lowers its price, that firm will earn $50,000 in added profit because sales rise. Some of this increase in sales comes from those of the other firm and some comes from the added quantity demanded at the lower price. Both firms, of course, can see that each firm can gain by lowering price. But if both firms lower their price, each will see its profits fall (to $75,000). What is the new equilibrium point? Both firms will lower price, anticipating that the other will lower the price as well. This strategy maximizes their minimum profit (they each make at least $75,000). If their competitor lowers price, they cannot do better.

***Advertising: Lowe's and Home Depot*** Firms, politicians, special interest groups, and, it often seems, *everyone* advertises. The decision to advertise or not can be put in the Prisoner's Dilemma game theory framework as well.

Advertising costs money, but firms hope to garner market share and greater profits. However, if their competitors advertise as well, little is gained unless the impact of all the advertising is to grow the entire market sufficiently to compensate for the higher costs. Two home improvement big-box operations—Lowe's and Home Depot—face this dilemma.

Table 3 on the next page presents hypothetical numbers for the advertising decisions that Lowe's and Home Depot must make. If neither firm advertises, both will earn

**TABLE 3** Payoff Matrix for Advertising by Lowe's and Home Depot

| | Home Depot | |
|---|---|---|
| **Lowe's** | Don't advertise | Advertise |
| Don't advertise | \$100,000,\$100,000 | \$50,000,\$120,000 |
| Advertise | \$120,000,\$50,000 | \$80,000,\$80,000 |

\$100,000 in profit. If either Lowe's or Home Depot decides to spend the \$30,000 required to advertise, it will take \$50,000 in business away from the other, and its net profit will be \$120,000, leaving \$50,000 for the other. If both advertise, the market grows a little, but each firm's costs have risen, and profits drop to \$80,000 for both firms. If the decision must be made simultaneously without either firm having information about the decision of the other, the equilibrium is that both will advertise, and both will earn \$80,000 in profits.

## Dynamic Games

The static analysis above inherently assumes that pricing and advertising decisions are irreversible, occur simultaneously, and occur before the other knows what has happened. But most markets are dynamic, and firms are constantly trying new prices and other sales techniques to increase profits. This reality has led to the development of **dynamic games.**

Dynamic games: Sequential or repeated games where the players can adjust their actions based on the decisions of other players in the past.

***Price Discounting Reconsidered*** Another way to look at the pricing outcome in Table 2 is to assume that each firm knows these payoffs and will respond as soon as the other firm lowers its price. This makes the decision process a sequential process. Each firm waits for the other firm to alter price, then it follows suit. Since each firm has perfect knowledge and knows what each payoff is, a new equilibrium is reached; neither firm lowers prices for its banana splits, and profits remain at \$100,000. Neither firm would be inclined to lower price since profits would drop for both firms. This outcome is similar to the kinked demand curve model discussed earlier.

***Advertising: Another Look*** Once the game becomes dynamic and sequential, the outcome between Lowe's and Home Depot shown in Table 3 will be that neither firm advertises, and profits for each firm remain at \$100,000. You have probably noticed that Lowe's and Home Depot tend to locate near each other, and both firms tend to advertise only at specific times of the year mostly in spring and fall. Both tend to focus on competing on the basis of service and somewhat on price. Both have come to the conclusion that spending huge amounts on advertising does not pay, given the nature of the competition.

## Predatory Pricing

Predatory pricing: Selling below cost to consumers in the short run, hoping to eliminate competitors so that prices can be raised in the longer run to earn economic profits.

**Predatory pricing** involves offering sufficiently low prices to consumers in the short run to eliminate competitors, so that eventually prices can be increased in the longer run once the competitors are gone. Firms with monopoly power in a market can use price wars or threaten their use to keep firms from entering the market. Such was the case involving American Airlines and several low-cost carriers at Dallas-Fort Worth Airport (DFW) in the mid-1990s.[7]

American Airlines is the dominant air carrier at DFW, and several low-cost carriers (Vanguard, Western Pacific, and SunJet) entered the market. As the court noted:

[7] *U.S. v. AMR et al.*, 140 F. Supp. 2d (2001).

*During this period, these low-cost carriers created a new market dynamic, charging markedly lower fares on certain routes. For a certain period (of differing length in each market) consumers of air travel on these routes enjoyed lower prices. The number of passengers also substantially increased. American responded to the low-cost carriers by reducing some of its own fares and increasing the number of flights serving the routes. In each instance, the low-fare carrier failed to establish itself as a durable market presence, and so eventually moved its operations or ceased its separate existence entirely. After the low-fare carrier ceased operations, American generally resumed its prior marketing strategy, and in certain markets reduced the number of flights and raised its prices, roughly to levels comparable to those prior to the period of low-fare competition.*[8]

Table 4 captures the essence of the case using hypothetical data.

**TABLE 4** Payoff Matrix for American Airlines and Low-Cost Carriers

| **Low-Cost Carriers (potential entrants)** | **American Airlines (incumbent)** | |
|---|---|---|
| | Normal | Price war |
| Enter | \$100,000,\$100,000 | −\$100,000,−\$100,000 |
| Do not enter | \$0,\$400,000 | \$0,\$400,000 |

Without the entry of the low-cost carriers, American earns \$400,000 in profit. When they enter, American has a choice: continue to operate as normal and not slash prices (Normal column), or compete vigorously by lowering prices and offering more flights (Price War column). Normal activity results in profits to both parties of \$100,000, whereas engaging in a price war brings losses of \$100,000 to both, which ultimately the newly formed, lower-capitalized carriers probably cannot sustain. Once the low-cost carriers are gone, prices and routes can return to their original states.

This case raises an interesting issue: Was American just dropping fares to meet competition, or was it actually engaging in predatory behavior? Standard economic theory suggests that predatory behavior is unprofitable and unlikely. The argument goes like this: Suffering large losses to remove competition and then making it up through monopoly pricing is not likely to be profitable in the long run. Once the competitors are removed and high prices return, these same high prices provide a strong incentive for new firms to enter, and the monopoly is stuck continually lowering prices to maintain its monopoly. Modern game theory has challenged this view.

Table 4 and the American Airlines episode illustrate the new thinking by game theorists on predatory pricing. One possibility is that the profits from the monopoly are sufficient to offset the bouts of price wars required to maintain the monopoly. Second, this is a potentially repeatable game, and American (at least at DFW) has effectively shown that it stands ready to defend its turf. This *commitment* to lower prices (Price Wars) is a warning to other airlines that are considering whether to enter the market. Repeated games permit firms to demonstrate their strategic decisions, thereby creating a *reputation* for fierce competitive behavior, thus influencing the decisions of others. Ultimately, American won this case and also won on further appeal in 2003. The courts were not convinced that American did anything except match the prices of its competitors: In the words of the court, American engaged "only in bare, but not brass knuckle competition."

[8] *U.S. v. AMR*, p. 1141.

This case makes it clear that when the game is repeatable, the strategic matrix expands substantially. We now turn to some of the strategies that game theorists look at for repeated games.

## Repeated Game Strategies

Games can be endlessly (infinitely) repeated or repeated for a specific number of rounds. In either case, repeating opens the game to different types of strategies that are unavailable for the one-off game. These strategies can take into account the past behavior of rivals and can be more nuanced than one-off or limited sequential decisions. This section briefly explores these new strategies and some of their implications for understanding oligopoly behavior.

One possibility is simply to cooperate or defect from the beginning. These simple strategies, however, leave you at the mercy of your opponent, or lead to unfavorable outcomes where both firms earn less or suffer losses. A more robust set of strategies are **trigger strategies:** action is taken contingent on your opponent's past decisions. These strategies are described in the following sections.

Trigger strategies: Action is taken contingent on your opponent's past decisions.

### Grim Trigger

Let's start by considering an industry that is earning oligopoly profits. Suppose that all of a sudden, one firm lowers its price, maybe because it is in financial trouble and wants to increase sales right away. Under the grim trigger rule, the other firms lower their prices—but they do not stop there. They permanently lower their prices, making the financial condition of the original firm who reduced prices even more severe.

The grim trigger rule, thus, is this: Any decision by your opponent to defect (choose an unfavorable outcome) is met by a permanent retaliatory decision forever. This is a harsh decision rule. Its negative aspect is that it is subject to misreading. For example, has your competition lowered its price in an attempt to gain market share at your expense, or has the market softened for the product in general? This strategy can quickly lead to the unfavorable Prisoner's Dilemma result. To avoid this problem, researchers have developed the trembling hand trigger strategy.

### Trembling Hand Trigger

This strategy simply allows for one mistake by your opponent before you retaliate forever. This gives your opponent a chance to make a mistake and reduces misreads that are a problem for the grim trigger strategy. This approach can be extended to accept two nonsequential defects, and so on, but they can be exploited by clever opponents who figure out they can get away with a few "mistakes" before their opponent retaliates.

### Tit-for-Tat

This is a simple strategy that repeats the prior move of competitors. If one firm lowers its price, its rivals follow suit one time. If the same firm offers rebates or special offers, rivals do exactly the same in the next time period. This strategy has the efficient qualities that it rewards cooperation and punishes defection. It also offers forgiveness for defectors, so it avoids the misreading problems of the grim and trembling hand triggers. **Tit-for-tat strategies** also have been extended to include forgiveness of a single defection on a random basis.

Tit-for-tat strategies: Simple strategies that repeat the prior move of competitors. If your opponent lowers price, you do the same. This approach has the efficient quality that it rewards cooperation and punishes unfavorable strategies (defections).

This short list of strategies illustrates the richness of repeated games. Strategies tend to be more successful if they are relatively simple and easy to understand by competitors, tend to foster cooperation, have some credible punishment to reduce defections, and provide for forgiveness to avoid the costly mistakes associated with misreading opponents.[9]

Game theory took a long time to enter the profession, but it is now firmly entrenched. Its usefulness is in bringing forth insights for not only human behavior, but for oligopolistic market behavior, that is mutually interdependent.

[9] Nick Wilkinson, *Managerial Economics: A Problem Solving Approach* (Cambridge: Cambridge University Press), 2005, p. 373.

## *Issue:* Can We Use Game Theory to Predict the Future?

**Professor Bruce** Bueno de Mesquita of New York University thinks so. He has developed a game theory simulation program that he uses to predict the outcome of future negotiations as well as to suggest strategies to alter the likely outcome of negotiations.

His model quantifies the following four pieces of information using the opinions of participants and experts:

1. Catalog every individual or group with a meaningful stake or interest in the outcome (*stakeholders*).
2. Estimate what each of the stakeholders wants (*position*).
3. Approximate how important the issue is to each of these individuals or groups (*salience*).
4. Estimate how influential each of the players are relative to each other (*influence*).

First, he determines a numerical scale of outcomes and then assigns a numerical estimate for position, salience, and influence to each of the stakeholders.

As an example, most corporate firms face a large array of laws and regulations that pose potential legal tangles. Litigation is costly, time consuming, and typically involves threats of huge fines and/or criminal charges. Professor Bueno de Mesquita detailed a case of a firm embroiled in litigation with the Justice Department. The outcomes in this case were given numerical values and ranged from multiple severe felonies (100), to one severe felony (75), to several lesser felonies (60), to multiple misdemeanors (25), to just one misdemeanor (0). He then consulted participants and experts to estimate position, salience, and influence (using the same 100-point scale) for each stakeholder and created a table like the one below.

Corbis

This table represents only a sample of the stakeholders and outcomes Professor Bueno de Mesquita considered. He included nearly 50 stakeholders and 8 categories of outcomes. Using just this data, the initial run of the simulation suggested that a settlement would give a result around 80, one severe felony and several lesser felonies. This turned out to be what the executives and their lawyers feared would happen.

The firm did not consider this a fair outcome because they felt it was not obvious that they were responsible for the injuries, nor did they intend any harm to the victims. What could be done? By altering the firm's numbers and running the simulation over several times, a better outcome was suggested by the model. First, the attorney for one executive had to harden his initial settlement offer and demand misdemeanors only. Similarly, the company's directors who were eager to settle had to harden their initial demands to misdemeanors only. One thing that is clear in these types of negotiations is that whether criminal charges are warranted or not, they tend to encourage defendants to settle whether guilty or not.

By adopting the new negotiation strategy, the firm was able to achieve a settlement of one lesser felony and several misdemeanors (40 on the scale). This was roughly the outcome predicted when the modified positions were run through the game theory simulation.

Professor Bueno de Mesquita's model has been used to predict the results of such wide-ranging issues as Middle East peace negotiations, Securities and Exchange Commission investigations into fraud, and Environmental Protection Agency investigations of potential chemical harm when a firm suddenly introduces a "new and improved" version of a successful product where a significant chemical is absent in the new version. A declassified CIA study finds that his model "hit the bull's-eye about twice as often as the government's experts" who provided the data. While not useful for all types of predictions, his approach is highly useful for many negotiations.

| Stakeholder | Position | Salience | Influence |
|---|---|---|---|
| Affected individuals (plaintiffs) | 90 | 80 | 15.71 |
| Union | 85 | 80 | 5.61 |
| Senior executives (defendants) | 25 | 80 | 7.26 |
| Corporate council | 25 | 75 | 3.63 |
| Dept. of Justice attorney | 100 | 85 | 11.16 |
| OHSA representative | 25 | 65 | 16.43 |

Sources: Bruce Bueno de Mesquita, *The Predictioneer's Game: Using the Logic of Brazen Self-Interest to See and Shape the Future* (New York: Random House), 2009; and Nicholas Thompson, "Forecast: Self-Serving," *New York Times Magazine* November 8, 2009, p. 30.

## Summary of Market Structures

In this and the previous two chapters, we have studied the four major market structures: competition, monopolistic competition, oligopoly, and monopoly. As we move through this list, market power becomes greater, and the ability of the firm to earn economic profits in the long run grows.

Table 5 summarizes the important distinctions between these four market structures. Keep in mind that market structure analysis allows you to look at the overall characteristics of the market and predict the pricing and profit behavior of the firms. The outcomes for competition and monopolistic competition are particularly attractive for consumers because firms price their products equal to average total costs and earn just enough to keep them in the business over the long haul.

**TABLE 5** Summary of Market Structures

| | Competition | Monopolistic Competition | Oligopoly | Monopoly |
|---|---|---|---|---|
| **Number of Firms** | Many | Many | Few | One |
| **Product** | Homogeneous | Differentiated | Homogeneous or differentiated | Unique |
| **Barriers to Entry or Exit?** | No | No | Yes | Yes |
| **Strategic Interdependence?** | No | No | Yes | Not applicable |
| **Long-Run Price Decision** | P = ATC | P = ATC | P > ATC | P > ATC |
| **Long-Run Profits** | Zero | Zero | Usually economic | Economic |
| **Key Summary Characteristic** | Price taker | Product differentiation | Mutual interdependence | One-firm industry |

In contrast, the outcomes for oligopolistic and monopolistic industries are not as favorable to consumers. Concentrated markets have considerable market power, which shows up in pricing and output decisions. However, keep in mind that markets with market power (oligopolies) often involve giants competing with giants. Even though there is a mutual interdependence in their decisions, and they may not always compete vigorously over prices, they often are innovative because of some competitive pressures. We see this today especially in the electronics and automobile markets.

*Only the Paranoid Survive* is the title of a book by a former president of Intel Corporation, Andy Grove. His point is that you must keep ahead of the competition in innovation and technology if you want to remain in business. The last couple of years saw many large firms (Enron, WorldCom, Kmart, Lehman Brothers, and the Italian company Parmalat) fail or go bankrupt, costing their stockholders billions. Without the government bailouts during 2008–2009, many more large firms would have failed. Bigness does not make firms immune to market pressures.

### CHECKPOINT

#### GAME THEORY

- Game theory uses sophisticated mathematical analysis to model oligopolistic mutual interdependence.
- Game theory characteristics include (a) degrees of cooperation, (b) number of players, (c) simultaneous or sequential decision making, (d) information completeness, (e) discrete

or continuous strategies, (f) one-off or repeated games, and (g) zero-sum or non-zero-sum games.

- The Prisoner's Dilemma is a static noncooperative game where players minimize their maximum prison time by both confessing, a strategy that neither would have taken had they been able to communicate with one another.
- Nash equilibrium analysis showed that a solution exists for n-person games if each player chooses his optimal strategy, given that all other players have done the same.
- Games that are repeated lead to more nuanced trigger strategies, including grim trigger, trembling hand trigger, and tit-for-tat.

**QUESTION:** Game theory and sophisticated mathematical modeling can be used to develop PokerBots and chess software that consistently beat chess champions and will eventually probably beat poker champions. What might keep this same analysis from being used to beat the stock market?

Answers to the Checkpoint question can be found at the end of this chapter.

## Key Concepts

Monopolistic competition, p. 238
Product differentiation, p. 239
Oligopoly, p. 243
Mutual interdependence, p. 243
Cartel, p. 244
Kinked demand curve, p. 246
Game theory, p. 247
Prisoner's Dilemma, p. 249
Nash equilibrium, p. 251
Static games, p. 251
Dynamic games, p. 252
Predatory pricing, p. 252
Trigger strategies, p. 254
Tit-for-tat strategies, p. 254

## Chapter Summary

### Monopolistic Competition

Monopolistic competition assumes nearly the same characteristics as the competitive model, including the following:

- There are a large number of small firms with insignificant market share.
- There are no barriers to entry and exit.
- Unlike competition, the products sold by monopolistically competitive firms are similar, but differentiated. Product differentiation is the key to this market structure.

Although product differences are often modest, each firm nonetheless faces a downward sloping demand curve with an associated marginal revenue curve. This demand curve is, however, highly elastic.

Pricing and output behavior in the short run for the monopolistically competitive firm look a lot like that for a weak monopolist. Profit is maximized by selling an output where MR = MC.

In the long run, entry and exit of other firms will eliminate short-run profits or losses. If short-run profits exist, entry will reduce individual demand curves until the demand curve is just tangent to the average total cost curve. If short-run losses are the rule, exit will expand the demand curve of remaining firms until, again, the demand curve is tangent to the long-run average total cost (LRATC) curve.

At long-run equilibrium, P = ATC, and the firm earns normal profits. This output level is not, however, equal to the minimum point on the LRATC curve—it is lower than output needed to minimize costs. This is the cost to consumers from product differentiation. Costs of advertising, rapid innovation, and "me too" copying are all included in the price of the products we purchase.

### Oligopoly

Oligopoly industries are those in which the market is controlled by just a few firms. What constitutes a few firms is not precisely defined. Oligopoly products can be the same or differentiated, and barriers to entry are usually substantial.

Because there are only a few firms, decisions by one firm are dependent on what other firms in the industry decide to do. Economists refer to this as mutual interdependence. This is the key characteristic of oligopolies.

Cartels are illegal in the United States, but they are permitted in other parts of the world. Firms in cartels collude and agree to set monopoly prices and share the market according to some formula. Cartels are inherently unstable because cheating is profitable.

The kinked demand curve model of oligopoly answers the question of why oligopoly prices appear stable. The model assumes that if the firm raises its price, competitors will not react and raise theirs, but if the firm lowers its price, other firms will lower theirs in response. These reactions by competitors create a "kink" in the firm's demand curve and a discontinuity in the MR curve. This discontinuity permits marginal costs to vary considerably before the firm will change its pricing structure.

### Game Theory

Modern game theory owes its origins to the mathematician John von Neumann.

The Prisoner's Dilemma is a static, noncooperative game in which each player must anticipate whether the other is going to confess or not. Both players would be better off not confessing, but each will confess in the end. Both players end up minimizing their worst outcome (minimax solution).

John Nash showed that there is a solution in an *n*-person game if each player chooses his optimal strategy, given that all other players have done the same. This was an important result that allowed economists to develop realistic but complex games of market interactions, because they knew a solution existed.

Dynamic games allow for sequential decision making. This often changes the equilibrium outcome. When games are repeated, a host of new (more complex) strategies are introduced. They include trigger strategies such as grim trigger, trembling hand trigger, and tit-for-tat.

## Questions and Problems

### Check Your Understanding

1. How do monopolistic competitive markets differ from competitive markets? If monopolistically competitive firms are making economic profits in the short run, what happens in the long run?
2. Describe the assumption underlying the kinked demand curve model. Describe why marginal cost can vary, but price remains constant.
3. How many firms constitute an oligopoly? What else characterizes oligopoly markets?
4. When economists speak of "mutual interdependence" in oligopoly markets, what do they mean? Why is mutual interdependence such an important element of oligopoly markets?
5. What makes the strategies so different for repeated games than for one-off games?
6. Why is it difficult for cartels to effectively maintain high prices over the longer term?

## Apply the Concepts

7. Google has a huge share of the search activity on the Internet, as well as the online advertising revenue it generates. Microsoft had roughly the same percentage for operating system sales on microcomputers when the government filed its antitrust suit. Why hasn't the government filed a similar suit against Google?
8. Holding the industry constant, why does a monopolist earn more profits than a firm in an oligopolistic setting? Why does the oligopolist earn more than a monopolistic competitor?
9. "Monopolistic competition has a little of monopoly and a little of competition, hence its name." Do you agree? Why or why not?
10. We saw in the last chapter that the HHI (Herfindahl-Hirshman index) is used by the Department of Justice to measure industry concentration. Since domestically we have virtually no monopolies, some would argue that the HHI is really used to measure the degree of oligopoly. However, the HHI represents domestic concentration, and many of the products we purchase are made globally and sold in the United States by foreign firms. Has global competition made these HHI estimates less meaningful? Are old-line American oligopolies (autos, steel, and airlines) more like monopolistic competitors today? Why or why not?
11. In both competitive and monopolistically competitive markets, firms earn normal profits in the long run. What enables oligopoly firms to have the opportunity to earn economic profits in the long run?
12. As new firms enter a monopolistically competitive market, what happens to the average total cost curve for existing firms? What happens to the individual firm demand curve? What happens to individual firm profits?
13. The 1982 Export Trading Company Act and the 1918 Webb-Pomerene Act permit export cartels in the United States. Export cartels are groups of firms that can legally collude, set prices, and share marketing and distribution of their products in foreign countries. These cartels must register with the government, and their activities cannot affect domestic competition. Economic theory suggests that cartels are entities that exist to maximize monopoly profits for members. Given this, why would the United States permit these cartels to exist?
14. When trying to get tickets to a Broadway show recently, my wife may have had a chance to see game theory in action. Tickets for shows 6 months away went on sale online at 6:00 in the morning and she was there at 6:02. Every time she requested seats in a good area, she was informed they were unavailable, but others in much worse locations were available. No matter what day or which show, less attractive alternatives were suggested. Can you think of a game theory explanation that might suggest why this was happening?
15. Why does the U.S. Department of Justice successfully sue a cartel of leading foreign producers of LCD flat screens for price fixing in 2008, but not go after the OPEC (Organization of Petroleum Exporting Countries) cartel?

## In the News

16. As we have seen, cartels face a difficult time holding their group together. According to *The Economist* (March 31, 2007, p. 84), "Co-ordinating a price is one thing; sticking to it is another. Companies face the same dilemma that has undone countless hypothetical prisoners in economics textbooks." How is the incentive structure that leads to cheating in a cartel similar to that of the Prisoner's Dilemma?
17. John Gapper titled his article "Little Laptops Snap at the Oligopoly" (*Financial Times*, June 16, 2009, p. 9), and makes the point that netbooks (small, light, cheap laptop computers) are putting competitive pressure on the "three-way alliance

among Microsoft, Intel and Dell." He is suggesting that these three firms constitute an oligopoly. Do you agree that Microsoft, Intel, and Dell Computer constitute an oligopoly? Why or why not?

## Answers to Questions in CheckPoints

### Check Point: Monopolistic Competition

Clowns are unique; their acts are copyrighted and protected, and this is one way to differentiate your circus from others. Celebrity clowns draw crowds, especially youngsters, and are cheaper than buying, keeping, training, and insuring animals (not to mention the hassles from animal rights groups).

### Check Point: Oligopoly

The most recent example is the Internet. Barriers to entry in a large number of well-established industries (big and small) are affected. It is clearly changing the software, music, publishing, and entertainment industries. In a similar way, sequencing of DNA is another innovation that is rapidly changing the pharmaceutical industry.

### Check Point: Game Theory

Game theory is best used with a relatively small number of decision makers. Chess has a finite (but huge) number of moves, and computers can search for the optimal play. Poker involves a limited number of opponents. Games give insights into human behavior that can be used as inputs into stock market decisions. But when the number of participants, stocks, and economic variables are considered, the computing power required to solve the stock market problem probably prevents its use in real time.

# 11 Theory of Input Markets

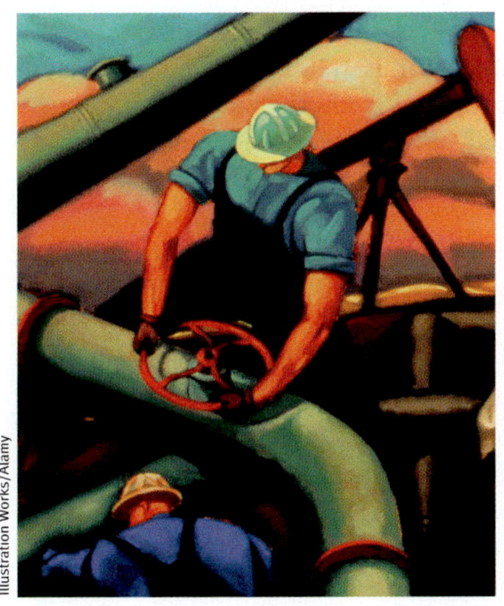

Illustration Works/Alamy

*The role model for indignant managers is the film director Alfred Hitchcock. When asked by anxious movie stars what their "motivation" was in a scene, his answer was blunt. "Your salary," he would say.*

—STEFAN STERN[1]

**Hardly a day goes by without** media reference to some celebrity's income or some CEO's astronomical salary laden with stock options. Rock stars and professional athletes command seven-figure salaries (that's millions of dollars), while your economics instructor labors away for a five-figure pittance that barely covers the costs of living. Meanwhile, shortages in nursing and elementary education seem to persist year after year, and we see numerous wage discrimination cases going to litigation. How are all these developments to be explained? Labor markets are complex institutions, and as usual, understanding the issues connected with them will require some simplification.

Input markets, also called factor markets, are extremely important to our economy. To this point in the book, we have focused on product markets, mentioning input markets only incidentally. Sitting behind the production of goods and services, however, are workers, machinery, and manufacturing plants. Few firms can operate without employees or capital. Similarly, few households could survive without the income that work provides.

The analysis of input markets in this chapter focuses on the labor and capital markets, while briefly touching on land rents and entrepreneurial profits. The first two sections look

[1] Stefan Stern, "The Meaning of Life at Work and Other Employee Perks," *Financial Times,* March 11, 2008, p. 16.

**After studying this chapter you should be able to:**

- ☐ Define and describe competitive labor markets.
- ☐ Derive a supply curve for labor.
- ☐ Describe the factors that can change labor supply.
- ☐ Describe the factors that can change labor demand.
- ☐ Determine the elasticity of demand for labor.
- ☐ Derive the market demand for labor.
- ☐ Describe monopoly and monopsony power and their impact on imperfect labor markets.
- ☐ Determine the present value of an investment.
- ☐ Compute the rate of return of an investment.
- ☐ Describe the impact of the supply of land on markets.
- ☐ Describe the impact of economic profits on entrepreneurs and markets.

at competitive labor markets where the participants—firms and employees—are price takers. We examine some imperfections in the labor market and look for differences in outcomes. We then turn to the role that capital markets play in the economy. The chapter closes with a brief examination of land and entrepreneurship, the source of rents and profits. In the following chapter, we will return to the labor market and take a closer look at several pressing labor issues, including human capital, economic discrimination, and the economics of labor unions.

Competitive labor markets are similar to competitive product markets. First, we assume that firms operate in competitive industries with many buyers and sellers, a homogeneous product, and easy entry and exit to the industry. As you will recall, moreover, the firms in competitive industries are price takers. Each firm is so small that it has no perceptible impact on industry price; all firms can do is adjust their output in response to changes in industry price.

A second assumption of competitive labor markets, inhumane as it may sound, is that workers are considered homogeneous, and labor is treated as a homogeneous commodity. One unit of labor is a perfect substitute for another in the competitive market, and no potential employees are "special." More precisely, all employees are regarded as equally productive, such that firms have no preference for one employee over another.

Third, a competitive labor market assumes that information in the industry is widely available and accurate. Everyone knows what the going wage rate is, so well-informed decisions about how much labor to supply are made by workers, and firms can wisely decide how many workers to hire.

A firm's demand for labor is a derived demand; it is derived from consumer demand for the firm's product and the productivity of labor. The labor supply, on the other hand, is determined by the individual preferences of potential workers for work or leisure. Like all competitive markets, supply and demand interact to determine equilibrium wages and employment. Much of this analysis you have seen before, but we now apply these analytical techniques to labor markets. We begin by looking at how the decisions by individuals to participate in labor markets generate the supply of labor.

## Competitive Labor Supply

When you decide to work, you are giving up leisure, understood broadly as nonwork activity, in exchange for the income that work brings. Economists assume people prefer leisure activities to work. This may not be entirely true, since work can be a source of personal satisfaction and a network of social connections, as well as provide many other benefits. For our discussion, however, we follow the practice of economists in simply dividing individual or household time into work and leisure. Note that the term *leisure* encompasses all activities that do not involve paid work, including caring for children, doing household chores, and activities that are truly leisurely.

### Individual Labor Supply

**Supply of labor:** The amount of time an individual is willing to work at various wage rates.

The **supply of labor** represents the time an individual is willing to work—the labor the individual is willing to supply—at various wage rates. On a given day, the most a person can work is 24 hours, though clearly such a schedule could not be sustained for long, given that we all need rest and sleep. For high wages, you would probably be willing to work horrendous hours for a short time, whereas if wages were low enough, you might not be willing to work at all. Between these two extremes lies the normal supply of labor curve for most of us.

Panel A of Figure 1 shows a typical labor supply curve for individuals. This individual is willing to supply $l_1$ hours of work a day when the wage is $W_1$. What happens if the wage rate increases? Assume that wages increase to $W_2$: This individual now is willing to increase hours spent working from $l_1$ to $l_2$ (point *b*), reducing her hours of leisure.

## Karl Marx (1818–1883)

"Working men of all countries unite!" With this exhortation, Karl Marx ended his seminal *Communist Manifesto,* neatly summing up both his philosophy and his view of the world. The solution was revolution by the proletariat—the working class that was the hero of all Marx believed and proposed.

Karl Marx was born in Germany in 1818. He spent much of his adult life, however, in England, where he died in 1883. By the time of his death, Marx and Friedrich Engels had crafted the essence of communism—the last ideology to seriously challenge capitalism in the 20th century. In their two major works, *The Communist Manifesto* (1848) and *Das Kapital* (1867), Marx and Engels offered a severe critique of capitalism and extolled the virtues of proletariat rebellion and the utopia of a stateless world order.

Ivan Vdovin/Alamy

To preserve their privileges, the ruling class had always striven to oppress the underclasses. Marx saw a struggle between the bourgeoisie (or property owners) and the proletariat (or workers). Modern states were merely a way to repress workers for the benefit of the bourgeoisie.

This exploitation—the essence of capitalism—not only kept the bourgeoisie in power, but it also alienated the proletariat from its own labor, which to Marx was the true essence of all economic value. The only prescription to cure the monopolistic and monopsonistic exploitation of labor was proletariat revolution.

## Substitution Effect

When wages rise, people tend to substitute work for leisure since the opportunity cost of leisure grows. This is known as the **substitution effect.** The substitution effect for labor supply is always positive; it leads to more hours of work when the wage rate increases.

**Substitution effect:** Higher wages mean that the value of work has increased, and the opportunity costs of leisure are higher, so work is substituted for leisure.

Note that this effect is similar to the substitution effect consumers experience when the price of a product declines. When the price of one product falls, consumers substitute that

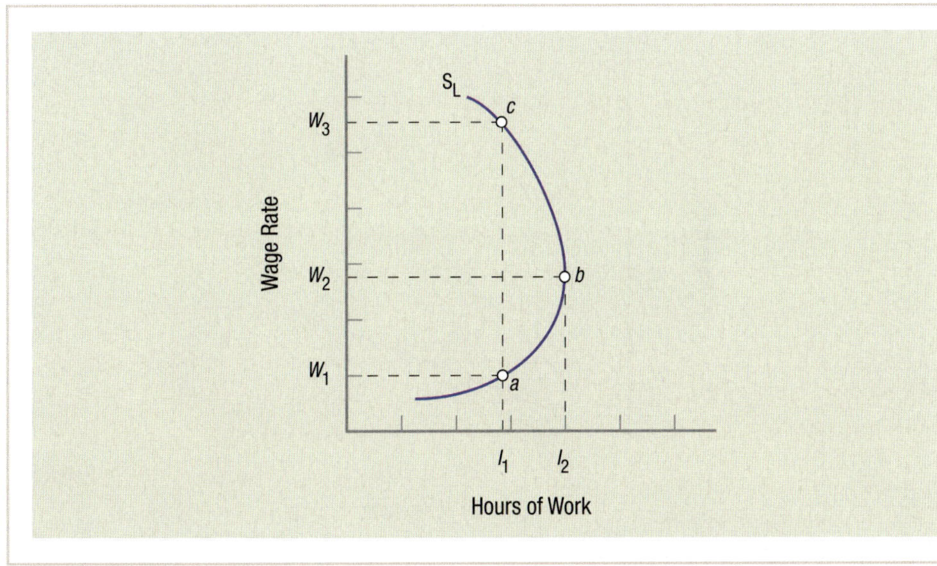


**FIGURE 1—Individual Supply of Labor**

When wages are $W_1$, this individual will work $l_1$ hours, but when the wage rate rises to $W_2$, her willingness to work rises to $l_2$. Over these two wage rates she is substituting work for leisure. Once the wage rises above $W_2$, the income effect begins to dominate, since she now has sufficient income that leisure is now more important and her labor supply curve is backward bending.

product for others. The substitution effect for consumer products, however, is negative (price falls and consumption rises), while it is always positive for labor (wages rise and the supply of labor increases).

## Income Effect

**Income effect:** Higher wages mean you can maintain the same standard of living by working fewer hours. The impact on labor supply is generally negative.

When wages rise, if you continue to work the same hours as before, your income will rise. When wage rates are very high, however, the income from working a few hours may be enough to support the lifestyle you wish. Higher wages may permit you to work fewer hours, but also enjoy a higher standard of living. This **income effect** on labor supply is normally negative—higher wages and income lead to fewer hours worked. As a result, the supply curve for *individuals* in Figure 1 is *backward bending*: At wages above $W_2$, workers increasingly elect to substitute leisure for the income that comes from additional work.

Once again, this is similar to the income effect consumers experience when the price of a common product drops. The falling price of this product permits consumers to purchase the same quantity as before and still have some added income left over to spend on other products. Higher wages mean a higher income, and with a higher income leisure looks more attractive.

The labor supply curve for individuals shows that, at wages below $W_2$, people will substitute work for leisure; income is more important than leisure at these wage levels. When wages are above $W_2$, workers will do the opposite, substituting leisure for work; they have enough income so leisure is more important.

When the labor supply curve is positively sloped, as it is below $W_2$ in Figure 1, the substitution effect is stronger than the income effect; thus, higher wages lead to more hours worked. Conversely, when the supply of labor curve bends backward, as it does above $W_2$, the income effect overpowers the substitution effect. In this case, higher wages mean fewer hours worked.

Backward bending labor supply curves have been observed empirically in developed and developing countries. Still, it takes rather high income levels before the income effect begins to overpower the substitution effect. People like to have incomes well beyond what is required to satisfy their basic needs before they select more leisure over work as wages rise.

## Market Labor Supply Curves

The labor supply for any occupation or industry is upward sloping; higher wages for a job mean more inquiries and job applications. Thus, although an individual's labor supply curve may be backward bending, market labor supply curves are normally positively sloped as shown in Figure 2. Note that this is true for all other inputs to the production process,

**FIGURE 2—Market Labor Supplies**

Market labor supplies are positively related to the wage rate. Increasing wages in one industry attract labor from other industries (a movement from point *d* to point e as the wage rises from $W_1$ to $W_2$). In contrast, market labor supply curves *shift* in response to demographic changes, changes in the nonwage benefits of jobs, wages paid in other occupations, and nonwage income.

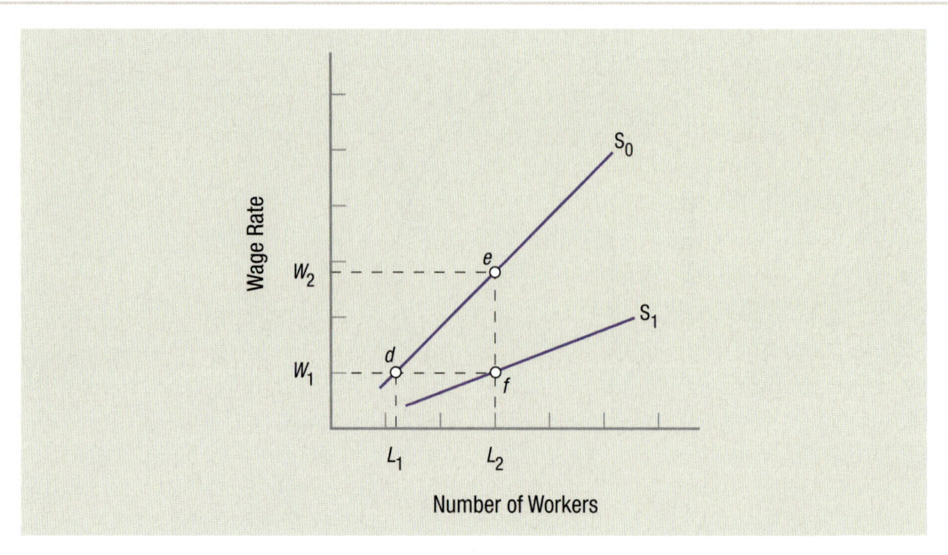

including raw materials such as copper, steel, and silicon, as well as for capital and land: Higher prices mean higher quantities supplied.

Changes in wage rates change the quantity of labor supplied. For example, increasing wages in one industry attract labor from other industries. This is a movement along the market labor supply curve, shown as a movement along $S_0$ from points $d$ to $e$ as wages (input prices) rise from $W_1$ to $W_2$.

## Factors That Change Labor Supply

But what factors will cause the entire market labor supply curve to shift from, say, $S_0$ to $S_1$ in Figure 2 so that $L_2$ workers are willing to work for a wage of $W_1$ (point $f$)? These include demographic changes, nonwage benefits of jobs, wages paid in other occupations, and nonwage income.

### Demographic Changes

Changes in population, immigration patterns, and labor force participation rates (the percentage of individuals in a group who enter the labor force) all change labor supplies by altering the number of qualified people available for work. Over the past three decades, labor force participation rates among women have steadily risen, continually adding workers to the expanding American labor force; dual-earner households are increasingly the norm. Today, both parents work in two-thirds of all married-couple households with children. Other demographic changes have shifted the labor supply curve by modifying the labor–leisure preferences among workers. Health improvements, for example, have lengthened the typical working life.

### Nonmoney Aspects of Jobs

Changes in the nonwage benefits of an occupation will similarly shift the supply of labor in that market. If employers can manage to increase the pleasantness, safety, or status of a job, labor supply will increase. Other nonmoney perks also help. The airline industry, for example, has greatly increased the number of people willing to work in mundane positions by allowing employees (and in some instances their immediate families) to fly anywhere for free on a standby basis.

### Wages in Alternative Jobs

When worker skills in one industry are readily transferable to other jobs or industries, the wages paid in those other markets will affect wage rates and the labor supply in the first industry. For example, Web and computer programming skills are useful in all industries, and their wages in one industry affect all industries. Because at least some of the skills that all workers possess will benefit other employers, all labor markets have some influence over each other. Rising wages in growth industries will shrink the supply of labor available to firms in other industries.

### Nonwage Income

Changes in income from sources other than working (such as income from a trust) will change the supply of labor. As nonwage income rises, hours of work supplied declines. If you have enough income from nonwork sources, after all, the retirement urge will set in no matter what your age. Maybe this is where the term "idle rich" came from.

The key thing to remember here is that market labor supply curves are normally positively sloped, even though an individual's labor supply curve may be backward bending. In the next section, we put this together with the other blade in the scissors: the demand for labor in competitive labor markets.

## *Issue:* Digital Bedouins and the World of Work

**Some people** suggest we are becoming "digital Bedouins," or nomads. Cell phones, Wi-Fi laptops, and Internet-connected smart phones (such as Blackberry and iPhone) are changing the way we work, where we live, and how we communicate with friends and family. As the table below shows, the impact of mobile technology is far greater for the young than those over 50.

Over half of the world's population subscribes to a mobile phone network. A growing number of people now use their smart phones and laptops as an office.

### Mobile Phone or PDA Use by Age Group

| | Age | |
|---|---|---|
| **Activity** | **18–29** | **50–64** |
| Send or receive text messages | 85% | 38% |
| Play a game | 47 | 13 |
| Play music | 38 | 5 |
| Access the Internet | 31 | 10 |
| Send or receive instant messages | 26 | 11 |
| Watch a video | 19 | 4 |

Firms are jettisoning cubicles and other office space for more in-demand mobile space and encouraging employees to work at home or on the road with only periodic get-togethers with colleagues.

MoveOn.org is an example of a purely nomadic organization. MoveOn has several dozen staffers, thousands of consultants, and several million volunteers, and a company rule that "no *two* people anywhere may share a physical office." This prevents organizational cliques. Through the use of instant messaging, they know who is available to help make a decision. Since MoveOn is an advocacy group, this process may be sufficient, and it clearly minimizes administrative expenses.

Josef Niedermeier/Photolibrary

But working at home or on the move also has its drawbacks. When people work together in physical offices, the interaction helps to cement relationships. Also, work presumably ends when you leave the office. Being a nomad has the potential to be isolating and, unless you have discipline, all-consuming.

Nomads are also changing how buildings are designed, how cities and parks are developed, and where many young people choose to live. Soon, entire cities will be Wi-Fied with WiMax or some other technology, and buildings will have specific areas for mobile computing. The world is changing to serve a new generation of digital Bedouins.

Source: Based on "Nomads at Last: A Special Report on Mobile Telecoms," *Economist*, April 12, 2008.

**CHECKPOINT**

### COMPETITIVE LABOR SUPPLY

- Competitive labor markets assume that firms operate in competitive product markets and purchase homogeneous labor, and that information is widely available and accurate.
- The supply of labor represents the time an individual is willing to work.
- The substitution effect occurs when wages rise, as people tend to substitute work for leisure because the opportunity cost of leisure is higher or vice versa when wages fall.
- When wages rise and you continue to work the same number of hours, your income rises. When wages rise high enough, an income effect occurs in which leisure is traded for income, and the supply of labor curve for individuals is backward bending.
- Industry or occupation labor supply curves are upward sloping.
- The labor supply curve shifts with demographic changes, changes in the nonwage aspects of an occupation, changes in the wages of alternative jobs, and changes in nonwage income.

**QUESTIONS:** Assume that you take a job with flexible hours, but initially your salary is based on a 40-hour week. Your salary begins at $15 an hour, or $30,000 a year. Assuming your salary rises, at what salary (hourly wage) would you begin to work fewer than 40 hours a week (remember, the job permits flexible hours)? If your rich aunt dies and leaves you $500,000, would this alter the wage rate where you cut your work hours? Do you think this wage rate will be the same when you are 35 and have two children?

Answers to the Checkpoint questions can be found at the end of this chapter.

## Competitive Labor Demand

The competitive firm's **demand for labor** is derived from the demand for the firm's product and the productive capabilities of a unit of labor.

**Demand for labor:** Demand for labor is derived from the demand for the firm's product and the productivity of labor.

### Marginal Revenue Product

Assume a firm wants to hire an additional worker, and that worker is able to produce 15 units of the firm's product. Further, assume that the product sells for $10 a unit, and labor is the only input cost (such as blackberry picking in Oregon), with this cost including a normal return on the investment. The last worker hired is therefore worth $150 to the firm (15 × $10 = $150). If the cost of hiring this worker is $150 or less (remember, a normal profit is included in the wage), then the firm will hire this person. If the wage rate for labor exceeds $150, a competitive firm will not hire this marginal worker.

To see how this works in greater detail, look at Table 1. The production function here is similar to the one used earlier in the chapter on production. Column 1 (L) is labor input, Column 2 (Q) is total output, and Column 3 ($MPP_L$) is the **marginal physical product of labor.** This last value is the additional output a firm receives from employing an added unit of labor ($MPP_L = \Delta Q \div \Delta L$). For example, adding a fourth worker raises output from 25 to 40 units, so the marginal physical product of labor for this additional worker is 15 units.

**Marginal physical product of labor:** The additional output a firm receives from employing an added unit of labor ($MPP_L = \Delta Q \div \Delta L$).

**TABLE 1** Competitive Labor Market

| (1) L | (2) Q | (3) $MPP_L$ | (4) P | (5) $MRP_L = VMP_L$ | (6) W |
|---|---|---|---|---|---|
| — | 0 | — | 10 | — | 100 |
| 1 | 7 | 7 | 10 | 70 | 100 |
| 2 | 15 | 8 | 10 | 80 | 100 |
| 3 | 25 | 10 | 10 | 100 | 100 |
| 4 | 40 | 15 | 10 | 150 | 100 |
| 5 | 54 | 14 | 10 | 140 | 100 |
| 6 | 65 | 11 | 10 | 110 | 100 |
| 7 | 75 | 10 | 10 | 100 | 100 |
| 8 | 84 | 9 | 10 | 90 | 100 |
| 9 | 90 | 6 | 10 | 60 | 100 |
| 10 | 95 | 5 | 10 | 50 | 100 |

In this example, the firm is operating in a competitive market, so it can sell all the output it produces at the prevailing market price of $10. The value of another worker to the firm, called the **marginal revenue product** ($MRP_L$), is equal to the marginal physical product of labor times marginal revenue:

**Marginal revenue product:** The value of another worker to the firm is equal to the marginal physical product of labor ($MPP_L$) times marginal revenue (MR).

$$MRP_L = MPP_L \times MR$$

In our example, adding a fourth worker leads to a marginal revenue product of $150; we multiply the marginal physical product of labor of 15 units by the marginal revenue—or price in this competitive market—of $10 per unit.

Column 5 contains the firm's $MRP_L$. Additional workers add this value to the firm. Thus, the marginal revenue product curve is the firm's demand for labor, which is graphed in Figure 3 on the next page. Note how the marginal revenue product reaches a maximum at four workers, as shown in column 5 of the table and in the figure.

**FIGURE 3—The Competitive Firm's Demand for Labor**

This figure reflects the data from columns 5 and 6 from Table 1. In this example, the firm is operating in a competitive market, so it can sell all the output it produces at the prevailing market price. The value of the additional worker to the firm, the value of the marginal product ($VMP_L$), is equal to the marginal physical product of labor times price (or marginal revenue in this case). $VMP_L$ is the competitive firm's demand for labor. If wages are equal to $100, the firm will hire seven workers (point *e*).

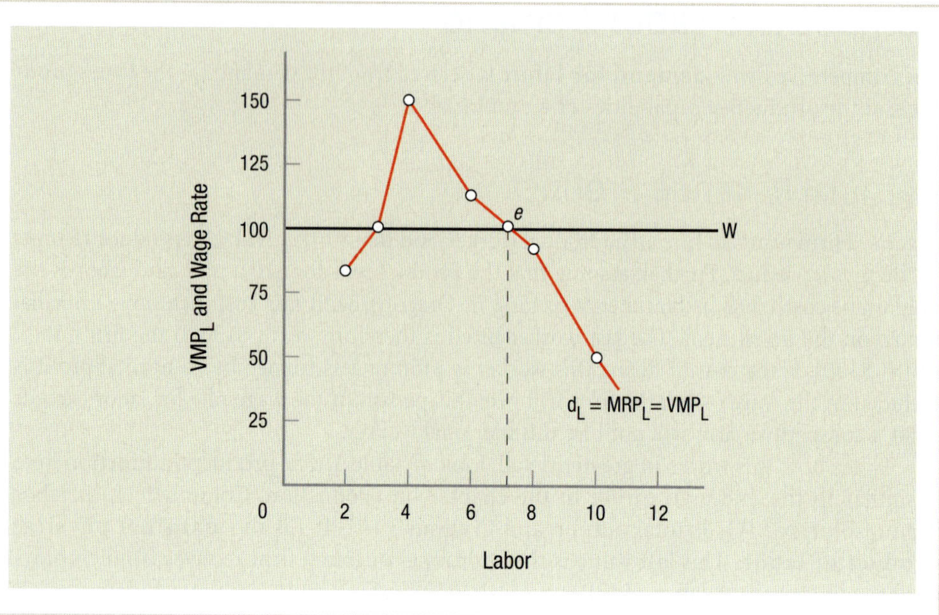


## Value of the Marginal Product

**Value of the marginal product:** The value of the marginal product of labor ($VMP_L$) is equal to price multiplied by the marginal physical product of labor, or P × $MPP_L$.

Competitive firms are price takers for whom marginal revenue is equal to the price of the product (MR = P). The **value of the marginal product** is defined as $VMP_L = MPP_L \times P$. For the fourth worker in Table 1, the value of the marginal product of labor is 15 units times $10, or $150. This is the same as the marginal revenue product of labor we just calculated. In the competitive case, MR = P, hence $VMP_L = MRP_L$. The distinction between VMP and MRP is of little importance here, but when we look at imperfect labor markets, these two will differ because marginal revenue will not equal price and the difference will have policy implications.

Competitive firms hire labor from competitive labor markets. Because each firm is too small to affect the larger market, it can hire all the labor it wants at the market-determined wage. Remember, we are assuming labor is a homogeneous commodity, and one unit of labor is the same as all others.

Table 1 and Figure 3 assume that the going wage for labor (W) is $100. For our firm, this results in seven workers being hired at $100 (point *e*), since this is the employment level at which $W = VMP_L$. Note that $W = VMP_L$ at three workers as well, but since the value of the marginal product is greater than the wage rate for workers four to six, the firm would hire seven workers, not three, to maximize its gains. The value to the firm of hiring the seventh worker is just equal to what the firm must pay this worker. Profits are maximized for the competitive firm when workers are hired out to the point where $VMP_L = W$.

However, if market wages were to fall to $90, the firm would hire an eighth worker to maximize profits, since with eight employees, $VMP_L$ is also equal to $90.

## Factors That Change Labor Demand

The demand for labor is derived from product demand and labor productivity—how much people will pay for the product and how much each unit of labor can produce. It follows that changes in labor demand can arise from changes in either product demand or labor productivity. Because most production also requires other inputs, changes in the price of these other inputs also change the demand for labor.

### Change in Product Demand

A decline in the demand for a firm's product will lead to lower market prices reducing $VMP_L$, and vice versa. As $VMP_L$ for all workers declines, labor demand will shift to the left. Anything that changes the price of the product in competitive markets will shift the firm's demand for labor.

### Changes in Productivity

Changes in worker productivity (usually increases) can come about from improving technology or because a firm uses more capital or land along with its workforce. As $MPP_L$ rises, the demand for the marginal worker rises, and thus the firm is willing to pay higher wages for a workforce of the same size, or else to expand its workforce at the same wage rate. As more capital is employed—say, an excavation company shifts from shovels to back loaders—the demand for labor will rise. To be sure, the number of workers hired for a job may decline with mechanization, but the workers running the digging equipment, since they are more productive, will earn higher wages. This is why capital-intensive industries often employ fewer workers than other industries, but their workers are usually high-skill, high-wage employees.

### Changes in the Prices of Other Inputs

An increase in the price of capital will drive up the demand for labor. More expensive capital means that labor will be substituted for capital in new projects, thus increasing the demand for labor.

More labor will be hired when wages fall, but how much more? The answer depends on the elasticity of demand for labor.

## Elasticity of Demand for Labor

The **elasticity of demand for labor** ($E_L$) is the percentage change in the quantity of labor demanded ($Q_L$) divided by the percentage change in the wage rate (W). This elasticity is found the same way we calculated the price elasticity of demand for products, except that we substitute the wage rate for the price of the product:

**Elasticity of demand for labor:** The percentage change in the quantity of labor demanded divided by the percentage change in the wage rate.

$$E_L = \frac{\%\Delta Q_L}{\%\Delta W}$$

The elasticity of demand for labor measures how responsive the quantity of labor demanded is to changes in wages. An inelastic demand for labor is one where the absolute value of the elasticity is less than 1. Conversely, an elastic curve's computed elasticity is greater than 1.

The time firms have to adjust to changing wages will affect elasticity. In the short run, when labor is the only truly variable factor of production, elasticity of demand for labor is more inelastic. In the long run, when all production factors can be adjusted, elasticity of demand for labor tends to be more elastic.

### Factors That Affect the Elasticity of Demand for Labor

Although time affects elasticity, three other factors also affect the elasticity of demand for labor: elasticity of product demand, ease of substituting other inputs, and labor's share of the production costs. Let's briefly consider each of these.

***Elasticity of Demand for the Product*** The more elastic the price elasticity of demand for a product, the greater the elasticity of demand for labor. Higher wages result in higher product prices, and the more easily consumers can substitute away from the firm's product, the greater the number of workers who will become unemployed. An elastic demand for labor means that employment is more responsive to wage rates. The opposite is true for products with inelastic demands.

***Ease of Input Substitutability*** The more difficult it is to substitute capital for labor, the more inelastic the demand for labor will be. At this point, computers cannot yet substitute for pilots in commercial airplanes, which results in an inelastic demand for pilots. As a result, pilots have been able to secure high wages from airlines through their union representatives. The easier it is to substitute capital for labor, the less bargaining power workers have, and labor demand tends to be more elastic.

***Labor's Share of Total Production Costs*** The share of total costs associated with labor is another factor determining the elasticity of demand for labor. If labor's share of total costs is small, the demand for labor will tend to be rather inelastic. In the example of airline pilots above, the percentage of costs going to pilot wages is small, perhaps 10%. Thus, a 20% increase in pilot wages, though a major raise, would increase ticket prices by only 2%. The resulting change in the demand for air travel would be small, and thus its effect on the demand for pilot labor is small. The opposite is true when labor's share of costs is large.

## Competitive Labor Market Equilibrium

Generalized market equilibrium in competitive labor markets requires that we take into account the industry supply and demand for labor. The market supply for labor ($S_L$) is the horizontal sum of the individual labor supply curves in the market.

The market demand for labor, however, is not simply a summation of the demand for labor by all the firms in the market. When wages fall, for instance, this affects all firms—all want to hire more labor and produce more output. This added production reduces market prices for their output and negatively affects the demand for labor. For our purposes it is enough to be aware that market demands for labor are not simply the horizontal summation of individual firm demands.

Turning to Figure 4, we have put both sides of the market together. In panel A, the competitive labor market determines equilibrium wage ($100 per day) and employment (300 workers) based on market supply and demand. Individual firms, in light of their own situation, hire 6 workers where this equilibrium wage is equal to marginal

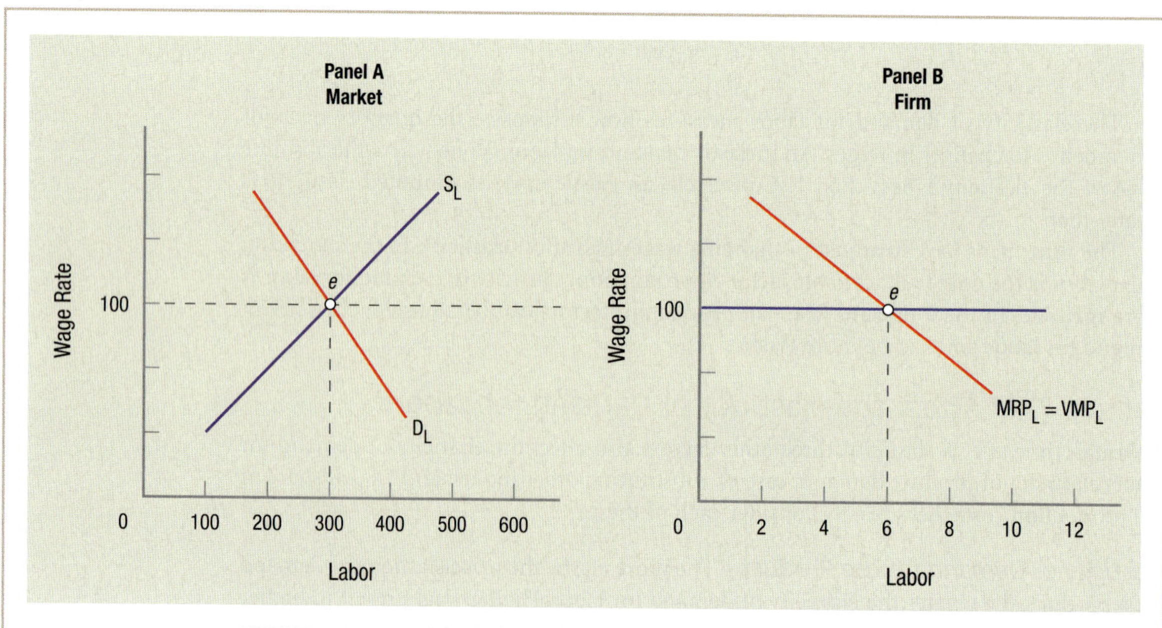


**FIGURE 4—Competitive Labor Markets**

In panel A, the competitive labor market determines equilibrium wages ($100 per day) and employment (300 workers). Individual firms hire six workers, where this equilibrium wage is equal to marginal revenue product ($MRP_L$), point *e* in panel B.

revenue product ($MRP_L$), point *e* in panel B. Much like the product markets we discussed in earlier chapters, the invisible hand of the marketplace sets wages and in the end determines employment.

CHECKPOINT

### COMPETITIVE LABOR DEMAND

- The firm's demand for labor is a derived demand—derived from consumer demand for the product and the productivity of labor.
- Marginal revenue product is equal to the marginal physical product of labor times marginal revenue.
- Value of the marginal product is equal to marginal physical product of labor times the price of the product.
- Since MR = P for the competitive firm, $VMP_L = MRP_L$.
- The demand for labor is equal to the value of the marginal product of labor for competitive firms.
- The demand for labor curve will change if there is a change in the demand for the product, if there is a change in labor productivity, or if there is a change in the price of other inputs.
- The elasticity of demand for labor is equal to the percentage change in quantity of labor demanded divided by the percentage change in the wage rate.
- The elasticity of demand for labor will be *more* elastic the greater the elasticity of demand for the product, the easier it is to substitute other factors for labor, and the larger the share of total production costs attributed to labor.
- Market equilibrium occurs where market labor demand and supply intersect.

**QUESTIONS:** Individuals are different in terms of ability, attitude, and willingness to work. Given this fact, does it make sense to assume labor is homogeneous? Does this model better fit firms such as Wal-Mart that hire 800+ employees at each store at roughly standardized wages than, say, firms such as Google that look for high-skilled computer geeks?

Answers to the Checkpoint questions can be found at the end of this chapter.

# Imperfect Labor Markets and Other Input Markets

The previous two sections focused on conditions in competitive product and input markets. In this section, we are going to relax our assumptions and look at imperfect labor markets. We also will consider the three other inputs in some depth: capital, land, and entrepreneurship.

## Imperfect Labor Markets

In the world as we know it, markets are not perfectly competitive. Product markets and labor markets contain *monopolistic* and *oligopolistic* elements. In many product markets, a few firms control the bulk of market share. They may not be monopolies, but they do have some monopoly power, through brand loyalty if nothing else.

Similarly, in most communities, there is only one government hiring firefighters and police officers. When the market contains only one buyer of a resource, economists refer to this lone buyer as a *monopsonist. Monopsony power,* meanwhile, is the control over input supply that the monopsonist enjoys. Before we look at the impact of **monopsony** on the labor market, let us first consider monopoly power in the product market.

Monopsony: A labor market with one employer.

## Monopoly Power in Product Markets

As we know, firms that enjoy monopoly power in product markets are price makers, not price takers. Because P > MR, it follows that $VMP_L > MRP_L$. Figure 5 shows why. The firm depicted has monopoly power in the product market, but buys inputs in a competitive environment.

As Figure 5 shows, a competitive firm would equate wage and value of the marginal product ($VMP_L$), hiring $L_C$ workers and paying the going wage of $W_0$ (point *c*). The firm with monopoly power, however, will equate wage and marginal revenue product ($MRP_L$), thus hiring $L_0$ workers, though again paying the prevailing wage $W_0$ (point *a*). So, although both firms hire workers at the same wage, the firm with monopoly power hires fewer workers.

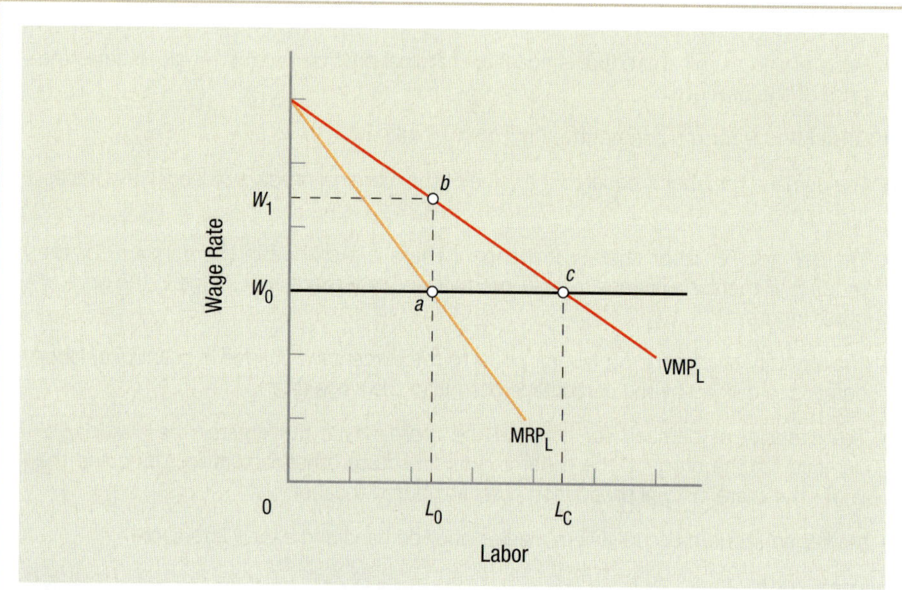


**FIGURE 5—Monopoly Firm in Product Market Employing Labor from a Competitive Market**

Firms with monopoly power in product markets are price makers. Because P > MR, it follows that $VMP_L > MRP_L$. A competitive firm would equate wages and value of the marginal product ($VMP_L$), hiring $L_C$ workers and paying the going wage of $W_0$ (point *c*). A firm with monopoly power, however, will equate wages and marginal revenue product ($MRP_L$), thus hiring $L_0$ workers, though again paying the prevailing wage $W_0$ (point *a*). Hence, although both firms hire workers at the same wage, the firm with monopoly power hires fewer workers. Also, the value of the marginal product ($VMP_L$) of workers in the monopolistic firm is much higher than what they are paid; their value to the firm is $W_1$ (point *b*), though they are only paid $W_0$ (point *a*). This difference is called monopolistic exploitation of labor.

This means the value of the marginal product ($VMP_L$) of workers in the monopolistic firm is much higher than what they are paid. Their value to the firm (point *b*) is $W_1$, though they are only paid $W_0$. This difference is referred to as **monopolistic exploitation of labor.** The term is loaded, but what economists mean by it is simply that workers get paid less than the value of their marginal product when working for a monopolist. This is, as you might expect, a source of monopoly profits.

Monopolistic exploitation of labor: When a firm has monopoly power in the product market, marginal revenue is less than price (MR < P) and the firm hires labor up to the point where $MRP_L$ = wage. Because $MRP_L$ is less than the $VMP_L$, workers are paid less than the value of their marginal product, and this difference is called monopolistic exploitation of labor.

## Monopsony

A monopsony is a market with one buyer or employer. The Postal Service, for instance, is the sole employer of mail carriers in this country, just as the armed forces are the only employer of military personnel. Single-employer towns used to dot the American landscape, and some occupations still face monopsony power regularly. Nurses and teachers, for example, often have only a few hospitals or local school districts where they can work.

Since a monopsonist is the only buyer of some input, it will face a positively sloped supply curve for that input, such as supply curve $S_L$ in Figure 6. This firm could hire 14 workers for $10 (point *a*), or it could increase wages to $11 and hire 15 workers (point *b*). Since the supply of labor is no longer flat, however, as it was in the competitive market, adding one more worker will cost the firm more than simply the new worker's higher wage. But just how much more?

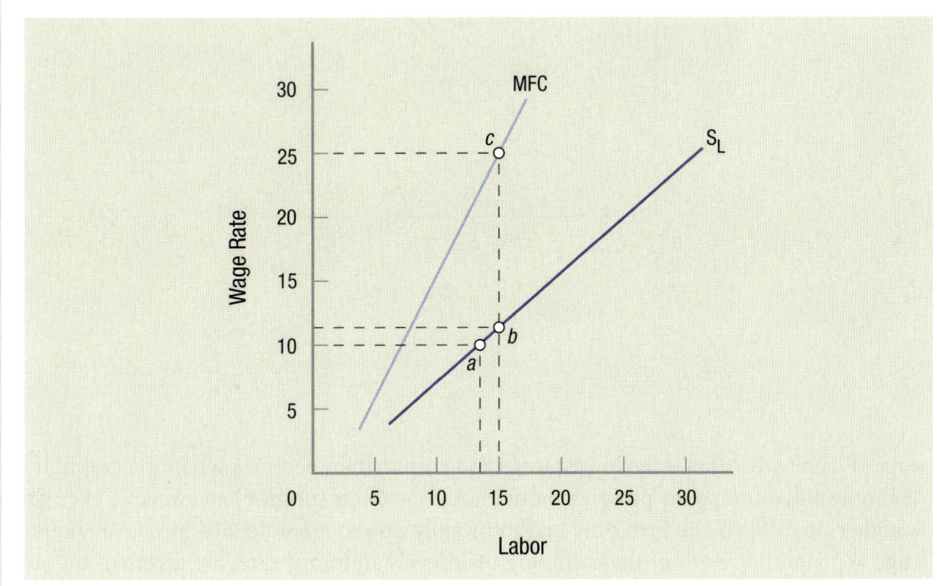


**FIGURE 6—Marginal Factor Cost**

This monopsonistic firm faces a positively sloped supply curve, $S_L$. The firm could hire 14 workers for $10 an hour (point *a*), or it could increase wages to $11 an hour and hire 15 workers (point *b*). Since the supply curve is positively sloped, however, adding one more worker will cost the firm more than simply the cost of a new worker. To hire an added worker requires a higher wage, and all current employees also must be paid the higher wage. Therefore, the total wage bill rises by more than just the added wages of the last worker hired. The marginal factor cost curve reflects these rising costs.

**Marginal factor cost (MFC)** is the added cost associated with hiring one more unit of labor. In Figure 6, assume that 14 workers earn $10 an hour (point *a*), and hiring the 15th worker requires paying $11 an hour (point *b*). Assume that you decide to go ahead and hire a 15th worker. When you employed 14 workers, total hourly wages were $140 ($10 × 14). But when 15 workers are employed at $11 an hour, all workers must be paid the higher hourly wage, and thus the total wage bill rises to $165 ($11 × 15). The total wage bill has risen by $25 an hour, not just the $11 hourly wage the 15th worker demanded. The marginal factor cost of hiring the 15th worker, in other words, is $25. This is shown as point *c*. Because the supply of labor curve is positively sloped, the MFC curve will always lie above the $S_L$ curve.

Marginal factor cost (MFC): The added cost associated with hiring one more unit of labor. For competitive firms, it is equal to the wage; but for monopsonists, it is higher than the new wage (W) because all existing workers must be paid this higher new wage, making MFC > W.

How does being a monopsonist in the labor market affect the hiring of a firm that is competitive in the product market? The monopsonist shown in Figure 7 on the next page is a competitor in the product market and has a demand for labor equal to its $VMP_L$. This firm faces the supply of labor, $S_L$. It will hire at the level where MFC = $VMP_L$ (point *a*), thus hiring $L_0$ workers at wage $W_1$ (point *b*). Note that these $L_0$ workers, though paid $W_1$, are actually worth $W_0$. Economists refer to this disparity as the **monopsonistic exploitation of labor.** Again, the term is loaded, but to economists it simply describes a situation in which labor is paid less than the value of its marginal product.

Monopsonistic exploitation of labor: Because monopsonists hire less labor than competitive firms, and workers are paid less than the value of their marginal products, this difference is referred to as monopsonistic exploitation of labor.

Note that the wages paid in the monopsony situation ($W_1$) are less than those paid under competitive conditions ($W_C$), and that monopsony employment ($L_0$) is similarly lower than competitive hiring ($L_C$). As was the case with monopoly power, monopsony power leads to results that are less than ideal when compared to competitive markets.

To draw together what we have just discussed, Figure 8 on the next page portrays a firm with both monopoly and monopsony power. The firm's equilibrium hiring will be at the point where MFC = $MRP_L$ (point *a*), and thus the firm will hire $L_0$ workers, though at

**FIGURE 7—Competitive Firm in the Product Market That Is a Monopsonist in the Input Market**

The monopsonist in this figure is a competitor in the product market and has a demand for labor equal to its $VMP_L$, while facing supply of labor, $S_L$. The firm will hire at the level where MFC = $VMP_L$ (point *a*), hiring $L_0$ workers at wage $W_1$ (point *b*). Note that these $L_0$ workers, though paid $W_1$, are worth $W_0$. This is called the monopsonistic exploitation of labor. Note also that the wages paid in this monopsony situation ($W_1$) are less than those paid under competitive conditions ($W_C$), and that monopsony employment ($L_0$) is lower than competitive employment ($L_C$).

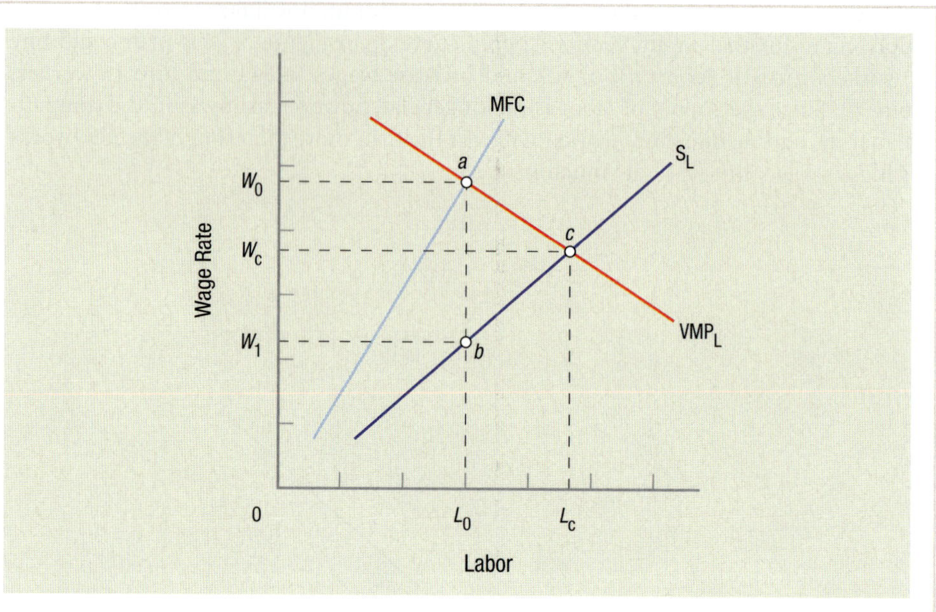


wage $W_0$. Note that this is the lowest wage and employment level shown in the graph. If the firm only had monopsony power, it would hire $L_1$ workers (point *b*) at a wage of $W_1$, which is higher than $W_0$. If the firm only had monopoly power, it would also hire $L_1$ workers for wage $W_1$ (point *c*). Both of these employment levels and wage rates are less than the competitive outcome of $L_C$ and $W_C$ (point *d*).

The key lesson to remember here is that competitive input (factor) markets are the most efficient, since inputs in these markets are paid precisely the value of their marginal products, and the highest employment results. This translates into the lowest prices for consumers at the highest output, assuming efficient production. Thus, just as competition is good for product markets, so too is it good for labor and other input markets.

**FIGURE 8—Monopolist Firm in the Product Market That Is a Monopsonist in the Input Market**

This firm has both monopoly and monopsony power. The firm's equilibrium hiring will be at the point where MFC = $MRP_L$ (point *a*), and thus the firm will hire $L_0$ workers, though at wage $W_0$. Note that this is the lowest wage and employment level shown in the graph. If the firm only had monopsony power, it would hire $L_1$ workers (point *b*) at a wage of $W_1$. If the firm only had monopoly power, it would also hire $L_1$ workers for wage $W_1$ (point *c*). Both of these employment levels and wage rates are less than the competitive outcome of $L_C$ and $W_C$ (point *d*).

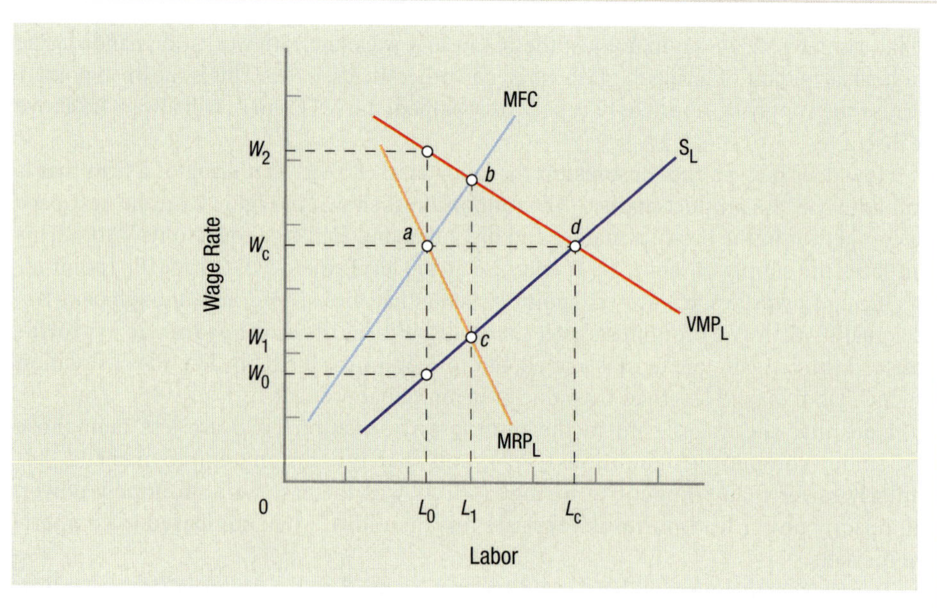

## *Issue:* Are Minimum Wage Laws Good Public Policy?

**In 2007, Congress** passed a whopping 40% increase in the minimum wage: Between 2007 and 2009, it shot up from $5.15 to $7.25. Passed while the economy was booming, this rapid rise in the minimum wage has many people concerned about its impact during the subsequent recession. As the figure below shows, the real minimum wage (adjusted for inflation) was around $4.00 per hour until the mid-1980s. After that, the real minimum wage fell to around the $3.00 an hour range.

The first minimum wage laws were passed in New Zealand and Australia in the 1890s, adopted in England in the early 1900s, and became part of the Fair Labor Standards Act in the United States in 1938.

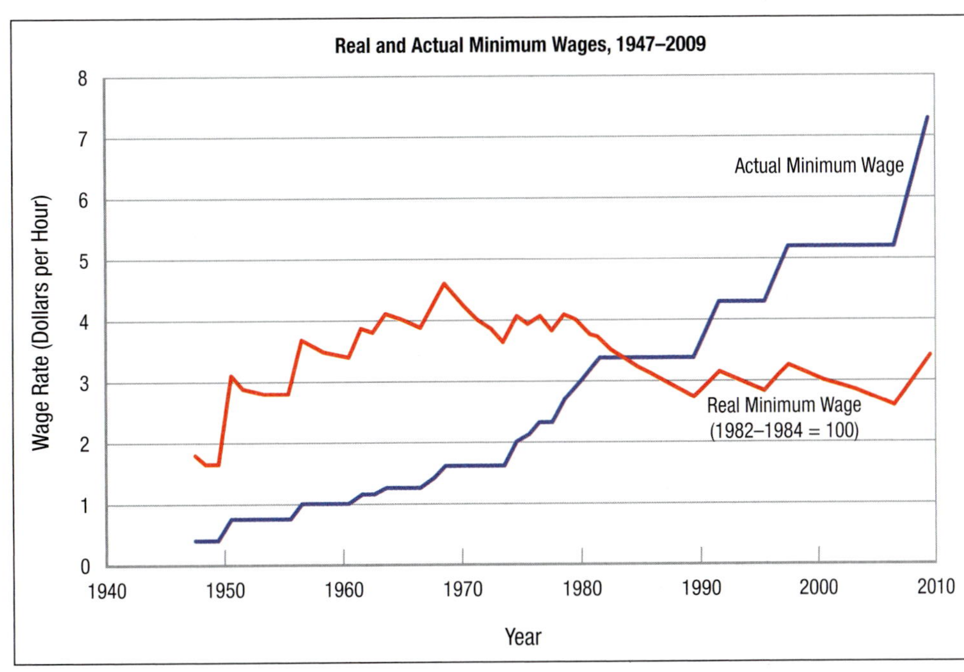


Because minimum wage laws have a 100-year history, the question of whether they are good public policy would seem to be moot. But recent research raises questions about the benefits and costs of laws mandating minimum wages.

These laws were originally passed to prevent "sweatshops" from employing women and young people at substandard wages. Minimum wage workers tend to be young, female, part-time workers who are not very well educated. As a result, minimum wage laws have other goals, including:

- Balancing the bargaining power between employers and workers to help ensure workers are paid a "fair" wage.
- Raising the incomes of low-income families and reducing poverty.
- Reducing wage inequality in the marketplace.

How well minimum wage laws stack up on these goals will give us a way to determine their effectiveness.

Like any other public policy, minimum wage laws involve tradeoffs. As we saw in Chapter 3, if labor markets are competitive, establishing a wage floor (the minimum workers can be paid) will lead to lower employment. At the other extreme, if the employer is a monopsonist and the minimum wage is set above the monopsony wage, employment will rise.

These two extremes are shown in the figure on the next page. In the competitive market in panel A, initial equilibrium is at point *e*, with 20,000 people hired. Employment falls from 20,000 to 15,000 (point *a*) when the minimum wage is set at $7.25.

In the monopsony case, initially wages are set by the firm at $4.00 an hour and 13,000 workers are hired at a MFC of around

Andrew Holbrooke/Corbis

$8 per hour (point *e* in panel B). When the government imposes a minimum wage of $7.25 an hour, the cost of an additional worker is now just $7.25 an hour, so the firm's supply of labor (the marginal factor cost) is the darkened horizontal line at $7.25 per hour as far out as 26,000 workers; then continues as the remainder of the supply of labor curve, $S_L$. In this case, the firm now hires 15,000 workers at the minimum wage (point *a*).

Whether employment rises or falls has been the subject of numerous studies and some controversy. David Neumark and William Wascher, in their book *Minimum Wages,* examined over 40 studies of the impact of minimum wages on low-wage workers, and they concluded that "our overall sense of the literature is that the preponderance of evidence supports the view that minimum wages reduce the employment of low-wage workers." For roughly every 10% increase in the minimum wage, employment of minimum wage workers falls by roughly 2%, which is more similar to the explanation in panel A.

But the low-wage workers who remain employed gain a 10% pay raise. Neumark and Wascher looked at the other goals of minimum wage legislation and concluded, "The research on the distribution effects of

*(continued)*

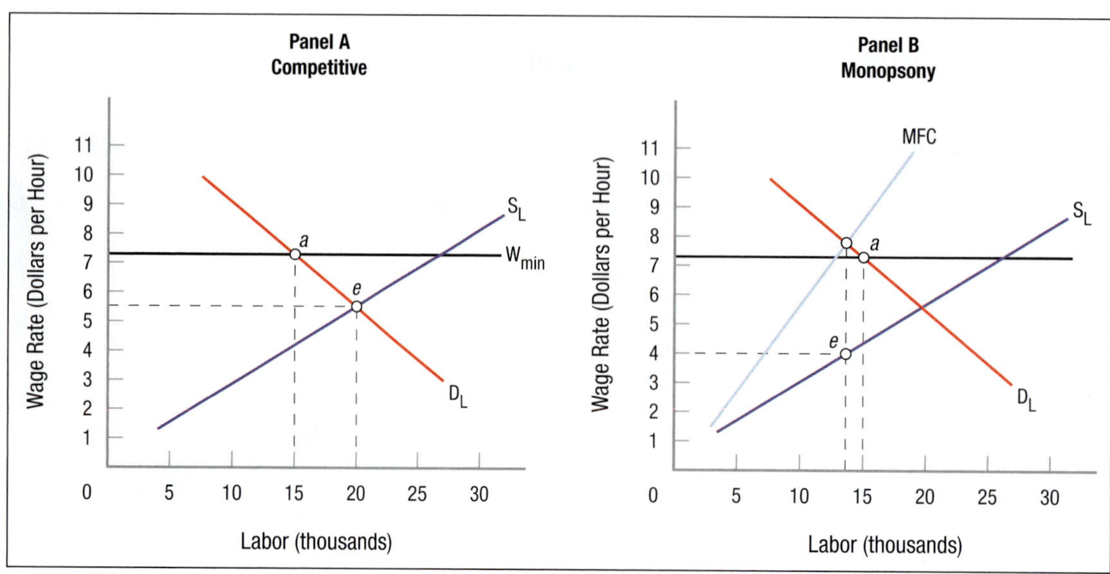


minimum wages, though far less extensive [than research on employment changes], finds virtually no evidence that minimum wages reduce the proportion of families with income near or below the poverty line, and some of it indicates that minimum wages adversely affect low-income families. Finally minimum wages appear to inhibit skill acquisition by reducing education attainment and perhaps training, resulting in lower adult wages and earnings."

If minimum wage laws cause loss of employment for low-wage people, have virtually no impact on poverty and the distribution of income, and may act as a disincentive for acquiring human capital, why do they continue to exist? The short answer is that they are popular. Surveys consistently show that over three-quarters of Americans support minimum wage laws and nearly every time state voters are given the chance to raise their state minimums above federal minimums, they approve the measures. Liberal advocacy groups and labor unions support minimum wages and people generally want to help low-income workers and their families. Finally, since the number of people earning minimum wages is small, roughly 1 to 2% of the workforce, the impact of raising minimum wages is trivial for most family budgets. These laws are so popular that even if people were aware of their potential to reduce employment and the other negative effects, they might still be supported.

Labor markets for minimum wage workers are generally quite competitive and it would be a mistake for policymakers to use the monopsony model in panel B, to suggest the impacts of minimum wage legislation on employment of minimum wage workers.

Sources: Based on David Neumark and William Wascher, *Minimum Wages* (Cambridge, MA: The MIT Press), 2008; and Guillaume Rocheteau and Murat Tasci, "The Minimum Wage and the Labor Market," *Economic Commentary,* Federal Reserve Bank of Cleveland, May 1, 2007.

## Capital Markets

**Capital:** All manufactured products that are used to produce goods and services.

**Capital** includes all manufactured products that are used to produce goods and services. *Capital markets* are those markets in which firms obtain financial resources to purchase capital goods. Financial resources come from the savings of households and other firms. Suppliers of funds and the demanders of these funds interact through what is called the *loanable funds market.* As with competitive labor markets, in which the market determines wages, each individual firm determines how many workers to employ, and the loanable funds market determines interest rates, leaving individual firms to calculate how much they should borrow.

Through their interactions in the loanable funds market, suppliers and demanders determine the interest rates to be charged for funds. Individual firms then evaluate their investment opportunities to determine their own investment levels. Figure 9 shows how this process works. The demand and supply of loanable funds is shown in panel A, where equilibrium interest rates equal $i_0$. Note that the demand for loanable funds looks just like a normal demand curve. Its downward slope shows that, as the price of funds declines—as interest rates go down—the quantity of funds demanded rises. The supply of funds is positively sloped since individuals will be willing to supply more funds to the market when their price (interest rate) is higher.

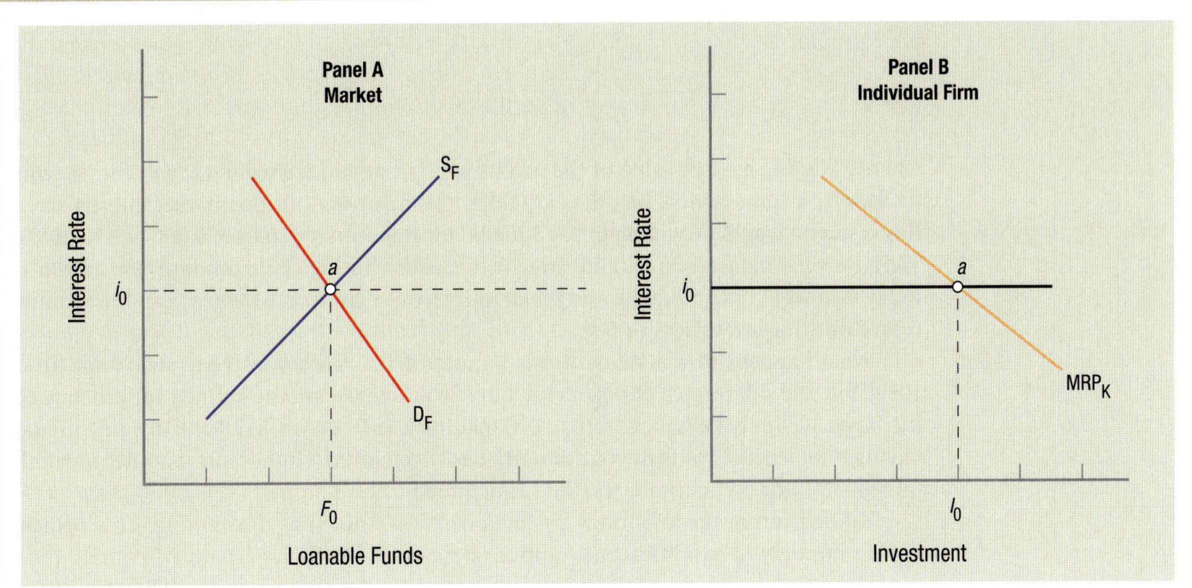


**FIGURE 9—Loanable Funds Market and Individual Firm Investment**

Panel A shows the market demand and supply of loanable funds, with equilibrium interest rates equal to $i_0$. Individual firms like the one shown in panel B will take this rate of interest, or cost of capital, and determine how much to invest. Firms make their best investments first, and then continue investing (to $I_0$) until the cost of capital ($i_0$) is equal to the $MRP_K$.

## Investment

Once the market has determined an equilibrium rate of interest, an individual firm like the one shown in panel B will take this rate of interest, or cost of capital, and determine how much to invest. The marginal revenue product of capital ($MRP_K$) is downward sloping, showing that the returns a firm earns on its investments diminish as more capital is invested. Firms make their best investments first, and then continue investing until the cost of capital ($i_0$) is equal to the $MRP_K$. This admittedly simplifies the investment process, but it is a good general model of investment decisions. Next, we turn to two more precise ways in which investment is determined, the present value approach and the rate of return approach.

## Present Value Approach

When a firm considers upgrading its information system or purchasing a new piece of equipment, a building, or a manufacturing plant, it must evaluate the returns it can expect over time. Firms invest money today, but earn returns over years. To compare investments having different income streams and different levels of required investment, firms look at the *net* **present value** of the investment.

**Present value:** The value of an investment (future stream of income) today. The higher the discount rate, the lower the present value today, and vice versa.

One hundred dollars *a year from now* is worth *less* than one hundred dollars *today.* This is illustrated by the fact that you could put less than a hundred dollars in the bank today, earn interest on this money over the next year, and still end up with one hundred dollars at year's end. Yet, just how much less than one hundred dollars would you be willing to take for one hundred dollars a year from today? To answer this question, let us begin by looking at the simplest form of financial assets, annuities.

An annuity is a financial instrument that pays the bearer a certain dollar amount forever. Assume that the market rate of interest is 5%, and you are offered an annuity that pays you or the holder of the annuity $1,000 a year indefinitely. How much would you be willing to pay for this annuity? If you want to follow the market in earning 5% a year, then the simple question you must ask is this: On what amount of money does \$1,000 a year forever represent a 5% return? The answer is found through the simple formula:

$$PV = X/i$$

where PV is the present value of the investment (what you are willing to pay for the annuity today), *X* is the annual income (\$1,000 in this case), and *i* is the market interest rate. In this case, you would be willing to pay \$20,000 for this annuity, since \$20,000 = \$1,000/0.05. We have thus reduced an infinite stream of income to the finite amount you would pay today. You would pay \$20,000, and the annuity would give you \$1,000 a year, for an annual return on your investment of 5%.

What happens to the value of this annuity if the market interest rate should rise to 10%? You will still receive \$1,000 a year, but if you want to sell the annuity to someone else, the buyer will only be willing to pay \$10,000 for it (\$10,000 = \$1,000/0.10). Interest rates having doubled, the value of your annuity has been halved. Higher interest rates mean that income in future years is not worth as much today.

Valuing future income today by this process is known as *discounting*. This principle applies not only to annuities, but computing for years less than perpetuity requires a more complex formula. For example, assume that someone agrees to pay you \$500 in two years, and that the going interest rate is 5%. What would you be willing to pay today for this future payment of \$500? The answer is found using the following formula:

$$PV = X/(1 + i)^n$$

Again, PV is the present value of the future payment, *X* is the future payment of \$500, *i* is the interest rate (5%), and *n* is the number of years into the future before the payment is made. In this case the calculations are

$$\begin{aligned} PV &= \$500/(1 + 0.05)^2 \\ &= \$500/[(1.05)(1.05)] \\ &= \$500/1.1025 \\ &= \$453.51 \end{aligned}$$

Hence, you would be willing to pay only \$453.51 for this \$500 payment coming two years in the future. Again, the higher the interest or discount rate, the lower your price.

When only one future payment is at stake, computing the present value of that payment is fairly simple. When future streams of income are involved, however, things get more complicated. We must compute the present value of each individual future payment. The general formula looks nearly the same as before:

$$PV = \Sigma\, X_n/(1 + i)^n$$

Here, the Greek letter Σ (sigma) stands for "sum of," and $X_n$ is the individual payment received at year *n*. Assume, then, that you are going to receive \$500, \$800, and \$1,200 over the next three years, and that the interest rate is still 5%. The present value of this income stream is therefore

$$\begin{aligned} PV &= \$500/(1.05)^1 + \$800/(1.05)^2 + \$1{,}200/(1.05)^3 \\ &= \$500/(1.05) + \$800/(1.1025) + \$1{,}200/(1.1576) \\ &= \$476.19 + \$725.62 + \$1{,}036.63 \\ &= \$2{,}238.44 \end{aligned}$$

Given the complexity of such computations, economists often use computers to solve for present value, especially when the annual income stream is complicated. When the annual income is constant, tables of discount factors are also available. In any case, the point to note is that payments to be made in the future are worth a lower dollar amount today.

Firms often use present value analysis to determine if potential investments are worthwhile. Assume a machine will yield a stream of income exceeding operating costs over a given period. The present value of this income is then compared to the cost of the machine. The machine's *net present value* (NPV) is equal to the difference between the present value of the income stream and the cost of the machine. If NPV is positive, the firm will invest; if it is negative, the firm will decline to invest.

When interest rates are high, firms will find fewer investment opportunities where NPV is positive since the higher discount rate reduces the value of the income streams for investments. As interest rates fall, more investment is undertaken by firms.

## Rate of Return Approach

An alternative approach to determining whether an investment is worthwhile involves computing the investment's rate of return. This rate of return is also known as a firm's *marginal efficiency of capital*, or its *internal* **rate of return.**

**Rate of return:** Uses the present value formula, but subtracts costs, then finds the interest rate (discount rate) at which this investment would break even.

Computing an investment's rate of return requires using essentially the same present value formula for income streams introduced above with a slight modification: You have to explicitly consider the cost of capital in the calculation. This new formula is

$$PV = [\Sigma X_n/(1 + i)^n] - C$$

where $C$ represents the cost of capital. The question we must ask is: At what rate of interest ($i$) will the investment just break even? You would compute the present value of the income streams, then subtract the cost of the capital investment, and finally find the rate of interest ($i$) where the present value equals zero. This discount rate is the rate of return on the investment.

The calculated rate of return can be compared to the firm's required rate of return on investments to determine whether the investment is worthwhile. The firm might require, say, a 20% yield on all projects, in which case investments yielding returns of less than 20% are deemed not worthwhile. Risk in investment projects is usually managed by adding a risk premium to the required rate of return for risky projects. This risk premium can vary by project type or with the business cycle. Some investments, such as drilling for oil or researching innovative new drugs, are risky and require high rates of return if they are to be undertaken.

# Land

For economists, the term *land* includes both land in the usual sense and other natural resources that are inelastically supplied. **Rent,** sometimes called *economic rent,* is any return or income that flows to land as a factor of production. This is a different meaning than when we speak of the rent on an apartment. Land is unique among the factors of production because of its inelasticity of supply.

**Rent:** The return to land as a factor of production. Sometimes called economic rent.

In some instances, the supply of land is perfectly inelastic. Finding an empty lot on which to build in San Francisco is virtually impossible. The land available to San Franciscans is fixed by the terrain; it cannot be added to nor moved from one place to another.

Figure 10 on the next page shows how rent is determined when the available supply of land is fixed. In this example, the number of acres of usable land is fixed at $L_0$ (or supply $S_0$). If the demand for land is $D_0$, the economic rent will be $r_0$ (point *a*). When demand rises to $D_1$, rent increases to $r_1$ (point *b*). Notice that because the supply of land in this example is perfectly inelastic, rent depends entirely on demand. If demand were to fall, rent would fall as well.

In a strict sense, land is not perfectly fixed in supply. Land can be improved. Land that is arid, like the deserts of Arizona, can be improved through irrigation. Jungles can be cleared, swamps can be drained, and mountains can be terraced, making land that was once worthless productive. Still, even if the supply of land is not perfectly inelastic, it is quite inelastic when compared to other production inputs.

The supply inflexibility in land led Henry George (1839–1897) to propose a single tax on land to finance government needs. In his 1879 book *Progress and Poverty,* George argued that

**FIGURE 10—Determination of Rent**

This figure shows how rent is determined when the available supply of land is fixed. The acres of usable land are fixed at $L_0$ (supply $S_0$). If the demand for land is $D_0$, the economic rent is $r_0$ (point *a*). When demand rises to $D_1$, rent increases to $r_1$ (point *b*). Notice that because the supply of land in this example is perfectly inelastic, rent depends entirely on demand. If demand were to fall, rent would fall as well.

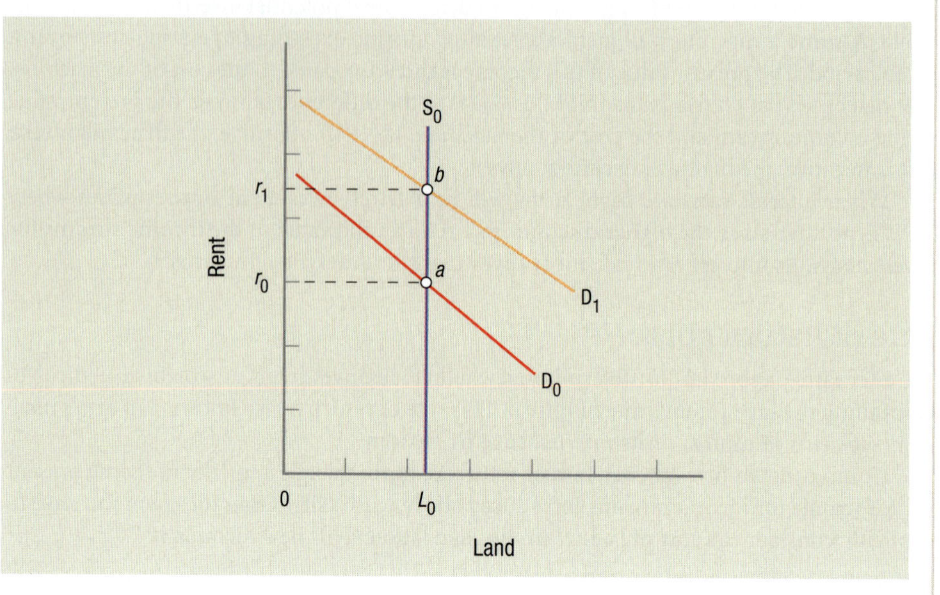


increases in rents and land values were the result of speculation, population growth, and public improvements in the community's infrastructure (raising demand to $D_1$ in Figure 10). Since landholders apparently do nothing to earn these rental increases, George thought they could and should be taxed away. His approach became known as the single-tax movement, since he thought all government spending could be financed from the revenue of this tax.

It should be added that George proposed to tax only the pure ground rent of land, not the improvements made on land. Thus, his tax is also sometimes called a "site tax." Although such a tax would probably not cover all government spending today, some economists are sympathetic to the concept. Nobel Prize winner Milton Friedman has noted, "In my opinion, the least bad tax is the property tax on the unimproved value of land, the Henry George argument of many, many years ago."[2]

As a final note, land will theoretically continue to earn rent forever. To quickly approximate the value of a piece of land, we can use our annuity formula ($PV = X/i$). Given a 5% rate of interest, a parcel of land earning \$10,000 a year in rent will be worth \$200,000 (\$200,000 = \$10,000/0.05). To apply to the real world, this simple approximation would require a few qualifications. Even so, it gives us a first approximation of how land is valued.

## Entrepreneurship

Profits are the rewards entrepreneurs receive for (1) combining land, labor, and capital to produce goods and services and (2) assuming the risks associated with producing these goods and services. Entrepreneurs must combine and manage all the inputs of production; make day-to-day production, finance, and marketing decisions; innovate constantly if they hope to remain in business over the long run; and simultaneously bear the risks of failure and bankruptcy.

As we saw at the turn of the century—just a few years ago in 2000, not 1900—large firms that have become household names can implode within months. Enron, Arthur Anderson, and more recently Lehman Brothers, General Motors, and Chrysler come to mind. Even for large firms, business is risky. Bankruptcy or business failure, meanwhile, can be exceedingly painful for business owners, stockholders, employees, and communities. Still, a free economy requires such failures. If firms were guaranteed never to fail, perhaps

[2] Mark Blaug, *Great Economists before Keynes: An Introduction to the Lives & Works of One Hundred Great Economists of the Past* (Atlantic Highlands, NJ: Humanities Press International), 1986, p. 86.

through government subsidies (bailouts), they would have little incentive to be efficient or innovate, or to worry about what consumers want from them.

When a firm earns economic profits—profits exceeding normal profits—this is a signal to other firms and entrepreneurs that consumers want more of the good or service the profitable firm provides, and that they are willing to pay for it. Profit signals shift resources from areas of lower demand to the products and services consumers desire more highly.

By far, the largest part of national income—roughly 70%—goes to labor, the smallest goes to rental income, and the remainder is split between interest and profits. Labor is thus the most important factor of production, and labor issues are often paramount for policymakers. The next chapter will look into some specific labor issues, including investment in human capital, economic discrimination, and labor unions.

**CHECKPOINT**

## IMPERFECT LABOR MARKETS AND OTHER INPUT MARKETS

- When a firm is a monopolist in the product market and hires labor from competitive markets, the firm will hire labor where the marginal revenue product is equal to the competitive wage.
- Monopolistic exploitation results because the monopolist pays less than the value of the marginal product of labor.
- Monopsony is a market with one employer. A monopsonist who sells its product in a competitive market hires labor where the value of the marginal product is equal to the marginal factor cost.
- Monopsonistic exploitation occurs when the monopsonist pays labor less than the value of its marginal product.
- Capital markets are markets in which firms get financial resources to purchase capital goods.
- Firms will use either the net present value approach or the rate of return approach to compare investments with different income streams.
- Land includes both land and natural resources and is inelastically supplied. Returns on land are called rents (or economic rent).
- Because land is inelastically supplied, the rent on land is determined by demand.
- Entrepreneurs earn profits for combining other inputs to produce products and for assuming the risks of producing goods and services.

**QUESTIONS:** Are public schools in rural areas a monopsony? Do they set wages in a way that is different from how wages are set in large urban areas?

Answers to the Checkpoint questions can be found at the end of this chapter.

## Key Concepts

Supply of labor, p. 262
Substitution effect, p. 263
Income effect, p. 264
Demand for labor, p. 267
Marginal physical product of labor, p. 267
Marginal revenue product, p. 267
Value of the marginal product, p. 268
Elasticity of demand for labor, p. 269
Monopsony, p. 271
Monopolistic exploitation of labor, p. 272

Marginal factor cost (MFC), p. 273
Monopsonistic exploitation of labor, p. 273
Capital, p. 276
Present value, p. 277
Rate of return, p. 279
Rent, p. 279

# Chapter Summary

## Competitive Labor Supply

Competitive labor markets comprise firms that are price takers; these firms compete with other firms in the wider market for labor. Labor is assumed to be a homogeneous input; one unit of labor is just as productive as all others. Information about prices and wages is assumed to be widely available, and supply and demand interact to determine the equilibrium wage for the industry. Each firm then decides how much labor to purchase at the going wage rate.

The supply of labor is the time an individual is willing to work (the labor the person is willing to supply) at various wage rates. The supply of labor is positively sloped, since at higher wages, workers will substitute work for leisure. When wages rise high enough, however, the income effect may swamp the substitution effect. Workers may elect more leisure over greater income, resulting in a backward-bending supply of labor curve.

Changes in wage rates will change the quantity of labor supplied, or cause movements along the market supply of labor curve. Demographic changes and changes in the nonmoney aspects of a job, the wages for alternative jobs, and nonwage income will all shift the supply of labor curve. Such a shift might be precipitated, for instance, by a change in the labor force participation rates, a reduction in the riskiness of a job, or a change in nonwage incomes of workers.

## Competitive Labor Demand

The demand for labor is a derived demand; it is derived from the productive capabilities of labor and the demand for the good or service produced. The demand for labor is equivalent to the marginal revenue product ($MRP_L$) curve. Marginal revenue product is equal to marginal physical product of labor times the product's marginal revenue.

Because competitive firms are price takers, marginal revenue is equal to price. So the competitive firm's demand for labor is equal to what economists call the value of the marginal product ($VMP_L$). The value of the marginal product is equal to marginal physical product times price.

Since the demand for labor is a derived demand, changes in labor demand will come about because of changes in labor productivity or changes in product demand. Anything that changes the price of a firm's product will change its labor demand.

The elasticity of demand for labor is the percentage change in the quantity of labor demanded divided by the percentage change in the wage rate. Elasticity of demand for labor is determined by the elasticity of demand for the product, the ease of input substitutability, and the size of labor's share in production costs.

Competitive labor markets determine an equilibrium wage, then individual firms must look at their own needs and hire employees up to the point where equilibrium wage is equal to marginal revenue product (or, equivalently for competitive markets, equal to the value of the marginal product of labor).

## Imperfect Labor Markets and Other Input Markets

If wages are determined in a competitive market, a firm will hire labor until $MRP_L = W$. But if the firm enjoys some monopoly power in the product market, marginal revenue product will be less than the value of the marginal product because $MR < P$. The difference between the value of the marginal product and marginal revenue product is known as monopolistic exploitation of labor.

A monopsony is a market with a single buyer or employer. Marginal factor cost (MFC) is the added cost associated with hiring one more unit of labor. For the monopsonist, the MFC curve lies above the supply of labor curve because the firm must increase the wages of all workers to attract added labor. If the monopsonist purchases labor from a competitive market, it hires labor up to the point where MRP = MFC > W. At this point, the value of labor's marginal product exceeds the wage rate; economists refer to this as monopsonistic exploitation of labor.

Capital includes all manufactured goods that are used to produce other goods and services. Capital markets are those markets where financial resources are available for the purchase of capital goods. The loanable funds market determines equilibrium interest rates for these funds. Firms look at their potential investment projects and borrow money to invest when the rate of return on a project is greater than or equal to the market interest rate.

Two approaches are used to determine whether investments are potentially profitable. The present value approach discounts projected future streams of income to determine their present value. This is then compared to the cost of the investment to determine whether the investment will be profitable. The rate of return approach uses the same present value formula, but looks for the rate of return, or discount rate, where the potential income stream and investment costs will be just equal.

Land, to the economist, means land and other natural resources that are nearly fixed in supply, or inelastically supplied. Because the supply of land is fixed, the rent on land is determined by demand.

Profits are rewards to entrepreneurs for combining the other inputs of production—land, labor, and capital—in ways that produce goods and services and for assuming the risks associated with production. Economic profits are profits that exceed normal levels. They act as signals to other entrepreneurs and firms that consumers want more of the profitable product. These signals produce shifts in resources toward those goods that consumers want.

# Questions and Problems

## Check Your Understanding

1. How do the income and substitution effects related to labor supply differ?
2. Why does a monopolist in the product market hire fewer workers than if the industry is competitive?
3. If the interest rate is 6% and you are offered a bond that will pay you $2,000 in two years, but no interest between now and then, what would you be willing to pay for this bond today?
4. What factors will increase the demand for labor?
5. Why are individual supply curves of labor potentially backward bending, but market and industry supply curves are always positively sloped?

## Apply the Concepts

6. As the baby boomer generation—those born between 1946 and 1964—begins retiring in earnest in the near future, wealthy economies like the United States and Europe will need to replace these skilled workers. These workers are an immense storehouse of knowledge and specialized skills that are not easily replaced. This is particularly acute in the engineering fields where college enrollments are falling (*Economist,* March 4, 2006). Would it make sense for America, as *The Economist* (November 5, 2005, p. 86) noted, to "no longer welcome the tired and the huddled; [but] to compete ever more fiercely for the bright and the qualified"? What could companies do to encourage these older workers to remain on the job?

7. Adam Smith, in the *Wealth of Nations,* noted that, "The wages of labour vary with the ease or hardship, the cleanliness or dirtiness, the honourableness or dishonourableness of the employment." He is referring to the nonwage or "amenities" aspect of employment. By making the "job" more enjoyable, cleaner, or more honorable, or adding more amenities, employers should be able to pay lower wages, since the positive attributes compensate for higher wages. If so, why don't all employers offer amenities to lower their wage bill?

8. Fifty years ago, married women age 35 to 44 worked for pay only 10 hours per week on average; today they work over 26 hours on average. During the same period, the workweek for married men of the same age has been relatively constant, between 42 and 44 hours. Can you think of reasons why women's working hours have nearly tripled in the last half century?

9. Since 1970 the number of dual-earning households as a percent of total U.S. households has grown from 39% to nearly 65% today. Do you think there is a relationship between this growth in dual-earning households and the rapid growth in restaurants?

10. How do times of growth in the general economy encourage capital investments? How do recessions discourage capital investments? What happens to the cost of capital in boom times when the economy is growing? What happens in recessionary times?

11. Why do college professors who usually spend five to seven years in graduate school and play such an important role in shaping our society make so much less than a Hollywood producer such as Jerry Bruckheimer, who most people don't even know (he has produced over 40 films and a dozen TV shows)?

12. Since all college professors mostly teach classes and do research, why are they not all paid the same wage?

13. We often hear that America needs cheap unskilled foreign workers to do the jobs that Americans will not do. But Professor Barry Chiswick (*New York Times,* June 3, 2006, p. A23) suggested, "If the number of low-skilled foreign workers were to fall, wages would increase. Low-skilled American workers and their families would benefit, and society as a whole would gain from a reduction in income inequality." Is Professor Chiswick's argument consistent with the competitive labor market described in this chapter? Why or why not?

14. In 2008, IBM paid $65 million to settle a lawsuit regarding overtime pay (*Wall Street Journal,* January 24, 2008, p. B6). Salaried ($80,000 per year) technicians who installed and repaired computers averaged 45 hours a week, 5 hours over the Fair Labor Standards Act that requires hourly employees be paid time-and-a-half for hours over 40. As part of its program to reclassify employees who were previously incorrectly classified as "exempt" salaried employees, IBM announced that over 7,000 employees would have their base pay cut by 15%, but with overtime their overall compensation should remain roughly the same. Does this action by IBM seem consistent with W = MRP = VMP for competitive markets discussed in this chapter?

15. Some employees feel locked into their jobs because employer benefits like health insurance are not transferrable to other companies. This "job lock" phenomenon is especially severe with health insurance coverage for employees if someone in their family has a severe preexisting condition that prevents them from getting private health insurance at reasonable rates. What are the impacts of this type of inflexibility on labor markets? What would be the impact if some form of health care reform eliminated the potential loss of health insurance for workers?

## In the News

16. Tightened visa rules since 9/11 have reduced the number of high-skill legal immigrants. Stiffer security rules and insufficient personnel have substantially increased the waiting time (and certainty) of visas. Spencer Ante (*Business Week,* November, 2004, pp. 90–94) quotes Nobel Prize winner Gary Becker: "We benefit enormously from high-skilled immigration . . . we have to try to maintain that." He further suggests that the United States should "give the highest priority to people with high skills and allow large numbers to come in, maybe unlimited numbers." Do you agree with Becker? If so, what might be some of the obstacles to implementing such a policy? If not, why not?

17. "Where labour is scarce and expensive, businesses have an incentive to invest in labour-saving technology, which boosts productivity growth by enabling fewer workers to produce more" (Michael Lind, *Financial Times,* June 9, 2006, p. 13). Do you agree with this statement? Why or why not? Would bringing in a large number of unskilled workers improve productivity and living standards?

## Solving Problems

18. The figure below shows the supply of labor, marginal factor costs, and the demand for labor for a firm that is large enough that it is essentially a monopsonist in the community where it operates. Assume that all workers are paid the same wage and that they work 2,000 hours per year (40 hours a week for 50 weeks).

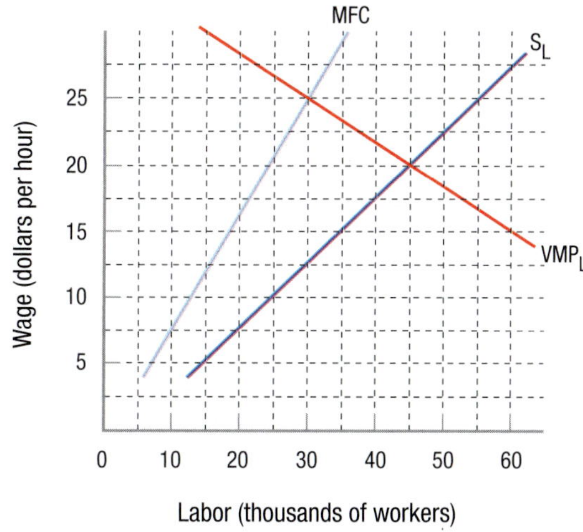


a. What is the total wage bill (total wages paid by the firm) for this monopsonistic firm?
b. If the firm was actually hiring from a competitive labor market, what would be the total wage bill for the firm?
c. What is the total value of the monopsonistic exploitation of labor by this firm?
d. Is the firm a competitor or a monopolist in the product market?

# Answers to Questions in CheckPoints

## Check Point: Competitive Labor Supply

Each person will have a different wage where their supply of labor curve bends backward. Getting a large inheritance will generate substantial nonwage income and typically lead to fewer hours worked. Having a family will probably raise the income required before you will cut your hours.

## Check Point: Competitive Labor Demand

For many jobs, firms have standardized procedures that each employee follows. Therefore, the difference in productivity between individuals is relatively narrow. While homogeneous labor is a simplification, taking in everyone's difference would make analysis impractical. No, the model explains both since markets exist for each broad category of workers.

## Check Point: Imperfect Labor Markets and Other Input Markets

Yes, they are monopsonists when it comes to hiring teachers. Generally, there is only one school district in rural areas. They probably act more like monopsonists when setting wages when compared to their urban counterparts, which have competition for teachers from other districts and private schools.

# Labor Market Issues

# 12

imagebroker/Alamy

**Why are some people paid** more than others? Is there a relationship between your earnings and your education? Does discrimination explain wage differences between groups? Why are there different wages for different occupations? What role will unions play in the 21st-century economy?

To get a better sense of what this chapter covers, let us pause for a moment on the last question: What role will unions play in the 21st century? Many of us already have some familiarity with unions, which are legal associations of employees that bargain with employers over terms and conditions of work. Unions use strikes and the threat of strikes to achieve their goals. You may have heard of craft unions such as the Teamsters, which represents truck drivers, or industry unions, such as the UAW (United Auto Workers), which represents auto workers.

One of the fastest growing labor groups is made up of part-time and independent contract workers. They freelance in graphic design, in Web design services and programming, as nannies, and in many other areas. Pay and terms of work are typically set by individual negotiation. This group clearly could use a union, since they are rarely provided benefits beyond the agreed-upon compensation.

But how could a union serve such a diverse group of people in terms of skills, compensation, locations, industries, and working conditions? Sara Horowitz asked herself that question and decided that a union could provide self-employed workers with similar services that full-time employees take for granted. She formed the Freelancers Union in New York and provides her members with health insurance, 401(k)-type retirement plans,

**After studying this chapter you should be able to:**

- ☐ Describe the relationship between education and earnings.
- ☐ Understand how the rate of return on a college degree is computed.
- ☐ Know how market equilibrium levels for human capital are determined.
- ☐ Understand the different theories of human capital.
- ☐ Describe the difference between general and specific training.
- ☐ Describe Becker's theory of economic discrimination.
- ☐ Describe the concept of segmented labor markets and how they affect wage levels.
- ☐ Describe federal laws and policies regarding discrimination.
- ☐ Describe the history, costs, and benefits of trade unions.
- ☐ Discuss the evolution of labor markets.

redress for employer or client nonpayment, and other benefits.[1] This union does not strike like traditional unions, but the union has grown to 13,000 members and is an advocacy organization for freelance workers.

Labor markets in the 21st century are changing dramatically. Adjustments are being made: flexible hours, job sharing, working at home instead of in a centralized office, and more part-timers and freelancers in the market. In this chapter, we will address these labor market issues, and more.

## Investment in Human Capital

Let us first consider the role education and on-the-job-training (OJT) play in determining wage levels in labor markets. Workers, students, and firms all invest in themselves or their employees to increase productivity. This is called **investment in human capital.** Workers invest by accepting lower wages while they undertake apprenticeships. Students invest by paying for tuition and books, and by forgoing job opportunities, to learn new skills. Firms invest in their workers through OJT and in-house training programs that involve workers being paid to attend classes. These investments entail costs in the current period that are borne in the interest of raising future productivity. They can be analyzed using the investment analysis we developed in the last chapter.[2]

**Investment in human capital:** Investments such as education and on-the-job training that improve the productivity of human labor.

### Education and Earnings

One of the surest ways to advance in the job world and increase your income is by investing in education. The old saying, "To get ahead, get an education," still holds true. Table 1 shows the age/earnings profiles for all Americans between 25 and 64 for 2006. It provides strong evidence that education and earnings are related.

Average earnings for those without a high school education peaked at $25,688 a year, while those completing high school peaked at $37,173, a 44% increase. Getting a college degree bumped peak earnings up to $66,061, over a 150% rise. Going on to get a professional degree moved the peak all the way up to $133,151, over a 100% increase over a bachelor's degree alone. These figures represent average earnings. It is easy to see that earnings in all age groups were much higher for those with higher levels of education.

Table 1 suggests that education is a good investment. But like any investment, future earnings must be balanced against the cost of obtaining that education. The costs of education must be borne today, but the earnings benefits do not arrive until later. Evaluating educational decisions therefore requires that we use some of the tools developed in the last chapter when we studied investment in the capital markets.

**TABLE 1** Average Earnings by Highest Degree Earned, 2006

| Age Grouping | No HS Diploma | HS Diploma | Some College | College Degree | Professional |
|---|---|---|---|---|---|
| 25–34 | $21,153 | $28,448 | $31,026 | $48,724 | $78,119 |
| 35–44 | 24,333 | 35,083 | 40,943 | 63,335 | 133,151 |
| 45–54 | 25,438 | 37,173 | 43,027 | 66,061 | 131,011 |
| 55–64 | 25,688 | 34,845 | 40,968 | 60,393 | 123,759 |

**Source:** U.S. Census Bureau, *Statistical Abstract of the United States, 2009* (Washington, DC: U.S. Government Printing Office), 2009, Table 224.

[1] "Face Value: Freelancers of the World Unite," *Economist,* November 11, 2006, p. 76; and see the Freelancers Union Web site at www.freelancersunion.org.

[2] Gary S. Becker, *Human Capital,* 2nd ed. (New York: National Bureau of Economic Research), 1975. Becker won the Nobel Prize in 1992 for this and other work in economics.

## Education as Investment

To keep our analysis simple, we will focus on the decision to attend college for four years. The basic approach outlined in this section will nonetheless apply to other investments in education or training.

Figure 1 presents a stylized graph showing the benefits and costs of a college education. For simplicity, we will assume students go to college at age 18. If an individual chooses not to go to college, the high school earnings path applies: On leaving high school, the person enters the labor market immediately, and earnings begin rising along the path labeled "High School." Note that the earnings are positive throughout the individual's working life.

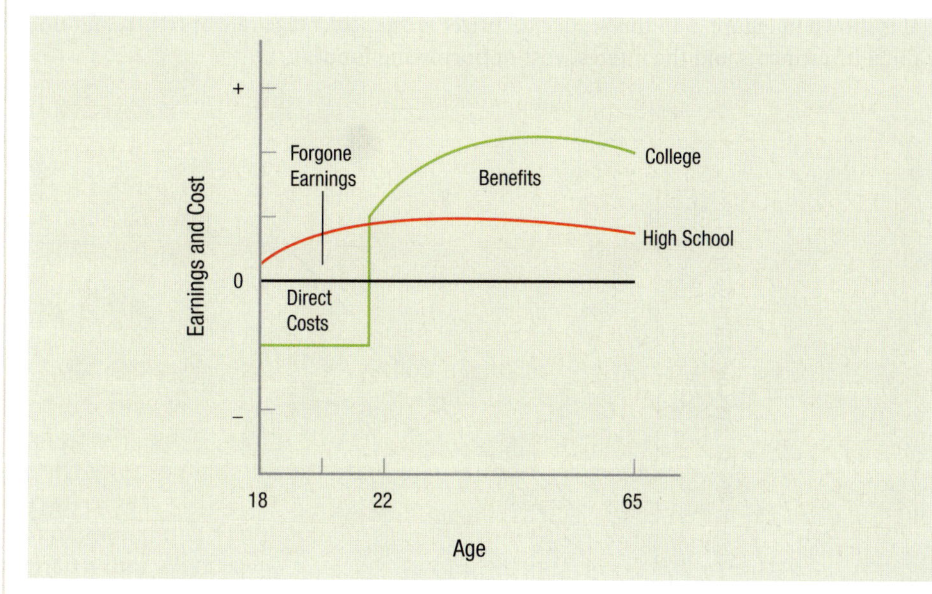


**FIGURE 1—Benefits and Costs of a College Education**

If an individual chooses not to go to college at age 18, he or she enters the labor market on leaving high school, and earnings rise and fall along the path labeled "High School." The college student incurs the direct costs of education, such as tuition and books, and the forgone earnings of not immediately entering the job market. The benefits of the college education show up as the difference in earnings from ages 22 to 65.

A college student immediately incurs costs in two forms. First, tuition, books, and other fees must be paid. These direct costs exclude living expenses, such as food and rent, since these must be paid whether you work or go to college. Tuition varies substantially depending on whether you attend a private or public university.

Second, students give up earnings as they devote full time to their studies (and to the occasional party). These costs can be substantial when compared to the direct costs of an education at a state-supported institution, since the average earnings for high school graduates range between $15,000 and $20,000 a year.

The benefits from a college degree show up as the difference in earnings from ages 22 to 65. If the return on a college degree is to be positive, this area must offset the direct costs of college and the forgone earnings. We must also keep in mind that a large part of the income high school and college graduates earn will not come until well into the future. For college graduates, this is especially important, since they will not see income for at least four years. How can we tell if this sacrifice is worth it? The fact that the median earnings of college graduates in 2007 exceeded that of high school graduates by over 80% suggests a college education is worth it.[3]

An alternate way to decide which of the two career paths is best is by computing the rate of return on a college degree. If the annual return on a college education over the course of one's working life is 10% a year, the earnings of the college graduate in middle

[3]U.S. Census Bureau, *Statistical Abstract of the United States, 2010* (Washington D.C.: U.S. Government Printing Office), 2010.

age will exceed those of the high school graduate by enough to generate a 10% return. A lower return would mean that the difference in earnings is smaller, while a higher return suggests the difference in earnings is greater. An extensive study[4] of rates of return to higher education in nearly 100 countries put the average return at nearly 20%. That is, college graduates around the world earn on average nearly 20% more per year over the course of their working lifetime than high school graduates, taking into consideration all of the costs of going to college.

## Equilibrium Levels of Human Capital

Each of us must decide how much to invest in ourselves. This decision, like so many in economics, ultimately depends on supply and demand, in this case, the supply of, and demand for, funds to be used for human capital investment. A hypothetical market for human capital is shown in Figure 2. In this scenario, "price" is the percentage rate of return on human capital investments and the interest cost of borrowing funds.

**FIGURE 2—Equilibrium Levels of Investment in Human Capital**

This graph portrays a hypothetical market for human capital; the percentage rates of return and the interest costs of borrowing funds are shown on the vertical axis. With demand $D_0$ and supply $S_0$, equilibrium will be at point *e*. If the supply of funds is reduced ($S_1$), interest rates and the cost of investment increase, resulting in less investment. Reduced demand for education ($D_1$) similarly reduces human capital investment.

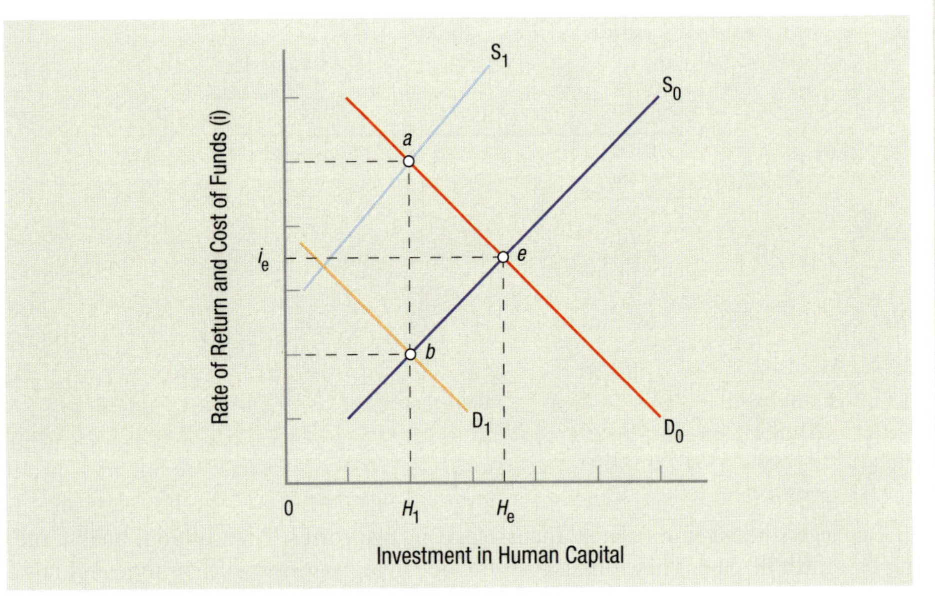


The demand for human capital investment slopes down and to the right, reflecting the diminishing returns of more education and that more time in school leaves you less time to earn back its costs. Students pursuing a Ph.D. or a medical degree are often well into their thirties before they can begin paying back their student loans. As a result, they require higher salaries to bring their rates of return up above those of college-educated workers.

The supply of investable funds, meanwhile, is positively sloped, since students will use the lowest-cost funds first—mom and dad paying for college—then turn to government-subsidized funds, and finally use private market funds, if needed.

With demand ($D_0$) and supply ($S_0$), equilibrium in this market is at point *e*. Human capital investment is equal to $H_e$, with the rate of return equaling the interest rate ($i_e$). Notice that reducing the supply of funds, or shifting the supply curve to $S_1$, will increase interest rates and the cost of investment. This results in lower investments in education.

[4] G. Psacharopoulos and H. Patrinos, "Returns to Investment in Education: A Further Update," *Education Economics*, 2004.

Similarly, anything reducing the demand for funds, or shifting the demand curve to $D_1$, will result in reduced human capital investment. Let us briefly consider some of the factors that might cause these curves to shift.

The most important factor determining the supply of investable funds for students consists of family resources. Students from well-off families can draw on a pool of inexpensive funds, but students from poorer families must scratch together funds that are often expensive. At the aggregate level, reductions in federally subsidized low-interest student loans will result in a shift in the supply curve to $S_1$, meaning lower investments in human capital ($H_1$). Conversely, the GI Bills enacted after World War II and the Vietnam War greatly increased college enrollments and the stock of human capital in America.

The demand for human capital is influenced by an individual's abilities and learning capacity: the more able the person, the larger the expected benefits of human capital investment.

Discrimination in the labor market also plays an important role in determining whether an investment in education is worthwhile or not, since expected earnings are affected by wage or occupational discrimination. Assume $D_0$ represents the demand for human capital investment for individuals facing no discrimination in the labor market. If these same people were to face a reduced wage in the market from wage discrimination, their demand for education would fall to $D_1$, reflecting the reduced return on investment in human capital. A similar decline in demand would result if the choice of jobs is limited by occupational discrimination. We look at discrimination more closely in the next section.

## Implications of Human Capital Theory

Individuals are more productive because of their investment in human capital, and thus they are capable of earning more during their working lives. Because younger people have longer earning horizons, they are more likely to invest in human capital and education. As workers get older and gain labor market experience and higher wages, their opportunity costs for attending college grow larger, while their potential postcollege earning period shrinks. This explains why most students in college classrooms are young.

The greater the market earnings differential between high school and college graduates, the more people will attend college, since a higher earnings differential raises the return on college educations. Similarly, reductions in the cost of education lead to greater educational investment.

Last, the more an individual discounts the future—the higher $i$ is in present value formulas—the less investment in human capital we would expect. If your discount rate is high, this means you value the present highly but do not place as much value on future outcomes. People with high discount rates often are not willing to pursue doctoral or medical degrees because the time between the beginning of the training process and the point when earnings begin is simply too long.

## Human Capital as Screening or Signaling

Human capital theorists see investments in human capital as improving the productivity of individuals. This higher productivity then translates into higher wages. There is another view why higher educational levels lead to higher wages: Higher education acts as a **screening/signaling** device for employers.

**Screening/signaling:** The argument that higher education simply lets employers know that the prospective employee is intelligent and trainable and has the discipline to potentially be a good employee.

Economists who advocate this view concede that some education will undoubtedly lead to higher productivity. But these economists argue that higher education is largely an indicator to employers that the college graduate is trainable, has discipline, and is intelligent. In their view, the job market is one big competition where entry-level workers compete for on-the-job training. As a result, earning a college degree does little more than give the college graduate a leg up in this competition.

One implication of this view is the controversial suggestion that the social benefits for more public spending on education may be low. If college educations do not enhance productivity but simply trigger competitive pursuits for resume items, then the return to public funds will be low. In the words of *The Economist,*

> *How can more education fail to make a country more prosperous? A first crucial point is that education is a "positional good": that is, getting yourself tagged for high wages is not just about being educated, it is also about being better educated than the next man. To some extent, education is a race: if everybody runs faster, that may be good in itself, but it does not mean that more people can finish in the top 10%. In that sense, much of the extra effort may be wasted. In weighing the social benefits of higher spending on education against the cost, this needs to be borne in mind.*[5]

Still, it is doubtful that screening is the only purpose served by higher education. If it were, the high costs of college education and the higher wages employers must pay college graduates would create tremendous incentives for workers and employers to develop an alternative, less expensive screening device.

## On-the-Job Training

**On-the-job training:** Training typically done by employers, ranging from suggestions at work to sophisticated seminars.

**On-the-job training** (OJT) can take many different forms. Often training amounts to nothing more than receiving instructions from a supervisor on how to help customers, operate a machine, or retrieve items from inventory. Sometimes this training takes place in a more formal setting away from the job, almost like a college course.

Today, spending on OJT approaches $80 billion a year, including training costs and the wages paid to employees during training. The costs of OJT are usually borne by employers, but workers may bear some of the costs through reduced wages throughout the training period. Firms benefit from OJT by gaining more productive workers, and workers gain by becoming more versatile, and thus more competitive, in labor markets.

### General Versus Specific Training

Nobel Prize winner Gary Becker was one of the pioneers of human capital theory. In his book, *Human Capital,* he outlined two distinct forms of OJT: general training and specific training.

**General training:** Training that improves a worker's productivity in all firms.

**Specific training:** Training that improves a worker's productivity in a specific firm.

**General training** improves productivity in all firms. Learning to use computers, word processors, and spreadsheets, for example, raises your productivity no matter where you work. The same is true for a college education, as well as for the apprenticeships electricians, plumbers, and carpenters undertake.

**Specific training,** in contrast, increases a worker's productivity only within the particular firm. Firm-specific training might cover the way a firm handles such issues as order flow, inventory control and purchasing, or familiarization of workers with the firm's specific products.

Firms usually will not provide general training. Since productivity is increased equally for all firms, workers must acquire these skills at their own expense. Firms will provide specific training, however, if the returns from this investment compare favorably to other investment alternatives.

Because investing in OJT is just one of many investments a firm can undertake, the rate of return to OJT must equal or exceed those of other investments if it is to be worthwhile. On-the-job investments entail present costs meant to yield future benefits. These

[5] "Economic Focus: The Education Shibboleth," *The Economist,* June 8, 2002, p. 73. See Alison Wolf, *Does Education Matter? Myths About Education and Economic Growth,* (London: Penguin Books), 2002.

## *Nobel Prize*

### Gary Becker

The 1992 winner of the Nobel Prize in Economic Sciences, Gary Becker, applied the theory of "rational choice" to areas of human behavior not ordinarily associated with economic analysis and research. Through his academic work and columns in *Business Week* magazine, he has offered provocative insights on a broad array of subjects, including family relations, racial discrimination, and the criminal justice system.

Born in Pottsville, a coal-mining community in eastern Pennsylvania, Becker completed his undergraduate degree in three years at Princeton University. He then entered the University of Chicago, where he studied under economist Milton Friedman.

In 1957, he published his dissertation, *The Economics of Discrimination,* an analysis of the effects of racial prejudice on earnings and employment among minorities. The book was favorably reviewed in journals but failed to make an impact on mainstream economics. The support of Friedman and other economists at the University of Chicago, however, encouraged Becker to continue along this line of research. Becker taught for several years at Chicago and then Columbia. In 1970, he rejoined the faculty at Chicago and befriended George Stigler, collaborating with him on two influential papers. His work with Stigler rekindled an interest in the relationship between economics and politics. In the 1980s, he wrote two papers that analyzed the impact of special interest groups on the political process.

Jim West/Alamy

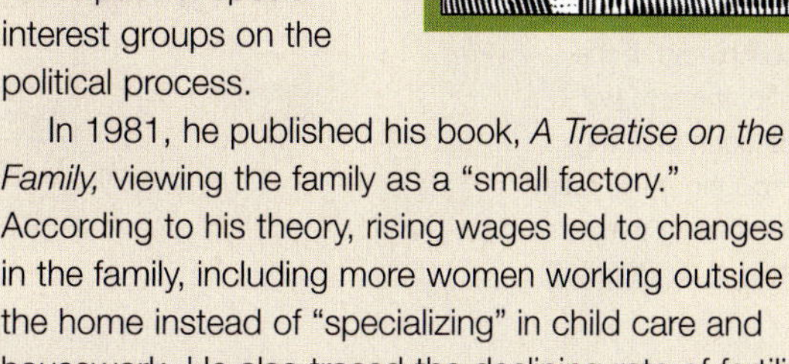

In 1981, he published his book, *A Treatise on the Family,* viewing the family as a "small factory." According to his theory, rising wages led to changes in the family, including more women working outside the home instead of "specializing" in child care and housework. He also traced the declining rate of fertility to a rational choice of having fewer children and investing more in education for the individual child.

On questions of crime and punishment, Becker suggested that most criminals react in predictable ways to the costs and benefits of illegal activity. His empirical studies indicated that the probability of being caught and punished was a greater deterrent than the harsh nature of the punishment. On the question of race, Becker viewed discrimination as a "tax wedge" between social and private returns, concluding that prejudice tends to be economically detrimental to all parties concerned.

investments can be analyzed just like those involving college education that we looked at earlier. Figure 3 on the next page shows the benefits and costs of OJT.

Wages and productivity (marginal revenue product, or MRP) are shown on the vertical axis. For simplicity, individuals without training are assumed to have productivity (MRP) and earn wages equal to $W_0$ throughout their working careers. Further, we will assume that workers are provided training at the beginning of their careers, which improves their productivity in that firm for the remainder of their working lives. The heavy line labeled "With Training" reflects this increased productivity.

If OJT is general training, workers will be expected to accept reduced wages during the training period, and then earn wages equal to $W_2$ once the training is completed. In Figure 3, the area below $W_0$ and above $W_1$ represents the costs workers bear during the training period. Historically, this is how apprenticeship programs in the trades have operated. Today, professional internships provide college students with OJT at reduced wages over the summer. Hiring summer interns is a good way for firms to get an extended look at potential employees. The internships provide students, meanwhile, with

**FIGURE 3—Benefits and Costs of On-the-Job Training**

Individuals without training are assumed to earn wages $W_0$ throughout their working careers. Trained workers have an increased productivity for the remainder of their working lives, as shown by the heavy line labeled "With Training." If OJT is general, workers will get reduced wages during the training period, then earning wages equal to $W_2$ once the training is completed. If the training is specific, the firm will often absorb the cost, keeping wages at $W_0$ throughout the training process, then raising wages to somewhere between $W_2$ and $W_0$.

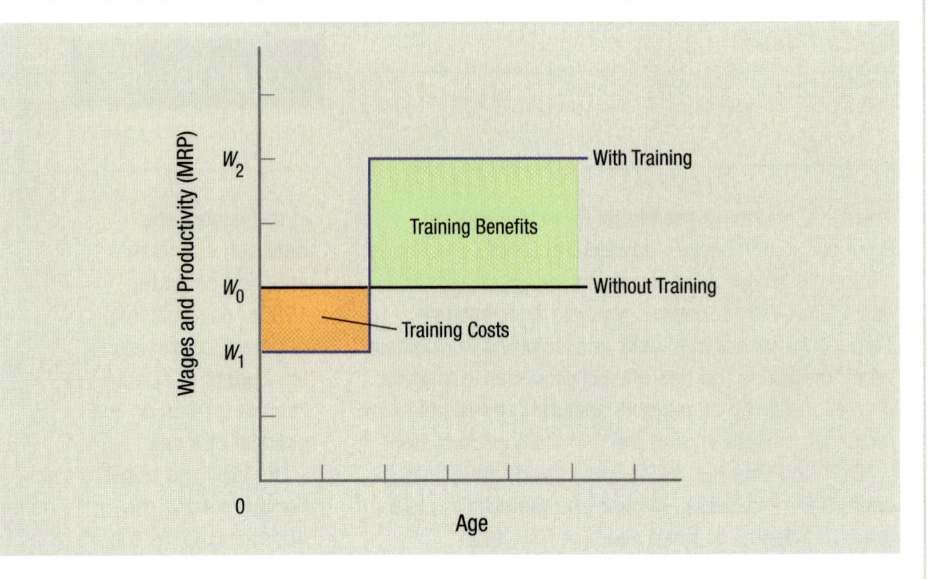


a look at several different firms and industries before graduating and entering the job market.

Specific training is usually handled differently. Because this training increases productivity only within the firm providing the training, the firm will usually absorb the cost of this training, keeping wages at $W_0$ throughout the training process. Once workers have completed the training, their productivity rises to $W_2$. The firm will not, however, raise their pay all the way to $W_2$, since then it would not recoup the training costs. Instead, the firm will share the benefits of specific training with the newly trained workers, raising their pay to somewhere between $W_2$ and $W_0$. Paying these workers something more than $W_0$ will reduce turnover, since the workers could expect to earn only $W_0$ if they went to another firm, given that specific training only increases productivity in the firm providing the training.

As we have seen, investments in human capital go a long way toward explaining why people are paid different wages. Education and earnings are closely related. Human capital theorists believe that this is because education and productivity are closely related. Other economists question whether more education translates into higher productivity; they view education as little more than a screening device for employers. In any case, the investment in human capital is just one of the reasons for wage differentials. Economic discrimination is another, as we will see next.

## CHECKPOINT

### INVESTMENT IN HUMAN CAPITAL

- Investment in human capital includes all investments in human beings such as education and on-the-job training.
- There is a positive relationship between education and earnings.
- The rate of return to education is computed by comparing the streams of income of two levels of education.
- The greater the wage differential between two levels of education, the more people will pursue that next level of education.
- The higher the rate of return to education, the more people will attain that level.

- Higher education may just be a screening or signaling device telling potential employers that this individual is trainable, has discipline, and is smart.
- Firms will provide specific training (training that enhances productivity in the firm only) but usually will not provide general training (training that enhances productivity in all firms).

**QUESTIONS:** If the United States decided, as part of an immigration reform package, to restrict immigration only to those with college degrees, and thus decided to allow only 500,000 foreigners a year to enter, what would happen to the rate of return on college education? Alternatively, if, as part of a reform package, 500,000 low-skilled people were permitted to enter the United States, what would happen to the rate of return on college education?

Answers to the Checkpoint questions can be found at the end of this chapter.

# Economic Discrimination

**Economic discrimination** takes place whenever workers of equal ability and productivity are paid different wages or are otherwise discriminated against in the workplace because of their race, color, religion, gender, age, national origin, or disability. This can mean that one group is paid lower wages than another for doing the same job, or that members of different groups are segregated into occupations that pay different wages.

**Economic discrimination:** When workers of equal ability are paid different wages or in any other way discriminated against because of race, color, religion, gender, age, national origin, or disability.

Economic theories of discrimination generally take one of two approaches. The first, developed by Gary Becker, rests on the notion that bias is articulated in the *discriminatory tastes* of employers, workers, and consumers. The second approach, the *segmented markets approach,* maintains that labor markets are divided into segments based on race, gender, or some other category. This approach is often referred to as the *job crowding hypothesis,* or the *dual labor market hypothesis.*

## Becker's Theory of Economic Discrimination

Gary Becker's main contribution to economics is that he vastly broadened the issues that economists study. This was no small feat. Before Becker's influence, economists focused almost exclusively on the production and exchange of material goods and services. One early example shows the difficulties Becker faced in broadening this focus.

In 1955, Becker was asked to speak at Harvard about his dissertation on the economics of discrimination. Becker noted that his audience was perplexed. "They thought I would discuss price discrimination"—that is, the analysis of why businesses charge different prices for the same goods. "No one conceived that an economist would talk about race discrimination in those days."[6]

Published in 1957, *The Economics of Discrimination* was not warmly received by the profession. Not until the mid-1960s, when the civil rights movement gained momentum, did the book get the recognition it deserved. Surprisingly enough, Becker challenged the conventional view that discrimination benefits the person who discriminates. Let's see why he thought the conventional wisdom was wrong.

Becker argued that employers who discriminate against women will lose market share and profit opportunities, both because they do not hire the best employees available, and because they must pay mostly high-wage male employees. Nondiscriminating firms, in contrast, will have lower labor costs, having more low-wage women on the payroll. Nondiscriminating firms will attract the most productive managers and employees, many of whom will likely be women. Profits for the nondiscriminating firm should therefore be higher. Becker concluded that the cost of wage differentials and the pressures of the marketplace should drive discrimination down to zero in the long run.

[6] Peter Passell, "New Nobel Laureate Takes Economics Far Afield," *New York Times,* October 14, 1992, p. D1.

In practice, we know that wage discrimination still exists. Why might competition fail to erase wage differentials? For one thing, the adjustment costs of firing unproductive workers, giving them severance pay, then recruiting and training new workers can be extremely high, especially considering the protections unions and the legal system offer workers. Second, women may be less mobile than men when it comes to work. They may be less willing to move to accommodate employer preferences, and thus be forced to accept lower wage positions. Third, if women continue to choose occupations with more flexible career paths that do not heavily penalize extended absences from the labor market, wage differentials between men and women may always exist. Note, however, that such differentials could also be caused by discrimination that precedes labor market entry, as when social norms direct girls toward lower-wage occupations such as elementary education or social work.

## Segmented Labor Markets

**Segmented labor markets:** Labor markets split into separate parts. This leads to different wages paid to different sectors even though both markets are highly competitive.

Economists who advocate **segmented labor market** theories argue that discrimination does not arise due to a lack of competitive labor markets, but rather because these markets, though competitive, are segmented into a variety of constituent parts. And these different parts, while interacting, are noncompeting sectors. Segmented labor market theories have been developed along several different lines.

- The *dual labor market hypothesis* splits the labor market into primary and secondary sectors. As Doeringer and Piore wrote, "Jobs in the primary market possess several of the following characteristics: high wages, good working conditions, job stability, chances of advancement, equity and due process in the administration of work rules. Jobs in the secondary market, in contrast, tend to have low wages and fringe benefits, poor working conditions, high labor turnover, little chance of advancement, and often arbitrary and capricious supervision."[7]
- The *job crowding hypothesis* breaks occupations into predominately male and female jobs. In 1922, Edgeworth recognized this problem when he wrote, "The pressure of male trade unions appears to be largely responsible for that crowding of women into a comparatively few occupations, which is universally recognized as a main factor in the depression of their wages. Such crowding is prima facie a flagrant violation of that free competition which results in maximum production in . . . equal pay for equal work."[8]
- The *insider-outsider theory* maintains that workers are segregated into those who belong to unions and those who are unemployed or non-union workers. Alternatively, economists have recognized that large firms use internal promotion and job security to inspire loyalty to the firm. Company customs, norms, and policies provide loyal workers with clear advancement paths. The preference given to promotion from within can be a good recruiting vehicle for a firm, but it can also become an indirect method of segregating the labor market.

These hypotheses all predict that separate job markets will emerge for different groups. Figure 4 shows how segregated markets can lead to significant wage differentials, such as those we see for men and women.

In a world without discrimination, equilibrium wages for everyone would be $W_e$, with total employment at $M_0 + F_0$. If some form of discrimination in male-dominated jobs is present, labor supply to that segment will decline to $S_1$, wages will rise to $W_1$, and hiring will fall to $M_1$ (point *a*). Those women who are excluded from jobs in this sector will have to move to jobs available in the female-dominated sector, thus increasing the supply of

[7] P. Doeringer and M. Piore, *Internal Labour Markets and Manpower Analysis* (1971), p. 165, cited in Stephen Smith, *Labour Economics* (New York: Routledge), 1994, p. 104.

[8] F. Y. Edgeworth, "Equal Pay to Men and Women for Equal Work" (1922), p. 439, cited in Stephen Smith, *Labour Economics* (New York: Routledge), 1994, p. 102.

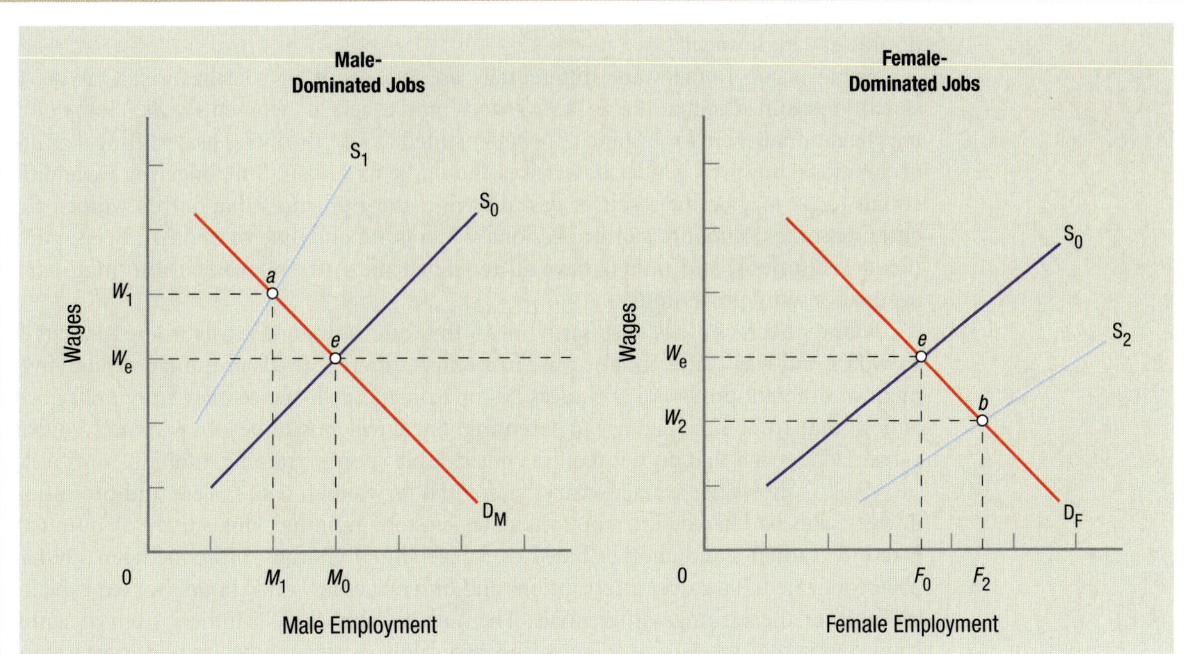


**FIGURE 4—Job Crowding and a Dual Labor Market**

Segregated markets can lead to significant wage differentials between men and women. Absent discrimination, equilibrium wages will be $W_e$ for everyone, with total employment at $M_0 + F_0$. If, however, there is some form of discrimination in male-dominated jobs, the supply of labor to that segment will decline to $S_1$, wages will rise to $W_1$, and employment will fall to $M_1$ (point *a*). Those women who are excluded from jobs in this sector will have to move to available jobs in the female-dominated sector, thus increasing the labor supplied for these jobs to $S_2$, raising employment to $F_2$, but reducing wages to $W_2$ (point *b*). The result is a wage differential equal to $W_1 - W_2$.

labor there to $S_2$ and reducing wages to $W_2$, employment climbing to $F_2$ (point *b*). The result is a wage differential equal to $W_1 - W_2$.

Notice that once such a wage differential is established, the firms in competitive markets have no real incentive to eliminate the gap. Men and women are both being paid their marginal revenue products, so no profits are gained by substituting workers.

Wage differentials can arise for a variety of reasons. Some people may simply prefer one occupation to another. If such preferences have their roots in specific social groups, groupwide wage differentials can be expected to arise. Wages will vary between occupations, moreover, because of differences in their attractiveness, difficulty, riskiness, social status, and the human capital investments required.

Markets may naturally gravitate toward different equilibrium wage levels for different occupations. Two occupations may require the same skills and effort, for instance, but be valued differently by consumers. Finally, government policies that promote or restrict entry into occupations or professions affect wages. Licensing requirements for everything from hair styling to surgery today create wage differentials in over 700 different occupations.

Occupational segregation may also arise from disparate degrees of labor force attachment. Female labor force participation is often interrupted when women take a break from working to have children. Skills and other forms of human capital depreciate during these interruptions, which influences the occupational choices of women and employer decisions concerning which employees to offer specific training. For women who anticipate spells out of the labor force, jobs that mostly involve general training—nursing, teaching, retail sales, and secretarial or administrative work—may look attractive. These occupations do not require climbing long career ladders, so women can leave their jobs, later returning or finding a new employer, with little loss in salary or benefits. The downside to these occupations, however, is that most of them do not pay high wages.

Some occupational wage differentials are the result of socialization: Our culture stereotypes some occupations as "men's work" and others as "women's work." Some of this may be rational; men, for instance, are better suited to jobs involving heavy lifting. For most occupations, however, gender differences should be irrelevant. Still, lingering wage differentials today may be the result of past discriminatory practices that barred women from entering some occupations or professional schools. At one time or another, firms, educational institutions, and unions have all restricted the entry of women into high-paying occupations and professions.

Do wage differentials necessarily mean that discrimination exists in the market? Job crowding and wage differentials could just reflect different levels of human capital investment or different professional choices. Many women, for instance, may truly prefer occupations that are complementary to parenting. These will tend to be jobs without significant career ladders and that do not require considerable specific training, mobility, or travel.

Table 2 shows the average salary differential for women with college and professional degrees who had career interruptions of at least 18 months. This survey of over 6,000 Harvard graduates and another based on University of Chicago MBAs between 1990 and 2006 confirmed that career interruptions and differences in weekly hours worked explained the bulk of the earnings differentials. The authors note that, "Mothers seem to actively choose jobs that are family friendly and avoid jobs with long hours and greater career advancement opportunities." They also found that, "Mothers with high-earning spouses reduce their labor supply much more [than] mothers with lower earning spouses . . ."

**TABLE 2** Financial Cost to Women from an 18-Month Career Interruption

| | |
|---|---|
| MBA | −41% |
| J.D. | −29 |
| Ph.D. | −29 |
| B.A. only | −25 |
| M.D. | −16 |
| Other/master's | −13 |

**Sources:** Claudia Goldin and Lawrence Katz, "Transitions: Career and Family Life Cycles of the Educational Elite," *American Economic Review: Papers & Proceedings,* 2008, pp. 363–369; Marianne Bertrand, Claudia Goldin, and Lawrence Katz, "Dynamics of the Gender Gap for Young Professionals in the Financial and Corporate Sectors," unpublished working paper, January 2009; and David Leonhardt, "Careers That Work for Families," *New York Times,* May 27, 2009, p. B1.

Although initially both men and women were paid the same, women were working and earning considerably less than their male counterparts 10 years later. Balancing careers and family responsibilities for today's dual-earner households continues to be a challenge for both families and employers.

## Public Policy to Combat Discrimination

For the first half of the last century, the inequities associated with various forms of discrimination were simply accepted as a part of life in the United States. Gradually, however, a groundswell developed to end racial segregation and other forms of discrimination, culminating in passage of the Civil Rights Act in 1964. In what follows, we briefly outline the major acts and public policies that have been implemented with the goal of ending discrimination. Because of these policies, discrimination, wage differentials, and segmented labor markets have declined markedly over the past four decades.

### The Equal Pay Act of 1963

Equal Pay Act of 1963 amended the Fair Labor Standards Act of 1938; it requires that men and women receive equal pay for equal work. Equal work is defined as work performed under similar circumstances requiring equal effort, skill, and responsibility. Some argue that the Equal Pay Act was a hollow victory because occupational segregation forced women into specific occupations, causing them to earn less than men for essentially comparable work.

## Civil Rights Act of 1964

Title VII of the Civil Rights Act of 1964 makes it unlawful to "refuse to hire or to discharge any individual, or otherwise to discriminate against any individual with respect to his compensation, terms, conditions, or privileges of employment, because of such individual's race, color, religion, sex, or national origin." The act also created the Equal Employment Opportunity Commission (EEOC) to administer the Act.

To date, most of the litigation brought under this statute has focused on the meaning of the phrase *to discriminate.* Amendments to the statute and court cases have ruled that, to show discrimination, a plaintiff must show that an employment practice inflicts a "disparate" or unequal impact on members of a minority group, as compared to its impact on others. Once this has been demonstrated, the burden shifts to the defendant (the employer) to show that its employment practices—seniority rules, prehiring examinations or other screening devices, weight or height requirements—are related to employee performance or are otherwise a matter of "business necessity." Plaintiffs may sue for a full range of remedies, including back pay, reinstatement, court costs, attorney's fees, and punitive damages.

## Executive Order 11246—Affirmative Action

In 1965, President Lyndon Johnson issued Executive Order 11246. This order established the Office of Federal Contract Compliance Programs (OFCCP) in the Department of Labor. A key provision of this order required that firms doing at least $50,000 in business with the federal government submit an affirmative action program that includes a detailed analysis of their labor force.

Affirmative action programs have been controversial from the outset. Critics see such programs as "enforced quotas," whereas supporters see them as a way of breaking down discriminatory hiring barriers.

In the summer of 2003, the U.S. Supreme Court ruled in the University of Michigan case (*Gratz v. Bollinger*) that adding a large specific numerical adjustment for minority group status to university admission criteria was unacceptable. The undergraduate admissions program automatically added 20 points (out of a total of 100) to minority candidates for admission. The Law School at Michigan, on the other hand, simply took race into account in a nuanced approach to improving diversity of the class. The Supreme Court found this approach acceptable (*Grutter v. Bollinger*).

## Age and Disabilities Acts

Two other acts were designed to reduce discrimination based on age and physical or mental disabilities. The Age Discrimination in Employment Act of 1967 protects workers over age 40 from discrimination based on age. The Americans With Disabilities Act of 1990 prohibits discrimination against people with a physical or mental disability who could still perform a job with reasonable accommodation by an employer. What constitutes "reasonable accommodation" has been a point of contention in many recent court cases.

**CHECKPOINT**

### ECONOMIC DISCRIMINATION

- Economic discrimination occurs whenever workers of equal ability and productivity are paid different wages or otherwise discriminated against because of their race, color, religion, gender, age, national origin, or disability.
- Becker's analysis of discrimination assumed that employers had a taste for discrimination, and he showed that both parties were harmed by discrimination.

- Segmented labor markets assume that separate markets lead to wage differentials that represent discrimination.
- Public policy to eliminate discrimination has included the Equal Pay Act of 1963, Civil Rights Act of 1964, Executive Order 11246 (Affirmative Action), Age Discrimination in Employment Act of 1967, and Americans With Disabilities Act of 1990.

**QUESTION:** The Civil Rights Act of 1964 made defendants liable for the plaintiffs attorney's fees if they lost the case, but it did not have the same provision for plaintiffs if they lost the case. Why do you think Congress wrote this part of the law this way? (Hint: Who did Congress assume would be plaintiffs and who would be defendants under the Civil Rights Act?)

Answers to the Checkpoint question can be found at the end of this chapter.

## Labor Unions and Collective Bargaining

A friend who had been working for a large construction company for eight years as an engineer and project coordinator recently staged a one-man strike. He had been training new employees on various aspects of cost estimating and job specification, and he noticed that these new people were being hired at salaries approaching his own. He requested a raise several times, but was essentially ignored. Exasperated, he refused to go to work one day, informing his boss that he would not return without a raise. He did not quit; he simply staged a walkout and refused to return until given a raise. He was out for 2 weeks before his supervisor called and asked him how much he wanted. They settled on a raise of over 20%.

This story is unique in that one-person strikes are rarely successful; more often they are career busters. In most instances, individual employees have little control over wages or job conditions, essentially being at the mercy of employers and the market. This is the primary reason that unions exist: Collective action is more powerful than the action of one individual. As individuals, we can easily be replaced (except, apparently, my friend above). To replace an entire workforce, on the other hand, imposes serious costs to an employer. This section looks at the role unions play in our economy, their history, and their effects.

### Types of Unions

Labor unions are legal associations of employees that bargain with employers over terms and conditions of work, including wages, benefits, and working conditions. They use strikes and threats of strikes, as well as other tactics, to try to achieve their goals. Elections determine union representatives who negotiate on the workers' behalf, and employers are legally required to "bargain in good faith" with the union.

Unions are usually defined by industry, or by craft or occupation. A *craft* union represents members of a specific craft or occupation, such as air traffic controllers (PATCO), truck drivers (Teamsters), and teachers (AFT). An *industrial* union represents all workers employed in a specific industry. Examples include auto workers (UAW) and public employees (AFSCME).

### Benefits and Costs of Union Membership

Without a union, each individual employee would have to bargain with management for his or her own wages, benefits, and working conditions. Unions bring collective power to this bargaining arrangement. The source of this power is ultimately the willingness of the union to strike if no agreement is reached during negotiations. Collective bargaining often leads to a more equitable pay schedule than individual negotiation. It also provides workers with greater job security by protecting them against arbitrary or vindictive decisions by management.

Management's unilateral authority is curbed by the union contract, specifically through restrictions on job assignments and restrictions that severely limit the ability of management to fire employees without good cause and due process. These rules are subject to an elaborate grievance procedure laid out in the union contract's work rules.

Union membership, like everything else, has its price. First, union members must pay monthly dues. Then, if negotiations break down and a strike is called, wages are lost and the possibility exists, however remote, that management will refuse to settle with the union and replace the entire workforce. Finally, union workers must give up some individual flexibility since their work rules are more rigid.

## Brief History of American Unionism

Labor unions date from the late 18th century in England. In this country, public attitudes toward unions were highly unfavorable until the Great Depression. In the early part of the 20th century, employers could easily secure legal injunctions against union organization by arguing that unions behaved like monopolies, in violation of antitrust laws. Employers often required employees to sign enforceable *yellow dog contracts,* in which they agreed not to join a union as a condition of employment.

Figure 5 shows union membership as a percentage of total employment since 1930. Going into the 1930s, unions represented just over 7% of workers because of public attitudes and legal restrictions. With the onset of the Depression, attitudes about collective bargaining began to change. In 1932, Congress passed the Norris-LaGuardia Act, which outlawed yellow dog contracts and prohibited injunctions against union organizing. Then, in 1935, Congress passed a sweeping reform by enacting the Wagner Act, or the National Labor Relations Act (NLRA). It prohibited a variety of unfair labor practices by employers,

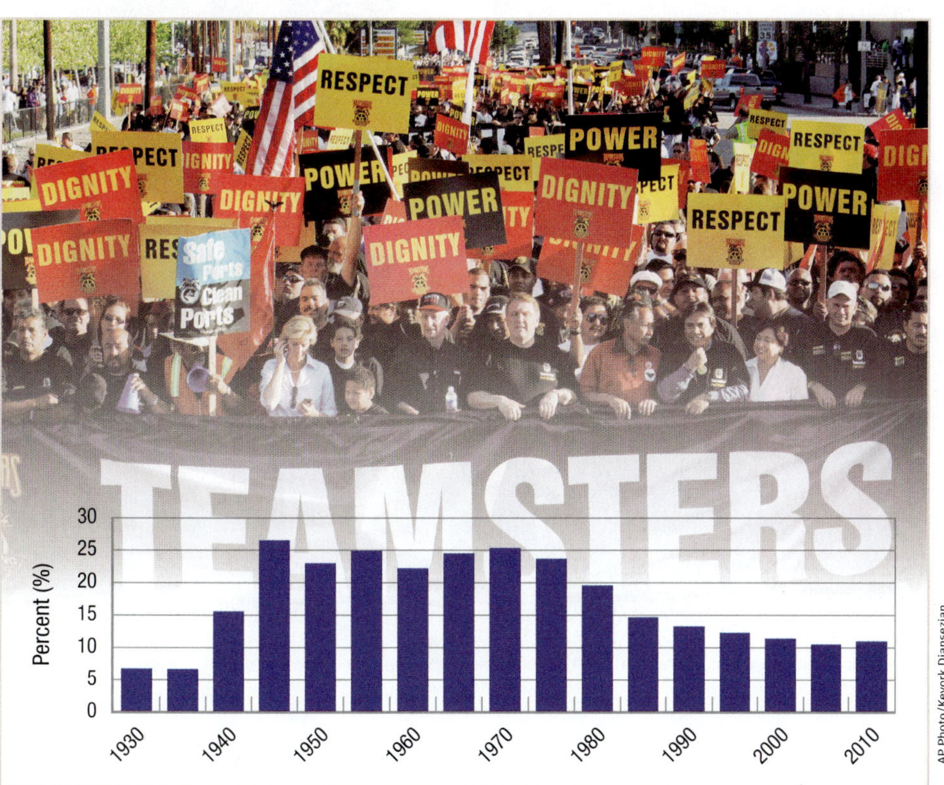


**FIGURE 5—Union Membership as a Percent of Employment**

Union membership grew dramatically from the mid-1930s until after World War II. Following the war, over one-quarter of American workers were unionized. Union membership has fallen because benefits obtained by unions for union members spread throughout the wider workforce, making the benefits of joining a union less valuable. Also, the changing economy led to faster growth in the more difficult-to-unionize service sector.

including firing employees for engaging in union activities. The Act also required employers to "bargain in good faith" with those unions that had won recognition through a majority vote of the firm's workers.

The NLRA also established the National Labor Relations Board (NLRB) to oversee union certification elections. These elections were to be held to determine which union, if any, would represent employees. The NLRB was also given the power to investigate complaints by labor and management about elections and the bargaining process.

As Figure 5 illustrates, union membership grew dramatically from the mid-1930s until after World War II. Following the war, union membership covered over one-quarter of American workers. It was concentrated in a few major industries.

Figure 6 shows work stoppages, or strikes, since 1950. In 1946 a rash of strikes turned public opinion against the unions; many people felt unions had become too powerful. Because of this swing in popular opinion, in 1947 Congress passed the Taft-Hartley Act, which prohibits some unfair labor practices by unions. Unions could no longer coerce or discriminate against workers who chose not to join the union, and unions were required to

AP Photo/Elaine Thompson

**FIGURE 6—Work Stoppages (Strikes)**

This figure shows work stoppages, or strikes, since 1950. In 1946, numerous strikes turned public opinion against the unions. In 1947, Congress reacted by passing the Taft-Hartley Act, seeking a balance between unions and management. After this, the use of work stoppages by unions gradually began to decline.

bargain in good faith, just like employers. With the passage of this Act, the prolabor aspects of the 1935 Wagner Act were balanced.

Taft-Hartley changed the collective bargaining landscape dramatically by ending secondary boycotts and closed shops, and establishing procedures for decertification elections. A **secondary boycott** occurs when unions clash with one firm—the primary firm—but put pressure on neutral secondary firms by getting their union members to refuse to process the products of the primary firm. A **closed shop** is a workplace where workers are required to be union members before they can be hired.

**Secondary boycott:** Occurs when unions clash with one firm and put pressure on a neutral, second firm to enlist the help of the second firm to obtain the union's objectives with the original firm.

**Closed shop:** Workers must belong to the union before they can be hired.

A **union shop** is one where nonunion hires must join the union within a specified period, usually 30 days. In an **agency shop,** employees are not required to join the union, but they must pay union dues to compensate the union for its services. The Taft-Hartley Act outlawed closed shops outright, while permitting states to pass *right-to-work statutes* that prohibit union shops. Today, over 20 states have **right-to-work laws.**

**Union shop:** Nonunion hires must join the union within a specified period of time.

**Agency shop:** Employees are not required to join the union, but must pay dues to compensate the union for its services.

**Right-to-work laws:** Laws created by the Taft-Hartley Act that permitted states to outlaw union shops.

Near the end of the 1950s, union corruption had become a serious issue, as various union leaders were accused of taking kickbacks, committing pension fund fraud, and engaging in a variety of other illegal activities. In response to these problems, Congress in 1959 passed the Labor Management Reporting and Disclosure Act, or the Landrum-Griffin Act. This Act protects union members from their leaders by promoting union democracy and requiring financial transparency.

Until 1962, all collective bargaining statutes focused on the private sector; public employees were prohibited from organizing. In 1962, however, President Kennedy signed Executive Order 10988, giving federal workers the right to bargain collectively. Still, public employees are not permitted to strike. Rather, when an impasse is reached, both sides must submit to binding arbitration in which a neutral arbitrator resolves the dispute.

## *Issue:* Why Are Unions Pushing for Pledge Card Organizing?

**As if declining** membership wasn't enough trouble for labor, in the summer of 2005 several big unions broke away from the AFL-CIO in a disagreement over whether extensive political involvement or a focus on organizing new members was the best long-run strategy for the union movement. The breakaway unions, essentially led by the Service Employees International Union (SEIU), want to emphasize organizing new members and they are fighting with new strategies.

Under the National Labor Relations Act, the union creation process starts with pledge cards. Either employees of a nonunion firm contact a union or a union contacts employees of a firm and offers to represent them. Interest in a union is revealed by employees signing pledge cards. Nothing official occurs until employee "interest" in a union is shown by obtaining pledge cards from 30% of employees. A petition is then filed with the NLRB, and a secret ballot is held. This often results in a heavily contested brawl with employers, and unions typically win fewer than half of the elections. As a result, unions employ new strategies and tactics that emphasize "pledge card check recognition," neutrality agreements, public relations, and advertising to win new members.

Pledge cards are the size of index cards, which workers sign to indicate that they would like to have a union represent them. Before organizing begins, unions approach employers for voluntary recognition if more than 50% of workers sign pledge cards. If employers insist on following NLRB election certification rules, the union tries to get employers to sign neutrality agreements whereby employers are restricted from actively campaigning against union recognition.

Now, why would an employer want to voluntarily recognize a union or agree to remain neutral during the election campaign? Here's where the second half of the union's new tactics, the "corporate campaign," comes into play. Firms who refuse the unions' overtures will face public relations and advertising campaigns to harm their corporate image as well as grassroots community opposition to new facilities, mergers, or requests for regulatory relief.

These tactics have proven quite successful. When unions get neutrality agreements signed, the organizational success rate climbs to 45%; when card check agreements are added, the union success rate exceeds 75% of their attempts to organize. In 2006, janitors at the University of Miami staged walkouts, sit-ins, and hunger strikes to get the university service contractor to agree to pledge card recognition if the union got 60% of the workers to sign cards, thus avoiding a secret ballot election. Some students supported the janitors. During the walkout, the service contractor increased wage rates by one-third at the request of the university. Media attention was directed at university president Donna Shalala, President Clinton's former Secretary of Health and Human Services, who tried to remain neutral. In the end, the service contractor agreed to the union's demands.

Anderson Ross/Jupiter Images

These strategies are effective. With labor union membership such a small fraction of the workforce, unions are using these new tactics to increase membership and influence.

Sources: See "Unions Favor Card Check Recognition in Organizing," *National Law Journal,* January 10, 2005; and Timothy Aeppel, "Not-So-Big Labor Enlists New Methods for Greater Leverage," *Wall Street Journal,* August 29, 2005, p. A2.

Why has union membership declined as a percentage of wage and salary workers since World War II? The answer lies partly with the changes in labor laws just discussed, the country's changing economy—notably, a larger service sector that is hard to organize—and ironically, the very success of labor at pushing its agenda through Congress and the courts. In addition, management has become more aggressive and sophisticated in defeating certification elections along with the rising labor force participation of women who historically have been difficult to organize.

Before unionization, employees were *hired at will*, which meant they could be fired "for a good reason, a bad reason, or no reason at all." Unions and their supporters pressed Congress and the courts for work safety legislation, minimum wage laws, Social Security, antidiscrimination statutes, restrictions on firing employees, laws that put restrictions on plant closures, and many other statutes and rules that protect workers.

Each of these successes resulted in union membership being a little less valuable. Over this same period, the service sector has become a bigger share of our economy. This sector has always been difficult for labor to organize, and as a result, union membership may continue to shrink as a percentage of the workforce.

## Union Versus Nonunion Wage Differentials

Why join a union? The primary benefit to unionization should be higher wages, given the union's collective bargaining power. The general theoretical argument for union–nonunion wage differentials is illustrated in Figure 7.

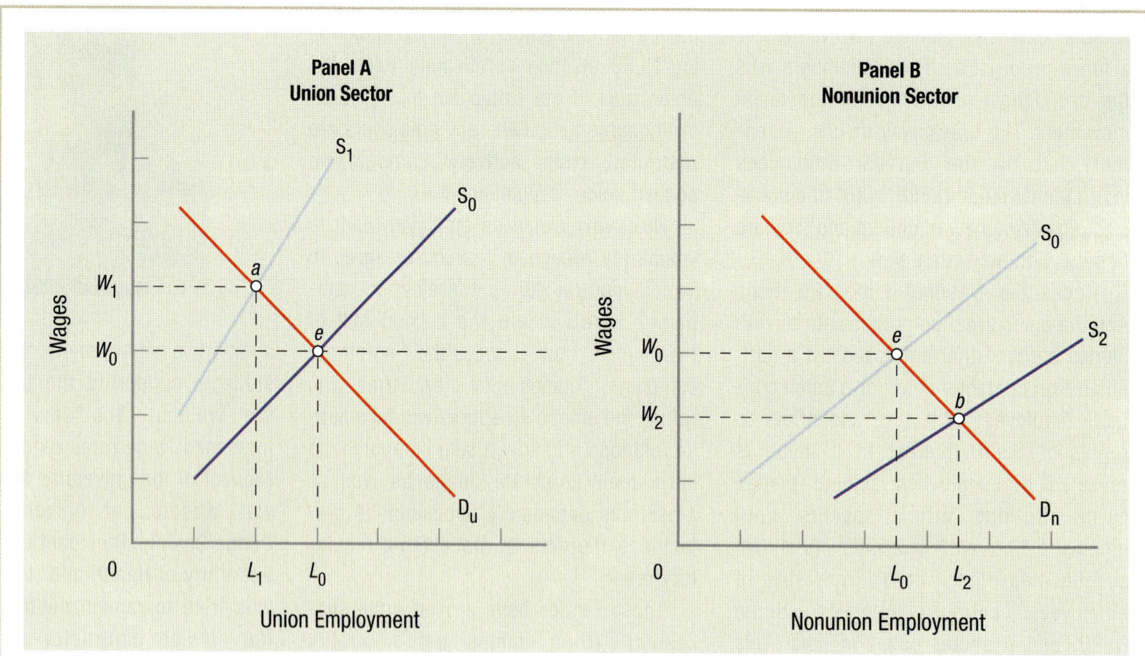


**FIGURE 7—Union Versus Nonunion Wage Differentials**

This figure illustrates the argument for union–nonunion wage differentials. Unions increase wages in their sectors by restricting entry into union jobs. Assuming the markets for unionized and nonunionized jobs begin at equilibrium, at point *e* in both panels, union and nonunion wages are initially $W_0$. If the union successfully restricts supply to $S_1$ in panel A, union wages will rise to $W_1$, but employment will fall to $L_1$ (point *a*). Those workers released will have no choice but to move to the nonunion sector represented in panel B, thus increasing its supply to $S_2$. Equilibrium in the nonunion sector thus moves to point *b*, where more workers ($L_2$) are employed at a lower wage ($W_2$). The result is a wage differential equal to $W_1 - W_2$.

This figure shows how unions are able to increase the wages in their sectors by restricting entry into union jobs. The markets for both unionized and nonunion labor begin at equilibrium, at point *e* in both panels of Figure 7. Thus, union and nonunion wages are initially equal, at $W_0$. If the union successfully restricts supply to $S_1$ in panel A, union wages will rise to $W_1$, but employment will fall to $L_1$ (point *a*). Those workers who are released have no choice but to move over to the nonunion sector represented in panel B, thus shifting its supply to $S_2$. Equilibrium in the nonunion sector moves to point *b*, where more workers ($L_2$) are employed at lower wages ($W_2$). The resulting wage differential, $W_1 - W_2$, is caused by successful collective bargaining in the union sector. Notice that this analysis is substantially the same as that for discrimination in the segmented labor force described in Figure 4 earlier.

Unions also have several ways of negotiating higher wages without losing members to unemployment. They can engage in activities that increase demand for their firm or industry's products, reduce the elasticity of demand for the product, or increase union productivity. One approach, advertisements encouraging consumers to buy the union label, fell flat.

More successful activities have included featherbedding, or forcing companies to hire redundant personnel. Examples include the firemen kept on trains long after diesels had replaced coal-burning steam engines, and the backup orchestras required by union contracts in New York City. This approach works in industries with significant pricing power, and in which labor costs are a small fraction of total costs. Under such conditions, it is simply not worth it for a firm to fight union demands for a few extra positions.

Union–nonunion wage differentials vary by the union, occupation, industry, and historical period. In general, average union wages are 10% to 20% higher than the average nonunion wage. Union wage effects are most pronounced among blue-collar workers and service employees. These differentials suggest that unionization may tend to reduce the inequities inherent in labor markets.

## Evolving Labor Markets and Issues

Labor markets, like all other markets, change with time and the wishes of their participants. Over the last three decades, the entry of women into the labor force has been a major factor spurring economic growth. Over this same period, two-earner families increased so that today over half of all families with small children are two-earner households.

These demographic changes have shifted the focus of labor politics from union bargaining to issues such as telecommuting, family leave policies, affirmative action, and the question of how much employers should pay for medical benefits. As Social Security begins to look more fragile and the baby boomers begin flooding the retirement ranks, employer retirement packages will undoubtedly receive even more attention.

Immigration, legal and illegal, has caught the attention of labor economists. The United States, unlike Europe, has relatively open borders. Some argue that we need new immigrants to do the work that most Americans are unwilling to do. Other economists suggest that, in the absence of such inflows, salaries in these low-skill occupations would be high enough to attract the needed labor. In any case, immigrants are doing what they have done for centuries: entering the economy at lower skill levels and hoping that circumstances will be better for their children.

This great tide of immigrants into low-skilled, low-wage jobs, together with the growth of high-skilled, high-wage, high-tech jobs and the rise in dual-earner households, has resulted in growing income inequality. Executive pay scales compared to average salaries have exploded in the last decade. These pressures have renewed the debate surrounding income distribution and the welfare system. We discuss these issues in more detail in a later chapter.

CHECKPOINT

### LABOR UNIONS AND COLLECTIVE BARGAINING

- Unions are typically organized around a craft or an industry.
- Unions and the managers of firms must bargain "in good faith."
- Secondary boycotts occur when unions put pressure on a neutral second firm to not process the products of the intended target. They were outlawed by the Taft-Hartley Act.
- In a closed shop, only union members are hired. In a union shop, nonunion workers can be hired, but they must join the union within a specified period. An agency shop permits both union and nonunion workers, but the nonunion workers must pay union dues.
- Union wage differentials are between 10% and 20% higher.

**QUESTION:** Union negotiations always seem to run up against a "strike deadline." Are there incentives for both sides to put off a settlement until the very last moment?

Answers to the Checkpoint question can be found at the end of this chapter.

## Key Concepts

Investment in human capital, p. 288
Screening/signaling, p. 291
On-the-job training, p. 292
General training, p. 292
Specific training, p. 292
Economic discrimination, p. 295
Segmented labor markets, p. 296
Secondary boycott, p. 302
Closed shop, p. 302
Union shop, p. 303
Agency shop, p. 303
Right-to-work laws, p. 303

## Chapter Summary

### Investment in Human Capital

Workers invest in themselves by going to school or learning a trade. Firms invest in workers through OJT or in-house training for employees. The value of these activities can be analyzed using investment analysis.

Investments in education involve the direct costs of education and forgone earnings. The benefits of such investments are then spread over the individual's working life.

Anything that reduces the availability of funds will reduce investments in human capital. The demand for human capital, meanwhile, is influenced by an individual's abilities and learning capacity. Human capital improves an individual's productivity, thereby resulting in higher lifetime earnings. Productivity thus links education and earnings.

Some economists suggest that investments in human capital do little more than serve as screening or signaling devices for employers. With this view, a college degree is merely a proxy for trainability, discipline, good work habits, and intelligence.

On-the-job training falls into two categories: general and specific training. General training improves productivity at all firms, while specific training improves productivity only at one specific firm. Firms rarely provide general training, but firms will provide specific training if the returns are high enough.

## Economic Discrimination

Economic discrimination occurs whenever workers of equal ability and productivity are paid different wages or otherwise discriminated against in the workplace because of their race, color, religion, gender, age, national origin, or disability. Lower wages, segregation into different occupations, and restrictions on entry into professions are all examples of economic discrimination.

Gary Becker concluded that employers who discriminate lose profit opportunities, so competitive pressures should end this discrimination. Competitive forces, however, may not be enough to end discrimination because of the significant costs associated with hiring and firing and otherwise restructuring a firm's workforce. Some workers, moreover, are less mobile than others. If this is true of a group of workers, such as women, this could lead to wage differences that are not clearly discriminatory.

Another approach to analyzing economic discrimination in labor markets rests on the existence of segmented markets. Various forces can segment workers from different groups into different, noncompeting sectors of the labor market. The labor market can be split into primary and secondary markets (the dual labor market hypothesis); it can be broken into predominantly male and female jobs (the job crowding hypothesis); or it can be split into union and nonunion or unemployed workers (insider-outsider theory).

## Labor Unions and Collective Bargaining

Labor unions are legal associations of employees formed to bargain collectively with employers over the terms and conditions of employment.

Collective bargaining provides workers with increased job security, a more structured work environment, and potentially higher wages. In return, monthly dues must be paid to the union, flexibility on the job is often restricted, and infrequently strikes are required, resulting in a loss of wages and possible job loss.

# Questions and Problems

## Check Your Understanding

1. Would unions be more likely to successfully organize firms in highly competitive markets or firms with monopsony power? Why or why not?
2. Why are colleges filled with young people rather than middle-aged individuals? If interest rates rose to over 10%, would this have any impact on the number of people attending college or its composition?
3. Why would it be so difficult to unionize part-time and contract employees (independent contractors)?
4. When there is discrimination in the labor market, who loses? Why? Why is it harder to discriminate when both labor and product markets are competitive?

## Apply the Concepts

5. When a company uses resources to train staff or subsidize tuition for employees, it is clearly investing in human capital. However, this investment is treated as current spending (cost of selling or producing goods) rather than investment. Should these activities be treated as investments and be reflected in the investment statistics of the economy?
6. Why do we all work Monday through Friday? Why not stagger the workweek and reduce highway congestion and pollution?
7. Americans work on average 400 hours more (roughly 10 weeks) each year than German or French workers. What might be some of the reasons for this?

8. Has globalization made it more difficult for unions to negotiate higher wages? Why or why not?

9. We saw in the previous chapter that wage rates rose when productivity rose. Unions now face serious foreign competition that restricts its ability to simply use its bargaining strength to increase wages. What can unions do to increase the productivity of its members to make it easier to bargain for higher wages?

10. Does it seem reasonable that a certain portion of the benefits of a college education is essentially a way to show prospective employers that you are reasonably intelligent, trainable, and have a certain degree of discipline?

11. Some politicians during any election campaign offer proposals to make college more affordable by increasing subsidies through higher Pell grants and subsidizing reduced rate loans. If these policies come to pass, and college becomes less expensive, more people will attend college. What will this do to the rate of return on a college education?

12. If unions can raise wages 10% to 20%, as suggested by empirical studies, why doesn't everyone join a union?

13. The airline pilots union has been very successful in negotiating six-figure salaries for pilots. The unions representing flight attendants have not been nearly as successful. What probably accounts for the difference?

14. Why do we permit price discrimination with different ticket prices at movies based on age, or ladies' nights at bars (when women get in free or get cheaper drinks) or insurance where women sometimes pay more (health) or less (automobile), but we do not permit discrimination in wage rates?

15. It is often suggested that American businesses are at a competitive disadvantage because other countries supply health care to workers via the central government while big American companies have to pay for their employees' health insurance. If labor markets are essentially national and workers are paid wages and benefits, explain why American companies might only gain a short-term advantage if the government implemented a national health care alternative to health care insurance being part of the wage package. (Hint: If health care was provided nationally and workers had to buy insurance from the government or pay higher taxes, would they expect to get higher wages?)

## In the News

16. Two decades ago, General Motors was the top automobile firm in the United States, and as such a strong company, its profits seemed secure. During negotiations with the United Auto Workers (UAW), GM gave workers wage and benefit packages that were unsustainable, including the "job bank" that gave laid-off employees full pay until they were brought back. General Motors filed for bankruptcy in June 2009. As reported by the *New York Times* (January 25, 2010), "G.M. sold its good assets to a new government-owned company," and "The federal government will hold nearly 61 percent of the new company, with the Canadian government, a health care trust for the United Autoworkers union and bondholders owning the balance." How does this new ownership structure change the bargaining process for the UAW?

17. *The Economist,* March 4, 2006, reported that "a woman with middling skills who has a baby at age 24 loses $981,000 in lifetime earning compared with one who remains childless." If the woman waits a few years before having a baby, the figure is lower, but still large. What are the reasons that having children reduces women's earnings so much?

# Answers to Questions in CheckPoints

## Check Point: Investment in Human Capital

Letting in a large number of college-educated immigrants would drive the rate of return on college down as wages of college graduates would not grow very rapidly. The opposite would occur when unskilled immigrants enter, holding down the wages of those without college educations, leading to a growing gap between those with college degrees, increasing the rate of return to a college degree.

## Check Point: Economic Discrimination

Congress felt that most people who were discriminated against were unlikely to be able to afford an attorney. This provision encourages lawyers to take on these cases knowing that if they prevail, they will be paid.

## Check Point: Labor Unions and Collective Bargaining

Both sides work hard to get the best bargain for their constituents. There are incentives to continue negotiations up to the last moment to get the most and to appear to be driving a hard bargain. Strikes involve costs, and both sides use the threat of imposing these costs as a bargaining chip.

# Public Goods, Externalities, and Environmental Economics

Tim Foley Illustration

*We humans are about as subtle as the asteroid that wiped out the dinosaurs. . . . The damage we do is increasing. In the next 20 years, the population will increase by 1.5 billion. These people will need food, water and electricity, but already our soils are vanishing, fisheries are being killed off, wells are drying up, and the burning of fossil fuels is endangering the lives of millions. We are heading for cataclysm.*

APRIL 2001 GLOBAL SUPPLEMENT FROM *NEW SCIENTIST*

*Psychologically, the population explosion first sunk in on a stinking hot night in Delhi. The streets were alive with people. People eating, people washing themselves, people sleeping, people working, arguing and screaming. People reaching their hands in through taxi windows to beg. People sitting, people pissing. People hanging off buses. People driving animals through the streets. People, people, people.*

PAUL EHRLICH, *THE POPULATION BOMB*, 1968

*This is my long-run forecast in brief: The material conditions of life will continue to get better for most people, in most countries, most of the time, indefinitely. Within a century or two, all nations and most of humanity will be at or above today's western living standards. I also speculate, however, that many people will continue to think and say that the conditions of life are getting worse.*

JULIAN SIMON (1932–1998)

*At its most basic, all environmental policy involves a rearrangement of property rights.*

CHARLES PEARSON, *ECONOMICS AND THE GLOBAL ENVIRONMENT*, 2000

**After studying this chapter you should be able to:**

- ☐ Describe the market failures that lead to environmental problems.
- ☐ Describe the impact of negative and positive externalities on society.
- ☐ Describe the Coase theorem on social costs and the role transaction costs play in the optimal allocation of resources.
- ☐ Describe government failures in dealing with market failures.
- ☐ Recognize the importance of the discount rate in assessing the costs and benefits of environmental policies.
- ☐ Use marginal analysis to determine the optimal level of pollution.
- ☐ Describe the differences between command and control policies and market-based approaches to environmental regulation.
- ☐ Understand the economic issues surrounding global climate change.

**As the quotes above illustrate,** people have radically different ideas about how well we live and what impact human existence is having on the globe. Many environmentalists and others see the Earth as wasting away as human beings exhaust its natural resources, foul its air and water, and decimate animal species. Others optimistically regard advancing technologies, newfound efficiencies, and rising standards of living as signs that people are taking ever better care of the planet.

In 1980, Julian Simon offered the following bet:

> *This is a public offer to stake $10,000, in separate transactions of $1,000 or $100 each, on my belief that mineral resources (or food or other commodities) will not rise in price in future years adjusted for inflation. You choose any mineral or other raw material (including grain and fossil fuels) that is not government controlled, and the date of settlement.*

The bet was an open offer, but Simon aimed it at environmental activist Paul Ehrlich, author of *The Population Bomb.* Ehrlich and two other Stanford University colleagues accepted the bet in October 1980, selecting copper, chrome, nickel, tin, and tungsten for a 10-year period. Ehrlich noted that he would "accept Simon's astonishing offer before other greedy people jumped in," since the "lure of easy money can be irresistible."[1]

Ten years later, in October 1990, Ehrlich sent Simon a check for $576.07. The real value (adjusted for inflation) of the basket of minerals had gone down over the decade by $576.07. New sources of supply had been discovered, the tin cartel collapsed during the intervening period, and other minerals had become substitutes for some in the original five. Not only had the value of the five resources declined, the price of each one of the metals had fallen. Simon offered the same bet again, but Ehrlich declined.

Are there lessons to be drawn from this bet? Surely one is that forecasting economic and market conditions far into the future is difficult, at best. Another is that overly pessimistic predictions about growth and the environment almost always turn out to be wrong.[2] It is true that the Earth is finite in size, and the natural resources it contains are limited. Even so, economic growth is often accompanied by increasing efficiencies in resource use. Rising incomes and standards of living, moreover, are typically accompanied by falling population growth rates. Were it not for immigration, population would be declining in the United States today.

Many trends involving living standards and the environment are moving in the right direction, yet that does not mean all is well. Clearly, we still have many environmental problems that must be addressed, including global climate change, species extinction, overharvesting of fisheries, and overcrowding of our highways and parks at the national level.

Environmental economics is a discipline that applies the principles and methods of economics to the study of the environment and natural resources. This marriage of economics and the environment may seem like a stretch to some, but economists must already deal with the environment regularly; environmental and natural resources are frequently inputs into economic production, and at times are economic products or services. Resources such as coal, iron, and oil, for instance, are extracted from the Earth and moved directly into the production process. National parks and the restrictions on their use, meanwhile, show that the natural environment is itself a product that has value to us.

## Public Goods

We saw in Chapter 4 that markets do not always provide the socially optimal amount of a good at the socially optimal price. Either too much or too little of the good is produced, or it is offered at too high or too low a price. Before we dive into our discussion of how

[1] Bjorn Lomborg, *The Skeptical Environmentalist: Measuring the Real State of the World* (Cambridge: Cambridge University Press), 2001, p. 137.

[2] Both Simon's book *The Ultimate Resource 2* and Lomborg's book *The Skeptical Environmentalist* provide numerous examples.

## By the *Numbers*

### The Environment and Sustainability

Having a sustainable economy will likely require a focus on energy other than fossil fuels, finding better methods to recycle waste, and developing methods to manage the natural environment.

**Hybrid car sales** have been rising since 2000 and are slated to grow even faster in the near future.

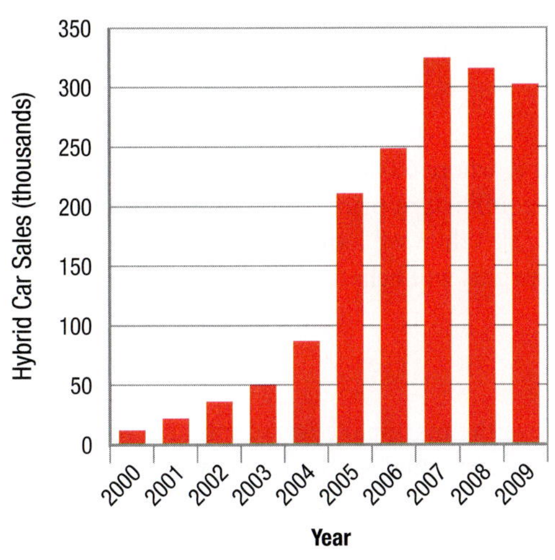


**80,000 European fishing boats** are fishing out Atlantic cod using advanced technology that makes finding and catching fish easier.

Jeff Rotman/Alamy

**120 million**
Number of electric bicycles in China

**342%**
Increase in wind energy generated in the United States between 2004 and 2009

**$39**
Annual savings from replacing five 60-watt bulbs with compact fluorescents

**1.5 (0.2)**
Acres of arable land per person in the United States (and China)

**40¢**
Gasoline tax in the United States

**$4.25**
Gasoline tax in Britain

**Millions of tons of solid waste** fill landfills, while some is recovered and recycled. To be sustainable, the United States must recover more in the future.

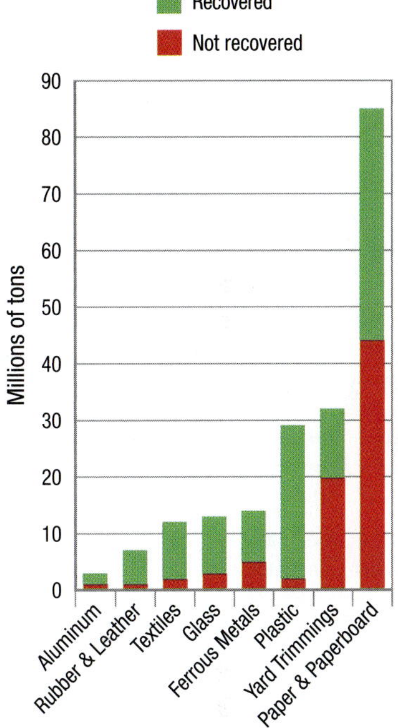


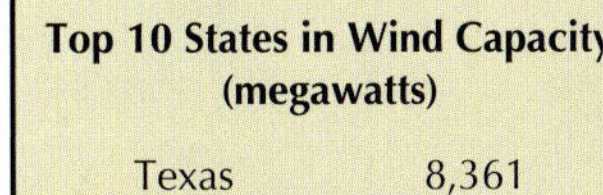

**Top 10 States in Wind Capacity (megawatts)**

|  |  |
|---|---|
| Texas | 8,361 |
| Iowa | 3,043 |
| California | 2,787 |
| Minnesota | 1,805 |
| Washington | 1,575 |
| Oregon | 1,408 |
| New York | 1,264 |
| Colorado | 1,068 |
| Kansas | 1,014 |
| Illinois | 915 |

Panoramic Images/Getty Images

market failures can lead to environmental problems, let us first briefly review the concepts of consumer and producer surplus. These two concepts are often used to measure the impact environmental policies have on social welfare.

## A Brief Refresher on Producer and Consumer Surplus

Recall that demand curves represent, in dollar terms, the utility consumers receive from a given product. Supply curves represent the marginal cost to producers of producing goods and services; a supply curve similarly represents the opportunity cost to society of producing and distributing a given product. Figure 1 depicts a market for a product that has no environmental impacts. The supply curve thus represents the full marginal cost to society of producing this product.

### Consumer Surplus

**Consumer surplus:** The difference between what consumers (as individuals or the market) would be willing to pay and the market price. It is equal to the area above market price and below the demand curve.

Equilibrium in Figure 1 is found at point *e*, where 6,000 units are sold for $30 each. The area under the demand curve and above equilibrium price is **consumer surplus** and is equal to $90,000 [(($60 − $30) × 6,000)/2]. When we look at changes in environmental policy, monitoring changes in consumer surplus will help us measure the gains or losses to consumers from policy changes.

### Producer Surplus

**Producer surplus:** The difference between market price and the price at which firms would be willing to supply the product. It is equal to the area below market price and above the supply curve.

The area below equilibrium price and above the marginal cost (supply) curve is **producer surplus,** the revenue firms get over the costs they would willingly bear to supply the product. It is equal to the triangle shown in Figure 1 and is equal to $60,000 [(($30 − $10) × 6,000)/2].

### Social Welfare

**Social welfare:** The sum of consumer and producer surplus.

**Social welfare** is equal to consumer surplus plus producer surplus. This is the value produced over what would be required for the product to be brought to market; it is equal to $150,000 in Figure 1. This is often referred to as the net welfare resulting from the production and consumption of this product. An activity or policy that increases net welfare is considered efficient.

Markets provide us with most of the products and services we consume. Under competitive conditions, as we have seen, markets will provide consumers with what they want

**FIGURE 1—Consumer and Producer Surplus**

The product in this market has no environmental impacts. Supply represents the full marginal costs to society of producing this product. The area under the demand curve but above the equilibrium price of $30 is consumer surplus. The area above the marginal cost curve and below equilibrium price is producer surplus. Total social welfare is equal to consumer surplus plus producer surplus.

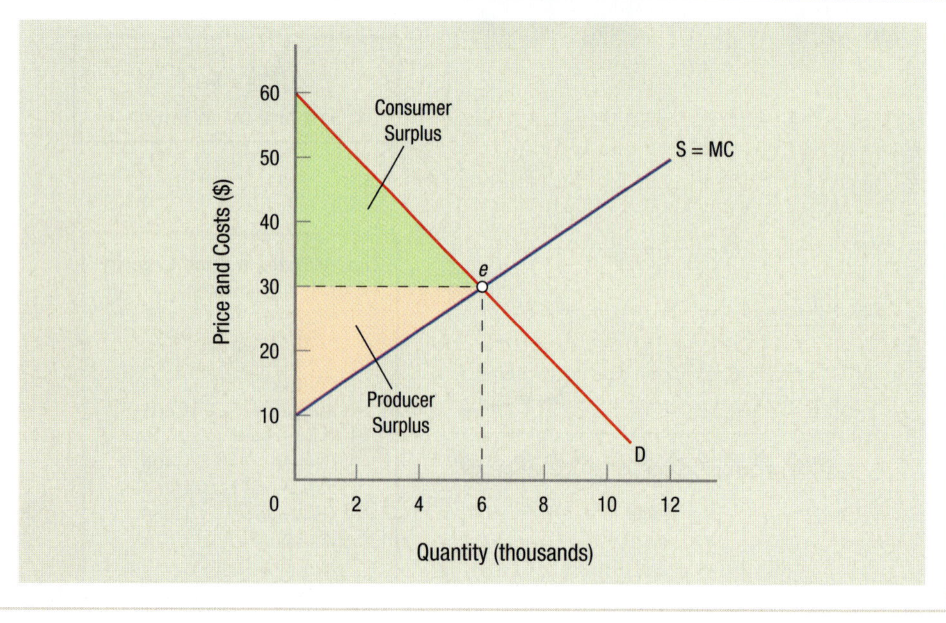

at the lowest possible opportunity costs. In what follows, we examine some of the reasons why a competitive market allocation may not always be the best solution for society. These reasons all fall under the heading of **market failures,** and they underpin our environmental laws and regulations.

**Market failures:** When markets are not competitive or involve public goods, externalities, or common property resources, markets will fail to provide the optimal level of output, and will provide output at too high or low a price.

As noted earlier, market failure occurs when a market does not provide the socially optimal amount of a good at the socially optimal price. Either too much or too little of the good is produced, or it is offered at too high or too low a price. There are three main causes of market failure: The product or service in question is a *public good,* the good is a *common property resource,* or the production or consumption of the product or service creates *externalities.*

## What Are Public Goods?

Pure **public goods** are nonrival in consumption, and exhibit nonexcludability. **Nonrivalry** means that the consumption of a good or service by one person does not reduce the utility of that good or service to others. **Nonexcludability** means that it is not feasible to exclude some consumers from using the good or service once it has been provided.

**Public goods:** Goods that, once provided, no one person can be excluded from consuming (i.e., nonexclusion), and one person's consumption does not diminish the benefit to others from consuming the good (i.e., nonrivalry).

**Nonrivalry:** The consumption of a good or service by one person does not reduce the utility of that good or service to others.

**Nonexcludability:** Once a good or service is provided, it is not feasible to exclude others from enjoying that good or service.

By way of contrast, a can of Coke is a rival product. When you drink a can of Coke, no one else can drink that same can. Airline flights exhibit excludability—when a flight is full, no one else is allowed to board the plane. But consider a lighthouse. Once it is built and in operation, all ships can see the lighthouse and use the light to avoid obstacles. One captain's use of the lighthouse does not prevent another from using it, nor can a ship realistically be excluded from using the lighthouse's services. Hence, the lighthouse is a public good. Other examples of public goods include national defense, accumulated knowledge, standards such as a national currency, protection of property rights, vaccinations, mosquito spraying, and clean air. Table 1 provides a taxonomy of private and public goods.

**TABLE 1** Taxonomy of Private and Public Goods

| | Property Rights | |
|---|---|---|
| **Characteristics of Goods** | **Exclusive** | **Nonexclusive** |
| **Rival** | Pure private good<br>■ Airline seat<br>■ Ice cream bar | Common property resource<br>■ Ocean fishery<br>■ Highways |
| **Nonrival** | Public good with exclusion<br>■ Cable TV<br>■ National park | Pure public good<br>■ National defense<br>■ Law enforcement |

Since consumers cannot be excluded from a public good once it is provided, they have little incentive to pay for the good in question. Instead, most will essentially be free riders. Think of the lighthouse again. If you have a ship and cannot be excluded from the benefits the lighthouse provides, why should you contribute anything to its upkeep? But if everyone took this position, there would be no support for the lighthouse, and it would go out of business. With free riders, private producers cannot hope to sell many units of a good, and so they have no incentive to produce it. Private markets will therefore fail to provide public goods, even if the goods are things everyone would like to see produced. This is why the government must get involved in the provision of products and services that have significant public good characteristics.

## The Demand for Public Goods

Assessing the public's demand for public goods is clearly different from that of private goods where we found market demand by horizontally summing private demands. But the fact that once a public good is supplied, no one can be excluded from consuming it, and

**FIGURE 2—Demand for Public Goods: Vertical Summation of Individual Demand Curves**

For public goods, exclusion is not possible, individuals can consume the good simultaneously, and market demand is found by summing vertically. Market demand for public goods is really a willingness to pay curve since the government will have to provide the good and levy taxes to pay the cost. The total demand for the public good is shown by the heavy line labeled $D_{Public\ Goods}$ and is the vertical summation of individual demands.

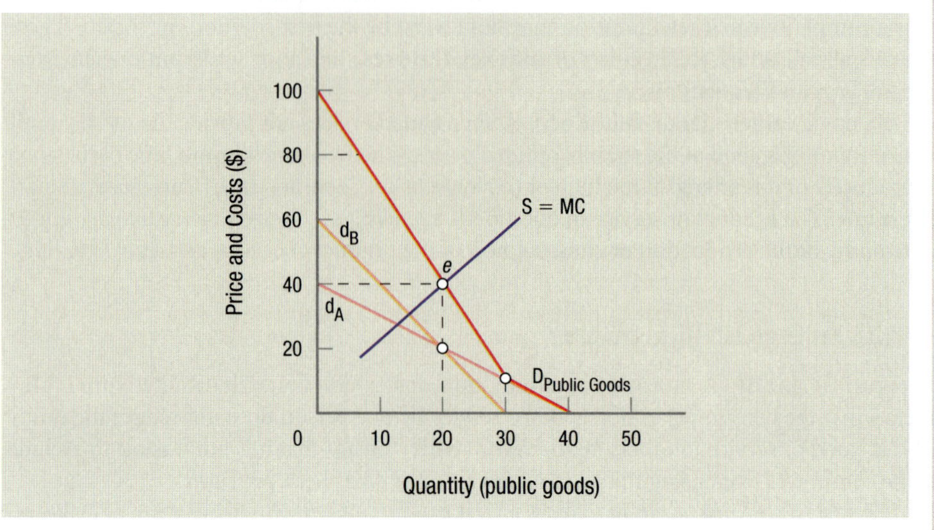


one person's consumption does not affect another's, plays a crucial role. Figure 2 provides a solution to finding the demand for public goods.

Figure 2 shows demand for a public good by two different consumers. Individual A wants none when the price is $40 and is willing and able to buy 40 units when the price approaches zero. Individual B wants none when price is $60 and only is willing to buy 30 units when the price nears zero. Because each consumer can consume any given amount of a public good at the same time, the total demand for a public good is found by summing the individual demands *vertically.* To see why, consider when both individuals demand 20 units. This is the point where the two demand curves cross, and both are willing to pay $20 for 20 units. Thus, total demand for 20 units is $40. The total demand for the public good in Figure 2 is shown by the heavy line labeled $D_{Public\ Goods}$ and is the vertical summation of individual demands.

Notice how this differs from our discussion of market demand curves for private goods. There others could be excluded from consuming any good we bought, so demands were horizontally summed. In contrast, with public goods, exclusion is not possible, so we both can consume the good simultaneously, and market demand is found by summing vertically. Market demand for public goods is really a *willingness to pay curve,* because the government will have to provide the good and levy taxes to pay the cost.

## Optimal Provision of Public Goods

Providing the optimal amount of public goods is easy in theory and is illustrated in Figure 2. The supply of public goods is equal to the marginal cost curve (S = MC) shown in the figure. Just like the competitive market equilibrium we covered earlier, optimal allocation is where MC = P, and in this instance, it is 20 units of the good at a total price of $40 (point *e*). In this example, the taxes are split equally between individuals A and B. Determining how much tax each person should (or would be willing to) pay is hampered by the fact that once the public good is provided, no one can be excluded, so individuals will be unwilling to reveal their true preferences for the good because it might mean they would have to pay a higher tax.

In reality, providing public goods involves the political process. This means that politicians, bureaucrats, special interest groups, and many others generate the decisions on how much of any particular public good to provide. The typical provision process uses some form of **cost-benefit analysis** (CBA). Since the demand for a public good represents the benefits to society and the supply curve represents society's costs, equating marginal benefits and marginal costs yields the optimal amount. But estimating the demand (benefits)

**Cost-benefit analysis:** A methodology for decision making that looks at the discounted value of the costs and benefits of a given project.

from public goods and their costs can be a complex process. Since people cannot be excluded from the good, once provided, people have little incentive to reveal their true preferences. Cost-benefit analysis was developed to help policymakers bridge this gap. The following section is a brief overview of CBA to give you an idea of the issues involved.

## Cost-Benefit Analysis

Cost-benefit methodology was introduced into the Flood Control Act of 1936 and eventually grew more sophisticated; by 1960, it became an important element of the decision-making process of the Office of Management and Budget (OMB). The OMB's circular A-94 provides a straightforward summary of what CBA is designed to accomplish:

> *The standard criterion for deciding whether a government program can be justified on economic principles is net present value—the discounted monetized value of expected net benefits (i.e., benefits minus costs). Net present value is computed by assigning monetary values to benefits and costs, discounting future benefits and costs using an appropriate discount rate, and subtracting the sum total of discounted costs from the sum total of discounted benefits. Discounting benefits and costs transforms gains and losses occurring in different time periods to a common unit of measurement. Programs with positive net present value increase social resources and are generally preferred. Programs with negative net present value should generally be avoided. Although net present value is not always computable (and it does not usually reflect effects on income distribution), efforts to measure it can produce useful insights even when the monetary values of some benefits or costs cannot be determined.*

Cost-benefit analysis provides a rational model for policy decisions, forces a focus on alternatives (opportunity costs), draws conclusions about the optimal *scale* of projects, makes the intergenerational aspects explicit through discounting, and takes into account the explicit preferences of individuals. The explicit steps of a CBA are:[3]

- Specify the set of alternative projects.
- Decide whose benefits and costs count (the standing question).
- Catalogue the impacts and select measurement indicators.
- Predict the impacts quantitatively over the life of the project.
- Monetize (attach dollar values to) all impacts.
- Discount benefits and costs to obtain present values.
- Compute the net present value of each alternative.
- Perform sensitivity analysis (change some variables to see impacts).

One of the major difficulties with CBA for big public projects and environmental programs is measuring nonmarket or intangible aspects of projects. Economists have developed several different approaches to measuring these intangibles.[4] Some environmental goods have a bundle of characteristics, and some of them resemble market traded goods, so determining values in this way provides an estimate. Another approach looks at the travel costs people incur to recreational sites. The operating assumption is that these costs infer something about the value of parks and other recreational sites. Another approach is to look to the funds and effort people expend to avert harm. If you live by an airport and install double-pane glass to reduce noise, or purchase safety equipment (helmets, car seats, or bigger automobiles) to avoid injury from auto accidents, you are providing some evidence of the value (cost) of the harm.

---

[3] Anthony E. Boardman et al., *Cost-Benefit Analysis: Concepts and Practice* (Upper Saddle River, NJ: Pearson-Prentice Hall), 2006, p. 8.

[4] Organisation for Economic Co-operation and Development, *Cost-Benefit Analysis and the Environment* (OECD), 2006.

A more controversial method is contingent valuation. This method uses direct surveys to determine the value of such environmental qualities as species and forest preservation, biodiversity, and water quality projects. Those surveyed are provided an open-ended willingness-to-pay question or an iterative bidding questionnaire. The open-ended approach might ask how much you would pay (in increased taxes) to keep the Preble's meadow jumping mouse from going extinct. The iterative approach provides an initial value: If you agree with that number, then the number is iteratively increased until you say no; if you initially answer no, the number is reduced until you express willingness to pay. The numbers are then aggregated by the population to get total values.

Cost-benefit analysis, then, is a rational approach to valuing some things that are hard to put a price on, because people have no incentive to reveal their willingness to pay. This is what makes the decision to provide public goods so difficult.

## Common Property Resources

Commonly held resources are subject to nonexclusion but are rival in consumption. The market failure associated with commonly owned resources is often referred to as "the **tragedy of the commons.**"[5] The tragedy here is the tendency for commonly held resources to be overused and overexploited. Because the resource is held in common, individuals race to "get theirs" before others can grab it all.

**Tragedy of the commons:** Resources that are owned by the community at large (e.g., parks, ocean fish, and the atmosphere) and therefore tend to be overexploited because individuals have little incentive to use them in a sustainable fashion.

One example of commonly held resources giving rise to problems involves oil fields. Oil reservoirs often span the surface property of many landowners. Because oil reservoirs are regarded as common property, each surface owner has an incentive to drill as many wells as possible and to pump out oil as rapidly as possible. Having too many wells pumping too quickly, however, reduces the oil field's water and gas pressure, thus reducing the total recoverable oil from the reservoir. Each owner's decision to drill a well therefore imposes an external cost on the other owners of land over the reservoir. At one point, this problem grew so severe that it resulted in passage of the 1935 Connolly "Hot Oil" Act. This Act restricted drilling, regulated the number and location of oil wells, and capped pumping rates.[6]

Road congestion is another illustration of the tragedy of the commons. Figure 3 shows a market for usage of a road that is fully used and is right at the tipping point

**FIGURE 3—Road Congestion**

Assume this road is fully used and is right at the tipping point before becoming congested. Demand for driving on this road is $D_0$, and the marginal cost of using the road—gas, time, and auto expenses—is $MC_0$. Equilibrium is at point *e*, with $Q_0$ miles a day being driven. Consumer surplus is area $P_0ae$ for the typical driver. When a new driver begins using the road, this increases the marginal cost of driving to $MC_1$ for everyone, since the tipping point has been passed, and the road is now congested. Consumer surplus shrinks because of overuse of this common good.

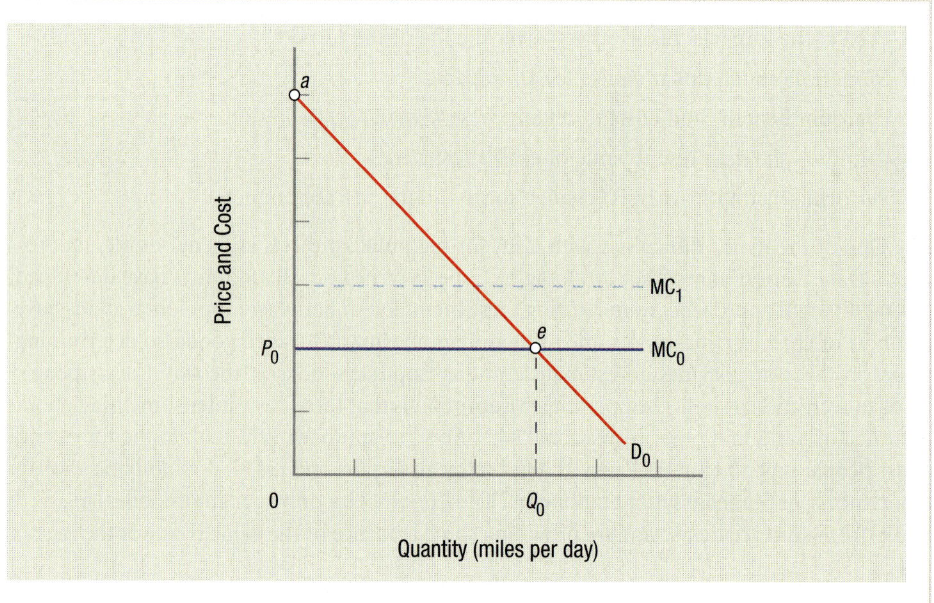


[5] Garrett Hardin, "The Tragedy of the Commons," *Science* 162, 1968, pp. 1243–1248.

[6] Daniel Yergin, *The Prize* (New York: Simon & Schuster), 1991.

## *Issue:* Tragedy of the Commons: The Perfect Fish

**Ocean fisheries** are another good example of the problem of common property resources. Fish in the ocean were once in excess supply; there was no need to restrict the use of this resource. As the global demand for fish has risen, improved fishing technologies have allowed fishing boats to increase their hauls. Because many of the world's fisheries are still unregulated, one population after another has been fished out. Each fishing fleet grabbed as much as they could, and there was no incentive to hold back. The situation is clearly unsustainable, and indeed, as fish populations have shrunk, so have fishing fleets.

The Patagonian toothfish, as it is known, lives up to 50 years and can weigh over 200 pounds. This big, ugly, gray-black fish lives in the cold deep waters of the Southern Ocean near Antarctica, and in the 1990s, it became the signature dish of top restaurants in the United States, Japan, and Europe. It became so popular that during the mid-1990s, the annual catch was estimated at 100,000 metric tons.

How did such an ugly fish with such an unappetizing name become so popular? In the late 1970s, Lee Lantz, a Los Angeles fish merchant, visited the docks in Valparaiso, Chile, and spotted a toothfish. He bought a sample and cooked it, but the oily flesh had little taste. Most fish have bladders that they inflate to adjust their buoyancy, reducing the energy it takes to move up and down in the water. Toothfish do not have bladders, but use oil (lighter than water) secreted to create buoyancy. Also, Patagonian toothfish are predators, waiting in ambush for prey. Thus, they do not need a lot of blood rushing through their system. As a result, toothfish meat is oily and white like cod. It is this oiliness—along with the fact that it absorbed any spice—that made the toothfish a hit with restaurants. No matter what you do, you can't overcook it, and this made it popular with busy restauranteurs and chefs.

As the reputation of the toothfish spread, so did the take in the ocean. Because this fish is found in the Southern Ocean, where it is cold and where few venture, it was highly susceptible to poaching. A full hold of toothfish could bring a million dollars wholesale!

Soon it became clear to many that the species was being seriously overharvested, and chefs began to notice that the filets were getting smaller. The tragedy of the commons was playing out again. So the chefs from the best restaurants organized a boycott campaign called "Take a Pass on Chilean Sea Bass." (The Patagonian toothfish was renamed Chilean sea bass by Lee Lantz in 1977.)

Rodez/Getty Images

Today, limits are set on the catch, and Chilean sea bass is coming back from the brink of extinction. But as G. Bruce Knecht reported in his book *Hooked,* keeping pirates from poaching the toothfish is a dangerous job for the Australian Customs patrols. The toothfish's problem is that it is the perfect fish.

Source: G. Bruce Knecht, *Hooked: Pirates, Poaching, and the Perfect Fish* (Emmaus, PA: Rodale), 2006.

before becoming congested. In Figure 3, demand for driving on this road is $D_0$, and the marginal cost to use the road—gas, time, and auto expenses—is initially $MC_0$. Equilibrium is at point *e*, with $Q_0$ miles per day driven. Consumer surplus is area $P_0ae$ for the typical driver.

Now assume a new driver begins using the road. This increases the marginal costs of driving to $MC_1$ for everyone, since the tipping point has been passed, and the road is now congested. Consumer surplus shrinks because of overuse of the commons. Note that the new driver did not take these external costs into consideration; the driver assumed that MC would be equal to $MC_0$, not $MC_1$.

Possible solutions to common property resource problems can involve establishing private property rights, using government policy to restrict access to the resource, or informal organizations that restrict each user's benefits from the resource. Reduced congestion, for example, could be achieved by raising the tax on gasoline, subsidizing bus or rapid transit travel, or privatizing roads and allowing the owners to charge tolls.

## *Nobel Prize*

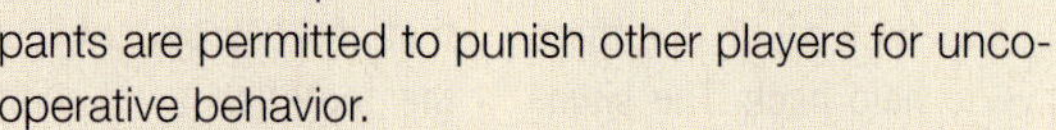

### Elinor Ostrom

When economists talk about common property (or pool) resources, they typically discuss the tragedy of the commons and suggest a solution that involves privatization or central government takeover and management of the resource. Elinor Ostrom was awarded the 2009 Nobel Prize in Economics for challenging this conventional wisdom. The Nobel committee noted that her studies of *user-managed* "fish stocks, pastures, woods, lakes, and groundwater basins" led to the conclusion that the outcomes often do not lead to the "tragedy" forecasted by conventional theory.

Born in 1933 at the depth of the Great Depression and growing up during World War II when her family and others had a victory garden, she began to see how people could cooperate to solve a resource issue. In high school while on the debate team, she concluded that "debate was a fabulous thing to learn . . . especially for appreciating that there are at least two positions to every issue." Completing her doctorate in political science in 1965, her dissertation looked at a case where saltwater was seeping into western Los Angeles' water basin. A group of individuals formed a water association to solve the problem by creating rules and injected water along the coast. Without the efforts of this group, the water basin would have been irreparably harmed. This experience led her to look at other common resource problems from a new perspective.

Luciano Leon/Alamy

She used field studies and thousands of case studies by other social scientists along with game theory to determine how these informal organizations evolved and what conditions make them successful. The game that consistently reflected her case studies was a repeated *n*-person prisoner's dilemma where participants are permitted to punish other players for uncooperative behavior.

Her work has determined the requirements for sustainable user-managed common pool property, including (a) rules must clearly define entitlement to the resource, (b) adequate conflict resolution measures must exist, (c) an individual's duty to maintain the resource must be in proportion to their benefits, (d) monitoring and sanctioning must be by users or accountable to users, (e) sanctions should be graduated—mild for a first violation and stricter as violations are repeated, (f) governance and decision processes must be democratic, and (g) self-organization is recognized by outside authorities. When these institutional conditions are met, user management of common pool resources typically is successful.

Professor Ostrom's insights and research have opened up a third policy alternative to prevent the tragedy of the commons. Her work will be particularly important as nations begin working together to reduce the potential harm from global climate change, maybe our biggest common resource problem to date.

**CHECKPOINT**

### PUBLIC GOODS

- Social welfare is equal to consumer plus producer surplus.
- Pure public goods are nonrival in consumption, and once the good is provided, no one can be excluded from using it.

- The demand for public goods is found by vertically summing individual demand curves.
- Optimal provision of public goods is found where the marginal benefit of public goods (demand) is equal to the marginal cost of provision.
- Determining the optimal provision of public goods is easy in theory, but difficult in practice. Cost-benefit analysis (CBA) helps policymakers allocate scarce public funds to competing projects.
- Common property resources have the characteristics of nonexcludability but are rival. This typically leads to overuse and overexploitation.

**QUESTIONS:** In the June 1, 2006, issue of the *New York Times,* the Humane Society ran a full-page ad with a picture of a baby harp seal and the headline, "Did You Know That Over 300,000 Baby Seals Were Killed in Canada This Year for Their Fur?" Below the picture, it reads, "Over 1,000 U.S. Restaurants, Grocers and Seafood Distributors Do and They're Doing Something to End It." The ad then asks you to join them and 256,000 individuals who are boycotting Canadian seafood until commercial seal hunting ends. Is this essentially the equivalent of a secondary boycott that labor unions once used but was subsequently outlawed by the Taft-Hartley Act? Does this boycott seem fair to Canadian fishermen who do not hunt seals? How does this boycott differ from the one by restaurants to save the Chilean Sea Bass?

Answers to the Checkpoint questions can be found at the end of this chapter.

## Externalities

**Externalities,** often called *spillovers,* arise when two parties engage in a transaction, yet some third party uninvolved in the transaction either benefits or is harmed. If the market exchange imposes costs on others, it is called a *negative externality* or an *external cost.* If a third party benefits, this is a *positive externality* or an *external benefit.* Negative externalities include air and water pollution, littering, and chemical runoff that affect fish stocks. Some examples of activities that generate positive externalities are education, beehives next to apple orchards, and quieter lawn equipment.

**Externalities:** The impact on third parties of some transaction between others where the third parties are not involved. An external cost (or negative externality) harms the third parties, whereas external benefits (positive externalities) result in gains to them.

Both producers and consumers can create externalities and can feel the effects of them. The matrix in Table 2 identifies the origin and impact of some common external effects. The effects are negative unless otherwise noted.

**TABLE 2 Externalities by Origin and Impact**

| Origin of Externality | Impact: Victims and Beneficiaries of Externality — Consumers | Producers |
|---|---|---|
| **Consumers** | ■ Auto air pollution<br>■ Littering<br>■ Park congestion<br>■ Smoking<br>■ Private schools and colleges (beneficial) | ■ Private auto use that adds to road congestion, slowing down commercial traffic |
| **Producers** | ■ Factory air pollution on wilderness hikers<br>■ Clear cutting of forest trees<br>■ Agricultural pesticide runoff affecting trout fishing | ■ Honey bees and apple orchards (beneficial)<br>■ Commercial pollution that harms commercial fishing |

## Negative Externalities

Again, when a market transaction harms people not involved in the transaction, negative externalities exist. Pollution of all sorts is the classic example. Firms and consumers rarely consider the impact their production or consumption will have on others. For simplicity, we focus on the pollution caused by production. Figure 4 shows a typical market.

**FIGURE 4—The Negative Externality Case**

Supply curve $S_P$ represents the manufacturer's supply when only its private costs are considered, ignoring the external costs imposed on others through pollution. Market equilibrium is 30 units sold at \$6 each (point *e*). If each unit of production results in \$2 in pollution costs, then supply curve $S_S$ represents the true social costs to manufacture the product. Socially optimal output is 20 units sold at \$7 each (point *g*).

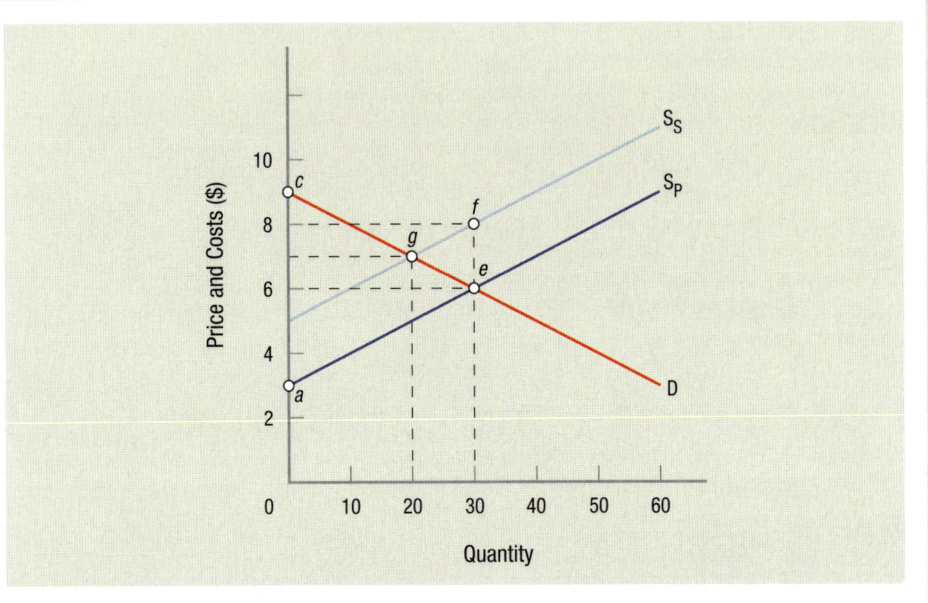


Supply curve $S_P$ represents the manufacturer's supply curve when only its private costs are considered (the subscript P stands for private). This supply curve ignores the external costs imposed on others from the pollution generated during production. These external costs might include toxic wastes dumped into lakes or streams, smokestack soot, or the clear cutting associated with timber harvests. Ignoring these costs, market equilibrium is at point *e*, where the product is priced at \$6 and 30 units are sold. Total consumer surplus plus producer surplus is equal to \$90 [((\$9 − \$3) × 30)/2] or area *ace*.

Now let's assume that for every unit of the product produced, pollution costs (or effluent) equal to \$2 is generated. Thus, at an output level of 30 units (point *e*), \$60 in pollution costs (or negative externalities) is generated. Subtracting this \$60 in pollution from total consumer and producer surplus results in \$30 of real social benefit from this output.

This means the true marginal cost of producing the product, including pollution costs, is equal to supply curve $S_S$ (the subscript S stands for social). This new supply curve incorporates both the private and social costs of production, thus shifting supply upward by an amount equal to *ef*, or \$2. Equilibrium moves to point *g*, where 20 units of the product are sold at \$7. This is the socially optimal production for this product given the pollution it creates.

So why is it better for society than when 30 units were produced? First, notice that when output is 20, the cost of the last unit produced—including the cost of pollution—is \$7 (point *g*). This is just equal to the value society attributes to the product. Hence, consumers get just what they want when all costs are considered. Second, notice that consumer and producer surplus at an output of 20 units is \$40 [((\$9 − \$5) × 20)/2]. More important, it is now higher than the \$30 of consumer and producer surplus minus the pollution costs when output was 30 units (point *e*).

Each unit of output produced beyond 20 costs more—taking both private and social costs into account—than its value to consumers.

Imagine a situation in which external costs exceed the consumer and producer surplus from consuming the good. Such a situation might arise when an extremely toxic substance is a by-product of production. Society is better off not permitting production of this good.

What has this analysis shown? First, when negative externalities are present, an unregulated market will produce too much of a good at too low a price. Second, optimal pollution levels are not zero, except in the case just mentioned of extremely toxic agents. In Figure 4, the socially optimal production is 20 units with total pollution costs of \$40. Pollution reduction as a good has no price. Even so, we can infer a price, known as a shadow price, equal to the marginal damages—\$2 in this case. As we will see later, prices for the "rights to pollute" will provide us with better approximations of the costs of pollution.

## The Coase Theorem

Ronald Coase was awarded the Nobel Prize in Economics for his seminal paper, "The Problem of Social Cost." Coase has written few articles—less than a dozen—but, as economist Robert Cooter noted, though "most economists maximize the amount they write, Coase maximized the amount others wrote about his work."[7] Indeed, Coase's paper on social cost is one of the most cited works in economics.

Reducing output to the optimal level results in gains to "victims" because pollution is reduced. The reduction in output, however, causes losses to producers. The presence of losses and gains to two distinct parties, Coase argued, introduces the possibility of bargaining, provided the parties are awarded the property rights necessary for negotiation.

The **Coase theorem** states that if transaction costs are minimal (near zero), the resulting bargain or allocation of resources will be efficient—output will decline to the optimal level—regardless of the initial allocation of property rights. The socially optimal level of production will be reached, that is, no matter whether polluters are given the right to pollute or victims are given the right to be free of pollution.

**Coase theorem:** If transaction costs are minimal (near zero), a bargain struck between beneficiaries and victims of externalities will be efficient from a resource allocation perspective. As a result, the socially optimal level of production will be reached.

Even so, the distribution of benefits or income will be different in these two cases. If victims, for example, are assigned the property rights, their income will grow, but if polluters are assigned these rights, the income of victims will decline.

As Coase noted, for these efficient results to be achieved, transaction costs must approach zero. This means it must be possible for polluters and victims to accurately determine their collective interests, then negotiate and enforce an agreement. In many situations, however, this is simply not feasible. In cases involving air pollution, for instance, polluters and victims are so widely dispersed that negotiating is impracticable. In other cases, individuals may be both victims and polluters, making it difficult for an agreement to be reached and enforced.

Another problem associated with assigning rights to one party or another might be called *environmental mugging*. Polluters might at first threaten to pollute more than they anticipate, for instance, simply to increase their bargaining leverage and, ultimately, their income. Victims, in like manner, might assert exaggerated environmental concerns, again simply to bid up their compensation. Alternatively, if negotiations should prove unfruitful, polluters might start lobbying for legal relief, thus devoting their money to rent-seeking behaviors rather than buying pollution-abatement equipment.

Although the private negotiations Coase proposed have their limitations, his insights proved to be a turning point in environmental policy. Coase challenged the prevailing practice of assuming victims had a right to be pollution-free. His analysis stressed that a clear assignment of rights and responsibilities by the law might not be needed. No matter how property rights were assigned, if information was good and transaction costs were low, efficiency would result. Given the costs of pollution, affected parties have an incentive to work out efficient agreements.

This idea was so radical when Coase published "The Problem of Social Cost" in 1960 that another Nobel Prize winner, George Stigler, wondered "how so fine an economist

[7] Peter Passell, "Economics Nobel to a Basic Thinker," *New York Times*, October 16, 1991, p. D6.

## *Nobel Prize*

### Ronald Coase

University of Chicago professor Ronald Coase won the Nobel Prize in Economic Sciences in 1991 for "his discovery and clarification of the significance of transaction costs and property rights" in the institutional structure and functioning of the economy. According to his analysis, traditional microeconomic theory was incomplete because it neglected the costs of executing contracts and managing firms. To Coase, these "transaction costs" were the principal reason that firms existed. Economic actors found it cost efficient to create a more complex organization to minimize transaction costs.

Coase also analyzed the economy in terms of the *rights* to use goods and factors (inputs) of production rather than the actual goods and factors themselves. These "property rights" could be defined in different ways according to contracts and rules within organizations. Coase introduced the concept of property rights as an important element of economic analysis. His work stimulated interest in the intersection between economics and legal theory for which the University of Chicago is well known.

JG Photography/Alamy

Born in 1910 in Willesden, a suburb of London, Coase attended the London School of Economics (LSE), where he earned a Bachelor of Commerce degree in 1932. During 1931–1932 he was awarded the Sir Ernest Cassel Traveling Scholarship by the University of London to research industrial organization in the United States. During that year he traveled throughout America to visit business and industrial plants.

From the fall of 1932 to 1939, he taught at the Dundee School of Economics, the University of Liverpool, and the London School of Economics. Returning to LSE after the war, he earned a Doctor of Science degree in economics in 1951. Coase later cited his first seminar in economics with the commerce professor Arnold Plant as a life-changing experience. "What Plant did was to introduce me to Adam Smith's hidden hand," he wrote. "He made me aware of how a competitive economic system could be coordinated by the pricing system."

Becoming disillusioned with the future of British socialism and taking "a liking for life in America," he migrated to the United States in 1951 and taught at the University of Buffalo. Coase's 1960 article on "The Problem of Social Cost" questioned whether governments could efficiently allocate resources for social purposes through taxes and subsidies. He argued that arbitrarily assigning property rights and using markets to reach a solution was usually better than costly government regulation. This was instantly controversial and led to a lengthy exchange of papers in economics journals.

In 1964, Coase joined the faculty at the University of Chicago and became editor of the *Journal of Law and Economics*. The journal was an important catalyst in developing the economic interpretation of legal issues.

could make such an obvious mistake." Coase was later invited to the University of Chicago to discuss his ideas; Stigler described what transpired:

> *We strongly objected to this heresy. Milton Friedman did most of the talking, as usual. He also did much of the thinking, as usual. In the course of two hours of argument the vote went from twenty against and one for Coase to twenty-one for Coase. What an exhilarating event! I lamented afterward that we had not had the clairvoyance to tape it.*

The Coase theorem has changed the way economists look at many issues, not just environmental problems. In cases where the costs of negotiation are negligible and the number of parties involved is small, economists and jurists have begun to look more closely at legal rules assigning liability.

## Positive Externalities

When private market transactions generate benefits for others, a situation opposite to that just described results. Figure 5 illustrates a positive externality. Market supply curve S and private demand curve $D_P$ represent the market for private college education. Equilibrium is at point *e*, with $Q_e$ students enrolling. Society would clearly benefit, however, if more people earned college educations: Tax revenues would rise, crime rates would fall, and a better-informed electorate might produce a better-operating democracy.

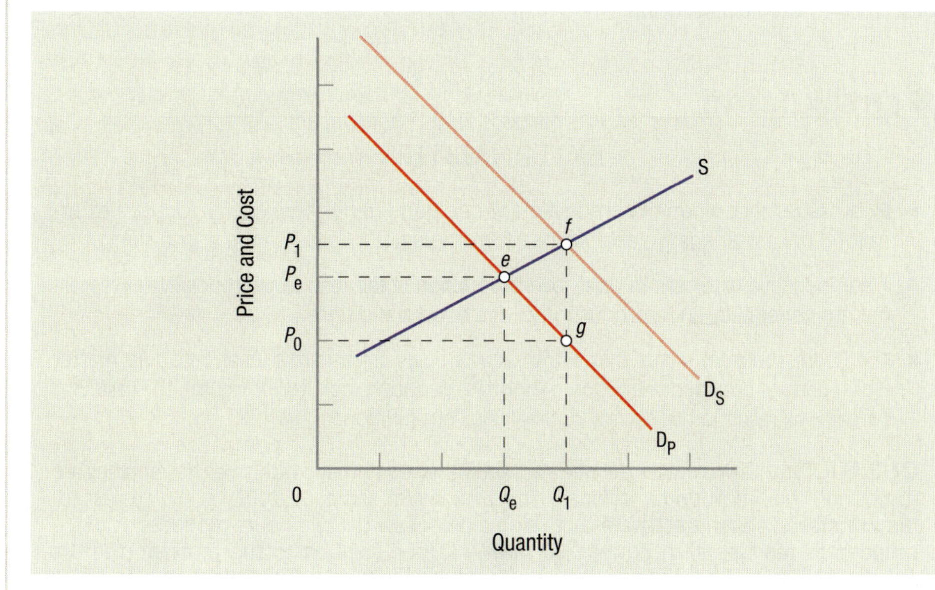


**FIGURE 5—The Positive Externality Case**

Market supply curve S and private demand curve $D_P$ represent the market for private college education. Equilibrium is at point e, and students enrolled are $Q_e$. Society would benefit, however, if more people would go to college. Social demand curve $D_S$ represents the private demand for college education plus the external benefits that flow from it. Socially optimal enrollment would be $Q_1$ (point *f*).

Taking these considerations into account, social demand curve $D_S$ is the private demand for college education plus the external benefits that flow from it. Socially optimal enrollment would be $Q_1$ (point *f*). How can society tweak the market so that more students will attend college? Students will demand $Q_1$ levels of enrollment only if its price is $P_0$ (point *g*). The public must therefore subsidize private education by *fg* to draw its price down to $P_0$.

The U.S. government recognizes that private education benefits society at large when it provides low-interest student loans, grants, and scholarships to students attending private colleges and universities.

## Limitations

Some caveats about our analysis of externalities need to be noted. First, producer and consumer surpluses are good measures of society's welfare if all incomes are weighted equally or the distribution of income is optimal. When income is unequally distributed, gross unfairness created throughout society swamps any improvements from efficiency. Thus, measures of efficiency like consumer and producer surplus can become unconvincing for public policy. Since no one can agree on the correct distribution of income, economists generally ignore this question and focus on efficiency.

Second, the discussion has focused on the pollution that arises from production, not consumption. The results applied to congestion and littering, however, would be substantially the same.

Third, the examples presented here have assumed, moreover, that pollution has no cumulative effects. And, indeed, smaller amounts of pollution effluence may just flow into the ocean, for instance, with no lasting effects. But the same will not hold true for sustained higher pollution levels.

Fourth, for convenience, we have assumed we can assign specific amounts to the damages resulting from pollution. In practice, this is not always easy to do.

Fifth, we have assumed pollution can be reduced only by reducing output, but in real markets, there are other ways to reduce pollution.

Despite these limitations, the analysis presented here helps us focus our attention on ways of reducing the harm done to society by negative externalities.

In summary, the market failures associated with public goods, externalities, and commonly held resources all lead to overuse of resources and environmental degradation. To address these problems, collective or government action is required. Solutions range from privatization—assigning property rights—to government regulations or prohibitions, described in the next section.

**CHECKPOINT**

### EXTERNALITIES

- Externalities arise when the production of one good generates benefits (positive externalities) or costs (negative externalities) for others not involved in the transaction.
- When negative externalities exist, overproduction is the result. When positive externalities are generated, underproduction of the good is the norm.
- The Coase theorem states that if transaction costs are minimal (near zero), no matter which party is provided the property rights to pollution (polluter or victim), the resulting bargain will result in the socially optimal level of pollution.

**QUESTION:** Lawn mowers, chainsaws, and other equipment with small gas engines are surprisingly high-polluting machines. *The Economist* (June 9, 2007, p. 36) reported, "Regulators in California estimate that using a chain-saw for two hours produces as much pollution as ten cars each driving 250 miles." As one solution to the problem, the Los Angeles air quality management district offered residents a $400 electric lawn mower for $100 if they traded in an old gas burning mower. Describe and show graphically why the Los Angeles air quality district is making this offer.

Answers to the Checkpoint question can be found at the end of this chapter.

## Environmental Policy

We have seen that market failure can lead to excessive amounts of products that pollute or generate other negative externalities. This section looks at the broad approaches to environmental policy available to the government, focusing on emissions. First, we look briefly at government failure. Government policies can fail to improve such situations if the incentives of politicians and policymakers are not aligned with the public interest. Balanced public policies must take intergenerational effects into account. Then, we look at the actual policies used by government regulators to reduce pollution, ranging from direct intervention and control to the use of various market instruments to reduce emissions. Policymakers also occasionally use publicity and moral suasion to encourage polluters to voluntarily reduce emissions.

### Government Failure

**Government failure:** The result when the incentives of politicians and government bureaucrats do not align with the public interest.

Market failure is one reason unregulated markets may produce inequitable or inefficient results. Government policies, however, do not always make things better. The terrible environmental record the Eastern Bloc countries accumulated during the Soviet era illustrates that, in environmental policy as elsewhere, governments—like markets—can fail.

**Government failure** occurs when (1) public policies do not bring about an optimal allocation of resources and/or (2) the incentives of politicians and government bureaucrats are not in line with the public interest. As Nobel Prize winner George Stigler has argued, economic regulation often benefits the group being regulated at the expense of the larger public. Government failures are often more acute in nondemocratic societies. Yet, even in the United States, public policy formation involves a struggle among interest groups, lobbyists, politicians, large corporate interests, and the public at large. The sausage calling itself "public policy" that results from this tug-of-war is often not pretty.

Government failure may result from the practical inability of policymakers to gather enough information to set good policies. Water pollution, for instance, is well understood, resulting in fairly obvious regulatory policies, but the same is not true for issues like global climate change. Even if we all agree that the Earth is getting warmer and humans are partly to blame, controversy remains about the adequacy of public policy to address this problem. Though calls for government action—"there ought to be a law"—are often justified, we do well to maintain a healthy skepticism about the ability of the public sector to solve our problems.

## Intergenerational Questions

Should politicians consider the interests of voters whose great-grandparents have not yet been born? Environmental issues raise complex questions involving how resources are to be allocated across generations. Some resources, such as sunlight, are continual and renewable. Others, like forests, fisheries, and the soil are exhaustible yet renewable, though they can be exhausted if overexploited. And some resources are nonrenewable, such as oil and coal. These resources are finite and cannot be renewed, but their available stock can be expanded through exploration or the use of new technologies that allow greater extraction or more efficient use.

When we develop environmental policies, we need to consider and evaluate different possible futures. Discounting was discussed earlier, but Figure 6 is a reminder of the effects discount rates have on the present value of a fixed payment that will come due at some date in the future. For environmental policies, the discount rate we choose is crucially important.

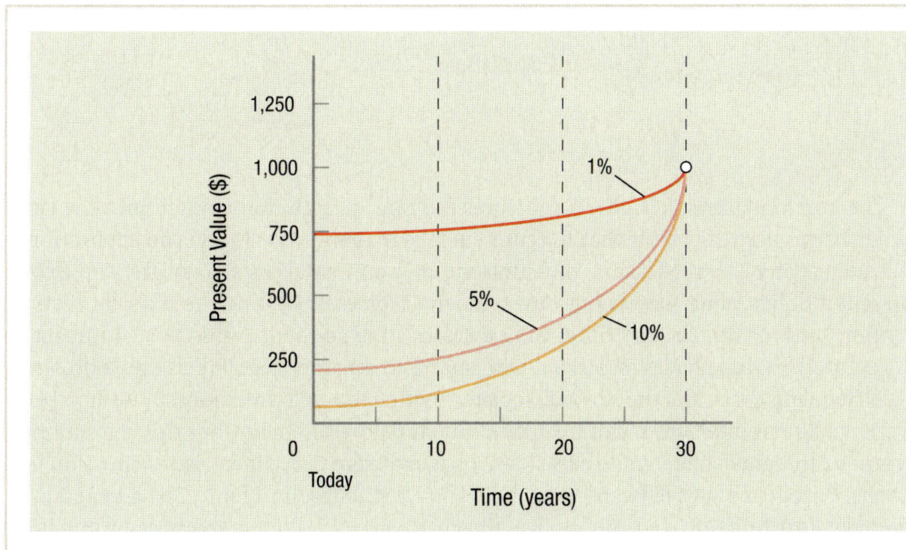


**FIGURE 6—Present Value of $1,000 to Be Paid in 30 Years Discounted at 1%, 5%, and 10%**

This figure is a reminder of the effects discount rates have on the present value of a fixed payment that will come due at a future date. A higher discount rate means the value today of a future payoff will be lower. The higher the discount rate we choose, the lower the value we place on the environmental damage to be suffered by future generations. The lower our discount rate, the more we are willing to protect the health of the future environment.

A higher discount rate means the value today of a future payoff will be less. At a 10% discount, a payment of $1,000 in 30 years is worth only $42 today, whereas discounting the same $1,000 at 1% yields a present value of $748. The higher the discount rate we choose, the lower the value we place on the environmental damage to be suffered by future generations. The lower our discount rate, conversely, the more we are willing to protect the health of the future environment. As always, crafting good public policies requires striking a balance between the two.

## Socially Efficient Levels of Pollution

We have already seen that some pollution is acceptable to society. To require that no one pollute, period, would bring most economic activity as we know it to a halt. Yet, pollution damages our environment. The harmful effects of pollution range from direct threats to our health coming from air and water pollution to reductions in species from deforestation.

In general terms, the more pollution we create, the greater the harm to the environment. The damages that come from pollution are a cost we incur for living: To be alive is to generate some pollution. Our focus is on marginal damage, which resembles the marginal cost curves we have studied earlier. The marginal damage (MD) curve in Figure 7 shows the change in damages that come from a given change in emission levels. Notice that as emissions levels rise, the added damages rise.

**FIGURE 7—Marginal Damages and Marginal Abatement Costs**

The marginal damage curve (MD) shows the *change* in damages that come from a given *change* in emission levels. The horizontal axis measures pollution. Note that $E_0$ is the maximum pollution that can occur without environmental cleanup. The vertical axis measures the environmental costs of this pollution. Marginal abatement costs curve (MAC) begins at zero at $E_0$, then rises as emission levels are reduced (moving leftward from $E_0$). Socially optimal pollution is $E_S$, at a cost to society of $C_e$ (point *e*).

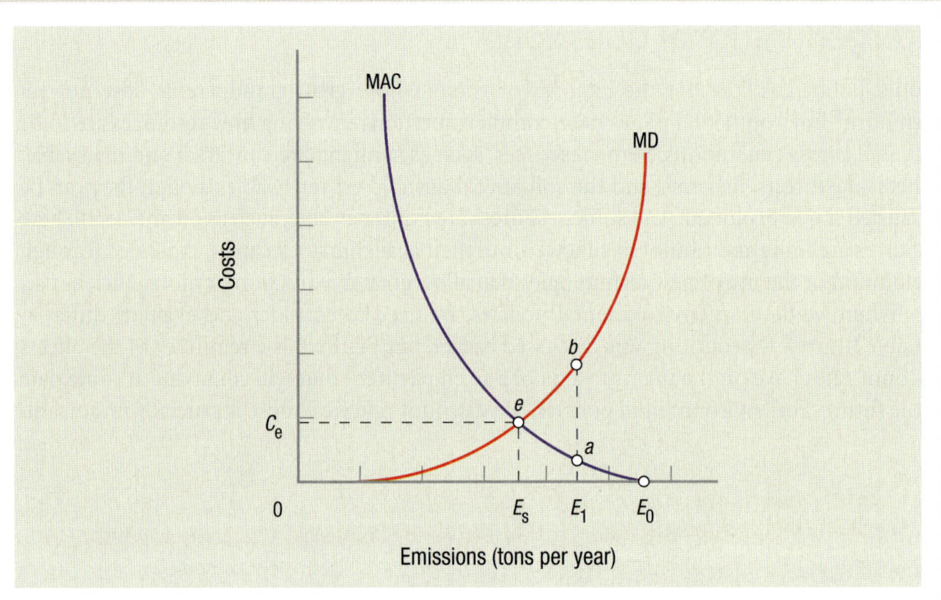


The horizontal axis of Figure 7 measures the tons of pollution emitted into the environment (tons per year). Note that $E_0$ represents the maximum pollution (no environmental cleanup at all). The vertical axis measures the environmental costs in dollars. These costs represent a dollar value for various environmental losses, including the physical costs of pollution (asthma attacks and other lung diseases), the aesthetic losses (visual impact of clear cutting), and the losses associated with species reduction (we all miss the dodo bird).

Abatement costs are the costs associated with reducing emissions. A utility plant dumping effluent into a river can treat the effluent before discharge, but this costs money. In Figure 7 marginal abatement costs (MAC) begin at zero at $E_0$, then rise as emission levels are reduced (moving leftward from $E_0$). The MAC curve in Figure 7 is a generalized abatement cost function, but in practice, the costs vary for different sources of pollution and the technologies available for reducing them. Chemical plants face different problems than utilities that release hot water into rivers. Cooling the water before release clearly requires a different technology—and is much easier—than eliminating toxic chemicals from effluent flow.

The socially optimal level of pollution in Figure 7 is $E_S$, at a cost to society of $C_e$ (point *e*). To see why this is so, assume we are at pollution level $E_1$. The cost to reduce another unit of emissions is equal to point *a* (measuring on the vertical axis), while the damage that would result from this pollution is shown at point *b*. Since $b > a$, society is better off if emissions are reduced. Once we begin reducing emissions below $E_S$, however, abatement costs overtake marginal damages, or the costs of cleanup begin to outweigh the benefits.

The total damage from pollution in Figure 7 is represented by the area beneath the marginal damages curve and to the left of $E_S$. Total abatement costs, meanwhile, are equal to the area beneath the marginal abatement costs curve and to the right of $E_S$. Combined, these two costs represent the total social costs from emissions. We turn now to consider how environmental policy can ensure that emissions approach this optimal level.

## Overview of Environmental Policies

Over the years, many types of environmental policies have been developed in response to different problems, covering the spectrum from centralized control to decentralized economic incentives. To be effective, all environmental policies must be efficient, fair, and enforceable, and they must provide incentives for improvement in the environment.

As a general rule, the more centralized an environmental policy, the more likely it represents a **command and control** philosophy. This means a centralized agency sets the rules for emissions, including levels of effluents allowed, usable technologies, and enforcement procedures. Command and control policies usually set standards of conduct that are enforced by the legal and regulatory system. Abatement costs at this point become compliance costs of meeting the standards. Standards are popular because they are simple, they treat all firms in an industry the same way, and they prevent competing firms from polluting.

**Command and control policies:** Environmental policies that set standards and issue regulations, which are then enforced by the legal and regulatory system.

At the other end of the spectrum are **market-based policies,** which use charges, taxes, subsidies, deposit-refund systems, or tradable emission permits to achieve the same ends. Examples of this approach include water effluent charges, user charges for water and wastewater management, glass and plastic bottle refund systems, and tradable permits for ozone reduction. We begin with a brief look at command and control policies, contrasting them with abatement taxes, then look at the case for tradable emission permits.

**Market-based policies:** Environmental policies that use charges, taxes, subsidies, deposit-refund systems, or tradable emission permits to achieve environmental ends.

### Command and Control Policies

Policymakers determine the pollution control or abatement that is best, then introduce the most efficient policies to achieve those ends. Figure 8 shows the supply and demand for pollution abatement. Demand curve $D_A = MB_A$ represents society's demand for abatement; it is a reflection of the marginal damage curve we looked at earlier. Note that the demand curve for abatement is negatively sloped because the *marginal benefit* from abatement declines as the environment becomes cleaner. The gains from an ever cleaner environment eventually become smaller and smaller because of the law of diminishing returns.

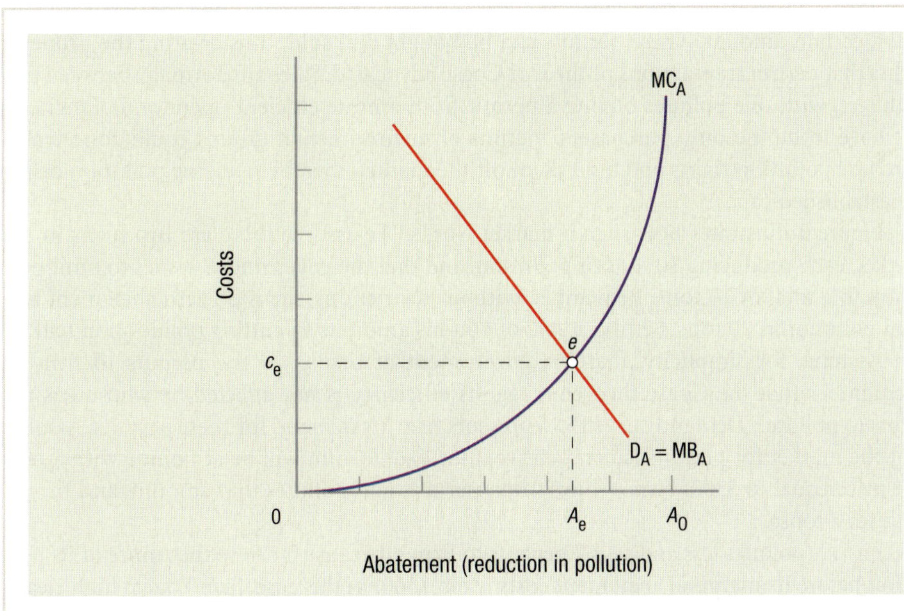


**FIGURE 8—Marginal Cost of Abatement and Abatement Demand**

Demand curve $D_A$ represents society's demand for abatement. The marginal benefit from abatement ($MB_A$) declines as the environment becomes cleaner, since the gains from an ever cleaner environment become smaller and smaller (diminishing returns). The marginal costs of abatement are the costs of reducing pollution. These costs rise with abatement efforts and become high as zero pollution $A_0$ is approached (again, because of the law of diminishing returns, or increasing costs). Optimal abatement is $A_e$, costing $c_e$. This means optimal pollution, $A_0 - A_e$, is greater than zero.

The marginal costs of abatement are the costs of cleaning up pollution. These costs rise with abatement efforts and become high as zero pollution, $A_0$, is approached. Optimal abatement comes at $A_e$, costing $c_e$. This means optimal pollution, $A_0 - A_e$, is greater than zero. Command and control policies could set $A_e$ as the abatement requirement and then set the right standards to meet this requirement. Aiming for abatement higher than $A_e$ would be inefficient, since marginal costs would exceed benefits.

Setting abatement requirements (or standards) equal to $A_e$ in Figure 8 is a classic example of command and control policies. Alternatively, policymakers could enact an effluent tax equal to $c_e$ per unit of pollution. Firms would adopt pollution controls up to $A_e$, because the costs to reduce pollution to this point are less than the tax. Firms would emit only $A_0 - A_e$ pollution.

Again, command and control policies that set rigid standards for polluters have long been a favorite of policymakers. Yet, this approach can lead to inefficiencies, since different industries may emit the same (or equivalently dangerous) substances but face different technical problems and costs in reducing their pollution. To minimize the cost of reducing pollution, each source of pollution needs to be reduced to the point where the marginal cost of abatement is equal for all sources.

## Market-Based Policies

Economists have increasingly begun to argue that market-oriented, or indirect, approaches to environmental policy are more efficient than command and control policies. One of the most popular and effective of these indirect approaches is marketable or tradable permits.

***Marketable or Tradable Permits*** Economists first proposed marketable or tradable permits when environmental laws were first being debated and enacted in the 1960s and 1970s. Environmental regulators essentially ignored this suggestion until the 1990s.

Today, tradable permits are used to reduce water effluents in the Fox River in Wisconsin, Tar-Pamlico River in North Carolina, and Dillon Reservoir in Colorado. One of the most successful uses of marketable permits for air pollution has reduced the sulfur dioxide ($SO_2$) emissions in the Midwest that create acid rain in the East. Originally, the cost of this cleanup was expected to be significant, and the price of permits did start out fairly high. As the cleanup has progressed, however, technical advances have steadily reduced abatement costs, causing the price of the permits to decline sharply. This success with $SO_2$ has spawned the use of similar permits in Europe, where opposition to marketable permits historically was strong.

Marketable permits require that a regulatory body set a maximum allowable quantity of effluents allowed, typically called the "cap," and issue permits granting the "right" to pollute a certain amount. These permits can be bought and sold, thus creating the property rights that permit transactions of the sort Coase advocated. Sales are normally between two polluters, with one polluter buying a permit from a more efficient operator. Polluters do not have to be the only purchasers: victims or environmental groups could conceivably purchase pollution rights and hold them off the market, thereby reducing pollution below the established cap.

Figure 9 illustrates how such a market works. We assume there are two firms in the market, each producing 10 tons of pollution, and that the government wishes to limit pollution to a total of 10 tons. Remember, without restrictions, firms do zero abatement and total pollution is 20 tons. Setting a goal of 10 tons amounts to cutting pollution in half.

Assume, for simplicity, that the government at first gives the permits to firm X. (Remember that the Coase theorem suggests efficiency is not affected by who owns the rights to pollute.) Demand curve $D_Y$ represents firm Y's demand for these permits. Assume that the market for permits is competitive, thus equilibrium will be at point *e* with a permit price equal to \$300. Firm Y buys seven permits and pollutes that amount, and firm X pollutes 3 tons.

Firm X pollutes less and sells 7 permits to firm Y because it can reduce more of its pollution before its marginal abatement costs reach \$300. In this case, firm Y faces high cleanup costs that reach \$300 a ton at 3 tons. Thus, it buys 7 tons of abatement from firm X.

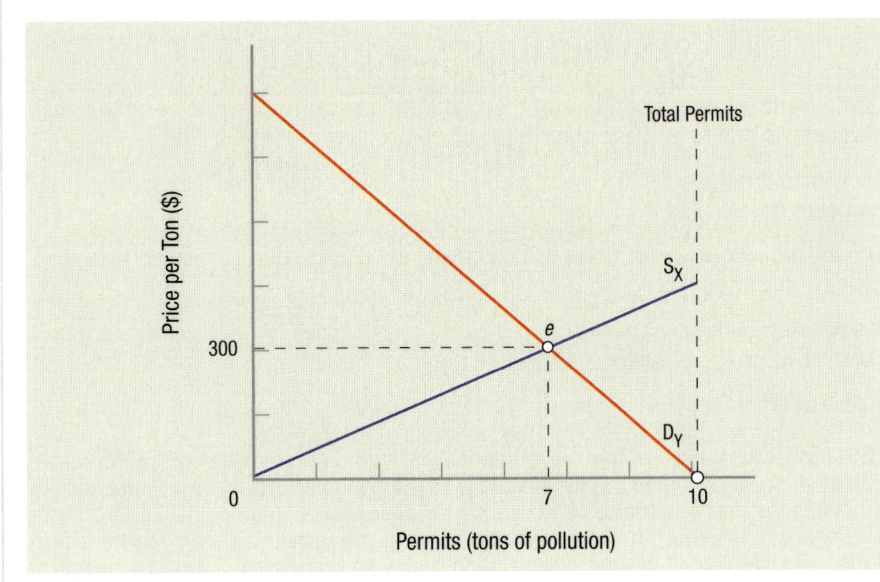


**FIGURE 9—Tradable Permits**

This figure illustrates how a market for tradable pollution permits works. Again, assume there are only two firms (X and Y) in the market and the government wishes to limit total pollution to 10 tons. Without restrictions, both firms do zero abatement and pollution is 20 tons. Setting a goal of 10 tons therefore amounts to cutting pollution in half. Assume the government gives the permits to firm X. Demand curve $D_Y$ represents firm Y's demand for these permits. Given a competitive market for permits, equilibrium will be at point *e* with a permit price equal to $300. Firm Y buys seven permits and pollutes that amount, and firm X emits 3 tons of pollution.

Firm X in this example ends up with the revenue from permit sales, while firm Y's income declines by the same amount ($2,100). Auctioning off the permits produces the same result, but the government gets the revenue.

Keep in mind that regulators could have set a $300 per ton tax on effluents and achieved the same result. One advantage of permits over taxes is that no knowledge of marginal abatement costs is needed to ensure that the tax rate is optimal. The market price of permits will adjust to variances in abatement costs; all the regulator must determine is how much to reduce pollution levels. If reducing pollution by a certain amount, regardless of the cost, is the goal, permits will achieve this goal.

***Other Market-Based Policies*** We have looked at two of the most frequently used market-based policies, taxes/charges and marketable permits. Emission taxes and charges have been used for water effluents, waste management, pesticide packaging, batteries, tires, and other products and processes. User charges are the most common way to finance wastewater treatment facilities.

Federal subsidies, the flip side of taxes or charges, are used when local communities do not have the resources for pollution control. Marketable permits have been most successful in programs to reduce air pollution, as well as those targeting acid rain and ozone reduction. Deposit-refund systems have been used mainly for recyclable products such as cans, bottles, tires, and batteries.

Over the years, most environmental policies have been of the command and control variety. The 1969 Clean Air Act focused on specific forms of air pollution—particulates, carbon dioxide ($CO_2$), and so forth—and established air quality standards. Standards were set for vehicles and stationary sources of pollution including power plants and factories.

Today, economic or market-based approaches to environmental policy are considered more efficient than command and control policies. Most environmental agencies, however, in this country and abroad, have not used these tools until recently.

One reason for this is probably that many people in the regulatory and environmental communities resist viewing environmental resources as commodities to be subjected to market forces of supply and demand. It is market failures, after all, that led to environmental decay in the first place; why would we want to put the environment on the market? Many pollutants, moreover, are frequently mixed together and their individual impacts are difficult to determine. Consequently, setting the right tax rate or issuing the right number of allowable permits is difficult. Finally, some policymakers balk at giving corporations the right to pollute, even for a limited amount of pollution.

**CHECKPOINT**

### ENVIRONMENTAL POLICY

- Government failure can occur when politicians and government do not have the right incentives to bring about an optimal allocation of resources.
- The discount rate chosen for environmental policies determines the intergenerational impact of policy.
- The socially optimal level of pollution occurs where the marginal damage is equal to the marginal abatement costs.
- Policymakers determine the optimal pollution levels and then often use command and control policies to set the most efficient regulations or levels of abatement.
- Tradable permits use market forces to bring pollution within limits set by regulators.

**QUESTION:** In the 1960s, the Environmental Protection Agency (EPA) initially focused on pollution, principally air and water. In a similar way, the Bureau of Land Management initially honed in on multiple-use of public lands with an emphasis on timber harvests. Today both agencies have a much broader focus that looks at maintaining an ecological balance, and their activities extend beyond pollution and timber to species and habitat protection. Is this just another example of bureaucratic mission creep?

Answers to the Checkpoint question can be found at the end of this chapter.

## Economic Aspects of Climate Change

Antar Dayal/Getty Images

Global warming may turn out to be the mother of all market failures.[8] There is a growing scientific consensus that "without big changes in emission rates, global warming from the buildup of greenhouse gases is likely to lead to substantial, and largely irreversible, transformations of climate, ecosystems and coastlines later this century."[9] The economics surrounding this issue are complex and require almost all of the tools of microeconomics we have studied, and then some.

A sense of urgency surrounds climate change because the state of climate science has advanced to the point where scientists can now put probability estimates on certain impacts of warming, some of which are catastrophic. Current levels of greenhouse gases are roughly 430 parts per million (ppm). This compares to 280 ppm before the Industrial Revolution. If the annual levels of emissions remain constant at today's levels across the world, levels of greenhouse gases will rise to 550 ppm by 2050. And if emissions increase, the level of greenhouse gases will be greater than 550 ppm.

What will happen as greenhouse gases increase and lead to global warming? Table 3 estimates these effects. The top part of the table shows a range of greenhouse gases from 400 ppm to 800 ppm, with predicted effects on temperature below it. The bottom panel estimates the impacts likely to arise with each increase in temperature. The estimated effects of a difference of just 1 or 2 degrees raise serious concerns.

### Unique Timing Aspects

Global climate change is essentially a huge global negative externality. But what makes analysis and decision making so difficult is the long time horizon that must be considered. Most cost-benefit studies do not look out 50 to 100 years and beyond. This extended time horizon adds a host of difficulties and uncertainties.

---

[8] Nicholas Stern, *The Economics of Climate Change* (Cambridge: Cambridge University Press), 2007. This section draws heavily from this study, also known as the "Stern Review."

[9] Andrew C. Revkin, "Yelling 'Fire' on a Hot Planet," *New York Times*, April 23, 2006, p. wk1.

**TABLE 3** Greenhouse Gases, Likely Temperature Changes, and Estimated Impacts

| | Greenhouse Gases (ppm) | | | | |
|---|---|---|---|---|---|
| | 400 | 450 | 550 | 700 | 800 |
| | Eventual Temperature Change (relative to preindustrial) | | | | |
| | 1°C | 2°C | 3°C | 4°C | 5°C |
| **Food** | Rising crop yields in high-latitude developed countries | Rising number of people at risk from hunger | Falling crop yields in developing regions | Major decline in crop yields in all regions | ? |
| **Water** | Small mountain glaciers disappear | Over a 30% drop in runoff in South Africa and the Mediterranean | Large numbers of people suffer water shortages | Billions of people affected by water shortages | Sea level rise threatens major cities, including New York, Hong Kong, and London |
| **Ecosystems** | Ocean coral reef systems damaged | Many ecosystems unable to maintain their current form | Part of Amazon rain forest begins to collapse | 20% to 50% species extinction possible | ? |
| **Extreme Weather Events** | Rising levels of storms, fires, droughts, floods, and heat waves → | | | | |
| | | Rising hurricane intensity → | | | |
| **Major Irreversible Impacts** | Risk of weakening the natural carbon absorption system → | | | | |
| | | Rising risk of large-scale shifts in climate system → | | | |

**Source:** *Stern Review*

Air or water pollution is something that we can see on the horizon, can be measured, is typically localized, and can be altered in a short period of time by some of the approaches discussed earlier. Global warming, in contrast, is not something we can generally see; it is cumulative (this year's $CO_2$ adds to that from the past to raise concentrations in the future); and once it reaches a certain level, it may lead to extreme consequences that cannot be reversed.

Cleaning up pollution problems typically involves finding that level of abatement where the marginal costs of abatement equal the marginal benefits from abatement and either taxing, assigning (or auctioning) marketable permits, or using command and control policies to require the optimal level of abatement. However, reducing global warming gases is not a onetime change, but a cumulative process across many years. As a result, the abatement process is dynamic, and the marginal benefits of abatement depend on the future stock of emissions. To find the optimal abatement in any one period (say, the current period) requires that we look at the optimum path of abatement across many years and assume in the future that abatement will be set optimally for all future periods.

Because of the cumulative nature of greenhouse gases, our short-run decisions will have immense impacts in the long run (50 to 100 years out). Small changes in emissions today will have little impact immediately or even for the current generation, but will have sizable effects many decades out. This aspect of the problem seriously complicates any policymaking and economic analysis.

## Public Good Aspects

To further compound the problem, global climate change is a public good. Greenhouse gas emissions "are the purest example of a negative public good; nobody can have less of them because someone else has more; and nobody can be excluded from their malign consequences or the efforts of others to ameliorate them."[10] One of the solutions is technical innovation that reduces our output of $CO_2$. But knowledge and technology have large public good aspects, so private firms will find it difficult to collect the full returns on their innovation investments that reduce greenhouse gases. Other firms and countries will to some extent be free riders on private innovation, so society (and the world) may get less than the socially optimal level of innovation. This will mean that a substantial amount of climate change research and development will have to be financed by governments. Since the governments of developed nations have more resources than the governments of less-developed nations, the burden will fall on them.

## Equity Aspects

*Why should I do anything for posterity? What has posterity ever done for me?*

GROUCHO MARX

Much of what we do today will have little immediate impact on our lives. The impacts will show up in the latter half of the century. So any action taken today principally benefits our great-grandchildren. Groucho Marx's joke not withstanding, this fact makes it more difficult to get a political consensus to act.

Also, rich countries will have to make the biggest sacrifices, yet they will not get the biggest benefits from efforts to reduce the impacts of global warming. Let us say that the United States reduces its dependence on carbon. What about China and India? They may decide that growth is worth more than a cleaner environment. At that point, the United States would have to be willing to pay China and India large sums to get them to decarbonize their economies. How well will that sell to American voters? Probably not well, but it may be what is ultimately necessary. After all, the developed world is responsible for three-quarters or more of all greenhouse gasses emitted since the Industrial Revolution began.

People in developing countries living along bodies of water will face floods if current climate forecasts come to pass. These are some of the world's poorest people, and adapting to flooding will be extremely difficult given their hopelessly limited resources. In addition, developing nations rely heavily on agriculture, one industry that will be hardest hit as the warming of the Earth inevitably leads to famines.

The long time horizon for policymaking and global climate change puts a different light on the discounting process typically used in cost-benefit analysis. When you use any reasonable discount rate (3% to 5%) on benefits 75 to 100 years into the future, they become miniscule numbers today. Nicholas Stern argued that "there is no compelling reason to value the welfare of future generations much below our own."[11] As a result, the Stern Review adopts a discount rate near zero.

## Finding a Solution

Since climate change is global, it will take a concerted international effort and cooperation. According to the Stern Review, it will take cooperation "in creating price signals and markets for carbon, spurring technology research, development and deployment, and promoting adaptation, particularly in developing countries."[12]

[10] Martin Wolf, "Curbs on Emissions Will Take a Change of Political Climate," *Financial Times*, November 8, 2006, p. 15.

[11] Martin Wolf, "After the Arguments, the Figures Still Justify Swift Climate Action," *Financial Times*, November 15, 2006, p. 15.

[12] Stern Review, p. i.

A temperature rise of 3°C to 4°C will likely lead to serious consequences for food and water shortages in developing nations, and increase the rate of species extinction and possibly more extreme weather events (see Table 3). If the temperature increase is large, the events become catastrophic. Since there is a positive probability that these extreme events will occur, we should invest in ways to reduce the risks of this happening. Consider it a form of insurance.

Many economists, including Nicholas Stern, argue that using smaller levels of resources now will result in lower spending in the future. The Stern Review estimates that the costs of stabilizing greenhouse gases at 550 ppm will cost roughly 1% of world gross domestic product (GDP) if we begin soon.

This will require a transition to a low-carbon economy that will only be accomplished by establishing a worldwide price for carbon that includes its external costs. This can be done using carbon taxes or tradable permits. Permits for acceptable levels of carbon emissions could be auctioned and then traded on open markets on exchanges such at the EU-ETS (Emissions Trading Scheme) and the US-CCX (Chicago Climate Exchange). Europe's system has been plagued by national governments issuing too many permits (for free and to specific industries), so the resulting market price for carbon offsets was a fraction of what was needed to provide the right incentives to reduce emissions. Firms bought permits at these cheap prices rather than attempting to reduce their emissions. There is the problem of having too many permits: Prices are too low. For carbon markets to operate effectively and provide the right incentives to reduce emissions, "countries need independent agencies to issue the permits, just as there are independent central banks to issue money."

Robert Socolow of Princeton University has suggested that much of the technology needed to reduce our carbon footprint is available today.[13] He and several colleagues suggest that we could use techniques such as the following to keep our carbon emissions constant over the next 50 years:

- Use more efficient vehicles and reduce use.
- Build more efficient buildings.
- Capture $CO_2$ at power plants.
- Use nuclear power.
- Exchange biomass fuels for fossil fuels.
- Use wind and solar power.
- Reduce deforestation.

Each of these has the capacity to reduce $CO_2$ emissions by 1 billion tons per year by 2057. The wedges shown in Figure 10 on the next page would prevent our $CO_2$ emissions from doubling over the next 50 years.

Clearly, undertaking some policies to reduce our carbon footprint as a nation represents an insurance policy on the future. All of the activities suggested in Figure 10 are sufficiently flexible such that as new climate change information becomes available, we can adjust our policies. And making some moves now will reduce the potential costs in the future.

To that end, the Obama administration tried to put carbon dioxide emissions on the political agenda. Unfortunately, the recession made it harder to get people's attention on this issue. Furthermore, questions arose about the initial grant of permits in any cap-and-trade program. Do large established companies with huge capital resources get permits? What about smaller, possibly more innovative alternative energy companies? Do permits get auctioned off, and does this then favor the richer, more established companies? Political issues combine with economic issues to make this a thorny problem for the future.

[13] Robert Socolow et al., "Solving the Climate Problem: Technologies Available to Curb $CO_2$ Emissions," *Environment*, December 2004, p. 8–19.

**FIGURE 10—Stabilization Wedges**

This figure, based on the work of Robert Socolow and colleagues, shows the contribution to reduction in carbon emissions that seven wedges can make. Each approach can reduce our carbon footprint by 1 billion tons per year by 2057. Adopting these changes will stabilize our carbon emissions to roughly 7 or 8 billion tons per year.

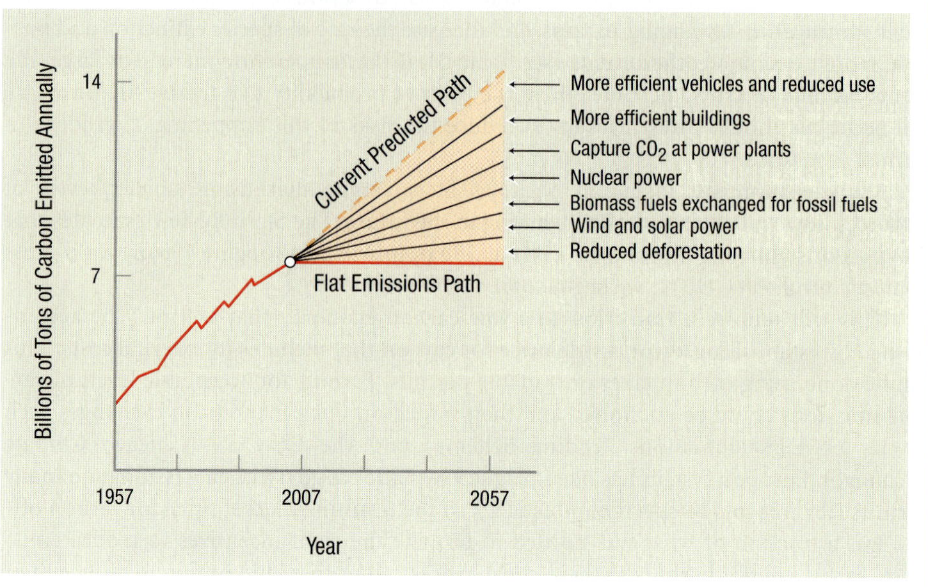


## CHECKPOINT

### ECONOMIC ASPECTS OF CLIMATE CHANGE

- Global climate change is essentially a huge negative externality with an extremely long time horizon.
- The public goods aspects of climate change make it a truly global problem.
- Balancing the current generation's costs and benefits against the potential harm to future generations raises difficult economic issues.
- Actions taken today to reduce a potential future calamity are a form of insurance.

**QUESTION:** Professor Wilfred Beckerman, writing in the *Financial Times* (April 22, 2009, p. 10) puts the most difficult aspect presented by climate change policy into perspective when he writes, "How much certain sacrifice is one prepared to impose on people living today, most of whom are desperately poor, in the interests of future generations who, as it happens, are projected to be much richer?" He cites two studies about peoples' attitudes toward discounting the future that showed one group (Washington, DC, and Maryland) would "trade 45 lives in 100 years time against one life today" and another similar study from Sweden showed that they were willing to trade off 243 lives. Just how important to the global climate change policymaking issue is the discount rate used for the potential harm to future generations?

Answers to the Checkpoint question can be found at the end of the chapter.

## Key Concepts

# Chapter Summary

## Public Goods

Consumer surplus is the difference between what people are willing to pay for a product and what they actually pay for it. Producer surplus is the difference between the revenues firms earn from a product and the costs they would be willing to bear to supply it.

Market failure occurs whenever a market does not provide the socially optimal quantity of a product at the socially optimal price. Market failure can occur because of public goods, externalities, or common property resources.

Public goods exhibit both nonrivalry in consumption and nonexcludability. Nonrivalry means that one person's consumption of a good does not reduce the availability of that good to others. Nonexcludability means that once a product has been provided, no consumers can be excluded from consuming the product. Candy bars are a rival and exclusive product; clean air is nonrival and nonexclusive.

Because common property resources are owned by the community, individuals tend to overuse and overexploit them, as has happened with ocean fishing. Solutions to such problems involve either direct government regulation or establishing private property rights.

## Externalities

Externalities, or spillovers, arise when a transaction benefits or harms parties not involved in the transaction. Pollution and littering are examples of negative externalities, or external costs. Positive externalities, or external benefits, include education and vaccinations.

The Coase theorem suggests that if transaction costs are near zero, how property rights are allocated (to pollute or to be free from pollution) will not affect the efficiency of the ultimate allocation of resources. The resulting bargain between the parties will lead to an optimal allocation of resources. Benefits, however, will be distributed differently, depending on the original assignment of property rights.

## Environmental Policy

Sometimes government policies do not make things better. Government failures occur when the incentives of policymakers and bureaucrats do not coincide with the public interest. Government regulators are often captured by the industries they regulate, resulting in regulations that benefit the industry rather than consumers.

When developing environmental policies, policymakers must consider and evaluate different possible futures. This intergenerational aspect of environmental issues depends on the discount rate chosen. The higher the discount rate, the lower the value we place on events farther into the future, which can result in significant burdens being placed on future generations. Conversely, if we select a low discount rate, the current generation may be overburdened in paying for benefits to be enjoyed by future generations.

Some pollution is acceptable to society. Optimal pollution levels are found where marginal abatement costs equal the marginal benefits. These costs and benefits vary for different types of pollution, industries, and regions of the country.

Environmental policy in the United States has been based on command and control policies that set standards for polluters, which are systematically enforced through inspections and reports. Another option is to enact effluent taxes that lead to optimal pollution levels.

More recently, market-based policies have been recognized as being more efficient than command and control policies. First, the government determines a permissible pollution level; then firms are allocated permits to pollute, which they may buy, sell, and trade.

## Economic Aspects of Climate Change

Global climate change is a huge global externality accompanied by public goods aspects and extremely long time horizons. These issues complicate the solution, and the fact that the developed countries will have to bear the brunt of containing the impacts from climate change—but will get few of the benefits—introduces equity issues into the policymaking equation. The solution to this problem must include global carbon pricing that is credible and covers the full costs of carbon-based products.

## Questions and Problems

### Check Your Understanding

1. What makes public goods so different from private goods?
2. Put the following list of goods and services in order of mostly public goods in nature to mostly private: National Public Radio, a slice of pizza, cable TV, music downloaded from iTunes, your economics class, a seat in a sports bar for Monday Night Football, summer spraying for mosquitoes, the Coast Guard, a ski patrol on Aspen mountain, and an Oklahoma toll road.
3. Assume that you are convinced that if something isn't done now, global warming is going to create extensive problems and damage at the end of this century. If you were preparing a CBA of the impacts and had a 100-year horizon for your projections, would you use a 3% or an 8% discount rate?
4. What is the tragedy of the commons? How can it be solved?
5. When trying to estimate the external benefits of a college education, what kinds of specific benefits would you include?
6. How might the government use market forces to encourage recycling?

### Applying the Concepts

7. As a way to increase the funds for wildlife conservation, why don't we just auction off (say, on eBay) the right to name a new species when it is discovered? Why not do the same for existing species?
8. We can estimate the emissions caused in one year from automobile use. What can you do to offset these emissions? Buy a *green tag.* These voluntary purchases are akin to carbon offsets traded in Europe. For a small fee, individuals can purchase carbon offsets for their cars or SUVs, or companies can use them as a way to purchase wind power for their stores. Organizations selling the green tag (both for-profit and nonprofit) provide a decal; most of the fee collected is provided to alternative energy producers as a subsidy, which then can lower their prices to the market to encourage use. Is this a public good being sold privately? Why would someone or a business buy a tag when they can free ride?
9. One's home (or apartment) is typically thought of as one's castle. But not so in the condominiums with homeowners associations (HOAs) in Jefferson County, Colorado. In an older four-unit condo, the HOA voted 3–1 to adopt a no-smoking rule (inside the individual condos) after smokers bought one of the units and smoke permeated the walls of the structure. In 2006, a district judge ruled that the HOA's adoption of no-smoking rules were reasonable restrictions on ownership rights, stating that the rules were designed to prevent the odor of cigarettes from penetrating the walls of neighboring condos.

   Since there are a small number of people involved (3 nonsmoking units, 1 smoking), you would think that transaction costs would be minimal. Why do you think the homeowners could not work out an agreement (à la Coase) and ended up in court? According to the Coase theorem, would it have made any difference if the judge had ruled against the HOA?
10. Internalizing the cost of negative externalities means that we try to set policies that require each product to include the full costs of its negative spillovers in its price. How do such policies affect product price and industry output and employment? Are these kinds of policies easy to implement in practice? How has globalization of production affected our ability to control pollution?

11. Garbage dumps are a particular source of a potent global-warming gas, the methane that bubbles up as the garbage decomposes. Does it make sense for companies in the European Union (EU) to help Brazilian garbage dumps reduce their releases of methane as a way of meeting their Kyoto obligations?
12. The Presidio, previously a military base in San Francisco, is now a national park. It sits in the middle of San Francisco on some of the most valuable real estate in the United States. Congress, when it created the park, required that it rehabilitate the aging buildings and be self-sufficient within a decade or so, or the land would be sold off to developers. The park appears to be well on its way to self-sufficiency by leasing the land to private firms—Lucas Films has built a large digital animation studio, and other firms have undertaken similar projects. These projects all must maintain the general character of the park and generate rent that will cover the park's expenses in the future. Would this privatization approach work with most of America's other national parks? Why or why not?
13. Nobel Prize winner Simon Kuznets once suggested that poor nations tend to pollute more as they grow—until they reach a certain level of income per capita—after which they pollute less. Does this observation by Kuznets seem reasonable? Why or why not?

## In the News

14. Environmental regulation is undergoing change as many companies seek to be part of the regulatory process and get ahead of regulation. *The New York Times* (May 17, 2006, p. 10) reported that

    > *The Environmental Protection Agency has long been concerned about the possible toxicity of perfluorooctanoic acid (usually called PFOA), a chemical in waterproof clothing and nonstick cookware. Regulating the substance could take years, said Susan B. Hazen, acting assistant administrator for the agency's Office of Prevention, Pesticides and Toxic Substances. So last year, the agency called together a group of chemical companies and environmentalists to discuss how to control PFOA's. Each company voluntarily curtailed its use of the substance. "Everyone set aside their parochial interests, and we reached agreement in a few months," Ms. Hazen said.*

    Does knowing that regulations are inevitable make it easier for companies to get on board early? What is the benefit to companies from adapting their production to reduce toxic waste and pollution?
15. Some environmentalists suggest that the airline industry is contributing greatly to global warming. This is because aircraft emit greenhouse gases at high altitudes, and these gases have several times the impact of the same gases emitted at ground level. Air travel alone could account for roughly 5% of our total impact on climate change. Aside from restricting air travel, there doesn't appear to be much that can be done about it. Other nonfossil fuels are not technically or safely possible, and the other small fixes (towing aircraft to the runway, filling all seats in the plane, etc.) don't really reduce fuel consumption enough. Could this just be a situation where society is better off with more pollution? In general, when are we better off with more pollution?

# Answers to Questions in CheckPoints

## Check Point: Public Goods

Yes, it is a secondary boycott, designed to get the Canadian seafood industry to put pressure on the government to eliminate the hunts. No, it does not seem fair. Chilean sea bass was one product that chefs focused on. Since most sea bass was sold to restaurants, the boycott was successful. Also, the price of sea bass rose as supply declined (as the result of overfishing), making it easier for restaurants to substitute other fish.

## Check Point: Externalities

The social benefits from homeowners using electric lawn mowers are shown in the figure below as $D_S$, while the private benefits are much less (shown as $D_P$). Fewer electric mowers are sold ($Q_P$) than is socially desirable ($Q_S$), so the Los Angeles air quality district is subsidizing electric mowers by $300 to encourage their use.

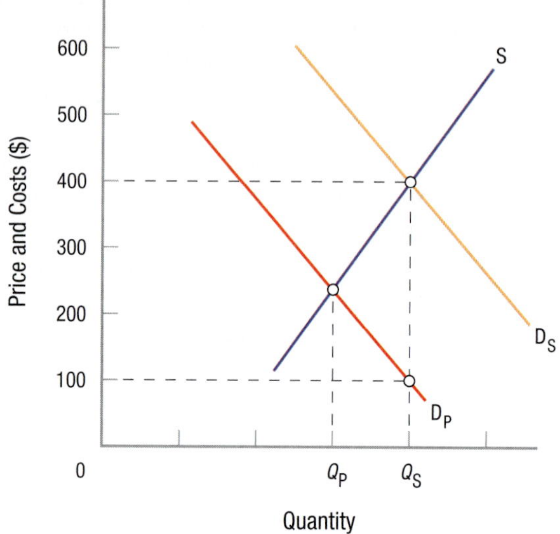


## Check Point: Environmental Policy

In the last 50 or so years, as the United States has become richer, environmental issues and our willingness to pay have grown. Simultaneously, science has developed new insights, changing approaches to managing natural environments. Also, when the EPA was formed, pollution was a high-priority item because many streams and cities were fouled. Yes, the EPA probably has suffered mission creep, but it probably reflects the public's desire for a cleaner environment as the U.S. economy has become more prosperous.

## Check Point: Economic Aspects of Climate Change

The discount rate used to determine the costs and benefits for global climate policymaking is quite important. If set too high, the benefits to future generations will look trivial in today's dollars. But if set too low, future harm, no matter how trivial when discounted to today, will be huge because of the time span involved. Ultimately, how much we are willing to do today depends crucially on the sacrifice the developed nations of the world (including China and India) are willing to make on behalf of future generations. Perhaps Professor Beckerman said it best when he argued, "But perhaps the whole of this debate is irrelevant. We are confronted with a minute but totally unquantifiable risk of some unquantifiable catastrophe in the distant future. There is no algorithm in cost-benefit analysis that can make this judgment for us. We must each make up our own minds on the basis of our own intuitions and sensibilities."

# 14 Poverty and Income Distribution

Ross Pictures/Corbis

**Income inequality and poverty** are among the most contentious issues facing economists and other social scientists today. Many people have trouble accepting that baseball pitchers earn millions, while teachers earn only thousands (and just a few at that) and many others eke out wages that just barely permit subsistence.

Is it fair that some people earn so much when others have so little? Questions of fairness are normative questions. They can only be answered through individual value judgments; economics has no right or wrong answers to offer in this area. Still, economists can contribute *something* to our discussions of economic fairness. What might this be?

Earlier, we saw that when input and product markets are competitive, wages are determined by worker productivity and the market value of output produced. The supply of people willing and able to work and the demand for labor sets the prevailing wages. Many of us are willing to play professional baseball, but few are called, and those who do reach "The Show" are so much more skilled than the rest of us that they command huge contracts.

The teaching profession, in contrast, requires far fewer specific skills and less training. Besides, hundreds of thousands of positions are always available. The result is that teacher salaries are much closer to what average folks earn. Clearly, teachers perform a valuable service, arguably more valuable than the service performed by professional baseball players. Still, there is no real shortage of people willing and able to teach at prevailing wages. But there is a real shortage of people able to throw a 95 mph fastball.

It must also be remembered that our economy contains people whose skill levels and discipline are so low that their income-earning possibilities are dismal. High school dropouts, transients, and many other people with all variety of problems are of little

**After studying this chapter you should be able to:**

- ☐ Describe the difference between wealth and income.
- ☐ Describe the effects of life cycles on income.
- ☐ Analyze functional, personal, and family income distributions.
- ☐ Use a Lorenz curve and Gini coefficient to graphically depict the distribution of wealth and income.
- ☐ Describe the impact of income redistribution efforts.
- ☐ Describe the causes of income inequality.
- ☐ Describe the means for determining poverty thresholds.
- ☐ Describe the two measures for determining depth of poverty for families.
- ☐ Describe the prevailing theories on how to deal with poverty and income inequality.

economic value in a market economy. Society has various safety net programs designed to provide these people with basic services to help them become more self-sufficient.

Economic analysis gives us some insight into why income inequality exists. We have already seen how monopoly, monopsony, unions, and discrimination can potentially skew income distribution. Even when public policy focuses on reducing these market imperfections, inequalities persist.

This chapter looks at income inequality, its trends, its causes, and how it is measured. We then take a brief historical look at income inequality and the policies designed to reduce it. Next, we turn our attention to poverty, focusing on how poverty is traditionally measured, and the U.S. Census Bureau's new approach to measuring poverty. Finally, we look at current poverty trends and the causes of poverty. Throughout this chapter, we use economics to provide a framework for analyzing income distribution, poverty, and the public policies used to combat poverty and to change the distribution of income.

## The Distribution of Income and Wealth

**Income** is a *flow,* **wealth** is a *stock.* Income measures the receipts of funds by individuals or households over time, usually a week, month, or year. Income is a *flow of funds* measure. Wealth, in contrast, measures a family's assets and net liabilities at a given point in time. You may earn a certain income in 2011, but your net wealth is measured on a specific day, say, December 31, 2011. Many people were wealthy on January 1, 2000, but after twice suffering the ravages of a falling stock market, they were considerably less wealthy on July 1, 2003.

You can be wealthy with low income if you do not work and your assets are in low-yielding certificates of deposit. Alternately, you can have little wealth, yet a high income, like a rookie professional ball player who earns a seven-figure salary but has not yet accumulated assets.

**Income:** A flow measure reflecting the funds received by individuals or households over a period of time, usually a week, month, or year.

**Wealth:** A stock measure of an individual's or family's assets, net of liabilities, at a given point in time.

### Life Cycle Effects

Family and individual incomes vary significantly over the course of people's lives. Young people just starting their careers and their families often earn only modest incomes. Over their working careers, they become more experienced and their salaries increase, with income peaking roughly between the ages of 45 and 55. At some point between ages 45 and 60, family size begins to decline as the kids grow up and leave home. Somewhere approaching 60, income also begins declining, though household saving rises as the family prepares for retirement. Incomes decline with retirement, but then again, so do family responsibilities.

One result of this economic life cycle is that a society that is growing older can expect to see changes in income distribution as greater numbers of households fall into lower income brackets. The life cycle also has implications for the economic effects of immigration. Newcomers to the United States are often unskilled, so when the country admits more immigrants, it can expect more low-income households. The children of immigrants, however, move up the income distribution ladder.

### The Distribution of Income

Income distribution can be considered from several different perspectives. First, we can look at the **functional distribution of income,** which splits income among the inputs (factors) of production. The functional distribution for the United States between 1929 and 2009 is shown in Table 1.

**Functional distribution of income:** The distribution of income for resources or factors of production (land, labor, capital, and entrepreneurial ability).

Labor's share of national income rose from 1929 to become relatively stable from the 1970s onward, but falling slightly each decade. The share of income going to small businesses, called "proprietor's income," has declined over this period. Rental income has grown recently to where it was in 1970. The share accruing to corporate profits has hovered around 10%.

As Table 1 illustrates, the biggest fluctuations in income share have been associated with income from interest. It declined into the 1960s, then rose again in the last decade.

**TABLE 1** Functional Distribution of Income (absolute dollars in billions, numbers in parentheses are percentages)

| Year | Wages | Proprietor's Income | Rent | Corporate Profits | Net Interest |
|---|---|---|---|---|---|
| 1929 | 51.1 (60.3) | 14.9 (17.6) | 4.9 (5.8) | 9.2 (10.8) | 4.7 (5.5) |
| 1940 | 52.1 (65.4) | 12.9 (16.2) | 2.7 (3.4) | 8.7 (10.9) | 3.3 (4.1) |
| 1950 | 154.8 (65.5) | 38.4 (16.3) | 7.1 (3.0) | 33.7 (14.3) | 2.3 (1.0) |
| 1960 | 296.4 (69.4) | 51.9 (12.1) | 16.2 (3.8) | 52.3 (12.2) | 10.7 (2.5) |
| 1970 | 617.2 (73.7) | 79.8 (9.5) | 20.3 (2.4) | 81.6 (9.7) | 38.4 (4.6) |
| 1980 | 1651.7 (73.6) | 177.6 (7.9) | 31.3 (1.4) | 198.5 (8.8) | 183.9 (8.2) |
| 1990 | 3351.7 (72.2) | 381.0 (8.2) | 49.1 (1.1) | 408.6 (8.8) | 452.4 (9.7) |
| 2000 | 5715.2 (71.6) | 715.0 (9.0) | 141.6 (1.8) | 876.4 (11.0) | 532.7 (6.7) |
| 2009 | 7727.8 (70.1) | 1028.0 (9.3) | 262.0 (2.4) | 1226.5 (11.1) | 784.4 (7.1) |

**Source:** Bureau of Economic Analysis.

## Personal or Family Distribution of Income

When most people use the term "the distribution of income," they typically mean **personal or family distribution of income.** This distributional measure is concerned with how much income, in percentage terms, goes to specific segments of the population.

**Personal or family distribution of income:** The distribution of income to individuals or family groups (typically quintiles, or fifths, of the population).

To analyze personal and family income distribution, the Census Bureau essentially arrays households from the lowest incomes to the highest. It then splits these households into quintiles, or fifths, from the lowest 20% of households to the highest 20%. After totaling and averaging household incomes for each quintile, the Census Bureau computes the percentage of income flowing to each quintile.

Today, the United States contains just over 100 million households. So the 20 million households with the lowest incomes compose the bottom quintile, and the 20 million households with the highest incomes compose the upper quintile.

Table 2 shows the official income distribution estimates for the United States since 1970. These estimates are based "solely on *money income before taxes* and do not include the value of employment based fringe benefits nor of government-provided noncash benefits such as food stamps, Medicaid and public or subsidized housing."[1]

**TABLE 2** Share of Aggregate Income Received by Each Household Quintile: 1970–2008 and the Gini Coefficient

| Year | Lowest | Second | Third | Fourth | Highest | Gini Coefficient |
|---|---|---|---|---|---|---|
| 1970 | 4.1 | 10.8 | 17.4 | 24.5 | 43.3 | 0.394 |
| 1975 | 4.4 | 10.5 | 17.1 | 24.8 | 43.2 | 0.397 |
| 1980 | 4.3 | 10.3 | 16.9 | 24.9 | 43.7 | 0.403 |
| 1985 | 4.0 | 9.7 | 16.3 | 24.6 | 45.3 | 0.419 |
| 1990 | 3.9 | 9.6 | 15.9 | 24.0 | 46.6 | 0.428 |
| 1995 | 3.7 | 9.1 | 15.2 | 23.3 | 48.7 | 0.450 |
| 2000 | 3.6 | 8.9 | 14.9 | 23.0 | 49.6 | 0.462 |
| 2008 | 3.4 | 8.7 | 14.8 | 23.4 | 49.7 | 0.463 |

**Source:** U.S. Census Bureau, Current Population Reports, P60-236, *Income, Poverty, and Health Insurance in the United States: 2008* (Washington, DC: U.S. Government Printing Office), 2009.

[1] U.S. Census Bureau, *Money Income in the United States: 2004–05*, p. 2.

Note that if the income distribution were perfectly equal, all quintiles would receive 20% of aggregate income. A quick look at these income distributions over the past three decades suggests that our distribution of income has been growing more unequal. Keep in mind that these numbers ignore taxes and transfers (direct payment to households such as welfare and food stamps).

Compressing distribution data into quintiles allows us to see how distribution has evolved. Economists have developed two primary measures that allow comparisons to be drawn with ease across time and between countries. These measures are Lorenz curves and the Gini coefficient.

## Lorenz Curves

**Lorenz curves:** A graphical method of showing the income distribution by cumulating families of various income levels on the horizontal axis and relating this to their cumulative share of total income on the vertical axis.

**Lorenz curves** cumulate families of various income levels on the horizontal axis, relating this to their cumulated share of total income on the vertical axis. Figure 1, for simplicity, shows a two-person economy. Assume that both people earn 50% of the total income, or that income is divided evenly. Point *a* in Figure 1 marks out this point, resulting in equal distribution curve 0*ac*.

The second curve in Figure 1 shows a two-person economy where the low-income person earns 25% of the total income and the upper income person receives 75% (point *b*). This graph is skewed to the right (curve 0*bc*), indicating an unequal distribution. If this two-person income distribution were as unequal as possible (0% and 100%), the Lorenz curve would be equal to curve 0*dc*.

**FIGURE 1—Lorenz Curves (two-person economy)**

If both people in this two-person economy earn 50% of the total income, income will be distributed perfectly equally, shown by the equal distribution curve 0*ac*. Curve 0*bc* represents the same economy in which the low-income person earns 25% of the total income and the upper-income person earns 75%. This curve is skewed to the right, indicating an unequal distribution. The most extreme distribution between these two individuals (0% and 100%) is represented by the Lorenz curve 0*dc*.

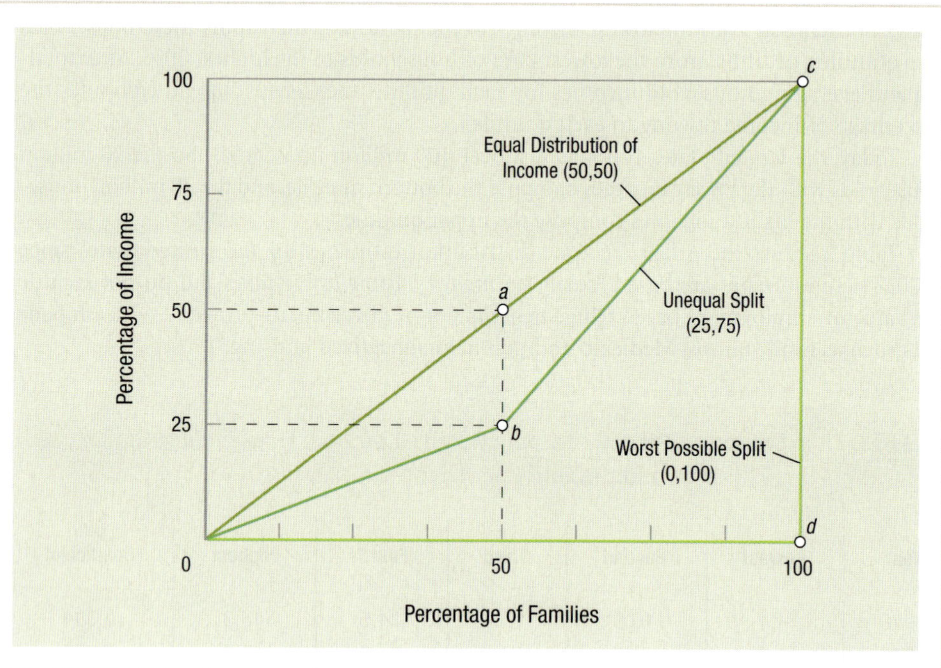


Figure 2 and its accompanying table offer more realistic Lorenz curves for income and wealth data for the United States. The quintile income distribution in the second column of the table is cumulated in the third column and plotted in Figure 2. (To *cumulate* a quintile means to add its percentage of income to the percentages earned by all lower quintiles.)

In Figure 2, for instance, the share of income received by the lowest fifth is 3.5%; it is plotted as point *a*. Next, the lowest two quintiles are summed (3.5 + 8.7 = 12.2) and plotted as point *b*. The process continues until all quintiles have been plotted to create the Lorenz curve.

Figure 2 also plots the Lorenz curve for wealth; it shows how wealth is much more unequally distributed than income. The wealthiest 20% of Americans control over 80% of wealth, even though they earn only half of all income.

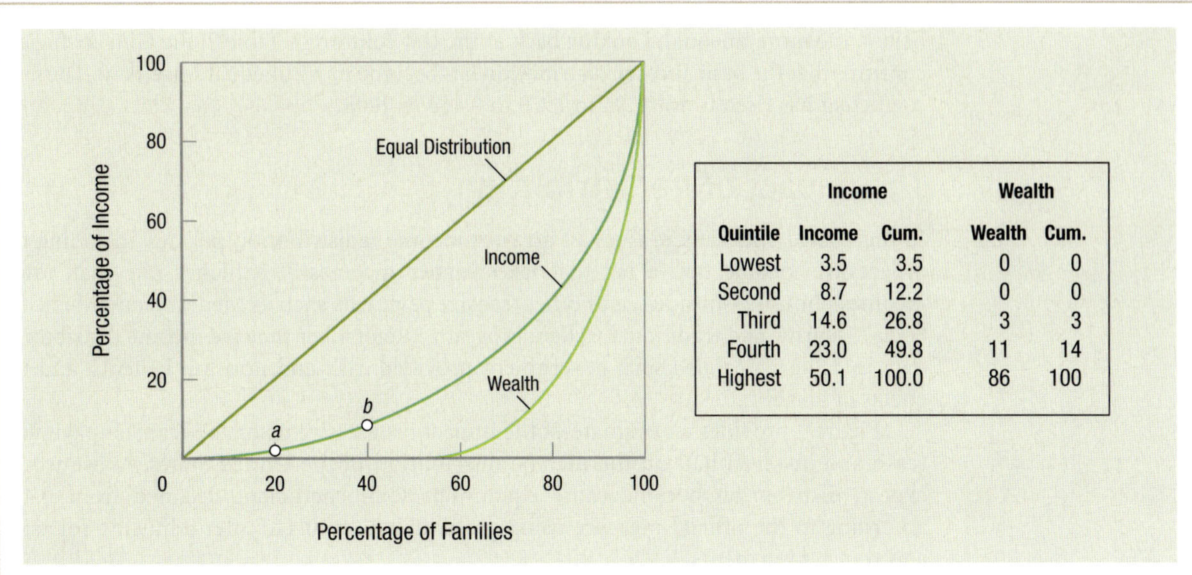


| | Income | | Wealth | |
|---|---|---|---|---|
| **Quintile** | **Income** | **Cum.** | **Wealth** | **Cum.** |
| Lowest | 3.5 | 3.5 | 0 | 0 |
| Second | 8.7 | 12.2 | 0 | 0 |
| Third | 14.6 | 26.8 | 3 | 3 |
| Fourth | 23.0 | 49.8 | 11 | 14 |
| Highest | 50.1 | 100.0 | 86 | 100 |

**FIGURE 2—Lorenz Curves**

The graph shows the most recent Lorenz curves for income and wealth in the United States. The quintile distribution of income, found in the second column of the accompanying table, is cumulated in the third column and then plotted as a Lorenz curve. Notice how wealth is much more unequally distributed than income.

## Gini Coefficient

Lorenz curves give us a good graphical summation of income distributions, but they can be inconvenient to use when comparing distributions between different countries or across time. Economists would like one number that represents an economy's income inequality. The **Gini coefficient** provides such a number.

The Gini coefficient provides a precise method of measuring the position of the Lorenz curve. It is defined as the ratio of the area between the Lorenz curve and the equal distribution line, in the numerator, and the total area below the equal distribution line, in the denominator. In Figure 3, the Gini coefficient is the ratio of area *A* to area ($A + B$).

If the distribution were equal, area *A* would disappear (equal zero), so the Gini coefficient would be zero. If the distribution were as unequal as possible, with one individual or household earning all national income, area *B* would disappear, so the Gini coefficient would be 1.

**Gini coefficient:** A precise method of measuring the position of the Lorenz curve, defined as the area between the Lorenz curve and the equal distribution line divided by the total area below the equal distribution line.

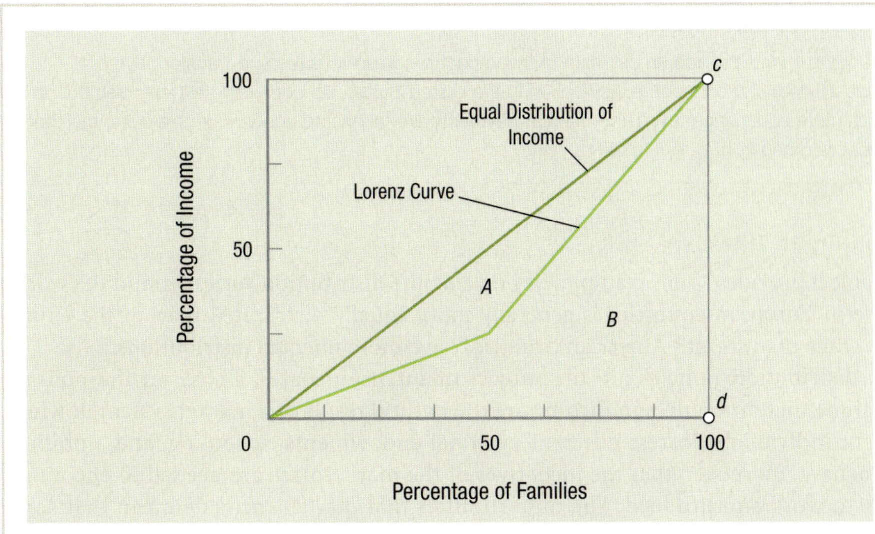


**FIGURE 3—The Gini Coefficient**

The Gini coefficient is a precise method of measuring the position of the Lorenz curve. It is defined as the ratio of the area between the Lorenz curve and the equal distribution line, and the total area below the equal distribution line. Thus, the Gini coefficient is equal to the ratio between area *A* and area ($A + B$). If distribution were equal, area *A* would be zero, and the Gini coefficient would equal zero. If distribution were as unequal as possible, area *B* would disappear, so the Gini coefficient would be 1.

As a rule, the lower the coefficient, the more equal the distribution; the higher the coefficient, the more unequal. Looking back at the last column in Table 2, the Gini coefficient confirms that the basic income distribution has become more unequal since 1970. The Gini coefficient has risen from 0.394 in 1970 to 0.463 in 2008.

## The Impact of Redistribution

In the United States, there is a vast array of income redistribution policies, including the progressive income tax (a tax that taxes higher incomes at a higher rate than lower incomes), housing subsidies, and other transfer payments such as Medicaid and Medicare, Social Security, and traditional welfare programs. Remember that the income distribution data in Table 2 *excluded* such government-provided cash and noncash benefits, and the effects of taxation.

Figure 4 provides an estimate of the impact progressive taxes and transfer payments (cash and in-kind) had on the income distribution in the United States. As we would expect, distribution became more equal: The Gini coefficient declined from 0.463 according to the official measure using gross income to 0.412 after adjusting for taxes and transfer payments.

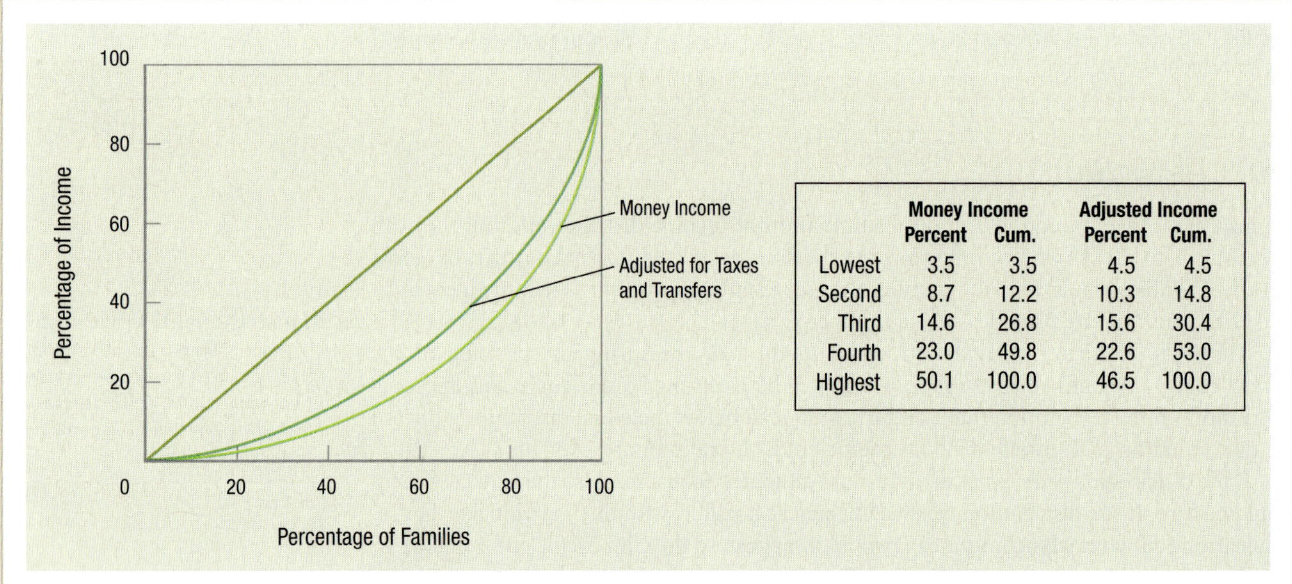


| | Money Income | | Adjusted Income | |
|---|---|---|---|---|
| | Percent | Cum. | Percent | Cum. |
| Lowest | 3.5 | 3.5 | 4.5 | 4.5 |
| Second | 8.7 | 12.2 | 10.3 | 14.8 |
| Third | 14.6 | 26.8 | 15.6 | 30.4 |
| Fourth | 23.0 | 49.8 | 22.6 | 53.0 |
| Highest | 50.1 | 100.0 | 46.5 | 100.0 |

**FIGURE 4—Lorenz Curves for the United States: Money Income and Income Adjusted for Taxes and Transfer Payments**

These Lorenz curves provide an estimate of the impact progressive taxes and transfer payments (cash and in-kind) had on income distribution in the United States. As one would expect, distribution becomes more equal once taxes and transfer payments are taken into account. In this case, the Gini coefficient declined from 0.463 to 0.412.

Table 3 provides some examples of how income distribution varies around the world. Income in European countries is generally more equally distributed than in the United States, while many South American countries have more unequal distributions.

Redistribution policies are the subject of intense debates. Those on the political right argue that differences in income are the natural result of a market system in which different individuals possess different personal endowments, schooling, and ambition. They believe, moreover, that the incentives of the marketplace are needed to encourage people to work and produce. The opportunities that markets provide mean that some

**TABLE 3** Gini Coefficients for Various Countries, 2007

| Country | Gini Coefficient |
|---|---|
| Australia | 0.352 |
| Bolivia | 0.582 |
| Brazil | 0.550 |
| Canada | 0.326 |
| Chile | 0.520 |
| China | 0.415 |
| Denmark | 0.247 |
| France | 0.327 |
| Israel | 0.392 |
| Italy | 0.360 |
| Japan | 0.249 |
| Mexico | 0.481 |
| New Zealand | 0.362 |
| South Africa | 0.578 |
| Spain | 0.347 |
| Sweden | 0.250 |
| United Kingdom | 0.360 |
| United States | 0.408 |

**Source:** World Bank, *World Development Indicators* (Washington, DC: World Bank), 2009.

people will be winners and others will lose. These analysts are unconcerned about the distribution of income unless it becomes so unequal that it discourages incentives and reduces efficiency.

Those on the political left argue that public policy should ultimately be guided by human needs. They see personal wealth as being the product of community effort as much as individual effort, and therefore they favor greater government taxation of income and wealth. By and large, European nations have found this argument more compelling than has the United States. This is reflected in the breadth of European social welfare policies. Because there is no correct answer (except possibly keeping distribution away from the extremes), this debate continues.

## Causes of Income Inequality

Many factors contribute to income inequality in our society. First, as just mentioned, people are born into different circumstances with differing natural abilities. Families take varying interest in the well-being of their children, with some kids receiving immense inputs of family time and capital, while others receive little. These family choices largely fall outside the realm of public policy.

### Human Capital

The guarantee of a free public education through high school and huge subsidies to public colleges and universities for all Americans are designed to even out some of the economic differences among families. Still, public education does not eliminate the disparities. Some parents plan their children's educations long before they are born, while other parents ignore education altogether.

Table 4 on the next page provides evidence of the impact investments in education have on earnings. Those without high school diplomas earned the least, roughly a third less than high school graduates. A college degree resulted in mean earnings nearly 3 times higher than what individuals without high school diplomas earned.

**TABLE 4** Mean Earnings by Highest Degree Earned, 2006

| | Mean Earnings by Highest Degree | | | |
|---|---|---|---|---|
| | No High School Diploma | High School Graduate | College Graduate | Professional |
| All Persons | $20,873 | $31,071 | $56,788 | $116,214 |
| Male | 24,072 | 37,356 | 69,818 | 132,991 |
| Female | 15,352 | 23,236 | 43,302 | 86,010 |
| White | 21,464 | 32,083 | 57,932 | 117,718 |
| Black | 17,823 | 26,368 | 47,903 | 101,374 |
| Hispanic | 20,581 | 27,508 | 45,371 | 82,627 |

**Source:** U.S. Census Bureau, Current Population Survey, *2009 Statistical Abstract of the United States,* Table 224.

The U.S. economy has become more technologically complex. Manufacturing jobs have dwindled, reducing the demand for these workers, reducing their real wages. Several decades ago, people with low education levels could find highly productive work in manufacturing, with good wages and benefits. Globalization and increased capital mobility, however, have caused many of these jobs to migrate to lower-wage countries. The result: Real wages have declined for Americans in many manufacturing occupations.

Our economy is increasingly oriented toward service industries, making investments in human capital more important than ever. The service industry spans more than just burger flipping, maid service, and landscaping. The United States is still the world leader in the design and development of new products, basic scientific research and development, and other professional services. All these industries and occupations have one thing in common: the need for highly skilled and highly educated employees.

## Other Factors

In an earlier chapter, we saw that economic discrimination (dual labor markets or segmented markets) leads to an income distribution skewed against those subject to discrimination. Reduced wages then reduce an individual's incentive to invest in human capital since the returns are lower, perpetuating a vicious circle.

Table 5 outlines some characteristics of households occupying two different income quintiles. By comparing the lowest quintile with the highest, we can see some of the reasons for income inequality. As the Census Bureau summarizes these differences, "High-income households tended to be family households that included two or more earners, lived in the suburbs of a large city, and had a working householder between 35 and 54 years old. In contrast, low-income households tended to be in a city with an elderly householder who lived alone and did not work."

The rise in two-earner households over the last two decades accounts for a large part of the growing inequality in income. Note in Table 5 that only 5.8% of the lowest-quintile households had two earners, while 76.4% of the highest quintile did. Also, only 3% of top quintile householders did not work, but 58.6% of those in the bottom quintile were not working.

It is hardly surprising that households with two people working should tend to have higher incomes than households with only one person or none working. In most households, whether one or two people work represents a choice. Today, clearly more couples are opting for two incomes. This is significant, given that rising income inequality is often cited as evidence that the United States needs to change its public policies to reduce inequalities. Yet, if the rise in inequality is due largely to changes in household attitudes toward work and income, with more couples choosing dual-career households, changes in public policy may not be needed. Rising inequality may simply be a reflection of the changing personal choices of many households.

This overview of income distribution and inequality provides a broad foundation for the remainder of the chapter, which focuses on poverty, its causes, and possible cures.

**TABLE 5** Distribution of Households by Selected Characteristics within Income Quintiles, 2008

| Characteristic | Lowest Quintile | Highest Quintile |
|---|---|---|
| **Type of Residence** | | |
| Inside metropolitan area | 79.4% | 90.2% |
| Inside central city | 39.5 | 29.3 |
| Outside central city | 39.8 | 60.8 |
| Outside metropolitan area | 20.6 | 9.9 |
| **Type of Household** | | |
| Family households | 40.5 | 87.4 |
| Married-couple families | 18.1 | 79.3 |
| Nonfamily households | 59.5 | 12.6 |
| Householder living alone | 59.5 | 12.6 |
| **Age of Householder** | | |
| 15 to 34 years | 22.1 | 15.0 |
| 35 to 54 years | 26.8 | 53.6 |
| 55 to 64 years | 14.7 | 21.3 |
| 65 years or older | 36.4 | 10.0 |
| **Number of Earners** | | |
| No earners | 58.6 | 3.0 |
| One earner | 35.6 | 20.6 |
| Two or more earners | 5.8 | 76.4 |
| **Work Experience of Householder** | | |
| Worked | 35.5 | 88.4 |
| Worked full-time, year-round | 21.5 | 78.8 |
| Worked part-time or part year | 14.0 | 9.6 |
| Did not work | 64.5 | 11.6 |

**Source:** U.S. Census Bureau, Current Population Reports, P60-236, *Income, Poverty, and Health Insurance Coverage in the United States: 2008* (Washington, DC: U.S. Government Printing Office), 2009.

**CHECKPOINT**

## THE DISTRIBUTION OF INCOME AND WEALTH

- The functional distribution of income splits income among factors of production.
- The family or personal distribution of income typically splits income into quintiles.
- Lorenz curves cumulate families of various income levels on the horizontal axis and their cumulative share of income on the vertical axis.
- The Gini coefficient is the ratio of the area between the Lorenz curve and the equal distribution line to the total area below the equal distribution line. It is used to compare income distribution across time and between countries.
- Income redistribution activities such as progressive taxes, Medicare, Medicaid, and other transfer and welfare programs reduce the Gini coefficient and reduce the inequality in the distribution of income.
- Income inequality is caused by a number of factors, including individual investment in human capital, natural abilities, and discrimination.

**QUESTIONS:** Economist Charles Murray suggested doing away with all social insurance, including Social Security, Medicare, Medicaid, and other welfare programs, and instead simply giving $10,000 a year to every citizen of the United States over 21 years of age. The purpose of the idea was to reduce bureaucracy and the government's role in the decision making of families. Expand his idea slightly by eliminating the age restriction. Would this improve the income distribution in America? Why or why not?

Answers to the Checkpoint questions can be found at the end of this chapter.

# Poverty

Thus far, we have examined income distribution in general terms, looking at the spectrum from the top to the bottom. This section focuses on the bottom of the income spectrum—those who live in poverty. First, we look at poverty thresholds and how they are defined. Then we turn to the incidence of poverty and its trends. Last, we take a brief look at some experimental measures of poverty, considering their impact on measured rates of poverty.

## Measuring Poverty

**Poverty thresholds:** Income levels for various household sizes, below which people are considered to be living in poverty.

**Poverty thresholds** were developed by Mollie Orshansky in the 1960s. They were based on the Agriculture Department's Economy Food Plan, the least expensive plan by which a family could feed itself. The Agriculture Department first surveyed the food-buying patterns of low-income households, using these data to determine the cost of a nutritionally balanced food plan on a low-income budget. Orshansky then extrapolated these costs to determine the cost of maintaining such a food plan for households of various compositions. Finally, to determine the official poverty threshold, Orshansky multiplied the cost of the food plan, adjusted for family size, by 3. This multiplier was based on an earlier household survey that had shown the average family of three or more spends roughly a third of its income on food.[2]

Since the 1960s, the poverty thresholds have been updated every year for changes in inflation using the consumer price index (CPI). Table 6 shows the poverty thresholds for 2008. If a family's income is less than the threshold, every person in the household is considered poor. Official thresholds do not vary geographically. "Income" includes all money income before taxes, including cash benefits, but not capital gains or noncash benefits such as public housing, food stamps, and Medicaid. Later, we will briefly look at some new alternative measures that do adjust for these factors.

**TABLE 6** Average Poverty Thresholds, 2008

| | |
|---|---|
| One person | $10,991 |
| Two people | 14,051 |
| Three people | 17,163 |
| Four people | 22,025 |
| Five people | 26,049 |
| Six people | 29,456 |
| Seven people | 33,529 |
| Eight people | 37,220 |
| Nine people | 44,346 |

**Source:** U.S. Census Bureau, Current Population Reports, P60-236, *Income, Poverty, and Health Insurance in the United States: 2008* (Washington, DC: U.S. Government Printing Office), 2009.

[2] See Constance F. Citro and Robert T. Michael, *Measuring Poverty: A New Approach* (Washington DC: National Academy Press), 1995, p. 13 and Chap. 2 for more detail on how thresholds are measured.

## *Issue:* Why Do We Use an Outdated Measure of Poverty?

**Why does the** United States still define poverty as 3 times the cost of a *1963* low-income food budget adjusted for inflation? You might think that government policymakers could design a measure that reflects a family's well-being by looking at more than just money income based on some old formula nearly a half-century old.

Based on this measure, poverty rates have fluctuated between 10% and 15% over the four decades. But in that time, antipoverty programs were generously increased to include reduced tax burdens on the poor, as well as the expansion of food stamp and housing programs, the earned income tax credit, and Medicare, Medicaid, and other programs that have undoubtedly helped the poor. But the measure doesn't reflect this success and as a result provides little guidance to solving poverty. As Professor Rebecca Blank at the University of Michigan observes, "In a very fundamental way, our poverty statistics failed us and made it easy to claim that public spending on the poor had little effect."

Aurora Photos/Alamy

Why has the Census Bureau failed to update our poverty measure in the same way that employment, unemployment, consumer prices, national income accounts, and many other economic statistics have been improved? The answer is straightforward and surprising. Through a historical accident, the Executive Office of the President is in charge of the measure. The decision resides at the Office of Management and Budget (OMB), and the president must ultimately approve any change. To date, no White House has been willing to approve any change. If a change in measurement results in falling poverty rates, some will claim manipulation. If a change results in higher poverty rates, the administration risks being seen as a failure on this front. Ultimately, we will probably not see improvement until Congress gives the Census Bureau responsibility for the statistic.

Source: Rebecca Blank, "Presidential Address: How to Improve Poverty Measurement in the United States," *Journal of Policy Analysis and Management,* 2008, pp. 233–254.

## The Incidence of Poverty

Poverty rates for the United States since 1960 are shown in Figure 5 on the next page. Poverty fell rapidly between 1960 and 1975 but has remained roughly stable ever since, fluctuating with the business cycle: rising around recessions (the shaded vertical bars) and falling when times are good.

Poverty rates vary considerably along racial and ethnic lines. Figure 6 on the next page charts the poverty rate since 1970. Over most of this time, the poverty rate for blacks and Hispanics was roughly twice the rate for whites. Both of these minority groups benefited, however, from the strong economic growth of the 1990s, their poverty rates dropping from around 30% at the beginning of the decade to below 25% today. White poverty remained fairly steady over the 1990s, fluctuating between 10% and 11%.

These data suggest that robust economic growth is a major force for reducing poverty. The expression "a rising tide floats all boats" would appear to have something to it.

Table 7 on page 353 shows other characteristics that contribute to poverty. Single parent households have 2 to 5 times the poverty rate of married couples. Not surprisingly, working part-time or not working at all leads to higher poverty rates. And, as we saw in Figure 6, black and Hispanic poverty rates are roughly twice that of whites.

## Depth of Poverty

It is one thing to say that a certain percentage of the population is poor. It is another to determine just how poor they are. The poverty threshold for a family of four today is over $22,000. If most poor families have incomes approaching this threshold, we could be confident poverty was just a transitory stage—one phase of the life cycle—and that many people who are poor today would have higher incomes tomorrow.

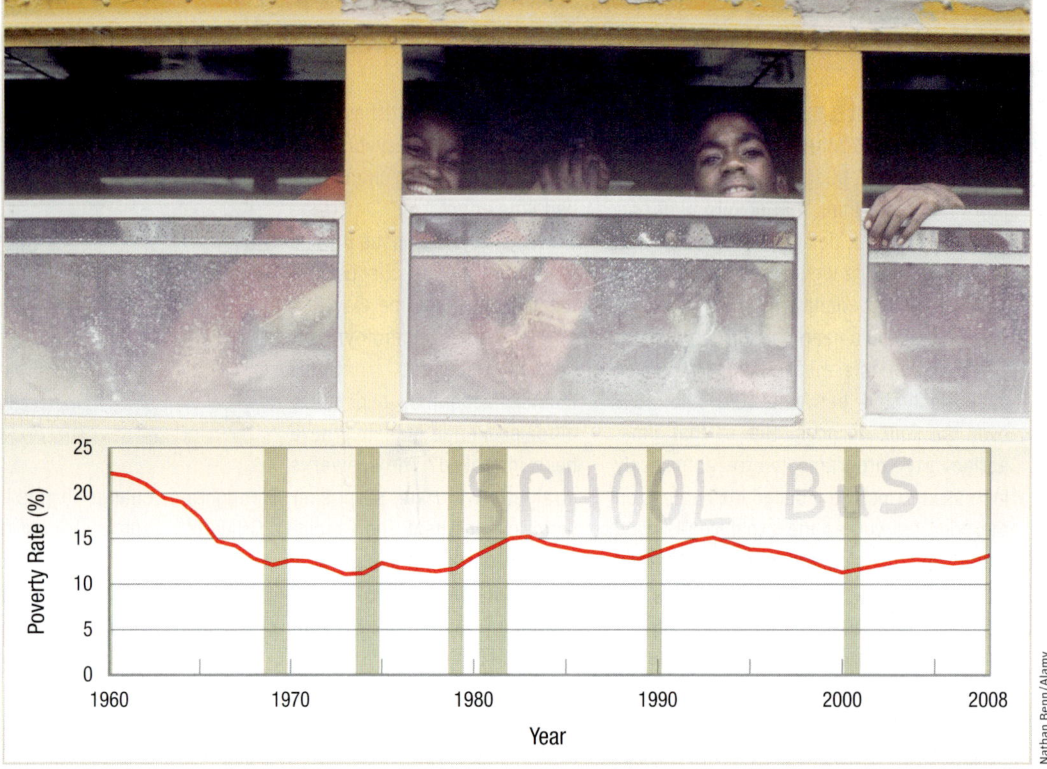


**FIGURE 5—Poverty Rates in the United States, 1960–2008**

Poverty fell rapidly between 1960 and 1975 but has remained roughly stable ever since.

Source: U.S. Census Bureau, Current Population Reports, P60-236, *Income, Poverty, and Health Insurance in the United States: 2008* (Washington, DC: U.S. Government Printing Office), 2009.

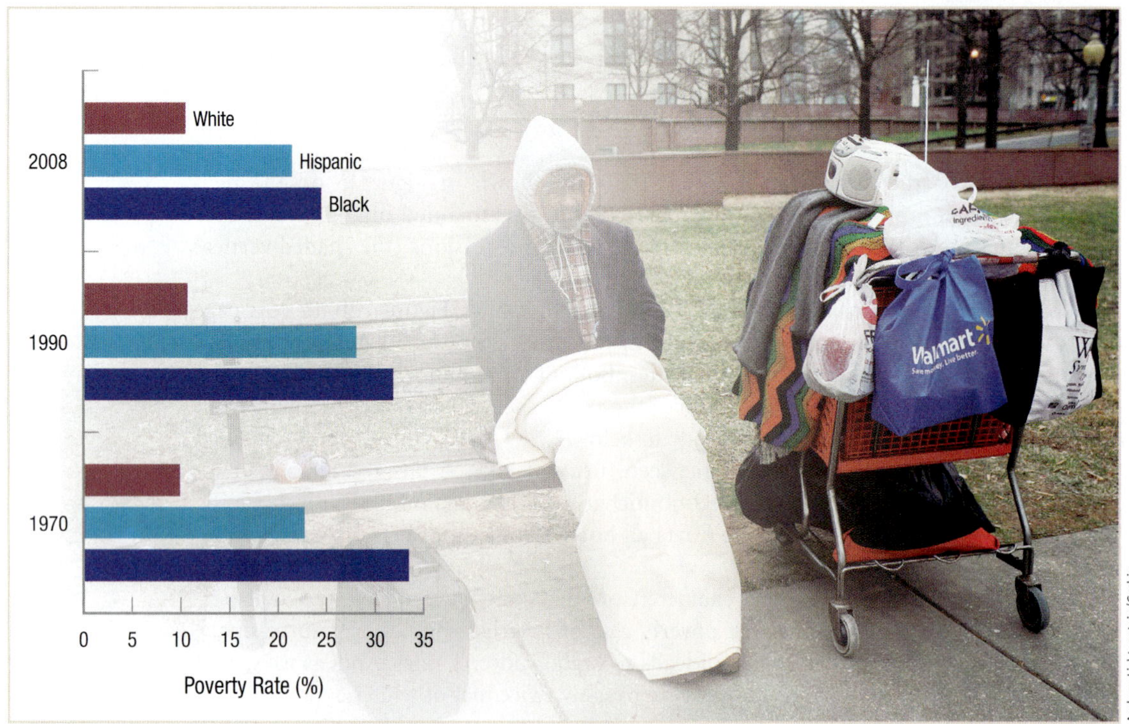


**FIGURE 6—Poverty Rates by Race and Ethnic Origin, 1970–2008**

Poverty rates vary considerably along racial and ethnic lines. Over most of this period, the poverty rate for blacks and Hispanics was roughly twice the rate for whites. Both of these minority groups benefited, however, from the strong economic growth of the 1990s, their poverty rates dropping from around 30% at the beginning of the decade to below 25% today. White poverty remained fairly steady over the 1990s, fluctuating between 10% and 11%.

Source: U.S. Census Bureau, Current Population Reports, P60-236, *Income, Poverty, and Health Insurance in the United States: 2008* (Washington, DC: U.S. Government Printing Office), 2009.

**TABLE 7** People and Families in Poverty by Selected Characteristics, 2008

| Characteristic | Poverty Rate |
|---|---|
| **Type of Household** | |
| Married-couple households | 5.5% |
| Female households (no husband) | 28.7 |
| Male households (no wife) | 13.8 |
| **Work Experience** | |
| Worked full time, year round | 2.6 |
| Worked part-time, year round | 13.5 |
| Did not work | 22.0 |
| **Race** | |
| White | 11.2 |
| Black | 24.7 |
| Asian | 11.8 |
| Hispanic | 23.2 |

**Source:** U.S. Census Bureau, Current Population Reports, P60-236, *Income, Poverty, and Health Insurance in the United States: 2008* (Washington, DC: U.S. Government Printing Office), 2009.

But if, conversely, many poor families have incomes below $10,000, our view of poverty would be different, and our public policies aimed at reducing poverty would need to be considerably more robust.

To gain a view of the broad spectrum of poverty, economists have developed two *depth of poverty* measures that describe the economic well-being of lower-income families. One measure, the **income deficit,** tells us how far below the poverty threshold a family's income lies. In 2008, the income deficit for families living in poverty averaged just over $9,100.

Income deficit: The difference between the poverty threshold and a family's income.

The second measure of poverty, the one we will focus on, is the **ratio of income to poverty.** It compares family income to the poverty threshold and expresses this comparison as a ratio. Thus, the ratio for families with incomes equal to the poverty threshold equals 1.0; the ratio for those living at half the threshold income is 0.5. The Census Bureau considers people who live in families with ratios below 0.5 to be "severely or desperately poor." Those with ratios between 0.5 and 1.0 are "poor," and people with ratios above 1.0 but less than 1.25 (less than 25% above the poverty threshold) are considered to be "near poor."

Ratio of income to poverty: The ratio of family income to the poverty threshold. Families with ratios below 0.5 are considered severely poor, families with ratios between 0.5 and 1.0 are considered poor, and those families with ratios between 1.0 and 1.25 are considered near poor.

Of the nearly 40 million poor people in 2008, over 17 million of them were desperately poor, and an additional 14 million were categorized as near poor. These measures (income deficit and the ratio of income to poverty) provide us with a more nuanced picture of poverty.

## Alternative Measures of Poverty

Many researchers have questioned the relevance of the current method for determining poverty thresholds. The National Academy of Sciences studied the official approach to poverty thresholds and concluded that the measure is flawed because "[it] counts taxes as income, [and] is flawed in the adjustments to the households for different family circumstances."[3]

The study further concluded that the current poverty measure does not distinguish well among working parents, workers generally, nonworkers, or people with higher versus lower health care needs and costs. Finally, noting that the current thresh-

[3] Citro and Michael, *Measuring Poverty,* pp. 97–98.

old is simply the threshold from "1963 updated for price changes," the panel questioned the value of such a simplistic approach, given how much the U.S. standard of living has changed.

Given the Academy's findings, the Census Bureau developed some new ways of measuring poverty. These alternative measures of poverty differ from the old in basing their estimates on after-tax income plus capital gains and counting as income such noncash benefits as food stamps and housing subsidies plus imputed return on home equity.

The Census Bureau derived its new estimates of income thresholds from a survey of expenditures on food, clothing, housing, utilities, and other necessities for the typical family of four (two adults and two kids). These figures were then adjusted to reflect differences in family composition and size, given that children consume less than adults, some household economies are associated with larger families, and the first child in a one-adult family costs more to support than the first child in a two-adult family. Under these measures, poverty rates fell by roughly a quarter.

## Eliminating Poverty

Poverty can be a relative or an absolute measure. As we saw in the previous section, the official measure of poverty in the United States is based on an absolute number, the poverty threshold. Some researchers, however, think a relative measure would be more useful, such as labeling the bottom 20% of American households "poor."

If we decide to use such a measure, poverty will never be eliminated, no matter how wealthy our country might become. A relative measure obscures the fact that poverty in the United States means something different than it does in the developing world. The official U.S. poverty threshold for an individual is an income of roughly $25 a day. In the developing world, by contrast, the World Bank and other agencies define poverty as incomes of less than $2 a day. By World Bank standards, poverty has already been eradicated in the United States.

### Reducing Income Inequality

Regardless of how poverty is defined, the question of how to reduce it is controversial. The political left views income and wealth redistribution as the chief means of reducing poverty. Social justice, they argue, requires that the government provide an extensive safety net for the poor. In their view, services the government already provides, including public education, housing subsidies, Medicaid, and unemployment compensation, should be greatly expanded.

They say these policies should be supplemented, moreover, by increasing the progressivity of the tax system. This would reduce the inequalities in wealth and income. By increasing the tax burden on the well-to-do, people of modest incomes could lead more meaningful and just lives.

### Increasing Economic Growth

The opposite side of the political spectrum argues that such programs, when allowed to become too expansive, can be disastrous. Welfare significantly reduces the incentive to work and produce, thereby reducing the economy's output. A vibrant market economy accommodates the wishes of those who want full-time, upwardly mobile careers as well as those who only want just enough work to pursue other goals.

Since wages provide 70% of all income, those on the political right note, there inevitably will be some inequality in a market system. Some people, after all, make bad choices and fail to invest enough in their education or job skills. Yet, the possibility of failure itself provides an incentive to work hard and invest, and the political right sees this sort of efficiency in the economy as being more important than equity or fairness. The best way to cure poverty, they argue, is by implementing policies that increase the economic pie shared by all, not just by splitting up the pie more evenly.

This political dispute has fueled a controversy in economics. One group of economists argues that economic growth raises low incomes at a rate similar to that of average incomes, such that the poor benefit from growth just as much as anyone else.[4] Other economists reply that the shift toward freer markets around the world, combined with the resulting economic growth, has widened inequalities, causing the poor to fall further behind.

Who is right? Economist Richard Adams launched a major study to determine whether policies designed to foster growth or policies geared toward reducing income and wealth inequalities do more to reduce poverty in developing countries.[5] His basic conclusions are

> *Economic growth represents an important means for reducing poverty in the developing world. . . . Economic growth reduces poverty because first and foremost growth has little impact on income inequality. . . . Since income distributions are relatively stable over time, economic growth—in the sense of rising incomes—has the general effect of raising income for all members of society, including the poor.*

Adams's study also notes that "for any given rate of economic growth, the more inequality falls, the greater is the reduction in poverty." For income redistribution to reduce poverty, there must be a significant economic pie to redistribute. For most developing nations, the size of the pie is not large enough to measurably reduce poverty.

## Rawls and Nozick

Unfortunately, there is no unified theory of income distribution that takes the various issues we have discussed into account. Earlier chapters suggested that income depends on productivity—in competitive markets, each input (factor) is paid the value of its marginal product.

Human capital analysis adds that as people invest in themselves, their productivity and income rise. Analysis of imperfect input markets, however, shows that income distribution advantages accrue more to those with monopoly or monopsony power.

Our analysis of economic discrimination and dual labor or segmented markets suggested several more reasons why incomes may be skewed in favor of some groups rather than others. The bargaining strength of labor unions is yet another factor that can skew income distribution, in this case in favor of union members.

These analyses have focused, in one way or another, on whether certain patterns of income distribution are economically efficient. Yet, how do we know whether various income distributions are equitable or fair? Is there anywhere to turn for theoretical help in addressing this question? The answer is a qualified "yes." Two philosophers, John Rawls and Robert Nozick, published competing views on this subject in the early 1970s.[6]

John Rawls proposed the "maximin principle," in which he argued that society should maximize the welfare of the least well-off individual. He asks us to conduct a thought experiment: Assume you must decide on the income distribution for your society, without knowing where in the distribution you will end up. Since chance could lead to you being the least well-off individual in the society, Rawls suggests people would favor significant income redistribution under these circumstances.

Robert Nozick argued that it is "illegitimate to use the coercive power of the state to make some better off at the expense of others." To Nozick, justice requires protecting property rights "legitimately acquired or legitimately transferred."[7] Nozick argued strongly for competitive market equilibriums, suggesting that the state has no role in selecting which equilibrium is best.

This debate highlights the perennial tradeoff in economic policy between equity and efficiency, a tradeoff that serves as a bone of contention in nearly every discussion of economic and public policy. Though microeconomics is sometimes beset by controversy itself, at its best it provides us with a dispassionate framework in which to analyze and discuss many issues.

---

[4] David Dollar and Aart Kraay, "Growth Is Good for the Poor," *World Bank Policy Research Working Paper #2587* (Washington, DC: World Bank), August 2001.

[5] Richard Adams, "Economic Growth, Inequality and Poverty: Findings for a New Data Set," *World Bank Policy Research Working Paper #2972* (Washington, DC: World Bank), February 2002.

[6] John Rawls, *A Theory of Justice* (Oxford: Clarendon), 1972; and Robert Nozick, *Anarchy, State and Utopia* (Oxford: Blackwell), 1974.

[7] John Kay, *The Truth about Markets: Their Genius, Their Limits, Their Follies* (London: Penguin Books), 2003, p. 187.

## *Issue:* How Mobile Are Poor Families?

**The poverty rates** and income distribution data provide a snapshot in time. How about over time? What is the human side to this? Do people start in poverty or fall into poverty and then stay there, or is there movement out of poverty?

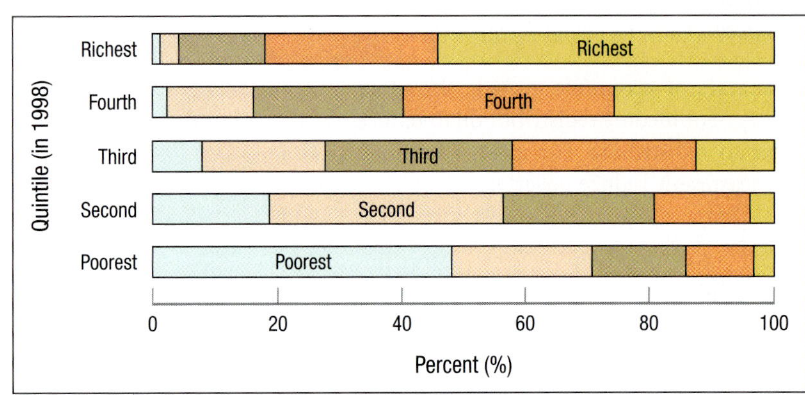


A study tracking over 180,000 workers in California from 1988 to 2000 provides an answer. People in all quintiles moved up the economic ladder, but those workers who started out at the lowest wages had the greatest real wage gains. More than 80% of workers in the bottom bracket moved up to a higher earnings quintile. In particular, those with the lowest wages gained the most when they switched industries, searching for better career and earnings potential. This finding points to the dynamism in the economy, and the recognition of opportunity by all income classes.

Another study used data from the University of Michigan's Panel Study of Income Dynamics, which has followed 5,000 families since 1968. It shows how fluid the income distribution really is and the important role played by working wives.

The figure shows the mobility of under-55, married-couple families between 1988 and 1998. Each color represents a different quintile in 1988.

Here is how we read the graph. First, focus on the poorest quintile. The poorest quintile in 1988 is shown as a light blue bar. Start with the bar on the bottom. Reading across the bar, we see that almost half of the married-couple families in the poorest quintile at the beginning of 1988 remained in this poorest quintile 10 years later. But the other half in this poorest quintile moved up. Following the light blue bars up, we see that almost 20% moved up to the second quintile in 1998. Some in the poorest quintile in 1988 even made it up to the highest quintile in 1998.

Using this same procedure to look at the other quintiles, note that almost 20% of the married-couple families in the second quintile at the beginning of the period dropped down to the poorest quintile by 1998 (follow the pink quintile). The third and fourth quintiles show similar amounts of mobility.

In just one decade, over half of the poorest families moved up the income distribution ladder, but nearly half remained in the poorest quintile. The richest quintile was surprising, roughly a mirror image of the poorest quintile. Slightly less than half dropped out and were replaced by families from the other quintiles. Looking at all quintiles, only one-third to one-half remained in their original quintile after a decade.

The families that remained in the lowest quintile after a decade are the most worrisome. Research by Richard B. Freeman of Harvard tells us that there is a core of poor people who stay poor. This core has physical disabilities, suffers from substance abuse, or is unable to work for a host of other reasons.

This finding suggests that poverty will never be totally eradicated. It also suggests that policies to deal with core poverty should be different from policies that deal with people who start or who have fallen into poverty but are highly likely to escape.

Sources: Based in part on the article by Alan B. Krueger, "After 40 Years, What Are Some Results and Lessons of America's War on Poverty?" *New York Times,* January 8, 2004, p. C2. See also Michael Dardia, Elisa Barbour, Akhtar Khan, and Colleen Moore, "Moving Up? Earnings Mobility in California, 1988–2000," *California Policy Review* 1:4, April 2002; "An Embarrassment of Riches," *Wall Street Journal,* November 12, 2002, p. A20; and Katharine Bradbury and Jane Katz, "Wives' Work and Family Income Mobility," *Public Policy Discussion Papers,* Federal Reserve Bank of Boston, May 12, 2005.

**CHECKPOINT**

### POVERTY

- Poverty thresholds were developed in the 1960s based on a food budget, adjusted for family size, that was then multiplied by 3.
- Economic growth is a major force in reducing poverty.
- The income deficit measures how far below the poverty threshold a family's income lies.
- The other depth of poverty measure is the ratio of income to poverty. If the ratio is below 0.5, the family is considered "severely or desperately poor." A ratio greater than 1.0 but less than 1.25 indicates the family is "near poor."

- The Census Bureau has introduced new measures of poverty that consider health care costs, transportation needs, and child care costs.
- The controversy surrounding reducing poverty centers on whether reducing income inequality or increasing economic growth is the best approach.
- Philosopher John Rawls proposed a "maximin principle" that suggests society should maximize the welfare of the least well-off individual.
- Robert Nozick argued that the state should not use its coercive power to make some people better off at the expense of others.
- Income mobility is quite robust in the United States, with more than half of all families moving up and down the income distribution ladder in any decade.

**QUESTIONS:** Return to the suggestion by economist Charles Murray that the United States should eliminate all social insurance, including Social Security, Medicare, Medicaid, and other welfare programs, and instead give $10,000 each year to each citizen over 21 years of age. Again, expand his idea by eliminating the age restriction. Would this eliminate poverty in America? Would this satisfy those on the left who wish to reduce inequality in income distribution? What do you think would be the response to such an idea by those on the political right?

Answers to the Checkpoint questions can be found at the end of this chapter.

## Key Concepts

Income, p. 342
Wealth, p. 342
Functional distribution of income, p. 342
Personal or family distribution of income, p. 343
Lorenz curves, p. 344
Gini coefficient, p. 345
Poverty thresholds, p. 350
Income deficit, p. 353
Ratio of income to poverty, p. 353

## Chapter Summary

### The Distribution of Income and Wealth

Income is a flow; it measures the receipts of funds by individuals or households over time. Wealth is a stock; it measures a family's assets and net liabilities at a given point in time.

Family and individual incomes vary significantly over the course of the life cycle. Young people just starting their careers and their families usually have modest incomes. As people grow older and gain experience, their incomes usually rise, peaking between the ages of 45 and 55. Incomes then normally decline with retirement, as do family responsibilities.

The functional distribution of income refers to the income distribution among inputs (factors) of production. The share of national income going to labor has gradually risen since 1929; it is now fairly stable at around 70%. The remainder of the national income is divided among proprietor's income (small business profits), rent, corporate profits, and net interest.

Personal or family income distribution refers to the percentage of income flowing to families in specific segments of the population. To analyze family income distribution, the Census Bureau arranges households in quintiles, or fifths, ranging from the 20% of households with the lowest incomes to the 20% with the highest. After totaling and averaging household incomes for each quintile, the Census Bureau computes the percentage of income flowing to each quintile. Since the 1970s, the income distribution in the United States has become more unequal.

Economists have developed two primary methods of measuring inequality. Lorenz curves cumulate and plot the percentage of people below various income levels on the horizontal axis, relating this to their share of income on the vertical axis. A perfectly equal distribution results in a Lorenz curve that bisects the axes, and deviations from this equal distribution curve indicate inequality.

The Gini coefficient is another method of measuring income inequality. The Gini coefficient is used to compare income distribution across time and countries.

Income distribution is influenced by redistribution policies that include progressive taxes and cash and in-kind transfer payments. Redistribution policies are contentious. Those on the political left tend to push for greater redistribution of income and wealth, while those on the right argue that such policies hurt incentives.

Income inequality in our society has many causes. Different education levels are a major factor determining inequalities in income and wealth. Economic discrimination can lead to an income distribution skewed against those suffering the discrimination. The growth of two-earner households over the last three decades is a major reason for rising income inequality.

## Poverty

The poverty threshold was first determined by the U.S. Department of Agriculture. When the Census Bureau calculates the official poverty rate, it counts as income all money income before taxes, including cash benefits, but does not include capital gains or noncash benefits such as public housing or food stamps.

The poverty rate in the United States fell rapidly between 1960 and 1975, but it has remained roughly stable since then, fluctuating around 12% to 15%, following the business cycle. Over most of this period, the poverty rate for blacks and Hispanics was roughly twice the rate for whites.

Economists have developed two depth-of-poverty measures that describe the economic well-being of lower-income families. The first, the income deficit, measures how far below the poverty threshold a family's income lies. The ratio of income to poverty compares family income to the poverty threshold and expresses this comparison as a ratio. In 2008, over 5% of Americans lived in severely poor families.

Many researchers have criticized the Census Bureau's official method of determining poverty thresholds. In response, it has developed experimental measures that differ from the old in basing their estimates on after-tax income and counting as income such noncash benefits as food stamps and housing subsidies. Work-related expenses, such as transportation and child care, are deducted from income, as are out-of-pocket medical expenses. When these new measures were applied, poverty rates fell by almost one-quarter.

The question of how to go about reducing poverty is controversial. The political left sees income and wealth redistribution as the main tool for curing poverty. They suggest expanding welfare-related programs and enhancing the progressivity of the tax system. Those on the right argue that such an approach is too expensive, and it significantly reduces the incentives to work and produce, thereby reducing the economy's output. These people maintain that the best way to cure poverty is by implementing policies that increase the economic pie shared by all, not just by splitting the current pie more evenly.

There is no unified theory of income distribution that takes all issues into account, or that tells us which distribution is the fairest. John Rawls argued that low inequality is the fairest, since this is what everyone would choose if he or she did not know where in the income distribution he or she would fall. Robert Nozick replied that it is unfair to use the coercive power of the state to deprive people of their private property to redistribute it to others.

Studies of income mobility suggest that there is a lot of shifting by individuals and families between quintiles of the income distribution. Roughly half of all families move out of their quintile into others over a decade.

# Questions and Problems

## Check Your Understanding

1. If you look at income distribution over the life cycle of a family, would it be more equally distributed than for one specific year?

2. List some of the reasons why household incomes differ.

3. How does the Gini coefficient differ from the Lorenz curve?

## Apply the Concepts

4. Is there an efficiency-equity tradeoff when income is redistributed from the rich to the poor? Explain.

5. Currently the poverty threshold for a family of four is over $22,000 a year. Does this seem about right to you? This family would also probably qualify for food stamps, Medicaid, and subsidized housing. Does the poverty threshold still seem about right?

6. What do you think has been the impact on the distribution of income in the United States from the combined impact of the huge number of unskilled illegal immigrants and the growing number of dual-earner households?

7. It is probably fair to say that when we classify people as rich or poor at any given moment in time, we are simply describing similar people at different stages in life. Does this life cycle of income and wealth make the income distribution concerns a little less relevant? Why or why not?

8. What would be the change in the distribution of income (Gini coefficient) if the United States decided to permit 10 million new immigrants into the United States who were highly skilled doctors, engineers, executives of large foreign firms, and wealthy foreigners who just want to migrate to the United States? How would the Gini coefficient change if, instead, the United States decided to permit 10 million unskilled foreign workers to enter?

9. If the poverty threshold is roughly $22,000 for a family of four, why don't we just raise the minimum wage to $12.50 an hour and eliminate poverty?

10. Roughly half of all marriages in the United States end in divorce. What is the impact of this divorce rate on the distribution of income and poverty?

11. According to the U.S. Department of the Treasury, people in the top income quintile (20%) pay roughly 75% of all personal income taxes, with the remaining 80% paying less than 25%. Further, the bottom half of the population pays less than 4% of all personal income taxes. Many politicians often assert that they want to bring tax relief (presumably with the idea of redistributing income) to "middle- and lower-income" families. Given this distribution of income tax payments, what would middle- and lower-income tax relief look like?

12. Are the poor in 2011 just as poor as the poor in 1950? What, if anything, has changed in 60 years to make poverty different today?

13. What are some of the reasons for income inequality? Is income inequality necessarily a bad thing?

14. Poverty rates have declined for blacks and have been relatively stable for everyone else over the last 40 years. But the poverty rate still hovers around 13%. What makes it so difficult to reduce poverty below 10% to 15% of the population?

## Solving Problems

15. Use the two different distributions of income in the table below to answer the questions that follow.

| Quintile | A | B |
|---|---|---|
| Poorest | 11.2 | 10.5 |
| Second | 12.0 | 11.6 |
| Middle | 21.2 | 20.3 |
| Fourth | 26.0 | 25.7 |
| Richest | 29.6 | 31.9 |

a. Use the grid below and graph the two Lorenz curves.

b. Which curve has the least unequal distribution?

c. Are these distributions more or less equal than that for the United States today?

# Answers to Questions in CheckPoints

## Check Point: The Distribution of Income and Wealth

It would clearly improve (make more equal) the before-tax and benefits distribution of income. The impact on the distribution of income after adjusting for current benefits of such a policy would depend on the explicit value of current benefits. Murray suggested that his proposal would cost more for a decade and then begin saving money.

## Check Point: Poverty

Based on the poverty thresholds, poverty would almost be eliminated by this proposal. In general, the political left would welcome this redistribution except for the elimination of the social safety net. Some people would make bad decisions and not save for retirement or purchase health care, and the political left would still want these services to exist, defeating the idea of the proposal. The political right would worry that once the redistribution scheme is introduced, enough people would reduce their working hours to harm economic growth. Further, the political right would worry that after the redistribution, the safety net would creep back into existence, eroding the benefits of the original idea.

# Introduction to Macroeconomics

Tim Foley Illustration

**Over the last 150 years, the U.S.** economy has suffered through more than 33 recessions (downturns)—on average one every four to five years. Every president could expect a downturn during his presidency. In recent years this has been true for presidents Nixon, Carter, Reagan, George H. W. Bush, George W. Bush, and Obama; Clinton was the only exception in nearly 40 years.

Before the Great Depression of the 1930s, presidents and their administrations had no consistent approach or agreed upon method to restore the economy to prosperity during a downturn, and the study of macroeconomics and macroeconomic policy that we take for granted today did not exist. Nearly all of what you will study in the rest of this book is about as old as your grandparents. Further, macroeconomics as a specific discipline—meaning the study of the *overall* economy—is due primarily to one man, John Maynard Keynes, whom we will meet in later chapters.

Managing a $15,000,000,000,000 (that's $15 trillion) economy is no easy task. In a market economy, some markets and firms may be doing well while others are in the dumps. To keep track of the economy as a whole requires data on income, output, employment, inflation, and a host of other areas. Several times a week, the government announces the latest level of some macroeconomic variable or another. These data help firms, markets, consumers, and government policymakers gauge the general condition of the economy. Most data are released monthly, although some are released only quarterly. When a drop in the unemployment rate is reported, we all feel better and have more confidence in the economy, even if we know someone who has just lost their job.

One measure of the success of macroeconomic analysis as a tool to guide policymakers is that most of you reading this book are currently living through your first *real*

**After studying this chapter you should be able to:**

- ☐ Describe the scope of macroeconomics.
- ☐ Describe the big events that shaped the study of macroeconomics.
- ☐ Describe the goals of macroeconomic policy.
- ☐ Describe the business cycle and some of the important macroeconomic variables that affect the level of economic activity.
- ☐ Describe the national income and product accounts (NIPA).
- ☐ Describe the circular flow of income and discuss why GDP can be computed using either income or expenditure data.
- ☐ Describe the four major expenditure components of GDP.
- ☐ Describe the major income components of national income.
- ☐ Describe the shortcomings of GDP as a measure of our standard of living.

recession. Since the early 1980s, the United States experienced two very minor recessions in 1990–1991 and 2001. Both lasted eight months, employment barely fell, and aggregate output dropped only slightly. It wasn't until 2008 that the current downturn, a deep recession, put nearly one in ten of the labor force out of work. Collapses in the financial, automobile, and housing sectors set the economy on its back. So if you are under 40, this is your first experience with the impacts of a serious recession. If history is any evidence, you likely will see more in your lifetime.

Unfortunately, the impacts of recessions are not just economic. Recessions adversely affect suicide rates and divorce rates among upper income couples.[1] Sales of laxatives go up because, as one wag put it, "people are under stress, and holding themselves back."[2] Sales at McDonald's and Wal-Mart rise and sales of inexpensive Hershey candy bars rise while sales of upscale Godiva chocolates drop. But recessions also have their benefits. Some see recessions as a way to "empty the bird cage," a euphemism for a downturn's way of winnowing out weak firms that booms permit but recessions force into bankruptcy.[3] Also, as unemployment rates rise, people eat out less and spend more time with their families. They also exercise more and smoke and drink less.[4] So recessions can potentially be beneficial by improving overall health. On balance, however, they create far more costs than benefits.

This chapter briefly introduces you to why macroeconomics developed as a specific discipline, how we define and measure business fluctuations, and what the major statistics are that are collected by government to keep track of the economy.

In the first section of this chapter, we consider some of the major events that have accelerated the development of macroeconomics. We then turn to the primary macroeconomic goals our nation has set for itself and look at how business cycles are defined and measured.

The second major section of this chapter looks at the system of national income accounts. These accounts give us our primary measures of income, consumer and government spending, business investment, and foreign transactions, including exports and imports. To conclude the chapter, we raise the question of how well these accounts measure our standard of living.

Together, these two sections will give you an introduction to the study of macroeconomics. The foundation established here will apply to the remainder of the course.

# The Scope of Macroeconomics

Macroeconomics studies economic activity from the broadest of perspectives, that of the entire economy. Macroeconomics focuses on such issues as economic growth, output of the economy (called gross domestic product [GDP]), inflation rates, employment, unemployment, and interest rates. These are the dominant variables that define our macroeconomy. Several major events have shaped the way we study macroeconomics and focused attention on these specific variables.

## Major Events That Shaped Macroeconomic Ideas

The study of macroeconomics has developed out of a series of real-world experiences. To better understand these major economic events or catastrophes, economists have been forced to produce macroeconomic analysis that explains how the macroeconomy works. Three major events of the past century—the Great Depression, episodes of hyperinflation, and massive budget deficits—helped form much of the macroeconomic analysis presented in the following chapters.[5]

---

[1] "Divorce and Economic Growth: Negatively Correlated," *The Economist*, July 26, 2008, p. 67.

[2] Tamar Lewin, "A Hemline Index, Updated," *New York Times*, October 19, 2008, p. 4.

[3] Tom Miller, "China's Plan to Empty the Bird Cage," *Financial Times*, June 10, 2009, p. 8.

[4] Lewin, "A Hemline Index, Updated."

[5] These three major events (and others) are described and analyzed in detail in Rudiger Dornbusch, et al., *Macroeconomics* (New York: McGraw-Hill Irwin), 2004, Chap. 18, p. 452.

## By the *Numbers*

### A Long, Deep Recession?

The 2008–2009 downturn was the longest since the Great Depression in the 1930s. While not as severe as the 1930s Depression, it was about as severe as any since 1950.

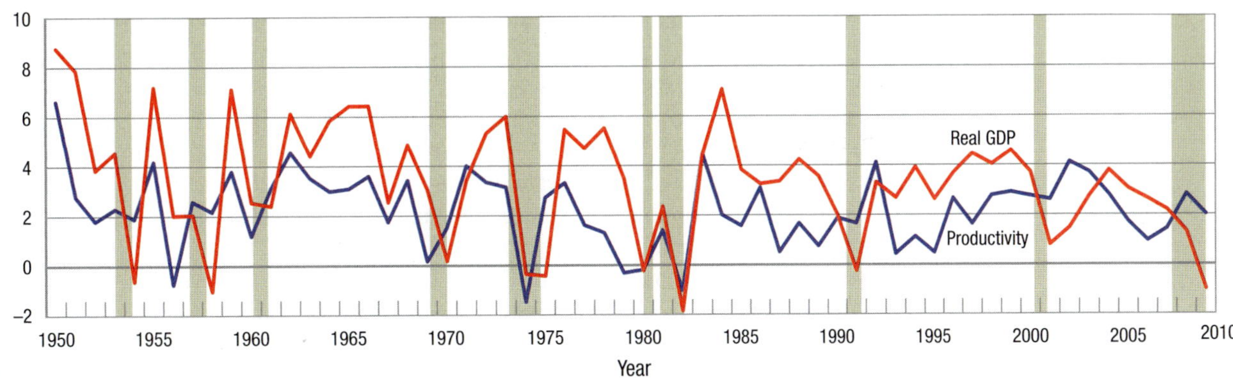


**During the 2008–2009 recession,** economic growth (real GDP) was negative and productivity (output per hour worked) was down. These two measures are usually positive with small negative dips near recessions (shown in the vertical shaded bars). During the last recession, growth was negative for the first time in 20 years.

**Savings rates have steadily fallen;** high unemployment and income anxiety meant consumers tightened their belts and increased savings, which deepened the recession.

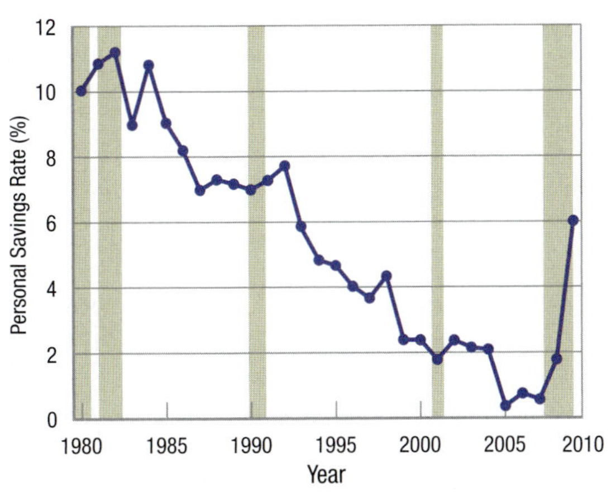


**Housing prices have fallen** since 2006. High mortgage default rates reduced construction activity, helping to make this a deep recession.

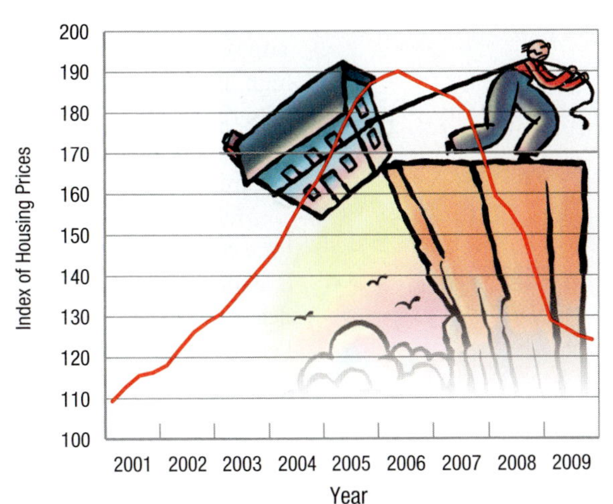


**77%**
Drop in consumer confidence since January 2007

**31%**
Reduction in business investment since January 2007

**438%**
Increase in number of people unemployed six months or longer since January 2007

**Regional impact is uneven.** The industrial East and far West have been hit the hardest.

## The Great Depression

The first and most important event—the event that really put macroeconomics on the map as a discipline of consideration and study—was the Great Depression of the 1930s. Between 1929 and 1933, a $1,000 investment in the stock market fell to a value of $150. Massive bank failures and unemployment rates approaching 25% devastated the American economy, with similar downturns spreading all over the world. Business investment dropped from nearly 18% of gross domestic product in 1929 to under 4% in 1933. Government spending doubled during this period, but it was still not enough to pull the economy out of the Depression.

The collapse of economies around the world during the Depression changed our whole approach to macroeconomics. Before the Depression, macroeconomics was regarded as an extension of the microeconomics of markets. It was assumed that labor, capital, and output markets would keep the economy near full employment, with small fluctuations in wages, prices, and interest rates helping the economy to adjust to disruptions. The Depression forced economists to reconsider—and for several decades to scrap—this earlier way of looking at the macroeconomy.

British economist John Maynard Keynes led the profession in providing an explanation for the Depression. He shifted the entire focus of economic analysis. He didn't begin by studying individual markets, then assuming the economy would behave in similar fashion. Instead, Keynes began by looking at the broader economy, focusing on such aggregate data as spending by consumers, business, and government. His analysis serves as the foundation of modern macroeconomics; it underlies much of what follows in the rest of this book. After Keynes, macroeconomics became a subject in its own right, not just a small extension of microeconomics.

## Episodes of Hyperinflation

The second major event to influence macroeconomic analysis was episodes of extremely high inflation, or hyperinflation. These high inflationary episodes, which include the hyperinflation in Germany in the 1920s, the inflation crises many South American countries experienced during the last part of the 20th century, and most recently the inflation in Zimbabwe, involved inflation rates of over 1,000% a year.

Episodes of high inflation cripple economies by forcing people to spend much of their time coping with rapidly changing prices, until finally the economy collapses. Hyperinflation is associated with a rapid increase in the money supply, usually because governments finance deficits by pulling out all the stops on the printing presses—printing more and more money. Periods of high inflation, therefore, tend to be associated with high budget deficits, which many governments finance by printing money. Several chapters in this book consider the link between the quantity of money in the economy and changes in output and inflation.

These inflationary episodes and the havoc they wreaked have convinced monetary authorities such as the Federal Reserve to carefully manage the money supply. As you will see, nudging the growth rate of the money supply up can lead to short-term gains in employment and output, but increasing the money supply too rapidly simply leads to higher prices in the longer term, or inflation. Modern monetary theory and policy has developed out of this cauldron of past episodes of high inflation.

## Budget Deficits

A third influence on macroeconomic analysis has been the huge swings in federal budget deficits over the past two or three decades. Massive deficits in many developing countries devastated their economies, focusing attention on the long-run consequences of mismanaging the economy.

High budget deficits must be financed by either borrowing from the public or printing money. Borrowing huge sums of money in the capital markets drives up interest rates and often crowds out the private investment in new plants and equipment that must occur if the economy is to grow and prosper. Just as you are less likely to take out a mortgage when interest rates are 15% as compared to 6%, so businesses are far less likely to invest in production capacity when interest rates climb into double digits. And as noted earlier, running the printing presses to finance a deficit simply generates inflation. The higher the deficit relative to the size of the economy, the higher inflation rates go, and the more devastating the results.

It is not surprising that major economic problems such as a depression, hyperinflation, and massive budget deficits focus the attention of economists, much as a 1,000-foot drop straight down focuses the attention of a mountain climber. In times of economic trouble, economists are not just engaged in academic research. They desperately try to solve problems that, if not corrected, can bring massive hardship to millions of people and whole nations. Later, with the benefit of hindsight, economists can develop more complete explanations of what has happened. These theories help economists prevent the future occurrence of similar events. These theories also help achieve future macroeconomic goals.

## Macroeconomic Goals

Before the Great Depression and World War II, no one talked about macroeconomic goals. Government policy revolved around a few limited responsibilities, such as national defense, tax and tariff collection, road building, and the maintenance of a stable legal environment. During the Depression, the Roosevelt administration expanded the role of government by enacting a wide variety of employment and spending programs, collectively known as the New Deal, and establishing the Social Security Administration to ensure a minimal standard of living for the elderly.

Following World War II, many people assumed that the economy would shrink back to its prewar recession levels, possibly ushering in another depression. To avert such a downturn, Congress passed the Employment Act of 1946, which mandated a national goal of providing full employment to all Americans who are willing and able to work. Rationing and the focus on producing armaments during the war years, however, left consumers with huge pent-up demands for cars, appliances, and housing. As a result, the economy mushroomed after the war, much to the surprise of many Americans.

Congress passed the Full Employment and Balanced Growth Act of 1978, also known as the Humphrey-Hawkins Act, to augment the original Act passed in 1946. Besides full employment, this Act directs the government to pursue policies designed to stimulate economic growth and reduce inflation. Because inflation had reached double digits by the 1970s, it was only natural that Congress should add price stability to the nation's economic goals.

Figures 1 and 2 (on the next page) show how well these major macroeconomic goals have been met over the last three decades (the vertical shaded areas represent recessions). The rate of economic growth has been negative in only three periods and averaged around 3% in the rest (Figure 1). The most recent recession represented the biggest decline in real

**FIGURE 1—Percent Change in Real GDP and the Federal Deficit as a Percent of GDP**

Real GDP grows on average around 3%, but has been negative in the early 1980s and in 2009. The federal budget was in surplus between 1997–1999, though normally it is in deficit by approximately 3% to 4% of GDP. The deficit jumped to 13% of GDP in 2009 as the Obama administration used deficit spending to stimulate the economy and pay for new programs.

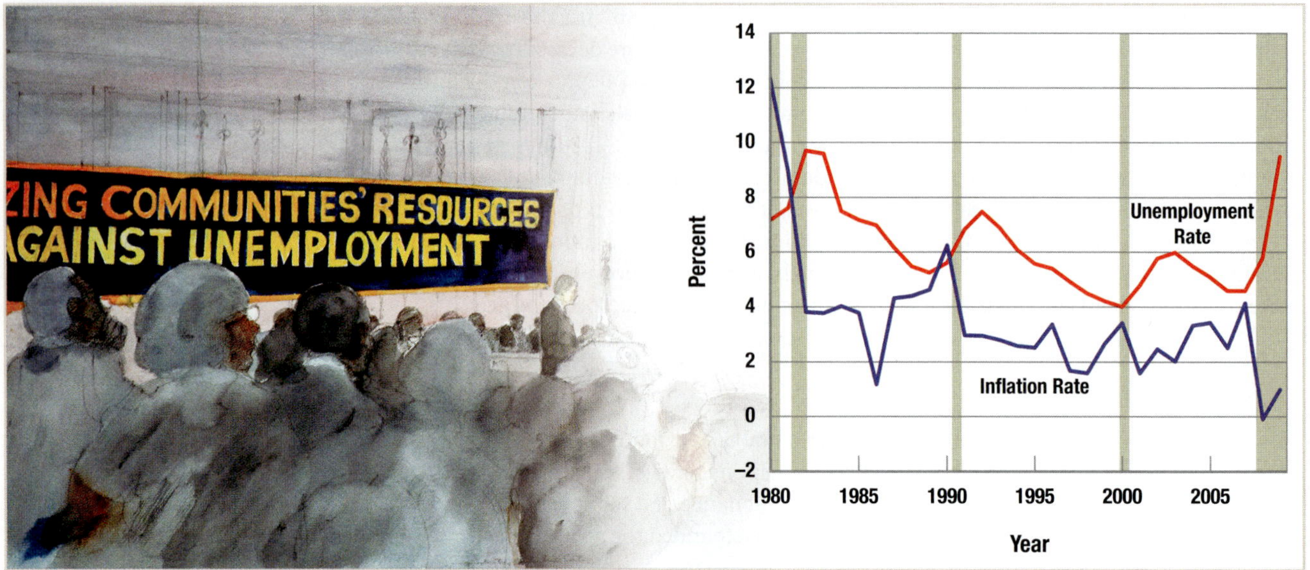


**FIGURE 2—Unemployment and Inflation Rates**

Unemployment rates rise during and for a while after recessions (the vertical shaded areas), with the annual average rate approaching 10% in the early 1980s and in 2009. Inflation was high during the late 1970s and early 1980s, but fell to roughly 2% to 3% annually by the early 1990s and generally has stayed in this relatively low range.

GDP in half a century. The federal budget was in surplus (tax revenue exceeded spending) in 1997–1999 during the tech boom of the late 1990s. The rest of the time, deficits have been roughly 3% to 4% of GDP, with the notable exception of our current deficit that is over 13% but is expected to decline as the economy rebounds.

As Figure 2 shows, annual unemployment rates have been high in the early 1980s and in 2009 when the economy was in a deep recession. The rest of the time it was in the 5% to 7% range. Inflation was clearly a problem in the 1970s and early 1980s, but has been low ever since. On the whole, the economy performed well during the 20 plus years before 2008. The recession of 2008–2009 deviated from this trend and has resulted in an extraordinary policy response from the federal government, as we will see in the chapters that follow.

In summary, the major economic goals our nation has set for itself include full employment, price stability, and high economic growth. And, as we will see, moreover, full employment and low inflation involve tradeoffs: It is difficult to have both for long. We will leave this issue, however, for a later chapter. Let's turn now to a brief look at business cycles.

## Business Cycles

America's economic growth over the past century has been little short of phenomenal. Even so, the general upward rise in economic activity and standard of living has been punctuated by periods of downturn, recession, and one outright depression. These fluctuations around the long-run growth trend are called business cycles, and they are a common feature of industrialized economies.

### Defining Business Cycles

Business cycles: Alternating increases and decreases in economic activity that are typically punctuated by periods of downturn, recession, recovery, and boom.

**Business cycles** are defined as alternating increases and decreases in economic activity. As economists Arthur Burns and Wesley Mitchell wrote,

> *Business cycles are a type of fluctuation found in the aggregate economic activity of nations that organize their work mainly in business enterprises: a cycle consists of expansions occurring at about the same time in many economic activities, followed by similarly general recession, contractions and revivals which merge into the expansion phase of the next cycle.*[6]

[6] Arthur Burns and Wesley Mitchell, *Measuring Business Cycles* (New York: National Bureau of Economic Research), 1946, p. 3.

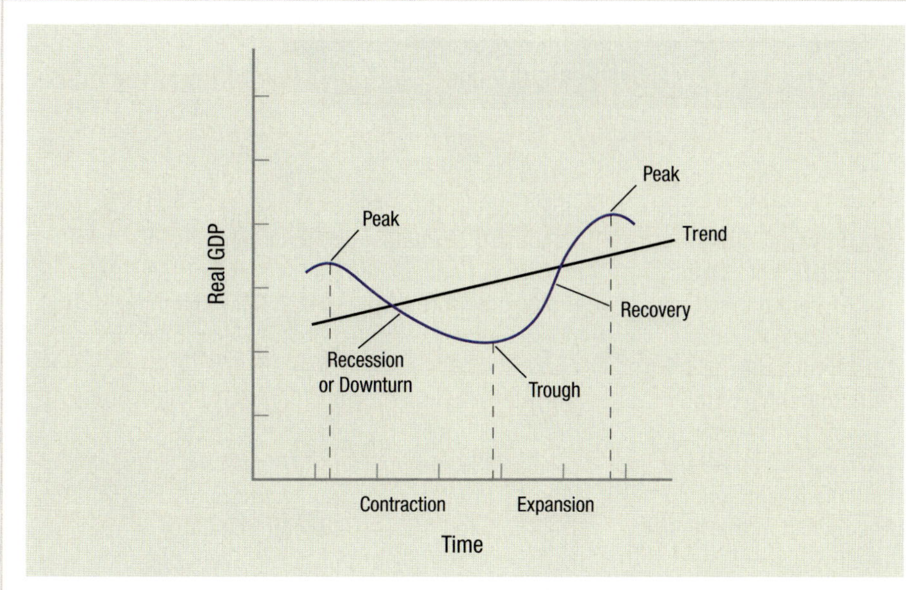


**FIGURE 3—Typical Business Cycle**

The four phases of the business cycle are the peak or boom, followed by a recession (often called a downturn or contraction), leading to the trough or bottom of the cycle, followed by a recovery or an expansion leading to another peak. Note that although this diagram suggests business cycles have regular movements, in reality the various phases of the cycle vary widely in duration and intensity.

Figure 3 shows the four phases of the business cycle. These phases, around an upward trend, include the peak (sometimes called a boom), followed by a recession (often referred to as a downturn or contraction), leading to the trough or bottom of the cycle, finally followed by a recovery or an expansion to another peak.

A peak in the business cycle usually means the economy is operating at its capacity. Peaks are followed by downturns or recessions. This change can happen simply because the boom runs out of steam and business investment begins to decline, thereby throwing the economy into a tailspin, as we will see in later chapters.

Once a recession is under way, business reacts by curtailing hiring and perhaps even laying off workers, thus adding to the recession's depth. Eventually, however, a trough is reached, and economic activity begins to pick up as businesses and consumers become more enthusiastic about the economy. Often, the federal government or the Federal Reserve institutes fiscal or monetary policies to help reverse the recession. Again, this analysis is the focus of future chapters.

Figure 3 suggests that business cycles are fairly regular, but in fact the various phases of the cycle can vary dramatically in duration and intensity. As Table 1 shows, the recessions of the last half century have lasted anywhere from 6 months to 18 months. Expansions or

**TABLE 1 Selected Data for U.S. Business Cycles Since 1950**

| Years | Peak | Trough | Recession Length (months) | Expansion Length (months) | Percentage Change in Real GDP | Maximum Unemployment Rate (%) |
|---|---|---|---|---|---|---|
| 1953–54 | Jul-53 | May-54 | 10 | 39 | −2.2 | 5.9 |
| 1957–58 | Aug-57 | Apr-58 | 8 | 24 | −3.6 | 7.4 |
| 1960–61 | Apr-60 | Feb-61 | 10 | 106 | −0.6 | 7.1 |
| 1969–70 | Dec-69 | Nov-70 | 11 | 36 | +0.2 | 6.1 |
| 1973–75 | Nov-73 | Mar-75 | 16 | 58 | −1.8 | 9.0 |
| 1980 | Jan-80 | Jul-80 | 6 | 12 | −2.3 | 7.8 |
| 1981–82 | Jul-81 | Nov-82 | 16 | 92 | −2.2 | 10.8 |
| 1990–91 | Jul-90 | Mar-91 | 8 | 120 | −1.0 | 6.9 |
| 2001 | Mar-01 | Nov-01 | 8 | 73 | +1.0 | 5.8 |
| 2007–09 | Dec-07 | Jun-09 | 18 | — | −4.1 | 10.4 |

## Joseph Schumpeter (1883–1950)

Joseph Schumpeter drew attention to the critical role of the entrepreneur in the process of economic development. He famously coined the term "creative destruction" to describe the innovative dynamism of capitalism but came to the surprising conclusion that the system he exalted was ultimately doomed by the forces it helped create.

Born in Triesch, Moravia, in 1883, Schumpeter was the son of a cloth manufacturer. He attended an elite private school and then studied law and economics at the University of Vienna. After graduating, he practiced law in Cairo and provided financial advice to an Egyptian princess. In 1909 he returned to Europe and began teaching at the University of Czernowitz and later at the University of Graz.

AP Photo/Dick Fung

At 28, he wrote his first important book, entitled *The Theory of Economic Development,* in which he emphasized the importance of the innovator as distinct from the inventor. Innovators made use of the benefits of technology and scientific discovery to advance economic progress. This book was greeted with enthusiasm and helped him to land the position of minister of finance for Austria. Seven months later he resigned, stating, "I have no wish to remain minister of finance for a country which is about to go bankrupt." Unbelievably, he was then appointed president of a private bank that he bankrupted two years later by borrowing to speculate in high-risk stocks. In 1932, he emigrated to the United States, where he would finish his career as an influential economics professor at Harvard University.

Schumpeter was a confirmed elitist who suffered from self doubt and depression. Although he enjoyed telling audiences that he "aspired to become the greatest economist, horseman [he often lectured in riding attire], and lover in the world," he would then throw in the punchline, "but things are not going well with the horses." Even though his career was in the shadow of the more famous John Maynard Keynes, he considered himself to be the greater economist.

In 1939, he published *Business Cycles,* which linked entrepreneurial activity to business cycles. He identified a first wave of innovation in the 1780s with the advent of steam power and textile manufacturing. The second wave of innovation came with railways and steel production. The third wave was concerned with electricity and the automobile. Paradoxically, Schumpeter connected innovation with the downturns or depressions in the business cycle, as new products competed with the old. Depressions, in his view, were part of the process of adapting to new innovations. As entrepreneurs spent their capital to pay off debts, the result was deflation. Economic recovery would come when adaptation was completed and the deflationary forces ended.

In 1942, Schumpeter published *Capitalism, Socialism and Democracy,* considered by many to be his masterpiece. He wrote about the future of capitalism, which he described as creative destruction. In an odd exercise in devil's advocacy, he praised the economic thinking of Karl Marx and came to a similar conclusion about the ultimate fate of capitalism. In Schumpeter's view, however, it was the "bourgeoisie" and not the working class that would destroy the system, as the role of the individual entrepreneur was supplanted by the bureaucratic administration of large corporations.

Sources: Thomas McCraw, *Prophet of Innovation: Joseph Schumpeter and Creative Destruction* (Cambridge, MA: Harvard University Press), 2007; and Paul Strathern, *A Brief History of Economic Genius* (New York: Texere), 2001.

recoveries have varied even more, lasting from 1 year to as many as 9 years. Some recessions, moreover, have been truly intense, bringing about major declines in income, while others have been little more than potholes in the road, causing no declines in real income.

Unemployment has shown a similar variability: The more severe the recession, the higher the unemployment rate goes. In our previous two recessions (1990–91 and 2001), the economy as a whole showed remarkable resiliency, but the recoveries were termed "jobless recoveries" because the early rate of employment increase was well below the average for past recoveries.

## Dating Business Cycles

Business cycles are officially dated by the National Bureau of Economic Research (NBER), a nonprofit research organization founded in 1920. The NBER assigns a committee of economists the task of dating "turning points"—points at which the economy switches from peak to downturn or from trough to recovery. The committee looks for clusters of aggregate data pointing either up or down. Committee members date turning points when they reach a consensus that the economy has switched directions.

The committee's work has met with some criticism because their decisions rest on the consensus of six eminent economists, who often bring different methodologies to the table. The committee's deliberations, moreover, are not public; the committee announces only its final decision. Finally, the NBER dates peaks and troughs only after the fact: Their decisions appear several months after the turning points have been reached.[7] By waiting, the panel can use updated or revised data to avoid premature judgments. But some argue that the long lag renders the NBER's decisions less useful to policymakers.

## National Activity Index

To some degree, to overcome these considerations, the Federal Reserve Bank of Chicago developed its National Activity Index, a weighted average of 85 indicators of national economic activity. These indicators are drawn from categories such as production, income, employment, unemployment, hours worked, personal consumption, housing, sales, orders, and inventories. This data clearly covers a huge swath of economic activity.

Figure 4 shows the index since 1985. When the index has a zero value, the economy is growing at its historical trend. Negative values mean the economy is growing slower and

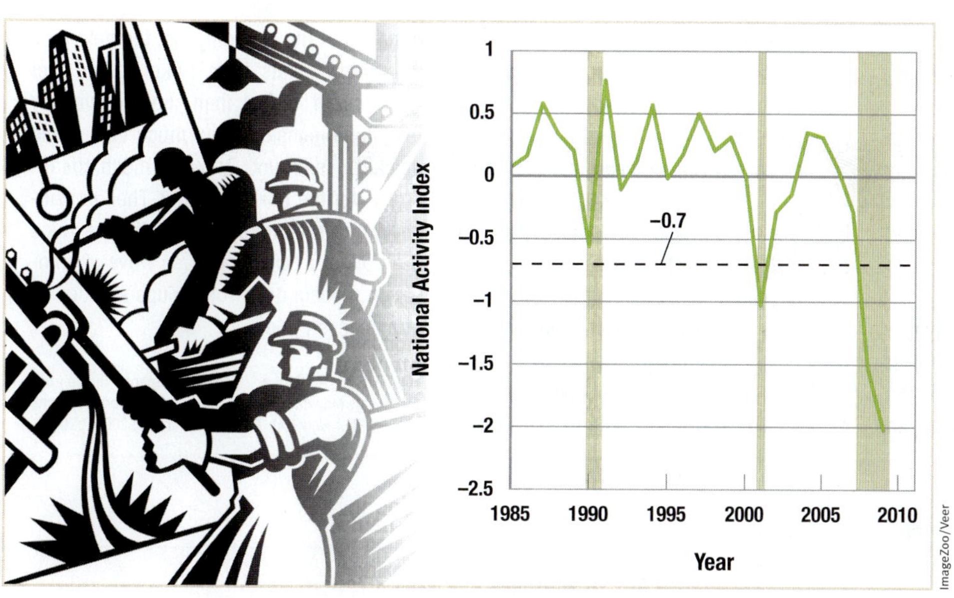


**FIGURE 4—The Federal Reserve Bank of Chicago's National Activity Index**

The National Activity Index is a weighted average of 85 economic indicators of economic activity in the economy. When the index moves below −0.70 (dashed line), the economy is probably moving into a recession. This index appears to track the official NBER peak turning points.

[7] Marcelle Chauvet and Jeremy Piger, "Identifying Business Cycle Turning Points in Real Time," *Review* (St. Louis: The Federal Reserve Bank of St. Louis), March/April 2003, pp. 47–61.

positive rates imply it's growing faster than its long-term trend. When the index moves below –0.70 following a period of expansion, this suggests a high likelihood the economy has moved into recession. If the index exceeds +0.70 after a substantial period of expansion, this suggests the economy may face a period of increasing inflation.

The index has done a remarkable job of pinpointing the signs of recession in a reasonably current time frame. Official NBER peak dates indicating the beginning of a downturn coincide closely with the Chicago Fed's index falling below –0.70. This index is one more tool in economists' arsenal to help them guide policymakers.

The duration and intensity of business cycles are measured using data collected by the Bureau of Economic Analysis and U.S. Department of Labor. These data for aggregate income and output come from the national income and product accounts. We turn in a moment to see how these data are collected and analyzed and consider how well they measure our standard of living. Keep in mind that these data are the key ingredients economists use to determine the state of the macroeconomy and to decide whether our national macroeconomic goals are being met.

## *Issue:* Do Waves of Innovation Explain Business Cycles?

**Economist Joseph Schumpeter** used the phrase "creative destruction" to describe waves of innovations that are the driving force behind business cycles. Writing in the late 1930s and early 1940s, he saw innovations such as steam power and railroads as forces that were at first engines of economic growth. Then once they were widely adopted, stagnation followed as the economy waited for the next great innovation and boom.

The effect of information technology (our current innovation wave) on manufacturers is easy enough to see. It is obvious that computer-aided design has streamlined product creation in the automobile, airline, and heavy-machinery industry.

What have not been so obvious are the beneficial effects of information technology on the labor-intensive service sector of the economy. Preliminary studies have revealed that productivity in services grew at a greater rate than for goods-producing sectors.

This growth in services productivity due to information technology has been almost across the board. So far, nearly all of the service industries studied have witnessed growth in labor productivity after 1995. The service industry laggards are hotels, health, education, and entertainment, possibly because these industries are especially labor-intensive.

It is fairly clear how information technology has helped service industries that have seen significant growth. The telephone industry, wholesale and retail trade, and finance have all benefited from being better able to track inventory and communicate with customers. Think of bar-coded merchandise and scanners at grocery stores or retail stores. These stores know immediately what is selling, what is not, what stock is on hand, and what needs to be replenished quickly. And the ubiquity of bar codes on products and the plummeting cost of "smart" cash registers mean that your local 7-Eleven is practically as efficient in tracking customer demand and inventory as the big Wal-Mart down the road.

The preliminary view is that the rapid decline in the price of information technology in the 1990s brought this technology to medium- and small-size service enterprises. This led to productivity growth throughout most of the economy. So, the next time you order tickets from Ticketmaster over the Internet rather than the old way by telephone, consider how much easier and quicker it is for you, and how much cheaper it is for the ticket provider. Then consider how this change might just be a good example of a Schumpeterian wave of innovation, a main driver of the ups and downs of business cycles.

Peter Siu/Getty Images

Source: Hal R. Varian, "Economic Scene: Information Technology May Have Been What Cured Low Service-Sector Productivity," *New York Times*, February 12, 2004, p. C2.

**CHECKPOINT**

### THE SCOPE OF MACROECONOMICS

- Three major events have shaped macroeconomic ideas in the last century: the Great Depression, episodes of hyperinflation, and large budget deficits.

- The Great Depression and John Maynard Keynes completely changed the focus of macroeconomics from an extension of microeconomic theory to an analysis in its own right.
- The Employment Act of 1946, later amended to become the Full Employment and Balanced Growth Act of 1978 (Humphrey-Hawkins Act), directs the government to pursue policies that generate full employment with economic growth while maintaining price stability.
- Business cycles are alternating increases and decreases in economic activity.
- The four phases of the business cycle include the peak, recession (or contraction), trough, and recovery (or expansion).
- Business cycles are dated by the National Bureau of Economic Research (NBER). Business cycles are usually dated some time after the trough and peak have been reached.
- The Chicago Federal Reserve Bank's National Activity Index is more of a real-time estimate of where the economy is in the business cycle.

**QUESTION:** Do you think the business cycle has a bigger impact on automobile and capital goods manufacturers or on grocery stores?

Answers to the Checkpoint question can be found at the end of this chapter.

## National Income Accounting

The national income and product accounts (NIPA) let economists judge our nation's economic performance, compare American income and output to that of other nations, and track the economy's condition over the course of the business cycle. Many economists would say these accounts represent one of the greatest inventions of the 20th century.[8]

Before World War I, estimating the output of various sectors of the economy—and to an extent the output of the economy as a whole—was a task left to individual scholars. Government agencies tried to measure various sorts of economic activity, but little came of these efforts. When the Great Depression struck, the lack of reliable economic data made it difficult for the administration and Congress to design timely and appropriate policy responses. Much of the information that was available at the time was anecdotal: newspaper reports of plant shutdowns, stories of home and farm foreclosures, and observations of the rapid meltdown of the stock market.

In 1933, Congress directed the Department of Commerce to develop estimates of "total national income for the United States for each of the calendar years 1929, 1930, and 1931, including estimates of the portions of national income originating from [different sectors] and estimates of the distribution of the national income in the form of wages, rents, royalties, dividends, profits and other types of payments." This directive was the beginning of the NIPA.

In 1934, a small group of economists working under the leadership of Simon Kuznets and in collaboration with the NBER produced a report for the Senate. The report defined many standard economic aggregates still in use today, including gross national product, gross domestic product, consumer spending, and investment spending. Kuznets was later awarded a Nobel Prize for his lifetime of work in this area.

Work continued on NIPA through World War II, and by 1947 the basic components of the present day income and product accounts were in place. Over the years, the Department of Commerce (DOC) has modified, improved, and updated the data it collects. These data are released on a quarterly basis, with preliminary data being put out in

[8] William Nordhaus and Edward Kokkelenberg (eds.), *Nature's Numbers: Expanding the National Economic Accounts to Include the Environment* (Washington, DC: National Academy Press), 1999, p. 12.

## Nobel Prize

### Simon Kuznets

Simon Kuznets was awarded the Nobel Prize in 1971 for devising systematic approaches to the compilation and analysis of national economic data. Kuznets is credited with developing gross national product as a measurement of economic output.

Born in the Ukraine in 1901, Kuznets emigrated to the United States in 1922 and taught himself English in one summer. He attended Columbia University where he earned a Ph.D. in 1926. He then worked at the National Bureau of Economic Research, conducting studies of national income and capital formation. For many, World War II interrupted their professional lives, but for Kuznets, who served on the Bureau of Planning and Statistics of the War Production Board, it was a chance to apply his work measuring output.

Kuznets developed methods for calculating the size and changes in national income known as the national income and product accounts. Caring little for abstract models, he sought to define concepts that could be observed empirically and measured statistically. Thanks to Kuznets, economists have had a large amount of data with which to test their economic theories. Starting in 1931, he taught economics at the University of Pennsylvania, Johns Hopkins University, and then Harvard University until his death in 1985.

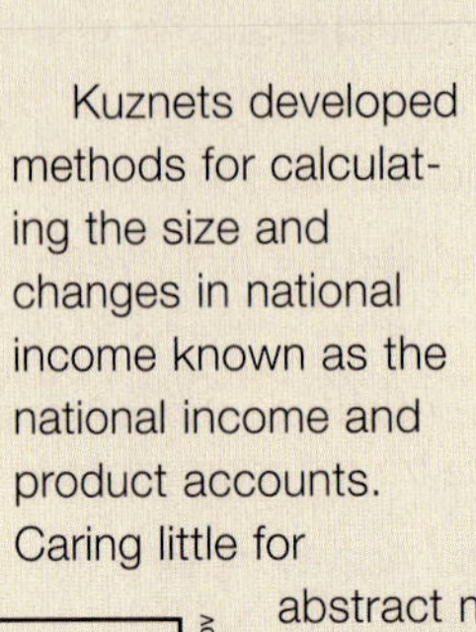


Office of Management and Budget, www.budget.gov

the middle of the month following a given quarter. By the end of a given quarter, the DOC will have collected about two-thirds of the survey data it needs, allowing it to estimate the remaining data to generate preliminary figures.

## The Core of the NIPA

The major components of the NIPA can be found in either of two ways: by adding up the income in the economy or by adding up spending. A simple circular flow diagram of the economy shows why either approach can be used to determine the economy's level of economic activity.

### The Circular Flow Diagram

**Circular flow diagram:** Illustrates how households and firms interact through product and resource markets and shows that economic aggregates can be determined by either examining spending flows or income flows to households.

Figure 5 is a simple **circular flow diagram** that shows how businesses and households interact through the product and resource markets.

Let us first follow the arrows that point in a clockwise direction. Begin at the bottom of the diagram with households. Households supply labor (and other inputs or factors of production) to the resource market; that is, they become employees of businesses. Businesses use this labor (and other inputs) to produce goods and services that are supplied to the product markets. Such products in the end find their way back into households through consumer purchases. The arrows pointing clockwise show the flow of real items: hours worked, goods and services produced and purchased.

The arrows pointing counterclockwise, in contrast, represent flows of money. Businesses pay for inputs (factors) of production: land, labor, capital, and entrepreneurship. Factors are paid rents, wages, interest, and profits. These payments become income for the economy's households, which use these funds to purchase goods and services in the product market. This spending for goods and services becomes sales revenues for the business sector.

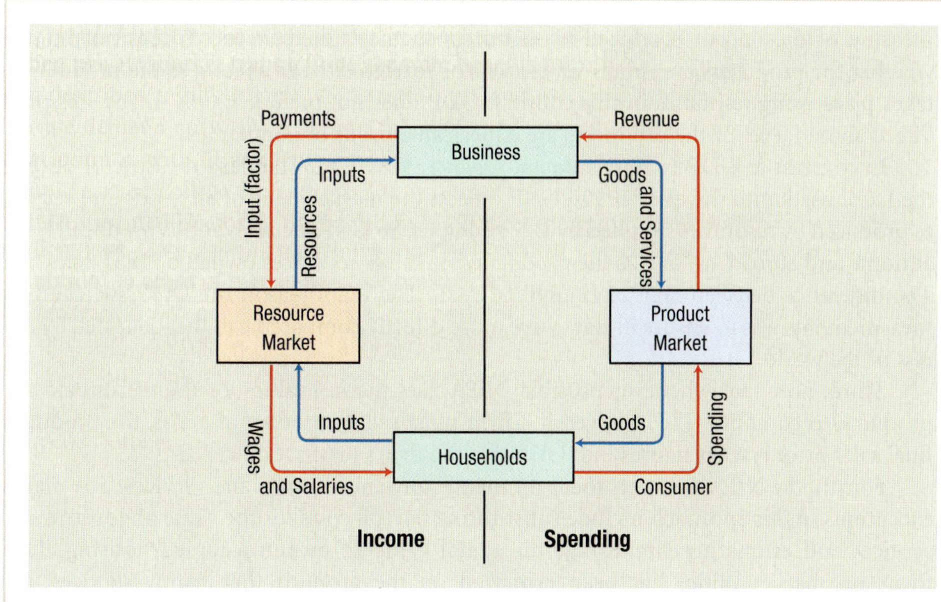


**FIGURE 5—A Simple Circular Flow Diagram**

This simple circular flow diagram illustrates why the economic aggregates in our economy can be determined in either of two ways. Spending flows through the right side of the diagram, while the left side of the diagram shows incomes flowing to households. Note that one person's spending is another person's income.

## Spending and Income: Looking at GDP in Two Ways

This simple circular flow diagram illustrates why economic aggregates in our economy can be determined in either of two ways. The spending in the economy accrues on the right side of the diagram. In this simple diagram, all spending is assumed to be consumer spending for goods and services. We know, however, that businesses spend money on investment goods such as equipment, plants, factories, and specialized vehicles to increase their productivity. Also, government buys goods and services, as do foreigners. This spending shows up in the NIPA, though it is not included in our simple circular flow diagram.

Second, similar income is generated equal to the spending in the product market. This is shown on the left side of the diagram. Wages and salaries constitute the bulk of income in our economy (roughly three-quarters of it), with rents, interest, and profits comprising the rest. Everything that is spent on the right side represents income on the left side; all spending must equal input (factor) incomes. We now define the major aggregates in the NIPA.

## Gross Domestic Product

**Gross domestic product (GDP)** is a measure of the economy's total output; it is the most widely reported value in the NIPA. Technically, the nation's *GDP is equal to the total market value of all final goods and services produced by resources in the United States in a given year.* A few points about this definition need to be noted.

Gross domestic product (GDP): A measure of the economy's total output; it is the most widely reported value in the national income and product accounts (NIPA) and is equal to the total market value of all final goods and services produced by resources in the United States in a given year.

First, GDP reflects the *final* value of goods and services produced. So measurements of GDP do not include the value of intermediate goods used to produce other products. This distinction helps prevent what economists call "double counting," since a good's final value includes the intermediate values going into its production.

To illustrate, consider a box of toothpicks. The firm producing these toothpicks must first purchase a supply of cottonwood, let's say for \$0.22 a box. The firm then mills this wood into toothpicks, which it puts into a small box purchased from another company at \$0.08 apiece. The completed box is sold to a grocery store wholesale for \$0.65. After a markup, the grocery retails the box of toothpicks for \$0.89. The sale raises GDP by \$0.89, *not* by \$1.84 (0.22 + 0.08 + 0.65 + 0.89), since the values of the cottonwood, the box, and the grocery store's services are already included in the toothpicks' final sales price. Thus, by including only final prices in GDP, double counting is avoided.

A second point to note is that, as the term gross *domestic* product implies, GDP is a measure of the output produced by resources in the United States. It does not matter whether the producers are American citizens or foreign citizens as long as the production takes place using resources in this country. GDP does not include goods or services produced abroad, even if the producers are American citizens or companies.

In contrast to GDP is *gross national product* (GNP), the standard measure of output the DOC used until the early 1990s. GNP reflects the market value of all goods and services produced by resources supplied by U.S. residents. So GNP includes goods produced both at home and abroad, as long as the production involves resources owned by U.S. residents. The difference between GDP and GNP is small. The main reason the DOC switched its measurements was to ensure its data were more directly comparable to that collected by the rest of the world.

Third, note that whenever possible, NIPA uses market values, or the prices paid for products, to compute GDP. So even if a firm must sell its product at a loss, the product's final sales price is what figures into GDP, not the firm's production costs.

Fourth, the NIPA accounts focus on market-produced goods and services. The major exceptions to this approach include substituting payroll costs for the value of government services and estimating (imputing) the rental value of owner-occupied housing. This focus on market values has been criticized on the grounds that nanny services, for instance, are figured into GDP, while the values for these same services when performed by parents are not.

## The Expenditures Approach to Calculating GDP

Again, GDP can be measured using either spending or income. With the expenditures approach, all spending on final goods and services is added together. The four major categories of spending are personal consumer spending, gross private domestic investment (GPDI), government spending, and net exports (exports minus imports).

### Personal Consumption Expenditures

Personal consumption expenditures: Goods and services purchased by residents of the United States, whether individuals or businesses; they include durable goods, nondurable goods, and services.

**Personal consumption expenditures** are goods and services purchased by residents of the United States, whether individuals or businesses. Goods and services are divided into three main categories: durable goods, nondurable goods, and services. Durable goods are products that can be stored or inventoried; they have an average life span of three years. Automobiles, major appliances, books, CDs, and firearms are all examples of durable goods. Nondurable goods include all other tangible goods, such as canned soft drinks, frozen pizza, toothbrushes, and underwear (all of which should be thrown out before they are three years old). Services are commodities that cannot be stored and are consumed at the time and place of purchase, for example, legal, barber, and repair services. Table 2 gives a detailed account of U.S. personal consumption spending in 2009. Notice that personal consumption is roughly 70% of GDP, far and away the most important part of GDP, and services are two-thirds of personal consumption.

### Gross Private Domestic Investment

Gross private domestic investment (GPDI): Investments in such things as structures (residential and nonresidential), equipment, and software, and changes in private business inventories.

The second major aggregate listed in Table 2 is **gross private domestic investment (GPDI),** which at nearly 11% of GDP, refers to *fixed investments,* or investments in such things as structures (residential and nonresidential), equipment, and software. It also includes changes in private inventories.

Residential housing represents about a quarter of GPDI, and nonresidential structures make up the rest since inventory changes are small. Nonresidential structures include such diverse structures as hotels and motels, manufacturing plants, mine shafts, oil wells, and fast-food restaurants. Improvements to existing business structures and new construction are counted as fixed investments.

**TABLE 2** The Expenditures Approach to GDP (2009)

| Category | Billions of $ | % of GDP |
|---|---|---|
| **Personal Consumption Expenditures** | **10,132.90** | **71.15** |
| Durable goods | 1,051.30 | 7.38 |
| Nondurable goods | 2,241.00 | 15.74 |
| Services | 6,840.60 | 48.03 |
| **Gross Private Domestic Investment** | **1,556.10** | **10.93** |
| Fixed nonresidential | 1,353.90 | 9.51 |
| Fixed residential | 358.80 | 2.52 |
| Change in inventories | −156.50 | −1.10 |
| **Government Purchases of Goods and Services** | **2,955.40** | **20.75** |
| Federal | 1,164.30 | 8.18 |
| State and local | 1,791.10 | 12.58 |
| **Net Exports** | **−402.20** | **−2.82** |
| Exports | 1,573.80 | 11.05 |
| Imports | 1,976.00 | 13.87 |
| **Gross Domestic Product** | **14,242.10** | **100.00** |

**Source:** U.S. Department of Commerce, Bureau of Economic Analysis, www.bea.doc.gov.

A "change in inventories" refers to a change in the physical volume of the inventory a private business owns, valued at the average prices over the period. If a business increases its inventories, this change is treated as an investment since the business is adding to the stock of products it has ready for sale.

Private investment is a key factor driving economic growth and an important determinant of swings in the business cycle. Figure 6 tracks GPDI as a percentage of GDP since 1980. Recessions are represented by vertical shaded areas. Notice that during each recession, GPDI turns down, and when the recession ends, GPDI turns up. Investment is, therefore, an important factor shaping the turning points of the business cycle, especially at the troughs, and an important determinant of how severe recessions will be.

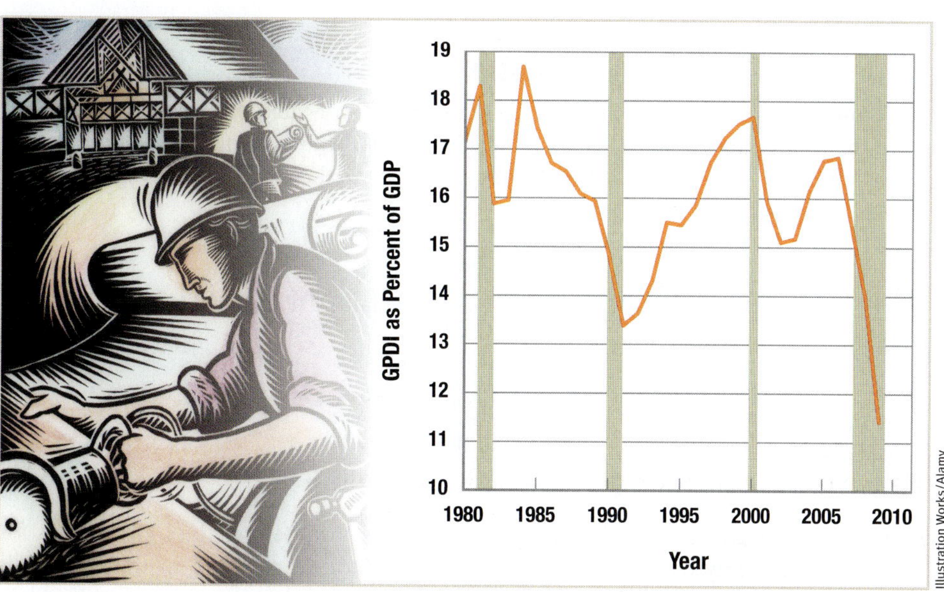


**FIGURE 6—Gross Private Domestic Investment (GPDI) as a Percent of GDP**

Private investment is a key factor driving economic growth and an important determinant of swings in the business cycle. This graph tracks GPDI as a percentage of GDP since 1980.

**Government spending:** Includes the wages and salaries of government employees (federal, state, and local); the purchase of products and services from private businesses and the rest of the world; and government purchases of new structures, equipment, and software.

## Government Purchases

The government component of GDP measures the impact **government spending** has on final demand in the economy. As Figure 7 illustrates, at over 20% of GDP, government spending is now a relatively large and growing component of GDP. It includes the wages and salaries of government employees (federal, state, and local) and the purchase of products and services from private businesses and the rest of the world. Government spending also includes the purchase of new structures, equipment, and software.

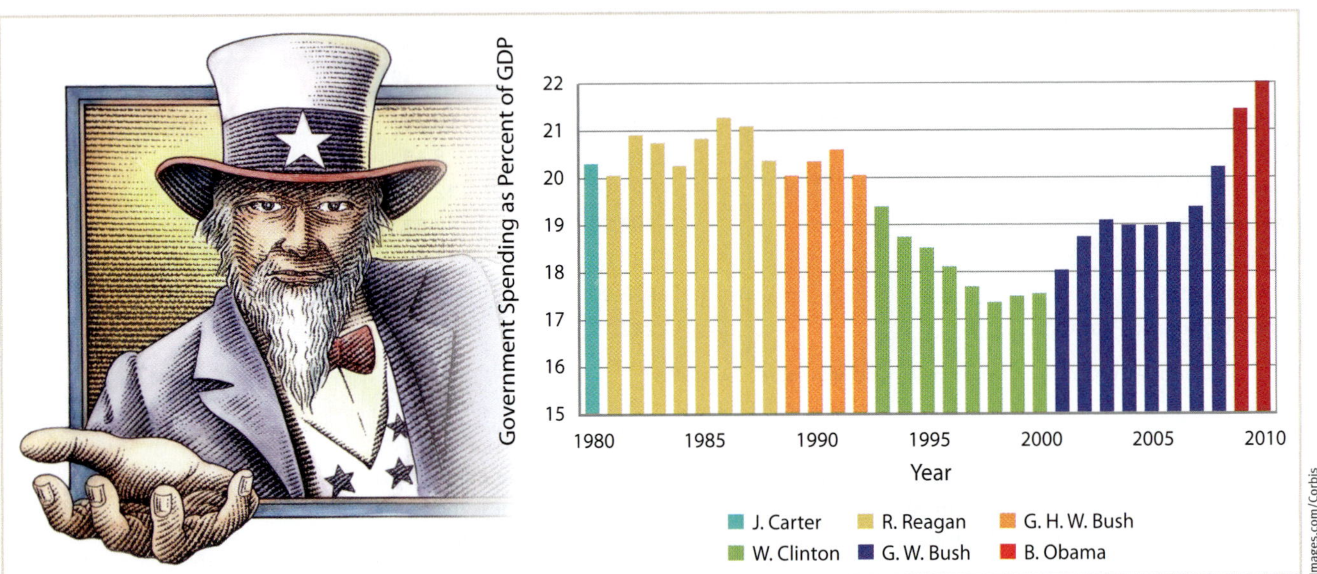


**FIGURE 7—Government Spending as a Percent of GDP**

Since the late 1990s, government spending as a percent of the economy has been rising.

## Net Exports of Goods and Services

**Net exports** of goods and services are equal to exports minus imports for the current period. Exports include all the items we sell overseas: items such as agricultural products, movies, and technology products such as computers and software. Our imports are all those items we bring into the country, including vegetables from Mexico, clothing from the Far East, and cars from Japan. Most years our imports exceed our exports, so net exports are a minus percentage of GDP.

**Net exports:** Exports minus imports for the current period. Exports include all the items we sell overseas such as agricultural products, movies, and technology products. Imports are all those items we bring into the country such as vegetables from Mexico, wine from Italy, and cars from Germany.

## Summing Aggregate Expenditures

The four categories just described are commonly abbreviated as C (consumption), I (investment), G (government), and X − M (net exports; exports minus imports). Together, these four variables constitute GDP. We often summarize this by the following equation:

$$GDP = C + I + G + (X - M)$$

Using the information from Table 2, we can calculate GDP for 2009 (in billions of dollars) as

$$14{,}242.1 = 10{,}132.9 + 1{,}556.1 + 2{,}955.4 + (-402.2)$$

# The Income Approach to Calculating GDP

As we have already seen, spending that contributes to GDP provides an income for one of the economy's various inputs (factors) of production. And in theory, this is how this process works. In practice, however, the national income accounts need to

**TABLE 3** The Income Approach to GDP (2009)

| Category | Billions of $ | % of GDP |
|---|---|---|
| **Compensation of Employees** | **7,751.5** | 54.43 |
| Wages and salaries | 6,249.2 | 43.88 |
| Employer contribution for social insurance | 456.2 | 3.20 |
| Employer contribution to pensions and insurance | 1,046.1 | 7.35 |
| **Proprietors' Income** | **1,037.9** | 7.29 |
| **Corporate Profits** | **1,358.9** | 9.54 |
| **Rental Income** | **277.9** | 1.95 |
| **Net Interest** | **759.7** | 5.33 |
| **Miscellaneous Adjustments** | **1,073.8** | 7.54 |
| **National Income** | **12,259.7** | 86.08 |
| **Adjustments to National Income** | | 0.00 |
| Capital consumption allowance | 1,032.5 | 7.25 |
| Statistical and other adjustments | 994.9 | 6.99 |
| **Gross Domestic Product** | **14,242.1** | 100.00 |

**Source:** U.S. Department of Commerce, Bureau of Economic Analysis, www.bea.doc.gov.

be adjusted to fully account for GDP when we switch from the expenditures to the income approach. Let's work our way through the income side of NIPA, which Table 3 summarizes.

## Compensation of Employees

Compensation to employees refers to payments for work done, including wages, salaries, and benefits. Benefits include the social insurance payments made by employers to various government programs, such as Social Security, Medicare, and workers' and unemployment compensation. Some other benefits that count as labor income are employer-provided pensions, profit-sharing plans, group health insurance, and in-kind benefits such as day care services. Employee compensation is nearly 55% of GDP.

## Proprietors' Income

Proprietors' income represents the current income of all sole proprietorships, partnerships, and tax-exempt cooperatives in the country. It includes the imputed (estimated) rental income of owner-occupied farm houses. Proprietors' income is adjusted by a capital consumption allowance to account for depreciating equipment (equipment that is used up while producing goods and services). Although there are a lot of proprietorships in the United States, their combined income is less than 8% of GDP.

## Corporate Profits

Corporate profits are defined as the income that flows to corporations, as adjusted for inventory valuation and capital consumption allowances. Most corporations are private enterprises, although this category also includes mutual financial institutions, Federal Reserve banks, and nonprofit institutions that mainly serve businesses. Despite the huge profit figures reported in the news media, corporate profits are less than 10% of GDP.

## Rental Income

Rental income, less than 2% of GDP, is the income that flows to individuals engaged in renting real property. This does not include the income of real estate agents or brokers, but it does include the imputed value of owner-occupied homes, along with royalties from patents, copyrights, and rights to natural resources.

## Net Interest

Net interest is the interest paid by businesses less the interest they receive, from this country and abroad, and is over 5% of GDP. Interest expense is the payment for the use of capital. Interest income includes payments from home mortgages, home improvement loans, and home equity loans.

## Miscellaneous Adjustments

Both indirect business taxes (sales and excise taxes) and foreign income earned in the United States are part of GDP, but must be backed out of payments to factors of production in this country. Neither is paid to U.S. factors of production.

## National Income

**National income:** All income, including wages, salaries and benefits, profits (for sole proprietors, partnerships, and corporations), rental income, and interest.

**National income** is all income, including wages, salaries, and benefits; profits (for sole proprietors, partnerships, and corporations); rental income; and interest. Pay to employees represents nearly two-thirds of national income, whereas corporate profits compose over 11%, with rental income and interest making up the rest.

## From National Income to GDP

National income is the income that accrues to U.S.-supplied resources, whether at home or abroad. Getting from national income to GDP requires a few adjustments. Specifically, one major item (and some minor ones that we will ignore) plus a statistical discrepancy must be added to national income to arrive at the GDP figures listed on the bottom of Table 3.

An allowance for the depreciation (or consumption) of fixed capital is added back, since gross domestic product is gross of depreciation to fixed capital.

This adjusted sum is known as *gross domestic income.* Once a small statistical discrepancy has been corrected, it is equal to GDP. When these adjustments are completed, GDP is the same whether it is derived from spending or income.

## Net Domestic Product

**Net domestic product:** Gross domestic product minus depreciation, or the capital consumption allowance.

As firms and individuals generate GDP, they use up some capital, which must be replaced if future production is to continue at similar levels. A more realistic measure of sustainable output, **net domestic product,** is defined as GDP minus depreciation, or the capital consumption allowance. Equipment wears out as output is produced. Motor graders, cranes, trucks, and automobiles do not last forever. Therefore, net domestic product represents the output the economy produced after adjusting for capital used up in the process.

## Personal Income and Disposable Personal Income

**Personal income:** All income, including wages, salaries, and other labor income; proprietors' income; rental income; personal interest and dividend income; and transfer payments (welfare and Social Security payments) received, with personal contributions for social insurance subtracted out.

**Disposable personal income:** Personal income minus taxes.

**Personal income** includes all income—wages, salaries, and other labor income; proprietors' income; rental income; personal interest and dividend income; and transfer payments (welfare and Social Security payments) received, with personal contributions for social insurance subtracted out.

People can do three things with the money they receive as personal income: pay taxes, spend the money (engage in consumption), or put the money into savings. **Disposable personal income** is defined as personal income minus taxes. Disposable income (Y) can be either spent (C) or saved (S); thus,

$$Y = C + S$$

This simple equation, which you will see again, led John Maynard Keynes to some powerful ideas about the workings of our economy.

We have seen how the national income and product accounts determine the major macroeconomic aggregates. But what does NIPA tell us about our economy? When GDP rises, are we better off as a nation? Do increases in GDP correlate with a rising standard of living? What impact does rising GDP have on the environment and the quality of life? We conclude this chapter with a brief look at some of these questions.

## GDP and Our Standard of Living

After World War II, GDP growth was viewed universally as a positive event for the economy. Today, Americans have become increasingly concerned with the impact economic activity has on the natural world. These days, it is difficult to watch a nightly newscast without seeing a report about some ecological disaster or looming environmental problem. Government, consumers, and businesses in the United States spend hundreds of billions of dollars annually to protect the environment at home and abroad. Surprisingly, however, our national income and production statistics do little to account for the environmental benefits or harmful impacts of economic activity.

In 1992, the Bureau of Economic Analysis decided to develop an experimental set of economic accounts known as the Integrated Environmental and Economic Satellite Accounts. Preliminary versions of these green GDP accounts were published in 1994, and later Congress directed the Department of Commerce (DOC) to set up an outside panel of experts to study this issue in greater depth. The DOC asked the National Academy of Sciences to look at green economic accounting, which it did, appointing a select panel.

The DOC panel concluded that "extending the U.S. NIPA to include assets and production activities associated with natural resources and the environment is an important goal." The panel concluded, "Developing nonmarket accounts to address such concerns as environmental impacts, the value of nonmarket natural resources, the value of nonmarket work, the value of investments in human capital, and the use of people's time would illuminate a wide variety of issues concerning the economic state of the nation."[9]

The panel's recommendations highlight some of the broader shortcomings of NIPA. For example, the national accounts ignore nonmarket transactions. If a maid cleans your apartment, GDP rises, but if you did the same job yourself, GDP is unaffected. The same is true for babysitting, lawn care, and car maintenance. Nor is the notion of augmenting the national accounts to account for nonmarket activities anything new; NIPA already imputes (estimates) the rental value of owner-occupied homes and adds this to GDP. The panel proposed that further measures be developed to reflect "not merely what consumers buy in stores, but also what they produce for themselves at home; the government services they 'buy' with their taxes; and the flow of services that are produced by environmental capital such as forests, national parks, and ocean fisheries."[10]

Many people believe NIPA should be an index of the well-being found within our economy. In that case, it would ideally need to take into account the implications of economic activity the DOC panel noted and more, perhaps including data on life expectancy; business spending on research and development; the stock of human capital, including education and health; greenhouse gas emissions; income distribution; poverty rates; and unemployment rates.

It is important, however, to keep NIPA's original purpose in mind. As the DOC panel noted, "The modern national income and product accounts are among the great inventions of the twentieth century. Among other things, they are used to judge economic performance over time, to compare the economies of different nations, to measure a nation's saving and investment, and to track the business cycle. Much as satellites in space can show the weather across an entire continent, the national accounts can give an overall picture of the state of the economy."[11]

To be sure, NIPA has served us well. Still, adjusting the current accounts to account for various environmental and other nonmarket considerations might provide us with an even better picture of the health of our economy. But we must keep in mind that an aggregate measure of the economy cannot be all things to all people. As we add complexity to an already complex undertaking, the NIPA may lose some of their effectiveness as a measure of economic activity. This is a difficult balancing act facing policymakers.

[9] Nordhaus and Kokkelenberg, *Nature's Numbers*, pp. 2–3.
[10] Ibid., p. 22.
[11] Ibid., p. 12.

The NIPA allow us to track business cycles, compare the domestic economy with that of other nations, and take a crude measure of our standard of living. In the next chapter, we will see how two other important policy variables, unemployment and inflation, are measured.

In the next several chapters, our focus will be on developing explanations of short-term movements in the business cycle and long-term economic growth (the trend line in Figure 3). If we can understand why upturns and downturns occur, we may be able to devise policies that reduce the severity of business cycle swings while promoting economic growth. These investigations and policy objectives form the essence of modern macroeconomic analysis.

## CHECKPOINT

### NATIONAL INCOME ACCOUNTING

- The circular flow diagram shows how households and firms interact through product and resource markets.
- GDP can be computed as spending or as income.
- GDP is equal to the total market value of all final goods and services produced by labor and property in an economy in a given year.
- Personal consumption expenditures are goods and services purchased by residents of the United States, both by individuals and businesses.
- Gross private domestic investment (GPDI) refers to fixed investments such as structures, equipment, and software.
- GDP is equal to consumer expenditures, investment expenditures, government purchases, and exports minus imports. In equation form, $GDP = C + I + G + (X - M)$.
- GDP can also be computed by adding all of the payments to factors of production. This includes compensation to employees, proprietors' income, rental income, corporate profits, and net interest, along with some statistical adjustments.
- While not perfect, GDP is a good measure of economic activity in our economy.

**QUESTIONS:** Each individual has a sense of how the macroeconomy is doing. Is it a mistake to extrapolate from one's own experience what may be happening in the aggregate? How might individual experiences lead one astray in thinking about the macroeconomy? How might it help?

Answers to the Checkpoint questions can be found at the end of this chapter.

## Key Concepts

Business cycles, p. 366
Circular flow diagram, p. 372
Gross domestic product (GDP), p. 373
Personal consumption expenditures, p. 374
Gross private domestic investment (GPDI), p. 374
Government spending, p. 376
Net exports, p. 376
National income, p. 378
Net domestic product, p. 378
Personal income, p. 378
Disposable personal income, p. 378

# Chapter Summary

## The Scope of Macroeconomics

Macroeconomics is the study of economic activity from the perspective of the entire economy. It focuses on such issues as economic growth, output of the economy, employment levels, inflation, unemployment, and interest rates.

The study of macroeconomics was driven by three major events of the 20th century: the Great Depression, episodes of hyperinflation, and extensive budget deficits. In each case, major economic problems forced economists to focus their attention on the economy as a whole.

Macroeconomic policy goals include stimulating economic growth, maintaining full employment, and price stability (low inflation).

Business cycles are the alternating increases and decreases in economic activity typical of market economies. These fluctuations take place around a long-run growth trend.

Business cycles contain four phases: the peak or boom, followed by a recession or downturn, leading to the trough of the cycle, followed by a recovery leading to another peak. Although the business cycle has regularity in its movements, business cycles vary dramatically in duration and intensity.

Business cycles are officially dated by the National Bureau of Economic Research, which assigns a committee of economists the task of dating "turning points," or points at which the economy switches from peak to downturn or from trough to recovery.

## National Income Accounting

The national income and product accounts (NIPA) allow economists to judge our nation's economic performance, compare American income and output to that of other nations, and track the economy's condition over the course of the business cycle. The NIPA were first developed in the early 1930s by the Department of Commerce, which has refined them over the years.

The major components of NIPA can be constructed in either of two ways: by summing the income of the economy or by summing spending.

Gross domestic product (GDP) is equal to the total market value of all final goods and services produced by resources in the United States. Gross national product (GNP) measure the market value of all goods and services produced by resources supplied by U.S. residents. The difference between GDP and GNP is small.

GDP can be measured by adding together either spending or income. With the expenditures approach, all spending on final goods and services is added together. The four major categories of spending are personal consumer spending, gross private domestic investment, government spending, and net exports (exports minus imports).

Personal consumption expenditures account for 70% of GDP.

Gross private domestic investment (GPDI) currently accounts for just under 11% of GDP, but it fluctuates significantly.

The government component of GDP measures the impact government spending has on final demand in the economy and accounts for over 20% of GDP.

The net export of goods and services is equal to exports minus imports for the current period. Currently, net exports account for under −3% of GDP (imports are greater than exports, hence the negative sign).

The four spending categories are commonly abbreviated as C (consumption), I (investment), G (government), and X − M (exports minus imports, or net exports). Together, these four variables constitute GDP:

$$GDP = C + I + G + (X - M)$$

Using the income approach to measure GDP, the major categories of income are compensation of employees, proprietors' income, rental income, corporate profits, and net interest. Several adjustments are required to the national accounts to fully account for GDP.

Compensation to employees is nearly 55% of GDP. Proprietors' income is less than 8% of GDP. Rental income is less than 2% of GDP. Corporate profits are less than 10% of GDP. Net interest is over 5% of GDP.

NIPA has some shortcomings. For instance, the national accounts ignore most nonmarket transactions and fail to account for the environmental impact of economic activity.

## Questions and Problems

### Check Your Understanding

1. Describe why GDP can be computed using either expenditures or income.

2. What accounts for the difference between personal income and disposable personal income?

3. Describe the three major goals of macroeconomics. How well has the United States economy performed in accomplishing these three goals in the last few years?

4. How are business cycles defined? Describe the four phases of business cycles. Business cycles are dated by which federal agency?

5. What is the difference between a recession and a depression?

6. Describe the circular flow diagram. Why must all income equal spending in the economy?

7. Why does GDP accounting only include the final value of goods and services produced? What would be the problem if intermediate products were included?

8. What are some of the limitations of the national income accounts in how they represent our standard of living?

### Apply the Concepts

9. Assume the federal government runs huge budget deficits today to finance, say, Social Security, Medicare, and other programs for the elderly, and finances these deficits by selling bonds, which raises interest rates. Since business often borrows money to invest, and interest is the cost of borrowing, these higher interest rates will reduce investment. Describe why this scenario is likely to be bad for the macroeconomy.

10. Critics of the NIPA argue that they are outdated and fail to account for "intangibles" in our new knowledge economy. For example, many firms create copyrighted materials (movies, books, etc.) that when completed are much more valuable than just the value of the marketplace inputs that went into their production. What might be some of the problems associated with trying to include these intangibles in the NIPA?

11. Assume that we are able to accurately account for environmental degradation in the NIPA. Rank the following countries by the percent reduction to their GDP (from least to most percentage reduction): the United States, China, and Norway.

12. Gross domestic product and its related statistics are published quarterly and are often revised in the following quarter. Do you think quarterly publication and revision in the next quarter would present problems for policymakers trying to control the business cycle? Why or why not?

13. Gross private domestic investment (GPDI) includes new residential construction as investment. Why is new housing included? Isn't this just another consumer purchase of housing services? How would the sale of an existing house be treated in the GDP accounts?

## Solving Problems

14. The table below lists gross domestic product (GDP), consumption (C), gross private domestic investment (I), government spending (G), and net exports (X − M). Compute each as a percent of GDP for the five years presented.

| Year | GDP | C | I | G | X − M | C(%) | I(%) | G(%) | X − M(%) |
|---|---|---|---|---|---|---|---|---|---|
| 1965 | 719.1 | 443.8 | 118.2 | 151.5 | 5.6 | ____ | ____ | ____ | ____ |
| 1975 | 1638.3 | 1034.4 | 230.2 | 357.7 | 16 | ____ | ____ | ____ | ____ |
| 1985 | 4220.3 | 2720.3 | 736.2 | 879 | −115.2 | ____ | ____ | ____ | ____ |
| 1995 | 7397.7 | 4975.8 | 1144 | 1369.2 | −91.4 | ____ | ____ | ____ | ____ |
| 2005 | 12455.8 | 8742.4 | 2057.4 | 2372.8 | −716.7 | ____ | ____ | ____ | ____ |

a. Which component of GDP is the most stable? Look for the smallest change from the year with the smallest contribution to GDP to the year with the largest contribution.

b. Which is the most volatile as a percent of GDP?

c. Ignoring net exports, which component has grown the fastest as a percent of GDP since 1965?

15. Using the data below, compute GDP, national income, and net domestic product.

| | |
|---|---|
| Corporate profits | 1,200 |
| Gross private domestic investment | 2,000 |
| Nondurable goods | 3,000 |
| Exports | 1,200 |
| Proprietors' income | 900 |
| Taxes, imports, and miscellaneous adjustments | 800 |
| Services | 4,000 |
| Net interest | 550 |
| Compensation of employees | 7,000 |
| Change in inventories | 80 |
| Imports | 1,800 |
| Rental income | 150 |
| Government spending | 2,000 |
| Durable goods | 1,000 |
| Capital consumption allowance | 1,500 |

# Answers to Questions in CheckPoints

## Check Point: The Scope of Macroeconomics

Big-ticket (high-priced, high-margin) items like automobiles are affected by a recession more than grocery stores where the margins are less and prices are lower. When the economy turns down, investment falls, so the capital goods industry is one of the first to feel the pinch.

## Check Point: National Income Accounting

In general, it is probably a bad idea to extrapolate how the aggregate economy is doing by your personal situation. Just because you are having trouble finding a job does not mean that everyone else is. The recent downsizing by General Motors and Chrysler means that auto workers are having problems, even though the rest of the economy may be growing steadily or may not have fallen as much. There might be times when your situation (such as a layoff in an important industry) may be a leading indicator of what is coming for the economy as a whole. In general, anecdotal evidence is not particularly helpful in forecasting where the aggregate economy is going. When times are uncertain, anecdotal evidence may mislead. Even in recessions, some firms do well, so anecdotal evidence is suspect.

# 16 Measuring Inflation and Unemployment

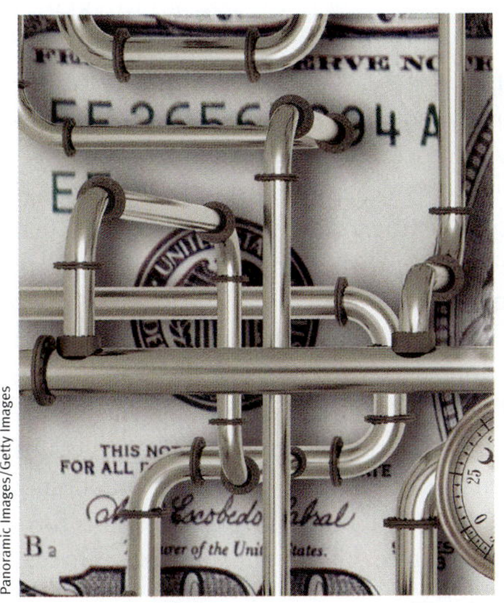

Panoramic Images/Getty Images

**Two primary goals of macroeconomic** policy are full employment and low inflation. After two decades of a steady decline in unemployment and inflation rates, a deep recession in 2008–2009 pushed unemployment over 10%. Fears of inflation (rising prices) receded, but they were still in the background. Once the employment situation improved, would inflation come roaring back? Unemployment and inflation can cause economic and social problems, as we will discover in this chapter.

Every month, the Department of Labor, through its Bureau of Labor Statistics (BLS), issues updates on unemployment and the price level. Both numbers are considered important indicators of how the economy is doing and where it is headed. Stock markets can immediately change direction on the release of this data.

Measures of employment, unemployment, consumer prices, and producer prices have been estimated on a monthly basis only since the Great Depression. The lack of historical and timely data in the early 1930s made it difficult to track the impact of fiscal and monetary policies during the Depression. At the time, the data produced on the severity of the Depression were anecdotal (newspaper accounts of layoffs, plant closings, and bankruptcies) that did not lend themselves to systematic analysis for policymakers.

Because economists and policymakers had so much trouble making sense of the economy during the Depression, the government began to systematically collect data on aggregate (economy wide) variables. The Departments of Commerce and Labor began tracking things such as aggregate output (GDP), unemployment, and inflation.

**After studying this chapter you should be able to:**

- ☐ Define inflation and the various terms associated with inflation.
- ☐ Describe the methods for measuring inflation used by the Bureau of Labor Statistics.
- ☐ Describe the GDP deflator.
- ☐ Use an escalator formula to determine future values.
- ☐ Convert a nominal value to a real or constant dollar value.
- ☐ Describe the economic consequences of the different forms of inflation.
- ☐ Describe the differences between the labor force, employment, unemployment, and underemployment.
- ☐ Describe the different forms of unemployment and their economic consequences.
- ☐ Define what full employment means.

To understand changes that are happening to the economy and to make good policy, we must know just what these numbers represent and how they are calculated. Are they accurate? Are they biased? Do they reflect the political philosophy of the party holding the White House? Why do they sometimes seem to get better just before an election and get worse afterward? How can these numbers be used for economic policymaking? These and other questions are the focus of this chapter. Let's begin with a look at the various measures of inflation, then go on to measures of unemployment.

## Inflation

*"[Inflation is] as violent as a mugger, as frightening as an armed robber and as deadly as a hit-man."*

—RONALD REAGAN

**Inflation** is a measure of changes in the cost of living. In an economy like ours, prices are constantly changing. Some go up as others go down, and some prices rise and fall seasonally. What we need, however, is a measure of how the cost of living is changing.

Why do we need such a measure? Why is it such a big deal if the cost of living is changing? Everyone has some intuitive sense of the cost of unemployment, in the waste that occurs when people want to work but cannot find a job, or when there are huge layoffs in a time of recession. Inflation, however, is a little harder to grasp.

Here is a simple example of inflation's destructive effects in the hope this gives you some intuitive sense of why inflation is bad. Say you work hard at a job after graduation and after your first year, your effort is rewarded with a 3% raise when the average wage increase in your company is 2%. You feel happy, that is, until the government releases its inflation report and says that inflation is running at 5%. In effect, you have lost purchasing power. You may not consider the 2% difference to be much, but keep going like this for a few years, and you will find that inflation is taking a big bite out of your standard of living. Inflation has many other bad effects, as we will soon see.

Because inflation can be harmful, we need a precise measure of how the cost of living is changing. If gas prices rise, rents hold steady, and the prices of electronic components decline, determining the overall change in consumer prices can be complicated. What follows is a description of how the Bureau of Labor Statistics collects and analyzes the prices of various products to construct an index that measures inflation in our economy.

### Defining Inflation Terms

Around the middle of each month, the BLS announces the change in retail prices over the previous month. These updates in the consumer price index (CPI) provide us with our principal measure of inflation. Before we discuss how this index is arrived at and used, however, let us briefly examine some of the terms often used to discuss inflation-related topics.

**Inflation:** A measure of changes in the cost of living. A general rise in prices throughout the economy.

**Price level:** The absolute level of a price index, whether the consumer price index (CPI; retail prices), the producer price index (PPI; wholesale prices), or the GDP deflator (average price of all items in GDP).

**Disinflation:** A reduction in the rate of inflation. An economy going through disinflation typically is still facing inflation, but at a declining rate.

- *Price level:* The **price level** is the absolute level of a price index, whether this is the CPI (retail prices), the producer price index (PPI; wholesale prices), or the GDP deflator (average price of all items in GDP).
- *Inflation:* A general rise in prices throughout the economy. A rise in the CPI or GDP deflator is usually referred to as inflation.
- *Rate of inflation:* The percentage increase in prices over a 12-month period. An inflation rate of 3% for 2008 means price levels increased by that rate in 2008 over 2007.
- *Disinflation:* A reduction in the rate of inflation. Note that an economy going through **disinflation** may still be facing inflation, but at a declining rate. This was the case from the mid-1980s throughout the 1990s.

## By the *Numbers*

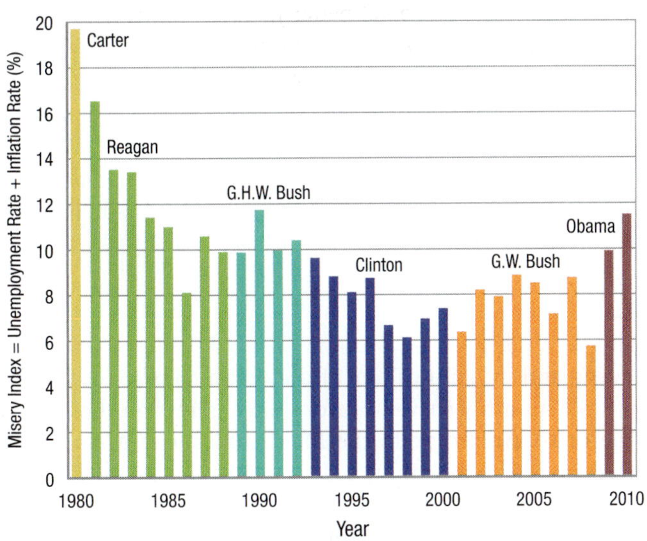


### Do Unemployment and Inflation Measure Our Misery?

The **misery index** was created by economist Arthur Okun, an adviser to President Lyndon Johnson. It is the *sum* of the unemployment and inflation rates. The higher the number, the more misery the economy is suffering. Running against Gerald Ford for the presidency in 1976, Jimmy Carter made an issue of the misery index: it was 13%. He argued that no one should be reelected as president when the misery index is that high. When Carter sought reelection in 1980, the misery index approached 20%; he lost to Ronald Reagan.

**53%**

**Increase in government employment between 2008 and 2009 in Zimbabwe**

**231,000,000%**

**Inflation rate in Zimbabwe in 2008. The $100 trillion bill shown here was worth US$20 when it was issued.**

**20%**

**Percent of immigrants with college degrees working as unskilled labor in Zimbabwe**

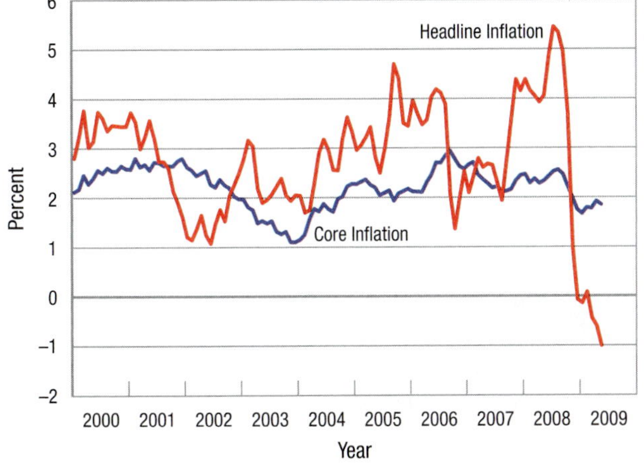


**Headline inflation (the CPI) was negative in 2009** (not necessarily good), but core inflation (the CPI minus price changes in food and energy) was positive. Core inflation is more stable because the two most volatile components are not included.

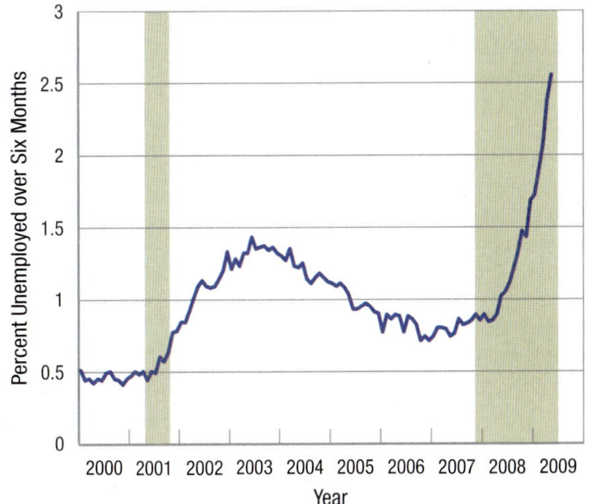


**Nearly 3% of the labor force was out of work for over six months in 2009.** Even the mild recession in 2001 put a lot of people out of work for a long time.

**Deflation:** A decline in overall prices throughout the economy. This is the opposite of inflation.

**Hyperinflation:** An extremely high rate of inflation; above 100% per year.

- *Deflation:* A decline in overall prices throughout the economy. **Deflation** is the opposite of inflation. During deflationary periods, such as the early 1930s, average prices in the economy fall.
- *Hyperinflation:* An extremely high rate of inflation. At first, **hyperinflation** was defined as an inflation rate of at least 50% per month. In 2008 in Zimbabwe, prices were more than doubling *every day,* for an annual inflation rate of 231,000,000 percent. Today, most economists refer to inflation above 100% a year as hyperinflation. Hungary experienced the highest rate of inflation on record during World War II. By the end of the war, in August 1946, it took over 800 octillion (8 followed by 29 zeros) Hungarian pengos to equal 1 prewar pengo. We will discuss hyperinflation in greater detail later in this chapter.

## Measuring Inflation

Measuring consumer spending and inflation is one of the oldest data-collection functions of the BLS. Unlike today's monthly surveys, before the Depression these surveys were collected every decade or so. According to the *BLS Handbook of Methods,* "The first nationwide expenditure survey was conducted in 1888–91 to study workers' spending patterns as elements of production costs. With special reference to competition in foreign trade, it emphasized the worker's role as a producer rather than as a consumer."[1]

During World War I, several other economic surveys were conducted, including one that weighted various areas of consumer spending to compute a cost of living index. During the Great Depression, more extensive consumer surveys were used to study the welfare of selected groups, notably farmers, rural families, and urban families. The BLS began regular reports of the modern CPI during the late 1930s. Today, the CPI is the measure of inflation with which the average American is most familiar. There are, however, four measures of inflation in use today.

**Consumer price index (CPI):** A measure of the average change in prices paid by urban consumers for a typical market basket of consumer goods and services.

**Personal consumption expenditures (PCE) index:** A measure of the changes in consumer prices focusing on consumer expenditures in the GDP accounts.

**Producer price index (PPI):** A measure of the average changes in the prices received by domestic producers for their output.

**GDP deflator:** An index of the average prices for all goods and services in the economy, including consumer goods, investment goods, government goods and services, and exports. It is the broadest measure of inflation in the national income and product accounts (NIPA).

The **consumer price index (CPI)** is a measure of the average change in prices paid by urban consumers for a typical market basket of consumer goods and services. The **personal consumption expenditures (PCE) index** measures changes in consumer prices by focusing on consumer expenditures in the GDP accounts. The **producer price index (PPI),** originally known as the wholesale price index (WPI), measures the average changes in the prices received by domestic producers for their output. A fourth index, the **GDP deflator,** is a measure of the average change in prices of the components in GDP. The GDP deflator is the broadest measure of inflation, but it is not as well known as the CPI.

In the sections that follow, we discuss how each of these indexes is constructed and measured, how each is used to adjust nominal values of income and output, and some other conceptual issues surrounding indexes.

### The Consumer Price Index (CPI)

The CPI measures the average change in prices paid by urban consumers (CPI-U) and urban wage earners (CPI-W) for a market basket of consumer goods and services. The CPI-U covers roughly 87% of the population.

***Cost-of-Living Versus Cost-of-Goods*** The CPI is often referred to as a "cost-of-living" index, but the current CPI differs from a true cost-of-living measure. A cost-of-living index compares the cost of maintaining the same standard of living in the current and base periods. It is a complex index that requires knowing a good deal more

[1] U.S. Department of Labor, Bureau of Labor Statistics, *BLS Handbook of Methods,* 1997. Available at www.bls.gov

than just prices and quantities of products purchased in a market basket of goods and services. It also requires information on how consumers will respond to changes in product prices and income.

A cost-of-goods index, in contrast, merely measures the cost of a fixed bundle of goods and services from one period to the next. Such an index is calculated by dividing the market basket's cost in the current period by its cost in the base period. The current CPI is a cost-of-goods index, since it measures changes in the price of a fixed basket of goods. The reference or base period used today for the CPI is 1999, but any base year would work just as well. The index simply measures the percentage change from one period to the next, so the selection of the base year does not fundamentally alter the index.

***How the Bureau of Labor Statistics Measures Changes in Consumer Prices.***[2] Measuring consumer prices requires the work of many people. Thousands of individuals complete household surveys and help collect retail prices in stores, the result of which BLS economists then analyze and publish. According to the BLS, the "cycle begins during the first week of the month when BLS data collectors (called economic assistants) gather price information from selected department stores, supermarkets, service stations, doctors' offices, rental units, and so on for the entire month, about 80,000 prices are recorded in 87 urban areas."

The BLS does not have enough resources to price all goods and services in all retail outlets, so it uses three scientifically selected sample groups to approximate the spending behavior of all urban consumers. These include a

> *Consumer Expenditure Survey from a national sample of over 30,000 families, which provides detailed information on spending habits. This information enables BLS to construct the CPI market basket of goods and services and to assign each item in the market basket a weight or importance based on total family expenditures. Another national sample of about 16,800 families serves as the basis for a Point-of-Purchase survey that identifies the places where households purchase various types of goods and services. Finally, BLS uses 1990 Census of Population data to select the urban areas where prices are collected, and to determine the housing units within each urban area that are eligible for use in the shelter (housing) component of the CPI.*

Goods and services are divided into more than 200 categories, with each category specifying over 200 items for monthly price collection. After these data have been checked for accuracy, the data from the three surveys are combined, weighted, and used to compute the index. The result is the cost in the current period required to purchase the fixed market basket of goods. This cost is then compared to the base period and put into percentage form using the following formula:

$$\text{CPI} = (\text{Cost in Current Period} \div \text{Cost in Base Period}) \times 100$$

For example, assume the market basket of goods cost \$5,000 in 1999 and that same basket of goods now costs \$5,750. The CPI for today, using 1999 for the base year, is 115.0 ([\$5,750 ÷ \$5,000] × 100). So the cost of goods has risen by 15%, since the index in 1999 was 100.0 ([\$5,000 ÷ \$5,000] × 100 = 1 × 100 = 100).

Given that this method is the way the BLS collects and computes the CPI, how accurately does this index reflect the changes in our cost of living? As we have seen, the BLS has the establishment of a *cost-of-living* index as its ultimate measurement goal, yet

[2] The following is based on material from the BLS Web site.

the CPI is a *cost-of-goods* index. Indeed, crafting a true cost-of-living index is difficult. We now take a quick look at some of the problems inherent in the current approach to measuring the CPI.

## Problems in Measuring Consumer Prices

The CPI is a *conditional* cost-of-goods index in that it measures only private goods and services; public goods and services are excluded. Other background environmental factors, meanwhile, are held constant. The current CPI, for instance, does not take into account such issues as the state of the environment, homeland security, life expectancy, crime rates, climate change, or other conditions affecting the quality of life. For these reasons alone, the CPI will probably never be a true cost-of-living index.

But even being free of the broader domain of environmental factors and public services, the CPI still has problems. The CPI uses a fixed market basket determined by consumer expenditures surveys that are often three to five years old. Inherent in a fixed-market-basket approach is the assumption that, as prices change, consumers continue to purchase the same basket of goods as before. We know, however, that when the price of one good rises, consumers substitute other goods that have fallen in price, or at least did not rise as much. To the extent that the CPI does not account for product substitution, it will overstate inflation.

In a given year, about 30% of the products in the market basket will disappear from store shelves.[3] Data collectors can directly substitute other products for roughly two-thirds of these products. This means nearly a third of the dropped products, or 10% of the original market basket, must be replaced by products that have been improved or modified in some important way. Old and new products are often not directly comparable. Some adjustment must be made in the index to account for these changes in quality.

Adjusting the index to account for products that have undergone quality changes is difficult, but it is easier than accounting for new products. Cellular phones and the rapid conversion of taped content (video and audio) to CDs, DVDs, and now digital delivery are examples of the challenges facing the BLS.

In some instances, a new product does not fit properly into any existing category, so it gets overlooked. Another question raised by new products is when to add them to the CPI product mix. New products often have high prices initially as producers "skim" the market for the most interested consumers. (Apple dropped the iPhone's price by $200 a couple of months after it was introduced.) Cell phones were expensive in the beginning, used only by some consumers, and available only in selected local markets. Only in the last few years have many people begun to replace their landlines with cell phones. Including cell phones in the index fifteen years ago would have been premature, because the market was still small. As a result, the BLS often waits until a product matures and is used by a significant number of consumers before including it in the market basket.

Another factor to consider is that stores, like goods, come and go. This means the BLS must adjust its selection of retail outlets frequently. Yet, even this adjustment presents problems. When consumers go shopping at an upscale department store such as Neiman Marcus, where prices are higher, the whole shopping experience is different from that of a discount store like Wal-Mart—at least, we would hope so. Thus, when a new retail store enters the sample, it may sell some product that the store it replaces sold at a different price. The BLS assumes this price difference reflects the differences in the quality of the shopping experience at the two stores and does not change the CPI. This assumption may not be completely accurate, but it does keep the CPI from showing a change in prices just because one firm left the sample.

---

[3] National Research Council, *At What Price? Conceptualizing and Measuring Cost-of-Living and Price Indexes* (Washington, DC: National Academy Press), 2002, p. 28.

One final difficulty to note has to do with measuring the changing costs of health care. The CPI looks only at consumers' out-of-pocket spending on health care. This number represents roughly 6% of total consumer spending. The current CPI does not track changes in medical costs paid by Medicare, Medicaid, or employer-financed health insurance policies. Yet, because total health care spending is roughly 18% of consumer spending, this means the CPI only considers about a third of the overall health care charges. To the extent that price changes are different in the two areas of health care spending, the CPI will be inaccurate.

## Personal Consumption Expenditures Index

The CPI does a good job of measuring inflation for urban consumers and is the most widely reported inflation measure. Policymakers, however, especially the Federal Reserve, have been focusing attention on the personal consumption expenditures index (PCE). The PCE focuses on consumer expenditures in the GDP accounts and is a little broader index of consumer inflation than the CPI.

The major difference between the CPI and the PCE is the weighting of individual components. For example, the PCE has a heavier weighting on medical care, apparel, and recreation, but lighter weights on food and housing. The CPI is a fixed market basket that is updated every two years based on surveys, whereas the PCE, based on GDP components, is updated each period. The CPI reflects out-of-pocket expenses of households; the PCE includes expenditures made by businesses on behalf of households. For example, business spending on employee health care is included in the PCE, but only household out-of-pocket spending on health care is included in the CPI.

The CPI is released about two weeks before the PCE, so it gets the most media attention. Which is best is up for debate, but the Federal Reserve has given the PCE a boost since it announced that Federal Reserve inflation policy will focus on the PCE as a key indicator of inflation.

Finally, make a note that you will often see inflation measured by the CPI referred to as "headline" inflation, which is often contrasted with a "core" version that excludes food and energy costs. Since food and energy costs are quite volatile, the core indexes are considered more reflective of underlying inflationary trends. But keep in mind that if, for example, energy prices remain high or continue to grow, these prices will eventually filter back into the economy as a whole and increase inflationary pressures.

## The Producer Price Index

The producer price index (PPI) measures the average changes in the prices received by domestic producers for their output. Before 1978 this index was known as the wholesale price index (WPI). The PPI is compiled by doing extensive sampling of nearly every industry in the mining and manufacturing sectors of our economy.

The PPI contains the following:

- Price indexes for roughly 500 mining and manufacturing industries, including over 10,000 indexes for specific products and product categories
- Over 3,200 commodity price indexes organized by type of product and end use
- Nearly 1,000 indexes for specific outputs of industries in the service sector, and other sectors that do not produce physical products
- Several major aggregate measures of price changes, organized by stage of processing, both commodity based and industry based[4]

The PPI measures the net revenue accruing to a representative firm for specific products. Because the PPI measures net revenues received by the firm, excise taxes

[4] This listing is excerpted from Chapter 14 of the *BLS Handbook of Methods*, 1997, found on the BLS Web site (www.bls.gov).

are excluded, but changes in sales promotion programs such as rebate offers or zero-interest loans are included. Since the products measured are the same from month to month, the PPI is plagued by the same problems discussed above for the CPI. These problems include quality changes, deleted products, and some manufacturers exiting the industry.

### The GDP Deflator

The GDP deflator shown in Figure 1 is our broadest measure of inflation. It is an index of the average prices for all goods and services in the economy, including consumer goods, investment goods, government goods and services, and exports. The prices of imports are excluded. Note that *deflation* occurred in the Great Depression. The spike in inflation occurred just after the end of World War II, when price controls were lifted. Since the mid-1980s, the economy has witnessed disinflation—inflation was present but generally at a decreasing rate.

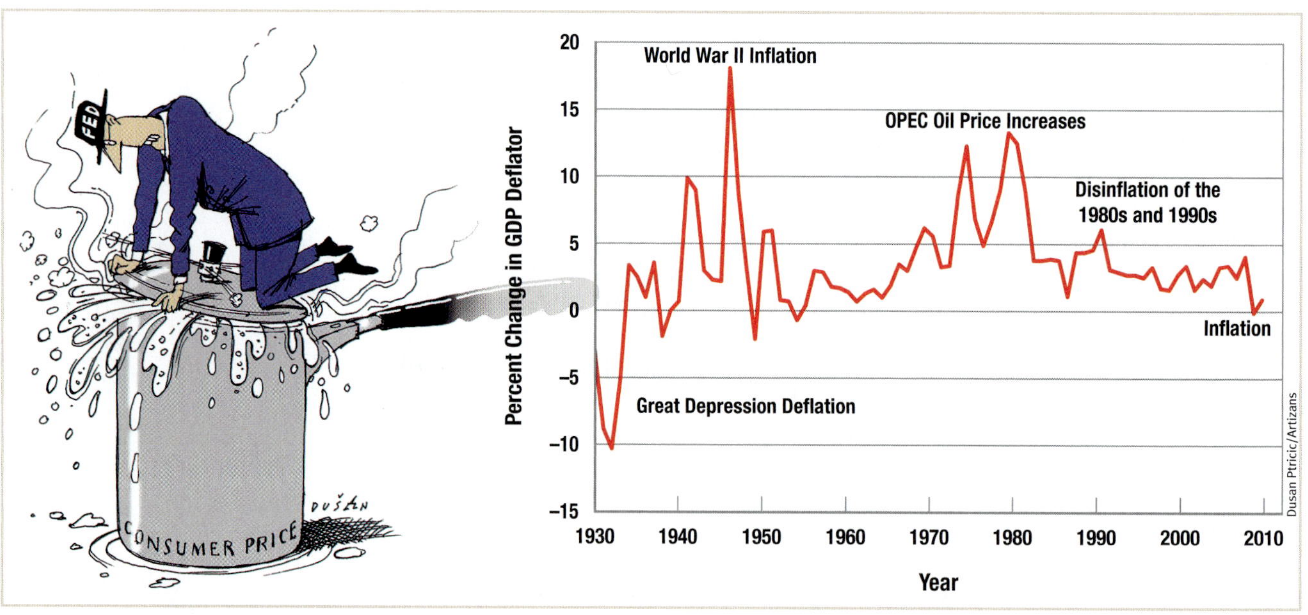


**FIGURE 1—Inflation from 1930 to Today—GDP Deflator**

The broadest measure of inflation, the GDP deflator, is used to graph inflation from 1930 to the present. Deflation occurred during the Great Depression. The spike in inflation occurred after World War II ended, when price controls were lifted. Since then, inflation has existed in a 1% to 13% range. Since the mid-1980s, the U.S. economy has generally faced disinflation (inflation, but generally at a decreasing rate).

## Adjusting for Inflation: Escalation and Deflation

Price indexes are used for two primary purposes: escalation and deflation. An escalator agreement modifies future payments, usually increasing them, to take the effects of inflation into account. Deflating a series of data with an index involves adjusting some current value (often called the nominal value) for the impact of inflation, thereby creating what economists call a *real value.* Using the GDP deflator, for instance, to deflate annual GDP involves adjusting nominal GDP to account for inflation, thereby yielding real GDP, or GDP adjusted for inflation.

### Escalator Clauses

Many contracts, including commercial rental agreements, labor union contracts, and Social Security payments are subject to escalator clauses. An escalator clause is designed to adjust payments or wages for changes in the price level. Social Security payments, for example, are adjusted upward every year to account for the rate of inflation. The general formula for an escalator clause adjustment is

$$\text{New} = \text{Original} \times (\text{Current Year Index} \div \text{Original Year Index})$$

To see how escalators work, let us assume your wages are tied to the CPI in such a way that your current wage is automatically adjusted by last year's inflation rate every April 1. (Can you guess why I chose this date?) Assume that you are earning $45,000 per year and that the CPI went from 115.0 to 118.5 last year. This means that the inflation rate for last year was about 3.0%:

$$(118.5 - 115) \div 115 = 0.0304$$

To calculate your new salary, simply divide the current year's CPI figure by the previous year's figure, and multiply this ratio by your current salary; thus, (118.5/115) × $45,000 = $46,369. Alternately, if the inflation rate is already known, just multiply the sum of 1 plus this figure by your current salary to produce the same result: $45,000 × 1.0304 = $46,369. Note that we are simply increasing your current salary by a little over 3%.

Escalator clauses become important in times of rising or significant inflation. These clauses protect the real value of wages. For example, a 10% pay raise is great when there is little inflation, but if the inflation rate is 12%, you are worse off than before even with your 10% raise. In times of low inflation, as in the United States in the past 10 years, escalator clauses have been used infrequently.

### Deflating Series: Nominal Versus Real Values

GDP has grown by nearly 13% from 2005 to 2009, but should we be celebrating? Not quite, because inflation has eroded the purchasing power of that increase. So how much did GDP really increase?

First, remember that every index is grounded on a base year, and that the value for this base year is always 100. The base year used for the GDP deflator, for instance, is 2005. The formula for converting a nominal value, or *current dollar value,* to real value, or *constant dollar* value, is

$$\text{Real} = \text{Nominal} \times (\text{Base Year Index} \div \text{Current Year Index})$$

To illustrate, nominal GDP in 2009 was $14,242.1 billion. The GDP deflator, having been 100 in 2005, was 109.7 in 2009. Real GDP for 2009 was therefore equal to $12,997.4 billion ($12,997.4 = $14,242.1 × [100.0 ÷ 109.7]) in real 2005 dollars. Note that because the economy has faced some inflation—9.7% from 2005 to 2009—the nominal value of GDP has been reduced by this same amount to arrive at the real value.

## The Consequences of Inflation

Why do so many policymakers, business people, and consumers dread inflation? Your attitude toward inflation will depend in large part on whether you live on a fixed income, whether you are a creditor or debtor, and whether you have properly anticipated inflation.

Many elderly people live on incomes that are fixed; often, only their Social Security payments are indexed to inflation. People on fixed incomes are harmed by inflation, since the purchasing power of their income declines. If people live long enough on fixed incomes, inflation can reduce them from comfortable living to poverty.

Creditors, meanwhile, are harmed by inflation because both the principal on loans and interest payments are usually fixed. Inflation reduces the real value of the payments they receive, while the value of the principal declines in real terms. This means that debtors benefit from inflation; the real value of their payments declines as their wages rise with inflation. Many homeowners in the 1970s and 1980s saw the value of their real estate rise from inflation. At the same time, their wages rose, again partly due to inflation, but their mortgage payment remained fixed. The result was that a smaller part of the typical family's income was needed to pay the mortgage, and thus the real value of mortgages had declined. Inflation thus redistributes income from creditors to debtors.

This result takes place only if the inflation is unanticipated. If lenders foresee inflation, they will adjust the interest rates they offer to offset the inflation expected over the period of the loan. Suppose, for instance, the interest rate during zero inflation periods is roughly 3%. Now suppose a lender expects inflation to run 5% a year over the next 3 years, the life of a proposed loan. The lender will demand an 8% interest rate to adjust for the expected losses caused by inflation. Only when lenders fail to anticipate inflation does it harm them, to the benefit of debtors.

Note the adjustment costs that inflation brings on an economy. In times of low inflation, this inflation is virtually ignored. In times of rising or significant inflation, people start to worry about diminished purchasing power and a falling standard of living. Workers seek escalator clauses. Mortgage lenders seek inflation adjustments. In the early 1980s when inflation was in double digits in the United States, mortgage lenders began offering adjustable-rate mortgages, with interest rates that adjusted every year. Many potential borrowers faced a choice between a 15% fixed-rate mortgage and a 13% adjustable-rate mortgage with its annual uncertainty about what the interest rate would be. It is much better for everyone when inflation is low and does not have to be brought into every financial consideration.

## Hyperinflation

Hyperinflation is an extremely high rate of inflation. Historically it was defined as an inflation rate of at least 50% a *month.* Today, however, most economists refer to an inflation rate above 100% a *year* as hyperinflation. But in most episodes of hyperinflation, the inflation rates dwarf 100% a year.

Hyperinflation is not new. It has been around since paper money and debt were invented. During our war of independence, the Continental Congress issued money until the phrase "not worth a continental" became part of the language. Germany experienced the first modern hyperinflation after World War I. The wholesale price index went from 100 in the summer of 1922 to nearly 200,000 in July 1923, then soared to nearly 800,000,000,000 three months later in November 1923.

The causes of hyperinflation are usually an excess of government spending over tax revenues (extremely high deficits) coupled with the printing of money to finance these deficits. Post–World War I Germany faced billions of dollars in war reparations that crippled the country. The German government found it difficult to collect enough taxes to pay the reparations (which were viewed by Germans as unfair), so it embarked on the forced taxation of hyperinflation. As more money was printed and circulated, the value of the currency fell as prices rose. Over time, financial assets in banks and pension accounts became worthless and were essentially taxed away.

When hyperinflation is at its worst, workers are paid hourly, and they or their families take the money and rush out and buy anything the money will purchase. Eventually, the monetary system breaks down and barter takes over. People no longer trust the money, so they are unwilling to accept it in exchange for goods or services. At the peak of hyperinflation in Germany, retail stores essentially closed and refused to part with their inventory except by barter. In the end, the economic system collapses.

Stopping hyperinflation requires restoring confidence in the government's ability to bring the budgetary process under control. It usually requires a change in regime and a new currency. However, a new administration and new currency are not sufficient unless the government is ready to rein in the deficit and reduce the growth of the money supply.

Hyperinflation is an extreme case, yet it shows how inflation can have detrimental effects on an economy. This is why it is important to keep track of inflation and, in turn, reveals the importance of having an accurate way to measure inflation.

Inflation is one important measure of the health of an economy. Another is employment and unemployment, to which we now turn.

## *Issue:* Does It Matter if the CPI Overstates Inflation?

**Many federal benefits** and income tax rates are indexed to the CPI, which means that if inflation (as measured by the CPI) goes up by 3%, these benefits are increased by 3%. As a result, if the CPI overstates inflation, federal revenues are lower and expenditures are higher. So, for example, Social Security payments are higher than they should have been. This is an important problem for economic policy.

Two commissions, one from the Senate Finance Committee and another by the National Research Council, concluded that the CPI substantially overstated inflation and recommended changes to the Department of Labor. The Senate Finance Committee found the CPI overstatement ranged from 0.8 to 1.6 percentage points per year.

Consider the impact of overstating inflation by a small amount on average weekly earnings since 1970. We often hear that the middle class (presumably earning the average each week) is worse off today than in the past. This analysis is often based on showing that *real* (adjusted for inflation) earnings have declined. In 1970, average weekly earnings were $126 while today they are $590, or 4.68 times as much. Using the CPI to adjust the data, today's wage of $590 is only $110 in 1970 dollars. So adjusting for inflation, average earnings today are less than they were in 1970.

For policymakers, the implication is that standards of living have declined for the middle class. Even though average earnings have grown by over 4 times, inflation has actually reduced what can be bought with those earnings. But life in 2009 involves a vastly different lifestyle than in 1970. Many of the products we consume today—computers, the Internet, mobile phones, life-saving drugs and medical technology—didn't exist in 1970. Many others, such as larger houses, better cars, and cheap air travel, all suggest a better lifestyle today.

So what if the CPI doesn't do an adequate job of accounting for these changes and overstates inflation a little? The figure shows that a small error in the CPI can have profound long-run impacts.

To easily see percentage changes, the graph shows average weekly earnings indexed to $100 in 1970. The lower line adjusts earnings by the CPI. To see the impact of an overstated CPI, the two top lines represent adjustments with the CPI − 0.5 (CPI reduced by half a percentage point) and the CPI − 1.0 (CPI reduced by 1 percentage point).

Adjusted by the CPI alone, real wages (bottom line) have fallen, so workers earn roughly 14% *less* in real income today compared to 1970. But once we eliminate a 1-percentage point overstatement (top line), workers are nearly 30% *better off* now, a more than 40% difference in reality. Maybe the middle class hasn't evaporated. This leads to quite a different set of issues for policymakers and our economy.

Like any compound interest issue, the magnitude of the problem gets larger as the time frame expands. The inset in the figure shows the relative changes in real average earnings since 2000. Even though there is a difference, the amounts are small.

Economist Robert Gordon reports that the Department of Labor has implemented many of the changes suggested by the Senate committee and the National Research Council. As a result, today's CPI is a more accurate measure of inflation.

Sources: Based on Senate Finance Committee, *Toward a More Accurate Measure of the Cost of Living,* 1996; National Research Council, *At What Price? Conceptualizing and Measuring Cost-of-Living and Price Indexes* (Washington, DC: National Academy Press), 2002; and Robert Gordon, "The Boskin Commission Report and Its Aftermath," National Bureau of Economic Research, 1999.

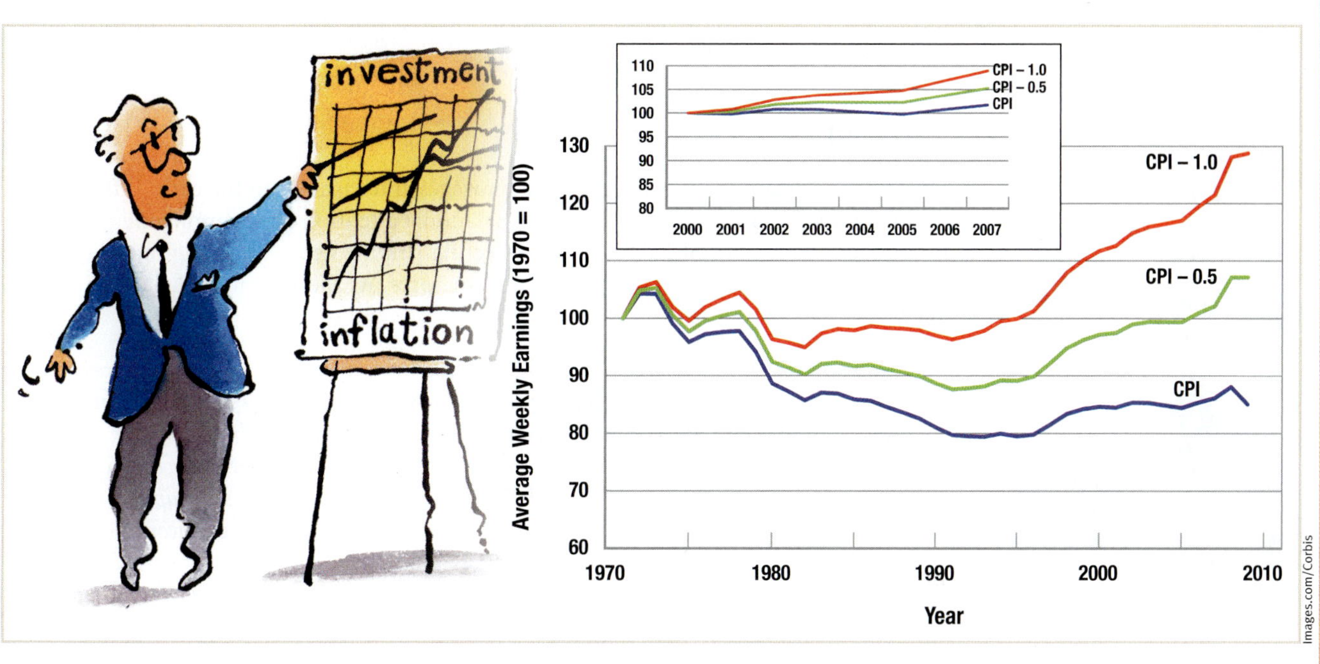

**CHECKPOINT**

### INFLATION

- Inflation is a measure of the change in the cost of living.
- Inflation is a general rise in prices throughout the economy.
- Disinflation is a reduction in the rate of inflation, and deflation is a decline in overall prices in the economy.
- Hyperinflation is an extremely high rate of inflation.
- The consumer price index (CPI) measures inflation for urban consumers and is based on a survey of a fixed market basket of goods and services each month.
- The personal consumption expenditures index (PCE) is based on consumer expenditures in the GDP accounts. This index is a little more broadly based than the CPI.
- The producer price index (PPI) measures price changes for the output of domestic producers.
- The GDP deflator is the broadest measure of inflation and covers all goods and services in GDP.
- Escalator clauses adjust payments (wages, rents, and other payments) to account for inflation.
- Real (adjusted for inflation) values are found by multiplying the nominal (current dollar) values by the ratio of the base year index to the current year index.

**QUESTION:** If you lived in a country where you saw the signs of a government beginning to spend excessively relative to its tax base and was funding this immense spending by printing new money, what would you do to protect yourself and your monetary assets?

Answers to the Checkpoint question can be found at the end of this chapter.

## Unemployment

When people are unemployed, individual workers, their families, and the economy all suffer. Workers lose wages, and the economy loses what they could have produced. Consumer spending drops, and as we will see later, this drop in consumer spending can have a ripple effect, leading other workers to lose their jobs.

A 1946 Census Bureau poster encouraging compliance with the initial unemployment survey.

### The Historical Record

The Census Bureau began collecting data on wages and earnings in the early 19th century, but it took the Great Depression to focus national attention on unemployment. By the 1940s, the Department of Labor began collecting employment data using monthly surveys to get a more detailed picture of the labor force. As the Bureau of Labor Statistics has noted,

> *To know about unemployment—the extent and nature of the problem—requires information. How many people are unemployed? How did they become unemployed? How long have they been unemployed? Are their numbers growing or declining? Are they men or women? Are they young or old? Are they white or black or of Hispanic origin? Are they skilled or unskilled? Are they the sole support of their families, or do other family members have jobs? Are they more concentrated in one area of the country than another?*[5]

[5] This is from the BLS Web site.

Once the BLS has collected and processed the current employment statistics, policymakers use this information to craft economic policies. Before we discuss how these statistics are defined, collected, used, and made accurate, let's briefly look at the historical record of unemployment and its composition.

Figure 2 shows unemployment rates for the last century. Unemployment has varied from a high of 25% of the labor force in the middle of the Great Depression to a low of just over 1% during World War II. Unemployment during the past 50 years has tended to hover around the 5% to 6% range, although it approached 10% during the 1981–1982 and 2008–2009 recessions.

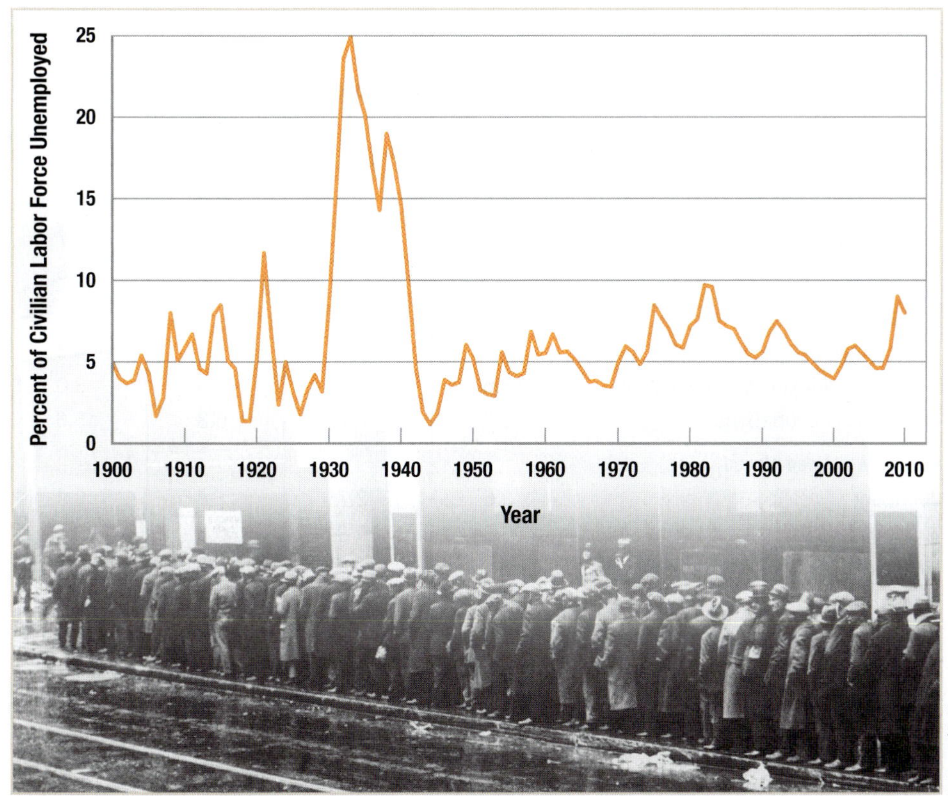


**FIGURE 2—A Century of Unemployment (1900–2010)**

Over the last century, unemployment has varied from a high of 25% of the labor force in the middle of the Great Depression to a low of just over 1% during World War II. Unemployment during the past 50 years has tended to hover around the 5% to 6% range.

Table 1 on the next page shows a breakdown of unemployment among various groups by gender, race, and education for 1980, 1990, 2000, and 2009. For blacks, unemployment has tended to be about double the rate of white unemployment, and the unemployment rate for Hispanics has usually exceeded that for whites by roughly 50%. Unemployment for college graduates is consistently low. Roughly half of all unemployment is normally from job losses, but this rose to two-thirds during the 2008–2009 downturn. The next largest group involves people who have not worked in some time and are looking to reenter the labor force. Finally, those people who quit their jobs or are new entrants into the labor force constitute a small percentage of the unemployed.

Now that we have some idea of the composition of the unemployed, let us consider just how these numbers are compiled. First, we need to see how people get categorized as employed or unemployed.

## Defining and Measuring Unemployment

The three major monthly numbers the BLS reports are the size of the labor force, number of people employed, and number unemployed. The unemployment rate is the number of people unemployed divided by the labor force.

**TABLE 1** Unemployment Rates by Gender, Race, Education, Occupation, and Reason for Unemployment, 1980–2009

| | 1980 | 1990 | 2000 | 2009 |
|---|---|---|---|---|
| Total unemployment | 7.1 | 5.6 | 4.0 | 9.4 |
| **Gender** | | | | |
| Men | 6.9 | 5.7 | 3.9 | 10.5 |
| Women | 7.4 | 5.5 | 4.1 | 8.0 |
| **Race or Ethnicity** | | | | |
| White | 6.3 | 4.8 | 3.5 | 8.6 |
| Black | 14.3 | 11.4 | 7.6 | 14.9 |
| Hispanic | 10.1 | 8.2 | 5.7 | 12.7 |
| **Education** | | | | |
| Less than high school diploma | 8.4 | 9.6 | 7.9 | 15.5 |
| High school graduate | 5.1 | 4.9 | 3.8 | 10.0 |
| Less than bachelor's degree | 4.3 | 3.7 | 3.0 | 7.7 |
| College graduate and higher | 1.9 | 1.9 | 1.5 | 4.8 |
| **Occupation** | | | | |
| Managerial and professional | 2.5 | 2.1 | 1.7 | 4.3 |
| Office and administrative support | 3.6 | 4.3 | 3.6 | 8.0 |
| Production occupations | 6.5 | 8.7 | 6.3 | 15.6 |
| **Reason Why Unemployed** | | | | |
| Job loser | 3.6 | 2.7 | 1.8 | 6.2 |
| Job leaver | 0.8 | 0.8 | 0.5 | 0.6 |
| Reentrant | 1.8 | 1.5 | 1.4 | 2.1 |
| New entrant | 0.8 | 0.5 | 0.3 | 0.6 |

**Source:** U.S. Department of Labor, Bureau of Labor Statistics.

## Employed

People are counted as *employed* if they have done any work at all for pay or profit during the survey week. Regular full-time work, part-time work, and temporary work are all included. People who have a job, but are on vacation, ill, having child care problems, on maternity or paternity leave, on strike, prevented from working because of bad weather, or engaged in some family or personal obligation are treated as employed. These people are considered to be employed since they have jobs to return to once their temporary situations have been resolved.

One other group, called *unpaid family workers,* is considered to be employed. These are people who work 15 or more hours a week in a family enterprise; they usually show up in agriculture and retail. Unpaid family workers who work fewer than 15 hours a week are deemed not to be members of the labor force.

## Unemployed

People are counted as *unemployed* if they do not have a job, but are available for work and have been *actively* seeking work for the previous 4 weeks. Actively looking for work means doing things like responding to help-wanted ads, sending off résumés, scheduling job interviews, visiting school placement centers, and contacting private or public employment agencies.

Note the emphasis on being active in the job search. A *passive* job search that merely involves looking in the want ads or talking to friends about jobs is not enough to characterize someone as unemployed. One exception involves workers who have been laid off but are expecting to be recalled; they do not need to seek other work to count as unemployed. Aside from the only other exception—namely, people suffering a temporary illness—individuals must be engaged in a job search to be counted as unemployed.

### Labor Force

The **labor force** is the total number of those employed and unemployed. The unemployment rate is the number of unemployed divided by the labor force, expressed as a percent.

**Labor force:** The total number of those employed and unemployed. The unemployment rate is the number of unemployed divided by the labor force, expressed as a percent.

As the Bureau of Labor Statistics has noted,

> *Because of the complexities of the American economic system and the wide variety of job arrangements and job seeking efforts, the definitions of employment and unemployment must be specific so as to ensure uniformity of reporting at any given time and over any period of time. When all of the details are considered, definitions may seem rather complicated. The basic concepts, however, are still the same: people with jobs are employed, people who do not have jobs and are looking for jobs are unemployed, and people who meet neither labor market test are not in the labor force. The qualifying conditions are necessary to cover the wide range of labor force patterns and to provide an objective set of standards for consistent treatment of cases.*[6]

## The Two Employment Surveys

The Census Bureau and the Department of Labor conduct different surveys to measure employment. The Census Bureau surveys households and the Labor Department focuses on the payrolls of businesses and government agencies.

### The Household Survey

Every month the Census Bureau, as part of the Current Population Survey, contacts roughly 60,000 households to determine the economic activity of people. The sample is drawn from over 700 geographical areas intended to represent the entire country, including urban and rural areas. The survey includes self-employed, unpaid family workers, agricultural workers, private household workers, and workers absent without pay.

The Census Bureau does not directly ask interviewees if they are employed. Rather, it asks a series of factual questions designed to elicit information that permits the Bureau to determine by its own standards whether people are employed or unemployed and whether they are in the labor force.

### The Payroll Survey

The payroll or "establishment" survey focuses on roughly 400,000 companies and government agencies that are asked how many employees they currently have. If jobs are cut, this survey will immediately show a decrease in the number of employees.

According to the Labor Department, "Both the payroll and household surveys are needed for a complete picture of the labor market. The payroll survey provides a highly reliable gauge of monthly change in nonfarm payroll employment. The household survey provides a broader picture of employment including agriculture and the self employed."

The household survey provides a detailed demographic picture of the labor market and captures entrepreneurial activity missed by the payroll survey. In contrast, the payroll survey provides detailed information by industry and region of the country. Because the payroll survey has a larger sample, it is generally viewed as the most accurate gauge of employment and unemployment changes, but both surveys closely track each other.

[6] See BLS Web site.

## Problems with Unemployment Statistics

Trying to measure personal situations as complex as employment, unemployment, and job seeking can be expected to generate its share of controversy and criticism. When the Department of Labor announces its results each month, commentators often note that these numbers understate unemployment, since they do not include chronically unemployed workers who have grown so frustrated and discouraged they have dropped out of the labor force. Newspaper and television pundits agonize over the plight of discouraged workers or the underemployed while discussing the impact of the latest numbers on the stock market.

How unemployment is measured depends on the intended use of the resulting measurements. Various uses for unemployment statistics include (1) gauging the state of the economy, (2) determining the divergence of supply and demand in labor markets, and (3) assessing the distribution of unemployment and the extent to which people are suffering from being out of work. In the United States, most unemployment statistics have been developed to gauge the state of the economy. The Bureau of Labor Statistics does, however, publish data about underemployment and discouraged workers.

### Underemployment and Discouraged Workers

It is not uncommon for people to take jobs that do not fully use their skills. In the early 1990s, many engineers and skilled workers who were employed in the defense industry saw their careers fall apart with the collapse of the Soviet Union. The "peace dividend" most of us enjoyed generated excess supplies in defense-related labor markets. In the early 2000s, the collapse of many Internet start-ups and telecommunications firms threw many highly skilled workers out of work. More recently, the recession caused by the collapse of automobile demand, the mortgage meltdown, and the subsequent financial crisis, put large numbers of auto, construction, and Wall Street workers out of work.

The result of these shake-ups has been that many people are unable to find jobs that enable them to duplicate their past standards of living. These individuals are *underemployed* in that they are forced to take jobs that do not fully—or in some cases even remotely—exploit their education, background, or skills.

Consider the following situation. After being laid off at the beginning of a recession, you spend several months looking for work, until finally you conclude that landing a job in the current downturn is impossible. And so you give up looking for work. Are you still unemployed? Not according to official statistics. Clearly, you would like to resume working; you have simply despaired of doing so anytime soon. Sufficiently discouraged to have quit *actively seeking work,* the BLS classifies you as being out of the labor force; part of the leisure class.

**Discouraged workers:** To continue to be counted as unemployed, those without work must actively seek work (apply for jobs, interview, register with employment services, etc.). Discouraged workers are those who have given up actively looking for work and, as a result, are not counted as unemployed.

The deeper a recession is, the more **discouraged workers** there will be. Today, the Census Bureau asks other questions of respondents to determine whether they fit into the discouraged worker category, listing these results separately.

Data from the Department of Labor in Figure 3 shows a breakdown of underemployment and discouraged workers. Discouraged workers increase unemployment rates by a small amount. The same is true for marginally attached workers—those who were available for work and actively looked for work in the last 12 months, but *not* in the last 4 weeks of the survey. The biggest group missing from the reported unemployment rate is those working part time for economic reasons. They would prefer a full-time job but have been unable to land one. Adding all of these categories nearly doubles the unemployment rate.

Other countries have different definitions of actively seeking work, classifying individuals engaged in passive job searches as unemployed. Notably, Canada and Europe have more relaxed search standards than the United States.

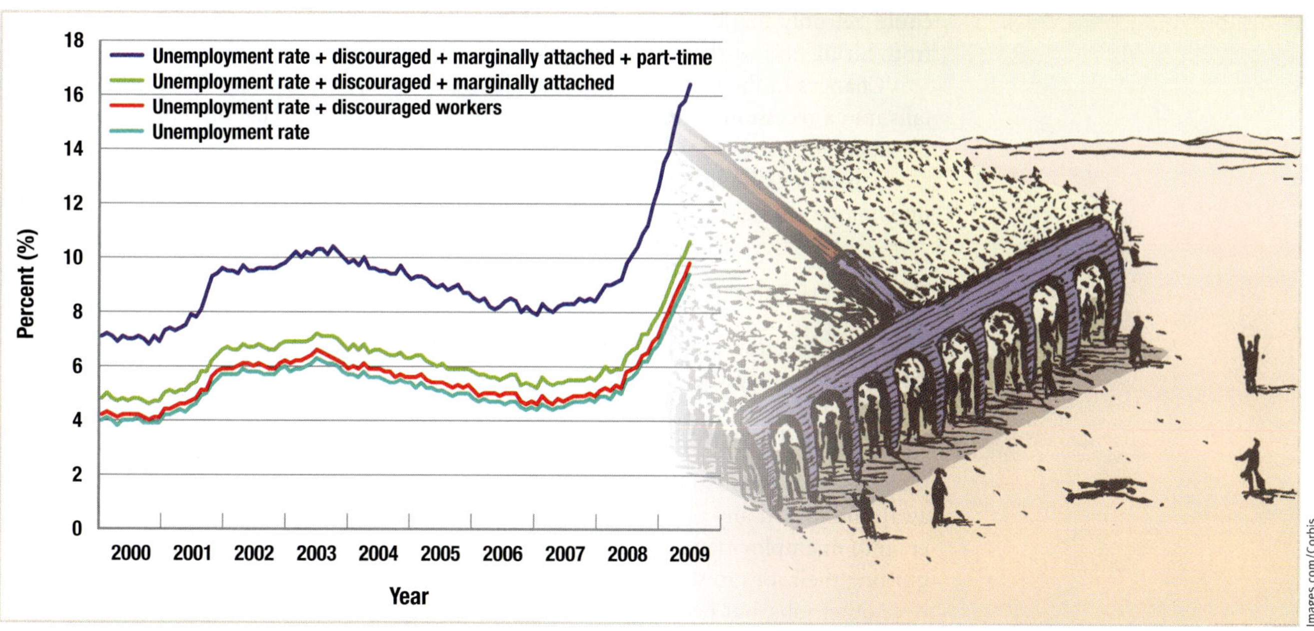


Images.com/Corbis

**FIGURE 3—Unemployment Categories (2000–2009)**

The Department of Labor categorizes unemployment into those unemployed and still actively seeking work, those who are discouraged (have quit looking), those who are marginally attached (those who looked for work in the past 12 months but not the last 4 weeks), and those working part time but who would prefer full-time work.

### CHECKPOINT

#### UNEMPLOYMENT

- People are counted as employed if they worked for pay or profit during the survey week.
- People are unemployed if they do not have a job but are available for work and have been actively seeking work for the previous 4 weeks.
- The labor force is the sum of the employed and unemployed. The unemployment rate is the number of unemployed divided by the labor force.
- Unemployment statistics do not account for underemployed and discouraged workers.

**QUESTIONS:** Does it seem reasonable to require that to be counted as unemployed, a person must be actively seeking work? Why not simply count those who do not have a job but indicate they would like to work?

Answers to the Checkpoint questions can be found at the end of this chapter.

## Unemployment and the Economy

Inevitably, our economy will contain some unemployment. People who are reentering the workforce or entering it for the first time will often find that landing their first job can take some time. Then they may find, moreover, that taking the first available job is not always in their best interests—that it might be better to take the time to search for another position better matching their skills and personality. Getting information and searching more extensively can extend the period people remain unemployed.

Unemployment can occur because wages are artificially set above the market clearing or equilibrium wage. Both minimum wage laws and union bargaining can have this effect, helping those workers who are employed to earn more, but shutting some potential workers out of jobs.

Employers often keep wages above market equilibrium to reduce turnover, boost morale, and increase employee productivity. These *efficiency wages* give employees an incentive to work hard and remain with their present employers, since at other jobs, they could get only market wages. These higher wages, however, can also prevent employers from hiring new workers, thus contributing to unemployment.

Changes in the business cycle will also generate unemployment. When the economy falls into a recession, sales decline, and employers are forced to lay off workers, so unemployment grows.

Separating different types of unemployment into distinct categories will help us apply unemployment figures to our analysis of the economy.

## Types of Unemployment

There are three types of unemployment: frictional, structural, and cyclical. Each type has different policy ramifications.

### Frictional Unemployment

Businesses and industries are born; sometimes they thrive, but just as often they waste away and die. At any given moment, some business is closing its doors, forcing its workers into unemployment. Similarly, there will always be some workers who are voluntarily quitting their jobs to search for better positions. In some cases, these people may already have other jobs, but it may still take several days or weeks before they can report to their new employers. In these cases, people moving from one job to the next are said to be frictionally unemployed.

**Frictional unemployment:** Unemployment for any economy that includes workers who voluntarily quit their jobs to search for better positions, or are moving to new jobs but may still take several days or weeks before they can report to their new employers.

**Frictional unemployment** is natural for our economy and, indeed, necessary and beneficial. People need time to search for new jobs, and employers need time to interview and evaluate potential new employees.

### Structural Unemployment

**Structural unemployment:** Unemployment caused by changes in the structure of consumer demands or technology. It means that demand for some products declines and the skills of this industry's workers often become obsolete as well. This results in an extended bout of unemployment while new skills are developed.

**Structural unemployment** is roughly the opposite of frictional unemployment. Whereas frictional unemployment is assumed to be of rather short duration, structural unemployment is usually associated with extended periods of unemployment.

Structural unemployment is caused by changes in the structure of consumer demands or technology. Most industries and products inevitably decline and become obsolete, and when they do, the skills honed by workers in these industries often become obsolete as well.

Declining demand for cigarettes, for instance, has changed the labor market for tobacco workers. Farm work, textile finishing, and many aspects of manufacturing have all changed drastically in the last several decades. Farms have become more productive, and many sewing and manufacturing jobs have moved overseas because of lower wages there. People who are structurally unemployed are often unemployed for long periods and then become discouraged workers.

To find new work, those who are structurally unemployed must often go through extended periods of retraining. The more educated those displaced are, the more likely they will be able to retrain easily and adjust to a new occupation. One benefit of a growing economy is that retraining is more easily obtained when labor markets are tight.

### Cyclical Unemployment

**Cyclical unemployment:** Unemployment that results from changes in the business cycle, and where public policymakers can have their greatest impact by keeping the economy on a steady, low-inflationary, solid growth path.

**Cyclical unemployment** is the result of changes in the business cycle. If, for example, business investment or consumer spending declines, we would expect the rate of economic growth to slow, in which case the economy would probably enter a recession, as we will examine in later chapters. Cyclical unemployment is the difference between the current unemployment rate and what it would be at full employment, defined below.

Frictional and structural unemployment are difficult problems, and macroeconomic policies provide only limited relief. Cyclical unemployment, most economists agree, is where public policymakers can have their greatest impact. By keeping the economy on a steady, low-inflationary, solid growth path, policymakers can minimize the costs of cyclical unemployment. Admittedly, this is easier said than done given the various shocks that can affect the economy.

## Defining Full Employment

Economists often describe the health of the economy by comparing its performance to *full employment.* We know full employment cannot be zero unemployment, since frictional and structural unemployment will always be present. Full employment today is generally taken to be equivalent to the natural rate of unemployment.

### The Natural Rate of Unemployment

The **natural rate of unemployment** has come to represent several ideas to economists. First, it is often defined as that level of unemployment where price and wage decisions are consistent—a level at which the actual inflation rate is equal to people's inflationary expectations. Natural unemployment is also considered to be the unemployment level where unemployment is only frictional and structural, or cyclical unemployment is zero.

**Natural rate of unemployment:** That level of unemployment where price and wage decisions are consistent; a level at which the actual inflation rate is equal to people's inflationary expectations and where cyclical unemployment is zero.

Economists often refer to the natural rate of unemployment as the nonaccelerating inflation rate of unemployment (NAIRU). This is defined as the unemployment rate most consistent with a low rate of inflation. It is the unemployment level where inflationary pressures in the economy are at their minimum. We will discuss these issues in greater detail throughout the remainder of the book. For now, it is enough to remember that the natural rate of unemployment, or NAIRU, is the unemployment rate consistent with low inflation and low unemployment.

Full employment, or the natural rate of unemployment, is determined by such institutional factors as the presence or absence of employment agencies and their effectiveness. For many technology workers, Internet employment agencies like Monster.com represent efficient job search engines. Other factors might include the demographic makeup of the labor force and the incentives associated with various unemployment benefit programs and income tax rates.

Inflation, employment, unemployment, and gross domestic product (GDP) are the key macroeconomic indicators of our economic health. Our rising standards of living are closely tied to GDP growth. In the next chapter, we will investigate what causes our economy and living standards to grow over the long term.

### CHECKPOINT

#### UNEMPLOYMENT AND THE ECONOMY

- Frictional unemployment is inevitable and natural for any economy as people change jobs and businesses open and close.
- Structural unemployment is typically caused by changes in consumer demands or technology. It is often of long duration and often requires that the unemployed become retrained for new jobs.
- Cyclical unemployment is the result of changes in the business cycle. When a recession hits, unemployment rises, then falls when an expansion ensues.
- Macroeconomic policies have the most effect on cyclical unemployment.
- Full employment is typically defined as that level where cyclical unemployment is zero or that level associated with a low nonaccelerating inflation rate.

**QUESTIONS:** After the Berlin Wall fell and the Soviet Union split into several countries, the defense industry in the United States underwent a serious decline as part of the so-called peace dividend. Many high-skilled engineers and other workers became unemployed as the industry retrenched. For many, their skills were so specialized that they were unable to find new jobs at their old salaries. Were these people frictionally, structurally, or cyclically unemployed? What policies might the government implement to reduce the impact of this type of unemployment?

Answers to the Checkpoint questions can be found at the end of this chapter.

## Key Concepts



## Chapter Summary

### Inflation

Inflation is a general rise in prices throughout the economy. Disinflation is a reduction in the rate of inflation, whereas deflation is a decline in prices throughout the economy. Hyperinflation is an extremely high rate of inflation. Most economists refer to inflation above 100% per year as hyperinflation.

Four major price indexes are used to measure inflation in the United States. The consumer price index (CPI) is a measure of the average change in prices paid by urban consumers for a market basket of consumer goods and services. The personal consumption expenditures (PCE) index measures the change in prices of consumption expenditures in the GDP accounts and is used by the Federal Reserve as its primary measure of inflation because it is broader than the CPI. The producer price index (PPI)—originally known as the wholesale price index (WPI)—measures the average change in prices received by domestic producers for their output. The GDP deflator is the broadest measure of inflation; it is a measure of the average change in prices of the components in GDP.

To adjust for inflation, nominal (current) values are calculated against a base year, providing a real (inflation adjusted) value.

People who live on fixed incomes and creditors are harmed by unanticipated inflation, since it decreases the purchasing power of their incoming funds. By the same token, inflation helps debtors: It decreases the real value of their debts. These effects are amplified during periods of hyperinflation.

### Unemployment

People are counted as employed if they have done any work at all for pay or profit during the survey week. Regular full-time work, part-time work, and temporary work are all included.

People are counted as unemployed if they do not have a job, but are available for work and have been actively seeking work for the previous 4 weeks. Actively looking for work requires doing things such as sending off résumés, contacting employers directly, going on job interviews, visiting school placement centers, or contacting private or public employment agencies.

The labor force is the sum of those people employed and unemployed. It does not include people who may have lost their jobs and are not actively seeking work. The unemployment rate is the number of people unemployed divided by the labor force, expressed as a percent.

### Unemployment and the Economy

The economy inevitably contains some unemployment. Unemployment is split into three types. When people are temporarily unemployed because they are switching jobs, they are said to be frictionally unemployed. Frictional unemployment is short term, and it exists because there are always some workers who are voluntarily or involuntarily changing jobs.

Structural unemployment is unemployment brought about by changes in the structure of consumer demands or technology. It is often long term, with workers requiring considerable retraining before they can find work again.

Cyclical unemployment is unemployment that arises because of downturns in the business cycle. This type of unemployment has the best chance of being affected by changes in government policy.

The natural rate of unemployment, or full employment, is that rate of unemployment where price and wage decisions are consistent, and thus the inflation rate is equal to people's inflationary expectations. It is also where unemployment is only frictional and structural; cyclical unemployment is zero. Economists often refer to the natural rate of unemployment as the nonaccelerating inflation rate of unemployment (NAIRU). This is defined as the unemployment rate most consistent with a low rate of inflation.

## Questions and Problems

### Check Your Understanding

1. In the beginning of a recovery after a recession, employment begins to rise and the news media report these data on job growth. Would such a report have an impact on the labor force? Would it affect the unemployment rate?
2. How could a decline in the unemployment rate actually reflect a deteriorating economy?
3. Why is frictional unemployment important to have in any economy?
4. Explain why hyperinflation has such a devastating impact on economies. Explain what it takes to stop hyperinflation.
5. Describe the possible losses to our society and the economy when people are unemployed.
6. Why do teenagers and young people have high unemployment rates?
7. Describe the three types of unemployment. What types of government programs would be most effective in combating each type of unemployment?
8. Describe the four measures of inflation in use today and the focus of each measure.
9. Describe who loses from unanticipated inflation.
10. What is required for a person to be considered unemployed? How is the unemployment rate computed?

### Apply the Concepts

11. Since 1980, the U.S. population has grown 37%, while employment has risen by 44%, or nearly 20% faster than population. How can it be true that employment grows faster than population? Further, the number of people unemployed has only risen 5%. Are all of these indicators a sign of a strong or weak labor market?
12. Assume you just lost your job and you have decided to take a month-long break to travel to Europe before looking for a new position. Just as you return home from your trip, you are interviewed by the Department of Labor about your employment status. How would you be classified (employed, unemployed, or not in the labor force)?
13. The Bureau of Labor Statistics categorizes unemployed people into several groups, including job leavers, job losers, and discouraged workers. During a mild recession, which group would tend to increase the most? During a deep recession? During a boom?

### Solving Problems

14. In January 1980, the CPI stood at 77.8, and by January 2006, it was 198.3. By what percent have consumer prices increased over this period? Assume college graduates entering the job market were being paid on average $1,200 a month in 1980, and in

January 2006 the average was $3,000. Are these newer graduates paid more or less after adjusting for inflation?

**15.** In 2000, median household income was $40,816. By 2004, it had grown to $44,389. The personal consumption expenditures index for 2004 (2000 = 100) was 108.37. Has median household income, adjusted for inflation, grown or declined since 2000?

**16.** Given the data for the United States between 1960 and 2000, complete the table below and answer the questions that follow.

| Year | GDP (billions of dollars) | GDP Deflator (2000 = 100) | Real GDP (billions of 2000 dollars) | Population (millions) | Real GDP per Capita (billions of 2000 dollars) |
|---|---|---|---|---|---|
| 1960 | 526.4 | 20.04 | _______ | 180.7 | 14,537 |
| 1970 | 1,038.5 | _______ | 3,772.3 | 205.1 | _______ |
| 1980 | _______ | 54.06 | 5,109.0 | _______ | 22,437 |
| 1990 | _______ | 81.61 | _______ | 250.1 | 28,432 |
| 2000 | 9,817.0 | _______ | 9,817.0 | 282.4 | _______ |

a. Between 1960 and 2000:
   (1) GDP was how many times larger in 2000 than in 1960?
   (2) The price level was how many times larger in 2000 than in 1960?
   (3) Real GDP was how many times larger in 2000 than in 1960?
   (4) What is the relationship between these values?

b. What was the percentage change in real GDP per capita between 1960 and 2000? Are people in the United States better off today than in 1960?

c. What are some of the problems associated with using real GDP per capita as a measure of our well-being?

## Answers to Questions in CheckPoints

### Check Point: Inflation

If you see the hyperinflation coming, you are in a position to protect monetary assets by purchasing hard or real assets such as real estate, gold, or diamonds. Early on, you might convert your monetary assets to the currency of other stable countries. If this is not possible, you would buy hard assets.

### Check Point: Unemployment

The reason for the requirement that a person actively seek work is to empirically differentiate those who profess to want a job (at possibly a higher wage than they can earn in the market) from those who are actively trying to obtain work.

### Check Point: Unemployment and the Economy

Most would be structurally unemployed. Since many of these people have significant skills and education, retraining funds would go a long way to helping these people find new careers.

# Economic Growth

# 17

Duravitski/Alamy

*Is there some action a government of India could take that would lead the Indian economy to grow like Indonesia's or Egypt's? If so, what, exactly? If not, what is it about the "nature of India" that makes it so? The consequences for human welfare involved in questions like these are simply staggering: Once one starts to think about them, it is hard to think about anything else.*

ROBERT LUCAS (1988)

**The quote by Nobel Prize winner** Robert Lucas in 1988 argues that economic growth is of paramount importance. At that time Egypt's growth was over double that of India's, and India's GDP per capita was half of Egypt's. But a lot has happened in the last two decades: Egypt's growth rate faltered while India's accelerated. Today, India's growth rate is roughly twice that of Egypt and India's GDP per capita is nearly the same, but India's population at 1.13 billion people is 14 times that of Egypt. What has India done right and where has Egypt let down? That is a difficult question to answer. We can try to answer it in this chapter by looking at many of the characteristics that promote long-run economic growth.

In Chapter 1, we suggested that reducing real growth by 1 percentage point per year in the last century would result in our standard of living today equaling Mexico's. Alternatively, *adding* 1 percentage point to the annual economic growth rate over this same period would mean that our standard of living today would be *tripled,* resulting in a per capita GDP in excess of $100,000 and median family income over $120,000 annually. Clearly, the annual rate of economic growth is important.

For most of human history, per capita income was virtually unchanged. People lived a subsistence life and not a very long one at that. As Figure 1 shows and Angus Maddison noted, "From the year 1000 to 1820 the advance in per capita income was a slow crawl—

**After studying this chapter you should be able to:**

- ☐ Describe the aggregate production function in terms of classical economic theory.
- ☐ Analyze labor supply and demand and the role of flexible wages.
- ☐ Explain Say's law.
- ☐ Use supply and demand to analyze the relationships among interest rates, savings, and investment.
- ☐ Describe the implications and limitations of classical economic theory.
- ☐ Describe the sources of long-term growth.
- ☐ Describe the sources of productivity growth.
- ☐ Describe modern growth theory.
- ☐ Define infrastructure and explain its importance.
- ☐ Describe the importance of tangible and intangible infrastructure.

the world average rose about 50 per cent. Most of the growth went to accommodate a fourfold increase in population."[1]

It has only been in the last century that standards of living have risen substantially and life expectancy has tripled. Even so, much of the world still leads a subsistence life. Looking at Figure 1, it is clear that development has been uneven, even for neighbors.

Although standards of living have progressed nicely in the United States, Mexico lags way behind. Japan and Western Europe both made dramatic recoveries after World War II, whereas much of the Middle East and Africa did not. Today, 4 billion people, mostly in Africa and Asia, still live on less than $2 a day. Understanding why these changes have taken place in the Western world and not everywhere else is one of the great challenges of macroeconomics.

Much of macroeconomics is focused on the short-term goal of keeping the economy near full employment with low inflation. In the short run, individuals can improve their lives through human capital investments such as education and training. These investments make them more productive and have huge impacts on their wages and incomes. Also, in the short run, governments can provide safety nets for people, but if the safety nets become too extensive, they can have negative effects on the society's standard of living over the longer term.

In the short run, government policies cannot appreciably alter the standard of living of citizens. They can improve the quality of life at the margin through various policies such as free health care and education. Developing countries in the short run cannot expect to raise all citizens out of poverty and bring living standards up to those of Western Europe and the United States. Such changes require a combination of good policies, quite a lot of time, and often some luck.

This chapter focuses on long-term **economic growth** and describes the conditions needed to sustain economic growth and improve standards of living. In the long run, all variables in the economy can adjust to changing conditions. The models in this chapter are a good framework for evaluating policies meant to encourage economic growth in the *long run*. These models also suggest policies we should *not* undertake to deal with short-run fluctuations because their long-term effects are so deleterious. Having a good sense of what

**Economic growth:** Usually measured by the annual percentage change in real GDP, reflecting an annual improvement in the standard of living.

**FIGURE 1—Per Capita GDP (1500–2006)**

It has only been in the last century that economic growth and standards of living have shown significant improvement, but this improvement has been uneven. The United States and Western Europe have progressed nicely, while much of the rest of the world is still living at a subsistence level.

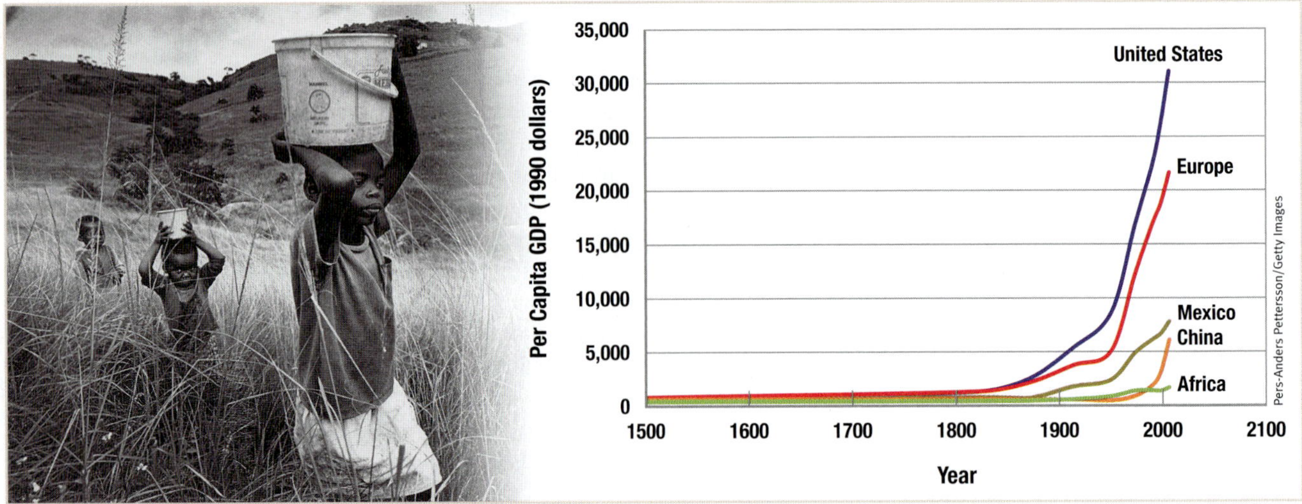


[1] Angus Maddison, *The World Economy, Vol. 1: A Millennial Perspective, Vol. 2: Historical Statistics* (Paris: Organisation for Economic Co-Operation and Development [OECD]), 2009.

## By the Numbers

### Why Should We Care about Economic Growth?

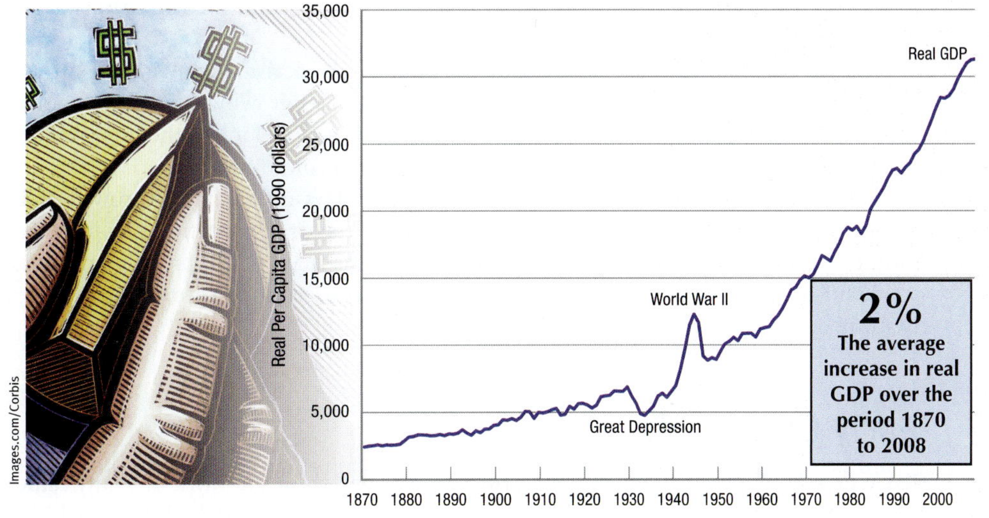


**Real per capita GDP has grown 13 times** since 1870 in the United States. After adjusting for inflation, growth has averaged 2% per year over this period and accounts for the higher U.S. standard of living. Economic growth results from increases in the labor force and its productivity, increases in capital, and improvements in technology.

**The Benefits of Growth in the United States (1980 to 2008)**

- 38% reduction in property crime
- 12% increase in college graduates as a percent of the population
- 29% increase in high school graduates as a percent of the population
- 6.7% decline in the death rate
- 36% reduction in the poverty rate of blacks
- 400% increase in federal outlays for science, space, and technology
- 32% increase in the number of colleges

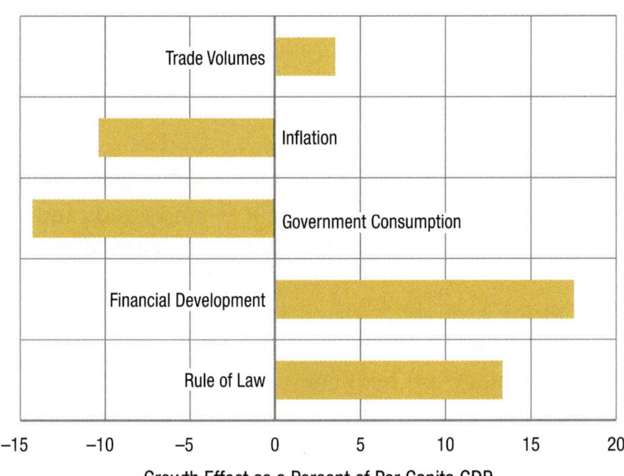


**Good public policies promote growth.** Implementing the rule of law, improving financial markets, and trading with other nations all promote growth. Higher government consumption and higher inflation harm growth.

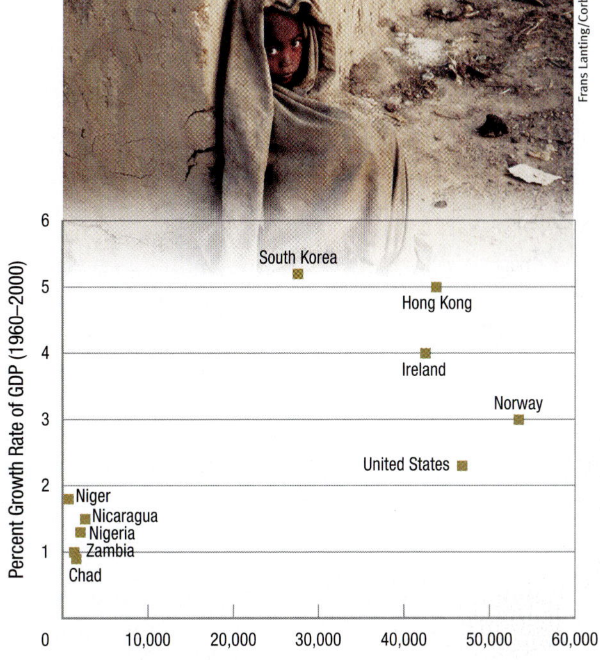


**Growth in poor countries is well below that of highly developed and high-income countries.** Given the growth in low-income countries, it is unlikely that they will ever catch up.

causes economic growth in the long run should help us later when we look at the economy in the short run.

The classical tradition of economic analysis began with Adam Smith's publication of *The Wealth of Nations* in 1776, and the classical model continued to be the dominant tool of economic analysis until the Great Depression. Classical economists took a long-run view of the economy that predicted relatively stable economic conditions around full employment.

In this chapter, we begin with a look at the early classical model. We then turn to a broader view of the sources of economic growth—such as a growing labor force—and we show why labor's productivity is so important. We take a close look at the important role of ideas and technology and how their spread generates economic growth.

The last section looks at the role infrastructure plays in facilitating growth. Public infrastructure includes economy-wide attributes such as transportation facilities, communications networks, education systems, legal systems that protect property rights and stable financial institutions. Without good infrastructure, economic growth will be greatly stunted.

## Early Growth Theory

**Classical model:** A model of the economy that relied on competitive conditions in product, labor, and capital markets, and flexible prices, wages, and interest rates to keep the economy operating around full employment. Anyone unemployed simply was unwilling to work at the prevailing real wage.

Early growth theory—the **classical model**—was based on the work of many famous economists, including Adam Smith, Thomas Malthus, Alfred Marshall, and Karl Marx. Classical economists broke the aggregate economy into three markets: a product market, a labor market, and a capital market. All three markets were thought to be highly competitive, with product prices, wages for labor, and interest on loanable funds being set by the forces of supply and demand in each market. The competitive interaction of these three markets, according to classical economists, kept the economy operating near full employment.

We will employ a simple example of preparing invoices to be sent to customers, which in days past was done by individuals and typewriters. Today, computers spit these out by the thousands each hour. Keep in mind that our simple example (assuming that all activity is invoice preparing) can be expanded to cover all products and services produced in the economy.

### Aggregate Production

In Chapter 2, we briefly discussed production, the process by which individual firms turn inputs (factors)—land, labor, capital, and entrepreneurial ability—into goods and services. At this point, we consider aggregate production, or the production carried out by an entire economy.

For our purposes, aggregate output is directly related to an economy's technology (typewriters) and to the quantities of inputs it uses in the production process. If capital (the number of typewriters) and technology are held constant, increasing labor inputs (people) will result in rising output. In the long run, all these variables can change. As we will see later, this production relationship provides us with a straightforward approach for determining which policies will enhance growth in the long run. Note that land and entrepreneurship are not ignored, just assumed to be encapsulated in capital.

### Product Markets

Early economists focused on the microeconomics of markets applied to an aggregate economy. Consumer choices determine demand, and competitive markets determine supply, as we discussed in Chapter 3. This leads to a market equilibrium price and output for invoices as shown in Figure 2. The market sets a price of $2.00 per invoice. The classical school argued that output and flexible prices from these competitive markets would absorb any changes in demand or supply.

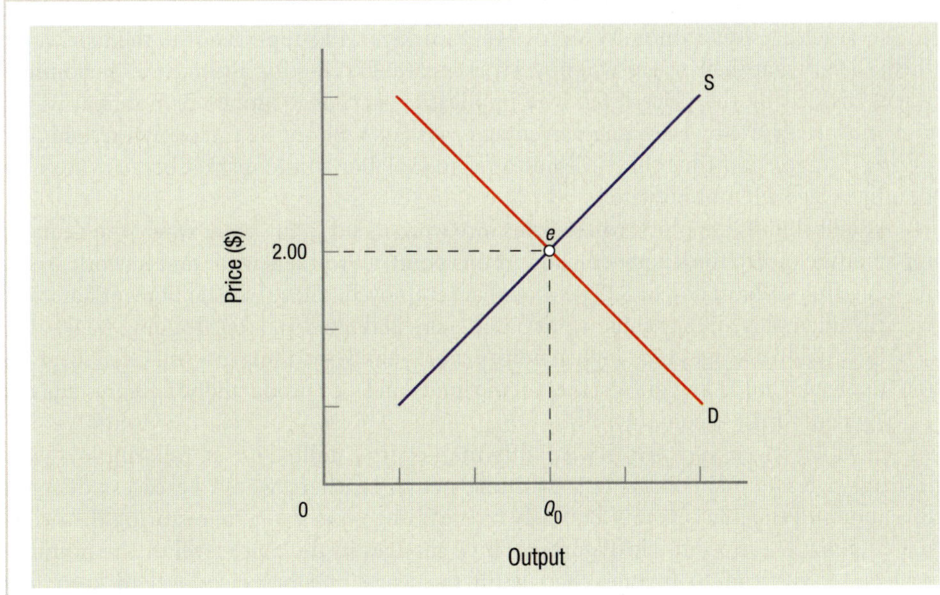


**FIGURE 2—Competitive Product Market**

The competitive product market would equate supply and demand and set market price

## Labor Markets

How did early economists get from product markets to the demand for and supply of labor? The product market determined that each invoice drafted, printed, and mailed is worth $2.00 to firms. If you can produce 100 letters in an 8-hour day, you will be worth $200.00 a day to your employer. Thus, your wage will be $200 a day, or $25.00 an hour, as shown in Figure 3.

The demand for labor curve reflects diminishing returns for much the same reasons that the production possibilities curves in Chapter 2 were bowed out from the origin. If more workers are hired and all are employed in the same office, each worker's output will fall, given that the firm's capital is fixed in the short term—printers become overloaded, workers get in each others' way or begin to gossip, and so forth. Now each worker produces less, so real wages must fall for the firm to be willing to hire more workers.

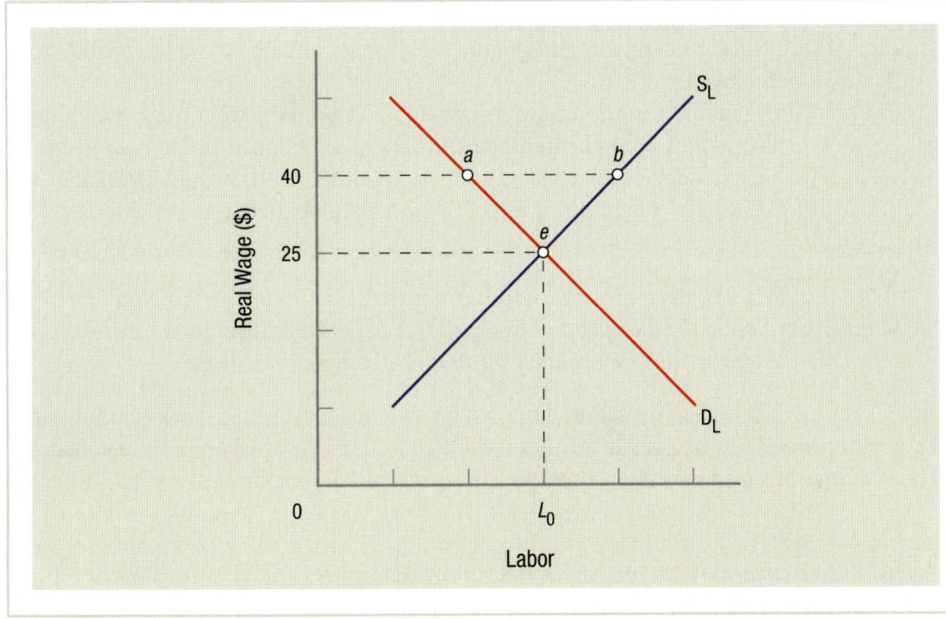


**FIGURE 3—Competitive Labor Market**

Competitive labor markets stay at full employment by equating supply and demand for labor to determine the equilibrium real wage (what the money wages will purchase). Unemployment (distance *ab*) could result if wages were artificially held above equilibrium.

The supply of labor curve illustrates the tradeoff workers face between working and leisure. Classical economists argued that workers will supply labor to the market on the basis of what their wages will buy. Workers are working for a *real wage,* or nominal wages divided by the price level. The implication is that if money or nominal wages rise, but prices rise by the same percentage, workers will not be fooled by these higher nominal wages, and thus they will not offer more labor to the market because the new nominal wage will not buy more.

Equilibrium is at point *e* where firms hire workers up to the point where the demand for labor is equal to the supply of labor. At this point, all workers who want to work at this real wage rate ($200 a day, or $25 per hour) are employed. Those who do not work are voluntarily unemployed; they could work but are unwilling to do so for the going wage.

Clearly, if real wages were higher, more people would be willing to work. Even so, given the supply of labor facing the market and the limits on labor productivity, $L_0$ represents full employment for this economy.

Flexible wages and prices keep this market in equilibrium at full employment. If real wages were somehow less than $25 per hour, there would be excess demand for labor and the market would quickly bid real wages back to $25, restoring the original equilibrium at point *e* in Figure 3. Thus, changes in the price level or the nominal wage rate will lead to further changes in the wage rate or price level to keep real wages constant.

In the long run, $L_0$ will remain the equilibrium employment level unless technology improves or more capital is employed, increasing the demand for labor and shifting the curve to the right, increasing real wages. Alternatively, if the labor force grows, the supply of labor will shift to the right, increasing employment; but note that unless the demand for labor rises, real wages would fall. Keep in mind that this is what happened in the world before 1820 (see Figure 1). Population growth kept per capita income virtually constant.

Notice also that all unemployment in this economy is voluntary. Classical economists recognized that if some artificial barrier were to keep wages above the equilibrium level, unemployment could result. In Figure 3, for instance, persistent unemployment would result if real wages were artificially maintained at a wage of $320 a day through minimum wage laws or union collective bargaining, for example. At a wage of $40.00 ($320/8) an hour, unemployment would equal *ab,* since businesses would only be willing to hire to point *a,* but *b* workers would like to work. Before the Depression, however, minimum wage laws and unions were rare.

In summary, individuals supply labor to the market for real wages (what the money wages will purchase). Firms demand labor, hiring more when real wages are lower, resulting in equilibrium where business wants the same number of employees supplied. At this point, all those who want to work at the going real wage can, and those not working are voluntarily unemployed.

The classical school's assumption was that people worked for what wages would purchase and that all earnings would be translated into spending (demand). This would ensure that there was no deficiency in consumption (demand), which would guarantee full employment. This has become known as **Say's law,** named after Jean Baptiste Say, who argued that

**Say's law:** The act of production produces income that leads to an equivalent amount of consumption spending; it is often paraphrased as "supply creates its own demand."

> *A product is no sooner created, than it, from that instant, affords a market for other products to the full extent of its own value . . . the mere circumstance of the creation of one product immediately opens a vent for other products.*[2]

Say argued, in other words, that there can be no deficiency in aggregate spending since the act of production also produces an income that leads to an equal amount of consumption. "Supply creates its own demand," as Say's law is often paraphrased.

[2] Jean B. Say, *A Treatise on Political Economy,* 1821, quoted in Brian Snowdon et al., *A Modern Guide to Macroeconomics: An Introduction to Competing Schools of Thought* (Brookfield, VT: Edward Elgar), 1994, p. 52.

But what about saving? Some people saved money from their income, and this offered the potential for underconsumption, which would lead to reduced incomes and employment below full employment. To counter this situation, classical economists turned to capital markets, which equated saving by households with investment by business.

## Capital Markets: Saving and Investment

To early economists, saving and investment decisions were influenced primarily by interest rates. Saving reflects a willingness to abstain from current consumption; this abstention is then rewarded by the interest earned on saved funds. Higher interest rates represent higher rewards, and thus, consumers can be expected to save more as interest rates rise.

Figure 4 portrays the market for loanable funds, or the capital market. The supply curve for loanable funds, $S_0$, is positively sloped, like most supply curves. As interest rates rise, the quantity of savings supplied rises as consumers choose to save more money rather than spend it.

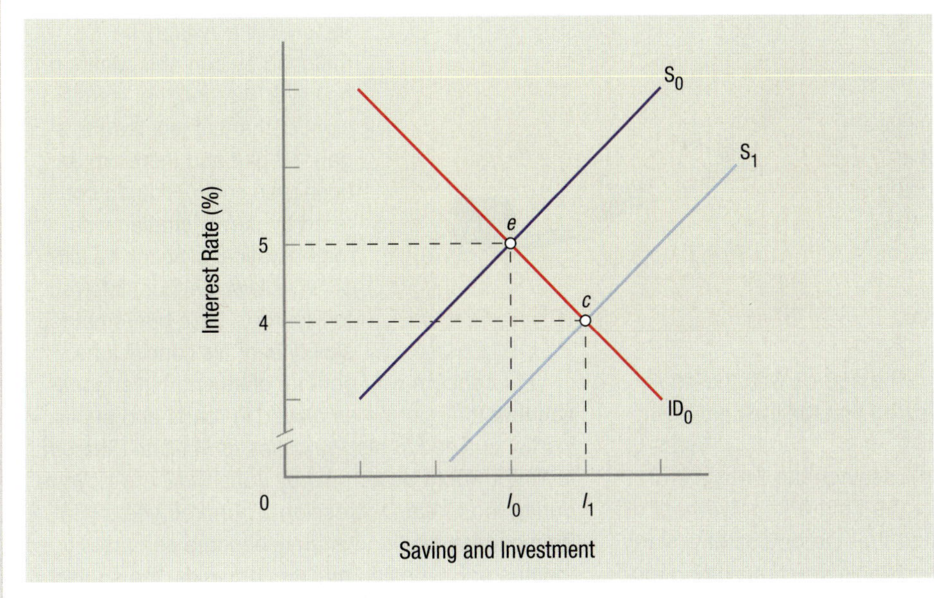


**FIGURE 4—Competitive Capital Markets**

Competitive loanable funds (capital) markets determine equilibrium interest rates (point *e*). If consumers decide to save more, the supply of loanable funds increases to $S_1$, causing interest rates to fall and investment to rise.

Curve $ID_0$ represents the demand for loanable funds, or investment demand. As interest rates decline, the cost of investing falls, so borrowing for investment purposes will rise. We can think of the investment curve, $ID_0$, as an array of possible capital projects. When interest rates are 5%, investment projects up to $I_0$ will be undertaken, since they earn the required rate of return. As interest rates decline, more such projects become profitable.

But just how do saving and investment ward off insufficient demand to keep the economy at full employment? Assume the economy is initially at full employment in the labor market, and savings and investment are equal at $S_0 = ID_0$ (point *e*), and interest rates are at the equilibrium level (5%).

Suppose consumers decide to purchase fewer goods than before, so that consumption falls below the level needed to maintain full employment. The entire saving schedule now increases (shifts to the right) to $S_1$; at all interest rates, consumers want to spend less and save more.

Equilibrium moves to point *c*, where interest rates are lower (4%), but investment increases. This additional spending on business investment will increase demand

## Thomas Malthus (1766–1834)

Thomas Malthus was raised in Surrey, England, the son of a wealthy eccentric country gentleman. Home-schooled by his father and a tutor he had learned enough to be accepted to Cambridge University. After attending Cambridge, he spent several years as a clergyman before accepting a teaching post in political economy at the college of the East India Company, making him the first academic economist in history.

In 1793, the pamphleteer William Godwin published *Political Justice,* describing a utopian future with no war, poverty, crime, injustice, or disease. Malthus argued against the book's conclusions during a lengthy discussion with his father, who agreed with the book, but nevertheless suggested that Malthus set down his ideas in print.

The result was "An Essay on the Principle of Population as It Affects the Future Improvement of Society." Malthus argued that the origins of poverty were rooted in an unavoidable contradiction: population, when allowed to grow without limits, increases geometrically, while the food supply could only increase arithmetically. He argued that English Poor Laws spread pauperism because any improvement in conditions of the poor would simply lead to population increases and to rising food prices and scarcities.

He even went so far as to suggest that "a proclamation should be read out at marriage ceremonies warning couples that they would have to bear the financial burden and consequences of their passion."

Malthus met David Ricardo in 1809 after the stockbroker-turned-economist wrote a series of articles criticizing protectionist agricultural policies. The two became lifelong friends and professional antagonists. One of their most significant debates was over Say's law, which held that a "general glut" in goods and services was a logical impossibility because supply will inevitably be matched by demand. Malthus, however, worried that insufficient demand might lead to a general glut and therefore an economic crisis. Ricardo countered by demonstrating with mathematical logic the validity of Say's law. Malthus deferred to Ricardo's logic but remained skeptical of his conclusions.

AGStockUSA/Alamy

His concern with general gluts and his suggestion that the poor be employed in roads and public works, outlined in his *Principles of Political Economy* in 1820, would be echoed by John Maynard Keynes during the Great Depression a hundred years later. These ideas would ultimately become central to the themes of Keynesian macroeconomics, the subject of the next chapter.

Sources: Paul Strathern, *A Brief History of Economic Genius* (New York: Texere), 2002; Howard Marshall, *The Great Economists: A History of Economic Thought* (New York: Pitman Publishing), 1967; and Donald Winch, "Malthus," in *Three Great Economists* (Oxford: Oxford University Press), 1997, pp. 105–218.

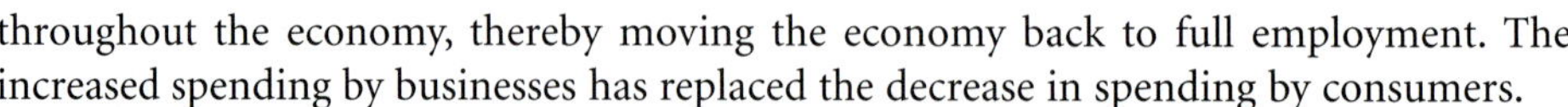

throughout the economy, thereby moving the economy back to full employment. The increased spending by businesses has replaced the decrease in spending by consumers.

The result of classical analysis is that the economy will be at full employment all the time. Flexible wages, interest rates, and prices ensure that the economy hovers around full employment.

During the 18th and 19th centuries, as we have seen, per capita income rose very little. This led early economists to be pessimistic about future standards of living. Most famous is Thomas Malthus, whose analysis that population would grow substantially faster than the food supply has often been wrongly attributed to economics, causing it to be dubbed the "dismal science."

## Implications for Economic Growth

If the economy is always operating at full employment, how does the economy grow? The implications for economic growth from classical economics are very straightforward. Anything that improves the productivity of labor, the amount of capital employed with labor, or new productivity-enhancing technology will result in economic growth. This is very much like our conclusion on economic growth from production possibilities analysis in Chapter 2.

The primary limitations of classical analysis are its exclusive focus on the long run and its stylistic assumptions. In the real world, most of the politicians who are responsible for economic policy face reelection every few years. They will often support policies to assure their reelection, and not be as concerned with the long-run effects of short-term policies.

Second, as the Great Depression illustrated, high unemployment levels can last a long time. A long recession may be required before the competitive mechanisms that early economists envisioned bring the economy back to full employment. Consequently, a focus on shorter time frames is often needed.

Despite these limitations, most contemporary economists see the classical model as representative of the economy's long-run course.

**CHECKPOINT**

### EARLY GROWTH THEORY

- Early economists relied on competitive conditions in product, labor, and capital markets, and flexible prices, wages, and interest rates to keep the economy operating around full employment. Anyone unemployed simply was unwilling to work at the prevailing real wage.
- Economic growth in the classical model results from improvements in labor productivity, increases in capital, and productivity-enhancing technological change.

**QUESTION:** The classical model relies on competitive markets for labor, products, and capital to keep the economy near full employment and output. Before 2008, the United States enjoyed nearly three decades of high employment, high growth, and low inflation, interrupted by two short and mild recessions. Has the recent growth in globalization and trade liberalization introduced more competition into labor, capital, and product markets, making our economy look and act like early economists envisioned?

Answers to the Checkpoint question can be found at the end of this chapter.

# Long-Run Economic Growth: Productivity

We have seen that economic growth can come from three sources: increases in capital, increases in labor, and improvements in technology. Communications and computers provide recent examples of industries that have experienced such high rates of technical change and improved productivity that prices have fallen off a cliff, even as output has ballooned. Both industries have powered much of the economic growth that we have seen over the last two decades.

## Productivity Is Key

As we saw earlier, the demand for labor and the equilibrium real wage is determined by the marginal productivity of labor. When worker **productivity** grows, real wages rise. The primary reason the American standard of living is so high is that American workers produce so much more per worker than do workers throughout most of the rest of the world. Many people in the developing world eke out a living using tools that would remind us of an earlier century. This lower productivity is reflected in their standard of living: Many of these people lead 19th-century lives.

**Productivity:** How effectively inputs are converted into outputs. Labor productivity is the ratio of the output of goods and services to the labor hours devoted to the production of that output. Higher productivity and higher living standards are closely related.

The more you produce and the higher the value of the goods or services you produce, the higher will be your earnings and your standard of living. People whose skills are in high demand—entertainers, movie stars, and professional athletes—earn immense fortunes. The moment their star fades, however, whether because of age or changing public tastes, their incomes plummet. In the world of athletics or rock music, stars are often has-beens by age 35. Although their salaries are not as high as sports superstars, highly skilled executives, supercomputer systems programmers, and doctors all are highly productive, and their earnings reflect the value of their skills.

Higher productivity and higher standards of living similarly go hand in hand for nations as a whole. Highly productive places like the United States, Japan, and Europe are also places with high standards of living. At the opposite end of the spectrum, countries like Chad, Nigeria, and Pakistan have less productive labor forces with low incomes, along with the problems this lower living standard entails.

## Sources of Productivity Growth

Productivity growth raises wages and incomes. Let's look at some of the factors that increase labor productivity.

### Increasing the Capital-to-Labor Ratio

When a farmer in Nigeria plows his field with a crude plow hitched to a buffalo, the amount of land he can plant and harvest is miniscule. American farmers, in contrast, use farm equipment that allows them to plow, plant, fertilize, water, and harvest thousands of acres; they have a high **capital-to-labor ratio.** This raises U.S. farm productivity many orders of magnitude above that of poor Nigerian farmers. The ultimate result of this vastly superior productivity is that American farmers earn a far higher income than their counterparts in the developing world.

Capital-to-labor ratio: The capital employed per worker. A higher ratio means higher labor productivity and, as a result, higher wages.

Developing countries have large labor forces, but little capital. Developed nations like the United States, on the other hand, have limited labor supplies, and each worker works with a large array of capital equipment. As a rule, the more capital employed with workers, the greater their productivity and the higher their earnings.

### Growth of the Labor Force

One part of the phenomenal economic growth of the United States over the past century can be tied to its population growth, and specifically to its immigration policies. Historically, U.S. immigration policies have been some of the most open of any country in the world.

Over the last few decades, the U.S. labor force—those working and looking for work—has grown faster than the population. Women have entered the labor force in increasing numbers. The demand for their labor has led many companies to introduce more family-friendly policies such as day care, increased opportunities for job sharing, and more flexible working hours and locations, sometimes from home.

Government policies designed to enhance labor-force participation have included day care subsidies, enhanced protections for pension funds, support for retirement benefits, and tax incentives that make work more attractive. For instance, the progressivity of the income tax has been reduced over the past several decades. This raises the take-home pay of the second worker in the family, thereby increasing the benefits for both adults in a family from work.

### Increasing the Quality of the Labor Force

Another source of productivity growth comes from improvements to the labor force from **investment in human capital.** Human capital is a term economists use to describe skills, knowledge, and the quality of workers. On-the-job training and general education can improve the quality of labor by improving productivity. In many ways, increasing capital and a highly skilled labor force go together: Well-trained workers are needed to run the

Investment in human capital: Improvements to the labor force from investments in skills, knowledge, and the overall quality of workers and their productivity.

highly productive, often highly complex, machines. Unskilled workers are given the least important jobs and earn the lowest wages.

By investing in human capital, nations can ultimately raise their growth rates by improving worker productivity. Government programs that raise the literacy rate, such as universal public education, also raise the rate of economic growth.

### Improvements in Technology

Technological improvements can come from various sources and play the major role in improving productivity, raising the standard of living and increasing economic growth. These include enterprising individuals who discover innovative new ways to produce a product, such as Henry Ford and the assembly line, and the inventors of new products, such as Thomas Edison, who invented the lightbulb and hundreds of other products.

Over the past few decades, microcomputers and their associated software have improved productivity immensely. Hardly a business or government office exists today that does not use a computer to automate some office task. Spreadsheets and modern database programs have revolutionized the way businesses manage, plan, and keep track of their customers.

The telecommunications industry and the Internet have further raised productivity by improving information flow and reducing the costs of producing and distributing products to consumers. Advances in biotech research will reduce the costs of developing new drugs and improve their efficacy. As researchers learn more about DNA, they may one day be able to target new drugs to specific individuals with unique genetic characteristics. This process will lower the cost of producing drugs, reduce the time needed for government approval, and enhance the healing power of the drugs.

Technological progress is the primary explanation for the extraordinary economic growth the United States has enjoyed over the last century. The technologies that kept the economy expanding have also helped many other countries to grow. In the developing world, however, growth most often comes from foreign companies building factories that employ locals at low wages. These companies often pay more than workers could have hoped to earn on their own. These higher earnings become the grubstake to better education and earnings for their children.

Today, new technologies are helping many developing nations to jump-start their growth. Cheap cellular service has improved communications, inexpensive vaccinations and health education programs have reduced mortality rates, and the global movement of capital and production facilities has created new job opportunities. Trade liberalization has helped many countries to develop.

## Modern Growth Theory

The seeds for modern growth theory, developed by Nobel Prize winner Robert Solow in the 1950s, introduced a more robust production relationship and added a relationship for technical progress that assumed the technical progress had occurred, but did not explain it. These refinements led to the conclusion that technical change is an important driver of economic growth. Unfortunately, technology was not explained by the model.

Since the mid-1980s a new approach to understanding the process of technical change in economic growth has focused on increases in knowledge. Specifically, modern growth theory argues that economic growth is driven primarily by new knowledge produced by technical change.

In a groundbreaking 1986 article, Paul Romer focused on the "public good" characteristics of knowledge. He argued that research and development by one firm necessarily has positive spillovers on production in other firms. Examples include just-in-time inventory systems, which reduced operating costs and quickly spread throughout industry, and Netscape's development of the graphical Internet browser that revolutionized Internet communications, which nearly everyone takes for granted today. The crucial point is that many innovations developed by individual firms have these *public good* aspects, which mean that these firms are unable to completely internalize the benefits; some benefits spill over to the economy at large.

New knowledge discovered by one firm quickly becomes public, and in this way, the acquisition of capital (human and physical) exhibits increasing returns instead of the earlier assumption of diminishing returns. Instead of one firm exploiting its discovery or innovation, the benefits are shared among hundreds or thousands of firms, amplifying the returns to the economy. Again, modern consumer electronics are a clear example of this phenomenon, as new, more complex, and powerful products are released every year at lower and lower prices. Moore's law that computing power doubles every 18 months (and at lower prices) has been a driving force behind increasing returns in the digital revolution of so many products and industries. These forces have also been driving rising levels of labor productivity and the standard of living.

Notice that all of this is just the "unintentional by-product of capital accumulation by individual firms,"[3] but with millions of firms engaging in huge amounts of research and development, this adds up to a force that drives economic growth. Once ideas and knowledge have been created, they can be spread to others for nearly nothing. In the digital world of software, instructions (computer code) can be used over and over, virtually for free.

As growth theories evolve, they lead economists to direct their attention to different reasons and sources of economic growth.

To summarize this section, economic growth comes from increases in capital, increases in labor, and improvements in technology. Increases in the capital-to-labor ratio tend to increase productivity. Increasing the size of the labor force and increasing the quality of the labor force turn directly into economic growth. Improvements in technology in this information age have led to the most dramatic increases in economic growth. Although labor and capital are important elements for economic growth, it is technological change and its spread that is the most important source. The speed at which ideas and technology are now created and shared between firms and countries has created unprecedented improvements in standards of living.

## CHECKPOINT

### LONG-RUN ECONOMIC GROWTH: PRODUCTIVITY

- Growth can come from increases in capital or labor resources or from improvements in technology.
- Growth in labor is important, but the productivity of that labor is more important for growth and future standards of living.
- Increased productivity of labor can come from increases in the capital-to-labor ratio, improvements in the quality of the labor force, and improvements in technology.
- Modern growth theory suggests that research and development improve technology, which in turn drives economic growth through its huge public good aspects and positive spillovers.

**QUESTION:** In June 2010, Warren Buffett, the world's second richest individual, pledged that 'more than 99% of my wealth will go to philanthropy during my lifetime or at death' and noted that he would give this approximately $30 billion in installments to the Bill & Melinda Gates Foundation. The foundation focuses on grants to developing nations, helping the poorest of the poor. What suggestions would you give the foundation to help these developing nations grow?

Answers to the Checkpoint question can be found at the end of this chapter.

[3] Brian Snowdon and Howard Vane, *Modern Macroeconomics: Its Origins, Development and Current State* (Cheltenham, UK: Edward Elgar), 2005, p. 627.

## Infrastructure and Economic Growth

What are the reasons that some nations are rich and others are poor? Economists have been struggling to answer this question for several centuries. Today, we know that part of the answer lies in the different levels of infrastructure development among various countries. In essence, the focus on infrastructure means that there is something important that lies behind our aggregate production: We do not just increase capital, increase labor, improve technology, and turn a crank to obtain economic growth.

### Public Capital

**Infrastructure** is defined as a country's public capital. It includes dams, roads, and bridges; transportation networks, such as air and rail lines; power-generating plants and power transmission lines; telecommunications networks; and public education facilities. These items are tangible public goods that can easily be measured. All are crucial for economic growth.

**Infrastructure:** The public capital of a nation, including transportation networks, power-generating plants and transmission facilities, public education institutions, and other intangible resources such as protection of property rights and a stable monetary environment.

### Protection of Property Rights

Less tangible yet equally important national resources include a stable legal system that protects property rights. As mentioned in Chapter 4, many developing countries do not systematically record the ownership of real property: land and buildings. Though ownership is often informally recognized, without express legal title, the capital locked up in these informal arrangements cannot be used to secure loans for entrepreneurial purposes. As a result, valuable capital sits idle; it cannot be leveraged for other productive purposes.[4]

### Enforcement of Contracts

The legal enforcement of contract rights is another important component of an infrastructure that promotes economic growth and well-being. Patent and copyright laws that protect innovators for specified lengths of time are needed to promote invention and innovation. Every country has its innovators; the only question is whether these people are offered enough of an incentive to devote their efforts to coming up with the innovations that drive economic growth. In today's digital world, protecting copyrights is especially important, since the cost of duplicating digital products is nearly zero. Yet, without some sort of protection, producers of these goods would have little incentive to produce them.

### Stable Financial System

Another important component of a nation's infrastructure is a stable and secure financial system. Such a financial system keeps the purchasing power of the currency stable, facilitates transactions, and permits credit institutions to arise. The recent global financial turmoil caused by subprime mortgage defaults and the subsequent severe credit crunch is an example of the problems caused by financial instability. Further, bank runs, like those that caused major economic disruption in Uruguay and Argentina in 2001–2002, are less likely when a nation's financial environment is stable.

Unanticipated inflations or deflations are both detrimental to economic growth. Consumers and businesses rely on the money prices they pay for goods and services for information about the state of the market. If these price signals are constantly being distorted by inflation or deflation, the quality of business and consumer decisions suffers.

[4] For an extensive discussion of this issue, see Hernando de Soto, *The Mystery of Capital: Why Capitalism Triumphs in the West and Fails Everywhere Else* (New York: Basic Books), 2000.

Unanticipated price changes further lead to a redistribution of income between creditors and debtors. Financial instability is harmful to improving standards of living and generating economic growth.

## Economic Freedom

Because it is both tangible and intangible, a nation's infrastructure is difficult to measure. The country's roads, dams, and other public capital do not present much of a measurement problem, but trying to measure intangibles often requires subjective judgments. One reasonably objective measure for infrastructure is the 2009 Index of Economic Freedom.[5]

This index incorporates information about freedoms in 10 categories, including business, trade, fiscal policy, government size, monetary policy, investment, finance, property rights, corruption, and labor.

Clearly, assigning some of these items a numeric value requires some subjective judgment. Even so, this index is one reasonable approach to measuring the infrastructure of a country.

Figure 5 portrays the relationship between economic freedom and per capita GDP measured by purchasing power parity (what income will buy in each country). Those nations with the most economic freedom have the highest per capita GDP and also the highest growth rates (not shown).

**FIGURE 5—Economic Freedom and Per Capita GDP**

The relationship between economic freedom and per capita GDP is shown here. Those nations with the most economic freedom also have the highest per capita GDP.

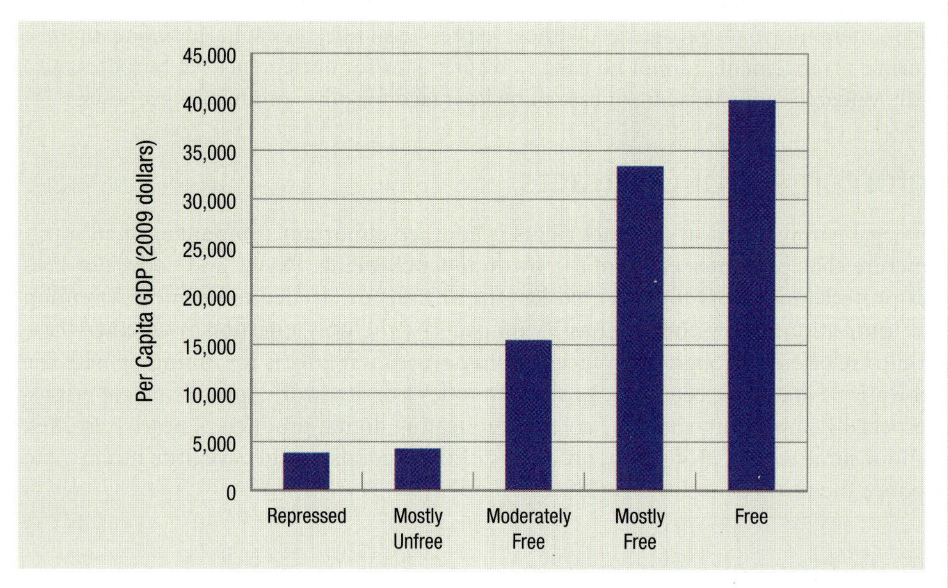


This idea that economic freedom and economic development go hand in hand has not always been popular. After World War II, the dominant view was that richer countries should provide capital (foreign aid) to poorer countries, and that this capital, when spent by the governments of the poorer countries, would generate economic growth. This money, however, often went into large infrastructure projects such as dams and power plants that did little to stimulate growth, or else the money was siphoned off into the pockets of the powerful ruling elite.

One economist, Peter Bauer from the London School of Economics, argued that "opportunities for private profit, not government plans, held the key to development. Governments had the limited though crucial role of protecting property rights, enforcing

[5] Terry Miller and Kim Holmes, *2009 Index of Economic Freedom* (Washington, DC: Heritage Foundation), 2009.

## *Issue:* Are Innovation Waves Accelerating?

**As we saw in** an earlier chapter, Joseph Schumpeter viewed the economy as being hit with shocks of innovation over long periods of time. He referred to these waves of innovation as "creative destruction," in which a lone inventor creates a major new idea or process that propels the economy to ever greater heights, but once the innovation has spread across the economy, the economy begins a decline until another innovation occurs and the economy booms again. These new ideas create a surge in investment that stimulates the business cycle and last—according to Schumpeter—roughly 50 to 60 years.

Before World War II, innovation came primarily from lone inventors and innovators, but after the war, business began establishing research and development departments that focused strictly on innovation. Bell Labs, a part of American Telephone and Telegraph (AT&T), was responsible for many innovations, including the transistor that ushered in the digital age. Another was the Palo Alto Research Center (PARC), a subsidiary of Xerox Corporation, which brought us technologies such as laser printing and the first graphical user interface (GUI), forerunner of the Mac and Windows operating systems.

It took 60 years to go from water power to steam power, then just 50 years to electricity as our major source of power. It took 50 years to get from steam to the internal combustion engine and then 40 years for commercial aviation to take its place in the transportation system. In the 1950s, electronic equipment became commonplace, and within 40 years it was replaced by digital equipment, software, and the Internet. Since 1990, digital computing has spurred the development of biotechnology, sequencing of human DNA, and the development of nanotechnology. Any of these may become the next major innovation of the near future. All of this suggests that the time between waves of innovation is becoming shorter. The figure shows the important innovations during each wave and illustrates how the waves are becoming smaller. Why is this?

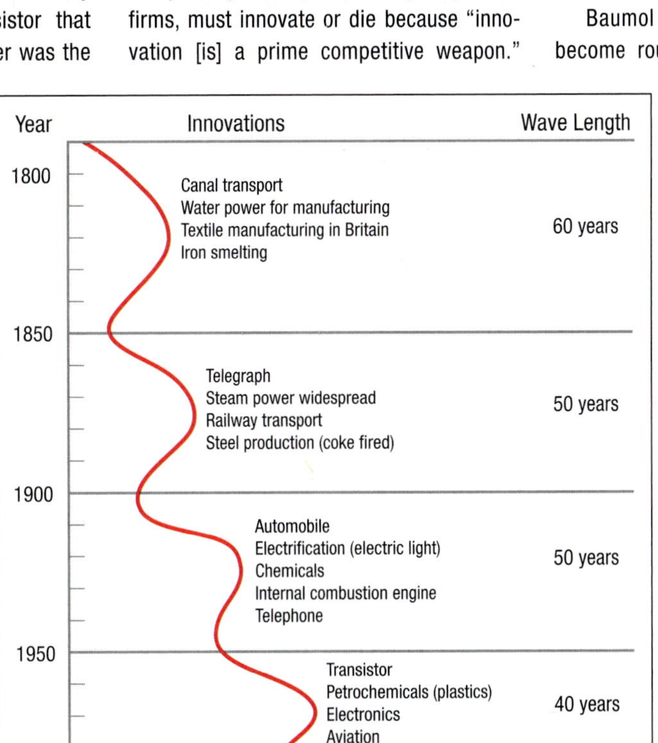


Princeton economist William Baumol suggests that capitalism's ability to produce a steady stream of new ideas and processes has made capitalism not only the most efficient growth machine but also the best economic system for generating economic growth. He suggests that enforcement of contracts, protection of property (both physical and intellectual), and the rule of law all provide the right incentives to innovate. Further, he suggests that large oligopolistic (an industry with a few large companies) firms, especially high-tech firms, must innovate or die because "innovation [is] a prime competitive weapon."

Andy Zito/Getty Images

Clear examples of this competition are seen in computer chips (Intel and AMD), operating systems (Microsoft, Apple, and Linux), digital music players (iPod and other MP3 players), drug makers in their rush to bring new (patented) pharmaceuticals to the market, and movie companies with the use of more and better special effects.

Baumol argues that innovation has become routine in large companies that want to survive, and the incentives established by patents and licensing have meant that firms often license their innovations to technology-exchange partnerships where cross licensing is the norm. As modern growth theory suggests, Baumol estimates that roughly 20% of the total economic benefits accrue to the original investors of the innovation, with the rest spilling over into the broader economy and society. For all of these reasons, the innovation cycle may be going from a long wave to a much shorter cycle.

Sources: "Catch the Wave: The Long Cycles of Industrial Innovation Are Becoming Shorter," *The Economist*, February 19, 1999; and William J. Baumol, *The Free-Market Innovation Machine: Analyzing the Growth Miracle of Capitalism* (Princeton, NJ: Princeton University Press), 2002.

contracts, treating everybody equally before the law, minimizing inflation and keeping taxes low. It was a tragedy that countries neglected this role."[6] Today, his ideas are part of a new conventional wisdom.

In this chapter, we have seen that economic growth in the long run comes from growth of the labor force, improvements in labor's productivity, increases in capital, or improvements in technology. Investments in human capital and greater economic freedom also lead to higher growth rates and higher standards of living. Modern growth theory tells us that knowledge and technological improvements spread rapidly throughout the economy because they are essentially public goods, making them key drivers of economic growth.

In the long run, all of these factors generate growth and higher standards of living. Yet, what are we to do if the economy collapses in the shorter term? The Great Depression of the 1930s was to prove that for a reasonably long period (a decade), the economy could be mired in a slowdown with high unemployment rates and negative growth. A deep economy-wide downturn inflicts high costs on both today's citizens and future generations. In the next chapter we turn to the first of our discussions on managing the economy in the shorter term.

**CHECKPOINT**

### INFRASTRUCTURE AND ECONOMIC GROWTH

- Infrastructure is a country's public capital, including dams, roads, transportation networks, power-generating plants, and public schools.
- Other less tangible infrastructure elements include protection of property rights, enforcement of contracts, and a stable financial system.
- The Index of Economic Freedom measures a country's infrastructure that supports economic growth.

**QUESTION:** Imagine a country with a "failed government" that can no longer enforce the law. Contracts are not upheld and lawlessness is the order of the day. How well could an economy operate and grow in this environment?

Answers to the Checkpoint question can be found at the end of this chapter.

## Key Concepts

Economic growth, p. 408
Classical model, p. 410
Say's law, p. 412
Productivity, p. 415
Capital-to-labor ratio, p. 416
Investment in human capital, p. 416
Infrastructure, p. 419

## Chapter Summary

### Early Growth Theory

Early (Classical) economists argued that competitive conditions in product, labor, and capital markets, combined with flexible prices, wages, and interest rates, would keep the economy operating near full employment. Everyone willing to work at the prevailing real wage would be employed.

---
[6] "Economic Focus: A Voice for the Poor," *The Economist*, May 4, 2002, p. 76.

Economic growth and rising standards of living in the classical model results from improvements in the productivity of labor, increases in the capital stock, and technological change that improves productivity.

## Long-Run Economic Growth: Productivity

Modern growth theories consider the growth in knowledge as key. Incentives for research and development result in processes that quickly spread to the entire economy. Knowledge has public good and spillover aspects that lead to increasing returns that drive modern economic growth.

Another key factor in American economic growth over the past century has been the expansion of its labor force from population growth and increased labor force participation. These trends have been encouraged by open immigration policies and increased incentives for entering the workforce, such as lower marginal tax rates.

The marginal productivity of labor is the most significant determinant of real wages, and high productivity is the primary reason the standard of living is so high. Sources of productivity growth include increases in the capital-to-labor ratio, increases in the quality of the labor force, and improvements in technology. Technological progress has been the most significant source of the enormous productivity gains the United States and many other countries have enjoyed over the past century.

## Infrastructure and Economic Growth

One of the key reasons some nations are rich and others are poor is the different levels of infrastructure in various countries. Infrastructure is defined as a country's public capital. It includes not only tangible assets, such as dams, roads, and bridges, but also intangible goods, such as secure property rights, legally enforced contract rights, and a stable financial system.

Despite the difficulties of measuring infrastructure, the Index of Economic Freedom is a fairly objective means of assessing a country's infrastructure. Those countries with the most economic freedom also have the highest real per capita GDP. It is widely believed that investing in human capital and promoting greater economic freedom will lead to higher growth rates and higher standards of living in the developing world.

# Questions and Problems

## Check Your Understanding

1. Describe how early economists saw competitive markets keeping the economy near full employment.
2. Explain why the level of economic growth today is more important to your great-grandchildren than to you.
3. Although abundant natural resources can be a blessing to a country, are they necessary to ensure economic growth and a prosperous economy?
4. In the quote that begins this chapter, Nobel Prize winner Robert Lucas in 1988 suggested that differences in growth rates between Egypt and India raise the most fundamental economic question of what causes economic growth. What makes this issue of growth so important? Is a long-term growth rate of 1.4% so different from 3.4%?
5. Why might a lack of economic freedom hold back development and keep living standards low?
6. Why is investment in human capital good for both individuals and fostering economic growth for the economy as a whole?
7. Why is a stable financial system important to economic growth?

## Apply the Concepts

8. The airline industry has struggled with unions in adapting to deregulation over the last two decades. Competitive pressures have resulted in lower wages for industry employees, but several airlines have had to invoke bankruptcy proceedings to eliminate their union contracts and reduce payroll costs. How do these activities square with the assumption of competitive labor markets and flexible wages assumed by classical economists?
9. The standard of living we enjoy today is largely due to the investments of earlier generations of Americans. Do you agree? Why or why not?
10. What role might foreign investment play in helping developing nations improve their growth rate and increase income levels?
11. Higher levels of savings and investment lead to greater rates of economic growth. What can government do to encourage more savings and investment?
12. Per capita income (or output) is the general measure used to compare the standards of living between countries. If a country's population growth is higher than its economic growth, what happens to per capita income? What are some of the limitations to using per capita income as a measure to compare the well-being of different countries?
13. One of the potential negative consequences of both economic and population growth is that we will eventually exhaust the Earth's natural resources, leading to our demise. What kind of activities might prevent this from happening?
14. Early economists assumed that highly competitive labor and capital markets would keep the economy around full employment. Which of these two markets in our economy is the most like classical analysis? If these markets are not highly competitive, what might that mean for the conclusion by classical economists that full employment will typically prevail?

## Solving Problems

15. The Chinese economy currently produces a GDP of roughly $10 trillion with over 1.3 billion people, so its GDP per capita is roughly $7,500. Contrast this with the United States, which produces over $13 trillion GDP with a population of roughly 300 million, or nearly $44,000 per person. If an economy, adjusted for inflation, grows at 3% annually, it will be 4.4 times bigger in 50 years; at 5% growth, it will be 11.5 times bigger, and if it grows at 10% annually, it will be 117.4 times larger in 50 years. If the United States grows at an average annual rate of 3% over the next 50 years and China grows at 10%, will China's standard of living or per capita income catch up to that of the United States? Under what assumptions would China have a larger economy than the United States in 50 years? Answer the same questions if China only grows at a real rate of 5% and the United States grows at 3%. Considering the classical model in the chapter and the factors that contribute to long-run growth, is 10% or 5% growth for China more likely?

# Answers to Questions in CheckPoints

## Check Point: Early Growth Theory

A credible case could be made that globalization and trade liberalization have made world product, labor, and capital markets more competitive than ever before. The revolutions in communications, data processing, the Internet, and health care are introducing competitive pressures in all markets. In this way, the world economy may reflect the working of the classical model more today than in the past.

## Check Point: Long-Run Economic Growth: Productivity

An organization like the Gates Foundation can help people improve their health through vaccinations, clean water, and sanitation, thereby enabling them to improve their productivity and earning power. Then, focus can be put on schools and improving education. All of this focus on human capital broadly can be accomplished with grants to communities or parents (by subsidizing them to send their kids to school) in developing nations.

## Check Point: Infrastructure and Economic Growth

Not very well. Large-scale business that we are accustomed to could not exist. What's left is small individual businesses that serve small local populations. Growth is stymied, and everyone ekes out a small living. Countries like Somalia are in this no-win situation.

# Keynesian Macroeconomics 18

Panoramic Images/Getty Images

*We have involved ourselves in a colossal muddle having blundered in the control of a delicate machine, the working of which we do not understand.*

JOHN MAYNARD KEYNES, 1930

**If you hadn't heard of** John Maynard Keynes before the recent financial crisis, you most likely have heard of him by now. The nearly $787 billion stimulus spending recommended by the Obama administration and passed by Congress in 2009 was largely based on his analysis of the macroeconomy. That analysis is the focus of this chapter. When economists suspect an economy is sinking into a deep recession, Keynesian macroeconomics often becomes the framework that they use to understand what is going on and to give policy advice.

Pre-Depression economic analysis essentially ignored the role of the government in macroeconomic stabilization. To be sure, the government was seen as providing the necessary framework in which the market could operate, maintaining competition, providing central banking services, providing for the national defense, administering the legal system, and so forth. But government was not expected to play a role in promoting full employment, stabilizing prices, or stimulating economic growth—the economy was supposed to do this on its own. The prevailing thought of economists before the 1930s was that a *laissez-faire* (leave it alone) approach to the economy was the best approach for government. Competitive markets for labor, products, and financial assets would lead to flexible wages, prices, and interest rates that would keep the economy humming along near full employment, with only a minor recession here and there.

The Great Depression changed political and economic thinking in the United States. Before the Depression, government spending (federal, state, and local) was roughly 10% of

**After studying this chapter you should be able to:**

- ☐ Name the components of aggregate spending.
- ☐ Analyze consumption using the average propensity to consume (APC) and the marginal propensity to consume (MPC).
- ☐ Analyze savings using the average propensity to save (APS) and the marginal propensity to save (MPS).
- ☐ Describe the determinants of consumption, saving, and investment.
- ☐ Determine aggregate equilibrium in the simple Keynesian model of the private domestic economy.
- ☐ Explain why, at equilibrium, injections equal withdrawals in the economy.
- ☐ Explain the multiplier process, how it is computed, and why it operates in both directions.
- ☐ Describe macroeconomic equilibrium in the full Keynesian model when government and the foreign sectors are added.
- ☐ Explain why the balanced budget multiplier is equal to 1.
- ☐ Describe the differences between recessionary and inflationary gaps.

the economy. Today, that figure has tripled to around 30%. The government, moreover, has added a vast number of laws, rules, and regulations to the books.

Since the Depression, the U.S. population has more than doubled, growing from 121 million to more than 300 million, yet over this same period, *real* gross domestic product has risen to nearly 14 times its 1929 level. With government spending at 30% of this gross domestic product number today, our economy can truly be called a mixed economy where the government plays a huge role.

Most of the changes in post-Depression economic thinking can be traced back to one book, *The General Theory of Employment, Interest and Money,* by John Maynard Keynes, published in 1936. In this book, Keynes moved out of the classical framework, which had viewed the economy as three separate and distinct competitive markets, and focused his attention on the economy as a whole and on aggregate spending.

In this chapter, we are going to develop the Keynesian model that can be used to analyze short-run macroeconomic fluctuations. This model will give you the tools to understand why policymakers took such an aggressive approach to the 2008–2009 downturn. Keynes's focus is on aggregate expenditures. Keynes's operating assumption, given that he was writing to explain the economic consequences of the Great Depression, was that if consumers demanded a given level of output, it would be provided by business. Thus, consumer spending is a key component to explaining how the economy reaches short-term equilibrium employment, output, and income. Using this model, we will see why an economy can get stuck in an undesirable place. So let us get started with Keynes and his focus on aggregate expenditures.

## Aggregate Expenditures

Recall that when we discussed measuring gross domestic product (GDP), we concluded that it could be computed by adding up either all spending or all income in the economy. We saw that the expenditures side consists of consumer spending, business investment spending, government spending, and net foreign spending (exports minus imports); thus, **aggregate expenditures** are equal to:

$$GDP = AE = C + I + G + (X - M)$$

**Aggregate expenditures:** Consist of consumer spending, business investment spending, government spending, and net foreign spending (exports minus imports): GDP = C + I + G + (X − M).

### Some Simplifying Assumptions

In this chapter, we first will focus on a simple model of the private economy that includes only consumers and businesses. Later in the chapter, we will incorporate government spending, taxes, and the foreign sector into our analysis. Second, we will assume, moreover, that all saving is personal saving. And since our initial model has no government sector at this point, GDP and national income, as well as personal income and disposable personal income, are all regarded as equal because there are no taxes in this simple model.

Third, because Keynes was modeling a depression economy, we follow him in assuming that there is considerable slack in the economy. Unemployment is high and other resources are sitting idle. There is excess plant capacity, which means that if demand were to rise, business could quickly and without added cost increase output. We will assume, therefore, that the aggregate price level (the CPI, PCE, PPI, or GDP deflator) is fixed; output can grow without putting upward pressure on prices. With these assumptions in mind, let us begin by looking at consumption and saving.

### Consumption and Saving

Personal consumption expenditures (C) represent roughly 70% of GDP, and for this reason **consumption** is a major ingredient in our model. Figure 1 shows personal consumption expenditures for the years since 1980. Notice how closely consumption parallels disposable income.

**Consumption:** Spending by individuals and households on both durable goods (e.g., autos, appliances, and electronic equipment) and nondurable goods (e.g., food, clothes, and entertainment).

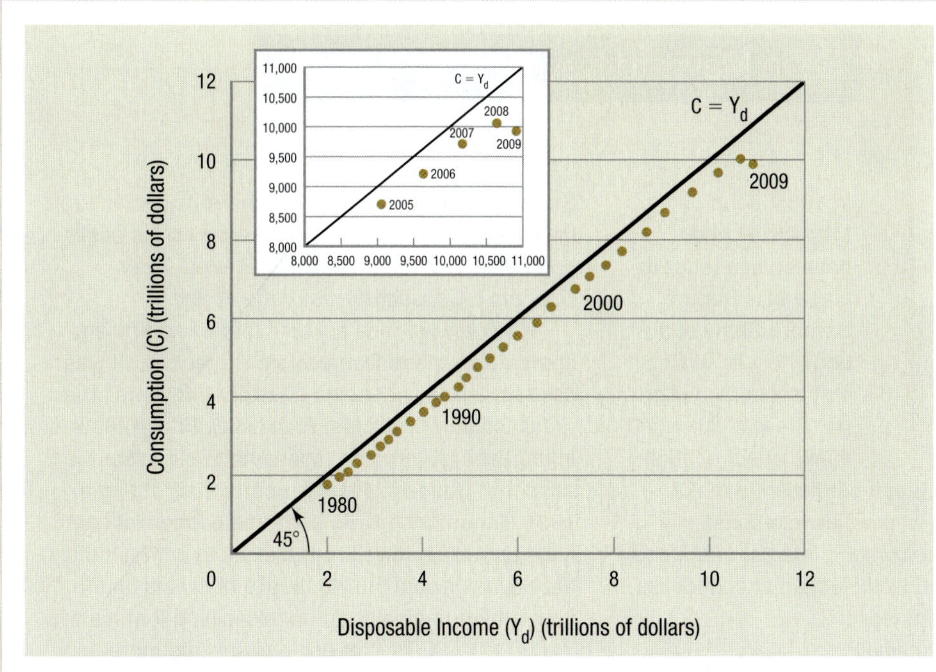


**FIGURE 1—Consumption and Disposable Income**

This graph shows personal consumption spending (C) for the years since 1980. The 45° line inserted in the figure represents the points where consumption is equal to disposable income ($Y_d$). If you spent your entire annual income, saving nothing, the 45° line would represent your consumption. Annual saving (S) is equal to the vertical difference between the 45° reference line and your annual consumption ($S = Y_d - C$).

The 45° line inserted in the figure represents all points where consumption is equal to disposable income ($Y_d$). If you spent your entire annual income, saving nothing, the 45° line would represent your consumption. Consequently, your annual **saving** (S) is equal to the vertical difference between the 45° reference line and your annual consumption ($S = Y_d - C$). After all, what can you do with income except spend it or save it?

**Saving:** The difference between income and consumption; the amount of disposable income not spent.

Notice that consumption spending increased every year since 1980 except in 2009, when disposable income rose but consumption dropped. This was an important contributor to the depth of the 2008–2009 recession.

Keynes began his theoretical examination of consumption by noting the following:

> *The fundamental psychological law, upon which we are entitled to depend with great confidence both a priori from our knowledge of human nature and from the detailed facts of experience, is that men are disposed, as a rule and on the average, to increase their consumption as their income increases, but not by as much as the change in their income.*[1]

Consumption spending grows, in other words, as income grows, but not as fast. So, as income grows, saving will grow as a percentage of income. Notice that this approach to analyzing saving differs from the classical approach. Classical economists assumed that the *interest rate* is the principal determinant of saving and, by extension, one of the principal determinants of consumption. Keynes, in contrast, emphasized *income* as the main determinant of consumption and saving.

Table 1 on page 431 portrays a hypothetical consumption function of the sort Keynes envisioned. As income grows from \$4,000 to \$4,200, consumption increases by \$150 (\$4,150–\$4,000) and saving grows from 0 to \$50. Thus, the *change* in income of \$200 is divided between consumption (\$150) and saving (\$50). Note that at income levels below \$4,000, saving is negative; people are spending more than their current income either by using credit or drawing on existing savings to support consumption.

[1] John Maynard Keynes, *The General Theory of Employment, Interest and Money* (New York: Harcourt Brace Jovanovich) 1936, p. 96.

## John Maynard Keynes (1883–1946)

In 1935, John Maynard Keynes boasted in a letter to playwright George Bernard Shaw of a book he was writing that would revolutionize "the way the world thinks about economic problems." This was a brash prediction to make, even to a friend, but it was not an idle boast. His *General Theory of Employment, Interest and Money* did change the way the world looked at economics. Arguably, it changed the world.

Keynes belongs in a small class of economic earth-shakers such as Karl Marx and Adam Smith. His one-man war on classical theory launched a new field of study known as macroeconomics. His ideas would have a profound influence on theorists and government policies for decades to come. Keynes also led an enviable life outside of economics, achieving success as a speculator, theater impresario, journalist, public servant, and member of an exclusive literary circle, the Bloomsbury group.

AP Photo/The Plain Dealer, Scott Shaw, File

Keynes grew up in the university town of Cambridge, England. His father, John Neville Keynes, was a leading economist; his mother, a former town mayor. He attended the best British schools, Eton and King's College, Cambridge.

During World War I, Keynes was assigned by the British Treasury to work on problems of wartime finances. Knowledgeable observers considered his contribution to have been indispensable to the war effort. Difficulties arose, however, after the peace, when Keynes was enlisted to advise the British government in negotiations over the Versailles Treaty. Strenuously objecting to the punitive financial terms imposed on Germany, Keynes resigned his position and published a brilliant analysis titled *The Economic Consequences of the Peace.*

Keynes was once asked if there was any era comparable to the Depression. He replied, "It was called the Dark Ages and it lasted 400 years." His prescription to President Franklin D. Roosevelt was to increase government spending to stimulate the economy. Sundeep Reddy reports that "during a 1934 dinner in the U.S., after one economist carefully removed a towel from a stack to dry his hands, Mr. Keynes swept the whole pile of towels on the floor and crumpled them up, explaining that his way of using towels did more to stimulate employment among restaurant workers." (*Wall Street Journal, January 8, 2009,* p. A10.)

During the world economic depression in the early 1930s, Keynes became alarmed when unemployment in England continued to rise after the first few years of the crisis. "I shall argue that the postulates of classical theory are applicable to a special case only and not to a general case," he wrote in the introduction to the *General Theory of Employment, Interest and Money.* "Moreover, the characteristics of the special case assumed by the classical theory happen not to be those of the economic society we live in." Keynes argued that *aggregate expenditures,* the sum of investment, consumption, government spending, and net exports, determined the levels of economic output and employment. When aggregate expenditures were high, the economy would foster business expansion, higher incomes, and high levels of employment. With low aggregate spending, businesses would be unable to sell their inventories and would cut back on investment and production.

### Average Propensities to Consume and Save

**Average propensity to consume:** The percentage of income that is consumed (C/Y).

The percentage of income that is consumed is known as the **average propensity to consume** (APC); it is listed in column 4 of Table 1. It is calculated by dividing consumption spending by income (C/Y). For example, when income is $5,000 and consumption is $4,750, APC is 0.95, meaning that 95% of the income is spent.

**TABLE 1** Hypothetical Consumption and Saving and Propensities to Consume and Save

| (1) Income or Output Y | (2) Consumption C | (3) Saving S | (4) APC C ÷ Y | (5) APS S ÷ Y | (6) MPC ΔC ÷ ΔY | (7) MPS ΔS ÷ ΔY |
|---|---|---|---|---|---|---|
| 3,000 | 3,250 | −250 | 1.08 | −0.08 | 0.75 | 0.25 |
| 3,200 | 3,400 | −200 | 1.06 | −0.06 | 0.75 | 0.25 |
| 3,400 | 3,550 | −150 | 1.04 | −0.04 | 0.75 | 0.25 |
| 3,600 | 3,700 | −100 | 1.03 | −0.03 | 0.75 | 0.25 |
| 3,800 | 3,850 | −50 | 1.01 | −0.01 | 0.75 | 0.25 |
| 4,000 | 4,000 | 0 | 1.00 | 0.00 | 0.75 | 0.25 |
| 4,200 | 4,150 | 50 | 0.99 | 0.01 | 0.75 | 0.25 |
| 4,400 | 4,300 | 100 | 0.98 | 0.02 | 0.75 | 0.25 |
| 4,600 | 4,450 | 150 | 0.97 | 0.03 | 0.75 | 0.25 |
| 4,800 | 4,600 | 200 | 0.96 | 0.04 | 0.75 | 0.25 |
| 5,000 | 4,750 | 250 | 0.95 | 0.05 | 0.75 | 0.25 |
| 5,200 | 4,900 | 300 | 0.94 | 0.06 | 0.75 | 0.25 |
| 5,400 | 5,050 | 350 | 0.94 | 0.06 | 0.75 | 0.25 |
| 5,600 | 5,200 | 400 | 0.93 | 0.07 | 0.75 | 0.25 |

The **average propensity to save** (APS) is equal to saving divided by income (S/Y); it is the percentage of income saved. Again, if income is $5,000 and saving is $250, APS is 0.05, or 5% is saved. The APS is shown in column 5 of Table 1.

**Average propensity to save:** The percentage of income that is saved (S/Y).

Notice that if you add columns 4 and 5 in Table 1, the answer is always 1. That is because Y = C + S, so all income is either spent or saved. Similar logic dictates that the two percentages spent and saved must total 100%, or that APC + APS = 1.

## Marginal Propensities to Consume and Save

*Average* propensities to consume and save represent the proportion of income that is consumed or saved. *Marginal* propensities measure what part of *additional* income will be either consumed or saved. This distinction is important because changing policies by government policymakers means that income changes and consumers' reactions to their *changing* incomes is what we will see later drives changes in the economy.

The **marginal propensity to consume** (MPC) is equal to the change in consumption associated with a given change in income. Denoting change by the delta symbol (Δ), MPC = ΔC/ΔY. Thus, for example, when income grows from $5,000 to $5,200 (a $200 change), and consumption rises from $4,750 to $4,900 (a $150 change), MPC is equal to 0.75 ($150/$200).

**Marginal propensity to consume:** The change in consumption associated with a given change in income (ΔC/ΔY).

Notice that this result is consistent with Keynes's fundamental psychological law quoted earlier, holding that "men [and women] are disposed, as a rule and on the average, to increase their consumption as their income increases, but not by as much as the change in their income." In Table 1, the MPC for all changes in income is 0.75, as shown in column 6.

The **marginal propensity to save** (MPS) is equal to the change in saving associated with a given change in income; MPS = ΔS/ΔY. So, when income grows from $5,000 to $5,200, and saving grows from $250 to $300, MPS is equal to 0.25 ($50/$200). Column 7 lists MPS.

**Marginal propensity to save:** The change in saving associated with a given change in income (ΔS/ΔY).

Note once again that the sum of the MPC and the MPS will always equal 1, since the only thing that can be done with a change in income is to spend or save it. A small word of warning, however: Though APC + APS = 1 and MPC + MPS = 1, most of the time APC + MPS ≠ 1 and APS + MPC ≠ 1. Try adding a few different columns from Table 1 and you will see that this is true. These little equations often show up on exams as wrong answers.

**FIGURE 2—Consumption and Saving**

The consumption and saving schedules from Table 1 are graphed here. Panel A extends the consumption schedule back to zero income, where consumption is equal to $1,000 and saving is equal to −$1,000. At the point where the consumption schedule crosses the reference line (point *a,* Y = $4,000), saving is zero. The saving schedule in panel B simply plots the difference between the 45° reference line and the consumption schedule in panel A. Thus, when income = $5,000, saving = $250 [line (*b* − *c*) in panel A, point *g* in panel B].

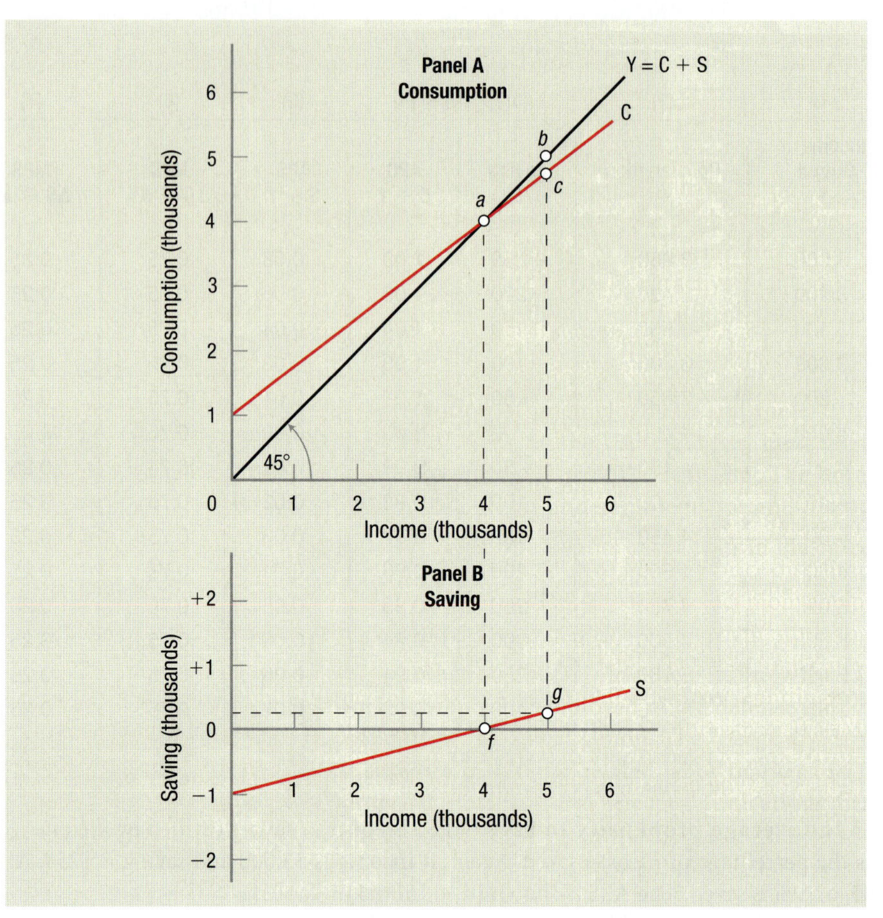


Figure 2 graphs the consumption and saving schedules from Table 1. The graph in Panel A extends the consumption schedule back to zero income, where consumption is equal to $1,000 and saving is equal to −$1,000. (Remember that Y = C + S, so if Y = 0 and C = $1,000, then S must equal −$1,000. With no income, people in this economy would continue to spend, either borrowing money or drawing down their accumulated savings to stay alive.) The 45° line in panel A is a reference line where Y = C. At the point where the consumption schedule crosses the reference line (point *a,* Y = $4,000), saving is zero, since consumption and income are equal.

The saving schedule in panel B simply plots the difference between the 45° reference line (Y = C) and the consumption schedule in panel A. For example, if income is $4,000, saving is zero (point *f* in panel B), and when income equals $5,000, saving equals $250 [line (*b* − *c*) in panel A, point *g* in panel B]. Saving is positively sloped, again reflecting Keynes's fundamental law; the more people earn, the greater percentage of income they will save (the average propensity to save rises as income rises). Make a mental note that the saving schedule shows how much people *desire* to save at various income levels.

How much people will *actually* save depends on equilibrium income, or how much income the economy is generating. We are getting a bit ahead of the story here, but planting this seed will help you when we get to the section where we determine equilibrium income in the economy.

Note finally that the consumption and saving schedules in our example are straight-line functions. This need not be the case, but it simplifies some of the relationships to graph them like this at this point. When the consumption and saving schedules are linear, the MPC is the slope of the consumption function, and the MPS is the slope of the saving schedule. In this case, MPC = 0.75 and MPS = 0.25, which tells us that every time income changes by $1,000, consumption will change by $750 and saving will change by $250.

## Other Determinants of Consumption and Saving

Income is the principal determinant of consumption and saving, but other factors can shift the saving and consumption schedules. These factors include the wealth of a family, their expectations about the future of prices and income, family debt, and taxation.

***Wealth*** The more wealth a family has, the higher its consumption at all levels of income. Wealth affects the consumption schedule by shifting it up or down, depending on whether wealth rises or falls. When the stock market was soaring in the late 1990s, policymakers—most notably the Federal Reserve Board—were continually worried about the "wealth effect" that the rising stock market might have on consumption spending. The concern was that, as many households saw their wealth dramatically expanding, rising consumption might have an adverse impact on the economy's inflation rate.

As it turned out, the stock market collapsed in 2000, again in 2008–2009, and the economy moved into recession. Then, economists began worrying about the negative impact of this wealth effect. With $6 to $7 trillion of wealth evaporating from the stock market in 2000, the concern was that consumers would reduce their consumption even more than would otherwise be expected. The 2008–2009 financial crisis and the falling stock market reduced wealth and consumption, contributing to the severity of the ensuing recession.

***Expectations*** Expectations about future prices and incomes help determine how much a family will spend today. If you anticipate that prices will rise next week, you will be more likely to purchase more products today. What are sales, after all, but temporary reductions in price designed to entice customers into the store today? Similarly, if you anticipate that your income will soon rise—perhaps you are about to graduate from medical school—you will be more inclined to incur debt today to purchase something you want, as was the case with high school student LeBron James, driving around in a Hummer, knowing that when he was drafted into the NBA, he would be making a fortune. Lotto winners who receive their winnings over a 20-year span often spend much of the money early on, running up debts. Few winners spend their winnings evenly over the 20 years.

***Household Debt*** The more debt a family has, the less it will spend in the current period. Though the household might want to spend more money on goods now, its debt level restricts its ability to get more credit.

***Taxes*** Taxes reduce disposable income, so taxes result in reduced consumption and saving. When taxes are increased, spendable income falls, so consumption is reduced by the MPC times the reduction in disposable income, and saving falls by the reduction in disposable income times the MPS. Tax reductions have the opposite impact, as we will see later in this chapter.

## Investment

Though consumer spending, at 70%, is by far the largest component of GDP, until recently it held fairly steady from year to year. In contrast, *gross private domestic* ***investment*** (the "I" in the GDP equation), is volatile. The annual percentage changes in consumption and investment spending from 1980 to 2009 are shown in Figure 3 on the next page.

**Investment:** Spending by business that adds to the productive capacity of the economy. Investment depends on factors such as its rate of return, the level of technology, and business expectations about the economy.

Notice that although consumption until 2009 plodded along with annual increases between 3% and 10%, investment spending has undergone annual fluctuations ranging from −20% to +30%. Investment constitutes roughly 15% of GDP, so its volatility often accounts for our recessions and booms.

The economic boom of the 1990s, for instance, was fueled by investments in information technology infrastructure, including massive investments in telecommunications. In the 1990s, people believed Internet traffic would grow by 1,000% a year, doubling every 3 months or so. This belief led many companies to lay millions of miles of fiber optic cable. When the massive investments made in computer hardware and software over that same decade are taken into account, it is no wonder that the economy grew at a breakneck pace.

**FIGURE 3—Changes in Consumption and Gross Private Domestic Investment**

The annual percentage changes in consumption and gross private domestic investment (GPDI) are shown here. Consumption is relatively stable, but investment spending is highly volatile, with annual fluctuations ranging from −20% to +30%. The shaded bars represent recessions.

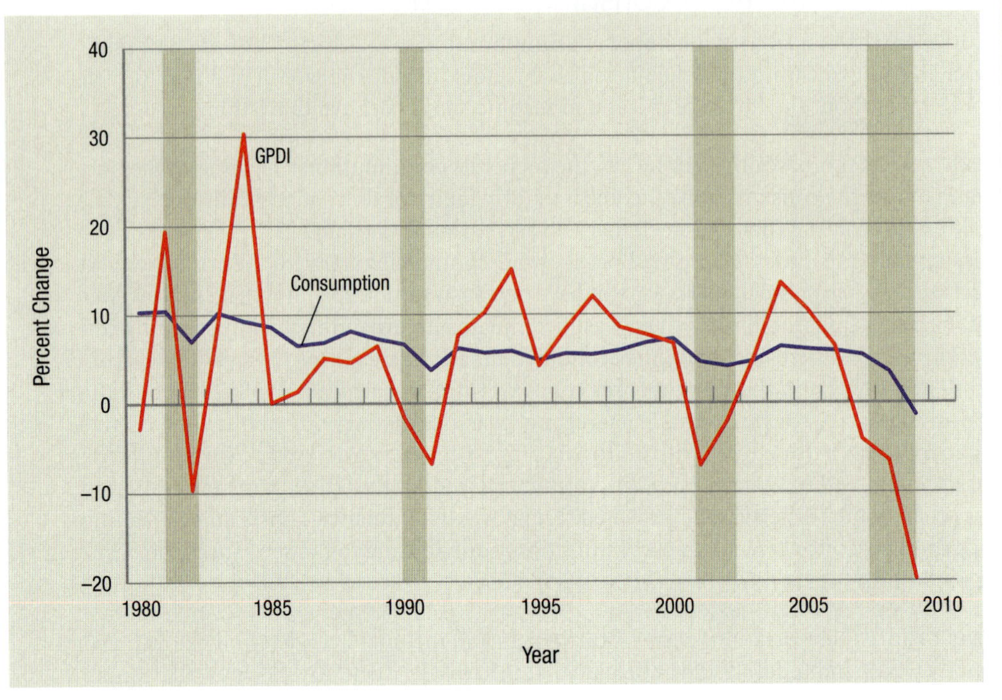


But this increase came to a halt in the early 2000s, when businesses—especially the telecoms—discovered they had built up a massive excess capacity, and thus bandwidth prices plummeted. The resulting plunge in investment between 2000 and 2001 can be seen in Figure 3. Investment recovered by 2003, then collapsed in 2007–2009 as the housing and financial crises took their toll.

## Investment Demand

Investment levels depend mainly on the rate of return on capital. Investments earning a high rate of return are the investments undertaken first (assuming comparable risk), with those projects offering lower returns finding their way into the investment stream later. Interest rate levels also are important in determining how much investment occurs, since much of business investment is financed through debt.

Figure 4 shows a hypothetical investment demand schedule, $ID_0$. When the interest rate is $i_0$, firms will invest an amount equal to $I_0$. When interest rates fall to $i_1$, investment rises to $I_1$ (a movement from point *a* to point *b*). As the rates for borrowing drop, more projects will become feasible, since the projected profit required to meet this lower interest rate is now less.

## Other Determinants of Investment Demand

The rate of return on investments is the main determinant of investment spending, but other factors shift the investment schedule shown in Figure 4.

***Expectations*** Projecting the rate of return on investment is not an easy task. Returns are forecasted over the life of a new piece of equipment or factory, yet many changes in the economic environment can alter the actual return on these investments. As business expectations improve, the investment schedule will shift to the right—businesses think returns will be going up, so they are willing to invest more at any given interest rate. Figure 4 illustrates this as a shift in the investment demand schedule from $ID_0$ to $ID_1$. Even though the interest rate is still equal to $i_0$, investment will be greater at $I_1$ (point *c*).

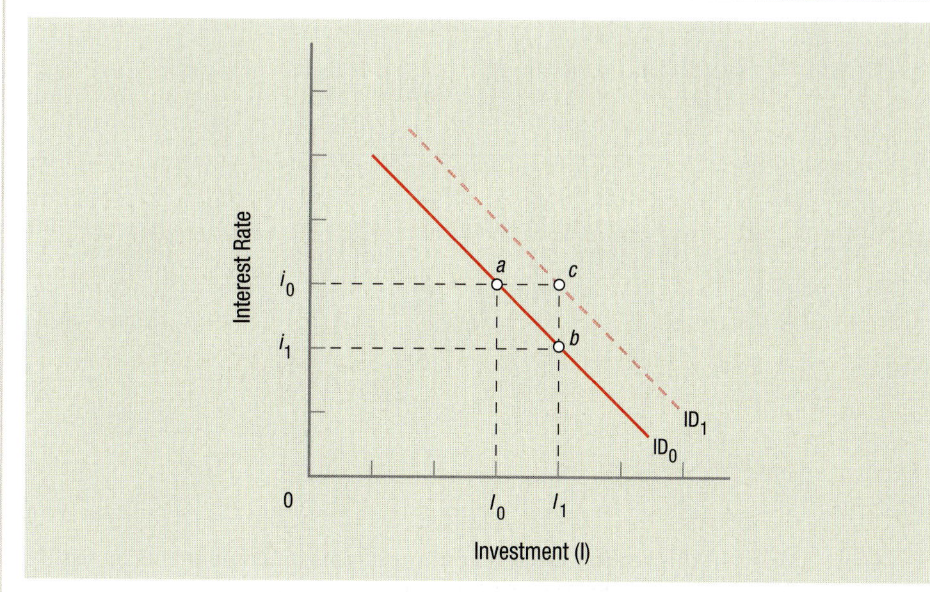


**FIGURE 4—The Investment Demand Curve**

Investment demand curve $ID_0$ illustrates that when the interest rate is $i_0$, firms will invest an amount equal to $I_0$, and when the rate falls to $i_1$, investment will rise to $I_1$. As the rates for borrowing drop, more investment projects become feasible, since the rate of return required to earn a profit declines. If business expectations improve, investment demand increases, shifting the curve out to $ID_1$.

***Technological Change*** It is clear (with the benefit of hindsight) that business expectations about technology and the Internet in the 1990s were exuberant. Technological innovations periodically spur investment. Electrification, automobiles, and phone service at the beginning of the 20th century and, most recently, microchips and the new products they have spawned are examples.

Producing brand new products requires massive investments in plant, equipment, and research and development. For example, Intel is expected to invest over $7 billion in new chip fabrication plants in 2009–2010. These investments often take a long time before their full potential is realized. Many economists expect that the investments in Internet and telecommunications technology are just in their beginning stages of boosting economic growth here and abroad.

***Capital Goods on Hand and Operating Costs*** The more capital goods a firm has on hand, including inventories of the products they sell, the less the firm will want to make new investments. Until existing capacity can be fully used, investing in more equipment and facilities will do little to help profits. When the costs of operating and maintaining machinery and equipment rise, the rate of return on capital equipment declines and new investment will be postponed. Most firms will wait until demand for their products grows enough to justify increasing production in the face of higher operating costs. However, unlike most firms, Intel has a history of increasing investment during recessions to be ready for the subsequent upturn.

## Aggregate Investment Schedule

To simplify our analysis, we will assume that rates of return and interest rates fully determine investment in the short run. But once that level of investment has been determined, it remains independent of income, or *autonomous,* as economists say. Therefore, in Figure 4, if interest rates are $i_0$ and investment demand is $ID_0$, investment will be $I_0$ in the short run (point *a*). Figure 5 on the next page shows the resulting aggregate investment schedule that plots investment spending with respect to income.

Because we have assumed that aggregate investment is $I_0$ at all income levels, the curve is a horizontal straight line. Investment is unaffected by different levels of income. This is a simplifying assumption that we will change in later chapters when we look at its implications.

**FIGURE 5—The Investment Schedule**

The aggregate investment schedule, relating investment spending to income, is shown here. Because aggregate investment is $I_0$ at all income levels, the curve is a horizontal straight line. This assumption simplifies the Keynesian model.

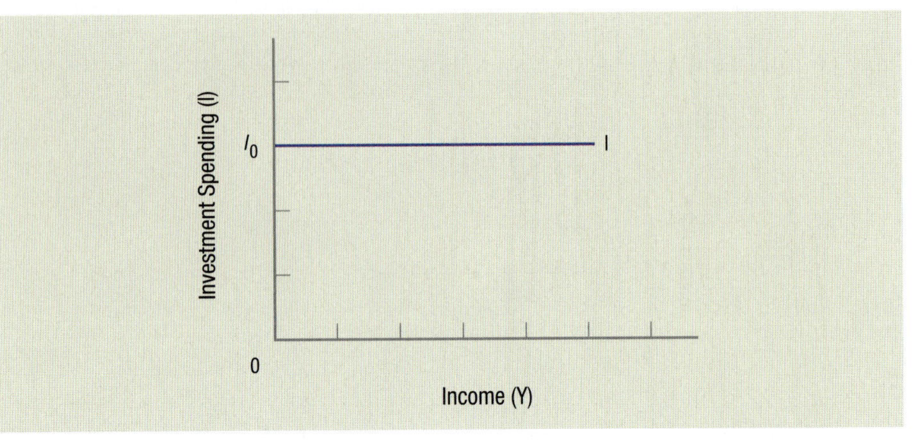


Our emphasis in this section has been on two important components of aggregate spending: consumption and investment. Consumption is 70% and investment is 15% of aggregate spending. Consumption is relatively stable, but investment is volatile and especially sensitive to expectations about conditions in the economy. We have seen that, on average, some income is spent (APC) and some is saved (APS). But, it is that portion of *additional* income that is spent (MPC) and saved (MPS) that is most important for where the economy settles or where it reaches equilibrium, as we will see in the next section.

## CHECKPOINT

### AGGREGATE EXPENDITURES

- Before the Great Depression, economists looked at three primary markets and thought these markets would keep the economy operating around full employment. Keynes analyzed the economy by first looking at aggregate expenditures.
- Aggregate expenditures are equal to C + I + G + (X − M), with consumption being roughly 70% of aggregate spending.
- Keynes argued that saving and consumption spending are related to income and that they grow with income but not as fast.
- The average propensities to consume (APC) and save (APS) are equal to C/Y and S/Y, respectively.
- The marginal propensities to consume (MPC) and save (MPS) are equal to $\Delta C/\Delta Y$ and $\Delta S/\Delta Y$, respectively. They represent the change in consumption and saving associated with a change in income.
- Other factors affecting consumption and saving include wealth, expectations about future income and prices, the level of household debt, and taxes.
- Investment levels depend primarily on the rate of return on capital.
- Other determinants of investment demand include business expectations, technology change, operating costs, and the amount of capital goods on hand.
- Consumption is relatively stable, and investment is volatile.

**QUESTION:** Figure 3 shows that investment spending is much more volatile than consumption spending. Why is this?

Answers to the Checkpoint question can be found at the end of this chapter.

## The Simple Keynesian Model

Since we have stripped the government and foreign sectors from our analysis at this point, aggregate expenditures (AE) will consist of the sum of consumer and business investment spending (AE = C + I). Aggregate expenditures based on the data in Table 1 are shown in panel A of Figure 6; panel B shows the corresponding saving and investment schedules.

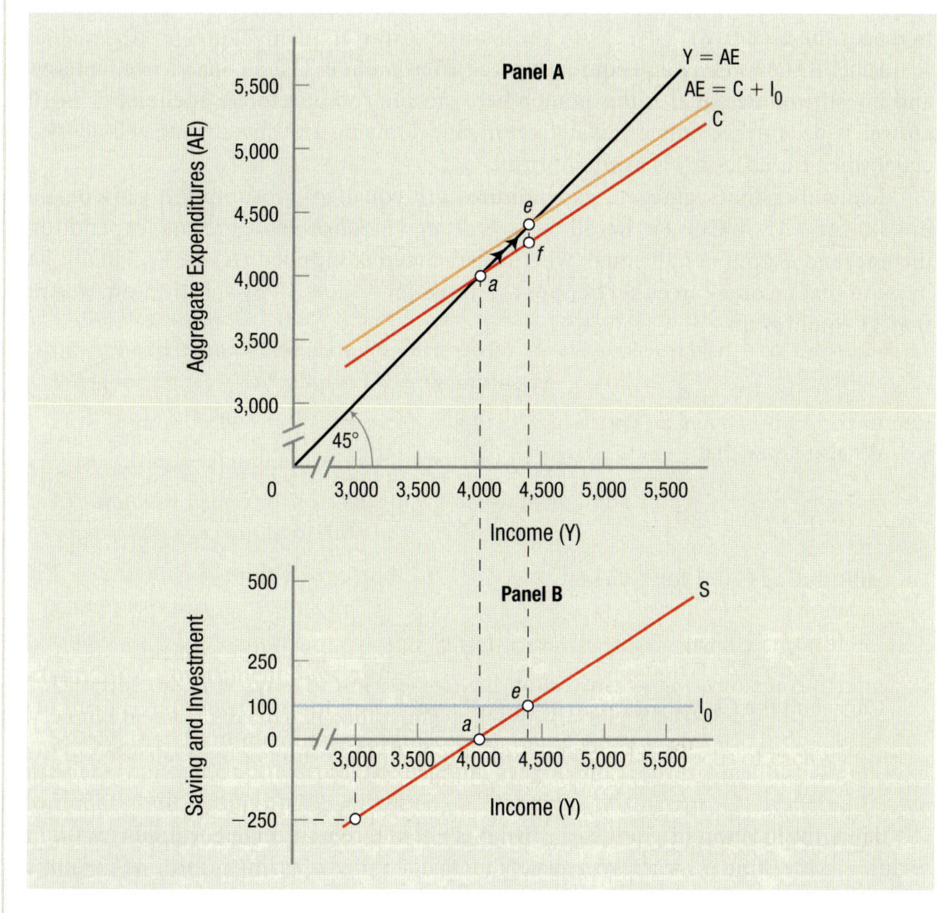


**FIGURE 6—Equilibrium in the Keynesian Model**

Ignoring government spending and net exports, aggregate expenditures (AE) consist of consumer spending and business investment (AE = C + I). Panel A shows aggregate spending; panel B shows the corresponding saving and investment schedules. Point *a* in both panels shows where income equals consumption and saving is zero. Therefore, saving is positive for income levels above $4,000 and negative at incomes below $4,000. The vertical distance *ef* in panel A represents investment ($100); it is equal to $I_0$ in panel B. Equilibrium income and output is $4,400 (point *e*), since this is the level at which businesses are producing just what other businesses and consumers want to buy.

Let us take a moment to remind ourselves what these graphs represent. Point *a* in both panels is that level of income ($4,000) where saving is zero and all income is spent. Saving is, therefore, positive for income levels above $4,000 and negative at incomes below. The vertical distance *ef* in panel A represents investment ($I_0$) of $100; it is equal to $I_0$ in panel B. Note that the vertical axis of panel B has a different scale from that of panel A.

## Macroeconomic Equilibrium in the Simple Model

The important question to ask is where this economy will come to rest. Or, in the language of economists, at what income will this economy reach **Keynesian macroeconomic equilibrium**? By equilibrium, economists mean that income at which there are no net pressures pushing the economy to move to a higher or lower level of income and output.

**Keynesian macroeconomic equilibrium:** In the simple model, the economy is at rest; spending injections (investment) are equal to withdrawals (saving), or I = S, and there are no net inducements for the economy to change the level of output or income. In the full model, all injections of spending must equal all withdrawals at equilibrium: I + G + X = S + T + M.

To find this equilibrium point, let's begin with the economy at an income level of $4,000. Are there pressures driving the economy to grow or decline? Looking at point *a* in panel A of Figure 6, we see that the economy is producing $4,000 worth of goods and services and $4,000 in income. At this income level, however, consumers and businesses want to spend \$4,100 (\$4,000 in consumption and \$100 in investment). Since aggregate expenditures (AE) exceed current income and output, there are more goods being demanded (\$4,100) than are being supplied at \$4,000. As a result, businesses will find it in their best interests to produce more, raising employment and income and moving the economy toward income and output level \$4,400 (point *e*).

Once the economy has moved to \$4,400, what consumers and businesses want to buy is exactly equal to the income and output being produced. Business is producing \$4,400, aggregate expenditures are equal to \$4,400, and there are no pressures on the economy to move away from point *e*. Income of \$4,400, or point *e*, is an equilibrium point for the economy.

Panel B shows this same equilibrium, again as point *e*. Is it a coincidence that saving and investment are equal at this point where income and output are at equilibrium? The answer is no. In this simple private sector model, saving and investment will always be equal when the economy is in equilibrium.

Remember that aggregate expenditures are equal to consumption plus business investment (AE = C + I). Recall also that *at equilibrium,* aggregate expenditures, income, and output are all equal; what is demanded is supplied (AE = Y). Finally, keep in mind that income can either be spent or saved (Y = C + S). By substitution, we know that, at equilibrium,

$$AE = Y = C + I$$

We also know that

$$Y = C + S$$

Substituting C + I for Y yields

$$C + I = C + S$$

Canceling the Cs, we find that, *at equilibrium,*

$$I = S$$

Thus, the location of point *e* in panel B is not just coincidental; at equilibrium, actual saving and investment are always equal. Note that at point *a*, saving is zero, yet investment spending is \$100 at $I_0$. This difference means businesses desire to invest more than people desire to save. With *desired* investment exceeding *desired* saving, this cannot be an equilibrium point, since saving and investment must be equal for the economy to be at equilibrium. Indeed, income will rise until these two values are equal at point *e*.

What is important to take from this discussion? First, when intended (or desired) saving and investment differ, the economy will have to grow or shrink to achieve equilibrium. When desired saving exceeds desired investment—at income levels above \$4,400 in panel B—income will decline. When intended saving is below intended investment—at income levels below \$4,400—income will rise. Notice that we are using the words "intended" and "desired" interchangeably.

Second, at equilibrium all **injections** of spending (investment in this case) into the economy must equal all **withdrawals** (saving in this simple model). Spending injections increase aggregate income, while spending withdrawals reduce it. This fact will become important as we add government and the foreign sector to the model.

**Injections:** Increments of spending, including investment, government spending, and exports.

**Withdrawals:** Activities that remove spending from the economy, including saving, taxes, and imports.

## The Multiplier Effect

Given an initial investment of \$100 ($I_0$), equilibrium is at an output of \$4,400 (point *e*). Remember that at equilibrium, what people *withdraw* from the economy (saving) is equal to what others are willing to *inject* into the spending system (investment). In this

may inadvertently make the recession worse. As they pull more of their money out of the spending stream, *withdrawals* increase, and income is reduced by a multiplied amount as other agents in the economy feel the effects of this reduced spending. The result can be a more severe or longer-lasting recession.

This was the case when consumer spending peaked in the summer of 2008. After that, auto sales plummeted and housing prices and sales fell. As the recession that started in December 2007 progressed and jobs were lost, consumers reduced their spending. As their confidence in the economy evaporated, households began to save more, consumer spending declined further, and the economy sunk into a deeper recession. Figure 9 shows how consumer spending (downward arrow) fell and saving rose (upward arrow) after September 2008. Leading up to the recession, saving was less than 1% of personal income, but by mid-2009 it had grown to 7%. Before the recession, aggregate household debt had soared, and part of what we are seeing in Figure 9 may reflect households spending less in order to pay off debt and return to more sustainable levels of debt.

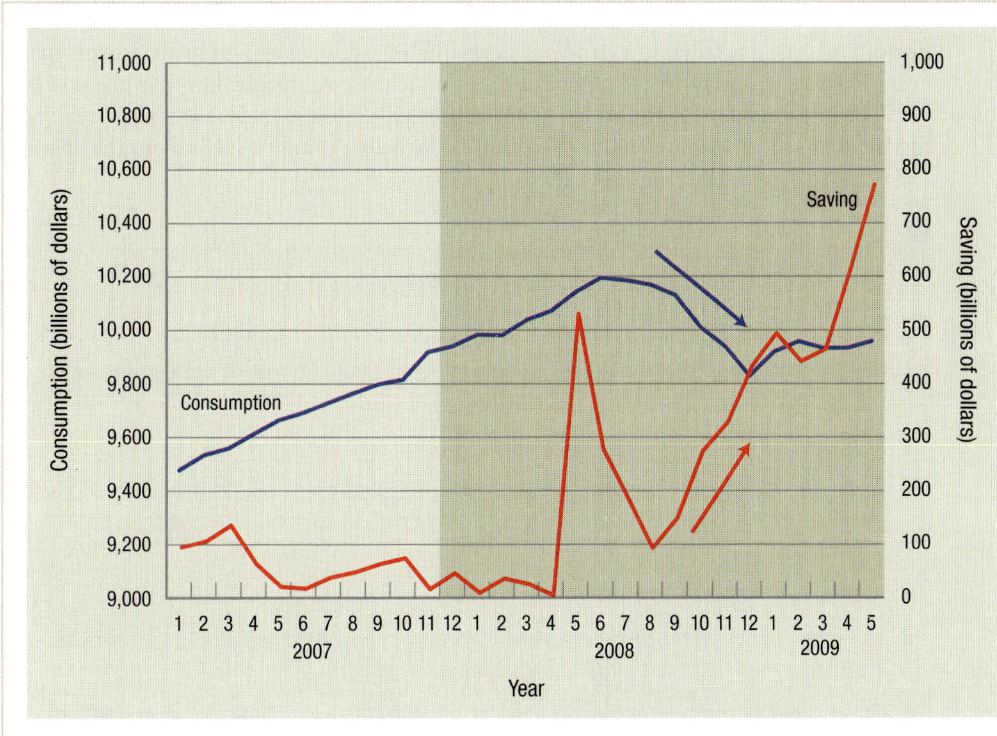


**FIGURE 9—Consumption and Saving, 2007–2009**

Consumption declined as the recession developed, and consumer worries about job losses and the decline in housing prices resulted in households saving more. The shaded area on the right represents the recession.

## Paradox of Thrift

The implication of Keynesian analysis for actual aggregate household saving and household intentions regarding saving is called the **paradox of thrift.** As we saw in Figure 9, if households *intend* (or desire) to save more, they will reduce consumption, thereby reducing income and output, resulting in job losses and further reductions in income, consumption, business investment, and so on. The end result is an aggregate equilibrium with lower output, income, investment, and in the end, lower *actual* aggregate saving.

**Paradox of thrift:** When investment is positively related to income and households *intend* to save more, they reduce consumption, income, and output, reducing investment so the result is that consumers *actually* end up saving less.

Notice that we have modified our assumption about investment—it now varies with economic conditions and is positively related to income. When the economy improves and income (or output) rises, investment expands as well, and vice versa when the economy sours. This is shown in our simple Keynesian framework in Figure 10 on the next page.

Initially the economy is in equilibrium at point *e* with saving equal to $S_0$. If households *desire* to save more because they feel insecure about their jobs, the savings curve will shift to the left to $S_1$. Now at all levels of income households *intend* to save more. This sets up

**FIGURE 10—Paradox of Thrift**

When consumers intend to save more and consume less (the saving schedule shifts from $S_0$ to $S_1$), and if investment is a rising function of income, the end result is that at equilibrium, households actually end up saving less (point *a*).

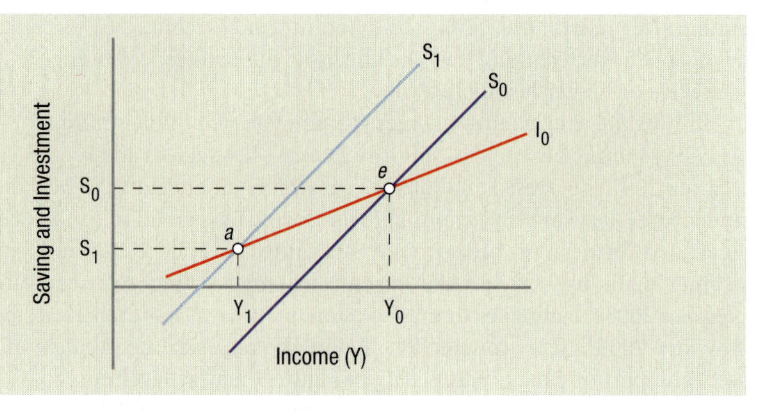


the chain reaction we described above, leading to a new equilibrium at point *a* where equilibrium income has fallen to $Y_1$ and *actual* saving has declined to $S_1$. The paradox is that if everyone tries to save more (even for good reasons), in the aggregate they may just save less.

The important question for policymakers is whether households will continue this saving trend after the recession ends. It will be a while before economists find out the answer.

## CHECKPOINT

### THE SIMPLE KEYNESIAN MODEL

- Ignoring both government and the foreign sector in our simple Keynesian model, macroeconomic equilibrium occurs when aggregate expenditures are just equal to what is being produced.
- At equilibrium, aggregate saving equals aggregate investment.
- The multiplier process amplifies new spending because some of the new spending is saved and some becomes additional spending. And some of that spending is saved and some is spent, and so on.
- The multiplier is equal to $1/(1 - MPC) = 1/MPS$.
- The multiplier works in both directions. Changes in spending are amplified, changing income by more than the initial change in spending.
- The paradox of thrift results when households *intend* to save more, but at equilibrium they end up saving less.

**QUESTION:** Business journalists, pundits, economists, and policymakers all pay attention to the results of the Conference Board's monthly survey of 5,000 households, called the consumer confidence index. When the index is rising, this is good news for the economy, and when it is falling, concerns are often heard that it portends a recession. Why is this survey important as a tool in forecasting where the economy is headed in the near future?

Answers to the Checkpoint question can be found at the end of this chapter.

## The Full Keynesian Model

With the simple Keynesian model of the domestic private sector (individual consumption and private business investment), we concluded that at equilibrium, saving would equal investment, and that changes in spending changed income by more than the change in spending. This multiplier effect was an important insight by Keynes. To build the full Keynesian model, we now turn our attention to adding government spending and taxes and the impact of the foreign sector.

## Adding Government Spending and Taxes

Although government spending and tax policy can get complex, for our purposes it involves simple changes in government spending (G) or taxes (T). As we have seen in the previous section, any change in aggregate spending causes income and output to rise or fall by the spending change times the multiplier.

Figure 11 illustrates a change in government spending. Initially, investment is $100, so equilibrium income is $4,400 (point *e*), just as in Figure 7 earlier. Rather than investment rising by $100, let's assume the government decides to spend an added $100. As Figure 11 shows, the new equilibrium is $4,800 (point *b*). This result is similar to the one in Figure 7, confirming that spending is spending; the economy does not care where it comes from.

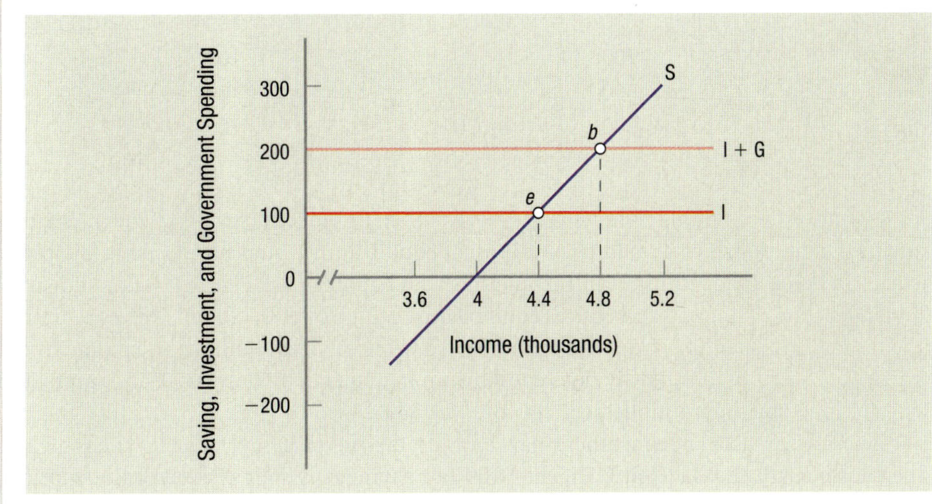


**FIGURE 11—Saving, Investment, and Government Spending**

A change in government spending (G) causes income and output to rise or fall by the spending change times the multiplier.

A quick summary is now in order. Equilibrium income is reached when *injections* (here I + G = $200) equal *withdrawals* (in this case S = $200). It did not matter whether these injections came from investment alone or from investment and government spending together. The key is spending.

Changes in spending modify income by an amount equal to the change in spending times the multiplier. How, then, do changes in taxes affect the economy? The answers are not as simple in that case.

### Tax Changes and Equilibrium

When taxes are increased, money is withdrawn from the economy's spending stream. When taxes are reduced, money is injected into the economy's spending stream because consumers and business have more to spend. Thus, taxes form a wedge between income and that part of income that can be spent, or disposable income. Disposable income ($Y_d$) is equal to income minus taxes ($Y_d = Y - T$). For simplicity, we will assume that all taxes are paid in a lump sum, thereby removing a certain fixed sum of money from the economy. This assumption does away with the need to worry now about the incentive effects of high or lower tax rates. These supply-side issues will be discussed in a later chapter.

Returning to the model of the economy we have been developing, consumer spending now relates to disposable income (Y − T) rather than just to income. Table 3 on the next page reflects this change, using disposable income to determine consumption. With government spending and taxes (fiscal policy) in the model, spending *injections* into the economy equal government spending plus business investment (G + I). *Withdrawals* from the system include saving and taxes (S + T).

Again, equilibrium requires that *injections* equal *withdrawals,* or in this case,

$$G + I = S + T$$

**TABLE 3** Keynesian Equilibrium Analysis with Taxes

| Income or Output (Y) | Taxes (T) | Disposable Income $Y_d$ | Consumption (C) | Saving (S) | Investment (I) | Government Spending (G) |
|---|---|---|---|---|---|---|
| 4,000 | 100 | 3,900 | 3,925 | −25 | 100 | 100 |
| 4,100 | 100 | 4,000 | 4,000 | 0 | 100 | 100 |
| 4,200 | 100 | 4,100 | 4,075 | 25 | 100 | 100 |
| 4,300 | 100 | 4,200 | 4,150 | 50 | 100 | 100 |
| 4,400 | 100 | 4,300 | 4,225 | 75 | 100 | 100 |
| 4,500 | 100 | 4,400 | 4,300 | 100 | 100 | 100 |
| 4,600 | 100 | 4,500 | 4,375 | 125 | 100 | 100 |
| 4,700 | 100 | 4,600 | 4,450 | 150 | 100 | 100 |
| 4,800 | 100 | 4,700 | 4,525 | 175 | 100 | 100 |
| 4,900 | 100 | 4,800 | 4,600 | 200 | 100 | 100 |
| 5,000 | 100 | 4,900 | 4,675 | 225 | 100 | 100 |

In our example, Table 3 shows that G + I = S + T at income level $4,500 (the shaded row in the table). If no tax had been imposed, equilibrium would have been at the point where S = G + I, and thus at an income of $4,800 (point *b* in Figure 11, not shown in Table 3). So, imposing the tax reduces equilibrium income by $300. Because taxes represent a withdrawal of spending from the economy, we would expect equilibrium income to fall when a tax is imposed. Yet, why does equilibrium income fall by only $300, and not by the tax multiplied by the multiplier, which would be $400?

The answer is that consumers pay for this tax, in part, by *reducing* their saving. Specifically, with the MPC at 0.75, the $100 tax payment is split between consumption, reduced by $75, and saving, reduced by $25. When this $75 decrease in consumption is multiplied by the multiplier, this yields a decline in income of $300 ($75 × 4). The *reduction* in saving of $25 *dampens* the impact of the tax on equilibrium income because those funds were previously withdrawn from the spending stream. Simply changing the withdrawal category from saving to taxes does not affect income: Both are withdrawals.

Equilibrium is shown at point *g* in Figure 12. At point *g*, I + G = S + T, with equilibrium income equal to $4,500 and taxes and saving equal to $100 each.

The result is that a tax increase (or decrease, for that matter) will have less of a direct impact on income, employment, and output than will an equivalent change in government spending. For this reason, economists typically describe the "tax" multiplier as being smaller than the "spending" multiplier.

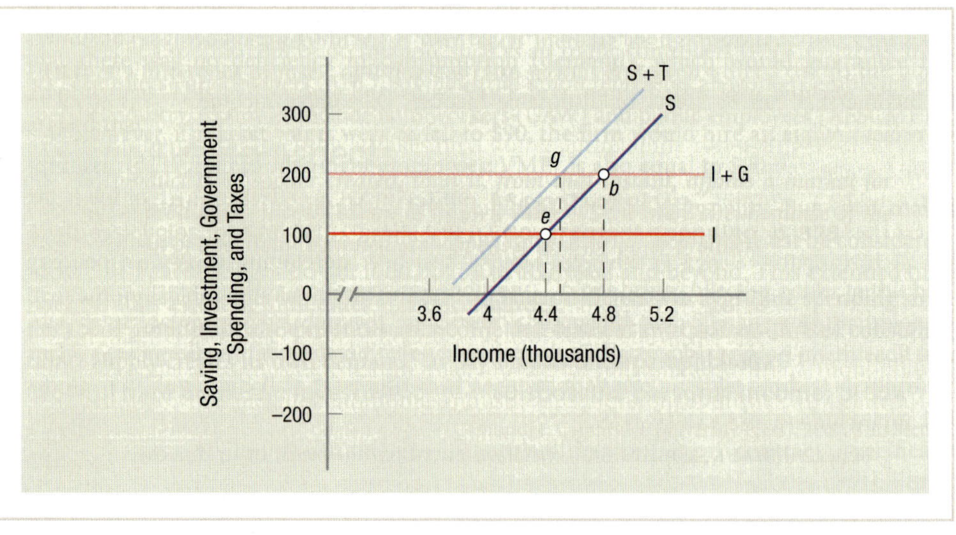


**FIGURE 12—Saving, Investment, Government Spending, and Taxes**

Tax increases or decreases have less of a direct impact on income, employment, and output than an equivalent change in government spending. Some of a tax increase will come from saving and some of a tax decrease will go into saving, thereby reducing the effect of these tax changes.

## The Balanced Budget Multiplier

By now you have probably noticed a curious thing. Our original equilibrium income was \$4,400, with investment and saving equal at \$100. When the government was introduced with a balanced budget (G = T = \$100), income rose by \$100 to \$4,500, while equilibrium saving and investment remained constant at \$100.

This has led to what economists call the **balanced budget multiplier.** Equal changes in government spending and taxation (a balanced budget) lead to an equal change in income. Equivalently, the balanced budget multiplier is equal to 1. If spending and taxes are increased by the same amount, income grows by this amount, hence a balanced budget multiplier equal to 1. Note that the balanced budget multiplier is 1 no matter what the values of MPC and MPS.

**Balanced budget multiplier:** Equal changes in government spending and taxation (a balanced budget) lead to an equal change in income (the balanced budget multiplier is equal to 1).

## Adding Net Exports

Thus far we have essentially assumed a closed economy by avoiding adding foreign transactions: exports and imports. We now add the foreign sector to complete the Keynesian model.

The impact of the foreign sector in the Keynesian model is through net exports: exports minus imports (X − M). Exports are *injections* of spending into the domestic economy, and imports are *withdrawals.* When Africans purchase grain from American farmers, they are injecting new spending on grain into our economy. Conversely, when we purchase French wine, we are withdrawing spending (as saving does) and injecting these funds into the French economy.

Figure 13 adds net exports to Figure 11 with investment and government spending. By adding \$100 of net exports to the previous equilibrium at point *b*, equilibrium moves to \$5,200 (point *c*). Again, we see the multiplier at work as the \$100 in net exports leads to a \$400 increase in income.

With the foreign sector included, all injections into the economy must equal all withdrawals, so at equilibrium,

$$I + G + X = S + T + M$$

Thus, if we import more and all other spending remains the same, equilibrium income will fall. This is one reason so may people focus on the trade deficit or net exports (X − M) figures each month. In later chapters, we will look more deeply into the relationship between the trade deficit (M − X), the budget deficit (G − T), as well as the impact on private savings and investment.

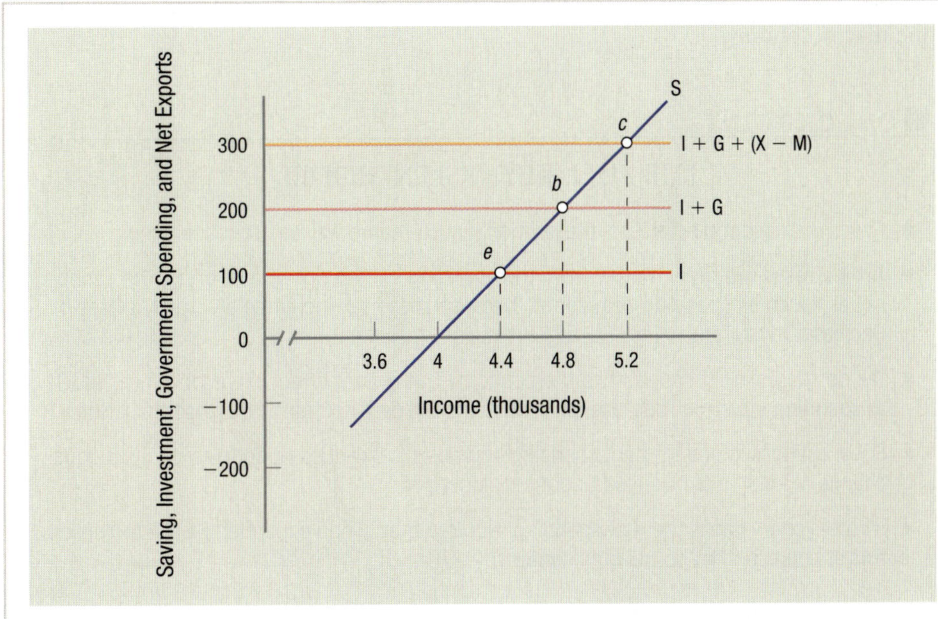


**FIGURE 13—Saving, Investment, Government Spending, and Net Exports**

Adding investment (I), government spending (G), and net exports (X − M) causes income and output to rise or fall by the spending change times the multiplier. In this figure, we have added net exports (X − M) of \$100 to the investment and government spending in Figure 11 to get I + G + (X − M). Thus, an increase in investment spending, government spending, and net exports have the same effect on income and output.

The Keynesian model illustrates the importance of spending in an economy. Investment, government spending, and exports all increase income, whereas saving, taxes, and imports reduce it. Further, the fact that consumers spend and save some of the *changes* in income (MPC and MPS) gives rise to a spending multiplier that exaggerates the impact of changes in spending on the economy.

## Recessionary and Inflationary Gaps

Keynesian analysis illustrated what was needed to get the economy out of the Great Depression: an increase in aggregate spending. Keynes argued that if consumers, businesses, and foreigners were unwilling to spend (their economic expectations were clearly dismal), government should. This was also the basic rationale for the 2009 stimulus package passed by Congress and signed by President Obama. Finally, this leads to the question of just how much additional spending is needed to return the economy to full employment.

### Recessionary Gap

**Recessionary gap:** The increase in aggregate spending needed to bring a depressed economy back to full employment; equal to the GDP gap divided by the multiplier.

The **recessionary gap** is the increase in aggregate spending needed to bring a depressed economy back to full employment. Note that it is not the difference between real GDP at full employment and current real GDP, which is called the GDP gap. If full employment income is $4,400 and our current equilibrium income is $4,000, the recessionary gap is the added spending ($100) that when boosted by the multiplier (4 in this case) will close a GDP gap ($400).

### Inflationary Gap

**Inflationary gap:** The spending reduction necessary (again, when expanded by the multiplier) to bring an overheated economy back to full employment.

If aggregate spending generates income above full employment levels, the economy will eventually heat up, creating inflationary pressures. Essentially, the economy is trying to produce more output and income than it can sustain for very long. Thus, the excess aggregate spending exceeding that necessary to result in full employment is the **inflationary gap.** Using our previous example, if full employment is an income of $4,400 and our current equilibrium is $4,800, a reduction in aggregate expenditures of $100 with a multiplier of 4 would bring the economy back to full employment at $4,400.

This Keynesian approach to analyzing aggregate spending revolutionized the way economists looked at the economy and led to the development of the modern macroeconomics you will study for the remainder of this course. In the next chapter, we extend our analysis to the aggregate demand and supply model, a modern extension of this Keynesian model to account for varying price levels and the supply side of the macroeconomy.

**CHECKPOINT**

### THE FULL KEYNESIAN MODEL

- Government spending affects the economy in the same way as other spending.
- Tax increases withdraw money from the spending stream but do not affect the economy as much as spending reductions, because these tax increases are partly offset by decreases in saving.
- Tax decreases inject money into the economy but do not affect the economy as much as spending increases, because tax reductions are partly offset by increases in saving.
- Equal changes in government spending and taxes (a balanced budget) result in an equal change in income (a balanced budget multiplier of 1).
- A recessionary gap is the new spending required that, when expanded by the multiplier, moves the economy to full employment.

- An inflationary gap is the spending reduction necessary (again when expanded by the multiplier) to bring the economy back to full employment.

**QUESTION:** If the government is considering reducing taxes to stimulate the economy, does it matter if the MPS is 0.25 or 0.33?

Answers to the Checkpoint question can be found at the end of this chapter.

## *Issue:* Was Keynes Right about the Great Depression?

**There is little** disagreement that the Great Depression was one of the most important events for the United States in modern history. Good aggregate data were not yet available, but President Roosevelt and Congressional leaders knew something was very wrong.

Within a couple of years, 10,000 banks collapsed, farms and businesses were lost, the stock market fell to almost a tenth of its value at the beginning of the decade, and soup kitchens fed a growing horde as unemployment soared to nearly 25%, up from 3.2% in 1929. Worse, the Depression persisted: It did not look to be temporary; there was no end in sight.

The Keynesian model we have just studied provides some insight into the Depression. The figure plots hypothetical saving and investment curves over the actual data for 1929 and 1933. Both government and the foreign sector were tiny at this time, so the basic Keynesian model effectively illustrates why the Depression did not show signs of much improvement; by 1939, the unemployment rate was still over 17%.

Saving and investment were over $16 billion in 1929, or roughly a healthy 15% of GDP (point *a*). By 1933, investment collapsed to just over $1 billion (a 91% decline), and the economy was in equilibrium at an income of roughly half of that in 1929 (point *b*). Government spending remained at roughly the same levels while net exports, a small fraction of aggregate expenditures, fell by more than half of their previous levels.

Keynes had it right: Unless something happened to increase investment or exports (not likely given that the rest of the world was suffering economically as well), the economy would remain mired in the Depression (point *b*). He suggested that government spending was needed. Ten years later (1943), the United States was in the middle of World War II, and aggregate expenditures swelled as government spending rose by a factor of 10. The Depression was history.

Archive Holdings Inc./Getty Images

## Key Concepts

Aggregate expenditures, p. 428
Consumption, p. 428
Saving, p. 429
Average propensity to consume, p. 430
Average propensity to save, p. 431
Marginal propensity to consume, p. 431
Marginal propensity to save, p. 431
Investment, p. 433
Keynesian macroeconomic equilibrium, p. 437
Injections, p. 438
Withdrawals, p. 438

Multiplier, p. 439
Paradox of thrift, p. 441
Balanced budget multiplier, p. 445
Recessionary gap, p. 446
Inflationary gap, p. 446

## Chapter Summary

### Aggregate Expenditures

Gross domestic product (GDP) can be computed by adding up all spending or all income in the economy. The spending side consists of consumer spending (C), business investment spending (I), government spending (G), and net foreign spending, or exports minus imports, (X − M). Hence, GDP = C + I + G + (X − M).

Personal consumption expenditures represent roughly 70% of GDP. What consumers do not spend of their income, they save; thus, disposable income ($Y_d$) can be divided into consumption (C) and saving (S). Saving equals disposable income minus annual consumption ($S = Y_d - C$). In our simple Keynesian model we initially eliminated government and the foreign sector, so disposable income was just income or GDP.

Keynes observed that as disposable income increases, consumption will increase, though not as fast as income. Consequently, as income grows, saving will grow as a percentage of income. This Keynesian approach to analyzing saving differs sharply from the classical approach, which assumed the interest rate to be the principal determinant of saving, and by extension, a principal determinant of consumption.

The percentage of income people consume is known as the average propensity to consume (APC). The average propensity to save (APS) is the percentage of income people save. Because income (Y) equals consumption plus saving (Y = C + S), APC + APS = 1.

The marginal propensity to consume (MPC) is the change in consumption associated with a given change in income; thus, MPC = $\Delta C/\Delta Y$. The marginal propensity to save (MPS) is the change in saving associated with a given change in income, MPS = $\Delta S/\Delta Y$. Again, because Y = C + S, MPC + MPS = 1.

Income is the main determinant of consumption and saving, but other factors can shift the entire saving and consumption schedules. These factors include family wealth, expectations about future changes in prices and income, family debt, and taxation.

Gross private domestic investment (the "I" in the GDP equation) accounts for roughly 15% of GDP. It is volatile, sometimes increasing by 30% or falling by 20%; these investment swings often account for booms and recessions.

Investment levels depend mainly on the rate of return. Other determinants of investment spending include future expectations about returns, technological changes, the quantity of capital goods on hand, and operating costs. The aggregate investment schedule relates investment to income.

### The Simple Keynesian Model

Ignoring government spending and net exports, aggregate expenditures (AE) are the sum of consumer and business investment spending: AE = C + I. When an economy is at equilibrium, aggregate expenditures, income, and output will all be equal; just what is demanded is supplied (AE = Y). And because income can be either spent or saved (Y = C + S), we can determine that, at equilibrium, investment equals saving (I = S). However, if *intended* saving and *intended* investment differ, the economy will have to grow or decline to achieve equilibrium.

The multiplier is equal to 1/(1 − MPC) = 1/MPS. The multiplier process occurs because new spending sets up additional round-by-round spending based on the MPC that results in more total spending and income in the economy than the original change in spending. The multiplier expands the impact of both spending increases and decreases.

## The Full Keynesian Model

Government spending affects the economy just like other spending. Tax changes have less of an impact than spending because some of the money (the MPS) from tax changes comes from or goes into saving, reducing its multiplier effect. Equal doses of government spending and taxes (G = T) will increase income by the same amount, and vice versa for reductions in both. For this reason, the balanced budget multiplier is equal to 1.

The recessionary gap is the increase in aggregate spending (that is then multiplied) necessary to bring a depressed economy to full employment. When aggregate income exceeds full employment income, the inflationary gap is the reduction in aggregate expenditures (again expanded by the multiplier) needed to reduce income to full employment levels.

# Questions and Problems

## Check Your Understanding

1. Describe the impact of rising interest rates on consumer spending.
2. Describe the important difference between the average propensity to consume (APC) and the marginal propensity to consume (MPC).
3. Explain why we wouldn't expect investment to grow sufficiently to pull the economy out of a depression.
4. Define the simple Keynesian multiplier. Describe why a multiplier exists.
5. Explain why a $100 reduction in taxes does not have the same impact on output and employment as a $100 increase in government spending.

## Apply the Concepts

6. Explain why MPC + APS ≠ 1 and MPS + APC ≠ 1. Provide an example to show why.
7. Assume a simple Keynesian depression economy with a multiplier of 4 and an initial equilibrium income of $3,000. Saving and investment equal $400, and assume full employment income is $4,000.
   a. What is the MPC equal to? The MPS?
   b. How much would government spending have to rise to move the economy to full employment?
   c. Assume the government plans to finance any government spending by raising taxes to cover the increase in spending (it intends to run a balanced budget). How much will government spending and taxes have to rise to move the economy to full employment?
   d. From the initial equilibrium, if investment grows by $100, what will be the new equilibrium level of income and savings?
8. Other than reductions in interest rates that increase the level of investment by businesses, what other factors would result in higher investment at existing interest rates?
9. The simple Keynesian model discussed in this chapter concluded that one form of spending was just as good as any other; increases in all types of spending leads to equal increases in income. Is there any reason to suspect that private investment might be better for the economy than government spending?

10. Assume the economy is in equilibrium at $5,700, and full employment is $4,800. If the MPC is 0.67, how big is the inflationary gap?

11. How does the economy today differ from that of the Great Depression, the economy Keynes used as the basis for the macroeconomic model discussed in this chapter?

## Solving Problems

12. Using the aggregate expenditures table below, answer the questions that follow.

| Income (Y) | Consumption (C) | Saving (S) |
|---|---|---|
| 2,200 | 2,320 | −120 |
| 2,300 | 2,380 | −80 |
| 2,400 | 2,440 | −40 |
| 2,500 | 2,500 | 0 |
| 2,600 | 2,560 | 40 |
| 2,700 | 2,620 | 80 |
| 2,800 | 2,680 | 120 |
| 2,900 | 2,740 | 160 |
| 3,000 | 2,800 | 200 |

a. Compute the APC when income equals 2,300 and the APS when income equals 2,800.

b. Compute the MPC and MPS.

c. What does the simple Keynesian multiplier equal?

d. If investment spending is equal to 120, what will be equilibrium income?

e. Using the graph below, show saving, investment, and equilibrium income.

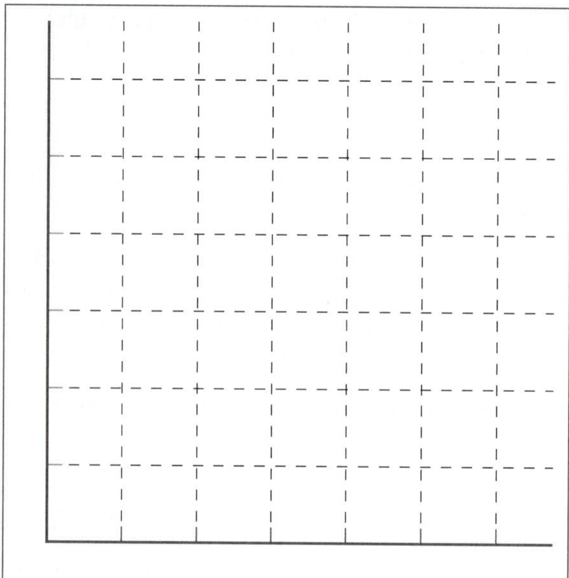

Use the figure below to answer questions 13–15.

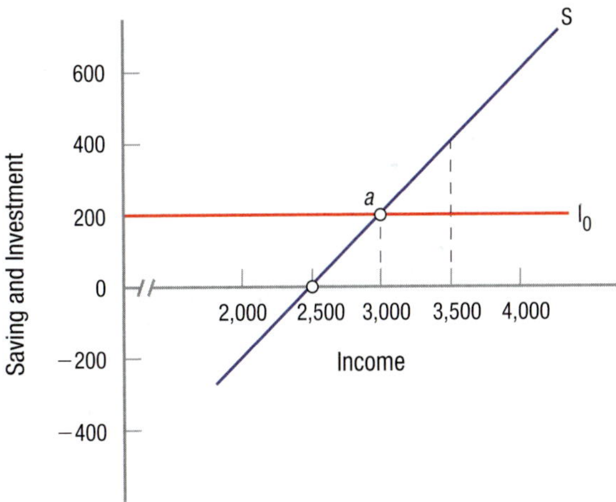


13. What are the MPC, the MPS, and the multiplier?
14. If the economy is currently in equilibrium at point *a* and full employment income is \$4,000, how much in *additional* expenditures is needed to move this economy to full employment? What is this level of spending called?
15. Assume the economy is currently in equilibrium at point *a* and full employment income is \$4,000. How much of a tax decrease would be required to move the economy to full employment?

## Answers to Questions in CheckPoints

### Check Point: Aggregate Expenditures

Consumer spending, while 4 times larger in absolute size than investment spending, involves many small purchases by households that do not vary much from month to month such as rent (or mortgage payment), food, fuel, and others. Consumers change habits, but slowly. Business investment expenditures are typically on big-ticket items like new plant and equipment, if businesses have favorable expectations about the economy. Further, these investments are often undertaken (or not) by business when the group as a whole sees the economy going in the same direction. When expectations sour, investment typically falls by all firms.

### Check Point: The Simple Keynesian Model

When consumer confidence is declining, this may suggest that consumers are going to spend less and save more. Since consumer spending is roughly 70% of aggregate spending, a small decline represents a significant reduction in aggregate spending and may well mean that a recession is on the horizon. Relatively small changes in consumer spending coupled with the multiplier can mean relatively large changes in income, and therefore forecasters and policymakers should keep a close eye on consumer confidence.

### Check Point: The Full Keynesian Model

Yes, it does matter. If the tax reduction is going to be \$100, for example, and the MPS is 0.25, the multiplier is 4, and the income increase will be \$75 × 4 = \$300. Keep in mind that in this case, one-fourth of the tax reduction will go into saving and will not be amplified by the multiplier. However, with a MPS of 0.33, the multiplier will be 3, and one-third will not be multiplied (will go into saving), so the increase in income will be \$67 × 3 = \$201.

## Answers to Questions in Checkpoints

# Aggregate Demand and Supply

# 19

Illustration Works/Alamy

**The Employment Act of 1946** charged policymakers with three goals: promoting economic growth, maintaining full employment, and achieving price level stability. This is a big charge for any administration.

Contrast two situations. First, imagine you are in an administration that takes office just as the stock market rallies because business investment spending has grown to new high levels in the race to implement new technologies, and the economy responds by producing ever greater employment opportunities without any real inflationary pressures. In this case, managing the economy looks easy. In contrast, if you join a new administration facing a collapse in the stock, real estate, automobile, and financial markets and a subsequent fall in consumer and business confidence that reduces consumer spending and business investment, plunging the economy into a deep recession, policymaking is not nearly as enjoyable.

Let's take a moment to remind ourselves of how macroeconomic analysis got to where it is today. This brief capsule summary sets the stage for our discussion of the development of modern macroeconomics, which is the focus of this chapter.

Before the Great Depression in the 1930s, economists viewed the overall economy as simply a set of small competitive markets driven by consumer and business interests that Adam Smith's "invisible hand" kept working in the public interest. Wages, prices, and interest rates were determined in labor, product, and capital markets, and the government's role was to set appropriate competitive rules. This *laissez-faire* (leave it alone) view meant that the best government was minimal government. These markets operate like those discussed in Chapter 3.

Furthermore, before the Depression, economists argued that these competitive markets would ensure that the economy operated near full employment with only relatively minor recessions in relation to the long-term growth trend. For example, if people started to save more and spend less because they were nervous about the economy, the increased

**After studying this chapter you should be able to:**

- ☐ Describe why the aggregate demand curve has a negative slope.
- ☐ Describe the effects of wealth, exports, and interest rates on the aggregate demand curve.
- ☐ List the determinants of aggregate demand.
- ☐ Analyze the aggregate supply curve and differentiate between the short run and long run.
- ☐ Describe the determinants of an aggregate supply curve.
- ☐ Define the multiplier and describe why it is important.
- ☐ Describe demand-pull and cost-push inflation.

savings would translate into lower interest rates, which would spur business investment. Adjustment would be relatively quick.

When the Depression hit in the United States, unemployment climbed to a quarter of the workforce. But because good data were unavailable at the time, economists continued to believe that the recovery was just around the corner. Figure 1 shows the extent of the Depression. Gross domestic product (GDP) fell nearly 40%, business investment fell by 80%, exports were cut nearly in half, and almost half of the banks existing in 1929 failed by 1933, sending many families' life savings down the drain (there was no federal deposit insurance at that time).

As Figure 1 shows, the economy was clearly broken, and for a decade, showed little sign of returning to prosperity. This brought a radical shift in economic thinking. This chapter develops a modern model of the macroeconomy based on the lessons learned in the 1930s.

British economist John Maynard Keynes convinced economists to turn away from focusing on individual competitive markets. Basing his analysis on a depression economy where there is immense slack (productive capacity), he argued that expenditures by consumers, business (in the form of investment), government, and foreigners (in the form of exports)—**aggregate expenditures,** also known as *aggregate spending*—was what determined employment and income.

His attention was drawn to the aggregate economy as a whole and not the individual markets that composed the basis for previous analysis. As such, Keynes created the beginnings of what we now call modern macroeconomics.

The Keynesian *fixed price* model we examined in the previous chapter essentially ignored aggregate supply since increasing production would occur without a rise in prices. Keynes's analysis was based on the facts of the Great Depression, in which significant industrial capacity was going unused and unemployment was high. He concluded that any amount of spending (demand) could and would be supplied without any pressure on costs (the aggregate price level would not change). Clearly, more labor could be hired without having to raise wages; in fact, firms with just a few openings were mobbed with job applicants.

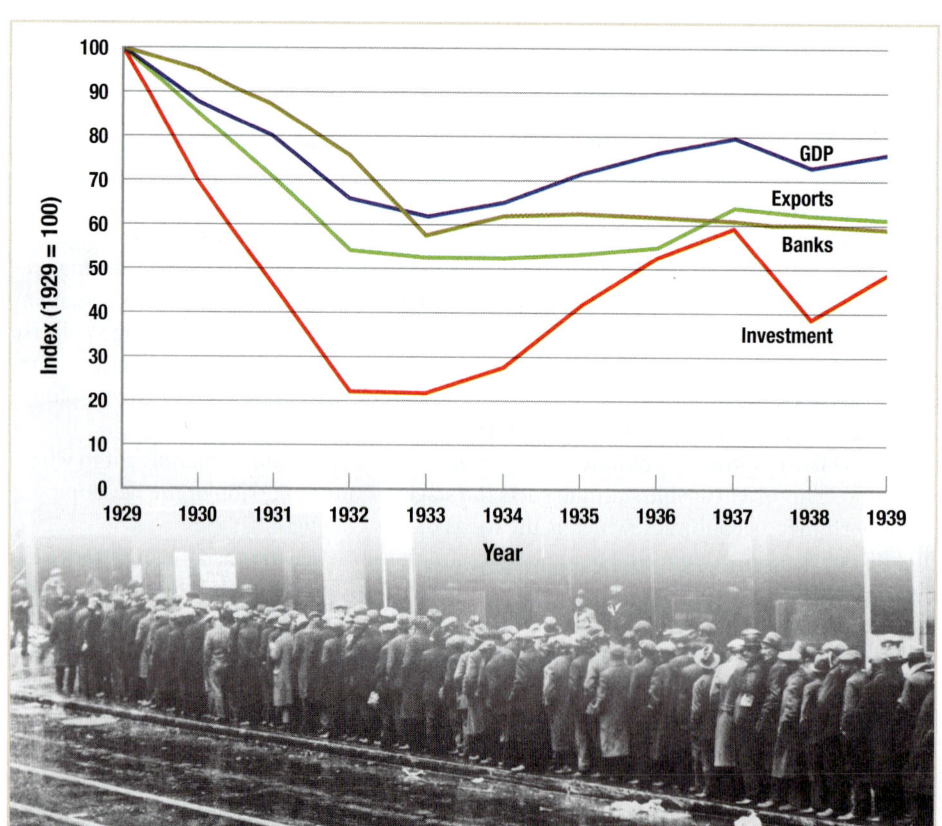


**FIGURE 1—GDP, Investment, Exports, and Operating Banks, 1929–1939**

Data for GDP, business investment, exports, and the number of operating banks are indexed to 1929 (1929 = 100). All fell precipitously after 1929 and didn't recover to 1929 levels within the decade. Aggregate spending and income fell nearly by half between 1929 and 1933.

Source: U.S. Census Bureau, *Historical Statistics of the United States,* p. 1019; and Pedro Amaral and Jim MacGee, "The Great Depression in Canada and the United States: A Neoclassical Perspective," *Review of Economic Dynamics,* 2002, Data Appendix.

The lessons learned from the Depression and the insights from Keynes form the foundation of the demand side of the modern macroeconomic model we develop in this chapter. This modern approach looks a lot like the supply-demand model developed in Chapter 3, but extended to the aggregate (overall) economy. Whereas the Keynesian model assumed that the price level was fixed, the aggregate demand and supply model developed in this chapter is a *flexible price* model. The model also introduces additional complexities to the aggregate supply side of the economy.

**Aggregate expenditures:** Consist of consumer spending, business investment spending, government spending, and net foreign spending (exports minus imports): GDP = C + I + G + (X − M).

Although the original Keynesian approach was focused on the Depression, this flexible price version expands the analysis to many more modern problems facing economies. It is worth keeping in mind however, that when economies face the potential of a deep recession like the one in 2008–2009, with high rates of joblessness, reduced consumer spending, and falling business investment, the policy prescriptions from Keynesian analysis return to the forefront. The beauty of this approach is that it builds on concepts and skills you already have: defining demand curves, supply curves, and equilibrium; assessing changes in economic facts; and determining a new equilibrium.

## Aggregate Demand

The **aggregate demand** (AD) curve (or schedule) shows the output of goods and services (real GDP) demanded at different price levels.[1] The aggregate demand curve in Figure 2 looks like the product demand curves we studied earlier. However, it's important to remember that these two curves and the reasons they slope downward are different.

**Aggregate demand:** The output of goods and services (real GDP) demanded at different price levels.

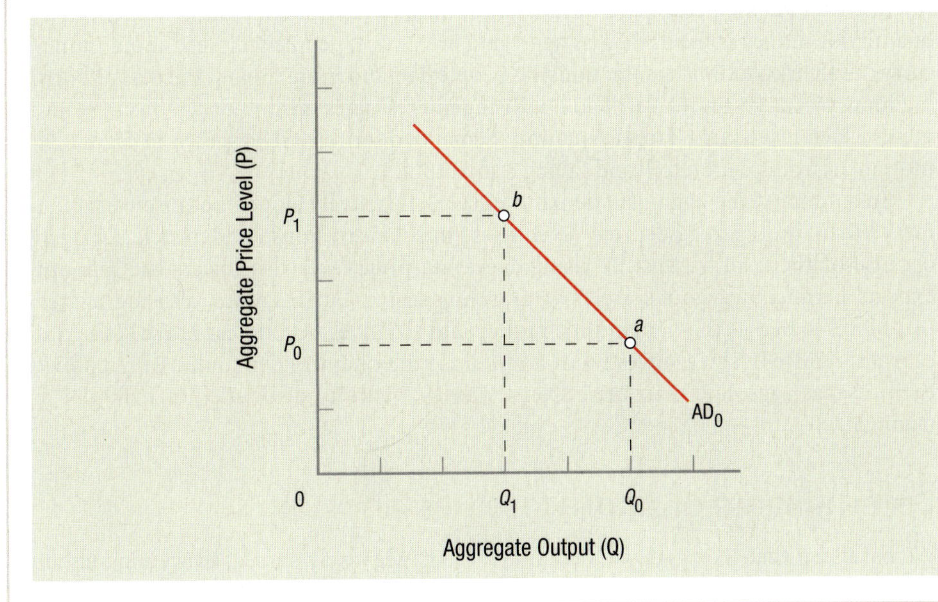


**FIGURE 2—The Aggregate Demand Curve**

The aggregate demand curve shows the amount of real goods and services (output = real GDP) that will be purchased at various price levels.

### Why Is the Aggregate Demand Curve Negatively Sloped?

Product demand curves slope downward for two reasons. First, when the price of a given product declines, consumers' spendable income rises, because it takes less income to purchase the same quantity of the product as before; rising prices have an opposite impact. This is known, once again, as the *income effect*. Second, when the price of a product falls,

[1] The derivation of the AD curve using the Keynesian fixed price model is shown in the Appendix to this chapter.

consumers will purchase more of the product as they substitute it for other, higher-priced, goods—when the price of chicken declines, consumers substitute chicken for beef and other meats in their diets. This is known as the *substitution effect*, which was discussed in Chapter 3. Yet, these explanations for specific products do not explain the slope of the demand curve for the aggregate economy.

### The Wealth Effect

**Wealth effect:** Families usually hold some of their wealth in financial assets such as savings accounts, bonds, and cash, and a rising aggregate price level means that the purchasing power of this money wealth declines, reducing output demanded.

One reason real output declines when the aggregate price level rises is the resulting reduction in household wealth, called the **wealth effect.** Families usually hold some of their wealth in financial assets such as savings accounts, bonds, and cash. A rising aggregate price level means that the purchasing power of this money wealth is declining. If, for example, you have $5,000 in a savings account and prices rise throughout the economy, that $5,000 will now purchase less than before. This reduction in household purchasing power means that some purchases are put on hold, thereby reducing output demanded. This is represented by a movement from point *a* to point *b* in Figure 2.

### Impact on Exports

When the American aggregate price level rises, American goods become more expensive in the global marketplace. Higher prices mean that our goods are less competitive with the goods made in other countries. The result is that foreigners purchase fewer American products, and our exports decline. As exports drop, the quantity demanded of domestically produced goods and services (real GDP) also declines, resulting in lower real output.

### Interest Rate Effects

Interest rates are the prices paid for the use of money. If we assume for a moment that the quantity of money is fixed, then as aggregate prices rise, people will need more money to carry out their economic transactions. As people demand more money, the cost of borrowing money—interest rates—will go up. Rising interest rates mean reduced business investment, which results in a drop in quantity demanded for real GDP, shown in Figure 2 as a movement from point *a* to *b* and falling real output.[2]

In summary, the aggregate demand curve is negatively sloped because of three factors. When the aggregate price level rises, this lowers household purchasing power because of the wealth effect. A rising aggregate price level also lowers the amount of exports because our goods are now more expensive. Furthermore, a rising aggregate price level increases the demand for money and so drives up interest rates. Rising interest rates reduce business investment and reduce the quantity demanded of real GDP. In each case, as aggregate prices rise from $P_0$ to $P_1$, quantity demanded of real GDP falls from $Q_0$ to $Q_1$.

## Determinants of Aggregate Demand

We have seen that the aggregate demand curve is negatively sloped. Everything else held constant, a change in the aggregate price level will change the quantity of real GDP demanded along the aggregate demand curve. The *determinants* of aggregate demand are those factors that shift the *entire* aggregate demand curve when they change. They are the "everything else held constant." These include the components of GDP: consumption, investment, government spending, and net exports.

If one of these components of aggregate spending changes, the aggregate demand curve will shift, as shown in Figure 3. At first, aggregate demand is $AD_0$, so a shift to $AD_1$ represents an increase in aggregate demand; more real output is demanded at the same

[2] The actual process is more complex than described here. Rising demand for money means individuals and businesses must sell bonds, reducing the price of bonds and raising interest rates. We will discuss this process in detail in future chapters.

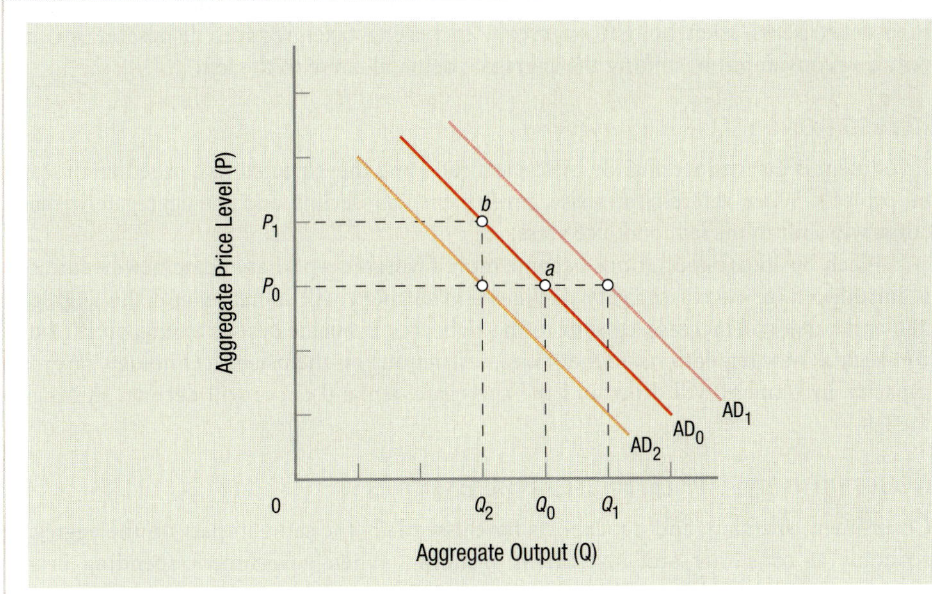


**FIGURE 3—Shifts in the Aggregate Demand Curve**

The determinants of aggregate demand include the components of GDP and aggregate spending: consumption, investment, government spending, and net exports. A change in one will shift the aggregate demand curve, as shown here. At first, aggregate demand is $AD_0$, so a shift to $AD_1$ represents an increase in aggregate demand; more real output is demanded at the same price level. A decline in aggregate demand to $AD_2$ means that less real output is being demanded at all price levels.

price level, $P_0$. If, for example, business decides to invest more in new technology, more real output is now demanded at the current price level, $P_0$, and at all other price levels. For similar reasons, a decline in aggregate demand to $AD_2$ means that less real output is being demanded. If consumers for some reason fear the onset of a recession and decide to reduce spending to increase their saving reserves, less output, $Q_2$, will be demanded at all price levels.

Now let's consider what might cause the various components of aggregate expenditures to change.

## Consumer Spending

Consumer spending is affected by four major factors: wealth, consumer confidence, household debt, and taxes. When any of these factors change, consumer spending patterns change. For example, when the technology-heavy NASDAQ stock market surged in the late 1990s, Federal Reserve Chairman Alan Greenspan became concerned that a consequent surge in consumer spending from the newly added wealth would increase aggregate demand to $AD_1$ in Figure 3, resulting in higher inflation. (We'll see why spending can lead to inflation a little later in the chapter.) When the NASDAQ collapsed in the early 2000s, the Federal Reserve then became worried that sinking consumer confidence (caused by declining wealth) would reduce consumption spending, thereby adding to recession woes. In late 2008 and early 2009, falling housing prices and a stock market slump reduced consumer spending and was an important factor in the depth of the subsequent recession. Changes in wealth change consumer confidence and spending.

Note that changes in wealth have two similar but distinct impacts on aggregate demand. First, as described earlier, when aggregate prices rise, the purchasing power of financial assets falls, reducing the *amount* of goods and services that can now be purchased with this money. This is a movement along an existing aggregate demand curve to a higher price level (point *a* to *b* in Figure 3).

Second, described here, is a decline in wealth (for example, caused by a stock market crash) that reduces consumption *at all price levels.* In this case, the entire aggregate demand curve shifts from $AD_0$ to $AD_2$ in Figure 3. This is the impact of changing wealth on consumer spending that is usually the focus of attention by the media and policymakers.

Consumer expectations and confidence about the economy play a significant role in determining the level of consumer spending. High confidence in the economy eases job security fears and stimulates consumer spending, shifting the aggregate demand curve to the right. High family debt ratios restrict access to future credit, reducing spending on high-ticket items often bought on credit. Increasing taxes reduces disposable income, reducing consumption, shifting the aggregate demand curve to the left.

## Investment

Investment is determined mainly by interest rates and the expected rate of return on capital projects. When interest rates rise, investment will decline and the aggregate demand curve will shift to the left, and vice versa.

When business expectations become more favorable—perhaps some new technology is introduced, or excess capacity declines—investment will increase, and the aggregate demand curve will increase, or shift to the right. But if businesses see clouds on the horizon such as new regulations, higher taxes, restrictions on the use of technology, or excess capacity, investment will drop, and the aggregate demand curve will decline, shifting to the left.

## Government Spending and Net Exports

Government spending and net exports have essentially the same impact on the aggregate economy as consumer and investment spending. When government spending or net exports rise, aggregate demand increases, and vice versa.

When the national income of a foreign country rises, this increases its demand for U.S. goods and services, thereby increasing our exports and our aggregate demand. A change in foreign exchange rates will also affect aggregate demand. An appreciation, or rise, in the value of the euro, for instance, will result in Europeans buying more U.S. goods since a euro will buy more. Again, this change increases American exports and aggregate demand.

A quick summary is now in order. The aggregate demand curve shows the quantities of real GDP demanded at different price levels. The aggregate demand curve slopes downward because of the wealth effect (the value of monetary assets declines when the price level rises), because exports fall as domestic prices rise, and because rising prices raise interest rates, which reduces investment. On the other hand, changes in one of the determinants

**TABLE 1** **The Determinants of Aggregate Demand (aggregate demand curve shifts when these change)**

| Determinant | AD Increases | AD Decreases |
|---|---|---|
| **Consumer Spending** | | |
| • Wealth | Wealth increases | Wealth decreases |
| • Consumer expectations | Expectations improve | Expectations worsen |
| • Household debt | Debt falls | Debt rises |
| • Taxes | Taxes are cut | Taxes increase |
| **Investment** | | |
| • Interest rates | Fall | Rise |
| • Expected rate of return on investment | Higher | Lower |
| **Government Spending** | Increases | Decreases |
| **Net Exports** | Increases | Declines |
| • Exports | | |
| • Income in other countries | Rising | Falling |
| • Exchange rate changes | Depreciating dollar | Appreciating dollar |
| • Imports | | |
| • Income in the United States | Falling | Rising |
| • Exchange rate changes | Depreciating dollar | Appreciating dollar |

of aggregate demand shift the aggregate demand curve. Table 1 summarizes the determinants of aggregate demand.

Again, the determinants of aggregate demand are those "other factors held constant": consumption, investment, government spending, and net exports. If one of those determinants changes, the entire aggregate demand curve will shift. Keep in mind that changes in the determinants are most important for policymaking. When a policy is enacted (say, lower tax rates), policymakers expect to stimulate consumer and investment spending, increasing aggregate demand, output, and employment.

But the aggregate demand curve only tells one part of the story. We have to consider the other part: aggregate supply.

**CHECKPOINT**

### AGGREGATE DEMAND

- The aggregate demand curve shows the relationship between real GDP and the price level.
- The aggregate demand curve has a negative slope because of the impact of the price level on financial wealth, exports, and interest rates.
- The determinants of aggregate demand are consumer spending, investment spending, government expenditures, and net exports. Changes in any of these determinants will shift the aggregate demand curve.

**QUESTION:** Consumer spending is related to disposable personal income (income minus taxes). Describe how changing tax rates would affect consumption and aggregate demand.

Answers to the Checkpoint question can be found at the end of this chapter.

## Aggregate Supply

The **aggregate supply** curve shows the real GDP that firms will produce at varying price levels. Even though the definition seems similar to that for aggregate demand, note that we have now moved from the spending side of the economy to the production side. We will consider two different possibilities for aggregate supply. The first possibility is the short run in which aggregate supply is positively sloped and prices rise when GDP grows. The second, long-run aggregate supply, reflects the long-run state of the economy and is vertical. Growth occurs in the economy by shifting this vertical aggregate supply curve to the right.

**Aggregate supply:** The real GDP that firms will produce at varying price levels. In the short run, aggregate supply is positively sloped because many input costs are slow to change, but in the long run, the aggregate supply curve is vertical at full employment since the economy has reached its capacity to produce.

### Short Run

As Figure 4 on the next page shows, the **short-run aggregate supply (SRAS) curve** is positively sloped because some input costs are slow to change in the short run. When prices rise, firms do not immediately see an increase in wages or rents since these are often fixed for a specified term; thus, profits will rise with the rising prices and firms will supply more output as their profits increase.

**Short-run aggregate supply (SRAS) curve:** The short-run aggregate supply curve is positively sloped because many input costs are slow to change in the short run.

This situation, however, cannot last for long. As an entire industry or the economy as a whole increases its production, firms must start hiring more labor or paying overtime. As each firm seeks more employees, wages are driven up, increasing costs and forcing higher prices.

For the economy as a whole, a rise in real GDP results in higher employment and reduced unemployment. Lower unemployment rates mean a tightening of labor markets. This often leads to fierce collective bargaining by labor, followed by increases in wages, costs, and prices. The result is that a short-run increase in GDP is usually accompanied by a rise in the price level.

**FIGURE 4—Aggregate Supply**

The short-run aggregate supply (SRAS) curve is positively sloped because many input costs are slow to change in the short run. The long-run aggregate supply (LRAS) curve is vertical, reflecting the assumptions of classical economic analysis. In the long run, all variables in the economy can adjust, and the economy will settle at full employment, shown at aggregate output $Q_f$.

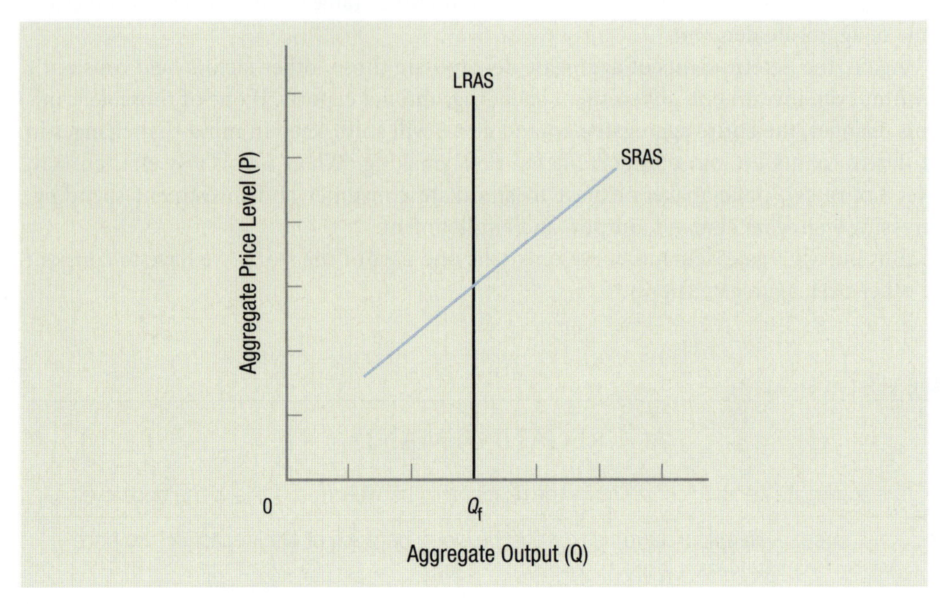


## Long Run

**Long-run aggregate supply (LRAS) curve:** The long-run aggregate supply curve is vertical at full employment because the economy has reached its capacity to produce.

The *vertical* **long-run aggregate supply (LRAS) curve** incorporates the assumptions of classical (pre-1930s) economic analysis. Classical analysis assumes that all variables are adjustable in the long run, where product prices, wages, and interest rates are flexible in the longer term. As a result, the economy will gravitate to the position of full employment shown as $Q_f$ in Figure 4.

Full employment is often referred to as the *natural rate of output* or *the natural rate of unemployment* by economists. This long-run output is an equilibrium level where inflationary pressures are minimal. Once the economy has reached this level, further short-term increases in output are extremely difficult to achieve; there is simply no one else to operate more machines, and no more machines to operate. As we will see later, attempts to expand beyond this output level simply produce higher prices and rising inflation.

In general terms, full employment is determined by the capital available, the size and quality of the labor force, and the technology employed; in effect, the productive capacity of the economy. Remember from Chapter 2 that these are also the big three factors driving economic growth (shifting the LRAS curve to the right) once a suitable infrastructure has been put in place.

## Determinants of Short-run Aggregate Supply

We have seen that, because the aggregate supply curve is positively sloped in the short run, a change in aggregate output, other things held constant, will result in a change in the aggregate price level. The determinants of short-run aggregate supply—those other things held constant—include changes in input prices, productivity, taxes, regulation, the market power of firms, or business and inflationary expectations. When any of these determinants change, the entire SRAS curve shifts, as Figure 5 illustrates.

### Input Prices

Changes in the cost of land, labor, capital, or entrepreneurship will change the output that firms are willing to provide to the market. As we have seen, when world crude oil prices rise, it is never long before gasoline prices rise at the pump. Rising input prices are quickly passed along to consumers, and the opposite is true, as well. New discoveries of raw materials result in falling input prices, causing the prices for products incorporating these inputs

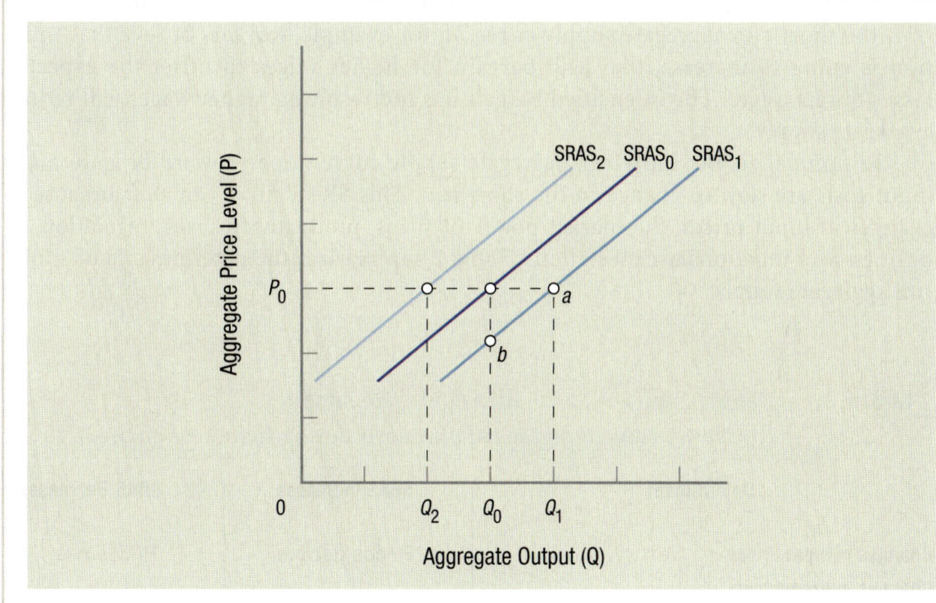


**FIGURE 5—Shifts in Short-Run Aggregate Supply**

The determinants of short-run aggregate supply include changes in input prices, the market power of firms, productivity, taxes, regulation, and business and inflationary expectations. If one of these determinants changes, the entire short-run aggregate supply curve shifts. Increasing productivity, for instance, will shift the short-run aggregate supply curve to the right, from $SRAS_0$ to $SRAS_1$. Conversely, raising taxes or adding inefficient regulations can shift the short-run aggregate supply curve to the left, from $SRAS_0$ to $SRAS_2$.

to drop. This means that more of these products can be produced at a price of $P_0$ in Figure 5 as short-run aggregate supply shifts to $SRAS_1$ (point *a*), or now output $Q_0$ can be produced at a lower price on $SRAS_1$ (point *b*).

## Productivity

Changes in productivity are another major determinant of short-run aggregate supply. Rising productivity will shift the short-run aggregate supply curve to the right—from $SRAS_0$ to $SRAS_1$ in Figure 5—and vice versa. This is why changes in technology that increase productivity are so important to the economy. Technological advances, moreover, often lead to new products that expand short-run aggregate supply. They also increase the productive capability of the economy, which shifts LRAS to the right.

## Taxes and Regulation

Rising taxes or increased regulation can shift the short-run aggregate supply curve to the left, from $SRAS_0$ to $SRAS_2$ in Figure 5. Excessively burdensome regulation, though it may provide some benefits, raises costs so much that the new costs exceed the benefits. This results in a decrease in short-run aggregate supply. Often, no one knows how much regulation has increased costs until some sort of deregulation is instituted.

## Market Power of Firms

Monopoly firms charge more than competitive firms. So, a change in the market power of firms can increase prices for specific products, thereby reducing short-run aggregate supply. When the Organization of Petroleum Exporting Countries (OPEC) finally coalesced in 1973, it formed an effective cartel and raised oil prices roughly 10-fold. Since at that time oil was an input in nearly all products, the SRAS curve shifted to the left.

## Expectations

A change in business expectations can also change short-run aggregate supply. If firms perceive that the business climate is declining, they may reduce their investments in capital equipment. This reduced investment results in reduced productivity, fewer new hires, or even the closing of marginally profitable plants, any of which can reduce aggregate supply in the short run.

A change in inflationary expectations by businesses, workers, or consumers can shift the short-run aggregate supply curve. If, for example, workers believe that inflation is going to increase, they will bargain for higher wages to offset the expected losses to real wages. The intensified bargaining and resulting higher wages will reduce aggregate supply.

To summarize, the short-run aggregate supply curve slopes upward because many input costs are slow to change in the short run. This SRAS curve can shift because of changes in input prices, the market power of firms, productivity, taxes, regulation, or business and inflationary expectations. Table 2 summarizes the determinants of short-run aggregate supply.

**TABLE 2** Determinants of Short-Run Aggregate Supply (the short-run aggregate supply curve shifts when these change)

| Determinant | SRAS Increases | SRAS Decreases |
|---|---|---|
| **Changes in Input Prices** | Prices decline | Prices rise |
| **Changes in Productivity** | | |
| • Technology | Improvements | Declines |
| • Changes in human capital | Improvements | Declines |
| **Changes in Taxes and Regulations** | | |
| • Tax rates | Lower | Higher |
| • Subsidies | Higher | Lower |
| • Change in burdensome regulations | Reductions | Additions |
| **Change in Market Power** | Reductions | Increases |
| **Changes in Business or Inflation Expectations** | | |
| • Business expectations | More positive | More negative |
| • Inflation expectations | Lower | Higher |

## The Shifting Long-Run Aggregate Supply Curve

The vertical LRAS curve represents the full employment capacity of the economy. This output level depends on the amount of resources available for production and the available technology. Increases in resources, productivity, or technology shift the LRAS curve to the right and represent economic growth.

### CHECKPOINT

#### AGGREGATE SUPPLY

- The aggregate supply curve shows the real GDP that firms will produce at varying price levels.
- The short-run aggregate supply (SRAS) curve is upward sloping, reflecting rigidities in the economy since input and output prices are slow to change.
- The vertical long-run aggregate supply (LRAS) curve represents the long-run full-employment capacity of the economy.
- The determinants of short-run aggregate supply include changes in input prices, the market power of firms, productivity, taxes, regulations, and business and inflationary expectations. Changes in these determinants shift aggregate supply in the short run.
- Increasing resources or improved technology shift the LRAS curve, which represents economic growth.

**QUESTION:** In Europe, nearly two-thirds of wages are covered by union collective bargaining agreements; wage rates are determined (or fixed) for a given period, typically two to four years. In the United States, only about one-sixth of wages are covered. Unemployment rates in Germany, France, and Italy are typically double that (8% to 12%) of those in the United States (4% to 6%). Do higher unemployment rates in Germany, France, and Italy mean that their SRAS curves are flatter than ours in the United States?

Answers to the Checkpoint question can be found at the end of this chapter.

## Macroeconomic Equilibrium

Let us now put together our aggregate demand and aggregate supply model. A *short-run* **macroeconomic equilibrium** occurs at the intersection of the short-run aggregate supply and aggregate demand curves; see point *e* in Figure 6. In this case, point *e* also represents *long-run macroeconomic equilibrium,* since the economy is operating at full employment, producing output $Q_f$.

**Macroeconomic equilibrium:** Occurs at the intersection of the short-run aggregate supply and aggregate demand curves. At this output level, there are no net pressures for the economy to expand or contract.

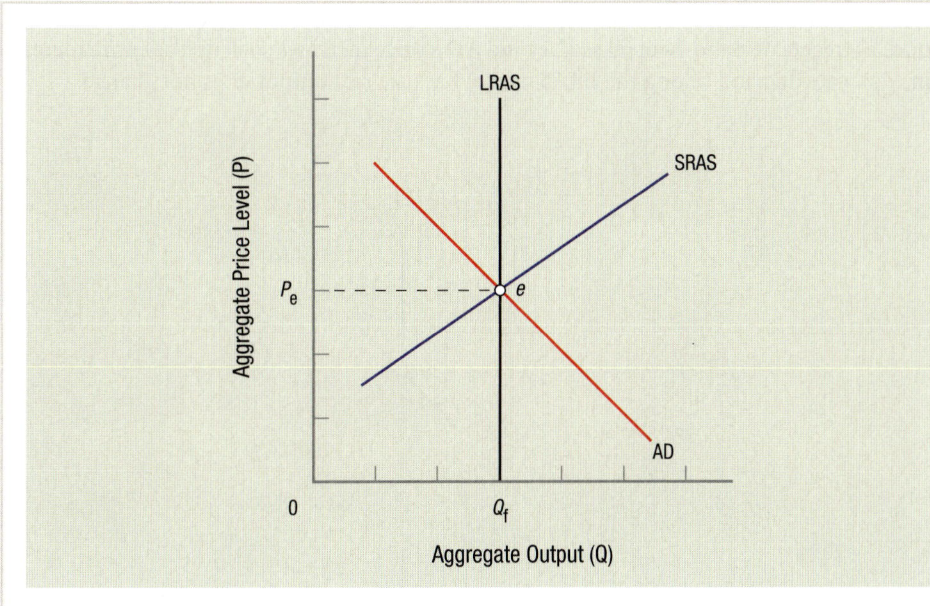


**FIGURE 6—Macroeconomic Equilibrium**

Point *e* represents a short-run macroeconomic equilibrium, the point at which the short-run aggregate supply and aggregate demand curves intersect. In this case, point *e* also represents a long-run macroeconomic equilibrium, since the economy is operating at full employment, producing output $Q_f$.

Output level $Q_f$ represents full employment. The SRAS curve assumes price level expectations equal to $P_e$, and thus $Q_f$ is the natural rate of unemployment or output. Remember that the natural rate of unemployment is that unemployment level where inflation is low and consistent with inflationary expectations in the economy.

### The Spending Multiplier

The spending **multiplier** is an important concept introduced into macroeconomics by John Maynard Keynes in 1936. The central idea is that new spending creates more spending, income, and output than just an amount equal to the new spending itself.

**Multiplier:** Spending changes alter equilibrium income by the spending change times the multiplier. One person's spending becomes another's income, and that second person spends some (the MPC), which becomes income for another person, and so on, until income has changed by $1/(1 - \text{MPC}) = 1/\text{MPS}$. The multiplier operates in both directions.

Let's assume, for example, consumers tend to spend three-quarters and save one-quarter of any new income they receive. If $100 of new spending is introduced into the economy, that initial spending adds $100 of new GDP (income to someone). Now $25 of that additional income will be saved, and $75 will be spent on additional products, creating $75 of new income to be spent and saved. Of this new $75 in income, $56.25

(\$75 × 0.75) will be spent, creating still more income, and \$18.75 (\$75 × 0.25) will be saved, and so on, round-by-round.

Adding up all of the new spending (\$100 + \$75 + 56.25 + . . .) from the initial \$100 results in GDP increasing by \$400. Adding up total new saving (\$25 + 18.75 + . . .) equals \$100, so that the initial \$100 in new spending has increased savings by the same amount.

**Marginal propensity to consume:** The change in consumption associated with a given change in income (ΔC/ΔY).

**Marginal propensity to save:** The change in saving associated with a given change in income (ΔS/ΔY).

The proportion of *additional* income that consumers spend and save is known as the **marginal propensity to consume** and the **marginal propensity to save** (MPC and MPS). In our example, MPC = 0.75 and MPS = 0.25. The multiplier is equal to 4, given that \$400 of new income was created with the introduction of \$100 of new spending. The formula for the spending multiplier is equal to 1/(1 − MPC) = 1/MPS, and in this case, is 1/(1 − 0.75) = 1/0.25 = 4. This formula works as long as the aggregate price level is stable.

When the economy has many unemployed resources and excess capacity, the price level will remain constant and output will increase by the full magnitude of the multiplier. However, when the economy moves up the SRAS curve in the short run, its response to the same increase in aggregate spending is not as great. In Figure 7, aggregate demand increases the same amount as before (the horizontal distance between $AD_0$ and $AD_1$ is \$100). The new equilibrium is at point *a* with output of $Q_f$. But, output grows less because price increases or inflation eat up some of each spending round, so less real output results. The multiplier is therefore less than the pure spending multiplier of 4 just discussed. Note that once aggregate demand is increased beyond $AD_1$, price increases soak up the entire increase in aggregate demand (along the LRAS curve) because real output does not change.

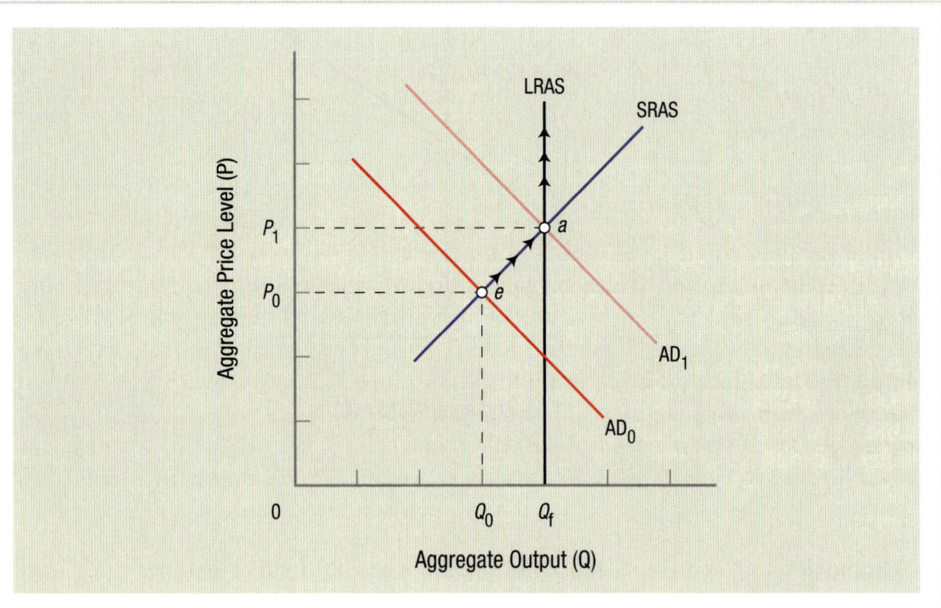


**FIGURE 7—The Multiplier and Aggregate Demand and Supply**

The spending multiplier magnifies new spending into greater levels of income and output because of round-by-round spending of a portion of each round of spending. Your spending becomes my income, and I spend some of that income, creating further income and consumption, and so on.

Let's take a moment to summarize where we are before we begin to use this model to understand some important macroeconomic events. Macroeconomic equilibrium occurs at the intersection of AD and SRAS. It can also happen that this equilibrium represents long-run equilibrium, but not necessarily; equilibrium can occur at less than full employment. As we will see shortly, the Great Depression is one example. Increases in spending are multiplied and lead to greater changes in output than the original change in spending. For policymakers, this means that the difference between equilibrium real GDP and full-employment GDP (the GDP gap) can be closed with a smaller change in spending.

This leads us to the point where we can use the AD/AS model to analyze past macroeconomic events. By looking at these events through the AD/AS lens, we begin to see the options open to policymakers that become the focus of the next chapter. In this next section, we look at what happened during the Great Depression, then examine both demand-pull and cost-push inflation. Each type of inflation presents unique challenges for policymakers.

## The Great Depression

Figure 6 conveniently showed the economy in long-run equilibrium and short-run equilibrium at the same point. The Great Depression demonstrated, however, that an economy can reach short-run equilibrium at output levels substantially below full employment.

The 1930s Depression was a graphic example of just such a situation. Real GDP dropped by nearly 40% between 1929 and 1933. Unemployment peaked at 25% in 1932 and never fell below 15% throughout the 1930s.

Figure 8 shows the actual data for the Depression with superimposed aggregate demand and SRAS curves for 1929 and 1933. Investment is the most volatile of the GDP components, and it fell nearly 80% from 1929 to 1933. This drop in investment reduced spending and therefore income and consumption, resulting in a deep depression. The increase in aggregate demand necessary to restore the economy back to 1929 levels was huge, and it was no wonder that a 6% increase in government spending had virtually no impact on the Depression. It wasn't until spending ramped up for World War II that the country popped out of the Depression.

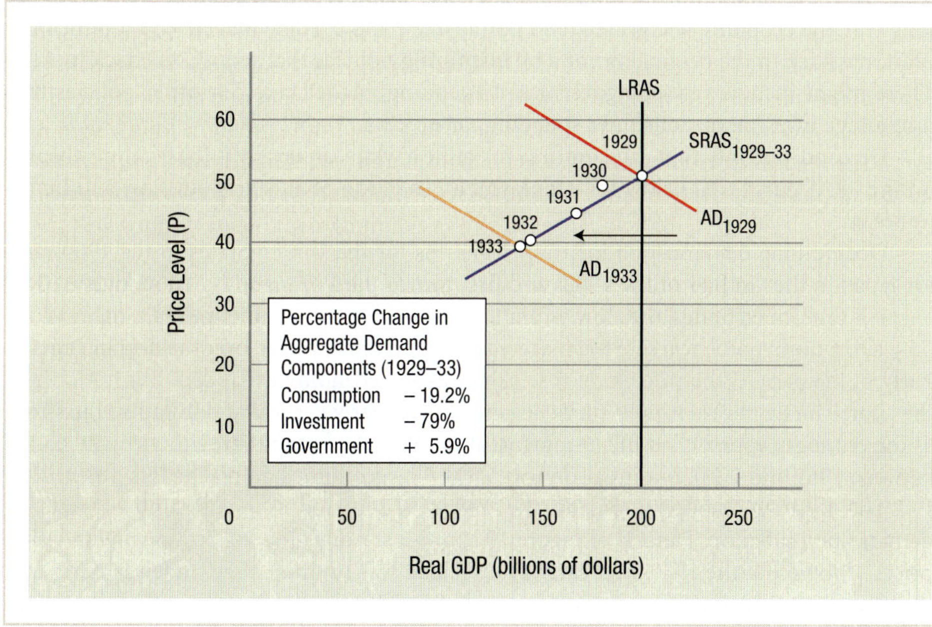


**FIGURE 8—Aggregate Demand, Short-Run Aggregate Supply, and the Investment Decline in the Depression**

In this figure, aggregate demand and short-run aggregate supply are superimposed on the real GDP and price level data for the Great Depression. Investment dropped nearly 80% and consumption declined nearly 20%. Together, these reductions in spending created a depression that was so deep that it took the massive spending for World War II to bring the economy back to full employment.

## Demand-Pull Inflation

**Demand-pull inflation** occurs when aggregate demand expands so much that equilibrium output exceeds full employment output. Turning to Figure 9 on the next page, assume the economy is initially in long-run equilibrium at point *e*. If business becomes irrationally exuberant and expands investments in some area (again, like telecommunications in the late 1990s), this expansion will push aggregate demand out to $AD_1$. The economy moves to a short-run equilibrium beyond full employment (point *a*), and the price level rises to $P_1$.

Demand-pull inflation: Results when aggregate demand expands so much that equilibrium output exceeds full employment output and the price level rises.

On a temporary basis, the economy can expand beyond full employment as workers incur overtime, temporary workers are added, and more shifts are employed. Yet, these activities increase costs and prices. And since long-run aggregate supply (LRAS) has not shifted, the economy will ultimately move to point *c* (if AD stays at $AD_1$), shifting

**FIGURE 9—Demand-Pull Inflation**

Demand-pull inflation occurs when aggregate demand expands and equilibrium output (point *a*) exceeds full employment output ($Q_f$). Since the LRAS curve has not shifted, the economy will in the end move into long-run equilibrium at point *c*. With the new aggregate demand at $AD_1$, prices have unexpectedly risen, so short-run aggregate supply shifts to $SRAS_2$ as workers, for example, adjust their wage demands upward, leaving prices permanently higher at $P_2$.

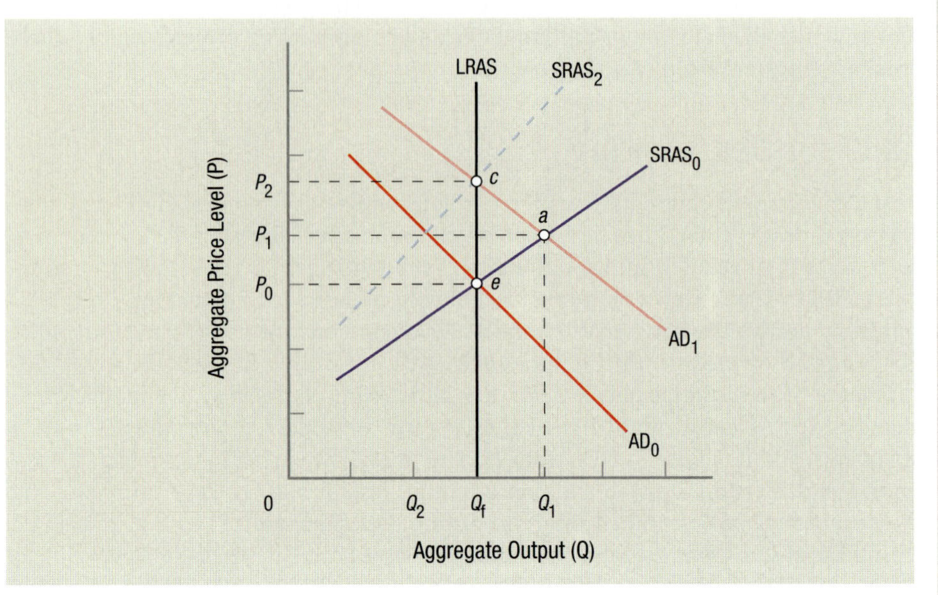


short-run aggregate supply to $SRAS_2$ and leaving prices permanently higher (at $P_2$). In the long run, the economy will gravitate to points like *e* and *c*. Policymakers could return the economy back to the original point *e* by instituting policies that reduce AD back to $AD_0$. These might include reduced government spending, higher taxes, or other policies that discourage investment, consumer spending, or exports.

Demand-pull inflation can continue for quite a while, especially if the economy begins on the SRAS curve well below full employment. Inflation often starts out slow and builds up steam.

Decade-long demand-pull inflation scenarios for the United States in the 1960s and for Japan in the last half of the 1980s and first half of the 1990s are shown in Figure 10.

For the United States, the slow escalation of the Vietnam conflict fueled a rising economy along the hypothetical short-run aggregate supply curve placed over the data in panel A. Early in the decade, the price level rose slowly as the economy expanded. But notice how the short-run aggregate supply curve began to turn nearly vertical and inflation rates rose as the economy approached full employment in 1969. Real output growth virtually halted between 1969 and 1970, but inflation was 5.3%. The economy had reached its potential.

The Japanese economy during the 1985–1995 period is a different example of demand-pull inflation. Panel B of Figure 10 shows a steadily growing economy with rising prices, throughout the 1980s and early 1990s. Japan was running huge trade surpluses and the yen was appreciating (becoming more valuable). A rising yen would eventually reduce exports (Japanese products would become too expensive). To keep this from happening, the Japanese government kept interest rates artificially low, reducing the pressure on the yen and encouraging investment. But these policies fueled a huge real estate and stock bubble that began collapsing in the beginning of the 1990s and led to a decade-long recession that has been called "the lost decade."

Demand-pull inflation can often take a while to become a problem. But once the inflation spiral gains momentum, it can pose a serious problem for policymakers, as we will see in later chapters.

## Cost-Push Inflation

**Cost-push inflation:** Results when a supply shock hits the economy, reducing short-run aggregate supply, and thus reducing output and increasing the price level.

**Cost-push inflation** occurs when a supply shock hits the economy, shifting the short-run aggregate supply curve leftward, as from $SRAS_0$ to $SRAS_2$ in Figure 11. The 1973 oil shock is a classic example. Because oil is a basic input in so many goods and services we purchase, skyrocketing oil prices affected all parts of the economy. After a bout of cost-

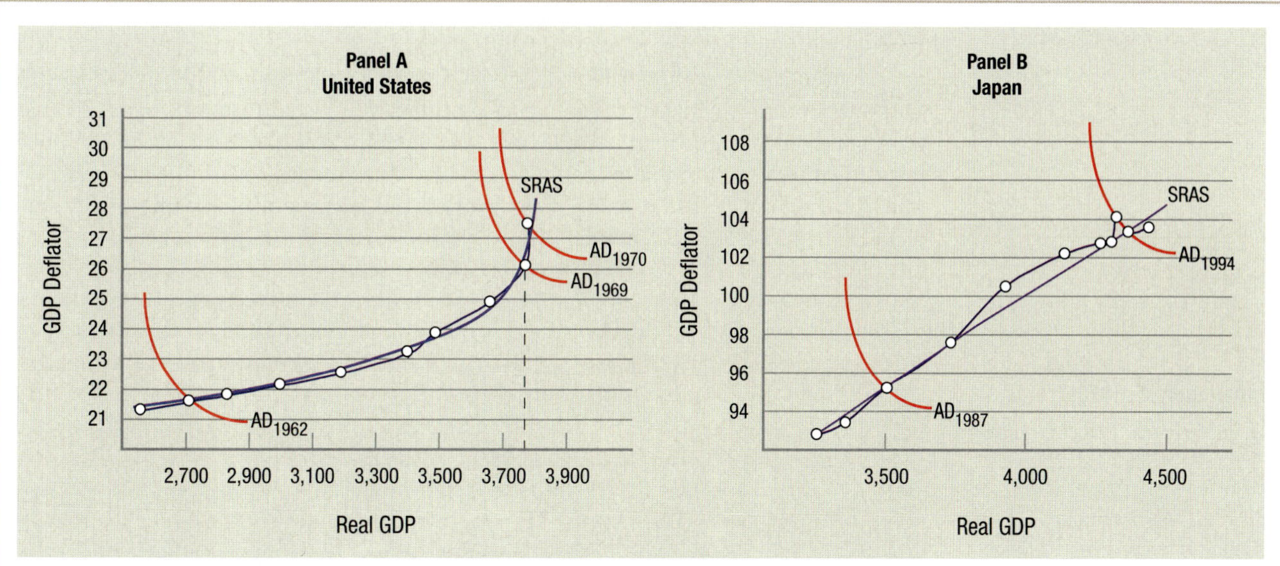


**FIGURE 10—Demand-Pull Inflation, United States (1960s) and Japan (1985–1995)**

This figure shows two examples of demand-pull inflation for the United States and Japan. Hypothetical aggregate demand and short-run aggregate supply curves are superimposed over the data for the two time periods. The Vietnam conflict expanded aggregate demand in the 1960s, and the U.S. economy experienced inflation over the entire decade and faced rising inflation rates as the economy approached full employment in 1969. Japan experienced demand-pull inflation as it enjoyed a huge trade surplus and its exports expanded the economy. Japanese policymakers kept interest rates artificially low, fueling a real estate and stock bubble that collapsed in the 1990s, resulting in a decade-long recession.

push inflation, rising resource costs push the economy from point *e* to point *b* in Figure 11. Note that at point *b,* real output has fallen (the economy is in a recession) and the price level has risen. Policymakers can increase demand to $AD_1$ and move the economy back to full employment at point *c.* For example, they might increase government spending, reduce taxes, or introduce policies that encourage consumption, investment, or net exports. But notice that this means an even higher price level. Alternatively, policymakers could reduce

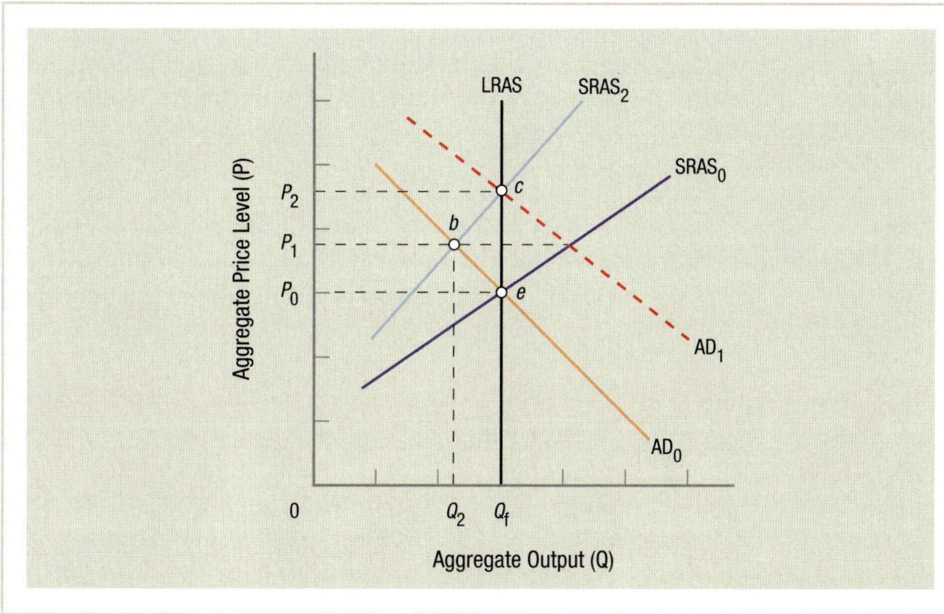


**FIGURE 11—Cost-Push Inflation**

Cost-push inflation is represented by an initial decline in short-run aggregate supply from $SRAS_0$ to $SRAS_2$. Rising resource costs or inflationary expectations will reduce short-run aggregate supply, resulting in a short-run movement from point *e* to point *b.* If policymakers wish to return the economy to full employment, they can increase aggregate demand to $AD_1$, but must accept higher prices as the economy moves to point *c.* Alternatively, they could reduce aggregate demand, but that would lead to lower output and employment.

inflationary pressures by reducing aggregate demand, but this leads to an even deeper recession as output and employment fall further.

Figure 12 shows the striking leftward shift in equilibrium points for 1973–1975. Output stood still, while prices rose as the economy adjusted to the new energy prices. Superimposed over the annual data are two hypothetical short-run aggregate supply curves. Notice that it took the economy roughly three years to absorb the oil shock. Only after the economy had adjusted to the new prices did it continue on a path roughly equivalent to the pre-1973 SRAS curve.

**FIGURE 12—Cost-Push Inflation in the 1970s**

The rise in equilibrium prices following the 1973 oil shocks was striking. From 1973 to 1975, prices rose, yet output stood still as the economy adjusted to the new energy prices. Superimposed over the actual annual data are two hypothetical short-run aggregate supply curves. Notice that it took the economy roughly three years to absorb the oil shock.

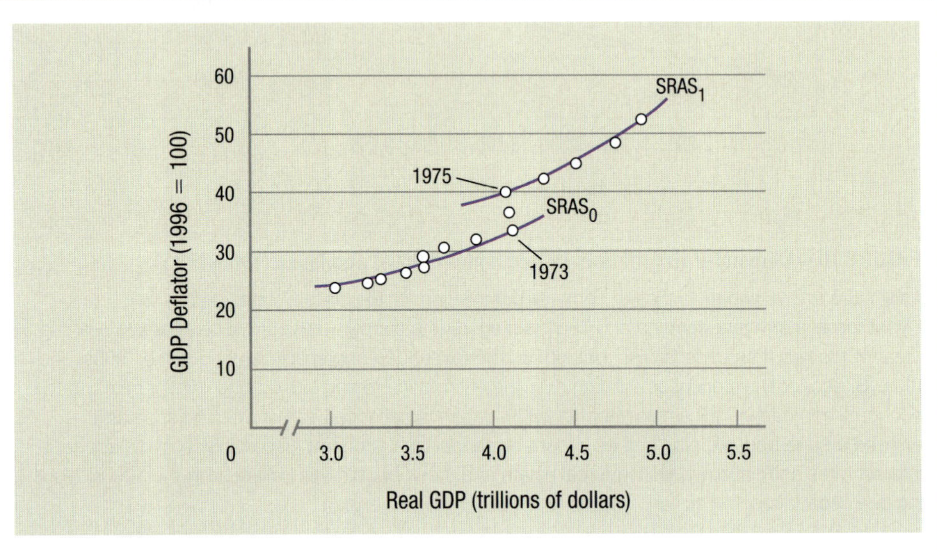


Before the Great Depression, economic analysis focused on the behavior of individuals, households, and businesses. Little attention was paid to the macroeconomic stabilization potential of government policies. The federal government had its responsibilities under the Constitution in areas such as national defense, the enforcement of contracts, and tax collection, but managing the economy was not among these.

The Great Depression of the 1930s and John Maynard Keynes's *The General Theory* drastically changed how economists viewed the role of the federal government. During the Depression, when unemployment reached 25% and bank failures wiped out personal savings, federal intervention in the economy became imperative. After the 1930s, the federal government's role grew to encompass (1) expanded spending and taxation and the resulting exercise of fiscal policy, (2) extensive new regulation of business, and (3) expanded regulation of the banking sector, along with greater exercise of monetary policy.

The next chapter focuses on how government spending and taxation combine to expand or contract the macroeconomy. When the economy enters a recession, fiscal policy can be used to moderate the impact and prevent another depression. Later chapters will explore the monetary system and the use of monetary policy to stabilize the economy and the price level. As you read these chapters, keep in mind that the long-run goals of fiscal and monetary policy are economic growth, low unemployment, and modest inflationary pressures.

## CHECKPOINT

### MACROECONOMIC EQUILIBRIUM

- Macroeconomic equilibrium occurs where short-run aggregate supply and aggregate demand cross.

- The spending multiplier exists because new spending generates new round-by-round spending (based on the marginal propensities to consume and save) that creates additional income.
- The formula for the spending multiplier is $1/(1 - MPC) = 1/MPS$.
- The multiplier is larger when the economy is in a deep recession or a depression.
- Policymakers can increase output by enacting policies that expand government spending, consumption, investment, or net exports, or reduce taxes.
- Demand-pull inflation occurs when aggregate demand expands beyond that necessary for full employment.
- Cost-push inflation occurs when short-run aggregate supply shifts to the left, causing the price level to rise along with rising unemployment.

**QUESTIONS:** Between 2004 and 2008, the price of petroleum products in the United States more than doubled, and gasoline and diesel fuel peaked at over $4.00 a gallon. Describe the impact of this price increase on short-run aggregate supply. How might it affect employment, unemployment, and the price level? Would the impact depend on whether consumers and business thought the price increase was permanent?

Answers to the Checkpoint questions can be found at the end of this chapter.

## Key Concepts

**Aggregate expenditures**, p. 455
**Aggregate demand**, p. 455
**Wealth effect**, p. 456
**Aggregate supply**, p. 459
**Short-run aggregate supply (SRAS) curve**, p. 459
**Long-run aggregate supply (LRAS) curve**, p. 460
**Macroeconomic equilibrium**, p. 463
**Multiplier**, p. 463
**Marginal propensity to consume**, p. 464
**Marginal propensity to save**, p. 464
**Demand-pull inflation**, p. 465
**Cost-push inflation**, p. 466

## Chapter Summary

### Aggregate Demand

The aggregate demand curve shows the quantities of goods and services (real GDP) demanded at different price levels.

The aggregate demand curve is downward sloping for several reasons. When price levels rise, household wealth is reduced because the purchasing power of money held in savings accounts, bonds, and cash declines. Some purchases are thus put on hold, thereby reducing output demanded. This is known as the *wealth effect.* Second, when the country's aggregate price level rises, U.S. goods become more expensive in the global marketplace, so foreigners purchase fewer U.S. products, and thus exports decline. Third, as aggregate prices rise, people need more money to carry out transactions. This added demand for money drives up interest rates, which reduces business investment.

The determinants of aggregate demand include the components of aggregate spending—consumption, investment, government spending, and net exports. Changing any one of these aggregates will shift the aggregate demand curve.

## Aggregate Supply

The aggregate supply curve shows the real GDP that firms will produce at varying price levels. The aggregate supply curve has two regions: a positively sloped section, where prices rise when GDP grows (SRAS curve); and a vertical region (LRAS curve), where output cannot grow.

The short-run aggregate supply (SRAS) curve is positively sloped because many input costs are slow to change in the short run. When prices rise, firms do not immediately need to increase wages or rents, because these are often fixed for a specified term. However, as an industry or the economy as a whole increases its production, firms must start hiring more labor or paying overtime. As each firm seeks more employees, wages are driven up, increasing costs and forcing higher prices.

The vertical long-run aggregate supply (LRAS) curve reflects classical economic analysis. Over the long run, all variables in the economy, including prices, wages, and interest rates, can adjust. This means that an economy in the long run will gravitate to an equilibrium position at full employment.

The determinants of the short-run aggregate supply curve include changes in input prices, the market power of firms, productivity, taxes, regulation, and business and inflationary expectations. If one of these determinants changes, the entire short-run aggregate supply curve shifts.

## Macroeconomic Equilibrium

A short-run macroeconomic equilibrium occurs at the intersection of the short-run aggregate supply and aggregate demand curves. When an economy is operating at full employment, this also represents a point of long-run macroeconomic equilibrium. The Great Depression demonstrated, however, that an economy can reach short-run equilibrium at output levels substantially below full employment. Unless something happens to change aggregate demand or short-run aggregate supply, the economy could remain mired in a recession.

The spending multiplier exists because new round-by-round spending generates more spending and income (based on the marginal propensities to consume and save) that creates additional income.

Demand-pull inflation occurs when aggregate demand expands so much that equilibrium output exceeds full employment output. On a temporary basis, the economy can expand beyond full employment as workers incur overtime, temporary workers are added, and more shifts are added. All these components increase costs and prices. Without a reduction in aggregate demand, the economy will move to a new equilibrium where prices are permanently higher.

Cost-push inflation occurs when a supply shock hits the economy, shifting the short-run aggregate supply curve leftward. Cost-push inflation makes using policies to expand aggregate demand to restore full employment difficult because of the additional inflationary pressures added to the economy.

# Questions and Problems

## Check Your Understanding

1. Describe the impact of rising interest rates on consumer spending.
2. When the economy is operating at full employment, why is an increase in aggregate demand not helpful to the economy?
3. When the economy is hit with a supply shock, such as oil prices rising from $25 a barrel to $75, why is this doubly disruptive and harmful to the economy?
4. Explain why the aggregate supply curve is positively sloped during the short run and vertical in the long run.
5. List some examples of factors that will shift the aggregate demand curve.
6. List some examples of factors that will shift the long-run aggregate supply curve.

## Apply the Concepts

7. There is little doubt that computers and the Internet have changed our economy. Information technology (IT) can boost efficiency in nearly everything: Markets are more efficient, IT is global, and IT improves the design, manufacture, and supply chain of products we produce. Use the aggregate demand and supply framework discussed in this chapter to show the impact of IT on the U.S. economy.
8. Unemployment can be caused by a reduction in aggregate demand or short-run aggregate supply. Both changes are represented by a leftward shift in the curves. Does it matter whether the shift occurs in aggregate demand or short-run aggregate supply? Use the AD/AS framework to show why or why not.
9. Why is cost-push inflation a more difficult problem for policymakers than demand-pull?
10. Why is consumer confidence so important in determining the equilibrium level of output and employment?
11. As the Japanese yen appreciated in value during the 1980s and 1990s, more Japanese auto companies built auto manufacturing plants in other parts of Asia and the United States. What impact did this have on net exports for the United States? Why did Japanese automakers build plants in the United States? Were the reasons similar to the reasons that American firms build plants (or outsource production) to China and other parts of Asia?
12. Some advocates have suggested that the United States should move to a universal health care plan paid for at the federal level like Medicare, which would be funded out of general tax revenues. Such a plan, it is argued, would guarantee quality health care to all. Ignoring all the controversy surrounding such a plan, would the introduction of universal health care paid for from general revenues have an impact on short-run aggregate supply? Long-run aggregate supply? Why or why not?

## Solving Problems

13. In the figure below, the economy is initially in equilibrium at full employment at point *e*. Assume aggregate demand declines by 100 (shifts from $AD_0$ to $AD_1$).

    a. What is the new short-run equilibrium?

    b. How large is the simple Keynesian multiplier in this case?

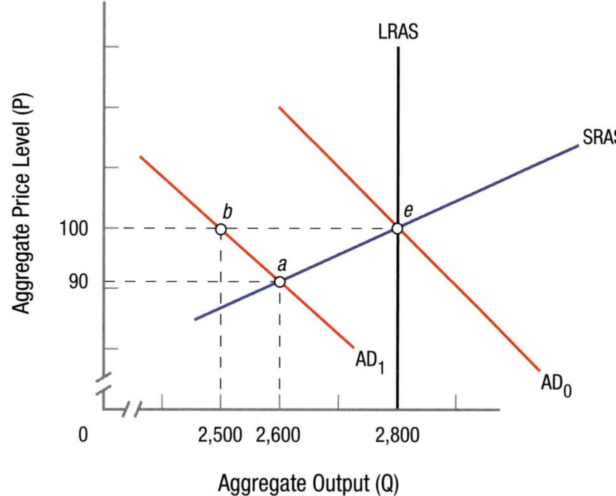


14. In the figure below, assume the economy is initially at full employment equilibrium at point *e*. Now assume that aggregate demand rises to $AD_1$, creating demand-pull

inflation. Describe what happens to the economy in both the short run and the long run.

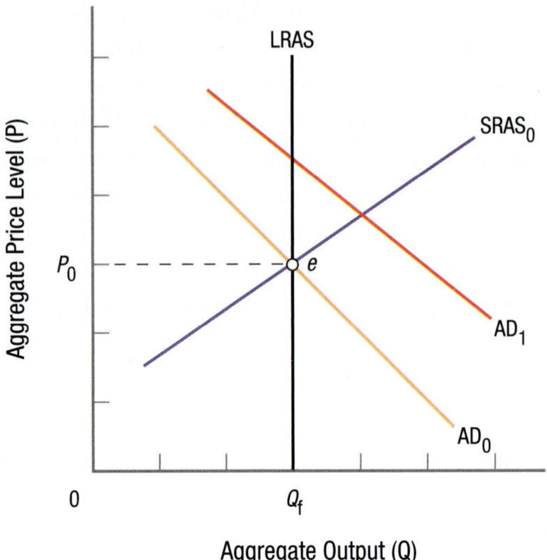


15. Use the table and grid below to answer the following questions:
    a. In the grid, graph the aggregate demand and short-run aggregate supply curves (label them $AD_0$ and $SRAS_0$). What is equilibrium output and the price level?
    b. Assume aggregate demand grows by 100% (doubles; so that output doubles at each price level). Graph the new aggregate demand curve and label it $AD_1$. What is the new equilibrium output and price level?
    c. If full employment output is 600, what will be the long-run output and price level given the new aggregate demand curve?

| Price Level | Output (short-run aggregate supply) | Output (aggregate demand) |
|---|---|---|
| 150 | 1,000 | 200 |
| 125 | 800 | 400 |
| 100 | 600 | 600 |
| 75 | 400 | 800 |
| 50 | 200 | 1,000 |

# Answers to Questions in CheckPoints

## Check Point: Aggregate Demand

An increase in taxes (or tax rates) would reduce disposable income and consumption, shifting aggregate demand to the left. In a similar way, decreasing taxes would raise disposable income and shift aggregate demand to the right. Since government spending is an element of aggregate demand, what the government does with the revenue also affects aggregate demand (more about this in later chapters).

## Check Point: Aggregate Supply

Probably not. Because of the greater extent of collective bargaining, European labor markets are less competitive, and "full employment" may be reached at higher unemployment levels than in the United States. Hiring additional workers in Europe costs more initially, and laying off workers is much harder by law. This added inflexibility in labor markets probably leads to a steeper short-run aggregate supply curve in Europe than in the United States.

## Check Point: Macroeconomic Equilibrium

Petroleum products are an important input in our economy. Higher oil prices will increase costs of transportation, and where oil is an important input (plastics), it will increase costs and reduce short-run aggregate supply. Over time, these cost increases will show up as a higher price level, reduced employment, and higher unemployment. If the economy continues to grow, these impacts will be masked, but will simply reduce the growth numbers. After the oil price shocks in the 1970s, the United States became much more energy efficient, so today's price increases may not have quite the shock effect on the economy as was experienced in the 1970s. If the change is seen as permanent, consumers and firms will begin making long-run adjustments to higher prices. For example, consumers will begin switching to more fuel-efficient cars (hybrids and smaller cars), and business will look at investing in energy-saving methods of distribution and production. If the price increases are just viewed as temporary, both groups might not adjust much at all.

# Appendix: Deriving the Aggregate Demand Curve

**The aggregate demand curve** shows the quantities of goods and services (real GDP) demanded at different price levels. It can be derived using the aggregate expenditures model described in Chapter 18. To illustrate, panel A of Figure APX-1 shows aggregate expenditures (AE) curves at two different price levels. Remember that AE curves are drawn assuming fixed prices.

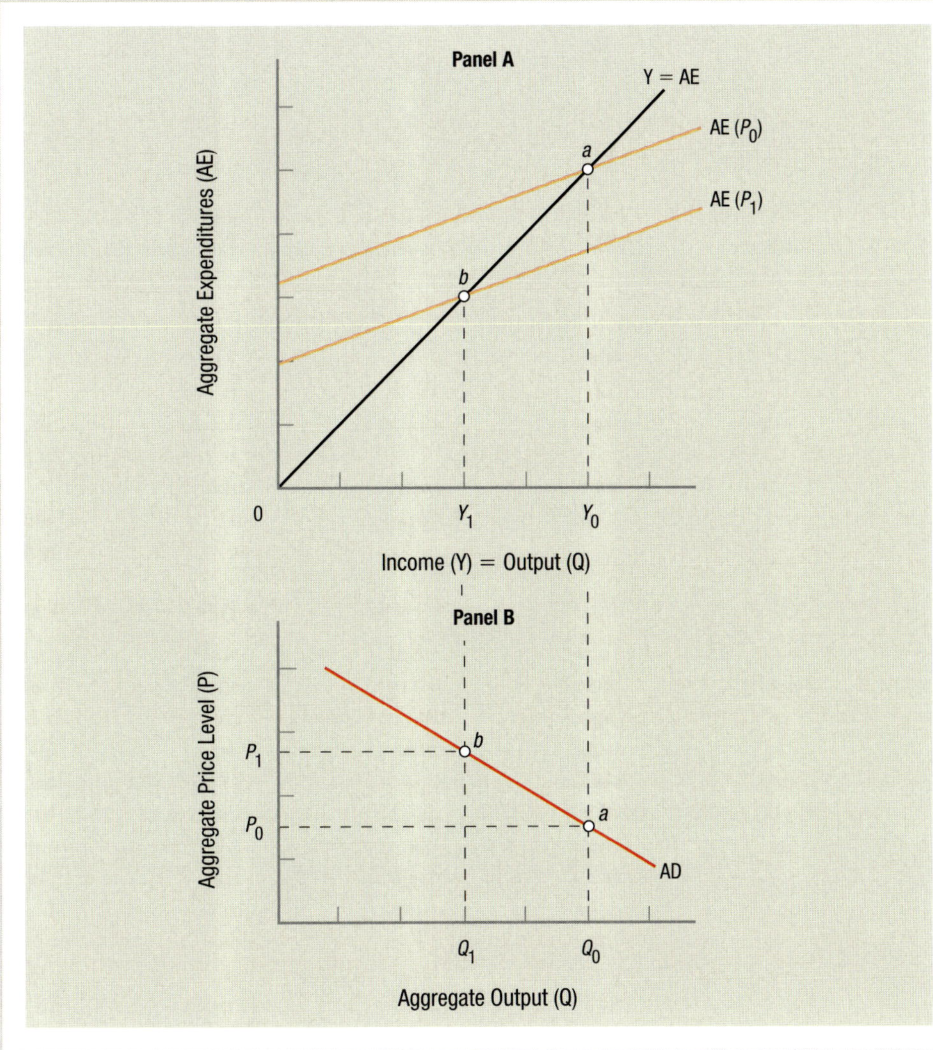


**FIGURE APX-1—Deriving the Aggregate Demand Curve**

The aggregate demand curve, which shows the quantities of goods and services demanded at different price levels for the entire economy, can be derived using the aggregate spending model. Panel A shows aggregate expenditures curves at two different price levels. Point *a* on aggregate expenditures curve AE($P_0$) represents equilibrium income $Y_0$, equivalent to a real output of $Q_0$. Point *a* in panel B shows real output of $Q_0$ that is associated with equilibrium point *a* and its price level $P_0$. If the aggregate price level rises to $P_1$, aggregate spending will decline to AE($P_1$) in panel A. The result is a new equilibrium at point *b* in both panels. Connecting points *a* and *b* in panel B results in aggregate demand curve AD.

First, consider equilibrium point *a* on aggregate expenditures curve AE($P_0$). This point shows an equilibrium income of $Y_0$, which is equivalent to a real output of $Q_0$. Point *a* in panel B, therefore, represents a real output of $Q_0$ and a price level of $P_0$. However, if the aggregate price level rises to $P_1$, aggregate expenditures will decline to AE($P_1$) because at these higher prices, the same level of expenditures will not buy as much real output as before. The result is a new equilibrium at point *b* in both panels. Connecting points *a* and *b* in panel B, we have constructed aggregate demand curve AD that represents the relationship between the price level and aggregate output.

# Fiscal Policy

Murat Taner/Getty Images

**There is nothing like a housing** bubble followed by a financial meltdown and a deep and prolonged recession to make almost everyone in America familiar with the term "fiscal policy." The pending bankruptcy in late 2008 of major insurance companies, auto makers, and commercial and investment banks, along with the first decline in housing prices in decades and a 40% drop in stock prices, forced policymakers to quickly broaden their usual set of policy tools.

Fiscal policy involves adjusting government spending (on goods and services), transfer payments, and taxes with the express purpose of managing the macroeconomy. The severity of the 2008–2009 macroeconomic downturn led policymakers to increase the magnitude of fiscal policy. Congress (at the urging of the president) passed a huge ($787 billion) stimulus package that included tax reductions and rebates with a large dose of infrastructure spending.

Fiscal policy, massive as it became, was not the only tool that policymakers had available to them. They also implemented monetary policy. We will hold off discussing monetary policy until later chapters. Here we focus on fiscal policy: using government spending and taxing to manage the macroeconomy.

Figure 1 on the next page shows the distribution of the nearly $4 trillion U.S. federal budget. The biggest source of revenues is individual income and Social Security taxes, which constitute over 80% of revenues. Social Security, national defense, and Medicare represent nearly half of all spending.

We will focus on three aspects of fiscal policy. First, we will examine government tools for influencing aggregate demand. Second, we will look at how government can influence aggregate supply. You will use the aggregate demand and aggregate supply model that we

**After studying this chapter you should be able to:**

- ☐ Describe the tools that governments use to influence aggregate demand.
- ☐ Describe mandatory and discretionary government spending.
- ☐ Describe the multiplier effect of increased government spending on the equilibrium output of an economy.
- ☐ Describe expansionary and contractionary fiscal policy.
- ☐ Describe why tax changes have a smaller impact on the economy than changes in government spending.
- ☐ Describe the fiscal policies that governments use to influence aggregate supply.
- ☐ Describe the impact of automatic stabilizers, lag effects, and the crowding out effects in fiscal policymaking.
- ☐ Describe the debate over the size of government and economic policy.

**FIGURE 1—Federal Government Revenues and Expenditures, 2009**

The pie charts show the percentage distribution of federal revenues and expenditures. The bulk of revenues come from individual income taxes and Social Security payroll taxes. Spending is much more diversified; most of the funds go to national defense, health, Social Security, energy and the environment, and income security (welfare).

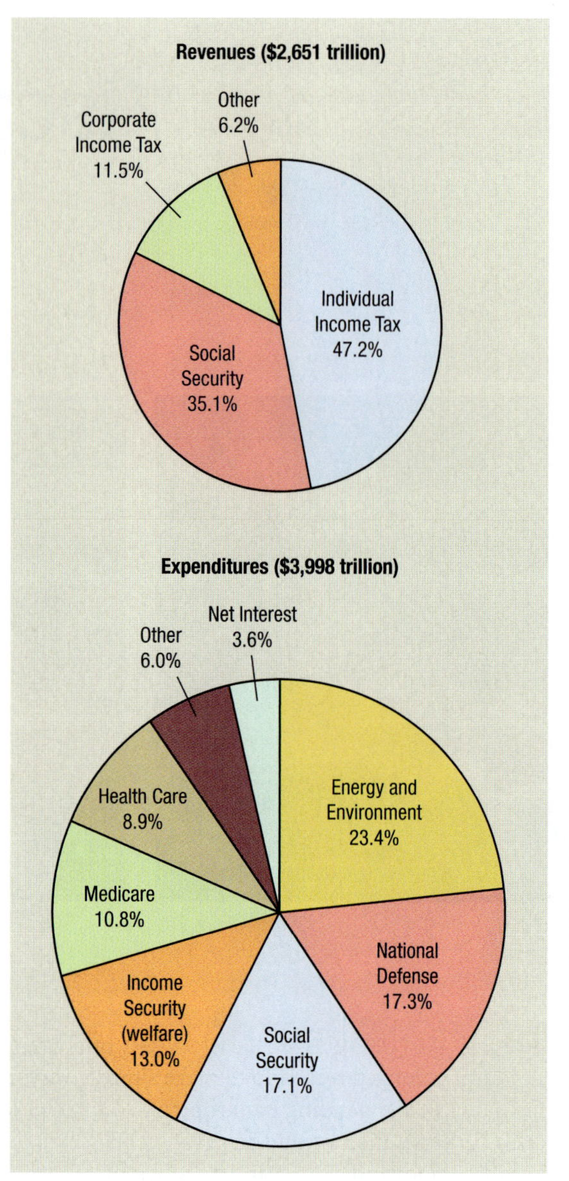


developed in the previous chapter in both of these sections. Finally, we will look at how implementing the demand-side and supply-side policies that government believes necessary can generate its own problems.

## Fiscal Policy and Aggregate Demand

When an economy faces underutilization of resources because it is stuck in equilibrium well below full employment, we saw that increases in aggregate demand can move the economy toward full employment without generating excessive inflation pressures. However, influencing aggregate demand brings with it a tradeoff: Output is increased at the expense of raising the price level. When the economy is in an inflationary equilibrium *above full employment,* contracting aggregate demand brings about other tradeoffs: Decreasing output dampens inflation but leads to unemployment. Before we examine the theory behind how government influences aggregate demand by using fiscal policy, let's take a brief look at what categories of spending fiscal policy typically alters.

## Discretionary and Mandatory Spending

The federal budget can be split into two distinct types of spending: discretionary and mandatory. Discretionary spending is the part of the budget that works its way through the appropriations process of Congress each year. **Discretionary spending** includes such programs as national defense (essentially the military), transportation, science, environment, income security (some welfare programs such as Medicaid), education, and veterans benefits and services. As Figure 2 shows, discretionary spending is now under 40% and has steadily declined as a percent of the budget since the 1960s, when it was over 60% of the budget.

**Discretionary spending:** The part of the budget that works its way through the appropriations process of Congress each year and includes such programs as national defense, transportation, science, environment, and income security.

**Mandatory spending** is authorized by permanent laws and does not go through the same appropriations process as discretionary spending. To change one of the entitlements of mandatory spending, Congress must change the law. Mandatory spending includes such programs as Social Security, Medicare, interest on the national debt, and some means-tested income-security programs, including food stamps and TANF (Temporary Assistance to Needy Families). This part of the budget has been growing, as Figure 2 illustrates, and now accounts for over 60% of the budget.

**Mandatory spending:** Spending authorized by permanent laws that does not go through the same appropriations process as discretionary spending. Mandatory spending includes such programs as Social Security, Medicare, and interest on the national debt.

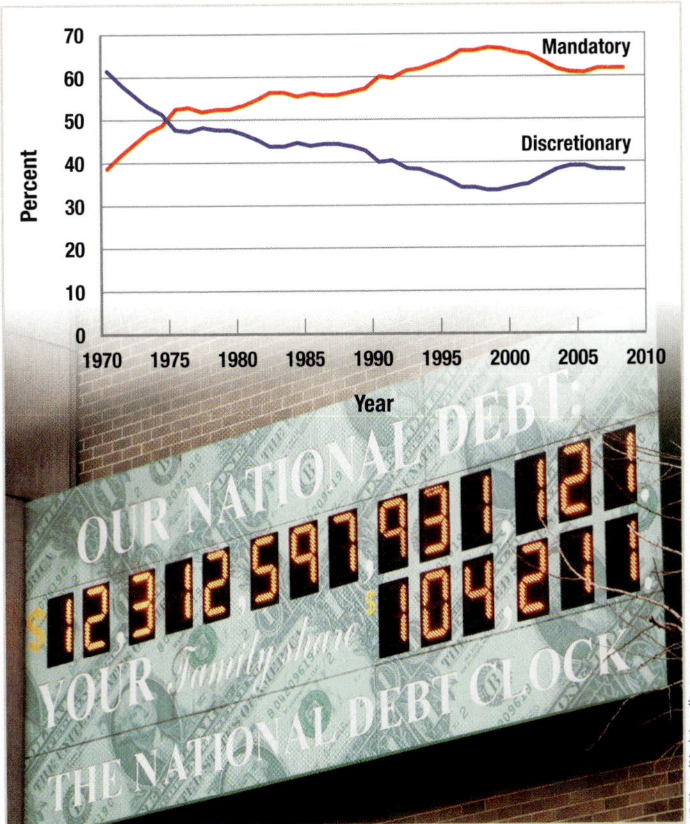


FIGURE 2—Discretionary and Mandatory Federal Spending

Mandatory spending includes programs authorized by law (also called entitlements) such as Social Security, Medicare, and food stamps. Mandatory programs do not go through the normal congressional appropriations process and have been growing. Discretionary programs are authorized each year by the appropriations process of Congress and include national defense, transportation, environment, and education spending. Discretionary spending has been steadily declining as a percent of the budget.

Even though discretionary spending is only 38% of the budget, this is still roughly $1.5 trillion, and the capacity to alter this spending is a powerful force in the economy. Further, the 60% of the budget that is on auto-pilot may well act as a stabilizing force. So we are mainly concerned with discretionary spending when we consider fiscal policy.

## Discretionary Fiscal Policy

The exercise of **discretionary fiscal policy** is done with the express goal of influencing aggregate demand. It involves adjusting government spending and tax policies with the express short-run goal of moving the economy toward full employment, encouraging economic growth, or controlling inflation.

**Discretionary fiscal policy:** Involves adjusting government spending and tax policies with the express short-run goal of moving the economy toward full employment, expanding economic growth, or controlling inflation.

Some examples of the use of discretionary fiscal policy include tax cuts enacted during the Kennedy, Reagan, and George W. Bush administrations. These tax cuts were designed to expand the economy, both in the near term and the long run—they were meant to influence both aggregate demand and aggregate supply. Tax increases were enacted under the George H. Bush and Clinton administrations in the interest of reducing the government deficit and interest rates. The Roosevelt administration used increased government spending, although small amounts by today's standards, to mitigate the impact of the Depression.

## Government Spending

Though discretionary fiscal policy can get complex, the impact of changes in government spending is relatively simple. As we know, a change in government spending or other components of GDP will cause income and output to rise or fall by the spending change *times* the multiplier.

This is illustrated in Figure 3 with the economy initially in equilibrium at point *e*, with real output equaling $Q_0$. If government spending increases, shifting aggregate demand from $AD_0$ to $AD_1$, aggregate output will increase from $Q_0$ to $Q_f$. Because the short run aggregate supply curve is upward sloping, some of the increase in output is absorbed by rising prices, reducing the pure spending multiplier discussed in earlier chapters.

**FIGURE 3—The Multiplier and Government Spending**

The economy is initially in equilibrium at point *e*. New government spending works its way through the economy round-by-round, both income and output are multiplied, but price increases absorb some of the increase in AD. Once the economy reaches full employment (point *a*), price increases absorb all of the increase in AD.

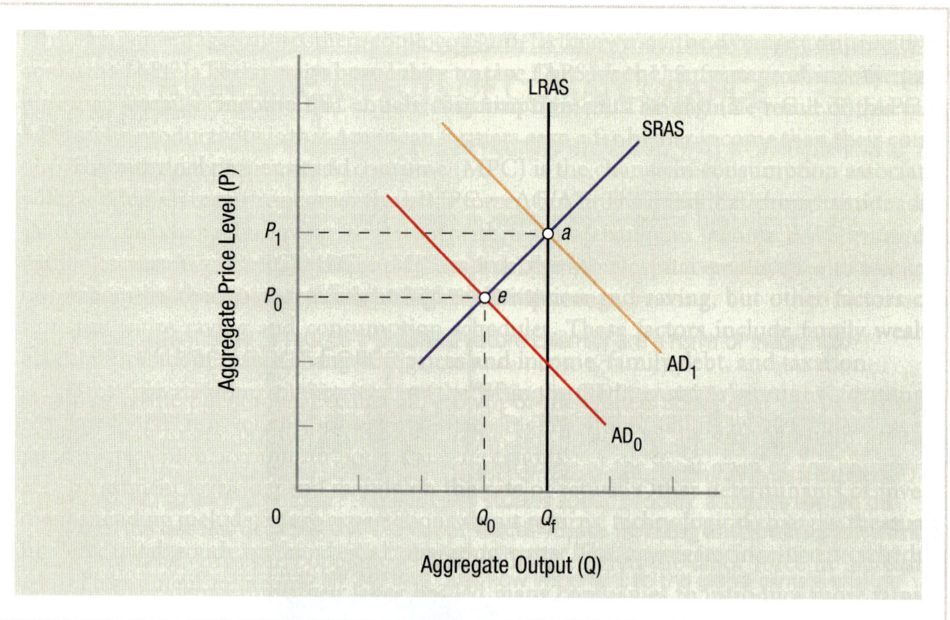


Once the economy reaches full employment (point *a*), further spending is not multiplied as the economy moves along the LRAS curve, and price increases absorb it all. Finally, keep in mind that the multiplier works in both directions.

## Taxes

Changes in government spending modify income by an amount equal to the change in spending *times* the multiplier. How, then, do changes in taxes affect the economy? The answer is not quite as simple. Let's begin with a reminder of what constitutes spending equilibrium.

When the economy is in equilibrium,

$$GDP = C + I + G + (X - M)$$

At equilibrium, all spending *injections* into the economy equal all *withdrawals* of spending. To see why, let's simplify the above equation and begin with only a private economy, eliminating government (G) and the foreign sector, or net exports (X − M). Thus,

$$\text{GDP} = \text{C} + \text{I}$$

Gross domestic product (GDP) is equal to consumer plus business investment spending. Without government and taxes, GDP is just income (Y), so

$$\text{Y} = \text{C} + \text{I}$$

or, subtracting C from each side of the equation,

$$\text{Y} - \text{C} = \text{I}$$

Now, income minus consumption (Y − C) is just saving (S), so at equilibrium,

$$\text{S} = \text{I}$$

or

$$\text{I} = \text{S}$$

This simple equation represents a very important point: At equilibrium, *injections* (in this case, I) are just equal to *withdrawals* (S in this instance). Investment represents spending where saving is the removal of income from the spending-income-spending stream.

Now, without going through all of the algebra, when we add government spending (G), taxes (T), and the foreign sector (X − M) to the equation, we have simply added some *injections* (G) and (X) and subtracted some *withdrawals* (T) and (M), so the equilibrium equation becomes

$$\text{I} + \text{G} + \text{X} = \text{S} + \text{T} + \text{M}$$

Now let's focus on taxes. When taxes are increased, money is withdrawn from the economy's spending stream. When taxes are reduced, consumers and business have more to spend. Thus, taxes form a wedge between income and the part of income that can be spent, or disposable income. Disposable income ($Y_d$) is equal to income minus taxes ($Y_d = Y - T$). For simplicity, we will assume that all taxes are paid in a lump sum, thereby removing a certain fixed sum of money from the economy. This assumption does away with the need to worry now about the incentive effects of higher or lower tax rates. These supply-side issues will be discussed later in the chapter.

Because taxes represent a withdrawal of spending from the economy, we would expect equilibrium income to fall when a tax is imposed. Consumers pay a tax increase, in part, by *reducing* their saving. If we initially increase taxes by $100, let's assume that consumers draw on their savings for $25 of the increase in taxes. Since this $25 in savings was already withdrawn from the economy, only the $75 in reduced spending gets multiplied, reducing the change in income. The *reduction* in saving of $25 dampens the effect of the tax on equilibrium income because those funds were previously withdrawn from the spending stream. Simply changing the withdrawal category from saving to taxes does not affect income. A tax decrease has a similar but opposite impact because only the MPC part is spent and multiplied, and the rest is saved and thus withdrawn from the spending stream.

The result is that a tax increase (or decrease, for that matter) has less of a direct impact on income, employment, and output than an equivalent change in government spending. Another way of saying this is that the government tax multiplier is *less* than the government spending multiplier. So, added spending leads to a larger increase in GDP when compared to the same reduction in taxes. The 2009 $787 billion stimulus package was more heavily structured toward spending partly for this reason.

## Issue: How Big Are Spending and Tax Multipliers?

**President Obama's** $787 billion 2009 stimulus package set off a flurry of discussion among economists about the actual size of the Keynesian spending and tax multipliers. It is one thing in our simple models to show that these multipliers exist and assert the value based on the MPC (a multiplier of 4 in our model with an MPC of 0.75). But the economy is a complex machine and there are various leakages that keep the multiplier from reaching its theoretical Keynesian "depression" potential. Leakages are those funds of additional income not saved but also that do not find their way into the domestic consumption-income multiplication stream.

The first and important leakage is taxes. Income generated from one person's consumption is taxed, reducing the amount available for further consumption and income generation. Second, purchases of imports reduce income generated domestically. When consumers buy imported goods, that money flows overseas and is not multiplied here. Both taxes and imports withdraw money from the spending stream, reducing the actual value of the multiplier. This explains why Congress and the president wanted to include a "Buy American" clause in the 2009 stimulus plan.

So what empirical value best represents the short-term government spending and tax multipliers for our economy?

Estimates by Susan Woodward, Robert Hall, and Valerie Ramey suggest that the multiplier for government spending is around 1.4, or that the increase in GDP is roughly equal to or slightly larger than the increase in government spending. They looked at periods where government spending ramped up quickly (mostly wars). This study ignored the fact that taxes were raised during the periods studied, so their estimate probably understates the true value of the spending multiplier. But it shows how quickly the leakages reduce the impact of additional government spending.

These relatively small estimates created a controversy, as other economists suggested that tax rate reduction targeted to business investment might have a bigger impact.

What about the tax multiplier? Christina and David Romer did an exhaustive analysis of 49 tax laws that resulted in 104 quarterly tax changes to estimate the impact of federal tax changes on output and employment. They estimated that the long-run multipliers for tax increases (and by implication tax reductions) approach 3 when the increases were addressing a budget deficit or promoting long-run economic growth. Their estimates were considerably less when tax increases were used to contract the economy or used to pay for increases in government spending (moving toward a balanced budget).

Empirically estimating spending and tax multipliers is extremely difficult and controversial. The spending multiplier is likely less than 2 but greater than 1, with the short-run tax multiplier in that same range but probably less than the spending multiplier. The controversy is really in comparing the long-run tax multiplier with short-run spending multipliers. There is evidence that the long-run tax multiplier may approach 3 because tax reductions have a longer running impact on the economy than short-run spending increases, given the leakages discussed above.

Sources: Susan Woodward and Robert Hall, "Measuring the Effect of Infrastructure Spending on GDP," online paper: woodwardhall.wordpress.com; and Valerie Ramey, "Identifying Government Spending Shocks: It's All in the Timing," NBER Working Paper, October 2009; and Christina Romer and David Romer, "The Macroeconomic Effects of Tax Changes: Estimates Based on a New Measure of Fiscal Shocks," working paper, March 2007.

### Transfers

Transfer payments are money payments directly paid to individuals. These include payments for such items as Social Security, unemployment compensation, and welfare. In large measure, they represent our social safety net. We will ignore them as part of the discretionary fiscal policy, since most are paid as a matter of law, but we will see later in the chapter that they are very important as a way of stabilizing the economy.

## Expansionary and Contractionary Fiscal Policy

Expansionary fiscal policy: Involves increasing government spending, increasing transfer payments, or decreasing taxes to increase aggregate demand to expand output and the economy.

**Expansionary fiscal policy** involves increasing government spending; increasing transfer payments such as Social Security, unemployment compensation, or welfare payments; or decreasing taxes—all to increase aggregate demand. These policies put more money into the hands of consumers and business. In theory, these additional funds should lead to higher spending. The precise effect expansionary fiscal policies have, however, depends on whether the economy is at or below full employment.

When the economy is below full employment, an expansionary policy will move the economy to full employment, as Figure 4 shows. The economy begins at equilibrium at point *e*, below full employment. Expansionary fiscal policy increases aggregate demand from $AD_0$ to $AD_1$, and equilibrium output rises to $Q_f$ (point $f$) as the price level rises to $P_1$.

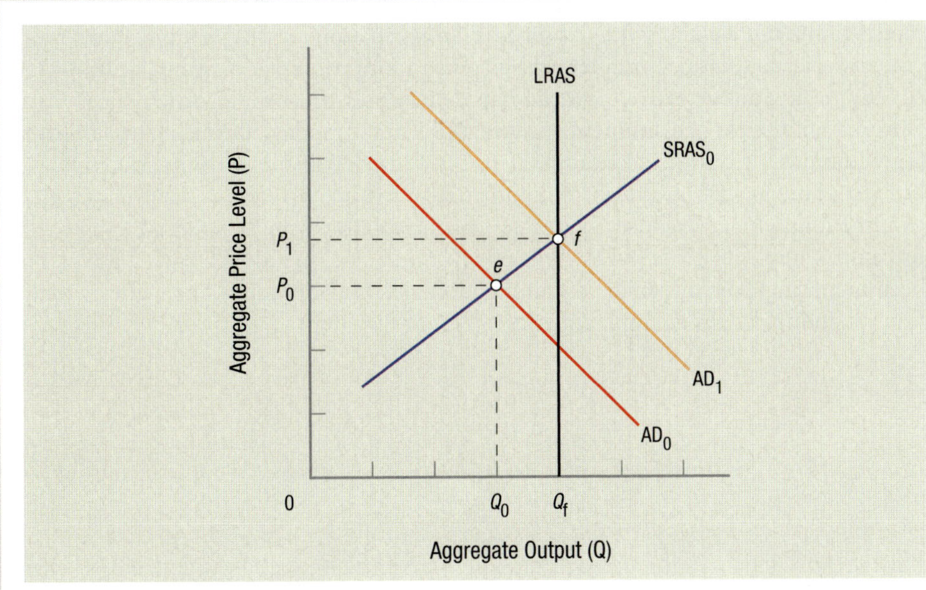


**FIGURE 4—Expansionary Fiscal Policy below Full Employment**

When the economy is below full employment, expansionary policies move it to full employment. Here, the economy begins at equilibrium at point *e*, below full employment. Expansionary fiscal policy increases aggregate demand from AD$_0$ to AD$_1$, raising equilibrium output to $Q_f$ and the price level to $P_1$ (point *f*).

In this case, one good outcome results—output rises to $Q_f$—though it is accompanied by one less desirable result, the price level rises to $P_1$.

Figure 5 shows what happens when the economy is at full employment: An expansionary policy raises prices without producing any long-run improvement in real GDP. In this figure, the initial equilibrium is already at full employment (point *e*), so increasing aggregate demand moves the economy to a new output level above full employment (point *a*), thereby raising prices to $P_1$. This higher output is only temporary, however, as workers and suppliers adjust their expectations to the higher price level, thus shifting short-run aggregate supply upwards to SRAS$_2$. Short-run aggregate supply declines because workers and other resource suppliers realize the prices they are paying for products have risen; hence, they demand higher wages or prices for their services. This higher demand just pushes prices up further, until finally workers adjust their inflationary expectations and the economy settles into equilibrium at point *b*. At this point, the economy is again at full employment, but at a higher price level ($P_2$) than before.

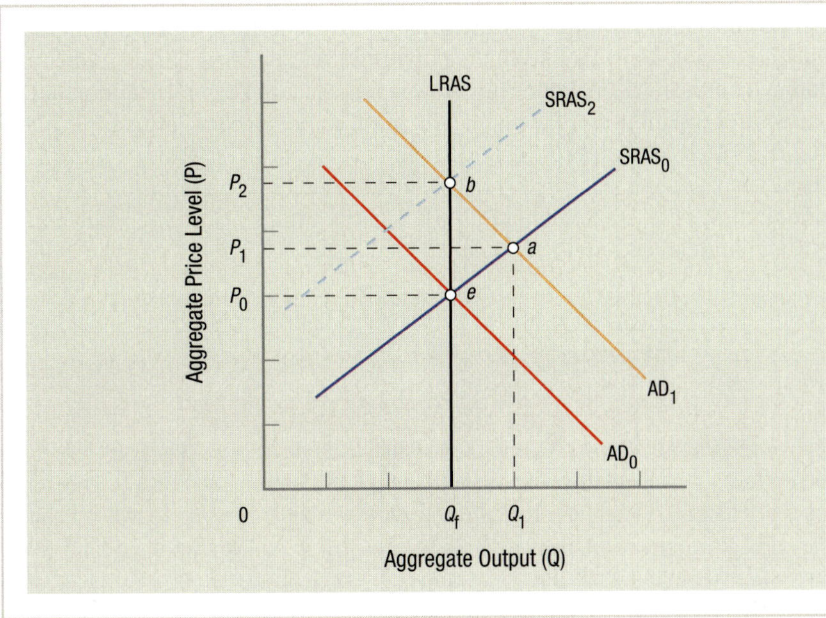


**FIGURE 5—Expansionary Fiscal Policy at Full Employment**

When an economy is already at full employment, expansionary policies lead to no long-run improvement in real GDP. Beginning at full employment (point *e*), increasing aggregate demand moves the economy to an output level above full employment (point *a*). This higher output is only temporary, however, as workers and suppliers adjust their expectations to the higher price level ($P_1$), thus shifting short-run aggregate supply left toward SRAS$_2$. But this just pushes prices up further, until finally workers adjust their inflationary expectations, and the economy settles into a new long-run equilibrium at point *b*, where the economy is once again at full employment, but at a higher price level ($P_2$).

**Contractionary fiscal policy:** Involves increasing withdrawals from the economy by reducing government spending, transfer payments, or raising taxes to decrease aggregate demand to contract output and the economy.

When an economy moves to a point beyond full employment, as just described, economists say an *inflationary spiral* has set in. The explanation for this phenomenon was suggested earlier, but a later chapter will give it a more extensive treatment. Still, we can already see that one way to reduce such inflationary pressures is by a **contractionary fiscal policy**: reducing government spending, transfer payments, or raising taxes (increasing withdrawals from the economy). Figure 6 shows the result of contractionary policy. The economy is initially overheating at point *e*, with output above full employment. Contractionary policy reduces aggregate demand to $AD_1$, bringing the economy back to full employment at price level $P_1$. This policy reduces the inflationary pressures that had been mounting, thereby staving off an inflationary spiral, but the fall in aggregate output leads to an increase in unemployment.

**FIGURE 6—Contractionary Fiscal Policy to Reduce Inflation**

In this figure, the economy is overheating at point *e*, with output above full employment. Contractionary policies reduce aggregate demand to $AD_1$, bringing the economy back to full employment at price level $P_1$. These policies prevent an inflationary spiral, but the fall in aggregate output leads to an increase in unemployment.

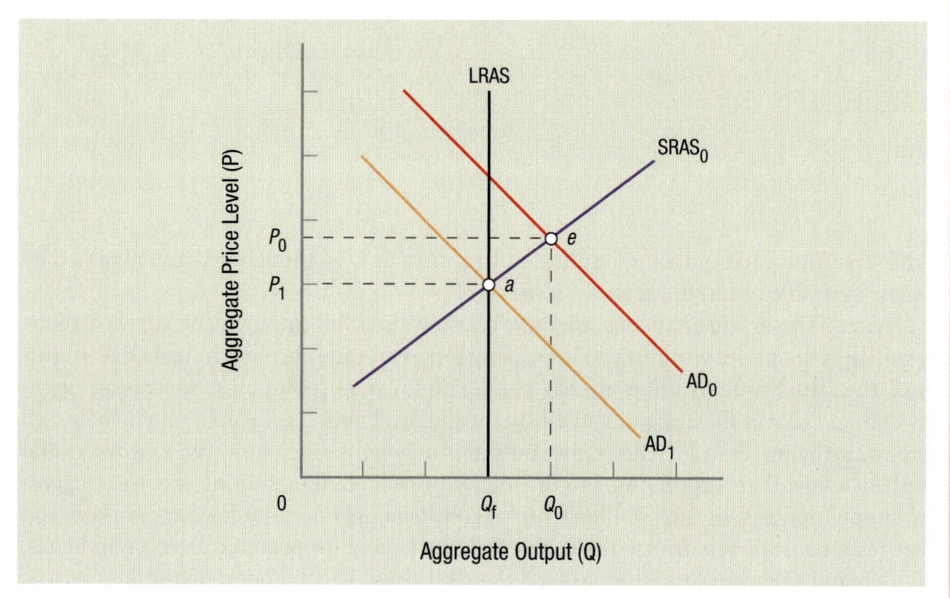


Exercising demand-side policy requires tradeoffs between increasing output at the expense of raising the price levels, or else lowering price levels by accepting a lower output. When recession threatens, the public is often happy to trade higher prices for greater employment and output. One would think the opposite would be true when an inflationary spiral loomed on the horizon. Politicians, however, are loath to support contractionary policies that control inflation by reducing aggregate demand, since high unemployment can cost politicians their jobs. As a result, the demand-side fiscal policy tools—government spending, transfer payments, and taxes—may remain unused. In these instances, politicians often look to the Federal Reserve to use its tools and influence to keep inflation in check. We will examine the Federal Reserve in later chapters.

## CHECKPOINT

### FISCAL POLICY AND AGGREGATE DEMAND

- Demand-side fiscal policy involves using government spending, transfer payments, and taxes to change aggregate demand and equilibrium income, output, and the price level in the economy.
- In the short run, government spending raises income and output by the amount of spending times the multiplier. Tax reductions have a smaller impact on the economy

than government spending because some of the reduction in taxes is added to saving and is therefore withdrawn from the economy.

- Expansionary fiscal policy involves increasing government spending, increasing transfer payments, or decreasing taxes.
- Contractionary fiscal policy involves decreasing government spending, decreasing transfer payments, or increasing taxes.
- When an economy is at full employment, expansionary fiscal policy may lead to greater output in the short term, but will ultimately just lead to higher prices in the longer term.

**QUESTION:** The 2009 $787 billion stimulus package cost roughly $2,500 per person or $10,000 for a family of four. The time required for the government to spend that sum on infrastructure projects (funding approvals, environmental clearances, and so on) means that the spending will likely stretch over two to four years. Why didn't Congress just send a $2,500 check to each man, woman, and child in America to speed up the impact on the economy?

Answers to the Checkpoint question can be found at the end of this chapter.

## Fiscal Policy and Aggregate Supply

Fiscal policies that influence aggregate supply are different from policies that influence aggregate demand, as they do not always require tradeoffs between price levels and output. That is the good news. The bad news is that **supply-side fiscal policies** require more time to work than do demand-side fiscal policies. The focus of fiscal policy and aggregate supply is on long-run economic growth.

**Supply-side fiscal policies:** Policies that focus on shifting the long-run aggregate supply curve to the right, expanding the economy without increasing inflationary pressures. Unlike policies to increase aggregate demand, supply-side policies take longer to have an impact on the economy.

Figure 7 shows the impact that fiscal policy can have on the economy over the long run. The goal of these fiscal policies is to shift the long-run aggregate supply curve to the right, here from $LRAS_0$ to $LRAS_1$. This shift moves the economy's full employment equilibrium from point *a* to point *b*, thereby expanding full-employment output while keeping inflation in check. In Figure 7, the price level declines as output expands. In practice, this would be an unusual, though by no means impossible, result of fiscal policies. If, for example, aggregate demand remained the same, the price level would fall. But this is rarely the case because aggregate demand typically expands as the economy grows, keeping prices from falling.

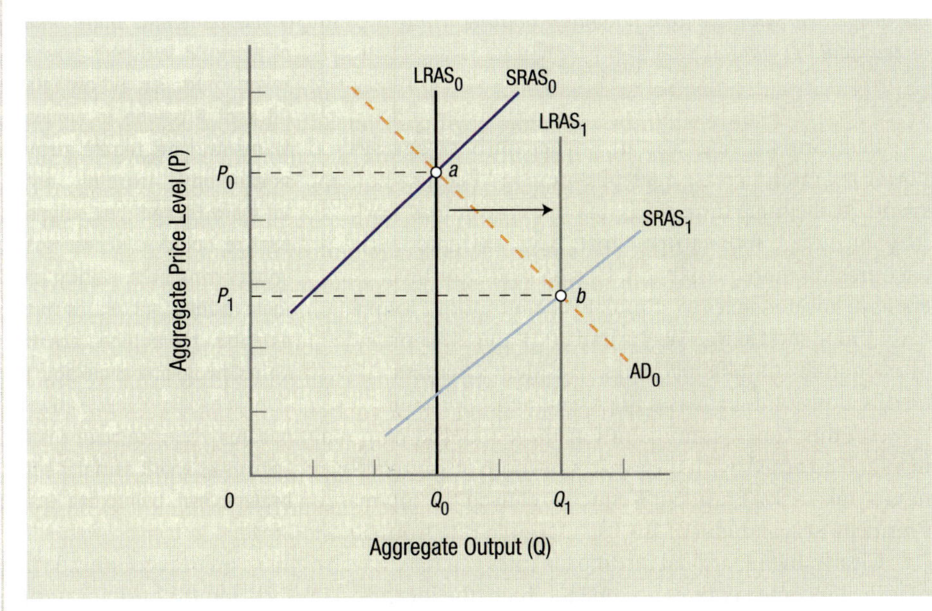


**FIGURE 7—Fiscal Policy and Aggregate Supply**

The ultimate goal of fiscal policy directed at aggregate supply is to shift the long-run aggregate supply curve from $LRAS_0$ to $LRAS_1$. This moves the economy's full employment equilibrium from point *a* to point *b*, expanding output while keeping inflation in check. With these fiscal policies, the inflationary pressures are reduced as output expands, but these policies take a longer time to have an impact.

Figure 7 may well reflect what happens in general as the world economy embraces trade and globalization. Improvements in technology and communications increase productivity to the point that global long-run aggregate supply shifts outward. These changes, along with freer trade, help increase economic growth and keep inflation low.

Just what fiscal policies will allow the economy to expand without generating price pressures? First, there are the government policies advocated by economists Robert Lucas and Paul Romer, the architects of modern growth theory, that we examined earlier. These policies encourage investment in human capital (education) and policies that encourage the development and transfers of new technologies. Second, there are the fiscal policies that focus on reducing tax rates. Third, there are policies that promote investment in new capital equipment, encourage investment in research and development, and trim burdensome business regulations. These policies are intended to expand the supply curves of all businesses and industries.

## Infrastructure Spending

Modern growth theory suggests governments can do a lot to create the right environment to encourage economic growth. We already have seen the benefits of building and maintaining a nation's infrastructure, including roads, bridges, dams, and communications networks, or setting up a fair and efficient legal system and stable financial system. Lucas and Romer have shown that the higher the levels of human capital and the easier technology is transferred to other firms and industries (the public good aspect of technology), the more robust is economic growth. Thus, they stress the long-run growth benefits of things such as higher education and research and development.

## Reducing Tax Rates

*Macroeconomics in its original sense has succeeded: Its central problem of depression prevention has been solved. . . . There remain important gains in welfare from better fiscal policies, but I argue that these are gains from providing people with better incentives to work and save, not from better fine-tuning of spending flows. Taking U.S. performance over the past 50 years as a benchmark, the potential for welfare gains from better long-run, supply-side policies exceeds* by far *the potential from further improvements in short-run demand management.*

ROBERT LUCAS, JR. (2003)

*The best summary of supply-side economics I know was uttered by Charles Schultze, who some of you will know as former Chairman of the Council of Economic Advisers, and a former director of the budget. He said, "There is absolutely nothing wrong with supply-side economics that dividing by ten wouldn't cure."*

ROBERT SOLOW (2000)

Reducing tax rates has an impact on both aggregate demand and aggregate supply. Lower tax rates increase aggregate demand because households now have more money to spend. At the same time, lower tax rates mean that workers' take-home wages rise and this may encourage more work effort. Also, entrepreneurial profits are taxed at lower rates, encouraging more people to take risks and start businesses. At different times, policymakers have lowered taxes to stimulate consumption: John F. Kennedy reduced tax rates in the early 1960s and George W. Bush in 2001 and 2008 provided tax rebates to taxpayers as part of economic stimulus packages. President Obama's 2009 stimulus program included tax credits along with increases in government spending.

At other times, administrations have reduced marginal tax rates, the rate paid on the next dollar earned, with the express purpose of stimulating incentives to work and for business to take risks. President Kennedy reduced the top marginal rate from 70% to 50%, and President Reagan reduced the top marginal rate from 50% to 28%.

Clearly, high marginal income tax rates can have adverse effects on the economy. When marginal income tax rates become too high, the incentives to work and for business to take on added risk can be harmed. This is the economic rationale for reducing tax rates.

Unfortunately, this economic rationale has become clouded by a political dimension because "supply-side economics" became associated with a political movement in the 1980s.

As the quotes by the two Nobel Prize winners Robert Lucas and Robert Solow illustrate, there is still considerable controversy regarding the benefits of the supply-side approach to macroeconomic fiscal policy. The supply-side movement that resulted in the marginal tax rate reductions in the 1980s by the Reagan administration was partially driven by reference to a simple tax revenue curve drawn by economist Arthur Laffer.

## The Laffer Curve

Economist Arthur Laffer first drew the curve in the photo below for a member of Congress to illustrate how reducing tax *rates* could increase tax *revenues*. The curve plots hypothetical tax revenues at various income tax rates and has become known as the **Laffer curve**. If tax rates are zero, tax revenues will be zero as well. If rates are 100%, revenues will again be zero, since there will be no incentive to earn income; everything just gets taxed away. In between these two extreme tax rates, tax revenues will be positive, reaching their maximum at point *E*.

**Laffer curve:** Plots hypothetical tax revenues at various income tax rates. If tax rates are zero, tax revenues will be zero; if rates are 100%, revenues will also be zero. As tax rates rise from zero, revenues rise, reach a maximum, and then decline.

AP Photo

Art Laffer with the graph that bears his name. The Laffer curve plots hypothetical tax revenues at various income tax rates. If tax rates are zero, tax revenue will be zero. If rates are 100%, revenue will also be zero, since there will be no incentive to earn income; it would just be taxed away. In between these two extremes, tax revenues will be positive, reaching their maximum at point *E*. If the economy is somewhere around point *C*, raising tax rates would reduce tax revenues, whereas lowering tax rates would increase tax revenues.

The Laffer curve further suggests that if the economy is at point *B*, policymakers can increase tax revenues by raising tax rates. When Laffer developed the curve in the 1980s, however, he argued that the economy was found somewhere around point *C*, where further raising tax rates would reduce tax revenues. He felt that the incentives to work and produce were being hampered by high federal marginal income tax rates, which topped 50% in some cases. If you already earn a high income, what incentive do you have to work more if Uncle Sam is going to take away 50% of your added earnings? (This is to say nothing about the state and local taxes you must pay plus Social Security taxes.)

The Laffer curve has something to say about the disincentive effects of high marginal tax rates. But critics zeroed in on two things. First, was the shape of the Laffer curve correct? If the curve were flatter, then the effects of lowering tax rates would be less. Second, how could we be sure where we were on the Laffer curve? These are tough questions to answer. Now throw in political considerations, with those on the political right looking for ways to limit government by reducing government revenue and those on the political left looking for ways to increase government spending and government revenue, and one can imagine how heated the discussion became in the 1980s, and can see why this controversy creates a partisan divide in Washington.

## *Issue:* Do High Marginal Income Tax Rates Affect the Labor Supply of Women?

**In the 1960s** and 1970s, women who were married to successful men found it difficult to justify working when income taxes (state, local, and federal) and Social Security taxes claimed well over half of their entire salaries. In the mid-1980s, the Reagan administration reduced top marginal income tax rates to 28%, making second incomes more valuable. Three decades ago women were more likely to be secondary earners and not the primary earner in the household. Reducing marginal tax rates had an impact on their decision whether to work or not. This raised the incentive for married women to work. But how much did these lowered marginal tax rates lead to more women joining the work force?

The figure shows labor force participation rates (LFPR) for women over age 20 and between 16 and 19, along with the top marginal tax rates since 1970. Women over 20 entered the labor force in increasing numbers in the 1970s, and this trend accelerated after the Reagan marginal tax rate cuts. The LFPR for women age 16 to 19 dropped as marginal rates were reduced, possibly encouraging women to extend their education beyond high school. With lower tax rates, the return from this added investment is greater. Today, more women attend college than men.

Two people now work in over half of all American families, and the LFPR of women has risen markedly over the last several decades. How much of this resulted from reduced marginal income tax rates? Clearly, part of the increase in the LFPR of women has been due to changing social norms and expansion of educational and occupational opportunities for women. Also, the LFPR for working age women has been steadily rising from 30% just after World War II to roughly 60% today. Economist Jonathan Gruber has summarized the evidence and concluded, "For secondary earners, each 1% rise in after-tax wages increases labor supply from 0.5% to 1%. Most of the response of secondary earners comes from the decision to work at all . . .". However, it is still difficult to determine the precise effects of the Reagan tax cuts on economic incentives.

Source: Jonathan Gruber, *Public Finance and Public Policy* (New York: Worth Publishers), 2005, p. 590.

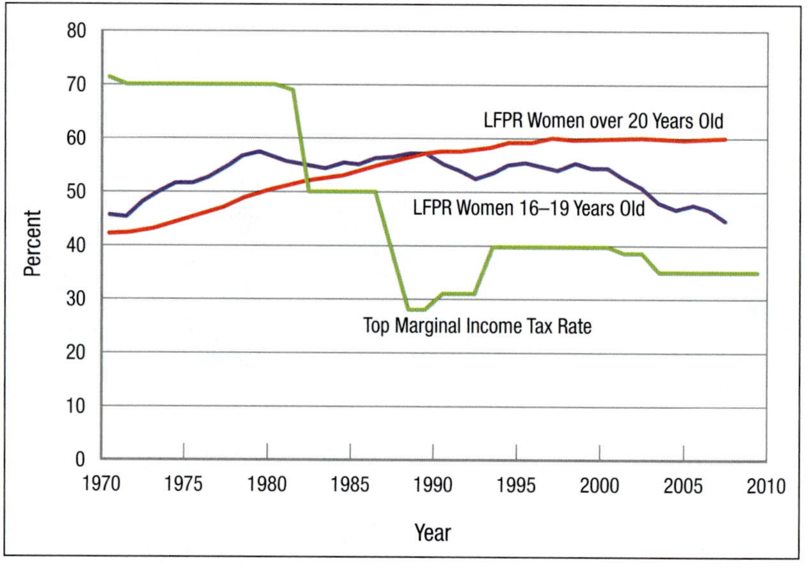


## Expanding Investment and Reducing Regulations

We have already seen how closely standards of living are tied to productivity. Investment increases the capital with which labor works, thereby increasing productivity. Rising productivity drives increased economic growth and raises the average standard of living, shifting the long-run aggregate supply curve to the right.

Investment can be encouraged by such policies as investment tax credits (direct reductions in taxes for new investment) and more rapid depreciation schedules for plant and equipment. When a firm can expense (depreciate) its capital equipment over a shorter period of time, it cuts its taxes now rather than later, and so earns a higher return on the capital now. Similarly, government grants for basic research help firms increase their budgets for research and development, which results in new products and technologies brought to market.

Nowhere is this impact more evident than in the health care field. The Human Genome Project, largely supported by public funds, is already enabling new medicines to be developed at a much faster rate than previously. And beyond the obvious benefits this has for the people who require such medicines, investments of this sort pay dividends for the entire economy. As health care improves, workers' absentee rates are less and productivity rises.

Another way of increasing long-run aggregate supply involves repealing unnecessarily onerous regulations that simply hamper business and add to costs. Clearly, some regulation of business activities is needed, as the recent financial industry meltdown has shown. Still, these regulations should be subjected to rigorous cost-benefit analysis. Otherwise, excessive regulations end up simply adding to the costs of the products we buy, without yielding significant benefits. Examples of excessively regulated industries have included trucking and the airlines. When these industries were deregulated in the 1980s, prices fell and both industries expanded rapidly. Today, some economists argue that the Federal Drug Administration's drug approval process is too long and costly; bringing a new drug to market can cost over $1 billion.

Fiscal policies to increase aggregate supply are promoted mainly through the government's encouragement of human capital development and technology improvements, its power to tax, its ability to promote investment in infrastructure and research, and the degree and efficiency of regulation. Cutting marginal tax rates, offering investment tax credits, and offering grants for research are the favored policies. The political fervor of the 1980s supply-side movement has largely dissipated as marginal income tax rates have declined. But fiscal policies to encourage growth in long-run aggregate supply are still an important part of the government's long-term fiscal policy arsenal.

**CHECKPOINT**

### FISCAL POLICY AND AGGREGATE SUPPLY

- The goal of fiscal policies that influence aggregate supply is to shift the long-run aggregate supply curve to the right.
- Modern growth theory stresses the importance of expanding long-run aggregate supply through higher investments in human capital and a focus on technological infrastructure with "public good" benefits.
- The Laffer curve suggested that reducing tax rates could lead to higher revenues in some cases.
- Other fiscal policies to increase long-run aggregate supply include providing incentives for business investment and reducing burdensome regulation.
- The major limitation of fiscal policies to influence long-run aggregate supply is that they take a longer time to have an impact.

**QUESTIONS:** In 1962 at a speech before the Economic Club of New York, President Kennedy argued that ". . . it is a paradoxical truth that taxes are too high today and tax revenues are too low—and the soundest way to raise revenues in the long run is to cut rates now." Is President Kennedy's argument consistent with supply side economics? Why or why not?

Answers to the Checkpoint questions can be found at the end of this chapter.

## Implementing Fiscal Policy

Implementing fiscal policy is often a complex and time-consuming process. Three disparate groups—the Senate, House, and the executive branch—must collectively agree on specific spending and tax policies. Ideally, these decisions are made in the open with the public fully informed. The complexities of the budgeting process and its openness (not a bad thing in itself) give rise to several inherent difficulties. We will briefly consider some problems having to do with the timing of fiscal decisions and the crowding-out effect, after first looking at the automatic stabilization mechanisms contained in the federal budgeting process.

### Automatic Stabilizers

There is a certain degree of stability built into the U.S. macroeconomic system. Tax revenues and transfer payments are the two principal **automatic stabilizers**; without any overt action by Congress or other policymakers, these two components of the federal budget expand or contract in ways that help counter movements of the business cycle.

When the economy is growing at a solid rate, tax receipts rise, since individuals and firms are increasing their taxable incomes. At the same time, transfer payments decline, because fewer people require welfare or unemployment assistance. Rising tax revenues and

**Automatic stabilizers:** Tax revenues and transfer payments automatically expand or contract in ways that reduce the intensity of business fluctuations without any overt action by Congress or other policymakers.

declining transfer payments have contractionary effects, so in this case, they act as a brake to slow the growth of GDP, helping to keep the economy from overheating, or keeping it from generating inflationary pressures. When the economic boom ends, and the economy goes into a downturn, the opposite happens: Tax revenues decline and transfer payments rise. These added funds getting pumped into the economy help cushion the impact of the downturn, not just for the recipients of transfer payments, but for the economy as a whole.

The income tax is a powerful stabilizer because of its progressivity. When incomes fall, tax revenues fall faster since people do not just pay taxes on smaller incomes, but they pay taxes at lower rates as their incomes fall. Disposable income, in other words, falls more slowly than aggregate income. But when the economy is booming, tax revenues rise faster than income, thereby withdrawing spending from the economy. This helps to slow the growth in income, thus reducing the threat of an inflationary spiral.

The key point to remember here is that automatic stabilizers reduce the intensity of business fluctuations. Automatic stabilizers do not eliminate fluctuations in the business cycle, but they render business cycles smoother and less chaotic. Automatic stabilizers act on their own, whereas discretionary fiscal policy requires overt action by policymakers, and this fact alone creates difficulties.

## Fiscal Policy Timing Lags

Using discretionary fiscal policy to smooth the short-term business cycle is a challenge because of several lags associated with its implementation. First, most of the macroeconomic data that policymakers need to enact the proper fiscal policies are not available until at least one quarter (three months) after the fact. Even then, key figures often get revised for the next quarter or two. The **information lag**, therefore, creates a one- to six-month period before informed policymaking can even begin.

**Information lag:** The time policymakers must wait for economic data to be collected, processed, and reported. Most macroeconomic data are not available until at least one quarter (three months) after the fact.

**Recognition lag:** The time it takes for policymakers to confirm that the economy is trending in or out of a recession. Short-term variations in key economic indicators are typical and sometimes represent nothing more than randomness in the data.

**Decision lag:** The time it takes Congress and the administration to decide on a policy once a problem is recognized.

**Implementation lag:** The time required to turn fiscal policy into law and eventually have an impact on the economy.

Compounding this lag, even if the most recent data suggest the economy is trending into a recession, it may take several quarters to confirm this fact. Short-term (month-to-month or quarter-to-quarter) variations in key indicators are common and sometimes represent nothing more than randomness in the data. This **recognition lag** is one reason recessions and recoveries are often well under way before policymakers fully acknowledge a need for action on their parts.

Third, once policymakers recognize that the economy has turned downward, fiscal policy requires a long and often contentious legislative process, referred to as a **decision lag**. Not all legislators have the same goals for the economy, so any new government spending must first survive an arduous trip through the political sausage machine. Once some new policy has become law, it often requires months of planning, budgeting, and implementation to set up a new program. This process, the **implementation lag**, rarely consumes *less* than 18 to 24 months.

The problem these lags pose is clear: By the time the fiscal stimulus meant to jump-start a sputtering economy kicks in, the economy may already be on the mend. And if so, the exercise of fiscal policy can compound the effects of the business cycle by overstimulating a patient that is already recovering.

Some of these lags can be reduced by expediting spending already approved for existing programs rather than implementing new programs. This was the approach Congress and the administration wanted to take with the 2009 stimulus package. Congress allocated part of the increased spending to "shovel-ready" projects to reduce the time for this spending to have an impact on the economy. Also, the lags associated with tax changes are much shorter, given that new rates can go into withholding tables and take effect within weeks of enactment. Therefore, policymakers often include tax changes because of their shorter implementation lags.

## Crowding-Out Effect

**Crowding-out effect:** Arises from deficit spending requiring the government to borrow, which drives up interest rates, which in turn reduces consumer spending and business investment.

The **crowding-out effect** of fiscal policy arises from deficit spending, which requires the government to borrow. This borrowing can drive up interest rates. A greater demand for loanable funds, whether by the government or the private sector, means higher interest rates. The result of these higher interest rates is often reduced consumer spending on

## *Issue:* How Big Should Government Be?

**Often, fiscal policy** debates have little to do with the state of the macroeconomy. Underlying all the rhetoric about the economic benefits or dangers of tax cuts, budget deficits, and spending priorities lies a long-standing philosophical debate about the proper size of government. As a rule, those on the left of the political spectrum favor a larger and more active government, while those on the right are constantly looking for ways to limit the size and power of the government.

The figure shows federal receipts and spending as a percentage of GDP from the 1970s through the present. Throughout the 1970s, the 1980s, and much of the 1990s, spending significantly exceeded tax receipts; spending was usually more than 20% of GDP, and taxes barely topped 18%. It was only the collapse of the Soviet Bloc in the late 1980s—which permitted a decrease in defense spending, led to the stock market boom of the late 1990s, and boosted federal capital gains tax revenues—that finally brought government spending back into line with tax receipts.

The resulting government surpluses were brief. The bull market collapsed in 2000, and along with tax rate cuts, caused a steep decline in tax revenues, while the mini-recession and national security concerns that dogged the opening years of this century increased the demand for government spending. The predictable result has been rising deficits. With the aging of the population, moreover, federal spending will undoubtedly grow as a percent of GDP as the proportion of the population receiving Social Security and Medicare increases, and the proportion of those of working age decreases.

Increases in government spending can help an economy during a recession, and an economy facing strong growth can afford to cut back in government spending. The robust growth the economy experienced during the 1980s and 1990s accrued during a period when the trend of federal government outlays as a percent of GDP was declining and revenues were slowly rising.

Dick Palulian/Getty Images

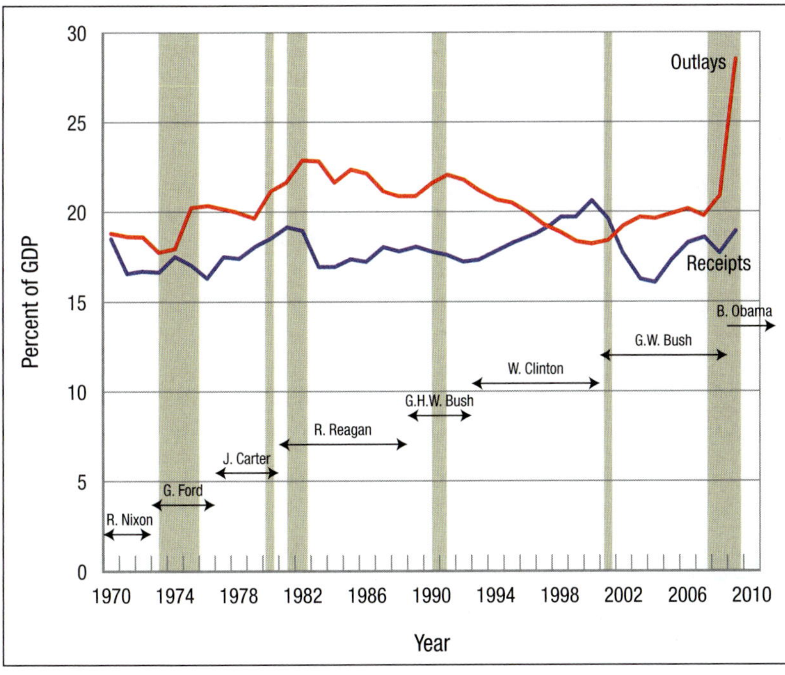


Those on the political right point to this period and argue that minimal government interference with market activities led to higher economic growth and living standards. Those on the political left look at this period and argue that income inequality increased and set the stage for the mess we're in now. They prefer to have government provide more services and level the field with higher taxes on those with high incomes.

The deep 2008–2009 recession has significantly widened the spread between outlays and receipts, as the new administration and Congress have pushed the deficit to new heights. Bringing outlays back to historic levels as the economy grows will be a challenge because Congress will have to determine what programs are going to be cut.

Put another way, which voters are going to be hurt? So there is a natural tendency to spend more and more. The real question, year after year, is how much more? Government spending is often a blunter tool of fiscal policy than policymakers might hope.

durable goods such as cars or refrigerators, often bought on credit, and reduced business investment. While deficit spending is usually expansionary, its impact can be partially offset by reductions in private spending.

When an economy is at full employment and private borrowers are already competing vigorously for funds, we would expect the crowding-out effect to be large. In a severe recession, when consumers are not buying durable goods and firms do not feel much like borrowing for the sake of investing anyway, the crowding-out effect will be less pronounced. When crowding-out is minimal, fiscal policy is at its most powerful.

With current budget deficits in the trillions of dollars, the question is how much leeway fiscal policymakers have to cut taxes. Will they be forced to raise taxes regardless of the state of the economy? This action we now know could have perverse effects if taxes are raised during a recession. What will be the impact on the economy if we continue to run huge budget deficits at the federal level and significantly increase the national debt? That is the focus of the next chapter.

**CHECKPOINT**

### IMPLEMENTING FISCAL POLICY

- Automatic stabilizers reduce the intensity of business fluctuations. When the economy is booming, tax revenues are rising and unemployment compensation and welfare payments are falling, dampening the boom. When the economy enters a recession, tax revenues fall and transfer payments rise, cushioning the decline. This happens automatically.
- Fiscal policymakers face information lags (the time it takes to collect, process, and provide data on the economy), recognition lags (the time required to see that a recession has in fact begun), decision lags (the time it takes for Congress and the administration to decide on a policy), and implementation lags (the time required by Congress to pass a law and see it put in place).
- These lags can often result in government policy being mistimed. For example, expansionary policy taking effect when the economy is well into a recovery or failing to take effect when a recession is underway can make stabilization worse.
- Crowding-out occurs when the government runs a deficit and then sells bonds to finance the deficit. This drives interest rates up and reduces private investment. Lower investment now means reduced income and output in the future.

**QUESTION:** Until we entered a deep recession in 2008, we rarely heard Congress discuss the budget in terms of fiscal policy (passing a spending and taxing package for macroeconomic purposes). Most of the discussion is on particular spending priorities for specific programs and bringing home projects for each politician's district. Would it be fair to say that Congress essentially abandoned fiscal policy and left macroeconomic stabilization to the Federal Reserve and the setting of monetary policy?

Answers to the Checkpoint question can be found at the end of this chapter.

## Key Concepts

Discretionary spending, p. 479
Mandatory spending, p. 479
Discretionary fiscal policy, p. 479
Expansionary fiscal policy, p. 482
Contractionary fiscal policy, p. 484
Supply-side fiscal policies, p. 485
Laffer curve, p. 487
Automatic stabilizers, p. 489
Information lag, p. 490
Recognition lag, p. 490
Decision lag, p. 490
Implementation lag, p. 490
Crowding-out effect, p. 490

# Chapter Summary

## Fiscal Policy and Aggregate Demand

Governments try to influence aggregate demand by using fiscal policy. The government's main fiscal policy tools are spending on goods and services, transfer payments, and taxes.

Fiscal policy can be powerful because of the multiplier effect. The multiplier tells us that added government spending will raise equilibrium income and output by the multiplier times the added spending and vice versa.

The exercise of discretionary fiscal policy involves changing government spending, transfer payments, or tax policies with the short-run goal of moving the economy toward full employment, encouraging economic growth, or controlling inflation.

When government fiscal policy is added to our model of the economy, equilibrium is achieved when government spending plus business investment (*injections*) into the economy equal saving plus taxes (*withdrawals*); thus, at equilibrium, G + I = S + T.

A change in government spending (G) will cause short-run equilibrium income and output to rise or fall by the spending change times the multiplier. The effect of a change in taxes (T) is not as large. But in the longer run, tax changes might have a larger impact on the economy.

Expansionary fiscal policies include increasing government spending; increasing transfer payments such as Social Security, unemployment compensation, and welfare payments; and decreasing taxes. These policies put more money into the hands of consumers and business. The opposite policies are contractionary, taking money out of the hands of consumers and business.

The multiplier has its full effect when an economy is in a depression or a deep recession. Price pressures will be small, and thus the effects of spending increases are multiplied throughout the economy, without being absorbed by higher prices. When the same economy begins to recover, its short-run aggregate supply curve will be positively sloped, and thus higher prices will absorb some of the effects of increased spending. When the economy reaches full employment, its long-run aggregate supply curve will be vertical. Spending increases will simply raise the price level without raising equilibrium income or output. When an economy moves beyond full employment, driving up wages and prices, an inflationary spiral sets in.

Exercising demand-side fiscal policy requires tradeoffs between output and price levels except when the economy is in a deep recession. Output can be increased, but only by raising the price level, or prices can be stabilized, but only by reducing output and increasing unemployment.

## Fiscal Policy and Aggregate Supply

Supply-side policies do not require such tradeoffs; they can expand output without raising prices. Supply-side policies, however, take much longer to work than demand-side policies.

The goal of supply-side economics is to shift the long-run aggregate supply curve to the right, thereby expanding output without raising the price level, and perhaps even lowering prices. Some of the specific policies that might help achieve this goal include reducing tax rates, encouraging investment in new capital equipment, encouraging investment in research and development, and ending burdensome regulations.

Economist Arthur Laffer argued that high marginal tax rates discourage working. Lowering tax rates might increase tax revenues. Raising tax rates too high reduces tax revenues, because high marginal tax rates reduce the incentives to work and take risks.

## Implementing Fiscal Policy

Without overt action by policymakers, tax revenues and transfer payments expand or contract in ways that help counteract the movements of the business cycle. These are called automatic stabilizers. When the economy is growing briskly, tax receipts rise and transfer payments sink, withdrawing spending from the economy. This decrease in spending acts as a brake to slow the growth of GDP, keeping the economy from overheating. When the economy goes into recession, the opposite occurs.

Using fiscal policy to smooth out the short-term business cycle is difficult because of several lags associated with implementing it: an information lag, a recognition lag, a decision lag, and an implementation lag. Consequently, by the time fiscal policy is enacted, the economy may well have moved to a different point in the business cycle, where the policy enacted could be detrimental.

The crowding-out effect arises when the government engages in deficit spending, thereby driving up interest rates. Deficit spending has an expansionary effect on the economy, but this effect can be diminished by offsetting reductions in private spending.

## Questions and Problems

### Check Your Understanding

1. Explain why government spending theoretically gives a bigger boost to the economy than tax cuts.
2. Explain why increasing government purchases of goods and services is expansionary fiscal policy. Would increasing taxes or reducing transfer payments be contractionary or expansionary? Why?
3. Changes in tax rates affect both aggregate demand and aggregate supply. Explain why this is true.

### Apply the Concepts

4. A balanced budget amendment to the Constitution is introduced in Congress every so often. Congress would be required to balance the budget every year. What sort of problems would this introduce for policymakers and the economy? What would be the benefit of such an amendment?
5. The macroeconomy has shown less variability in the last several decades—GDP has fluctuated, but less violently than in the past. Would the fact that over one-quarter of the federal budget goes to Social Security and Medicare have any impact on the variations in GDP? Why or why not?
6. One argument often heard against using fiscal policy to tame the business cycle is that the lags associated with getting a fiscal policy implemented are so long that when the program is finally passed and implemented, the business cycle has moved on to the next phase and the new program may not be necessary and may even be potentially destabilizing at that point. Does this argument seem reasonable? What counterarguments can you make in support of using fiscal policy?
7. As mandatory federal spending becomes increasingly a larger share of the budget, should we worry that the economic stabilization aspects of fiscal policy are becoming so limited as to be ineffective?
8. Individual income tax rates vary from zero (if your income is low enough) to 35% (for high-income individuals). Explain how this progressive tax structure acts as an automatic stabilizer for the economy.
9. Our current personal income tax system is progressive: Income tax rates rise with rising incomes and are lower for low-income individuals. Some policymakers have favored a "flat tax" as a replacement to our modestly progressive income tax system. Most exemptions and deductions would be eliminated, and a single low tax rate would be applied to personal income. Would such a change in the tax laws alter the automatic stabilization characteristics of the personal income tax?

10. In the 2000 presidential election, candidate Bush's platform included a promise to cut income taxes. The economy entered a recession just after he was elected in 2001. In early 2001, Congress passed a tax cut package that included tax rate reductions and \$300 to \$600 rebates to all taxpayers. In general, was this an appropriate exercise of fiscal policy given that the economy was headed into a recession? Why?
11. During the late 1990s, the Clinton administration had very low deficits and actually ran three years of surpluses. As a result, interest rates were low and private investment was vibrant. When the government runs large deficits, as it has done since the early 2000s, interest rates inevitably rise, crowding-out private investment. In the aggregate demand and supply model, spending is spending; income and output rise the same amount no matter whether the government spent on goods and services or business spent on investment. Why then are economists concerned with the crowding-out of private investment?

## In the News

12. At the beginning of the 2001 recession, Robert Dunn, writing in the August 19, 2001, issue of the *New York Times,* noted that "an absurd debate is going on in Washington over who is to blame for the horrors of a declining federal budget surplus. The truth is that the fall in the surplus should be welcomed, given the current state of the economy, and politicians should be trying to take credit for it." Does Robert Dunn have it right? Why or why not?
13. The informal or underground economy operates off the books and typically for cash. Estimates of the underground economy in the United States are usually less than 10%. However, William Lewis (*The Power of Productivity,* 2004), reports that half of Brazil's workers labor in the "informal" sector. The Brazilian government represents nearly 40% of GDP, and corporations pay 85% of all taxes collected. Could lowering tax rates actually lead to higher tax revenues for the Brazilian government (a Laffer curve experiment)?
14. Referring to the 2001 recession, an editorial in *The Economist* titled "Restoring the Fiscal Option" (January 17, 2002) argued that "in the United States, 9 months after the recession began, Republicans and Democrats are quarrelling over which ill-conceived measures to include in their stimulus package—as if to prove right those who say that fiscal expansion always comes too late to be any use." Is that right? Is fiscal policy often too late to be helpful?

## Solving Problems

15. In late 2004, economists Gregory Mankiw and Matthew Weinzierl, using dynamic scoring that accounts for the added economic growth from tax cuts on tax revenue, concluded that tax cuts can be partially self-financing. Roughly 17% of the cut in labor taxes and roughly half of the cuts in capital gains taxes are recouped through economic growth. Looking back to the Laffer curve on page 487, is their study consistent with being at point *A, B, C,* or *D*?

# Answers to Questions in CheckPoints

## Check Point: Fiscal Policy and Aggregate Demand

Although the money would have hit the economy sooner, a significant portion of the proceeds would have been saved or used to pay existing bills, potentially limiting the stimulative impact of *added* spending. The other benefit of the infrastructure package is that by being spread out over several years, it won't just be a big jolt to the economy that ends as fast as it began. Thus, the impact on employment and business planning will likely be smoother.

## Check Point: Fiscal Policy and Aggregate Supply

In general, President Kennedy's statement is consistent with the arguments of supply-siders who feel that a reduction in tax rates will yield higher revenues, depending where tax rates are on the Laffer curve. When President Kennedy made his address, marginal tax rates were as high as 70%. Today, top marginal rates are 35%, so it is less clear that rate reductions will lead to higher long-run revenues.

## Check Point: Implementing Fiscal Policy

To some degree, Congress did leave macroeconomic stabilization to monetary policy and the Federal Reserve, a subject left to the next few chapters. Congress mostly focuses on what programs and services are needed and funds those programs, generally ignoring macroeconomic conditions unless they are quite bad. But once the 2008 recession deepened, Congress moved quickly to use fiscal policy to stimulate the economy.

# Federal Deficits and Public Debt

# 21

Randy Miramontez/Alamy

*Some people have compared the federal government to an infant: It has a limitless appetite at one end and no sense of responsibility at the other.*

—Todd Buchholz

**Alexander Hamilton,** Secretary of the Treasury in George Washington's administration, fought to establish a National Bank and to allow the federal government to borrow funds. His goal was to establish a powerful central government that would manage the economy and the money supply, promote industrialization, and finance public infrastructure projects such as roads and canals.

Thomas Jefferson, on the other hand, viewed public debt as a serious threat to the country and proposed that a balanced budget amendment be added to the Constitution.[1] Jefferson and other Democrats feared that deficit spending and a high national debt would encourage the national government to "subvert the national balance of society, by empowering the central administration to dole out financial favors that would enable it to dominate the legislature and to achieve, on behalf of itself and its allies in the moneyed aristocracy . . . a tyrannical preeminence over the rest of society."[2] A quick read of any newspaper is enough to see that, two centuries later, American politicians are still divided into those who take Hamilton's view of deficit spending and those who follow in Jefferson's footsteps.

[1] Arthur Benavie, *Deficit Hysteria: A Common Sense Look at America's Rush to Balance the Budget* (Westport, CT: Praeger), 1998, p. 16.

[2] Daniel Shaviro, *Do Deficits Matter?* (Chicago: University of Chicago Press), 1997, pp. 18–19.

**After studying this chapter you should be able to:**

- ☐ Define deficits and the national debt.
- ☐ Describe public choice analysis.
- ☐ Describe the various approaches to balancing budgets.
- ☐ Analyze the relationship between budget and trade deficits.
- ☐ Explain the difference between internally and externally held debt.
- ☐ Describe the crowding-out effect.
- ☐ Analyze the sustainability of federal deficits.

As federal deficits now go over $1 trillion each year, most of us have a little bit of Jefferson inside of us. We know that each of us cannot have our spending overwhelm our revenues year after year. There are recognized periods when we can run a deficit—going to college is one—yet each of us knows we cannot have such a spending imbalance for the rest of our lives. With our personal situations in mind, we tend to project this spending imbalance on the federal deficit. It makes most of us uneasy. How much is too much?

In this chapter, we are going to explore the issue of whether deficits and debt will eventually destroy the economy. First, we define what the public debt is, look at why deficits are persistent in our government, and then show what follows from a call to balance the budget. Second, we examine how deficits are financed, exploring the implications of the methods used today. Finally, we look at the burden of the public debt, especially on future generations, and we analyze the fiscal sustainability of the federal budget. By the time this chapter is finished, you should have a good sense of the effect that deficits and public debt have on the economy.

## Financing the Federal Government

We saw in the last chapter that discretionary fiscal policy may call for increased government spending or tax reductions during times of recession. When the economy is expanding so rapidly that it risks overheating, government spending cuts or a tax increase may be warranted.

In the late 1990s, some economists argued that spending should be reduced, taxes increased, or a contractionary monetary policy implemented to cool down an economy and stock market that were overheating. Their advice was partly heeded, in that tax rates were increased as the economy entered a boom, and the federal budget ended the 1990s in surplus. The recession of 2001, caused in part by the fall in the stock market and a reduction in investment, moved the budget back into deficit. Let's first define deficits, surpluses, and public debt before going on to consider if our government is prone to deficits.

### Defining Deficits and the National Debt

**Deficit:** The amount by which annual government spending exceeds tax revenues.

**Surplus:** The amount by which annual tax revenues exceed government expenditures.

A **deficit** is the amount by which annual government spending exceeds tax revenues. A **surplus** is the amount by which annual tax revenues exceed government expenditures. In 2000, the budget surplus was $236.4 billion. By 2002, tax cuts, a recession, and new commitments for national defense and homeland security had turned the budget surpluses of 1998–2001 into deficits—a deficit of roughly $250 billion for fiscal year 2007. The election of Barack Obama and a Democratic-controlled Congress, together with a deep recession in 2008–2009, changed the magnitude of the deficit picture again. Government intervention and support for the financial and automobile industries and a nearly $800 billion stimulus package to soften the recession resulted in a 2009 deficit of $1.5 trillion.

**Public debt:** The total accumulation of past deficits and surpluses; it includes Treasury bills, notes, and bonds, and U.S. savings bonds.

The **public debt**, or *national debt*, is the total accumulation of past deficits and surpluses. Gross public debt in 2009 was nearly $12 trillion, but public debt held by the public was only three-quarters of that amount (almost $8 trillion). Some agencies of government, such as the Social Security Administration, the Treasury Department, and the Federal Reserve, hold some debt; one agency of government owes money to another. Debt held by the public (including foreign governments) is debt that represents a claim on government assets, not simply intergovernmental transfers.

Figure 1 shows the public debt held by the public as a percentage of gross domestic product (GDP) since 1940. During World War II, public debt exceeded GDP. It then trended downward until the early 1980s, when public debt began to climb again. Public debt held by the public as a percentage of GDP fell from the mid-1990s until 2000, first because of growing budget surpluses in the late 1990s, then because of falling interest rates (what the government has to pay on the debt), but it has risen since then. Public debt held by the public (as opposed to government institutions) is now approaching 60% of GDP.

Public debt is held as U.S. Treasury securities, including Treasury bills, notes, bonds, and U.S. savings bonds. Treasury bills, or T-bills, as they are known, are short-term

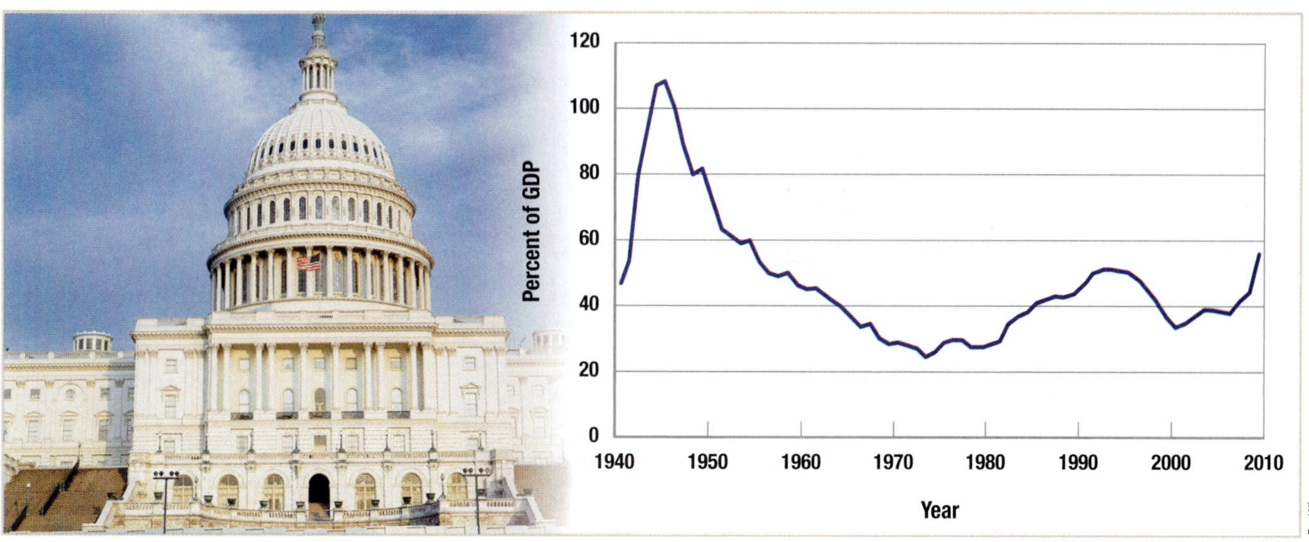


**FIGURE 1—Public Debt Held by the Public as a Percent of GDP**

The public debt as a percentage of GDP has varied considerably since 1940. During World War II, public debt exceeded GDP. It then trended downward until the early 1980s, when public debt began to climb again. Today, public debt held by the public (as opposed to government institutions) is approaching 60% of GDP.

instruments with a maturity period of a year or less that pay a specific sum at maturity. T-bills do not pay interest. Rather, they are initially sold at a discount, and their yields are then determined by the time to maturity and the discount. T-bills are the most actively traded securities in the U.S. economy, and they are highly liquid, providing the closest thing there is to risk-free returns.

Treasury notes are financial instruments issued for periods ranging from 1 to 10 years, whereas Treasury bonds have maturity periods exceeding 10 years. Both of these instruments have stated interest rates and are traded sometimes at discounts and sometimes at premiums. The discount or premium depends on interest rates and the coupon rates of the bonds.

Today, interest rates on the public debt are between 4% and 6%. This relatively low rate has not always been the case. In the early 1980s, interest rates varied from 11% to nearly 15%. Inflation was high and investors required high interest rates as compensation. When rates are high, government interest costs on the debt soar.

Interest on the debt as a percentage of GDP, as shown in Figure 2 on the next page, was steady from 1950 to 1980, hovering around 1.50%. This percentage more than doubled during the 1980s because of inflation, interest rates in the double digits, and rising budget deficits, along with a growing national debt. Since the mid-1990s, interest rates have dropped and deficits have fallen, even becoming surpluses for a short time. Consequently, interest as a percentage of GDP has declined to approach the level it was in the 1950s.

Now that we know what deficits and the public debt are, we can consider why deficits seem to persist in our government.

## Public Choice Analysis

Why has deficit spending become almost endemic to our system of government? What impact do deficits have on the size and character of the federal government? These are the sorts of questions being asked by public choice economists.

**Public choice theory** involves the economic analysis of public and political decision making. It looks at such issues as voting, the relationship between voting and policy outcomes, the impact of election incentives on politicians, the influence of special interest groups, rent-seeking behaviors, and the effects of "rational ignorance" (Why do people take so much time and effort to vote when their votes count for so little?).

**Public choice theory:** The economic analysis of public and political decision making, looking at issues such as voting, the impact of election incentives on politicians, the influence of special interest groups, and rent-seeking behaviors.

Public choice theorists often conclude that collective decision making is inherently flawed and inefficient. They view the government as a huge monopolist attempting to increase its size and power through higher taxes and other policies that end up devaluing its debt through unexpected inflation. Unanticipated inflation acts as a tax on debt holders as interest rates rise and bond values fall, creating capital losses.

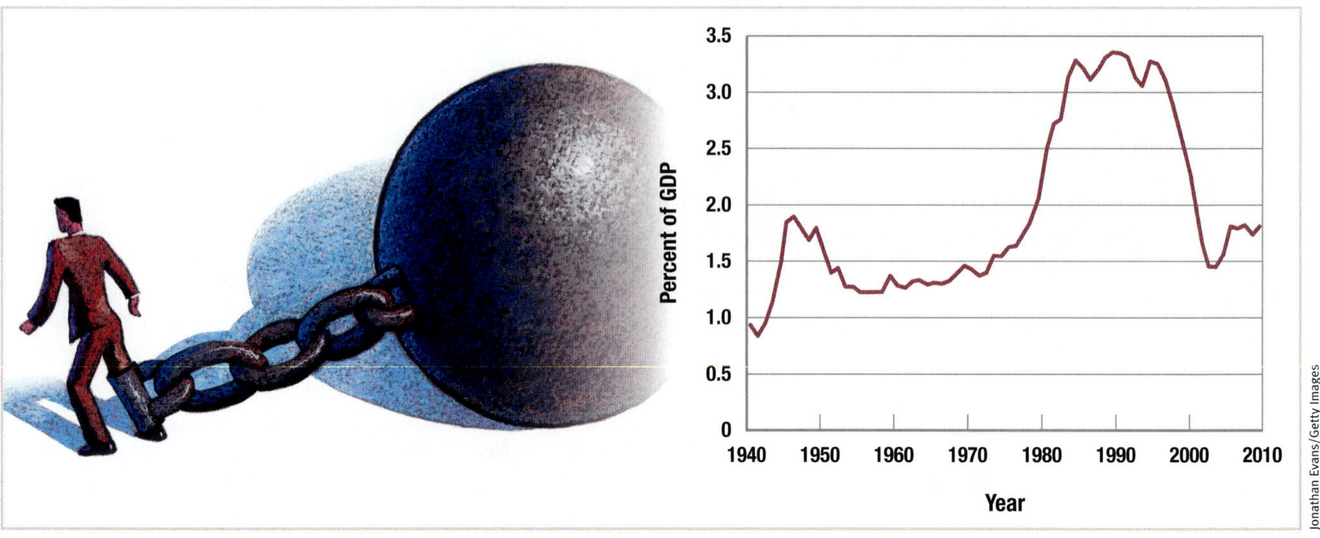


**FIGURE 2—Public Debt Interest as a Percent of GDP**

Interest on the debt as a percentage of GDP was steady from 1950 to 1980, hovering around 1.50%. This percentage more than doubled during the 1980s because of high inflation and high interest rates, along with growing budget deficits and a rising debt. Since the mid-1990s, interest as a percentage of GDP has declined to just above the level it was in the 1950s.

James Buchanan, considered the father of public choice theory, essentially fused the disciplines of economics and political science. He was awarded the Nobel Prize in 1986 for "his development of the contractual and constitutional bases for the theory of economic and political decision making." Buchanan's analysis assumes that politicians and bureaucrats consider their own self-interest when making public policy. In this sense, they behave no differently than other economic actors, and this means our public policies may not always be guided by the "public interest."

As economist Robert Hershey noted, "Public choice can be considered the doctrine of the invisible foot; a negative analogue to Adam Smith's wealth-creating invisible hand."[3] Buchanan contrasted Adam Smith's description of social benefits that arise from private individuals acting in their own self-interest with the harm that frequently results from politicians doing the same thing. Competition among individuals and firms for jobs, customers, and profits creates wealth, and thus it benefits the entire society. Self-interested politicians, however, often instigate government interventions that are harmful to the larger economy. Driven by their own desire for reelection, politicians frequently cave in to pressure from special interest groups in ways that magnify market imperfections. Public choice analysis, therefore, suggests that government action should be limited.

Public choice economists like Buchanan argue that deficit spending reduces the perceived cost of current government operations. The result is that taxpayers permit some programs to exist that they would oppose if required to pay the full cost today. But this situation, public choice economists charge, amounts to shifting the cost of government to the next generation. And this intergenerational burden shifting, they argue, has led to the steady expansion of the federal government.

Public choice analysis helps us to understand why deficits seem inevitable: We do not pay the full costs of today's programs. Keep in mind the intergenerational issue as we examine the implications of balancing the budget.

## Approaches to Federal Finance

Federal budget deficits have been the norm for the past 50 years, leading some observers to propose that the federal government, like state governments, should be required to balance its budget every year. Many economists argue that balancing the budget over the business cycle is a better approach, while still others have suggested that the federal

[3] Robert Hershey, "Man in the News; an Austere Scholar: James M. Buchanan," *New York Times*, October 17, 1986, p. D4.

government should focus on promoting full employment with stable prices, treating the budget deficit or surplus as a secondary concern. Let us examine each of these three approaches in greater detail.

## Annually Balanced Budget

That the federal government should have an **annually balanced budget**, which means it would have to equate its revenues and expenditures every year, was the prevailing economic wisdom before the 1930s. The massive unemployment of the Great Depression, however, along with the appearance of Keynes's *General Theory* in 1936, caused many economists and policymakers to rethink their views. Today, we know that balancing the federal budget yearly would undercut fiscal policies aimed at maintaining full employment.

**Annually balanced budget:** Federal expenditures and taxes would have to be equal each year. Annually balanced budgets tend to be procyclical.

When an economy begins to fall into recession, output, income, and employment all start to decline. Before long, tax revenues begin to fall, even as government spending increases because of rising unemployment, which triggers increased payments for unemployment compensation. Both of these anticyclical automatic mechanisms tend to move the federal budget toward a deficit. But this is a welcome trend, since reducing taxes or increasing spending at the expense of running a deficit is often the best response to a looming recession. Such an expansionary fiscal policy is most likely to dampen the effects of the recession and restore the economy to its potential growth rate.

To insist on balancing the budget as recession looms by reducing spending or increasing taxes, would mandate a contractionary policy that would undoubtedly worsen the economic situation and thus ultimately increase the deficit. This is essentially what happened in the early 1930s. Many economists believe contractionary policies aimed at balancing the budget turned what probably would have been a modest recession into the global Depression.

As a result, few economists today favor annually balancing the federal budget, as the result would be incompatible with countercyclical fiscal policy.

## Cyclically Balanced Budget

To get around the procyclical aspects of annually balancing the budget, some economists have recommended having a **cyclically balanced budget**: balancing the budget over the course of the business cycle. The basic idea is to restrict spending or raise taxes when the economy is booming. By slowing spending growth or raising tax rates as the economy approaches the peak of the business cycle, overheating is reduced. These measures prevent inflationary pressures from taking hold, thereby heading off the need later to enact extreme contractionary policy measures. Surpluses, moreover, should accumulate during boom periods that can be used to offset deficits during downturns and recessions, when deficit spending is appropriate.

**Cyclically balanced budget:** Balancing the budget over the course of the business cycle by restricting spending or raising taxes when the economy is booming and using these surpluses to offset the deficits that occur during recessions.

Balancing the budget over the business cycle is good in theory, and to an extent, this probably happens automatically as long as fiscal policy is held constant. When discretionary spending levels and tax rates are held reasonably stable, tax revenues will rise and spending will decline during booms, thereby creating either surpluses or smaller deficits. Conversely, tax revenues will fall and spending will rise during recessions, bringing on deficits. Automatic stabilizers, thus, tend to roughly equate spending and taxes over the course of the business cycle.

In practice, perfectly balancing the budget over the course of the business cycle is difficult and politically risky. Raising taxes during boom periods to create surpluses and dampen economic growth may be acceptable to the public and the political establishment, since everyone is more flexible during periods of economic expansion. Incomes are rising, so added taxes do not seem so onerous. And some of these added funds can be used to expand government services into areas of perceived need, while others are retained to build surpluses. But the political fact of life is that politicians are reluctant to raise taxes even when the economy is booming.

When recession arrives, however, the rhetorical knives are also sharpened and tax cuts and spending increases are called unfair. What is naturally occurring and what is needed to correct the recession become the subject of rhetoric.

In addition, different phases of the business cycle are not of equal length or severity. Historically, booms tend to last longer than recessions. This complicates balancing the federal budget over a given cycle. Furthermore, forecasting turning points in business cycles along with their uncertain duration and extent is nearly impossible. Finally, and most problematic for a long-term balanced budget, politicians are always looking for new ways to serve their constituencies and find it difficult to ever cut spending.

## Functional Finance

**Functional finance:** Essentially ignores the impact of the budget on the business cycle and focuses on fostering economic growth and stable prices, while keeping the economy as close as possible to full employment.

Economists who favor a **functional finance** approach to the federal budget believe the first priority of policymakers should be to keep the economy at full employment with stable prices. Whether the budget is in surplus or deficit is a secondary concern. Their view is that the government's primary macroeconomic responsibility is to foster economic growth and stable prices, while keeping the economy as close as possible to full employment.

The government's primary microeconomic job, meanwhile, is to provide those public goods and services that citizens want. These include national defense, a stable legal environment, and many other services we take for granted. Economists favoring a functional finance approach feel that if the government is successful in providing the right microeconomic mix and successful macroeconomic fiscal policies, deficits and surpluses will be unimportant. Rapidly growing and fully employed economies do not have significant public debt or deficit issues.

In sum, balancing the budget annually or over the business cycle may be either counterproductive or difficult to do. Furthermore, from public choice theory, we saw that balancing the budget is even more difficult when we consider politicians' incentives to spend and not raise taxes. Budget deficits begin to look like a normal occurrence in our political system.

### CHECKPOINT

#### FINANCING THE FEDERAL GOVERNMENT

- A deficit is the amount that government spending exceeds tax revenue in a particular year.
- The national debt is the total accumulation of past deficits and surpluses.
- Public choice analysis suggests that collective decision making is inherently flawed and inefficient, and deficit spending reduces the perceived cost of the current government operations.
- Approaches to financing the federal government include annually balancing the budget, balancing the budget over the business cycle, and ignoring the budget deficit and focusing on promoting full employment and stable prices.

**QUESTION:** Is the absolute size of the national debt or the national debt as a percent of GDP the best measure of its importance to our economy? Explain.

Answers to the Checkpoint question can be found at the end of this chapter.

# Financing Debt and Deficits

Seeing as how deficits may be persistent, we now turn to the methods used by the federal government to finance debt and deficits. How does the government deal with debt, and what does this imply for the economy?

Government deals with debt in two ways. It can either borrow or sell assets. In borrowing, government sells bonds to government agencies, the Federal Reserve (the central bank of the United States, which we will cover in detail in the next chapter), and the public.

## The Government Budget Constraint

Given its power to print money and collect taxes, the federal government cannot go bankrupt. But it does face what economists call a **government budget constraint**:

**Government budget constraint:** The government budget is limited by the fact that $G - T = \Delta M + \Delta B + \Delta A$.

$$G - T = \Delta M + \Delta B + \Delta A$$

where

$G$ = government spending

$T$ = tax revenues, thus $(G - T)$ is the federal budget deficit

$\Delta M$ = the change in the money supply (selling bonds to the Federal Reserve)

$\Delta B$ = the change in bonds held by public entities, domestic and foreign

$\Delta A$ = the sales of government assets

The left side of the equation, $G - T$, represents government spending minus tax revenues. A positive $(G - T)$ value is a budget deficit, and a negative $(G - T)$ value represents a budget surplus. The right side of the equation shows how government finances its deficit. It can sell bonds to the Federal Reserve, sell bonds to the public, or sell assets. Let's look at each of these options.

## The Role of the Federal Reserve

First, the government can sell bonds to government agencies, especially the Federal Reserve. When the Federal Reserve buys bonds, it is exchanging cash for bonds. Where does the Federal Reserve get the money to pay for the government's bonds? As we will see in the next chapter, the Federal Reserve creates it out of thin air: it credits the government's account. This part of the government's debt is therefore "monetized." With the Federal Reserve pumping new money into the money supply, the government is financing the deficit by "printing money" ($\Delta M > 0$).

If the Federal Reserve does not purchase the bonds, they may be sold to the public, including corporations, banks, mutual funds, individuals, and foreign entities. This also has the effect of financing the government's deficit ($\Delta B > 0$).

Asset sales ($\Delta A > 0$) represent only a small fraction of government finance in the United States. These sales include auctions of telecommunications spectra and offshore oil leases. Europe and many developing nations have used asset sales, or privatization, in recent years to bolster sagging government revenues and to encourage efficiency and development in the case where a government-owned industry is sold.

Thus, when the government runs a deficit, it must borrow funds from somewhere, assuming it does not sell assets. If the government borrows from the public, the quantity of publicly held bonds will rise; if it borrows from the Federal Reserve, the quantity of money in circulation will rise.

## Budget and Trade Deficits

In earlier chapters, we learned that when an economy is at equilibrium (using budget and national income accounting arithmetic), all injections and withdrawals are equal, thus:

$$G + I + X = T + S + M$$

In other words, government spending plus investment plus exports equals taxes plus savings plus imports.

By subtracting $T$ from each side, we get

$$G - T + X + I = S + M$$

Now subtracting $I$ and $X$ from both sides and regrouping, this leaves

$$G - T = (S - I) + (M - X)$$

If the economy is at equilibrium, therefore, budget deficits (a positive number on the left side of the equation) must be made up by private savings ($S > I$) or a trade deficit ($M > X$). **Budget and trade deficits** are linked.

**Budget and trade deficits:** These are related by the following equation: $G - T = (S - I) + (M - X)$. So, budget deficits must be covered by net domestic saving (private plus corporate) or by net foreign saving (imports minus exports).

## Implications of Deficit Financing in an Open Economy

Assume for a moment that investment and saving are equal, such that $(S - I) = 0$. With this constraint in place, the link between budget deficits and trade deficits becomes clear. If $T > G$ (a surplus) then $(M - X)$ must also be in surplus ($X > M$). Conversely, when the budget turns to deficit ($T < G$), a trade deficit will follow ($X < M$).

The intuition here is this: If the United States runs a budget deficit, who buys its bonds? If savings and investments are equal, then bond purchases have to come from abroad. When we import, we send dollars abroad to pay for the goods and services we obtain. These dollars held abroad wind up as bond purchases. For there to be a surplus of dollars held abroad to soak up these U.S. deficit bonds, imports must be greater than exports, which is the definition of a trade deficit. Thus, budget deficits and trade deficits are linked.

Next, assume that exports and imports are equal ($X = M$) such that the trade balance is zero. Budget deficits ($G > T$) must be met by higher private saving ($S > I$). This illustrates the crowding-out effect of government deficits. If $G$ grows, with $T$ and $S$ remaining constant, investment must fall. Increased deficit spending by the government, therefore, crowds out private investment.

All this tells us that rising federal deficits must be paid for with rising trade deficits, rising private savings, falling investment, or some combination of these three. For example, in 2000 the government ran a *surplus* of nearly $200 billion in the National Income and Product Accounts and the trade deficit was under $400 billion, with investment exceeding saving by nearly $600 billion. Contrast this with 2005, when the government ran a $300 billion *deficit*, the trade deficit exceeded $700 billion, and investment was just $400 billion more than saving. During this five-year period, our federal deficit worsened, our trade deficit became larger, and our investment-to-saving ratio worsened, just as the simple equation above suggests.

What do trillion-dollar federal deficits for the next several years portend for the economy? First, trade deficits have been falling as imports have declined. As a result, these federal deficits will necessarily have to be paid for by saving exceeding investment by a large amount. If $(G - T)$ is large and $(M - X)$ is small, then $(S - I)$ must be large, so saving must exceed investment. Households will save more and their spending will essentially be replaced by government spending. This happened in 2009 as households cut spending and savings rose.

We have seen two key ideas in this section. First, to finance the deficit, government can either borrow or sell assets, but it is limited by the budget constraint. Second, rising deficits must be paid for by a combination of rising trade deficits, rising private savings, and falling investment.

**CHECKPOINT**

### FINANCING DEBT AND DEFICITS

- The federal government's deficit must be financed by selling bonds to the Federal Reserve ("printing money" or "monetizing the deficit"), by selling bonds to the public, or by selling government assets. This is known as the government budget constraint.
- Budget deficits and trade deficits are related by the following equation: $G - T = (S - I) + (M - X)$. So budget deficits must be covered by net domestic saving (private plus corporate) or by net foreign saving (imports minus exports).

**QUESTION:** The deep recession in 2009 caused federal policymakers to run a deficit of $1.410 trillion, which included the nearly $800 billion stimulus package. Gross private domestic investment for 2009 was $1.623 trillion. Due to the recession, both imports and exports fell (imports were $1.950 trillion; exports were $1.560 trillion). Given these economic results for 2009, what was total private saving?

Answers to the Checkpoint question can be found at the end of this chapter.

## The Burden of the Public Debt

Politicians and other professional alarmists frequently warn that the federal government is going bankrupt, or that we are burdening future generations with our own enormous public debt. After all, total (gross) public debt exceeds $12 trillion and private debt held by the public totals almost $8 trillion, meaning that every baby born in the United States begins life saddled with over $25,000 in public debt. Such numbers are enough to scare anyone. Anyone but an economist, that is. Let's examine the burden of the public debt.

### Internally Versus Externally Held Debt

*The great advantage of citizens being creditors as well as debtors with relation to the public debt is obvious. Men readily perceive that they can not be much oppressed by a debt which they owe to themselves.*

—Abraham Lincoln (1864)

Consider first, as Abraham Lincoln noted in 1864, much of the national debt held by the public is owned by American banks, corporations, mutual funds, pension plans, and individuals. As a people, we essentially own this debt—this is **internally held debt.** Hence, the taxes collected from a wide swath of the American public to pay the interest on the debt are simply paid back out to yet another group of Americans. As Table 1 shows, however, foreigners do now own nearly half of the public debt held by the public. This is **externally held debt.**

**Internally held debt:** Public debt owned by U.S. banks, corporations, mutual funds, pension plans, and individuals.

**Externally held debt:** Public debt held by foreigners, which is roughly equal to half of the outstanding U.S. debt held by the public.

**TABLE 1 Distribution of National Debt, as of December 2009 (trillions)**

| | | |
|---|---|---|
| Held by Federal Reserve and government agencies | $5.277 | 42.9% |
| Held by the public | 7.034 | 57.1 |
| Held by foreigners | 3.497 | 49.7 |
| Held domestically | 3.537 | 50.3 |
| Total national debt | 12.311 | 100.0 |

Of the interest paid on the $12 trillion gross public debt, roughly 40% goes to federal agencies holding this debt—the Social Security Administration, the Federal Reserve, and other federal agencies—30% goes to the American private sector, and roughly 30% goes to foreigners.

The interest paid on externally held debt represents a real claim on our goods and services, and thus can be a real burden on our economy. Public debt held by the public has grown, and the portion of the debt held by foreigners has expanded. Until the mid-1990s, foreigners held roughly 20% of publicly held debt.

Traditionally much of the U.S. debt is held internally, but this is changing. In just a decade, foreign holdings have doubled to nearly 50% of debt held by the public, and over half of this is held by China, Japan, and oil-exporting countries. Why such a rapid expansion of foreign holdings since the 1990s? The reason seems to be that these countries are buying our debt to keep their exchange rates constant or keep their currencies from rising relative to the dollar. When their currencies rise, their exports to America are more costly, and as a result sales fall, hurting their economies. Better to accumulate U.S. debt than see their export sectors suffer.

## Interest Payments

The national debt held by the public is large (nearly $8 trillion), resulting in interest costs of just over $250 billion in 2009, representing over 6% of the federal budget. If the national debt is so enormous, wouldn't it be wise to simply pay the debt down or pay it off? Not necessarily so. Many people today "own" some small part of the public debt in their pension plans, but many others do not. If taxes were raised across the board to pay down the debt, those who did not own any public debt would be in a worse position than those who did.

Servicing the debt requires taxing the general public to pay interest to bondholders. Most people who own part of the national debt (or who indirectly own parts of entities that hold the debt) tend to be richer than those who do not. This means money is taken from those across the income or wealth distribution and given to those near the top. Still, the fact that taxes are mildly progressive mitigates some, and perhaps even all, of this reverse redistribution problem.

In contrast to internally held debt, externally held debt makes up the bulk of debt of many developing countries. These countries have discovered that relying on externally held public debt has its limits. The typical result of such policies has been that a country's debt as a percentage of GDP becomes so high that it can no longer service the debt; it can only pay the interest. In some developing nations, the entire public debt is held by foreigners. Many large banks invest in the public debt of small nations since the yields are high, given the high risk of default.

Figure 3 shows the debt of mostly developed nations. Japan and Italy have a large debt relative to their GDP. Although most countries have debt below 100% of GDP and deficits below 6% of GDP, Japan, Britain, and the United States are notable exceptions. China, Russia, and Chile have low debt ratios (debt/GDP) and both Russia and Chile actually had surpluses in 2008.

**FIGURE 3—Public Debt and Deficits as a Percent of GDP**

This figure shows the relationship between public debt and deficits for several developed nations. Those countries with high deficits tend to have high debt-to-GDP ratios.

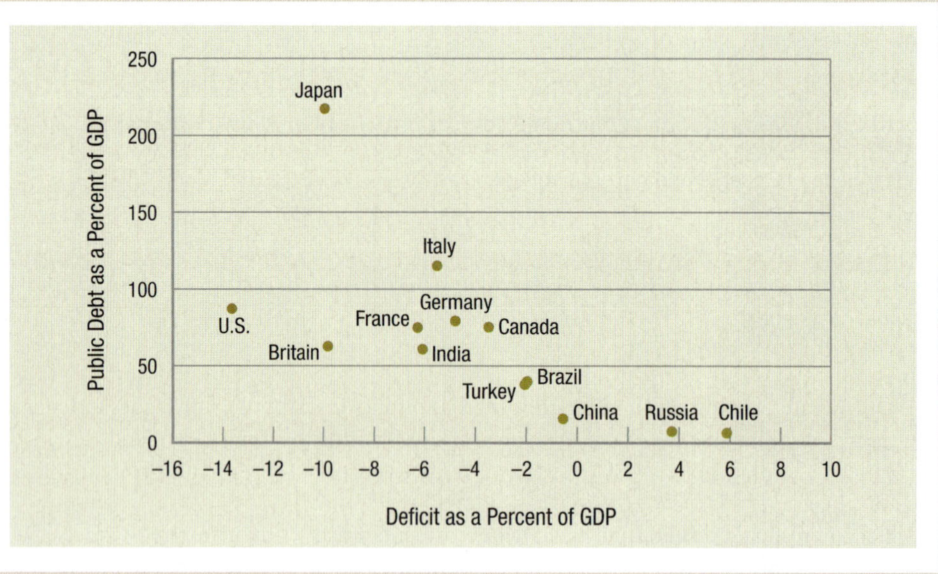


As an economy moves toward the upper left in Figure 3, problems begin to rise. This topic is discussed in detail in the Issue box later in the chapter.

## Crowding-Out Effect

As we saw in the budget constraint section above, when the government runs a deficit, it must sell bonds to either the public or the Federal Reserve. If it sells bonds to the Federal Reserve (prints money) when the economy is near full employment, the money supply will grow and inflation will result. Note, the Fed doesn't actually *print* money. By buying the bonds from the federal government, it puts cash into the economy. The next two chapters focus on this and the role of the Fed in detail.

Alternatively, when the federal government spends more than tax revenues permit, it can sell bonds to the public. But as interest rates rise, private investment declines. The result is that future generations will be bequeathed a smaller and potentially less productive economy, resulting in a lower standard of living. This is the **crowding-out effect** of deficit spending. We will see more about this issue in the next few chapters.

**Crowding-out effect:** Arises from deficit spending requiring the government to borrow, thus driving up interest rates and reducing consumer spending and business investment.

### Public Investment and Crowding-Out

The crowding-out effect can be mitigated if the funds from deficit spending are used for public investment. Improvements in the nation's transportation infrastructure, education establishment, and research facilities, for instance, are all aimed at improving the economy's future productive capacity. Politicians have become adept, however, at labeling the most arcane pork-barrel spending projects "investments." Many are no more investments than are family cars.

Think of the decision to run deficits and increase the national debt as an investment decision. When running a deficit, the government is borrowing money and spending it on a mix of public investments and consumption. The important question concerns how profitable the investments are for the economy. If the investments expand the nation's productive capacity enough, growth will be such that the debt-to-GDP ratio may fall. But if all or most of the deficit is spent on current consumption, growth in GDP may be weak and the debt-to-GDP ratio will most likely rise.

Some public investments are complementary with private investments. Cleaning up a superfund environmental disaster site using government funds, for example, may permit that site to be redeveloped using private funds. The result is that some or possibly all of the crowding-out effect is offset.

## Intergenerational Burdens of Fiscal Policy

*John Kenneth Galbraith's greatest contribution to economics is the concept of the bezzle—the increment to wealth that occurs during the magic interval when a confidence trickster knows he has the money he has appropriated but the victim does not understand that he has lost it. The gross national bezzle has never been larger than in the past decade.*

—John Kay[4]

Accounting scandals of the early 2000s caused an uproar as people lost their pension and retirement funds and cries rang out to extend prison terms for crooked executives. The Sarbanes-Oxley bill shot through Congress, adding stiffer penalties to corporate governance laws. Lawsuits began against the accounting firms that had audited the books of the collapsed companies in the hope of recovering some of the lost funds.

For all the vigor and indignation with which politicians and government prosecutors have pursued the wrongdoers in that wave of accounting scandals, many economists today suspect that federal accounting is no better. Why is there not a similar outrage? In what follows, we look at the recent controversy surrounding federal budget accounting and look at some of the intergenerational burdens imposed by budgetary and fiscal policy. Our earlier discussion of public choice analysis will provide us with some help.

## Fiscal Sustainability of the Federal Budget

*Unless we demonstrate a strong commitment to fiscal sustainability in the longer term, we will have neither financial stability nor healthy economic growth.*

—Ben Bernanke (2009)

[4] John Kay, "America's Borrowing Bonanza Will End in Tears," *Financial Times*, May 26, 2004, p. 15.

## *Issue:* Is America Heading into a Debt Trap?

*Arithmetically, a government's debt burden is sustainable if it can pay the interest without borrowing more. Otherwise the government will eventually fall into a debt trap, borrowing ever more just to service earlier debt.*

*The Economist* (June 2009)

**Over the next** decade, the gross public debt is expected to rise between $5 and $8 trillion, and this follows a $2 trillion increase during President George W. Bush's tenure. The annual deficits for the last three presidents, the 2009 deficit of nearly $1.5 trillion, and the Congressional Budget Office's (CBO) forecast of deficits out to 2015 are shown in the figure at right.

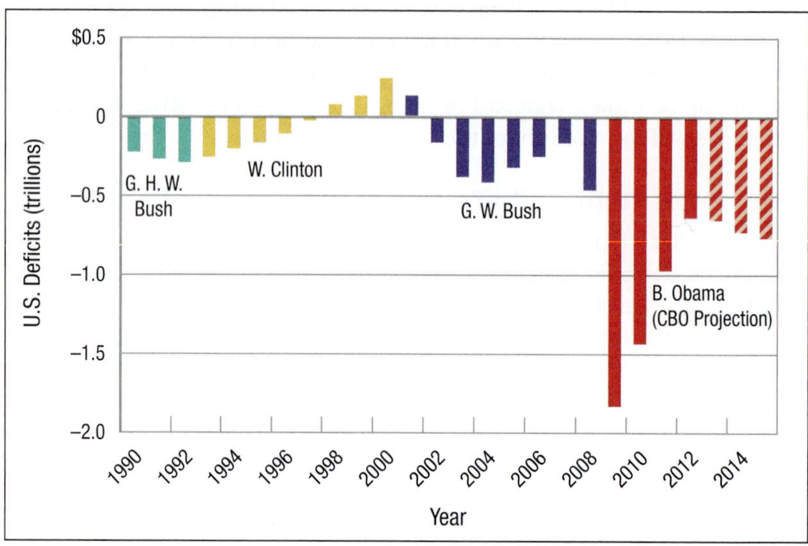


Earlier, we saw that these deficits will have to be financed by selling bonds or printing money. Neither of these options is particularly attractive when deficits are sizeable. Printing money (or monetizing the debt) leads eventually to inflation, and selling bonds leads to rising interest rates and crowding-out of private investment, reducing long-run economic growth.

As noted earlier, China, Japan, and oil-exporting countries currently hold half of the debt held by foreigners, and the 2008–2009 recession has forced these countries to focus on domestic investment rather than buying our debt. If this results in a softer market for U.S. debt, interest rates will have to rise to attract buyers. China is worried about U.S. government policy because it holds nearly $1 trillion of our debt. So much so that Richard Fisher, president of the Dallas Federal Reserve, noted that on a 2009 trip to China, "senior officials in the Chinese government wanted to know if the United States was going to generate a lot of inflation."

Second, we have seen that deficits affect saving, investment, and the trade deficit. These high deficits will result in higher saving (or lower consumption), lower investment, a bigger trade deficit, or some combination of the three.

GDP actually fell in 2009 (a negative growth rate) and is not expected to soar in the near future. The figure at right shows gross public debt as a percent of GDP since 1990. It uses the deficits projected by CBO (from the previous figure) and the assumption that GDP will grow at a 3% annual rate between 2010 and 2015 (the shaded area). Our debt-to-GDP ratio will likely approach 100% during this period—not necessarily a bad thing in and of itself, but significantly higher than our historical norm. It will introduce an added burden on federal finances.

Assume that the debt-to-GDP ratio is 100% and the interest rate on the debt is 3%. If the economy grows by 3% and if the federal government runs a balanced budget, the debt-to-GDP ratio will not change. With high deficits, the more likely result is a growing debt-to-GDP ratio. But if interest rates rise, then in order to keep the debt-to-GDP ratio constant, the federal government will have to reduce spending on other programs to cover the added interest on the debt.

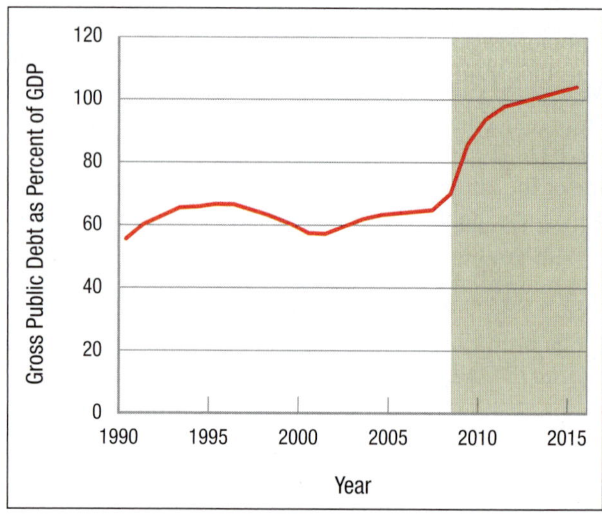


When the debt-to-GDP ratio is lower, economic growth and interest rate pressures on fiscal policy are less, and vice versa as the ratio rises. Imagine the problems some countries face when their debt-to-GDP ratios get well above 200%. Interest on the previous debt begins to dominate the budget and, eventually, lenders either demand extremely high interest rates for new debt or refuse to lend. The country is then left with printing money as the only option to finance deficits, often leading to hyperinflation. This is how countries essentially go bankrupt.

If the CBO projections turn out to be in the ballpark, the United States will face a difficult set of budget decisions over the next decade.

Sources: Peter Goodman, "A Sinking Sound, and a Test of Nerve," *New York Times,* July 8, 2009, p. B1; John Taylor, "Exploding Debt Threatens America," *Financial Times,* May 27, 2009, p. 9; Mary Anastasia O'Grady, "Don't Monetize the Debt," *Wall Street Journal,* May 23, 2009, p. A9; and "The Big Sweat," *The Economist,* June 13, 2009, p. 71–73.

Economists Jagadeesh Gokhale and Kent Smetters have proposed two different measures to assess the **fiscal sustainability** of the federal budget.[5] For a fiscal policy to be fiscally sustainable, the present value of all projected future revenues must be equal to the present value of projected future spending. By converting the estimates to present values, the sustainability of today's fiscal policies can be evaluated using estimates of current dollar imbalances.

**Fiscal sustainability:** A fiscal imbalance equal to zero.

**Fiscal imbalance** (FI), one of the measures Gokhale and Smetters propose, computes the difference between the present value of future obligations and expected revenues, assuming current policies remain unchanged. Fiscal imbalance is defined as follows:

**Fiscal imbalance:** The difference between the present value of future obligations and expected revenues, less government assets, assuming current policies remain unchanged.

$$FI = PVE - PVR - A$$

The present value of expenditures (PVE) and revenues (PVR) are discounted at the government's long-term interest rate to reflect the true values today. Assets of the government are represented by A. To be sustainable, FI must equal zero.

Note that just because a given (or proposed) fiscal policy's fiscal imbalance is zero does not necessarily mean that it is sustainable. As *The Economist* has noted, "A law that lavished new spending on today's citizens, but fully paid for it by levying a 90% income tax on everybody born after this year, would have an FI of zero. It would not, however, be sustainable—future taxpayers would surely rebel—and it would also be monstrously unfair."[6]

Recognizing this, Gokhale and Smetters developed a second measure of sustainability, **generational imbalance** (GI), to estimate how much of the fiscal imbalance is being shifted to future generations. Clearly, some tax burden shifting is sensible. When current fiscal policy truly invests in the economy, future generations benefit, so some of the present costs may justifiably be shifted to them. Investments in infrastructure, education, research, national defense, and homeland security are good examples.

**Generational imbalance:** An estimate of how much of any fiscal imbalance is being shifted to future generations.

As Gokhale and Smetters point out,

> *suppose Congress creates a new Medicare benefit and finances it by raising payroll taxes such that each year's additional outlay is matched by additional revenue. By construction, this policy has no impact on Medicare's FI and, therefore, no impact on the federal government's total FI. . . . Nevertheless, this policy could potentially shift a substantial amount of resources away from future generations and toward current generations.*[7]

Our current budget accounts measure and report debt and deficits on roughly a cash basis. These measures were developed and worked fine when government liabilities were mainly short-term projects such as road and dam building. Even military spending, agricultural price supports, and other programs of this sort were straightforward and short term enough to account for on a cash basis.

Today, the federal government has immense obligations that extend over long periods. Its two largest programs, Social Security and Medicare, account for over one-quarter of all federal spending. People entering their 60s, who are just beginning to enter retirement, can expect to live for two or three more decades. Add to this the fact that medical costs are growing at rates significantly higher than economic growth as new and more sophisticated treatments are developed and demanded.

So, you might ask, since we all get old and eventually need these services, how do these programs have an intergenerational impact? If each generation were to pay into a fund that accumulated enough to cover its own medical and Social Security costs, there would be no burden shifting. But that is not how these programs are structured.

Social Security and Medicare are pay-as-you-go programs. The current working generation, in other words, funds the older generation's benefits; there are no pooled funds

[5] J. Gokhale and K. Smetters, *Fiscal and Generational Imbalances: New Budget Measures for New Budget Priorities* (Washington, DC: AEI Press), 2003. Reprinted by the Federal Reserve Bank of Cleveland, December 2003.

[6] "Economic Focus: Hidden Dangers," *The Economist*, August 2, 2003, p. 65.

[7] Gokhale and Smetters, *Fiscal and Generational Imbalances*, p. 5.

waiting to be tapped as needed. Thus, these two programs represent huge unfunded liabilities to younger (and yet to be born) generations.

The two measures proposed by Gokhale and Smetters are designed "to reveal the consequences of current practices and to clarify the nature of the choices we face."

The current national debt held by the public is roughly $8 trillion. To most people, this is an immense amount—over $25,000 per person in America. And, indeed, the fiscal imbalance (FI) of the federal government is enormous when its liabilities, estimated by the Dallas Federal Reserve to be over $90 trillion, are considered.[8] Keep in mind that this is the present value of the government's liabilities, not just a sum of future dollar liabilities. A dollar of pension liability 75 years into the future has a present value of less than a nickel today.

What are the implications of this estimate for future budgeting? First, it means that bringing fiscal policy into sustainability today would require that the government "expropriate the nation's entire gross domestic product for the next four years to meet the Social Security and Medicare commitments it has already made."

Second, it suggests that relying too heavily on present measures of deficits and public debt can mislead policymakers. Government accounting measures should help policymakers accurately see the real choices we face. If a program's future liabilities are seriously underestimated, future generations will get stuck with the bill.

Third, without some significant change in economic or demographic growth, taxes will have to be increased on a massive scale at some point, or else the benefits for Social Security and Medicare will have to be drastically cut. Gokhale and Smetters estimate that the 15.3% combined payroll tax would have to be doubled, or Medicare and Social Security benefits would need to be cut roughly in half.

If these estimates of fiscal imbalance are in the ballpark, fiscal policy is headed for a train wreck as the baby boomers keep retiring. The public choice analysis discussed above suggests that politicians will try to keep this issue off the agenda for as long as possible, one side fighting tax increases while the other resists benefit reductions. Clearly, given the magnitudes discussed here, this problem will be difficult to solve once it reaches crisis proportions.

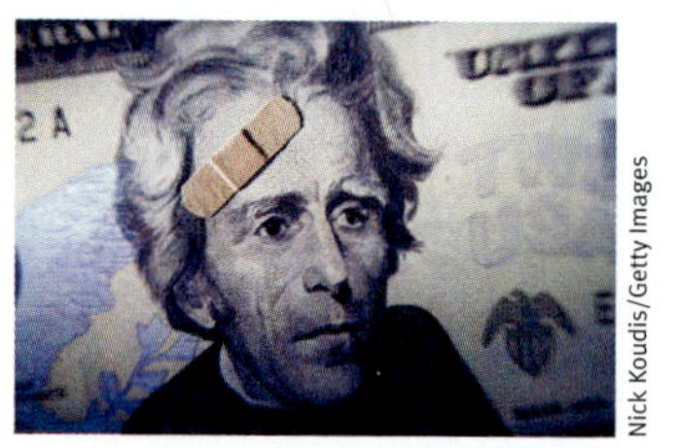
Nick Koudis/Getty Images

We started this chapter by talking about our individual uneasiness with personal debt, and projected this on to the federal government's position as a debtor running large budget deficits. We saw that, unlike individuals, the federal government has the ability to incur debt for some time because of its ability to print money and borrow from the public. Further, we saw that some of this debt is being financed by foreign entities through trade deficits. So the federal government can run up debts long after such magnitudes would sink individuals. Yet we did not try to quantify just how much debt the federal government could safely take on, though it is clear that it is far from that point at the present time. Some time down the road, this picture may change as Social Security and Medicare liabilities continue to grow. The implication is that we are better off dealing with this future problem now rather than later.

## CHECKPOINT

### THE BURDEN OF THE PUBLIC DEBT

- About half of the public debt held by the public is held by domestic individuals and institutions, and half is held by foreigners. The domestic half is internally held and represents transfers among individuals, but that part held by foreigners is a real claim on our resources.
- Interest on the debt approaches 6% of the federal budget, and these funds could have been spent on other programs. Again, half is paid domestically (as transfers among individuals), and half goes to foreigners—and this half is the real cost of the public debt.
- When the government pays for the deficit by selling bonds, interest rates rise, crowding out some private investment and reducing economic growth. To the extent that these funds are for public investment and not current consumption, this effect is mitigated.

[8] Jason Saving, "Fiscal Fitness: The U.S. Budget Deficit's Uncertain Prospects," *Economic Letter,* Federal Reserve Bank of Dallas, April 2007; and Mary Anastasia O'Grady, "Don't Monetize the Debt," *Wall Street Journal,* May 23, 2009, p. A9.

- For fiscal policy to be fiscally sustainable, the present value of all projected future revenues must equal the present value of projected future spending.

**QUESTION:** The deficit is \$1.5 trillion, total public debt is \$12 trillion, and the fiscal imbalance (including Social Security and Medicare) is approaching \$100 trillion. Why is seemingly little being done to solve this problem of long-term fiscal imbalance?

Answers to the Checkpoint question can be found at the end of this chapter.

## Key Concepts

Deficit, p. 498
Surplus, p. 498
Public debt, p. 498
Public choice theory, p. 499
Annually balanced budget, p. 501
Cyclically balanced budget, p. 501
Functional finance, p. 502
Government budget constraint, p. 503
Budget and trade deficits, p. 504
Internally held debt, p. 505
Externally held debt, p. 505
Crowding-out effect, p. 507
Fiscal sustainability, p. 509
Fiscal imbalance, p. 509
Generational imbalance, p. 509

## Chapter Summary

### Financing the Federal Government

A deficit is the amount by which annual government spending exceeds tax revenues. A surplus, when it occurs, is the amount by which the year's tax revenues exceed government spending.

The public debt, or national debt, is the total accumulation of past deficits and surpluses. Public debt consists of U.S. Treasury securities, including Treasury bills, notes, and bonds, and U.S. savings bonds.

Public choice theory involves the economic analysis of public and political decision making. Public choice theorists often conclude that collective decision making is flawed and inefficient, and politicians and bureaucrats consider their own self-interest when making public policy.

Public choice economists argue that deficit spending reduces the perceived cost of current government operations, and therefore shifts the cost of government to the next generation.

Some observers believe the federal government, like state governments, should balance its budget every year. Others argue that balancing the budget over the business cycle is a better approach, while still others have suggested that the federal government should focus on promoting full employment with stable prices, treating the budget deficit or surplus as a secondary concern.

We know that annually balancing the federal budget would undercut fiscal policies aimed at maintaining full employment.

Balancing the budget over the course of the business cycle is extremely difficult and politically risky.

Economists who favor a functional finance approach to the federal budget believe the first priority of policymakers should be to keep the economy at full employment with stable prices.

### Financing Debt and Deficits

Given its power to print money and collect taxes, the federal government cannot go bankrupt. It does, however, face what economists call a budget constraint:

$$G - T = \Delta M + \Delta B + \Delta A$$

To finance a deficit, the government can sell bonds to the Federal Reserve and other government agencies, sell bonds to the public, or sell government assets.

When an economy is at equilibrium, all injections and withdrawals are equal; thus $G + I + X = T + S + M$. Budget deficits must be made up by private savings ($S > I$) or a trade deficit ($M > X$).

## The Burden of the Public Debt

Almost half of the national debt held by the public is owned by U.S. banks, corporations, mutual funds, pension plans, and individuals. The interest paid on externally held debt (the interest paid to foreigners) represents a real claim on our goods and services; it can thus be a real burden on our economy.

Increased deficit spending by the government ultimately crowds out private investment. The crowding-out effect can be mitigated if the funds from deficit spending are used for public investment.

Two measures have been proposed to assess the fiscal sustainability of the federal budget: fiscal imbalance and generational imbalance.

Today, the federal government has immense obligations that extend over long periods. Its two largest programs, Social Security and Medicare, account for over one-quarter of all federal spending and represent huge unfunded liabilities to future generations.

# Questions and Problems

## Check Your Understanding

1. Since 1950 the federal government has run a surplus on average roughly one year in each decade. Why is it so difficult for the federal government to run a budget surplus?
2. What is one benefit to business when the government budget is in surplus?
3. How might interest paid on the national debt lead to greater income inequality?
4. Since balancing the budget over the business cycle seems like such a sensible idea, why haven't public policymakers (Congress and the executive branch) implemented a program to do this?

## Apply the Concepts

5. Economists generally agree that Americans save too little, and if they saved more, net foreign borrowing would fall. Explain why this is true. What incentives might the government introduce to get people to save more?
6. Government accounting rules for corporations require that the present value of pensions and other long-term liabilities be included in their annual reports and on their balance sheets. Several airlines and steel companies became insolvent partly because of these liabilities and went through bankruptcy. In the fall of 2007, General Motors got the UAW to accept responsibility for GM's retiree health care fund to get this less than fully funded liability off GM's books. Why doesn't the federal government add the present value of its long-term liabilities for Social Security and Medicare to its budget reports each year?
7. If the economy (gross domestic product and income) are growing faster than the federal debt held by the public (both domestic and foreign), is a huge government debt any real problem?
8. In the late 1990s, along with the budget surpluses in 1998 to 2001, some policymakers were talking about retiring the entire federal debt outstanding (in private hands) by the early part of the next decade (2012–2015). Today that discussion looks

a little quaint. Leaving aside whether it is possible or not, is it a good idea to retire all federal debt held by the public?

9. When someone argues that the national debt is bankrupting the country, what arguments can you use to rebut this assertion?

10. Assume that the U.S. balances its federal budget, and savings and investment remain where they are today. What impact would this have on the economies of Europe?

## In the News

11. Robert Dunn, in the August 19, 2001, issue of the *New York Times,* noted that "a federal budget surplus should decline in an economic downturn like this one, and attempts to "protect the surplus" by cutting expenditures, as some Republicans wish or by increasing taxes, as Democratic leaders in Congress have suggested, is madness." Is he right? Why or why not?

12. Ben Stein wrote an open letter to Henry Paulson, just after Paulson was appointed U.S. Treasury Secretary in May 2006, arguing that America was facing a dire economic future:

    *Just to give you an idea what you are up against, Standard & Poor's issued a warning not long ago. The caution was that if the United States government did not seriously alter fiscal policy, Treasury bonds would be downgraded to BBB, slightly above junk status, by 2020. This is a stunning piece of news for the world's most highly rated security denominated in its primary reserve currency. The S&P report said further that if the nation did not make serious changes after that, by 2025 Treasuries would be junk bonds, like the bonds of less successful emerging-markets nations.*[9]

    What kind of problems implied here would reduce U.S. government bonds to "junk" status? What policies enacted today could eventually eliminate these problems?

13. Professors Leszek Balcerowicz and Andrzej Rzonca (*Financial Times,* December 10, 2008) wrote that "consumers are guided by expectations. They take a longer term view in making their spending and saving decisions. This limits the stimulating effect of most temporary tax cuts relative to permanent ones." They also suggest that "when the ratio of public debt to gross domestic product is already high, the multiplier effect of fiscal stimulus is low. . . . This fact should reduce the number of countries that undertake fiscal stimulus, especially if one considers their unfunded liabilities and the fiscal consequences of the public interventions taken so far."

    Does it seem reasonable that consumers are guided by expectations such that consumption spending may not respond much to stimulus by government (tax rebates and added government spending)? Is it reasonable to lump government debt and unfunded liabilities into the same category?

# Answers to Questions in CheckPoints

## Check Point: Financing the Federal Government

The debt-to-GDP ratio is the measure that best illustrates the debt's impact. Gross domestic product represents the economy's earning (producing) potential and puts the debt relative to GDP in perspective. A small national debt alongside a smaller GDP would be much worse than our large debt associated with a huge economy.

[9] Ben Stein, "Everybody's Business: Note to the New Treasury Secretary: It's Time to Raise Taxes," *New York Times*, June 25, 2006, p. 3.

## Check Point: Financing Debt and Deficits

We use the equation $G - T = (S - I) + (M - X)$ to find the value for $S$. Plugging in the numbers, we get 1.410 = (? − 1.623) + (1.950 − 1.560). Working through it logically, 1.410 = (? − 1.623) + (0.390). For the equation to balance, 1.410 = (2.643 − 1.623) + 0.390. So total private saving was $2.643 trillion.

## Check Point: The Burden of the Public Debt

Most likely the answer lies in the fact that the fiscal imbalance is a *long-term* issue, and politicians with a two-, four-, or six-year time frame between elections see little benefit in taking on hard problems. Second, because they are so huge, the tradeoffs are so severe that making these decisions is extremely difficult.

# Money and the Financial System

# 22

Panoramic Images/Getty Images

**We have looked at how the** federal government tries to manage the macroeconomy through fiscal policy, by using government taxation and spending. We now want to look at the government's other policy approach—monetary policy. To analyze how government uses monetary policy to influence the macroeconomy, we first have to examine the financial system and the role of money, which is the subject of this chapter. After laying this foundation, we then look at modern monetary policy in the following chapter.

In discussing money and the financial system, we begin by looking at money: what it is and what it does. We then examine why people save and why firms borrow. We next show how the market for loanable funds brings these two groups together, and how the financial system makes this process easier and better for all. We then go on to the surprising ability of banks to create money, as if out of thin air. Finally, we introduce the Federal Reserve, which is the guarantor of our money and our financial system.

## What Is Money?

*Anything can serve as money, from the cowrie shells of the Maldives to the huge stone disks used on the Pacific islands of Yap. And now, it seems, in this electronic age nothing can serve as money too.*

NIALL FERGUSON, *THE ASCENT OF MONEY*

**Money:** Anything that is accepted in exchange for other goods and services or for the payment of debt.

**Money** is anything that is accepted in exchange for other goods and services or for the payment of debt. We are familiar with currency and coins; we use them every day. Over the ages, however, a wide variety of commodities has served as money—giant circular stones

**After studying this chapter you should be able to:**

- ☐ Describe the functions of money.
- ☐ Define the money supply according to M1 and M2.
- ☐ Use the simple loanable funds model to show how savers and borrowers are brought together.
- ☐ Explain how the financial system makes it easier for savers and borrowers.
- ☐ Describe the relationship between the price of bonds and interest rates.
- ☐ Describe the money creation process.
- ☐ Describe the history and structure of the Federal Reserve System.
- ☐ Understand the Federal Reserve's principal monetary tools and target.
- ☐ Explain why the Federal Reserve's policies take time to affect the economy.

on the island of Yap, wampum (trinkets) among early Native Americans, and cigarettes in prisoner-of-war camps during World War II.

First, for a commodity to be used as money, its value must be easy to determine. Therefore, it must be easily standardized. Second, it must be divisible, so that people can make change. Third, money must be durable. It must be easy to carry (so much for the giant circular stones). Fourth, a commodity must be accepted by many people as money if it is to act as money. As Niall Ferguson makes clear in the quote above, today we have "virtual" money, in the sense that digital money is moved from our employer to the bank and then to the retailer for our goods and services in nothing but a series of electronic transactions. We never touch the stuff. This is really the ultimate in **fiat money:** money without any intrinsic value but accepted as money because the government has made it legal tender.

Money is so important that nearly every society has invented some form of money for its use. We begin our examination of money by looking at its functions.

## The Functions of Money

Money has three primary functions in our economic system: as a medium of exchange, as a measure of value (unit of account), and as a store of value. These uses make money unique among commodities.

### Medium of Exchange

Let us start with a primitive economy. There is no money. To survive, you have to produce everything yourself: food, clothing, housing. It is a fact that few of us can do all of these tasks equally well. Each one of us is better off specializing, providing those goods and services where we are more efficient. Say I specialize in dairy products and you specialize in blacksmithing. We can engage in **barter,** which is the direct exchange of goods and services. I can give you gallons of milk if you make me a pot for cooking. A *double coincidence of wants* occurs if, in a barter economy, I find someone who not only has something I want, but who also wants something I have. What happens if you, the blacksmith, are willing to make the cooking pot for me but want clothing in return? Then I have to search out someone who is willing to give me clothing in exchange for my milk; I will then give you the clothing in exchange for the cooking pot. You can see that this system quickly becomes complicated. This is why barter is restricted to primitive economies.

Consider what happens when money is introduced. Everyone can spend their time producing goods and services, rather than running around trying to match up exchanges. Everyone can sell their products for money, and then can use this money to buy cooking pots, clothing, or whatever else they want. Thus, money's first and most important function is as a **medium of exchange.** Without money, economies remain primitive.

**Fiat money:** Money without intrinsic value but nonetheless accepted as money because the government has decreed it to be money.

**Barter:** The direct exchange of goods and services for other goods and services.

**Medium of exchange:** Money is a medium of exchange because goods and services are sold for money, then the money is used to purchase other goods and services.

### Unit of Account

Imagine the difficulties consumers would have in a barter economy where every item is valued in terms of the other products offered—12 eggs are worth 1 shirt, 1 shirt equals 3 gallons of gas, and so forth. A 10-product economy of this sort, assigning every product a value for every other product, would require 45 different prices. A 100-good economy would require 4,950 prices.[1] This is another reason why only the most primitive economies use barter.

Once again, money is able to solve a problem inherent to the barter economy. It reduces the number of prices consumers need to know to the number of products on the market; a 100-good economy will have 100 prices. Thus, money is a **unit of account,** or a measure of value. Dollar-prices give us a yardstick for measuring and comparing the values of a wide variety of goods and services.

**Unit of account:** Money provides a yardstick for measuring and comparing the values of a wide variety of goods and services. It eliminates the problem of double coincidence of wants associated with barter.

[1] The formula for determining the number of prices needed when $N$ goods are in an economy is $[N(N - 1)]/2$. Thus, for 10 goods, the result is $[10(10 - 1)]/2 = 90/2 = 45$.

Admittedly, ascribing a dollar-value to some things, such as human life, love, and clean air, can be difficult. Still, courts, businesses, and government agencies manage to do so every day. For example, if someone dies and the court determines this death was due to negligence, the court tries to determine the value of the life to the person's survivors—not a pleasant task, but one that has to be undertaken. Without a monetary standard, such valuations would be not just difficult, but impossible.

### Store of Value

Using cherry tomatoes as a medium of exchange and unit of account might be handy, except that they have the bad habit of rotting. Money lasts, enabling people to save the money they earn today and use it to buy the goods and services they want tomorrow. Thus, money is a **store of value.** It is true that money is not unique in preserving its value. Many other commodities, including stocks, bonds, real estate, art, and jewelry are used to store wealth for future purchases. Indeed, some of these assets may rise in value, so they might be preferred to money as a store of value. Why, then, use money as a store of wealth at all?

Store of value: The function that enables people to save the money they earn today and use it to buy the goods and services they want tomorrow.

The answer is that every other type of asset must be converted into money if it is to be spent or used to pay debts. Converting other assets into cash involves transaction costs, and for some assets, these costs are significant. An asset's **liquidity** is determined by how fast, easily, and reliably it can be converted into cash.

Liquidity: How quickly, easily, and reliably an asset can be converted into cash.

Money is the most liquid asset because, as the medium of exchange, it requires no conversion. Stocks and bonds are also liquid, but they do require some time and often a commission fee to convert into cash. Prices in stock and bond markets fluctuate, causing the real value of these assets to be uncertain. Real estate requires considerable time to liquidate, with transaction costs that often approach 10% of a property's value.

Money differs from many other commodities in that its value does not deteriorate in the absence of inflation. When price levels do rise, however, the value of money falls: if prices double, the value of money is cut in half. In times of inflation, most people are unwilling to hold much of their wealth in money. If hyperinflation hits, money will quickly become worthless as the economy reverts to barter.

Money, then, is crucial for a well-functioning modern economy. All of its three primary functions are important: medium of exchange, unit of account, and store of value.

## Defining the Money Supply

How much money is there in the U.S. economy? One of the tasks assigned to the Federal Reserve System (the Fed), the central bank of the United States, is that of measuring our money supply. The Fed has developed several different measures of monetary aggregates, which it continually updates to reflect the innovative new financial instruments our financial system is constantly developing. The monetary aggregates the Fed uses most frequently are M1, the narrowest measure of money, and M2, a broader measure.

Until March 2006, the Fed did publish another monetary aggregate called M3 that included M2 plus large-denomination time deposits and other large deposits. The Fed indicated that it quit publication of M3 data because

> *M3 does not appear to convey any additional information about economic activity that is not already embodied in M2 and has not played a role in the monetary policy process for many years. Consequently, the Board judged that the costs of collecting the underlying data and publishing M3 outweigh the benefits.*

More specifically, the Fed defines M1 and M2 as follows:

**M1** equals currency
+ Travelers checks
+ Demand deposits
+ Other checkable deposits

M1: The narrowest definition of money; includes currency (coins and paper money), demand deposits (checks), and other accounts that have check-writing or debit capabilities, such as stock market and money market accounts. The most liquid instruments that might serve as money.

**M2:** A broader definition of money that includes "near monies" that are not as liquid as cash, including deposits in savings accounts, money market accounts, and money market mutual fund accounts.

**M2** equals M1
+ Savings deposits
+ Money market deposit accounts
+ Small-denomination (less than $100,000) time deposits
+ Shares in retail money market mutual funds net of retirement accounts

## Narrowly Defined Money: M1

Because money is used mainly as a medium of exchange, when defined most narrowly it includes currency (coins and paper money), demand deposits (checks), and other accounts that have check-writing capabilities, such as stock market accounts. Currency represents roughly half of M1, with paper money constituting more than 90% of currency; coins form only a small part of M1. Checking accounts represent the other half of the money supply, narrowly defined. Currently, M1 is equal to roughly $1.7 trillion. It is the most liquid part of the money supply.

Checking accounts can be opened at commercial banks and at a variety of other thrift institutions, including savings and loan institutions, mutual savings banks, and credit unions. Also, some stock brokerage firms offer checking services on brokerage accounts.

## A Broader Definition: M2

A broader definition of money, M2, includes the "near moneys": money that cannot be drawn on instantaneously but that is nonetheless accessible. This includes deposits in savings accounts, money market deposit accounts, and money market mutual fund accounts. Many of these accounts have check-writing features similar to demand deposits.

Certificates of deposits (CDs) and other small-denomination time deposits can usually be cashed in at any time, though they often carry heavy penalties for early liquidation. Thus, M2 includes the highly liquid assets in M1 and a variety of accounts that are less liquid, but still easy and inexpensive to access. This broader definition of money brings the current money supply up to nearly $8.5 trillion.

When economists speak of "the money supply," they are usually referring to M1, the narrowest definition. Even so, the other measures are sometimes used. The index of leading economic indicators, for instance, uses M2, adjusted for inflation, to gauge the state of the economy. For the remainder of this book, the money supply will be considered to be M1 unless otherwise specified.

The near financial meltdown the United States experienced in 2008–2009 illustrates the complexity of our financial system. At its essence, it channels funds from savers to borrowers. In the next section, we look at a simple model of loanable funds and examine in some detail the financial system as a whole.

### CHECKPOINT

#### WHAT IS MONEY?

- Money is anything accepted in exchange for other goods and services and for the payment of debts.
- The functions of money include: a medium of exchange, a unit of account, and a store of value.
- *Liquidity* refers to how fast, easily, and reliably an asset can be converted to cash.
- M1 is currency plus demand deposits plus other checkable deposits.
- M2 is equal to M1 plus savings deposits plus other savings-like deposits.

**QUESTION:** Gresham's Law says that bad money drives out the good money from the marketplace. One example was the 1965 U.S. Coinage Act that replaced silver quarters with "sandwich" coins made of a cheaper silver-nickel alloy. The pre-1965 quarters

## *Issue:* Where Did All the Dollar Coins Go?

**When is the last** time you got a Sacagawea or Susan B. Anthony dollar as change for some purchase you made? For most of us, the answer approaches never. Why don't dollar coins circulate in the United States?

The benefits of a dollar coin are clear: coins last much longer than dollar bills, which tend to deteriorate within 18 months. Annual savings from minting coins over printing dollar bills runs to $500 million a year, because although production costs are higher, coins circulate longer than bills, making total costs less for coins. This is why the Treasury has tried twice recently to introduce dollar coins.

Introducing dollar coins faces several serious hurdles. First, several industries will incur added costs. For example, banks will have additional costs to sort, store, and wrap the coins, and vending machines must be altered to accept the coins. The coins cannot be too big, or the public will reject them as too heavy; this was the problem with the Kennedy half-dollar and the silver dollars of the past. But a small dollar, roughly the size of a quarter, generates confusion—Is it a dollar or a quarter?—and again has been rejected by the public.

Other countries have successfully introduced dollar coins: Canada has $1 and $2 coins and Britain has a 1-pound coin. All are circulated widely. What do we need to do to launch a successful dollar coin in the United States?

After reviewing the experiences of other countries, the General Accounting Office (GAO) concluded that a successful introduction of a dollar coin would require that the government develop a substantial awareness campaign (a heavy, extended advertising campaign) to overcome initial public resistance. Second, the Treasury must mint sufficient coins for acceptance by the public. Third, and probably most important, the dollar bill would have to be eliminated. A key element in the general acceptance of the dollar coins in Canada was that the populace had no choice: the dollar bill was removed from circulation at the same time the dollar coin was introduced.

This being the case, why did the Treasury try once again in 2007 to launch a dollar coin without removing the paper dollar from circulation? These new coins were based on the popularity of the state quarters program, in which each year five state quarters were released for general circulation. The new dollar coins released in 2007 were engraved with an image of George Washington, and eventually over the years all of the presidents will be represented. But these are more collector's items than general issue, hence the continuance of the paper dollar bill.

United States Mint image

Given the potential annual savings, we will undoubtedly see further attempts at introducing a dollar coin in the United States until this coin is generally accepted.

Source: See Sebastien Lotz and Guillaume Rocheteau, "The Fate of One-Dollar Coins in the U.S.," *Economic Commentary*, Federal Reserve Bank of Cleveland, October 15, 2004.

quickly vanished from circulation. Where did all the pre-1965 silver quarters go? Is Gresham's Law much of a problem in today's economy with paper (fiat) money and credit cards?

Answers to the Checkpoint question can be found at the end of this chapter.

# The Financial System and the Market for Loanable Funds

The market for loanable funds is a simple model (much like those you have seen before) that describes the financial market for saving and investment. Initially, we will assume that savers deal directly with investors. This simplifies our analysis. We then will bring in financial intermediaries (banks, mutual funds, and other financial institutions) to describe the benefits of a well-functioning financial system.

## Supply and Demand for Loanable Funds

Why do people save? Why do they borrow?

People supply funds to the loanable funds market because they do not spend all of their income; they save. There are many reasons why individuals save. People save "for a rainy day": they put away some of their income when times are good to take care of them when times turn bad. Saving behavior is also a cultural phenomenon: many Asian countries have savings rates far higher than that in the United States.

The reward for not spending today is the *interest* received on savings, enabling people to spend more in the future. The supply of funds to the loanable funds market is directly related to the interest rate because at higher rates of interest, savers are rewarded more and are willing to provide more funds to the market. Since interest rates are the price (reward) that savers receive, this is just another example of people reacting to incentives. Higher prices (interest rates) result in more saving (funds) supplied to the market.

This supply of loanable funds is shown as $S_0$ in Figure 1. It relates the real (adjusted for inflation) rate of interest to loanable funds and is positively sloped like other supply curves we studied earlier. People in our simple scenario supply these funds to banks.

**FIGURE 1—The Market for Loanable Funds**

This market represents supply and demand for funds. Savers spend less than they earn and supply the excess funds to the market. Borrowers (firms) have potential profit-making investment opportunities, and this leads to their demand for funds. Equilibrium is at point *e*.

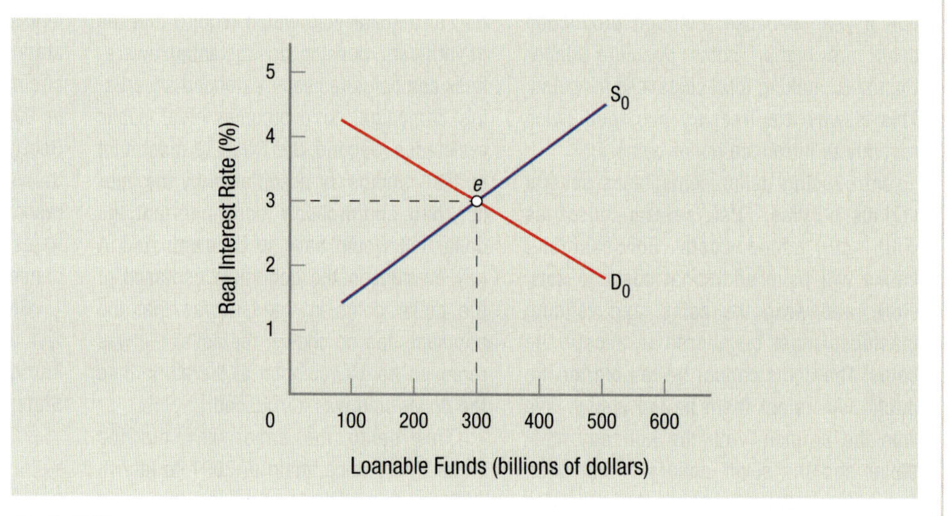


The demand for loanable funds comes from people who want to purchase goods and services, such as taking out a mortgage on a house, or who, as entrepreneurs, want to start or expand a business. Firms are borrowers, too. Firms may want to invest in new plants, additional equipment, expanded warehouse facilities, or engage in additional research and development on new products. The specific investment depends on the industry. For firms in the oil industry, it might be for an offshore oil platform or refinery. For Google, it might be for another server farm.

The demand for loanable funds is shown as $D_0$ in Figure 1. Notice that it slopes downward, reflecting the fact that when the real interest rate is high, only a few projects will have a rate of return high enough to justify the investment. A project will be undertaken only if its expected return is higher than the cost of funding the project. When oil prices are high, for example, an oil platform might have a high enough return to justify paying a high interest rate, but the expected returns on a new commuter airplane for a small airline may not be. As interest rates fall, more projects become profitable and the amount of funds demanded rises.

Keep in mind that when we refer to interest rates we are referring to *real* interest rates (adjusted for inflation) that reflect the real cost of borrowing and the real return to savers.

The loanable funds market reaches equilibrium in Figure 1 at a 3% real interest rate and $300 billion in funds traded in the market. If for some reason the real interest rate *exceeded* 3%, savers would provide more funds to the market than investors want and interest rates would fall until the market reached point *e*. In a similar way, if interest rates were somehow *below* 3%, investors would want more funds than savers would be willing to provide and, again, the market would push interest rates up to 3% at point *e*. Not surprisingly, this market is similar to the competitive markets for other goods and services we have discussed earlier. When compared to most markets, financial markets are typically more competitive and often reach equilibrium quicker if something changes in the market. Let's now use this model to analyze various impacts (private and public) on the market for loanable funds.

## Changes in Saving, Investment, and Interest Rates

Just as in other markets, when something happens to change the supply or demand for loanable funds, interest rates and the level of saving and investment also change.

Let's begin by asking what happens if households decide to save a larger proportion of their income because they fear job loss in a recession. If households decide to save more, the amount of funds provided to the market at all interest rates will grow, so the supply of loanable funds will shift from $S_0$ to $S_1$ in Figure 2. Equilibrium will move from point *e* to point *a*, real interest rates will fall, and both saving and investment will rise from \$300 billion to \$400 billion.

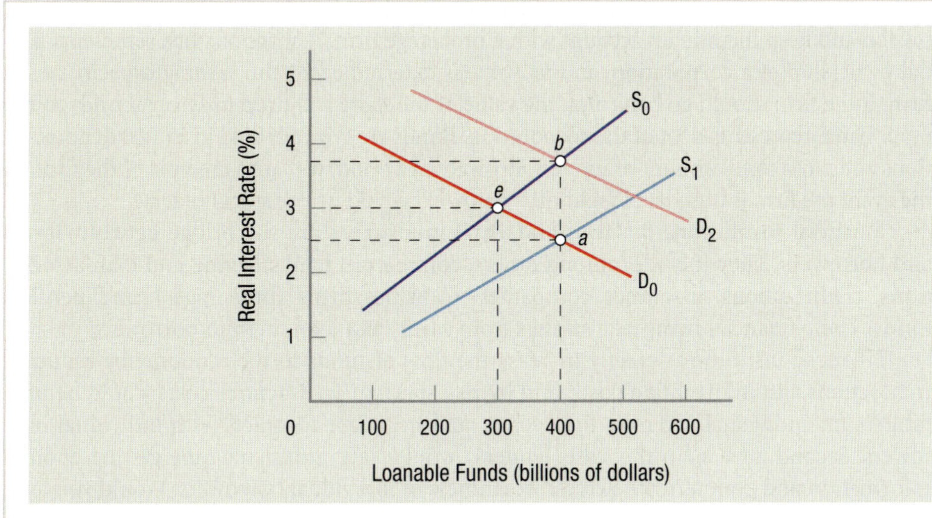


**FIGURE 2—Changes in Supply, Demand, and Interest Rates**

If savers decide to save more, the supply of funds will grow to $S_1$. At the new equilibrium, point *a*, interest rates fall and the amount of funds traded rises. Anything that increases the rate of return on investment (investment tax credits or increased demand for the firm's product) will result in the demand for funds increasing and a new equilibrium at point *b*.

Similarly, if a recession ends and people go on a buying spree, savings will fall. In Figure 2, this would be a shift in the supply curve from $S_1$ to $S_0$.

We have seen how changes in savings can shift the supply of loanable funds. Now let's turn our attention to the demand side. Anything that changes the rate of return on potential investment will cause the demand for loanable funds to change. Let's keep saving on the initial supply curve, $S_0$.

Investment tax credits effectively reduce tax payments for firms building new factories or buying new equipment. These laws give firms incentives to invest by increasing their *after-tax* rate of return. This results in a shift in the demand for loanable funds from $D_0$ to $D_2$ in Figure 2 and results in both higher real interest rates (3.75%) and higher investment (\$400 billion).

Technological advances that increase productivity or create new products also increase the demand for loanable funds. In a similar way, an increase in the demand for a firm's products gives the firm an incentive to increase production, which often results in plant expansion or the need to build an additional facility, increasing the demand for loanable funds.

One way to reduce the demand for funds is to increase business taxes or expand regulation, hindering plant expansion. Any other policy that has the potential to reduce returns on investment will lower the demand for loanable funds.

In summary, we have seen that when households decide to increase saving, real interest rates fall and investment rises. When the demand by firms for investment funds rises, real interest rates rise along with expanded investment. Together, savings and borrowings move toward equilibrium in the market for loanable funds.

## The Financial System

Our financial system is a complex set of institutions that, in the broadest sense, allocates scarce resources (financial capital) from savers, those who are spending less than they earn, to borrowers, those who want to use these resources to invest in potentially profitable projects. Both savers and borrowers can include households, firms, and governments, but our focus is on households as savers and firms as borrowers. As we have seen, savers expect to earn interest on their savings and borrowers expect to pay interest on what they borrow. Households may save for a down payment on a house or a new car, and firms borrow to invest in new plants, equipment, or research and development.

Savers can invest their funds *directly* by purchasing a bond or shares of stock from a firm. Savers can also invest *indirectly* by providing funds to a financial institution (bank or mutual fund, for example) that channels those funds to borrowers. Savers can purchase bonds or stocks from financial markets, storing them in safety deposit boxes, or not take physical possession and keep them in an account with a brokerage firm. A share of stock represents partial ownership of a corporation, and its value is determined by the earning capacity of the firm. If the firm should go bankrupt, the value of the share will drop to zero. A bond, on the other hand, represents debt of the corporation. Bonds are typically sold in $1,000 denominations and pay a fixed amount of interest. If you own a bond, you are a creditor of the firm; in the event the firm is liquidated (sold off), you will be paid before stockholders.

**Financial intermediaries:** Financial firms (banks, mutual funds, insurance companies, etc.) that acquire funds from savers and then lend these funds to borrowers (consumers, firms, and government).

Financial institutions or **financial intermediaries** are the bridge between savers and borrowers. They include, among others, commercial banks, saving and loan associations, credit unions, insurance companies, securities firms (brokerages), and pension funds. These financial firms take savings from savers and loan them to borrowers.

Financial institutions greatly increase the flow of funds to the economy by reducing transactions and information costs, and by risk sharing. Transactions costs would be prohibitive for individual savers to find, select, and negotiate contracts with individual borrowers. Second, savers (in this case, lenders) would have a difficult time getting enough information and evaluating the credit worthiness of individual borrowers. Would you lend to your neighbor down the block? You might know plenty about your neighbors, but have few ways to determine if a specific neighborhood business was safe to lend to or was unsound, or even just a fraud. Third, firms need funds for long-term investments, but savers want access to their money at a moment's notice and would want their funds invested in a number of diversified projects to reduce risk.

Financial institutions reduce transactions costs by providing standardized financial products, including savings accounts, stocks, bonds, annuities, mortgages, futures, and options. They reduce information costs by screening, evaluating, and monitoring firms to see that they are credit worthy and use the funds loaned in a prudent manner. And finally, financial institutions accept funds from savers and pool this money into a portfolio of diversified financial instruments (stocks, bonds, etc.), reducing overall risk and at the same time permitting savers access to their funds when needed. In addition, they can also offer securities with different risk profiles to savers, from relatively safe CDs and savings accounts to more risky domestic and foreign stocks. In so doing, these institutions allow a greater flow of funds between savers and borrowers, greatly increasing the efficiency of investment in the economy.

The role of financial institutions of funneling funds from savers to investors is essential, because the people who save are often not the same people with profitable investment opportunities. Without financial institutions, investment would be a pale version of what we see today, and the economy would be a fraction of its size.

Financial institutions are heavily regulated to ensure the soundness and safety of the financial system and to increase the transparency and information to investors. The agencies regulating financial markets include the Securities and Exchange Commission (SEC), the Federal Reserve System, the Federal Deposit Insurance Corporation (FDIC), and another half dozen or so federal agencies, along with all the state agencies regulating firms in this market.

Although heavily regulated, financial markets are complex environments that are occasionally subjected to meltdowns that can lead the economy into a recession and result in huge losses for the affected firms. We have more to say about this in the next chapter.

## Bond Prices and Interest Rates

We examined real interest rates when we described the loanable funds market, and we described several direct and indirect financial instruments such as stocks, savings accounts, and bonds. But most of the loanable funds are in the form of corporate or government *bonds,* and economists often look at financial markets from the viewpoint of the supply and demand for bonds. They often consider policy implications by their impact on the price of bonds and the quantity traded. It can be a little confusing because bond prices and interest rates are inversely related—when interest rates go up, bond prices go down, and vice versa. Let's take a quick look at the characteristics of bonds to help you see why interest rates and bond prices move in opposite directions. Understanding this will give you a better understanding of how monetary policy actually works.

To see why bond prices and interest rates are inversely related, we need to analyze bond contracts more closely. A bond is a contract between a seller (the company or government issuing the bond) and a buyer that determines the following items:

- Coupon rate of the bond
- Maturity date of the bond
- Face value of the bond

The seller agrees to pay the buyer a fixed rate of interest (the coupon rate) on the face value of the bond (usually $1,000 for a corporate bond, but much larger values for government bonds) until a future fixed date (the maturity date of the bond). So, if XYZ Company issues a bond with a face value of $1,000 at a coupon rate of 5%, it agrees to pay the bondholder $50 per year until the maturity date of the bond. Note that this $50 payment per year is *fixed* for the life of the bond.

Once a bond is issued, it is subject to the forces of the marketplace. As economic circumstances change, people may be willing to pay more or less for a bond originally sold for $1,000. The *yield* on a bond is the percentage return earned over the life of the bond. Yields change when bond prices change.

Assume, for instance, that when a $1,000 bond is issued, general interest rates are 5%, so that the bond yields an annual interest payment of $50. For simplicity, let's assume that the bond is a perpetuity bond—that is, the bond has no maturity date. The issuer of the bond has agreed to pay $50 a year *forever* for the use of this money.

Assume that market interest rates rise to 8%. Just how much would the typical investor now be willing to pay for this bond that returns $50 a year? We can approach this intuitively. If we can buy a $1,000 bond now that pays $80 per year, why would we pay $1,000 for a similar bond that pays only $50? Would we pay more or less for the $50-paying bond? Intuitively, if we can get an $80-paying bond for $1,000, we would pay *less* for a $50-paying bond.

There is a simple formula we can use for perpetuity bonds:

$$\text{Yield} = \frac{\text{Interest Payment}}{\text{Price of Bond}}$$

Or rearranging terms:

$$\text{Price of Bond} = \frac{\text{Interest Payment}}{\text{Yield}}$$

The new price of the bond will be $625 ($50 ÷ 0.08 = $625). Clearly, as market interest rates went up, the price of this bond fell. Conversely, if market interest rates were to fall, say, from 5% to 3%, the price of the bond would rise to $1,666.67 ($50 ÷ 0.03 = $1,666.67).

Keep this relationship between market interest rates and bond prices in mind when we focus on the tools of monetary policy.

**CHECKPOINT**

### THE FINANCIAL SYSTEM AND THE MARKET FOR LOANABLE FUNDS

- Households supply loanable funds to the market because they spend less than their income and because they are rewarded with interest for saving.
- Firms demand funds to invest in profitable opportunities.
- The supply curve of funds is positively sloped; higher real interest rates bring more funds into the market. The demand for loanable funds is negatively sloped, reflecting the fact that at higher real interest rates, fewer investment projects are profitable.
- Any policy that provides additional incentives for households to save will increase the supply of loanable funds, resulting in lower interest rates and greater investment.
- Anything that increases the potential profitability (rate of return) of business investments will increase the demand for loanable funds, resulting in higher interest rates and investment.
- Financial institutions are financial intermediaries that build a bridge between savers and borrowers.
- Financial institutions reduce transaction costs, information costs, and risk, making financial markets more efficient.
- Bond prices and interest rates are inversely related.

**QUESTION:** How do recessions affect the market for loanable funds? What happens to the supply of savings? What happens to the demand for borrowing? What happens to the supply and demand curves found in Figure 2?

Answers to the Checkpoint questions can be found at the end of this chapter.

## How Banks Create Money

The role banks and money play in the U.S. economy has a long history. Banks are essential for an economy to expand beyond the constraints of the barter system. The primary purpose of financial markets and financial institutions is to act as conduits for transferring funds from lenders to borrowers. By accepting deposits and making loans, however, banks and other financial institutions are also able to create money. Let us see how this happens.

Banks and other financial institutions offer consumers and businesses many services, including checking and savings accounts, ATM services, loans, estate management services, and safe deposit boxes. The most important of these is checking services, also known as *demand deposits,* since checking account balances are "due on demand."

As we have seen, money supply M1 includes currency and demand deposits, and other checkable deposits. This money supply splits roughly evenly between currency and checkable deposits. These checkable deposits are what allow banks and other financial institutions to create money through the issuance of loans. The whole process works because of a fractional reserve system.

## Fractional Reserve System

Most of M1 is used for transaction purposes. A bank will take our deposits, say, when we get a paycheck, then disburses these funds to sellers as we write checks, use our debit cards, or pay bills electronically for various goods and services.

Banks loan money for consumer purchases and business investments. Assume you deposit $1,000 into your checking account and the bank then loans this $1,000 to a local business to purchase some machinery. If you were to go to the bank the next day and ask to withdraw your funds, how would the bank pay you? The bank could not pay you if you were its only customer. Banks, however, have many customers, and the chance that all these customers would want to withdraw their money on the same day is small.

Such "runs on the bank" are rare, normally occurring only when banks or a country's currency are in trouble; the run by depositors on the Northern Rock bank in Britain in late 2007 is one recent example. The British government agreed to insure all deposits and the run ended. In the United States, the Federal Deposit Insurance Corporation (FDIC) protects bank deposits (up to $250,000 per account) from bank failure. When a bank gets in trouble, the FDIC typically arranges for another healthy bank to take over the failing bank so the result is virtually no interruption of services to the bank's customers. The bank takeover usually occurs late on Friday and the bank reopens on Monday morning under a new name. Since most accounts are insured, it is business as usual on Monday.

Courtesy of Author

A bit of unusual economic graffiti found on a Venice, California, ATM machine.

It was the possibility of bank runs that led to the **fractional reserve banking system.** When someone deposits money into a bank account, the bank is required to hold part of this deposit in its vault as cash, or else in an account with the regional Federal Reserve Bank. We will learn more about the Federal Reserve System at the end of this chapter, but for the moment, let us continue to concentrate on how fractional reserve banking permits banks to create money.

**Fractional reserve banking system:** To prevent bank runs (all depositors demanding their deposits in cash at the same time), a portion of bank deposits must be held as vault cash, or else in an account with the regional Federal Reserve Bank.

### The Money Creation Process

Banks create money by lending their excess reserves. When money is loaned out, it eventually is deposited back into the original bank or some other bank. The bank will again hold some of these new deposits as reserves, loaning out the rest. The whole process continues until the entire initial deposit is held as reserves somewhere in the banking system.

To illustrate this process of money creation, we will use a stylized bank balance sheet that ignores the capital requirements necessary to open a bank. Under these simplified conditions, a bank balance sheet reads as follows:

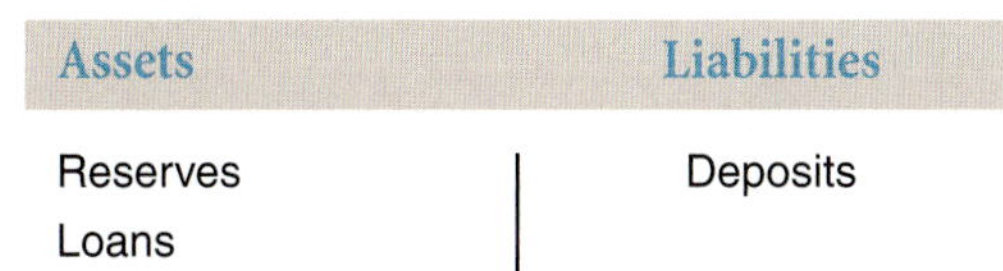

| Assets | Liabilities |
|---|---|
| Reserves | Deposits |
| Loans | |

Liabilities are shown on the right side of the balance sheet. When you deposit money into the bank, it becomes a liability for the bank—the bank owes you money. Specifically, the bank is obliged to give you the deposited money on demand. To balance out this liability, however, the bank now has an asset consisting of the funds from your deposit. Assets are shown on the left side of the balance sheet. In our simple banking world, the bank can either put your funds into reserves or loan out part of this money to business or consumers. These loans become assets of the bank, since borrowers have an obligation to pay the bank back.

Assume that the Federal Reserve sets the reserve requirement at 20%. So, by law, banks must hold 20% of each deposit as reserves, whether in their vaults or in accounts with the regional Federal Reserve Bank. Now assume that you dig $1,000 out of your mattress at home and take it to Bank A. Note that this money is considered "out of circulation," so we can consider it new money put into the system. Bank A puts 20% of your $1,000 into its vault and loans out the rest. Its balance sheet now reads:

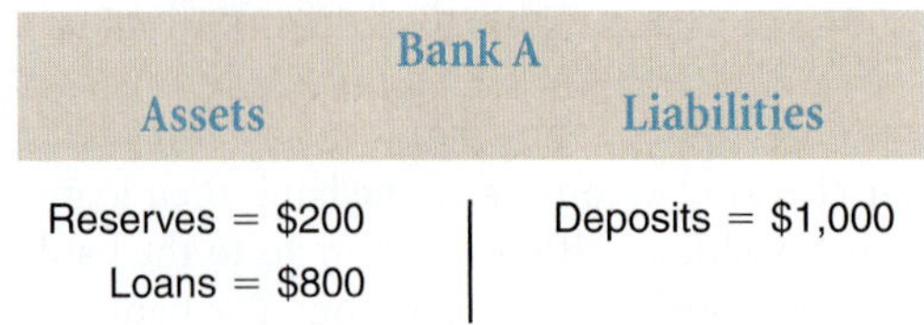

| Bank A | |
|---|---|
| **Assets** | **Liabilities** |
| Reserves = $200 | Deposits = $1,000 |
| Loans = $800 | |

As the balance sheet indicates, your $1,000 deposit is now a liability for Bank A. But the bank also has new assets, split between reserves and loans as required by the Fed. (In each of the transactions that follow, we assume banks become fully *loaned-up,* loaning out all they can and keeping in reserves only the amount required by law.)

Assume that Bank A loans out the $800 it has in excess funds to a local gas station, and assume this money is deposited into Bank B. Bank B's balance sheet now reads:

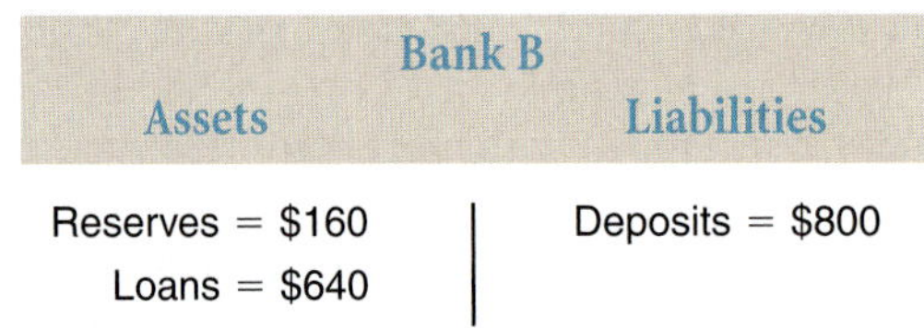

| Bank B | |
|---|---|
| **Assets** | **Liabilities** |
| Reserves = $160 | Deposits = $800 |
| Loans = $640 | |

Bank B, in other words, has new deposits totaling $800. Of this, the bank must put $160 into reserves; the remaining $640 it loans out to a local winery. The winery deposits these funds into its bank, Bank C. This bank's balance sheet shows:

| Bank C | |
|---|---|
| **Assets** | **Liabilities** |
| Reserves = $128 | Deposits = $640 |
| Loans = $512 | |

Summing up the balance sheets of the three banks shows that total reserves have grown to $488 ($200 + $160 + $128), loans have reached $1,952 ($800 + $640 + $512), and total deposits are $2,440 ($1,000 + $800 + $640). Your original $1,000 new deposit has caused the money supply to grow.

| Banks A, B, C | |
|---|---|
| **Assets** | **Liabilities** |
| Reserves = $488 | Deposits = $2,440 |
| Loans = $1,952 | |

This process continues until the entire $1,000 of the original deposit has been placed in reserves, thus raising total reserves by $1,000. By this point, all the banks together will have loaned out a total of $4,000. A summary balance sheet for all banks in the area reads:

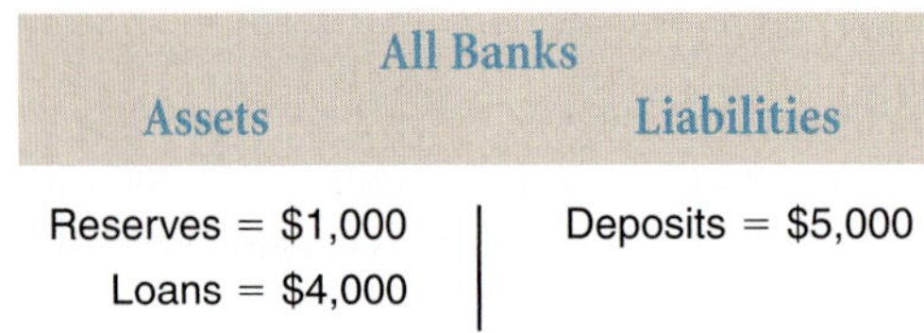

| All Banks | |
|---|---|
| **Assets** | **Liabilities** |
| Reserves = $1,000 | Deposits = $5,000 |
| Loans = $4,000 | |

Notice what has happened. Keeping in mind that demand deposits form part of the money supply, your original deposit of $1,000—new money injected into the banking system—has ended up increasing the money supply by $5,000. Bank reserves, in other words, have gone up by your initial deposit, but beyond this, an added $4,000 has been created. And this was made possible because banks were allowed to loan part of your deposit to consumers and businesses.

## The Money Multiplier

We have just seen how banks create new money when they accept deposits. The **money multiplier** measures the *potential* or maximum amount the money supply can increase (or decrease) when new deposits enter (exit) the system. The money multiplier is defined as:

**Money multiplier:** Measures the *potential* or *maximum* amount the money supply can increase (or decrease) when new deposits enter (exit) the system and is defined as 1 divided by the reserve requirement. The actual money multiplier will be less, since some banks hold excess reserves.

$$\text{Money Multiplier} = \frac{1}{\text{Reserve Requirement}}$$

Thus, if the reserve requirement is 20%, as in our example, the money multiplier is 1/0.20 = 5. And so an initial deposit of $1,000 ends up creating $5,000 in money.

Notice that this formula gives us the *potential* money multiplier. The actual money multiplier will be less because of leakages from the system. For one thing, not all the money loaned out is deposited back into banking accounts. Some people and businesses keep some of their loans in cash for transactions purposes. This action diminishes their deposits, thus reducing the actual multiplier.

Similarly, banks do not always want to be loaned-up. At times, they may choose to keep some excess reserves, or reserves above the legally required amount. Again, this action reduces the actual money multiplier, since issuing smaller loans recirculates less money back through the larger system.

The key point, though, is that banks can create money, almost out of thin air. This is a large power.

Now that we understand that banks influence the supply of money because they can create money, let us turn to a brief survey of the Federal Reserve System. We consider how it is organized, what purposes it serves, and what functions it has; the next chapter takes a closer look at the Fed in action.

**CHECKPOINT**

### HOW BANKS CREATE MONEY

- The fractional reserve system permits banks to create money through their ability to accept deposits and make loans.
- The potential money multiplier is equal to 1 divided by the reserve requirement. This is the maximum value for the multiplier. The actual money multiplier will be less, as some banks will hold excess reserves and not all of the funds from loans will be deposited in the banking system.

**QUESTION:** If the Federal Reserve did not have any reserve requirements for member banks, would those banks hold zero reserves? Why or why not?

Answers to the Checkpoint questions can be found at the end of this chapter.

## The Federal Reserve System

The **Federal Reserve System** is the central bank of the United States. It controls this huge power to create money.

**Federal Reserve System:** The central bank of the United States.

Early in U.S. history, banks were private and chartered by the states. In the 1800s and early 1900s, bank panics were common. After an unusually severe banking crisis in 1907,

Congress established the National Monetary Commission. This commission proposed one central bank with sweeping powers. But a powerful national bank became a political issue in the elections of 1912, and the commission's proposals gave way to a compromise that is today's Federal Reserve System.

The Federal Reserve Act of 1913 was a compromise between competing proposals for a huge central bank and for no central bank at all. The Act declared that the Fed is "to provide for the establishment of Federal reserve banks, to furnish an elastic currency, to afford means of rediscounting commercial paper, to establish a more effective supervision of banking in the United States, and for other purposes."

Since 1913, other acts have further clarified and supplemented the original act, expanding the Fed's mission. These acts include the Employment Act of 1946, the International Banking Act of 1978, the Full Employment and Balanced Growth Act of 1978, the Depository Institutions Deregulation and Monetary Control Act of 1980, and the Federal Deposit Insurance Corporation Improvement Act of 1991.

The original Federal Reserve Act, the Employment Act of 1946, and the Full Employment and Balanced Growth Act of 1978 all mandate national economic objectives. These acts require the Fed to promote economic growth accompanied by full employment, stable prices, and moderate long-term interest rates. As we will see in the next chapter, meeting all of these objectives at once has often proved difficult, if not downright impossible.

The Federal Reserve is considered to be an independent central bank, in that its actions are not subject to executive branch control. The entire Federal Reserve System is, however, subject to oversight from Congress. The Constitution invests Congress with the power to coin money and set its value, so the Federal Reserve Act delegated this power to the Fed, subject to congressional oversight. Though several presidents have disagreed with Fed policy over the years, the Fed has always managed to maintain its independence from the executive branch.

Experience in this country and abroad suggests that independent central banks are better at fighting inflation than are politically controlled banks. The main reason for this, in the words of the Council of Economic Advisers, "is that an independent central bank is less vulnerable to short-term political pressures to inflate than are those with closer links to the government. During recessions, governments may try to rely on too much expansionary monetary policy to hasten a recovery."[2]

## The Structure of the Federal Reserve

As noted earlier, the Federal Reserve System was a compromise between competing proposals for a massive central bank and no central bank at all. What Congress finally settled on were *regional* banks governed by a central authority. The intent was to provide the Fed with a broad perspective on the economy, with the regional Federal Reserve Banks contributing economic analysis from all parts of the nation, while still investing a central authority with the power to carry out a national monetary policy.

The Fed is composed of a central governing agency, the Board of Governors, located in Washington, D.C., and twelve regional Federal Reserve Banks in major cities around the nation. Figure 3 shows the twelve Fed districts and their bank locations.

### The Board of Governors

The Fed's Board of Governors consists of seven members who are appointed by the president and confirmed by the Senate. Board members serve terms of 14 years, after which they cannot be reappointed. Appointments to the Board are staggered so that one term expires on January 31 of every even-numbered year. The current chairman, Ben Bernanke, and the vice chairman of the Board must already be Board members; they are appointed to their leadership positions by the president, subject to Senate confirmation, for terms of four years. The Board of Governors' staff of nearly 2,000 helps the Fed carry out its responsibilities for monetary policy, and banking and consumer credit regulation.

[2] *Economic Report of the President,* 1993, p. 97.

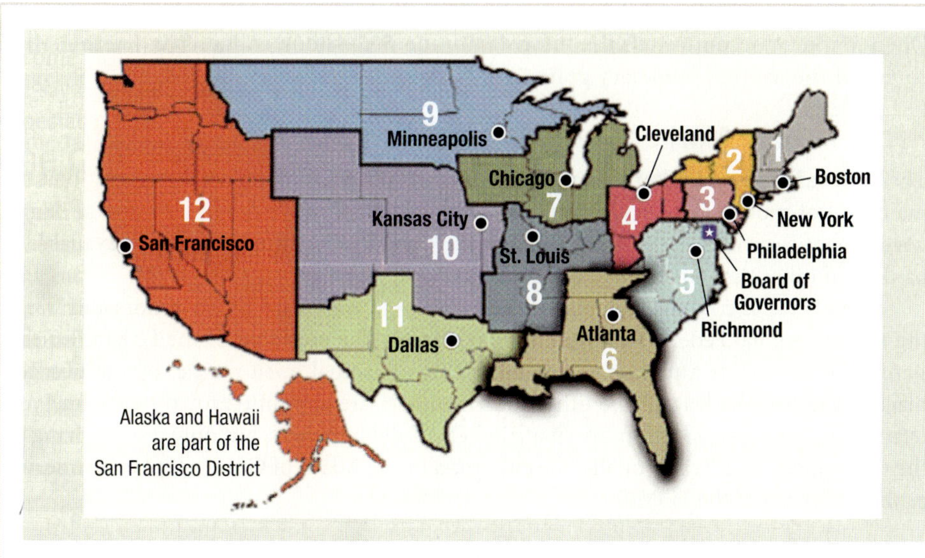


**FIGURE 3—Regional Federal Reserve Districts**

The twelve regional Federal Reserve districts and their bank locations.

## Federal Reserve Banks

Twelve Federal Reserve Banks and their branches perform a variety of functions, including providing a nationwide payments system, distributing coins and currency, regulating and supervising member banks, and serving as the banker for the U.S. Treasury. Table 1 lists all regional banks and their main locations. Each regional bank has a number and letter associated with it. If you look at your money, you will see that all U.S. currency bears the designation of the regional bank where it was first issued, as shown in Table 1.

Each regional bank also provides the Federal Reserve System and the Board of Governors with information on economic conditions in its home region. This information is compiled into a report—called the Beige Book—that details the economic conditions around the country. This report is provided to the Board a few weeks before policy

**TABLE 1** Federal Reserve Regional Banks

| Number | Bank | Letter |
|---|---|---|
| 1 | Boston | A |
| 2 | New York | B |
| 3 | Philadelphia | C |
| 4 | Cleveland | D |
| 5 | Richmond | E |
| 6 | Atlanta | F |
| 7 | Chicago | G |
| 8 | St. Louis | H |
| 9 | Minneapolis | I |
| 10 | Kansas City | J |
| 11 | Dallas | K |
| 12 | San Francisco | L |

decisions are required, and it is later released to the public. The Board and the Federal Open Market Committee use the information the Beige Book contains to determine the course of the nation's monetary policy.

### Federal Open Market Committee

**Federal Open Market Committee (FOMC):** This twelve-member committee is composed of members of the Board of Governors of the Fed and selected presidents of the regional Federal Reserve Banks; it oversees open market operations (the buying and selling of government securities), the main tool of monetary policy.

The **Federal Open Market Committee (FOMC)** oversees open market operations, the main tool of monetary policy. Open market operations involve the buying and selling of government securities. How these open market operations influence reserves available to banks and other thrift institutions will become clear shortly.

The FOMC is composed of the seven members of the Board of Governors and five of the twelve regional Federal Reserve Bank presidents. The president of the Federal Reserve Bank of New York is a permanent member because actual open market operations take place at the New York Fed. The other four members are appointed for rotating one-year terms. All regional presidents participate in FOMC deliberations, but only those serving on the Committee vote. Traditionally, the chairman of the Board of Governors has also served as the chairman of the FOMC.

### The Fed as Lender of Last Resort

The essence of banking, as we have seen, is that banks take in short-term loans (deposits) and make long-term, often illiquid, loans (assets). This puts banks in the unique position of facing extraordinary withdrawals when people panic and all want their money at the same time. Banks typically do not have sufficient reserves to stem a full-fledged financial panic. They cannot turn these long-term loans into cash. During a panic, banks would be forced to dump the securities or loans onto the market at a deep discount (or "take a haircut" in modern parlance), potentially forcing them into insolvency. Lending to banks during financial panics—being a lender of last resort—is a principal reason for the existence of central banks.

The value of the Fed's ability to provide loans during a financial crisis stood out during the financial panic in late 2008. The Fed extended credit where none was available. As markets collapse during financial panics, banks become reluctant to lend out money to businesses and to other banks that need cash in an emergency. This is when the Fed steps in.

In just a few months, the Fed extended more that $2 trillion in loans and altered its balance sheet in ways not seen since it was created in 1913. Had the Fed and its "lender of last resort" capability not been available, the 2008–2009 recession would have been much deeper and could possibly have resulted in another Great Depression. We say more about the financial panic of 2008 in the next chapter.

## Federal Reserve: Tools, Targets, and Policy Lags

How is monetary policy actually carried out? Setting monetary policy is the role of the Federal Reserve. It has three primary tools at its disposal for conducting monetary policy:

- **Reserve requirements**—the required ratio of funds that commercial banks and other depository institutions must hold in reserve against deposits.
- **The discount rate**—the interest rate the Federal Reserve charges commercial banks and other depository institutions to borrow reserves from a regional Federal Reserve Bank.
- **Open market operations**—the buying and selling on the open market of U.S. government securities, usually Treasury bonds, to adjust reserves in the banking system.

### Reserve Requirements

**Reserve requirements:** The required ratio of funds that commercial banks and other depository institutions must hold in reserve against deposits.

The Federal Reserve Act specifies that the Fed must establish **reserve requirements** for all banks and other depository institutions. As we have seen, this law gives rise to a fractional reserve system that enables banks to create new money, expanding demand deposits through loans. The potential expansion depends on the money multiplier, which in turn depends on the reserve requirement ratio. By altering the reserve ratio, the Fed can alter reserves in the system and alter the supply of money in the economy.

Banks hold two types of reserves: required reserves and excess reserves above what they are required to hold. Roughly 15,000 depository institutions, ranging from banks to thrift institutions, are bound by the Fed's reserve requirements. Reserves are kept as vault cash or in accounts with the regional Federal Reserve Bank. These accounts not only help satisfy reserve requirements, but are also used to clear many financial transactions.

Banks are assessed a penalty if their accounts with the Fed are overdrawn at the end of the day. Given the unpredictability of the volume of transactions that may clear a bank's account on a given day, most banks choose to maintain excess reserves. Interest earned on these excess reserves is then used to pay the cost of Fed services, such as check clearing.

At the end of the day, banks and other depository institutions can loan one another reserves or trade reserves in the Federal Funds Market. One bank's surplus of reserves can become loans to another institution, earning interest (the **federal funds rate**). A change in the federal funds rate reflects changes in the market demand and supply of excess reserves.

**Federal funds rate:** The interest rate financial institutions charge each other for overnight loans used as reserves.

When banks hold excess reserves, they reduce the actual money multiplier. By raising or lowering the reserve ratio, the Fed can add reserves to the system or squeeze reserves from it, thereby altering the supply of money. Yet, changing the reserve requirement is almost like doing surgery with a bread knife. The impact of changing the reserve requirement is so massive and imprecise that the Fed rarely uses this tool.

When the Fed does resort to changing the reserve requirement, moreover, it usually does so to accomplish other, non-monetary-policy objectives. Economists Scott Hein and Jonathan Stewart studied the Fed's reserve requirement reductions in 1992 and concluded that the Fed acted "to ease the credit crunch of that time and improve the profitability of depository institutions without expanding the money supply or lowering interest rates."[3]

## Discount Rate

The **discount rate** is the rate regional Federal Reserve Banks charge depository institutions for short-term loans to shore up their reserves. The discount window also serves as a backup source of liquidity for individual depository institutions.

**Discount rate:** The interest rate the Federal Reserve charges commercial banks and other depository institutions to borrow reserves from a regional Federal Reserve Bank.

The Fed extends discount rate credit to banks and other depository institutions typically for overnight balancing of reserves. The rate charged is roughly 1 percentage point higher than the FOMC's target federal funds rate. However, banks would typically use the federal funds market unless that market breaks down as it did in late 2008. As noted earlier, the federal funds rate is the interest rate that banks and other financial institutions with excess reserves charge other banks for overnight loans to help them shore up their reserves. As we will see below, this is an important target for Federal Reserve policy.

Neither the discount rate nor the reserve ratio, however, gives the Fed as much power to implement monetary policy as open market operations. Open market operations allow the Fed to alter the supply of money and system reserves by buying and selling government securities.

## Open Market Operations

When one private financial institution buys a government bond from another, funds are simply redistributed around the economy; the transaction does not change reserves in the economy. When the Fed buys a government security, however, it pays some private financial institution for this bond; thus, it adds to aggregate reserves by putting new money into the financial system.

**Open market operations** are powerful because of the dollar-for-dollar change in reserves that comes from buying or selling government securities. When the FOMC buys a $100,000 bond, $100,000 of new reserves are instantly put into the banking system. These new reserves have the potential to expand the money supply as banks make loans.

**Open market operations:** The buying and selling of U.S. government securities, usually Treasury bonds, to adjust reserves in the banking system.

[3] See Scott Hein and Jonathan Stewart, "Reserve Requirements: A Modern Perspective," *Economic Review*, Federal Reserve Bank of Atlanta, Fourth Quarter, 2002, pp. 41–52.

## The Federal Funds Target

The Fed cannot alter the price level or output directly. It can change bank reserves with open market operations, thereby altering the money supply, which will change interest rates and ultimately alter investment and other interest-sensitive components of consumption and net exports.

The target federal funds rate is the Fed's primary approach to monetary policy. The FOMC meetings result in a decision on the target federal funds rate, which is announced at the end of the meeting. Keep in mind that the federal funds rate is not something that the Fed directly controls. Banks lend overnight reserves to each other in this market, and the forces of supply and demand set the interest rate.

The Fed uses open market operations to adjust reserves and thus change nominal interest rates with the goal of nudging the federal funds rate toward the Fed's target. When the Fed buys bonds, its demand raises the price of bonds, lowering nominal interest rates in the market. The opposite occurs when the Fed sells bonds and adds to the market supply of bonds for sale, lowering prices and raising the nominal interest rate. The Fed has actually been pretty good at keeping the federal funds rate near the target, as Figure 4 illustrates.

**FIGURE 4—The Federal Funds Rate and Target Federal Funds Rate**

In the last two decades, the Fed has been very successful at hitting its federal funds target rate.

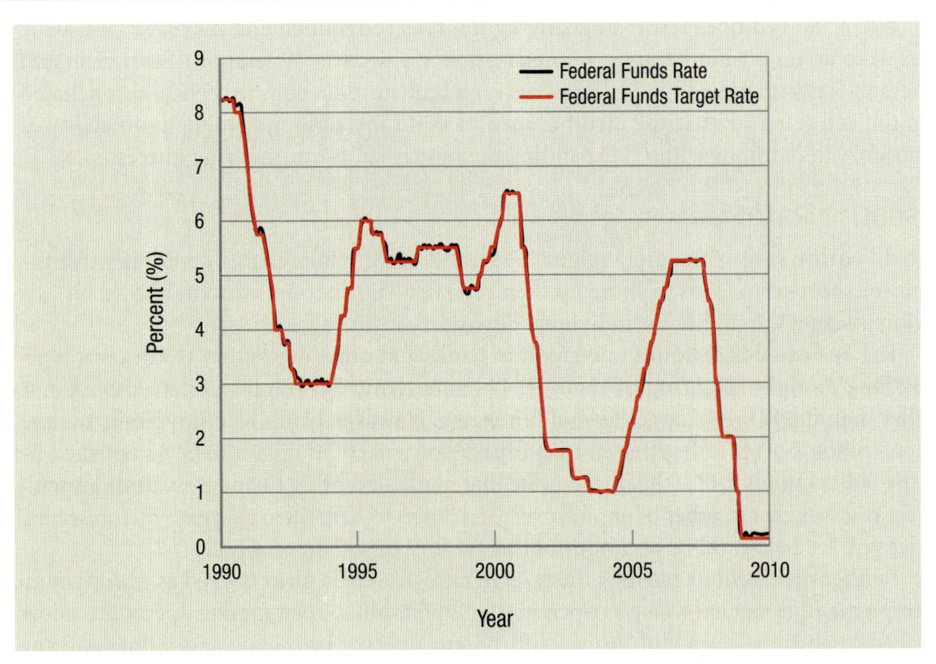


In summary, typically the Fed sets a target for the federal funds rate and then uses open market operations to manipulate reserves to alter the money supply. Changing the money supply alters market interest rates to bring the federal funds rate in line with the Fed's target. Open market purchases increase reserves, reducing the need for banks to borrow, lowering the federal funds rate, and vice versa for open market sales. The key thing to note here is that the Fed does not directly control the money supply: it proceeds indirectly, though it has been very successful in meeting its goals.

## Monetary Policy Lags

Though the Fed's tools have important impacts on interest rates, bank reserves, and the money supply, they take some time to have an effect on the economy, like the fiscal policy we discussed earlier. And like fiscal policy, monetary policy is subject to four major lags: information, recognition, decision, and implementation lags. The combination of these lags can make monetary policy difficult for the Fed. Not only does the Fed face a moving bull's-eye in terms of its economic targets, but often it can be difficult for the Fed to know when its own policies will take effect and what their effect will be.

***Information Lags*** We discussed information lags when we discussed fiscal policy lags: economic data are available only after a lag of one to three months. So when an economic event takes place, changes may ripple throughout the economy for up to three months before monetary authorities begin to see changes in their data. Many economic measures published by the government, moreover, are subject to future revision. It is not uncommon for these revisions to be so significant as to render the original number meaningless. Thus, it might take the Fed several quarters to clearly identify a changing trend in prices or output.

***Recognition Lags*** Simply seeing a decline in a variable in one month or quarter does not necessarily mean that a change in policy is warranted. Data revisions upward and downward are common. In the normal course of events, for instance, unemployment rates can fluctuate by small amounts, as can GDP. A quarter-percent decline in the rate of growth of GDP does not necessarily signal the beginning of a recession, although it could. Nor does a quarter-percent increase in GDP mean the economy has reached the bottom of a recession; double-dip recessions are always a possibility.

Because of this recognition lag, policymakers are often unable to recognize problems when they first develop. In the economy, as in life, small problems are usually easier to solve before they become big problems.

***Decision Lags*** The Federal Reserve Board meets roughly on a monthly basis to determine broad economic policy, so once a problem is recognized, decisions are forthcoming. Decision lags for monetary policy are shorter than for fiscal policy. Once the Fed makes a decision to, say, avert a recession, the FOMC can begin to implement that decision almost immediately. As Figure 4 illustrates, once the Fed decides on a federal funds target, nominal interest rates track that target in a hurry. In contrast, fiscal policy decisions typically require administrative proposals and then congressional action.

***Implementation Lags*** Once the FOMC has decided on a policy, there is another lag associated with the reaction of banks and financial markets. Monetary policy affects bank reserves, interest rates, and decisions by businesses and households. As interest rates change, investment and buying decisions are altered, but often not with any great haste. Investment decisions hinge on more than just interest rate levels. Rules, regulations, permits, tax incentives, and future expectations (what Keynes called "animal spirits") all enter the decision-making process.

Economists estimate that the average lag for monetary policy is between a year and 18 months, with a range varying from a little over one quarter to slightly over two years. Using monetary policy to fine-tune the economy requires not only skill, but possibly some luck. The next chapter looks more deeply into how the Fed uses monetary policies to balance its goals of keeping income growing and prices stable.

## CHECKPOINT

### THE FEDERAL RESERVE SYSTEM

- The Federal Reserve is the central bank of the United States.
- The Federal Reserve System is structured around twelve regional banks and a central governing agency, the Board of Governors.
- The Federal Open Market Committee oversees open market operations for the Fed.
- The Fed's tools include altering reserve requirements, changing the discount rate, and open market operations (the buying and selling of government securities).

- The Fed uses open market operations to keep the federal funds rate at target levels.
- The Fed's policies, as with fiscal policy, are subject to information, recognition, decision, and implementation lags.

**QUESTION:** The reserve requirement sets the required percentage of vault cash plus deposits with the regional Federal Reserve banks that banks must keep for their deposits. Many banks have widespread branches and ATMs. Would the existence of branches and ATMs affect the level of excess reserves (above those required) that banks hold? Why or why not? What would be the effect on the actual money multiplier?

Answers to the Checkpoint questions can be found at the end of this chapter.

## Key Concepts



## Chapter Summary

### What Is Money?

Money is anything that is accepted in exchange for other goods and services or for the payment of debts.

Money has three primary functions: as a medium of exchange, as a measure of value (unit of account), and as a store of value. Using money as a medium of exchange overcomes the double coincidence of wants problem that plagues barter economies. Using money as a measure of value drastically reduces the number of prices individuals must determine. Money is a durable store of value; it allows people to save the money they earn today and use it to buy goods and services tomorrow.

An asset's liquidity is determined by how fast, easily, and reliably it can be converted into cash. Money is the most liquid asset because it is the medium of exchange and requires no conversion.

The Federal Reserve System uses two different measures of the money supply. M1 includes currency (coins and paper money), demand deposits (checks), and other accounts that have check writing capabilities. M2 is composed of M1 plus the "near moneys": money that cannot be drawn upon instantaneously but is nonetheless accessible, including savings accounts, money market deposit accounts, and money market mutual fund accounts.

### The Financial System and the Market for Loanable Funds

The market for loanable funds describes the financial market for saving and investment. Households spend less than they earn and supply funds to the loanable funds market, earning interest as recompense. Firms demand funds for profitable investment opportunities. Savers increase the amount they provide the market if interest rates are higher, hence there is a positively sloped supply curve. At higher interest rates, fewer business investments are profitable, and as interest rates fall, more investments will be undertaken; hence, there is a negatively sloped demand curve for loanable funds. Market equilibrium real interest rates are determined by equating the supply and demand for loanable funds.

The supply of loanable funds changes in response to incentives to save. Demand for loanable funds responds to changes in the potential profitability of investments.

Financial institutions or financial intermediaries accept funds from savers and efficiently channel these to borrowers, including consumers, firms, and government. This role is essential because the people who save are typically not the same people who have profitable investment opportunities.

Financial intermediaries reduce transactions costs and information costs, and lower risk.

A bond is a contract between a seller (the company or government issuing the bond) and a buyer. As a general rule, as market interest rates rise, the value of bonds (paying fixed dollars of interest) fall. Conversely, if interest rates drop, the price of bonds rise.

## How Banks Create Money

Banks operate under a fractional reserve system that allows them to create money. Banks accept deposits and hold only a certain required fraction of these deposits, loaning out the rest. Most of the money loaned out is deposited back into the system. Part of these deposits is held as new reserves; the rest is again loaned out. This process continues until the entire initial deposit is held as reserves somewhere in the banking system. By this point, the new money in the economy has expanded to well beyond the size of the original deposit.

The money multiplier measures the potential or maximum amount the money supply can increase (or decrease) when new deposits enter (exit) the system. The money multiplier is defined as 1 divided by the reserve requirement.

## The Federal Reserve System

The Federal Reserve System is the central bank of the United States. It was established by the Federal Reserve Act of 1913 and is required by law to promote economic growth accompanied by full employment, stable prices, and moderate long-term interest rates.

The Federal Reserve is an independent central bank, in that its actions are not subject to executive branch oversight, although the entire Federal Reserve System is subject to oversight by Congress. Experience in the United States and other countries suggests that independent central banks are better at fighting inflation than are politically controlled banks.

The Fed is composed of a central governing agency—the Board of Governors—and twelve regional Federal Reserve Banks. The Board of Governors consists of seven members appointed by the president and confirmed by the Senate. The twelve regional Federal Reserve Banks and their branches provide a nationwide payments system, distribute coins and currency, regulate and supervise member banks, and serve as the banker for the U.S. Treasury.

The Fed is the guarantor of the financial system. It is the lender of last resort.

The Fed's major tools include changing reserve requirements, altering the discount rate, and open market operations (buying and selling government bonds).

The Fed targets the federal funds rate.

Monetary policy, just like fiscal policy, is subject to lags.

# Questions and Problems

## Check Your Understanding

1. Describe the three functions of money.
2. Describe why barter is inefficient and why no modern economy could exist on barter.
3. Besides being legal tender, what differentiates money from most of the goods we consume?

4. Describe the role required reserves play in determining how much money the banking system creates.
5. Why are checking accounts (demand deposits) considered a liability to the bank?
6. Explain why the actual money multiplier is less than its potential (1 divided by the reserve requirement).
7. The Federal Deposit Insurance Corporation (FDIC) insures individual bank accounts up to $250,000 per account. Does the existence of this insurance eliminate the need for reserve requirements? Does it essentially prevent "runs" on banks?
8. Explain the important difference between M1 and M2.
9. What gives our money its value if there is no gold or silver backing the currency?
10. What happens to savings if the real interest rate goes up? What happens to the demand for borrowing?
11. Explain why bond prices and interest rates are inversely related.

## Apply the Concepts

12. List the following assets from most liquid to least liquid: a house (real estate); cash; a one-carat diamond; a savings account; 100 shares of Google; a Harley Davidson motorcycle; a checking account; your old leather jacket.
13. Many central banks in the world are independent in the sense that they are partially isolated from short-run political considerations and pressures. How is this independence attained? How important is this independence to policymaking at the Federal Reserve?
14. Alan Greenspan, the former chairman of the Fed, noted that "the Federal Reserve has to be independent in its actions and as an institution, because if Federal Reserve independence is in any way compromised, it undercuts our capability of protecting the value of the currency in society." What is so important about protecting the value of the currency? How does Fed independence help?

## In The News

15. Eric Keetch offered an interesting anecdote in the *Financial Times* (August 12, 2009):

    *In a sleepy European holiday resort town in a depressed economy and therefore no visitors, there is great excitement when a wealthy Russian guest appears in the local hotel reception, announces that he intends to stay for an extended period and places a €100 note on the counter as surety while he demands to be shown the available rooms.*

    *While he is being shown the room, the hotelier takes the €100 note round to his butcher, who is pressing for payment.*

    *The butcher in turn pays his wholesaler who, in turn, pays his farmer supplier.*

    *The farmer takes the note round to his favorite "good time girl" to whom he owes €100 for services rendered. She, in turn, rushes round to the hotel to settle her bill for rooms provided on credit.*

    *In the meantime, the Russian returns to the lobby, announces that no rooms are satisfactory, takes back his €100 note and leaves, never to be seen again.*

    *No new money has been introduced into the local economy, but everyone's debts have been settled.*

    What's going on here? In the end, no new money was introduced into the town, but all debts were paid. Is the money multiplier infinite? How do you explain what has happened? Did local GDP increase as a result of all debts being paid?

## Solving Problems

**16.** Assume that First Purity Bank begins with the balance sheet below and is fully loaned-up. Answer the questions that follow.

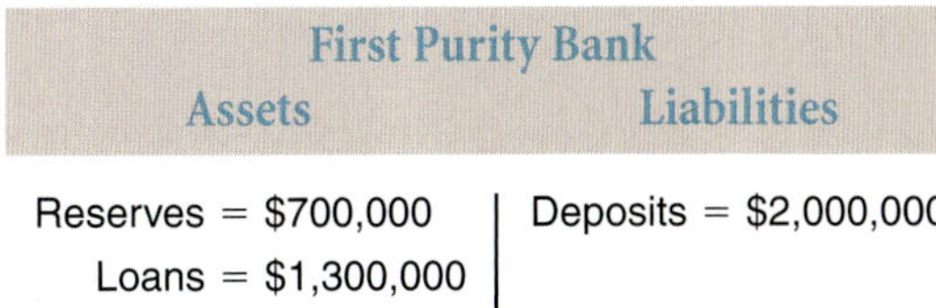

| First Purity Bank | |
|---|---|
| Assets | Liabilities |
| Reserves = \$700,000 | Deposits = \$2,000,000 |
| Loans = \$1,300,000 | |

a. What is the reserve requirement equal to?

b. If the bank receives a new deposit of \$1 million and the bank wants to remain fully loaned-up, how much of this new deposit will the bank loan out?

c. When the new deposit to First Purity Bank works itself through the entire banking system (assume all banks keep fully loaned-up), what will total deposits, total loans, and total reserves be equal to?

d. What is the potential money multiplier equal to in this case?

# Answers to Questions in CheckPoints

## Check Point: What Is Money?

Most of the quarters were withdrawn from circulation by the Fed or hoarded by individuals. When silver prices rose, many were sold and melted for bullion. Gresham's Law is not particularly important today since our money now is fiat money—money without intrinsic value.

## Check Point: The Financial System and the Market for Loanable Funds

In a recession, savings tend to increase and borrowings tend to fall. Supply shifts to the right and demand shifts to the left. Thus, real interest rates fall.

## Check Point: How Banks Create Money

Banks would still hold some reserves, just as banks currently hold excess reserves over the required limit. No bank would want to be at the mercy of a small bank run that would lead to its ruin, so it would keep some currency reserves on hand.

## Check Point: The Federal Reserve System

ATMs and branches require a lot of vault cash to maintain and might be expected to result in banks holding greater excess reserves. Thus, the actual money multiplier would be lower.

# Monetary Policy

REUTERS/Joe Pavel/Federal Reserve Board/Landov

**The Federal Reserve Act** mandates that the Federal Reserve implement monetary policies that will promote economic growth accompanied by high employment, stable prices, and moderate long-term interest rates. In the previous chapter, we saw how the financial system brings savers and borrowers together, how banks create money using a fractional reserve system, and how the Federal Reserve system is organized and what monetary policy tools it has. In this chapter, we look at monetary policy: why monetary policy can be effective, how the Federal Reserve actually undertakes monetary policy, and the financial crisis of 2008–2009.

The first part of this chapter considers several theories on how changes in the money supply affect the economy. We will see that money has no effect on the economy's real growth in the long run but can have sizeable effects in the short run. Having established that money can affect the economy in the short run, we examine the impact of monetary policy in controlling demand and supply shocks. In the second part of this chapter, we look at modern monetary policy to see how the Federal Reserve actually tries to manage the economy. We will see that the Fed's control over the economy is indirect and that good monetary policymaking is both art and science.

The last section looks at modern monetary policy in the context of the financial crisis of 2008–2009. What did the Fed do to deal with problems in the financial system?

Monetary policy is a key way that government influences the economy. As we will see, it can be more effective at some times than others. Furthermore, balancing the Fed's mandated goals is not an easy matter.

**After studying this chapter you should be able to:**

- ☐ Describe the equation of exchange and its implications for monetary policy.
- ☐ Describe the classical long-run monetary transmission mechanism.
- ☐ Describe Keynesian monetary analysis and the three motives for holding money.
- ☐ Describe the Keynesian monetary transmission mechanism and how it differs from classical theory.
- ☐ Describe the monetarist model of monetary theory.
- ☐ Describe the important differences in the three models of monetary theory and the implications of these differences for monetary policy.
- ☐ Describe why the Fed targets price stability in the long run and inflation rates and output in the short run.
- ☐ Determine the effectiveness of monetary policy when demand or supply shocks occur.
- ☐ Describe the controversy over whether the Fed should have discretion or be governed by simple monetary rules.
- ☐ Describe the federal funds target, the Taylor rule, and how they are used for modern monetary policy.

# Monetary Theories

In discussing the theories that justify monetary policy, it is best to differentiate the long run from the short run. We will see that money has no effect on the real economy (such as employment and output) in the long run but can have an effect in the short run.

## The Long Run: Quantity Theory

The *quantity theory of money* is a product of the classical school of economics. As we saw in an earlier chapter, classical economists focused on long-run adjustments in economic activity. In the long run, wages, prices, and interest rates are flexible, allowing the labor, product, and capital markets to adjust to keep the economy at full employment.

### The Equation of Exchange

Classical economists defined money narrowly, limiting it to currency and coins, while assuming that money is used for transactions purposes only. Money is held, they suggested, because spending and income do not occur at the same time: you receive income once or twice a month but spend that income over that entire period. The quantity theory was developed in a time of metallic currency when money was either gold or silver coins.

Quantity theory is defined by the **equation of exchange:**

$$M \times V = P \times Q$$

where $M$ is the supply of money, $V$ is the velocity of money (the average number of times per year a dollar is spent on goods and services, or the number of times it turns over in a year), $P$ is the price level, and $Q$ is the economy's real output level. Note that in contemporary terms, the right side of the equation—the aggregate price level times the level of output—is equal to nominal GDP.

**Equation of exchange:** The heart of classical monetary theory uses the equation $M \times V = P \times Q$, where $M$ is the supply of money, $V$ is the velocity of money (the average number of times per year a dollar is spent on goods and services, or the number of times it turns over in a year), $P$ is the price level, and $Q$ is the economy's output level.

For classical economists, the money supply consisted of currency, coins, and the beginnings of a banking sector. Velocity was determined by the quality of the prevailing monetary institutions and technology. Both of these were assumed to change slowly, meaning that velocity would also be slow to change.

In the long run, when the economy is at full employment, the implications for monetary policy are straightforward. Since velocity ($V$) is assumed to be fixed by existing monetary institutions and the state of technology, and aggregate output ($Q$) is assumed to be fixed at full employment, any change in the money supply ($\Delta M$) will translate directly to a change in prices ($\Delta P$).

In the long run, in other words, a change in the money supply will directly change the aggregate price level and have no effect on the real economy ($Q$). Alternatively, if the money supply increases by 10%, then the aggregate price level will rise by 10%. Since a 10% change in the aggregate price level is a 10% rate of inflation, the higher the rate of increase in the money supply the higher the rate of inflation the economy must endure.

Figure 1 on page 542 shows average monetary growth and inflation in thirty countries over the period 1970 to 2006. Notice the clear positive relationship between changes in the supply of money and inflation rates. This correlation is reasonably close over the entire period, confirming what Milton Friedman argued: "Inflation is always and everywhere a monetary phenomenon." It also makes clear that any central bank that wants to avoid high inflation must avoid rapid growth of its money supply.

### Long-Run Money Transmission Mechanism

What is the channel through which changes in the money supply influence prices in the long run? The equation of exchange suggests the process is quite direct: in the long run, any change in $M$ will be felt directly in $P$. Giving individuals more money

## Irving Fisher (1867–1947)

Irving Fisher was one of the ablest mathematical economists of the early 20th century. A staunch advocate of monetary reform, his theories influenced economists as different as John Maynard Keynes and Milton Friedman.

Born in upstate New York in 1867, Fisher studied mathematics, science, and philosophy at Yale University, receiving his B.A. in math in 1898 and his Ph.D. in economics—the first ever offered by the university—in 1901. In 1905, Fisher was in a phone booth in Grand Central Station in New York City when someone stole his briefcase with his manuscript of *The Nature of Capital and Income,* one of the first economics books on the stock market. He rewrote the book in the next year, making copies of each chapter as it was finished and always closing the doors to phone booths after that. The book made Fisher an instant celebrity.

RubberBall/Alamy

For three years he taught mathematics at Yale, only switching to economics after the international success of his book entitled *Mathematical Investigations and the Theory of Value and Prices.* The book made important advances in mathematical economics and developed a theory to measure the utility of commodities. Fisher also designed a hydraulic "machine" to illustrate general equilibrium in a multimarket economy.

Monetarists owe a great debt to Fisher's next great book, *The Purchasing Power of Money,* in which he offered an "equation of exchange": $MV = PT$, where $M$ is the amount of money in circulation, $V$ is the velocity of circulation of that money, $P$ is the average price level, and $T$ is the number of transactions taking place (output). Classical economists have used variations of the formula to suggest that inflation is caused by increases in the money supply.

In 1898, Fisher came down with tuberculosis, provoking a lifelong interest in health and nutrition that resulted in his best-selling self-help book called *How to Live: Rules for Healthful Living Based on Modern Science*. As a person, Fisher was "prim and straight-laced, disciplined in all matters, he did not drink alcohol or coffee or tea, smoke, eat chocolate, or use pepper. He followed a stern diet and rarely ate meat, but he was not quite a vegetarian. He was almost totally humorless. No extant picture even shows him smiling. Because of his seriousness, his personal code and habits, his sometimes controversial economic beliefs, as well as his dedication to crusades [world peace, prohibition, annual medical check-up, and 100% bank reserves] many regarded as strange, some people, including some of his colleagues in the economics profession, thought Fisher odd."

Among his many skills and interests, Fisher was a successful inventor and businessman. In 1925, he patented the "visible card index" system, an early version of the Rolodex, and earned a fortune when his firm merged with another company, which came to be known as Sperry Rand. Unfortunately, within a few years he would lose everything in the stock market crash of 1929, an event that he famously failed to predict.

In fact, Fisher's belief that the market had reached a "permanently high plateau" a few weeks before the crash and his insistence on an imminent recovery throughout the early Depression years caused irreparable damage to a well-earned reputation as one of America's greatest economists. Fisher taught at Yale until his retirement in 1935.

Sources: Justin Fox, *The Myth of the Rational Market* (New York: HarperCollins), 2009, p. 3; Robert Allen, *Irving Fisher: A Biography* (Cambridge, MA: Blackwell), 1993, p. 9.

to spend on goods and services when the economy is already at full employment—output ($Q$) is fixed—will lead to increases in aggregate prices as the additional money will go toward bidding up prices. In the end, prices will rise in exact proportion to the rise in the money supply. This is known as the **classical monetary transmission mechanism.**

**Classical monetary transmission mechanism:** Classical economists assumed a direct monetary transmission process: any change in $M$ would be felt directly in $P$.

**FIGURE 1—Money Growth and Inflation: Thirty Countries from 1970 to 2006**

Quantity theory predicts that $\Delta M = \Delta P$, or that, in the long run, a change in the money supply will bring about a directly proportionate change in the aggregate price level. Monetary growth and inflation for thirty countries from 1970 to 2006 supports this.

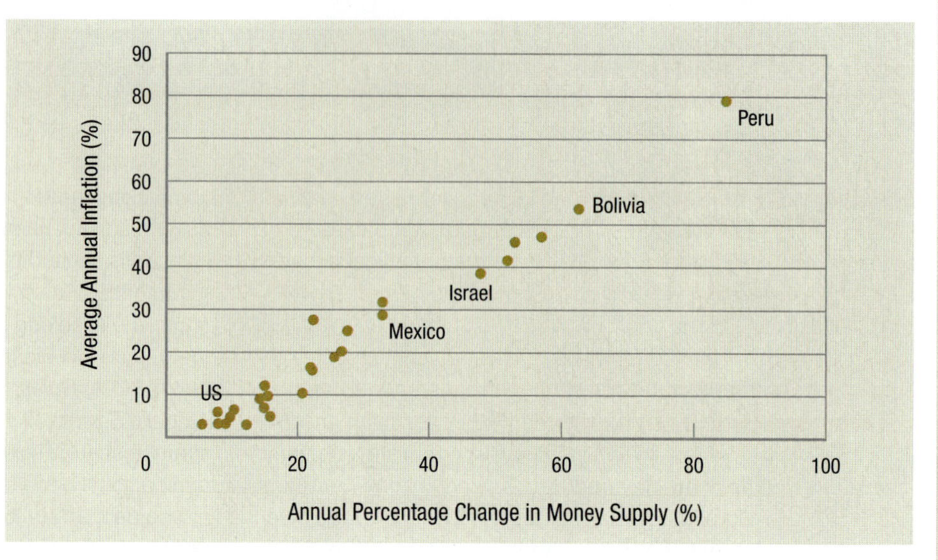


Figure 2 illustrates how the quantity theory works within an aggregate demand and supply context. The economy is initially in equilibrium at point *e*. The long-run aggregate supply curve is vertical, reflecting the long-run assumption of full employment (at $15 trillion), and the aggregate demand curve reflects an initial money level of $2.0 trillion. Increasing the money supply to $2.2 trillion (a 10% increase) shifts aggregate demand upward to $AD_{(\$2.2T)}$, resulting in a new equilibrium at point *b* where the aggregate price level (GDP deflator) increases to 110 (a 10% increase), yet real output remains constant at $15 trillion.

**FIGURE 2—The Impact of a Change in the Money Supply in the Long Run**

The long-run quantity theory of money is shown using aggregate demand and aggregate supply. The economy is initially in equilibrium at point *e*. The long-run aggregate supply curve is vertical (long-run full employment at $15 trillion), while the aggregate demand curve reflects a money supply of $2.0 trillion. Increasing the money supply to $2.2 trillion (a 10% increase) shifts aggregate demand upward to $AD_{(\$2.2T)}$, resulting in a new equilibrium at point *b* where the aggregate price level rises by 10%, yet real output remains constant. The price level rise is equal to the percentage increase in the money supply.

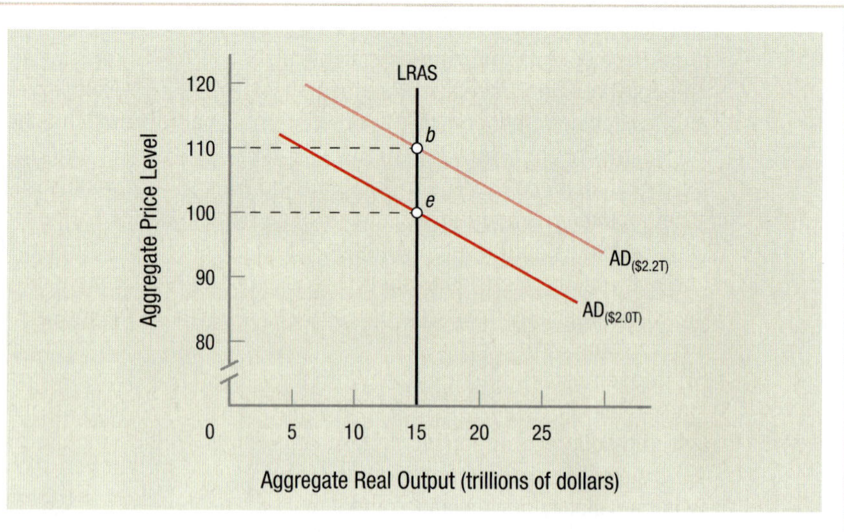


Quantity theory and the equation of exchange provide a good explanation of the long-run effects of the money supply on the larger economy. Indeed, when European explorers discovered massive new sources of gold and silver in the New World, economists accurately predicted what would happen: massive inflation. And even today, as Figure 1 illustrates, quantity theory still provides a good explanation of the *long-run* impact of monetary growth.

## The Short Run: Interest Rate Channels

If the short-run effects of money were the same as in the long run, that would be the end of the story. In contrast to the long run, changes in the money supply can have an effect on the real economy in the short run, not just on the price level. In this section, we look at two opposing views on the effectiveness of monetary policy in the short run.

### Keynesian Monetary Analysis

Developed by John Maynard Keynes during the Great Depression of the 1930s, Keynesian analysis has had a profound effect on policymakers and economists that continues today. Keynes thought that monetary policy could have an effect on the real economy in the short run, but would have no effect even in the short run when an economy is in the midst of a deep recession or depression.

In our earlier analysis, we ignored the relationship between the rate of interest and investment by assuming investment levels to be fixed. We now relax that assumption.

***Keynesian Monetary Transmission Mechanism*** Keynes identified three motives for holding money. In addition to the *transactions motive* that was the basis of classical analysis, he added a *precautionary motive:* people hold money to accommodate unforeseen circumstances. Keynes argued that both of these components of the demand for money are related to income. At higher income levels, more money is kept on hand for transactions and precautionary purposes.

To these, Keynes added a *speculative motive*. He asked why individuals would choose to hold money balances rather than holding their wealth in bonds, where it would earn interest. The answer is that people sometimes hold money for speculation against changes in interest rates or the price level.

When would money be a better investment than a bond? First, when interest rates have fallen to low levels. The expectation, after all, is that interest rates will eventually rise again. And when interest rates do rise, the price of bonds will fall, so bondholders will suffer capital losses that quickly wipe out the interest they receive.

Second, when the price level in the economy *falls,* money becomes a more valuable asset since its purchasing power increases. If deflation is expected, it's a good time to hold cash.

If the money supply increases, more money in the market means that people will want to convert more of it to interest-earning assets (bonds), causing the price of bonds to rise and the interest rate to fall. Lower interest rates should normally lead to an increase in investment. This increase in investment expands aggregate demand, which increases income, output, and employment. A decrease in the money supply would act in the opposite fashion. In simple symbols, the **Keynesian transmission mechanism** is:

**Keynesian transmission mechanism:** An increase in the money supply lowers interest rates, thus increasing investment; expanding aggregate demand; and increasing income, output, and employment. The opposite occurs when the money supply is reduced.

$$\uparrow M \rightarrow \downarrow i \rightarrow \uparrow I \rightarrow \uparrow AD \rightarrow \uparrow Q$$

Let's take a moment to contrast the *short-run* Keynesian approach to that of the *long-run* equation of exchange. Keynes emphasized the role of the speculative demand for money, whereas classical economists focused on the transactions demand. Speculative demand puts deflation fears and bond returns front and center. In the Keynesian model, changes in money affect the real economy only *indirectly* through changes in interest rates and investment, while in the long run (via the equation of exchange), monetary changes directly affect the price level through more money chasing a fixed (full employment) level of goods with no effect on the real economy.

But for Keynes, the Depression was not a normal time. Massive excess capacity meant that reducing interest rates might not lead to greater investment, since firms were unable to sell what they were currently producing. Further, increasing the money supply might not even reduce interest rates if the economy was in what Keynes described as a liquidity trap.

**Liquidity trap:** When interest rates are so low that people believe rates can only rise, they hold on to money rather than investing in bonds and suffer the expected capital loss.

***The Liquidity Trap*** If interest rates fall to very low levels, Keynes argued that people simply hoard money. Keynes referred to this phenomenon as the **liquidity trap.** Once interest rates sink so low that people start to believe rates can only go up, they hold on to all the money they can, rather than investing in bonds. They realize that when interest rates do rise, if they are holding bonds, bond prices will fall and they will suffer capital losses.

In the liquidity trap, an increase in money is hoarded and there is no change in interest rates; thus there is no change in investment, and consequently no change in income, output, or employment. Monetary policy is totally ineffective. This was one reason Keynes argued that fiscal policy, especially government spending—not monetary policy—was needed to get the economy out of the Depression.

After the Depression, the Keynesian view of the relative importance of fiscal policy dominated economic thinking well into the 1960s. Economists viewed the Fed's role as that of banking regulator and as the federal government's bank.

## Monetarist Model

Nobel Prize winning economist Milton Friedman challenged this orthodoxy with his monetarist approach to monetary policy and economic stabilization. Keynesian analysis was so ingrained into the economics profession that Friedman's efforts initially met with skepticism, but he was not deterred. His perseverance and immense analytical skills eventually persuaded nearly all economists that monetary policy is extremely important. Monetarists see the economy as self-stabilizing around full employment in the long run, as the classical economists did, but monetarists see monetary policy as being effective in the short run. Whereas the Depression gave birth to the Keynesian model, the monetarist approach was developed in more normal economic times, when full employment (or near it) was not an unreasonable assumption.

By the 1960s, studies of the influence of monetary policy had begun to appear. The most famous of these was *A Monetary History of the United States, 1867–1960,* written by Friedman and Anna Schwartz and published in 1963. This study and others showed statistically that monetary variables play an important role in determining short-run income and employment levels, as well as inflation. Although the studies of Friedman and Schwartz were often contested, they forced economists of all stripes to reconsider the role money plays in the real economy in the short run.

***Permanent Income*** Friedman pioneered the notion that consumption is not only based on income, but that wealth also plays a role. Two people with the same income but different levels of wealth, Friedman observed, will presumably consume at different levels; common sense says the wealthier individual will consume more.

Because empirical data on wealth and consumption was unavailable at the time, Friedman had to look for some proxy. To Friedman, wealth is composed of money, bonds, equities, real assets, and human capital. For most people in the United States in the 1960s, their wealth was their human capital (their skills and education level). A smaller percentage of people owned homes, and 401(k) accounts didn't exist. So most wealth was wrapped up in people's abilities and earning capacity.

Friedman developed the concept of *permanent income,* which is the present value of an individual's future stream of labor income. He eventually settled on a weighted average of past incomes to define permanent income, the proxy for wealth embedded in human capital.

Friedman suggested that the demand for real money balances will be higher if (1) wealth or permanent income is higher, (2) the rate of return on other assets is lower, and (3) the expected rate of inflation is lower. We will ignore the effects of the expected inflation rate until a later chapter.

***Monetarist Transmission Mechanism*** Friedman assumed that utility-maximizing individuals would allocate their wealth among various assets until their marginal rates of return are equal. This approach treats money as just one more asset within a generalized portfolio of assets that might include bonds, real estate, fine art, or consumer durables.

## Nobel Prize

### Milton Friedman

Milton Friedman may be the best known economist of the latter half of the 20th century. During the 1980s, his advocacy of free market economics and "monetarist" theories had a dramatic impact on policymakers, notably President Ronald Reagan and British Prime Minister Margaret Thatcher. His book, *A Monetary History of the United States, 1867–1960,* co-authored with Anna Schwartz, is considered a modern classic of economics. He also made important contributions to consumption analysis, exchange rates, and economic stabilization policy.

Born in 1912 in Brooklyn, New York, Friedman's parents were immigrants who struggled to make ends meet. Awarded a scholarship to Rutgers University, Friedman paid for his additional expenses by waiting on tables and clerking in a store.

AP Photo/Nati Harnik

In 1932, he entered the University of Chicago as a graduate student in economics. Thanks to economist Harry Hotelling, Friedman was offered a fellowship to study at Columbia University, where he honed his analysis of mathematical statistics. Professors Wesley Mitchell and John M. Clark introduced him to an empirical approach and view of theory that differed from the Chicago school.

In 1946, he accepted a professorship at the University of Chicago. At the same time, he accepted a position at the National Bureau of Economic Research, delving into the role of money in business cycles. At Chicago, Friedman established a "Workshop in Money and Banking." In 1950, Friedman worked in Paris for the Marshall Plan, studying a precursor to the Common Market. He came to believe in the importance of flexible exchange rates between members of the European community.

Friedman published a book entitled *Studies in the Quantity Theory of Money,* which laid out his views on the importance of money and monetary policy in determining the level of economic activity. His views were explicitly counter to the Keynesian belief in a range of activist government policies to stabilize the economy. Friedman advocated a consistent policy of steady growth in the money supply to encourage stability and economic growth.

Friedman was awarded the Nobel Prize in Economics in 1976. The prize-givers acknowledged his monetary theories but emphasized his work on rethinking Keynes's theory of the "consumption function," the tendency of people to save rather than spend a higher proportion of money when they reached higher income levels. The theory was important to the Keynesian explanation for economic downturns. Friedman's work suggested that people based their saving habits on "permanent income"—that is, the typical amount they earn instead of on increases or decreases they may view as temporary.

Milton Friedman died in 2006.

With Friedman's approach, when the money supply increases, more money will be held in the portfolio than is desired. These excess money balances will thus be exchanged for other financial and real assets, including bonds, real estate, and consumer durables such as cars and houses.

The **monetarist transmission mechanism** can be symbolically described as follows:

**Monetarist transmission mechanism:** An increase in money will reduce interest rates as portfolios rebalance, leading to a rise in investment or consumption and resulting in an increase in aggregate demand and thus an increase in income, output, or the price level.

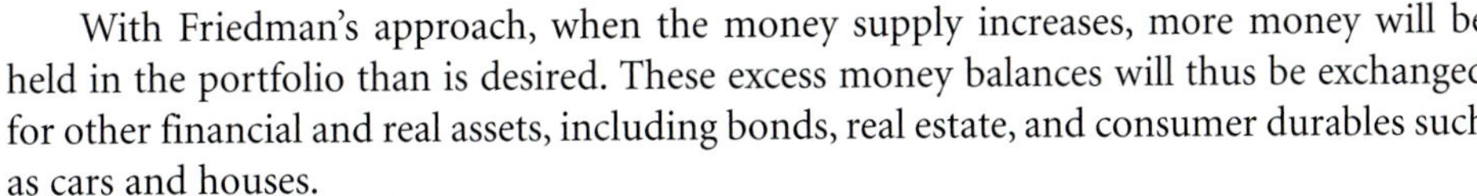

$$\uparrow M \rightarrow \downarrow i \rightarrow (\uparrow I \text{ and/or } \uparrow C) \rightarrow \uparrow AD \rightarrow \uparrow Q \text{ and/or } \uparrow P$$

An increase in money will reduce interest rates. Portfolios rebalance, leading to a rise in investment and/or consumption, which leads to an increase in aggregate demand and, thus, ultimately an increase in income, output, and/or the price level. Monetarists also assume that velocity is constant, so—with reference to the equation of exchange—any increase in $M$ will change either $P$ *or* $Q$, *or both.*

**FIGURE 3—Monetarist Transmission Mechanism**

Monetarists argue that a change in output will last only for the short run; in the long run, the economy will move back to full employment. The economy begins in equilibrium at point e. An increase in the money supply of 10% shifts the aggregate demand curve from $AD_0$ to $AD_1$, resulting in higher short-run output, \$16 trillion, and a higher price level (point *b*). Over time, the economy will move back to full employment (\$15 trillion), increasing the price level in the long run to 110 (a 10% increase). The long-run aggregate supply curve is therefore vertical at full employment output (\$15 trillion).

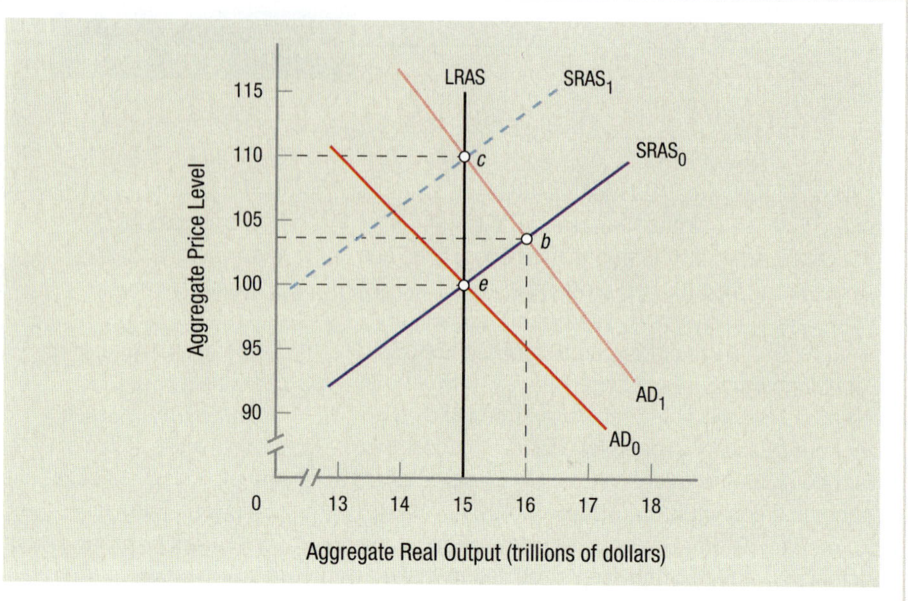


For monetarists, in the *short run,* either output or the price level *or both* can change because of the portfolio adjustments noted above. But, in the *long run,* an increase in money will ultimately increase prices just as the equation of exchange suggests. Figure 3 illustrates the monetarist approach that a change in output will operate only in the short run; in the long run, the economy will move back to its full employment output, \$15 trillion.

This economy is initially in equilibrium at point *e,* with price level 100 and output equal to the long-run potential output, \$15 trillion. A 10% increase in the money supply from \$2.0 trillion to \$2.2 trillion will shift the aggregate demand curve from $AD_0$ to $AD_1$, initially raising output to \$16 trillion and the aggregate price level to 104 (point *b*). Over time, the economy will move back to its full employment output (\$15 trillion), raising prices in the long run by 10% to 110 (point *c*).

In the short run, changes in the money supply affect output and/or the price level, unless the economy faces a Keynesian liquidity trap (is in a deep recession or depression and interest rates are extremely low). In the long run, changes in the money supply will affect the price level only. What is clear from this is that monetary policy normally is effective in the short run.

## Summary of the Effectiveness of Monetary Policy

It's time to summarize the theories of the effectiveness of monetary policy. First, in the *long run,* changes in the money supply will show up directly as increases in the price level. Since in the equation of exchange ($M \times V = P \times Q$), $V$ is assumed constant and $Q$ is assumed to be at (or near) full employment, changes in $M$ will directly change $P$. Keep in mind two points: in the long run, inflation is always a monetary phenomenon (changes in $M$ change $P$) and classical economists saw no use for monetary policy because the economy was always near full employment output.

Second, Keynes argued that the long run was not the appropriate yardstick because the economy was suffering and showed no sign of moving toward full employment. Writing on how to move the economy out of the Depression, Keynes argued that monetary policy was insufficient to accomplish the job, even in the short run. The Keynesian transmission mechanism posits that monetary policy can lower interest rates, which would normally increase investment, thereby increasing aggregate demand, employment, and output in the short run. However, he suggested that investment was more influenced by "animal spirits" (business expectations about the economy) than interest rates: lowering interest rates would only marginally increase investment and have almost no impact on the economy. Further, Keynes suggested that once interest rates get very low, monetary policy might confront a "liquidity trap," where increases in the money supply are just hoarded and interest rates do not change. Thus, for different reasons, Keynes saw little reason for using monetary policy to manage the business cycle even in the short run. He favored using fiscal policy to stimulate aggregate demand to move the economy toward full employment.

Third, monetarists see a role for monetary policy. In the long run, they see the Fed's role as keeping the growth in the money supply sufficient to keep the economy on a solid growth path with low rates of inflation. In the short run, changes in the money supply reduce interest rates that have an impact on both investment and consumption. Consumer spending is related to wealth, and any change in interest rates would induce portfolio adjustments that would alter consumer spending for durable goods.

## Monetary Policy and Economic Shocks

Monetary policy can be effective in the short run. When the economy goes into a recession, the Fed should use expansionary monetary policy to bring the economy back to full employment. Conversely, when the economy is running hot—the economy is operating above full employment and inflation is a problem—the Fed should use contractionary monetary policy to rein in the economy. Expansionary monetary policy includes lowering interest rates and buying government bonds to expand the money supply. Contractionary monetary policy is the opposite—the Fed raises interest rates or sells bonds to reduce the money supply.

Our discussion so far suggests that the Fed's approach to monetary policy should be based on both short- and long-run considerations. Low inflation represents a reasonable long-run goal, while income and output are more appropriate for the shorter term.

Economists generally agree that, in the long run, the Fed should focus on price stability, since low rates of inflation have been shown to create the best environment for long-run economic growth.

We have seen from the equation of exchange that, in the long run, aggregate supply is vertical and fixed at full employment, and changes in the supply of money result directly in changes in the price level. The Fed does seem to have low inflation rates as its long-term goal and has argued that this is the best policy for long-run economic growth.

But in the short run, demand and supply shocks to the economy may require differing approaches to monetary policy. The direction of monetary policy and its extent depends on whether it focuses on the price level or income and output, and whether the shock to the economy comes from the demand or supply side.

### Demand Shocks

Demand shocks to the economy can come from reductions in consumer demand, investment, government spending, or exports, or from an increase in imports. For example, the economy faced a demand shock in 2008 when households increased saving and reduced spending. The 2005–2007 housing bubble substantially increased mortgage indebtedness, but $4 per gallon gasoline in the summer of 2008 and falling housing prices reduced household wealth and caused households to tighten their belts, reducing consumption and adding to the depth of the recession. Turning to Figure 4 on the next page, let's consider an economy that is initially in full employment equilibrium at point *e*. A *demand shock* then reduces aggregate demand to $AD_1$. At the new equilibrium (point *a*), the price level and output both fall.

An expansionary monetary policy will increase the money supply, lower interest rates, thereby shifting aggregate demand back to $AD_0$ and restoring employment and output to full employment. In this case, targeting a stable price level or the original income and output level will bring the economy back to the same point of equilibrium, point *e*. If the Fed targets a stable price level, increasing aggregate demand enough to restore the price level to 100, full employment results. And if the Fed targets full employment, raising aggregate demand sufficiently to restore output to $15 trillion, this restores the price level to 100.

**FIGURE 4—Demand Shocks and Monetary Policy**

Monetary policy can be effective in counteracting a demand shock. The economy begins in full employment equilibrium at point *e* and then a demand shock reduces aggregate demand to $AD_1$, resulting in a new equilibrium (point *a*). Expansionary monetary policy will shift aggregate demand back to $AD_0$. This policy restores employment and output back to full employment ($15 trillion), while restoring prices to their original level (100). Notice that restoring either prices or output to their original levels also restores the other variable to its original level.

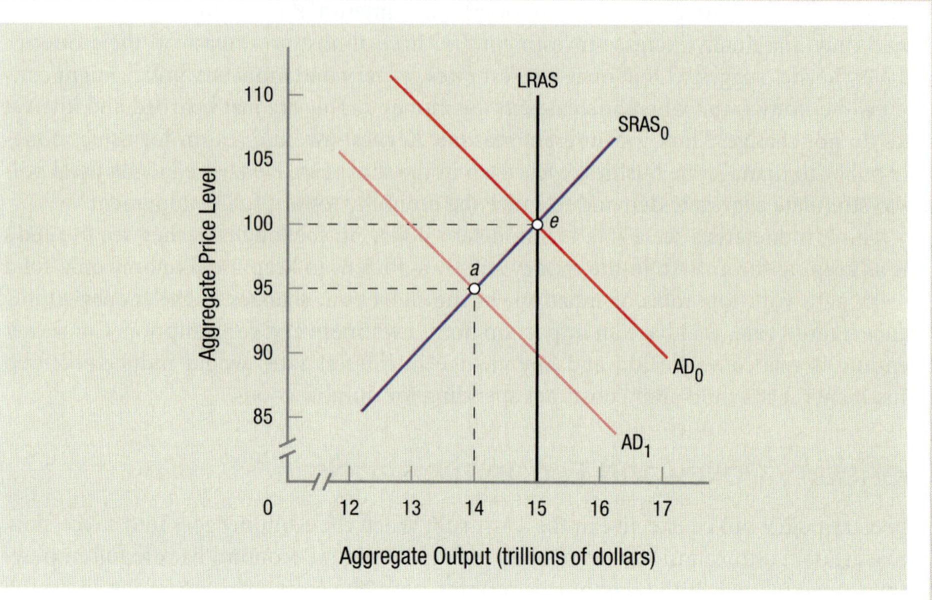


A positive demand shock produces a corresponding, though opposite, result. The positive demand shock will jolt output and the price level upward. Contractionary monetary policy will reduce both of them, restoring the economy to its original equilibrium.

For demand shocks, therefore, no conflict arises between the twin goals of monetary policy. Not only is the objective of full employment compatible with the objective of stables prices, but by targeting either one of these objectives, the Fed takes steps that work to bring about the other.

## Supply Shocks

Supply shocks can hit the economy for many reasons, including changes in resource costs such as a rise in oil prices, changes in inflationary expectations, or changes in technology. Looking at Figure 5, let us again consider an economy initially in full employment

**FIGURE 5—Supply Shocks and Monetary Policy**

Monetary policy is less effective in counteracting a supply shock than a demand shock. A negative supply shock shifts short-run aggregate supply from $SRAS_0$ to $SRAS_1$. The new equilibrium (point *a*) is at a *higher* price level, 105, and *lower* output, $14 trillion. This doubly negative result means a supply shock is nearly impossible to counter. The Fed could use expansionary monetary policy to shift $AD_0$ to $AD_1$; this would restore the economy to full employment output of $15 trillion (point *b*), but at an even higher price level (110). Alternatively, the Fed could focus on price level stability, using contractionary monetary policy to shift aggregate demand to $AD_2$, but this would further deepen the recession by pushing output down to $13 trillion (point *c*).

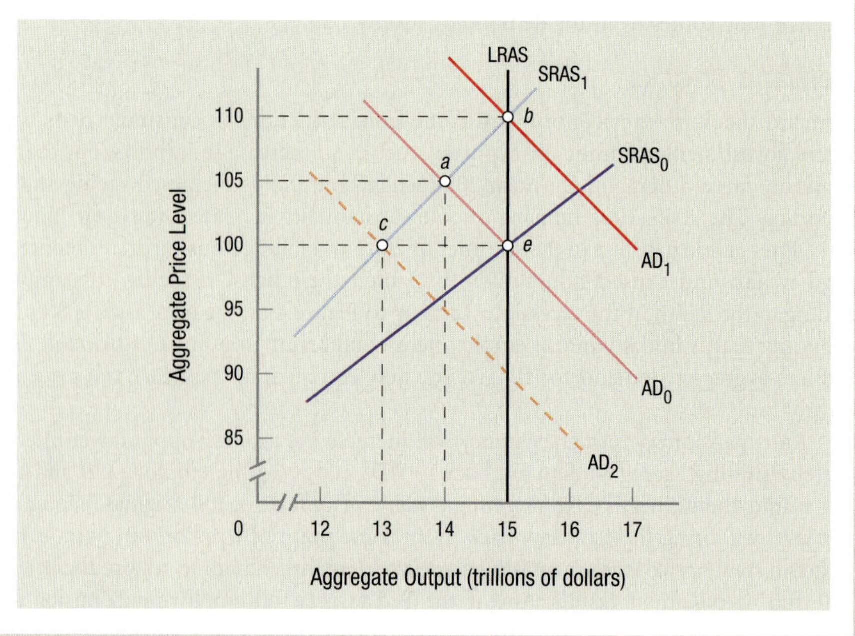

equilibrium at point *e*. Assume that a negative shock to the economy, say, an oil price spike, shifts short-run aggregate supply from $SRAS_0$ to $SRAS_1$. The new equilibrium (point *a*) occurs at a *higher* price level (105) and a *lower* output of $14 trillion.

This doubly negative result means a supply shock is nearly impossible to counter. The Fed could use expansionary monetary policy to shift $AD_0$ to $AD_1$; this would restore the economy to full employment output of $15 trillion (point *b*), but at an even higher price level (110). Alternatively, the Fed could focus on price level stability, using contractionary monetary policy to shift aggregate demand to $AD_2$, but this would further deepen the recession by pushing output down to $13 trillion (point *c*).

For a negative supply shock, not only has price level stability worsened, but so has output and income. Contrast this with the situation earlier, when a demand shock worsened the economy for one of its targets, but improved it for the other. Supply shocks are difficult to counteract because of their doubly negative results.

## Implications for Short-Run Monetary Policy

There is general agreement among economists that monetary policy should focus on price stability in the long run, while focusing on output or income in the short run. When a demand shock strikes, following this short-run policy course has the same effect as using price stability as the goal. When a supply shock occurs, however, targeting nominal income or output is preferable, since it permits the Fed to spread the shock's impact between income and output losses and price level increases. By increasing aggregate demand, the economy will suffer some added increase in the price level, but output will rise, reducing the severity of any recession. The Fed will probably not try to immediately push the economy back to full employment (from point *a* to point *b* in Figure 5), since this action would result in much higher inflation. Moving the economy back to full employment would be spread over several periods.

**CHECKPOINT**

### MONETARY THEORIES

- The classical long-run equation of exchange is: $M \times V = P \times Q$. In the long run, velocity ($V$) was considered set by institutional and technical considerations and the economy hovers around full employment so that output ($Q$) is fixed. Money ($M$) and the price level ($P$) are directly related, so that changes in the supply of money translated into changes in the price level: $\Delta M = \Delta P$.
- Keynes considered three motives for holding money: transactions, precautionary, and speculative motives.
- In the short run, Keynesian monetary analysis suggests that changes in the money supply change interest rates, leading to short-run changes in *investment,* changing aggregate demand, which in turn changes income, employment, and output. However, in a recession or depression, changes in the money supply would have no effect on the real economy.
- Monetarists suggest that in the long run, the economy functions in the way classical economists described, but by focusing on the demand for real money balances, they see monetary policy affecting both *investment and consumption* in the short run. Money supply changes affect interest rates in the short run, which in turn change investment *and/or* consumption, changing aggregate demand and thus affecting output *and/or* the price level.
- In the long run, the Fed targets price stability. Low rates of inflation are most conducive to long-run economic health.
- Monetary policy can focus on either a stable price level or output and income when the shock to the economy comes from the demand side. The objective of full employment is compatible with the objective of stable prices.

- Supply shocks present a more serious problem for monetary policy. A negative supply shock reduces output but increases the price level. Expansionary monetary policy to increase output further increases the price level, and contractionary policy to reduce the price level worsens the recession. Targeting nominal income is preferable, since it permits the Fed to spread the shock's impact between income losses and price level increases.

**QUESTION:** Of the three motives for holding money, which one is most important for monetary policy?

Answers to the Checkpoint question can be found at the end of this chapter.

## Modern Monetary Policy

**Easy money, expansionary monetary policy, or quantitative easing:** Fed actions designed to increase excess reserves and the money supply to stimulate the economy (expand income and employment).

**Tight money, restrictive, or contractionary monetary policy:** Fed actions designed to decrease excess reserves and the money supply to shrink income and employment, usually to fight inflation.

When the Fed buys bonds, it adds to bank reserves. This is called **easy money, expansionary monetary policy, or quantitative easing.** It is designed to increase excess reserves and the money supply, and ultimately reduce interest rates to stimulate the economy. Expansionary monetary policy, in other words, is intended to expand income and employment. The opposite of an expansionary policy is a **tight money, restrictive, or contractionary monetary policy.** Tight money policies are designed to shrink income and employment, usually in the interest of fighting inflation. The Fed brings about tight monetary policy by selling bonds, thereby pulling reserves from the financial system.

The Federal Reserve Act gives the Board of Governors significant discretion for conducting monetary policy. It sets out goals but leaves it up to the discretion of the Board how best to reach these objectives. As we have seen, the Fed attempts to frame monetary policy to keep inflation low over the long run, but also to maintain enough flexibility to respond in the short run to demand and supply shocks.

### Rules vs. Discretion

**Monetary rule:** Keeps the growth of money stocks such as M1 or M2 on a steady path, following the equation of exchange (or quantity theory), to set a long-run path for the economy that keeps inflation in check.

The complexities of monetary policy, especially in dealing with a supply shock, have led some economists, most notably Milton Friedman, to call for a **monetary rule** to guide monetary policymakers. Other economists argue that modern economies are too complex to be managed by a few simple rules. Constantly changing institutions, economic behaviors, and technologies mean that some discretion, and perhaps even complete discretion, is essential for policymakers. Also, if policymakers could use a simple and efficient rule on which to base successful monetary policy, they would have enough incentive to adopt it voluntarily, since it would guarantee success and their job would be much easier.

Milton Friedman argued that variations in monetary growth were a major source of instability in the economy. To counter this problem, which is compounded by the long and variable lags in discretionary monetary policy, Friedman advocated the adoption of monetary growth rules. Specifically, he proposed increasing the money supply by a set percentage every year, at a level consistent with long-term price stability and economic growth.

Remember that Friedman and other monetarists, like the Classical economists before them, believe the economy to be inherently stable. If they are correct, then generating a steady increase in the money supply should reduce the potentially destabilizing effects monetary policy can have on the economy.

If the change in aggregate demand is small or temporary, a monetary growth rule will probably function well enough. But if the shock is large, persistent, or continual, as was the case in the Great Depression and the recent financial crisis, a discretionary monetary policy aimed at bringing the economy back to full employment more quickly would probably be preferred.

In some cases, a monetary rule keeps policymakers from making things worse by keeping them from doing anything. Yet, the monetary rule also prevents policymakers from aiding the economy when a policy change is needed. Policymakers argue that they need to be able to balance one goal against another, rather than being tied down to strict rules that in the end do nothing.

Monetary targeting, the practice of setting a fixed rate for money supply growth, suggested by Milton Friedman, was the focus of the Fed from 1970 to 1980 but wasn't considered successful.

The alternative to setting money growth rules that monetary authorities around the world have tried is the simple rule of **inflation targeting,** which is setting targets on the inflation rate, usually around 2% per year. If inflation (or the forecasted rate of inflation) exceeds the target, contractionary policy is employed; if inflation falls below the target, expansionary policy is used. Inflation targeting has the virtue of explicitly reiterating that the long-run goal of monetary policy is price stability.

**Inflation targeting:** The central bank sets a target on the inflation rate (usually around 2% per year) and adjusts monetary policy to keep inflation in that range.

Assume once more that a negative demand shock hits the economy. Inflation targeting means that discretionary expansionary monetary policy will be used to bring the economy back to full employment. But now consider a negative supply shock from an increase in the price of energy or some other raw material. Inflation targeting means that contractionary monetary policy should be used to reduce the inflation spiral. As we saw, however, contractionary policy would deepen the recession, and in reality, few monetary authorities would stick to an inflation-targeting approach in this situation. They would be more likely to stimulate the economy slightly, hoping to move it back to full employment with only a small increase in inflation. The result is that inflation targeting could soon lose its credibility and effectiveness.

## The Federal Funds Target and the Taylor Rule

If not monetary targeting or inflation targeting, what other rule can the Fed use? We know that the Fed alters the federal funds rate as its primary monetary policy instrument. Under what circumstances will the Fed change its federal funds target? The Fed is concerned with two major factors: preventing inflation and preventing and moderating recessions. Professor John Taylor of Stanford University studied the Fed and how it makes decisions and he empirically found that the Fed tended to follow a general rule that has become known as the **Taylor rule** for federal funds targeting:

**Taylor rule:** A rule for the federal funds target that suggests that the target is equal to 2% + current inflation rate + ½(inflation gap) + ½(output gap). Alternatively, it is equal to 2% plus the current inflation rate plus ½ times the difference between the current inflation rate and the Fed's inflation target rate plus ½ times the output gap (current GDP minus potential GDP).

$$\text{federal funds target rate} = 2 + \text{current inflation rate} + \tfrac{1}{2}(\text{inflation gap}) + \tfrac{1}{2}(\text{output gap})$$

The Fed's inflation target is typically 2%, the inflation gap is the current inflation rate minus the Fed's inflation target, and the output gap is current GDP minus potential GDP. If the Fed tries to target inflation around 2%, the current inflation rate is 4%, and output is 3% below potential GDP, then the target federal funds rate according to the Taylor rule is:

$$\begin{aligned} FF_{\text{Target}} &= 2 + 4 + \tfrac{1}{2}(4 - 2) + \tfrac{1}{2}(-3) \\ &= 2 + 4 + \tfrac{1}{2}(2) + \tfrac{1}{2}(-3) \\ &= 2 + 4 + 1 - 1.5 \\ &= 5.5\%. \end{aligned}$$

Notice that the high rate of inflation (4%) drives the federal funds target rate upward while the fact that the economy is below its potential reduces the rate. If the economy was operating at its potential, the federal funds target would be 7%, because the Fed would not be worried about a recession and would be focused on controlling inflation.

Figure 6 on the next page shows how closely the Taylor rule tracks the actual federal funds rate. Some economists have blamed the large spread between the two rates during 2003 to 2007 for the housing boom that precipitated the financial crisis in 2008. They argue that the extremely low interest rates fueled the housing boom.

More important, what the Taylor rule tells us is that when the Fed meets to change the federal funds target rate, the two most important factors are whether inflation is different

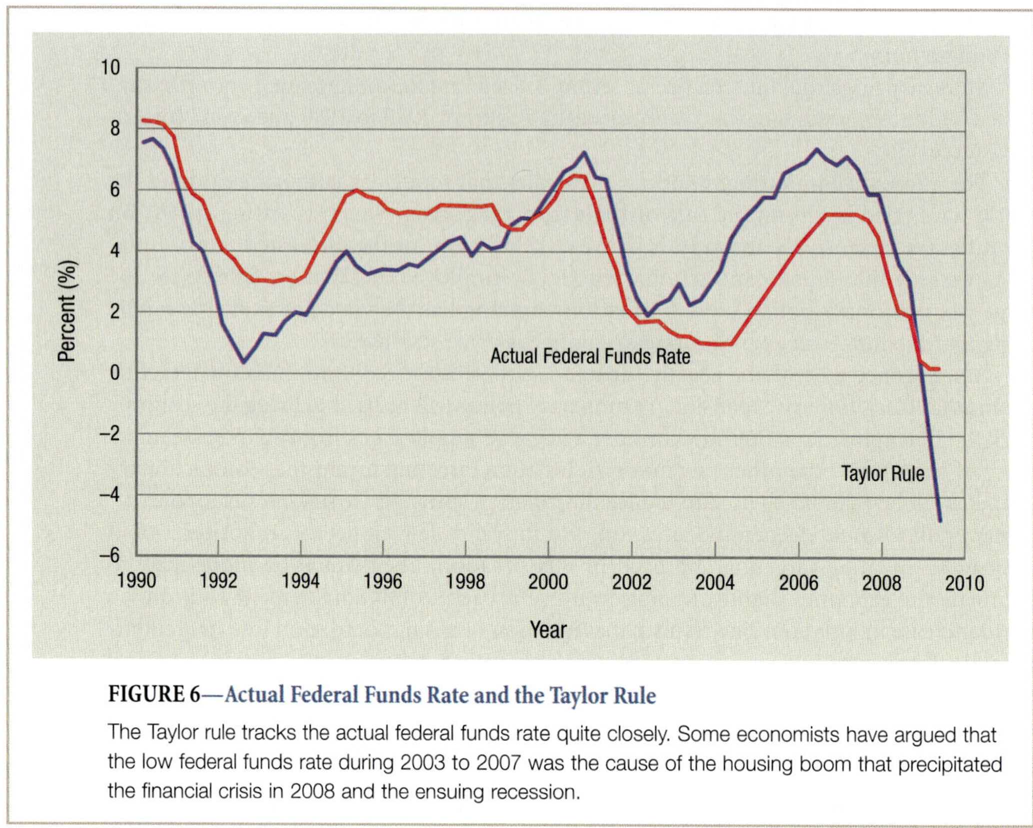


**FIGURE 6—Actual Federal Funds Rate and the Taylor Rule**

The Taylor rule tracks the actual federal funds rate quite closely. Some economists have argued that the low federal funds rate during 2003 to 2007 was the cause of the housing boom that precipitated the financial crisis in 2008 and the ensuing recession.

from the Fed's target (typically 2%) and whether output varies from potential GDP. If output is below its potential, a recession threatens and the Fed will lower its target, and vice versa when output exceeds potential and inflation threatens to exceed the Fed's target.

## Modern Monetary Policy

For policymakers, when the economy heats up and GDP exceeds potential GDP, inflationary pressures mount and the Fed reacts by using open market operations to shrink reserves (sells bonds), which increases interest rates and puts a damper on investment and other interest-sensitive components of aggregate demand. The result is that output growth slows, bringing the economy back toward its potential level.

When output drops below potential GDP and the economy begins to fall into a recession, inflationary pressures will subside, and the Fed takes just the opposite tactic: it lowers its federal fund target rate and uses expansionary monetary policy (buys bonds) to lower real interest rates, stimulating investment, consumption of durable goods, and net exports.

When the Fed lowers interest rates, American bonds become less attractive to foreign investors, and this often leads to a decline in the value of the dollar in foreign exchange markets. A falling dollar makes American products cheaper relative to foreign products. This stimulates exports and reduces imports, both of which soften recessionary tendencies.

In summary, when output exceeds potential output ($Q > Q_f$), firms are operating above their capacities and costs will rise, adding an inflationary threat that the Fed wants to avoid, so it increases the real interest rate to cool the economy. When output is below potential ($Q < Q_f$), the Fed's goal is to drive the economy back to its potential and avoid a recession and the losses associated with an economy below full employment. The Fed does this by lowering the real interest rate. This reflects the Fed's desire to fight recession when output is below full employment and fight inflation when output exceeds its potential.

Today, monetary authorities set a target interest rate and then use open market operations to adjust reserves and keep the federal funds rate near this level. The Fed's interest target is the level that will keep the economy near potential GDP and/or keep inflationary pressures in check. When GDP is below its potential and a recession is threatened and inflation falls below its target, the Fed uses expansionary policy to lower interest rates, expanding investment, consumption and exports, and vice versa when output is above potential GDP. When inflation threatens, the Fed again uses a higher interest rate target to slow the economy and reduce inflationary pressure.

When inflation becomes a problem in the short run (assuming initially no change in output), the Fed will act in a similar manner. It will increase interest rates to slow the economy and reduce inflationary pressures. Raising interest rates is never a politically popular act, but the Fed will be forced to balance future economic growth against rising inflationary expectations. As former Fed Chairman William McChesney Martin said, "The job of a good central banker is to take away the punchbowl just as the party gets going".

## Transparency and the Federal Reserve

How does the Fed convey information about its actions, and why is this important? For many years, decisions were made in secrecy, and often they were executed in secrecy: the public did not know that monetary policy was being changed. Since monetary policy affects the economy, the Fed's secrecy stimulated much speculation in financial markets about current and future Fed actions. Uncertainty often led to various counterproductive actions by people guessing incorrectly. These activities were highly inefficient.

When Alan Greenspan became head of the Fed in 1987, this policy of secrecy started to change. By 1994, the Fed released a policy statement each time it changed interest rates, and by 1998 it included a "tilt" statement forecasting what would probably happen in the next month or two. By 2000, the FOMC released a statement after each of its eight meetings even if policy remained the same.

This new openness has come about because the Fed recognized that monetary policy is mitigated when financial actors take counterproductive actions when they are uncertain what the Fed will do. In the words of William Poole, former president of the Federal Reserve Bank of St. Louis,

> *Explaining a policy action—elucidating the considerations that led the FOMC to decide to adjust the intended funds rate, or to leave it unchanged—is worthwhile. Over time, the accumulation of such explanations helps the market, and perhaps the FOMC itself, to understand what the policy regularities are. It is also important to understand that many—perhaps most—policy actions have precedent value. … One of the advantages of public disclosure of the reasons for policy actions is that the required explanation forces the FOMC to think through what it is doing and why.*[1]

Fed transparency helps the public understand why it is taking certain actions. This helps the market understand what the Fed does in certain circumstances, and what the Fed is likely to do in similar future situations. The Fed also includes a "looking forward" or "tilt" comment after each meeting, which provides a summary of the Fed's outlook on the economy and information on the target federal funds rate. Transparency helps the Fed implement its monetary policy.

Until very recently, the performance of monetary authorities over the previous several decades illustrated how effective discretionary monetary policy could be. Price stability was remarkable, unemployment and output levels were near full employment levels, interest rates were kept low, and economic growth was solid.

[1] William Poole, "Fed Transparency: How, Not Whether," The Federal Reserve Bank of St. Louis, *Review*, November/December 2003, p. 5.

## *Issue:* The Record of the Fed's Performance

**Determining how** to measure the impact of Federal Reserve policy on our huge, complex economy is not easy. The figure shows how three variables—unemployment, inflation, and interest rates—have fared during the tenure of the four Fed chairmen over the last three decades.

Before 1980, when Arthur Burns headed the Fed, inflation was rising. An oil supply shock in 1973 was met with accommodative monetary policy and aggregate demand expanded.

The economy was hit with a second oil price shock in the late 1970s. By the early 1980s, inflation rose to double digits, peaking at over 14% in 1980. Paul Volcker, the new head of the Fed, tightened monetary policy to induce a recession (1981–1982) to reduce inflation. By the end of his term, inflation had been reduced to little more than 4%, a remarkable feat.

During the 1990s, the Greenspan Fed alternated between encouraging output growth (mid-1990s) and fighting inflation (early and late 1990s). The Fed under Greenspan did a good job of keeping the economy near full employment. Interest rates trended down and inflation was moderate during the 1990s and early 2000s. But a housing bubble, partly the result of the extremely low interest rates from 2003 to 2007, followed by its collapse in 2008, brought on a financial panic and a deep recession. These problems have now become a challenge for the current Fed chairman, Ben Bernanke.

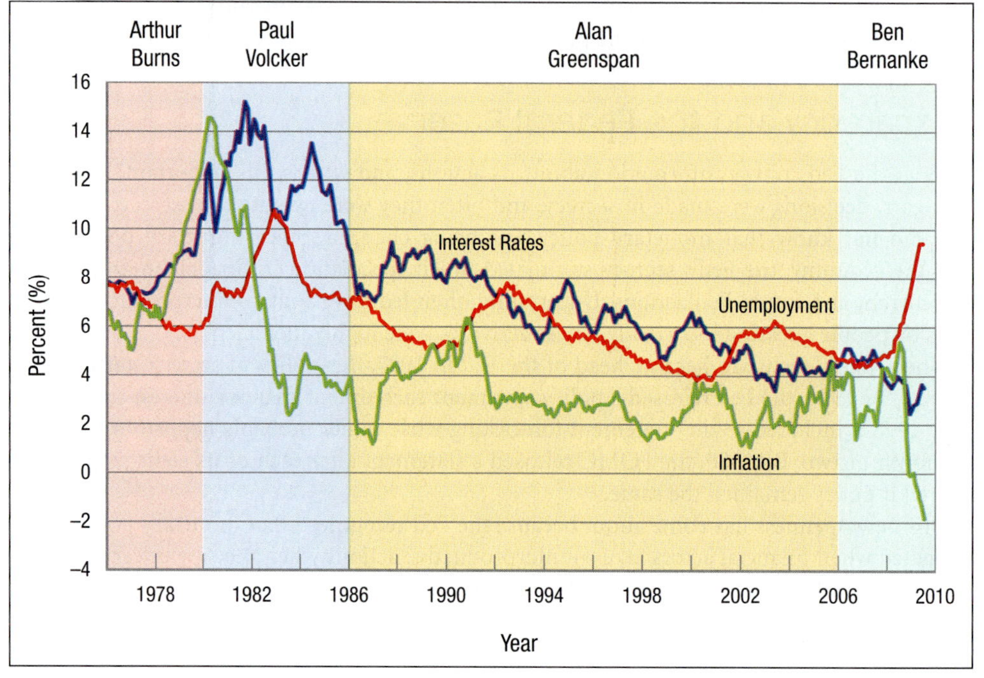


The most recent financial crisis is testing monetary authorities and reshaping the regulatory environment, as we will see in the concluding section of this chapter.

### CHECKPOINT

#### MODERN MONETARY POLICY

- In the long run, the Fed targets price stability. Low rates of inflation are most conducive to long-run economic growth.
- In the past, monetary targeting was used to control the rate of growth of the money supply. Inflation targeting was used that set targets on the inflation rate, usually around 2%.
- The Fed sets a target federal funds rate and then uses open market operations to adjust reserves and keep the federal funds rate near this level.
- Because inflation changes little in the short run, changing nominal interest rates alters real interest rates, which affects investment and the other interest-sensitive components of aggregate demand. Changes in aggregate demand change output, employment, and the price level.

- When inflation rises, the Fed uses contractionary monetary policy to increase the federal funds rate to slow the economy. When the economy drifts into a recession and inflationary pressures fall, the Fed does the opposite and reduces the federal funds rate, giving the economy a boost.
- Fed transparency helps us understand why the Fed makes particular decisions and also what the Fed will probably do in similar circumstances in the future.

**QUESTION:** "When central bankers aggressively bang the drum on inflation, bond investors quickly head for the exits. So it is not surprising that waves of selling have engulfed global government debt markets." (Michael Mackenzie, *Financial Times*, May 11, 2008, p. 23). Why should bond investors sell when the Fed or other central bankers decide that inflation is a growing problem?

Answers to the Checkpoint question can be found at the end of this chapter.

## The Financial Crisis of 2008–2009

A small number of home mortgage defaults starting in 2008 resulted in falling housing prices and culminated in a global recession more severe than any in the last half century. How did the fact that some homeowners with poor (subprime) credit began falling behind on their mortgage payments set in motion events that brought the world financial system to its knees and the world economy to the brink?

The short answer is that massive spending on credit by American consumers, government, and business brought large inflows of foreign capital into the United States, creating a huge demand for "safe" investment assets. Second, reduced lending standards for home mortgages, followed eventually by subprime mortgage defaults, caused housing prices to collapse. This should not have been a major problem, except for the financing which undergirded the housing market. Third, Wall Street's creation of supposedly safe "collateralized mortgage debt obligations" (CDOs; the bundling of millions of dollars of mortgages into bond-like packages), along with interest rates kept low by the Fed, created an asset price bubble in housing. Fourth, the widespread use of borrowing to increase the returns on CDOs magnified the losses when mortgage defaults spread. Fifth, extreme uncertainty surrounding the value of trillions of dollars of complex CDOs made them unmarketable except at extremely low prices, driving many financial institutions into insolvency and creating a credit crisis that resulted in a worldwide financial and economic meltdown.

As we will see, each part played a role in creating this "perfect storm" that put the economy in a deep recession. The financial panic in late 2008 has forever altered monetary policy, the role of the Fed, and the era of relative self-regulation of financial institutions.

As a result of the financial crisis of 2008–2009, the Federal Reserve stepped in and did many things to contain the damage. It used its recognized tools and powers, and then stretched its mandate. This section will consider in brief what caused the crisis and then examine the responses of the Fed and what these might mean for the future.

### Origins

In describing the origins of the financial crisis, we look at risk, savings, and interest rates, and show how all three contributed to the housing bubble in 2004–2007. The bursting of this bubble was the major factor in the financial crisis.

#### Risk

Risk is a fact of life. No one knows if they will become sick, get injured, or when they will die. To deal with risk, people take out insurance. In return for a payment called a premium, insurance companies provide insurance. Profits flow to insurance companies if they accurately predict the amount of future claims and offset them with premiums received, with some surplus remaining.

Let's say that you are married and have started to raise a family. Though both you and your spouse work, your family would endure financial hardship if you were to die now. So you take out life insurance: in return for a premium paid by you each year, the insurance company will pay your family a set amount of money should you die prematurely. The insurance company determines the premium amount by looking at your pertinent characteristics and then putting you in an insurance group. Do you smoke? The premium is raised. Do you exercise? The premium is lowered. Insurance companies have extensive data on the population as a whole: they have to, their profits depend on it. This system works to the benefit of both sides: you recognize the risk of premature death and offset this risk on the insurance company in return for a premium you pay, and the insurance company can accurately place you in an insurance group and so can be reasonably sure that it will make a profit based on the premiums it receives.

Several problems can cause trouble for the insurance company. For example, let's say that after taking on the insurance, you become active in dangerous sports such as hang-gliding. This changes your risk profile, but the insurance company knows nothing about it and has now *underpriced* your insurance premium. Or let's say that you have always been an avid hang-glider but failed to inform the insurance company before you sought out insurance. In this case, depending on the forms you filled out, you may have fraudulently withheld material information from the insurance company, again leading to the insurance company underpricing your insurance premium. One such person doing this will cause only minor problems for a large insurance company insuring thousands of people, but the problem can become greater if many people engage in the same behavior or suppress important information. If the insurance company has many more claims than forecasted, the premiums might not cover the claims and the insurance company could go bankrupt.

The point of this example is that risk is normal and offsetting risk is normal. Problems arise when those bearing the risk, such as insurance companies, do not properly account for risk. Furthermore, unaccounted-for risk can happen when behavior changes or when outright fraud occurs. If you keep this simple idea in mind, you will come a long way to understanding the financial crisis of 2008–2009.

## The World Savings Glut and Low Interest Rates

*Usually it's the rich country lending to the poor. This time, it's the poor country lending to the rich.*

—Niall Ferguson, *The Ascent of Money*

A key factor in the financial crisis was the worldwide savings glut. Fed Chairman Ben Bernanke has suggested that a savings glut in developing countries (principally China, India, and the Middle East oil producers) fueled demand for American financial assets. He concluded that the Chinese saved so much and invested overseas because they didn't have confidence in their own economies or the habits to spend. Our low saving rate (and high spending habits), along with steady and growing government deficits and investments by business, were financed by foreign capital inflows. In Figure 7, the negative numbers for our balance of payments reflect our levels of annual foreign capital inflows.

This huge flow of funds lowered interest rates. Professor John Taylor, as we saw earlier, argued that the Fed followed a highly accommodative monetary policy from 2002 to 2006, lowering interest rates beyond what they should have been based on the Taylor rule. This is illustrated by the gap between interest rates and the rate suggested by the Taylor rule in Figure 8. Overspending on credit and low interest rates both set in motion the events that would lead to the financial crisis.

## Cheap Credit and the Housing Market

Low interest rates had significant effects on the housing market. Demand for housing increased. People who owned houses but wanted more space bought larger houses. People who rented but aspired to own their own home found it easier to achieve their dream. Increased demand drove up the price of housing. After a few years of rising prices, people started to think prices could only go up. Some obvious behavior followed from this belief:

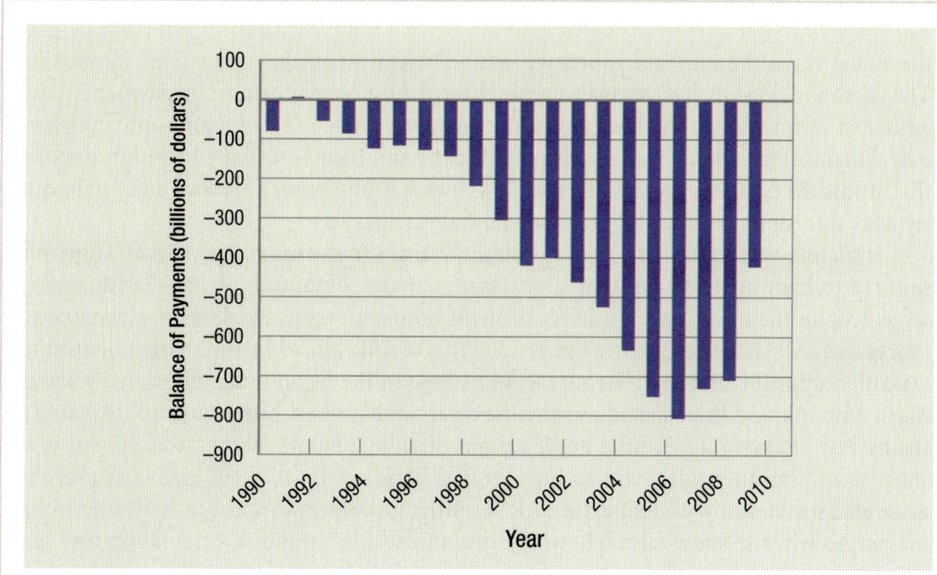


**FIGURE 7—U.S. Balance of Payments**

As Americans (consumers, government, and business) saved little and spent on credit, our balance of payments grew more unfavorable as foreign capital flowed into the United States to finance this spending.

some people became speculators, which led to house "flipping"—purchasing a home with the intention of selling it as soon as possible for a tidy profit. When television infomercials began advising people to join the house flipping craze, speculation had come from the fringes to the center of the housing market.

People wanted more houses and more people could afford more luxurious homes at the low interest rates, so luxury homebuilders such as Toll Brothers undertook large development projects. States such as Florida, Arizona, California, and Nevada enjoyed a huge building boom and a rapid rise in existing home prices. They also were the states to suffer the most when the financial crisis hit.

Builders provide homes, but usually a third party brings the transaction to a close: a financial intermediary provides the financing to home buyers in the form of a mortgage.

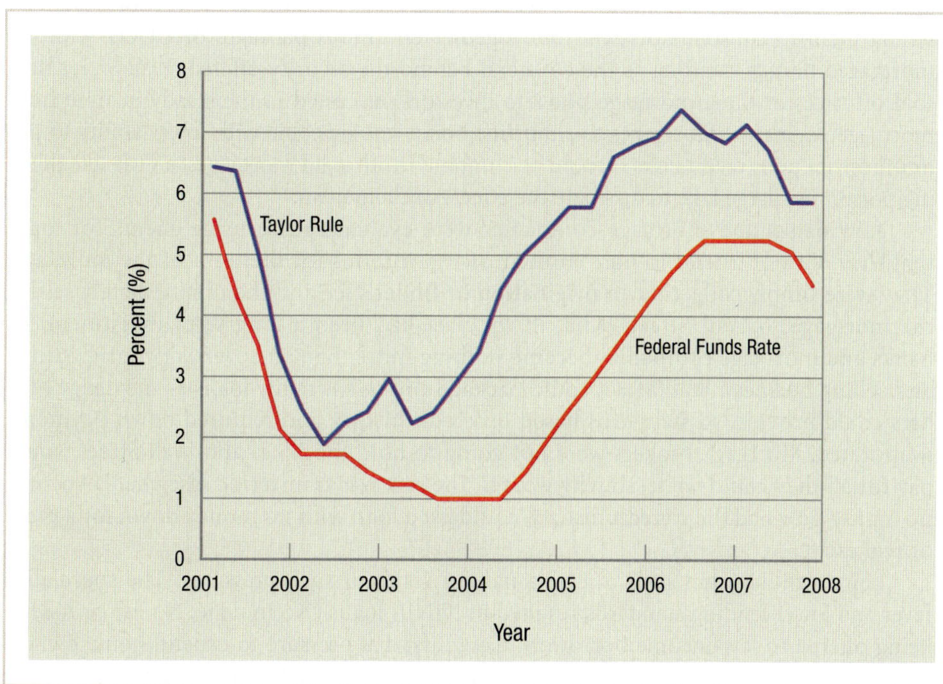


**FIGURE 8—The Taylor Rule and the Actual Federal Funds Rate**

Professor John Taylor argues that the Fed kept interest rates too low between 2002 and 2006, encouraging a housing bubble that eventually led to the financial meltdown of 2008–2009.

## Mortgage and Financial Market Developments

For many years, the standard mortgage was a 30-year mortgage with a fixed interest rate. The person taking out the mortgage to purchase the home made monthly payments, which consisted of interest on the loan and some payment toward the loan amount (the principal). Financial intermediaries—savings and loans and banks—usually had high standards that would-be home buyers had to meet. Further, a home buyer's income and credit quality were rigorously checked by the financial intermediaries.

High inflation in the early 1980s brought changes to the mortgage market. High inflation led to high interest rates that suppressed demand. Financial intermediaries, seeing a large drop in their mortgage business, brought home buyers in by offering adjustable-rate mortgages (ARMs). These mortgages tended to work like this: a below-market interest rate was offered for the first year; the rate would adjust in the second year, but only by a maximum amount; and then starting in the third year, the interest rate would adjust based on the market interest rate. From a buyer's point of view, a below-market rate, at least in the short term, was an inducement to buy. From a bank's point of view, below-market rates generated business: they could expect ARM mortgage holders to seek out fixed interest rate mortgages when interest rates fell, which meant a second round of origination fees (paid when every mortgage is taken out). Interest rates fell after the mid-1980s, and mortgage holders converted to fixed rate mortgages.

The housing boom of 2002 to 2007 saw further innovations in the mortgage market, and the ARM idea was taken to new lengths. Home prices were rising, demand for mortgages was rising, and financial intermediaries felt competitive pressure from new mortgage brokers and Wall Street firms who were only too happy to meet the growing demand. Two key things happened: the market for CDOs developed, and mortgage credit standards fell.

### Collateralized Debt Obligations and Lending Standards

Subprime mortgages were a small percentage of all mortgages when the market began collapsing in 2008. Why would rising defaults in these not-so-good mortgages beginning in 2007 bring havoc to the world economy? The answer lies in how Wall Street combined these higher-risk, higher-return mortgages with other prime mortgages in CDO packages.

CDOs are essentially bonds backed by a collection of prime, subprime, home equity, and other ARMs. Banks holding mortgages found they could offset the risk of default by selling them to consolidators who put together enormous packages of CDOs, with the mortgaged homes standing as the collateral behind the security offered. Wall Street then sold off slices of these mortgage pools to investors interested in the steady income from mortgage payments. Mortgages to subprime borrowers—people with lower ability to pay or otherwise poor credit risks—could be combined with solid mortgages, a little like diluting poison in a large lake to dissipate the effects of the poison.

Now banks and mortgage companies were evaluating mortgage clients for loans that they did not intend to hold in their own portfolios for the term of the mortgage. They were simply collecting an origination or finder's fee and then immediately selling the mortgage to Wall Street. What in the past had been a long-term investment for banks and mortgage companies became nothing more than an advertising, originating, and selling business. Wall Street could package and sell as many loans as mortgage brokers could provide, so standards based on credit history and required down payments evaporated. Mortgage brokers were not going to hold the notes and Wall Street would pay for all they could write, so why worry? The risk was transferred elsewhere. Anyone, no matter how bad their credit history, could get a loan with no money down for a piece of real estate.

Lower lending standards can be a natural result of such pressures. The speculative fever and lower lending standards resulted in NINJA loans (No Income, No Job or Assets) being offered to low-income borrowers. Congressional pressure to expand home ownership, and the growing sense that housing prices would never fall, convinced many that any future payment problems could be finessed with a simple refinancing to lower monthly payments. The market became so crazy that a farm laborer with an annual income of $14,000 was given a $720,000 loan on a Bakersfield, California, home.[2]

Trouble started when some of the people who took on subprime mortgages started to default in 2007. These people simply were stretched too thin. When their ARMs reset, they faced higher payments, sometimes double or triple the original monthly payments. Even with rising housing prices, they could not refinance away such a large increase in the face of rising interest rates (see Figure 8).

Subprime mortgages of $3 trillion represented only a small part of all mortgages when the market began collapsing in 2008. Why would rising defaults in these mortgages be such a problem? In the past, default rates on such CDO securities were miniscule.

## Inadequate Risk Ratings

One answer lies with the bond rating agencies whose job it is to rate packages of mortgages. Wall Street knew the minimum requirements needed for a rating agency to assign a AAA rating, and they manipulated the components to get that all-important rating. The ratings models had a relatively low historical default rate based on past default-foreclosure rates when loan standards were stricter. Also, rating firms were paid 6 times their normal fee to give the AAA rating to the mortgage packages, and were only paid *if the CDO got the AAA rating*. This led Wall Street to shop around for ratings, and all this new business led to high rating agency profits. Investors wanted the security of a AAA rating, giving these bonds the appearance of high-yield, low-risk investments. They sold well all over the world. The risk of each CDO was underestimated because of the overly rosy ratings.

## Leverage

The second answer lies in leverage (the ratio of debt to capital). Because the mortgage packages were seen as low-risk investments, many investors borrowed money at the low prevailing interest rates to purchase greater quantities, leveraging their capital and earning high returns. The difference between what they paid in interest on borrowed funds and what they earned in the mortgage pool significantly raised the return on their capital. But with leverage comes another risk. If you borrow 90% and only put 10% of your own capital in an investment (a leverage ratio of 10 to 1) and prices fall (considered an unlikely event for a AAA-rated investment), they would only need to fall by 10% to wipe out an investor's total investment. Many financial firms loaded up with bonds backed by these mortgage pools with leverage of more than 30 to 1. For these firms, a market reversal of a little over 3% would wipe them out.

## Credit Default Swaps

It gets worse. For those investors who were leveraged (and even for those who weren't) and who were concerned that there was always a possibility of default, no matter how remote, the financial industry developed another instrument that acted as insurance against default. Credit default swaps permitted investors to pay a small monthly fee to a counterparty who would compensate investors in the event of default. (The fees were small because the risk of default was assumed to be extremely low.)

The biggest issuer of credit default swaps, the American Insurance Group (AIG), sold several *trillion* dollars of these swaps with only a few *billion* dollars in capital to back them up. As Michael Lewis and David Einhorn note, credit default swaps are "more like buying fire insurance on your neighbor's house, possibly for many times the value of that house—from a company that probably doesn't have any real ability to pay you if someone sets fire to the whole neighborhood."[3] Here again we see risk underestimated, and so mispriced.

[2] Michael Lewis, "The End," *Portfolio.com*, November 11, 2008.

[3] Michael Lewis and David Einhorn, "How to Repair a Broken Financial World," *The New York Times*, January 4, 2009.

## Collapsing Markets

This brings us to the central event that brought down the financial system. By 2007, $25 trillion of American CDOs were in investment portfolios of banks, pension funds, mutual funds, hedge funds, and other financial institutions worldwide. The rate of subprime mortgage defaults was on the rise. In essence, up to a quarter of the mortgages in CDOs could default, representing a default rate 10 times greater than that anticipated by the AAA rating models. Because investors did not know what exactly was in their CDOs (the prospectuses were impenetrable), they panicked and tried to sell these investments.

Because the CDOs were too complex, and often investors didn't know what they held, the market collapsed. Buyers evaporated, markets became thin (lightly traded) at prices well below the CDOs' intrinsic values. Some investors were able to turn to their credit default swaps to recover their losses. But because AIG had sold trillions of dollars of swaps on only a few billion dollars in capital, AIG was soon insolvent and unable to pay off the losses.

For banks, this was a catastrophe. Their CDOs were virtually worthless because getting good information and differentiating between good and bad assets was impossible. Banking regulators require that banks retain a certain amount of capital, and the value of this capital must be "marked to market," or valued on their balance sheets at current market values. Now, however, at current prices, an important part of the banks' capital was wiped out. To raise capital, banks called in loans and reduced lines of credit to business, which reduced the money supply, contracted the economy, caused job losses, and deepened the recession.

So there you have it. A savings glut led to low interest rates, which fueled a housing boom. Wall Street created CDOs that packaged bad loans with good ones and was able to get these new investments premium ratings. Risk was underestimated, and so mispriced. Highly leveraged credit default swaps provided the illusion of insurance in the unlikely event of default, so many investors used leverage to boost returns. This meant that only a small decline in the price of CDOs could result in total loss. All of this created a financial house of cards. When one card at the bottom (subprime loans) collapsed, the entire edifice fell. Since most investors could not assess the riskiness of their CDO portfolio, the market was flooded and froze. Because all types of financial institutions worldwide were investors in CDOs, credit dried up, creating a credit crisis that precipitated a worldwide recession.

# The Government's Response

*The ultimate result of shielding man from the effects of folly is to people the world with fools.*

—Herbert Spencer

As long as the financial system takes on risks that it misperceives, we will have financial crises. In looking at the government's response to the financial crisis, we raise three issues. First, do financial firms have an incentive to take on large risks? Second, what government body is charged with recognizing untoward risk in the system? Third, do certain government actions in dealing with the financial crisis make a financial crisis more likely in the future?

The answers to these three questions are fairly straightforward. First, incentive schemes on Wall Street encourage the taking of large risks. If you are playing with other people's money and your bonus is based on your returns, why not take larger risks in the hope of gaining a larger bonus, in some cases a staggeringly larger bonus? If financial firms do not provide the right incentives, maybe regulatory bodies have to do this. Second, the Fed was the prime mover in dealing with the financial crisis, once it recognized it. One can argue that it took too long for the Fed to recognize the problem, and the Fed may have encouraged the housing bubble by keeping interest rates very low for too long, but what other government body could have had a key role in mitigating the effect of the financial crisis? Third, as Fed Chairman Ben Bernanke said, if your neighbor's house is on fire because he was smoking in bed, you deal with the fire first because if you don't, your own house can burn down. You deal with your neighbor's smoking problem later.

Let's look at the government's response to the financial crisis.

## Bear Stearns

Trouble began in 2007. On April 2, a large subprime lender, New Century Financial Corporation, filed for bankruptcy protection. By July, Bear Stearns, a large Wall Street investment bank, liquidated two hedge funds that invested in mortgage-backed securities. Two other large subprime lenders faced financial difficulties at this time. By August and September, the Fed started to lower interest rates in an attempt to stimulate the economy. By the end of the year, the Fed had established a Term Auction Facility to auction off funds in return for various types of collateral in the hope of providing liquidity to the system. This was only one type of program that the Fed created to bring funds into the financial system.

By March 2008, the Fed had cut interest rates further, though this action did not stem the tide. Also in March, with Bear Stearns likely to go bankrupt because of losses in its holdings of mortgage-backed securities, the Fed engineered a takeover of Bear Stearns by Chase Bank. The novel thing about the takeover was this: Chase would assume the first $1 billion in losses, and the Fed would take on the next $29 billion in potential losses. In essence, the Fed was bailing out a rogue bank. This kept a lid on things for a while, but not for long.

## Lehman Brothers

We reached the depths of the financial crisis in September 2008. Stung by criticism of its Bear Stearns bailout, the Fed let Lehman Brothers, the fourth largest commercial bank, fail on September 15, the same day that Bank of America announced its intention to buy the venerable stock broker Merrill Lynch, which was reeling under mortgage-backed securities losses. The Fed and the Treasury thought they were sending a message to the financial markets that imprudent behavior such as Lehman's would result in harsh costs to stockholders and executives. Unfortunately, this decision sent the financial markets into a tailspin, quickly changing the viewpoint of policymakers.

Subprime mortgage default rates were rising, and the overnight lending facilities that banks use to maintain and balance required reserves were frozen. Banks no longer had faith in other banks' ability to pay back *overnight* loans. Prices on CDOs plummeted and insolvencies were on the rise throughout the entire financial sector, not just banks. To counter this credit crisis, the Fed opened the discount window to some nonbank financial firms. At the same time, to reassure the public, the Treasury Department guaranteed all mutual fund money market accounts.

Also in September, the market received another shock when AIG announced it was bankrupt. AIG had vastly misperceived the riskiness of its credit default swaps. AIG was one of the biggest sellers of credit default swaps, and news of its bankruptcy turned AAA-rated CDO bonds into highly discounted junk bonds. Because CDO packages were highly complex, the market had difficulty valuing these bonds and buyers vanished. To stem the panic, the Fed lent AIG $85 billion to prevent insolvency. Interest rates were now down to 2%.

## Controlling Contagion

Amazingly, just one month later, in October 2008 Congress responded to the crisis by passing the $700 billion Troubled Asset Relief Program (TARP), authorizing the Treasury Department to purchase CDOs from banks to shore up their capital. Less than 60 days later, Treasury announced it would not purchase the bad assets, but would instead invest in banks by injecting government money for preferred equity (stock), thereby increasing bank capital and eliminating insolvency. Treasury had decided that paying "fair market value" for toxic assets would not solve the banks' problems. They would just be exchanging cash for the now highly discounted assets, resulting in no real change to bank balance sheets. They also concluded that determining fair market value was extremely difficult given the market's collapse, and paying more would not look good to auditors and taxpayers.

At this point, policymakers were starting to be concerned about public confidence in banks and worried that depositors might begin withdrawing funds, putting banks at further risk of failure. The Federal Deposit Insurance Corporation (FDIC) temporarily increased its guarantee on deposits from $100,000 to $250,000 per depositor per bank (this guarantee has now been extended until January 1, 2014).

Further deterioration in the CDO market required the Fed to put $38 billion more into AIG. The Treasury announced a $250 billion capital investment program in the nation's troubled banks. Initially, nine big banks soaked up $125 billion in funds. Over the next several months, hundreds of banks traded preferred stock for capital. The federal government is now a significant owner of the private banking system. Over time, when the economy improves and bank stocks rise in price, the government is expected to sell the stock, reducing the cost of the crisis to taxpayers.

These extraordinary efforts kept bank failures to around 100; in contrast, 9,000 banks failed between 1930 and 1933. For Bernanke and the Fed, it was crucial to maintain public confidence and keep the recession from becoming a full-blown depression.

By mid-December 2008, the Fed had essentially lowered its federal funds target rate to *zero*. The National Bureau of Economic Research officially dated the start of the recession to December 2007, confirming what many already knew—that the economy had already been declining for a year. Treasury loaned General Motors and Chrysler nearly $18 billion to keep them afloat. The last four months of 2008 will likely go down in history as one of the most frenetic times for policymaking since the Great Depression. The Fed stepped far outside of its usual role of managing the money supply, interest rates, inflation, and unemployment, and took extraordinary, out-of-the-box measures to prevent a financial sector meltdown.

## Stimulating the Economy

The inauguration of Barack Obama as president in January 2009 brought additional stimulus in the form of the $787 billion American Recovery and Reinvestment Act signed into law in February. By March, $30 billion more was loaned to AIG, and Treasury now guaranteed $3 trillion in money market funds. By the summer, AIG converted $25 billion of loans into equity (stock) and ten large banks repaid nearly $70 billion in TARP loans. The New York Fed's portfolio of equity and bonds had grown so large that it announced it would double its trading staff to handle the load.

This brief summary of the responses from policymakers in the first year of the financial crisis outlines the breadth and depth of fiscal and monetary policies designed to avert a catastrophe. They have succeeded, but the cost may not be known for a decade.

## Long-Term Policy Actions

*Instruct regulators to look for the newest fad in the industry and examine it with great care. The next mistake will be a new way to make a loan that will not be repaid.*

William Seidman, past head of the FDIC and Resolution Trust Corporation

The banking industry is different from other nonfinancial sectors because it is subject to systemic (system-wide) risks of illiquidity. A loss of confidence in one bank can affect all. As we saw during this most recent financial crisis, even banks can lose confidence in other banks. Further, a banking failure or financial crisis has serious consequences for the broader economy. Recessions that follow a banking crisis are typically twice as long and result in nearly 4 times the loss in GDP.[4]

[4] Financial Services Authority, *The Turner Review: A Regulatory Response to the Global Banking Crisis* (London: FSA), 2009.

Any new regulation will also have to confront the fact that nonbank financial firms, hedge funds, insurance companies, bond rating agencies, and so on, all contribute to system-wide risk. They will have to be brought under the new regulatory umbrella. The concerns that many economists expressed before the financial crisis became obvious did come true in practice: if you bail out big banks because they are "too big to fail" (their failing will have catastrophic effects on the entire financial system), how do you keep them from taking on even riskier actions in the future? Because policymakers could not afford a system-wide collapse, they saved firms that should have failed. Now, more inclusive regulations are required to prevent excessive risk-taking in the pursuit of higher short-term returns. Employment contracts in these firms must ultimately provide incentives that marry compensation with the long-term health of the firm.

Congress provided a new financial regulatory environment with the passage of the Restoring American Financial Stability Act of 2010. The Act creates a 9-member Financial Stability Oversight Council that together with the Federal Deposit Insurance Corporation is given the authority to seize and liquidate large firms (just as the FDIC does now with banks) that get into trouble. The Act also creates a Consumer Financial Protection Bureau to protect consumers from unfair, deceptive and abusive financial practices. New regulations also were put on over-the-counter derivatives, hedge funds and mortgage brokers.

Hundreds of new rules will have to be written and it will be several years before the Act is fully implemented.

## *Issue:* Moral Hazard and the Bernanke Put

**Initially it** was called the Greenspan Put; now it is the Bernanke Put. First, a little background. A *put* (on a stock) gives the holder the right to sell a stock at a set (strike) price, for a given period of time. For this right, the buyer of the put pays a premium. If the stock falls in price, the put rises in price and the holder collects the difference between the strike price and market price of the stock. Puts are typically used to insure against losses from market declines.

Critics of the Fed suggest that the Fed has created a belief in financial markets that if stock and bond prices fall too much, the Fed will quickly lower interest rates to prop up prices, reducing losses. The Fed under Greenspan kept the economy on an even keel during several crises, including a stock market crash in 1987, the recessions of 1990 and 2001, as well as several international financial meltdowns in the 1990s. Subprime mortgage defaults and housing foreclosures have created major problems (losses) for Wall Street firms. This has led to bailouts and sizable loans to private firms. To critics, the Bernanke put is that the Fed seems to be rewarding risk-taking by huge nonbank financial institutions, creating incentives to take even bigger risks in the future, knowing that the Fed will bail them out. This is a moral hazard problem that future policymakers will have to contend with.

Maybe this is just the Fed doing a good job. Between 1918 and 1936, the economy was in recession 41% of the time; between 1940 and 1985, roughly 18%; and since 1986, only 6% of the time. As Harvey Rosenblum, executive vice president and director of research at the Federal Reserve Bank of Dallas, has argued, the real moral hazard in the United States today is that "Americans spend, save and invest in the belief that recessions, if they occur, will be short, mild and infrequent. People believe that unemployment is something that happens to someone else." The latest recession, which has seen unemployment rise to 10%, may change household attitudes about saving and spending for some time to come.

Balancing the mandated goals assigned to the Fed may require decisions that give the appearance of creating a system where risk is privatized for the poor but socialized for the rich; however, it may simply be the natural outcome of preventing recessions. As Mervyn King, the governor of the Bank of England, said just before the bank stepped in to quell a run on Northern Rock Bank, "There must be strong grounds for believing that [central-bank inaction] would lead to economic costs on a scale sufficient to ignore the moral hazard."

The Fed's actions in 2008–2009 may have kept the economy from descending into a depression, but in the process it gave the impression that it had saved many large financial institutions from their imprudent and overly risky investment decisions. The result is that Congress will pass more restrictive regulations on all financial firms.

Sources: Harvey Rosenblum, "Fed Policy and Moral Hazard," *The Wall Street Journal,* October 18, 2007, p. A17; David Wessel, "Has Fed Risked Creating Moral Hazard?," *Wall Street Journal,* September 20, 2007, p. A2.

**CHECKPOINT**

### THE FINANCIAL CRISIS OF 2008–2009

- Financial risk was not properly accounted for in the period leading up to the financial crisis.
- A world savings glut and unusually low interest rates during 2002–2007 led to a housing price bubble. When it collapsed, foreclosures on subprime mortgages sent the economy into a recession.
- The incentives surrounding mortgages (package and sell) and pressure from Congress on financial firms to loan to low-income people led to a reduction in lending standards.
- Investors were lulled into thinking that collateralized debt obligations (CDOs) were relatively risk-free, even though they included a lot of subprime assets in the pool.
- Ratings companies gave too many CDOs a AAA rating that wasn't deserved.
- Because CDOs were considered relatively safe, financial firms and others used leverage to purchase them. When the market turned sour, it didn't take much of a downturn to bankrupt these firms.
- Credit default swaps were a form of insurance for those holding CDOs, but the firms providing the swaps were so leveraged that they were unable pay off on the contracts.
- To control the panic, the Fed used its normal monetary policy tools and some that it hadn't used since the 1930s.
- New rules imposed on financial firms will probably include higher capital requirements, restrictions on leverage, and much tighter regulations.

**QUESTION:** The collapse of the financial markets in late 2008 resulted in the Fed reducing interest rates to near zero. Was it likely that the U.S. economy in 2009 sank into a Keynesian liquidity trap?

Answers to the Checkpoint question can be found at the end of this chapter.

## Key Concepts

Equation of exchange, p. 540
Classical monetary transmission mechanism, p. 541
Keynesian transmission mechanism, p. 543
Liquidity trap, p. 544
Monetarist transmission mechanism, p. 545
Easy money, expansionary monetary policy, or quantitative easing, p. 550
Tight money, restrictive, or contractionary monetary policy, p. 550
Monetary rule, p. 550
Inflation targeting, p. 551
Taylor rule, p. 551

## Chapter Summary

### Monetary Theories

The long-run quantity theory of money is a product of the classical school of thought that concludes that the economy will tend toward equilibrium at full employment in the long run.

Classical quantity theory is defined by the equation of exchange:

$$M \times V = P \times Q.$$

In this equation, $M$ is the supply of money, $V$ is its velocity, $P$ is the price level, and $Q$ is the economy's output. Classical theorists considered the velocity of money to be limited by the prevailing monetary institutions and technology, and aggregate output to be fixed at full employment. The result is that a change in the money supply translates directly into a change in prices, or $\Delta M = \Delta P$. Thus, classical quantity theory predicts that, in the long run, changes in the money supply will bring about directly proportionate changes in the aggregate price level.

Keynesian monetary analysis was developed during the 1930s. It examines the short-run effects that changes in the money supply have on interest rates and subsequently on investment, consumption, and output.

Keynes identified three motives that people have for holding money in their portfolios: transactions, precautionary, and speculative motives.

Keynes thought an increase in the money supply causes the price of bonds to rise and interest rates to fall. Falling interest rates boost investment, which raises aggregate demand and thus increases aggregate income, output, and employment. However, in a recession or depression, there was so much slack that monetary policy would be ineffective.

Monetarism first arose in the 1960s as a response to Keynesian monetary analysis; it was pioneered by Milton Friedman. Monetarism assumes the economy will ultimately stabilize itself around full employment in the long run.

Friedman pioneered the notion that consumption levels are determined not only by income but also by wealth. Friedman assumed that utility-maximizing individuals will allocate their wealth among various assets until the marginal rates of return are equal. Thus, when the money supply increases, people will discover that they are holding more money than they desire, and the additional supply of money decreases the return on money. Excess money balances will thus be exchanged for other financial and real assets, including bonds, real estate, and consumer durables such as cars and houses. Eventually, portfolios will rebalance and markets will return to equilibrium.

In conducting monetary policy, the Fed has the broad option of targeting either a stable price level or full employment income and output. Most economists agree that, in the long run, the Fed should target price stability, since low rates of inflation have been shown to provide the best environment for long-run economic growth.

In the short run, demand and supply shocks to the economy may need differing approaches to monetary policy. When a demand shock hits the economy, no conflict arises between the twin goals of monetary policy. Not only is the aim of full employment compatible with the objective of stable prices, but in targeting either one of these objectives, the Fed will take steps that help to bring about the other.

When a supply shocks hits the economy, in contrast, both price stability and output worsen. If the Fed then increases the money supply to restore the economy to full employment, this action only drives inflation up further, whereas if the Fed enacts a contractionary policy to stabilize prices, this move will just lead to a deeper recession. Most economists agree that when a supply shock occurs, an expansionary policy is best since it permits the Fed to spread the shock's impact between income and output losses and price level increases.

## Modern Monetary Policy

Some economists, notably Milton Friedman, have called for monetary rules to guide monetary policymakers. Other economists argue that modern economies are too complex to be managed by a few simple rules. Changing institutions, economic behaviors, and technologies require some discretion by policymakers.

Monetary targeting aims to secure the steady growth of money stocks. Experience with monetary targets has not proven successful.

Inflation targeting involves setting targets on the inflation rate, usually of around 2% a year. If inflation (or the forecasted rate of inflation) then exceeds this target, the Fed implements a contractionary policy, and vice versa. Inflation targeting has the virtue of explicitly acknowledging that the long-run goal of monetary policy is price stability.

Today, the Fed sets a target federal funds rate and then uses open market operations to alter excess reserves, and ultimately alters interest rates. Changing interest rates change investment and other interest-sensitive components of consumption, exports, and imports.

The Fed changes its federal funds target in response to two major factors: inflation and output that varies from its potential level.

### The Financial Crisis of 2008–2009

Financial risk was not properly accounted for in the period leading up to the financial crisis.

A world savings glut and unusually low interest rates during 2002–2007 led to a housing price bubble. When it collapsed, foreclosures on subprime mortgages sent the economy into a recession.

The incentives surrounding mortgages (package and sell) and pressure from Congress on financial firms to loan to low-income people led to a reduction in lending standards.

Investors were lulled into thinking that collateralized debt obligations (CDOs) were relatively risk-free, even though they included a lot of subprime assets in the pool.

Ratings companies gave too many CDOs a AAA rating that wasn't deserved.

Because CDOs were considered relatively safe, financial firms and others used leverage to purchase them. When the market turned sour, it didn't take much of a downturn to bankrupt these firms.

Credit default swaps were a form of insurance for those holding CDOs, but the firms providing the swaps were so leveraged that they were unable pay off on the contracts.

To control the panic, the Fed used its normal monetary policy tools and some that it hadn't used since the 1930s.

New rules imposed on financial firms will probably include higher capital requirements, restrictions on leverage, and much tighter regulations.

## Questions and Problems

### Check Your Understanding

1. Why is it important for the Federal Reserve Board to be independent of the executive branch of the federal government?
2. The equation of exchange, $M \times V = P \times Q$, helps explain ____________.
3. Describe how open market operations alter the supply of money.
4. When the interest rate falls, people desire higher money balances. Why?
5. How is the impact of expansionary monetary policy different when the economy is considerably below full employment than when it is at full employment?

### Apply the Concepts

6. If oil (or energy) prices double and then remain steady at the new higher price, and the Fed *does nothing,* will inflation rise and continue at the new higher rate, or will it rise temporarily and then fall back to its former rate?
7. It seems that each time the Fed raises interest rates, the stock market has an awful few days. Why do higher interest rates have such an impact on the stock market?
8. If the Fed persistently pursues an easy money policy, what is the likely outcome?
9. When NASA scientists were operating the Mars rovers to get them to drive across the Martian landscape and collect and analyze rocks and crevices, the scientists complained that the 20-minute delay between when they issued a command and when the rovers responded made their job more challenging. Isn't this somewhat similar to what monetary policymakers face? How is it different?

## In the News

**10.** "There are two forces that cause the economy to grow. One is real, the other is an illusion. The real force—entrepreneurial innovation and creativity—comes naturally as long as government policies do not drive it away. The artificial force is easy money. An increased supply of money, by creating an illusion of wealth, can increase spending in the short run, but this eventually turns into inflation. Printing money cannot possibly create wealth; if it could, counterfeiting would be legal."[5] Does this quote illustrate the short-run versus the long-run aspects of monetary policy? Why or why not?

**11.** The *Financial Times* (June 8, 2006) reported that "the European Central Bank has lost patience with inflation that has remained persistently higher than its 2 per cent definition of price stability. It is almost certain to raise the cost of borrowing today, perhaps by 0.5 percentage points." Explain why increasing the "cost of borrowing" is an appropriate policy in this case.

**12.** In 2004–2005, when the Fed reduced the discount rate to around 2.25%, some commentators became concerned that the interest rate was so low that the Fed's ability to conduct monetary policy might be compromised. But Ben Bernanke, then a Fed governor, earlier had suggested:

> *As I have mentioned, some observers have concluded that when the central bank's policy rate falls to zero—its practical minimum—monetary policy loses its ability to further stimulate aggregate demand and the economy. At a broad conceptual level, and in my view in practice as well, this conclusion is clearly mistaken. Indeed, under a fiat (that is, paper) money system, a government (in practice, the central bank in cooperation with other agencies) should always be able to generate increased nominal spending and inflation, even when the short-term nominal interest rate is at zero.*

Do you agree? Why or why not?

**13.** The May 13, 2006, issue of *The Economist* noted that "rather than worrying about being predictable—indicating to markets precisely what they are going to do next—central bankers ought to worry about being transparent—explaining how they think and why they choose their policies." How transparent can central banks be in explaining their reasoning for policy? Would it be easier for monetary authorities to be more transparent if they have an explicit framework such as inflation targeting?

**14.** William Poole, former president of the Federal Reserve Bank of St. Louis, has suggested that,"we may face more inflation pressure than currently shows up in the formal data. . . . Statistical studies to detect pass-through from recent energy price increases have failed to show significant effects in U.S. price data. . . . But stories about widespread pass-through are becoming increasingly common." Another Fed policymaker, Randall Kroszner, concludes, "We want to try to look where inflation is going. We don't want to look in the rearview mirror at what has happened to inflation."[6] What policymaking problems are these two Fed members alluding to? Why are these problems important?

**15.** Writing in the *Financial Times* (April 7, 2009), John Thornhill asks, "To what extent would today's unprecedented economic intervention undermine tomorrow's recovery?" He is, of course, referring to the Obama administration's considerable fiscal stimulus along with a nearly $4 trillion budget combined with the Fed's low interest rate policy and its huge monetary jolt to the economy. In the short term, these policies are designed to reenergize the economy, but they are also expected to lead to

---

[5] Brian Wesbury, "Economic Rehab," *Wall Street Journal,* June 7, 2006, p. A14.

[6] "Data May Not Fully Reflect Inflation, Fed Officials Say," *New York Times,* June 17, 2006.

huge deficits, rapidly rising public debt, and an increase in government's share of national output.

Thornhill suggests that over the longer term, there are only four options to address these changes in our public sector finances: "default, inflation, increased taxes, or decreased spending." Is he right? How economically palatable or politically feasible are these options?

### Solving Problems

16. Why are supply shocks so much harder than demand shocks for monetary policy to adjust to? Use the grid below to show your answer to this question.

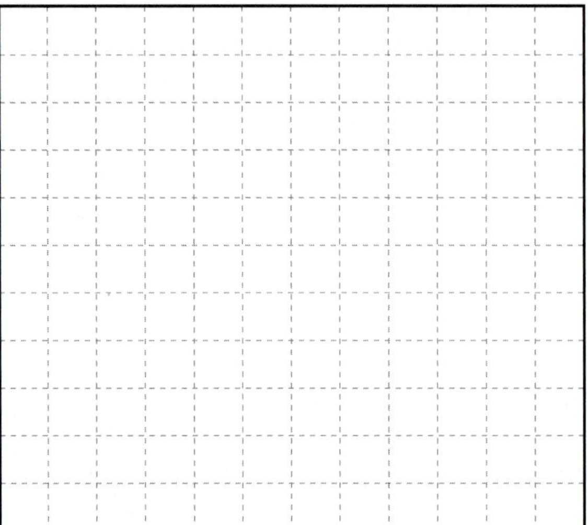

## Answers to Questions in CheckPoints

### Check Point: Monetary Theories

The speculative demand for money influences interest rates and is most important for monetary policy because interest rates affect consumption and investment spending.

### Check Point: Modern Monetary Policy

When the Fed begins to view inflation as a growing problem, it usually means that some form of contractionary monetary policy is to follow. This typically means that interest rates will rise and, most important for bond investors, bond prices will *fall* and bondholders will incur capital losses.

### Check Point: The Financial Crisis of 2008–2009

Reducing interest rates to low levels to stimulate credit and the economy was probably not sufficient by itself. But as consumer spending dropped off, business avoided new investments as markets declined or disappeared, suggesting that the economy may have been in a liquidity trap. Keynesian analysis got the nod from policymakers with the $787 billion fiscal stimulus package.

# Macroeconomic Policy Challenges 24

Andy Rain/epa/Corbis

**Before the 1930s,** the common wisdom held that the economy was best left alone, since it would hover around full employment as flexible wages, prices, and interest rates kept business humming. The Great Depression, however, made mincemeat of the common wisdom. With the publication of Keynes's *General Theory,* the government's role in economic stabilization was substantially expanded. Today, the government routinely seeks to control the business cycle and the major macroeconomic variables of employment, unemployment, output, economic growth, and inflation.

The 1950s and 1960s provided economists with the nearest thing possible to a laboratory for testing Keynesian aggregate demand policies. In 1958, British economist A. W. Phillips found empirical evidence of a relatively stable negative correlation between changes in wages and unemployment. Later, a similar negative relationship between inflation and unemployment was discovered by U.S. economists, with lower rates of unemployment being associated with higher rates of inflation. This latter relationship has been dubbed the *Phillips curve* by economists.

This stable tradeoff between unemployment and inflation was soon translated into a menu of policy options among which policymakers could choose. Politicians would select a desired unemployment level, and economists could then tell them what inflation rate would be required.

In the late 1960s, however, Milton Friedman and Edmund Phelps advanced theoretical arguments maintaining that any direct relationship between inflation and unemployment would be short-lived. By the early 1970s, Friedman and Phelps had been proven correct, as something had gone terribly wrong with the economy and the Phillips curve predictions.

**After studying this chapter you should be able to:**

- ☐ Explain what Phillips curves are and what relationship they postulate between inflation and unemployment.
- ☐ Describe the natural rate of unemployment.
- ☐ Describe stagflation.
- ☐ Describe how inflationary expectations can take on a life of their own and stymie policymakers.
- ☐ Describe adaptive expectations and its major drawback.
- ☐ Describe rational expectations and its implications for policymakers.
- ☐ Critique the rational expectations theory.
- ☐ Describe what jobless recoveries are.
- ☐ Explain why jobless recoveries might arise.
- ☐ Explain when monetary policy or fiscal policy might be an appropriate response to macroeconomic downturns.

The breakdown of the stable Phillips curve led to the development of the concept of the *natural rate of unemployment.* Determined by such factors as technology, social and economic customs, regulations, and demographics, the natural rate of unemployment is that level of unemployment at which there are no inflationary pressures on the economy. If the economy might deviate from its natural level in the short run due to incorrect inflationary expectations, it should return to this level over the long run. The result, as Friedman and Phelps argued, is that there is no long-run tradeoff between inflation and unemployment. As for policymaking, this meant that any beneficial short-term effects would soon be dissipated and then show up as harmful long-term effects.

Before the 1970s were over, Robert Lucas, Thomas Sargent, and Neil Wallace were arguing that the *rational expectations* of economic actors (consumers and business) would eliminate even the short-run relationship thought to exist between inflation and unemployment. Taken to its logical conclusion, this *new classical* model suggests that public macroeconomic policy is totally ineffective, incapable of influencing either unemployment or output. No profession stands idly by as its very reason for being is logically assaulted from within. Thus, several *new Keynesian* economists challenged the rational expectations model, striking up a debate that continues to this day.

In this chapter we consider modern challenges to macroeconomic policymaking. The first section focuses on the connection between inflation and real economic activity. This section explores Phillips curve analysis, along with the enhancements provided by Friedman and Phelps. Is there a tradeoff between inflation and unemployment?

The second section looks at the rational expectations debate and the new Keynesian response, coming face to face with the issue of whether macroeconomic policy can be effective at all.

The last section of this chapter puts the concepts from these two sections and other parts of this text to work to examine the recession of 2008–2009. What do the data tell us about this recession? What does theory suggest are appropriate policies to undertake? Is there something special about financial crises? Finally, what does the future have in store for us?

## Unemployment and Inflation: Phillips Curves

**Phillips curve:** The original curve posited a negative relationship between wages and unemployment, but later versions related unemployment to inflation rates.

In his early work, A. W. Phillips[1] compared the rate of change in money wages to unemployment rates in Britain over the years 1861 to 1957. The nonlinear, negatively sloped curve shown in Figure 1 on page 572 reflects his estimate of how these variables were related and has been called a **Phillips curve** in his honor. As you can see, when unemployment rises, wage rates fall.

What explains this negative relationship between wages and unemployment? Labor costs or wages are typically a firm's largest cost component; in our economy, wages represent nearly three-quarters of total costs. As the demand for labor rises, labor markets will tighten, making it difficult for employers to fill vacant positions. Hence, when unemployment falls, wages go up as firms bid up the price of labor to attract more workers. The opposite happens when labor demand falls: unemployment rises and wages decline.

Telecommunications workers in the 1990s were in short supply, and many were earning six-figure salaries. For nearly five years, this labor market remained extremely tight; résumés flew around the Internet, and employees took the jobs of their choice. But when the dot-coms collapsed, unemployment in the telecommunications sector soared, and salaries plummeted for those workers lucky enough to find jobs. A similar impact was felt by workers in the current downturn. Collapsing financial and housing sectors, along with reduced consumer spending, put 10% of the labor force out of work. Many people exhausted their unemployment benefits after being unemployed for over a year.

[1] A. W. Phillips, "The Relation Between Unemployment and the Rate of Change of Money Wages in the United Kingdom, 1861–1957," *Economica*, 1958, pp. 283–299.

By the *Numbers*

## Anatomy of a Recession

The Federal Reserve and fiscal policymakers look at a range of economic indicators to judge when a recession begins and to measure its depth. Here is a sampling of data from the current recession (indicated by the shaded areas).

**Real GDP growth began dropping** in the last quarter of 2007, tanked in 2008, and then began recovering in 2009.

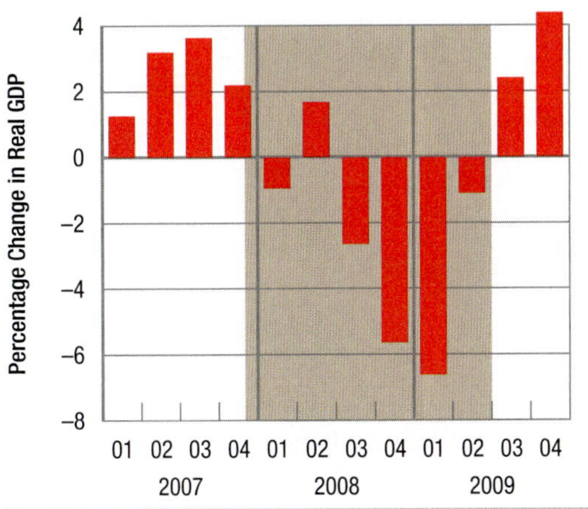


**Consumer sentiment fell** for two years. It rose in early 2009, possibly signaling the beginning of the end of the recession.

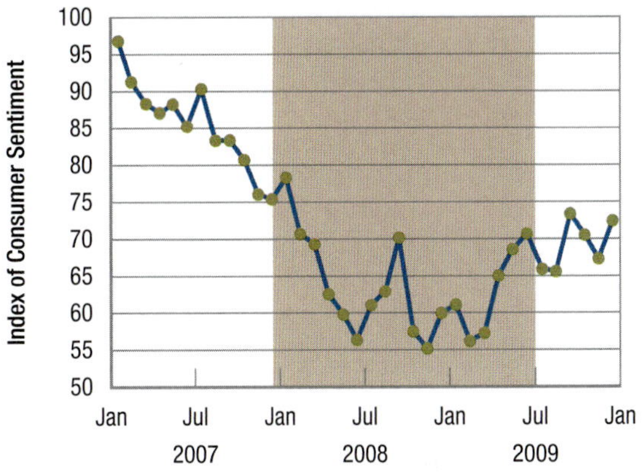


**The good news** is that inflation expectations are down.

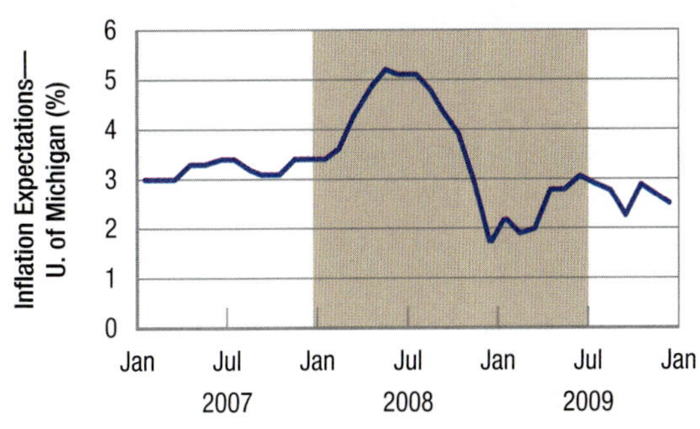


**Real retail sales fell** roughly 7% since January 2007.

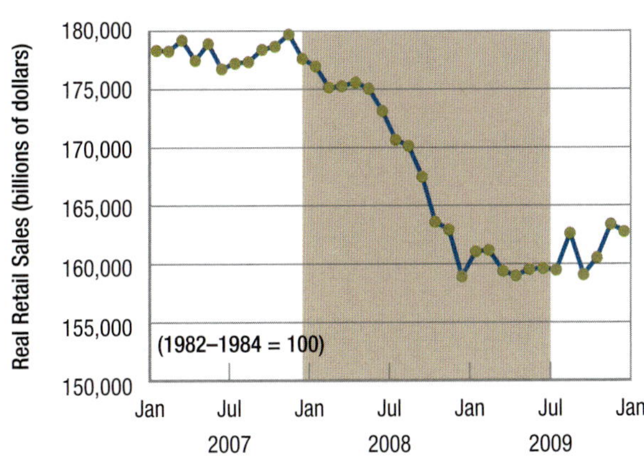


**Both the unemployment rate** and the number of people unemployed for more than 27 weeks rose dramatically since the recession began. This was the deepest recession in 75 years.

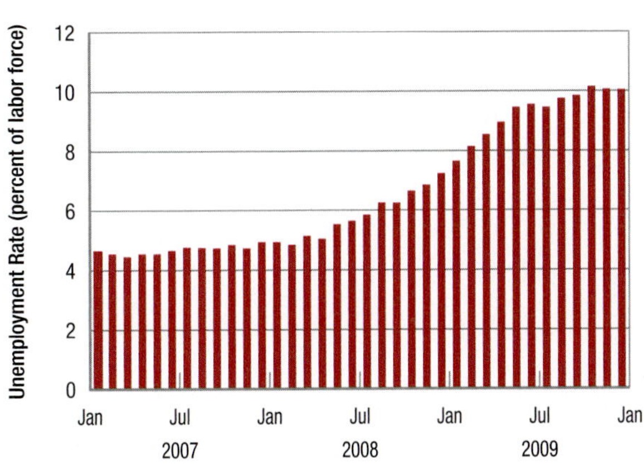


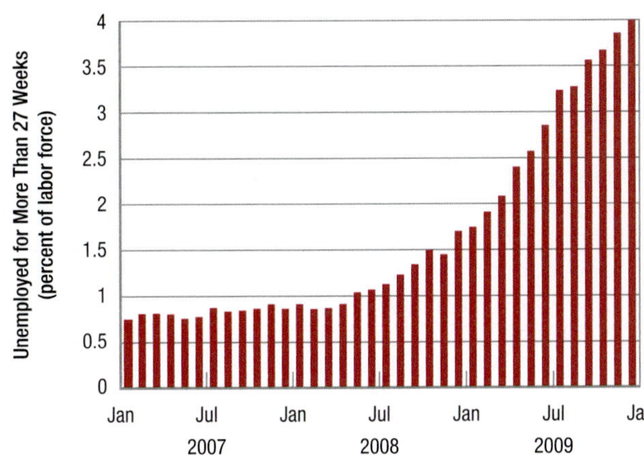

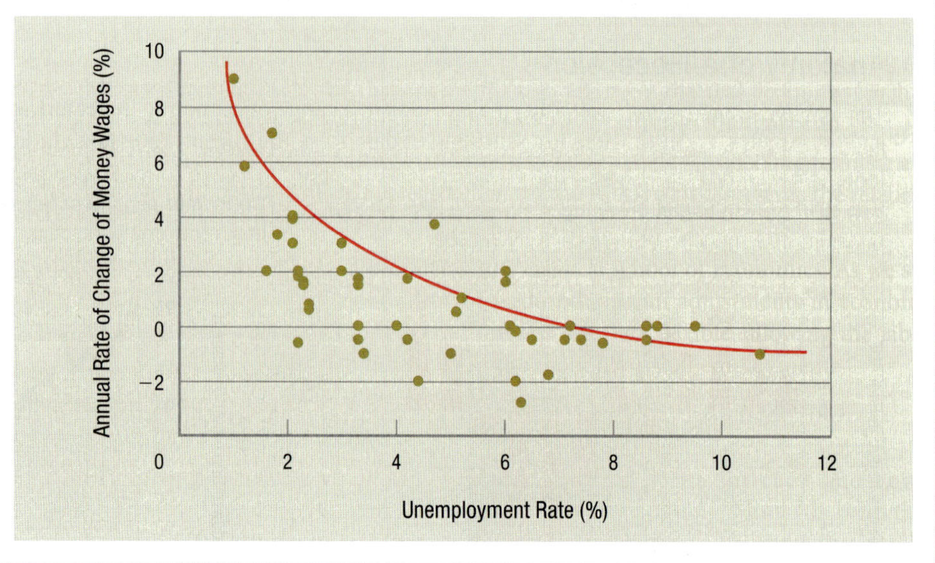


**FIGURE 1—The Original Phillips Curve for Britain (1861–1957)**

A. W. Phillips compared the rate of change in money wages to unemployment rates in Britain from 1861 to 1957. The resulting nonlinear, negatively sloped curve is the first example of a Phillips curve. When unemployment rises, wage rates fall, and vice versa. Note, some dots represent multiple years.

The market relationship between wages and unemployment will clearly affect prices. But worker productivity also plays an important role in determining prices.

## Productivity, Prices, and Wages

We might think that whenever wages rise, prices must also rise. Higher wages mean higher labor costs for employers—costs that businesses then pass along as higher prices. But this is not always the case. If worker productivity increases enough to offset the wage increase, then product prices can remain stable. The basic relationship among wages, prices, and productivity is

$$p = w - q$$

where $p$ is inflation, $w$ is the rate of increase in nominal wages, and $q$ is the rate of increase in labor productivity. For example, when wages increase by 5% and productivity increases by 3%, inflation is 2%.

Given this relationship, the Phillips curve can be adapted to relate productivity to inflation and unemployment, as shown in Figure 2.

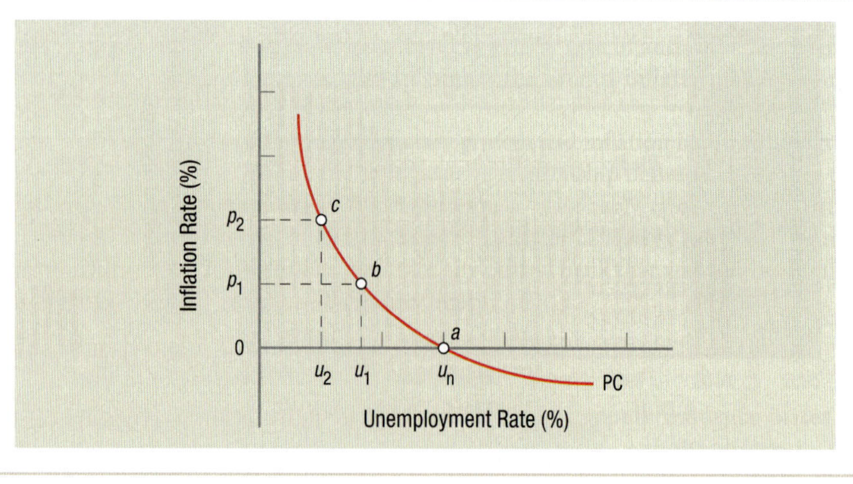


**FIGURE 2—The Phillips Curve**

A rise in wages may cause a rise in prices, but if worker productivity increases sufficiently to offset the wage increase, product prices can remain stable. When the rates of change in productivity and wages are equal, inflation is zero (point *a*). This is the natural rate of unemployment. If policymakers want to use expansionary policy to reduce unemployment from $u_n$ to $u_1$, they must be willing to accept inflation of $p_1$. Reducing unemployment further to $u_2$ would raise inflation to $p_2$ as labor markets tighten and wages rise more rapidly than productivity.

Notice that when the rates of change in productivity and wages are equal ($w = q$), inflation is zero (point $a$). This level of unemployment is known as the **natural rate of unemployment,** the unemployment rate when inflationary pressures are nonexistent. This unemployment rate, for reasons that we will discuss below, is also known as the *nonaccelerating inflation rate of unemployment (NAIRU)*. Note that higher rates of productivity growth mean that for a given level of unemployment, inflation will be less (the Phillips curve would shift in toward the origin).

**Natural rate of unemployment:** The level of unemployment where price and wage decisions are consistent; a level at which the actual inflation rate is equal to people's inflationary expectations, and cyclical unemployment is zero.

If policymakers want to use expansionary policy to reduce unemployment from $u_n$ to $u_1$, then according to the curve shown in Figure 2, they must be willing to accept inflation of $p_1$. To reduce unemployment further to $u_2$ would raise inflation to $p_2$ as labor markets tightened and wages rose more rapidly.

Figure 3 shows the Phillips curve for the United States during the 1960s. Notice the nearly smooth negative relationship between the two variables, much like that in the last two figures. As unemployment fell, inflation rose. This empirical relationship led policymakers to believe that the economy presents them with a menu of choices. By accepting a minor rise in inflation, they could keep unemployment low. Alternatively, by accepting a rise in unemployment, they could keep inflation near zero. Using the data found in Figure 3, policymakers concluded that an inflation rate of 3% to 4% was required to keep unemployment below 4%.

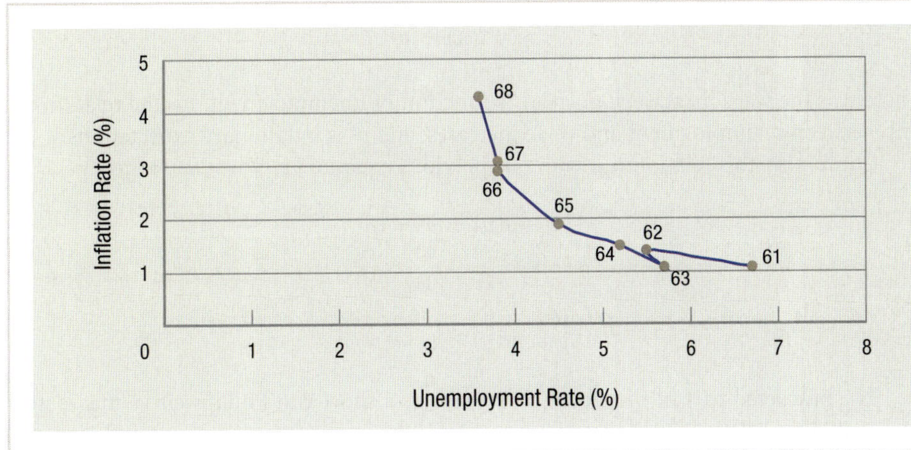


**FIGURE 3—The Phillips Curve—1960s**

The Phillips curve for the United States during the 1960s gives a smooth negative relationship between inflation and unemployment, much like that found in the last two figures. Using this relationship, policymakers concluded that an inflation rate of 3% to 4% was required to keep unemployment below 4%.

But just as policymakers were getting used to accepting moderate inflation in exchange for lower unemployment rates, the economy played a big trick on them. As Figure 4 shows, the entire Phillips curve began shifting outward during the early 1970s.

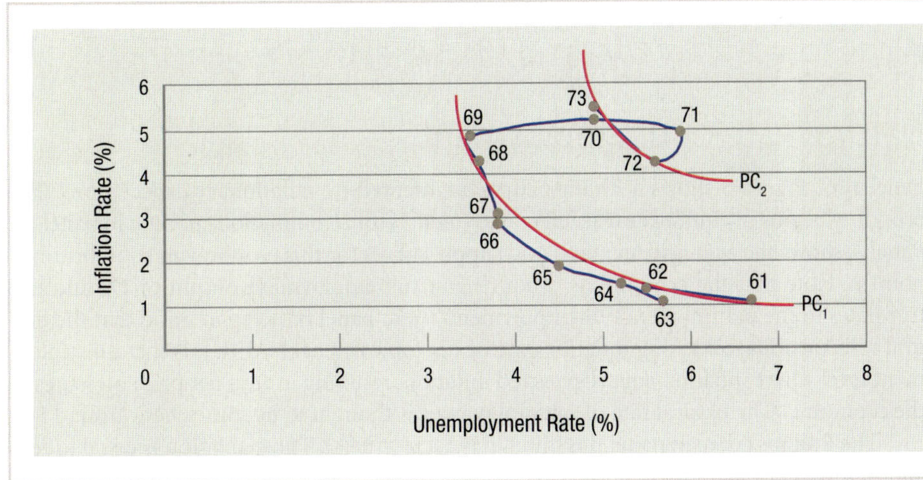


**FIGURE 4—The Phillips Curve in 1961–1973—Instability**

Just as policymakers were getting used to accepting moderate inflation in exchange for lower unemployment rates, the economy surprised them. The entire Phillips curve began shifting outward during the early 1970s. Unemployment rates that, in the 1960s, had been associated with modest inflation of 2% to 3% quickly began requiring twice that rate.

What looked to be an easy task for those in charge—just select the desired rate of inflation and unemployment from the 1960s menu—turned into a nightmare. Unemployment rates that, in the 1960s, had been associated with modest inflation of 2% to 3% quickly began requiring twice that rate in the early 1970s, and as we will see in a few moments, by the late 1970s, these same unemployment rates were generating annual inflation rates approaching the double digits. The reason for these shifts turned out to be the oil supply shocks of the mid-1970s and the rising inflationary expectations that followed.

## The Importance of Inflationary Expectations

As discussed in earlier chapters, workers do not work for the sake of earning a specific dollar amount, or a specific nominal wage. Rather, they work for the sake of earning what those wages will buy—for real wages. Consequently, when they bargain for wage increases, workers will take their past experiences with inflation into account. Furthermore, if workers failed to anticipate the inflation that occurred when they negotiated their previous contract, such that their real wages declined over the course of this contract, they will be looking to correct for this loss in the new contract—the new wages will have to make up the loss.

**Inflationary expectations:** The rate of inflation expected by workers for any given period. Workers do not work for a specific nominal wage but for what those wages will buy (real wages), so their inflationary expectations are an important determinant of what nominal wage they are willing to work for.

Taking **inflationary expectations** into account, wage increases can be connected to unemployment and expected inflation as follows:

$$w = f(u) + p^e$$

where $w$ is the wage increase, $f(u)$ (read "a function of unemployment") is the relationship between unemployment and wage increases, and $p^e$ is inflationary expectations.

Combining this relationship with our previous equation, $p = w - q$, we get

$$p = f(u) + p^e - q$$

or

$$p = [f(u) - q] + p^e$$

The bracketed part of this equation represents a short-run Phillips curve that is now augmented by inflationary expectations $p^e$. This is the same tradeoff between inflation and unemployment that we saw before, but there is a unique tradeoff for each level of inflationary expectations.

For example, let's assume that when unemployment is 4%, inflation will normally be 5%. If productivity is growing at a 2% rate, then the Phillips curve part $[f(u) - q]$ will be 3%, similar to the inflation rate on Phillips curve $PC_1$ in Figure 4 for the 1960s. However, if inflationary expectations ($p^e$) grow to, say, 4%, the Phillips curve will shift to $PC_2$ in Figure 4, and the inflation rate now associated with 4% unemployment will be

$$p = [f(u) - q] + p^e = 3\% + 4\% = 7\%$$

## Natural Rate of Unemployment

Panel B of Figure 5 shows a Phillips curve augmented by inflationary expectations. The economy begins in equilibrium at full employment with zero inflation (point $a$ in panel B). Panel A shows the aggregate demand and supply curves for this economy in equilibrium at point $a$. Note that the economy is producing at full employment output of $Q_f$, and this translates to the natural rate of unemployment, $u_n$, in panel B. (Keep in mind that the natural rate, or nonaccelerating inflation rate of unemployment [NAIRU], is that unemployment level where inflation equals expected inflation, resulting in zero net price pressures in the economy.) The natural rate of unemployment is thought to be somewhere around 5%.

The Phillips curve in panel B is initially $PC_0$ ($p^e = 0\%$). Thus, inflation is equal to zero and so are inflationary expectations ($p^e$).

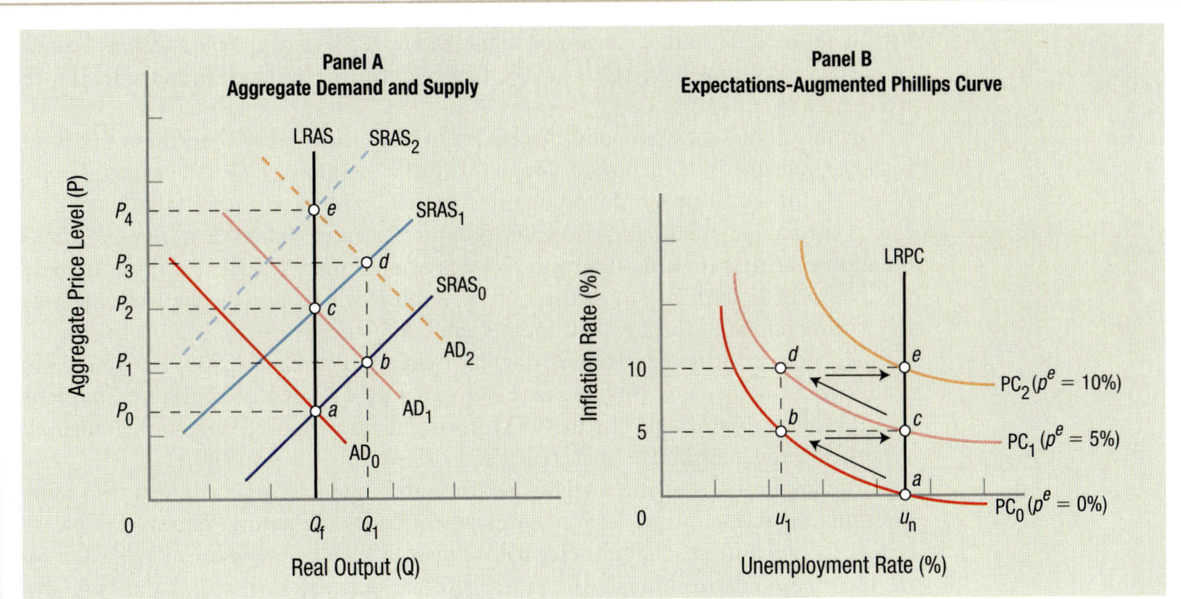


**FIGURE 5—Aggregate Demand, Aggregate Supply, and the Expectations-Augmented Phillips Curve**

Panel A shows the economy's aggregate demand and supply curves, and panel B shows the economy's Phillips curve, augmented by inflationary expectations. Using expansionary policies to reduce unemployment below $u_n$, policymakers shift aggregate demand in panel A from $AD_0$ to $AD_1$. This moves the economy to point *b*, with real output and the price level rising to $Q_1$ and $P_1$. Unemployment declines to $u_1$ (point *b* in panel B), but inflation rises to something approaching 5%. If policymakers attempt to hold unemployment below the natural rate, the economy will endure accelerating inflation. The long-run Phillips curve (LRPC) in panel B shows the relationship between inflation and unemployment when the inflation rate is just equal to inflationary expectations.

Now assume, however, that policymakers are unhappy with the economy's performance and want to reduce unemployment below $u_n$. Using expansionary policies, they shift aggregate demand in panel A from $AD_0$ to $AD_1$. This moves the economy to point *b*; real output and the price level rise, to $Q_1$ and $P_1$.

In panel B, meanwhile, the unemployment rate has declined to $u_1$ (point *b*), but inflation has risen to something around 5%. Workers had anticipated zero inflation, or that prices would remain stable at $P_0$ in panel A. As a result, inflation exceeds expected inflation. This *unanticipated inflation* means that real wages have fallen. Unionized workers will demand adjustments to their contracts to provide for higher nominal earnings. Workers who are not in unions will begin asking for raises, and employers wanting to keep turnover at a minimum may well begin offering higher wages.

### The Long-Run Phillips Curve

The long-run Phillips curve (LRPC), shown in panel B of Figure 5 as the vertical line at full employment (unemployment = $u_n$), shows the long-term relationship between inflation and unemployment when the inflation rate and the expected inflation rate are equal. The LRPC is the Phillips curve counterpart to the vertical long-run aggregate supply curve (LRAS) in panel A.

## Accelerating Inflation

As nominal wages rise, the result in panel A is that, over time, the short-run aggregate supply curve shifts leftward to $SRAS_1$, thus moving the economy back to full employment at point *c*. In panel B, with inflation now running at 5%, the Phillips curve shifts outward to $PC_1$ ($p^e = 5\%$). Workers, however, now expect 5% inflation, and the economy moves back to point *c*. Unemployment has moved back to its natural rate, but inflationary expectations have risen to 5%. The aggregate price level, meanwhile, has risen from $P_0$ to $P_2$, or 5%.

By this point, however, policymakers are in trouble. To move the economy back to $u_1$ (or $Q_1$), policymakers must move along $PC_1$. Again, expanding aggregate demand in panel A to $AD_2$ moves the economy to point *d* in panel A and toward point *d* in panel B. This causes output and inflation to rise, while dropping unemployment to $u_1$. But this time, the inflation rate rises toward 10%, with workers again failing to fully anticipate the rise in prices. Processes similar to those described previously will then move the economy back to the natural rate of unemployment (points *e* in both panels).

The end result is that workers now have inflationary expectations of 10%, and the economy settles on a new Phillips curve $PC_2$ ($p^e = 10\%$). Thus, policymakers are presented with the uncomfortable fact that the rate of inflation required to maintain unemployment below the natural rate keeps rising and rising.

The implications of this analysis for fiscal and monetary policymakers who want to fine-tune the economy and keep unemployment below the natural rate are not pleasant. For one thing, it means that if policymakers want to keep unemployment below the natural rate, they must continually increase aggregate demand so that inflation will always exceed what is expected. Thus, policymakers must be willing to incur a permanently *accelerating* rate of inflation—hardly a popular idea.

In 1968, Friedman and Phelps predicted such trends of accelerating inflation and outward-shifting Phillips curves. These predictions proved accurate, as Figure 6 shows. The inflation-unemployment tradeoff worsened throughout the 1970s and into the early 1980s, largely because of the oil price shocks and rising inflationary expectations. Inflation and unemployment continued to rise, creating what economists call **stagflation.** Where under the original Phillips curve the conclusion was that rising unemployment would be met by *falling* inflation, the 1970s witnessed rising unemployment and *rising* inflation (stagflation).

**Stagflation:** Simultaneous occurrence of rising inflation and rising unemployment.

**FIGURE 6—The Phillips Curve in 1972–1981—Supply Shocks**

In 1968, Friedman and Phelps predicted accelerating inflation and outward-shifting Phillips curves. These predictions proved accurate, as this figure shows. The inflation-unemployment tradeoff worsened throughout the 1970s and into the early 1980s, largely due to oil price shocks and rising inflationary expectations. Inflation and unemployment continued to rise, creating stagflation. By 1980, annual inflation was over 9%, and unemployment was over 7%.

Stagflation is the simultaneous occurrence of inflation and unemployment, with both approaching double digits. By 1980, as Figure 6 shows, annual inflation was over 9%, and unemployment was over 7%. This bout of stagflation probably cost President Carter his reelection bid in 1980, and solving the problem kept President Reagan occupied until well into his presidency.

## Phillips Curves and Disinflation

To eliminate inflationary pressures when they arise, policymakers must be willing to curtail growth in aggregate demand and accept the resulting higher rates of unemployment for a certain transition period. How long it takes to reduce inflation and return to the natural rate of unemployment will depend on how rapidly the economy adjusts its inflationary expectations. Policymakers can speed this process along and reduce the transition costs by ensuring their policies are credible, for instance, by issuing public announcements that are consistent with contractionary policies in both the monetary and fiscal realms.

Figure 7 illustrates how inflationary expectations are reduced to bring about a more favorable tradeoff. Initially, the economy is in equilibrium at point *a*, with the economy at natural rate of unemployment 6% and inflation at 10%.

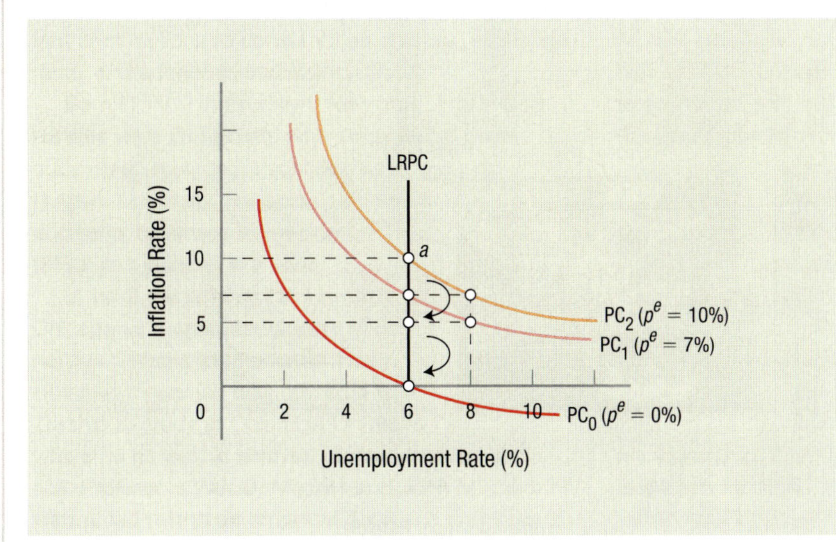


**FIGURE 7—Phillips Curves and Disinflation**

In the disinflation process, the economy initially is in equilibrium at point *a*. To reduce inflationary expectations, policymakers must reduce aggregate demand and push the economy into a recession, increasing unemployment to 8%. As aggregate demand slumps, wage and price pressures soften, reducing inflationary expectations. As these expectations decline, the entire Phillips curve shifts inward, from $PC_2$ to $PC_1$. If the process goes on long enough, the Phillips curve will shift back to $PC_0$. The arrows here show the path the economy must take back to roughly stable prices at the natural unemployment rate.

To reduce inflationary expectations, policymakers must be willing to reduce aggregate demand and push the economy into a recession, thereby increasing unemployment to 8%. As aggregate demand slumps, wage and price pressures will soften, reducing inflationary expectations. As these expectations decline, the Phillips curve shifts inward, from $PC_2$ to $PC_1$, and if the process goes on long enough, the Phillips curve will eventually shift back to $PC_0$. The arrows in Figure 7 show the path the economy must take back to lower inflation rates. How fast this occurs will depend on the severity of the recession and the confidence the public has that policymakers are willing to stay the course.

In 1981, the Reagan administration launched a long-term program designed to increase economic growth and reduce inflation. The long-term nature of the program and the reasons for it were summarized in the 1982 *Economic Report of the President*. "The major failure of the late 1960s and 1970s was to give insufficient weight to the long-term effects of economic policies. For example, the so-called Phillips curve . . . and its implication that a tradeoff is possible was one of the key notions relied on by economic advisers."

The Reagan administration took the view that stagflation had arisen from a "substantial increase in the Federal Government's role in the economy." Administration officials lamented that federal spending and taxes were absorbing a growing share of national output, that federal regulations had been growing in scope and burden, and that the money supply was growing at too rapid a rate.

The key points of the Reagan administration's long-term plan to increase economic growth and reduce inflation were to reduce the rate of growth of government spending, reduce tax rates to encourage work and business investment, and reduce burdensome regulations.

This aggressive plan of wringing stagflation out of the U.S. economy took the better part of the 1980s, as panel A of Figure 8 shows. The movement of equilibrium points is consistent with the theoretical model we saw depicted in Figure 7: Inflation that took over a decade to develop required nearly another decade to be resolved. After the recession of 1982–1983, which was the deepest since the Great Depression (unemployment exceeded 10%), inflationary pressures were heading downward. Federal Reserve Chairman Paul Volcker, who insisted on keeping interest rates high in the face of fierce public opposition, deserves much of the credit for this triumph over inflation, which was also a victory for the theories of Friedman and Phelps.

This lesson about the importance of restraining monetary growth and focusing on stable prices was not lost on the next Federal Reserve chairman, Alan Greenspan. Throughout the decade of the 1990s, the Federal Reserve maintained a tight watch on inflation, and as panel B of Figure 8 shows, reduced inflation from around 4% to near 1%.

**FIGURE 8—The Phillips Curve in the 1980s and 1990s—Disinflation**

Wringing stagflation out of the American economy took the better part of the 1980s and 1990s, as shown here. The movement of equilibrium points is consistent with the theoretical model depicted in Figure 7.

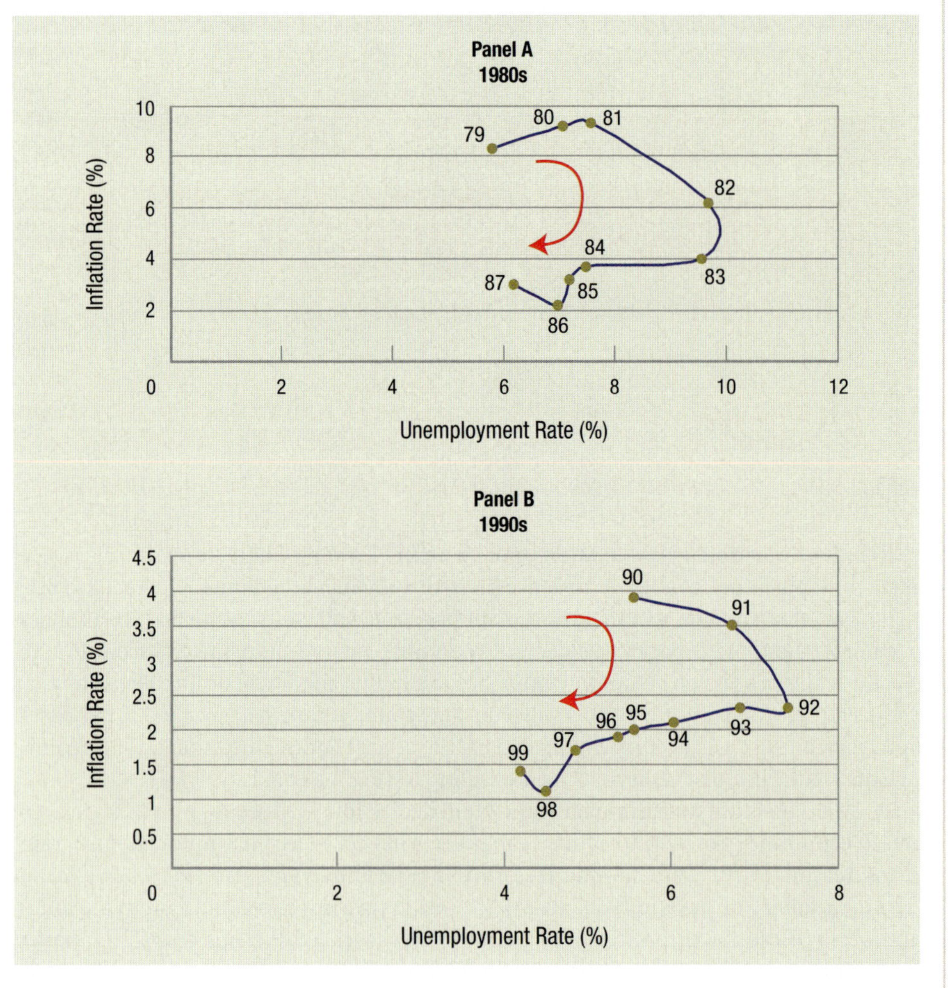


The legacy of the Reagan plan in the early 1980s, except for the failure to reduce government spending, has been followed over the last two decades and extends to policymaking today. The natural rate analysis just discussed assumes that inflation expectations adjust with a noticeable lag. Some economists, however, argue that consumers and business adapt their expectations so rapidly that their behavior tends to nullify much of policymakers' actions. We turn to this critique in the next section.

## *Issue:* Anchored Inflation Expectations

*Anchors Aweigh, my boys*
*Anchors Aweigh . . .*

**"Anchors Aweigh"** is the unofficial song of the U.S. Navy, but it could easily be the Federal Reserve's biggest nightmare. Fed Chairman Ben Bernanke has described anchored inflation expectations to mean "relatively insensitive to incoming data," while others at the Fed understand "anchored" to mean that businesses, consumers, investors, and other economic actors are confident that the Fed will not let inflation get out of control.

Anchored inflation expectations are particularly important when the Fed faces supply shocks caused by rising commodity prices that put inflationary pressures on the economy while at the same time leading to a recession. When oil prices rise, for example, *headline inflation* (the consumer price index rates reported in the media) rises, but the core rate often remains relatively stable. Remember that the core rate excludes food and energy prices. If the public's inflation expectations are immune or relatively resistant to changes in food and energy inflation and based more on changes in core inflation, this permits the Fed to lower interest rates to resist the recession. It can worry about inflation a little later.

But if inflation expectations change rapidly in response to changes in headline inflation, the Fed's job is manifestly complicated. Returning the economy to a steady growth path with *low* inflation as the economy recovers from the 2008–2009 recession may be a difficult task. Both monetary and fiscal policy used a lot of cash and debt to stem the downturn, which will have to be financed in the future. Raising interest rates to prevent inflation could short-circuit the recovery. If inflationary expectations get out of control, the short-run aggregate supply curve could shift to the left, slowing the recovery.

One way to keep inflation expectations in check, or anchored, is for the Fed to clearly announce its intentions to maintain inflation at reasonable levels. As long as the Fed comes through, the Fed's credibility is maintained and these types of communications are helpful to policymaking. But if the Fed fails to follow up and keep inflation in check, it is anchors aweigh.

Stephen F. Hayes/Getty Images

Source: See talks by Ben Bernanke on July 10, 2007, and Charles Plosser on July 22, 2008 www.federalreserve.gov.

## CHECKPOINT

### UNEMPLOYMENT AND INFLATION: PHILLIPS CURVES

- The Phillips curve represents the negative relationship between the unemployment rate and the inflation rate. When the unemployment rate goes up, inflation goes down, and vice versa.
- The natural rate of unemployment is that level where inflation or inflationary pressures are nonexistent.
- Phillips curves are affected by inflationary expectations. Rising inflationary expectations by the public would be reflected in a shift in the Phillips curve to the right, worsening the tradeoff between inflation and unemployment.
- If policymakers use monetary and fiscal policy to attempt to keep unemployment continually below the natural rate, they will face accelerating inflation.
- This inflation requires that policymakers curtail aggregate demand and accept higher rates of unemployment during the transition period back to low inflation.

**QUESTION:** In the last decade, productivity growth has been unusually high, arguably because of technical advances in microcomputers, cellular phones, and Internet service. Have these advances made it easier for the Federal Reserve to contain inflationary pressures?

Answers to the Checkpoint question can be found at the end of this chapter.

## Rational Expectations and Policy Formation

The use of expectations in economic analysis is nothing new. Keynes devoted a chapter to expectations in the *General Theory*, focusing on investors. In his usual colorful way, he asserted, "A conventional valuation which is established as the outcome of the mass psychology of a large number of ignorant individuals is liable to change violently as the result of a sudden fluctuation of opinion due to factors which do not really make much difference to the prospective yield."[2]

Keynes believed that expectations are driven by emotions. In the passage just cited, he suggested investors in the stock market will jump on board trends without attempting to understand the underlying market dynamics. Keynes might well have smiled at the technical analysts who appear on CNN and CNBC today purporting to predict what the stock market will do by referring to such chart formations as "head-and-shoulders," "double tops," and "double bottoms."

**Adaptive expectations:** Inflationary expectations are formed from a simple extrapolation from past events.

Friedman developed his natural rate of unemployment theory using what are known as **adaptive expectations.** In this model of expectations, people are assumed to perform a simple extrapolation from past events. Workers, for example, are assumed to expect that past rates of inflation, averaged over some time period, will continue into the future. Other economists have developed far more complex formulations of adaptive expectations. The key point to note, however, is that adaptive expectations are represented by a *backward-looking* model of expectations, which contrasts with the rational expectations model.

### Defining Rational Expectations

In 1961, John Muth suggested that "expectations since they are informed predictions of future events are essentially the same as the predictions of the relevant economic theory."[3] William Poole explained rational expectations by noting that "market outcomes have characteristics as if economic agents are acting on the basis of the correct model of how the world works and that they use all available information in deciding on their actions."[4]

**Rational expectations:** Rational economic agents are assumed to make the best possible use of all publicly available information, then make informed, rational judgments on what the future holds. Any errors in their forecasts will be randomly distributed.

In the **rational expectations** model developed by Robert Lucas, rational economic agents are assumed to make the best possible use of all publicly available information. Before reaching a decision, people are assumed to consider all relevant information before them, then make informed, rational judgments on what the future holds. This does not mean that every individual's expectations or predictions about the future will be correct. Those errors that do occur will be randomly distributed, such that the expectations of large numbers of people will average out to be correct.

To illustrate, assume the economy has been in an equilibrium state for several years with low inflation (2% to 3%) and low unemployment (5.5% to 6%). In such a stable environment, the average person would expect the inflation rate to stay right about where it is indefinitely. But now assume the Federal Reserve announces it is going to significantly increase the rate of growth of the money supply. Basic economic theory tells us an increase in the money supply will translate into higher prices, such that increasing the annual rate of growth of the money supply should bring about higher future inflation rates. Knowing this, households and businesses will revise their inflationary expectations upward.

As this simple example shows, people do not rely only on past experiences to formulate their expectations of the future, as adaptive expectations theory would suggest. Rather, people use all information available to them in judging what the future will hold. This information can include past data, but it will also include current policy announcements and all other information that give them reason to believe the future

[2] John Maynard Keynes, *The General Theory of Employment, Interest, and Money* (New York: Harcourt Brace Jovanovich), 1964 (first published in 1936), p. 154.

[3] John Muth, "Rational Expectations and the Theory of Price Movements," *Econometrica*, July 1961, pp. 315–335.

[4] William Poole, "Expectations," *Review of the Federal Reserve Bank of St. Louis*, March–April 2001, pp. 1–10.

## Nobel Prize

### Robert Lucas

In the 1970s, a series of articles by Robert E. Lucas changed the course of contemporary macroeconomic theory and profoundly influenced the economic policies of governments throughout the world. His development of the rational expectations theory challenged decades of assumptions about how individuals respond to changes in fiscal and monetary policies.

Lucas was born in 1937 in Yakima, Washington. His father was a welder, who advanced through the ranks to become president of a refrigeration company. Lucas was awarded a scholarship to the University of Chicago. He had wanted to be an engineer, but Chicago did not have an engineering school, so he studied history. He attained a Woodrow Wilson Doctoral Fellowship in history at the University of California, Berkeley. There he developed a strong interest in economics and returned to the University of Chicago, earning his Ph.D. in 1964. One of his professors was Nobel laureate Milton Friedman, whose skepticism about interventionist government policies influenced a generation of economists. Lucas began his teaching career at Carnegie-Mellon University and later became a professor of economics at the University of Chicago.

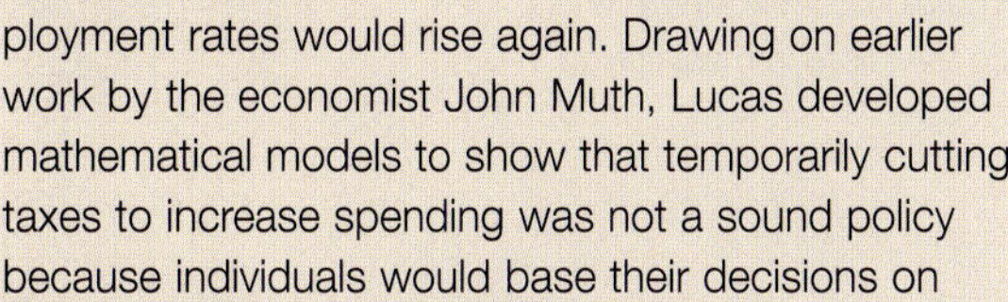
Visions of America, LLC/Alamy

Before Lucas, economists accepted the Keynesian idea that expansionary policies could lower the unemployment rate. Lucas, however, argued that the rational expectations of individual workers and employers would adjust to the changing inflationary conditions, and unemployment rates would rise again. Drawing on earlier work by the economist John Muth, Lucas developed mathematical models to show that temporarily cutting taxes to increase spending was not a sound policy because individuals would base their decisions on expectations about the future, and these temporary tax cuts would find their way into savings and not added spending. In other words, individuals were rational, forward thinking, and perfectly able to adapt to changing economic information. He also suggested that the fluctuations of fiscal and monetary policy could have harmful effects on the economy.

When the Royal Swedish Academy of Sciences awarded Lucas the Nobel Prize in 1995, it credited Lucas with "the greatest influence on macroeconomic research since 1970." In recent years, Lucas has turned his attention to issues of demographics and understanding the dynamics of economic growth.

might hold certain changes. If adaptive expectations are backward looking, rational expectations are *forward looking*, in that they assume people will use all of the information available to them.

## Policy Implications of Rational Expectations

Do economic actors really form their future expectations as the rational expectations hypothesis suggests? If so, the implications for macroeconomic policy would be enormous; indeed, it could leave macroeconomic policy ineffective. This was the proposition advanced by economists Thomas Sargent and Neil Wallace in the mid-1970s.[5]

To illustrate, let us assume that the economy in Figure 9 on the next page is operating at full employment at point *a*. Short-run aggregate supply curve $SRAS_0$ ($P = 100$) reflects

[5] Thomas Sargent and Neil Wallace, "Rational Expectations, the Optimal Monetary Instrument and the Optimal Money Supply Rule," *Journal of Political Economy*, April 1975; and "Rational Expectations and the Theory of Economic Policy," *Journal of Monetary Economics*, April 1976.

**FIGURE 9—Rational Expectations: The Policy Ineffectiveness Hypothesis**

Rational expectations theory suggests that macroeconomic policy will be ineffective, even in the short term. Assume the economy is operating at full employment (point *a*) and short-run aggregate supply curve $SRAS_0$ ($P$ = 100). Now suppose the Federal Reserve announces it intends to increase the money supply. Expanding the money supply will shift aggregate demand from $AD_0$ to $AD_1$, and this will increase the demand for labor and raise nominal wages. Yet, as soon as the Fed announces it is going to increase the money supply, rational economic agents will use this information to immediately raise their inflationary expectations. Thus, output will remain unchanged, though the price level rises immediately to 110.

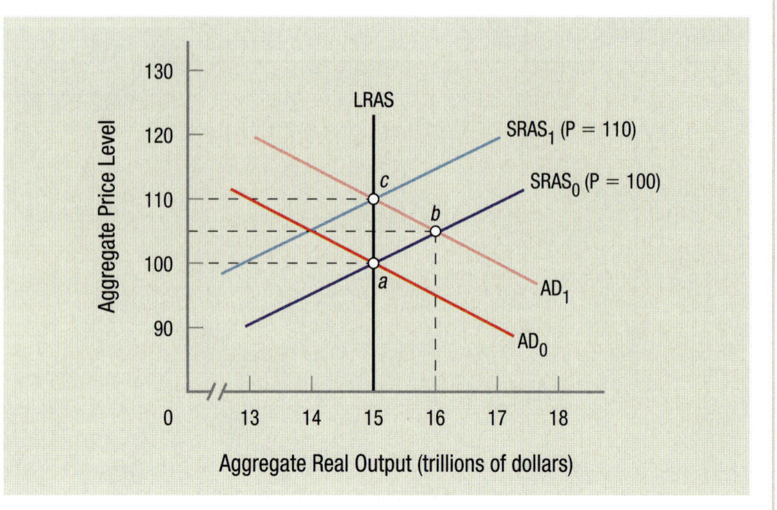


current inflationary expectations. Suppose the Federal Reserve announces it intends to increase the money supply (or to increase its rate of growth).

Expanding the money supply will shift aggregate demand from $AD_0$ to $AD_1$. This will increase the demand for labor and raise nominal wages. But what happens next?

Natural rate theorists, using adaptive expectations, would argue that workers will be fooled into thinking the increase in money wages represents a real raise, thus driving output and employment up to $16 trillion (point *b*). After a time, however, workers will realize that real wages have not risen since prices have risen by at least as much as wages. Aggregate supply will then fall to $SRAS_1$ ($P$ = 110) as price expectations climb and the economy gradually moves back to full employment at a higher price level (point *c*). In this scenario, the Fed's policy succeeds in raising output and employment in the short term, but only at the expense of a long-term rise in the cost of living.

Contrast this with the picture rational expectations theorists paint of the same scenario. When the Federal Reserve announces it is going to increase the money supply, perfectly rational economic agents will heed this information and immediately raise their inflationary expectations. Since the model of the economy they use to determine their future expectations matches that shown in Figure 9, output will remain unchanged, but the price level will rise immediately to 110. No one gets fooled into temporarily increasing output or employment, even though the increase in the money supply still drives up prices.

In the rational expectations model, whenever the Federal Reserve announces a policy change, rational individuals and firms will anticipate the long-term results and move immediately to that new equilibrium, leaving the short-term aspects of the policy change ineffective.

This suggests that if the Federal Reserve wants to use an increase in the money supply to raise output and employment in the short term, the only way it can do so is by *not* announcing its plans; it must essentially force economic actors to make decisions with substantially incomplete information. Rational expectations theory suggests that the Federal Reserve and other policymakers must fool the public if its policies are to have short-term benefits.

## A Critique of Rational Expectations

To date, empirical assessments of Sargent and Wallace's policy ineffectiveness proposition have yielded mixed results. In general, these studies do not support the policy ineffectiveness proposition. That is, macroeconomic policies do have a real impact on the economy, and monetary policies are credited for reducing inflation over the past two decades.

New Keynesian economists have taken a different approach to critiquing rational expectations theory. Both the adaptive and the rational expectations models assume that labor and product markets are highly competitive, with wages and prices adjusting quickly to expansionary or contractionary policies. The new Keynesians point out, however, that labor markets are often beset with imperfect information, and that efficiency wages often bring about short-term wage stickiness.

**Efficiency wage theory** disputes the notion that labor markets are like commodity markets: highly competitive markets in which homogeneous goods are exchanged at market-clearing prices. For all labor is not equal. Just because people show up to work for eight hours a day does not mean they all work equally hard. For this, people need incentives, and higher wages are one form of motivation. By paying their employees an efficiency wage, or a wage above the market-clearing level, employers can hope to improve morale and productivity, as well as create a disincentive for employees to shirk their duties. After all, if well-paid employees get caught shirking and are laid off, they would have to look for work elsewhere, most likely at lower, more competitive, market-clearing wage levels.

**Efficiency wage theory:** Employers often pay their workers wages above the market-clearing level to improve morale and productivity, reduce turnover, and create a disincentive for employees to shirk their duties.

Nobel laureate George Akerlof noted,

> *Such wages [efficiency wages] cause rationing in the labor market. If employers pay above the market-clearing wage, more workers are going to apply for jobs than there are jobs available. Employers will pay such high wages for a variety of reasons. A leading reason comes from asymmetric information—that the employers cannot watch workers all the time and know everything they do. Employers cannot completely monitor them. So employers pay workers a higher wage so that, should they be caught shirking, they would lose something if they had to seek employment elsewhere.*[6]

Imperfect information and efficiency wages suggest that wages and prices may be sticky and not instantly clear in the market. This means that neither workers nor firms can react quickly to changes in monetary or fiscal policy. And this would give such policies a chance of a short-term impact.

Though the policy ineffectiveness proposition has not found significant empirical support, rational expectations as a concept has profoundly affected how economists approach macroeconomic problems. Nearly all economists agree that policy changes affect expectations, and that this affects the behavior of economic agents. In turn, these expectations have the potential to reduce the effectiveness of monetary and fiscal policy.

So far, we have considered two challenges to the effectiveness of policy while taking the stylized model of the business cycle for granted. First, we looked at Phillips curves with the policymaker pressing a button, picking the amount of unemployment in column A and obtaining the amount of inflation in column B. We saw that this was overly optimistic, as Friedman's critique was to prove when stagflation hit in the 1970s. Second, we looked at rational expectations and showed how expectations could mitigate the effectiveness of policy. We now want to apply these concepts and examine the recession of 2008–2009.

## CHECKPOINT

### RATIONAL EXPECTATIONS AND POLICY FORMATION

- Adaptive expectations assume economic agents extrapolate from past events. It is a *backward-looking* model of expectations.
- Rational expectations assume economic agents make the best possible use of all publicly available information.

[6] "On Making Economics Realistic: Interview with George Akerlof," *Challenge*, November–December 2002, p. 11.

- Rational expectations are *forward looking;* economic agents use all available information to forecast the impact of public policy.
- Rational expectations analysis leads to the conclusion that policy changes will be ineffective in the short run because individuals will immediately adjust to the long-run consequences of the policy.
- Market imperfections and asymmetric information are two reasons why the policy ineffectiveness conclusions of rational expectations analysis have met with mixed results empirically.

**QUESTION:** If efficiency wages are widespread throughout the economy but most workers feel they are significantly underpaid, will paying workers more prevent them from shirking?

Answers to the Checkpoint question can be found at the end of this chapter.

## Putting It All Together: The Recession and the Future

Macroeconomic theory developed over the last 200 years, especially in the 70 years after Keynes. Until recently, economists thought they had the understanding and the tools to make depressions or deep recessions a thing of the past. For the last 30 years, a general consensus grew among economists that monetary policy should handle most of the task of keeping the economy on a steady low-inflation growth path. The recent financial crisis and subsequent recession has made the profession question that conclusion. This downturn has reinvigorated those who felt that fiscal policy should have more of a role.

In this section we will use the theories and tools we have learned to try to understand the 2008–2009 recession. First, what do the data tell us? Next, what do macroeconomic theories tell us policymakers can do? Finally, what does the future have in store for us? As you will see (and probably already realize), there is no one policy prescription for any macroeconomic problem, just like there is no one medicine for all ills.

### Using Data: The 2008–2009 Recession

The economy grew nicely between 2005 and the beginning of 2008. Inflation was low and the economy grew at about 2.5% a year. When we discussed lags in a previous chapter, we saw how it takes time to ascertain when an economy enters a recession. In hindsight, it is easy to see when this recession started. Figure 10 shows hypothetical aggregate demand and short-run aggregate supply curves superimposed over the actual data for the years 2005 to 2009. Follow the dots and you can see progressive growth in real GDP until 2008. This recession began at the beginning of 2008 and accelerated in the middle of 2008 throughout 2009. Real GDP declined by nearly 4% and unemployment reached 10% of the labor force.

How can we explain this shift in aggregate demand and short-run aggregate supply? The recession was brought on by the financial crisis, which in turn was brought on, as we discussed in the previous chapter, by the mispricing of the risk of subprime mortgages and by excessive consumer debt. At the onset of the financial crisis, jobs were cut as consumers cut their spending: they tightened their belts in an effort to reduce household debt levels and hunkered down for what they perceived as a severe recession on the way. As a result, 7 million people lost their jobs during this two-year period. Job losses reduced consumer confidence, further reducing consumer spending, which shifted aggregate demand from $AD_{2008}$ toward $AD_{2009}$. As demand dropped, business reduced its production capacity through layoffs and plant closings, shifting short-run aggregate supply leftward from its original trajectory at $SRAS_{2005-2007}$ to that shown as $SRAS_{2009}$.

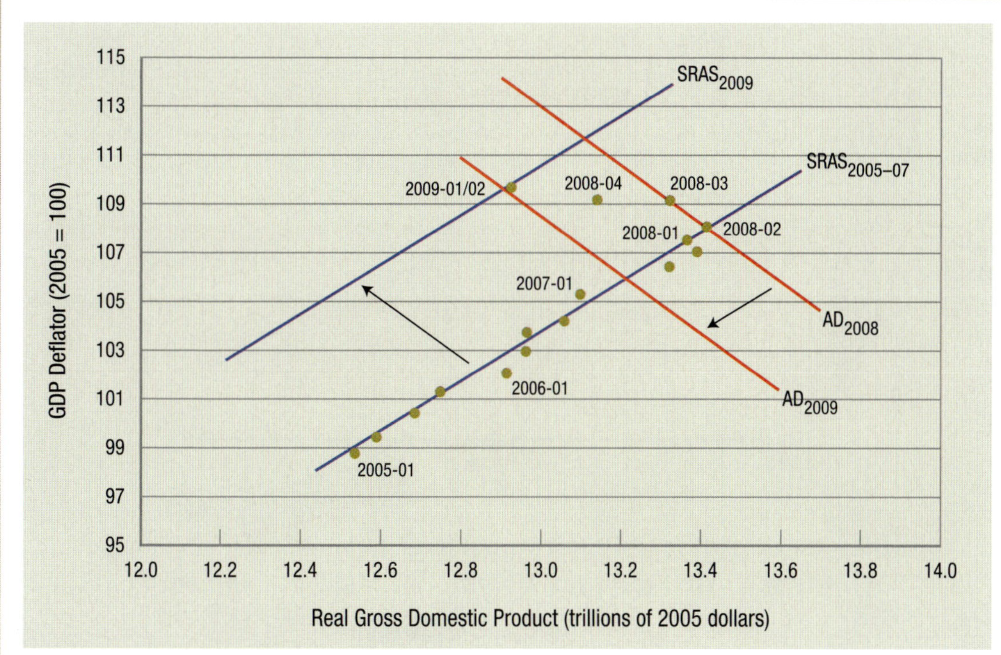


**FIGURE 10—The 2008–2009 Recession**

This figure illustrates the recent downturn by using real GDP and the GDP deflator data for 2005 through 2009 and superimposing hypothetical aggregate demand and short-run aggregate supply curves on the data. Because of the financial crisis, consumer spending declined, reducing aggregate demand in 2008 and 2009. Layoffs ensued and short-run aggregate supply declined as well. During this period, real output declined by nearly 4%.

What else do the data tell us? We started this chapter with a discussion of Phillips curves. Figure 11 on the next page provides a Phillips curve for the 2008–2009 recession. The data reveal a standard Phillips curve path from August 2008 through 2009. More important, *deflation* has been the case for most of 2009. We have spent a considerable time in this book studying the harmful effects of inflation, yet now we face deflation. Deflation can be a problem because it increases the *real* value of existing debt, making the debt more burdensome and requiring more purchasing power to make interest payments or pay off the debt. Policymakers now face the problem of preventing debt from becoming a more serious burden on households, which would further reduce aggregate demand and deepen the recession.

## Using Macroeconomic Theory and Policy

As we have seen in this book, macroeconomic theories have developed and changed in response to major economic events. Throughout the 1800s and early 1900s, economists thought that, left alone, markets would adjust to changing economic circumstances and keep the economy on a relatively steady growth path. Flexible wages, prices, and interest rates would work to deflect any downturn back toward full employment. This long-run approach to the economy neglected short-term policy.

In the long run, the economy would gravitate toward full employment, and inflation would be determined by the rate of growth of the money supply. Economic growth was related to resources and technology. Even today, economists still generally accept this long-run view.

Policymaking with a focus on the long run is therefore fairly straightforward. Policies should be directed at increasing resources, improving the productivity of those resources, and improving technology and its spread throughout the economy. Examples include such

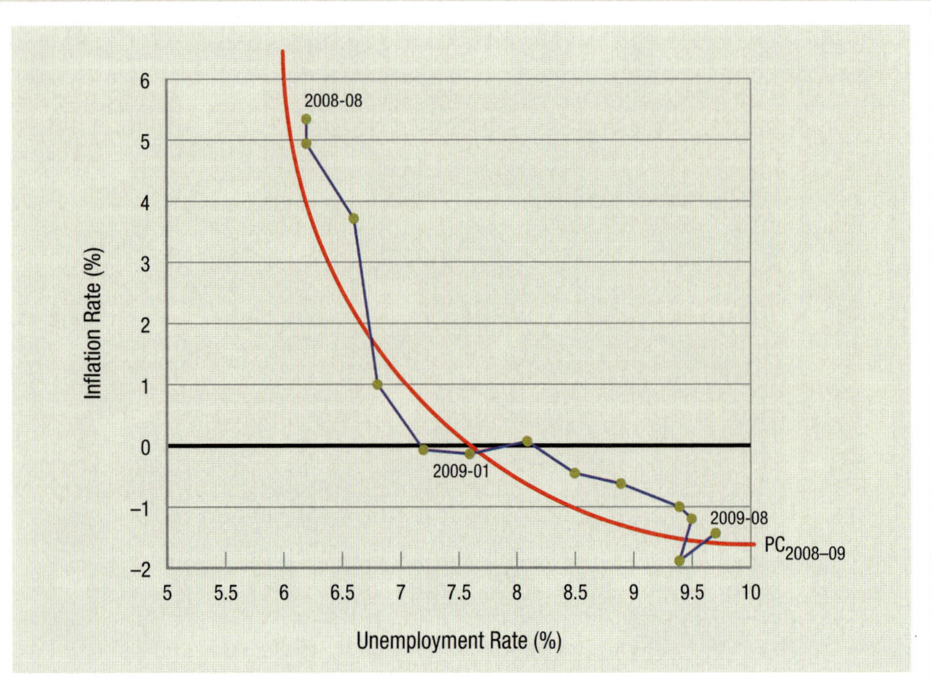


**FIGURE 11—Inflation and Unemployment, 2008–2009 (Phillips Curve)**

This figure illustrates the Phillips curve during the recent downturn by using unemployment and inflation data for 2008 through 2009 and superimposing a hypothetical Phillips curve on the data. Over this year, the economy closely tracked the hypothetical short-run Phillips curve into its deflationary zone.

policies as capital investment incentives (investment tax credits and rapid expensing of investment expenditures), policies that encourage investment in human capital (college grants and low-interest loans), and research grants to develop new technologies.

While in the long run the economy may approach full employment, the Great Depression of the 1930s showed that an economy could be mired in a slump for a long time. Because of the profession's long-run focus, economic advisers in the 1930s often suggested policies that made the Depression worse. These included raising taxes to balance the federal budget and the Fed's failure to provide liquidity to banks.

When Keynes published the *General Theory* in 1936, his attention was on the aggregate economy and not markets. He drew attention to uncertainty in the economy and explained why private spending (consumer spending and business investment) would not respond to lower interest rates. His analysis meant that government would have to pick up the ball and increase aggregate demand with its spending. He preferred infrastructure projects, but argued for all kinds of spending because spending had a multiplier.

Thus, when the economy faces a depression or a deep recession, the Keynesian policy prescription is clear. Private spending will be insufficient to pull the economy out of recession in the short run and government deficit spending will be necessary.

After World War II, the economics profession adopted Keynesian demand management as a way of keeping the economy growing and unemployment low. Monetary policy was largely relegated to a bank regulation role. All went reasonably well until the stagflation of the 1970s. Milton Friedman argued that money did matter in the short run and that inflationary expectations play an important role in determining inflation rates.

The Keynesian model had neglected inflation because of the huge excess capacity during the Depression: production could expand with little or no pricing pressures. But Friedman was able to show that if policymakers continued to use demand management policies to keep unemployment below the natural rate of unemployment (roughly 5% to 6%), inflation expectations would lead to accelerating inflation.

As a result of simultaneous double-digit inflation and unemployment in the 1970s, keeping inflation low became a priority and monetary policy ascended. Fiscal policy faded to the background and economic growth policies moved to center stage. Here again, a significant stagflation had brought about a new policy model that gained general acceptance.

The policy implications from the 1970s for economists were clear. Expanding aggregate demand to push the economy beyond full employment results not only in inflation (up the existing Phillips curve), but *accelerating* rates of inflation. Thus, monetary policy should be used to keep inflation low, and fiscal authorities should focus on policies that promote economic growth. The results were remarkable: low inflation rates coupled with steady economic growth and just two minor recessions.

Getting government out of the way of markets dominated policy from 1980 until just recently. The recent collapse of the economy with its drop in consumer spending and business investment brought the Keynesian model back from relative obscurity. Popular magazines and newspapers featured articles on Keynes, and his model became the rationale for the $787 billion stimulus package passed in 2009.

What accounts for the Keynesian comeback? Monetary policy could only go so far. In response to the financial crisis, the Fed and the Treasury did several things, all meant to prevent a complete collapse of the financial sector and aggregate demand. It bailed out large insolvent financial, insurance, and automobile companies deemed "too big to fail." It expanded bank liquidity by injecting capital and taking an equity (stock) interest in many banks. It lowered the target federal funds rate to essentially zero. In September 2008, when it became clear that the federal funds market was frozen because banks were unwilling to lend to each other to temporarily shore up reserves, the Fed flooded the market with liquidity. All of these Fed actions helped, but as Figure 10 shows, aggregate demand did not snap back. More was needed. Keynesian fiscal policy then made its comeback.

If you take one idea away from this course it should be that there is *not* one economic model or one economic policy that fits all occasions or circumstances. It often seems that one set of policymakers see "cutting taxes" as the universal cure-all while others see "more government spending" as the only solution. Both are wrong. Different circumstances call for different approaches. Cutting taxes will not likely solve depressions or deep recessions. In the same vein, as the economy approaches full employment, additional deficit spending by government will just crowd out private spending or lead to inflation.

We have laid out the different models and the circumstances in which each is most effective. Use this framework to reach your own conclusions about which policy is appropriate given the times.

## A Special Case: Financial Crises and Macroeconomic Policy

For most college students, the 2008–2009 financial crisis and the accompanying recession represents their first experience with a *serious* downturn in the economy. As we will see shortly, the previous two slumps (1990 and 2001) were shallow and lasted only eight months, but were followed by a period of slow job growth.

The savings and loan collapse (our last banking crisis) is now more than 25 years old, so most people under 40 cannot recollect its impact. Over the last 35 years, Europe, the United States, Australia, and New Zealand have endured a total of 18 bank-centered financial crises.

Studying more than 350 banking crises since 1800, Carmen Reinhart and Kenneth Rogoff came to the conclusion that "if there is one common theme to the vast range of crises we consider in this book, it is that excessive debt accumulation, whether it be by the government, banks, corporations, or consumers, often poses greater systemic [system wide] risks than it seems during a boom."[7] They go on to explain that large infusions of cash (credit) into an economy can make government appear to be providing stronger economic growth than is the case, make business appear more profitable, and inflate housing and stock prices. They note that "such large-scale debt buildups pose risks because they

[7] See Carmen Reinhart and Kenneth Rogoff, *This Time Is Different: Eight Centuries of Financial Folly* (Princeton, NJ: Princeton University Press), 2009.

make an economy vulnerable to crises of confidence, particularly when debt is short term and needs to be constantly refinanced."

For policymakers, the last major banking crisis was in the 1930s. This is fortunate because Reinhart and Rogoff find that when they do occur, housing prices tend to drop substantially over roughly half a decade, output drops an average of 9%, unemployment rises on average by 7%, and government debt on average nearly doubles. Bailouts are expensive and recessions are costly both for the government and for the people unemployed. More distressing for today's recession is that recessions associated with bank-centered financial crises tend to last much longer.

## The Future: Are Recoveries Becoming "Jobless Recoveries"?

Globalization, new technologies, and improved business methods are making the jobs of policymakers much more difficult and may even be changing the nature of the business cycle. The 1990 and 2001 recessions deviated significantly from what has happened in past business cycles in that they have been followed by jobless recoveries. This suggests that recovery from the recession of 2008–2009 may follow the same slow job-growth path.

Taming the business cycle has proven to be just as much art as science. Whenever economists believe they have finally gotten a handle on controlling the economy, some new event or transformation of the economy has taken place, humbling the profession. There is no doubt that between 1983 and 2007, the federal government and the Federal Reserve did a remarkable job of keeping the economy on a steady upward growth path, with only two minor recessions. The 1990 and 2001 recessions were mild, but the recoveries coming out of these recessions were weak, especially for those out of work and looking for a job.

Just what is a jobless recovery? When output begins to grow after a trough, employment usually starts to grow. But when output begins to rise yet employment growth does not resume, the recovery is called a **jobless recovery.**

**Jobless recovery:** Takes place after a recession, when output begins to rise, but employment growth does not.

We have already seen that business cycles vary dramatically in their depth and duration. The Great Depression was the worst downturn in American history, while the 2001 recession was one of the mildest. In that recession, the unemployment rate never rose above 6% and real output (GDP) actually increased throughout the downturn, though at a diminished rate. But if the recession was mild, the recovery was not as strong as in typical business cycles.

Figure 12 shows how the 2008–2009 recession compares to the two previous downturns and their recoveries. It indexes real output for all three downturns so the current recession and recovery can be compared to those previous business cycles. Specifically, real GDP for each business cycle is indexed to the peak of the cycle. This involves dividing each quarter's output by output at the peak and multiplying by 100 to index the values to 100. Thus, if one quarter after the peak, output has fallen by 1%, the index would be 99 at that point. In this way we can get a graphical picture of how output is doing throughout the course of each cycle.

Notice in this figure that both the 1990 and 2001 recessions lasted only just under three quarters (eight months each). For the 1990 recession, this is shown by the two-quarter drop in real GDP to a little below 99, then the economy resumed an upward path. The 2001 downturn shows a slight dip in the second quarter, but the index itself never drops below 100. Clearly, both of these recessions were mild indeed.

In contrast, the 2008–2009 recession is considerably more severe than both of the previous downturns. A year and a half into this recession, real output fell by nearly 4% and the decline in the economy was just leveling off.

Figure 13 presents the same type of indexed graph for employment, though indexing the values monthly. Notice that for both of the previous recessions, employment had not reached its prior peak even after two years. In fact, employment took nearly three years to

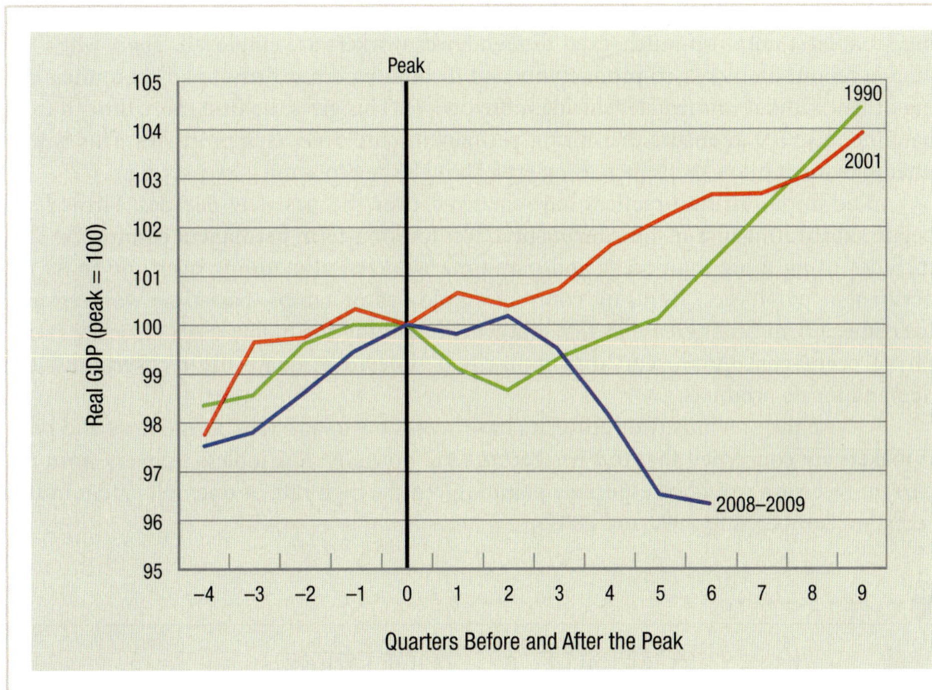


**FIGURE 12—Real GDP Growth Relative to the Peak of the Business Cycle**

The 2008–2009 recession is compared to the previous two recessions in 1990 and 2001 by indexing real output to the peak of the business cycle. The current downturn is deeper; in both of the previous recessions, GDP was back to the previous peak at this point in the cycle.

return to peak levels after the 1990 recession, and nearly four years after the 2001 recession. In the past, the turnaround in employment to the previous peak was typically reached in two years. This will obviously not be the case with the current recession. Many economists suggest it will likely be a jobless recovery as well.

Several factors seem to be driving jobless recoveries: rapid increases in productivity, a change in employment patterns, and outsourcing. Productivity increases arising from computers, Internet services, and cellular phones make labor far more flexible than ever before. Now when the economy contracts, employers can more easily lay off workers and

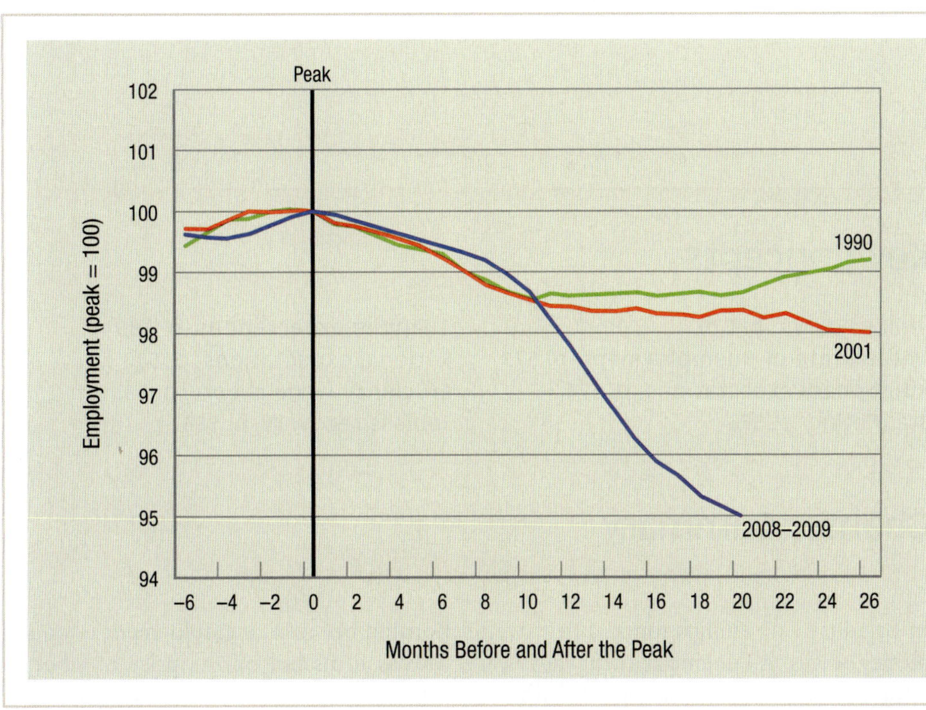


**FIGURE 13—Employment Growth Relative to the Peak of the Business Cycle**

Employment in the 2008–2009 recession is compared to the previous two recessions in 1990 and 2001 by indexing employment to the peak of the business cycle. This downturn is deeper than the previous recessions, when it took three to four years to get back to peak employment levels.

shift their responsibilities to the workers who remain. As a result, output may keep growing, or at least not drop much, even though fewer workers are employed. Then, when the market rebounds, increased productivity and flexibility permit firms to adjust to their rising orders without immediately hiring more people. This gives the firm more time to evaluate the recovery to ensure that hiring permanent employees is appropriate. This is why unemployment often keeps increasing even though the economy is recovering.

In addition, hiring practices have changed over the past few decades. Firms have begun substituting just-in-time hiring practices for long-term permanent employees. This includes using more temporary and part-time workers, and adding overtime shifts for permanent employees. By using contract employees or temps, part-time workers, and overtime, a firm can increase its flexibility while limiting the higher costs associated with hiring permanent employees until it has had time to evaluate the recovery and the demand for its products.

Because the previous two recoveries have been slow to add jobs, economists and policymakers are concerned that this has become the norm. A slow jobless recovery from the current recession would be especially painful given the high rate of unemployment in this recession compared to 1990 and 2001.

## CHECKPOINT

### PUTTING IT ALL TOGETHER: THE RECESSION AND THE FUTURE

- Use of monetary policy or fiscal policy, or both, depends on the type of downturn.
- Severe financial crises are usually followed by long recovery times.
- Future recessions might be followed by jobless recoveries.

**QUESTION:** Looking back at Figure 11, you see that 2009 was a year in which inflation was negative; average prices *fell*. The 2008–2009 recession was partly the result of American households carrying too much debt (both in mortgages and on credit cards). Households set out to reduce their debt levels by reducing spending, causing a deeper recession in 2009. Is deflation a help or hindrance to using monetary and fiscal policy to stimulate the economy? Why?

Answers to the Checkpoint question can be found at the end of this chapter.

## Key Concepts

Phillips curve, p. 570
Natural rate of unemployment, p. 573
Inflationary expectations, p. 574
Stagflation, p. 576
Adaptive expectations, p. 580
Rational expectations, p. 580
Efficiency wage theory, p. 583
Jobless recovery, p. 588

## Chapter Summary

### Unemployment and Inflation: Phillips Curves

In Britain, A. W. Phillips found a negative relationship between unemployment rates and money wages. As unemployment falls, wages rise as firms bid up the price of labor to attract more workers, and wages fall when unemployment rises. Unemployment was later connected to inflation, and the tradeoff between inflation and unemployment has become known as the Phillips curve.

A rise in wages may lead to a rise in prices, but if worker productivity increases enough to offset the wage increase, product prices can remain stable. The basic relationship among wages, prices, and productivity is $p = w - q$, where $p$ is the rate of inflation, $w$ is the rate of increase in nominal wages, and $q$ is the rate of increase in labor productivity.

The natural rate of unemployment is that unemployment rate at which inflationary expectations match inflation, and thus inflationary pressures in the economy are nonexistent. This unemployment rate is also known as the nonaccelerating inflation rate of unemployment (NAIRU), and it is often thought to be around 5%.

A negative relationship between unemployment and inflation is represented by the Phillips curve. It suggests that the economy presents policymakers with a menu of choices. By accepting modest inflation, they can keep unemployment low.

Phillips curves are affected by inflationary expectations. Rising inflationary expectations by the public would be reflected in a shift in the Phillips curve to the right, worsening the tradeoff between inflation and unemployment. If policymakers use monetary and fiscal policy to attempt to keep unemployment continually below the natural rate, they will face accelerating inflation. This inflation requires that policymakers curtail aggregate demand and accept higher rates of unemployment during the transition period back to low inflation.

## Rational Expectations and Policy Formation

The adaptive expectations model assumes that people form their future expectations by performing a simple extrapolation from past events. Therefore, it is a backward-looking model of expectations.

The rational expectations model assumes that rational economic agents use all publicly available information in forming their expectations. In this sense, rational expectations theory is a forward-looking model of expectations.

If the rational expectations hypothesis is correct, the implications for policymakers will be enormous. It will mean that policymakers cannot stimulate output in the short run by raising inflation unless they keep their actions secret.

Market imperfections and asymmetric information are two reasons why the policy ineffectiveness conclusions of rational expectations analysis have met with mixed results empirically.

## Putting It All Together: The Recession and the Future

Use of monetary policy or fiscal policy, or both, depends on the type of downturn. Severe financial crises are usually met with long recovery times. Future recessions might be followed by jobless recoveries.

# Questions and Problems

## Check Your Understanding

1. The Phillips curve for the United States in the 1960s shown in Figure 3 becomes very steep after unemployment drops below 4%, and rather shallow as unemployment exceeds 6%. Why is a typical Phillips curve shaped this way?

2. Does the long-run Phillips curve make it difficult (if not impossible) for policymakers to increase output and employment beyond full employment in the long run?

3. Explain why inflation accelerates if policymakers use monetary and fiscal policy to keep unemployment below the natural rate.

4. Does having rational expectations mean that all economic actors act rationally and are always correct?

5. Would policymakers prefer a Phillips curve with a steep or shallow slope? Why?

6. A negative supply shock (a huge natural disaster or significant energy price spike) would do what to the short-run Phillips curve? To the long-run Phillips curve?

## Apply the Concepts

7. Why would policymakers want to drive unemployment below the natural rate, given that inflation will result?

8. Why couldn't the problems of inflation be solved by simply requiring that wages, rents, profits, product prices, and interest rates are subject to "cost-of-living" increases each year?

9. Explain why those who favor the rational expectations approach to modeling the economy do not favor discretionary policymaking.

10. Why are inflationary expectations so important for policymakers to keep under control? When a supply shock such as an oil price spike hits the economy, does it matter how fast policymakers attempt to bring the economy back to full employment?

11. How are the long-run Phillips curve (LRPC) and the long-run aggregate supply (LRAS) curve related?

12. Would the credibility of policymakers' (Congress and the Fed) commitment to keeping inflation low have an effect on inflationary expectations when the economy is beset by a supply shock?

13. America's employment practices are much more flexible than most of those in the European countries. Does the fact that our labor markets are more flexible and more competitive than those of Europe make our Phillips curve tradeoffs more reasonable?

## In the News

14. Ben Bernanke, the chairman of the Fed, recently noted that "in the 1970s the public had little confidence that the Fed would keep inflation low and stable." As a result, when oil prices rose, wages and prices quickly followed. This caused the Fed to have to sharply increase interest rates to curtail inflation. Do people have a different perspective on the Fed than in the past?

## Solving Problems

15. In Canada, the consensus estimate of the natural rate of unemployment was 4.5% in 1970 and 7% in 2005. A minority view has claimed that the change to 7% is beyond explanation and must be too high. A similar change has taken place in the United States over this period, but the consensus estimate of the natural rate of unemployment is closer to 5% today. What would be the result if the Bank of Canada (the central bank in Canada) and the Federal Reserve in the United States assumed that the natural rate was 7% when it really was closer to 5%?

16. When the recessions of 1990 and 2001 ended, unemployment kept rising and it took roughly two and a half years before unemployment returned to where it was at the

*trough* of the recession. The figure below shows the path of unemployment (indexed to 100 = trough level) after the recession had officially ended.

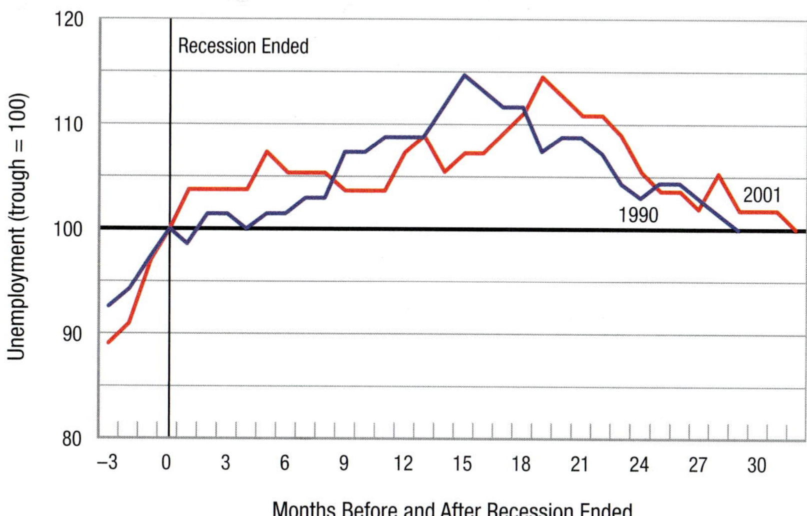


Following the 1990 recession, unemployment only returned to its lowest level (at the peak before the recession) after four and a half years, and with the recession of 2001, unemployment never returned to its lowest level. Does this phenomenon of unemployment continuing to rise after a recession has ended help foster the conclusion that these two recoveries were jobless recoveries?

# Answers to Questions in CheckPoints

## Check Point: Unemployment and Inflation: Phillips Curves

Since we have seen that $p = w - q$, if $q$ is high, wage increases ($w$) can be high without any real pressures on inflation ($p$). High productivity growth along with globalization and lower wages in many other countries have helped to keep inflationary pressures in the United States in check.

## Check Point: Rational Expectations and Policy Formation

If employees are convinced they are significantly underpaid (or they are worth more than they are paid), efficiency wages may have little impact on shirking, productivity, or turnover. If true, it probably doesn't do much for the rational expectations theory's ineffectiveness conclusion because there are a number of other inefficiencies in labor markets such as collective bargaining and information problems. Even those who think they are underpaid and begin looking for a new position often must face the reality that they are overpaid when no offers are forthcoming, or when information filters back to them about those who quit and ended up with lower-paying jobs.

## Check Point: Putting It All Together: The Recession and the Future

On balance, it is a hindrance when households and businesses are attempting to reduce debt levels. Falling prices increase the real value of debt, while declining real income makes it harder to pay off. Declining demand and prices for output provides little incentive for business to invest and expand. Deflation is a symptom of a declining economy and was a concern of monetary policymakers at the onset of the financial crisis in 2008. It is a factor that policy stimulus must overcome.

# International Trade

# 25

BananaStock/Jupiter Images

**The world economy is becoming** increasingly intertwined. Capital, labor, goods, and services all flow across borders. Most Americans wear foreign-made clothing, over half of us drive foreign cars, and even American cars contain many foreign components. Australian wines, Swiss watches, Chilean sea bass, and Brazilian coffee have become common in the United States. At the same time, Apple iPods, Nike athletic shoes, and Intel Pentium computers with Microsoft Windows can be found in abundance overseas. Trade is now part of the global landscape.

Worldwide foreign trade has quadrupled over the past 25 years. In the United States today, the combined value of exports and imports approaches $3.5 trillion a year. Twenty-five years ago, trade represented just over 15% of gross domestic product (GDP); today it accounts for more than a quarter of GDP. Nearly a 10th of American workers owe their jobs to foreign consumers. Figure 1 on the next page shows the current composition of U.S. exports and imports. Note that the United States imports and exports a lot of capital goods—that is, the equipment and machinery used to produce other goods. Also, we export nearly 50% more services than we import. Services include, for example, education and health care. Third, petroleum products represent approximately 14% of imports, totaling $273 billion a year.

Improved communications and transportation technologies have worked together to promote global economic integration. In addition, most governments around the world have reduced their trade barriers in recent years. But free trade has not always been so popular.

In 1929–1930, as the Great Depression was just beginning, many countries attempted to protect their domestic industries by imposing trade restrictions that discouraged imports. In 1930, the United States enacted the Smoot-Hawley tariffs, which imposed an

**After studying this chapter you should be able to:**

- ☐ Describe the benefits of free trade.
- ☐ Distinguish between absolute and comparative advantage.
- ☐ Describe the economic impacts of trade.
- ☐ Describe the terms of trade.
- ☐ List the ways in which trade is restricted.
- ☐ Discuss the various arguments against free trade.
- ☐ Describe the issues surrounding increasing global economic integration.

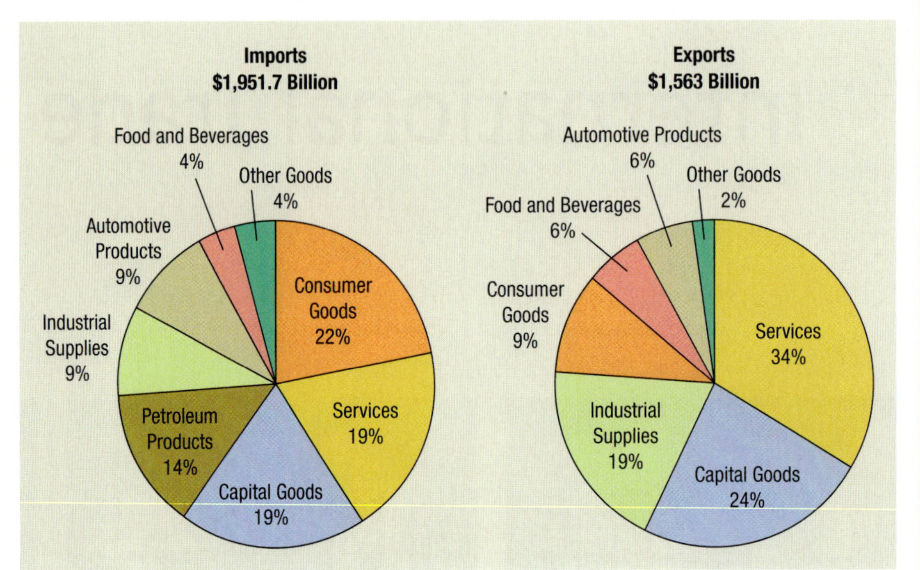


**FIGURE 1—U.S. Trade by Sector (2009)**

This figure shows trade by sector. The United States imports and exports large amounts of capital goods, the equipment and machinery used to produce other goods. Also, over one-third of United States exports are services such as education and health care.

average tax of 60% on imported goods. This move deeply hurt industries around the world, and it has been credited with adding to the severity of the global depression. Since World War II, in the wake of Smoot-Hawley's obvious failure, governments have steadily reduced trade barriers through a series of international agreements.

Trade must yield significant benefits or it would not exist. After all, there are no laws requiring countries to trade, just agreements permitting trade and reducing impediments to it. This chapter begins with a discussion of why trade is beneficial. We look at the terms of trade between countries. We then look at the tariffs and quotas sometimes used to restrict trade, calculating their costs. Finally, we will consider some arguments critics have advanced against increased trade and globalization.

## The Gains from Trade

Economics studies voluntary exchange. People and nations do business with one another because they expect to gain through these transactions. Foreign trade is nearly as old as civilization. Centuries ago, European merchants were already sailing to the Far East to ply the spice trades. Today, people in the United States buy cars from Japan and electronics from South Korea, along with millions of other products from countries around the world.

Many people assume that trade between nations is a zero-sum game: a game in which, for one party to gain, the other party must lose. Poker games fit this description; one person's winnings must come from another player's losses. This is not true of voluntary trade. Voluntary exchange and trade is a positive-sum game meaning that both parties to a transaction can gain.

Library of Congress, Prints and Photographs Division

The United States's first foreign trade zone opened on Staten Island, City of New York, February 1, 1937. This poster was commissioned by the Works Project Administration (WPA) in 1937.

To understand how this works, and thus, why nations trade, we need to consider the concepts of absolute and comparative advantage. Note that nations per se do not trade; individuals in specific countries do. We will, however, refer to trade between nations, but recognize that individuals, not nations, actually engage in trade. We covered this earlier in Chapter 2, but it is worthwhile to go through it again.

## By the *Numbers*

### International Trade

Most economists would agree that trade has been a net benefit to the world. The 1947 General Agreement on Tariffs and Trade (GATT) lowered tariffs and led to expanded trade and higher standards of living around the world.

**Trade deficits** (exports minus imports) were not a problem until the mid-1970s, when the United States began importing more than it exported. The recent recession has resulted in exports rising while imports fell.

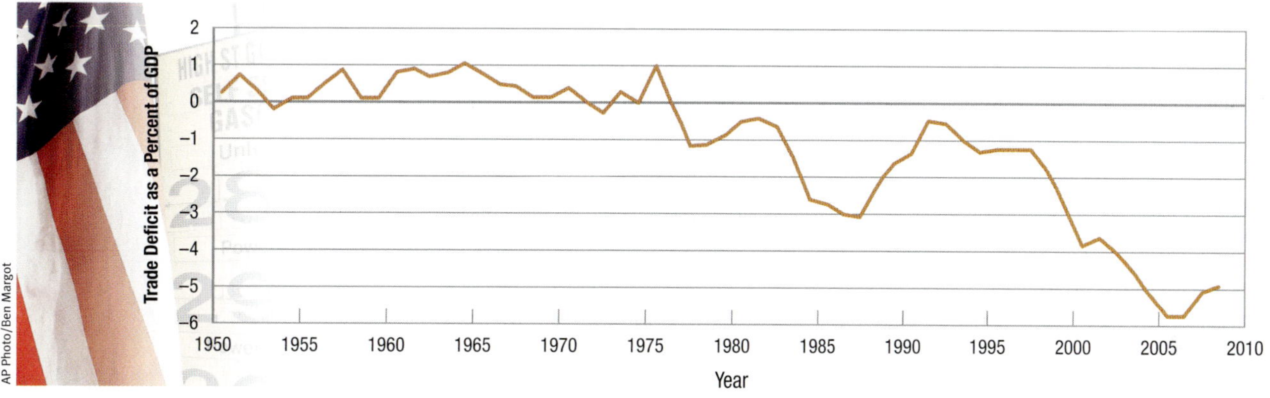


AP Photo/Ben Margot

**Tariff barriers** (a tax on imports) are relatively low in most countries.

Jon Feingersh/Blend Images/Corbis

**Medical tourism is growing** because health costs are less expensive overseas, even including the costs of travel.

**Cost of Various Medical Procedures**

| Procedure | United States | Thailand | Singapore |
|---|---|---|---|
| Heart Bypass | $130,000 | $22,000 | $16,300 |
| Heart Valve | 140,000 | 25,000 | 22,000 |
| Hip Replacement | 57,000 | 12,700 | 12,000 |
| Knee Replacement | 53,000 | 11,500 | 9,600 |
| Prostate Surgery | 16,000 | 4,400 | 5,300 |

**128%**

Increase in Chinese life expectancy from 1960 to 2008

**5%**

Growth in U.S. manufacturing capacity from 2000 to 2007, (while U.S. economy grew over 17%)

**U.S. public sentiment** about lowering trade barriers is mixed, and some even oppose helping displaced workers.

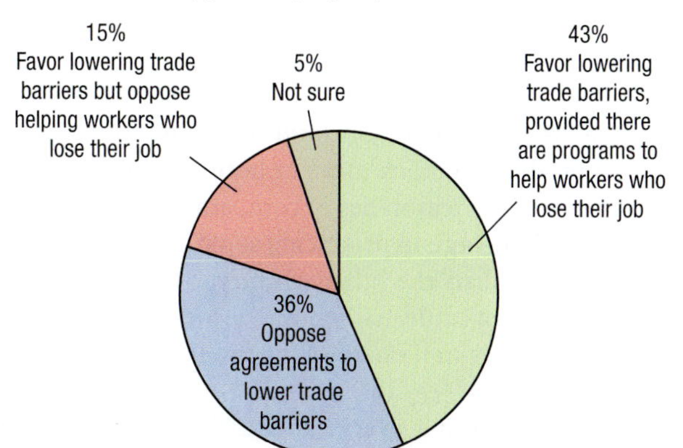


**China, once a world powerhouse,** slipped in the 20th century but is coming back.

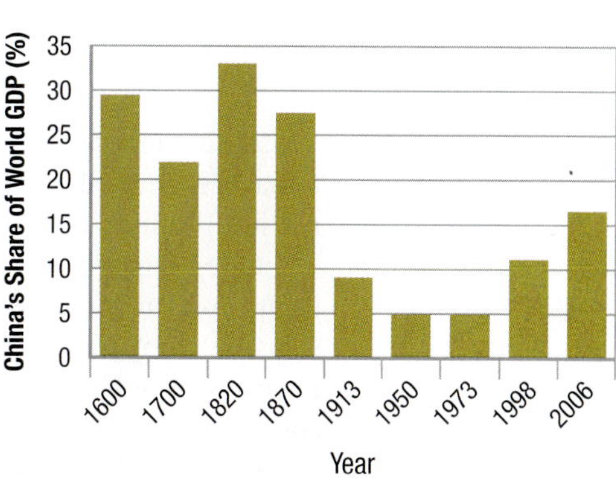

## Absolute and Comparative Advantage

**Absolute advantage:** One country can produce more of a good than another country.

Figure 2 shows hypothetical production possibilities curves for the United States and Canada. For simplicity, both countries are assumed to produce only beef and digital cameras. Given the production possibility frontiers (PPFs) in Figure 2, the United States has an absolute advantage over Canada in the production of both products. An **absolute advantage** exists when one country can produce more of a good than another country. In this case, the United States can produce 4 times as much beef and 10 times as many cameras as Canada.

**FIGURE 2—Production Possibilities for the United States and Canada**

The production possibilities frontier (PPF) curves shown here assume that the United States and Canada produce only beef and digital cameras. In this example, the United States has an absolute advantage over Canada in producing both products; the United States can produce 4 times as many cattle and 10 times as many cameras as Canada. Canada nonetheless has a comparative advantage over the United States in producing beef.

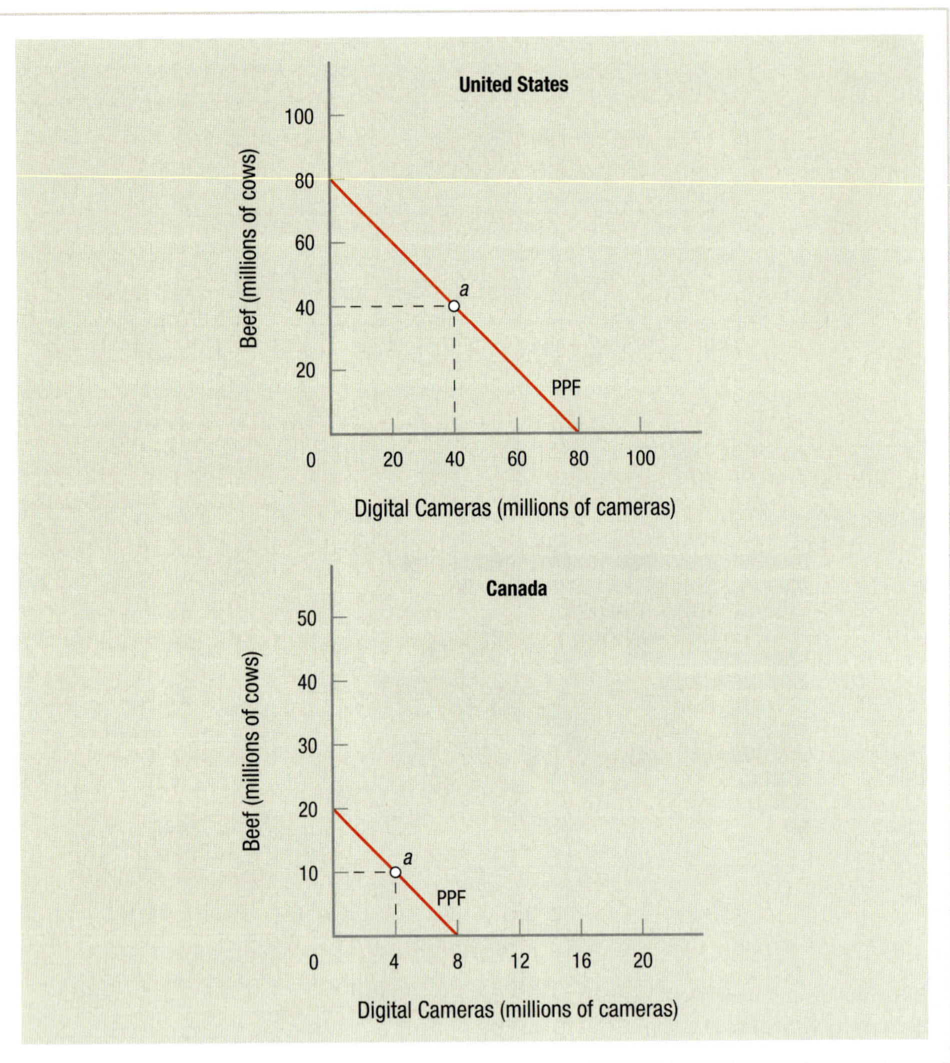


At first glance, we may wonder why the United States would be willing to trade with Canada. Because the United States can produce so much more of both commodities, why not just produce its own cattle and cameras? The reason lies in comparative advantage.

**Comparative advantage:** One country has a lower opportunity cost of producing a good than another country.

One country enjoys a **comparative advantage** in producing some good if its opportunity costs to produce that good are lower than the other country's. In this example, Canada's comparative advantage is in producing cattle. As Figure 2 shows, the opportunity cost for the United States to produce another million cows is 1 million cameras; each added cow essentially costs 1 camera.

Contrast this with the situation in Canada. For every camera Canadian producers forgo producing, they can produce 2.5 more cows. This means cows cost only 0.4 camera in Canada ($1/2.5 = 0.4$). Canada's comparative advantage is in producing cattle, since a cow costs 0.4 camera in Canada, while the same cow costs an entire camera in the United States.

By the same token, the United States has a comparative advantage in producing cameras: 1 camera in the United States costs 1 cow, but the same camera in Canada costs 2.5 cows. These relative costs suggest that the United States should focus its resources on digital camera production and that Canada should specialize in beef.

## Gains from Trade

To see how specialization and trade can benefit both countries even when one has an advantage in producing more of both goods, assume that the United States and Canada at first operate at point *a* in Figure 2, producing and consuming their own beef and digital cameras. As we can see, the United States produces and consumes 40 million cattle and 40 million digital cameras. Canada produces and consumes 10 million cattle and 4 million digital cameras. This initial position is similarly shown as points *a* in Figure 3.

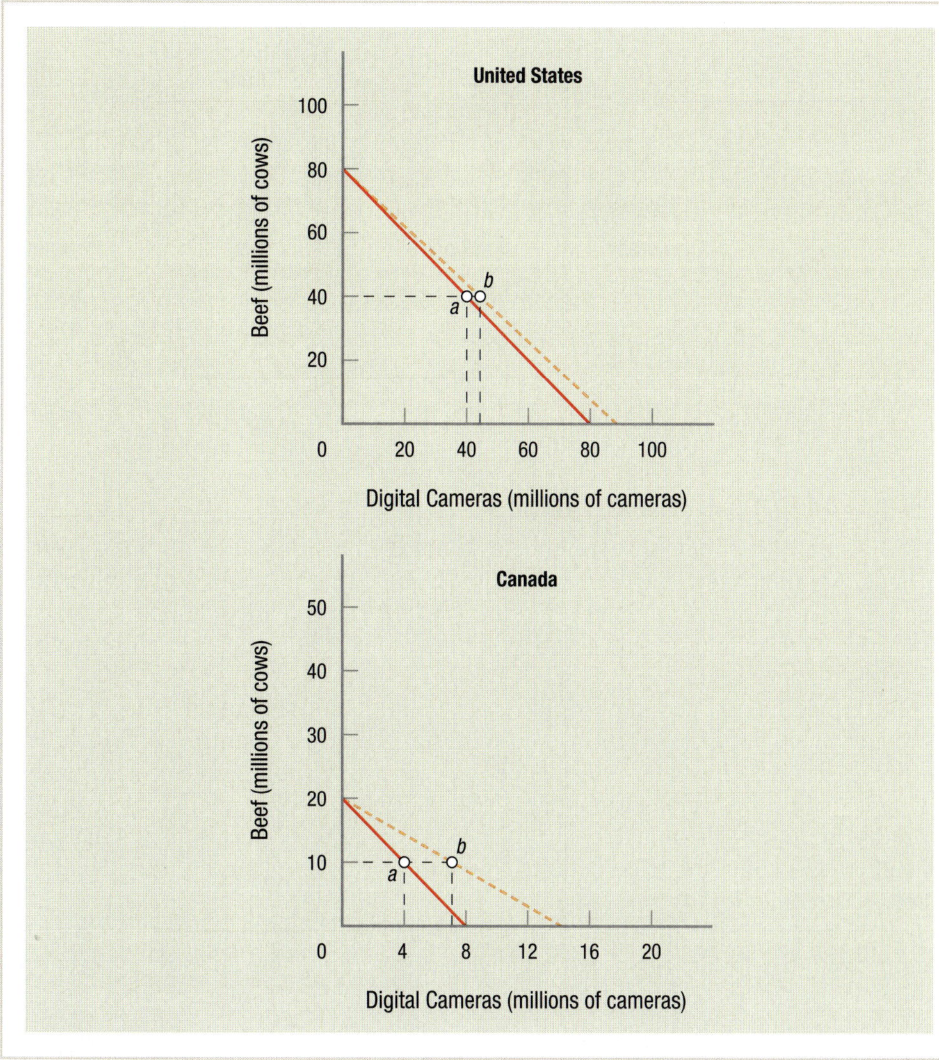


**FIGURE 3—The Gains from Specialization and Trade to the United States and Canada**

Assume Canada specializes in cattle. If the two countries want to continue consuming 50 million cows between them, the United States needs to produce only 30 million. This frees up resources for the United States to begin producing more digital cameras. Since each cow in the United States costs 1 camera to produce, reducing beef output by 10 million cattle means that 10 million more cameras can be produced. When the two countries trade their surplus products, both are better off than before.

Assume now that Canada specializes in producing cattle, producing all that it can—20 million cows. We will assume the two countries want to continue consuming 50 million cows between them. This means the United States needs to produce only 30 million cattle, since Canada is now producing 20 million. This frees up some American resources to produce digital cameras. Since each cow in the United States costs a digital camera, reducing beef output by 10 million cattle means that 10 million more cameras can now be produced.

So, the United States is producing 30 million cattle and 50 million cameras. Canada is producing 20 million cattle and no cameras. The combined production of cattle remains the same, 50 million, but camera production has increased by 6 million (from 44 to 50 million).

The two countries can trade their surplus products and will be better off. This is shown in Table 1. Assuming they agree to share the added 6 million cameras between them equally, Canada will trade 10 million cattle in exchange for 7 million digital cameras. Points *b* in Figure 3 show the resulting consumption patterns for each country. Each consume the same quantity of beef as before trading, but each country now has 3 million more digital cameras: 43 million for the United States and 7 million for Canada. This is shown in the final column of the table.

**TABLE 1** The Gains from Trade

| Country and Product | | Before Specialization | After Specialization | After Trade |
|---|---|---|---|---|
| United States | Cows | 40 million | 30 million | 40 million |
| | Cameras | 40 million | 50 million | 43 million |
| Canada | Cows | 10 million | 20 million | 10 million |
| | Cameras | 4 million | 0 | 7 million |

One important point to remember is that even when one country has an absolute advantage over another, countries still benefit from trade. The gains are small in our example, but they will grow as the two countries approach one another in size and their comparative advantages become more pronounced.

## Practical Constraints on Trade

At this point, we should take a moment to note some practical constraints on trade. First, every transaction involves costs. These include transportation, communications, and the general costs of doing business. Over the last several decades, however, transportation and communication costs have declined all over the world, resulting in growing world trade.

Second, the production possibilities curves for nations are not linear; rather, they are governed by increasing costs and diminishing returns. Countries find it difficult to specialize only in one product. Indeed, specializing in one product is risky since the market for the product can always decline, new technology might replace it, or its production can be disrupted by changing weather patterns. This is a perennial problem for developing countries that often build their exports and trade around one agricultural commodity.

Although it is true that trading partners benefit from trade, some individuals and groups within each country may lose. Individual workers in those industries at a comparative disadvantage are likely to lose their jobs, and thus may require retraining, relocation, or other help if they are to move smoothly into new occupations.

When the United States signed the North American Free Trade Agreement (NAFTA) with Canada and Mexico, many U.S. workers experienced this sort of dislocation. Some U.S. jobs went south to Mexico because of low wages. Still, by opening up more markets for U.S. products, NAFTA has stimulated the U.S. economy. The goal is that displaced workers, newly retrained, will end up with new and better jobs, although there is no guarantee this will happen.

## CHECKPOINT

### THE GAINS FROM TRADE

- An absolute advantage exists when one country can produce more of a good than another country.
- A comparative advantage exists when one country can produce a good at a lower opportunity cost than another country.
- Both countries gain from trade when each specializes in producing goods in which they have a comparative advantage.
- Transaction costs, diminishing returns, and the risk associated with specialization all place some practical limits on trade.

**QUESTIONS:** When two individuals voluntarily engage in trade, they both benefit or the trade wouldn't occur (one party wouldn't choose to be worse off after the trade). Is the same true for nations? Is everyone in both nations better off?

Answers to the Checkpoint questions can be found at the end of this chapter.

# The Terms of Trade

How much can a country charge when it sells its goods to another country? How much must it pay for imported goods? The terms of trade determine the prices of imports and exports.

To keep things simple, assume each country has only one export and one import, priced at $P_x$ and $P_m$. The ratio of the price of the exported goods to the price of the imported goods, $P_x/P_m$, is the terms of trade. Thus, if a country exports computers and imports coffee, with two computers trading for a ton of coffee, the price of a computer must be one half the price of a ton of coffee.

When countries trade many commodities, the **terms of trade** are defined as the average price of exports divided by the average price of imports. This can get a bit complicated, given that the price of each import and export is quoted in its own national currency, while the exchange rate between the two currencies may be constantly changing. We will ignore these complications by translating currencies into dollars, focusing our attention on how the terms of trade are determined and the impact of trade.

**Terms of trade:** The ratio of the price of exported goods to the price of imported goods ($P_x/P_m$).

## Determining the Terms of Trade

To get a feel for how the terms of trade are determined, let us consider the trade in computers between the United States and Japan. We will assume the United States has a comparative advantage in producing computers; all prices are given in dollars.

Panel A of Figure 4 on the next page shows the demand and supply of computers in the United States. The upward sloping supply curve reflects increasing opportunity costs in computer production. As the United States continues to specialize in computer production, resources less suited to this purpose must be employed. Thus, ever-increasing amounts of other goods must be sacrificed, resulting in rising costs for computer production. Because of this rise in costs as ever more resources are shifted to computers, the United States will eventually lose its comparative advantage in computer production. This represents one limit on specialization and trade.

Let us assume the United States begins in pretrade equilibrium, with the price of computers at \$600 each. Panel B shows Japan initially in equilibrium with a higher computer price of \$1,000. Since prices for computers from the United States are lower, when trade begins, Japanese consumers will begin buying U.S. computers.

American computer makers will increase production to meet this new demand. Japanese computer firms, conversely, will see the sales of their computers decline in Japan as prices begin to fall. For now, let us ignore transport costs, such that trade continues until

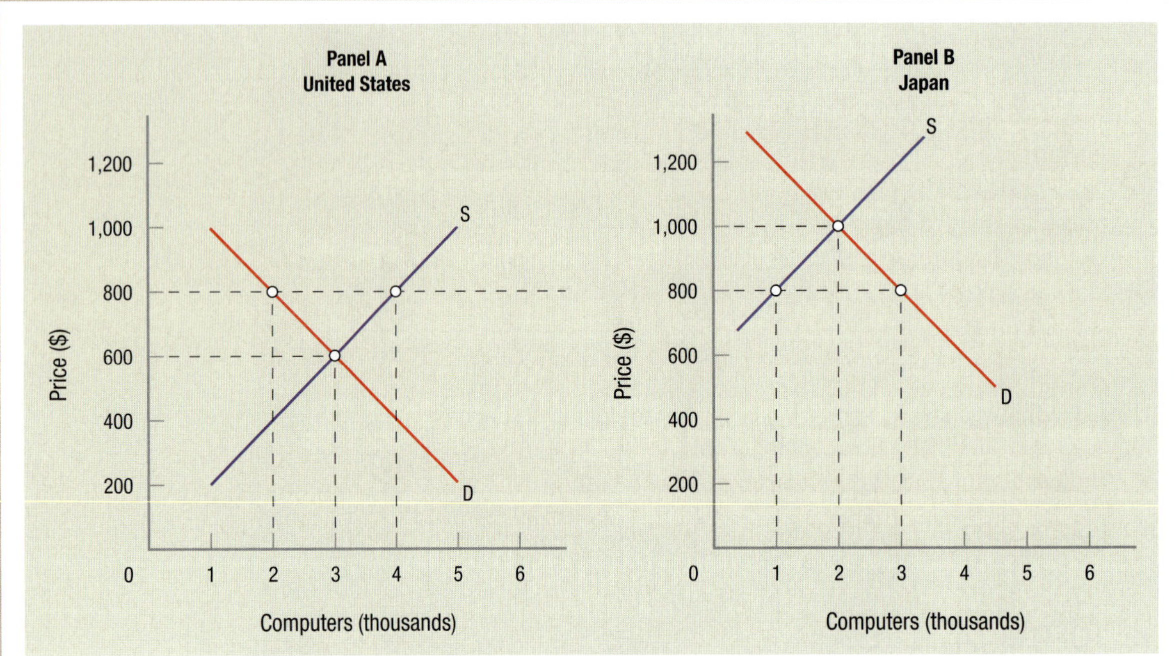


**FIGURE 4—Determining the Terms of Trade**

Panel A shows the demand and supply of computers in the United States; the upward slope of the supply curve reflects increasing opportunity costs to produce more computers. The United States begins in pretrade equilibrium at $600 and Japan's initial equilibrium is at $1,000. With trade, Japanese consumers will begin buying American computers because of their lower price. American computer makers will increase production to meet this new demand. Japanese computer firms will see sales of their computers decline as prices begin to fall. Ignoring transport costs, trade will continue until prices reach $800. At this point, American exports (2,000) are just equal to Japanese imports (2,000).

prices reach $800. At this point, U.S. exports (2,000 computers) are just equal to Japanese imports. Both countries are now in equilibrium, with the price of computers somewhere between the two pretrade equilibrium prices ($800 in this case).

Imagine this same process simultaneously working itself out with many other goods, including some at which the Japanese have a comparative advantage, such as cameras and electronic components. As each product settles into an equilibrium price, the terms of trade between these two countries is determined.

## The Impact of Trade

Our examination of absolute and comparative advantage has thus far highlighted the blessings of trade. A closer look at Figure 4, however, shows that trade produces winners and losers.

Picking up on the previous example, computer producers in the United States are happy, having watched their sales rise from 3,000 to 4,000 units. Predictably, management and workers in this industry will favor even more trade with Japan and the rest of the world. Yet, domestic consumers of computers are worse off, since after trade they purchase only 2,000 computers at the higher equilibrium price of $800. Computer users will likely oppose increased trade, and may even look to Congress to restrict trade.

Contrast this situation in the net exporting country, the United States, with that of the net importer, Japan. Japanese computer producers are worse off than before since the price of computers fell from $1,000 to $800, and their output was reduced to 1,000 units. Consequently, they must cut jobs, leaving workers and managers in the Japanese computer industry unhappy with its country's trade policies. Japanese consumers, however, are beneficiaries of this expanded trade, since they can purchase 3,000 computers at a lower price of $800.

These results are not merely hypothetical. This is the story of free trade, which has been played out time and again: Some sectors of the economy win, and some lose. American consumers have been happy to purchase Japanese cameras such as Minolta and Nikon, given their high quality and low prices. American camera makers such as Kodak and Polaroid have not been so pleased, nor have their employees. These firms, watching their prices, sales, and employment decline, have had to adapt to the competition from abroad.

Similarly, the ranks of American textile workers have been decimated over the past two decades as domestic clothing producers have increasingly become nothing but designers and marketers of clothes, shifting their production overseas to countries where wages are lower. American-made clothing is now essentially a thing of the past.

To be sure, American consumers have enjoyed a substantial drop in the price of clothing, because labor forms a significant part of the cost of clothing production. Still, being able to purchase inexpensive T-shirts made in China is small consolation for the unemployed textile worker in North Carolina.

The undoubted pain suffered by the losers from trade often is translated into pressure put on politicians to restrict trade in one way or another. The pain is often felt more strongly than the "happiness" felt by those who benefit from trade.

## How Trade Is Restricted

Trade restrictions can range from subsidies provided to domestic firms to protect them against lower-priced imports to embargoes in which the government bans any trade with a country. Between these two extremes are more intermediate policies, such as exchange controls that limit the amount of foreign currency available to importers or citizens who travel abroad. Regulation, licensing, and government purchasing policies are all frequently used to promote or ensure the purchase of domestic products. The main reason for these trade restrictions is simple: The industry and its employees actually feel the pain and lobby extensively for protection, while the huge benefits of lower prices are diffused among millions of customers whose benefits are each so small that fighting against a trade barrier isn't worth their time.

The most common forms of trade restrictions are tariffs and quotas. Panel A of Figure 5 on the next page shows the average U.S. tariff rates since 1900. Some economists have suggested that the tariff wars that erupted in the 1920s and culminated in the passage of the Smoot-Hawley Act in 1930 were an important factor underlying the severity of the Great Depression. Panel B shows the impact of higher tariffs on worldwide imports from 1930 to 1933. The higher tariffs reduced trade, leading to a reduction in income, output, and employment, and added fuel to the worldwide depression. Since the 1930s, the United States has played a leading role in trade liberalization, with average tariff rates declining to a current rate of roughly 2%.

### Effects of Tariffs and Quotas

What exactly are the effects of tariffs and quotas? **Tariffs** are often ad valorem taxes. This means the product is taxed by a certain percentage of its price as it crosses the border. Other tariffs are unit taxes: A fixed tax per unit of the product is assessed at the border. Tariffs are designed to generate revenues and to drive a wedge between the domestic price of a product and its price on the world market. The effects of a tariff are shown in Figure 6 on page 605.

Tariff: A tax on imported products. When a country taxes imported products, it drives a wedge between the product's domestic price and its price on the world market.

Domestic supply and demand for the product are shown in Figure 6 as S and D. Assume that the product's world price of $400 is lower than its domestic price of $600. Domestic quantity demanded (4,000 units) will consequently exceed domestic quantity supplied (2,000 units) at the world price of $400. Imports to this country will therefore be 2,000 units.

Now assume that the firms and workers in the industry hurt by the lower world price lobby for a tariff and are successful. The country imposes a tariff of $100 on this product. The results are clear. The product's price in this country rises to $500 and imports fall to 1,000 units

**FIGURE 5—Average U.S. Tariff Rates, 1900–2004, and the Downward Spiral of World Imports, 1930–1933**

Tariffs and quotas are the most common forms of trade restrictions. Panel A shows that tariff rates in the United States peaked during the Great Depression. For the last several decades, tariffs have stayed at roughly a rate of 2%. When tariffs jumped with the passage of the Smoot-Hawley Act in 1930, world imports spiraled downward as shown in panel B. As trade between nations declined, incomes, output, and employment also fell worldwide. In panel B, total monthly imports in millions of U.S. dollars for 75 countries is shown spiraling downward from $2,738 million in January 1930 to $1,057 million in March 1933.

Source: Charles Kindleberger, *The World Depression 1929–1939* (Berkeley: University of California Press), 1986, p. 170.

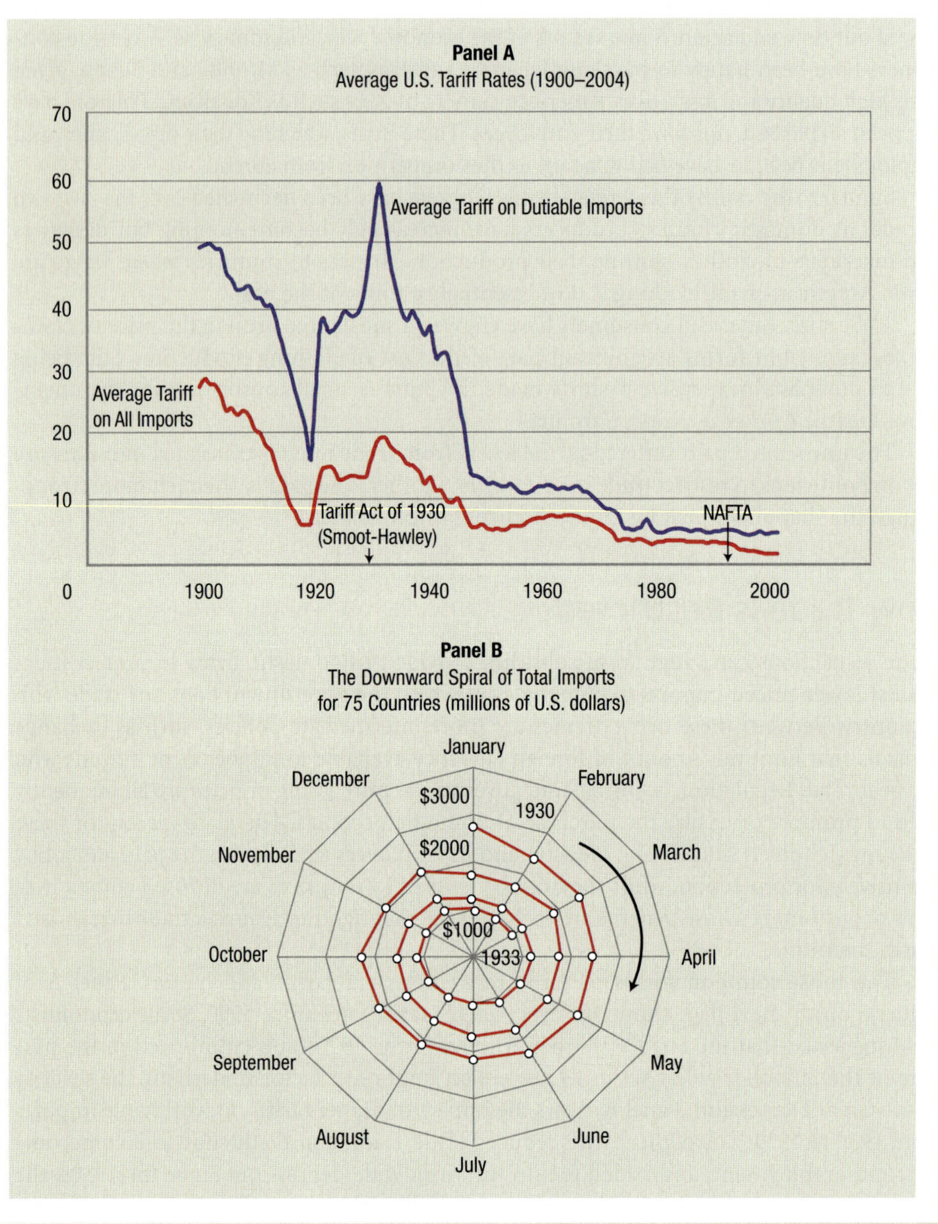


(3,500–2,500). Domestic consumers consume less of the product at higher prices. Even so, the domestic industry is happy, since its prices and output have risen. The government, meanwhile, collects revenues equal to $100,000 ($100 × 1,000), the shaded area in Figure 6. These revenues can be significant: In the 1800s, tariffs were the federal government's dominant form of revenue. It is only in the last century that the federal government has come to rely more on other sources of revenue, including taxes on income, sales, and property.

**Quota:** A government-set limit on the quantity of imports into a country.

Figure 7 shows the effects of a **quota.** They are similar to what we saw in Figure 6, except that the government restricts the quantity of imports into the country to 1,000 units. Imports fall to the quota level, and consumers again lose, because they must pay higher prices for less output. Producers and their employees gain as prices and employment in the domestic industry rise. For a quota, however, the government does not collect revenue. Then who gets this revenue? The foreign exporting company gets it in the form of higher prices for its products. This explains why governments prefer tariffs over quotas.

The United States imposed quotas on Japanese automobiles in the 1980s. The primary effect of these quotas was initially to dramatically raise the minimum standard

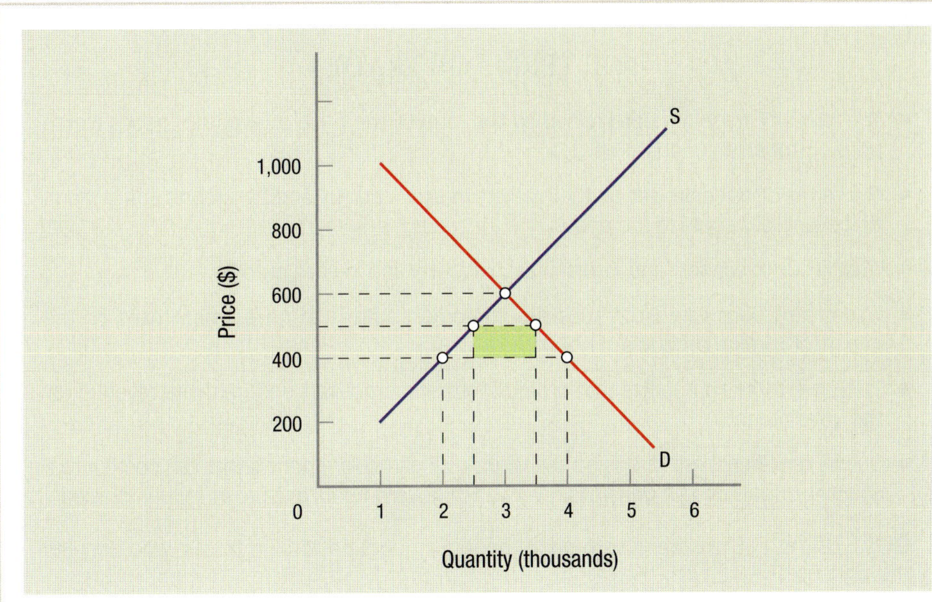


**FIGURE 6—Effects of a Tariff**

What are the effects of a typical tariff? Supply and demand curves S and D represent domestic supply and demand. Assume the product's world price of $400 is lower than its domestic price. Imports will therefore be 2,000 units. If the country imposes a tariff of $100 on this product, the domestic price rises to $500, and imports fall to 1,000 units. Domestic consumers now consume less of the product at higher prices. However, the domestic industry is happy since its prices and output have risen. Also, the government collects revenues equal to the shaded area.

equipment and price for some Japanese cars and to increase ultimately the number of Japanese cars made in American factories. If a firm is limited in the number of vehicles it can sell, why not sell higher-priced ones where the profit margins are higher? The Toyota Land Cruiser, for instance, was originally a bare-bones SUV selling for under $15,000. With quotas, this vehicle became a $60,000 luxury behemoth with all the extras standard.

One problem with tariffs and quotas is that when they are imposed, large numbers of consumers pay just a small amount more for the targeted products. Few consumers are willing to spend time and effort lobbying Congress to end or forestall these trade barriers from being introduced. Producers, however, are often few in number, and they stand to gain tremendously from such trade barriers. It is no wonder that such firms have large lobbying budgets and provide campaign contributions to congressional candidates.

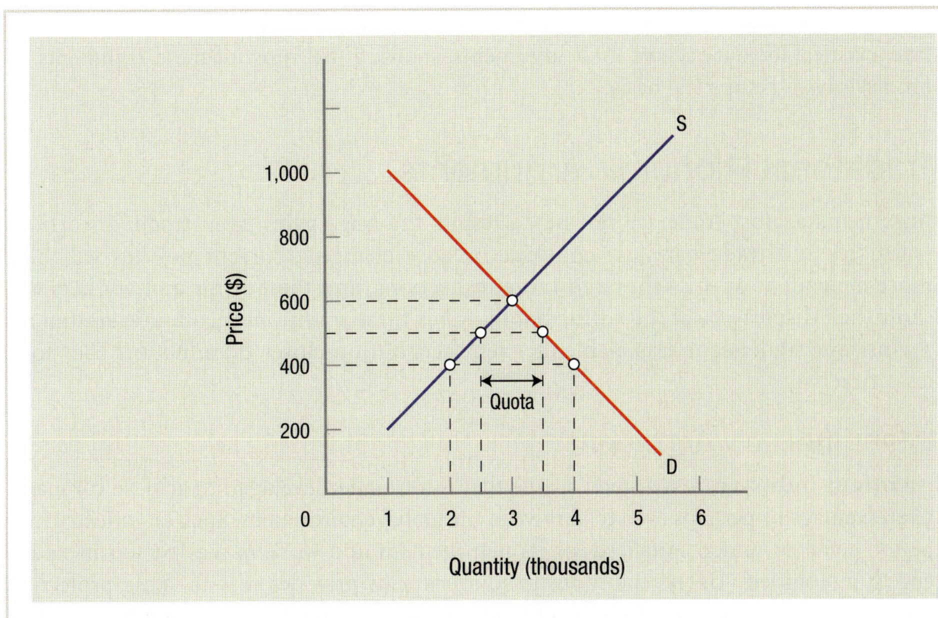


**FIGURE 7—Effects of a Quota**

What are the effects of a quota? They are similar to the effects of a tariff, except that the government restricts the quantity of imports into the country to 1,000 units. Imports fall to the quota level, and again consumers lose as they must pay higher prices for less output. Producers and their employees gain as prices and employment in the domestic industry rise. With a quota, however, the government does not collect revenues.

**CHECKPOINT**

## THE TERMS OF TRADE

- The terms of trade are determined by the ratio of the price of exported goods to the price of imported goods.
- The terms of trade are set by the markets in each country and by exports and imports that eventually equalize the prices.
- Trade leads to winners and losers in each country and in each market.
- Trade restrictions vary from subsidies to domestic firms to government bans on the import of foreign products.
- Tariffs are taxes on imports that protect domestic producers and generate revenue for the government.
- Quotas represent restrictions on the volume of particular imports that can come into a country. Quotas do not generate revenue for governments and are infrequently used.

**QUESTION:** When the government imposes a quota on foreign trucks, who benefits and who loses?

Answers to the Checkpoint question can be found at the end of this chapter.

# Arguments Against Free Trade

*"If goods do not cross borders, soldiers will."*

Frédéric Bastiat

We have seen the benefits of trade, and have looked at how trade undoubtedly benefits some and harms others. Those who are harmed by trade often seek to restrict trade, primarily in the form of tariffs and quotas. Because trade leads to some loss, those who are harmed by trade have made arguments against free trade.

The arguments against free trade fall into two camps. Traditional economic arguments include protection for infant industries, protection against dumping, low foreign wages, and support for industries judged vital for national defense. More recent arguments focus on globalization (social and economic) concerns that embody political-economy characteristics. These include domestic employment concerns, environmental concerns, and the impact of globalization on working conditions in developing nations. In what follows, we take a critical look at each of these arguments, showing that most of these arguments do not have a solid empirical basis.

## Traditional Economic Arguments

Arguments against trade are not new. Despite the huge gains from trade, distortions (subsidies and trade barriers) continue because changing current policies will hurt those dependent on subsidies and trade restrictions, and these firms and workers will show their displeasure at the voting booth. All of these traditional economic arguments against free trade seem reasonable on their face, but on closer examination, they look less attractive.

### Infant Industry Argument

**Infant industry:** An industry so underdeveloped that protection is needed for it to become competitive on the world stage or to ensure its survival.

An **infant industry,** it is argued, is one that is too underdeveloped to achieve comparative advantage or perhaps even to survive in the global environment. Such an industry may be too small or undercapitalized, or its management and workers may be too inexperienced, to compete. Unless the industry's government provides it with some protection through tariffs, quotas, or subsidies, it might not survive in the face of foreign competition.

In theory, once the infant industry has been given this protection, it should be able to grow, acquiring the necessary capital and expertise needed to compete internationally. Germany and the United States used high tariffs to protect their infant manufacturing sectors in the 1800s, and Japan continued to maintain import restrictions up until the 1970s.

Though the infant industry argument sounds reasonable, it has several limitations. First, protecting an industry must be done in a way that makes the industry internationally competitive. Many countries coddle their firms, and these producers never seem to develop into "mature," internationally viable firms. Once protection is provided (typically a protective tariff), it is difficult to remove after an industry has matured. The industry and its workers continue to convince policymakers of the need for continued protection.

Second, infant industry protection often tends to focus on capital manufacturing. Countries with huge labor supplies would do better to develop their labor-intensive industries first, letting more capital-intensive industries develop over time. Every country, after all, should seek to exploit its comparative advantages, but it is difficult to determine which industries have a chance of developing a comparative advantage in the future and should be temporarily protected.

Third, many industries seem to be able to develop without protections, so countries may be wasting their resources and reducing their incomes by imposing protection measures.

Clearly, the infant industry argument is not valid for advanced economies such as the United States, much of Europe, and Japan. The evidence for developing nations shows some benefits but is mixed for the reasons noted above.

## Antidumping

**Dumping** means that goods are sold at lower prices (often *below cost*) abroad than in their home market. This is typically a result of government subsidies.

**Dumping:** Selling goods abroad at lower prices than in home markets, and often below cost.

In the same way that price discrimination improves profits, firms can price discriminate between their home markets and foreign markets. Let's assume that costs of production are $100 a unit for all firms (domestic and foreign). A state subsidy of $30 a unit, for example, reduces domestic costs to $70 a unit and permits the firm to sell its product in world markets at these lower prices. These state subsidies give these firms a cost advantage in foreign markets.

Firms can use dumping as a form of predatory pricing, using higher prices in their domestic markets to support unrealistically low prices in foreign markets. The goal of predatory pricing is to drive foreign competitors out of business. When this occurs, the firm doing the dumping then comes back and imposes higher prices. In the long run, these higher prices thereby offset the company's short-term losses.

Dumping violates American trade laws. If the federal government determines that a foreign firm is dumping products onto the American market, it can impose antidumping tariffs on the offending products. The government, however, must distinguish among dumping, legitimate price discrimination, and legitimate instances of lower cost production arising from comparative advantage.

## Low Foreign Wages

Some advocates of trade barriers maintain that domestic firms and their workers need to be protected from displacement by cheap foreign labor. Without this protection, it is argued, foreign manufacturers that pay their workers pennies an hour will flood the market with low-cost products. As we have already seen, this argument has something to it: Workers in advanced economies can be displaced by low-wage foreign workers. This is what has happened in the American textile industry.

Once a handful of American clothing manufacturers began moving their production facilities overseas, thereby undercutting domestic producers, other manufacturers were forced to follow them. American consumers have benefited from lower clothing prices, but many displaced textile workers are still trying to get retrained and adapt to work in other industries. More recently, many manufacturing jobs have drifted overseas, and high-technology firms today are shifting some help desk facilities and computer programming to foreign shores.

On balance, however, the benefits of lower-priced goods considerably exceed the costs of lost employment. The federal government has resisted imposing protection measures for the sake of protecting jobs, instead funding programs that help displaced workers transition to new lines of work.

### National Defense Argument

In times of national crisis or war, the United States must be able to rely on key domestic industries, such as oil, steel, and the defense industry. Some have argued that these industries may require some protection even during peacetime to ensure that they are already well established when a crisis strikes and importing key products may be impossible. Within limits, this argument is sound. Still, the United States has the capacity to produce such a wide variety of products that protections for specific industries would seem to be unjustified and unnecessary.

So what are we to make of these traditional arguments? Although they all seem reasonable, they all have deficiencies. Infant industries may be helped in the short run, but protections are often extended well beyond what is necessary, resulting in inefficient firms that are vulnerable on world markets. Dumping is clearly a potential problem, but distinguishing real cases of dumping and comparative advantage has often proven difficult in practice. Low foreign wages are often the only comparative advantage a developing nation has to offer the world economy, and typically, the benefits to consumers vastly outweigh the loss to a particular industry. Maintaining (protecting) industries for national defense has merit and may be appropriate for some countries, but for a country as huge and diversified as the United States, it is probably unnecessary.

## Recent Globalization Concerns

Expanded trade and globalization have provided the world's producers and consumers with many benefits. Some observers, however, have voiced concerns about globalization and its effects on domestic employment, the global environment, and working conditions in developing nations. Let's look at each one of these globalization concerns.

### Trade and Domestic Employment

Some critics argue that increased trade and globalization spell job losses for domestic workers. We have seen that this can be true. Some firms, unable to compete with imports, will be forced to lay off workers or even close their doors. Even so, increased trade usually allows firms that are exporters to expand their operations and hire new workers. These will be firms in industries with comparative advantages. For the United States, these industries tend to be those that require a highly skilled workforce, resulting in higher wages for American workers.

Clearly, those industries that are adding workers and those that are losing jobs are different industries. For workers who lose their jobs, switching industries can be difficult and time consuming, and often it requires new investments in human capital. American trade policy recognizes this problem, and the Trade Adjustment Assistance (TAA) program provides workers with job search assistance, job training, and some relocation allowances. In some industries sensitive to trade liberalization, including textiles and agriculture, trade policies are designed to proceed gradually, thus giving these industries and their workers some extra time to adjust.

Possible employment losses in some noncompetitive industries do not seem to provide enough justification for restricting trade. By imposing trade restrictions such as tariffs or quotas in one industry, employment opportunities in many other industries may be reduced. Open, competitive trade encourages producers to focus their production on those areas in which the country stands at a comparative advantage. Free trade puts competitive pressure on domestic firms, forcing them to be more productive and competitive, boosting the flow of information and technology across borders, and widening the availability of inputs for producers. At the end of the day, consumers benefit from these efficiencies, having more goods to choose from and enjoying a higher standard of living.

## Trade and the Environment

Concerns about globalization, trade, and the environment usually take one of two forms. Some people are concerned that expanded trade and globalization will lead to increased environmental degradation as companies take advantage of lax environmental laws abroad, particularly in the developing world. Others worry that attempts by the government to strengthen environmental laws will be challenged by trading partners as disguised protectionism.

Domestic environmental regulations usually target a product or process that creates pollution or other environmental problems. One concern in establishing environmental regulations, however, is that they not unfairly discriminate against the products of another country. This is usually not a serious problem. Nearly all trade agreements, including the World Trade Organization Agreements and the NAFTA, have provisions permitting countries to enforce measures "necessary to protect human, animal or plant life or health" or to conserve exhaustible natural resources. Nothing in our trade agreements prevents the United States from implementing environmental regulations as long as they do not unreasonably discriminate against our trading partners.

Will free trade come at the expense of the environment? Every action involves a trade-off. Clearly, there can be cases where the benefits of trade accruing to large numbers of people result in harm to a more concentrated group. In 1995, however, President Clinton's Council of Economic Advisers concluded:

> *There are also complementarities between good trade policies and good environmental policies. Agricultural protection in industrialized countries is a case in point. The protection of developed-country agriculture leads to more intensive farming, often of lands that are of marginal use, causing unnecessary soil erosion, loss of biological diversity, and the excessive use of pesticides and chemicals. Liberalizing trade in agriculture and lowering agriculture production subsidies can lead to a pattern of world farming that causes less environmental damage.*
>
> *Also, high trade barriers to labor-intensive imports, such as clothing, from developing countries lead these countries instead to export products that are intensive in natural resources, causing environmental damage. In addition, high-value-added natural resource-based products such as wood or paper products often face high tariff barriers, whereas the raw natural resource itself does not; this forces developing countries to rely on exports of unprocessed natural resources while denying them the revenue gains from the downstream products.*[1]

We have seen that trade raises incomes in developed and developing countries. And environmental protection is an income elastic good: As incomes rise, the demand for environmental protections rises faster. Studies suggest that once a country's per capita income exceeds roughly $5,000, its environmental protection efforts begin to improve.

In poor, developing nations, environmental protection will not at first be a priority. Critics of globalization are concerned that because environmental and labor standards in many developing nations are well below those of the developed countries, there will be pressure to adopt these lower standards in rich nations due to trade and foreign direct investment. But as Bhagwati and Hudec argue, there has been no systematic "race to the bottom" and many corporations often have the highest environmental and labor standards in the developing world.[2] Also, it is worth noting that over time, as incomes rise, environmental protection takes on added importance even in poorer nations. On balance, trade probably benefits the environment over the longer term, as incomes grow in developing nations and environmental protections take on greater importance.

---

[1] *Economic Report of the President* (Washington, DC: U.S. Government Printing Office), 1995, p. 242.

[2] Jagdish Bhagwati and Robert Hudec (eds.), *Fair Trade and Harmonization, Vol. 1: Economic Analysis* (Cambridge, MA: MIT Press), 1996.

## Trade and Its Effect on Working Conditions in Developing Nations

Some antiglobalization activists argue that for the United States to trade with developing countries where wages are low and working conditions are deplorable simply exploits workers in these developing countries. Clearly, such trade does hurt American workers in low-wage, low-skilled occupations who simply cannot compete with the even lower-wage

## *Issue:* Is Outsourcing Just Another Form of Trade?

**Lawrence Summers,** President Obama's top economist, once argued that developed countries should consider moving "dirty" industries offshore to less developed countries (LDCs). Those countries have lower opportunity costs because pollution costs depend primarily on forgone earnings. He also suggested that developed nations should ship their solid waste to LDCs. He was roundly criticized for being "perfectly logical but totally insane." But what he suggested is just the logical extension of the generally agreed upon gains from comparative advantage and trade.

Professor N. Gregory Mankiw, who at the time headed President G.W. Bush's Council of Economic Advisers, suggested that outsourcing was only "the latest manifestation of the gains from trade that economists have talked about at least since Adam Smith. . . . More things are tradable than were tradable in the past, and that's a good thing."

These two highly respected economists seem to have few reservations about extending the benefits of comparative advantage and trade to seemingly unpopular sectors. For some time now, the popular media has blamed globalization and outsourcing for most of the United States's economic troubles. But are those critics correct?

Outsourcing became a hot topic right after the 2001 recession. The recovery was sluggish and job creation was anemic. Outsourcing, plant closings, and the shipping of production or services to low-cost areas has been going on in the United States for years. Manufacturing has been moving from north to south for a half-century. Nearly all new auto plants (both foreign and domestic) have been built in the South. Trade in products has been accepted throughout history, and manufacturing has been drifting offshore for several decades. But technological progress in computers, communications, and the Internet has made the process easier, sparking an intense debate about shipping jobs overseas.

Most of the arguments against outsourcing were based on anecdotal evidence—a plant closing here, a closing there, and so on. But in the mid-2000s, the Bureau of Labor Statistics developed a survey to quantify the levels of both outsourcing and insourcing (the flow of jobs to the United States by firms from other countries) and discovered that the *net* effect was that roughly 2 million jobs (around 1% of total jobs) were being outsourced over those insourced. Further studies by several economists found that rising employment by U.S. multinational firms at their foreign subsidiaries led to more employment in the United States as well.

As we have seen, there are both winners and losers in trade. But in general, economists found that there is a net increase in income to U.S. residents from outsourcing. When all impacts are considered, including savings to consumers from lower product costs, imports of U.S. goods by foreigners, profits to U.S. affiliates, and the value of labor reemployed, a dollar spent on outsourcing resulted in over a dollar of increased income to U.S. residents.

Clearly, those who lose their jobs to outsourcing suffer. But our policy approach should not be to curtail outsourcing, but rather to help displaced workers receive assistance and training to move to jobs in high demand. Also, when a firm saves money through outsourcing, it can redirect those savings to other activities, such as product design or research and development, activities that strengthen the firm in the long run.

However, outsourcing is not without its inherent problems. It requires good communication and coordination with the foreign firm. NCR outsourced the production of bank ATMs in 2007 to cut costs. But ATMs are complex and company engineers often had to fly around the world to solve production and design problems, leading to delays that frustrated customers. Two years later, because of these problems, NCR moved production for domestic sales to a new plant in Georgia, just two hours from its corporate headquarters and its research campus.

Andrew Holbrooke/Corbis

The issue of outsourcing became a heated political debate in the jobless recovery of the mid-2000s. In response, the Bureau of Labor Statistics undertook its effort to actually measure the impact of outsourcing and insourcing. Once economists had hard numbers, the issue didn't feel so damaging to the economy (just specific workers in specific industries) and the profile of the issue seems to have faded. Outsourcing is just another example of the net benefits to trade, but policymakers should not lose sight of the harm to individuals and policy should be directed to retraining and getting them back on their feet.

Sources: N. Gregory Mankiw and Phillip Swagel, "The Politics and Economics of Offshore Outsourcing," *AEI Working Paper #122,* December 7, 2005; Peter Engardio, "Why NCR Said 'Let's Go Back Home'," *Business Week,* August 24, 2009; and W. Michael Cox, Richard Alm, and Justyna Dymerska, "Labor Market Globalization in the Recession and Beyond," *Economic Letter,* Federal Reserve Bank of Dallas, December 2009.

workers overseas. But it is not clear that workers in developing countries would be helped if the United States were to cut off its trade with those countries that refuse to improve their wages or working conditions.

Restricting trade with countries that do not raise their wages to levels we think acceptable or bring working conditions up to our standards would probably do more harm than good. Low wages reflect, among other factors, the low investments in human capital, low productivity, and low living standards characteristic of developing nations. Blocking trade with these nations may deprive them of their key chance to grow and to improve in those areas where we would like to see change.

Liberalized trade policies, economic freedom, and a legal system that respects property rights and foreign capital investment probably provide the best recipe for rapid development, economic growth, environmental protection, and improved wages and working conditions.

In summary, trade does result in job losses in some industries, but the gain to consumers and the competitive pressures that trade puts on domestic companies is beneficial to the economy as a whole. Trade raises incomes in developing nations, resulting in a growing demand for more environmentally friendly production processes. Trade is not the reason for low environmental standards in developing countries; they result from low incomes, low standards of living, and poor governmental policies. Trade brings about higher levels of income and ultimately better working conditions.

**CHECKPOINT**

## ARGUMENTS AGAINST FREE TRADE

- The infant industries argument claims that some industries are so underdeveloped that they need protection to survive in a global competitive environment.
- Dumping involves selling products at different prices in domestic and foreign markets, often with the help of subsidies from the government. This is a form of predatory pricing to gain market share in the foreign market.
- Some suggest that domestic workers need to be protected from the low wages in foreign countries. This puts the smaller aggregate loss to small groups ahead of the greater general gains from trade. Also, for many countries, a low wage is their primary comparative advantage.
- Some argue that select industries need protection to ensure they will exist for national defense reasons.
- Clearly, globalization has meant that some U.S. workers have lost jobs to foreign competition, and some advocates would restrict trade on these grounds alone. But, on net, trade has led to higher overall employment. The U.S. government recognizes these issues and has instituted a Trade Adjustment Assistance (TAA) program to help workers who lose their jobs transition to new employment.
- Concern about the environment is often a factor in trade negotiations. Those concerned about globalization want to ensure that firms do not move production to countries with lax environmental laws, while others are concerned that environmental regulation not be used to justify protectionism. Trade ultimately raises income and environmental awareness in developing nations.
- Some antiglobalization activists consider shifting production to countries with low wages as exploitation and demand that wages be increased in other countries. Globalization has typically resulted in higher wages in developing nations, but not up to the standards of developed nations.

**QUESTION:** "The biggest gains in exports, imports, employment, and wages all occurred during the 1990s which was one of our greatest periods of economic growth. Thus it is clear that trade benefits both consumers and the economy." Evaluate this statement.

Answers to the Checkpoint question can be found at the end of this chapter.

## Key Concepts

Absolute advantage, p. 598
Comparative advantage, p. 598
Terms of trade, p. 601
Tariff, p. 603
Quota, p. 604
Infant industry, p. 606
Dumping, p. 607

## Chapter Summary

### The Gains from Trade

Worldwide foreign trade has quadrupled over the past 25 years. Improved communications and transportation technologies have worked together to promote global economic integration. Most governments around the world have reduced trade barriers in recent years.

Free trade has not always been popular. In 1929–1930, many countries attempted to protect their domestic industries by imposing trade restrictions that discouraged imports. In 1930, the United States enacted the Smoot-Hawley tariffs, which imposed an average tax of 60% on imported goods. This hurt industries around the world and has been credited with adding to the depth of the global depression.

In a zero-sum game such as poker, for one party to gain, the other party must lose. Voluntary exchange and trade is a positive-sum game, meaning that both parties to a transaction can gain. These gains arise because of comparative advantage.

One country has an absolute advantage over another if it can produce more of some good than the other country. A country has a comparative advantage over another if its opportunity cost to produce some good is lower than the other country's. Even when one country has an absolute advantage over another, both stand to benefit from trade if each focuses its production on the goods or industries with a comparative advantage.

### The Terms of Trade

The terms of trade determine the prices of imports and exports. When countries trade many commodities, the terms of trade are defined as the average price of exports divided by the average price of imports.

When two countries begin trading, the price charged for one good may be different in the two countries. As market forces lead each country to focus its production on the goods and industries at which it has a comparative advantage, that good's price will tend to equalize in the two countries, moving to an equilibrium level somewhere between the two original prices.

Though beneficial to both countries, trade produces winners and losers. Losers often seek trade restrictions.

The most common forms of trade restrictions are tariffs and quotas. A tariff is a tax on imports.

Tariffs generate revenues while driving a wedge between a product's domestic price and its price on the world market. When a tariff is imposed on a product, its price will rise. This benefits domestic producers, increasing their sales and the price they can charge, but the resulting price increase hurts domestic consumers. The government collects the tariff revenues.

Quotas restrict the quantity of imports into a country. Quotas have much the same effect as tariffs, except that they do not generate revenues for the government.

### Arguments Against Free Trade

Despite the many benefits of free trade, arguments continue for restricting trade. One is that infant industries exist and require some protection to survive. The problem is determining when these industries mature.

Some American trade laws target dumping, which occurs when a foreign firm sells its goods below cost in the United States or at a price below what it charges in its domestic market. If the federal government determines that a foreign firm is dumping products onto the American market, it can impose antidumping tariffs on the offending products.

Some advocates of trade barriers maintain that domestic firms and their workers need to be protected from displacement by cheap foreign labor. Most economists estimate that the benefits of lower-priced imported goods exceed the costs of lost employment. The federal government has resisted imposing measures to protect jobs, instead funding programs that help displaced workers transition to new lines of work.

In times of national crisis or war, the United States must be able to rely on key domestic industries such as oil, steel, and the defense industry. Some argue that these industries require some protection even during peacetime to ensure that they exist when a crisis strikes and importing resources may be difficult.

Some critics argue that increased trade and globalization spell job losses for domestic workers. Increased trade, however, allows firms that are exporters to expand their operations and hire new workers. For workers who lose their jobs, switching industries can be difficult and time consuming, and often requires new investments in human capital. American trade policy recognizes this problem. The Trade Adjustment Assistance (TAA) program provides workers with job search assistance, job training, and some relocation allowances.

Concerns about globalization, trade, and environmental degradation are countered by the rising income brought on by trade, which in turn increases the demand for environmental protections.

Some antiglobalization activists argue that for the United States to trade with developing countries where wages are low and working conditions are deplorable simply exploits workers in these developing countries. But restricting trade with these countries would probably do more harm than good. Low wages reflect low investments in human capital, low productivity, and low living standards characteristic of developing nations. Blocking trade with these nations may deprive them of their only chance to grow and thus improve in these areas.

## Questions and Problems

### Check Your Understanding

1. What is the difference between absolute and comparative advantage? Why would Michelle Wie, who is better than you at both golf and laundry, still hire you to do her wash?
2. Who are the beneficiaries from a large U.S. tariff on French and German wine? Who are the losers?

### Apply the Concepts

3. Brandeis University professor Stephen Cecchetti has argued that "if people understood the benefits of free trade as well as they do the rules of a favorite sport, there would be solid support for trade liberalization." Do you agree with Professor Cecchetti? Why or why not?
4. South Korean film production companies have been protected for half a century by policies enacted to protect an infant industry. But beginning in July 2006, the days that local films *must* be shown by any movie house was reduced to 73 from 146. South Korean film celebrities and the industry are fighting the changes even though local films command half the box office. Why would a country enact special protection for the local film industry? Who would be the major competitor threatening the South Korean film industry? If films made by the local industry must be shown 146 days a year, does the local industry have much incentive to develop good films and be competitive with the rest of the world?

5. Expanding trade in general benefits both countries, or they would not willingly engage in trade. But we also know that consumers and society often gain while particular industries or workers lose. Since society and consumers gain, why don't the many gainers compensate the few losers for their loss?
6. Some activist groups are calling for "fair trade laws" in which other countries would be required to meet or approach our environmental standards and provide wage and working conditions approaching those of developed nations in order to be able to trade with us. Is this just another form of rent seeking by industries and unions for protection from overseas competition?
7. Is outsourcing another example of the benefits of trade, in this case, trade between two companies? Many of the opponents of outsourcing are fans of the "open source" software movement that farms programming out to "volunteer" programmers or firms around the world. These individuals or firms must give their changes to the software to the open source community (run by a few people) and cannot sell the software, but can charge for services such as a help desk, technical improvements, or other services. Does the open source concept seem like trade between individuals?
8. Why is there free trade between states in the United States but not necessarily between countries?
9. Several decades ago, at the behest of the United Auto Workers (UAW) union and General Motors, Ford, and Chrysler, quotas were placed on the importation of Japanese cars to protect American auto manufacturers. Why didn't these quotas work? Would additional trade restrictions benefit American auto workers in the UAW? Would they benefit American consumers?
10. Remittances from developed countries are over $200 billion each year. These funds are sent to their home countries by migrants in developed nations. Is this similar to the gains from trade discussed in this chapter, or are these workers just taking jobs that workers in developed countries would be paid more to do in the absence of the migrants?
11. Why might protectionist trade barriers not save American jobs or benefit the economy?
12. Suppose Brazil developed a secret process that effectively quadrupled its output of coffee from its coffee plantations. This secret process enabled it to significantly undercut the prices of U.S. domestic producers. Would domestic producers receive a sympathetic ear to calls for protection from Brazil's lower-cost coffee? How is this case different from that of protection against cheap foreign labor?
13. Three economists estimated the benefits of trade to the American economy since 1950.[3] Looking at the benefits from comparative advantage, economies of scale, diffusion of production technology, and many other factors, they estimated that trade accounted for roughly 20% of the gains in GDP per person. With such gains from trade to the average household, why would so many people seem to be against trade and globalization?

## In the News

14. Economist Steven Landsburg (*New York Times* January 16, 2008, p. A23) makes the point that "bullying and protectionism have a lot in common. They both use force (either directly or through the power of the law) to enrich someone else at your involuntary expense. If you're forced to pay $20 an hour to an American for goods you could have bought from a Mexican for $5 an hour, you're being extorted." He also argues, "Surely we have fellow citizens who are hurt by those [trade] agreements, at least in the limited sense that they'd be better off in a world where trade

[3] Scott C. Bradford, Paul L. E. Grieco, and Gary Clyde Hufbauer, "The Payoff to America from Global Integration," in C. Fred Bergsten and the Institute for International Economics, *The United States and the World Economy* (Washington, DC: Institute for International Economics, 2005), Chap. 2.

flourishes, except in this one instance. What do we owe those fellow citizens?" The United States has programs to educate and retrain workers displaced from free trade agreements. Do we even owe them that? Why?

**15.** *The Economist* (November 21, 2009) suggests that in a highly globalized world where production is easily moved to other countries, there is an inherent tension between our desire to reduce carbon emissions to stem global climate change and our commitment to free trade. Do you agree? Why or why not?

## Solving Problems

**16.** The figure below shows the production possibilities frontiers (PPFs) for Italy and India for their domestic production of olives and tea. Without trade, assume that each is consuming olives and tea at point *a*.

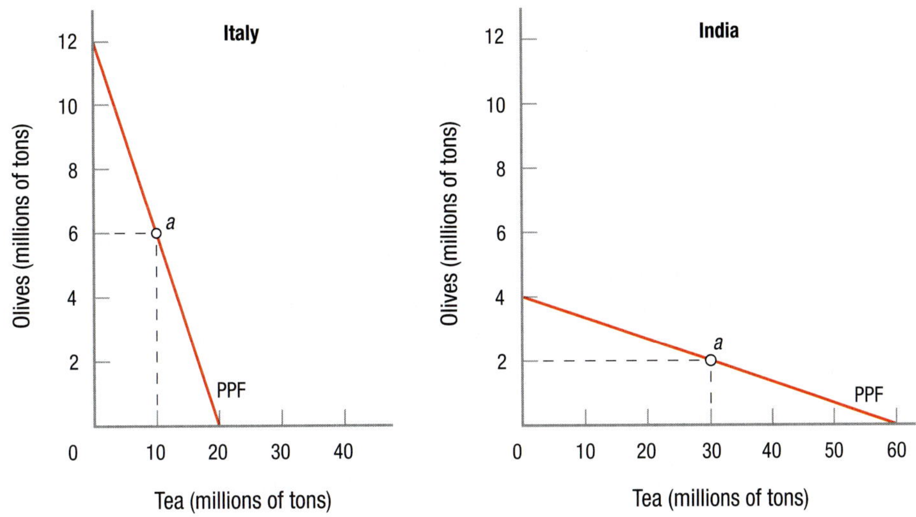


a. If Italy and India were to consider specialization and trade, what commodity would each specialize in? What is India's opportunity cost for tea and olives? What is Italy's opportunity cost for tea and olives?

b. Assume the two countries agree to specialize entirely in one product (the one in which each country has a comparative advantage), and agree to split the total output between them. Complete the table below. Are both countries better off after trade?

| Country and Product | | Before Specialization | After Specialization | After Trade |
|---|---|---|---|---|
| Italy | Olives | 6 million tons | _______ | _______ |
| | Tea | 10 million tons | _______ | _______ |
| India | Olives | 2 million tons | _______ | _______ |
| | Tea | 30 million tons | _______ | _______ |

**17.** The figure on the next page shows the annual domestic demand and supply for 2GB compact flash cards for digital cameras.

a. Assume the worldwide price of these 2GB cards is $10. What percent of United States sales would be imported?

b. Assume the U.S. government puts a $5 tariff per card on imports. How many 2GB flash cards would be imported into the United States?

c. Given the tariff in question b, how much revenue would the government collect from this tariff?

d. Given the tariff in question b, how much more sales revenue would domestic companies enjoy as a result of the tariff?

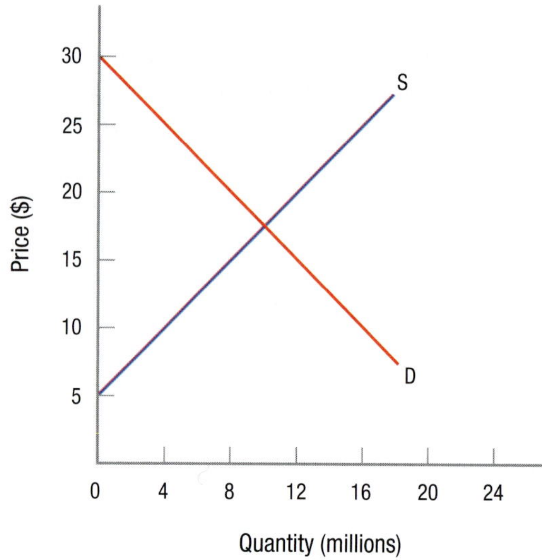


**18.** Most of the developed countries (Canada, Australia, the United States, Switzerland and Hong Kong) in the By-The-Numbers graph at the beginning of the chapter have relatively low tariff barriers while much the developing world still has high tariffs on imports. What reasons might account for why these countries continue to have high tariffs?

## Answers to Questions in CheckPoints

### Check Point: The Gains From Trade

Yes, in general, nations would not trade unless they benefit. However, as we have seen, even though nations as a whole gain, specific groups—industries and their workers who do not have a comparative advantage—lose.

### Check Point: The Terms of Trade

When a quota is imposed, the first beneficiary is the domestic industry. Competition from foreign competition is limited. If the market is important enough (as we saw with automobiles), the foreign companies build new plants in the United States and compete as if they are domestic firms. A second beneficiary is foreign competitors in that they can increase the price or complexity of their products and increase their margins. Losers are consumers and, to some extent, the government, because a tariff could have accomplished the same reduction in imports and the government would have collected some revenue.

### Check Point: Arguments Against Free Trade

Clearly the 1990s were a period of high growth in both trade and employment. The 1990s were also a time of heavy investment by businesses in technology and communications. Some industries and their employees were losers from trade, but the economy and other industries were clearly winners. Production employment has been on a steady decline over the last half-century as services have become more important. When the most recent recession led to lost jobs and unemployment rose, more attention was focused on trade and outsourcing as a source of those lost jobs.

# Open Economy Macroeconomics

# 26

Roussel Bernard/Alamy

**You probably are aware of** international finance if you have traveled abroad. To purchase goods and services in another country, you need to have an amount of that country's currency. True, you can use credit cards for major purchases, but you still need some currency for daily transactions. In Britain, you need to pay in British pounds; in France, you need euros. British and French shopkeepers and public transportation officials will not accept dollars. This means that sometime at the beginning of your trip, whether at the airport or a bank, you have to exchange your dollars for the currency of the country you are visiting.

As with tourism, so with international trade. You may pay dollars for your Burberry scarf or Louis Vuitton handbag in a store in the United States, but eventually your dollars have to be converted to foreign currency when your payments make their way back to the host country. And if U.S. companies export goods abroad, they will want to bring dollars back to the United States, whether they get paid originally in the host country's currency or not.

Furthermore, in today's open economies, individuals can hold domestic and foreign financial assets. Your own financial portfolio might include foreign stocks, bonds, and currency, as well as domestic stocks and bonds. Buying and selling foreign securities and goods involves the buying and selling of foreign currency, also known as foreign exchange.

We can see that foreign exchange transactions for tourism, trade, and investment would seem to be large in number and amount. Yet, foreign exchange transactions dwarf the volume of exports and imports, often by as much as 30 to 40 times, in the same way that the annual value of all stock transactions far surpasses the market value of all companies on the New York Stock Exchange. Most foreign exchange transactions are conducted not for trade but for financial or speculative purposes. The social benefit to emerge from this speculation is a highly liquid foreign exchange market that ensures the possibility of

**After studying this chapter you should be able to:**

- ☐ Define the current account and the capital account in the balance of payments between countries.
- ☐ Describe the difference between nominal and real exchange rates.
- ☐ Describe the effects of currency appreciation or depreciation on imports and exports.
- ☐ Describe the effects of changes in inflation rates, disposable income, and interest rates on exchange rates.
- ☐ Describe the differences between fixed and flexible exchange rate systems.
- ☐ Describe the implications for fiscal and monetary policies of fixed and flexible exchange rate systems.

trade. The large volume of speculative trade in currencies means that there will always be a market for international trade.

In this chapter, we want to look at foreign exchange markets to get a sense of how policymaking in the United States is affected by an open worldwide economy. We start with balance of payments accounts, which are to open economy macroeconomics what national income accounts are to an individual country's macroeconomic accounts. This accounting structure is the basis for open economy analysis. We then examine the foreign exchange market in detail, looking at both the trade and financial aspects of those common foreign currency events: currency appreciation and depreciation. Finally, we put this all together when we view fixed and flexible exchange rate systems and discuss how an open economy affects monetary and fiscal policymaking.

## The Balance of Payments

All open economies have balance of payments accounts. Open financial markets permit economies to run trade surpluses and deficits.

A simplified version of the U.S. balance of payments accounts for 2009 is shown in Table 1. These accounts were compiled by the Commerce Department's Bureau of Economic Analysis. The balance of payments represents all payments received from foreign countries and all payments made to them. Notice that the accounts are split into two broad divisions, the current account and the capital account.

**TABLE 1** The Balance of Payments 2009—Preliminary (billions of U.S. dollars)

| | | |
|---|---|---|
| **Current Account** | | |
| Exports | 1,554.7 | |
| Imports | −1,933.3 | |
| Balance of trade | | −378.6 |
| Income received (inflow) | 561.2 | |
| Income payments (outflow) | −472.2 | |
| Balance on income | | 89.0 |
| Net transfers | | −130.0 |
| Current account balance | | −419.6 |
| **Capital Account** | | |
| Increase in foreign-owned assets in the United States | 435.2 | |
| Increase in U.S.-owned assets abroad | −237.5 | |
| Net increase in foreign-owned holdings | | 197.7 |
| Statistical discrepancy | | 221.9 |
| Capital account | | 419.6 |

### The Current Account

**Current account:** Includes payments for imports and exports of goods and services, incomes flowing into and out of the country, and net transfers of money.

The **current account** includes payments for imports and exports of goods and services, incomes flowing into and out of the country, and net transfers of money.

#### Imports and Exports

In 2009, U.S. exports were $1,554.7 billion, with imports totaling $1,933.3 billion. This exchange produced a trade deficit of $378.6 billion because we imported more than we exported. Some balance of payments accounts break exports and imports into separate categories of goods and services; here they are combined. This component of the current account is known as the balance of trade.

### Income

Another source of foreign payments to the United States comprises income flows, which include wages, rents, interest, and profits that Americans earn abroad ($561.2 billion in 2009) minus the corresponding income foreigners earn in the United States ($472.2 billion). On balance, foreigners earned $89.0 billion less in the United States than U.S. citizens and corporations earned abroad in 2009.

### Transfers

Direct transfers of money also take place between the United States and other countries. These transfers includes foreign aid, funds sent to such international organizations as the United Nations, and stipends paid directly to foreign students studying in the United States or U.S. students studying abroad. These transfers also include the money that people working in the United States send back to their families in foreign countries. Net transfers for 2009 totaled –$130.0 billion.

Adding all current account categories for 2009 yields a current account deficit of $419.6 billion. In 2009, the United States paid out over $400 billion dollars more than it received. So, the United States had to borrow $419.6 billion from the rest of the world, or the net holdings of U.S. assets by foreigners must have increased by that same amount, or some combination of the two.

## The Capital Account

The **capital account** summarizes the flow of money into and out of domestic and foreign assets. This account includes investments by foreign companies in domestic plants or subsidiaries—a Toyota truck plant in Tennessee, for example. Note that the profits from such investments flow abroad, and thus they are in the income payments (outflow) category of the current account. Other foreign holdings of U.S. assets include portfolio investments such as mutual funds, stock, and bonds, and deposits in U.S. banks. American investors hold foreign financial assets in their portfolios, including foreign stocks and bonds. And American companies own plants and other assets in foreign countries.

**Capital account:** Summarizes the flow of money into and out of domestic and foreign assets, including investments by foreign companies in domestic plants or subsidiaries, and other foreign holdings of U.S. assets, including mutual funds, stock, bonds, and deposits in U.S. banks. Also included are U.S. investors' holdings of foreign financial assets, production facilities, and other assets in foreign countries.

Because the United States ran a current account deficit in 2009, it must run a capital account surplus. Net capital inflows into the United States must equal more than $400 billion to offset the current account deficit. Indeed, foreign-owned assets in the United States rose by $435.2 billion, while U.S. ownership of foreign assets increased by only $237.5 billion, resulting in a net inflow of capital of $419.6 billion. Note that because these are preliminary figures for 2009, the statistical discrepancy is particularly large.

The key point to remember is that balance of payments accounts have to show a balance: A deficit in the current account must be offset by a corresponding surplus in the capital account, and vice versa. Keep this point in mind as we go on to look at foreign exchange and policy implications of an open economy.

**CHECKPOINT**

### THE BALANCE OF PAYMENTS

- The balance of payments represents all payments received from foreign countries and all payments made to them.
- The balance of payments is split into two categories: current and capital accounts.
- The current account includes payment for exports and imports, income flows, and net transfers of money.
- The capital account summarizes flows of money into and out of domestic and foreign assets.
- The sum of the current and capital account balances must equal zero.

**QUESTION:** Ronald McKinnon (*Wall Street Journal*, April 20, 2006) noted, "China's saving is even higher than its own extraordinary high domestic investment of 40% of GDP. . . . The result is that China (like many other countries in Asia) naturally runs an overall current account surplus." Why would this be true? (*Hint:* Look back at the discussion on the relationship between federal and trade deficits in the chapter on federal deficits and public debt.)

Answers to the Checkpoint question can be found at the end of this chapter.

## Exchange Rates

As we saw in the introduction to this chapter, if you wish to go abroad or buy a product directly from a foreign firm, you need to exchange dollars for foreign currency. Today, credit cards automatically convert currencies for you, making the transaction more convenient. This conversion does not, however, alter the transaction's underlying structure.

But when you decide to travel abroad, the value of the dollar compared to the currency where you are going determines how expensive your trip will be. Figure 1 shows the trade-weighted exchange index value of the dollar compared to a wide range of currencies. The value of the dollar has generally been slowly rising until the early part of this century. This section looks at the issues of exchange rates and their determination.

**FIGURE 1—The Value of the Dollar**

The trade-weighted exchange index, a weighted average of the foreign exchange value of the dollar against a broad group of U.S. trading partners, is shown. Generally, the value of the dollar rose between 1975 and the early 2000s. After that, rising deficits and low interest rates put downward pressure on the dollar.

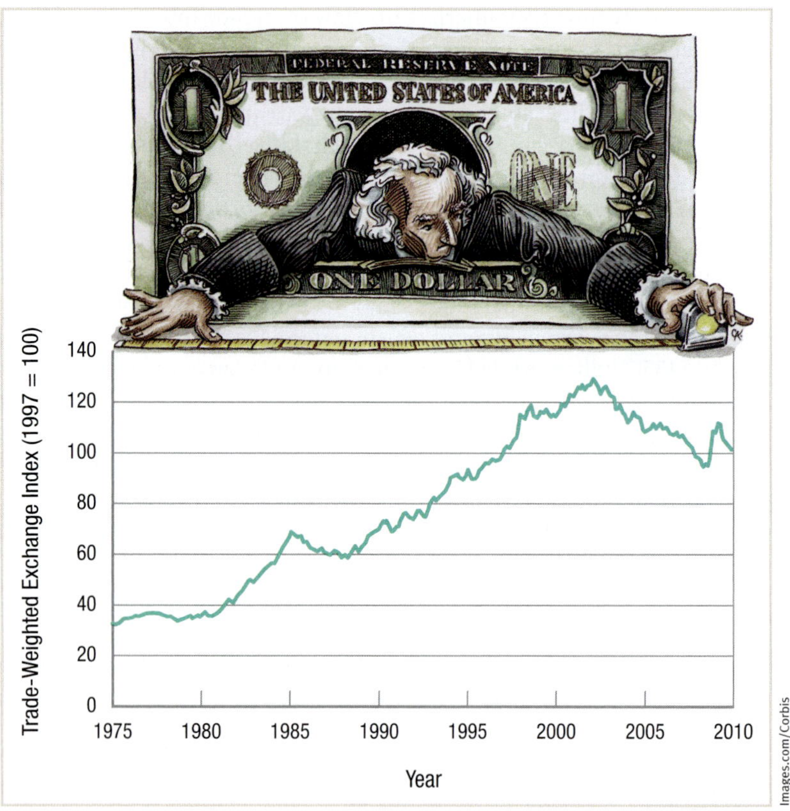


### Defining Exchange Rates

**Exchange rate:** The rate at which one currency can be exchanged for another, or just the price of one currency for another.

The **exchange rate** defines the rate at which one currency, such as U.S. dollars, can be exchanged for another, such as British pounds. The exchange rate is nothing more than the price of one currency for another. Table 2 shows exchange rates for selected countries for a specific date (April 9, 2010), as reported in the *Wall Street Journal*. Traditionally,

**TABLE 2** Exchange Rates (April 9, 2010)

| | Exchange Rates | |
|---|---|---|
| | U.S. Dollars | Currency Per U.S. Dollar |
| Argentina (peso) | 0.2580 | 3.876 |
| Australia (dollar) | 0.9328 | 1.072 |
| Brazil (real) | 0.5659 | 1.767 |
| Britain (pound) | 1.5379 | 0.650 |
| Canada (dollar) | 0.9960 | 1.004 |
| Japan (yen) | 0.0107 | 93.171 |
| Mexico (peso) | 0.0820 | 12.192 |
| Peru (new sol) | 0.3532 | 2.837 |
| Russia (ruble) | 0.0343 | 29.138 |

**Source:** *The Wall Street Journal.*

exchange rates were always quoted as the number of units of a foreign currency required to purchase one unit of domestic currency. As Table 2 illustrates, however, exchange rates are often listed from both perspectives.

## Nominal Exchange Rates

According to Table 2, 1 British pound will buy 1.54 dollars. Equivalently, 1 dollar will purchase 0.65 pound. These numbers are reciprocal measures of each other ($1 \div 1.54 = 0.65$).

## Real Exchange Rates

A **nominal exchange rate** is the price of one country's currency for another. The **real exchange rate** takes the price levels of both countries into account. Real exchange rates become important when inflation is an issue in one country. The real exchange rate between two countries is defined as

$$e_r = e_n \times (P_d/P_f),$$

where is $e_r$ is the real exchange rate, $e_n$ is the nominal exchange rate, $P_d$ is the domestic price level, and $P_f$ is the foreign price level.

The real exchange rate is simply the nominal exchange rate multiplied by the ratio of the price levels of the two countries. In a broad sense, the real exchange rate may be viewed as a measure of the price competitiveness between the two countries. When prices rise in one country, its products are not as competitive in world markets.

Let us take British and American cars as an example. Assume Britain suffers significant inflation that pushes the price of Land Rovers up by 15% in Britain. The United States, meanwhile, suffers no such inflation of its price level. If the dollar-to-pound exchange rate remains constant for the moment, the price of Land Rovers in the U.S. market will climb, while domestic auto prices remain constant.

Now Land Rovers are not as competitive as before, resulting in fewer sales. Note, however, that the resulting reduction in U.S. purchases of British cars and other items will reduce the demand for British pounds. This puts downward pressure on the pound, reducing its exchange value and restoring some competitiveness. Markets do adjust! We will look at this issue in more detail later in the chapter.

**Nominal exchange rate:** The rate at which one currency can be exchanged for another.

**Real exchange rate:** The price of one country's currency for another when the price levels of both countries are taken into account; important when inflation is an issue in one country; it is equal to the nominal exchange rate multiplied by the ratio of the price levels of the two countries.

## Purchasing Power Parity

**Purchasing power parity** (PPP) is the rate of exchange that allows a specific amount of currency in one country to purchase the same quantity of goods in another country. Absolute PPP would mean that nominal exchange rates equaled the same purchasing

**Purchasing power parity:** The rate of exchange that allows a specific amount of currency in one country to purchase the same quantity of goods in another country.

power in each country. As a result, the real exchange rate would be equal to 1. For example, PPP would exist if 4 dollars bought a meal in the United States, and the same 4 dollars converted to British pounds (say, roughly 2 pounds) bought the same meal in London.

If you have traveled abroad, you know that PPP is not absolute. Some countries, such as Malaysia and Thailand, are known as cheap countries, while others can be expensive, such as Denmark and Israel. The *Economist* annually publishes a "Big Mac Index," a lighthearted attempt to capture the notion of PPP.

Table 3 presents some recent estimates of PPP and the Big Mac Index. It also shows the PPP implied by the relative cost of Big Macs, along with the actual exchange rate. When comparing these two, we get an approximate over- or understating of the exchange rate. Keep in mind that the cost of a McDonald's Big Mac may be influenced by many unique local factors (trade barriers on beef, customs duties, taxes, competition), and therefore it may not reflect real PPP. Also, in some countries where beef is not consumed, chicken patties are substituted; and in still other countries, vegetarian patties are used. Note that a Big Mac is cheap in China and Thailand and expensive in Denmark.

**TABLE 3** Measures of Purchasing Power Parity

| | Big Mac Prices | | | | |
|---|---|---|---|---|---|
| | In Local Currency | In Dollars | Implied PPP of the Dollar | Actual Dollar Exchange Rate (July 2009) | Under(–)/Over (+) against the Dollar (%) |
| United States | $3.57 | 3.57 | | | |
| Argentina | Peso 11.5 | 3.03 | 3.22 | 3.81 | –15 |
| Britain | Pound 2.29 | 3.69 | 1.56 | 1.61 | +3 |
| China | Yuan 12.5 | 1.83 | 3.50 | 6.83 | –49 |
| Denmark | DK 29.5 | 5.53 | 8.62 | 5.34 | +55 |
| Japan | Yen 320 | 3.46 | 89.6 | 92.6 | –3 |
| Mexico | Peso 33 | 2.39 | 9.24 | 13.8 | –33 |
| Switzerland | CHF 6.5 | 5.98 | 1.82 | 1.09 | +68 |
| Taiwan | Taiwan $75 | 2.26 | 21.0 | 33.2 | –37 |
| Thailand | Bhat 64.49 | 1.89 | 18.1 | 34.2 | –47 |

Source: "The Big Mac Index," *The Economist*, July 16, 2009.

Although not perfect, changes in the Big Mac Index often are reflective of movements in true PPP, given that simultaneous changes in several of the factors that distort the index often reflect real changes in the economy.

## Exchange Rate Determination

We have seen that people and institutions have two primary reasons for wanting foreign currency. The first is to purchase goods and services and conduct other transactions under the current account. The second is to purchase foreign investments under the capital account. These transactions create a demand for foreign currency and give rise to a supply of domestic currency available for foreign exchange.

### A Market for Foreign Exchange

Figure 2 shows a representative market for foreign exchange. The horizontal axis measures the quantity of dollars available for foreign exchange, and the vertical axis measures the exchange rate in pounds per dollar. The demand for dollars as foreign exchange is down-

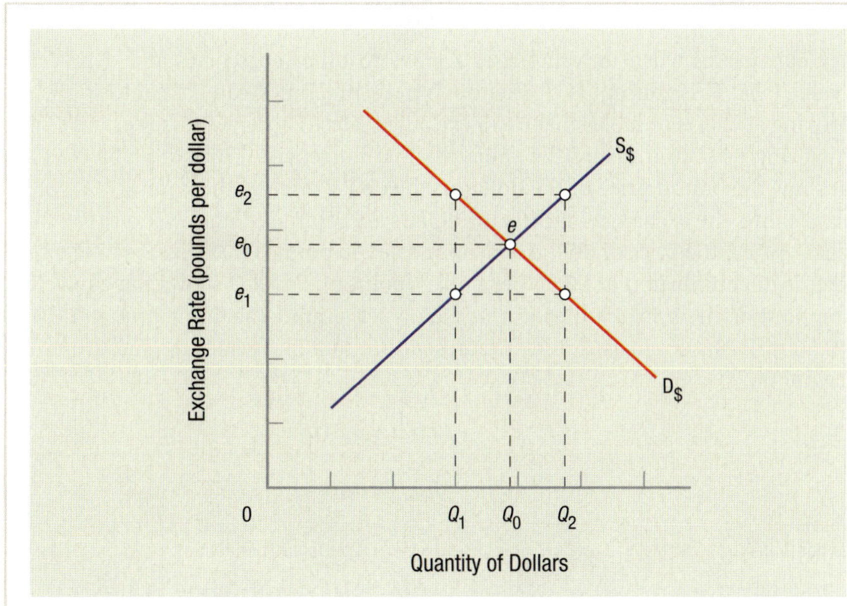


**FIGURE 2—The Foreign Exchange Market for Dollars**

A market for foreign exchange is shown here. The horizontal axis measures the quantity of dollars available for foreign exchange, and the vertical axis measures the exchange rate in pounds per dollar. If exchange rates are fully flexible and the exchange rate is initially $e_1$, there is excess demand for dollars: $Q_2$ minus $Q_1$. The dollar will appreciate and the exchange rate will move to $e_0$. Alternatively, if the exchange rate is initially $e_2$, there is an excess supply of dollars. Since there are more dollars being offered than demanded, the dollar will depreciate. Eventually, the market will settle into an exchange rate of $e_0$, where precisely the quantity of dollars supplied is the quantity demanded.

ward sloping; as the exchange rate falls, U.S. products become more attractive, and more dollars are desired.

Suppose, for example, that the exchange rate at first is \$1 = £1 and that the U.S. game company Electronic Arts manufactures and sells its games at home and in Britain for \$50 (£50). Then suppose the dollar *depreciates* by 50%, such that \$1.00 = £0.50. If the dollar price of a game remains at \$50 in the United States, the pound price of games in Britain will fall to £25 because of the reduction in the exchange rate. This reduction will increase the sales of games in Britain and increase the quantity of dollars British consumers need for foreign exchange. (Note that Figure 2 assumes a very elastic demand for games in Britain. Without this assumption, the analysis gets complicated, so we will assume highly elastic demands throughout this chapter.)

The supply of dollars available for foreign exchange reflects the demand for dollars, since to purchase pounds, U.S. firms or individuals must supply dollars. Not surprisingly, the supply curve for dollars is positively sloped. If the dollar were to *appreciate*, say, moving to \$1 = £2, British goods bought in the United States would look attractive since their dollar price would be cut in half. As Americans purchased more British goods, the demand for pounds would grow, and the quantity of dollars supplied to the foreign exchange market would increase.

## Flexible Exchange Rates

Assume that exchange rates are fully flexible, so the market determines the prevailing exchange rate, and that the exchange rate in Figure 2 is initially $e_1$. At this exchange rate, there is an excess demand for dollars since quantity $Q_2$ is demanded but only $Q_1$ is supplied. The dollar will **appreciate**, or rise in value relative to other currencies, and the exchange rate will move in the direction of $e_0$ (more pounds are required to purchase a dollar). As the dollar appreciates, it becomes more expensive for British consumers, thus reducing the demand for U.S. exports. Because of the appreciating dollar, British imports are more attractive for U.S. consumers, increasing U.S. imports. These forces work to move the exchange rate to $e_0$, closing the gap between $Q_2$ and $Q_1$.

**Currency appreciation:** When the value of a currency rises relative to other currencies.

Alternately, if the exchange rate begins at $e_2$, there will be an excess supply of dollars. Since more dollars are being offered than demanded, the value of dollars relative to British pounds will decline, or **depreciate**. American goods are now more attractive in Britain, increasing American exports and the demand for dollars, while British goods become more expensive for American consumers. Eventually, the market will settle into an exchange rate of $e_0$, at which precisely the quantity of dollars supplied is the quantity demanded.

**Currency depreciation:** When the value of a currency falls relative to other currencies.

## Currency Appreciation and Depreciation

A currency appreciates when its value rises relative to other currencies and depreciates when its value falls. This concept is clear enough in theory, but it can get confusing when we start looking at charts or tables that show exchange rates. The key is to be certain which currency is being used to measure the value of other currencies. Does the table you are looking at show the pound price of the dollar or the dollar price of the pound?

Figure 3 shows the exchange markets for dollars and pounds. Panel A shows the market for dollars, where the price of dollars is denominated in pounds (£/$), just as in Figure 2. This market is in equilibrium at £0.56 per dollar (point *e*). Panel B shows the equivalent market for pounds; it is in equilibrium at $1.78 per pound (again at point *e*). Note that 1 ÷ 0.56 = 1.78, so panels A and B represent the same information, just from different viewpoints.

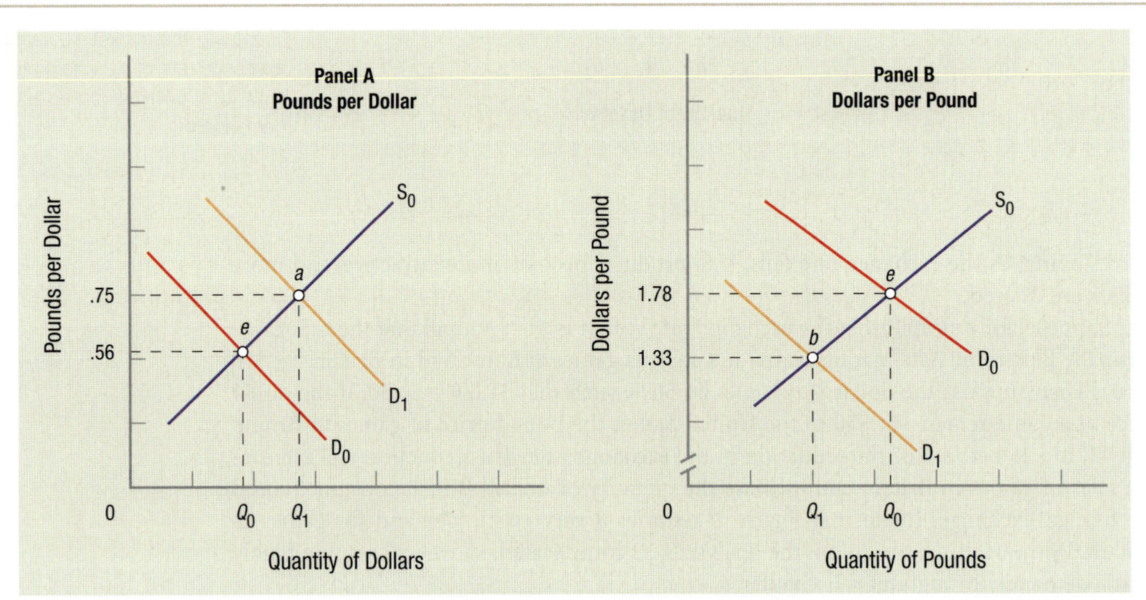


**FIGURE 3—The Foreign Exchange Market**

Data for dollars and pounds are graphically represented here. Panel A shows a market for dollars in which the price of dollars is denominated in pounds (£/$). In panel A, the market is in equilibrium at £0.56 per dollar (point e). Panel B shows the equivalent market for pounds in equilibrium at $1.78 per pound (again at point e). A rise in the demand for dollars means the dollar appreciates to £0.75 per dollar (point *a* in panel A). Panel B shows that the corresponding decline in demand for pounds (from $D_0$ to $D_1$) leads to a depreciation of the pound as the exchange rate falls from $1.78 to $1.33 per pound (point *b*).

Note that a depreciating pound in panel B indicates a decline in the exchange rate, but this simultaneously represents an appreciating dollar. Thus, graphs can be viewed as reflecting either appreciation or depreciation, depending on which currency is being used to establish the point of view.

Assume a rise in the demand for dollars. In panel A, the dollar appreciates to £0.75 per dollar (point *a*), thus leading to a rise in the exchange rate. In panel B, the corresponding decline in demand for pounds (from $D_0$ to $D_1$) leads to a depreciation of the pound and a fall in the exchange rate from $1.78 to $1.33 per pound (point *b*). Notice that the pound's depreciation in panel B produces a decline in the exchange rate, but this decline simultaneously results in appreciation of the dollar. These graphs could be viewed as showing either an appreciation or a depreciation, depending on which currency represents your point of view.

For our purposes, we will try to use figures that show the exchange rate rising when the focus currency appreciates. Still, you need to be aware that exchange rates can be represented in two different ways. Exchange rate graphs are difficult and sometimes confusing, so you will need to think through each graph you encounter. We now turn our discussion to the impact of changing exchange rates on current and capital accounts.

### Determinants of Exchange Rates

What sort of conditions will cause currencies to appreciate or depreciate? First, a change in our tastes and preferences as consumers for foreign goods will result in currency appreciation or depreciation. For example, if we desire to purchase more foreign goods, this will lead to an increase in the demand for foreign currency and result in the depreciation of the dollar.

Second, if our income growth exceeds that of other countries, our demand for imports will grow faster relative to the growth of other nations. This will lead again to an increase in demand for foreign currency, resulting in the depreciation of the dollar.

Third, rising inflation in the United States relative to foreign nations makes our goods and services relatively more expensive overseas and foreign goods more attractive here at home. This results in growing imports, reduced exports, and again leads to a depreciation of the dollar.

Fourth, falling interest rates in the United States relative to foreign countries makes financial investment in the United States less attractive. This reduces the demand for dollars, leading once again to a depreciation of the dollar. Note that if we reverse these stories in each case, the dollar will appreciate.

## Exchange Rates and the Current Account

As we have already seen, the current account includes payments for imports and exports. Also included are changes in income flowing into and out of the country. In this section, we focus on the effect that changes in real exchange rates have on both of these components of the current account. For our purposes, we will continue to assume that import and export demands are highly elastic for real exchange rates.

### Changes in Inflation Rates

Let's assume inflation heats up in Britain, such that the British price level rises relative to U.S. prices, or the dollar appreciates relative to the pound. Production costs rise in Britain, so British goods are more expensive. American goods appear more attractive to British consumers, so exports of American goods rise, improving the American current account. American consumers purchase more domestic goods and fewer British imports because of rising British prices, further improving the American current account. The opposite is true for Britain: British imports rise and exports fall, hurting the British current account.

These results are dependent on our assumption that import and export demands are highly elastic with real exchange rates. Thus, when exchange rates change, exports and imports will change proportionally more than the change in exchange rates.

### Changes in Domestic Disposable Income

If domestic disposable income rises, U.S. consumers will have more money to spend, and given existing exchange rates, imports will rise since some of this increased consumption will go to foreign products. As a result, the current account will worsen as imports rise. The opposite occurs when domestic income falls.

## Exchange Rates and the Capital Account

The capital account summarizes flows of money or capital into and out of U.S. assets. Each day, foreign individuals, companies, and governments put billions of dollars into Treasury bonds, U.S. stocks, companies, and real estate. Today, foreign and domestic assets are available to investors. Foreign investment possibilities include direct investment in projects undertaken by multinational firms, the sale and purchase of foreign stocks and bonds, and the short-term movement of assets in foreign bank accounts.

Because these transactions all involve capital, investors must balance their risks and returns. Two factors essentially incorporate both risk and return for international assets: interest rates and expected changes in exchange rates.

### Interest Rate Changes

If the exchange rate is assumed to be constant, and the assets of two countries are *perfectly substitutable*, then an interest rate rise in one country will cause capital to flow into it from the other country. For example, a rise in interest rates in the United States will cause capital to flow from Britain, where interest rates have not changed, into the United States, where investors can earn a higher rate of return on their investments. Since the assets of both countries are assumed to be perfectly substitutable, this flow will continue until the interest rates ($r$) in Britain and the United States are equal, or

$$r_{US} = r_{UK}$$

Everything else being equal, we can expect capital to flow in the direction of the country that offers the highest interest rate, and thus, the highest return on capital. But "everything else" is rarely equal.

### Exchange Rate Changes

Suppose that the exchange rate for U.S. currency is *expected to appreciate* ($\Delta\varepsilon > 0$). The relationship between the interest rates in the United States and Britain becomes

$$r_{US} = r_{UK} - \Delta\varepsilon$$

Investors demand a higher return in Britain to offset the expected depreciation of the U.K. pound relative to the U.S. dollar. Unless interest rates rise in Britain, capital will flow out of Britain and into the United States until U.S. interest rates fall enough to offset the expected appreciation of the dollar.

If capital is not perfectly mobile and substitutable between two countries, a *risk premium* can be added to the relationship just described; thus,

$$r_{US} = r_{UK} - \Delta\varepsilon + x$$

where $x$ is the risk premium. Expected exchange rate changes and risk premium changes can produce enduring interest rate differentials between two countries.

If the dollar falls relative to the yen, the euro, and the British pound, this is a sign that foreign investors were not as enthusiastic about U.S. investments. Low interest rates and high deficits may have convinced foreign investors that it was not a good time to invest in the United States. The United States is more dependent on foreign capital than ever before. Today, more than half of U.S. Treasury debt held by the public is held by foreigners. Changes in inflation, interest rates, and expectations about exchange rates are important.

## Exchange Rates and Aggregate Supply and Demand

How do changes in nominal exchange rates affect aggregate demand and aggregate supply? A change in nominal exchange rates will affect imports and exports. Consider what happens, for example, when the exchange rate for the dollar depreciates. The dollar is weaker, and thus the pound (or any other currency) will buy more dollars. American products become more attractive in foreign markets, so American exports increase and aggregate demand expands. Yet, because some inputs into the production process may be imported (raw materials, computer programming services, or call answering services), input costs will rise, causing aggregate supply to contract.

Let us take a more detailed look at this process by considering Figure 4. Assume the economy begins in equilibrium at point *e*, with full employment output $Q_f$ and the price level at $P_e$. As the dollar depreciates, this will spur an increase in exports, thus shifting

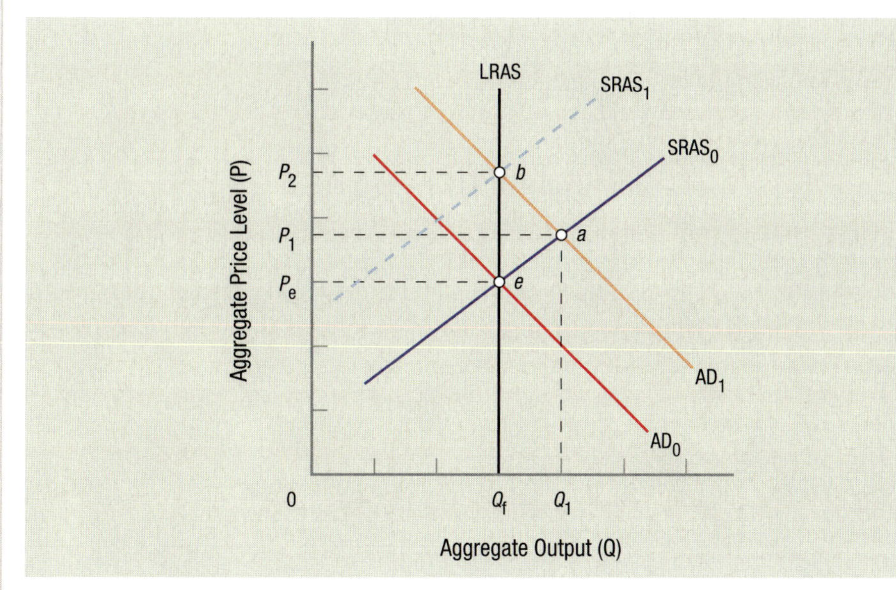


**FIGURE 4—Exchange Rates and Aggregate Demand and Supply**

Assume the economy initially begins in equilibrium at point *e*, with full employment output $Q_f$ and the price level at $P_e$. Assume the dollar depreciates. This will increase exports, shifting aggregate demand from $AD_0$ to $AD_1$ and raising prices to $P_1$ and output to $Q_1$ in the short run. In the long run, short-run aggregate supply will shift from $SRAS_0$ to $SRAS_1$, as workers readjust their wage demands in the long run, thus moving the economy to point *b*. As the economy adjusts to a higher price level, the benefits from currency depreciation are greatly reduced.

aggregate demand from $AD_0$ to $AD_1$ and raising prices to $P_1$ in the short run. Initially, output climbs to $Q_1$, but since some of the economy's inputs are imported, short-run aggregate supply will decline, mitigating this rise in output. In the short run, the economy will expand beyond $Q_f$, and prices will rise.

In the longer term, as domestic prices rise, workers will realize that their real wages do not purchase as much as before, since import prices are higher. As a result, workers will start demanding higher wages just to bring them back to where they were originally. This shifts short-run aggregate supply from $SRAS_0$ to $SRAS_1$, thereby moving the economy from point *a* in the short run to point *b* in the long run. As the economy adjusts to a higher price level, the original benefits accruing from currency depreciation will be greatly reduced.

Currency depreciation works because imports become more expensive and exports less so. When this happens, consumer income no longer goes as far, since the price of domestic goods does not change, but the cost of imports rises. In countries where imports form a substantial part of household spending, major depreciations in the national currency can produce significant declines in standards of living. Such depreciations (or devaluations) have occasioned strikes and, in some cases, even street riots; recent examples include Argentina, Brazil, Mexico, and Indonesia.

What are the implications of all this for policymakers? First, a currency depreciation or devaluation can, after a period, simply lead to inflation. In most cases, however, the causation probably goes the other way: Macroeconomic policies or economic events force currency depreciations.

Trade balances usually improve with an exchange rate depreciation. Policymakers can get improved current account balances without inflation by pursuing devaluation first, then pursuing fiscal contraction (reducing government spending or increasing taxes), and finally moving the economy back to point *e* in Figure 4. But here again, the real long-run benefit is more stable monetary and fiscal policies.

## CHECKPOINT

### EXCHANGE RATES

- Nominal exchange rates define the rate at which one currency can be exchanged for another.
- Real exchange rates are the nominal exchange rates multiplied by the ratio of the price levels of the two countries.

- Purchasing power parity (PPP) is a rate of exchange that permits a given level of currency to purchase the same amount of goods and services in another country.
- A currency appreciates when its value rises relative to other currencies. Currency devaluation causes a currency to lose value relative to others.
- Inflation causes depreciation of a country's currency, worsening its current account. Rising domestic income typically results in rising imports and a deteriorating current account.
- Rising interest rates cause capital to flow into the country with the higher interest rate, and expectations about a future currency appreciation or depreciation affect the capital account.
- Currency appreciation and depreciation have an effect on aggregate supply and demand. For example, currency depreciation expands aggregate demand as exports increase, but some (now high-priced) imported inputs are inputs into production, reducing aggregate supply.

**QUESTION:** If China were to revalue its currency by 10% so that, in effect, the yuan appreciated by 10%, would this have an impact on the U.S. current account?

Answers to the Checkpoint question can be found at the end of this chapter.

# Monetary and Fiscal Policy in an Open Economy

How monetary and fiscal policy is affected by international trade and finance depends on the type of exchange rate system in existence. There are several ways exchange rate systems can be organized. We will discuss the two major categories: fixed and flexible rates.

## Fixed and Flexible Exchange Rate Systems

**Fixed exchange rate:** Each government determines its exchange rate, then uses macroeconomic policy to maintain the rate.

**Flexible or floating exchange rate:** A country's currency exchange rate is determined in international currency exchange markets, given the country's macroeconomic policies.

A **fixed exchange rate** system is one in which governments determine their exchange rates, then adjust macroeconomic policies to maintain these rates. A **flexible or floating exchange rate** system, in contrast, relies on currency markets to determine the exchange rates consistent with macroeconomic conditions.

Before the Great Depression, most of the world economies were on the gold standard. According to Peter Temin, the gold standard was characterized by "(1) the free flow of gold between individuals and countries, (2) the maintenance of fixed values of national currencies in terms of gold and therefore each other, and (3) the absence of an international coordinating organization."[1]

Under the gold standard, each country had to maintain enough gold stocks to keep the value of its currency fixed to that of others. If a country's imports exceeded its exports, this balance of payments deficit had to come from its gold stocks. Since gold backed the national currency, the country would have to reduce the amount of money circulating in its economy, thereby reducing expenditures, output, and income. This reduction would lead to a decline in prices and wages, a rise in exports (which were getting cheaper), and a corresponding drop in imports (which were becoming more expensive). This process would continue until imports and exports were again equalized and the flow of gold ended.

In the early 1930s, the U.S. Federal Reserve pursued a contractionary monetary policy intended to cool off the overheated economy of the 1920s. This policy reduced imports and increased the flow of gold into the United States. With France pursuing a similar deflationary policy, by 1932 these two countries held more than 70% of the world's monetary gold.

[1] Peter Temin, *Lessons from the Great Depression: The Lionel Robbins Lectures for 1989* (Cambridge, MA: MIT Press), 1989, p. 8.

Other countries attempted to conserve their gold stocks by selling off assets, thereby spurring a worldwide monetary contraction. As other monetary authorities attempted to conserve their gold reserves, moreover, they reduced the liquidity available to their banks, thereby inadvertently causing bank failures. In this way, the Depression in the United States spread worldwide.

As World War II came to an end, the Allies met in Bretton Woods, New Hampshire, to design a new and less troublesome international monetary system. Exchange rates were set, and each country agreed to use its monetary authorities to buy and sell its own currency to maintain its exchange rate at fixed levels.

The Bretton Woods agreements created the International Monetary Fund to aid countries having trouble maintaining their exchange rates. In addition, the World Bank was established to loan money to countries for economic development. In the end, most countries were unwilling to make the tough adjustments required by a fixed rate system, and it collapsed in the early 1970s. Today, we operate on a flexible exchange rate system in which each currency floats in the market.

## Policies Under Fixed Exchange Rates

When the government engages in expansionary policy, aggregate demand rises, resulting in output and price increases. Figure 5 shows the result of such a policy as an increase in aggregate demand from $AD_0$ to $AD_1$, with the economy moving from equilibrium at point *a* to point *b* in the short run and the price level rising from $P_0$ to $P_1$. A rising domestic price level means that U.S. exports will decline as they become more expensive. As incomes rise, imports will rise. Combined, these forces will worsen the current account, moving it into deficit or reducing a surplus, as net exports decline.

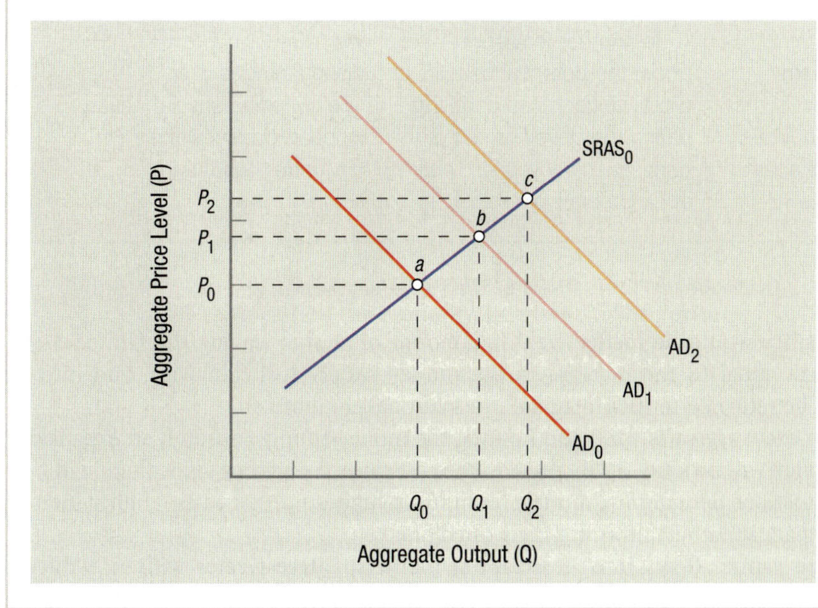


**FIGURE 5—Monetary and Fiscal Policy in an Open Economy**

When the government engages in expansionary policy, aggregate demand rises, resulting in output and price increases. A rising domestic price level means that U.S. exports will decline as they become more expensive. As incomes rise, imports will rise. Combined, these forces will worsen the current account, moving it into deficit or reducing a surplus, as net exports decline.

An expansionary monetary policy, combined with a neutral fiscal policy, will result in a rising money supply and falling interest rates. Lower interest rates result in capital outflow. This reduces the domestic money supply. The greater the capital mobility, the more the money supply is reduced, and the more aggregate demand moves back in the direction of $AD_0$.

An expansionary monetary policy, combined with a fiscal policy that is neither expansionary nor contractionary, will result in a rising money supply and falling interest rates. In Figure 5, this causes aggregate demand to rise to $AD_1$. Lower interest rates result in capital flowing from the United States to other countries. This reduces the U.S. money supply.

The greater the capital mobility, the more the money supply is reduced, and the more aggregate demand moves back in the direction of $AD_0$. With perfect capital mobility,

## Nobel Prize

### Robert Mundell

Awarded the Nobel Prize in 1999, Robert Mundell is best known for his groundbreaking work in international economics and for his contribution to the development of supply-side economic theory. Born in Canada in 1932, he attended the University of British Columbia as an undergraduate and studied at the University of Washington and the London School of Economics before earning his Ph.D. from the Massachusetts Institute of Technology in 1956. For a year, he served as a postdoctoral fellow at the University of Chicago, where he met the economist Arthur Laffer, his collaborator in the development of supply-side theory.

Hugh Threlfall/Alamy

Supply-side economists advocated reductions in marginal tax rates and stabilization of the international monetary system in an effort to overcome *stagflation,* the persistent combination of economic stagnation and inflation that plagued the United States and other countries during the 1970s. This approach was distinct from the two dominant schools of economic thought, Keynesianism and Milton Friedman's monetarism, though it shared some ideas with both. Mundell's work had a major influence on the economic policies of President Ronald Reagan, who cut taxes to spark an economic recovery, and on Federal Reserve Chairman Paul Volcker, whose tight money policies helped curb inflation.

Mundell's early research focused on exchange rates and the movement of international capital. In a series of papers in the 1960s that proved to be prophetic, he speculated about the impacts of monetary and fiscal policy if exchange rates were allowed to float, emphasizing the importance of central banks acting independently of governments to promote price stability. At the time, his work may have seemed purely academic. Within 10 years, however, the Bretton Woods system of fixed exchange rates tied to the dollar broke down, exchange rates became more flexible, capital markets opened up, and Mundell's ideas were borne out.

In another feat of near-prophecy, Mundell wrote about the potential benefits and disadvantages of a group of countries adopting a single currency, anticipating the development of the European currency, the euro, by many years. Since 1974, Mundell has taught at Columbia University.

monetary policy would be ineffective. The amount of capital leaving the United States would be just equal to the increase in the money supply to begin with, and interest rates would be returned to their original international equilibrium.

Keeping exchange rates fixed and holding the money supply constant, an expansionary fiscal policy will produce an increase in interest rates. As income rises, there will be a greater transactions demand for money, resulting in higher interest rates. Higher interest rates mean that capital will flow into the United States.

As more capital flows into U.S. capital markets, interest rates will be reduced, adding to the expansionary impact of the original fiscal policy. Expansionary fiscal policy is reinforced by an open economy with fixed exchange rates as aggregate demand moves to $AD_2$.

## Policies Under Flexible Exchange Rates

Expansionary monetary policy under a system of flexible exchange rates, again holding fiscal policy constant, results in a growing money supply and falling interest rates. Lower interest rates lead to a capital outflow and a balance of payments deficit, or a declining surplus. With flexible exchange rates, consumers and investors will want more foreign currency; thus, the exchange rate will depreciate. As the dollar depreciates, exports increase; U.S. exports are more attractive to foreigners as their currency buys them more. The net result is that the international market works to reinforce an expansionary policy undertaken at home.

Permitting exchange rates to vary and holding the money supply constant, an expansionary fiscal policy produces a rise in interest rates as rising incomes increase the transactions demand for money. Higher interest rates mean that capital will flow into the United States, generating a balance of payments surplus or a smaller deficit, causing the exchange rate to appreciate as foreigners value dollars more. As the dollar becomes more valuable, exports decline, moving aggregate demand back toward $AD_0$ in Figure 5. With flexible exchange rates, therefore, an open economy can hamper fiscal policy.

These movements are complex and go through several steps. Table 4 summarizes them for you. The key point to note is that under our flexible exchange rate system now, an open economy reinforces monetary policy and hampers fiscal policy. No wonder the Fed has become more important.

**TABLE 4** Summary of the Effects of an Open Economy on Monetary and Fiscal Policy in a Fixed and Flexible Exchange Rate System

| | Flexible Exchange Rate | Fixed Exchange Rate |
|---|---|---|
| Monetary policy (fiscal policy constant) | Reinforced | Hampered |
| Fiscal policy (monetary policy constant) | Hampered | Reinforced |

Several decades ago, Presidents and Congress could adopt monetary and fiscal policies without much consideration of the rest of the world. Today, economies of the world are vastly more intertwined, and the macroeconomic policies of one country often have serious impacts on others. Today, open economy macroeconomics is more important, and good macroeconomic policymaking must account for changes in exchange rates and capital flows.

## CHECKPOINT

### MONETARY AND FISCAL POLICY IN AN OPEN ECONOMY

- A fixed exchange rate is one in which governments determine their exchange rates and then use macroeconomic policy to maintain these rates.
- Flexible exchange rates rely on markets to set the exchange rate given the country's macroeconomic policies.
- Fixed exchange rate systems hinder monetary policy, but reinforce fiscal policy.
- Flexible exchange rates hamper fiscal policy, but reinforce monetary policy.

**QUESTION:** The United States seems to rely more on monetary policy to maintain stable prices, low interest rates, low unemployment, and healthy economic growth. Do the facts that the United States has really embraced global trade (imports and exports combined are over 25% of GDP) and we have a flexible (floating) exchange rate help explain why monetary policy seems more important than fiscal policy?

Answers to the Checkpoint question can be found at the end of this chapter.

## Key Concepts

Current account, p. 618
Capital account, p. 619
Exchange rate, p. 620
Nominal exchange rate, p. 621
Real exchange rate, p. 621
Purchasing power parity, p. 621
Currency appreciation, p. 623
Currency depreciation, p. 623
Fixed exchange rate, p. 628
Flexible or floating exchange rate, p. 628

## Chapter Summary

### The Balance of Payments

The current account includes payments for imports and exports of goods and services, incomes flowing into and out of the country, and net transfers of money.

The capital account includes flows of money into and out of domestic and foreign assets. Foreign investment in the United States includes foreign ownership of domestic plants or subsidiaries; investments in mutual funds, stocks, and bonds; and deposits in U.S. banks. In a similar fashion, U.S. investors hold foreign financial assets in their portfolios and own interests in foreign facilities and companies.

The sum of the current account and capital account balances must equal zero.

### Exchange Rates

The exchange rate defines the rate at which one currency can be exchanged for another. A nominal exchange rate is the price of one country's currency for another.

The real exchange rate takes price levels into account.

The real exchange rate is the nominal exchange rate multiplied by the ratio of the price levels of the two countries.

The purchasing power parity of a currency is the rate of exchange at which some currency in one country can purchase the same goods in another country.

If exchange rates are fully flexible, markets determine the prevailing exchange rate. If there is an excess demand for dollars, the dollar will appreciate, or rise in value. If there is an excess supply of dollars, the value of dollars will decline or depreciate.

It is important to keep in mind which currency is being used to measure the price of others. Graphs can be viewed as showing either an appreciation or a depreciation, depending on which currency is being considered.

Real exchange rates affect the payments for imports and exports, and also affect the current account. Inflation causes depreciation of a country's currency, worsening its current account.

Interest rates and exchange rate expectations affect the capital account. An interest rate rise in one country will cause capital to flow into it from the other country.

When capital is not perfectly mobile and substitutable between two countries, a risk premium will be added to interest rates. Expected exchange rate changes and risk premium changes can produce enduring interest rate differentials between two countries.

### Monetary and Fiscal Policy in an Open Economy

A fixed exchange rate system is one in which governments determine their exchange rates, then use macroeconomic adjustments to maintain these rates. A flexible or floating exchange rate system relies on currency markets to determine the exchange rates, given macroeconomic conditions.

Fixed exchange rate systems hinder monetary policy, but reinforce fiscal policy.

Flexible exchange rates hamper fiscal policy, but reinforce monetary policy.

# Questions and Problems

## Check Your Understanding

1. Describe the balance of trade. What factors contribute to our trade deficit?
2. Mexican immigrants working in the United States often send money back home (known as remittances) to help their families or to add to their savings account for the future. Today, these remittances approach $15 billion a year. How are these transfers recorded in the balance of payments accounts?
3. What is the important difference between the current account and the capital account, given that they are equal to the same dollar amount?
4. How are most exchange rates determined?
5. If the euro appreciates by 30%, what will happen to imports of Mercedes-Benz automobiles in the United States?
6. Describe the difference between fixed and flexible exchange rates.
7. When the world's economies are on a fixed gold standard and the discoveries of gold do not keep pace with the growing world GDP, what happens?
8. Describe the difference between the nominal and real exchange rates. What does rising inflation do to a country's real exchange rate?

## Apply the Concepts

9. Assume that global warming and especially high temperatures in Northern California have rendered it impossible for wine grapes in the Napa Valley (and all over California) to grow properly. Unable to get California wines, demand jumps dramatically for Australian wines. How would this affect the Australian dollar? Is this good for other Australian exports?
10. If the European economies begin having a serious bout of stagflation—high rates of both unemployment and inflation—will this affect the value of the dollar?
11. Trace through the reasoning why monetary policy is enhanced by a flexible exchange rate system.
12. Zimbabwe devalued its currency in mid-2006, essentially turning a $20,000 Zimbabwe bill into a $20 bill. People were permitted only three weeks to turn in their old currency for new notes; individuals were limited to $150 a day; and companies were restricted to $7,000. Who do you think were the losers from this devaluation, especially considering its limited turn-in period for the old currency?
13. Exchange rates and purchasing power parity should be the same between countries. If it costs $300 to purchase an iPod in the United States and 400 Australian dollars in Sydney, then the exchange rate between Australia and the United States should be 4:3. Why might purchasing power parity be different from the exchange rate?
14. When the dollar gets stronger against the major foreign currencies, does the price of French wine rise or fall in the United States? Would this be a good time to travel to Australia? What happens to U.S. exports?

## Solving Problems

15. Assume the following exchange rates prevail:

| | (U.S. $ Equivalent) |
|---|---|
| Argentina | 0.3253 (Peso) |
| Canada | 0.8812 (Dollar) |
| Mexico | 0.0914 (Peso) |
| Bahrain | 2.6526 (Dinar) |

How many Mexican pesos does it take to get one Bahrain Dinar? If you had 20 U.S. dollars, could you take a ferry ride in Canada if it cost $25 Canadian? If someone gave you 50 Argentinean pesos to settle a 150 Mexican pesos bet, would it be enough?

## Answers to Questions in CheckPoints

### Check Point: The Balance of Payments

The equation $G - T = (S - I) + (M - X)$ provides the answer. For simplicity, assume a balanced budget $(G - T = 0)$. If $S > I$, then $X > M$ to balance the equation. Large private saving is balanced by fewer imports in comparison to exports. China is a net exporter, which shows up as a current account surplus in their balance of payments accounts.

### Check Point: Exchange Rates

Yes, a 10% appreciation in the yuan would make China's output more expensive in the United States, and we would import less from China, improving the U.S. current account.

### Check Point: Monetary and Fiscal Policy in an Open Economy

As noted in this section, monetary policy is reinforced when exchange rates are flexible, while fiscal policy is hindered. This is probably only a partial explanation, because fiscal policy today seems driven more by "events" and other priorities, and less by stabilization issues.

The recent deep recession required heavy doses of both monetary and fiscal policy to keep the economy from a devastating downturn. Additional government spending, while huge, didn't seem to pack the punch many thought it would. Maybe flexible exchange rates kept it from being as effective as anticipated.

# Glossary

**Absolute advantage** One country can produce more of a good than another country.

**Adaptive expectations** Inflationary expectations are formed from a simple extrapolation from past events.

**Adverse selection** Occurs when products of different qualities are sold at the same price because of asymmetric information.

**Agency shop** Employees are not required to join the union, but must pay dues to compensate the union for its services.

**Aggregate demand** The output of goods and services (real GDP) demanded at different price levels.

**Aggregate expenditures** Consist of consumer spending, business investment spending, government spending, and net foreign spending (exports minus imports): GDP = C + I + G + (X − M).

**Aggregate supply** The real GDP that firms will produce at varying price levels. In the short run, aggregate supply is positively sloped because many input costs are slow to change, but in the long run, the aggregate supply curve is vertical at full employment since the economy has reached its capacity to produce.

**Allocative efficiency** The mix of goods and services produced is just what society desires. The price that consumers pay is equal to marginal cost and is also equal to the least average total cost.

**Annually balanced budget** Federal expenditures and taxes would have to be equal each year. Annually balanced budgets tend to be procyclical.

**Antitrust law** Laws designed to maintain competition and prevent monopolies from developing.

**Asymmetric information** Occurs when one party to a transaction has significantly better information than another party.

**Automatic stabilizers** Tax revenues and transfer payments automatically expand or contract in ways that reduce the intensity of business fluctuations without any overt action by Congress or other policymakers.

**Average cost pricing rule** Requires a regulated monopolist to produce and sell output where price equals average total costs. This permits the regulated monopolist to earn a normal return on investment over the long term and so remain in business.

**Average fixed cost** Equal to total fixed cost divided by output (TFC/Q).

**Average product** Output per worker, found by dividing total output by the number of workers employed to produce that output (Q/L).

**Average propensity to consume** The percentage of income that is consumed (C/Y).

**Average propensity to save** The percentage of income that is saved (S/Y).

**Average total cost** Equal to total cost divided by output (TC/Q). Average total cost is also equal to AFC + AVC.

**Average variable cost** Equal to total variable cost divided by output (TVC/Q).

**Balanced budget multiplier** Equal changes in government spending and taxation (a balanced budget) lead to an equal change in income (the balanced budget multiplier is equal to 1).

**Barter** The direct exchange of goods and services for other goods and services.

**Budget and trade deficits** These are related by the following equation: $G - T = (S - I) + (M - X)$. So, budget deficits must be covered by net domestic saving (private plus corporate) or by net foreign saving (imports minus exports).

**Budget line** Graphically illustrates the possible combinations of two goods that can be purchased with a given income, given the prices of both products.

**Business cycles** Alternating increases and decreases in economic activity that are typically punctuated by periods of downturn, recession, recovery, and boom.

**Capital** Includes manufactured products such as welding machines, computers, and cellular phones that are used to produce other goods and services. The payment to capital is referred to as interest.

**Capital account** Summarizes the flow of money into and out of domestic and foreign assets, including investments by foreign companies in domestic plants or subsidiaries, and other foreign holdings of U.S. assets, including mutual funds, stock, bonds, and deposits in U.S. banks. Also included are U.S. investors' holdings of foreign financial assets, production facilities, and other assets in foreign countries.

**Capital-to-labor ratio** The capital employed per worker. A higher ratio means higher labor productivity and, as a result, higher wages.

**Cartel** An agreement between firms (or countries) in an industry to formally collude on price and output, then agree on the distribution of production.

***Ceteris paribus*** Assumption used in economics (and other disciplines as well), where other relevant factors or variables are held constant.

**Change in demand** Occurs when one or more of the determinants of demand changes, shown as a shift in the entire demand curve.

**Change in quantity demanded** Occurs when the price of the product changes, shown as a movement along an existing demand curve.

**Change in quantity supplied** Occurs when the price of the product changes, shown as a movement along an existing supply curve.

**Change in supply** Occurs when one or more of the determinants of supply change, shown as a shift in the entire supply curve.

**Circular flow diagram** Illustrates how households and firms interact through product and resource markets and shows that economic aggregates can be determined by either examining spending flows from or income flows to households.

**Classical model** A model of the economy that relied on competitive conditions in product, labor, and capital markets, and flexible prices, wages, and interest rates to keep the economy operating around full employment. Anyone unemployed simply was unwilling to work at the prevailing real wage.

**Classical monetary transmission mechanism** Classical economists assumed a direct monetary transmission process: any change in *M* would be felt directly in *P*.

**Closed shop** Workers must belong to the union before they can be hired.

**Coase theorem** If transaction costs are minimal (near zero), a bargain struck between beneficiaries and victims of externalities will be efficient from a resource allocation perspective. As a result, the socially optimal level of production will be reached.

**Command and control policies** Environmental policies that set standards and issue regulations, which are then enforced by the legal and regulatory system.

**Common property resources** Resources that are owned by the community at large (parks, ocean fish, and the atmosphere) and therefore tend to be overexploited because individuals have little incentive to use them in a sustainable fashion.

**Comparative advantage** One country has a lower opportunity cost of producing a good than another country.

**Competition** Exists when there are many relatively small buyers and sellers, a standardized product, with good information to both buyers and sellers, and no barriers to entry or exit.

**Complementary goods** Goods that are typically consumed together. When the *price* of a complementary good rises, the *demand* for the other good declines, and vice versa.

**Complements** Goods that are typically consumed together, such as coffee and sugar. Complements have a negative cross elasticity of demand.

**Concentration ratio** The share of industry shipments or sales accounted for by the top four or eight firms.

**Constant cost industry** An industry that in the long run faces roughly the same prices and costs as industry output expands. Some industries can virtually clone their operations in other areas without putting undue pressure on resource prices, resulting in constant operating costs as they expand in the long run.

**Constant returns to scale** A range of output where average total costs are relatively constant. Fast-food restaurants and movie theatres are examples.

**Consumer price index (CPI)** A measure of the average change in prices paid by urban consumers for a typical market basket of consumer goods and services.

**Consumer surplus** The difference between market price and what consumers (as individuals or the market) would be willing to pay. It is equal to the area above market price and below the demand curve.

**Consumption** Spending by individuals and households on both durable goods (e.g., autos, appliances, and electronic equipment) and nondurable goods (e.g., food, clothes, and entertainment).

**Contestable markets** Markets that look monopolistic but have entry costs so low that the sheer threat of entry keeps prices low.

**Contractionary fiscal policy** Involves increasing withdrawals from the economy by reducing government spending, transfer payments, or raising taxes to decrease aggregate demand to contract output and the economy.

**Corporation** A business structure that has most of the legal rights of individuals, and in addition, the corporation can issue stock to raise capital. Stockholders' liability is limited to the value of their stock.

**Cost-benefit analysis** A methodology for decision making that looks at the discounted value of the costs and benefits of a given project.

**Cost-push inflation** Results when a supply shock hits the economy, reducing short-run aggregate supply, and thus reducing output and increasing the price level.

**Cross elasticity of demand** Measures how responsive the quantity demanded of one good is to changes in the price of another good. Substitute goods have positive cross elasticities: An increase in the price of one good leads consumers to substitute (buy more) of the other good whose price has not changed. Complementary goods have negative cross elasticities: An increase in the price of a complement leads to a reduction in sales of the other good whose price has not changed.

**Crowding-out effect** Arises from deficit spending requiring the government to borrow, thus driving up interest rates and reducing consumer spending and business investment.

**Currency appreciation** When the value of a currency rises relative to other currencies.

**Currency depreciation** When the value of a currency falls relative to other currencies.

**Current account** Includes payments for imports and exports of goods and services, incomes flowing into and out of the country, and net transfers of money.

**Cyclical unemployment** Unemployment that results from changes in the business cycle, and where public policymakers can have their greatest impact by keeping the economy on a steady, low-inflationary, solid growth path.

**Cyclically balanced budget** Balancing the budget over the course of the business cycle by restricting spending or raising taxes when the economy is booming and using these surpluses to offset the deficits that occur during recessions.

**Deadweight loss** The loss in consumer and producer surplus due to inefficiency because some transactions cannot be made and therefore their value to society is lost.

**Decision lag** The time it takes Congress and the administration to decide on a policy once a problem is recognized.

**Decreasing cost industry** An industry that in the long run faces lower prices and costs as industry output expands. Some industries enjoy economies of scale as they expand in the long run, typically the result of technological advances.

**Deficit** The amount by which annual government spending exceeds tax revenues.

**Deflation** A decline in overall prices throughout the economy. This is the opposite of inflation.

**Demand** The maximum amount of a product that buyers are willing and able to purchase over some time period at various prices, holding all other relevant factors constant (the *ceteris paribus* condition).

**Demand curve** Demand schedule information translated to a graph.

**Demand for labor** Demand for labor is derived from the demand for the firm's product and the productivity of labor.

**Demand-pull inflation** Results when aggregate demand expands so much that equilibrium output exceeds full employment output and the price level rises.

**Determinants of demand** Nonprice factors that affect demand, including tastes and preferences, income, prices of related goods, number of buyers, and expectations.

**Determinants of supply** Nonprice factors that affect supply, including production technology, costs of resources, prices of other commodities, expectations, number of sellers, and taxes and subsidies.

**Diminishing marginal returns** An additional worker adds to total output, but at a diminishing rate.

**Discount rate** The interest rate the Federal Reserve charges commercial banks and other depository institutions to borrow reserves from a regional Federal Reserve Bank.

**Discouraged workers** To continue to be counted as unemployed, those without work must actively seek work (apply for jobs, interview, register with employment services, etc.). Discouraged workers are those who have given up actively looking for work and, as a result, are not counted as unemployed.

**Discretionary fiscal policy** Involves adjusting government spending and tax policies with the express short-run goal of moving the economy toward full employment, expanding economic growth, or controlling inflation.

**Discretionary spending** The part of the budget that works its way through the appropriations process of Congress each year and includes such programs as national defense, transportation, science, environment, and income security.

**Diseconomies of scale** A range of output where average total costs tend to increase. Firms often become so big that management becomes bureaucratic and unable to efficiently control its operations.

**Disinflation** A reduction in the rate of inflation. An economy going through disinflation typically is still facing inflation, but at a declining rate.

**Disposable personal income** Personal income minus taxes.

**Dumping** Selling goods abroad at lower prices than in home markets, and often below cost.

**Dynamic games** Sequential or repeated games where the players can adjust their actions based on the decisions of other players in the past.

**Easy money, expansionary monetary policy, or quantitative easing** Fed actions designed to increase excess reserves and the money supply to stimulate the economy (expand income and employment).

**Economic costs** The sum of explicit (out-of-pocket) and implicit (opportunity) costs.

**Economic discrimination** When workers of equal ability are paid different wages or in any other way discriminated against because of race, color, religion, gender, age, national origin, or disability.

**Economic growth** Usually measured by the annual percentage change in real GDP, reflecting an annual improvement in the standard of living.

**Economic profits** Profits in excess of normal profits. These are profits in excess of both explicit and implicit costs.

**Economies of scale** As a firm's output increases, its LRATC tends to decline. This results from specialization of labor and management, and potentially a better use of capital and complementary production techniques.

**Economies of scope** By producing a number of products that are interdependent, firms are able to produce and market these goods at lower costs.

**Efficiency** How well resources are used and allocated. Do people get the goods and services they want at the lowest possible resource cost? This is the chief focus of efficiency.

**Efficiency wage theory** Employers often pay their workers wages above the market-clearing level to improve morale and productivity, reduce turnover, and create a disincentive for employees to shirk their duties.

**Elastic demand** The absolute value of the price elasticity of demand is greater than 1. Elastic demands are very responsive to changes in price. The percentage change in quantity demanded is greater than the percentage change in price.

**Elastic supply** Price elasticity of supply is greater than 1. The percentage change in quantity supplied is greater than the percentage change in price.

**Elasticity of demand for labor** The percentage change in the quantity of labor demanded divided by the percentage change in the wage rate.

**Entrepreneurs** Entrepreneurs combine land, labor, and capital to produce goods and services. They absorb the risk of being in business, including the risk of bankruptcy and other liabilities associated with doing business. Entrepreneurs receive profits for this effort.

**Equation of exchange** The heart of classical monetary theory uses the equation $M \times V = P \times Q$, where $M$ is the supply of money, $V$ is the velocity of money (the average number of times per year a dollar is spent on goods and services, or the number of times it turns over in a year), $P$ is the price level, and $Q$ is the economy's output level.

**Equilibrium** Market forces are in balance when the quantities demanded by consumers just equal the quantities supplied by producers.

**Equilibrium price** Market equilibrium price is the price that results when quantity demanded is just equal to quantity supplied.

**Equilibrium quantity** Market equilibrium quantity is the output that results when quantity demanded is just equal to quantity supplied.

**Equity** The fairness of various issues and policies.

**Exchange rate** The rate at which one currency can be exchanged for another, or just the price of one currency for another.

**Expansionary fiscal policy** Involves increasing government spending, increasing transfer payments, or decreasing taxes to increase aggregate demand to expand output and the economy.

**Explicit costs** Those expenses paid directly to another economic entity, including wages, lease payments, taxes, and utilities.

**External benefits** Positive externalities, such as education and vaccinations. Private markets provide too little at too high a price of goods with external benefits.

**External cost** (or **negative externality)** Occurs when a transaction between two parties has an impact on a third party not involved with the transaction. External costs are negative, such as pollution or congestion. The market provides too much of a product with negative externalities at too low a cost.

**Externalities** The impact on third parties of some transaction between others where the third parties are not involved. An external cost (or negative externality) harms the third parties, whereas external benefits (positive externalities) result in gains to them.

**Externally held debt** Public debt held by foreigners, roughly equal to half of the outstanding U.S. debt held by the public.

**Federal funds rate** The interest rate financial institutions charge each other for overnight loans used as reserves.

**Federal Open Market Committee (FOMC)** This twelve-member committee is composed of members of the Board of Governors of the Fed and selected presidents of the regional Federal Reserve Banks; it oversees open market operations (the buying and selling of government securities), the main tool of monetary policy.

**Federal Reserve System** The central bank of the United States.

**Fiat money** Money without intrinsic value but nonetheless accepted as money because the government has decreed it to be money.

**Financial intermediaries** Financial firms (banks, mutual funds, insurance companies, etc.) that acquire funds from savers and then lend these funds to borrowers (consumers, firms, and government).

**Firm** An economic institution that transforms resources (factors of production) into outputs for consumers.

**Fiscal imbalance** The difference between the present value of future obligations and expected revenues, less government assets, assuming current policies remain unchanged.

**Fiscal sustainability** A fiscal imbalance equal to zero.

**Fixed costs** Costs that do not change as a firm's output expands or contracts, often called overhead. These include items such as lease payments, administrative expenses, property taxes, and insurance.

**Fixed exchange rate** Each government determines its exchange rate, then uses macroeconomic policy to maintain the rate.

**Flexible or floating exchange rate** A country's currency exchange rate is determined in international currency exchange markets, given the country's macroeconomic policies.

**Fractional reserve banking system** To prevent bank runs (all depositors demanding their deposits in cash at the same time), a portion of bank deposits must be held as vault cash, or else in an account with the regional Federal Reserve Bank.

**Free rider** When a public good is provided, consumers cannot be excluded from enjoying the product, so some consume the product without paying.

**Frictional unemployment** Unemployment for any economy that includes workers who voluntarily quit their jobs to search for better positions, or are moving to new jobs but may still take several days or weeks before they can report to their new employers.

**Functional distribution of income** The distribution of income for resources or factors of production (land, labor, capital, and entrepreneurial ability).

**Functional finance** Essentially ignores the impact of the budget on the business cycle and focuses on fostering economic growth and stable prices, while keeping the economy as close as possible to full employment.

**Game theory** An approach to analyzing oligopoly behavior using mathematics and simulation by making different assumptions about the players, time involved, level of information, strategies, and other aspects of the game.

**GDP deflator** An index of the average prices for all goods and services in the economy, including consumer goods, investment goods, government goods and services, and exports. It is the broadest measure of inflation in the national income and product accounts (NIPA).

**General training** Training that improves a worker's productivity in all firms.

**Generational imbalance** An estimate of how much of any fiscal imbalance is being shifted to future generations.

**Gini coefficient** A precise method of measuring the position of the Lorenz curve, defined as the area between the Lorenz curve and the equal distribution line divided by the total area below the equal distribution line.

**Government budget constraint** The government budget is limited by the fact that $G - T = \Delta M + \Delta B + \Delta A$.

**Government failure** The result when the incentives of politicians and government bureaucrats do not align with the public interest.

**Government spending** Includes the wages and salaries of government employees (federal, state, and local); the purchase of products and services from private businesses and the rest of the world; and government purchases of new structures, equipment, and software.

**Gross domestic product (GDP)** A measure of the economy's total output; it is the most widely reported value in the national income and product accounts (NIPA) and is equal to the total market value of all final goods and services produced by resources in the United States in a given year.

**Gross private domestic investment (GPDI)** Investments in such things as structures (residential and nonresidential), equipment, and software, and changes in private business inventories.

**Herfindahl-Hirshman index (HHI)** A way of measuring industry concentration, equal to the sum of the squares of market shares for all firms in the industry.

**Horizontal summation** Market demand and supply curves are found by adding together how many units of the product will be purchased or supplied at each price.

**Hyperinflation** An extremely high rate of inflation; above 100% per year.

**Implementation lag** The time required to turn fiscal policy into law and eventually have an impact on the economy.

**Implicit costs** The opportunity costs of using resources that belong to the firm, including depreciation, depletion of business assets, and the opportunity cost of the firm's capital employed in the business.

**Incidence of taxation** Refers to who bears the economic burden of a tax. The economic entity bearing the burden of a particular tax will depend on the price elasticities of demand and supply.

**Income** A flow measure reflecting the funds received by individuals or households over a period of time, usually a week, month, or year.

**Income deficit** The difference between the poverty threshold and a family's income.

**Income effect** When higher prices essentially reduce consumer income, the quantity demanded for normal goods falls.

**Income effect, labor** Higher wages mean you can maintain the same standard of living by working fewer hours. The impact on labor supply is generally negative.

**Income elasticity of demand** Measures how responsive quantity demanded is to changes in consumer income.

**Increasing cost industry** An industry that in the long run faces higher prices and costs as industry output expands. Industry expansion puts upward pressure on resources (inputs), causing higher costs in the long run.

**Increasing marginal returns** A new worker hired adds more to total output than the previous worker hired, so that both average and marginal products are rising.

**Indifference curve** Shows all the combinations of two goods where the consumer is indifferent (gets the same level of satisfaction).

**Indifference map** An infinite set of indifference curves where each curve represents a different level of utility or satisfaction.

**Inelastic demand** The absolute value of the price elasticity of demand is less than 1. Inelastic demands are not very responsive to changes in price. The percentage change in quantity demanded is less than the percentage change in price.

**Inelastic supply** Price elasticity of supply is less than 1. The percentage change in quantity supplied is less than the percentage change in price.

**Infant industry** An industry so underdeveloped that protection is needed for it to become competitive on the world stage or to ensure its survival.

**Inferior goods** Goods that have income elasticities that are negative. When consumer income grows, quantity demanded falls for inferior goods.

**Inflation** A measure of changes in the cost of living. A general rise in prices throughout the economy.

**Inflation targeting** The central bank sets a target on the inflation rate (usually around 2% per year) and adjusts monetary policy to keep inflation in that range.

**Inflationary expectations** The rate of inflation expected by workers for any given period. Workers do not work for a specific nominal wage but for what those wages will buy (real wages), so their inflationary expectations are an important determinant of what nominal wage they are willing to work for.

**Inflationary gap** The spending reduction necessary (again, when expanded by the multiplier) to bring an overheated economy back to full employment.

**Information lag** The time policymakers must wait for economic data to be collected, processed, and reported. Most macroeconomic data are not available until at least one quarter (three months) after the fact.

**Infrastructure** The public capital of a nation, including transportation networks, power-generating plants and transmission facilities, public education institutions, and other intangible resources such as protection of property rights and a stable monetary environment.

**Injections** Increments of spending, including investment, government spending, and exports.

**Internally held debt** Public debt owned by U.S. banks, corporations, mutual funds, pension plans, and individuals.

**Investment** Spending by business that adds to the productive capacity of the economy. Investment depends on factors such as its rate of return, the level of technology, and business expectations about the economy.

**Investment in human capital** Investments such as education and on-the-job training that improve the productivity of human labor.

**Jobless recovery** Takes place after a recession, when output begins to rise, but employment growth does not.

**Keynesian macroeconomic equilibrium** In the simple model, the economy is at rest; spending injections (investment) are equal to withdrawals (saving), or $I = S$, and there are no net inducements for the economy to change the level of output or income. In the full model, all injections of spending must equal all withdrawals at equilibrium: $I + G + X = S + T + M$.

**Keynesian transmission mechanism** An increase in the money supply lowers interest rates, thus increasing investment; expanding aggregate demand; and increasing income, output, and employment. The opposite occurs when the money supply is reduced.

**Kinked demand curve** An oligopoly model that assumes that if a firm raises its price, competitors will not raise theirs; but if the firm lowers its price, all of its competitors will lower their price to match the reduction. This leads to a kink in the demand curve and relatively stable market prices.

**Labor** Includes the mental and physical talents of individuals who produce goods and services. The payment to labor is called wages.

**Labor force** The total number of those employed and unemployed. The unemployment rate is the number of unemployed divided by the labor force, expressed as a percent.

**Laffer curve** Plots hypothetical tax revenues at various income tax rates. If tax rates are zero, tax revenues will be zero; if rates are 100%, revenues will also be zero. As tax rates rise from zero, revenues rise, reach a maximum, and then decline.

**Land** Includes natural resources such as mineral deposits, oil, natural gas, water, and land in the usual sense of the word. The payment to land as a resource is called rent.

**Law of demand** Holding all other relevant factors constant, as price increases, quantity demanded falls, and as price decreases, quantity demanded rises.

**Law of diminishing marginal utility** As we consume more of a given product, the added satisfaction we get from consuming an additional unit declines.

**Law of supply** Holding all other relevant factors constant, as price increases, quantity supplied will rise, and as price declines, quantity supplied will fall.

**Liquidity** How quickly, easily, and reliably an asset can be converted into cash.

**Liquidity trap** When interest rates are so low that people believe rates can only rise, they hold on to money rather than investing in bonds and suffer the expected capital loss.

**Long run** Time period long enough for firms to alter their plant capacities and for the number of firms in the industry to change. Existing firms can expand or build new plants, or firms can enter or exit the industry.

**Long-run aggregate supply (LRAS) curve** The long-run aggregate supply curve is vertical at full employment because the economy has reached its capacity to produce.

**Long-run average total cost (LRATC)** In the long run, firms can adjust their plant sizes so LRATC is the lowest unit cost at which any particular output can be produced in the long run.

**Lorenz curves** A graphical method of showing the income distribution by cumulating families of various income levels on the horizontal axis and relating this to their cumulative share of total income on the vertical axis.

**Luxury goods** Goods that have income elasticities greater than 1. When consumer income grows, quantity demanded of luxury goods rises more than the rise in income.

**M1** The narrowest definition of money; includes currency (coins and paper money), demand deposits (checks), and other accounts that have check-writing or debit capabilities, such as stock market and money market accounts. The most liquid instruments that might serve as money.

**M2** A broader definition of money that includes "near monies" that are not as liquid as cash, including deposits in savings accounts, money market accounts, and money market mutual fund accounts.

**Macroeconomic equilibrium** Occurs at the intersection of the short-run aggregate supply and aggregate demand curves. At this output level, there are no net pressures for the economy to expand or contract.

**Macroeconomics** The broader issues in the economy such as inflation, unemployment, and national output of goods and services.

**Mandatory spending** Spending authorized by permanent laws that does not go through the same appropriation process as discretionary spending. Mandatory spending includes such programs as Social Security, Medicare, and interest on the national debt.

**Marginal cost** The change in total costs arising from the production of additional units of output ($\Delta TC/\Delta Q$). Since fixed costs do not change with output, marginal costs are the change in variable costs associated with additional production ($\Delta TVC/\Delta Q$).

**Marginal cost pricing rule** Regulators would prefer to have natural monopolists price where $P = MC$, but this would result in losses (long term) because $ATC > MC$. Thus, regulators often must use an average cost pricing rule.

**Marginal factor cost (MFC)** The added cost associated with hiring one more unit of labor. For competitive firms, it is equal to the wage; but for monopsonists, it is higher than the new wage (W) because all existing workers must be paid this higher new wage, making $MFC > W$.

**Marginal physical product of labor** The additional output a firm receives from employing an added unit of labor ($MPP_L = \Delta Q \div \Delta L$).

**Marginal product** The change in output that results from a change in labor ($\Delta Q/\Delta L$).

**Marginal propensity to consume** The change in consumption associated with a given change in income ($\Delta C/\Delta Y$).

**Marginal propensity to save** The change in saving associated with a given change in income ($\Delta S/\Delta Y$).

**Marginal revenue** The change in total revenue from selling an additional unit of output. Since competitive firms are price takers, $P = MR$ for competitive firms.

**Marginal revenue product** The value of another worker to the firm is equal to the marginal physical product of labor ($MPP_L$) times marginal revenue (MR).

**Marginal utility** The satisfaction received from consuming an additional unit of a given product or service.

**Marginal utility analysis** A theoretical framework underlying consumer decision making. This approach assumes that satisfaction can be measured and that consumers maximize satisfaction when the marginal utilities per dollar are equal for all products and services.

**Market failures** When markets are not competitive or involve public goods, externalities, or common property resources, markets will fail to provide the optimal level of output, and will provide output at too high or low a price.

**Market period** Time period so short that the output and the number of firms are fixed. Agricultural products at harvest time face market periods. Products that unexpectedly become instant hits face market periods (there is a lag between when the firm realizes it has a hit on its hands and when inventory can be replaced).

**Market structure analysis** By observing a few industry characteristics such as number of firms in the industry or the level of barriers to entry, economists can use this information to predict pricing and output behavior of the firm in the industry.

**Market-based policies** Environmental policies that use charges, taxes, subsidies, deposit-refund systems, or tradable emission permits to achieve environmental ends.

**Markets** Institutions that bring buyers and sellers together so they can interact and transact with each other.

**Medium of exchange** Money is a medium of exchange because goods and services are sold for money, then the money is used to purchase other goods and services.

**Microeconomics** The decision making by individuals, businesses, industries, and governments.

**Monetarist transmission mechanism** An increase in money will reduce interest rates as portfolios rebalance, leading to a rise in investment or consumption and resulting in an increase in aggregate demand and thus an increase in income, output, or the price level.

**Monetary rule** Keeps the growth of money stocks such as M1 or M2 on a steady path, following the equation of exchange (or quantity theory), to set a long-run path for the economy that keeps inflation in check.

**Money** Anything that is accepted in exchange for other goods and services or for the payment of debt.

**Money multiplier** Measures the *potential* or *maximum* amount the money supply can increase (or decrease) when new deposits enter (exit) the system and is defined as 1 divided by the reserve requirement. The actual money multiplier will be less, since some banks hold excess reserves.

**Monopolistic competition** Involves a large number of small firms and is similar to competition, with easy entry and exit, but unlike the competitive model, the firms have differentiated their products. This differentiation is either real or imagined by consumers and involves innovations, advertising, location, or other ways of making one firm's product different from that of its competitors.

**Monopolistic exploitation of labor** When a firm has monopoly power in the product market, marginal revenue is less than price ($MR < P$) and the firm hires labor up to the point where $MRP_L$ = wage. Because $MRP_L$ is less than the $VMP_L$, workers are paid less than the value of their marginal product, and this difference is called monopolistic exploitation of labor.

**Monopoly** A one-firm industry with no close product substitutes and with substantial barriers to entry.

**Monopoly power** A firm with monopoly power has some control over price.

**Monopsonistic exploitation of labor** Because monopsonists hire less labor than competitive firms, and workers are paid less than the value of their marginal products, this difference is referred to as monopsonistic exploitation of labor.

**Monopsony** A labor market with one employer.

**Moral hazard** Asymmetric information problem that occurs when an insurance policy or some other arrangement changes the economic incentives and leads to a change in behavior.

**Multiplier** Spending changes alter equilibrium income by the spending change times the multiplier. One person's spending becomes another's income, and that second person spends some (the MPC), which becomes income for another person, and so on, until income has changed by $1/(1 - MPC) = 1/MPS$. The multiplier operates in both directions.

**Mutual interdependence** When only a few firms constitute an industry, each firm must consider the reactions of its competitors to its decisions.

**Nash equilibrium** An important proof that an *n*-person game where each player chooses his optimal strategy, given that all other players have done the same, has a solution. This was important because economists now knew that even complex models (or games) had an equilibrium, or solution.

**National income** All income, including wages, salaries and benefits, profits (for sole proprietors, partnerships, and corporations), rental income, and interest.

**Natural monopoly** Large economies of scale mean that the minimum efficient scale of operations is roughly equal to market demand.

**Natural rate of unemployment** The level of unemployment where price and wage decisions are consistent; a level at which the actual inflation rate is equal to people's inflationary expectations, and cyclical unemployment is zero.

**Net domestic product** Gross domestic product minus depreciation, or the capital consumption allowance.

**Net exports** Exports minus imports for the current period. Exports include all the items we sell overseas such as agricultural products, movies, and technology products. Imports are all those items we bring into the country such as vegetables from Mexico, wine from Italy, and cars from Germany.

**Network externalities** Markets in which the network becomes more valuable as more people are connected to the network.

**Nominal exchange rate** The rate at which one currency can be exchanged for another.

**Nonexcludability** Once a good or service is provided, it is not feasible to exclude others from enjoying that good or service.

**Nonrivalry** The consumption of a good or service by one person does not reduce the utility of that good or service to others.

**Normal goods** Goods that have positive income elasticities of less than 1. When consumer income grows, quantity demanded rises for normal goods, but less than the rise in income.

**Normal profits** Equal to zero economic profits; where $P = ATC$. The return on capital necessary to keep investors satisfied and keep capital in the business over the long run.

**Oligopoly** A market with just a few firms dominating the industry where (1) each firm recognizes that it must consider its competitors' reactions when making its own decisions (mutual interdependence), and (2) there are significant barriers to entry into the market.

**On-the-job training** Training typically done by employers, ranging from suggestions at work to sophisticated seminars.

**Open market operations** The buying and selling of U.S. government securities, usually Treasury bonds, to adjust reserves in the banking system.

**Opportunity cost** The cost paid for one product in terms of the output (or consumption) of another product that must be forgone. The next best alternative; what you give up to do something or purchase something. For example, to watch a movie at a theater, there is not just the monetary cost of the tickets and refreshments, but the time involved in watching the movie. You could have been doing something else (knitting, golfing, hiking, or studying economics).

**Paradox of thrift** When investment is positively related to income and households *intend* to save more, they reduce consumption, income, and output, reducing investment so the result is that consumers *actually* end up saving less.

**Partnership** Similar to a sole proprietorship, but involves more than one owner who shares the management of the business. Partnerships are also subject to unlimited liability.

**Personal consumption expenditures** Goods and services purchased by residents of the United States, whether individuals or businesses; they include durable goods, nondurable goods, and services.

**Personal consumption expenditures (PCE) index** A measure of the changes in consumer prices focusing on consumer expenditures in the GDP accounts.

**Personal income** All income, including wages, salaries, and other labor income; proprietors' income; rental income; personal interest and dividend income; and transfer payments (welfare and Social Security payments) received, with personal contributions for social insurance subtracted out.

**Personal or family distribution of income** The distribution of income to individuals or family groups (typically quintiles, or fifths, of the population).

**Phillips curve** The original curve posited a negative relationship between wages and unemployment, but later versions related unemployment to inflation rates.

**Poverty thresholds** Income levels for various household sizes, below which people are considered to be living in poverty.

**Predatory pricing** Selling below cost to consumers in the short run, hoping to eliminate competitors so that prices can be raised in the longer run to earn economic profits.

**Present value** The value of an investment (future stream of income) today. The higher the discount rate, the lower the present value today, and vice versa.

**Price caps** Maximum price at which a regulated firm can sell its product. They are often flexible enough to allow for changing cost conditions.

**Price ceiling** A government-set maximum price that can be charged for a product or service. When the price ceiling is set below equilibrium, it leads to shortages.

**Price discrimination** Charging different consumer groups different prices for the same product.

**Price elasticity of demand** A measure of the responsiveness of quantity demanded to a change in price, equal to the percentage change in quantity demanded divided by the percentage change in price.

**Price elasticity of supply** A measure of the responsiveness of quantity supplied to changes in price. An elastic supply curve has elasticity greater than 1, whereas inelastic supplies have elasticities less than 1. Time is the most important determinant of the elasticity of supply.

**Price floor** A government-set minimum price that can be charged for a product or service. When the price floor is set above equilibrium, it leads to surpluses.

**Price level** The absolute level of a price index, whether the consumer price index (CPI; retail prices), the producer price index (PPI; wholesale prices), or the GDP deflator (average price of all items in GDP).

**Price system** A name given to the market economy because prices provide considerable information to both buyers and sellers.

**Price taker** Individual firms in competitive markets get their prices from the market since they are so small they cannot influence market price. For this reason, competitive firms are price takers and can produce and sell all the output they produce at market-determined prices.

**Prisoner's Dilemma** A noncooperative game where players cannot communicate or collaborate in making their decisions about whether to confess or not, which results in inferior outcomes for both players. Many oligopoly decisions can be framed as a Prisoner's Dilemma.

**Producer price index (PPI)** A measure of the average changes in the prices received by domestic producers for their output.

**Producer surplus** The difference between market price and the price at which firms are willing to supply the product. It is equal to the area below market price and above the supply curve.

**Product differentiation** One firm's product is distinguished from another's through advertising, innovation, and location, and so on.

**Production** The process of converting resources (factors of production)—land, labor, capital, and entrepreneurial ability—into goods and services. Also can be considered the process of turning inputs into outputs.

**Production efficiency** Goods and services are produced at their lowest resource (opportunity) cost.

**Production possibilities frontier (PPF)** Shows the combinations of two goods that are possible for a society to produce at full employment. Points on or inside the PPF are feasible, and those outside of the frontier are unattainable.

**Productive efficiency** Goods and services are produced and sold to consumers at their lowest resource (opportunity) cost.

**Productivity** How effectively inputs are converted into outputs. Labor productivity is the ratio of the output of goods and services to the labor hours devoted to the production of that output. Higher productivity and higher living standards are closely related.

**Profit** Equal to the difference between total revenue and total cost.

**Profit maximizing rule** Firms maximize profit by producing output where

MR = MC. No other level of output produces higher profits.

**Property rights** The clear delineation of ownership of property backed by government enforcement.

**Public choice theory** The economic analysis of public and political decision making, looking at issues such as voting, the impact of election incentives on politicians, the influence of special interest groups, and rent-seeking behaviors.

**Public debt** The total accumulation of past deficits and surpluses; it includes Treasury bills, notes, and bonds, and U.S. savings bonds.

**Public goods** Goods that, once provided, no one person can be excluded from consuming (nonexclusion), and one person's consumption does not diminish the benefit to others from consuming the good (nonrivalry).

**Purchasing power parity** The rate of exchange that allows a specific amount of currency in one country to purchase the same quantity of goods in another country.

**Quota** A government-set limit on the quantity of imports into a country.

**Rate of return** Uses the present value formula, but subtracts costs, then finds the interest rate (discount rate) at which this investment would break even.

**Rate of return regulation** Permits product pricing that allows the firm to earn a normal return on capital invested in the firm.

**Ratio of income to poverty** The ratio of family income to the poverty threshold. Families with ratios below 0.5 are considered severely poor, families with ratios between 0.5 and 1.0 are considered poor, and those families with ratios between 1.0 and 1.25 are considered near poor.

**Rational expectations** Rational economic agents are assumed to make the best possible use of all publicly available information, then make informed, rational judgments on what the future holds. Any errors in their forecasts will be randomly distributed.

**Real exchange rate** The price of one country's currency for another when the price levels of both countries are taken into account; important when inflation is an issue in one country; it is equal to the nominal exchange rate multiplied by the ratio of the price levels of the two countries.

**Recessionary gap** The increase in aggregate spending needed to bring a depressed economy back to full employment; equal to the GDP gap divided by the multiplier.

**Recognition lag** The time it takes for policymakers to confirm that the economy is trending in or out of a recession. Short-term variations in key economic indicators are typical and sometimes represent nothing more than randomness in the data.

**Rent** The return to land as a factor of production. Sometimes called economic rent.

**Rent seeking** Resources expended to protect a monopoly position. These are used for such activities as lobbying, extending patents, and restricting the number of licenses permitted.

**Reserve requirements** The required ratio of funds that commercial banks and other depository institutions must hold in reserve against deposits.

**Resources** Productive resources include land (land and natural resources), labor (mental and physical talents of people), capital (manufactured products used to produce other products), and entrepreneurial ability (the combining of the other factors to produce products and assume the risk of the business).

**Revenue** Equal to price per unit times quantity sold.

**Right-to-work laws** Laws created by the Taft-Hartley Act that permitted states to outlaw union shops.

**Saving** The difference between income and consumption; the amount of disposable income not spent.

**Say's law** The act of production produces income that leads to an equivalent amount of consumption spending; it is often paraphrased as "supply creates its own demand."

**Scarcity** Our unlimited wants clash with limited resources, leading to scarcity. Everyone faces scarcity (rich and poor) because, at a minimum, our time is limited on earth. Economics focuses on the allocation of scarce resources to satisfy unlimited wants.

**Screening/signaling** The argument that higher education simply lets employers know that the prospective employee is intelligent and trainable and has the discipline potentially to be a good employee.

**Secondary boycott** Occurs when unions clash with one firm and put pressure on a neutral, second firm to enlist the help of the second firm to obtain the union's objectives with the original firm.

**Segmented labor markets** Labor markets split into separate parts. This leads to different wages paid to different sectors even though both markets are highly competitive.

**Short run** Time period when plant capacity and the number of firms in the industry cannot change. Firms can employ more people, use overtime with existing employees, or hire part-time employees to produce more, but this is done in an existing plant.

**Short-run aggregate supply (SRAS) curve** The short-run aggregate supply curve is positively sloped because many input costs are slow to change in the short run.

**Short-run supply curve** The marginal cost curve above the minimum point on the average variable cost curve.

**Shortage** Occurs when the price is below market equilibrium, and quantity demanded exceeds quantity supplied.

**Shutdown point** When price in the short run falls below the minimum point on the AVC curve, the firm will minimize losses by closing its doors and stopping production. Since P < AVC, the firm's variable costs are not covered, so by shutting the plant, losses are reduced to fixed costs only.

**Social welfare** The sum of consumer and producer surplus.

**Sole proprietor** A type of business structure composed of a single owner who supervises and manages the business and is subject to unlimited liability.

**Specific training** Training that improves a worker's productivity in a specific firm.

**Stagflation** Simultaneous occurrence of rising inflation and rising unemployment.

**Static games** One-off games (not repeated) where decisions by the players are made simultaneously and are irreversible.

**Store of value** The function that enables people to save the money they earn today and use it to buy the goods and services they want tomorrow.

**Structural unemployment** Unemployment caused by changes in the structure of consumer demands or technology. It means that demand for some products declines and the skills of this industry's workers often become obsolete as well. This results in an extended bout of unemployment while new skills are developed.

**Substitute goods** Goods consumers will substitute for one another depending on their relative prices. When the *price* of one good rises and the *demand* for another good increases, they are substitute goods, and vice versa.

**Substitutes** Goods consumers substitute for one another depending on their relative prices, such as coffee and tea. Substitutes have a positive cross elasticity of demand.

**Substitution effect** When the price of one good rises, consumers will substitute other goods for that good, so the quantity demanded for the higher priced good falls.

**Substitution effect, labor** Higher wages mean that the value of work has increased, and the opportunity costs of leisure are higher, so work is substituted for leisure.

**Sunk costs** Those costs that have been incurred and cannot be recovered, including, for example, funds spent on existing technology that have become obsolete and past advertising that has run in the media.

**Supply** The maximum amount of a product that sellers are willing and able to provide for sale over some time period at various prices, holding all other relevant factors constant (the *ceteris paribus* condition).

**Supply curve** Supply schedule information translated to a graph.

**Supply of labor** The amount of time an individual is willing to work at various wage rates.

**Supply-side fiscal policies** Policies that focus on shifting the long-run aggregate supply curve to the right, expanding the economy without increasing inflationary pressures. Unlike policies to increase aggregate demand, supply-side policies take longer to have an impact on the economy.

**Surplus** Occurs when the price is above market equilibrium, and quantity supplied exceeds quantity demanded.

**Surplus, budgetary** The amount by which annual tax revenues exceed government expenditures.

**Tariff** A tax on imported products. When a country taxes imported products, it drives a wedge between the product's domestic price and its price on the world market.

**Taylor rule** A rule for the federal funds target that suggests that the target is equal to 2% + current inflation rate + ½(inflation gap) + ½(output gap). Alternatively, it is equal to 2% plus the current inflation rate plus ½ times the difference between the current inflation rate and the Fed's inflation target rate plus ½ times the output gap (current GDP minus potential GDP).

**Terms of trade** The ratio of the price of exported goods to the price of imported goods ($P_x/P_m$).

**Tight money, restrictive, or contractionary monetary policy** Fed actions designed to decrease excess reserves and the money supply to shrink income and employment, usually to fight inflation.

**Tit-for-tat strategies** Simple strategies that repeat the prior move of competitors. If your opponent lowers price, you do the same. This approach has the efficient quality that it rewards cooperation and punishes unfavorable strategies (defections).

**Total revenue** Price times quantity demanded (sold). If demand is elastic and price rises, quantity demanded falls off significantly and total revenue declines, and vice versa. If demand is inelastic and price rises, quantity demanded does not decline much and total revenue rises, and vice versa.

**Total utility** The total satisfaction that a person receives from consuming a given amount of goods and services.

**Tragedy of the commons** Resources that are owned by the community at large (e.g., parks, ocean fish, and the atmosphere) and therefore tend to be overexploited because individuals have little incentive to use them in a sustainable fashion.

**Trigger strategies** Action is taken contingent on your opponent's past decisions.

**Union shop** Non-union hires must join the union within a specified period of time.

**Unit of account** Money provides a yardstick for measuring and comparing the values of a wide variety of goods and services. It eliminates the problem of double coincidence of wants associated with barter.

**Unitary elastic supply** Price elasticity of supply is equal to 1. The percentage change in quantity supplied is equal to the percentage change in price.

**Unitary elasticity of demand** The absolute value of the price elasticity of demand is equal to 1. The percentage change in quantity demanded is just equal to the percentage change in price.

**Utility** A hypothetical measure of consumer satisfaction.

**Utility maximizing rule** Utility is maximized where the marginal utility per dollar is equal for all products, or $MU_a/P_a = MU_b/P_b = \ldots = MU_n/P_n$.

**Value of the marginal product** The value of the marginal product of labor ($VMP_L$) is equal to price multiplied by the marginal physical product of labor, or $P \times MPP_L$.

**Variable costs** Costs that vary with output fluctuations, including expenses such as labor and material costs.

**Wealth** A stock measure of an individual's or family's assets, net of liabilities, at a given point in time.

**Wealth effect** Families usually hold some of their wealth in financial assets such as savings accounts, bonds, and cash, and a rising aggregate price level means that the purchasing power of this money wealth declines, reducing output demanded.

**Withdrawals** Activities that remove spending from the economy, including saving, taxes, and imports.

**X-inefficiency** Protected from competitive pressures, monopolies do not have to act efficiently. Spending on corporate jets, travel, and other perks of business represent x-inefficiency.

# Index

Note: page numbers followed by *f* indicate figures; those followed by *n* indicate notes; those followed by *t* indicate tables.